Football Outsiders Almanac 2012

THE ESSENTIAL GUIDE TO THE 2012 NFL AND COLLEGE FOOTBALL SEASONS

Edited by Aaron Schatz

With Andy Benoit, Bill Connelly, Brian Fremeau, Tom Gower, Matt Hinton, Sean McCormick, Rivers McCown, Brian McIntyre, Mike Tanier, Danny Tuccitto, Vince Verhei, and Robert Weintraub

Copyright 2012 Football Outsiders, Inc.

ISBN-10: 1478201525

ISBN-13: 978-1478201526

All rights reserved

Without limiting the rights under copyright reserved above, no part of this publication may be reproduced, stored in or introduced into a retrieval system, or transmitted, in any form, or by any means (electronic, mechanical, photocopying, recording, or otherwise), without the prior written permission of both the copyright owner and the above publisher of this book.

Contents

Introduction	v	Indianapolis Colts	110
Pregame Show 2012	vii	Jacksonville Jaguars	118
Statistical Toolbox	xiii	Kansas City Chiefs	127
The Year In Quotes	xxxix	Miami Dolphins	137
		Minnesota Vikings	145
		New England Patriots	153
NFL Team Chapters		New Orleans Saints	163
Arizona Cardinals	1	New York Giants	171
Atlanta Falcons	10	New York Jets	180
Baltimore Ravens	17	Oakland Raiders	188
Buffalo Bills	25	Philadelphia Eagles	196
Carolina Panthers	34	Pittsburgh Steelers	206
Chicago Bears	42	St. Louis Rams	215
Cincinnati Bengals	50	San Diego Chargers	224
Cleveland Browns	58	San Francisco 49ers	233
Dallas Cowboys	68	Seattle Seahawks	243
Denver Broncos	77	Tampa Bay Buccaneers	253
Detroit Lions	85	Tennessee Titans	261
Green Bay Packers	94	Washington Redskins	270
Houston Texans	102		

Player Comments

Quarterbacks	278
Running Backs	314
Wide Receivers	355
Tight Ends	413
2012 Kicker Projections	438
2012 Fantasy Defense Projections	439

College Football

Introduction and Statistical Toolbox	440
Atlantic Coast Conference	446
Big East Conference	457
Big Ten Conference	464
Big 12 Conference	475
Pac-12 Conference	484
Southeastern Conference	496
Non-AQs and Independents	508

Further Research

Turning the Tide: Big Plays and Psychological Momentum in the NFL	518
The Curse of 25 Carries and Questionable	523
FO Rookie Projections	528
Top 25 Prospects	530
Statistical Appendix	536
Author Bios	553

Introduction

It was December 2002 when I first started analyzing football stats. It began with me trying to figure out whether "establishing the run" meant anything. I had to go to the Internet and copy-paste all the play-by-play from the 2002 season into a spreadsheet so that I could do the analysis. When I was done, there was nowhere to publish it. ESPN.com and SI.com weren't running articles on football statistics. Pro-football-reference.com was in its infancy back then. There was no NFL Network to watch replays of important games. Nobody was charting games to provide public information on blitzes, dropped passes, or quarterback knockdowns. There were very few stats available other than the usual yards, carries, passes, and touchdowns. And everybody knew that the Tennessee Titans were a great team because Eddie George established the run.

Now here we are, ten years later, and each year the idea of advanced statistical analysis for football has become more and more mainstream. There are a number of people and websites doing analysis, both play-by-play breakdown similar to what we do with DVOA and the creation of additional stats off tape, similar to what we do with our game charting project. If you go to pro-football-reference.com, all the basic stats from ten years ago are joined by in-depth lists of starting lineups throughout NFL history, defensive stats like tackles and passes defensed where available, and even expected points per play analysis. If you want to chart games yourself, we have NFL Game Rewind online, where you can call up any play from any game during the season. Beginning in September, we'll finally have access to the holy grail of football analysis, the coaches' all-22 film. ESPN even gave one prominent football stat analyst a regular twice-a-week spot on a daily debate program last fall.[1] And now everybody knows that a running back with 3.3 yards per carry isn't helping you win anything.

If this is your first *Football Outsiders Almanac*, you've probably been told that Football Outsiders are "those football stats guys." That's true, but that's not all we're about. At its heart, the football analytics revolution is about learning more about the intricacies of the game instead of just accepting the boilerplate storylines produced by color commentators, lazy beat reporters[2], and crotchety old players from the past. It's about not accepting the idea that some guy "just wins." It's about understanding that the "skill players" aren't the only guys on the team with skills. It's about gaining insight into the complexity behind the modern offense, and that you don't just shove the ball into the line hoping to gain yardage. It's about accepting that the pass dominates the run in the National Football League, and that it's been that way for 30 years.

Everybody who writes about football uses both statistics (whether they be basic yardage totals or more advanced stats like ours) and scouting (whether scouting reports by professionals or just their own eyes). The same goes for us, except that the statistics portion of our analysis is far more accurate than what you normally see from football coverage. Those numbers are based on two ideas:

1) Conventional football statistics are heavily dependent on context. If you want to see which teams are good and which are bad, which strategies work and which do not, you first need to filter out that context. Down and distance, field position, the current score, time left on the clock, the quality of the opponent—all of these elements influence the objective of the play and/or its outcome. Yet, the official NFL stats add together all yardage gained by a specific team or player without considering the impact of that particular yardage on wins and losses.

A close football game can turn on a single bounce of the ball. In a season of only 16 games, those effects

---

[1] Happily for both my ego and my mortgage, it was me. For those who are curious, despite some changes in the format, there's a good chance I will be returning to Numbers Never* Lie this fall in some capacity.

[2] This group, thankfully, constitutes a much smaller percentage of beat reporters than it did ten years ago.

can have a huge impact on a team's win-loss record, thus obscuring the team's true talent level. If we can filter out these bits of luck and random chance, we can figure out which teams are really more likely to play better for the rest of the season, or even in the following season.

2) On any one play, the majority of the important action is not tracked by the conventional NFL play-by-play. That's why we started the Football Outsiders game charting project in 2005. A cadre of football-obsessed volunteers watches every single game and adds new detail to our record of each play. We know how many pass rushers teams send on each pass, how often teams go three-wide or use two tight ends, how often teams use a play-fake or a zone blitz, and which defensive backs are in coverage, even when they don't get a tackle in the standard play-by-play.

As we remind people each year, Football Outsiders is not founded on the idea that statistics are all-encompassing or can tell us everything about football. There's a lot more to our analysis than numbers, and two well-known writers who are joining our staff will be a big part of that moving forward. This book contains the first Football Outsiders work from both Andy Benoit and Matt Hinton. Andy has been writing professionally about the NFL since he was a teenager, and brings a scouting perspective that will often explain our statistics—and will occasionally bring up new questions about whether we're interpreting them correctly. Matt happens to be one of the most well-respected and funniest college football writers on the Internet, and we're very happy to have him aboard to summarize the weekend on the college gridiron each Monday and preview the upcoming games each Thursday.

As with past books, *Football Outsiders Almanac 2012* starts off with "Pregame Show" (reviewing the most important research we've done in past books) and "Statistical Toolbox" (explaining all our stats). Once again, we preserve the ridiculousness of the NFL for posterity with another version of "The Year in Quotes" and we introduce you to some of the more promising (and lesser-known) young bench players with our sixth annual list of Top 25 Prospects chosen in the third round or later.

Each NFL team gets a full chapter covering what happened in 2011 and our projections for the upcoming season. Are there reasons to believe that the team was actually better or worse than its record last year? What did the team do in the offseason, and what does that mean for the team's chances to win in 2012? Each chapter also includes all kinds of advanced statistics covering 2011 performance and strategic tendencies, plus detailed commentary on each of the major units of the team: Offensive line, defensive front seven, defensive secondary, special teams, and coaching staff.

"Skill players" (by which we mean "players who get counted in fantasy football") get their own section in the back of the book. We list the major players at each position alphabetically, along with commentary and a 2012 KUBIAK projection that will help you win your fantasy football league. We also have the most accurate projections anywhere for two fantasy football positions that people wrongly consider impossible to predict: kickers and team defense.

Next comes our preview of the college football season. We preview every team from the six BCS conferences as well as the top independents and mid-majors. Just like with our NFL coverage, the goal of our college previews is to focus as much as possible on "why" and "how," not just "which team is better." We're not just here to rank the Football Bowl Subdivision teams from 1 to 124. We break things down to offense and defense, pass and run, and clutch situations compared to all plays.

In the back of the book, you will find a number of extra research essays, including analysis of whether big defensive plays really launch offensive momentum, further examination of running back injuries, and updates of our methods for projecting college wide receivers and edge rushers into the NFL.

We hope our book helps you raise your level of football expertise, win arguments with your friends, and win your fantasy football league. We hope you enjoy reading our book as much as we enjoy writing it every year.

Aaron Schatz
Framingham, MA
July 9, 2012

P.S. Don't forget to visit FootballOutsiders.com every day for fresh coverage of the NFL and college football, plus the most intelligent football discussion threads on the Internet.

Pregame Show 2012

It has now been nearly ten years since we launched Football Outsiders. In that time, we've done a lot of primary research on the National Football League, and we reference that research in many of the articles and comments in *Football Outsiders Almanac 2012*. New readers may come across an offhand comment in a team chapter about, for example, the idea that fumble recovery is not a skill, and wonder what in the heck we are talking about. We can't repeat all our research in every new edition of *Football Outsiders Almanac*, so we start each year with a basic look at some of the most important precepts that have emerged from Football Outsiders research. You will see these issues come up again and again throughout the book.

You can also find this introduction online at http://www.footballoutsiders.com/info/FO-basics, along with links to the original research in the cases in which that research appeared online.

Our various methods for projecting NFL success for college prospects are not listed below, but are referenced at times during the book. Those methods are detailed in an essay on page 528.

You run when you win, not win when you run.

If we could only share one piece of anti-conventional wisdom with you before you read the rest of our book, this would be it. The first article ever written for Football Outsiders was devoted to debunking the myth of "establishing the run." There is no correlation whatsoever between giving your running backs a lot of carries early in the game and winning the game. Just running the ball is not going to help a team score; it has to run successfully.

There are two reasons why nearly every beat writer and television analyst still repeats the tired old school mantra that "establishing the run" is the secret to winning football games. The first problem is confusing cause and effect. There are exceptions, but for the most part, winning teams have a lot of carries because their running backs are running out the clock at the end of wins, not because they are running wild early in games.

The second problem is history. Most of the current crop of NFL analysts came of age or actually played the game during the 1970s. They believe that the run-heavy game of that decade is how football is meant to be, and today's pass-first game is an aberration. As we addressed in an essay in *Pro Football Prospectus 2006* on the history of NFL stats, it was actually the game of the 1970s that was the aberration. The seventies were far more slanted towards the run than any era since the arrival of Paul Brown, Otto Graham, and the Cleveland Browns in 1946. Optimal strategies from 1974 are not optimal strategies for 2012.

A sister statement to "you have to establish the run" is "team X is 5-1 when running back John Doe runs for at least 100 yards." Unless John Doe is ripping off six-yard gains Jamaal Charles-style, the team isn't winning because of his 100-yard games. He's putting up 100-yard games because his team is winning.

A great defense against the run is nothing without a good pass defense.

This is a corollary to the absurdity of "establish the run." With rare exceptions, teams win or lose with the passing game more than the running game—and by stopping the passing game more than the running game. Ron Jaworski puts it best: "The pass gives you the lead, and the run solidifies it." The reason why teams need a strong run defense in the playoffs is not to shut the run down early; it's to keep the other team from icing the clock if they get a lead. You can't mount a comeback if you can't stop the run.

Note that "good pass defense" may mean "good pass rush" rather than "good defensive backs."

Running on third-and-short is more likely to convert than passing on third-and-short.

On average, passing will always gain more yardage than running, with one very important exception: when a team is just one or two yards away from a new set of downs or the goal line. On third-and-1, a run will convert for a new set of downs 36 percent more often than a pass. Expand that to all third or fourth downs with 1 or 2 yards to go, and the run is successful 40 percent more often. With these percentages, the possibility of a long gain with a pass is not worth the tradeoff of an incomplete that kills a drive.

This is one reason why teams have to be able to both run and pass. The offense also has to keep some semblance of balance so they can use their play-action fakes, and so the defense doesn't just run their nickel and dime packages all game. Balance also means that teams do need to pass occasionally in short-yardage situations; they just need to do it less than they do now. Teams pass roughly 60 percent of the time on third-and-2 even though runs in that situation convert 20 percent more often than passes. They pass 68 percent of the time on fourth-and-2 even though runs in that situation convert twice as often as passes.

Standard team rankings based on total yardage are inherently flawed.

Check out the schedule page on NFL.com, and you will find that each game is listed with league rankings based on total yardage. That is still how the NFL "officially" ranks teams, but these rankings rarely match up with common sense. That is because total team yardage may be the most context-dependent number in football.

It starts with the basic concept that rate stats are generally more valuable than cumulative stats. Yards per carry says more about a running back's quality than total yardage, completion percentage says more than just a quarterback's total number of completions. The same thing is true for teams; in fact, it is even more important because of the way football strategy influences the number of runs and passes in the game plan. Poor teams will give up fewer passing yards and more rushing yards because opponents will stop passing once they have a late-game lead and will run out the clock instead. For winning teams, the opposite is true. Who had a better pass defense last year: San Francisco or St. Louis? The answer is obviously San Francisco, yet according to the official NFL rankings, St. Louis (3,301 yards allowed on 484 passes) was a better pass defense than San Francisco (3,695 yards allowed on 579 passes).

Total yardage rankings are also skewed because some teams play at a faster pace than other teams. In 2010, for example, Tampa Bay (5,362) had roughly the same number of yards as the Washington Redskins (5,392). However, the Bucs were the superior offense and much more efficient; they gained those yards on only 163 drives while the Redskins needed 200 drives.

A team will score more when playing a bad defense, and will give up more points when playing a good offense.

This sounds absurdly basic, but when people consider team and player stats without looking at strength of schedule, they are ignoring this. In 2004, Carson Palmer and Byron Leftwich had very similar numbers, but Palmer faced a much tougher schedule than Leftwich did. Palmer was better that year, and better in the long run.

Matt Forte's 2011 season is another fine example. One reason his year looked so good is that he had to play only two games against teams that ranked among the top dozen in run defense DVOA. His four 100-yard games came against the defenses ranked 18th (Detroit), 19th (Philadelphia), 30th (Tampa Bay), and dead last (Carolina) in run defense DVOA.

If their overall yards per carry are equal, a running back who consistently gains yardage on every play is more valuable than a boom-and-bust running back who is frequently stuffed at the line but occasionally breaks a long highlight-worthy run.

Our brethren at Baseball Prospectus believe that the most precious commodity in baseball is outs. Teams only get 27 of them per game, and you can't afford to give one up for very little return. So imagine if there was a new rule in baseball that gave a team a way to earn another three outs in the middle of the inning. That would be pretty useful, right?

That's the way football works. You may start a drive 80 yards away from scoring, but as long as you can earn 10 yards in four chances, you get another four chances. Long gains have plenty of value, but if those long gains are mixed with a lot of short gains, you are going to put the quarterback in a lot of difficult third-and-long situations. That means more punts and more giving the ball back to the other team rather than moving the chains and giving the offense four more plays to work with.

The running back who gains consistent yardage is also going to do a lot more for you late in the game, when the goal of running the ball is not just to gain yardage but to eat clock time. If you are a Titans fan watching your team with a late lead, you don't want to see three straight Chris Johnson stuffs at the line followed by a punt. You want to see a game-icing first down.

A common historical misconception is that our preference for consistent running backs means that "Football Outsiders believes that Barry Sanders was overrated." Sanders wasn't just any boom-and-bust running back, though; he was the greatest boom-and-bust runner of all time, with bigger booms and fewer busts. Sanders ranked second in DYAR three times (1994, 1996, and 1997), although his first two seasons have still not been broken down for DVOA/DYAR.

Rushing is more dependent on the offensive line than people realize, but pass protection is more dependent on the quarterback himself than people realize.

Some readers complain that this idea contradicts the previous one. Aren't those consistent running backs just the product of good offensive lines? The truth is somewhere in between. There are certainly good running backs who suffer because their offensive lines cannot create consistent holes, but most boom-and-bust running backs contribute to their own problems by hesitating behind the line whenever the hole is unclear, looking for the home run instead of charging forward for the 4-yard gain that keeps the offense moving.

As for pass protection, some quarterbacks have better instincts for the rush than others, and are thus better at getting out of trouble by moving around in the pocket or throwing the ball away. Others will hesitate, hold onto the ball too long, and lose yardage over and over.

Note that "moving around in the pocket" does not necessarily mean "scrambling." In fact, a scrambling quarterback will often take more sacks than a pocket quarterback, because while he's running around trying to make something happen, a defensive lineman will catch up with him.

Shotgun formations are generally more efficient than formations with the quarterback under center.

Over the past four seasons, offenses have averaged 6.0 yards per play from Shotgun, but just 5.2 yards per play with the quarterback under center. This wide split exists even if you analyze the data to try to weed out biases like teams using Shotgun more often on third-and-long, or against prevent defenses in the fourth quarter. Shotgun offense is more efficient if you only look at the first half, on every down, and even if you only look at running back carries rather than passes and scrambles.

Clearly, NFL teams have figured the importance of the Shotgun out for themselves. In 2001, NFL teams only used Shotgun on 14 percent of plays. Five years later, in 2006, that had increased slightly, to 20 percent of plays. Last year, Shotgun was used on a record-setting 41 percent of plays (not counting the Wildcat or other college-style option plays). Before 2007, no team had ever used Shotgun on more than half its offensive plays. Last year, six different teams used Shotgun more than 50 percent of the time, led by Detroit which used Shotgun on an NFL-record 68 percent of plays. It is likely that if teams continue to increase their usage of the Shotgun, defenses will adapt and the benefit of the formation will become less pronounced.

But it certainly isn't happening yet; the difference between success on Shotgun and non-Shotgun plays last year was bigger than in 2008, 2009, or 2010.

A running back with 370 or more carries during the regular season will usually suffer either a major injury or a loss of effectiveness the following year, unless he is named Eric Dickerson.

Terrell Davis, Jamal Anderson, and Edgerrin James all blew out their knees. Larry Johnson broke his foot. Earl Campbell and Eddie George went from legendary powerhouses to plodding, replacement-level players. Shaun Alexander broke his foot *and* became a plodding, replacement-level player. This is what happens when a running back is overworked to the point of having at least 370 carries during the regular season.

The "Curse of 370" was expanded in our book *Pro Football Prospectus 2005*, and now includes seasons with 390 or more carries in the regular season and postseason combined. Research also shows that receptions don't cause a problem, only workload on the ground.

Plenty of running backs get injured without hitting 370 carries in a season, but there is a clear difference. On average, running backs with 300 to 369 carries and no postseason appearance will see their total rushing yardage decline by 15 percent the following year and their yards per carry decline by two percent. The average running back with 370 or more regular-season carries, or 390 including the postseason, will see their rushing yardage decline by 35 percent, and their yards per carry decline by eight percent.

It's worth noting that the return to the committee backfields that dominated the '60s and '70s may mean an end to the Curse of 370. No running back has gone over 370 carries since Michael Turner in 2008. However, the Curse of 370 is not a hard and fast line where running backs suddenly become injury risks. It is more of a concept where 370 carries is roughly the point at which additional carries start to become more and more of a problem.

Wide receivers must be judged on both complete and incomplete passes.

In 2011, for example, Dwayne Bowe had 1,188 receiving yards, while Marques Colston was close behind with 1,169 yards. Both players ran routes of roughly the same average length. But there was a huge difference between them: Bowe caught 57 percent of passes, while Colston had a catch rate of 75 percent. We don't yet know enough to precisely parse the blame for incomplete passes, but we know that wide receiver catch rates are almost as consistent from year to year as quarterback completion percentages. However, it is also important to look at catch rate in the context of the types of routes each receiver runs. Two years ago, we expanded on this idea with a new plus-minus metric, which is explained in the introduction to the chapter on wide receivers and tight ends.

The total quality of an NFL team is three parts offense, three parts defense, and one part special teams.

There are three units on a football team, but they are not of equal importance. Our DVOA ratings provide good evidence for this. The special teams ratings are turned into DVOA by comparing how often field position on special teams leads to scoring compared to field position and first downs on offense. After figuring out these numbers, the top ratings for special teams are roughly one-third as high as the top ratings for offense or defense.

Offense is more consistent from year to year than defense, and offensive performance is easier to project than defensive performance. Special teams is less consistent than either.

Nobody in the NFL understands this concept better than former Indianapolis Colts general manager Bill Polian. Both the Super Bowl champion Colts and the four-time AFC champion Buffalo Bills of the early 1990s were built around the idea that if you put together an offense that can dominate the league year after year, eventually you will luck into a year where good health and a few smart decisions will give you a defense good enough to win a championship. (As the Colts learned in 2006, you don't even need a year, just four weeks.) Even the New England Patriots, who are led by a defense-first head coach in Bill Belichick, have been more consistent on offense than on defense since they began their run of success in 2001.

Field-goal percentage is almost entirely random from season to season, while kickoff distance is one of the most consistent statistics in football.

This theory, which originally appeared in the *New York Times* in October 2006, is one of our most controversial, but it is hard to argue against the evidence. Measuring every kicker from 1999 to 2006 who had at least ten field goal attempts in each of two consecutive years, the year-to-year correlation coefficient for field-goal percentage was an insignificant .05. Mike Vanderjagt didn't miss a single field goal in 2003, but his percentage was a below-average 74 percent the year before and 80 percent the year after. Adam Vinatieri has long been considered the best kicker in the game. But even he had never enjoyed two straight seasons with accuracy better than the NFL average of 85 percent until last year, when he followed up his 26-for-28 2010 campaign by going 23-for-27 (85.2 percent).

On the other hand, the year-to-year correlation coefficient for kickoff distance, over the same period as our measurement of field-goal percentage and with the same minimum of ten kicks per year, is .61. The same players consistently lead the league in kickoff distance. In recent years, that group includes Olindo Mare, Stephen Gostkowski, Pat McAfee, and David Akers. Bill Cundiff, who has led the league in gross kickoff value the last two years, is a bit of an exception since he changed his style in 2010, but we expect him to be consistently near the top of the league going forward.

Teams with more offensive penalties generally lose more games, but there is no correlation between defensive penalties and losses.

Specific defensive penalties of course lose games; we've all sworn at the television when the cornerback on our favorite team gets flagged for a 50-yard pass interference penalty. Yet overall, there is no correlation between losses and the total of defensive penalties or even the total yardage on defensive penalties. One reason is that defensive penalties often represent *good* play, not bad. Cornerbacks who play tight coverage may be just on the edge of a penalty on most plays, only occasionally earning a flag. Defensive ends who get a good jump on rushing the passer will gladly trade an encroachment penalty or two for ten snaps where they get off the blocks a split-second before the linemen trying to block them.

In addition, offensive penalties have a higher correlation from year to year than defensive penalties. The penalty that correlates highest with losses is the false start, and the penalty that teams will have called most consistently from year to year is also the false start.

Recovery of a fumble, despite being the product of hard work, is almost entirely random.

Stripping the ball is a skill. Holding onto the ball is a skill. Pouncing on the ball as it is bouncing all over the place is not a skill. There is no correlation whatsoever between the percentage of fumbles recovered by a team in one year and the percentage they recover in the next year. The odds of recovery are based solely on the type of play involved, not the teams or any of their players.

Fans like to insist that specific coaches can teach their teams to recover more fumbles by swarming to the ball. Chicago's Lovie Smith, in particular, is supposed to have this ability. However, in Smith's first three seasons as head coach of the Bears, their rate of fumble recovery on defense went from a league-best 76 percent in 2004 to a league-worst 33 percent in 2005, then back to 67 percent in 2006.

Fumble recovery is equally erratic on offense. In 2010, the Houston Texans recovered nine of 15 fumbles on offense. Last year, they recovered only seven of 18 fumbles.

Fumble recovery is a major reason why the general public overestimates or underestimates certain teams. Fumbles are huge, turning-point plays that dramatically impact wins and losses in the past, while fumble recovery percentage says absolutely nothing about a team's chances of winning games in the future. With this in mind, Football Outsiders stats treat all fumbles as equal, penalizing them based on the likelihood of each type of fumble (run, pass, sack, etc.) being recovered by the defense.

Other plays that qualify as "non-predictive events" include two-point conversions, blocked kicks, and touchdowns during turnover returns. These plays are not "lucky," per se, but they have no value whatsoever for predicting future performance.

Field position is fluid.

As discussed in the Statistical Toolbox, every yard line on the field has a value based on how likely a team is to score from that location on the field as opposed to from a yard further back. The change in value from one yard to the next is the same whether the team has the ball or not. The goal of a defense is not just to prevent scoring, but to hold the opposition so that the offense can get the ball back in the best possible field position. A bad offense will score as many points as a good offense if it starts each drive 5 yards closer to the goal line.

A corollary to this precept: The most underrated aspect of an NFL team's performance is the field position gained or lost on kickoffs and punts. This is part of why players like Devin Hester and Patrick Peterson can have such an impact on the game, even when they aren't taking a kickoff or punt all the way back for a touchdown.

The red zone is the most important place on the field to play well, but performance in the red zone from year to year is much less consistent than overall performance.

Although play in the red zone has a disproportionately high importance to the outcome of games relative to plays on the rest of the field, NFL teams do not exhibit a level of performance in the red zone that is consistently better or worse than their performance elsewhere, year after year. The simplest explanation why is a small(er) sample size and the inherent variance of football, with contributing factors like injuries and changes in personnel.

Defenses which are strong on first and second down, but weak on third down, will tend to improve the following year. Defenses which are weak on first and second down, but strong on third down, will tend to decline the following year. This trend also applied to offenses through 2005, but may or may not still apply today.

We discovered this when creating our first team projection system in 2004. It said that the lowly San Diego Chargers would have one of the best offenses in the league, which seemed a little ridiculous. But looking closer, our projection system treated the previous year's performance on different downs as different variables, and the 2003 Chargers were actually good on first and second down, but terrible on third.

Teams get fewer opportunities on third down, so third-down performance is more volatile—but it's also is a bigger part of a team's overall performance than first or second down, because the result is usually either very good (four more downs) or very bad (losing the ball to the other team with a punt). Over time, a team will play as well in those situations as it does in other situations, which will bring the overall offense or defense in line with the offense and defense on first and second down.

This trend is even stronger between seasons. Struggles on third down are a pretty obvious problem, and teams will generally target their off-season moves at improving their third-down performance ... which often leads to an improvement in third-down performance.

However, we have discovered something surprising over the past few years: The third-down rebound effect seems to have disappeared on offense, as we explained in the Philadelphia chapter of *Football Outsiders Almanac 2010*. We don't know yet if this change is temporary or permanent, and there is no such change on defense.

Injuries regress to the mean on the seasonal level, and teams that avoid injuries in a given season tend to win more games.

There are no doubt teams with streaks of good or bad health over multiple years. However, teams who were especially healthy or especially unhealthy, as measured by our Adjusted Games Lost (AGL) metric, almost always head towards league average in the subsequent season. Furthermore, injury—or the absence thereof—has a huge correlation with wins, and a significant impact on a team's success. There's no doubt that a few high-profile teams have resisted this trend in recent years. The Patriots seem to overcome injuries every year, and the last three Super Bowl champions were among the most-injured teams in the league in each of those seasons. Nonetheless, the overall rule still applies. The Patriots and Giants made it to the Super Bowl despite being among the most injured teams in the league last year, but they also were the only two teams in the top 15 of our AGL metric that made the playoffs at all. In 2010, four of the six least-injured teams in the league made the playoffs, including surprise division champions Chicago and Kansas City. Last year, the least injured teams included surprise playoff teams Detroit and San Francisco.

In general, teams with a high number of injuries are a good bet to improve the following season. This year, that list would include Carolina, New England, and the entire NFC West outside of San Francisco. However, while injury totals tend to regress towards the mean, there's also no doubt that certain teams have a record of staying healthier than others. We need to do more research on this issue, but teams with a consistent record of poor health include Indianapolis, New England, and St. Louis, while teams with a consistent record of good health include Tennessee, Kansas City (with last year clearly a gigantic exception), and the New York Jets.

By and large, a team built on depth is better than a team built on stars and scrubs.

Connected to the previous statement, because teams need to go into the season expecting that they will suffer an average number of injuries no matter how healthy they were the previous year. The Redskins go into every season with a number of stars, and generally end up 5-11 because they have no depth. You cannot concentrate your salaries on a handful of star players because there is no such thing as avoiding injuries in the NFL. The game is too fast and the players too strong to build a team based around the idea that "if we can avoid all injuries this year, we'll win."

Running backs usually decline after age 28, tight ends after age 29, wide receivers after age 30, and quarterbacks after age 32.

This research was originally done by Doug Drinen (editor of pro-football-reference.com) in 2000. In recent years, a few players have had huge seasons above these general age limits (most notably Tony Gonzalez), but the peak ages Drinen found a few years ago still apply to the majority of players.

As for "non-skill players," research we did in 2007 for *ESPN the Magazine* suggested that defensive ends and defensive backs generally begin to decline after age 29, linebackers and offensive linemen after age 30, and defensive tackles after age 31. However, because we still have so few statistics to use to study linemen and defensive players, this research should not be considered definitive.

The strongest indicator of how a college football team will perform in the upcoming season is their performance in recent seasons.

It may seem strange because graduation enforces constant player turnover, but college football teams are actually much more consistent from year to year than NFL teams. Thanks in large part to consistency in recruiting, teams can be expected to play within a reasonable range of their baseline program expectations each season. Our Program F/+ ratings, which represent a rolling five-year period of play-by-play and drive efficiency data, have an extremely strong (.76) correlation with the next year's F/+ rating.

Championship teams are generally defined by their ability to dominate inferior opponents, not their ability to win close games.

Football games are often decided by one or two plays: a missed field goal, a bouncing fumble, the subjective spot of an official on fourth-and-1. One missed assignment by a cornerback or one slightly askew pass that bounces off a receiver's hands and into those of a defensive back 5 yards away and the game could be over. In a blowout, however, one lucky bounce isn't going to change things. Championship teams—in both professional and college football—typically beat their good opponents convincingly and destroy the cupcakes on the schedule.

Aaron Schatz

Statistical Toolbox

After nearly ten years of Football Outsiders, some of our readers are as comfortable with DVOA and ALY as they are with touchdowns and tackles. Yet to most fans, including our newer readers, it still looks like a lot of alphabet soup. That's what this chapter is for. The next few pages define and explain all of all the unique NFL statistics you'll find in this book: how we calculate them, what the numbers mean, and what they tell us about why teams win or lose football games. We'll go through the information in each of the tables that appear in each team chapter, pointing out whether those stats come from advanced mathematical manipulation of the standard play-by-play or simple counting of what see on television with the Football Outsiders game charting project. This chapter covers NFL statistics only. College metrics such as Adjusted POE and F/+ are explained in the introduction to the college football section on page 440.

We've done our best to present these numbers in a way that makes them easy to understand. This explanation is long, so feel free to read some of it, flip around the rest of the book, and then come back. It will still be here.

Even if you are a veteran reader of *Football Outsiders Almanac*, and usually skip this section, you may want to catch up on a number of changes this year, including the new normalized DVOA v7.0, a new method for calculating Pythagorean wins, and new tables reflecting performance by personnel group on both offense and defense.

Defense-Adjusted Value Over Average (DVOA)

One running back runs for three yards. Another running back runs for three yards. Which is the better run?

This sounds like a stupid question, but it isn't. In fact, this question is at the heart of nearly all of the analysis in this book.

Several factors can differentiate one three-yard run from another. What is the down and distance? Is it third-and-2, or second-and-15? Where on the field is the ball? Does the player get only three yards because he hits the goal line and scores? Is the player's team up by two touchdowns in the fourth quarter and thus running out the clock, or down by two touchdowns and thus facing a defense that is playing purely against the pass? Is the running back playing against the porous defense of the Raiders, or the stalwart defense of the Bears?

Conventional NFL statistics value plays based solely on their net yardage. The NFL determines the best players by adding up all their yards no matter what situations they came in or how many plays it took to get them. Now, why would they do that? Football has one objective—to get to the end zone—and two ways to achieve that, by gaining yards and achieving first downs. These two goals need to be balanced to determine a player's value or a team's performance. All the yards in the world won't help a team win if they all come in six-yard chunks on third-and-10.

The popularity of fantasy football only exacerbates the problem. Fans have gotten used to judging players based on how much they help fantasy teams win and lose, not how much they help *real* teams win and lose. Typical fantasy scoring further skews things by counting the yard between the one and the goal line as 61 times more important than all the other yards on the field (each yard worth 0.1 points, a touchdown worth 6). Let's say Larry Fitzgerald catches a pass on third-and-15 and goes 50 yards but gets tackled two yards from the goal line, and then Beanie Wells takes the ball on first-and-goal from the two-yard line and plunges in for the score. Has Beanie Wells done something special? Not really. When an offense gets the ball on first-and-goal at the two-yard line, they are going to score a touchdown five out of six times. Wells is getting credit for the work done by the passing game.

Doing a better job of distributing credit for scoring points and winning games is the goal of **DVOA**, or Defense-adjusted Value Over Average. DVOA breaks down every single play of the NFL season, assigning each play a value based on both total yards and yards towards a first down, based on work done by Pete Palmer, Bob Carroll, and John Thorn in their seminal book, *The Hidden Game of Football*. On first down, a play is considered a success if it gains 45 percent of needed yards; on second down, a play needs to gain 60 percent of needed yards; on third or fourth down, only gaining a new first down is considered success.

We then expand upon that basic idea with a more complicated system of "success points," improved over the past few years with a lot of mathematics and a bit of trial and error. A successful play is worth one point, an unsuccessful play zero points with fractional points in between (for example, eight yards on third-and-10 is worth 0.54 "success points"). Extra points are awarded for big plays, gradually increasing to three points for 10 yards (assuming those yards result in a first down), four points for 20 yards, and five points for 40 yards or more. Losing three or more yards is -1 point. Interceptions average -6 points, with an adjustment for the length of the pass and the location of the interception (since an interception tipped at the line is more likely to produce a long return than an interception on a 40-yard pass). A fumble is worth anywhere from -1.7 to -4.0 points depending on how often a fumble in that situation is lost to the defense—no matter who actually recovers the fumble. Red zone plays get a bonus: 20 percent for team offense, five percent for team defense, and 10 percent for individual players. There is a bonus given for a touchdown that acknowledges that the goal line is significantly more difficult to cross than the previous 99 yards (although this bonus is nowhere near as large as the one used in fantasy football).

(Our system is a bit more complex than the one in *Hidden Game* thanks to our subsequent research, which added larger penalty for turnovers, the fractional points, and a slightly higher baseline for success on first down. The reason why all fumbles are counted, no matter whether they are recovered by the offense or defense, is explained in the essay "Pregame Show.")

Every single play run in the NFL gets a "success value" based on this system, and then that number gets compared to the average success values of plays in similar situations for all players, adjusted for a number of variables. These include down and distance, field location, time remaining in game, and the team's lead or deficit in the game score. Teams are always compared to the overall offensive average, as the team made its own choice whether to pass or rush. When it comes to individual players, however, rushing plays are compared to other rushing plays, passing plays to other passing plays, tight ends to tight ends, wideouts to wideouts, and so on.

Going back to our example of the three-yard rush, if Player A gains three yards under a set of circumstances in which the average NFL running back gains only one yard, then Player A has a certain amount of value above others at his position. Likewise, if Player B gains three yards on a play on which, under similar circumstances, an average NFL back gains four yards, that Player B has negative value relative to others at his position. Once we make all our adjustments, we can evaluate the difference between this player's rate of success and the expected success rate of an average running back in the same situation (or between the opposing defense and the average defense in the same situation, etc.). Add up every play by a certain team or player, divide by the total of the various baselines for success in all those situations, and you get VOA, or Value Over Average.

Of course, the biggest variable in football is the fact that each team plays a different schedule against teams of disparate quality. By adjusting each play based on the opposing defense's average success in stopping that type of play over the course of a season, we get DVOA, or Defense-adjusted Value Over Average. Rushing and passing plays are adjusted based on down and location on the field; passing plays are also adjusted based on how the defense performs against passes to running backs, tight ends, or wide receivers. Defenses are adjusted based on the average success of the *offenses* they are facing. (Yes, technically the defensive stats are actually "offense-adjusted." If it seems weird, think of the "D" in "DVOA" as standing for "opponent-Dependent" or something.)

The biggest advantage of DVOA is the ability to break teams and players down to find strengths and weaknesses in a variety of situations. In the aggregate, DVOA may not be quite as accurate as some of the other, similar "power ratings" formulas based on comparing drives rather than individual plays, but, unlike those other ratings, DVOA can be separated not only by player, but also by down, or by week, or by distance needed for a first down. This can give us a better idea of not just which team is better, but why, and what a team has to do in order to improve itself in the future. You will find DVOA used in this book in a lot of different ways—because it takes every single play into account, it can be used to measure a player or a team's performance in any situation. All Pittsburgh third downs can be compared to how an average team does on third down. Kevin Kolb and John Skelton can each be compared to how an average quarterback performs in the red zone, or with a lead, or in the second half of the game.

Since it compares each play only to plays with similar circumstances, it gives a more accurate picture of how much better a team really is compared to the league as a whole. The list of top DVOA offenses on third down, for example, is more accurate than the conventional NFL conversion statistic because it takes into account that converting third-and-long is more difficult than converting third-and-short, and that a turnover is worse than an incomplete pass because it eliminates the opportunity to move the other team back with a punt on fourth down.

One of the hardest parts of understanding a new statistic is interpreting its scale, or what numbers represent good performance or bad performance. We've made that easy with DVOA. In all cases, 0% represents league-average. A positive DVOA represents a situation that favors the offense, while a negative DVOA represents a situation that favors the defense. This is why the best offenses have positive DVOA ratings (last year, Green Bay led the league at +33.8%) and the best defenses have negative DVOA ratings (with Baltimore number one in 2011 at -17.1%).

In general, the scale of offensive ratings is slightly wider than the scale of defensive ratings, although 2011 was a bit of an outlier in this regard, with the standard deviation of defenses particularly low. On offense, three different teams from 2011 rank among the top 10 offenses of the DVOA era (1991-2011). On defense, no team from 2011 ranked among either the top 30 or bottom 30 defenses of the DVOA era. In most years, the best and worst offenses tend to rate around +/- 30%, while the best and worst defenses tend to rate around +/- 25%. For starting players, the scale tends to reach roughly +/-40% for passing and receiving, and +/- 30% for rushing. As you might imagine, some players with fewer attempts will surpass both extremes.

Team DVOA totals combine offense and defense by subtracting the latter from the former because the better defenses will have negative DVOA ratings. (Special teams performance is also added, as described later in this essay.) Certain plays are counted in DVOA for offense and not for defense, leading to separate baselines on each side of the ball. Some other important notes about DVOA:

• Only four penalties are included in DVOA. Two penalties count as pass plays on both sides of the ball: intentional grounding and defensive pass interference. The other two penalties are included for offense only: false starts and delay of game. Because the inclusion of these penalties means a group of negative plays that don't count as either passes or runs, the league averages for pass offense and run offense are higher than the league averages for pass defense and run defense.

• Aborted snaps and incomplete backwards lateral passes are only penalized on offense, not rewarded on defense.

• Adjustments for playing from behind or with a lead in the fourth quarter are different for offense and defense, as are adjustments for the final two minutes of the first half when the offense is not near field-goal range.

• Offense gets a slight penalty and defense gets a slight bonus for games indoors.

Special Teams

The problem with a system based on measuring both yardage and yardage towards a first down is what to do with plays that don't have the possibility of a first down. Special teams are an important part of football and we needed a way to add that performance to the team DVOA rankings. Our special teams metric includes five separate measurements: field goals and extra points, net punting, punt returns, net kickoffs, and kick returns.

The foundation of most of these special teams ratings is the concept that each yard line has a different value based on the likelihood of scoring from that position on the field. In *Hidden Game*, the authors suggested that the each additional yard for the offense had equal value, with a team's own goal line being worth -2 points, the 50-yard line 2 points, and the opposing goal line 6 points. (-2 points is not only the value of a safety, but also reflects the fact that when a team is backed up in its own territory, it is likely that its drive will stall, forcing a punt that will give the ball to the other team in good field position. Thus, the negative point value reflects the fact that the defense is more likely to score next.) Our studies have updated this concept to reflect the actual likelihood that the offense or defense will have the next score from a given position on the field based on actual results from the past few seasons. The line that represents the value of field position is not straight, but curved, with the value of each yard increasing as teams approach either goal line.

Our special teams ratings compare each kick or punt to league average based on the point value of the position of the kick, catch, and return. We've determined a league average for how far a kick goes based on the line of scrimmage for each kick (almost always the 35-yard line for kickoffs, variable for punts) and a league average for how far a return goes based on both the yard line where the ball is caught and the distance that it traveled in the air.

The kicking or punting team is rated based on net points compared to average, taking into account both the kick and the return if there is one. Because the average return is always positive, punts that are not returnable (touchbacks, out of bounds, fair catches, and punts downed by the coverage unit) will rate higher than punts of the same distance which are returnable. (This is also true of touchbacks on kickoffs.) There are also separate individual ratings for kickers and punters that are based on distance and whether the kick is returnable, assuming an average return in order to judge the kicker separate from the coverage.

For the return team, the rating is based on how many points the return is worth compared to average, based on the location of the catch and the distance the ball traveled in the air. Return teams are not judged on the distance of kicks, nor are they judged on kicks that cannot be returned. As explained below, blocked kicks are so rare as to be statistically insignificant as predictors for future performance and are thus ignored. For the kicking team they simply count as missed field goals, for the defense they are gathered with their opponents' other missed field goals in Hidden value (also explained below).

Field goal kicking is measured differently. Measuring kickers by field goal percentage is a bit absurd, as it assumes that all field goals are of equal difficulty. In our metric, each field goal is compared to the average number of points scored on all field goal attempts from that distance over the past 15 years. The value of a field goal increases as distance from the goal line increases. Kickoffs, punts, and field goals are then adjusted based on weather and altitude. It will surprise no one to learn that it is easier to kick the ball in Denver or a dome than it is to kick the ball in Buffalo in December. Because we do not yet have enough data to tailor our adjustments specifically to each stadium, each one is assigned to one of four categories: Cold, Warm, Dome, and Denver. There is also an additional adjustment dropping the value of field goals in Florida (because the warm temperatures allow the ball to carry better) and raising the value of punts in San Francisco (because of those infamous winds).

The baselines for special teams are adjusted in each year for rule changes such as the introduction of the special-teams-use-only "k-ball" in 1999 as well as the move of the kickoff line from the 35 to the 30 in 1994 and then back to the 35 in 2011. Baselines have also been adjusted each year to make up for the gradual improvement of kickers over the last two decades.

Once we've totaled how many points above or below average can be attributed to special teams, we translate those points into DVOA so the ratings can be added to offense and defense to get total team DVOA.

There are three aspects of special teams that have an impact on wins and losses, but don't show up in the standard special teams rating because a team has little or no influence on them. The first is the length of kickoffs by the opposing team, with an asterisk. Obviously, there are no defenders standing on the 35-yard line, ready to block a kickoff after the whistle blows. However, over the past few years, some teams have deliberately kicked short in order to avoid certain top return men, such as Devin Hester and Josh Cribbs. The special teams formula now includes adjustments to give teams extra credit for field position on kick returns if kickers are deliberately trying to avoid a return.

The other two items that special teams have little control over are field goals against your team, and punt distance against your team. Research shows no indication that teams can influence the accuracy or strength of field-goal kickers and punters, except for blocks. As mentioned above, although blocked field goals and punts are definitely skillful plays, they are so rare that they have no correlation to how well teams have played in the past or will play in the future, thus they are included here as if they were any other missed field goal or botched punt, giving the defense no additional credit for their efforts. The value of these three elements is listed separately as "Hidden" value.

Special teams ratings also do not include two-point conversions or onside kick attempts, both of which, like blocks, are so infrequent as to be statistically insignificant in judging future performance.

DVOA v7.0

Football Outsiders Almanac 2012 introduces the latest iteration of our DVOA formula, which we are calling DVOA v7.0.

The biggest change in DVOA v7.0 is the normalization of DVOA ratings so that the league average for all years is now 0%. As you may know, offensive levels in the NFL have gone up and down over the years. Right now, the overall level of offense in the league is probably at its highest level of all time. This had created a big problem in recent years. Because DVOA baselines were created using the years 2002-2007, recent years were significantly slanted towards offense, and most of the years we have broken down from the 1990s were slanted towards defense.

For example, in a league where the average is 0%, roughly the half the teams should be positive and the other half should be negative. However, using the previous version of DVOA, 18 teams in 2011 had positive offensive ratings, and 22 teams had positive (i.e. worse than average) defensive ratings. On the other hand, in 1993, only nine out of 28 teams had positive offensive ratings, and only nine teams had positive defensive ratings.

With the new DVOA v7.0, each year's ratings have been normalized so that the league average for team offense and team defense is 0%. These ratings include all plays, however, so the league averages for team passing and team rushing are *not* 0%. Because passing is more efficient than rushing, the average for team passing is almost always positive and the average for team rushing is almost always negative. The variables for normalization were created by looking at how the league average compared to our multi-year baseline by different down-and-distance combinations. To give an example, in a season where teams had trouble gaining yardage on first down but were better than usual converting short third downs, teams would see their first-down performance adjusted upwards but their third-and-short performance adjusted downwards.

Individual DVOA ratings have also been normalized using the same methods. Unlike with team ratings, the individual ratings only compare passes to other passes and runs to other runs, so the league average for individual passing is 0%, as are the league averages for rushing and the three separate league averages for receiving by wide receivers, tight ends, and running backs. We've also worked to normalize each year's special teams numbers so that the league total value for each element of special teams is close to 0.0 points. However, we don't yet have a method to perfectly normalize each year of special teams, so the league totals for special teams are generally off by somewhere between 0.0% and 0.5%. (Nevertheless, this is much lower than the previous year-to-year differences in the league average for special teams.)

We have kept "raw VOA" numbers so that we can still track how strong the overall offensive levels are in a particular season. Figure 1 tracks two different numbers over the past 21 seasons: raw VOA, and the efficiency advantage of passing over rushing. We've

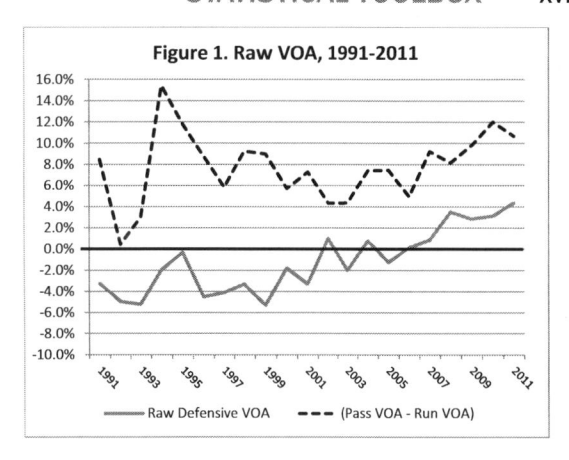

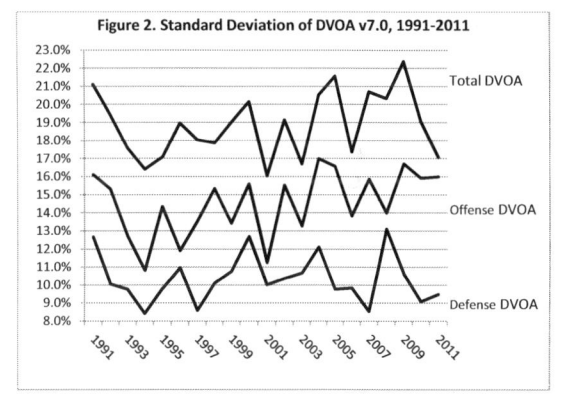

Figure 1. Raw VOA, 1991-2011

Figure 2. Standard Deviation of DVOA v7.0, 1991-2011

used defensive VOA for this graphic so we wouldn't need to worry about non-passing/rushing plays.

As we noted earlier, 2011 was a year with a particularly low standard deviation when it came to defenses, but a high standard deviation when it came to offenses. Figure 2 graphs the standard deviation of DVOA in each of the last 21 years for offense, defense, and total team performance (including special teams).

Normalization of the ratings does not really improve the predictive ability of DVOA, or its correlation to wins. However, it makes our comparisons of current teams and players to past teams and players much more accurate. It also improves our ratings of players by properly moving replacement level around from year to year (as explained further below in the section on DYAR).

In addition to the normalization of each year's ratings, a few other changes were made as part of DVOA v7.0, as follows:

• Based on research showing that red-zone performance is much less consistent from year-to-year than overall performance, the red zone bonus for team DVOA was dropped from 25 percent on both sides of the ball to 20 percent on offense and five percent on defense. We considered removing the red zone bonus entirely, but found that these rates made DVOA slightly more predictive than no red zone bonus at all.

• The coefficient used to translate special teams "points over average" into DVOA was increased slightly.

• A fix was added so that fourth-down interceptions now have no penalty whatsoever in the final two minutes of a game. Other fourth-down interceptions are still penalized based on the distance of the pass, although fourth-down interceptions have a much smaller penalty than interceptions on first through third down.

• A number of fixes were made to older years of play-by-play, including a change where we have decided to count lateral passes as pass plays rather than running plays where we have that information.

• The formulas for "estimated wins" and "Pythagorean wins" were changed slightly, as described later in this chapter.

How well does DVOA work? Using correlation coefficients, we can show that only actual points scored are better than DVOA at indicating how many games a team has won (Table 1) and DVOA does a better job of predicting wins in the coming season than either wins or points scored in the previous season (Table 2).

(Correlation coefficient is a statistical tool that measures how two variables are related by using a number between 1 and -1. The closer to -1 or 1, the stronger the relationship, but the closer to 0, the weaker the relationship.)

Table 1. Correlation of Various Stats to Wins, 2000-2011

Stat	Offense	Defense	Total
Points Scored/Allowed	.744	-.678	.917
DVOA	.696	-.496	.856
Yards Gained/Allowed	.560	-.421	.694
Yards Gained/Allowed per Play	.540	-.363	.728

Table 2. Correlation of Various Stats to Wins Following Year, 2000-2011

Stat	Correlation
DVOA	.374
Point Differential	.329
Pythagorean Wins	.324
Yards per Play Differential	.313
Wins	.290
Yardage Differential	.286

Defense-Adjusted Yards Above Replacement (DYAR)

DVOA is a good stat, but of course it is not a perfect one. One problem is that DVOA, by virtue of being a percentage or rate statistic, doesn't take into account the cumulative value of having a player producing at a league-average level over the course of an above-average number of plays. By definition, an average level of performance is better than that provided by half of the league and the ability to maintain that level of performance while carrying a heavy work load is very valuable indeed. In addition, a player who is involved in a high number of plays can draw the defense's attention away from other parts of the offense, and, if that player is a running back, he can take time off the clock with repeated runs.

Let's say you have a running back who carries the ball 300 times in a season. What would happen if you were to remove this player from his team's offense? What would happen to those 300 plays? Those plays don't disappear with the player, though some might be lost to the defense because of the associated loss of first downs. Rather those plays would have to be distributed among the remaining players in the offense, with the bulk of them being given to a replacement running back. This is where we arrive at the concept of replacement level, borrowed from our partners at Baseball Prospectus. When a player is removed from an offense, he is usually not replaced by a player of similar ability. Nearly every starting player in the NFL is a starter because he is better than the alternative. Those 300 plays will typically be given to a significantly worse player, someone who is the backup because he doesn't have as much experience and/or talent. A player's true value can then be measured by the level of performance he provides above that replacement level baseline, totaled over all of his run or pass attempts.

Of course, the *real* replacement player is different for each team in the NFL. Last year, the second-string running back in Washington (Roy Helu) had a higher DVOA than the original starter (Tim Hightower), and the third-string running back (Evan Royster) had a higher DVOA than either of them. Sometimes a player like Ryan Grant or Danny Woodhead will be cut by one team and turn into a star for another. On other teams, the drop from the starter to the backup can be even greater than the general drop to replacement level. The 2011 Indianapolis Colts will now be the hallmark example of this until the end of time. The choice to start an inferior player or to employ a sub-replacement level backup, however, falls to the team, not the starter being evaluated. Thus we generalize replacement level for the league as a whole as the ultimate goal is to evaluate players independent of the quality of their teammates.

Our estimates of replacement level are computed differently for each position. For quarterbacks, we analyzed situations where two or more quarterbacks had played meaningful snaps for a team in the same season, then compared the overall DVOA of the original starters to the overall DVOA of the replacements. We did not include situations where the backup was actually a top prospect waiting his turn on the bench, since a first-round pick is by no means a "replacement-level" player.

At other positions, there is no easy way to separate players into "starters" and "replacements," since unlike at quarterback, being the starter doesn't make you the only guy who gets in the game. Instead, we used a simpler method, ranking players at each position in each season by attempts. The players who made up the final 10 percent of passes or runs were split out as "replacement players" and then compared to the players making up the other 90 percent of plays at that position. This took care of the fact that not every non-starter at running back or wide receiver is a freely available talent. (Think of Jonathan Stewart or Randall Cobb, for example.)

As noted earlier, the challenge of any new stat is to present it on a scale that's meaningful to those attempting to use it. Saying that Tony Romo's passes were worth 131 success value points over replacement in 2011 has very little value without a context to tell us if 131 is good total or a bad one. Therefore, we translate these success values into a number called "Defense-adjusted Yards Above Replacement," or DYAR. Thus, Romo was fourth among quarterbacks with 1,344 passing DYAR. It is our estimate that a generic replacement-level quarterback, throwing in the same situations as Romo, would have been worth 1,344 fewer yards. Note that this doesn't mean the replacement level quarterback would have gained exactly 1,344 fewer yards. First downs, touchdowns, and turnovers all have an estimated yardage value in this system, so what we are saying is that a generic replacement-level quarterback would have fewer yards and touchdowns (and more turnovers) that would total up to be equivalent to the value of 1,344 yards.

One of the advantages of our new normalized DVOA v7.0 is an improvement to our measurement of player value compared to replacement level. The definition of replacement level now moves up and down in conjunction with our calculation of the league average. To give an example from last year, Jermaine Gresham in 2011 had a season which came very close to the baseline for tight ends. With our old method, this meant he had value above replacement level, 42 DYAR to be exact. However, tight ends had more success in 2011 than in any season we have tracked. The league-wide raw VOA for tight ends was 7.3%. Once we normalize, Gresham is now a below-average tight end, and in fact his total value comes in slightly below replacement level, at -8 DYAR. Because Gresham is targeted more than most other tight ends, this means his rank among tight ends in DYAR has dropped from 26th to 31st.

Problems with DVOA and DYAR

Football is a game in which nearly every action requires the work of two or more teammates—in fact, usually 11 teammates all working in unison. Unfortunately, when it comes to individual player ratings, we are still far from the point at which we can determine the value of a player independent from the performance of his teammates. That means that when we say, "In 2011, Matt Forte had a DVOA of -5.6%, what we are really saying is "In 2011, Matt Forte, playing in Mike Martz's offensive system with the Chicago offensive line blocking for him and Jay Cutler or Caleb Hanie selling the fake when necessary, had a DVOA of -5.6%."

DVOA is limited by what's included in the official NFL play-by-play or tracked by the Football Outsiders game charting project (introduced below). Because we need to have the entire play-by-play of a season in order to compute DVOA and DYAR, these metrics are not yet ready to compare players of today to players throughout the league's history. As of this writing, we have processed 21 seasons, 1991 through 2011, and we add seasons at a rate of roughly two per year (the most recent season, plus one season back into history.)

STATISTICAL TOOLBOX
Pythagorean Projection

The Pythagorean projection is an approximation of each team's wins based solely on their points scored and allowed. This basic concept was introduced by baseball analyst Bill James, who discovered that the record of a baseball team could be very closely approximated by taking the square of team runs scored and dividing it by the sum of the squares of team runs scored and allowed. Statistician Daryl Morey, now general manager of the Houston Rockets, later extended this theorem to professional football, refining the exponent to 2.37 rather than 2.

The problem with that exponent is the same problem we've had with DVOA in recent years: the changing offensive levels in the NFL. 2.37 worked great based on the league 20 years ago, but in the current NFL it ends up slightly underprojecting teams that play high-scoring games. The most accurate method is actually to adjust the exponent based on the scoring environment of each individual team. Saints games have a lot of points. Jaguars games feature fewer points.

This became known as Pythagenport when Clay Davenport of Baseball Prospectus started doing it with baseball teams. In the middle of the 2011 season, we switched our measurement of Pythagorean wins to a Pythagenport-style equation, modified for the NFL.[1] The improvement is slight, but noticeable with the high-scoring teams that have dominated the last few years. The projection for the 2011 Saints moves from 12.1 wins to 12.4 wins. The projection for the Packers moves from 11.9 wins to 12.2 wins. Losing teams in higher-scoring environments, in turn, will drop: Oakland goes from a projection of 6.3 wins to one of 6.1 wins. Overall, winning teams in higher scoring environments and losing teams in lower scoring environments get better projections, and teams with the opposite combinations see their projections drop.

Unfortunately, this improved Pythagorean projection system still can't do anything about last season's remarkable historical anomaly. The 2011 Giants are the first team in NFL history to make the Super Bowl, let alone win it, despite being outscored by opponents during the regular season. Since 1950, the Giants are only the third team in the four major American team sports to win a title despite being outscored during the regular season. (The others are the 1987 Minnesota Twins and the 1966-67 Toronto Maple Leafs; it has never happened in the NBA.)

For a long time, Pythagorean projections did a remarkable job of predicting Super Bowl champions. From 1984 through 2004, using our new formula, 10 of 21 Super Bowls were won by the team that led the NFL in Pythagorean wins. Seven other Super Bowls during that time were won by the team that finished second. Super Bowl champions that led the league in Pythagorean wins but not actual wins include the 2004 Patriots, 2000 Ravens, 1999 Rams, and 1997 Broncos.

From 2005 through 2008, as readers know, the results of the postseason did not quite look like the results of the regular season. As of 2004, the 1980 Oakland Raiders held the mark for the fewest Pythagorean wins by a Super Bowl champion, 9.7. The 2006 Colts broke that record, although just by a tiny decimal. The next year, the Giants shattered that record with 8.6 Pythagorean wins. The 2008 Cardinals didn't win the Super Bowl, but did set a record for conference champions with 8.0 Pythagorean wins.

For a couple of years, it looked like good ol' Pythagoras was reasserting himself. The 2009 Saints were second in the league in Pythagorean wins, and the Colts would have been first if Bill Polian hadn't pulled the plug on Peyton Manning midway through Week 16. In 2010, Green Bay and Pittsburgh were tied for second with 12.1 Pythagorean wins, behind New England at 12.6. For the Packers in particular, who lost six games by four points or less, Pythagorean wins were a more accurate portrayal of the team's postseason chances than their actual 10-6 record.

Then the 2011 Giants came along and shot that out of the water. The NFC was the clearly dominant conference last year, with the teams that finished 1-2-3 in Pythagorean wins (New Orleans, San Francisco, and Green Bay), but the NFC team that ended up winning it all was ranked 19th with 7.8 projected wins.

We don't know whether these last two Giants Super Bowl titles really say something about the usefulness of the Pythagorean projection when it comes to forecasting the postseason. Nonetheless, Pythagoras is also still a valuable predictor of year-to-year improvement. Teams that win a minimum of one full game more than their Pythagorean projection tend to regress the following year; teams that win a minimum of one

---

[1] The equation for the exponent for each team, for those curious, is $1.5 \times \log((PF+PA)/G)$.

full game less than their Pythagorean projection tend to improve the following year, particularly if they were at or above .500 despite their underachieving. For 2012, the team that clearly stands out in this fashion is Philadelphia, which had 9.8 Pythagorean wins but went just 8-8. On the other hand, three of the four AFC West teams (San Diego is the exception) had at least 1.9 more wins than their Pythagorean projection would otherwise suggest.[2]

Adjusted Line Yards

One of the most difficult goals of statistical analysis in football is isolating the degree to which each of the 22 men on the field is responsible for the result of a given play. Nowhere is this as significant as the running game, in which one player runs while up to nine other players—including wideouts, tight ends, and a fullback—block in different directions. None of the statistics we use for measuring rushing—yards, touchdowns, yards per carry—differentiate between the contribution of the running back and the contribution of the offensive line. Neither do our advanced metrics DVOA and DYAR.

We do, however, have enough play-by-play data amassed that we can try to separate the effect that the running back has on a particular play from the effects of the offensive line (and other offensive blockers) and the opposing defense. A team might have two running backs in its stable: RB A, who averages 3.0 yards per carry, and RB B, who averages 3.5 yards per carry. Who is the better back? Imagine that RB A doesn't just average 3.0 yards per carry, but gets exactly 3 yards on every single carry, while RB B has a highly variable yardage output: sometimes 5 yards, sometimes -2 yards, sometimes 20 yards. The difference in variability between the runners can be exploited not only to determine the difference between the runners, but the effect the offensive line has on every running play.

At some point in every long running play, the running back passes all of his offensive line blocks as well as additional blocking backs or receivers. From there on, the rest of the play is dependent on the runner's own speed and elusiveness and the speed and tackling ability of the opposing defense. If Frank Gore breaks through the line for 50 yards, avoiding tacklers all the way to the goal line, his offensive line has done a great job—but they aren't responsible for the majority of the yards gained. The trick is figuring out exactly how much they *are* responsible for.

For each running back carry, we calculated the probability that the back involved would run for the specific yardage on that play based on that back's average yardage per carry and the variability of their yardage from play to play. We also calculated the probability that the offense would get the yardage based on the team's rushing average and variability using all backs *other* than the one involved in the given play, and the probability that the defense would give up the specific amount of yardage based on its average rushing yards allowed per carry and variability. For example, based on his rushing average and variability, the probability in 2004 that Tiki Barber would have a positive carry was 80 percent while the probability that Giants would have a positive carry without Barber running was only 73 percent.

A regression analysis breaks the value for rushing yardage into the following categories: losses, 0-4 yards, 5-10 yards, and 11-plus yards. In general, the offensive line is 20 percent more responsible for lost yardage than it is for positive gains up to four yards, but 50 percent less responsible for additional yardage gained between five and ten yards, and not at all responsible for additional yardage past ten yards.

By applying those percentages to every running back carry, we were able to create **Adjusted Line Yards**, a statistic that measured offensive line performance. (We don't include carries by receivers, which are usually based on deception rather than straight blocking, or carries by quarterbacks, which are almost always busted passing plays unless they involve someone like Tim Tebow or Cam Newton.) Those numbers are then adjusted based on down, distance, situation, opponent and whether or not a team is in the shotgun. (Because defenses are generally playing pass when the quarterback is in shotgun, the average running back carry from shotgun last year gained 5.36 yards, compared to just 4.16 yards on other carries.) The adjusted numbers are then normalized so that the league average for Adjusted

---

[2] Perhaps the sentence earlier in this paragraph should have read "Teams that win a minimum of one full game more than their Pythagorean projection tend to regress the following year, unless they sign one of the five greatest quarterbacks who ever played professional football."

Line Yards per carry is the same as the league average for RB yards per carry (in 2011, 4.31 yards).

The NFL distinguishes between runs made to seven different locations on the line: left/right end, left/right tackle, left/right guard, and middle. Further research showed no statistically significant difference between how well a team performed on runs listed as having gone up the middle or past a guard, so we separated runs into just five different directions (left/right end, left/right tackle, and middle). Note that there may not be a statistically significant difference between right tackle and middle/guard either, but pending further research (and for the sake of symmetry) we still list runs behind the right tackle separately. These splits allow us to evaluate subsections of a team's offensive line, but not necessarily individual linemen, as we can't account for blocking assignments or guards who pull towards the opposite side of the line after the snap.

Success Rate

Success rate is a statistic for running backs that measures how consistently they achieve the yardage necessary for a play to be deemed successful. Some running backs will mix a few long runs with a lot of failed runs of one or two yards, while others with similar yards-per-carry averages will consistently gain five yards on first down, or as many yards as necessary on third down. This statistic helps us differentiate between the two.

Since Success Rate compares rush attempts to other rush attempts, without consideration of passing, the standard for success on first down is slightly lower than those described above for DVOA. In addition, the standard for success changes slightly in the fourth quarter when running backs are used to run out the clock. A team with the lead is satisfied with a shorter run as long as it stays in bounds. Conversely, for a team down by a couple of touchdowns in the fourth quarter, four yards on first down isn't going to be a big help.

The formula for Success Rate is as follows:

• A successful play must gain 40 percent of needed yards on first down, 60 percent of needed yards on second down, and 100 percent of needed yards on third or fourth down.

• If the offense is behind by more than a touchdown in the fourth quarter, the benchmarks switch to 50 percent, 65 percent, and 100 percent.

• If the offense is ahead by any amount in the fourth quarter, the benchmarks switch to 30 percent, 50 percent, and 100 percent.

The league-average Success Rate in 2010 was 46.4 percent. Success Rate is not adjusted based on defenses faced, and is not calculated for quarterbacks and wide receivers who occasionally carry the ball.

Similarity Scores

Similarity scores were first introduced by Bill James to compare baseball players to other baseball players from the past. It was only natural that the idea would spread to other sports as statistical analysis spread to other sports. NBA analyst John Hollinger has created his own version to compare basketball players, and we have created our own version to compare football players.

Similarity scores have a lot of uses, and we aren't the only football analysts who use them. Doug Drinen of the website Footballguys.com has his own system that is specific to comparing fantasy football performances. The major goal of our similarity scores is to compare career progressions to try to determine when players have a higher chance of a breakout, a decline, or—due to age or usage—an injury (much like Baseball Prospectus's PECOTA player projection system). Therefore we not only compare numbers such as attempts, yards, and touchdowns, but also age and experience. We often are looking not for players who had similar seasons, but for players who had similar two- or three-year spans in their careers.

Similarity scores have some important weaknesses. The database for player comparison begins in 1978, the year the 16-game season began and passing rules were liberalized (a reasonable starting point to measure the "modern" NFL), thus the method only compares standard statistics such as yards and attempts, which are of course subject to all kinds of biases from strength of schedule to quality of receiver corps. For our comparisons, we project full-season statistics for the strike years of 1982 and 1987, although we cannot correct for players who crossed the 1987 picket line to play more than 12 games.

In addition to our similarity scores for skill players, we also have a similarity score system for defensive players based on FO's advanced statistics going back to 1997. It measures things like average distance on run tackles or pass tackles, as well as Stops and Defeats. It does not account for game-charting stats like hurries or Success Rate in coverage.

If you are interested in the specific computations behind our similarity scores system, we have listed the standards for each skill position online at http://www.footballoutsiders.com/stats/similarity. (The defensive system is not yet listed.) In addition, as part of our online premium package, all player pages for current players—both offensive and defensive—list the top ten similar players over one-, two-, and three-year spans.

KUBIAK Projection System

Most "skill position" players whom we expect to play a role this season receive a projection of their standard 2012 NFL statistics using the KUBIAK projection system. KUBIAK takes into account a number of different factors including expected role, performance over the past two seasons, age, height, weight, historical comparables, and projected team performance on offense and defense. When we named our system KUBIAK, it was a play on the PECOTA system used by our partners at Baseball Prospectus—if they were going to name their system after a long-time eighties backup, we would name our system after a long-time eighties backup. Little did we know that Gary Kubiak would finally get a head coaching job the very next season. After some debate, we decided to keep the name, although discussing projections for Houston players can be a bit awkward.

To clear up a common misconception among our readers, KUBIAK projects individual player performances only, not teams.

2012 Win Projection System

In this book, each of the 32 NFL teams receives a **2012 Mean Projection** at the beginning of its chapter. These projections stem from three equations that forecast 2012 DVOA for offense, defense, and special teams based on a number of different factors including the previous two years of DVOA in various situations, improvement in the second half of 2011, recent draft history, coaching experience, injury history, specific coaching styles, and the combined tenure of the offensive line.

These three equations produce precise numbers representing the most likely outcome, but also produce a range of possibilities, used to determine the probability of each possible offensive, defensive, and special teams DVOA for each team. This is particularly important when projecting football teams, because with only 16 games in a season, a team's performance may vary wildly from its actual talent level due to a couple of random bounces of the ball or badly timed injuries. In addition, the economic structure of the NFL allows teams to make sudden jumps or drops in overall ability more often than in other sports.

This year's simulation works a bit differently from previous years. We used the range of DVOA possibilities to produce 1,000 different simulated seasons with 32 sets of DVOA ratings. We then plugged those season-long DVOA ratings into the same equation we use during the season to determine each team's likely remaining wins for our Playoff Odds Report. The simulation takes each season game-by-game, determining the home or road team's chance of winning each game based on the DVOA ratings of each team as well as home-field advantage, warm-weather or dome-stadium teams playing in the cold after November 1, and several other variables that can affect the outcome of each game. Then a random number between 0 and 100 determines whether the home or road team has won that game. Further tweaks adjust the simulation further to produce results closer to the historic distribution of wins in the NFL. While 8-8 is still more likely than any other record, historically more NFL teams end up with records between 2-14 and 4-12 or between 12-4 and 14-2 than you would otherwise expect from a normal distribution. We ran 1,000 simulations with each of the 1,000 sets of DVOA ratings, creating a million different simulations.

The resulting possible win totals are then separated into four categories:
- On the Clock (0-4 wins; NFL average 11%)
- Mediocrity (5-7 wins; NFL average 33%)
- Playoff Contender (8-10 wins; NFL average 38%)
- Super Bowl Contender (11+ wins; NFL average 19%)

The percentage given for each category is dependent not only on how good we project the team to be in 2012, but the level of variation possible in that projection, and the expected performance of the teams on the schedule. (Green Bay, Miami, and the New York Jets were teams with a high standard deviation in their DVOA projections; St. Louis, Arizona, and Washington had the lowest standard deviations.) In response to reader requests, we also list the mean projection for each team. We do not expect any teams to win the exact number of games in their mean projection, however—particularly since no team can win 0.8 of a game. This year, in addition, we are listing the odds that each team will make it to the postseason based on our simulation. The average team will make the playoffs in 37.5 percent of simulations.

A big thank you to Mike Harris for working on the season simulation, as Ben Alamar, who did the simulation in years past, was busy in his capacity as a consultant for the Oklahoma City Thunder.

Football Outsiders Game Charting Project

Each of the formulas listed above relies primarily on the play-by-play data published by the NFL. When we began to analyze the NFL, that was all that we had to work with. Just as a television broadcast has a color commentator who gives more detail to the facts related by the play-by-play announcer, so too we need some color commentary to provide contextual information that breathes life into these plain lines of numbers and text. The Football Outsiders Game Charting Project is our attempt to provide color for the simple play-by-play.

Providing color to 512 hours of football is a daunting task. To put it into perspective, there were more than 54,000 lines of play-by-play information in the 2011 NFL season and our goal is to add several layers of detail to nearly all of them. We recruited more than 50 volunteers to collectively chart each week's NFL games. Unfortunately, we have not in the past had access to the coaches' film the NFL provides to the 32 teams. That tape includes a sideline and end zone perspectives for each play, and shows all 22 players at all times, making it easier to see the cause-and-effect of certain actions taken on the field. Without access to coaches' film, we had to chart games using regular broadcast footage. Broadcast footage is not as definitive, but it served our purposes. In the end, we have data on nearly every play since 2005.

Through trial-and-error, we have narrowed our focus to charting things both traceable and definitive. We are limited by the camera angles on standard television broadcasts and the time constraints of our volunteers. Charting a game, and rewinding to make sure mistakes are minimized, can take two to three hours. More than a couple of these per week can be hazardous to one's marriage. Our goal was to provide comprehensive information while understanding that our charters were doing this on a volunteer basis.

We want to emphasize that all data from the charting project is unofficial. (For this reason, we will usually mention the charting project when using this data in comments later in the book.) Other sources for football statistics may keep their own measurements of yards after catch or how teams perform against the blitz. Our data will not necessarily match theirs. However, any other group that is publicly tracking this data is also working off the same television broadcast footage, and thus will run into the same issues of difficulty.

As you may know, the NFL has finally in 2012 decided to make the all-22 coaches' film available to the public. This is very exciting, and we have a lot of ideas about how this might improve our game charting. Unfortunately, those ideas are somewhat limited by our available time and monetary resources, and of course that kind of data isn't ready for this book anyway.

Football Outsiders has built our game charting project so that we are only tracking events, not rating players. We believe that it is not possible to grade player performance on a play without knowledge of the proper assignment or the coach's play call.

The Football Outsiders game charting project tracks the following information:

FORMATION/PERSONNEL: For each play, charters recorded the number of running backs, wide receivers, and tight ends. The formation was recorded in the moment prior to the snap. Therefore, it does not include any pre-snap motion. Formations have become more fluid in recent years, so these numbers should not be considered gospel. It can be hard to tell where to draw the distinction between an H-back and an offset fullback, or between a flex tight end and a slot receiver. We ask game charters to mark tight ends in the slot as tight ends, because defensive coordinators think of these players as flexed tight ends and assign coverage accordingly. Tight ends are only marked as wide receivers when they actually line up wide, outside the numbers. Charters were asked to specifically mark when a non-running back lined up in the backfield, or when a running back or tight end lined up wide.

Although game charters mark players based on where they line up in the formation, we know that defenses tend to think in terms of personnel, identifying players on the field by their listed position rather than where they lined up. When the offense sends its players onto the field, the defense has to decide on its personnel based solely on the identity of those players without knowing whether they will stand on the line of scrimmage or in the backfield. This year, for the first time, we went through our charting data from the last two seasons and also marked each play with the specific personnel package. Personnel packages were marked using the NFL standard of two digits, the first digit being the number of running backs and the second digit being the number of tight ends. To give an example, if the New England Patriots were to line up with Aaron Hernandez in the backfield, Rob Gronkowski and Danny Woodhead lined up wide, and Wes Welker and Deion Branch in the slot, our game charter would mark this as 1 RB / 0 TE / 4 WR, listing specifically that Hernandez was lined up as RB and that Gronkowski and Woodhead were lined up as WR. However, when we translate this into personnel, this comes out as "12" personnel, with one running back and two tight ends.

We'll specify below, but some figures which we previously reported based on formation are now based on personnel instead.

In 2011, for the first time, we also asked game charters to mark defensive formations by listing the number of linemen, linebackers, and defensive backs. There will be mistakes—a box safety may occasionally be confused for a linebacker, for example—but for the most part this data should be accurate. For the most part, we distinguished linemen from linebackers based on whether the player lined up with his hand on the ground before the snap. We did make an exception when defensive tackles stood up in an "everybody stand up to confuse the quarterback" style formation like Pittsburgh's "11 Angry Men." Linebackers were distinguished from defensive backs based on their listed roster position, so players like Bryan Scott and Deon Grant were always listed as defensive backs (barring a charter error). Players not on the screen were always assumed to be defensive backs.

RUSHERS AND BLOCKERS: Blitz is a rather ubiquitous word in football, and a standard definition is difficult to nail down. Rather than asking charters to determine when a team was blitzing, we asked them to record the number of blockers and rushers on passing plays. Counting rushers was easy, but counting blockers proved to be an art as much as a science. Offenses base their blocking schemes on how many rushers they expect. A running back or tight end's assignment may depend on how many pass-rushers cross the line at the snap. Therefore, an offensive player was deemed to be a blocker if he engaged in an actual block, or there was some hesitation before running a route. A running back that immediately heads out into the flat is not a blocker, but one who waits to verify that the blocking scheme is working and then goes out to the flat would, in fact, be considered a blocker.

We also ask charters to mark down when a defense used a "zone blitz." This was originally defined as any play where at least one down lineman dropped into pass coverage while at least one linebacker or defensive back rushed the passer. In 2009, we expanded the definition of zone blitz to also include plays where a 3-4 defense dropped both outside linebackers into coverage while an inside linebacker or defensive back rushed the passer. Note that this definition of zone blitz isn't entirely accurate, as it isn't actually dependent on whether the defense is playing zone coverage behind the pass rush. We are considering a new term for tracking these plays in the future.

QUARTERBACK ACTION: In passing situations, the charters recorded the movement of the quarterback. This consisted of three items:
• Marking plays which began with a play-action fake, including a fake end-around or a flea flicker.
• Marking when the quarterback left the pocket. Charters marked rollouts and bootlegs. (A rollout has the quarterback moving behind his blockers, while a bootleg has the quarterback moving one way and his blockers the other, usually in connection with a play-action fake.) Charters also marked when a quarterback run past the line of scrimmage was a sneak, a draw, or a scramble. We asked the charters to differentiate between designed runs and plays on which the quarterback originally intended to pass, although this is often a judgment call.
• Marking a defender with a "hurry" if he clearly caused the quarterback to rush his motion or leave the pocket after originally setting up in the pocket to throw. We have asked charters to think of hurries from the defensive perspective more than the offensive, so if the quarterback stood tall and delivered the pass with defenders in his face, this counted as a hurry. However, defenders are coming towards the quarterback from behind and he does not see them, that is not a hurry. Charters were allowed to list two names if necessary, and could also attribute a hurry to Overall Pressure. In addition, if the quarterback wasn't under pressure but ran anyway, the play could be marked either as Coverage Scramble (if the quarterback ran because there were no open receivers) or Hole Opens Up (if the quarterback ran because he knew he could gain significant yardage).

STATISTICAL TOOLBOX

PASS DETAILS: We divided all pass yardage into two numbers: distance in the air and yards after catch. You will see much of this information throughout the team chapters and in each of the individual player tables. Distance in the air was based on the distance from the line of scrimmage to the place where the receiver either caught or was supposed to catch the pass. We did not count how far the quarterback was behind the line or horizontal yardage if the quarterback threw across the field. All touchdowns were counted to the goal line, so that distance in the air added to yards after catch always equals the official yardage total kept by the league. Charters also marked screen passes and tried to differentiate between passes to running backs that were standard pass routes, swing passes, or dumpoffs.

DEFENDERS: The NFL play-by-play lists tackles and, occasionally, tipped balls, but it does not definitively list the defender on the play. Charters were asked to determine which defender was primarily responsible for covering either the receiver at the time of the throw or the location to which the pass was thrown, regardless of whether the pass was complete or not.

Every defense in the league plays zone coverage at times, some more than others, which leaves us with the question of how to handle plays without a clear man assigned to that receiver. We gave charters three alternatives:

• We asked charters to mark passes that found the holes in zone coverage as Hole in Zone, rather than straining to assign that pass to an individual defender. We asked the charter to also note the player who appeared to be responsible for that zone, and these defenders are assigned half credit for those passes. Some holes were so large that no defender could be listed along with the Hole in Zone designation.

• Charters were free to list two defenders instead of one. This could be used for actual double coverage, or for zone coverage in which the receiver was right between two close defenders rather than sitting in a gaping hole. When two defenders are listed, ratings assign each with half credit.

• Screen passes and dumpoffs are marked as Uncovered unless a defender (normally a linebacker) is obviously shadowing that specific receiver on the other side of the line of scrimmage.

Since we began the charting project in 2005, nothing has changed our analysis more than this information on pass coverage. However, we want to be upfront: It was often the most difficult information to chart.

Broadcast camera angles often do not show the setup of the secondary, making it impossible to identify before the play if there is man coverage. On passes longer than a few yards, the camera won't show the receiver until the pass is in the air. The sideline view of network cameras makes seeing the specific numbers on some jerseys difficult. (At this point, we would like to give a big shout out to all the defensive backs with dreadlocks that come out of their helmets, making them easier to identify.) Zone coverage makes things even twice as difficult. That being said, reviewing tape kept mistakes to a minimum and, if two cornerbacks might have been confused for one other once or twice, such mistakes tend to cancel out.

INCOMPLETE PASSES: Quarterbacks are evaluated based on their ability to complete passes. However, not all incompletes should have the same weight. Throwing a ball away to avoid a sack is actually a valuable incomplete, and a receiver dropping an otherwise quality pass is hardly a reflection on the quarterback. Therefore, our charters marked the reason for every incomplete pass. Possible entries included Overthrown, Underthrown, Thrown Away, Tipped/ Batted at Line, Hit in Motion (indicating the quarterback was hit as his arm was coming forward to make a pass), Defensed, Dropped, and a few others. Defensed was listed when the pass was incomplete as the direct result of actions by the defender. That action can include balls tipped or batted in coverage or hard hits that jar a ball loose. We also ask charters to track dropped interceptions by defenders.

(Note: Our count of passes defensed will be different from the unofficial totals kept by the league, as explained below in the section on Defensive Secondary tables.)

ADDITIONAL DETAILS: Charters marked each quarterback sack with one of the following terms: Blown Block, Coverage Sack, QB Fault, or Blitz/Overall Pressure. Blown Blocks were listed with the name of a specific offensive player who allowed the defender to come through. Coverage Sack denotes when the quarterback has plenty of time to throw but cannot find an open receiver. QB Fault represents "self sacks" listed without a defender, such as when the quarterback drops back, only to find the ball slip out of his hands with no pass-rusher touching him.

All draw plays were marked, whether by halfbacks or quarterbacks.

"Broken tackles" are tracked on all runs or pass plays. We define a "broken tackle" as one of two events: Either the ballcarrier escapes from the grasp of the defender, or the defender is in good position for a tackle but the ballcarrier jukes him out of his shoes. If the ballcarrier sped by a slow defender who dived and missed, that did not count as a broken tackle. If the defender couldn't bring the ballcarrier down but slowed him and still had his hand on him when another player made a tackle, this did not count as a broken tackle. It was possible to mark multiple broken tackles on the same play. Occasionally, the same defender would get a broken tackle, then recover, run upfield, and get a tackle on the same play, but we went through after the season to make sure no charter marked a broken tackle for contact that the league determined was an actual tackle.

Beginning in 2010, we tracked which defensive players drew the most offensive holding calls. This year, Cameron Wake led the league with 13; a list of the defenders who drew the most flags can be found in the appendix.

An additional column called Extra Comment allowed the charters to add any description they wanted to the play. These comments might be good blitz pickup by a running back, a missed tackle, a great hit, a description of a pass route, an angry tirade about the poor camera angles of network broadcasts, or a number of other possibilities.

Finally, we asked the game charters to mark when a mistake was made in the official play-by-play. These mistakes include missing quarterback hits, incorrect names on tackles or penalties, missing direction on runs or passes, or the absence of the "scramble" designation when a quarterback ran on a play that began as a pass. Thanks to the diligence of our volunteer game charters and a friendly contact at the league office, the NFL corrected more than 300 mistakes in the official play-by-play based on the data collected by our game charters.

SACK TIMING PROJECT: Separate from the regular game charting project is J.J. Cooper's sack timing project, which began as a series of columns for AOL Fanhouse in 2009-2010 and continued with Football Outsiders in 2011. Cooper has timed every sack in the NFL from the time of the snap to the time of initial contact on the sack. The median sack time is roughly 2.8 seconds. The project also assigns blame for blown blocks that lead to sacks or designates a sack as "QB/Play Call," roughly akin to when the regular game charting project designates a sack as "Rusher Untouched" or "QB Fault."

ACKNOWLEDGEMENTS: None of this would have been possible without the time spent by all the volunteer game charters. There are some specific acknowledgements at the end of the book, but we want to give a general thank you here to everyone who has helped collect data over the last few seasons. Without your unpaid time, the task of gathering all this information would have been too time-consuming to yield anything useful. If you are interested in participating in next year's charting project, please e-mail your contact information to info@footballoutsiders.com with the subject "Game Charting Project." Please make sure to mention where you live, what team you follow, and whether or not you have the Sunday Ticket package.

How to Read the Team Summary Box

Here is a rundown of all the tables and stats that appear in the 32 team chapters. Each team chapter begins with a box in the upper-right hand corner that gives a summary of our statistics for that team, as follows:

2011 Record gives each team's actual win-loss record. **Pythagorean Wins** gives the approximate number of wins expected last year based on this team's raw totals of points scored and allowed, along with their NFL rank. **DVOA** gives the team's total DVOA rating, with rank. **Offense**, **Defense**, and **Special Teams** list the team's DVOA rating in each category, along with NFL rank. Remember that good offenses and special teams have positive DVOA numbers, while a negative DVOA means better defense, so the lowest defensive DVOA is ranked number one (last year, Baltimore).

Variance measures a team's consistency over the 2011 season. Teams are ranked from most consistent (Atlanta, first) to least consistent (Buffalo, 32nd).

2012 Mean Projection gives the average number of wins for this team based on the 2012 Win Projection System described earlier in this chapter. The next few lines give the team's chances of finishing in the four different win categories and odds of making the postseason.

Projected Average Opponent gives the team's strength of schedule for 2012 based not on last year's record but on the mean projected DVOA for each opponent. A positive schedule is harder, a negative schedule easier. Teams are ranked from the hardest projected schedule (Denver, first) to the easiest (Chicago, 32nd). This strength of schedule projection does not take into account which games are home and which are away, or the timing of the bye week.

You'll also find a table with the team's 2012 schedule placed within each chapter, along with a graph showing each team's week-to-week performance by single-game DVOA. The second, dotted line on the graph represents a five-week moving average of each team's performance, in order to show a longer-term view of when they were improving and declining. After the essays come statistical tables and comments related to that team and its specific units.

Weekly Performance

The first table gives a quick look at the team's week-to-week performance in 2011. (Table 3) This includes the playoffs for those teams that made the postseason, with the four weeks of playoffs numbered 18 (wild card) through 21 (Super Bowl). All other tables in the team chapters represent regular-season performance only unless otherwise noted.

Looking at the first week for the Philadelphia Eagles in 2011, the first five columns are fairly obvious: the Eagles beat St. Louis, 31-13. **YDF** and **YDA** are net yards on offense and net yards against the defense. These numbers do not include penalty yardage or special teams yardage. **TO** represents the turnover margin. Unlike other parts of the book in which we consider all fumbles as equal, this only represents actual turnovers: fumbles lost and interceptions. So, for example, the Eagles had forced two more turnovers than Washington did in Week 6, but had one more turnover than Washington in the Week 17 rematch.

Finally, you'll see DVOA ratings for this game: Total **DVOA** first, then offense (**Off**), defense (**Def**), and special teams (**ST**). Note that these are DVOA ratings, adjusted for opponent, so the Eagles are listed with a higher DVOA for their close loss to the playoff-bound Falcons in Week 2 than they are for their win over the Rams in Week 1.

Trends and Splits

Next to the week-to-week performance is a table giving DVOA for different portions of a team's performance, on both offense and defense. Each split is listed with the team's rank among the 32 NFL teams. These numbers represent regular season performance only.

Total DVOA gives total offensive, and defensive DVOA in all situations. **Unadjusted VOA** represents the breakdown of play-by-play considering situation but not opponent. A team whose offensive DVOA is higher than its offensive VOA played a harder-than-average schedule of opposing defenses; a team with a lower defensive DVOA than defensive VOA player a harder-than-average schedule of opposing offenses.

Weighted Trend lowers the importance of earlier games to give a better idea of how the team was playing at the end of the regular season. The final four weeks of the season are full strength; moving backwards through the season, each week is given less and less weight until the first three weeks of the season, which are not included at all. **Variance** is the same as noted above, with a higher percentage representing less consistency. This is true for both offense and defense: Jacksonville, for example, was very consistent on offense (3.6% variance, fifth) but one of the league's *least* consistent defenses (10.0% variance, which ranked 30th).

Passing and **Rushing** are fairly self-explanatory. Note that rushing includes all rushes, not just those by running backs, including quarterback scrambles that may have began as pass plays.

The next three lines split out DVOA on **First Down**, **Second Down**, and **Third Down**. Third Down here includes fourth downs on which a team runs a regular offensive play instead of punting or attempting a field goal. **First Half** and **Second Half** represent the first two quarters and last two quarters (plus overtime), not the first eight and last eight games of the regular sea-

Table 3: 2011 Eagles Stats by Week

Wk	vs.	W-L	PF	PA	YDF	YDA	TO	Total	Off	Def	ST
1	@STL	W	31	13	403	335	0	11%	24%	11%	-2%
2	@ATL	L	31	35	447	318	-1	19%	19%	-4%	-4%
3	NYG	L	16	29	376	334	-3	-46%	-25%	25%	4%
4	SF	L	23	24	513	442	-2	-9%	37%	33%	-13%
5	@BUF	L	24	31	489	331	-4	-6%	-7%	2%	3%
6	@WAS	W	20	13	422	287	2	33%	-1%	-29%	5%
7	BYE										
8	DAL	W	34	7	495	267	1	71%	45%	-30%	-4%
9	CHI	L	24	30	330	372	0	-7%	21%	30%	1%
10	ARI	L	17	21	289	370	0	-14%	-27%	-6%	7%
11	@NYG	W	17	10	391	278	-1	52%	-10%	-50%	12%
12	NE	L	20	38	466	457	-1	-25%	-1%	25%	1%
13	@SEA	L	14	31	330	347	-4	-42%	-9%	41%	8%
14	@MIA	W	26	10	239	204	1	26%	-19%	-62%	-17%
15	NYJ	W	45	19	420	241	0	95%	56%	-48%	-10%
16	@DAL	W	20	7	386	238	-1	46%	25%	-28%	-7%
17	@WAS	W	34	10	390	377	-1	47%	44%	15%	18%

son. Next comes DVOA in the **Red Zone**, which is any offensive play starting from the defense's 20-yard line through the goal line. The final split is **Late and Close**, which includes any play in the second half or overtime when the teams are within eight points of each other in either direction. (Eight points, of course, is the biggest deficit that can be made up with a single score, a touchdown and two-point conversion.)

Five-Year Performance

This table gives each team's performance over the past five seasons. (Table 4) It includes win-loss record, Pythagorean Wins, **Estimated Wins**, points scored and allowed, and turnover margin. Estimated wins are based on a formula that estimates how many games a team would have been expected to win based on 2011 performance in specific situations, normalized to eliminate luck (fumble recoveries, opponents' missed field goals, etc.) and assuming average schedule strength. The formula emphasizes consistency and overall DVOA as well as DVOA in a few specifically important situations. The next columns of this table give total DVOA along with DVOA for offense, defense, and special teams, and the rank for each among that season's 32 NFL teams.

The final four columns give the Adjusted Games Lost for starters on both offense and defense. (Our total for starters here includes players who take over as starters due to another injury, such as Matt Leinart or Dan Connolly last year, as well as important situational players who may not necessarily start, such as pass-rush specialists and slot receivers.) Adjusted Games Lost was introduced in *Pro Football Prospectus 2008*; it gives a weighted estimate of the probability that players would miss games based on how they are listed on the injury report. Unlike a count of "starter games missed," this accounts for the fact that a player listed as questionable who does in fact play is not playing at 100 percent capability. Teams are ranked from the fewest injuries (2011: Baltimore on offense, New Orleans on defense) to the most (2011: St. Louis on offense, Carolina on defense).

Individual Offensive Statistics

Each team chapter contains a table giving passing and receiving numbers for any player who either threw five passes or was thrown five passes, along with rushing numbers for any players who carried the ball at least three times. These numbers also appear in the player comments at the end of the book (except for wide receiver rushing attempts). By putting them together in the team chapters we hope we make it easier to compare the performances of different players on the same team.

Players who are no longer on the team are marked with an asterisk. New players who were on a different team in 2011 are in italics. Changes should be accurate through at least June 15. Rookies are not included.

All players are listed with DYAR and DVOA. Passing statistics then list total pass plays (**Plays**), net yardage (**NtYds**), and net yards per pass (**Avg**). These numbers include not just passes (and the positive yardage from them) but aborted snaps and sacks (and the negative yardage from them). Then comes average yards after catch (**YAC**), as determined by the game charting project. This average is based on charted receptions, not total pass attempts. The final three numbers are completion percentage (**C%**), passing touchdowns (**TD**), and interceptions (**Int**).

It is important to note that the tables in the team chapters contain Football Outsiders stats, while the tables in the player comments later in the book contain official NFL totals, at least when it comes to standard numbers like receptions and yardage. This results in a number of differences between the two:

• Team chapter tables list yardage from Defensive Pass Interference; in the player comments, Defensive

Table 4: Detroit Lions' Five-Year Performance

Year	W-L	Pyth	Est W	PF	PA	TO	Total	Rk	Off	Rk	Def	Rk	ST	Rk	Off AGL	Rk	Def AGL	Rk
2007	7-9	5.5	4.9	346	444	-1	-29.0%	29	-10.3%	24	15.2%	32	-3.5%	23	24.5	23	4.7	2
2008	0-16	2.5	2.1	268	517	-9	-48.4%	32	-25.3%	30	24.3%	32	1.3%	15	44.3	27	60.7	32
2009	2-14	2.7	0.0	262	494	-18	-51.6%	32	-28.4%	31	17.9%	32	-5.3%	31	20.4	14	55.1	31
2010	6-10	7.8	7.5	362	369	+4	-1.1%	18	-0.8%	19	2.9%	22	2.6%	11	26.6	16	24.4	17
2011	10-6	10.1	9.4	474	387	+11	10.1%	11	7.1%	10	-8.1%	9	-5.1%	29	13.3	4	14.8	8

STATISTICAL TOOLBOX

Pass Interference is reflected in DVOA and DYAR but not listed in yardage.

- Team chapter tables listed aborted snaps as passes, not runs, although aborted handoffs are still listed as runs. Net yardage for quarterbacks in the team chapter tables includes the lost yardage from aborted snaps, sacks, and intentional grounding penalties.
- Football Outsiders stats omit kneeldowns from run totals and clock-stopping spikes from pass totals.
- In the Football Outsiders stats, we have changed a number of lateral passes to count as passes rather than runs, under the theory that a pass play is still a pass play, even if the receiver is standing five inches behind the quarterback. This results in some small differences in totals. For example, Ryan Fitzpatrick and C.J. Spiller are each listed with an additional 18 yards due to a Week 2 screen pass that was scored by the league as a lateral.

Table 5: Miami Dolphins' Passing

Player	DYAR	DVOA	Plays	NtYds	Avg	YAC	C%	TD	Int
M.Moore	135	-5.7%	388	2266	6.0	4.1	60.6%	16	9
C.Henne*	67	-2.7%	123	801	6.8	5.2	57.1%	4	4
J.P.Losman*	-66	-96.0%	15	22	1.5	3.8	60.0%	0	0

Rushing statistics start with DYAR and DVOA, then list rushing plays and net yards along with average yards per carry and rushing touchdowns. The final two columns are fumbles (**Fum**)—both those lost to the defense and those recovered by the offense—and Success Rate (**Suc**), explained earlier in this chapter. Fumbles listed in the rushing table include all quarterback fumbles on sacks and aborted snaps, as well as running back fumbles on receptions, but not wide receiver fumbles.

Table 6: Oakland Raiders' Rushing

Player	DYAR	DVOA	Plays	Yds	Avg	TD	Fum	Suc
M.Bush*	65	-2.7%	256	980	3.8	7	1	45%
D.McFadden	87	11.6%	113	616	5.5	4	1	44%
M.Reece	38	45.2%	17	112	6.6	0	0	59%
T.Jones	3	-1.6%	16	73	4.6	0	0	38%
J.Campbell*	-6	-19.1%	13	67	5.2	2	2	--
C.Palmer	-16	-32.1%	12	22	1.8	1	0	--
K.Boller	-14	-45.7%	7	34	4.9	0	1	--
L.Murphy	52	133.6%	6	69	11.5	1	0	--
D.Moore	43	164.7%	5	61	12.2	1	0	--

Receiving statistics start with DYAR and DVOA and then list the number of passes thrown to this receiver (**Plays**), the number of passes caught (**Catch**) and the total receiving yards (**Yds**). Yards per catch (**Y/C**) includes total yardage per reception, based on standard play-by-play, while yards after catch (**YAC**) is based on information from our game charting project. Finally we list total receiving touchdowns, and catch percentage (**C%**), which is the percentage of passes intended for this receiver which were caught. Wide receivers, tight ends, and running backs are separated on the table by horizontal lines.

Table 7: Indianapolis Colts' Receiving

Player	DYAR	DVOA	Plays	Ctch	Yds	Y/C	YAC	TD	C%
P.Garcon*	-48	-17.1%	134	70	950	13.6	5.1	6	52%
R.Wayne	143	1.2%	131	75	960	12.8	3.7	4	57%
A.Collie	-9	-13.8%	97	54	514	9.5	3.9	1	56%
D.Avery	10	-2.6%	11	3	45	15.0	7.0	1	27%
D.Clark*	-84	-25.5%	65	34	352	10.4	4.4	2	52%
J.Tamme*	-29	-20.8%	31	19	177	9.3	4.8	1	61%
B.Eldridge	-12	-24.1%	10	9	45	5.0	1.7	0	90%
J.Addai*	-6	-19.3%	22	15	93	6.2	6.8	0	68%
D.Brown	-6	-19.8%	19	16	86	5.4	5.9	0	84%
D.Carter	-30	-79.3%	8	5	18	3.6	6.8	0	63%
J.Felton*	8	6.6%	7	4	40	10.0	7.3	0	57%

Performance Based on Personnel

These tables provide a look at performance in 2011 based on personnel packages, as defined above in the section on marking formation/personnel as part of the Football Outsiders game charting project. There are four different tables, representing:

- Offense based on personnel
- Offense based on opponent's defensive personnel
- Defense based on personnel
- Defense based on opponent's offensive personnel

Most of these tables feature the top five personnel groupings for each team. Occasionally, we will list the personnel group which ranks sixth if the sixth group is either particularly interesting or nearly as common as the fifth group. Each personnel group is listed with its frequency among 2011 plays, yards per play, and DVOA. Offensive personnel are also listed with how often the team in question called a running play instead of a pass play from given personnel. (Quarterback scrambles are included as pass plays, not runs.)

Offensive personnel are given in the standard two-digit format where the first digit is running backs and the second digit is tight ends. You can figure out wide receivers by subtracting that total from five, with a couple of exceptions. Plays with six or seven offensive linemen will have a three-digit listing such as "611" or "622." Any play with a direct snap to a non-quarterback, or with a specific running quarterback taking the snap instead of the regular quarterback, was counted as "Wildcat." Surprisingly given its popularity only a couple years ago, no team ends up with Wildcat listed among its top five offensive personnel groups.

When defensive players come in to play offense, defensive backs are counted as wide receivers, linebackers as tight ends, and defensive linemen as offensive linemen, even if they are blocking fullbacks.

Defensive personnel are listed in the format "4-3-4," where the first number is defensive linemen, the second number is linebackers, and the third number is defensive backs. All personnel groups with at least six defensive backs are grouped together under the heading "Dime+" *except* on the table for the New York Jets, where formations with seven defensive backs are listed separately as "Quarter." In addition, except for 4-4-3 and 3-5-3, all personnel groups with fewer than four defensive backs are combined and listed as "G-Line."

You'll find a table listing all personnel groups on the bottom of this page, along with league-wide performance in 2011.

Strategic Tendencies

The Strategic Tendencies table presents a mix of information garnered from both the standard play by play and the Football Outsiders game charting project. It gives you an idea of what kind of plays teams run in what situations and with what personnel. Each category is given a league-wide **Rank** from most often (1) to least often (32) except as noted below. The sample table shown on the next page lists the NFL average in each category for 2011.

The first column of strategic tendencies lists how often teams ran in different situations. These ratios are based on the type of play, not the actual result, so quarterback scrambles count as "passes" while quarterback sneaks and draws count as "runs."

The first three entries are self-evident: **Runs** on **all plays**, in the **first half**, and on **first down**. **Runs, second-and-long** is the percentage of runs on second down with seven or more yards to go, giving you an idea of how teams follow up a failed first down. **Runs, power situations** is the percentage of runs on third or fourth down with 1 or 2 yards to go, or at the goal line with 1 or 2 yards to go. **Runs, behind 2H** tells you how

Table 8: NFL Performance by Offensive Personnel, 2011

Personnel	Freq	Yds	DVOA	Run%
11	40.4%	5.8	5.5%	24%
12	20.9%	5.7	6.8%	45%
21	16.8%	5.7	5.9%	59%
22	7.0%	4.4	-9.0%	77%
10	3.2%	6.4	10.5%	12%
20	2.3%	5.8	-4.8%	31%
13	2.3%	5.0	-3.0%	62%
01	1.4%	5.7	5.2%	6%
02	1.2%	7.0	45.0%	9%
611	1.0%	6.3	6.0%	59%
621	0.6%	3.7	-13.1%	81%
622	0.6%	0.8	8.3%	79%
612	0.6%	4.8	13.5%	77%
Other 6/7 OL	0.4%	3.2	4.7%	73%
23	0.3%	0.6	11.4%	71%
Wildcat	0.3%	4.2	-4.7%	92%
All 3RB Sets	0.2%	4.6	22.2%	69%
00	0.2%	5.2	14.9%	2%
620	0.2%	4.1	-2.4%	76%
Unknown	0.2%	4.6	6.5%	65%
03/04	0.1%	8.5	-30.3%	13%

Table 9: NFL Performance by Defensive Personnel, 2011

Personnel	Freq	Yds	DVOA
4-3-4	30.5%	5.4	-0.1%
4-2-5	25.2%	5.8	1.1%
3-4-4	17.0%	5.4	-1.4%
Dime+	10.3%	6.4	4.1%
3-3-5	8.1%	5.9	2.3%
2-4-5	6.5%	5.7	-1.1%
Goal Line	1.3%	0.9	-4.8%
4-4-3	0.6%	3.2	-19.4%
5-2-4	0.2%	2.7	-14.0%
10 Men/Unknown	0.2%	3.7	-5.9%
1-5-5	0.1%	5.2	-44.6%
5-1-5	0.1%	3.9	-41.8%
3-5-3	0.0%	1.9	-58.8%
2-5-4	0.0%	3.5	-40.5%

STATISTICAL TOOLBOX

Table 10: League Average Strategic Tendencies

Run/Pass		Rank	Offense		Rank	Pass Rush		Rank	Defense/Other		Rank
Runs, all plays	42%	16	Form: Single Back	63%	16	Rush 3	7.3%	16	4 DB	48%	16
Runs, first half	42%	16	Form: Empty Back	6%	16	Rush 4	62.3%	16	5 DB	40%	16
Runs, first down	51%	16	Pers: 3+ WR	49%	16	Rush 5	21.9%	16	6+ DB	10%	16
Runs, second-long	36%	16	Pers: 4+ WR	5%	16	Rush 6+	8.5%	16	CB by Sides	78%	16
Runs, power sit.	58%	16	Pers: 2+ TE/6+ OL	35%	16	Zone Blitz	5.5%	16	Go for it on 4th	0.92	16
Runs, behind 2H	31%	16	Play action	19%	16	Sacks by LB	34.1%	16	Offensive Pace	30.5	16
Pass, ahead 2H	43%	16	Max protect	11%	16	Sacks by DB	8.2%	16	Defensive Pace	30.5	16

often teams ran when they were behind in the second half, generally a passing situation. **Pass, ahead 2H** tells you how often teams passed when they had the lead in the second half, generally a running situation.

In each case, you can determine the percentage of plays that were passes by subtracting the run percentage from 100 (the reverse being true for "Pass, ahead 2H," of course).

The second column gives information about offensive formations, personnel, and strategy, as tracked by our game charters.

The first two entries detail formation, i.e. where players were lined up on the field. **Form: Single Back** lists how often the team lined up with only one player in the backfield, and **Form: Empty Back** lists how often the team lined up with no players in the backfield.

The next three entries were based on formation in previous books, but are now based on personnel. This means that players like Aaron Hernandez and Jimmy Graham are marked as tight ends no matter where they have lined up in the formation. **Pers: 3+ WR** marks how often the team plays with three or more wide receivers. **Pers: 4+ WR** marks how often the team plays with four or more wide receivers. (Although announcers will often refer to a play as "five-wide," formations with five wide receivers are actually quite uncommon.) **Pers: 2+ TE/6+ OL** marks how often the team plays with either more than one tight end or more than five offensive linemen.

Play action: The percentage of pass plays (including quarterback scrambles) which began with a play-action fake to the running back. This percentage does not include fake end-arounds unless there was also a fake handoff. It does include flea flickers.

Max protect: The percentage of this team's passing plays (including quarterback scrambles) on which blockers outnumber pass rushers by at least two, with a minimum of seven blockers.

The third column shows how the defensive **Pass Rush** worked in 2011.

Rush 3/Rush 4/Rush 5/Rush 6+: The percentage of pass plays (including quarterback scrambles) on which our game charters recorded this team rushing the passer with three or fewer defenders, four defenders, five defenders, and six or more defenders. These percentages do not include goal-line plays on the one- or two-yard line.

Zone blitz: The percentage of pass plays where this defense ran a zone blitz, as defined earlier in this chapter.

Sacks by LB/Sacks by DB: The percentage of this team's sacks that came from linebackers and defensive backs. To figure out the percentage of sacks from defensive linemen, simply subtract the sum of these numbers from 100 percent.

The fourth column has more data on defensive backs and coaching styles.

4 DB/5 DB/6+ DB: The percentage of plays where this defense lined up with four, five, and six or more defensive backs.

CB by Sides: One of the most important lessons from game charting is that each team's best cornerback does not necessarily match up against the opponent's best receiver. Most cornerbacks play a particular side of the field and in fact cover a wider range of receivers than we assumed before we saw the charting data. This metric looks at which teams prefer to leave their starting cornerbacks on specific sides of the field. It replaces a metric from previous books called "CB1 on WR1," which looked at the same question but through the lens of how often the top cornerback covered the opponent's top receiver.

To figure CB by Sides, we took the top two cornerbacks from each team and looked at the percentage of passes where that cornerback was in coverage on the left or right side of the field, ignoring passes marked as "middle." For each of the two cornerbacks, we took the higher number, right or left, and then we averaged the two cornerbacks to get the final CB by Sides rating. Teams which prefer to leave their cornerbacks in the same place, such as Seattle, Atlanta, and Philadelphia, will have high ratings. Teams that do more to move their best cornerback around to cover the opponent's top targets, such as Arizona and the two New York teams, will have low ratings.

Go for it on fourth: This is the aggressiveness index (AI) introduced by Jim Armstrong in *Pro Football Prospectus 2006*, which measures how often a team goes for a first down in various fourth-down situations compared to the league average. A coach over 1.00 is more aggressive, and one below 1.00 is less aggressive. Coaches are ranked from most aggressive to least aggressive. Contrary to popular wisdom, coaches on the whole have actually been less aggressive in recent seasons than they were five or six years ago, so the average Aggressiveness Index for 2011 was below 1.00, at 0.92.

Offensive Pace: Situation-neutral pace represents the seconds of game clock per offensive play, with the following restrictions: no drives are included if they start in the fourth quarter or final five minutes of the first half, and drives are only included if the score is within six points or less. Teams are ranked from quickest pace (New England, 26.4 seconds) to slowest pace (Tampa Bay, 33.5 seconds).

Defensive Pace: Situation-neutral pace based on seconds of game clock per defensive play. This is a representation of how a defense was approached by its opponents, not the strategy of the defense itself (an issue discussed in the Indianapolis chapter of *PFP 2006*). Teams are ranked from quickest pace (Pittsburgh, 28.6 seconds) to slowest pace (San Diego, 31.6 seconds).

Following each strategic tendencies table, you'll find a series of comments highlighting interesting data from that team's charting numbers. This includes DVOA ratings split for things like different formations, draw plays, or play-action passing. Please note that all DVOA ratings given in these comments are standard DVOA with no adjustments for the specific situation being analyzed, and the average DVOA for a specific situation will not necessarily be 0%. For example, the average offensive DVOA on play-action passes in 2011 was 19.6%. The average offensive DVOA when the quarterback was hurried was -80.6%; if we remove sacks, scrambles, and intentional grounding and only look at actual passes, the average offensive DVOA was -14.1%.

How to Read the Offensive Line Tables

The offensive line tables list the last three years of Adjusted Line Yards and other statistics for each team (Table 11).

The first column gives standard yards per carry by each team's running backs (**Yds**). The next two columns give Adjusted Line Yards (**ALY**) followed by rank among the 32 teams.

Power gives the percentage of runs in "power situations" that achieved a first down or touchdown. Those situations include any third or fourth down with one or two yards to go, and any runs in goal-to-go situations from the two-yard line or closer. Unlike the other rushing numbers on the Offensive Line table, Power includes quarterbacks. Second Level (**2nd Lev**) Yards and **Open Field** Yards represent yardage where the running back has the most power over the amount of the gain. Second Level Yards represent the number of yards per carry that come five to ten yards past the line of scrimmage. Open Field Yards represent the number of yards per carry that come 11 or more yards past the line of scrimmage. A team with a low ranking in Adjusted Line Yards but a high ranking in Open Field Yards is heavily dependent on its running back breaking long runs to make the running game work, and

Table 11: Cleveland Browns' Offensive Line

Year	Yards	ALY	Rank	Power	Rank	Stuff	Rank	2nd Lev	Rank	Open Field	Rank	F-Start	Cont.
2009	3.93	4.01	21	65%	14	18%	13	1.10	22	0.50	30	17	28
2010	3.95	4.04	17	74%	4	14%	4	0.93	30	0.55	24	12	31
2011	3.60	3.94	23	66%	9	16%	2	0.85	32	0.41	31	19	39

Year	LE	Rank	LT	Rank	Mid	Rank	RT	Rank	RE	Rank	Sacks	ASR	Rank	Short	Long
2009	5.21	4	3.73	26	3.97	23	4.09	17	2.69	30	30	6.1%	15	14	11
2010	3.34	29	4.56	8	3.84	21	4.74	5	4.00	15	36	7.6%	23	10	17
2011	2.02	31	4.45	13	3.91	22	4.71	6	1.47	32	39	6.4%	15	11	22

STATISTICAL TOOLBOX

therefore tends to have a less consistent running attack. Second Level Yards fall somewhere in between.

Stuff gives the percentage of runs that are stuffed for zero or negative gain. Since being stuffed is bad, teams are ranked from stuffed least often (1) to most often (32).

The next two columns give Adjusted Sack Rate (**ASR**) and its rank among the 32 teams. Some teams allow a lot of sacks because they throw a lot of passes; Adjusted Sack Rate accounts for this by dividing sacks and intentional grounding by total pass plays. It is also adjusted for situation (sacks are much more common on third down, particularly third-and-long) and opponent, all of which makes it a better measurement than raw sack totals. Remember that quarterbacks share responsibility for sacks, and two different quarterbacks behind the same line can have very different Adjusted Sack Rates. Particularly if one is named Rob Johnson.

F-start gives the number of false starts, which is the offensive penalty which best correlates to both wins and wins the following season. This total includes false starts by players other than offensive linemen, but it does not include false starts on special teams. False starts in 2011 ranged from seven (Denver) to 35 (Seattle), with the NFL average at 18.7. Finally, Continuity Score (**Cont.**) tells you how much continuity each offensive line had from game-to-game in that season. It was introduced in the Cleveland chapter of *Pro Football Prospectus 2007*. Continuity score starts with 48 and then subtracts:

• The number of players over five who started at least one game on the offensive line;
• The number of times the team started at least one different lineman compared to the game before; and
• The difference between 16 and that team's longest streak where the same line started consecutive games.

The perfect Continuity Score is 48, achieved last year by only one team, Denver. The lowest Continuity Score belonged to Pittsburgh and Indianapolis at 22. The NFL average was 32.75.

The second part of the Offensive Line table gives Adjusted Line Yards in each of the five directions with rank among the 32 teams. Note that the league average is higher on the left than the right. Specifically in 2011, the league average was 4.23 on left end runs (**LE**), 4.14 on left tackle runs (**LT**), 4.09 on runs up the middle (**MID**), 4.26 on right tackle runs (**RT**), and 3.63 on right end runs (**RE**).

How to Read the Defensive Front Seven Tables

Defensive players make plays. Plays aren't just tackles—interceptions and pass deflections change the course of the game, and so does the act of forcing a fumble or beating the offensive players to a fumbled ball. While some plays stop a team on third down and force a punt, others merely stop a receiver after he's caught a 30-yard pass. We still cannot measure each player's opportunities to make a tackle. We can measure a linebacker's opportunities in pass coverage, however, thanks to the Football Outsiders game charting project.

DEFENSIVE LINEMEN: Defensive linemen are listed in the team chapters if they made at least 15 plays during the 2011 season. Players are listed with the following numbers:

Age: The player's age, listed simply as the difference between birth year and 2012. Players born in January and December of the same year will have the same listed age.

Position (**Pos**): The player's position on the line.

Plays (**Plays**): The total defensive plays including tackles, pass deflections, interceptions, fumbles forced, and fumble recoveries. This number comes from the official NFL gamebooks and therefore does not include plays on which the player is listed by the

Table 12: Minnesota Vikings' Defensive Line

Defensive Line	Age	Pos	Plays	TmPct	Rk	Stop	Dfts	BTkl	St%	Rk	AvYd	Rk	Sack	Hit	Hur	Runs	St%	Yds	Pass	St%	Yds
Jared Allen	30	DE	67	8.0%	5	61	33	3	91%	4	-1.1	3	22	12	21.5	37	86%	1.8	30	97%	-4.8
Brian Robison	29	DE	45	5.4%	33	35	13	3	78%	40	0.8	22	8	6	20.5	31	71%	3.0	14	93%	-4.1
Kevin Williams	32	DT	40	5.5%	17	32	11	3	80%	29	1.6	22	5	5	11	31	77%	2.5	9	89%	-1.7
Fred Evans	29	DT	22	2.6%	65	19	9	1	86%	7	1.4	17	0	3	3.5	21	86%	1.6	1	100%	-2.0
Letroy Guion	25	DT	20	2.4%	69	13	4	0	65%	62	2.7	59	0	2	6	19	68%	2.4	1	0%	8.0
Remi Ayodele	29	DT	15	1.8%	--	12	2	1	80%	--	1.2	--	1.5	1	2	13	77%	2.4	2	100%	-6.5

Football Outsiders game charting project as in coverage, but does not appear in the standard play-by-play. Special teams tackles are also not included.

Percentage of Team Plays (**TmPct**): The percentage of total team plays involving this defender. The sum of the percentages of team plays for all defenders on a given team will exceed 100 percent, primarily due to shared tackles. This number is adjusted based on games played, so an injured player may be fifth on his team in plays but third in **TmPct**.

Stops (**Stop**): The total number of plays which prevent a "success" by the offense (45 percent of needed yards on first down, 60 percent on second down, 100 percent on third or fourth down).

Defeats (**Dfts**): The total number of plays which stop the offense from gaining first down yardage on third or fourth down, stop the offense behind the line of scrimmage, or result in a fumble (regardless of which team recovers) or interception.

Broken Tackles (**BTkl**): The number of broken tackles recorded by our game charters.

Stop Rate (**St%**): The percentage of all Plays that are Stops.

Average Yards (**AvYd**): The average number of yards gained by the offense when this player is credited with making the play. Note that passes defensed count as zero yards.

Sack: Standard NFL sack totals.

Hit: To qualify as a quarterback hit, the defender must knock the quarterback to the ground in the act of throwing or after the pass is thrown. We have listed hits on all plays, including those cancelled by penalties. (After all, many of the hardest hits come on plays cancelled because the hit itself draws a roughing the passer penalty.) Because official scorers are not entirely consistent, hits are adjusted slightly based on the home team of each game.

Hurries (**Hur**): The number of quarterback hurries recorded by the Football Outsiders game charting project. This includes both hurries on standard plays and hurries that force an offensive holding penalty that cancels the play and costs the offense yardage.

Finally, we split our stats for defensive linemen into **Run** plays and **Pass** plays. The latter category includes sacks, tackles after completions, and pass deflections.

Defensive linemen are ranked by percentage of team plays, Stop Rate, and average yards. The lowest number of average yards earns the top rank (negative numbers indicate the average play ending behind the line of scrimmage). Except for pass-rush specialists, most linemen do not have enough pass plays to make separate rankings of pass and run statistics viable. Defensive ends are ranked if they made 24 or more plays during 2011. There are 79 defensive ends who qualify. Defensive tackles are ranked if they made 20 or more plays during 2011, with 68 players ranked.

LINEBACKERS: Linebackers are listed in team chapters if they made at least 15 plays during the season. Most of the stats for linebackers are the same as those for defensive linemen. The listings of both total plays and percentage of team plays are based on standard play-by-play. Average yards on the left side of the table is also based on standard play-by-play, and gives us a good indication of which linebackers play closer to the line of scrimmage, and which players drop into coverage.

Linebackers are ranked in percentage of team plays, and also in Stop Rate and average yards for running plays specifically. Linebackers are ranked in these standard stats if they have a minimum of 48 plays or 10 games started. Outside, inside (3-4), and middle (4-3) linebackers are all ranked together, with 111 players ranked in total.

The final five columns in the linebacker stats come from the Football Outsiders game charting project.

Targets (**Tgts**): The number of pass players on which our game charters listed this player in coverage.

Success Rate (**Suc%**): The percentage plays of targeting this player on which the offense did not have a successful play. This means not only incomplete

Table 13: Green Bay Packers' Linebackers

				Overall						Pass Rush			vs. Run				vs. Pass				
Linebackers	Age	Pos	Plays	TmPct	Rk	Stop	Dfts	BTkl	AvYd	Sack	Hit	Hur	Runs	St%	Rk	Yds	Rk	Tgts	Suc%	Rk	AdjYd	Rk
Desmond Bishop	28	ILB	116	17.0%	9	45	16	4	6.8	5	4	4	67	45%	111	5.5	111	46	31%	78	9.6	73
A.J. Hawk	28	ILB	85	11.6%	43	44	11	6	4.9	1.5	1	5.5	51	55%	94	3.7	76	27	58%	14	6.2	27
Erik Walden	27	OLB	61	7.3%	91	29	11	3	5.2	3	15	9	39	49%	107	4.5	106	12	53%	--	7.9	--
Clay Matthews	26	OLB	58	7.4%	90	44	20	3	1.6	6	23	27.5	33	79%	10	1.6	3	14	64%	--	5.3	--
D.J. Smith	23	ILB	34	4.1%	--	15	5	2	4.8	0	0	3	21	52%	--	4.2	--	13	50%	--	4.3	--
Robert Francois	27	ILB	19	3.3%	--	9	5	2	5.0	0	0	0	6	50%	--	4.2	--	16	47%	51	5.0	10

STATISTICAL TOOLBOX

passes and interceptions, but also short completions which do not meet our baselines for success (45 percent of needed yards on first down, 60 percent on second down, 100 percent on third or fourth down). Success Rate is adjusted for the quality of the receiver covered.

Adjusted Yards per Pass (**AdjYd**): The average number of yards gained on plays on which this defender was the listed target, adjusted for the quality of the receiver covered.

These stats are explained in more detail below, in the section on secondary tables. Plays listed with two defenders or as "Hole in Zone" with this defender as the closest player count only for half credit in computing both Success Rate and Average Yards per Pass. Eighty linebackers are ranked in the charting stats, with a minimum of 16 charted passes. As a result of the different thresholds, some linebackers are ranked in standard stats but not charting stats, or vice versa.

FURTHER DETAILS: Just as in the offensive tables, players who are no longer on the team are marked with asterisks, and players who were on other teams last year are in italics. Other than the game charting statistics for linebackers, defensive front seven player statistics are not adjusted for opponent.

Numbers for defensive linemen and linebackers unfortunately do not reflect all of the opportunities a player had to make a play, but they do show us which players were most active on the field. A large number of plays could mean a strong defensive performance, or it could mean that the linebacker in question plays behind a poor part of the line. In general, defensive numbers should be taken as information that tells us what happened on the field in 2011, but not as a strict, unassailable judgment of which players are better than others—particularly when the difference between two players is small (for example, players ranked 20th and 30th) instead of large (players ranked 20th and 70th).

After the individual statistics for linemen and linebackers, the Defensive Front Seven section contains a table that looks exactly like the table in the Offensive Line section. The difference is that the numbers here are for all opposing running backs against this team's defensive front. As we're on the opposite side of the ball, teams are now ranked in the opposite order, so the number one defensive front seven is the one that allows the fewest Adjusted Line Yards, the lowest percentage in Power situations, and has the highest Adjusted Sack Rate. Directions for Adjusted Line Yards are given from the offense's perspective, so runs left end and left tackle are aimed at the right defensive end and (assuming the tight end is on the other side) weakside linebacker.

How to Read the Secondary Tables

The first few columns in the secondary tables are based on standard play-by-play, not game charting. **Age**, Total Plays, Percentage of Team Plays, Stops, and Defeats are computed the same way they are for

Table 14: Washington Redskins' Defensive Secondary

Secondary	Age	Pos	Plays	TmPct	Rk	Stop	Dfts	BTkl	Runs	St%	Rk	Yds	Rk	Tgts	Tgt%	Rk	Dist	Suc%	Rk	APaYd	Rk	PD	Int
DeAngelo Hall	29	CB	107	13.4%	4	41	16	6	25	56%	17	6.7	36	88	21.7%	10	11.2	42%	75	9.3	70	18	3
Reed Doughty	30	SS	78	9.7%	40	21	4	4	44	45%	24	5.8	16	20	4.9%	68	16.7	38%	73	13.0	74	1	0
Josh Wilson	27	CB	76	9.5%	22	27	12	6	18	28%	65	12.5	78	81	20.0%	24	13.6	61%	14	6.8	25	15	2
O.J. Atogwe*	31	FS	66	10.1%	36	21	10	1	30	23%	72	10.1	71	16	4.7%	69	14.4	43%	70	9.6	62	5	3
LaRon Landry*	28	SS	49	12.2%	15	26	7	7	33	55%	9	6.0	20	13	6.2%	53	13.2	41%	71	6.7	21	0	0
DeJon Gomes	23	SS	31	4.1%	--	15	1	2	20	60%	--	4.3	--	14	3.6%	--	12.1	50%	--	7.5	--	2	0
Kevin Barnes	26	CB	30	4.0%	--	11	7	6	3	67%	--	3.3	--	38	10.0%	--	9.1	59%	--	6.0	--	6	2
Cedric Griffin	30	CB	76	9.1%	27	28	8	5	20	40%	44	6.8	38	61	14.6%	61	11.6	41%	78	9.3	69	13	1
Tanard Jackson	27	FS	38	7.7%	61	12	3	16	23	22%	73	9.2	67	13	5.6%	62	12.4	63%	14	7.1	30	3	2
Brandon Meriweather	28	FS	34	6.0%	--	8	5	2	8	38%	--	8.0	--	13	3.7%	--	16.3	53%	--	10.5	--	2	0
Leigh Torrence	30	CB	18	2.9%	--	6	6	0	1	0%	--	12.0	--	19	4.8%	--	10.9	49%	--	10.4	--	3	1

Year	Pass D Rank	vs. #1 WR	Rk	vs. #2 WR	Rk	vs. Other WR	Rk	vs. TE	Rk	vs. RB	Rk
2009	20	3.7%	15	10.6%	26	-2.5%	12	0.8%	14	17.1%	25
2010	27	-5.6%	13	12.7%	24	21.7%	29	-9.7%	6	5.8%	17
2011	16	24.6%	25	-15.7%	9	-19.3%	10	23.7%	28	3.6%	20

other defensive players, so that the secondary can be compared to the defensive line and linebackers. That means that Total Plays here includes passes defensed, sacks, tackles after receptions, tipped passes, and interceptions, but not pass plays on which this player was in coverage but was not given a tackle or pass defense by the NFL's official scorer.

The middle four columns address each defensive back's role in stopping the run. Average Yardage and Stop Rate for running plays is computed in the same manner as for defensive linemen and linebackers.

The third section of statistics represents data from the game charting project:

Targets (**Tgts**): The number of pass plays on which our game charters listed this player in coverage. This number gives full credit to all passes, including those on which two defenders are listed and those listed as "Hole in Zone" with this player as the closest zone defender (both of those count as half credit in the other stats below). We do not count pass plays on which this player was in coverage, but the incomplete was listed as Thrown Away, Tipped at Line, or Hit in Motion.

Target Percentage (**Tgt%**): The number of plays on which this player was targeted divided by the total number of charted passes against his defense, not including plays listed as Uncovered. Like Percentage of Team Plays, this metric is adjusted based on number of games played.

Distance (**Dist**): The average distance in the air beyond the line of scrimmage of all passes targeted at this defender. It does not include yards after catch, and is useful for seeing which defenders were covering receivers deeper or shorter.

Success Rate (**Suc%**): The percentage plays of targeting this player on which the offense did not have a successful play. This means not only incomplete passes and interceptions, but also short completions which do not meet our baselines for success (45 percent of needed yards on first down, 60 percent on second down, 100 percent on third or fourth down). Success Rate is adjusted for the quality of the receiver covered. Defensive pass interference is counted as a failure for the defensive player, similar to a completion of equal yardage (and a new first down).

Adjusted Yards per Pass (**AdjYd**): The average number of yards gained on plays on which this defender was the listed target, adjusted for the quality of the receiver covered.

Passes Defensed (**PD**): This is our count of passes defensed, and will differ from the total found in NFL gamebooks. Our count includes:
- All passes listed by our charters as Defensed.
- All interceptions, or tipped passes leading to interceptions.
- All passes defensed listed in the NFL gamebooks for games which remain uncharted.
- Any pass on which the defender is given a pass defensed by the official scorer, and the game charter listed a reason for incomplete which can be hard to differentiate from a pass defensed, including: Dropped, Miscommunication, Alligator Arms, and Catch Out of Bounds.

Our count of passes defensed does not include passes marked as defensed in the official gamebooks but listed by our charters as Overthrown, Underthrown, or Thrown Away. It also does not include passes tipped in the act of rushing the passer.

Interceptions (**Int**): Standard NFL interception total.

Cornerbacks need 40 charted passes or eight games started to be ranked in the defensive stats, with 82 cornerbacks ranked in total. Safeties need 16 charted passes or eight games started to be ranked in the defensive stats, with 77 safeties ranked in total. Strong and free safeties are ranked together.

Just like the front seven, the secondary has a table of team statistics following the individual numbers. This table gives DVOA figured against different types of receivers. Each offense's wide receivers have had one receiver designated as number one, and another as number two. (Occasionally this is difficult, due to injury or an amorphous wide receiver corps like last year's Rams, but it's usually pretty obvious.) The other receivers form a third category, with tight ends and running backs as fourth and fifth categories. The defense is then judged on the performance of each receiver based on the standard DVOA method, with each rating adjusted based on strength of schedule. (Opponents with Roddy White and Larry Fitzgerald as top receivers, for example, are tougher than an opponent with Michael Crabtree as its number one receiver.) **Pass D Rank** is the total ranking of the pass defense, as seen before in the Trends and Splits table, and combines all five categories plus sacks and passes with no intended target.

The defensive secondary table should be used to analyze the defense as a whole rather than individual players. The ratings against types of receivers are generally based on defensive schemes, not specific cornerbacks, and the ratings against tight ends and running backs are in large part due to the performance of linebackers.

How to Read the Special Teams Tables

The special teams tables list the last three years of kick, punt, and return numbers for each team.

The first two columns list total special teams DVOA and rank among the 32 teams. The next two columns list the value in actual points of field goals and extra points (**FG/XP**) when compared to how a league average kicker would do from the same distances, adjusted for weather and altitude, and rank among the 32 teams. That is followed by the estimated point values of field position for net kickoffs (**Net Kick**) and kick returns (**Kick Ret**), and their respective ranks. Next, we list the estimated value in actual points of field position over or under the league average based on net punting (**Net Punt**) and punt returns (**Punt Ret**), and rank that value among the 32 teams.

The final two columns represent the value of "**Hidden**" special teams, plays which throughout the past decade have usually been based on the performance of opponents without this team being able to control the outcome. We combine the opposing team's value on field goals, kickoff distance, and punt distance, adjusted for weather and altitude, and then switch the sign to represent that good special teams by the opponent will cost the listed team points, and bad special teams will effectively hand them points. We have to give the qualifier of "usually" because, as explained above, certain returners such as Devin Hester will affect opposing special teams strategy. Nonetheless, the "hidden" value is still "hidden" for most teams, and they are ranked from the most hidden value gained (Jacksonville, 15.6 points) to the most value lost (Kansas City, -15.4 points). The best and worst individual values for kickers, punters, and returners are listed in the statistical appendix at the end of the book.

Administrative Minutiae

Receiving statistics include all passes intended for the receiver in question, including those that are incomplete or intercepted. The word "passes" refers to both complete and incomplete pass attempts. When rating receivers, interceptions are treated as incomplete passes with no penalty.

For the computation of DVOA and DYAR, passing statistics include sacks as well as fumbles on aborted snaps. We do not include kneeldown plays or spikes for the purpose of stopping the clock. Some interceptions which we have determined to be "Hail Mary" plays that end the first half or game are counted as regular incomplete passes, not turnovers.

All mentions of yards after catch, hurries, hits, blitzes, and screens come from the Football Outsiders game charting project and may be different from totals compiled by other sources.

Unless we say otherwise, when we refer to third-down performance in this book we are referring to a combination of third down and the handful of rushing and passing plays that take place on fourth down (primarily fourth-and-1).

Aaron Schatz

Table 14: Baltimore Ravens' Special Teams

Year	DVOA	Rank	FG/XP	Rank	Net Kick	Rank	Kick Ret	Rank	Net Punt	Rank	Punt Ret	Rank	Hidden	Rank
2009	1.8%	8	-4.7	24	9.8	6	9.8	4	-3.3	23	-0.6	16	-0.5	16
2010	5.1%	4	4.3	7	13.5	3	0.8	15	17.4	1	-5.7	26	-16.1	31
2011	-4.7%	30	-5.3	25	-7.4	28	-5.9	29	-7.7	27	-1.6	19	-8.2	25

The Year In Quotes

PIOLIROLLING: RICKROLLING WITH MORE CONDESCENSION

"I'm never going to give that up guys! Are you kidding me? Let me ask you: Back in your earlier life when you were single and asking girls out on dates—were you ever turned down? Did you run out to tell your buddies who the girls were that turned you down?"

—*Chiefs general manager Scott Pioli, when asked which players Kansas City targeted but could not sign in free agency.*

AFTER WATCHING SO MUCH TAPE OF DAVID CARR, SACKS ALL START TO BLEND TOGETHER

"That was the JaMarcus Russell year, with Brady Quinn, Trent Edwards, Kevin Kolb and Beck. So they asked me who I'd pick if I had the 10th pick in the draft. I told them Beck. They said he's not worth the 10th pick in the draft. I was standing on the table for him. I've never seen a guy play that well in college."

—*Redskins offensive coordinator Kyle Shanahan, on how much he loved then-Redskins quarterback John Beck in the 2006 draft.*

CLIFF'S NOT HERE, MAN

"We smoked it all."

—*Oregon defensive back Cliff Harris, responding to a police officer's question of why his car smelled of marijuana.*

BUT THE CAT CAME BACK, THE VERY NEXT DAY

"So I told our players, I tried to let it out the front door—'MEEEOOOW!'—the cat's still goin' crazy in there. And I told our players: You need to be more like a dog! We don't need a bunch of cats in here—'meeeooow!'—lookin' in the mirror. 'I look gooooood, I got my extra bands on, I got my other shoes'—Be a dog! We don't need no meows, we don't need no cats. We need more dogs."

—*Coastal Carolina head coach Steve Bennett, in a press conference, on ... something?*

LET'S NOW MOVE ON TO RESOLUTION 2011-83, THE REASONABLE ACCOMMODATION OF CROUTONS IN SALADS

"This proposal seeks to make a reasonable accommodation in allowing an institution to provide traditional bagel spreads to student-athletes in conjunction with the bagels it is already permitted to provide."

—*NCAA Proposal No. 2011-78*

AT LEAST SNYDER STILL HAS A NOSE TO CUT OFF

"The facts on the public record suggest that [Dan Snyder] is as likely to prevail on the merits here as Voldemort is to prevail over Harry Potter in their final battle."

—*ACLU court filing on Dan Snyder's libel lawsuit of Dave McKenna and the Washington City Paper.*

I ALWAYS PICTURED SHANG TSUNG AS MORE OF A QUARTERBACK.

"They've got fullbacks that want to block your soul."

—*Texas defensive coordinator Manny Diaz, on BYU's running game.*

POWERSTRIPE INVISIBLE SOLID OR POWERGEL?

"There is no right guard controversy in football that I'm aware of. I mean I could understand a quarterback controversy, I could understand us talking about that. But, I'm not aware of any right guard controversies, or how many times the defensive linemen play in a certain rotation, or how many snaps running backs play, and is there a rotation. That's just all part of football. But, I don't think there's a guard controversy."

—*49ers coach Jim Harbaugh, on why Chilo Rachal was losing snaps.*

QUI-GON JINN ORIGINALLY NAMED OUI-OUI JEAN

"I don't know what a Padawan is. You didn't call me a bad name did you? I don't speak French either."

—*Florida coach Will Muschamp, on the "teacher-Padawan" relationship between himself and Alabama coach Nick Saban.*

THE YEAR IN QUOTES

I DON'T THINK RIVALRIES OVER CONFERENCES IS A SENTIMENT THAT A COACH NAMED GARY PATTERSON CAN CO-SIGN, RILEY

"We're going to go on about our business, but they're not going to get the same help anymore—not about a ballgame, not about conferences, not about anybody. They're getting no help from Gary Patterson, period."

—*TCU head coach Gary Patterson (surprise!), on perceived disrespect shown to him by SMU.*

YOU MAY RUN LIKE MAYS, BUT...

"We're playing like s--t, that's what's going on. We're not playing good. We're not disciplined. We're not into our gaps. We're not physical. I don't know how many yards that kid had. He probably didn't even have 10 carries."

—*Bears linebacker Brian Urlacher, after Jahvid Best ran for 163 yards against them in a 24-13 Lions victory.*

LOOK, I'M ALL ABOUT LOYALTY. IN FACT, I FEEL LIKE PART OF WHAT I'M BEING PAID FOR HERE IS MY LOYALTY. BUT IF THERE WERE SOMEWHERE ELSE THAT VALUED LOYALTY MORE HIGHLY, I'M GOING WHEREVER THEY VALUE LOYALTY THE MOST

"By the way I was feeling, I just needed somebody else's opinion. If he'd have said, 'Peyton, you probably can do your thing,' I'd have listened to that. But he is my agent and he does help me out and I think we made the right choice, because I was definitely not healthy enough to play."

—*Browns running back Peyton Hillis, on missing a game with strep throat.*

IF THE ALTERNATIVE IS YOU, I LIKE HER CHANCES IN THE POWER-I

"I do stink. We all stink. When it comes to 0-6, everybody stinks. We've all, in some way, shape or form have not been good enough, and that's what I meant with those comments. I don't care if it's the front-desk secretary—she ain't doing a good enough job. Everybody's in this thing together."

—*Dolphins running back Reggie Bush, on his team's awful start.*

I DON'T KNOW YOU! THAT'S MY PURSE!

"From what I hear, it didn't show on the TV copy. But if you watch the game, you can clearly see he kind of picked me up in mid-air, put me on the back, and then presumed to come toward me. So automatically I went into defense mode."

—*Vikings defensive end Brian Robison, on why he kicked Packers lineman T.J. Lang in the crotch.*

OF COURSE, HE SAYS THAT EVERY SUNDAY HE HAS TO SIT NEXT TO TERRY BRADSHAW

"T.O. ... Tiki ... give me the bullet."

—*Ex-Cowboys and Dolphins coach Jimmy Johnson, on whether, at gunpoint, he'd rather employ Terrell Owens or Tiki Barber.*

IN FACT, HIS ONLY VIEWER LEFT AT THIS POINT IS RYAN MALLETT

"Yeah, I don't talk to Phil. Phil doesn't talk to me. He did text me after that, saying 'Hey, sorry to drag your name into this.' I wrote back, 'Phil I don't know what you're talking about.' He said, 'Well on my show, Inside the NFL, I made this statement.' I said, 'Phil, I hate to break it to you, but I don't watch your show, along with a lot of other people that I don't think watch that show.'"

—*then-Colts quarterback Peyton Manning, on speculative Phil Simms nonsense.*

WHAT'S WRONG WITH THIS COUNTRY? CAN'T A MAN WALK DOWN THE STREET WITHOUT BEING OFFERED A JOB?

"You know every quarterback that's gone down? Pretty much every team has called. They had me on flights ready to come out [saying,] 'Well, can he rehab here.' Every last one of them. And I've had to say 'no' every time. I don't even know if this is a record of how many quarterbacks have gone down in one season but for me to be sitting out here and not to be able to play? I've never not been able to play but there's nothing I can do. I'm good right now at getting in and out of chairs and helping my wife around the house but running around, throwing, and getting hit? I'm just not in that position at this time."

—*Dolphins quarterback David Garrard, on life during rehab.*

THE YEAR IN QUOTES

EVERY BEAST HAS HIS POISON, EVERY LINE HAS ITS VICTIM

"What happens when you take a lion out of the safari and try to take him to your place of residence and make him a house pet? It ain't going to happen. That's the type of person that I am. I'm that lion. The house that I'm in is somewhat of a tarnished house where losing is accepted. But I'm trying to change that, whether I'm going to have to turn that house into a safari, or I'm just going to have to get out of that house. I'm not saying I'm trying to leave this place. I'm just trying to get everybody on my level."

—*Panthers quarterback Cam Newton, on situations where he plays well but doesn't win.*

THREE BIG BAGS OF TRASH!

"That's the maturing process that you're seeing. Great defenses, if you're ever out there with them, it sounds almost like a stock market. Guys are saying, 'This guy's up! This guy's up! The tight's split! Tight's split! Closed split! Closed split.' And you have the linebackers saying, 'The back's far, the back's near.' That's great defenses. That's what happens. And then the secondary's talking about 'Cut split! This guy's split!' Well, first few weeks it was like a morgue out there. I mean, come on, talk!"

—*Michigan defensive coordinator Greg Mattison, on his unit's improvement last season.*

THEY PROBABLY SHOULD HAVE SAVED THIS GAME FOR DEEPER INTO THE WINTER

"Ravens-Steelers gets everybody's piss hot."

—*Ravens defender Terrell Suggs, on the rivalry between Baltimore and Pittsburgh.*

HALLOW VACUUM CHECK THE OXYGEN TANKS

"'Early retirement' sounds wonderful. It certainly did that cold night in Pittsburgh. I was going to use my time to conquer the world. Boy, was I wrong. Now I find myself in music chat rooms arguing the validity of Frank Zappa versus the Mars Volta. (If the others only knew Walkingpnumonia was the screen name for a former All-Pro football player and not some Oberlin College student trying to find his place in the world.)"

—*Former Broncos and Jets tackle Trevor Pryce, on the life of a bored retired athlete.*

JOHN MADDEN'S HEIR

"'Off' means he doesn't have a helmet on. I say him, but it's that whole group. We'll be in the locker room laughing, and we'll sit over there in practice and laugh and have a cut-up before practice starts, and you'll see them, watch their demeanor. It goes from boom to boom. It's just, boom! And I'm not saying the world of D-linemen is a normal place. It's not. And I get all that—it's the Muppets and bouncing off the walls, but it's like, Bam! You're on! If you ever see those kids in kindergarten, some of the kids take the colors and they put nice colors up and they try to draw squares—I think all the guys in my room were the ones with a big mess, a blob of stuff, you know? That's kind of the way it all is, because it's nuts in there! It's crazy! Stuff's flying around and you're like: 'Whoa man! Boom!' That's just the way it is. And they fit, but it's not for everybody. You don't want to talk about it too much because people will really think they're nuts. But they're normal. They are, they're normal outside. But you come in here and it's like, 'Boom!'"

—*49ers defensive line coach Jim Tomsula, on when defensive lineman Justin Smith is "on" or "off"*

I'M NOT GONNA LIVE IN A THIRD-WORLD COUNTRY WITH ALL THE CONFORMISTS

"I don't like going to Detroit. I'll be honest, it's gloomy, it sucks. Everything is brown and then there is snow on the ground. There's like brownstones everywhere and I'm like, 'Awesome.' I don't know, I couldn't do it. If I had to live in Detroit, I think I'd just drown myself in the river that was across the way."

—*Vikings defensive end Jared Allen, on his least favorite NFL city.*

NORMALLY I USE PROTECTION, BUT THEN I THOUGHT: WHEN AM I GOING TO MAKE IT BACK TO HAITI?

"It didn't work, so it was a bad idea. If it had worked, it would have been great."

—*then-Buccaneers head coach Raheem Morris, on a called Josh Johnson run against New Orleans that took Josh Freeman off the field.*

THE YEAR IN QUOTES

YOU WANNA KNOW SOMETHING? *ANYONE* CAN BECOME A KICKER. LIKE, THEY DON'T REGULATE

"I told the coaches, 'Hey—an intoxicated Brodus is better than nobody. Get him. Just get him here. Give him a Breathalyzer.' Fortunately he didn't do anything bad."

—Tennessee head coach Derek Dooley, solving an unprecedented kicker-injury crisis by getting a walk-on kicker out of a frat house.

NICE TRY, BUT BRETT KEISEL LOOKED MORE HOMELESS

"My grooming habits have nothing to do with the performance of our team. That's my own obsession, compulsive disorder, whatever they call it. You don't get to see me when I'm picking up pennies and how I do it and what pocket I put them in."

—then-Chiefs head coach Todd Haley, on his lucky beard.

PLAY US OUT, KEYBOARD CAT

"We were off to a 3-1 start and now we're 3-7 and I had pneumonia. And this whole thing just sucks."

—Redskins quarterback Rex Grossman, on the dwindling hopes in Washington.

THIS WAS A COPACETIC WAY OF DODGING THAT QUESTION

"It would be without propriety for me to make a determination about the history of college football."

—LSU head coach Les Miles, on his team's place in history.

THE NORVTASTROPHE HAS MOVED TO STAGE THREE

"We do the dumbest s--t. I've never been on a team that does the dumbest s--t all the time."

—Chargers linebacker Shaun Phillips, after the Broncos overcame San Diego in overtime.

OKAY McGUIRK, PEOPLE ARE PROBABLY LOOKING FOR YOU.

"These men are tired of being in the wilderness and they want to get out."

—New Ole Miss head coach Hugh Freeze, on where the program is going.

HIS GNOSIS MEANS HE CAN SURVIVE THE UMBRA

"More like a Lycan wolf ninja—like a ninja who been bit by a werewolf and then he's still a ninja but then transforms to the wolf come game time. And the wolf is the dog. And y'all know I got the dog, too."

—Texans defensive end Antonio Smith, on what kind of ninja he upgrades to in the playoffs.

IT'S ALWAYS SUNNY IN FLORIDA

"Those guys couldn't get a f---ing wide receiver if it hit them in the head. They haven't had anyone decent since Jimmy Smith."

—Falcons cornerback Dunta Robinson, on the state of affairs in Jacksonville.

"Fortunately, for us, the team didn't die on us like last week."

—Buccaneers head coach Raheem Morris, trying to take something positive from his team's loss to the Cowboys.

WHO NEEDS CHRIS PAUL WHEN YOU CAN HAVE RAMON SESSIONS?

"I can't believe they got him for the cheap price that they got him for replacing Reggie Bush. I think if it was the NBA, the commissioner might have stepped in and stopped that move."

—49ers defensive coordinator Vic Fangio, on Darren Sproles.

ANGRY BERNARD POLLARD SMASH BINARY GENDER CONCEPTS

"That's the pretty boy. That's the man of the NFL. That's Mr. Do-It-All. So everybody is going to hold that against me but I don't care. I don't play for men. I don't play for no woman. I play because I'm given the gift to play this game."

—Ravens safety Bernard Pollard, on his hit that ended Tom Brady's season years ago.

ONCE AGAIN, WAFFLE FRIES ARE THE DECIDER

"Um, kinda the environment, and like, you know, and plus they had no Chick-Fil-A on campus."

—Auburn recruit Cassanova McKinzy, on selecting Auburn over Clemson.

THE YEAR IN QUOTES

CMOA (CHARISMA-ADJUSTED MATRIMONY OVER AVERAGE)

"When you get two people in their mid-20s that are married and have wonderful wives, they're kind of like me because I think they were able to over-marry."

—*Jaguars general manager Gene Smith, on how their respective wives played a role in the signings of Laurent Robinson and Chad Henne.*

STOP OBJECTIFYING THE LOMBARDI TROPHY

"Being here, man, it's like watching porn. There's nothing bad about it at all."

—*then-Patriots reciever Chad Ochocinco on the Super Bowl.*

THIS MEANS MAX HALL IS CURLY

"We've got two guys that we feel like can play. They've shown at times that they can do things very well, they've shown at times that they are knuckleheads and it's our job to get the players that are there on our team to play better. That's what we're going to do and we're excited about that."

—*Cardinals coach Ken Whisenhunt, on John Skelton and Kevin Kolb.*

YOU'D REALLY THINK ALL THAT TIME ON A COLLEGE CAMPUS WOULD TEACH A COACH THAT VODKA IS THE DRINK TO GO CHEAP ON

"Nothing wrong with me that a little Grey Goose won't cure."

—*North Texas head coach Dan McCarney, following his stroke.*

LITERALLY!

"The coaches kind of messed me up. I didn't know if I would start a game or be benched. It hurt me, but I tried to fight through it."

—*Noted hothead and now-Bengals linebacker Vontaze Burfict, on his problems with the Sun Devils coaching staff.*

I, TOO, WOULD RELISH THE CHANCE TO GET MY ASS KICKED BY PEYTON MANNING

"Not offended at all. In fact, I would have relished the opportunity to compete for the starting quarterback job with Peyton Manning."

—*49ers quarterback Alex Smith, on San Francisco's interest in Peyton Manning.*

JOB SECURITY FIT FOR A KING

"Until they ship him out of here or shoot me dead in my office, the guy's the starting right tackle."

—*Jets offensive line coach Dave DeGuglielmo, on maligned offensive tackle Wayne Hunter.*

...NOT THAT THERE'S ANYTHING WRONG WITH THAT

"We ate a burrito together. Not the same burrito."

—*Redskins quarterback Robert Griffin III, on his relationship with fourth-round quarterback Kirk Cousins.*

HARD TO NEGOTIATE WITH A MAN WHO CAN CHANGE TENSES THAT FAST

"When I'm on the football field, I'm giving you everything. Do the Ravens know that? Yes they do. Did Ozzie know that Ed Reed was going to be playing against the Pittsburgh Steelers regardless of negotiating his contract? Yes he did. Did Ed Reed get the respect that he deserves? No he did not. Am I gonna get it? Probably won't. Hopefully he do. If I don't, then, hey man, I'm alright with me."

—*Ravens safety Ed Reed, on his lack of monetary respect from the front office.*

QUOTE OF THE YEAR

"Call me crazy, but I'm excited about Tyler Palko ... I've got to sell this."

—*ESPN announcer Ron Jaworski, behind the scenes, while preparing for Monday Night Football, according to an article in The New Yorker*

Compiled by Rivers McCown

A Note About The Printed Version Of Football Outsiders Almanac 2012

Due to a technical issue with Createspace, the company that handles our print-on-demand process, we are unable to fit this year's entire text into the published copy of the book that you hold in your hands. Three items have been cut from the original PDF version of Football Outsiders Almanac 2012 that is sold online.

First, an article detailing improvements to our college edge-rusher forecast system, SackSEER. Numbers for 2012 rookies can still be found in the section of the book marked "FO Rookie Projections." To read the full essay, please visit: http://www.footballoutsiders.com/files/sackseer.pdf.

Second, an article detailing improvements to our college wide receiver forecast system, Playmaker Score. Numbers for 2012 rookies can still be found in the section of the book marked "FO Rookie Projections." To read the full essay, please visit: http://www.footballoutsiders.com/files/playmaker.pdf.

Finally, the Fantasy Appendix listing the 2012 KUBIAK fantasy football projections in one large table; projections can still be found with each individual player comment.

We apologize for the inconvenience.

Arizona Cardinals

2011 Record: 8-8

Pythagorean Wins: 6.9 (21st)

DVOA: -19.7% (28th)

Offense: -18.4% (28th)

Defense: 2.4% (20th)

Special Teams: 1.2% (11th)

Variance: 8.7% (7th)

2012 Mean Projection: 5.9 wins

On the Clock (0-4): 24%

Mediocrity (5-7): 55%

Playoff Contender (8-10): 20%

Super Bowl Contender (11+): 1%

Postseason Odds: 17.2%

Projected Average Opponent: -1.6% (22nd)

2011: Arizona discovers that quarterback evaluation, much like pimping, ain't easy.

2012: Holes on the offensive and defensive lines will not be filled by rookie wide receiver Michael Floyd.

Once upon a time, the Arizona Cardinals stumbled across an undervalued Hall of Fame-caliber quarterback in free agency. That good fortune is now a distant memory, and the Cardinals are re-discovering the fact that finding a franchise quarterback is difficult. The club thought it had a solution when it drafted Matt Leinart following the 2005 season, but Leinart proved to be limited. When the Cardinals cut Leinart, they were stuck with Derek Anderson. That clearly was not a long-term solution. So the Cardinals made a big trade, sending their 2011 second-round pick (and cornerback Dominique Rodgers-Cromartie) to Philadelphia for longtime understudy Kevin Kolb. They signed Kolb to a five-year, $62.1 million contract, and handed him the starting job.

It did not go well.

Due to the lockout, Kolb only had a month to learn head coach Ken Whisenhunt's system and develop a relationship with his new receivers. Despite that, Kolb actually got off to a pretty good start with the Cardinals. It helped, of course, that Arizona's first three opponents were all teams that finished the season with losing records, but the Cardinals likely felt confident about Kolb after the first ten quarters of 2011. Kolb completed 49-of-75 pass attempts (65.3 percent) for 699 yards with five touchdowns and two interceptions. The second of those interceptions, however, came in Week 3, with the Cardinals entering field-goal range in the final 10 seconds of the first half. Kolb tried to force the ball to Larry Fitzgerald, who was bracketed by three Seattle defenders. One play doesn't turn an entire season, but damn if it didn't feel like it for Kevin Kolb. Over the rest of the season, he went 97-of-178 (54.5 percent) for 1,256 yards, throwing just four touchdowns with six interceptions and getting sacked once every 8.4 pass attempts.

Kolb also missed four games in the middle of the season with a toe injury and nearly four entire games at the end of the season with a concussion after being inadvertently kneed in the back of the head by San Francisco 49ers linebacker Ahmad Brooks following a strip-sack by Justin Smith. A concussion had ended Kolb's two-week reign as the Philadelphia Eagles' starter and his slow recovery from this latest head injury is a cause for concern. According to the *Arizona Republic*, when Kolb reported for the start of the offseason workout program, he admitted that he still experienced concussion symptoms for three weeks after the end of the season, a total span of seven weeks. During the OTAs, Kolb said that he was not concerned about another concussion, referring to them as "a freak deal," but will be wearing a new helmet that adds additional protection to the back of the head.

While Kolb was out, second-year player John Skelton took over as the starting quarterback. The 2010 fifth-round pick from Fordham had started four games

2012 Cardinals Schedule

Week	Opp.	Week	Opp.	Week	Opp.
1	SEA	7	at MIN	13	at NYJ
2	at NE	8	SF (Mon.)	14	at SEA
3	PHI	9	at GB	15	DET
4	MIA	10	BYE	16	CHI
5	at STL (Thu.)	11	at ATL	17	at SF
6	BUF	12	STL		

Figure 1. 2011 Arizona DVOA by Week

as a rookie, so he wasn't totally unprepared for the task, but he had been denied a full offseason by the lockout and had opened up the 2011 season as the No. 3 behind Kolb and the well-traveled Richard Bartel. Skelton ascended to the top backup spot a few weeks before Kolb's toe injury, which, combined with the Cardinals' schedule before and after Kolb's injury, proves that timing is everything. The Cardinals faced the New York Giants, Pittsburgh Steelers and Baltimore Ravens in three of four weeks before Kolb's injury. Skelton's first four starts included two games against the St. Louis Rams and a meeting with the 3-5 Philadelphia Eagles. The Cardinals won three of the games, including one over the Rams where Skelton took two safeties but Patrick Peterson returned a punt 99 yards for a touchdown in overtime. Overall, Skelton would start seven games and play most of an eighth game, and the Cardinals won six times to remain mathematically alive for the postseason despite their 1-6 start.

Whisenhunt's offseason comments about the quarterback position make it clear that he's a believer in "quarterback wins" as a viable statistic. Skelton will apparently open the training camp on equal footing with Kolb, although by our metrics Kolb (-18.5% DVOA, -133 DYAR) was better than Skelton (-27.6% DVOA, -326 DYAR) in 2011's battle of lame and lamer. "If it was up to me, I'd prefer we had a quarterback resolution two years ago," Whisenhunt said during the June minicamp, throwing grammar to the four winds. "But obviously that hasn't happened. When it happens, it happens. They're going to have to go through different tests. The next stage is going to be able to do that in training camp and being able to do that in preseason games."

Of course, the Cardinals were hoping to avoid a Kolb-Skelton quarterback competition. Glendale, Arizona was the second stop on the Peyton Manning Free Agent Tour 2012 (co-headlined by Kenny Chesney).

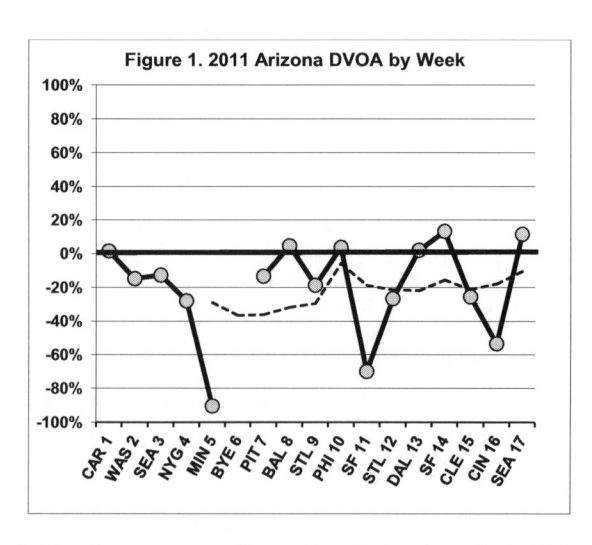

Whisenhunt personally retrieved the four-time NFL Most Valuable Player from the airport to chauffeur him to the team's facility where assistant coaches and Fitzgerald (the team's most important player) had gathered to meet face-to-face with Manning. The Cardinals had sought Fitzgerald's input before acquiring Kolb from the Eagles, so it only made sense for the team to include him in their attempt to woo a future Hall of Fame quarterback like Manning to the desert. Knowing that it was not a slam dunk, and that he might still be catching passes from Kolb, Skelton or a mystery quarterback, Fitzgerald wisely downplayed his involvement in the recruitment of Manning, saying those decisions were "above his pay grade." After signing a $113 million contract extension last August, however, little that goes on in the Cardinals' facility is above Fitzgerald's pay grade, particularly when it pertains to the personnel on the offensive side of the ball.

Financially, the Cardinals could afford to bring Manning on board, as they had a brief window to get out from under the five years and $51.5 million that remained on Kolb's contract. Kolb was due a $7 million roster bonus on the fifth day of the 2012 league year (March 17) and, had the Cardinals been successful in their pursuit of Manning, they could have released Kolb before that roster bonus was due, saving $2 million in cap space, and more importantly, $8.5 million in cash. The Cardinals will have a similar decision to make next offseason, when Kolb is due a non-guaranteed $2 million roster bonus on the fifth day of the league year. Parting ways with Kolb next offseason would save $11 million in cash and $7.5 million in salary cap space, so the pressure remains on the 28-year-old to stay healthy and productive in 2012.

Conventional wisdom said that the Cardinals would use the 13th overall pick in the draft to find Kolb or Skelton some desperately needed pass protection. The Cardinals did find some help for their quarterbacks, but not the kind of help most draft analysts were expecting. Instead, the Cardinals selected Notre Dame wide receiver Michael Floyd, a Twin Cities native and a player that Fitzgerald had advocated for. "In this league you have to be able to beat press man coverage on third down," Fitzgerald told the Arizona Republic on the night the team selected Floyd. "He is a big guy who has suddenness and can win on third down and make plays in the red zone." Clearly, Fitzgerald knew the Cardinals' offense had a -35.9% DVOA on third downs and -5.6% DVOA in the red zone in 2011. (OK, maybe he didn't know those exact numbers, but he had a good general idea of the problems.)

As much as Floyd's selection should help whoever ends up quarterbacking the Cardinals, it should also help Fitzgerald. The perennial Pro Bowler has produced solid traditional statistics since the departures of Kurt Warner (retirement) and Anquan Boldin (trade to Baltimore) after the 2009 season, but his DYAR and DVOA took a significant hit while playing with the Cardinals' four-headed quarterback monster in 2010. Those numbers returned to more Fitzgerald-like levels in 2011, but he is seeing more and more double and triple teams from opposing defenses, who haven't been concerned about being beaten by Steve Breaston or Andre Roberts the way they were with Boldin.

On the other hand, Floyd carries some off-field risks. During his four years at Notre Dame, Floyd was arrested three times for alcohol-related offenses, including a DUI on March 20, 2011. Floyd received a one-year sentence (suspended), had to install an ignition device into his car for six months, and was suspended by Irish coach Brian Kelly for four months before he was reinstated a month before his senior season was to begin. The off-field issues clearly did not hurt Floyd's production; he finished his college career by catching 100 passes for 1,147 yards and nine touchdowns last season. The Cardinals hope that his issues with alcohol are behind him, and that Fitzgerald, who has known Floyd since the latter was in high school, can keep him on the right path so he can be the high-quality No. 2 receiver the team has lacked since losing Boldin.

A potential added benefit to having another big, physical receiver on the outside is that opponents may be less inclined to blitz Kolb-Skelton, which would take some pressure off an offensive line that continues to struggle to protect the quarterback. Since the departure of Warner, the Cardinals' Adjusted Sack Rate has increased from 5.4 percent in 2009 to 9.0 percent in 2011. Perhaps the problem of pass protection was another factor in the pursuit of Manning, whose pre-snap reads and adjustments and quick release allowed the Indianapolis Colts to rank highly in ASR (first from 2008-10) despite lacking quality personnel. As for the Cardinals' offensive line, the decision to move Levi Brown from right to left tackle fared no better in year two than year one. Brown reached double-digits in blown blocks for a second straight season and was released for salary cap purposes in early March. Alas, with no suitable replacements available in free agency—they worked out Demetress Bell in March but didn't seem too excited by him—the Cardinals re-signed Brown to a five-year, $30 million contract on St. Patrick's Day.

The Cardinals did have the opportunity to select University of Iowa offensive tackle Riley Reiff with the No. 13 pick in the draft, which would have allowed them to move Brown back to his more natural position at right tackle, but opted to go with Floyd. Due to the Kolb trade, the Cardinals were without a second-round pick, and thus missed out on taking players such as Ohio State's Mike Adams and Stanford's Jonathan Martin. Then they passed on addressing the offensive line with their third-round pick, becoming one of two teams to have not used a first-, second- or third-round pick on an offensive lineman in five consecutive drafts (the Tennessee Titans are the other). The Cardinals would add multiple late-round offensive linemen to the roster, including fourth-round pick Bobby Massie, a 6-foot-6, 316-pounder who started 29 games at right tackle for Ole Miss and was projected by some draftniks to go as high as the second round. Massie has 35-inch arms, and he's very quick off the snap. He will get an opportunity to compete for a starting job right away.

Another need the Cardinals skipped so they could select Floyd was a pass-rushing outside linebacker. Though the Cardinals' 42 sacks from 2011 were tied for the seventh-most in the league, their Adjusted Sack Rate was only 6.4 percent, which ranked 22nd. The issue is one of schedule. The four NFC West teams were so bad at pass protection that all four ranked between 24th and 28th in offensive Adjusted Sack Rate. On top of that, the two opponents the Cardinals didn't share with their division rivals were Minnesota (32nd in ASR) and Carolina (21st). Not only was the Cardinals' sack total a bit overstated because of their schedule, but the outside linebackers didn't even account for much of the total, with just 14.5 sacks.

Even without the addition of a pass-rushing linebacker, Arizona's defense is the strength of the team and should improve with a full offseason under defensive coordinator Ray Horton. Hired last January, the lockout denied Horton the opportunity to fully implement his system before the start of the regular season. Horton's defense had to overcome the disappearance of Stewart Bradley, the unit's biggest free-agent addition after the lockout. Bradley struggled to adjust to a 3-4 scheme after spending the first four years of his career as a "Mike" in Philadelphia's 4-3 system, and ended up starting only two games all season. Horton was also hamstrung by the loss of his top cornerback with any game experience (Dominique Rodgers-Cromartie) in the Kolb trade, and was hit by a double whammy at the cornerback position when projected starter Greg Toler went down in the preseason with a torn ACL.

Those losses were a big reason why the Cardinals immediately threw Patrick Peterson into the crucible as a rookie. Not only did he start all 16 games, but he also covered the opponent's No. 1 receiver on 63 percent of his targets, fourth in the league behind only Darrelle Revis, Ike Taylor, and Champ Bailey. His fellow players may have voted Peterson No. 55 on the NFL Network's Top 100 Players list this offseason, but NFL quarterbacks certainly didn't give him that kind of respect. Peterson was targeted 108 times by our count, seventh-highest in the league. NFL officials also weren't swayed by his college exploits, flagging Peterson a team-high 10 times on defense, including six pass interference fouls totaling 106 yards. Peterson ended up 68th in Success Rate and 65th in Adjusted Yards per Pass, but there are clear indications of a learning curve here. In his first five starts, Peterson had a miserable 29 percent Success Rate with 11.1 adjusted yards per pass. After Arizona's bye in Week 5, Peterson had a much-improved 50 percent Success Rate with 8.0 adjusted yards per pass.

Peterson's inexperience and Bradley's struggles were among the numerous reasons why the Cardinals defense got off to a very slow start in 2011. In four of the first seven games of the season, opponents had more than 400 yards of total offense. Eventually, the unit would settle down and stop giving up so many big gains through the air. Over the final eight games of the season, the Cardinals allowed an average of 190 passing yards per game, and their DVOA rating against the pass improved dramatically (Table 1). The Cardinals will need this defensive improvement to carry over into 2012 if they want to return to the postseason. Certainly Peterson has the talent and desire to be a shutdown corner, and a full offseason of coaching from Horton should facilitate his development.

Table 1. Arizona Pass Defense Improvement in 2011

Weeks	Net Y/P	DVOA	Gains of 16+ Yds*
1-5	7.08	22.4%	33
7-9	6.66	23.8%	18
10-13	5.47	-12.1%	17
14-17	4.55	-23.0%	12

*includes Defensive Pass Interference

Still, no matter how well Peterson and the defense may play, quarterback play is likely to be the determining factor in the Cardinals beating our projection and possibly returning to the playoffs for the first time since 2009. Whisenhunt has been adamant that neither a player's acquisition price nor his current salary will be a factor in deciding who starts when the Seahawks come to town on September 9. Whichever passer plays the best during the preseason or has the best grasp of the system will get the job. While folks in the front office will certainly be privately pulling for Kevin Kolb, it is Whisenhunt's call, and since his seven-year career began as an unheralded 12th-round pick (No. 313 overall), he has some credibility when he says he's ignoring the players' price tags. The quarterback who wins the job should be more productive, aided by the arrival of Floyd and the addition of 2011 second-round pick Ryan Williams to an already decent running game, but the pass protection will still be faulty. If neither Kolb nor Skelton is able to get the job done, the Cardinals will be in the market for a franchise quarterback in the 2013 draft. Frankly, even if Kolb or Skelton does a reasonable job, the Cardinals will still be in the market for a franchise quarterback in the 2013 draft.

Brian McIntyre

ARIZONA CARDINALS

2011 Cardinals Stats by Week

Wk	vs.	W-L	PF	PA	YDF	YDA	TO	Total	Off	Def	ST
1	CAR	W	28	21	394	477	0	2%	-1%	13%	16%
2	@WAS	L	21	22	324	455	0	-15%	3%	9%	-9%
3	@SEA	L	10	13	324	261	1	-13%	-7%	-6%	-12%
4	NYG	L	27	31	368	360	0	28%	-12%	15%	-1%
5	@MIN	L	10	34	291	332	3	-90%	-56%	36%	2%
6	BYE										
7	PIT	L	20	32	330	445	1	-13%	18%	25%	-6%
8	@BAL	L	27	30	207	405	-1	5%	-24%	1%	30%
9	STL	W	19	13	262	383	-1	19%	-31%	14%	27%
10	@PHI	W	21	17	370	289	0	4%	-6%	-28%	-18%
11	@SF	L	7	23	229	431	4	-70%	-69%	6%	5%
12	@STL	W	23	20	374	272	1	-26%	-31%	-5%	0%
13	DAL	W	19	13	327	336	0	2%	1%	1%	2%
14	SF	W	21	19	325	233	3	-13%	-14%	-41%	-14%
15	CLE	W	20	17	363	333	0	-25%	-9%	13%	-3%
16	@CIN	L	16	23	316	301	1	-53%	-51%	0%	-3%
17	SEA	W	23	20	388	369	1	12%	-9%	-16%	5%

Trends and Splits

	Offense	Rank	Defense	Rank
Total DVOA	-18.4%	28	2.4%	14
Unadjusted VOA	-17.4%	28	0.0%	15
Weighted Trend	-20.1%	28	-2.4%	14
Variance	5.6%	9	7.0%	22
Average Opponent	-2.3%	7	-3.2%	25
Passing	-21.7%	29	3.2%	15
Rushing	-4.2%	17	1.5%	24
First Down	-5.0%	22	0.4%	17
Second Down	-23.7%	31	19.7%	32
Third Down	-35.9%	30	-22.1%	4
First Half	-33.2%	32	-0.3%	16
Second Half	-6.5%	22	5.5%	22
Red Zone	-5.6%	16	-31.8%	4
Late and Close	-3.9%	20	2.5%	19

Five-Year Performance

Year	W-L	Pyth	Est W	PF	PA	TO	Total	Rk	Off	Rk	Def	Rk	ST	Rk	Off AGL	Rk	Def AGL	Rk
2007	8-8	8.1	5.4	404	399	-7	-12.8%	23	-3.6%	19	4.7%	20	-4.5%	26	26.0	25	37.2	28
2008	9-7	8.0	7.2	427	426	0	-5.0%	21	4.6%	15	5.1%	21	-4.6%	28	23.5	14	14.3	8
2009	10-6	9.4	10.4	381	325	-7	11.2%	12	6.8%	13	-2.8%	11	1.7%	10	13.6	10	10.5	3
2010	5-11	4.3	3.1	289	434	-5	-37.1%	32	-35.6%	31	5.6%	25	4.2%	9	26.8	17	11.4	8
2011	8-8	6.9	4.9	312	348	-13	-19.7%	28	-18.4%	28	2.4%	20	1.2%	11	46.3	28	40.5	25

2011 Performance Based on Most Common Personnel Groups

Arizona Offense					Arizona Offense vs. Opp.				Arizona Defense				Arizona Defense vs. Opp.			
Pers	Freq	Yds	DVOA	Run%	Pers	Freq	Yds	DVOA	Pers	Freq	Yds	DVOA	Pers	Freq	Yds	DVOA
11	31%	5.7	-18.4%	19%	4-3-4	30%	5.1	-14.4%	3-4-4	50%	5.2	-0.2%	11	38%	5.5	1.2%
12	20%	4.8	-8.8%	49%	4-2-5	28%	5.3	-20.9%	2-4-5	36%	5.6	7.5%	12	26%	5.4	6.8%
21	17%	6.6	2.9%	58%	Dime+	15%	4.5	-36.4%	3-3-5	6%	5.9	-10.6%	21	13%	5.4	-1.9%
10	15%	5.1	-13.9%	11%	3-4-4	15%	6.3	2.6%	4-2-5	2%	6.5	6.6%	22	8%	5.4	11.1%
22	7%	3.3	-7.0%	79%	3-3-5	5%	6.3	-16.5%	Dime+	2%	5.5	-30.7%	13	6%	5.1	-2.1%

Strategic Tendencies

Run/Pass		Rank	Offense		Rank	Pass Rush		Rank	Defense/Other		Rank
Runs, all plays	38%	26	Form: Single Back	64%	14	Rush 3	5.6%	17	4 DB	51%	13
Runs, first half	39%	23	Form: Empty Back	6%	11	Rush 4	55.6%	24	5 DB	44%	13
Runs, first down	49%	20	Pers: 3+ WR	54%	12	Rush 5	27.9%	6	6+ DB	2%	25
Runs, second-long	29%	26	Pers: 4+ WR	18%	2	Rush 6+	10.8%	7	CB by Sides	59%	29
Runs, power sit.	57%	18	Pers: 2+ TE/6+ OL	32%	16	Zone Blitz	5.1%	17	Go for it on 4th	0.87	18
Runs, behind 2H	33%	10	Play action	15%	26	Sacks by LB	56.0%	9	Offensive Pace	30.5	16
Pass, ahead 2H	43%	19	Max protect	8%	25	Sacks by DB	11.9%	8	Defensive Pace	30.3	11

Arizona was massively boom-or-bust when it went with an empty backfield. The Cardinals had 8.4 yards per play, second in the NFL, but -13.8% DVOA, far below the league average from empty backfield of 20.4% DVOA. What happened? Kevin Kolb had three passes over 70 yards from empty sets, but the Cardinals as a team had only two other passes over 20 yards. The Cardinals also had three picks from empty sets (one by Kolb, two by John Skelton) and three passes from empty on third-and-long that gained at least 13 yards but still didn't convert. ⏺ Arizona went without a tight end on 19 percent of plays, which ranked third in the league. That sounds like a lot, but the Cardinals had gone without a tight end on at least 35 percent of plays in 2008, 2009, and 2010. ⏺ The Cardinals were a strong blitz team. With each successive additional pass rusher from three to six, their yards per play allowed went down by at least a yard. (However, they did allow 93 yards on the 10 plays where they brought seven.) ⏺ Only 15 percent of passes from Cardinals opponents were marked as being in the middle of the field; every other defense was at 19 percent or above. ⏺ Cardinals opponents threw a league-low 15 percent of passes to running backs.

Passing

Player	DYAR	DVOA	Plays	NtYds	Avg	YAC	C%	TD	Int
J.Skelton	-326	-27.6%	298	1745	5.9	5.4	55.3%	11	14
K.Kolb	-133	-18.5%	282	1698	6.1	6.2	58.6%	9	8
R.Bartel	-32	-32.2%	23	80	4.3	1.7	45.5%	1	1

Rushing

Player	DYAR	DVOA	Plays	Yds	Avg	TD	Fum	Suc
B.Wells	101	1.0%	245	1048	4.3	10	4	51%
L.Stephens-Howling	-14	-16.7%	43	167	3.9	0	0	40%
A.Smith	8	-3.3%	30	102	3.4	1	0	57%
C.Taylor*	2	-7.0%	20	77	3.9	1	0	40%
J.Skelton	34	19.8%	20	135	6.8	0	1	--
K.Kolb	-1	-14.2%	12	62	5.2	0	1	--

Receiving

Player	DYAR	DVOA	Plays	Ctch	Yds	Y/C	YAC	TD	C%
L.Fitzgerald	278	9.7%	154	80	1411	17.6	6.1	8	52%
E.Doucet	12	-11.1%	97	54	689	12.8	6.0	5	56%
A.Roberts	-22	-15.5%	97	51	586	11.5	4.4	2	53%
D.Sampson	4	-6.6%	8	3	36	12.0	2.3	0	38%
C.Stuckey*	-20	-45.5%	8	4	39	9.8	2.5	0	50%
T.Heap	-3	-8.7%	36	24	283	11.8	4.6	1	67%
J.King	53	14.6%	34	27	271	10.0	4.8	3	79%
R.Housler	-47	-39.7%	26	12	133	11.1	4.1	0	46%
C.Taylor*	-56	-65.6%	24	14	91	6.5	5.8	0	58%
L.Stephens-Howling	101	85.3%	17	13	234	18.0	16.2	2	76%
B.Wells	-22	-44.0%	16	10	52	5.2	1.9	0	63%
A.Sherman	20	22.8%	9	8	72	9.0	5.1	0	89%

Offensive Line

Year	Yards	ALY	Rank	Power	Rank	Stuff	Rank	2nd Lev	Rank	Open Field	Rank	F-Start	Cont.
2009	4.27	4.09	16	56%	28	23%	30	1.36	2	0.81	14	17	39
2010	4.31	3.84	21	74%	5	21%	22	1.20	11	1.00	7	14	39
2011	4.12	4.07	15	63%	16	20%	18	1.07	27	0.74	21	16	31

Year	LE	Rank	LT	Rank	Mid	Rank	RT	Rank	RE	Rank	Sacks	ASR	Rank	Short	Long
2009	5.47	2	3.81	22	3.94	24	4.27	9	3.72	24	26	5.2%	7	9	8
2010	5.18	2	2.84	31	3.68	25	4.41	7	3.84	19	50	8.4%	27	24	13
2011	3.38	25	4.25	15	4.02	17	4.65	10	3.33	21	54	9.0%	27	21	22

Levi Brown was briefly released for financial reasons in March, but the Cardinals felt that his play had improved over the second half of the season and that he was their best option in free agency. So Brown signed a five-year, $30 million contract on March 17 and is once again penciled in at left tackle. As was the case in his first season at left tackle, Brown's 2011 season was full of blown blocks. According to our game charters, Brown ranked second in the league with 12.5 blown blocks in 2010, and he had another 10.5 last season. With Daryn Colledge back at left guard and Lyle Sendlein at center, 60 percent of the offensive line will carry over to 2012. The right side of the line, however, will have a different look. Guards Deuce Lutui and Rex Hadnot both signed free agent deals elsewhere after the Cardinals gave a $5 million signing bonus to right guard Adam Snyder, who started the final 13 games of the 2011 season for the San Francisco 49ers. Brandon Keith was not re-signed after he started 11 games at right tackle; he battled injuries (knee, ankle) and inconsistency to the point where he and Jeremy Bridges saw the same amount of playing time. Now Bridges and 2012 fourth-round pick Bobby Massie (Ole Miss) will compete for the starting job. Massie was one of three offensive tackles the Cardinals took in the mid- to late rounds of the 2012 draft. He excelled in the SEC thanks to his long arms, quick feet, and nasty attitude, but he'll need to work on pass-blocking technique at the next level. He also sometimes struggles with losing his balance or executing blocks in space on run plays. Versatile and competitive Washington product Senio Kelemete was taken in the fifth round and is expected to be moved to guard, while seventh-rounder Nate Potter from Boise State could develop into a swing tackle.

Defensive Front Seven

Defensive Line	Age	Pos	Plays	TmPct	Rk	Stop	Dfts	BTkl	St%	Rk	AvYd	Rk	Sack	Hit	Hur	Runs	St%	Yds	Pass	St%	Yds
Calais Campbell	26	DE	82	9.4%	2	62	28	4	76%	52	2.1	59	8	10	17.5	51	71%	3.3	31	84%	0.2
Darnell Dockett	31	DE	49	5.6%	29	40	19	4	82%	30	0.9	24	3.5	16	23.5	36	83%	1.1	13	77%	0.3
Dan Williams	25	DT	22	4.0%	34	19	2	3	86%	7	1.6	24	0	1	1	20	85%	1.8	2	100%	0.0
David Carter	25	DT	18	2.1%	--	13	6	1	72%	--	1.9	--	1	1	1.5	13	69%	3.0	5	80%	-0.8
Vonnie Holliday	37	DE	17	2.0%	--	13	5	0	76%	--	2.2	--	0	4	3	15	73%	2.7	2	100%	-1.5

Linebackers	Age	Pos	Plays	TmPct	Rk	Stop	Dfts	BTkl	AvYd	Sack	Hit	Hur	Runs	St%	Rk	Yds	Rk	Tgts	Suc%	Rk	AdjYd	Rk
Daryl Washington	24	ILB	112	13.7%	25	61	30	10	4.5	5	2	15	62	56%	88	3.6	70	38	53%	26	7.6	64
Paris Lenon	35	ILB	96	11.0%	47	50	18	3	4.5	3	1	8.5	66	58%	84	3.6	69	33	52%	38	6.4	34
Clark Haggans	35	OLB	48	5.5%	106	30	8	0	3.3	3	5	15	27	63%	65	3.3	48	16	52%	34	5.6	19
Sam Acho	24	OLB	37	4.2%	110	25	11	0	3.2	7	0	6.5	21	62%	69	4.3	100	9	56%	--	6.2	--
O'Brien Schofield	25	OLB	25	2.9%	--	15	8	2	2.7	4.5	3	3.5	15	60%	--	4.4	--	4	0%	--	8.8	--
Stewart Bradley	29	ILB	22	2.5%	--	13	2	0	5.2	0	1	2.5	15	67%	--	3.8	--	9	42%	--	4.9	--
Joey Porter*	35	OLB	16	4.9%	--	7	3	0	5.9	1	1	2.5	9	56%	--	2.7	--	5	12%	--	16.2	--

Year	Yards	ALY	Rank	Power	Rank	Stuff	Rank	2nd Lev	Rank	Open Field	Rank
2009	4.72	3.95	11	61%	10	23%	8	1.26	27	1.31	32
2010	4.60	4.28	23	63%	17	20%	15	1.32	29	1.01	28
2011	4.23	4.11	19	71%	27	20%	13	1.27	23	0.69	10

Year	LE	Rank	LT	Rank	Mid	Rank	RT	Rank	RE	Rank	Sacks	ASR	Rank	Short	Long
2009	4.29	17	4.41	22	3.91	14	3.27	3	4.09	18	43	7.1%	10	13	17
2010	4.84	26	4.52	24	3.98	18	4.49	22	4.67	28	33	6.0%	19	14	9
2011	3.76	8	4.23	19	3.90	11	4.45	21	4.09	28	42	6.4%	22	12	15

The Cardinals arguably have the best pair of defensive ends among the league's 3-4 defenses. Darnell Dockett's three-year run of Pro Bowls came to an end and his 3.5 sacks were his lowest total since 2006, but he was solid against the run and led the Cardinals with 23.5 hurries. Opposite Dockett is Calais Campbell, a 6-foot-8, 300-pound monster who has led or tied for the team lead in sacks in each of the last three seasons. The Cardinals placed the franchise tag on Campbell in February before signing him to a five-year, $55 million contract in May. Depth behind Campbell and Dockett may be an issue, but the two rarely left the field in 2011, playing nearly 90 percent of the defensive snaps. Nose tackle Dan Williams' improvement against the run late in his rookie season was torpedoed by a lockout that kept him away from Tempe in the offseason. Williams was out of shape when training camp opened and had more broken tackles than defeats before breaking his left arm in Week 11. Williams has reportedly hit the gym and his playbook this offseason and is looking to become the anchor against the run the Cardinals envisioned him being when they chose him with the 26th overall pick in 2010. If he's not, 2011 sixth-round pick David Carter will get those snaps.

Improved play from the middle of the defensive line would help inside linebackers Daryl Washington, Paris Lenon, and Stewart Bradley. Washington and Lenon were nearly identical in every statistical category except Defeats, where Washington finished in the Top 5 with 30. Bradley was signed to five-year, $30 million contract after the lockout, but struggled to adapt to a new system and ended up making most of his impact on special teams. Bradley agreed to cut his pay in half this offseason and will be looking to wrestle a starting job away from Lenon. The Cardinals took the first step towards getting younger at outside linebacker when 2011 fourth-round pick Sam Acho replaced Joey Porter in the starting lineup opposite Clark Haggans. O'Brien Schofield, a 2010 fourth-round pick, led the team in special teams tackles while picking up 4.5 sacks in a reserve role. He is expected to start opposite Acho, although the Cardinals did decide to bring back Haggans in early June. Other than Haggans, there is so little depth behind Acho and Schofield that the Cardinals took a flier on Quentin Groves, a 2008 second-round bust who hasn't sacked a quarterback since December 14, 2008.

Defensive Secondary

Secondary	Age	Pos	Plays	TmPct	Rk	Stop	Dfts	BTkl	Runs	St%	Rk	Yds	Rk	Tgts	Tgt%	Rk	Dist	Suc%	Rk	APaYd	Rk	PD	Int
Richard Marshall*	28	CB	80	9.2%	25	36	16	2	35	43%	40	5.9	25	52	11.0%	77	11.2	63%	7	7.3	38	9	3
Adrian Wilson	33	SS	78	9.0%	50	49	19	6	47	57%	5	4.4	3	32	6.8%	43	13.1	73%	6	5.8	11	13	1
A.J. Jefferson	24	CB	77	8.8%	33	27	13	3	14	57%	12	6.2	29	96	20.2%	23	13.6	47%	63	7.4	41	11	1
Patrick Peterson	22	CB	77	8.8%	33	30	14	8	13	31%	60	6.9	40	108	22.7%	7	15.5	45%	68	8.9	65	15	2
Rashad Johnson	26	FS	43	4.9%	74	11	2	2	27	26%	67	7.3	46	9	1.9%	77	12.2	47%	61	13.4	75	2	0
Kerry Rhodes	30	FS	38	10.0%	39	15	6	0	17	35%	49	7.4	49	16	7.7%	29	13.1	45%	66	13.7	76	5	0
Michael Adams	27	CB	33	4.0%	--	18	5	5	8	63%	--	3.4	--	34	7.6%	--	10.3	55%	--	6.2	--	1	0
William Gay	27	CB	73	9.7%	19	36	14	4	21	57%	12	5.1	13	74	17.2%	42	10.3	53%	39	6.2	16	12	2
James Sanders	29	FS	42	5.8%	69	12	3	1	20	35%	50	8.1	55	16	4.0%	74	13.0	56%	38	9.1	51	3	0

Year	Pass D Rank	vs. #1 WR	Rk	vs. #2 WR	Rk	vs. Other WR	Rk	vs. TE	Rk	vs. RB	Rk
2009	12	19.7%	25	-26.4%	2	-14.1%	9	-3.2%	11	0.5%	17
2010	22	25.0%	28	10.3%	21	-9.3%	12	-6.4%	7	-6.9%	8
2011	14	10.7%	17	4.4%	16	6.0%	24	9.6%	17	-26.8%	2

The starting cornerback opposite Patrick Peterson will be determined in training camp. A.J. Jefferson and Richard Marshall split those duties in 2011, but the more effective (and versatile) Marshall signed with the Miami Dolphins as a free agent. Jefferson will compete for the starting job with a healthy Greg Toler as well as William Gay, a free-agent addition who spent the first four seasons of his career playing under Ray Horton with the Pittsburgh Steelers. Waiting in the wings is third-round rookie Jamell Fleming (Oklahoma).

Safety Adrian Wilson has long been a favorite of Football Outsiders, labeled as the "Best Safety in Football" on the cover of *Pro Football Prospectus 2007*. Wilson had a bounce back season in 2011, continuing to rank in the top five against the run and cutting down on his number of broken tackles (16 in 2010, only six in 2011) while improving significantly against the pass. What makes Wilson's 2011 performance even more impressive is that he played the entire season with a torn biceps tendon. Free safety Kerry Rhodes missed most of the second half of the year with a broken foot; 2009 third-round pick Rashad Johnson replaced Rhodes in the starting lineup and the two combined to give the Cardinals zero interceptions and just eight Defeats from the position. Marshall played some safety in sub packages for the Cardinals last season and that role could be filled by Fleming, an aggressive physical corner with good closing speed.

Special Teams

Year	DVOA	Rank	FG/XP	Rank	Net Kick	Rank	Kick Ret	Rank	Net Punt	Rank	Punt Ret	Rank	Hidden	Rank
2009	1.4%	10	4.6	8	-0.6	18	0.2	11	9.2	5	-5.2	24	4.5	8
2010	3.3%	9	9.1	2	7.3	8	13.8	4	0.7	17	-11.5	32	9.0	3
2011	1.0%	11	-5.2	24	-0.7	20	-3.5	24	-4.7	22	20.0	1	14.7	2

This was the Patrick Peterson Show. Peterson led the NFL in punt return yards, was second in punt return average, and tied an NFL record (in the process setting a rookie record) with four punt returns for touchdowns in 2011. By our metrics, the field position gained by Peterson meant an estimated 21 extra points for the Cardinals, who had ranked dead last in punt returns the year before. This year, opposing special teams coordinators will likely avoid giving Peterson many opportunities to flip the field.

Unfortunately, while Peterson was completely turning around the punt returns, the rest of the Arizona special teams slipped badly. Under the new rules in 2011, kick returner LaRod Stephens-Howling had just 36 return opportunities, compared to 55 in 2010, and did not have a return longer than 37 yards. After going 24-of-27 in 2010, with all three misses coming at 49 yards or more, Jay Feely was just 19-of-24 on field-goal attempts in 2011. Left-footed punter Dave Zastudil was added late in training camp and ended up beating out Ben Graham for the job. Zastudil had a 45.2-yard gross average, but the Cardinals' punt coverage unit was in the bottom five (allowing 7.6 estimated points of field position) as an area that was a strength in 2009 continued its decline. Feely, Zastudil and long-snapper Mike Leach were all unrestricted free agents this offseason, but all three veterans (average age: 35.3) received multi-year extensions.

Arizona's high "Hidden" value comes from a very bad year for opposing field-goal kickers. Opponents hit only 35 of 48 field-goal attempts against the Cardinals, making them a weather-adjusted 15 points worse than league average according to FO metrics. There will be some regression towards the mean here, although we should give the Cardinals credit: five of those 13 misses were blocked, three by Calais Campbell and two by Peterson. The Cardinals now have 11 blocked field goals in the last three seasons, fairly remarkable since the average team has less than one blocked field goal each season.

Coaching Staff

After replacing defensive coordinator Bill Davis with Ray Horton and promoting Mike Miller to offensive coordinator last offseason, head coach Ken Whisenhunt went to great lengths to keep most of his current staff intact for 2012. Horton interviewed for five hours for the St. Louis Rams opening that ultimately went to Jeff Fisher, and Whisenhunt may not be able to hold off the suitors much longer. Kevin Kolb and John Skelton's struggles cost quarterbacks coach Chris Miller his job, and receivers coach John McNulty was reassigned to coach the team's signal-callers. Before joining the Cardinals, McNulty spent five seasons on Greg Schiano's coaching staff at Rutgers. When Schiano was hired by the Tampa Bay Buccaneers, he sought permission to interview McNulty for offensive coordinator, but Whisenhunt denied the request. With McNulty reassigned to quarterbacks coach, the Cardinals hired former NFL quarterback Frank Reich to coach the team's receivers. Reich had filled that role with the Indianapolis Colts last season.

Atlanta Falcons

2011 Record: 10-6

Pythagorean Wins: 9.4 (10th)

DVOA: 13.9% (8th)

Offense: 6.1% (11th)

Defense: -9.1% (8th)

Special Teams: -1.3% (22nd)

Variance: 5.2% (1st)

2012 Mean Projection: 9.9 wins

On the Clock (0-4): 1%

Mediocrity (5-7): 11%

Playoff Contender (8-10): 48%

Super Bowl Contender (11+): 39%

Postseason Odds: 67.8%

Projected Average Opponent: 0.6% (18th)

2011: Judge our decisions based on process, not outcomes.

2012: An outcome that ends in the Super Bowl would be awfully nice right about now.

Sometimes, an organization can do everything right and still not reach the Super Bowl.

The Falcons have been a nearly textbook "best practices" example of how to run an NFL franchise since the start of the Tom Dimitroff-Mike Smith era in 2008. Dimitroff and Smith took over an organization whose former franchise quarterback was in jail and whose former coach quit via Dear John letter before the end of the previous season. They immediately started making all the right moves.

The Falcons identified and drafted their new franchise quarterback: Matt Ryan. They acquired workhorse back Michael Turner to take pressure off Ryan, while at the same time using the draft to build slowly instead of relying on the quick fix. They developed homegrown talents, some of whom were on the roster when they arrived and others who arrived through the draft: Roddy White, Jonathan Babineaux, Brent Grimes, Justin Blaylock, William Moore, Curtis Lofton, and others. They only resorted to free agency to patch specific holes with established stars like Tony Gonzalez and Dunta Robinson. The Falcons remained cap smart while acquiring and developing talent, allowing them to re-sign and retain the players they wanted to keep.

Dimitroff and Smith made smart quality-control decisions as the Falcons grew into contenders. Turner danced with the Curse of 370 while Ryan developed, but Smith and his assistants eased back on Turner's workload as Ryan and the offense grew up. When the 2010 Falcons were in obvious need of both a playmaking receiver and a bookend pass rusher to John Abraham, Dimitroff traded up to draft Julio Jones and jumped to sign Ray Edwards as soon as the lockout lifted. Both moves were prudent for a team coming off a 13-3 season, and while Edwards' effectiveness was limited by foot injuries, Jones was everything the Falcons could hope for.

When the Falcons reached the playoffs for the third time in four years, Smith faced two fourth-and-1 situations deep in Giants territory, one with a 2-0 lead and one while trailing 10-2. Smith elected to go for it both times. Going for it on fourth-and-short in both circumstances was the statistically correct decision, as independently studied and verified by Football Outsiders, our competitors, and anyone else who has seriously studied the issue. Smith's fourth-down decisions, like Dimitroff's trade for Jones, were a moderate-risk, high-yield gamble: an experienced, playoff-caliber offense should be able to gain one yard when it needs one.

Unfortunately, good decisions sometimes yield bad results. Go for it on fourth down, and you risk the chance of failing, twice. Acquire the "last big piece" of your roster, and you may just see other holes spring up in other places. Make the bold move to trade up to select an impact receiver in the draft, and you won't have a first-round pick the next year to address your

2012 Falcons Schedule

Week	Opp.	Week	Opp.	Week	Opp.
1	at KC	7	BYE	13	NO (Thu.)
2	DEN (Mon.)	8	at PHI	14	at CAR
3	at SD	9	DAL	15	NYG
4	CAR	10	at NO	16	at DET (Sat.)
5	at WAS	11	ARI	17	TB
6	OAK	12	at TB		

Figure 1. 2011 Atlanta DVOA by Week

next big problem. Bad luck and great opponents can undo the best plans.

The Falcons are now 0-3 in playoff games under Dimitroff-Smith, and it is easy to second guess even their wisest decisions. "Going for it" is all well and good, but quarterback sneaks into the teeth of the Giants defensive line may not have been the wisest play calls. Dimitroff's failure to add depth in the secondary became a huge problem when Grimes missed the final month of the season and Moore was knocked out early from the Giants game. Even Ryan is starting to collect doubters, as young quarterbacks often do after a few playoff losses.

Such criticisms are valid, to a degree, though they are all built upon 20-20 hindsight. They also miss the larger point: A window of success started to open for the Falcons in 2008. It gaped in 2010, making the Falcons look like the team of the next decade. Now, there is a risk that it will close prematurely.

The 2008 draft brought not just Ryan, but Lofton, Sam Baker, Harry Douglas, Kroy Biermann and Thomas DeCoud, among others. After two seasons, that class looked like it had the potential to be the best ever: Ryan was blossoming, Baker, DeCoud and Lofton starting, and the others were playing regular roles. Now, however, that class does not look nearly as impressive. Injuries threaten to derail Baker's career, and his last two seasons have been just short of disastrous. Lofton is now in New Orleans. DeCoud is an adequate-at-best starter. Biermann and Douglas peaked as role players. The 2009 and 2010 drafts were not very productive, with Weatherspoon and Corey Peters leading a cast of mostly reserves. Weatherspoon is the only true high-impact player the Falcons acquired between Ryan and Jones.

Meanwhile, core players are getting old, fast. Gonzalez, of course, continues to defy age. Abraham turned 34 in May. The Falcons lack obvious in-the-wings replacements for either of them. Babineaux and White turn 31 during the season. Turner turned 30 in February, and his odometer has flipped more than once. This core won't age overnight, but the Falcons cannot wait around until 2014 and expect it to still be intact. Because recent drafts have been lackluster, there is no obvious second wave of talent on the way. The Falcons have to win now, while the core is in its late prime and the Saints are being run out of the boiler room of a temp agency.

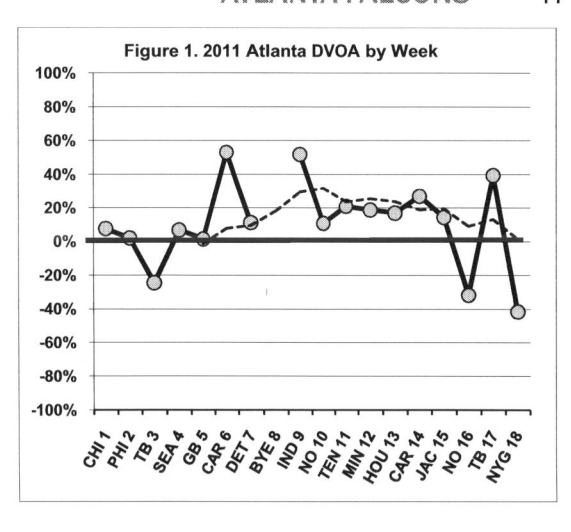

Dimitroff recognized this, but with no first-round pick to work with, he had to be creative about finding instant upgrades. Enter cornerback Asante Samuel, acquired from the Eagles for a mere seventh-round pick. Dimitroff's estimation of Samuel's value probably differed from Andy Reid's, just as the perception we get from our stats and tape study differs from those of Eagles fans and Philly columnists, who cast Samuel in the children's book *Diary of a Wimpy Cornerback*. Marcus Hayes condemned Samuel as "a fraud, wrapped in a mirage, inside an illusion" in a *Philadelphia Daily News* article after the trade. That was actually the nicest thing he said in an exit-interview article about a player who earned three Pro Bowl berths in Philly. Samuel's tackling has always been reminiscent of a mother daubing an infant's cheek with a cotton ball, but his performance in coverage has been excellent according to our data. Last year, he led the NFL in adjusted yards allowed per pass with 4.4 yards. He finished fourth in Success Rate, holding his receivers to an incomplete pass, interception, or minimal gain on 66 percent of pass attempts. Samuel finished first in both metrics in 2010. As for the tackling, in 2011 Samuel allowed an average of just 2.2 yards per catch after receptions, fifth best in the NFL, and could actually be seen delivering forceful blows on occasion.

Given the choice of dispassionate numbers and a columnist with a grudge preaching to the knockout-hungry base, erring on the side of the stats is always wise. Samuel still performs at or near a Pro Bowl level. He was the subject of trade rumors since the Eagles began Dream Teaming last August, so Samuel's attitude soured and the Eagles noticed. One trade later, Dimitroff filled the Falcons' biggest need on the cheap. Samuel, Grimes, and Dunta Robinson give the Falcons a deep cornerback corps that can withstand injuries and match up against pass-happy NFC contenders like the Packers and Saints.

The Falcons also signed Lofa Tatupu, another former All-Pro who ended up on the scrap heap during the post-lockout confusion. They selected center Peter Konz in the draft to eventually replace Todd McClure, but they also added veteran guard Vince Manuwai as an insurance policy on the interior offensive line. The Falcons are stocking up on veteran depth so they can make a short-term run.

As noted before, shifting into win-now mode is a wise move. A very clear window has opened at the top of the division. The Saints are in disarray. The Panthers are still learning to ride a big kid bike. The Buccaneers are rebuilding. The Falcons can, and should, win the division outright.

After that, they simply must play their brand of football and hope things break right in the playoffs. Neither the 2010 Packers loss nor last year's Giants loss started out as ugly games, but both unraveled after a few key plays: the pre-halftime pick-six against the Packers, the second failed sneak against the Giants. The Falcons have the talent to defeat the NFC contenders. They need things to break right, and they need better fallback plans if and when things break wrong. They solved the problem of being incapable of playing catch-up by grabbing Jones. The solution to the red zone and short-yardage problems could come from new offensive coordinator Dirk Koetter, who arrives from Jacksonville with a creative take on how to get the most from the running and screen games.

The prognosis beyond 2012 is cloudier. The "second nucleus" currently consists of Ryan, Jones, Weatherspoon, Peters, some developing prospects like Jacquizz Rodgers, and rookies like Konz. There are more blank spaces at places like tight end and defensive end then there are high draft picks to fill them in the next few seasons. Dimtroff has not built far beyond 2012 because it has not made sense to, but if the Falcons do not reach the Super Bowl in the next year, maybe two, they must refocus their priorities on acquiring additional high draft picks, purging veterans, and preparing for another success cycle during Ryan's prime.

The Falcons have made all of the right moves so far, and chances are they will keep making them. But whether it all results in a Super Bowl championship may be determined by forces beyond their control.

Mike Tanier

2011 Falcons Stats by Week

Wk	vs.	W-L	PF	PA	YDF	YDA	TO	Total	Off	Def	ST
1	@CHI	L	12	30	386	377	-2	8%	9%	4%	3%
2	PHI	W	35	31	318	447	1	2%	6%	0%	-4%
3	@TB	L	13	16	325	295	-1	-24%	-21%	-4%	-7%
4	@SEA	W	30	28	412	372	2	7%	29%	21%	-1%
5	GB	L	14	25	251	426	-1	2%	-5%	-5%	1%
6	CAR	W	31	17	325	368	3	53%	21%	-29%	2%
7	@DET	W	23	16	328	263	-1	11%	-21%	-16%	16%
8	BYE										
9	@IND	W	31	7	432	186	1	52%	9%	-34%	8%
10	NO	L	23	26	481	363	-1	11%	-5%	-24%	-9%
11	TEN	W	23	17	432	298	0	21%	21%	-1%	-1%
12	MIN	W	24	14	335	226	-1	19%	24%	-12%	-17%
13	@HOU	L	10	17	337	337	-1	17%	-10%	-23%	5%
14	@CAR	W	31	23	394	416	2	27%	15%	-12%	0%
15	JAC	W	41	14	373	207	4	14%	19%	-10%	-15%
16	@NO	L	16	45	469	463	1	-32%	-12%	14%	-5%
17	TB	W	45	24	428	294	2	39%	22%	-15%	2%
18	@NYG	L	2	24	247	442	0	-41%	-24%	20%	3%

Trends and Splits

	Offense	Rank	Defense	Rank
Total DVOA	6.1%	11	-9.1%	8
Unadjusted VOA	7.2%	10	-5.7%	11
Weighted Trend	7.0%	11	-13.1%	4
Variance	4.2%	3	3.3%	3
Average Opponent	3.3%	31	3.4%	3
Passing	23.2%	8	-1.8%	11
Rushing	-7.3%	23	-19.1%	3
First Down	-2.9%	20	-14.9%	6
Second Down	9.7%	10	-16.4%	2
Third Down	18.1%	11	12.7%	27
First Half	14.4%	7	-15.4%	5
Second Half	-2.6%	19	-2.9%	12
Red Zone	-1.9%	13	-41.1%	2
Late and Close	-4.2%	22	-13.1%	5

ATLANTA FALCONS

Five-Year Performance

Year	W-L	Pyth	Est W	PF	PA	TO	Total	Rk	Off	Rk	Def	Rk	ST	Rk	Off AGL	Rk	Def AGL	Rk
2007	4-12	3.9	4.8	259	414	+4	-25.9%	28	-16.2%	27	9.6%	28	-0.1%	15	26.4	27	20.4	17
2008	11-5	9.8	8.4	391	325	-3	4.7%	16	8.5%	9	7.5%	25	3.8%	7	15.5	11	13.3	7
2009	9-7	9.1	7.9	363	325	+3	0.5%	18	5.9%	14	4.1%	22	-1.3%	22	15.9	12	21.8	14
2010	13-3	11.4	11.3	414	288	+14	16.3%	7	8.0%	9	-2.1%	14	6.3%	3	5.2	1	10.9	6
2011	10-6	9.4	10.2	402	350	+8	13.9%	8	6.1%	11	-9.1%	8	-1.3%	22	22.2	13	26.4	16

2011 Performance Based on Most Common Personnel Groups

| Atlanta Offense ||||| Atlanta Offense vs. Opp. |||| Atlanta Defense |||| Atlanta Defense vs. Opp. ||||
Pers	Freq	Yds	DVOA	Run%	Pers	Freq	Yds	DVOA	Pers	Freq	Yds	DVOA	Pers	Freq	Yds	DVOA
11	43%	6.7	24.6%	24%	4-3-4	44%	5.4	-9.4%	4-3-4	46%	5.1	-22.2%	11	44%	6.0	5.0%
21	20%	6.9	18.5%	59%	4-2-5	29%	6.5	33.1%	4-2-5	44%	5.7	-1.3%	12	24%	5.1	-31.6%
12	13%	3.9	-43.0%	42%	3-3-5	8%	7.7	20.3%	3-3-5	6%	6.5	-16.7%	21	15%	6.3	-4.9%
22	8%	3.6	-36.7%	80%	Dime+	8%	6.6	25.6%	3-4-4	2%	9.8	51.7%	22	6%	3.2	-38.6%
13	3%	3.4	-5.0%	61%	3-4-4	5%	4.4	-0.2%	Dime+	2%	8.9	96.6%	01	2%	6.4	-4.6%

Strategic Tendencies

Run/Pass		Rank	Offense		Rank	Pass Rush		Rank	Defense/Other		Rank
Runs, all plays	41%	17	Form: Single Back	58%	23	Rush 3	6.7%	16	4 DB	48%	17
Runs, first half	45%	10	Form: Empty Back	7%	9	Rush 4	71.8%	8	5 DB	50%	8
Runs, first down	56%	8	Pers: 3+ WR	51%	16	Rush 5	17.1%	24	6+ DB	2%	29
Runs, second-long	33%	17	Pers: 4+ WR	4%	14	Rush 6+	4.5%	28	CB by Sides	98%	2
Runs, power sit.	56%	19	Pers: 2+ TE/6+ OL	30%	21	Zone Blitz	11.3%	2	Go for it on 4th	1.10	3
Runs, behind 2H	23%	30	Play action	17%	17	Sacks by LB	15.6%	21	Offensive Pace	31.6	27
Pass, ahead 2H	48%	7	Max protect	15%	4	Sacks by DB	4.7%	24	Defensive Pace	30.4	13

The Falcons were much less willing to run the ball when down in the second half compared to 2010 (when they ranked fifth at 32 percent runs). ☙ The Falcons were one of five teams that ran the running back screen pass less than once per game. ☙ The Falcons only handed the ball off on 3.7 percent of their plays from shotgun, the lowest rate in the league. ☙ By the count of our game charters, John Abraham dropped into coverage on a zone blitz more often than any defensive lineman in the league. ☙ Falcons opponents only threw 20 percent of their passes to their No. 1 receivers, tied with Miami for the lowest rate in the league. ☙ However, Atlanta was one of three defenses whose opponents threw to tight ends more than 25 percent of the time. ☙ Atlanta had the best defense in the league against passes to the deep middle by a HUGE amount. -60.8% DVOA. No other team was lower than -13.0%. The Falcons allowed just 10.1 yards per pass to the deep middle, with four picks. ☙ It won't surprise you that the Jets, with their great secondary, had the league's smallest gap between defensive DVOA bringing significant pass pressure and DVOA without pressure. But it may surprise you that the Falcons were a very close second. The Falcons brought pressure on 26.4 percent of pass plays (eighth in the NFL) with -40.5% DVOA (32nd) and 4.3 yards per play. Without pressure, they allowed 17.7% DVOA (fifth) with 7.3 yards per play. Every other team except the Falcons and Jets had a gap of more than 80% DVOA.

ATLANTA FALCONS

Passing

Player	DYAR	DVOA	Plays	NtYds	Avg	YAC	C%	TD	Int
M.Ryan	1118	18.7%	587	4011	6.9	5.0	62.1%	29	11
C.Redman	8	-6.2%	28	188	6.7	3.8	64.3%	0	1

Rushing

Player	DYAR	DVOA	Plays	Yds	Avg	TD	Fum	Suc
M.Turner	66	-3.4%	301	1349	4.5	11	3	45%
J.Rodgers	-3	-9.8%	56	195	3.5	1	1	46%
J.Snelling	-25	-22.9%	44	151	3.4	0	0	39%
M.Ryan	38	19.8%	21	107	5.1	2	0	--
J.Jones	31	40.9%	6	56	9.3	0	0	--

Receiving

Player	DYAR	DVOA	Plays	Ctch	Yds	Y/C	YAC	TD	C%
R.White	219	2.7%	180	100	1296	13.0	3.6	8	56%
J.Jones	164	9.9%	95	54	959	17.8	7.5	8	57%
H.Douglas	35	-4.9%	62	39	498	12.8	5.9	1	63%
E.Weems*	9	-4.4%	14	11	90	8.2	2.7	0	79%
T.Gonzalez	181	15.6%	116	80	875	10.9	3.0	7	69%
M.Palmer	-23	-28.8%	16	10	72	7.2	4.9	1	63%
J.Snelling	60	24.7%	32	26	179	6.9	6.3	1	81%
J.Rodgers	60	32.1%	28	22	199	9.0	6.5	1	79%
M.Turner	31	6.9%	26	17	168	9.9	8.6	0	65%
O.Mughelli	9	4.9%	8	4	25	6.3	4.5	2	50%

Offensive Line

Year	Yards	ALY	Rank	Power	Rank	Stuff	Rank	2nd Lev	Rank	Open Field	Rank	F-Start	Cont.
2009	4.36	4.26	10	63%	17	18%	12	1.12	17	0.89	10	15	34
2010	3.97	4.19	8	68%	9	19%	15	1.03	28	0.71	16	8	48
2011	4.21	3.83	27	59%	22	25%	31	1.16	17	1.05	6	13	34

Year	LE	Rank	LT	Rank	Mid	Rank	RT	Rank	RE	Rank	Sacks	ASR	Rank	Short	Long
2009	5.18	5	3.85	21	4.12	15	3.96	19	4.62	10	27	4.6%	6	9	13
2010	4.38	15	4.19	17	4.12	12	4.30	11	4.10	13	22	4.1%	3	9	8
2011	4.31	14	3.53	26	3.91	21	4.66	9	2.65	28	26	5.1%	7	13	9

Sam Baker suffered through another miserable season last year. He got pushed around at left tackle early in the year, was benched, had back surgery in October, moved briefly to right guard, then was benched again. Baker is penciled in as the starter at left tackle entering camp. Third-round pick Lamar Holmes (Southern Miss) has prototypical size for a left tackle, but a foot injury before rookie camp kept him from getting fast-tracked as an immediate challenger to Baker. If Baker struggles early in the season, journeyman Will Svitek will again step in.

Rookie Joe Hawley took over at right guard after Garrett Reynolds got destroyed by Ndamukong Suh and Brandon Mebane in early games and Baker proved no better. Hawley also started three games in relief of center Todd McClure, who signed a one-year deal for the veteran minimum and is clearly near the end of the line. Second-round pick Peter Konz is the obvious heir to McClure; Konz is a powerful drive blocker who can help in short-yardage situations, and he has the experience (three years as a starter at Wisconsin) to step right into the lineup if needed. Veteran Vince Manuwai adds an experienced, drive-blocking big body who could push Hawley.

Justin Blaylock renegotiated his contract in April so the team could sign Asante Samuel. He remains a fixture at left guard. There was talk in May of moving right tackle Tyson Clabo to the left side; if Baker struggles and Holmes is not ready, that could still be an option, with Svitek replacing Clabo on the right side.

Defensive Front Seven

Defensive Line	Age	Pos	Plays	TmPct	Rk	Stop	Dfts	BTkl	St%	Rk	AvYd	Rk	Sack	Hit	Hur	Runs	St%	Yds	Pass	St%	Yds
John Abraham	34	DE	37	5.1%	40	31	19	3	84%	23	0.0	11	9.5	10	35	20	80%	2.4	17	88%	-2.8
Ray Edwards	27	DE	36	4.7%	49	29	10	2	81%	33	1.6	48	3.5	6	15	26	77%	2.9	10	90%	-1.8
Corey Peters	24	DT	29	4.0%	35	26	9	1	90%	6	0.0	2	3	3	9.5	22	86%	1.2	7	100%	-3.9
Kroy Biermann	27	DE	28	3.6%	67	19	7	2	68%	73	1.9	54	2.5	7	18.5	23	65%	3.0	5	80%	-3.0
Jonathan Babineaux	31	DT	23	3.7%	47	15	4	0	65%	61	3.0	65	1	7	12.5	15	80%	2.1	8	38%	4.8
Vance Walker	25	DT	17	2.2%	--	15	4	1	88%	--	1.0	--	2	1	4.5	12	92%	1.3	5	80%	0.4

ATLANTA FALCONS

Linebackers	Age	Pos	Plays	TmPct	Rk	Stop	Dfts	BTkl	AvYd	Sack	Hit	Hur	Runs	St%	Rk	Yds	Rk	Tgts	Suc%	Rk	AdjYd	Rk
Curtis Lofton*	26	MLB	154	20.0%	2	84	21	6	4.7	1	2	9.5	87	69%	40	3.0	35	64	53%	28	5.3	13
Sean Weatherspoon	25	OLB	121	15.7%	16	76	26	13	3.5	4	1	8.5	57	81%	7	2.0	7	60	57%	16	4.9	9
Stephen Nicholas	29	OLB	32	6.7%	98	20	11	1	4.1	0	3	4.5	17	71%	31	2.5	21	11	45%	--	7.4	--
Mike Peterson*	36	OLB	25	3.5%	--	12	5	1	4.4	0	0	0	13	54%	--	3.8	--	11	64%	--	4.6	--

Year	Yards	ALY	Rank	Power	Rank	Stuff	Rank	2nd Lev	Rank	Open Field	Rank
2009	3.86	3.96	12	69%	24	21%	10	1.11	13	0.52	6
2010	4.28	3.83	13	64%	19	22%	5	1.19	22	0.92	22
2011	4.10	3.72	3	63%	17	23%	2	1.19	17	0.81	20

Year	LE	Rank	LT	Rank	Mid	Rank	RT	Rank	RE	Rank	Sacks	ASR	Rank	Short	Long
2009	4.51	19	4.18	18	3.80	12	4.15	15	3.68	10	28	5.6%	26	8	12
2010	4.31	19	3.40	7	3.58	4	3.83	11	4.69	29	31	5.8%	23	12	11
2011	3.52	7	3.62	5	4.29	25	2.96	1	2.41	2	33	6.0%	24	11	15

Lofa Tatupu is the likely replacement for Curtis Lofton at middle linebacker. Tatupu was a three-time Pro Bowler for the Seahawks before injuries and scheme changes derailed his career. He was not an ideal fit in Pete Carroll's defense, and when the Seahawks released him just after the lockout, Tatupu opted to sit out the season to rehab a chronically ailing knee and spend time with his newborn son. Tatupu does not turn 30 until November and may be another example of a Dimitroff bargain bin success. If not, 2011 third-rounder and popular local product Akeem Dent is waiting in the wings.

Weakside linebacker Sean Weatherspoon is expected to play a major role in Mike Nolan's new defense. Weatherspoon said in May that his responsibilities will include calling signals in the nickel package. A natural pass rusher and penetrator, Weatherspoon is also likely to attack the line of scrimmage if Nolan adds some 3-4 principles to the Falcons scheme. Stephen Nicholas, who missed much of last season with a quad injury, is expected to return on the strong side.

Weatherspoon finished tied for second on the Falcons with four sacks, so the Falcons desperately need a complementary pass rusher to John Abraham to emerge. Ray Edwards played through a knee injury last year and had minor surgery on the same knee in February. Jonathan Babineaux is now 30 years old and coming off an injury-plagued year. Corey Peters is developing into a fine nose tackle, but there is little depth behind him. Peria Jerry never developed into a difference maker, and Lawrence Sidbury and Kroy Biermann are try-hard guys off the bench at end. With Abraham (who signed a three-year, $17.5 million deal in the offseason), Babineaux, and Edwards healthy, this is a solid defensive line, but age and the odds are against all three playing 16 games. The only new face is fifth-round pick Jonathan Massaquoi, who recorded 13.5 sacks for Troy in 2010 but gained weight and lost his edge in 2011.

Defensive Secondary

Secondary	Age	Pos	Plays	TmPct	Rk	Stop	Dfts	BTkl	Runs	St%	Rk	Yds	Rk	Tgts	Tgt%	Rk	Dist	Suc%	Rk	APaYd	Rk	PD	Int
Thomas DeCoud	27	FS	91	11.8%	17	23	9	6	39	31%	56	7.4	50	33	7.6%	32	16.7	56%	42	9.3	56	7	4
William Moore	27	SS	63	10.9%	31	30	11	3	30	50%	15	6.0	22	25	7.6%	31	12.7	60%	21	6.8	24	7	2
Brent Grimes	29	CB	60	10.4%	16	28	9	7	16	38%	51	8.4	57	48	14.9%	58	15.5	66%	3	5.0	2	14	1
Dunta Robinson	30	CB	57	7.4%	56	21	9	9	15	33%	53	5.1	16	65	15.2%	55	15.0	55%	29	8.4	58	9	2
James Sanders*	29	FS	42	5.8%	69	12	3	1	20	35%	50	8.1	55	16	4.0%	74	13.0	56%	38	9.1	51	3	0
Chris Owens	26	CB	30	4.5%	--	11	5	2	3	100%	--	2.0	--	27	7.2%	--	13.9	40%	--	9.0	--	3	0
Kelvin Hayden*	29	CB	24	6.2%	--	11	3	2	10	50%	--	7.7	--	16	7.5%	--	9.9	55%	--	7.0	--	5	2
Dominque Franks	25	CB	20	3.0%	--	7	3	1	6	33%	--	5.2	--	27	7.1%	--	14.2	41%	--	10.0	--	8	2
Asante Samuel	31	CB	44	6.6%	65	20	10	8	9	56%	18	11.9	76	62	18.1%	35	13.7	66%	4	4.8	1	12	3

Year	Pass D Rank	vs. #1 WR	Rk	vs. #2 WR	Rk	vs. Other WR	Rk	vs. TE	Rk	vs. RB	Rk
2009	27	28.2%	31	-1.2%	16	20.5%	30	1.6%	15	24.5%	28
2010	10	7.4%	22	-11.3%	6	-6.9%	13	2.1%	13	3.1%	16
2011	10	30.9%	30	-5.6%	12	-32.1%	2	-16.9%	1	-13.2%	7

Mike Smith said in May that he plans to move Dunta Robinson to the slot, with Asante Samuel and Brett Grimes as the outside cornerbacks in the nickel package. Nine of Robinson's 52 tackle attempts were broken last year, but the Falcons face a Faustian bargain when deciding which kitten tackler they move inside. On the plus side, the Robinson-Grimes-Samuel trio will allow them to match up with the Saints' passing game. Dominique Franks, who started in place of Grimes late in the season, returns as the fourth cornerback.

Safety Thomas DeCoud re-signed with the Falcons in the offseason. DeCoud is fast and has good hands but can be broken down in the open field. William Moore, the other safety, is an injury-prone big hitter. Moore missed most of the Giants playoff game, and it showed; DeCoud's bad angles set up big plays for Brandon Jacobs and Hakeem Nicks, while backup James Sanders (now in Arizona) got burned on Mario Manningham's long touchdown. The new backup is sixth-round pick Charles Mitchell (Mississippi State), an in-the-box type with a reputation as a hitter.

Special Teams

Year	DVOA	Rank	FG/XP	Rank	Net Kick	Rank	Kick Ret	Rank	Net Punt	Rank	Punt Ret	Rank	Hidden	Rank
2009	-1.1%	22	-14.8	32	15.1	1	-0.4	13	-10.4	30	3.9	12	8.1	5
2010	5.4%	2	4.2	8	13.6	2	8.7	8	0.0	19	5.1	7	-9.8	28
2011	-1.1%	22	4.0	8	-8.0	29	-1.9	21	-1.4	17	0.9	14	-10.7	29

With Eric Weems in Chicago, the Falcons now lack an experienced kickoff or punt returner. Harry Douglas returned a punt for a touchdown in 2008 but has not been used as a specialist since. Dominique Franks is also in the mix, and Jacquizz Rodgers has the appropriate skill set. A team with a real shot at the Super Bowl cannot afford to train return men on the fly: one or two muffs can destroy a season, as the Niners can attest. If you are searching for the official Silly Thing the Falcons Overlooked that will cost them dearly in the playoffs, this may be it.

Rookie punter Matt Bosher looked very shaky early in last season but came around in the second half of the year. Bosher was responsible for some awful early-season punts, like a 40-yard line drive straight into Leon Washington's hands from his own end zone against the Seahawks, but by late in the year he was consistently grossing more than 50 yards per punt. Bosher also struggled on kickoffs, where he finished next-to-last in gross kickoff value, ahead of only Ryan Longwell. Veteran Matt Bryant hasn't kicked off since 2008, but he has only missed two field goals from inside 40 yards since 2006.

Coaching Staff

Dirk Koetter said in January that one element of the offense Mike Smith wanted him to improve was the screen game. The Falcons executed just nine running back screens last year, averaging just 3.7 yards per screen. Koetter's Jaguars executed 33 screens, averaging 5.1 yards per play for an offense with no one else to worry about except the recipient of most of those screens: Maurice Jones-Drew. The Falcons clearly need some remediation on this basic strategy. Michael Turner may have bad hands, but that does not explain a zero-screen-per-year workload, and scatback Jacquizz Rodgers was targeted just once. Other than the screens, everything else in Koetter's arsenal meshes with what the Falcons have done since Smith took over. Koetter is run-oriented, and he is not adverse to the no-huddle offense if he thinks his quarterback can handle it.

Mike Nolan's Dolphins defenses finished 10th in the NFL in DVOA last year and 11th in 2010, so he still has his chops. In 14 years as a coordinator, Nolan has used the 4-3 defense for seven seasons and the 3-4 for seven seasons, so adapting to Smith's preferred 4-3 will not be a major issue. Despite new coordinators, most of the Falcons position coaches return. Special teams coordinator Keith Armstrong, running backs coach Gerald Brown, secondary coaches Tim Lewis and Joe Danna, receivers coach Terry Robiskie, and others have been with the team since the start of the Smith-Dimitroff era. The mix of new ideas and continuity should benefit the Falcons. It's another example of the kind of "right moves" that never quite work out for the Falcons the way they should.

Baltimore Ravens

2011 Record: 12-4

Pythagorean Wins: 11.2 (5th)

DVOA: 14.5% (7th)

Offense: 2.9% (13th)

Defense: -17.1% (1st)

Special Teams: -5.6% (30th)

Variance: 23.5% (31st)

2012 Mean Projection: 9.2 wins

On the Clock (0-4): 3%

Mediocrity (5-7): 18%

Playoff Contender (8-10): 52%

Super Bowl Contender (11+): 28%

Postseason Odds: 50.8%

Projected Average Opponent: 2.5% (9th)

2011: Felled by the hand of Sterling Moore and the foot of Billy Cundiff.

2012: Hurry up, guys. The biological clock is ticking.

Baltimore Ravens Brand Pasteurized Football Food Product, a staple of your NFL diet since 2008, provides reliable, nutritious, playoff-caliber ball control-oriented football for fans who like things the old-fashioned way.

Ravens Football Product is made from a few simple, high-quality ingredients: an MVP-caliber running back, a handful of Hall of Fame defenders, a Pro Bowl nose tackle, several receivers who run fast, and a quarterback who throws far. Those ingredients are combined using a recipe that has stood the test of time: pass pressure, sound tackling, heady secondary play, I-formations, bombs, and play action. The result is a creamy, nourishing, somewhat bland concoction that fans of 24-10 victories find delectable. Whether you like a defense that generates 48 sacks or a running back who gains more than 2,000 yards from scrimmage, Ravens Football Product is the Sunday afternoon standby for you.

Warning: Ravens Football Product spoils in late January. And it is not freshness dated beyond the 2012 season.

Ravens football is reliable, consistent, predictable, and sometimes a bit of a drudge. On offense, Ray Rice takes handoffs and catches passes while Joe Flacco throws bombs to Torrey Smith and 12-yard outs to Anquan Boldin. On defense, Terrell Suggs pressures the edge, Haloti Ngata eats up the middle, Ed Reed patrols the secondary in search of cherries, and Ray Lewis scowls. You can set your watch by their schedule: two UFC-violent battles with the Steelers; sloppy, droopy wins over the other division opponents; two or three upset losses to teams like the Jaguars when the offense cannot meet its two-bomb-per game quota or the special teams mutiny.

Things run smoothly until the playoffs, when the Ravens inevitably come up short against some opponent with slightly better talent and a less formulaic approach to winning. The Ravens have spent four years establishing themselves as either the worst of the top-tier or the best of the second-tier AFC contenders, based on where you draw the line. They may be better than the Steelers one year and better than the Patriots in another, but they are never better than everyone in any year.

The 2011 season was just a slight variation on the 2008, 2009, and 2010 seasons. The strategies were familiar. Ray Rice rushed 291 times, with 239 of those carries from a two-back formation: the Ravens are one of the last NFL teams for whom you can pencil in 15 I-formation handoffs per game. Rice provided the jabs, Flacco and the receivers the roundhouse wallop. Flacco threw 78 passes that traveled 20 or more yards in the air (third in the league), completing 21 for 686 yards. The Ravens also drew five pass interference penalties for 219 yards on 20-plus-yard passes, fringe benefit yardage for a team that constantly challenges

2012 Ravens Schedule

Week	Opp.	Week	Opp.	Week	Opp.
1	CIN (Mon.)	7	at HOU	13	PIT
2	at PHI	8	BYE	14	at WAS
3	NE	9	at CLE	15	DEN
4	CLE (Thu.)	10	OAK	16	NYG
5	at KC	11	at PIT	17	at CIN
6	DAL	12	at SD		

Figure 1. 2011 Baltimore DVOA by Week

man defenders deep down the sidelines. When the receivers were covered, Flacco checked down to Rice: 61 of Rice's 104 targets were classified as "dumpoffs" by our game charters. Run, bomb, run, dumpoff, run, run, bomb. In an era when playbooks are downloaded onto iPads, offensive coordinator Cam Cameron keeps his on an 8-track.

The result is never a great offense, but one that takes care of the ball and provides enough big plays and clock-chewing capability to let the defense go to work. Last season, the Ravens defense allowed the fewest yards per drive of any team in the NFL (24.62). It finished second in the league in Adjusted Sack Rate (8.4 percent) and second in both Second Level Yards allowed (0.92) and Open Field Yards allowed (0.33). It allowed a negative DVOA against every category of receiver. You can see the influence of the Ravens' three levels of great defenders in those numbers: Ngata and Suggs driving the pass pressure, Lewis and Reed taking away easy open field yards, Reed and the pass rushers making opposing quarterbacks wary and ineffective, making life easier for a second tier of quality defenders like cornerback Lardarius Webb and linebacker Jameel McClain. Former defensive coordinator Chuck Pagano did not have to do anything exotic to get results from this group, and under normal circumstances Dean Pees, a veteran assistant promoted from within, could just wind the defenders up and cut them loose.

Ravens Football Product can be an important part of a balanced diet: After all, the Ravens came within a dropped pass and a missed field goal of the Super Bowl. But it is not an adaptable, versatile product. Elite teams can usually win in numerous ways, but the Ravens must stick to the script. They have obvious flaws: Flacco's immobility, their lack of a rhythm-based short passing game, their reliance on play-with-a-lead strategies. There is no good Plan B when things go wrong.

Unfortunately, things started to go wrong as soon as the offseason started. The team was forced to put the franchise tag on Rice, who reacted with predictable displeasure. The usually taciturn Flacco began grumbling about his desire for a contract extension while making an out-of-character boast about being a top-five quarterback. (Flacco's remark, like Eli Manning's, was ripped from its context; Flacco was asked point-blank if he was a top-five quarterback, said yes, explained that any NFL quarterback would say the same about himself and ... oh hell, you know how this tawdry little media game is played.) Worst of all, Suggs tore an Achilles tendon, potentially robbing the Ravens of their best defender for all of the 2012 season.

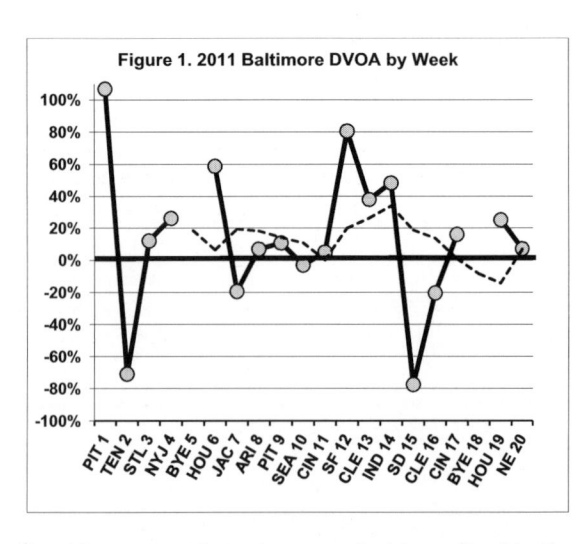

The Rice and Flacco problems are solvable. Flacco is unlikely to hold out or cause problems, and he is not the true catalyst of the offense, anyway. That would be Rice, who made soothing noises about contract progress in May. Rice is almost as irreplaceable as a Peyton Manning or Drew Brees: shave two-tenths of a yard per carry off the Ravens running game, or a half-yard per catch off those 61 dumpoffs, and opponents have no reason to keep a safety in the box or play the run honestly, turning the Flacco bomb game into a Flacco sack game. The contract progress suggests that the Ravens know this.

Suggs is another matter. Not only did he record 14 sacks and two interceptions, but our game charters listed him as applying pass pressure an additional 39 times. Those pressures led to three interceptions, two strip sacks, an intentional grounding penalty, and other offensive misadventures. Suggs also provided 36 run Stops and ten run Defeats. In other words, Suggs was good for three to five high impact plays per game. The Ravens have some good complementary pass rushers like Pernell McPhee and Paul Kruger, plus second-round pick Courtney Upshaw, but Suggs was the bringer of danger.

The Suggs injury is one major reason to expect the Ravens to fall short of last year's win total. Our projection system nudges them down for losing a pass-rushing Pro Bowler, but the nudge might not be strong enough to represent the impact of a borderline Hall of Famer in his late prime.

The second major issue is team age. Ray Lewis, of course, is two hundred and sixty-three years old. Reed turns 34 in September and has spent the last few seasons playing through the whole gamut of old guy ailments. Suggs will turn 30 before he returns to the field, if he returns to the field. Jarret Johnson, one of the Ravens' most dependable rank-and-file defenders for years, is now in San Diego. Ngata is still in his prime, and the rest of the defense is very young, but none of them other than Webb, up-and-coming cornerback Jimmy Smith, and perhaps McClain is anything but a supporting player. The Ngata-Lewis-Reed-Suggs core is one bout of sciatica and one concession to age from becoming the Ngata solo project.

A third, less critical issue is special teams, where the Ravens made no real upgrades. Cundiff was 1-of-6 from beyond 50 yards during the regular season and missed field goals of 34 and 36 yards before his 32-yard championship game miscue. Yes, field-goal percentages fluctuate wildly, but Cundiff's 2010 touchback record masks the fact that he has bounced around the league since 2002, and only in 2010 did he ever have a field-goal percentage above 80 percent. Kick and punt coverage units were woeful last year and lost gunner Haruki Nakamura to free agency. David Reed is still listed as the team's top kickoff returner despite several critical fumbles last year. A running-and-defense team cannot afford to miss chip-shot field goals or lose the field-position battle on special teams. The Ravens entered the draft with most of their roster positions set, affording them the luxury of using a late-round pick on a return man or a second kicker to handle field goals. They didn't, passing up an easy opportunity for a cheap upgrade.

The Ravens recipe for success is very delicate, and their margin for error in the AFC North is tiny. The absence of Suggs, some defensive erosion, and a special teams miscue is all the Steelers need to avenge the sweep they suffered last year, or for the young Bengals to take back a game. The Ravens are primed to slip back into the wild card pack, where they will be in the familiar position of trying to nip at the heels of the Patriots, Steelers, and a Peyton Manning-led team as underdogs. The last four years have shown that they are capable of beating any one of those teams, but never of running the table.

Look past 2012, and the Ravens' problems compound themselves. Lewis and Reed have an event in Canton scheduled before 2020, whether they like it or not. Suggs may also be reaching the end of the line. Flacco is not going to age well. One reason the Ravens are playing hardball with Flacco is that they know that he has already lost nearly all of his mobility and has a slow trigger, meaning it is only a matter of time before he becomes a Drew Bledsoe statue in the pocket. He is a short-window quarterback, a 26-year-old with the legs of a man five years older. With Flacco at his likely peak right now, it is hard to project anyone but Rice, Ngata, and perhaps a few newcomers like Torrey Smith as Super Bowl-caliber performers beyond next year or so.

And really, it is hard to imagine a future where Ray Lewis is not the Ravens middle linebacker, when the team is not trying to win with defensive dominance and ball control, a world where the Ravens change recipes like New Coke.[1] The team's stated offseason philosophy this year was to draft for depth, and their whole offseason approach was strangely passive for a team that finished 14 yards from the Super Bowl. They did little in free agency, traded out of the first round, and stocked up on offensive linemen and small-school defensive backs after landing Upshaw in the draft. Why didn't they draft a potential heir to Lewis? A field-stretching tight end? A quarterback for negotiating leverage? During this year's trade-happy draft, the Ravens could have moved up as easily as they moved down. They could have identified and landed that One Missing Piece.

Perhaps they have been following the recipe for so long that they cannot remember how to deviate from it. If so, they had better mix everything perfectly this year, because they are rapidly running out of ingredients.

Mike Tanier

---

[1] If you want to experience a sense of complete bewilderment, go to FootballOutsiders.com and look up DVOA stats for 1996, when the brand-new Ravens led the league in offensive DVOA and ranked 29th on defense. It's like watching a make-out session between Harry Reid and John Boehner.

BALTIMORE RAVENS

2011 Ravens Stats by Week

Wk	vs.	W-L	PF	PA	YDF	YDA	TO	Total	Off	Def	ST
1	PIT	W	35	7	385	312	7	107%	41%	-65%	1%
2	@TEN	L	13	26	229	432	-2	-71%	-68%	10%	7%
3	@STL	W	37	7	553	244	1	12%	18%	-10%	-16%
4	NYJ	W	34	17	267	150	1	26%	-24%	-78%	-27%
5	BYE										
6	HOU	W	29	14	402	293	-2	59%	15%	-33%	11%
7	@JAC	L	7	12	146	205	-1	-19%	-44%	-30%	-5%
8	ARI	W	30	27	405	207	-1	7%	2%	-24%	-19%
9	@PIT	W	23	20	356	392	1	11%	14%	3%	-1%
10	@SEA	L	17	22	323	327	-3	-3%	13%	-3%	-20%
11	CIN	W	31	24	373	483	2	5%	5%	0%	0%
12	SF	W	16	6	253	170	1	81%	37%	-42%	2%
13	@CLE	W	24	10	448	233	0	38%	15%	-22%	1%
14	IND	W	24	10	358	167	-1	48%	6%	-38%	4%
15	@SD	L	14	34	290	415	-2	-77%	-46%	28%	-3%
16	CLE	W	20	14	284	256	0	-20%	-1%	1%	-18%
17	@CIN	W	24	16	347	336	1	16%	21%	-1%	-6%
18	BYE										
19	HOU	W	20	13	227	315	4	25%	-28%	-40%	13%
20	@NE	L	20	23	398	330	2	7%	-13%	-19%	1%

Trends and Splits

	Offense	Rank	Defense	Rank
Total DVOA	2.9%	13	-17.1%	1
Unadjusted VOA	1.6%	15	-18.8%	1
Weighted Trend	5.1%	13	-12.2%	6
Variance	7.6%	16	5.1%	8
Average Opponent	-2.6%	6	-5.7%	28
Passing	14.2%	14	-20.2%	1
Rushing	3.8%	10	-13.4%	7
First Down	10.0%	9	-27.5%	2
Second Down	-15.1%	25	-5.4%	14
Third Down	18.3%	10	-15.9%	8
First Half	3.1%	14	-20.9%	2
Second Half	2.7%	12	-13.4%	5
Red Zone	1.5%	9	-38.8%	3
Late and Close	31.0%	4	-13.6%	4

Five-Year Performance

Year	W-L	Pyth	Est W	PF	PA	TO	Total	Rk	Off	Rk	Def	Rk	ST	Rk	Off AGL	Rk	Def AGL	Rk
2007	5-11	4.9	6.7	275	384	-17	-4.7%	19	-13.3%	25	-8.6%	5	0.1%	13	26.2	26	32.4	26
2008	11-5	12.0	11.7	385	244	+13	27.6%	2	-0.3%	19	-27.8%	2	0.1%	16	23.4	13	53.9	31
2009	9-7	11.6	12.0	391	261	+10	29.1%	1	12.8%	9	-14.2%	4	2.2%	8	8.4	5	22.2	15
2010	12-4	10.6	12.1	357	270	+7	21.7%	5	5.4%	12	-10.3%	6	6.0%	4	23.8	15	27.1	19
2011	12-4	11.2	10.6	378	266	+2	14.5%	7	2.9%	13	-17.1%	1	-5.6%	30	8.0	1	10.9	4

2011 Performance Based on Most Common Personnel Groups

Baltimore Offense				Baltimore Offense vs. Opp.				Baltimore Defense				Baltimore Defense vs. Opp.			
Pers	Freq	Yds	DVOA	Run%	Pers	Freq	Yds	DVOA	Pers	Freq	Yds	DVOA	Pers	Freq	Yds	DVOA
21	37%	5.8	12.8%	61%	4-3-4	34%	6.0	16.9%	3-4-4	25%	4.6	-24.3%	11	45%	4.8	-20.4%
11	25%	5.7	-5.7%	15%	3-4-4	25%	5.1	10.3%	3-3-5	22%	4.9	-15.2%	12	24%	5.3	1.9%
12	22%	5.9	18.1%	21%	4-2-5	16%	5.0	-13.6%	4-3-4	20%	4.8	-12.7%	21	13%	4.7	-38.6%
22	10%	5.2	19.8%	78%	Dime+	7%	5.9	8.5%	4-2-5	17%	4.4	-14.8%	22	6%	3.4	-6.4%
622	2%	0.2	-10.9%	65%	3-3-5	7%	6.8	50.7%	2-4-5	11%	5.8	3.5%	01	3%	5.8	1.1%
					2-4-5	7%	5.9	-7.7%								

Strategic Tendencies

Run/Pass		Rank	Offense		Rank	Pass Rush		Rank	Defense/Other		Rank
Runs, all plays	43%	12	Form: Single Back	41%	32	Rush 3	7.7%	13	4 DB	45%	22
Runs, first half	42%	20	Form: Empty Back	5%	18	Rush 4	56.7%	22	5 DB	50%	7
Runs, first down	53%	13	Pers: 3+ WR	28%	30	Rush 5	28.2%	5	6+ DB	2%	26
Runs, second-long	35%	16	Pers: 4+ WR	1%	28	Rush 6+	7.5%	16	CB by Sides	92%	6
Runs, power sit.	65%	8	Pers: 2+ TE/6+ OL	37%	10	Zone Blitz	7.8%	8	Go for it on 4th	0.75	28
Runs, behind 2H	17%	32	Play action	17%	18	Sacks by LB	43.8%	13	Offensive Pace	29.3	5
Pass, ahead 2H	38%	26	Max protect	12%	11	Sacks by DB	12.5%	7	Defensive Pace	30.4	15

Baltimore runs the "conventional" set of 21 personnel more than any other offense in the league. ◉ The Ravens ran only 21 percent of the time out of one-back formations, the lowest rate in the league. They ran 62 percent of the time from two-back formations, which was slightly above average. Yes, Vonta Leach is a good blocker, but it might help to switch up the play-calling a bit more. Overall, 80 percent of Baltimore's running back carries came from formations with two players in the backfield, the highest rate in the league. Surprisingly, given Leach's reputation, their rushing DVOA with two backs (2.4%) was not much higher than their rushing DVOA with one back (-3.2%). ◉ For the first time since John Harbaugh and Cam Cameron arrived, the Ravens were not near the top of the league in how often they used play-action. However, once again as in previous years, the Ravens were below average when using play-action, with 6.7 yards per play and 1.4% DVOA (compared to NFL averages of 7.5 yards per play and 19.6% DVOA). ◉ Baltimore threw a league-low five percent of passes to "other wide receivers" (third or lower on the depth chart). ◉ For the second straight year, the Ravens offense was better in the first quarter (sixth in DVOA) than it was the rest of the game (16th). ◉ Baltimore gave up a league-low 2.8 average yards and -58.3% DVOA to running back screens. ◉ Ravens opponents threw a league-high 22 percent of passes to their No. 2 receivers.

Passing

Player	DYAR	DVOA	Plays	NtYds	Avg	YAC	C%	TD	Int
J.Flacco	409	0.0%	574	3407	6.3	5.1	57.7%	20	12
C.Painter	-375	-33.3%	261	1412	5.6	5.7	54.5%	6	9

Rushing

Player	DYAR	DVOA	Plays	Yds	Avg	TD	Fum	Suc
R.Rice	129	2.1%	291	1364	4.7	12	2	45%
R.Williams*	15	-5.2%	108	445	4.1	2	2	51%
J.Flacco	34	19.3%	19	108	5.7	1	2	--
V.Leach	15	8.4%	12	35	2.9	0	0	83%
C.Painter	18	10.3%	13	109	8.4	0	0	--

Receiving

Player	DYAR	DVOA	Plays	Ctch	Yds	Y/C	YAC	TD	C%
A.Boldin	184	8.6%	106	57	887	15.6	3.9	3	54%
T.Smith	180	11.3%	96	51	851	16.7	4.7	7	53%
L.Evans*	-113	-67.4%	26	4	74	18.5	2.3	0	15%
L.Williams	-34	-45.7%	12	4	46	11.5	1.5	0	33%
J.Jones	41	-4.5%	64	32	515	16.1	4.4	2	50%
E.Dickson	31	-1.7%	89	54	528	9.8	2.9	5	61%
D.Pitta	72	12.2%	56	40	405	10.1	4.5	3	71%
R.Rice	236	29.0%	104	76	704	9.3	8.7	3	73%
V.Leach	-62	-51.7%	27	15	69	4.6	4.8	0	56%
R.Williams*	-5	-17.9%	20	13	83	6.4	5.2	0	65%

Offensive Line

Year	Yards	ALY	Rank	Power	Rank	Stuff	Rank	2nd Lev	Rank	Open Field	Rank	F-Start	Cont.
2009	5.00	4.45	4	68%	8	16%	7	1.29	6	1.27	3	17	29
2010	3.88	4.19	9	55%	24	15%	6	0.97	29	0.46	27	25	38
2011	4.47	4.25	7	63%	15	18%	11	1.05	30	1.06	5	23	36

Year	LE	Rank	LT	Rank	Mid	Rank	RT	Rank	RE	Rank	Sacks	ASR	Rank	Short	Long
2009	4.22	17	4.15	15	4.46	5	3.98	18	5.79	1	37	6.6%	19	12	17
2010	4.63	10	4.11	18	3.99	15	5.04	2	5.24	4	40	7.9%	25	8	27
2011	6.11	1	3.91	22	4.22	13	4.70	8	2.87	27	33	5.9%	12	4	19

Four of Baltimore's five starters will be returning for 2012, but the loss of Ben Grubbs (who signed with New Orleans) created a giant void at left guard. Grubbs is one of the best run-blocking guards in the league, and gave up only 5.0 blown-block sacks the past three seasons. The Ravens gave Eagles left guard Evan Mathis a look in free agency, but he ended up re-signing with Philadelphia, so the frontrunners to replace Grubbs are a pair of recent draft picks, both of whom played tackle in college: 2011 third-rounder Jah Reid (Central Florida) and 2012 second-rounder Kelechi Osemele (Iowa State). Reid was slated to start at tackle in his rookie year, but struggled enough to convince Baltimore to sign Bryant McKinnie in late August. Baltimore insists Reid can make the transition to guard because of the versatility he's shown in practice, but at 6-foot-7, he's more than three inches taller than the average starting left guard. Osemele, who scouts projected as an NFL guard because of his run-blocking prowess and lack of tackle-caliber mobility, seems like the more natural fit. Fortunately, the Ravens are set at the other guard position, where Marshal Yanda earned Pro Bowl and second-team All-Pro honors last season after signing a five-year contract extension when the lockout ended. At tackle, McKinnie and Michael Oher gave up nine blown-block sacks between them, but to be fair, it didn't help that they were blocking for a quarterback who holds onto the ball way too long, as evidenced by the line's absurd ratio of long sacks to short sacks. Finally, Matt Birk returns at center after starting all 16 games last season despite his age (now 36 years old) and preseason knee surgery. Birk re-signed for three more years and $8.525 million in March (though only $2.1 million was guaranteed), but Baltimore took no chances by selecting heir apparent Gino Gradkowski out of Delaware in the fourth round of April's draft.

Defensive Front Seven

Defensive Line	Age	Pos	Plays	TmPct	Rk	Stop	Dfts	BTkl	St%	Rk	AvYd	Rk	Sack	Hit	Hur	Runs	St%	Yds	Pass	St%	Yds
Haloti Ngata	28	DE	70	8.5%	3	53	12	1	76%	51	2.0	56	5	5	13.5	53	77%	2.2	17	71%	1.3
Cory Redding*	32	DE	44	5.7%	26	36	14	0	82%	29	0.8	21	4.5	6	6.5	37	78%	1.6	7	100%	-3.7
Terrence Cody	24	DT	32	3.9%	40	27	2	0	84%	14	2.5	55	0	0	3	29	83%	2.7	3	100%	0.3
Pernell McPhee	24	DE	25	3.0%	76	22	11	2	88%	9	1.0	26	6	3	16.5	13	92%	3.3	12	83%	-1.6
Arthur Jones	26	DT	19	2.6%	--	15	2	0	79%	--	2.5	--	0	3	2.5	18	83%	1.8	1	0%	14.0
Paul Kruger	26	DE	17	2.1%	--	15	13	1	88%	--	0.1	--	5.5	6	15.5	7	71%	5.0	10	100%	-3.4
Ryan McBean	28	DE	32	3.8%	65	22	11	0	69%	71	2.5	70	4	1	2.5	22	68%	2.7	10	70%	2.1

Linebackers	Age	Pos	Plays	TmPct	Rk	Stop	Dfts	BTkl	AvYd	Sack	Hit	Hur	Runs	St%	Rk	Yds	Rk	Tgts	Suc%	Rk	AdjYd	Rk
Ray Lewis	37	ILB	101	16.4%	13	69	18	6	4.1	2	3	6	71	70%	33	3.3	52	27	58%	9	7.1	47
Jameel McClain	27	ILB	85	10.4%	53	45	11	6	5.1	1	0	4.5	63	57%	85	3.7	75	25	44%	56	9.7	74
Terrell Suggs	30	OLB	74	9.0%	64	62	31	3	-0.2	14	14	38.5	47	77%	12	1.8	5	2	100%	--	-0.9	--
Jarrett Johnson*	31	OLB	59	7.2%	92	39	11	4	2.9	2.5	6	7.5	45	69%	42	2.6	26	11	58%	--	5.5	--
Brendon Ayanbadejo	36	ILB	27	3.3%	--	16	11	1	5.1	1.5	2	3	8	50%	--	5.1	--	17	73%	2	4.0	3
Dannell Ellerbe	27	ILB	17	3.7%	--	5	1	1	8.5	0	0	1	13	31%	--	8.2	--	4	22%	--	9.3	--

Year	Yards	ALY	Rank	Power	Rank	Stuff	Rank	2nd Lev	Rank	Open Field	Rank
2009	3.40	3.42	1	62%	11	20%	11	0.86	1	0.48	4
2010	3.84	3.81	12	67%	24	19%	17	1.04	8	0.56	10
2011	3.55	3.96	12	66%	22	17%	25	0.92	2	0.33	2

Year	LE	Rank	LT	Rank	Mid	Rank	RT	Rank	RE	Rank	Sacks	ASR	Rank	Short	Long
2009	3.07	6	3.19	4	3.80	13	2.80	1	3.07	3	32	5.8%	23	16	12
2010	2.36	2	4.21	19	3.67	7	4.75	28	4.84	31	27	5.5%	27	9	12
2011	4.11	12	3.35	3	4.06	14	4.06	14	3.93	23	48	8.4%	2	14	18

Last season, Baltimore was the only defense in the league to use a truly hybrid front as their base personnel package, splitting time almost evenly between 4-3 and 3-4 alignments. The key to the Ravens' hybrid is endbacker Terrell Suggs, who defends the run, rushes the passer, and drops into coverage on zone blitzes with equal proficiency. So when Suggs partially tore his Achilles tendon in May, Baltimore's defense not only lost one of its ingredients; it lost the straw that stirs the drink. The Ravens lost another ingredient when left outside linebacker Jarret Johnson signed with San Diego in March, although by the end of 2011 he was often replaced on nickel downs by backup Paul Kruger. Kruger, along with second-round pick Courtney Upshaw (Alabama), will be replacing Johnson and Suggs in the starting lineup, although early indications are that it will be Upshaw, not Kruger, manning the strong side. It's a curious choice given Kruger's success at the position last season and Upshaw's scouting profile (i.e., inexperience in coverage), but our guess is that, by starting Upshaw out on the strong side, the Ravens won't have to move or bench him when Suggs returns in midseason. On the inside, although Ray Lewis once again made the Pro Bowl and remains more of a playmaker at linebacker than Jameel McClain, McClain's total plays, stops, defeats, and hurries improved considerably in 2011 while Lewis' declined. Given their relative ages, that's not surprising, but Lewis' decline coupled with a four-game injury absence last season means it may finally be time to start looking for his replacement. After losing his starting job to McClain in 2010, Dannell Ellerbe has mostly played special teams, and the advanced statistics he posted at linebacker while filling in for Lewis suggest that a permanent replacement isn't currently on the roster.

Although he remained one of the most active defensive linemen in the league, Haloti Ngata had a down year statistically in 2011, both in terms of pass rush and run defense: His total of sacks, hits, and hurries fell by 25 percent from 2010, and his run stop rate was about almost 10 percent worse. A lingering quadriceps injury and differences in positioning were the primary reasons. Fortunately, defensive end Pernell McPhee, who will replace the departed Cory Redding, picked up much of the slack. In limited action, McPhee finished behind only Suggs in both sacks and hurries; the huge 2011 jump in Baltimore's Adjusted Sack Rate was mostly McPhee and Kruger. Terrence Cody mans the nose and was an upgrade in run defense over his predecessor, Kelly Gregg. Arthur Jones and Michael McAdoo provide depth along the line, with Jones providing a breather in running situations and McAdoo doing so in passing situations.

Defensive Secondary

Secondary	Age	Pos	Plays	TmPct	Rk	Stop	Dfts	BTkl	Runs	St%	Rk	Yds	Rk	Tgts	Tgt%	Rk	Dist	Suc%	Rk	APaYd	Rk	PD	Int
Cary Williams	28	CB	95	11.6%	6	33	12	4	20	30%	62	8.1	53	101	24.2%	2	12.9	52%	47	7.2	37	16	0
Lardarius Webb	27	CB	87	10.6%	13	42	18	4	18	28%	65	6.1	26	77	18.3%	33	11.3	53%	42	7.7	48	22	5
Bernard Pollard	28	SS	87	10.6%	33	42	14	7	42	45%	26	4.3	2	26	6.2%	51	11.8	63%	13	9.2	53	11	1
Ed Reed	34	FS	60	7.3%	65	17	8	5	14	43%	29	6.9	39	31	7.4%	33	14.7	36%	75	10.7	68	5	3
Jimmy Smith	24	CB	26	4.2%	--	14	7	0	5	40%	--	10.2	--	31	9.8%	--	12.2	68%	--	6.1	--	6	2
Chris Carr*	29	CB	22	4.8%	--	9	5	0	3	67%	--	6.0	--	18	7.7%	--	8.1	32%	--	8.3	--	2	0
Tom Zbikowski*	27	FS	16	2.2%	--	4	2	2	6	17%	--	8.5	--	6	1.5%	--	6.3	52%	--	8.4	--	0	0

Year	Pass D Rank	vs. #1 WR	Rk	vs. #2 WR	Rk	vs. Other WR	Rk	vs. TE	Rk	vs. RB	Rk
2009	8	-19.9%	8	-5.7%	13	7.1%	20	-26.4%	1	-19.3%	3
2010	6	-12.1%	8	5.2%	17	-29.6%	2	-14.0%	2	0.5%	12
2011	1	-4.5%	9	-4.2%	13	-28.8%	3	-0.4%	7	-18.0%	3

The (emerging) star among Baltimore cornerbacks is 2011 first-round pick Jimmy Smith. His ascension up the depth chart was impeded by an early-season high ankle sprain, but his adjusted success rate in coverage would have ranked first among cornerbacks if not for the fact that he fell nine targets short of qualifying. Even so, his performance as a nickel cornerback made Chris Carr expendable, and he was still far more successful than right cornerback Cary Williams, who is recovering from hip surgery and occupies the starting spot Smith is most likely to take. Opposite Smith will be Lardarius Webb, who led the Ravens in interceptions and passes defensed despite seeing 24 fewer targets than Williams. At safety, Bernard Pollard took over for a concussed Tom Zbikowski in Week 4 and proceeded to perform light years better in coverage, never relinquishing his starting strong safety job and allowing Baltimore to let Zbikowski walk in free agency. Even at 33 years old, Ed Reed is still one of the top free safeties in the league. His coverage stats dipped in 2011, but that may just be a one-year aberration given that he posted the fourth-best Success Rate among safeties in 2010. He spent much of the offseason waxing poetic about retirement, so this may be the last year we get to watch the first-ballot Hall of Famer. Free agent signees Corey Graham and Sean Considine will compete in training camp to replace Zbikowski in the Ravens' three-safety personnel package, but both played more special teams than defense in 2011.

Special Teams

Year	DVOA	Rank	FG/XP	Rank	Net Kick	Rank	Kick Ret	Rank	Net Punt	Rank	Punt Ret	Rank	Hidden	Rank
2009	1.8%	8	-4.7	24	9.8	6	9.8	4	-3.3	23	-0.6	16	-0.5	16
2010	5.1%	4	4.3	7	13.5	3	0.8	15	17.4	1	-5.7	26	-16.1	31
2011	-4.7%	30	-5.3	25	-7.4	28	-5.9	29	-7.7	27	-1.6	19	-8.2	25

Baltimore's poor performance on special teams is a bit surprising, because this is a team that devotes resources to the kicking game. By virtue of his shank in the AFC Championship game, kicker Billy Cundiff may be the consensus choice for AFC Special Teams Goat of Year. To be fair, though, he played through a calf injury late in the season, had the most gross kickoff value in the league (+6.4 expected points added), and Baltimore was just as bad or worse in the other four components of special teams DVOA. The Ravens' coverage units were especially bad, although they did improve from a combined -10.8 net expected points from Weeks 1 through 8 to -3.2 net expected points from Weeks 9 through 17. John Harbaugh attributed the problems to inexperience, so it's not surprising that Baltimore chose to re-sign the oldest of their special teams free agents, 36-year-old Brendon Ayanbadejo, while letting Tom Zbikowski (27 years old) and Haruki Nakamura (26) move on. Replacing them on the coverage units will be backup safeties Considine and Graham, the latter of whom made the Pro Bowl as a special teams player in 2011 and led the league in special teams tackles in 2010.

To handle punts, Baltimore signed Cundiff's runner-up in the STGOTY balloting, Jacoby Jones. It's delicious irony, given that Jones' infamous divisional-round muffed punt came against the Ravens. Like Cundiff, it's unfair to assess Jones' value based on one horrifically bad play, and his body of work (ranked eighth among punt returners with 5.4 net expected points added) suggests he's an above-average option. At the very least, signing Jones allows Baltimore to assign punt-return duties to a little-used offensive position (No. 3 wide receiver) rather than having starting cornerback Lardarius Webb moonlighting on special teams. Although Jones did not return a single kickoff last season, he's likely to also be the Ravens' primary kick returner in 2012. That's because the only other option is David Reed, who fumbled away his job midway through last season.

Coaching Staff

In what seems like an annual rite of winter, the Ravens were forced to once again replace their defensive coordinator after he left for a head coaching job elsewhere; this time it was Chuck Pagano taking helm of the Colts. The Ravens have been running similar hybrid defenses with complex pressure since Mike Nolan took over from Marvin Lewis, and there's no reason to believe new coordinator Dean Pees will diverge from the blueprint, especially since he spent four seasons coaching under hybrid aficionado Bill Belichick. However, there is one big difference between the defenses Pees coordinated in New England and the recent defenses in Baltimore: From 2008 to 2011, Baltimore ranked no lower than eighth in zone blitz frequency, but Pees' Patriots defenses ranked 29th in his final two seasons there. Without a jack-of-all-trades linebacker like Terrell Suggs at his disposal in New England, perhaps the lack of zone blitzing was personnel-driven. However, given Suggs' injury, Pees won't have such a player for at least the first half of 2012 either.

Buffalo Bills

2011 Record: 6-10

Pythagorean Wins: 6.4 (22nd)

DVOA: -9.7% (23rd)

Offense: 0.3% (16th)

Defense: 8.3% (24th)

Special Teams: -1.7% (24th)

Variance: 28.3% (32nd)

2012 Mean Projection: 9.7 wins

On the Clock (0-4): 1%

Mediocrity (5-7): 13%

Playoff Contender (8-10): 52%

Super Bowl Contender (11+): 34%

Postseason Odds: 54.8%

Projected Average Opponent: -3.6% (29th)

2011: After yet another strong start, we hop on the Buffalo bandwagon only to watch it crash and burn just like in every other year. That's it. Enough's enough. We're done believing in the Bills.

2012: Apparently, our spreadsheets did not receive the memo about no longer believing in the Bills, so here we go again. For crying out loud, Buffalo, don't make us look like idiots this time.

Bill Walsh, who knew a thing or two about offense, had some surprising views on the requirements for running a successful one. In Walsh's mind, a good coach did not need top of the line talent at the "skill positions," not even at quarterback. Good scheming could work around a lot of limitations, and an offensive coach who knew what his players could and couldn't do—and designed his system accordingly—would have no problem moving the ball. Michael Lewis compiled some convincing evidence in his book *The Blind Side*, as every quarterback Walsh came into contact with, from Virgil Carter to Kenny Anderson to Steve DeBerg to Dan Fouts to Joe Montana to Steve Young, became radically better in short order. Walsh was not nearly so sanguine about the impact of coaching on the other side of the ball. "There's just so much to offense that a coach really does have control of," he said. "Defense is just a matter of having the personnel."

More than any team in recent memory, the 2012 Buffalo Bills appear poised to test out Walsh's concepts. As they attempt to end a twelve-year playoff drought, the longest streak of futility in the league, Buffalo will go to war with an offense that would make Mel Kiper, Jr., reach for the index of his old draft guides. It's a development that began in 2010 with the hiring of Chan Gailey as head coach. The move was universally panned; the media (including us) snickered at owner Ralph Wilson's inability to land a big-name talent like Bill Cowher or Mike Shanahan, while to a lot of Bills fans, it looked simply like Dick Jauron 2.0. SI's Peter King, though critical of the hire, shed some light as to the reason for it in his Monday Morning Quarterback column. "I can guarantee you one of the things the Bills loved was Gailey's attitude about how you can win without stars in the NFL. In fact, it's the kind of team he prefers." With Buffalo rapidly turning into an NFL backwater that could only attract broken-down free agents with nowhere else to go (read: Terrell Owens), Gailey's philosophy was deeply attractive.

Most of Buffalo's skill position players have undistinguished draft pedigrees. Fred Jackson went undrafted after playing his college ball at tiny Coe College; so did starting wideout David Nelson, who played at not-so-tiny Florida. Newly minted star receiver Stevie Johnson was still on the board at pick 224 when the Bills finally ended his draft weekend wait. Tight end Scott Chandler was a fourth-round pick once upon a time, but general manager Buddy Nix signed him off the street in 2010 after three teams had given up on him. The only first-round pick

2012 Bills Schedule

Week	Opp.	Week	Opp.	Week	Opp.
1	at NYJ	7	TEN	13	JAC
2	KC	8	BYE	14	STL
3	at CLE	9	at HOU	15	SEA (Tor.)
4	NE	10	at NE	16	at MIA
5	at SF	11	MIA (Thu.)	17	NYJ
6	at ARI	12	at IND		

in sight is reserve halfback C.J. Spiller, a luxury pick who didn't see significant playing time until the unheralded Jackson got hurt.

And then, of course, there is the quarterback. Gailey waited all of two games before pulling the plug on the Trent Edwards era and hitching his star to Ryan Fitzpatrick, a former seventh-round pick of the Rams who seemed destined for career backup duty before injuries to Carson Palmer in Cincinnati and then Edwards in Buffalo got him an extended audition for a starting job. It's not like Fitzpatrick hit it out of the park, as his 2008-09 passing DVOA ranked 35th and 36th respectively, but his moxie won the respect of teammates and coaches alike. Fitz's two years as the Buffalo starter have been a mixed bag. His DYAR and DVOA have remained below average, and he has thrown 38 interceptions. On the other hand, the overall performance of the offense has improved in each of the last two years, and much of that has been due to Fitzpatrick's ability to make quick reads and be decisive with his throws. If you read the "Pregame Show" article earlier in the book, you know that pass protection is more dependent on the quarterback than most people realize. The Bills had the worst Adjusted Sack Rate in the NFL in 2009. In the first two games of the 2010 season, Trent Edwards was sacked seven times; in his 13 starts behind the same offensive line, Ryan Fitzpatrick was sacked only 24 times. Last year, with Fitzpatrick starting all 16 games, the Bills had the best Adjusted Sack Rate in the league despite constant upheaval along the offensive line. Fewer sacks means fewer three-and-outs, which means the offense has more opportunities to compile yardage, and that's exactly what Fitzpatrick did, boosting his attempts, completions and yardage totals without ever improving his efficiency. He was basically the same player as in 2010, there was just more of him.

Or was he? Fitzpatrick's numbers, and the offense's numbers as a whole, tailed off drastically in the second half of the season. Buffalo's pass DVOA was positive in every one of their first eight games, and negative in six of the final eight. After the season, it was reported that the downturn coincided with Fitzpatrick cracking two ribs in a win over Washington, and that he played out the season with the unreported injury. Now let's be honest, the effects of "unreported injuries" are often exaggerated. However, if the injury really did slow Fitzpatrick down, then a return to health would make Buffalo a top ten offense again. The Bills were seventh in offensive DVOA through Week 9 of last year, compared to 24th in Weeks 10-17.

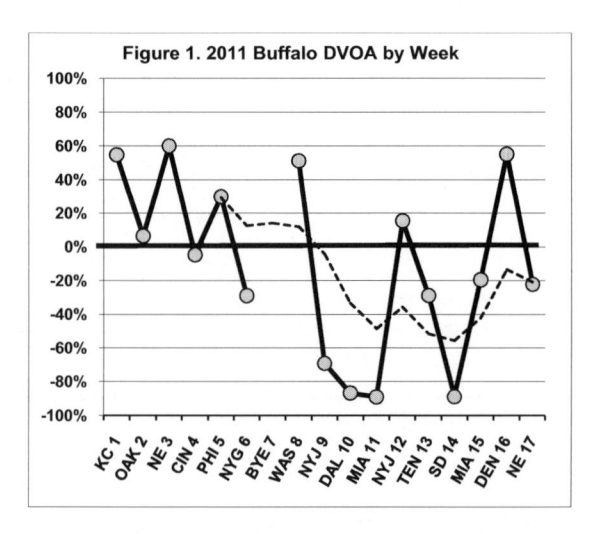

It's also possible that Fitzpatrick was playing a bit over his head in the first half of 2011, and even a healthy Fitzpatrick is unlikely to play at quite the same level again. In that case, the simplest way to improve the potency of the offense is to improve the other side of the ball. When a team generates a lot of yardage but fewer than expected points, field position is frequently the culprit, and it certainly was a factor for the 2011 Bills. The problem can be seen in a simple comparison of Buffalo's drive stats with those of the other AFC East teams (Table 1).

Table 1: AFC East Drive Stats

Team	Yards/Dr	Points/Dr	Avg Starting LOS	Net LOS*
NE	39.53 (2)	2.79 (3)	28.94 (9)	4.89 (2)
BUF	31.53 (12)	1.73 (18)	26.49 (27)	-2.94 (26)
MIA	27.54 (20)	1.68 (19)	29.29 (7)	1.45 (12)
NYJ	25.59 (28)	1.74 (17)	30.86 (3)	1.51 (10)

*Average starting line of scrimmage on offense minus average starting line of scrimmage on defense.

Obviously the Patriots are in a league of their own, but the other three teams finished in a tight cluster when it came to scoring points. Of the three, the Bills had by far the most productive offense, but they also had the worst starting field position, which was enough to cancel out the extra yardage gained. Put the offense another four or five yards closer to the end zone at the start of every possession and the effect would be dramatic.

Getting that extra four or five yards means improving the defense, and as Bill Walsh said, defense is a question of having the personnel. The Bills have spent the last few years chasing the latest rage on defense, jumping in on the back end of the Cover-2 years and then abruptly shifting to a 3-4 long after everyone else in the division was running it. When you are last to jump on the bandwagon, you end up trying to find the same kind of player as everyone else (making them both more expensive and less available) instead of looking for market inefficiencies. In the meantime, you are stuck playing a scheme that doesn't fit the talent already on the roster. Last year the Bills ended up running very little base 3-4 because they didn't have the key pieces to make the scheme work, particularly after Kyle Williams and Shawne Merriman got hurt. Instead, they flopped back and forth between different three- and four-man fronts, ultimately spending a lot of time in a modified 46 defense with Spencer Johnson and Chris Kelsay up on the line in a desperate attempt to plug the leaky run defense.

Dave Wannstedt replaces George Edwards as the defensive coordinator, and the assumption is that he will return to the traditional 4-3 base defense that he ran so successfully in Dallas and Miami. That's not a given; it's possible the team will continue to run a hybrid defense with a combination of three- and four-man fronts using an "elephant" player who can drop into coverage, and who can rush from a standing position or from a three-point stance. Even if Wannstedt is set on forcing the players he has into the system he wants, the transition shouldn't be as painful as it was when they moved to the 3-4 because many of the players have clear slots that fit their skill sets. Kyle Williams and Marcell Dareus were both able to play the nose tackle, but they project just as well if not better as 4-3 defensive tackles. Williams is an elite penetrator, which makes him a natural fit as a three-technique tackle, while the beefier Dareus can line up over the center, shut down running lanes, or push the pocket as needed.

Torell Troup, Dwan Edwards and Spencer Johnson are all good fits at defensive tackle, which gives Wannstedt a deep rotation to play around with. Chris Kelsay and Alex Carrington make for a good rotation at one of the end spots, particularly now that free-agent addition Mark Anderson is around to provide pass rush on third downs. Nick Barnett is one of the rare 3-4 inside linebackers with the speed and instincts to play weakside linebacker in a 4-3, a position that requires someone who can flow to the ball and make plays, while Kelvin Sheppard projects well to middle linebacker. For a defense that was one of the worst in football, there are actually a lot of pieces already in place.

To make it all work, Buddy Nix needed to find a pass rusher who could draw double teams and open up one-on-one matchups for the talented duo of Williams and Dareus inside. Everyone knew who the best player on the market was; the only question was whether the Bills would be able to lure Mario Williams to Buffalo when he would have his choice of half a dozen NFL cities. In the end all it took was $50 million in guaranteed salary, the most ever handed out to a defensive player. Insert Super Mario, a two-time Pro Bowler who has averaged just under nine sacks per year in his first six years in the league. At 6-foot-6 and 290 pounds, Williams is a freakish blend of size and speed, and he immediately provides a massive upgrade to both the run defense and the pass rush. Williams has spent most of his time as a down lineman, and he will primarily be used that way in Buffalo. However, he also has the versatility to rush from a two-point stance; in his one year at linebacker, Williams recorded five sacks in as many games before tearing his pectoral muscle and missing the rest of the season.

A better pass rush should make life easier for a secondary that is short on experience but high on draft pedigree. Nix surprised many people by using the tenth overall pick on South Carolina's Stephon Gilmore, who will team up with last year's second-round pick Aaron Williams to form a tall and athletic corner pairing. Jairus Byrd, another second-rounder, hasn't been able to duplicate the fireworks of his rookie year when he intercepted nine passes in as many games, but he's still one of the better free safeties in the AFC.

Buffalo teased us all last year with their 5-2 start before coming apart, but this year could be different. The defensive line is one of the best in the league on paper, and the combination of developing young talent and a quality defensive coordinator should result in a significant jump in performance. The schedule is going to help. Sure, there are two matchups against the mighty Patriots, but the out-of-division schedule is filled with punchless offenses like Cleveland, Indianapolis, Jacksonville, and St. Louis. The offense is going to be somewhere between acceptable and very good, depending on how healthy Ryan Fitzpatrick is and how successfully he avoids turnovers. The Bills close with four of their final five games at home (including one against Seattle at Rogers Centre in Toronto), where they could be playing in bad weather and before a rejuvenated crowd that smells an end to the franchise's 12-year absence from the postseason. They aren't going to close the gap on New England, but the Bills should be squarely in the hunt for a wild-card berth.

Sean McCormick

2011 Bills Stats by Week

Wk	vs.	W-L	PF	PA	YDF	YDA	TO	Total	Off	Def	ST
1	@KC	W	41	7	364	213	2	55%	27%	-23%	5%
2	OAK	W	38	35	481	454	1	7%	53%	42%	-5%
3	NE	W	34	31	448	495	2	60%	41%	-20%	-1%
4	@CIN	L	20	23	273	458	2	-5%	-1%	2%	-1%
5	PHI	W	31	24	331	489	4	30%	15%	-19%	-4%
6	@NYG	L	24	27	374	414	-2	-29%	1%	31%	1%
7	BYE										
8	WAS	W	23	0	390	178	0	51%	10%	-50%	-9%
9	NYJ	L	11	27	287	348	-1	-69%	-35%	36%	2%
10	@DAL	L	7	44	271	433	-4	-87%	-39%	44%	-3%
11	@MIA	L	8	35	245	242	-2	-89%	-63%	11%	-15%
12	@NYJ	L	24	28	336	318	2	16%	34%	25%	7%
13	TEN	L	17	23	386	317	-2	-29%	-2%	17%	-9%
14	@SD	L	10	37	281	366	-2	-89%	-62%	24%	-3%
15	MIA	L	23	30	404	448	0	-19%	6%	11%	-15%
16	DEN	W	40	14	351	285	3	55%	9%	-18%	29%
17	@NE	L	21	49	402	480	-3	-22%	-11%	6%	-5%

Trends and Splits

	Offense	Rank	Defense	Rank
Total DVOA	0.3%	16	8.3%	24
Unadjusted VOA	2.4%	14	9.5%	26
Weighted Trend	-12.1%	24	12.8%	30
Variance	14.0%	30	5.3%	10
Average Opponent	0.3%	18	2.3%	8
Passing	2.3%	19	11.1%	25
Rushing	4.5%	8	5.5%	28
First Down	4.1%	12	4.5%	21
Second Down	10.2%	9	14.9%	29
Third Down	-24.4%	25	5.8%	20
First Half	5.0%	12	6.1%	24
Second Half	-4.2%	20	11.0%	27
Red Zone	-3.9%	15	10.3%	30
Late and Close	9.4%	10	15.4%	29

Five-Year Performance

Year	W-L	Pyth	Est W	PF	PA	TO	Total	Rk	Off	Rk	Def	Rk	ST	Rk	Off AGL	Rk	Def AGL	Rk
2007	7-9	4.9	8.0	252	354	+9	-5.0%	21	-9.7%	23	0.2%	19	4.9%	6	22.6	18	43.6	30
2008	7-9	7.8	6.7	336	342	-8	-8.4%	23	-9.8%	24	5.8%	23	7.1%	1	13.3	8	34.9	25
2009	6-10	5.9	6.6	258	326	+3	-10.4%	24	-20.7%	29	-9.2%	8	1.1%	13	60.7	32	62.1	32
2010	4-12	4.3	5.5	283	425	-17	-21.3%	29	-14.5%	26	6.8%	28	-0.1%	17	10.4	5	31.2	22
2011	6-10	6.4	7.1	372	434	+1	-9.7%	23	0.3%	16	8.3%	24	-1.7%	24	33.8	20	37.1	21

2011 Performance Based on Most Common Personnel Groups

Buffalo Offense					Buffalo Offense vs. Opp.				Buffalo Defense				Buffalo Defense vs. Opp.			
Pers	Freq	Yds	DVOA	Run%	Pers	Freq	Yds	DVOA	Pers	Freq	Yds	DVOA	Pers	Freq	Yds	DVOA
11	49%	5.3	-9.0%	37%	4-2-5	33%	6.0	-1.2%	Dime+	31%	6.8	-2.6%	11	42%	6.2	1.7%
10	25%	7.0	16.8%	15%	Dime+	29%	6.5	8.6%	4-3-4	27%	6.2	19.6%	21	23%	6.6	29.0%
21	8%	5.9	-11.5%	54%	3-3-5	17%	5.4	-8.7%	4-2-5	21%	6.7	19.4%	12	13%	6.3	0.6%
12	7%	5.7	21.4%	53%	3-4-4	9%	4.8	10.6%	3-4-4	11%	5.6	8.7%	22	9%	5.2	13.8%
20	5%	9.2	22.5%	35%	4-3-4	7%	5.6	3.2%	3-3-5	5%	4.9	-38.9%	01	3%	6.8	-42.1%

Strategic Tendencies

Run/Pass		Rank	Offense		Rank	Pass Rush		Rank	Defense/Other		Rank
Runs, all plays	38%	27	Form: Single Back	70%	8	Rush 3	5.4%	19	4 DB	38%	28
Runs, first half	39%	24	Form: Empty Back	19%	1	Rush 4	74.1%	5	5 DB	27%	26
Runs, first down	49%	22	Pers: 3+ WR	82%	1	Rush 5	14.8%	29	6+ DB	31%	2
Runs, second-long	25%	32	Pers: 4+ WR	28%	1	Rush 6+	5.8%	24	CB by Sides	91%	7
Runs, power sit.	59%	14	Pers: 2+ TE/6+ OL	9%	32	Zone Blitz	1.0%	29	Go for it on 4th	1.00	8
Runs, behind 2H	29%	20	Play action	11%	32	Sacks by LB	46.4%	12	Offensive Pace	31.5	25
Pass, ahead 2H	44%	15	Max protect	5%	31	Sacks by DB	7.1%	15	Defensive Pace	30.4	14

The Bills may want to consider spreading things out a little less. They had the biggest advantage in the league when running from two-back sets (21.3% DVOA, 6.2 yards per carry) compared to one-back sets (-2.2% DVOA, 4.9 yards per carry). Yet only 21 percent of their RB carries came from two-back sets, which ranked 29th in the NFL. On the other hand, the Bills went without a tight end on a league-high 30 percent of plays, and were very good on those plays, with 20.6% DVOA and 7.4 yards per play. Buffalo's offense ranked fifth in DVOA in the first quarter, then 20th from the second quarter onwards. Bills opponents rushed three and dropped eight on 17 percent of pass plays, the highest rate in the league. No other offense was above 13 percent. It was a good strategy, as the Bills had just 4.7 yards per play against three pass rushers. Buffalo had the league's biggest gap between defense against the shotgun (-2.9% DVOA, 13th) and defense against standard formations (14.1% DVOA, 30th).

Passing

Player	DYAR	DVOA	Plays	NtYds	Avg	YAC	C%	TD	Int
R.Fitzpatrick	189	-6.2%	591	3702	6.5	5.3	62.5%	24	23
T.Thigpen	-49	-103.0%	8	25	3.1	3.3	37.5%	0	1
V.Young	-83	-21.7%	122	832	6.8	4.7	57.9%	4	9

Rushing

Player	DYAR	DVOA	Plays	Yds	Avg	TD	Fum	Suc
F.Jackson	161	13.7%	170	936	5.5	6	2	54%
C.J.Spiller	68	6.4%	106	538	5.1	3	2	51%
T.Choice	-7	-14.8%	23	69	3.0	1	1	48%
R.Fitzpatrick	38	5.2%	40	231	5.8	0	2	--
B.Smith	26	17.7%	20	87	4.4	1	0	60%
J.White	-2	-15.8%	12	38	3.2	0	0	25%
V.Young	2	-10.0%	15	83	5.5	0	0	--

Receiving

Player	DYAR	DVOA	Plays	Ctch	Yds	Y/C	YAC	TD	C%
S.Johnson	137	0.0%	134	76	1004	13.2	4.2	7	57%
D.Nelson	122	3.3%	98	61	658	10.8	3.3	5	62%
D.Jones	-86	-36.4%	46	23	231	10.0	3.0	1	50%
B.Smith	-41	-25.5%	42	23	240	10.4	4.6	1	55%
N.Roosevelt	32	3.4%	26	16	257	16.1	8.2	1	62%
D.Hagan	25	0.7%	22	13	138	10.6	1.9	1	59%
R.Martin	-17	-25.5%	16	7	82	11.7	4.3	0	44%
S.Chandler	113	27.0%	46	38	389	10.2	4.0	6	83%
M.Caussin	3	-0.7%	6	5	41	8.2	2.6	0	83%
C.J.Spiller	79	10.4%	54	40	289	7.2	6.3	2	74%
F.Jackson	95	22.5%	50	39	442	11.3	12.1	0	78%
T.Choice	-46	-76.0%	15	7	51	7.3	10.6	0	47%

Offensive Line

Year	Yards	ALY	Rank	Power	Rank	Stuff	Rank	2nd Lev	Rank	Open Field	Rank	F-Start	Cont.
2009	4.29	4.19	12	50%	31	16%	5	1.15	16	0.63	21	32	21
2010	4.05	3.85	20	65%	11	20%	21	1.10	19	0.66	19	20	26
2011	5.04	4.18	12	67%	7	18%	14	1.25	9	1.29	2	9	25

Year	LE	Rank	LT	Rank	Mid	Rank	RT	Rank	RE	Rank	Sacks	ASR	Rank	Short	Long
2009	3.27	26	4.21	13	4.39	7	3.22	30	4.78	7	46	9.9%	32	16	14
2010	3.57	22	5.25	1	3.85	20	3.11	30	3.65	23	34	6.5%	17	12	15
2011	4.57	10	4.10	20	4.27	11	3.21	30	5.02	2	23	3.8%	1	8	10

BUFFALO BILLS

The Bills never really acted as if they were interested in re-signing left tackle Demetress Bell, despite his anchoring a line that gave up only 23 sacks and led the league in Adjusted Sack Rate. Some of that indifference can be attributed to Buddy Nix believing that head coach Chan Gailey's scheme and quarterback Ryan Fitzpatrick's quick trigger were more responsible for the low sack numbers than anything Bell did. 2011 fourth-rounder Chris Hairston held up well in limited action and will begin training camp as the starter, but he's keeping the seat warm for second-round pick Cordy Glenn. Glenn played both inside and right tackle at Georgia before finishing up on the left side, which gives him the kind of positional flexibility the team craves. Nix considers Glenn to be very similar to former Charger standout Marcus McNeill, and obviously the team would be thrilled if that comparison proves valid. Should Glenn struggle early on, he can begin his career at guard, where he has the size and force to be a difference maker in the run game. Erik Pears inked a new three-year, $9.3-million deal this offseason that will keep him in the lineup through 2015. Pears looked to be the weakest link on the line heading into last season, but he provided consistent and reliable in pass protection. Fifth-round pick Zebrie Sanders (Florida State) should wind up backing up Pears and contributing in short-yardage situations.

Andy Levitre is not a jack of all trades; he's a left guard who was forced into other roles last season, subbing in at left tackle and at center as injuries mounted. The results were not pretty, as Levitre fumbled snaps and generally sent the ball spraying all over the place when the Bills lined up in shotgun. Levitre was playing as well as any guard in the league before the position switches, and with a plethora of other linemen on the roster who can move around, the Bills should do everything they can to keep Levitre in his natural position and let him do his thing. Right guard Kraig Urbik is one of those versatile players, and he ultimately came to the rescue with three solid weeks as the emergency center when it became clear that Levitre couldn't handle the position. Urbik also performed credibly at guard, which convinced the team to re-sign him for one more year. Eric Wood is still a developing talent at center. He shows flashes of dominance, but his technique is raw, perhaps because of a lack of reps. Wood has finished two of his first three seasons on injured reserve with major leg injuries, and so has only played in 33 games. Wood was running at full speed in March, so his ACL should be fully recovered in plenty of time for training camp. Chad Rinehart is the principal reserve, and while he won't challenge for a starting job, he provides insurance at all three interior line positions.

Defensive Front Seven

Defensive Line	Age	Pos	Plays	TmPct	Rk	Stop	Dfts	BTkl	St%	Rk	AvYd	Rk	Sack	Hit	Hur	Runs	St%	Yds	Pass	St%	Yds
Dwan Edwards	31	DE	52	6.4%	19	35	11	2	67%	75	3.0	76	2.5	5	2	47	66%	3.3	5	80%	0.2
Spencer Johnson	31	DE	48	5.9%	13	35	10	1	73%	51	2.3	49	2	2	9.5	43	74%	2.6	5	60%	0.4
Marcell Dareus	23	DT	45	5.6%	15	37	14	1	82%	24	1.4	14	5.5	4	13	34	82%	2.1	11	82%	-0.8
Kellen Heard	23	DT	20	2.6%	66	15	6	0	75%	45	2.2	45	2	1	2	18	72%	2.8	2	100%	-4.0
Alex Carrington	25	DE	18	2.2%	--	15	6	1	83%	--	0.9	--	1	1	4	12	92%	0.7	6	67%	1.3
Mark Anderson	29	DE	29	3.5%	69	25	16	1	86%	14	-1.6	1	10	6	16	16	75%	2.4	13	100%	-6.6

Linebackers	Age	Pos	Plays	TmPct	Rk	Stop	Dfts	BTkl	AvYd	Sack	Hit	Hur	Runs	St%	Rk	Yds	Rk	Tgts	Suc%	Rk	AdjYd	Rk
Nick Barnett	31	ILB	135	16.7%	11	76	26	6	4.0	3	0	2	91	58%	80	3.5	67	32	56%	19	4.1	4
Kelvin Sheppard	24	ILB	62	7.7%	87	32	8	2	4.6	0	2	0	46	59%	78	3.0	34	12	36%	--	13.5	--
Chris Kelsay	33	OLB	43	7.1%	94	29	10	1	2.7	5	3	12.5	30	73%	20	2.2	13	1	100%	--	0.8	--
Arthur Moats	23	OLB	20	2.8%	--	10	7	0	3.7	2.5	4	5.5	11	36%	--	4.6	--	0	0%	--	0.0	--
Danny Batten	25	OLB	17	2.1%	--	11	2	0	5.4	0.5	1	0	13	69%	--	4.9	--	1	0%	--	15.9	--

Year	Yards	ALY	Rank	Power	Rank	Stuff	Rank	2nd Lev	Rank	Open Field	Rank
2009	4.78	4.26	21	75%	30	18%	18	1.25	25	1.13	29
2010	4.73	4.88	32	65%	21	12%	32	1.32	31	0.71	13
2011	4.79	4.46	28	62%	14	15%	32	1.30	26	1.02	24

Year	LE	Rank	LT	Rank	Mid	Rank	RT	Rank	RE	Rank	Sacks	ASR	Rank	Short	Long
2009	3.54	9	3.84	11	4.26	23	4.90	29	5.16	27	34	7.1%	9	11	15
2010	4.86	27	4.96	29	4.86	32	4.30	18	6.15	32	27	5.7%	24	8	9
2011	5.29	30	4.68	27	4.43	29	4.50	23	3.23	12	29	5.9%	26	7	16

Six years and up to 100 million dollars. That's what Buffalo invested to lure Mario Williams to the east side of Lake Erie. Williams has bulked up to 300 pounds, and with the Bills switching to a purely 4-3 look, Williams won't have to worry about dropping into coverage except on the occasional zone blitz. The Texans were second in the league in Adjusted Line Yards when runners went at Super Mario, so in addition to his pass-rushing duties, he is expected to provide a significant bump to an underperforming Bills run defense. The other defensive end spot will probably belong to a rotation headed by fan whipping boy Chris Kelsay. Kelsay has been miscast for years as the team's top pass rusher, but he can be a solid complementary player who benefits from the attention Mario Williams will draw on the other side. More importantly, he is a good run defender and so should see time on early downs. The other option is Mark Anderson, the Chris Bosh of the Buffalo free agent signings. Anderson is a third-down specialist who is getting paid like an every-down player, and it is telling that the pass rush-starved Patriots showed absolutely no inclination to compete with Buffalo's offer. The ghost of Shawne Merriman is still haunting the roster and might push for playing time with a combination of better health and a good preseason showing.

Buffalo's starting defensive tackles are one of the best pairs in the league. Occasional inconsistency is to be expected from a rookie, but Marcell Dareus was on more than he was off, and the number three pick in the draft looked dominant when matched against poor offensive lines like Washington and San Diego. He'll be helped by the return of Kyle Williams, Buffalo's Pro Bowl defensive tackle, who missed 12 games last year with bone spurs in his left foot. Despite being undersized, Williams was a dominant penetrator at nose tackle because of his excellent technique and a non-stop motor. He should fit very naturally as a 3-technique defensive tackle in the new 4-3 scheme. Dareus also has some pass rushing chops, but as the bigger, stouter player, he will probably be used primarily as a run-stuffer.

The linebackers are an older group—starters Nick Barnett and Kirk Morrison and nickel linebacker Bryan Scott are all over age 30—and there isn't much depth behind them. The only youngster is 2011 third-rounder Kelvin Sheppard, who will take over the middle linebacker duties. Sheppard had an injury-plagued training camp and was slow out of the gate, but he picked up his game as the season went along, including a 14-tackle effort against San Diego. He's a two-down player and will come off the field in favor of hybrid safety/linebacker Scott on passing downs. There was some concern when Paul Posluszny left, as the defensive scheme was designed to let him flow to the ball and make tackles, but Nick Barnett was a more than adequate replacement. Barnett's 76 stops more than doubled any of his defensive teammates; more to the point, they surpassed Posluszny's 73 stops in 2010. Kirk Morrison was a reserve player for the first time last year, but the team re-signed him with an eye towards plugging him in at strongside linebacker. Arthur Moats is a situational pass rusher who is a longshot to push Morrison for playing time.

Defensive Secondary

Secondary	Age	Pos	Plays	TmPct	Rk	Stop	Dfts	BTkl	Runs	St%	Rk	Yds	Rk	Tgts	Tgt%	Rk	Dist	Suc%	Rk	APaYd	Rk	PD	Int
George Wilson	31	SS	110	16.7%	1	41	14	7	57	49%	16	6.7	34	38	11.5%	2	14.2	52%	47	6.5	18	5	4
Jairus Byrd	26	FS	105	13.0%	11	31	15	7	50	32%	54	8.9	62	30	7.3%	35	15.5	61%	19	7.6	37	7	3
Bryan Scott	31	SS	65	8.0%	58	30	11	8	17	65%	1	4.6	5	46	11.2%	4	6.5	60%	22	4.2	4	6	2
Drayton Florence*	32	CB	62	7.7%	53	20	7	3	16	6%	80	11.1	74	69	16.9%	43	15.2	47%	64	9.8	75	13	3
Leodis McKelvin	27	CB	43	5.3%	76	18	8	3	7	43%	40	8.1	54	41	10.0%	80	17.9	54%	34	11.0	80	8	1
Aaron Williams	23	CB	35	7.7%	--	13	5	2	15	40%	--	6.5	--	34	14.7%	--	13.9	52%	--	8.4	--	6	1
Terrence McGee	32	CB	30	9.9%	--	10	3	0	9	56%	--	3.2	--	28	18.4%	--	13.6	42%	--	6.7	--	2	0
Da'Norris Searcy	24	SS	30	3.7%	--	17	3	2	24	54%	--	4.4	--	7	1.7%	--	18.6	52%	--	7.0	--	2	1
Justin Rogers	24	CB	18	2.7%	--	8	4	1	4	25%	--	11.3	--	20	5.9%	--	11.3	63%	--	5.1	--	4	1

BUFFALO BILLS

Year	Pass D Rank	vs. #1 WR	Rk	vs. #2 WR	Rk	vs. Other WR	Rk	vs. TE	Rk	vs. RB	Rk
2009	3	-30.0%	4	-8.3%	10	-33.4%	1	-8.7%	8	-12.1%	8
2010	25	32.3%	31	9.9%	20	-43.5%	1	13.2%	23	-8.7%	7
2011	25	16.5%	22	33.3%	29	-41.0%	1	20.6%	23	5.1%	21

There is a youth movement afoot, which means this unit will look substantially different from a year ago. The two new starters will be second-year man Aaron Williams and first-round pick Stephon Gilmore. The scouting report on Gilmore is that he is exceptionally fast, that he closes quickly in zone coverage, and that his run defense is exceptional. South Carolina used Gilmore as the "force defender," allowing him to come off the edge on running plays and attack the weak side of the formation. That same aggressiveness made him a weapon when he came on the corner blitz, and he tallied seven career sacks. The downside is that Gilmore's technique is very raw, a flaw which is exacerbated when he is asked to play off coverage. Rookie corners always take their lumps, but it makes sense to throw Gilmore in, accept that he will make some bad plays, and hope that he makes enough good ones to balance things out. Aaron Williams was in and out of the lineup with injuries to both his collarbone and his knee. That's a problem, as what makes Williams attractive is his size and his physical play. Terrence McGee will operate as the nickelback and he received a new two-year deal that pays him like one. McGee is 31 years old, has missed 22 games the last three seasons, and as of press time he was nowhere near recovered from the torn patella tendon that ended his 2011 season. He is also the team's best corner when healthy, and it's entirely possible that he spends some of the season as one of the two starters. Justin Rogers and Ron Brooks will compete for dime corner duties, while former first-round pick Leodis McKelvin is on the outs with Chan Gailey and may not make the final roster.

George Wilson and Jairus Byrd are very different players who will have correspondingly different roles. Wilson is an effective box safety who had to come up and make plays all too frequently last year because runners were getting to the second level untouched. Byrd is a prototype centerfielder, a deep safety with range who can close on the ball quickly and is a threat to score when he gets his hands on it. People thought Byrd had a bad sophomore campaign because he only intercepted one pass, but the real problem was his lackluster 47 percent Success Rate on the 22 passes that went his way. Last year, Byrd was targeted 30 times, and his Success Rate jumped all the way up to 61 percent. The three interceptions and three forced fumbles were less a function of Byrd getting his playmaker mojo back than him simply playing sounder football and being in better position to force turnovers.

Special Teams

Year	DVOA	Rank	FG/XP	Rank	Net Kick	Rank	Kick Ret	Rank	Net Punt	Rank	Punt Ret	Rank	Hidden	Rank
2009	1.0%	13	3.7	10	4.7	12	-1.4	14	4.5	9	-5.8	25	2.3	12
2010	-0.1%	17	-0.5	18	3.4	10	-4.5	21	-0.4	21	1.6	14	0.2	14
2011	-1.4%	24	-7.1	28	4.6	7	-0.1	17	-10.6	29	4.7	6	-11.5	30

At age 36, Brian Moorman averaged 48.2 gross yards per punt, the best mark of his 12-year career. That sounds good until you realize he was routinely outkicking his coverage; Moorman's net average was a good ten yards lower than his gross average. Moorman also forced half as many fair catches as he did in 2010, and only angled four punts out of bounds. The Bills brought in undrafted rookie Shawn Powell from Florida State for a training camp battle, but we expect Moorman to keep his job. Age is also a potential issue at kicker. The Bills drafted rocket-legged John Potter (Western Michigan) in the seventh round as a kickoff specialist and eventual replacement for incumbent Rian Lindell. That didn't stop Buddy Nix from re-signing Lindell for another four years and $11 million, a deal that looks more like a reward to the franchise's second-leading scorer for service rendered than a smart future investment. Speaking of investments, it's surprising to see the Bills use a top-ten pick on C.J. Spiller and then not utilize him in the return game. Spiller only returned six kickoffs in 2011, down from 44 in 2010; he also made only half of Buffalo's punt returns. Chan Gailey would prefer to keep Spiller healthy and focused on offense, so Brad Smith will share return duties with either cornerback Justin Rogers or third-round rookie T.J. Graham.

Coaching Staff

When Chan Gailey was announced as the new Bills coach two years ago, SI's Peter King compared the hire to a batting practice pitcher getting sent out to pitch to Alex Rodriguez and Albert Pujols. Gailey's 10-22 record hasn't done anything to dispel that particular image, and the local media seemed to collectively sour on the coach late in the year, repeatedly questioning play-calling and even his personnel groupings. Buffalo isn't exactly New York or Boston, but there is no doubt that Gailey will feel the heat if the team is slow out of the gate. Dave Wannstedt was tucked away under a glass that read "Break in Case of George Edwards-related Emergency," and now he's both the defensive coordinator and the assistant head coach. Wannstedt's defensive philosophy has always been based on generating a pass rush with the front four and backing them up with undersized linebackers who can run to the ball, and he'll benefit from a roster that was a mismatch for the 3-4 from the start. Bob Sanders, who had been working with the outside linebackers, now gets to coach up the entire unit; it's the same job he had under Wannstedt when the two were in Miami. New quarterbacks coach David Lee has 37 years of coaching experience, most of it in college, including last year when he was both quarterbacks coach and offensive coordinator for Mississippi. Lee did a stint working with the Dolphins from 2008-10, which means he gets credit for Chad Pennington's final burst of productivity or blame for Chad Henne's lack of development, depending on how generous you're feeling. Lee also was instrumental in bringing the Wildcat to the NFL, and he shares Chan Gailey's willingness to raid the fertile college landscape for unconventional approaches to offense.

Carolina Panthers

2011 Record: 6-10

Pythagorean Wins: 7.4 (20th)

DVOA: -4.1% (20th)

Offense: 18.2% (4th)

Defense: 15.8% (32nd)

Special Teams: -6.5% (32nd)

Variance: 19.8% (26th)

2012 Mean Projection: 8.4 wins

On the Clock (0-4): 6%

Mediocrity (5-7): 28%

Playoff Contender (8-10): 48%

Super Bowl Contender (11+): 18%

Postseason Odds: 38.9%

Projected Average Opponent: 2.3% (10th)

2011: Cam Über Alles.

2012: A very likely "surprise" playoff team, though they just miss out in the majority of our simulations.

Dear Cam Newton,

On behalf of doubters everywhere, we would like to apologize. We thought you were just another spread-option scrambler destined to suffer through a rough rookie year on a last-place team. We assumed we would see a handful of exciting runs, a bomb or two to Steve Smith, and lots of bad reads and scared-squirrel behavior in the pocket.

We misjudged you. Badly.

We hope you understand why we made the mistakes we made, wrote the things we wrote and projected the numbers we projected. It had nothing to do with race. Well, maybe not quite nothing, because it is impossible to eliminate race from any discussion of a black quarterback. But it had little to do with race. It was about your limited experience, only one year as a starter at the Division I level. It was about the hinky, customized Auburn offense, with all of its option runs and tunnel screens that were essentially handoffs. It was about your evasive interview and press conference style: You sounded scripted and unprepared, mentally and emotionally, for life as an NFL starter. It was the high expectations and the short training camp. We are skeptics, by nature and profession, and we were forced to conclude that you were not ready to perform well, based on all available evidence.

We were not just wrong, but totally wrong. You did not just play well. You accomplished the unprecedented. The 2011 Panthers achieved the largest single-season offensive DVOA improvement in history, by a wide margin. Table 1 shows the teams with the greatest one-year offensive improvements of the last 20 years. It is an eclectic mix of offenses that suddenly exploded after a few seasons of simmering, like the Jon Gruden Raiders; teams that threw off the yokes of arch-conservative coaches, like the 1993 Broncos; teams recovering from multi-quarterback meltdowns, like the 1992 Eagles; and bad teams on the road from awful to mediocre, like the 2006 Niners.

Your Panthers fit into categories three and four of the list above, but you were the only rookie quarterback to spark such a DVOA turnaround. And while the final column shows that many teams gave up some of their offensive gains the next year, few gave up much of them, and a couple of teams actually improved more (Table 1).

Granted, other forces were at work to create such a turnaround. The Panthers offense had to be truly terrible for you to be able to improve it so completely. The final two seasons of the John Fox era almost looked like a concerted effort to destroy an offense. Fox's loyalty to his veterans, most obviously Jake Delhomme but also players like Muhsin Muhammad and Brad Hoover, went from laudable to a fetish to something close to necrophilia. When Fox finally parted ways with his old guard, his staff demonstrated a complete inability to identify and develop talent at quarterback, wide receiver, or tight

CAROLINA PANTHERS

2012 Panthers Schedule

Week	Opp.	Week	Opp.	Week	Opp.
1	at TB	7	DAL	13	at KC
2	NO	8	at CHI	14	ATL
3	NYG (Thu.)	9	at WAS	15	at SD
4	at ATL	10	DEN	16	OAK
5	SEA	11	TB	17	at NO
6	BYE	12	at PHI (Mon.)		

Figure 1. 2011 Carolina DVOA by Week

end. It's hard to imagine a rookie quarterback generating less enthusiasm than Jimmy Clausen produced during his brief tenure, and it didn't help that he had no one but Smith to throw to. By the time Fox resigned, the Panthers passing game was like the old Daffy Duck cartoon in which Bugs Bunny kept painting goofy backgrounds on a blank white canvas, with poor Steve Smith as Daffy. So you arrived, as did head coach Ron Rivera and offensive coordinator Rob Chudzinski. Rivera was a defensive coach. Coach Chud was just another NFL lifer, a former tight ends coach who served a not-too-distinguished tour as the Browns offensive coordinator. He wasn't Jon Gruden or anybody. Rivera and Chud looked nothing like a pair of quarterback development gurus. You worked on your delivery and mechanics with guru-for-hire Chris Weinke, but c'mon, it was *Chris Weinke*, for heaven's sake. This was not quite a recipe for disaster, but it was a recipe for 20 interceptions, 45 sacks, a few hundred rushing yards, and a 4-12 record.

No one knew that Weinke had reinvented himself as the Quarterback Whisperer who could teach proper

Table 1. Biggest Year-to-Year Improvement in Offensive DVOA, 1992-2011

Year	Team	DVOA Prev Yr	DVOA	Change	DVOA Next Yr	Change
2011	CAR	-35.8%	18.2%	+54.0%	--	--
1999	OAK	-24.2%	20.5%	+44.7%	17.3%	-3.2%
1998	BUF	-18.0%	19.4%	+37.4%	12.7%	-6.7%
1992	PHI	-24.6%	10.5%	+35.1%	6.3%	-4.2%
1993	SEA	-41.3%	-7.8%	+33.5%	-11.8%	-4.0%
2006	SF	-40.4%	-8.2%	+32.2%	-32.2%	-24.1%
1999	STL	-13.4%	17.7%	+31.0%	26.7%	+9.1%
1993	DEN	-15.7%	14.8%	+30.5%	1.0%	-13.8%
2007	NE	14.1%	43.5%	+29.4%	12.5%	-31.0%
2006	PHI	-7.5%	21.1%	+28.7%	12.4%	-8.7%
2003	HOU	-43.3%	-14.7%	+28.6%	-1.8%	+12.9%
1996	BAL	-5.0%	22.8%	+27.8%	1.8%	-21.0%

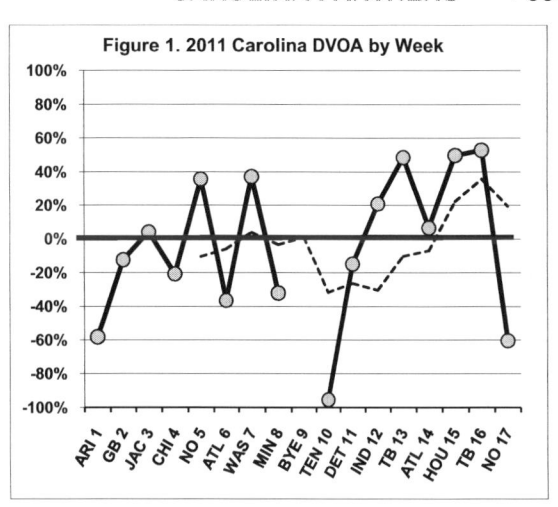

dropbacks and throwing motions in a few simple lessons. No one knew that Chud had an innovative two-tight end offense up his sleeve. The Panthers acquired Greg Olsen and Jeremy Shockey, and Chud put them to work in a two-tight end offense the Panthers used on 34 percent of snaps. Olsen, as he did in Chicago, lined up everywhere from fullback to wide receiver. Shockey split wide at times. You targeted your two tight ends 151 times, typically from the shotgun set from which you attempted 68 percent of your passes. The shotgun, two-tight end approach kept the Panthers from being personnel-package predictable while giving you both safe outlet receivers and additional pass protectors.

Meanwhile, Chud made sure to use your legs as well as your arm. You executed 70 designed rushing plays, averaging 5.05 yards per rush. Thirty-three of those runs came in the red zone, where you averaged an impressive 3.5 yards per carry. Ten others came in short-yardage situations, and you were 10-for-10 when you needed three or less yards for a first down. Then there were the shotgun handoffs to DeAngelo Williams and Jonathan Stewart: 93 of them, netting 6.3 yards per carry, with defenders wary of your rushing prowess and staying at home instead of chasing the running backs.

Chud created the perfect sandbox for the rookie quarterback. The designed runs made the most of your mobility, and they were fully integrated into the offense, not some "wrinkle" that appeared once every two weeks. The tight ends provided security. Smith proved that he can still go up and get deep passes thrown within a few yards of him. The backs and offensive line were never bad, they had just become impossible to evaluate when opponents had no fear whatsoever of the passing game.

So you landed in what turned out to be an ideal environment. But that does not minimize your accomplishments at all. If Weinke's teachings could turn anyone into a great quarterback, then Weinke would have used them. Chud's offense provided training wheels, but you added the jet engine. You proved that you were able to stay in the pocket and throw instead of taking off. You consistently found the second read, and sometimes found the third. There were some classic rookie mistakes, like out-routes thrown to open-looking receivers whose cornerbacks were baiting you for a pick-six, but those mistakes were surrounded by the kinds of plays a fourth-year All-Pro makes.

The Panthers became the most exciting team in the NFL last season, thanks to you. Now, they must go from "exciting" to "playoff worthy." That has little to do with you and nearly everything to do with the defense and special teams.

No one expected the Panthers defense to be great in 2011, but after a middle-of-the-pack (16th in DVOA) effort in 2010, it was expected to be competitive. Unfortunately, a defense with little depth to spare endured one of the most crippling injury rashes in history. Ron Edwards, the free agent signee who was supposed to stabilize the interior line, tore a triceps muscle in his very first Panthers practice. Middle linebacker Jon Beason tore his Achilles in the season opener. Thomas Davis blew an ACL the following week. Third-round picks Sione Fua and Terrell McClain became the starting defensive tackles until both of them hit the injured reserve in early December, forcing two more rookies into the fray.

The Panthers ended up with 55.4 Adjusted Games Lost on the front seven, the highest figure any team has endured since 2002. And those weren't just any games, but games by the team's only experienced defensive tackle, its All-Pro middle linebacker, and its second most-capable linebacker. With Beason and Davis out, Dan Connor and James Anderson were forced to grit through injuries, chasing the ball carriers who made it past a front line of Charles Johnson and walk-ons.

The special teams suffered a ripple effect from the defensive injuries: With a revolving cast of gunners, opponents returned three punts for touchdowns. Kicker Olindo Mare made matters worse by missing chip shots in close games: a 31-yarder in a 24-21 loss to the Vikings, a 36-yarder in a 31-23 loss to the Falcons, a blocked early extra point in a 30-27 loss to the Saints. With half the defense on injured reserve, punt returners running wild, and Mare stopping just short of open sabotage, you appeared to be carrying the team on your back at times. It's a wonder you carried them as far as you did.

You will not have to carry them as far this year. Beason and Davis are still rehabbing their injuries, but Beason should be at full speed for the start of the season, Davis a little later. Rookie Luke Kuechly gives the Panthers a ready-to-start playmaker as the third linebacker. Edwards is healthy, and McClain was growing into his role at defensive tackle before getting hurt. Either Mare will see his placekicking rebound, or Justin Medlock will replace him in training camp. Your secondary is not great and Johnson could use a complementary pass rusher, but the Panthers defense will climb to league average, and the special teams should also improve.

In fact, the improvements on defense and special teams should offset a likely dip in offensive production. Let's face it: What you did last year was unprecedented, and central tendency will join forces with defensive adjustments to pull your numbers back to earth a bit. The loss of Shockey may hurt, and you still lack a true second receiver, though Brandon LaFell came on at the end of last year and David Gettis will return from a torn ACL. As Table 1 showed, offenses that make huge DVOA leaps in one year typically tail off a bit in the second year. But if you and the offense decline a little, with the defense and special teams improving a lot simply by staying healthy, that's a net win for the Panthers, one that will keep you in the playoff hunt for the whole season.

The long-term prognosis is even better. You have revitalized your franchise. You have made a head coaching candidate out of Chud and helped soften Jerry Richardson's image after some ugly lockout remarks. You have the potential to turn the Panthers into one of the league's most attractive free agent destinations. You are the guy who gives the team a chance. And you have shown that you understand your role, apologizing for a handful of bouts of 2011 immaturity that the rest of the world has already forgiven and forgotten.

We hope you can forgive us. We will show that we have learned our lesson, not by fawning over every live-armed, scrambling rookie, but by digging deeper, studying more, and closing our ears a little more when we hear uninformed pre-draft static. And while we will keep scrutinizing your performance and pointing out flaws and areas in need of improvement, we promise to also appreciate the fun, exciting, and championship-worthy elements of your game. Because there are an awful lot of them, and you are probably going to develop more.

Mike Tanier

CAROLINA PANTHERS

2011 Panthers Stats by Week

Wk	vs.	W-L	PF	PA	YDF	YDA	TO	Total	Off	Def	ST
1	@ARI	L	21	28	477	394	0	-58%	10%	40%	-28%
2	GB	L	23	30	475	419	-3	-12%	-7%	10%	5%
3	JAC	W	16	10	265	257	1	4%	10%	3%	-2%
4	@CHI	L	29	34	543	317	0	-21%	50%	28%	-43%
5	NO	L	27	30	381	444	0	36%	26%	-8%	2%
6	@ATL	L	17	31	368	325	-3	-36%	-6%	30%	-1%
7	WAS	W	33	20	407	353	3	37%	28%	-2%	7%
8	MIN	L	21	24	405	361	-1	-32%	23%	32%	-23%
9	BYE										
10	TEN	L	3	30	279	383	-1	-95%	-53%	16%	-27%
11	@DET	L	35	49	409	495	-1	-15%	6%	41%	20%
12	@IND	W	27	19	377	323	1	21%	16%	0%	6%
13	@TB	W	38	19	385	285	1	49%	46%	-8%	-5%
14	ATL	L	23	31	416	394	-2	7%	27%	9%	-12%
15	@HOU	W	28	13	316	358	3	50%	48%	-12%	-10%
16	TB	W	48	16	433	317	4	53%	63%	21%	12%
17	@NO	L	17	45	301	617	-1	-60%	-4%	52%	-5%

Trends and Splits

	Offense	Rank	Defense	Rank
Total DVOA	18.2%	4	15.8%	32
Unadjusted VOA	17.5%	4	16.8%	31
Weighted Trend	19.6%	4	16.8%	32
Variance	8.6%	19	5.5%	11
Average Opponent	0.9%	22	0.3%	16
Passing	13.8%	15	20.5%	29
Rushing	32.1%	1	10.7%	32
First Down	1.5%	16	24.0%	32
Second Down	26.1%	4	15.3%	30
Third Down	46.2%	3	-0.5%	15
First Half	21.9%	4	3.0%	19
Second Half	14.1%	4	27.5%	32
Red Zone	1.8%	8	6.8%	25
Late and Close	14.2%	8	26.7%	32

Five-Year Performance

Year	W-L	Pyth	Est W	PF	PA	TO	Total	Rk	Off	Rk	Def	Rk	ST	Rk	Off AGL	Rk	Def AGL	Rk
2007	7-9	5.6	5.8	267	347	+1	-20.6%	26	-14.7%	26	0.0%	18	-5.8%	30	20.4	15	5.4	3
2008	12-4	10.2	10.3	414	329	+6	18.0%	6	12.9%	6	-2.4%	13	2.7%	10	14.4	9	5.6	4
2009	8-8	8.2	8.3	315	308	+6	7.1%	15	-2.0%	20	-12.8%	6	-3.7%	29	28.9	20	39.8	25
2010	2-14	2.4	2.2	196	408	-8	-36.2%	31	-35.8%	32	-1.1%	16	-1.5%	22	39.8	27	35.2	24
2011	6-10	7.4	6.9	406	429	+1	-4.1%	20	18.2%	4	15.8%	32	-6.5%	32	47.6	29	61.5	32

2011 Performance Based on Most Common Personnel Groups

Carolina Offense					Carolina Offense vs. Opp.				Carolina Defense				Carolina Defense vs. Opp.			
Pers	Freq	Yds	DVOA	Run%	Pers	Freq	Yds	DVOA	Pers	Freq	Yds	DVOA	Pers	Freq	Yds	DVOA
11	48%	7.0	34.4%	24%	4-3-4	44%	5.9	13.8%	4-3-4	59%	5.9	15.0%	11	36%	6.8	16.1%
12	23%	6.0	8.5%	42%	4-2-5	21%	6.8	30.2%	4-2-5	27%	7.3	17.6%	21	23%	7.4	28.4%
21	15%	5.9	15.1%	57%	3-4-4	17%	6.7	35.0%	3-4-4	6%	6.9	9.8%	12	17%	5.4	2.1%
22	6%	5.0	20.6%	70%	2-4-5	7%	7.7	25.6%	Dime+	3%	6.8	-20.1%	22	9%	4.7	8.0%
20	2%	8.1	58.4%	48%	3-3-5	5%	8.0	68.3%	3-3-5	2%	9.9	71.4%	20	3%	4.1	-64.4%

Strategic Tendencies

Run/Pass		Rank	Offense		Rank	Pass Rush		Rank	Defense/Other		Rank
Runs, all plays	44%	11	Form: Single Back	65%	11	Rush 3	5.6%	18	4 DB	66%	1
Runs, first half	43%	16	Form: Empty Back	3%	26	Rush 4	72.4%	7	5 DB	30%	25
Runs, first down	50%	18	Pers: 3+ WR	53%	13	Rush 5	15.9%	28	6+ DB	3%	24
Runs, second-long	30%	25	Pers: 4+ WR	0%	32	Rush 6+	6.0%	23	CB by Sides	85%	11
Runs, power sit.	72%	4	Pers: 2+ TE/6+ OL	34%	13	Zone Blitz	5.0%	19	Go for it on 4th	0.66	32
Runs, behind 2H	30%	17	Play action	20%	11	Sacks by LB	8.1%	28	Offensive Pace	32.0	30
Pass, ahead 2H	36%	28	Max protect	10%	17	Sacks by DB	9.7%	12	Defensive Pace	31.4	30

The Panthers were one of only three teams with a right-handed quarterback who threw more passes to the left side than to the right side of the field. The others were New England and Oakland. Cam Newton threw only two of his 17 interceptions on the right side of the field. ❧ The Panthers led the league with 7.2 yards per carry and 58.4% DVOA on designed runs on second-and-long (i.e., not scrambles). Yet they only ran 25 percent of the time in these situations. ❧ The Panthers also led the league with 6.4 yards per carry and 51.8% DVOA running from formations with three or four wide receivers. Overall, they had a better running game with a single back then they did with two or more backs, a big change from 2009-10 when they were a much better running team with multiple backs. ❧ However, the Panthers had a league-low -48.5% DVOA when they went empty backfield. ❧ Although the Panthers were the worst defense in the league by DVOA, they actually ranked 11th in the first quarter of games. ❧ Carolina gave up a league-high 9.7 average yards and 70.9% DVOA to running back screens. ❧ The Panthers were absolutely killed when they big-blitzed in 2011, allowing an astonishing 12.2 yards per play. That was three yards more than any other defense and almost five yards more than what the Panthers allowed otherwise. ❧ Carolina benefited from a league-low 15 dropped passes, just 3.1 percent of opposing passes. ❧ Panthers opponents threw a league-high 23 percent of passes to running backs.

Passing

Player	DYAR	DVOA	Plays	NtYds	Avg	YAC	C%	TD	Int
C.Newton	404	0.8%	551	3810	6.9	6.2	60.3%	21	17

Rushing

Player	DYAR	DVOA	Plays	Yds	Avg	TD	Fum	Suc
D.Williams	158	18.0%	155	831	5.4	7	0	46%
J.Stewart	194	23.4%	142	762	5.4	4	1	53%
C.Newton	188	14.5%	117	718	6.1	14	0	--
J.Vaughan	-14	-60.2%	7	24	3.4	0	0	43%
S.Smith	37	88.6%	6	56	9.3	0	0	--
M.Tolbert	30	-3.1%	121	492	4.1	8	1	48%

Receiving

Player	DYAR	DVOA	Plays	Ctch	Yds	Y/C	YAC	TD	C%
S.Smith	239	12.1%	129	79	1395	17.7	5.8	7	61%
L.Naanee*	-16	-15.5%	76	44	483	11.0	3.8	1	58%
B.LaFell	144	22.3%	56	36	614	17.1	6.5	3	64%
G.Olsen	-38	-13.9%	89	45	540	12.0	4.4	5	51%
J.Shockey*	36	1.6%	62	37	461	12.5	5.3	4	60%
J.Stewart	102	18.2%	61	47	413	8.8	10.3	1	77%
D.Williams	27	5.3%	25	16	135	8.4	9.8	0	64%
M.Tolbert	51	-2.6%	79	54	433	8.0	8.0	2	68%

Offensive Line

Year	Yards	ALY	Rank	Power	Rank	Stuff	Rank	2nd Lev	Rank	Open Field	Rank	F-Start	Cont.
2009	4.93	4.03	17	67%	11	22%	27	1.40	1	1.31	2	16	38
2010	4.29	3.74	27	62%	14	21%	23	1.22	9	0.99	9	22	36
2011	5.30	4.32	5	71%	4	17%	6	1.38	5	1.40	1	14	32

Year	LE	Rank	LT	Rank	Mid	Rank	RT	Rank	RE	Rank	Sacks	ASR	Rank	Short	Long
2009	4.05	21	4.83	6	3.98	22	3.66	27	3.54	26	33	6.5%	17	14	12
2010	2.52	32	3.59	27	3.97	17	3.67	25	4.59	8	50	9.9%	31	23	9
2011	5.85	2	4.13	18	3.87	23	4.03	24	5.56	1	35	7.2%	21	8	24

The Panthers dropped from a league-high 30 blown blocks leading to sacks in 2010 to just 19 in almost the same number of pass plays last year. The reasons, in order of importance: a) replacing Matt Moore, Jimmy Clausen, and various undesirables with Cam Newton, who was able to make good decisions and escape danger; b) replacing guard Geoff Schwartz, who committed six Blown Blocks in 2010, with Geoff Hangartner, who only blew one while maintaining the line's "Geoff" quota; c) staying healthy at running back so Mike Goodson (five Blown Blocks in 2010) was not asked to play much. But really, point "a" mostly covers it. The dramatic change in the ratio of short sacks to long sacks is pretty good evidence of what happens when you replace a series of statues with a quarterback like Newton.

Right tackle Bryan Bell blew five blocks last year, but he was effective in the running game and will battle Jeff Otah for the job in 2011. Otah has missed most of the last two seasons with various knee injuries. Bruce

Campbell, a 2010 Combine workout warrior originally drafted by (who else?) the Raiders will be groomed as a swing tackle and could get a look on the right side. Second-round pick Amini Silatolu will battle free agent Mike Pollak at left guard. Silatolu is a raw mauler from Midwestern State. *Pro Football Weekly* says he has "brute Polynesian strength," which sounds like some kind of antiperspirant. Pollak is a Colts-style lineman: quick and versatile, but not in any way brute or Polynesian.

Anchors Hangartner, center Ryan Kalil, and left tackle Jordan Gross are all back and pleased to be blocking for skill position players worthy of their efforts.

Defensive Front Seven

Defensive Line	Age	Pos	Plays	TmPct	Rk	Stop	Dfts	BTkl	St%	Rk	AvYd	Rk	Sack	Hit	Hur	Runs	St%	Yds	Pass	St%	Yds
Greg Hardy	24	DE	59	7.4%	9	45	14	0	76%	49	1.8	50	4	9	19.5	37	73%	2.6	22	82%	0.4
Charles Johnson	26	DE	44	5.9%	24	33	22	2	75%	53	-0.1	10	9	3	19	27	67%	1.7	17	88%	-2.8
Antwan Applewhite	27	DE	24	4.0%	63	17	5	2	71%	63	3.4	77	2	3	3.5	18	67%	4.3	6	83%	0.7
Andre Neblett	24	DT	22	3.7%	48	17	7	3	77%	42	1.0	9	2.5	0	2	19	74%	2.0	3	100%	-5.7
Terrell McClain	24	DT	18	3.0%	--	13	5	0	72%	--	3.1	--	1	2	9	17	71%	3.3	1	100%	0.0

Linebackers	Age	Pos	Plays	TmPct	Rk	Stop	Dfts	BTkl	AvYd	Sack	Hit	Hur	Runs	St%	Rk	Yds	Rk	Tgts	Suc%	Rk	AdjYd	Rk
James Anderson	29	OLB	153	19.2%	3	71	23	8	6.5	1.5	0	1	86	57%	87	4.3	93	43	53%	29	7.1	48
Dan Connor*	27	MLB	72	9.6%	58	44	6	1	4.1	0	0	0	63	65%	55	2.9	31	6	57%	--	5.8	--
Jordan Senn	28	OLB	66	8.3%	75	27	7	1	7.6	0	0	2	27	67%	48	4.2	90	22	31%	79	8.2	69
Omar Gaither*	28	MLB	30	6.0%	--	14	3	3	5.9	1	0	0	15	53%	--	3.7	--	7	47%	--	8.9	--
Jason Williams	26	OLB	15	2.2%	--	7	1	1	5.3	0	0	1	12	58%	--	3.8	--	2	0%	--	8.0	--

Year	Yards	ALY	Rank	Power	Rank	Stuff	Rank	2nd Lev	Rank	Open Field	Rank
2009	4.42	4.40	27	63%	14	17%	22	1.27	28	0.71	13
2010	4.02	3.77	10	62%	14	22%	6	1.15	18	0.87	20
2011	5.00	4.68	32	64%	18	17%	23	1.47	31	1.08	26

Year	LE	Rank	LT	Rank	Mid	Rank	RT	Rank	RE	Rank	Sacks	ASR	Rank	Short	Long
2009	4.99	27	4.23	19	4.26	22	4.93	31	3.96	16	31	6.9%	13	8	16
2010	4.35	20	3.87	12	3.84	12	3.01	1	3.50	7	31	6.2%	18	9	14
2011	4.04	10	3.96	13	4.53	31	5.62	32	5.64	32	31	6.7%	16	4	13

Jon Beason and Thomas Davis were extremely limited during May OTAs. In fact, they did not do much of anything, as the Panthers don't want to rush them back onto the field. Davis blew out his ACL two years ago while backpedaling during an OTA drill, so the extra precautions are warranted. Expect the Panthers to proceed gingerly throughout camp and the preseason. If Beason and Davis see their first live action in the season opener, the Panthers will consider it a win.

First-round pick Luke Kuechly focused on the weak side position during May activities but is also expected to get reps in the middle as Beason insurance. Kuechly was an incredibly productive defender at Boston College (532 tackles in three years) who makes up for being a step slow and a pound light with exceptional instincts. When you watch Kuechly's college game tape, the first tackle does not impress you at all, but the 14th tackle wears down your skepticism. James Anderson did his best as the Lone Healthy Linebacker last year and may start on the strong side while Davis eases back into his role. Jordan Senn proved that he can start in a pinch last year; he allowed just one broken tackle while making 58 stops.

Charles Johnson missed May OTAs due to arthroscopic surgery but will return as the Panthers' primary pass rusher. The other defensive end spot is wide open, with Greg Hardy battling Antwan Applewhite and a host of others. Ron Edwards (tricep) participated in OTAs and should be ready to erase memories of a lost 2011. Several of the youngsters who barely survived last year's extinction event at defensive tackle, like Sione Fua and Terrell McClain, are expected to evolve now that they are not stuck in a hopeless situation.

CAROLINA PANTHERS

Defensive Secondary

Secondary	Age	Pos	Plays	TmPct	Rk	Stop	Dfts	BTkl	Runs	St%	Rk	Yds	Rk	Tgts	Tgt%	Rk	Dist	Suc%	Rk	APaYd	Rk	PD	Int
Charles Godfrey	27	SS	87	12.5%	13	31	10	11	43	40%	36	8.0	54	37	10.8%	8	12.3	48%	56	8.6	49	6	2
Sherrod Martin	28	FS	73	9.2%	48	24	11	12	31	29%	60	9.6	70	31	8.0%	26	16.0	55%	43	10.2	64	9	3
Chris Gamble	29	CB	57	7.6%	54	26	11	9	15	40%	44	4.7	8	61	16.7%	46	13.4	67%	1	5.9	13	13	3
Captain Munnerlyn	24	CB	56	8.0%	47	22	10	3	16	31%	59	9.3	63	54	15.9%	51	11.5	43%	74	10.7	79	8	0
Darius Butler	26	CB	38	5.9%	74	15	5	3	10	40%	44	13.9	79	45	14.3%	63	12.8	45%	66	9.0	68	8	0
Jordan Pugh	24	FS	17	2.8%	--	4	2	2	4	0%	--	13.3	--	13	4.5%	--	10.2	40%	--	13.6	--	0	0

Year	Pass D Rank	vs. #1 WR	Rk	vs. #2 WR	Rk	vs. Other WR	Rk	vs. TE	Rk	vs. RB	Rk
2009	2	-27.9%	7	-21.4%	5	-27.8%	5	13.8%	22	-18.1%	5
2010	8	-8.4%	10	-27.4%	1	8.6%	24	35.1%	32	-17.5%	3
2011	29	26.5%	27	12.7%	22	-21.7%	8	40.2%	32	20.8%	27

Ron Rivera clearly hopes this unit will improve when the front seven in front of it improves. Better pass rush and basic competence from the defensive tackles and linebackers will help a little, but the Panthers failed to make some needed upgrades here.

Chris Gamble demonstrates one of the big discoveries since we started charting coverage seven years ago: The shocking year-to-year inconsistency of cornerbacks. Gamble was average in 2009, finished 87th in Adjusted Success Rate in 2010, and then had the number one Adjusted Success Rate in the entire league in 2011. In 2010, Gamble allowed a gain of over 20 yards roughly once every seven targets. Last year, it was once every 12 targets. Captain Munnerlyn will play opposite Gamble. His charting stats were as ugly as Gamble's were pretty in 2011: 10.7 yards per pass (fifth-worst in the league) and 6.4 average yards allowed after the catch (second-worst in the league). Munnerlyn is a pesky try-hard guy who blitzes well and would fit as a slot cornerback, but the Panthers have no obvious challenger for his starting job. Darius Butler was picked on as the third cornerback last year.

Wrapping up is a major problem in the Panthers secondary. Sherrod Martin had 12 tackles broken last year, one of the highest totals in the league for a defensive back, and is one of the main reasons that tight ends have run wild on the Panthers over the last couple seasons. Charles Godfrey also had double-digit broken tackles but is a more reliable all-around defender than Martin.

Special Teams

Year	DVOA	Rank	FG/XP	Rank	Net Kick	Rank	Kick Ret	Rank	Net Punt	Rank	Punt Ret	Rank	Hidden	Rank
2009	-3.2%	29	-1.1	20	-3.0	23	-6.3	25	-6.6	27	-1.5	19	3.6	10
2010	-1.3%	20	6.4	6	6.3	9	-9.5	28	-9.0	28	-1.7	18	-5.3	21
2011	-5.5%	32	-7.6	31	-0.8	21	2.2	10	-19.6	32	-6.7	24	6.7	8

When third-string defenders are forced to abandon their special teams assignments because they are needed in the starting lineup, it causes a ripple effect. That's part of the reason that the Panthers coverage and blocking teams were so terrible last year. The other is the simple reality of a rebuilding program: The Panthers had too many higher offseason priorities than kick coverage to worry about last year. Free-agent signee Haruki Nakamara gives the Panthers a career gunner to help incumbent specialist Kealoha Pilares and back-from-the-starting-lineup Jordan Senn settle things down in punt coverage. Fourth-round pick Joe Adams will take over on punts for Armanti Edwards, who never turned his nifty athleticism into production. Adams could also push Pilares on kickoffs.

Kicker Olindo Mare signed a big contract, then went out and was a dismal 22-for-28 on field goals. Remember our research, however: Kickoffs are consistent, and field goals are not. Mare finished second in the league in gross kickoff value for the second straight year, and his field-goal performance will likely rebound in 2012. At punter, Nick Harris will battle sixth-round pick Brad Nortman, a four-year starter for Wisconsin. Harris, the longtime Lions punter, signed with the Jaguars last year after the weird "Matt Turk doesn't match our punting philosophy, and we are seriously focused on our punting philosophy even though our rookie quarterback looks like he would be more comfortable bagging groceries at Safeway" controversy in Jacksonville. The Jaguars re-signed Harris in March, then drafted Bryan Anger in the third round, then released Harris, proving once again that punter indecision is a sign of insanity and/or Jaguars management.

Coaching Staff

Sean McDermott has inherited some terrible situations as a defensive coordinator, and he has not handled them well. Replacing mentor Jimmy Johnson for the Eagles in 2009 was not easy, and shepherding a rebuilding team through a historic injury rash did not look like much fun last year. But McDermott's deficiencies as a play caller were obvious in Philly—everyone knew when the big blitz was coming, and how to block it—and it is possible to battle though injuries like the ones the Panthers suffered last season without enduring 49-35 losses. There is a lot of offseason speculation that McDermott will experiment with more 3-4 fronts, or more stunts, or do something creative now that he is likely to have seven healthy linemen and linebackers to work with on a weekly basis. He will have to do something to keep from falling back to the ranks of the position coaches.

Mike Shula has gotten Weinke-blocked out of much of the credit for Cam Newton's development, but Shula deserves his due for helping turn a rookie into a superstar with a minimal amount of practice time. Newton and Shula get along well, playing their Alabama-Auburn rivalry for laughs, and Ron Rivera gives Shula credit for keeping things fresh in the classroom. "I don't care who you are—after 15 minutes, your eyes can glaze over. But Mike keeps those guys engaged," Rivera said to the Panthers' team website. "Mike is creative in ways where it's not always the same thing in meetings, where every time it's not a lecture where Mike talks ... It's not just about being on the board and watching tape. It's about asking direct questions, about having him draw on the board or lead certain discussions in meetings instead of just sitting there." Good heavens, are football coaches learning basic pedagogy? Next thing you know, Rex Ryan will institute Socratic Questioning.

Chicago Bears

2011 Record: 8-8	**2012 Mean Projection:** 10.2 wins
Pythagorean Wins: 8.3 (16th)	**On the Clock (0-4):** 1%
DVOA: 1.3% (15th)	**Mediocrity (5-7):** 8%
Offense: -21.4% (30th)	**Playoff Contender (8-10):** 46%
Defense: -14.2% (4th)	**Super Bowl Contender (11+):** 45%
Special Teams: 8.5% (1st)	**Postseason Odds:** 72.7%
Variance: 14.0% (16th)	**Projected Average Opponent:** -5.7% (32nd)

2011: For those who don't know, quarterback is the most important position in football.

2012: Once again, strong defense, strong special teams, and an offense that should be just mediocre enough for a playoff run.

You know that feeling you get when you witness someone throw out an entire piece of food just because a little corner of it was burnt? It's a weird feeling. You want to judge the person—criticize them, even. Salvaging the food seemed perfectly reasonable. Sure, the food may have required a little scraping or trimming, but overall, there wasn't really too much wrong with it. It was still edible. The problem is, in these instances, the food is almost always just flawed enough to keep you from speaking up. You think that if it had been your food, you would have been flexible enough to just eat ... but you're not 100 percent sure. So, you say nothing and just look on quietly as the person gets another plate.

This is what watching the Chicago Bears' 2012 offseason has felt like. In January, team CEO Ted Phillips, with ownership's blessing, made the decision to fire 11-year GM Jerry Angelo. Phillips said the move was difficult but that "at the same time, we need more. The decision was made that we need to keep up the pace with our division rivals. I'm not sure we're there yet, but our goal always has been to win championships ... we like our foundation."

Fair enough, but Phillips would have had a very hard time making this decision if the Bears had reached the playoffs in 2011. And the Bears would have very likely reached the playoffs had quarterback Jay Cutler (whom Angelo traded for in 2009) and Matt Forte (whom Angelo drafted in 2008) not gotten hurt late. Cutler's injury was a particularly big blow. In Weeks 1-to-11, when he was healthy, the Bears offensive DVOA was -7.5%, ranked 23rd in the league; in Weeks 12-to-17, with him out, it was -44.9%, dead last. The "with-Cutler" DVOA isn't great, of course, but the "without Cutler" DVOA would be the worst in history if it spanned over an entire season.

It wasn't just last season that ended in injury-propelled disappointment. There's also the chance that the Bears would have reached the Super Bowl the previous year had Cutler not hurt his knee in the NFC Championship. Over the last two years, with Cutler healthy, the Bears have gone 18-10 in the regular season. In other words, when bad luck hasn't intervened, this team has been just fine.

But like with the person who throws out the burnt food, it's difficult to formally condemn Phillips for making a front office change. Yes, the past two years the Bears had been successful when their quarterback was healthy. But in Angelo's 11-year run, the Bears had posted back-to-back winning seasons just once (2005-06). It may not have seemed completely rational for ownership and upper management to feel like making a change, but it by no means seemed *irrational*. If change was in store, Angelo was probably a more justifiable fall guy than head coach Lovie Smith.

Smith may have thrown out some slightly burnt food

2012 Bears Schedule

Week	Opp.	Week	Opp.	Week	Opp.
1	IND	7	DET (Mon.)	13	SEA
2	at GB (Thu.)	8	CAR	14	at MIN
3	STL	9	at TEN	15	GB
4	at DAL (Mon.)	10	HOU	16	at ARI
5	at JAC	11	at SF (Mon.)	17	at DET
6	BYE	12	MIN		

Figure 1. 2011 Chicago DVOA by Week

of his own this offseason. In January, he said goodbye to his long-time friend and, for the past two years, offensive coordinator, Mike Martz. Technically, Martz resigned after his contract expired, but the breakup was reportedly due to "philosophical differences" between the coordinator and head coach. Smith, who hails from Tony Dungy's "Cover-2" tree, has offensive philosophies that fall on the side of "conservative." Martz, who hails from Mike Martz's "Crazy downfield throwing without much concern for pass blocking" tree, had offensive philosophies that could be characterized as, well, more liberal.

Filling Martz's place is offensive line coach Mike Tice. The former Vikings head coach figures to install a system that features better run-pass balance and asks less of a front five that's been pilloried for its tumultuous play. Tice's more traditional scheme may be welcomed in the Windy City, but it will only be as effective as Cutler is. Blessed with arguably the strongest arm in the NFL, there isn't a throw the 29-year-old can't make. That's been Cutler's blessing and curse. He was starting to thrive in Martz's highly controlled system before breaking his thumb last season, but insiders will tell you that he also wasn't enjoying the system.

Tice will give Cutler more freedom at the line of scrimmage (which is to say, unlike Martz, Tice figures to give Cutler at least *some* freedom). He'll also lessen the burden on the offensive line in pass protection. That figures to help cut down on the beatings Cutler takes; the Bears ranked last and next-to-last in Adjusted Sack Rate during Martz's two years as co-ordinator. The scheme is being heavily counted on to engender drastic improvements to the blocking as Angelo's replacement, Phil Emery, surprised many fans by making no personnel changes to the offensive line other than the signing of disappointing former Niners second-round pick Chilo Rachal.

Emery was a scout for the Bears from 1998-2004.

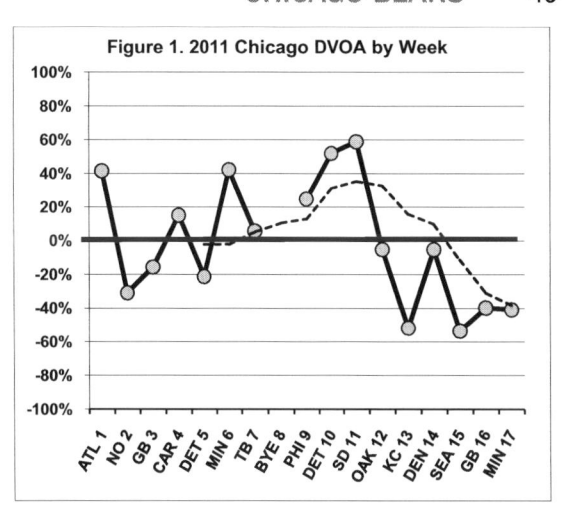

After that he served as Atlanta's director of college scouting until Thomas Dimitroff took over that front office. Dimitroff didn't have a place on his staff for Emery, but he was highly impressed with Emery's knowledge and character. Not surprisingly, Emery quickly found a new job in Kansas City, working for Dimitroff's close friend, Scott Pioli.

Since coming over from Kansas City this past winter, Emery's focus has been not on getting Cutler more protection but on getting him more weapons. He traded to Miami his 2012 and 2013 third-round picks to reunite Cutler with former Broncos teammate Brandon Marshall. The volatile but prolific seventh-year pro is easily the closest thing this century's Bears have had to a true No. 1 receiver. Emery also spent his second-round pick on wideout Alshon Jeffery who, like Marshall, is a high-risk, high-reward player with impressive size. Jeffery's weight and overall output were so inconsistent at South Carolina that, on draft night, ESPN's Jon Gruden—who has loved every "*this* guy" and "*that* guy" that he's ever talked publicly about—censured him.

If Jeffery has a strong enough training camp to earn the starting job opposite Marshall, then Devin Hester can finally become what he should have been all along: a full-time slot receiver. Or, if the Bears are willing to have three possession guys line up together at wide receiver, Hester can be more of a gadget No. 4 and Earl Bennett can handle the slot. A pecking order will be determined in due time, but the general point here is that we might actually be talking for once about genuine receiving depth in Chicago.

The only loose end Emery still needs to fix on offense is getting Matt Forte under contract long-term.

Then again, even though Forte, with his fluid lateral agility and diverse array of ground and aerial skills, is a critical component to Chicago's offense, it's possible Emery doesn't view him as a long-term necessity. After all, Forte will be 27 at the end of this season. The Bears just saw Marion Barber hit a wall and retire at 28. That isn't a great incentive for investing heavily long-term in their star running back. Even in the short-term, there may not be much incentive, as Emery brought in Michael Bush from Oakland to handle the No. 2 duties. Ideally, Bush will spell Forte. But should Forte hold out in protest of being franchise-tagged (he skipped the first OTAs), it's not unfathomable that the Bears would be comfortable simply making Bush their No. 1 back and Kahlil Bell, an ersatz Bush, the No. 2. Such a scenario is far from ideal, but pro football is always business first.

No matter how improved the offense turns out to be, if the Bears are to get over the hump that Ted Phillips alluded to after firing Angelo, they'll have to keep riding their defense. Lovie Smith, for basically the first time in his career, increased the aggressiveness of his scheme last season, shifting from some of the traditional Cover-2 base sets into more single-high safety fronts. "More aggressive" does not necessarily mean more blitzing. Rather, it meant more variety to the few blitzes Chicago did execute, and more press coverage and matchup-oriented concepts from the cornerbacks. This often added an extra safety to a run defense that already featured stud linebackers Brian Urlacher and Lance Briggs, as well as the best overall ground-stopping end in football, Julius Peppers.

Emery inherited those three front seven superstars from Angelo, and he hopes to milk at least one or two more good years out of the trio, and ideally, three years. That is the length of Briggs' new contract (worth $17.5 million, $8 million guaranteed). Urlacher is a free agent after this season. Many believe the Bears will take a wait-and-see approach with him, as he's 34 and coming off knee surgery. It's possible that re-signing him will carry about the same $500,000 or so per game cost that his contract is carrying this season. Urlacher is aging, but he's coming off one of his better seasons. He's been written off several times over the past five years but, in the end, has never lost his place amongst the best all-around defensive players in football.

A lot of people initially suggested that first-round pick Shea McClellin was brought in to be Urlacher's heir, but that's unlikely. The Bears have a defense that is supposed to be built around the pass rush, but that pass rush has ranked 20th or lower in Adjusted Sack Rate each of the last three years (including 29th last year). McClellan is here to help change that. He was only worth a first-round pick as an edge-rusher; that's what the Bears intend to make him. McClellan will have to adjust to playing with his hand in the dirt, but with the underrated Israel Idonije re-signed and defensive coordinator Rod Marinelli having a splendidly deep rotation to work with, he won't have to fully blossom right away.

In all, the Bears on both sides of the ball appear to be deeper and schematically more efficient than they were at this time last year. Whether that's to Angelo's credit or Emery's credit is debatable, but not something Chicagoans are too interested in figuring out. All they're interested in is what their team's CEO is interested in: this talented team finally becoming a champion.

Andy Benoit

CHICAGO BEARS

2011 Bears Stats by Week

Wk	vs.	W-L	PF	PA	YDF	YDA	TO	Total	Off	Def	ST
1	ATL	W	30	12	377	386	2	42%	8%	-22%	11%
2	@NO	L	13	30	246	382	0	-31%	-56%	-21%	4%
3	GB	L	17	27	291	392	0	-16%	-35%	-17%	3%
4	CAR	W	34	29	317	543	0	15%	10%	25%	30%
5	@DET	L	13	24	359	395	1	-21%	4%	23%	-2%
6	MIN	W	39	10	377	286	-1	42%	11%	-2%	30%
7	vs. TB	W	24	18	395	280	2	6%	-25%	-34%	-3%
8	BYE										
9	@PHI	W	30	24	372	330	0	25%	15%	-8%	1%
10	DET	W	37	13	216	393	5	52%	-29%	-59%	22%
11	SD	W	31	20	378	332	2	59%	16%	-26%	18%
12	@OAK	L	20	25	401	341	-2	-5%	-35%	-12%	18%
13	KC	L	3	10	181	252	-2	-52%	-66%	-13%	1%
14	@DEN	L	10	13	245	345	1	-5%	-25%	-11%	9%
15	SEA	L	14	38	221	286	-4	-53%	-60%	-10%	-3%
16	@GB	L	21	35	441	363	-2	-40%	-17%	20%	-3%
17	@MIN	W	17	13	209	301	0	-41%	-81%	-39%	1%

Trends and Splits

	Offense	Rank	Defense	Rank
Total DVOA	-21.4%	30	-14.2%	4
Unadjusted VOA	-18.2%	29	-11.7%	6
Weighted Trend	-26.2%	31	-17.6%	1
Variance	18.1%	31	7.8%	26
Average Opponent	3.5%	32	5.9%	1
Passing	-21.9%	30	-6.4%	8
Rushing	-7.9%	25	-26.5%	1
First Down	-31.4%	32	-17.6%	4
Second Down	-9.3%	21	-6.6%	11
Third Down	-20.2%	23	-19.4%	6
First Half	-10.8%	24	-17.9%	4
Second Half	-32.4%	32	-10.5%	7
Red Zone	-28.7%	27	-46.5%	1
Late and Close	-30.7%	30	.2%	18

Five-Year Performance

Year	W-L	Pyth	Est W	PF	PA	TO	Total	Rk	Off	Rk	Def	Rk	ST	Rk	Off AGL	Rk	Def AGL	Rk
2007	7-9	7.6	7.2	334	348	-1	-4.8%	20	-22.1%	30	-6.1%	10	11.2%	1	18.4	10	50.3	31
2008	9-7	8.7	9.0	375	350	+5	5.6%	15	-9.0%	22	-9.8%	7	4.7%	5	14.4	10	19.3	15
2009	7-9	6.7	6.1	327	375	-6	-18.1%	25	-19.7%	28	3.0%	21	4.7%	4	8.2	4	42.7	26
2010	11-5	9.5	8.3	334	286	+4	2.4%	14	-15.8%	28	-10.9%	4	7.4%	1	6.8	3	5.5	2
2011	8-8	8.3	7.3	353	341	+2	1.3%	15	-21.4%	30	-14.2%	4	8.5%	1	42.2	24	12.4	6

2011 Performance Based on Most Common Personnel Groups

Chicago Offense					Chicago Offense vs. Opp.				Chicago Defense				Chicago Defense vs. Opp.			
Pers	Freq	Yds	DVOA	Run%	Pers	Freq	Yds	DVOA	Pers	Freq	Yds	DVOA	Pers	Freq	Yds	DVOA
11	33%	5.3	-18.3%	38%	4-3-4	34%	4.2	-29.3%	4-2-5	52%	5.6	-16.1%	11	43%	5.5	-13.0%
12	19%	5.1	-18.7%	53%	4-2-5	31%	5.8	-10.4%	4-3-4	47%	5.3	-12.7%	12	22%	6.0	-12.3%
21	15%	5.4	-14.3%	58%	3-4-4	11%	6.1	-15.5%	Dime+	0%	10.4	115.1%	21	16%	5.4	-13.1%
10	14%	6.4	25.5%	10%	Dime+	9%	5.8	-1.0%					22	8%	4.4	-30.7%
22	8%	3.2	-34.2%	85%	2-4-5	7%	6.4	8.3%					20	3%	5.8	-10.1%
20	6%	5.4	-35.6%	24%	3-3-5	6%	4.8	-0.1%								

Strategic Tendencies

Run/Pass		Rank	Offense		Rank	Pass Rush		Rank	Defense/Other		Rank
Runs, all plays	46%	7	Form: Single Back	60%	18	Rush 3	2.1%	30	4 DB	47%	19
Runs, first half	48%	5	Form: Empty Back	5%	19	Rush 4	72.9%	6	5 DB	52%	6
Runs, first down	56%	7	Pers: 3+ WR	55%	9	Rush 5	17.9%	21	6+ DB	0%	32
Runs, second-long	38%	11	Pers: 4+ WR	15%	3	Rush 6+	7.1%	18	CB by Sides	71%	22
Runs, power sit.	59%	13	Pers: 2+ TE/6+ OL	29%	22	Zone Blitz	6.1%	14	Go for it on 4th	0.86	21
Runs, behind 2H	29%	19	Play action	15%	23	Sacks by LB	0.0%	32	Offensive Pace	31.1	24
Pass, ahead 2H	43%	18	Max protect	19%	3	Sacks by DB	6.3%	20	Defensive Pace	30.2	10

CHICAGO BEARS

As you can see from the table of stats by personnel group, the Bears are the very antithesis of "multiple" on defense. They don't even bring in extra linemen when they are on the goal line, and that "Dime+" listing represents a mere five plays. ☙ On offense, Chicago was one of only two teams to go without a tight end on at least 20 percent of plays (Buffalo was the other). That was probably a good idea, as the Bears offense was significantly better out of 10 personnel than it was from any other personnel group. ☙ Chicago ran out of 11 personnel more often than any team in the league. ☙ The Bears ranked 28th with -46.6% DVOA on running back screens. They were the only offense that ran the running back screen more than 30 times but had a negative DVOA on the play. ☙ It's probably not a surprise that Bears quarterbacks faced big blitzes on 13 percent of pass plays, the highest rate in the league. ☙ For the second year, the Bears used shotgun less than any other team in the NFL, 15 percent of plays. That's a Mike Martz thing, so expect to see Jay Cutler in the shotgun more often in 2012. So far in his career, Cutler doesn't have a strong record of being better in shotgun vs. under center, or vice versa. ☙ Ironically, Chicago had the only defense in the league that faced shotgun on a majority of opponent plays (51 percent).

Passing

Player	DYAR	DVOA	Plays	NtYds	Avg	YAC	C%	TD	Int
J.Cutler	157	-3.5%	339	2140	6.4	5.3	58.1%	13	7
C.Hanie*	-470	-78.7%	118	474	4.0	4.3	51.5%	3	8
J.McCown	-147	-50.6%	62	371	6.0	4.8	63.6%	2	4
J.Campbell	340	19.8%	169	1151	6.9	4.5	61.0%	6	3

Rushing

Player	DYAR	DVOA	Plays	Yds	Avg	TD	Fum	Suc
M.Forte	24	-5.6%	202	994	4.9	3	1	45%
M.Barber*	3	-7.9%	114	422	3.7	6	1	42%
K.Bell	-20	-15.1%	79	337	4.3	0	2	39%
A.Allen	-9	-23.9%	15	48	3.2	0	0	33%
C.Hanie*	25	36.4%	13	98	7.5	0	0	--
J.Cutler	-1	-14.5%	11	57	5.2	1	1	--
J.McCown	16	12.2%	10	70	7.0	0	0	--
M.Bush	65	-2.7%	256	980	3.8	7	1	45%
J.Campbell	-6	-19.1%	13	67	5.2	2	2	--

Receiving

Player	DYAR	DVOA	Plays	Ctch	Yds	Y/C	YAC	TD	C%
J.Knox	116	9.2%	69	37	729	19.7	4.4	2	54%
R.Williams*	96	6.4%	63	37	507	13.7	3.2	2	59%
D.Hester	-70	-29.6%	56	26	367	14.1	5.6	1	46%
D.Sanzenbacher	-22	-17.9%	54	27	276	10.2	2.1	3	50%
E.Bennett	42	1.0%	43	24	381	15.9	5.2	1	56%
S.Hurd*	-15	-26.2%	15	8	109	13.6	4.4	0	53%
B.Marshall	226	7.4%	143	82	1227	15.0	3.8	6	57%
E.Weems	9	-4.4%	14	11	90	8.2	2.7	0	79%
K.Davis	10	-2.9%	35	18	206	11.4	3.3	5	51%
M.Spaeth	5	-0.3%	11	7	50	7.1	2.6	2	64%
M.Forte	33	-5.7%	76	52	492	9.5	8.0	1	68%
K.Bell	-17	-29.6%	23	19	133	7.0	6.8	1	83%
T.Clutts	-16	-36.7%	10	8	48	6.0	4.6	0	80%
M.Barber	-4	-23.3%	9	5	50	10.0	9.8	0	56%
M.Bush	140	44.0%	47	37	418	11.3	8.6	1	79%

Offensive Line

Year	Yards	ALY	Rank	Power	Rank	Stuff	Rank	2nd Lev	Rank	Open Field	Rank	F-Start	Cont.
2009	4.04	4.01	19	58%	25	19%	16	0.95	30	0.81	15	26	33
2010	3.79	3.64	29	44%	32	25%	30	1.06	22	0.80	13	23	34
2011	4.39	3.92	24	61%	20	24%	30	1.24	11	1.03	8	27	31

Year	LE	Rank	LT	Rank	Mid	Rank	RT	Rank	RE	Rank	Sacks	ASR	Rank	Short	Long
2009	4.93	10	3.77	23	4.05	20	3.38	29	3.91	20	35	5.9%	13	9	19
2010	5.45	1	3.76	22	3.50	30	2.57	32	3.95	17	56	10.4%	32	20	26
2011	3.59	23	4.54	9	3.92	20	3.53	25	4.05	11	49	9.8%	31	23	14

This has been one of the most maligned units in all of football—right up there with the Patriots' secondary, Browns' receiving corps, and Dolphins' quarterbacks. When a group performs so resoundingly poorly yet its coach (Mike Tice) draws praise and, ultimately, a promotion, then obviously said group suffers from a paucity of talent. The Bears invested first-round picks in tackles Chris Williams and Gabe Carimi. So far, the former has been borderline soft, with his inconsistency leaving him subject to frequent position changes; the latter looked ill-prepared early in his rookie year before suffering a serious Week 2 knee injury from which he's still not fully recovered. If Carimi misses time in 2012, Williams will likely move from left guard back to right tackle (sigh). The original plan was for Williams to play left tackle, but that job now belongs to slow-footed, mistake-prone J'Marcus Webb. The 2010 seventh-round draft pick showed hints of improvements last season (he was given more one-on-one pass-blocking assignments than you would guess), but he also wound up leading the league with 15 offensive penalties. He also finished second with 11.5 blown blocks that led directly to either sacks or offensive holding flags.

Inside, Roberto Garza played with slightly better mobility after moving to center last season (likely because, in run-blocking, a center is usually less covered up off the snap than a guard is). Garza's 33 and still barely on the inside of his prime. The man next to him, Lance Louis, hasn't shown good enough footwork to stay at right tackle, but he seemed at least a little bit comfortable after moving to right guard last season. Louis shouldn't have too much trouble fending off lethargic ex-49ers bust Chilo Rachal during training camp. His real competition, in fact, is probably backup Edwin Williams, who started seven games in 2011 and proved a decent run-blocker at times. Williams also backs up left guard Chris Spencer, a player who, when healthy, moves well for his size.

Defensive Front Seven

Defensive Line	Age	Pos	Plays	TmPct	Rk	Stop	Dfts	BTkl	St%	Rk	AvYd	Rk	Sack	Hit	Hur	Runs	St%	Yds	Pass	St%	Yds
Israel Idonije	32	DE	50	6.1%	21	45	16	3	90%	6	1.0	26	5	7	22	40	95%	1.3	10	70%	-0.3
Julius Peppers	32	DE	40	4.9%	43	36	23	2	90%	6	-0.8	6	11	5	31	22	82%	1.4	18	100%	-3.4
Amobi Okoye*	25	DT	28	3.4%	51	22	10	2	79%	35	0.9	7	4	3	11	18	83%	2.3	10	70%	-1.8
Henry Melton	26	DE	24	3.1%	73	21	12	3	88%	11	0.0	13	7	9	18	17	82%	2.5	7	100%	-6.0
Matt Toeaina	30	DT	16	2.6%	--	13	2	2	81%	--	2.1	--	0	3	3	15	80%	2.1	1	100%	2.0
Anthony Adams*	32	DT	16	2.8%	--	15	3	1	94%	--	1.4	--	0	1	4.5	15	100%	1.1	1	0%	6.0

Linebackers	Age	Pos	Plays	TmPct	Rk	Stop	Dfts	BTkl	AvYd	Sack	Hit	Hur	Runs	St%	Rk	Yds	Rk	Tgts	Suc%	Rk	AdjYd	Rk
Lance Briggs	32	OLB	109	13.3%	28	71	26	7	4.1	0	2	7.5	61	80%	9	2.7	27	43	50%	45	5.8	23
Brian Urlacher	34	MLB	108	13.2%	30	61	22	3	5.8	0	0	2	58	69%	40	3.5	64	37	60%	8	7.3	52
Nick Roach	27	OLB	41	5.0%	109	26	9	3	4.4	0	3	5	19	68%	45	3.5	65	27	58%	12	5.6	17
Geno Hayes	25	OLB	65	8.3%	76	40	14	5	3.5	0	0	0	39	69%	39	2.1	8	23	51%	40	7.2	49

Year	Yards	ALY	Rank	Power	Rank	Stuff	Rank	2nd Lev	Rank	Open Field	Rank
2009	4.31	4.17	19	64%	15	23%	6	1.28	29	0.82	18
2010	3.95	3.54	2	72%	31	25%	1	1.16	20	0.80	18
2011	4.13	3.29	1	65%	20	26%	1	1.18	16	1.07	25

Year	LE	Rank	LT	Rank	Mid	Rank	RT	Rank	RE	Rank	Sacks	ASR	Rank	Short	Long
2009	5.08	28	4.72	26	3.64	8	4.43	25	3.90	14	35	5.9%	21	10	14
2010	3.82	10	4.45	22	3.28	1	3.48	9	3.65	11	34	6.0%	20	9	12
2011	2.90	4	3.87	12	3.36	1	3.54	4	2.55	3	33	5.2%	29	7	12

Year in and year out, the Bears manage to get as much out of their front seven as most defenses would get out of a front eight. The Bears led the league by allowing just 3.29 Adjusted Line Yards per carry; the gap between the Bears and the second-place Jets was equal to the gap between the Jets and the 15th place Steelers. Such is the reward for having talented veteran players who get to operate in a very familiar scheme. Since Brian Urlacher arrived in 2001, this has been primarily a Cover-2 defense. Urlacher's speed and ball recognition have had a large hand in Chicago's success with this approach. It remains to be seen whether a slower-than-expected recovery for Urlacher's Week 17 sprained MCL and PCL will impact his running come training camp. It shouldn't, but he remained sidelined for the initial slate of OTAs.

CHICAGO BEARS

Lance Briggs is essentially another Urlacher, only with slightly more point-of-attack intensity and slightly less football awareness. Thanks to Briggs' advanced age (32), the Bears got a good deal in re-signing him to a three-year, $17.5-million contract. Briggs and Urlacher alone are dominant enough to make this a great linebacking unit; it's just gravy that strongside linebacker Nick Roach (who would probably be a better fit in Briggs' weakside spot) is a fast, undervalued veteran. Roach should have no trouble holding off newcomer Geno Hayes for playing time.

Though Lovie Smith got more aggressive schematically last season, his defense still featured a four-man rush on 73 percent of pass plays, sixth most in the league. The Bears do a great job at creating one-on-one pass-rushing matchups through alignment variations before the snap. (One example: Urlacher and Briggs crowding the A-gaps makes it harder for running backs to get to their chip blocks outside, and it prevents a center from double-teaming defensive tackles right away.) After the snap, the Bears are very good with stunts. And there's talent across the board. Julius Peppers gets the headlines, and rightfully so, but the rest of the defensive linemen all have the right type of explosiveness for this one-gap scheme. That said, this defensive front's sack production has not matched its refinement and talent. To address this, the Bears spent their first-round pick on Boise State's Shea McClellin, whom many have compared to Clay Matthews. It remains to be seen how the more natural outside linebacker will adjust to playing a traditional defensive end position; fortunately, because the Bears re-signed the outlandishly underappreciated Israel Idonije, McClellin may not need to be much more than a third-down specialist in 2012.

To be fair, Chicago's low sack rate is not purely a reflection of the front four. A lot of it has to do with the fact that the Bears rarely blitz. Last season the Bears got 94 percent of their sacks from defensive linemen, the highest percentage in the league. Chicago's 30 defensive line sacks ranked seventh in the league. This isn't to say improvements still aren't needed. The Bears got pass pressure of some sort on just 22.9 percent of pass plays, which ranked 19th in the NFL.

Defensive Secondary

Secondary	Age	Pos	Plays	TmPct	Rk	Stop	Dfts	BTkl	Runs	St%	Rk	Yds	Rk	Tgts	Tgt%	Rk	Dist	Suc%	Rk	APaYd	Rk	PD	Int
Charles Tillman	31	CB	112	13.7%	2	47	20	6	24	63%	9	6.7	33	105	21.5%	12	12.0	48%	60	8.1	55	13	3
Tim Jennings	29	CB	86	10.5%	14	36	17	2	19	53%	25	7.6	49	95	19.5%	27	10.8	54%	33	6.5	21	8	2
Major Wright	24	SS	65	10.6%	34	21	9	6	23	35%	51	7.0	43	25	6.7%	44	14.1	46%	64	12.1	72	6	3
D.J. Moore	25	CB	51	7.7%	52	22	14	8	9	11%	78	10.2	69	51	12.9%	68	9.1	48%	58	7.1	34	8	4
Craig Steltz	26	SS	40	4.9%	--	18	6	3	27	52%	--	6.5	--	12	2.5%	--	9.5	48%	--	6.1	--	0	0
Brandon Meriweather*	28	FS	34	6.0%	--	8	5	2	8	38%	--	8.0	--	13	3.7%	--	16.3	53%	--	10.5	--	2	0
Chris Harris	30	SS	31	5.5%	71	9	1	4	13	38%	43	8.4	57	18	5.7%	60	16.4	47%	62	12.3	73	2	1
Chris Conte	23	FS	31	4.3%	76	6	4	3	12	25%	68	8.5	58	11	2.5%	76	15.5	74%	4	3.9	1	2	1
Jonathan Wilhite	28	CB	28	3.5%	--	13	8	1	1	0%	--	8.0	--	31	7.8%	--	8.9	40%	--	8.5	--	2	1
Kelvin Hayden	29	CB	24	6.2%	--	11	3	2	10	50%	--	7.7	--	16	7.5%	--	9.9	55%	--	7.0	--	5	2

Year	Pass D Rank	vs. #1 WR	Rk	vs. #2 WR	Rk	vs. Other WR	Rk	vs. TE	Rk	vs. RB	Rk
2009	24	13.8%	20	5.4%	22	-0.2%	16	-5.9%	10	13.2%	22
2010	5	-1.8%	15	16.6%	28	-22.1%	6	-0.9%	11	-17.6%	2
2011	7	-9.1%	6	-18.9%	4	-26.7%	7	0.9%	8	-5.5%	13

Lovie Smith last year drifted away a bit from the traditional Cover-2 designs he's always preferred and went with more matchup concepts, such as Cover-3 and even man-to-man. Charles Tillman was given a much heavier load than previous years, often shadowing the opposing team's top receiver. He held up well and had arguably a career year. This wasn't reflected in our game charting numbers, but those numbers don't reflect the way Tillman's heavier load leant more freedom to Chicago's once-conservative safeties. For the first time in ages, the Bears weren't regularly confined to playing two-deep coverages. Opposite Tillman, Tim Jennings, despite a temporary late-December benching, was solid facing the smaller receivers. Worth noting is that both corners were excellent in run support, which is critical in Chicago's defensive style.

This isn't to say the Bears don't have reason for concern about their secondary. If the pass rush stagnates, this unit can be easily dissected. Tillman, good as he was last season, lacks the catch-up speed to play trail technique coverage, and overall, he doesn't run well enough to consistently shadow elite targets man-to-man without safety help. This being Chicago, recent history says that the safety help is liable to be unreliable. Last year's third-round pick, Chris Conte, has a chance to change that. His comfort in centerfield and natural downhill speed were, presumably, big reasons why the Bears were willing to play more single-high concepts last season. Strong safety Major Wright will probably wind up competing with Craig Steltz for playing time at some point, as the Bears never seem to be able to settle on the same two starting safeties for an entire 16-game slate.

Even when in Cover-2, the Bears are willing to play man-to-man against the slot receiver for the sake of simplicity and spacing. The slot responsibilities will fall to D.J. Moore, who is a solid tackler and blitzer in the box (six hurries, four quarterback hits) and capable underneath pass defender. The miscellaneous corner who will likely find his way onto the field somehow (like Chicago's third safety, Chicago's fourth cornerback always seems to somehow crack the lineup at some point) is Kelvin Hayden, an experienced Cover-2 corner who flashed some playmaking prowess in Indianapolis. Hayden's playing time may depend on whether Lovie Smith continues to go with more coverage varieties or ultimately reverts back to his Cover-2 roots.

Special Teams

Year	DVOA	Rank	FG/XP	Rank	Net Kick	Rank	Kick Ret	Rank	Net Punt	Rank	Punt Ret	Rank	Hidden	Rank
2009	4.0%	4	4.8	7	-1.6	19	14.2	3	0.8	16	5.1	8	10.1	3
2010	6.3%	1	0.6	16	-4.0	24	14.6	3	-0.2	20	26.0	1	4.7	6
2011	7.2%	1	7.5	3	0.4	18	4.4	5	19.7	1	10.5	2	-5.1	23

The numbers say the Bears have had the best special teams in football the past two years. The film says those special teams are even more special than we know, as the numbers can't always account for the full amounts of field position that punters and kickers sacrifice in an effort to avoid Devin Hester. The best punt returner in NFL history is, surprisingly, not nearly as effective on kick returns (Hester's kickoff returns last season were worth 1.8 estimated points of field position; his punts were worth 10.6, second only to Patrick Peterson). This doesn't mean Hester's not worth putting back on kickoffs, of course. With Johnny Knox at risk of missing the 2012 season due to a back injury, Hester will share the kick return duties with newcomer Eric Weems. And yes, the rich have gotten embarrassingly richer here, as this is the same Eric Weems whose return prowess helped send him to the Pro Bowl as an all-purpose special teamer for the 2010 Falcons.

Robbie Gould is starting to look like an outlier to our general rule that field-goal kickers have no year-to-year consistency. He hasn't had negative value on field goals since his rookie year of 2005. Lovie Smith used to avoid field-goal attempts longer than 50 yards, but he started to let Gould kick those in 2009, and since then Gould is 11-for-13. By just about all measurements, punter Adam Podlesh ranked in the middle of the NFL's pack last season, but the Bears ranked first in net punting value thanks to phenomenal coverage teams. We estimate that punt returns against Chicago cost opponents more than two touchdowns worth of field position (-14.7 points) compared to what we would expect on average returns.

Coaching Staff

Just like Tom Coughlin in the NFL's largest market (or just like Tom Coughlin before Super Bowl XLVI, anyway), Lovie Smith, working in the NFL's second-largest market, feels constant heat under his britches. Smith signed a contract extension in 2011, but it only leaves him on the payroll through 2013. Many believe that Smith, at his core, is committed to the traditional black-and-blue, defense-oriented football that typifies most Tampa-2 aficionados. In reality, Smith is flexible enough to do whatever he has to do in order to win. Before this season, that meant being a high-risk/high-reward offense. Sure, Mike Martz's high-flying offensive system ultimately didn't work out, but most inside the NFL believe that Martz's departure was more about Jay Cutler's preferences than Smith's. Nevertheless, Smith now has a more traditional coordinator in Mike Tice, which he hopes will jive well with the defense that he and venerable assistant Rod Marinelli run.

Cincinnati Bengals

2011 Record: 9-7

Pythagorean Wins: 8.6 (12th)

DVOA: 0.1% (17th)

Offense: -1.4% (17th)

Defense: 0.8% (17th)

Special Teams: 2.3% (7th)

Variance: 7.0% (5th)

2012 Mean Projection: 8.8 wins

On the Clock (0-4): 4%

Mediocrity (5-7): 22%

Playoff Contender (8-10): 51%

Super Bowl Contender (11+): 22%

Postseason Odds: 41.9%

Projected Average Opponent: -1.3% (20th)

2011: The Kids Are Alright.

2012: Who Are You? Who? Who? (cause I really want to know)

The last four seasons in Cincinnati have been a thrill ride worthy of The Beast at nearby Kings Island amusement park. From the depths of 2008's injury-riddled 4-11-1, the striped coaster scaled the wooden slats to 2009's surprise division title. Then, with some national pundits putting the Bengals in the Super Bowl (step up, Mr. Mortensen), came a stomach-churning plummet to 2010's T.Ocho-induced 4-12. In 2011, with many of those same experts predicting an even worse disaster, the Bengals shot upward again, resulting in last season's wild-card run.

But while Bengals fans stagger woozily away in search of Dramamine, DVOA paints a different picture, one of a team that has spent the last three seasons walking an efficiency line so straight it would pass a field sobriety test. In 2009, Cincinnati finished 19th in DVOA at -0.1%. In 2010, the Bengals were 19th again, at -3.4%. Last year, when they made a playoff appearance, DVOA still ranked them only 17th overall at 0.1%.

Such consistent mediocrity isn't remarkable in and of itself. For example, take the 1995-97 Miami Dolphins, whose DVOA ratings went 1.0%/0.5%/2.2%. Or the 1993-95 Saints, who went -2.6%/-4.0%/-5.0%. Where the Bengals are unusual is in the volatility in their win-loss record. Those Fish won nine, eight, and nine games in the given stretch of DVOA similarity. The Saints won eight, seven, and seven. Cincinnati, on the other hand, bookended 2010's disappointing 4-12 record with playoff seasons of 10-6 and 9-7.

Schedule strength has been the main driver in the Bengals' ups and downs. With four annual games against Baltimore and Pittsburgh, it behooves Cincinnati to gorge on the league's cotton candy. In 2010, the Bengals went 1-7 against the AFC East and NFC South, and ended up with one of the ten hardest schedules in DVOA history. Last season, the schedule roulette wheel landed on "easy" and the Bengals fattened up on the AFC South and the NFC West, going 6-2. Overall, the Bengals took the phrase "borderline playoff team" to ridiculous extremes, winning all nine games against opponents that missed the postseason tournament, while losing all eight they played against playoff-bound opposition, including the loss in the wild card game at Houston.

Cincinnati also returned to form in close games after a 2-7 debacle in 2010. While their record in games decided by seven points or fewer was a pedestrian 5-5, that is deceptive. With the exception of a blowout loss at Pittsburgh in December, every single game was decided in the fourth quarter. In three straight October games, against the Jags, Colts and Seahawks, the Bengals delighted fans and maddened spread bettors with late defensive touchdowns that flattered them in the final score. On the other hand, Cincy fell just short on late drives against the Steelers, Ravens, and Broncos.

CINCINNATI BENGALS

2012 Bengals Schedule

Week	Opp.	Week	Opp.	Week	Opp.
1	at BAL (Mon.)	7	PIT	13	at SD
2	CLE	8	BYE	14	DAL
3	at WAS	9	DEN	15	at PHI (Thu.)
4	at JAC	10	NYG	16	at PIT
5	MIA	11	at KC	17	BAL
6	at CLE	12	OAK		

Figure 1. 2011 Cincinnati DVOA by Week

They twice won on field goals at the gun, and survived the Cardinals when a wide-open Early Doucet fell down in the end zone as he looked up for a potential tying touchdown pass. Pharmacies in southern Ohio and northern Kentucky reported a noticeable surge in Xanax prescriptions on Sundays in the fall.

Another key to a bounceback year in Cincinnati was rare good health. The Bengals training staff annually ranks near the bottom of our standings based on Adjusted Games Lost. But apparently Mike Brown finally started checking resumes for medical degrees, because the team improved from 25th to 13th in AGL. For the first time since 2003, the Bengals finished in the top half of the league in Adjusted Games Lost.

In *FOA 2011*, we wrote that the team had few holes in the traditional sense, but that it was time for the players in place to produce. One year later, the opposite seems true; while the overall talent level is as high as it has been in the Marvin Lewis era, many players are either fully untested or have yet to prove consistency. There are qualifiers or straight unknowns within virtually every position group. Only at tight end and defensive line are the Bengals seemingly set, and even those positions have newcomers looking to compete for snaps. While Lewis heads into his tenth season in charge (amazingly, only Bill Belichick and Andy Reid have more tenure), most everything else about the team is up in the air.

History doesn't help us predict Cincinnati's fortune. Of the 25 most consistent three-season teams by DVOA, 12 got better and 13 got worse. Most were significantly up or down (the aforementioned Dolphins improved by 22.1%, while those Saints worsened by 21.9%). On the other hand, two other recent teams that rode rookie quarterbacks to the playoffs a la the 2011 Bengals—the 2008 Falcons with Matt Ryan and the 2008 Ravens with Joe Flacco—both repeated as winning teams the following season, with Baltimore returning to the postseason and Atlanta just missing out.

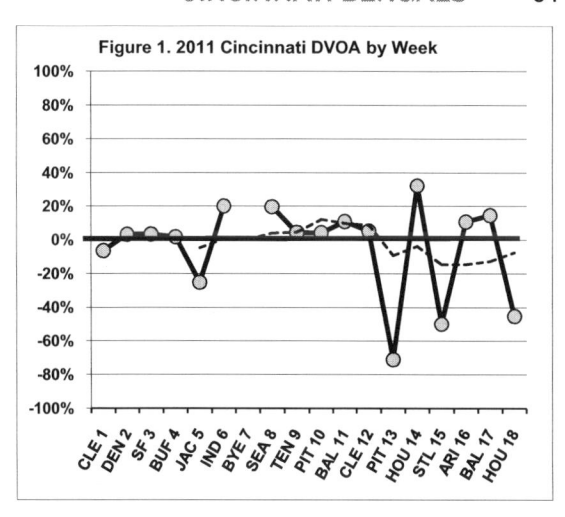

The Bengals project to be right within the margin of error of an exactly neutral DVOA team once again in 2012, and the schedule on paper looks less forgiving, with the formidable NFC North and the unpredictable AFC West on the docket. Will the team plunge toward the basement once again, remain in the stasis tube, or can they reach escape velocity at last?

Most of the answer is of course dependent on the development of second-year quarterback Andy Dalton. Cincinnati targeted the "Red Rifle" early in the pre-draft process for his smarts, athleticism, and unflappable nature, ignoring the low incidence of successful ginger-haired signal-callers. Those positive traits were on full display as the rookie piloted the team through the post-Carson Palmer shoals.

Dalton came of age in the season's second game. After missing the second half of the opener in Cleveland (won in the fourth quarter by backup Bruce Gradkowski), Dalton faced a rookie crucible: down by nine points in the fourth quarter at Denver, a howling crowd baying for further blood after a first-down sack put Dalton in a second-and-23 from his own seven-yard line. With most rookies, a screen and a give-up draw play were in order. Instead, Dalton dropped into his end zone and clotheslined a pass to Jerome Simpson on a deep-in route. Simpson wasn't hauled down until he reached the Broncos nine-yard line. Two plays later, the Bengals were in the end zone. They lost by a 24-22 margin, but the team had found its quarterback.

Two weeks later, after being encouraged to run more by the coaching staff, Dalton scrambled for the tying score, then lunged all out for the chains to convert an immense third down that set up a decisive field goal against Buffalo. That kick-started a five-game winning streak that catapulted Cincinnati into the playoffs.

The negatives on Dalton entering the draft were the lack of a cannon arm and the fact that as a shotgun spread passer at TCU he was slow in reading the whole field. The former complaint was borne out, particularly on deep passes outside the numbers, where Dalton was 17-of-49 for 560 yards. On deep balls thrown inside, he was much better: 11-of-16 for 362 yards. As the weather turned and the winds whipped, Dalton struggled to hit receivers downfield, and he had a tendency to loft balls.

As for the shotgun knock, Dalton made a concerted effort to stay in the pocket and make his reads. According to J.J. Cooper's timing stats, Dalton's average sack time was a lengthy 3.2 seconds, putting him 36th of 47 passers with more than 100 dropbacks. Indeed, Dalton was noticeably more effective under center, though he was in shotgun more often (Table 1).

Despite Dalton's initial success, doubts linger, at least among fans who saw Palmer, a far more talented physical specimen, deteriorate in Bengal-land. Dalton's 58.3 completion percentage is worrying, as are the five picks he threw in four winless games against the Steelers and Ravens. For the Bengals to turn a corner under Dalton's watch, he needs to prove he can pull out games against the league's big boys, not just keep them close.

Dalton may have been green, but at least he had Green—A.J., that is. The fourth overall pick proved a scintillating talent who was the exception to the maxim, "The quarterback makes the wide receiver." Green's playmaking ability and skill at mid-air adjustments gave Dalton a place to go at any time, confident that his fellow freshman would turn speculative throws into huge chunks of yardage. More stellar play in 2012 from Adriel Jeremiah is absolutely required, for there are few other reliable performers on the roster, especially on offense. Beyond Green and the sometimes spectacular, but less consistent, tight end Jermaine Gresham, the skill positions are laden with question marks.

Finding wideouts to relieve Green from triple-coverage will be a key plot to the 2012 season. The mercurial convict Jerome Simpson is gone to Minnesota, leaving a wide-open scramble for his starting gig. At press time, the only receiver on the roster with more than two years experience is Brandon Tate, who has 24 career catches and is foremost a returner. The rest of the corps includes sure-handed but oft-injured slot man Jordan Shipley, tiny (5-foot-7, 175-pound) Andrew Hawkins, speed-deprived Ryan Whalen, local guys Armon Binns and Vidal Hazelton (both played at University of Cincinnati), and rookies Mohamed Sanu and Marvin Jones, who have promise but aren't sure bets like Green. Don't be surprised if by the time you read this, or soon after, Braylon Edwards is wearing tiger stripes.

There is similar uncertainty at running back. BenJarvus Green-Ellis replaces the plodding Cedric Benson as the presumptive starter. The solid if unspectacular Law Firm seems an ideal candidate for a post-Belichick flop. If he does, the impact should be minimized by the team's stated and belated commitment to committee, which sounds like a Clyde Frazier formulation but is actually the new offensive gospel according to coordinator Jay Gruden. Bernard Scott is speedy but has yet to fulfill his promise; perhaps escaping Benson's shadow will be beneficial for the third-year runner.

Gruden's initial season in charge has to be considered a success, especially given the lack of offseason time he had to work with his new team (first and foremost the quarterback). But the statistical improvement was harder to see. In 2010, under the despised and deposed Bob Bratkowski, Cincinnati was 17th in offensive DVOA, 11th in passing. In 2011, with a West Coast system replacing Bratkowski's play-action based schemes, Cincy finished 17th in offensive DVOA, 11th in passing. Year One of the Gruden regime saw a slight uptick in rushing production, but otherwise the song remained the same. The general assumption among the Cincinnati media is that Gruden will open up the attack after using a necessarily arch-conservative approach in 2011.

Defensively, the team is similarly shy on bold-faced names, though much of that is by design, as defensive coordinator Mike Zimmer prefers to rotate players throughout games, especially in the front seven. The unit never fully recovered from the loss of its standard-bearer, cornerback Leon Hall, to an Achilles tendon tear in midseason. The team desperately needs Hall to heal fully and first-round pick Dre Kirkpatrick to develop into a worthy opposite number. Better play

Table 1. Andy Dalton Shotgun Splits, 2011

	DVOA	Passes.	Yards	Yd/Play
Shotgun	2.2%	350	2068	5.9
Under Center	10.4%	202	1368	6.8

from the linebackers, especially Rey Maualuga in the middle, and safeties would help as well.

The Bengals perennially have had a difficult time handling success and positive perceptions—witness 2010, or 2006, when the Bengals went 8-8 the year after their other recent AFC North title. Ironically, it is negative optics from last year that may propel the team forward. Despite the presence of what most considered a fun, overachieving squad to root for, Bengals Nation sent a loud message to ownership, failing to sell out six home games and leaving a yawning gap in the team's season ticket base and luxury box section. This wasn't apathy (the stadium was full for lean year after lean year) but a quiet revolt. The fans told the team they expected a greater commitment in exchange for hard-earned cash, and, surprisingly, Mike Brown appears to have heard them. For the first time in forever, the Bengals hired additional scouts, and have tightened up the football operations side of the franchise, paying as much attention to the off-field details, like better strength training and nutrition programs (unheralded keys to the aforementioned improvement in injury prevention), as to the on-field stuff.

Brown has taken less of a personnel role and given more voice to his daughter, team Executive Vice-President Katie Blackburn, one of the more prominent female executives in the league. (The fervent hope in Cincinnati is that football acumen skips a generation.) Meanwhile, the last year and change went much better than expected. The front office played the Carson Palmer situation just right, not giving in to a player-empowering panic move and sitting tight before finding a sucker (Oakland) in midseason to overpay for the aging vet. The Bengals' drafting has shown a pronounced upgrade of late. Cincinnati is the only team to draft a pair of Pro Bowlers in each of the last two drafts; that factoid required a number of AFC quarterbacks to drop out of last year's game and make room for Dalton, but let's not be picky. This April's haul included talented bulk on both lines and lower-round finds that sent the McKipers of the world into fits of ecstasy.

We're not talking Rooneyville here: The Bengals still don't have a practice bubble, still have more salary cap room than all but two teams, and still clip coupons and operate as though the league's TV deals didn't guarantee huge profits. The nature of the league and applied mathematics suggest that the Bengals could well improve in DVOA and not better their 2011 record. But should the Bengals defy history and make consecutive playoff appearances for the first time since 1982—and only the second time in the history of the franchise—2011 could be looked back upon as a defining moment in the team's history, signaled in bright red ink by the drafting of Dalton and Green.

Or another ride on The Beast beckons.

Robert Weintraub

2011 Bengals Stats by Week

Wk	vs.	W-L	PF	PA	YDF	YDA	TO	Total	Off	Def	ST
1	@CLE	W	27	17	294	285	1	-6%	-16%	-20%	-11%
2	@DEN	L	22	24	382	318	2	3%	22%	12%	-6%
3	SF	L	8	13	228	226	-2	3%	-25%	-29%	0%
4	BUF	W	23	20	458	273	-2	2%	-8%	-4%	6%
5	@JAC	W	30	20	239	296	1	-25%	-6%	18%	-1%
6	IND	W	27	17	358	273	3	20%	14%	4%	10%
7	BYE										
8	@SEA	W	34	12	252	411	0	20%	0%	8%	28%
9	@TEN	W	24	17	319	328	1	4%	19%	6%	-8%
10	PIT	L	17	24	279	328	-1	4%	-9%	-5%	8%
11	@BAL	L	24	31	483	373	-2	11%	20%	9%	1%
12	CLE	W	23	20	389	274	0	5%	0%	-4%	1%
13	@PIT	L	7	35	232	295	-2	-71%	-24%	22%	-25%
14	HOU	L	19	20	285	412	2	32%	1%	-12%	20%
15	@STL	W	20	13	283	305	-1	-50%	-45%	16%	11%
16	ARI	W	23	16	301	316	1	11%	-3%	-15%	-2%
17	BAL	L	16	24	336	347	-1	15%	28%	20%	7%
18	@HOU	L	10	31	300	340	-3	-45%	-9%	31%	-5%

Trends and Splits

	Offense	Rank	Defense	Rank
Total DVOA	-1.4%	17	0.8%	17
Unadjusted VOA	-1.2%	17	-3.4%	12
Weighted Trend	-0.4%	14	3.3%	19
Variance	7.3%	15	7.0%	23
Average Opponent	-3.9%	3	-6.0%	31
Passing	18.3%	11	6.7%	18
Rushing	-9.8%	26	-6.5%	16
First Down	-0.3%	17	-3.5%	12
Second Down	-17.3%	29	4.7%	18
Third Down	22.6%	9	2.6%	18
First Half	-2.9%	17	5.2%	23
Second Half	0.1%	16	-3.8%	10
Red Zone	-0.2%	10	2.9%	21
Late and Close	-7.7%	23	-12.4%	7

CINCINNATI BENGALS

Five-Year Performance

Year	W-L	Pyth	Est W	PF	PA	TO	Total	Rk	Off	Rk	Def	Rk	ST	Rk	Off AGL	Rk	Def AGL	Rk
2007	7-9	7.9	8.4	380	385	+5	1.7%	16	12.0%	7	9.5%	27	-0.8%	19	20.8	16	24.4	21
2008	4-11-1	3.3	4.6	204	364	-2	-20.7%	27	-18.3%	28	-0.3%	15	-2.8%	26	59.8	31	48.3	30
2009	10-6	8.4	8.0	305	291	0	-0.1%	19	-0.9%	19	-2.0%	13	-1.3%	21	34.1	24	36.5	24
2010	4-12	6.0	6.6	322	395	-8	-3.4%	19	1.7%	17	1.5%	17	-3.5%	28	14.9	7	47.5	30
2011	9-7	8.6	8.5	344	323	0	0.10%	17	-1.4%	17	0.80%	17	2.3%	7	25.2	15	26.5	17

2011 Performance Based on Most Common Personnel Groups

Cincinnati Offense					Cincinnati Offense vs. Opp.				Cincinnati Defense				Cincinnati Defense vs. Opp.			
Pers	Freq	Yds	DVOA	Run%	Pers	Freq	Yds	DVOA	Pers	Freq	Yds	DVOA	Pers	Freq	Yds	DVOA
11	43%	5.7	13.3%	21%	4-3-4	29%	5.2	1.3%	4-3-4	50%	5.5	5.5%	11	40%	4.9	-4.7%
12	19%	4.8	0.2%	53%	3-4-4	24%	5.5	6.5%	4-2-5	42%	4.9	-11.3%	12	18%	5.1	2.8%
21	15%	6.4	30.7%	62%	4-2-5	18%	4.8	2.9%	3-3-5	3%	3.8	7.9%	21	17%	6.4	-0.4%
22	8%	4.0	-15.7%	85%	2-4-5	10%	5.4	19.5%	Dime+	2%	8.5	168.6%	22	9%	5.7	23.1%
01	4%	6.1	22.2%	7%	3-3-5	8%	5.9	11.6%	G-line	2%	0.3	10.9%	10	5%	3.7	-29.3%
					Dime+	8%	6.3	18.7%								

Strategic Tendencies

Run/Pass		Rank	Offense		Rank	Pass Rush		Rank	Defense/Other		Rank
Runs, all plays	44%	9	Form: Single Back	64%	15	Rush 3	4.8%	22	4 DB	50%	15
Runs, first half	44%	14	Form: Empty Back	6%	15	Rush 4	64.6%	16	5 DB	45%	11
Runs, first down	58%	4	Pers: 3+ WR	51%	18	Rush 5	22.1%	15	6+ DB	2%	28
Runs, second-long	29%	28	Pers: 4+ WR	6%	8	Rush 6+	8.5%	13	CB by Sides	83%	13
Runs, power sit.	76%	3	Pers: 2+ TE/6+ OL	34%	14	Zone Blitz	7.0%	10	Go for it on 4th	0.87	19
Runs, behind 2H	36%	6	Play action	16%	20	Sacks by LB	6.7%	30	Offensive Pace	30.5	14
Pass, ahead 2H	41%	22	Max protect	11%	14	Sacks by DB	17.8%	2	Defensive Pace	30.4	16

The Bengals used six offensive linemen on 6.3 percent of plays, sixth in the league, but were awful on these plays: 3.7 yards per play and -35.8% DVOA. ◉ Cincinnati was second in the league with 69 offensive penalties (including declined and offsetting) but 29th with only 29 defensive penalties. ◉ Cincinnati allowed a league-high 7.9 yards per play and 31.3% DVOA when the opposing quarterback left the pocket. ◉ In 2009 and 2010, the Bengals defense was better when blitzing, but not in 2011; they allowed just 5.5 yards per play with four pass rushers, but 7.1 yards per play with five or more. ◉ Cincinnati was very strong against runs from shotgun, allowing a league-low 3.9 yards per carry with a second-ranked -17.1% DVOA.

Passing

Player	DYAR	DVOA	Plays	NtYds	Avg	YAC	C%	TD	Int
A.Dalton	575	5.6%	540	3224	6.2	4.4	58.3%	20	13
B.Gradkowski	-51	-58.5%	19	102	5.4	8.5	44.4%	1	1

Rushing

Player	DYAR	DVOA	Plays	Yds	Avg	TD	Fum	Suc
C.Benson*	-21	-10.4%	273	1065	3.9	6	5	49%
B.Scott	-11	-11.0%	112	380	3.4	3	0	43%
A.Dalton	-4	-14.6%	29	163	5.6	1	1	--
B.Leonard	18	18.5%	17	85	5.0	0	0	47%
A.Hawkins	23	35.6%	5	25	5.0	0	0	--
A.J.Green	8	-21.9%	5	53	10.6	0	1	--
B.Green-Ellis	106	3.9%	181	667	3.7	11	0	54%

Receiving

Player	DYAR	DVOA	Plays	Ctch	Yds	Y/C	YAC	TD	C%
A.J.Green	284	16.9%	115	65	1057	16.3	4.1	7	57%
J.Simpson*	47	-6.7%	105	50	725	14.5	4.6	4	48%
A.Caldwell*	-27	-17.9%	67	37	317	8.6	3.1	3	55%
A.Hawkins	23	-3.1%	34	23	263	11.4	6.3	0	68%
J.Gresham	-8	-8.5%	92	56	596	10.6	3.4	6	61%
D.Lee	15	9.3%	13	11	115	10.5	6.3	0	85%
C.Cochart	3	-2.0%	9	5	44	8.8	5.0	1	56%
B.Leonard	43	12.7%	31	22	210	9.5	8.5	0	71%
C.Benson*	-11	-23.5%	22	15	82	5.5	5.7	0	68%
B.Scott	-42	-62.9%	17	13	38	2.9	3.5	0	76%
B.Green-Ellis	64	72.6%	13	9	159	17.7	15.8	0	69%

CINCINNATI BENGALS

Offensive Line

Year	Yards	ALY	Rank	Power	Rank	Stuff	Rank	2nd Lev	Rank	Open Field	Rank	F-Start	Cont.
2009	4.14	3.97	24	79%	1	19%	17	1.20	12	0.74	16	24	27
2010	3.76	4.04	18	51%	28	23%	27	1.15	15	0.38	31	21	29
2011	3.81	3.99	20	56%	25	22%	27	1.12	23	0.51	28	25	32

Year	LE	Rank	LT	Rank	Mid	Rank	RT	Rank	RE	Rank	Sacks	ASR	Rank	Short	Long
2009	3.79	23	4.45	9	4.26	10	3.82	24	2.78	28	29	5.6%	10	13	12
2010	4.02	20	4.95	3	3.75	24	3.99	21	2.78	31	28	5.1%	7	14	6
2011	4.41	12	4.66	6	3.50	30	4.15	22	3.40	20	25	4.5%	4	10	11

For a team supposedly built around running the ball and wearing down the opposition, Cincinnati was mediocre on the ground, especially up the middle. As a result, the Bengals will be breaking in a pair of new guards. Veteran Travelle Wharton was signed from Carolina to take over the left side, with first-round draft choice Kevin Zeitler from Wisconsin taking over on the right. They should provide a significant upgrade over the Bobbie Williams/Nate Livings/Clint Boling trio that manned the middle in 2011. Wharton has started 99 games in his eight-year career, while Zeitler was a punishing earth-mover for the Badgers. Cohesion is a concern when you have two new starters, of course, as is depth after free-agent arrival Jacob Bell abruptly decided to retire in May.

While the Bengals' group of road graders is a work in progress, their pass blocking was superb, with just 25 sacks allowed and a mere 13 blown blocks that led directly to sacks (only Philly had fewer with 12). Andrew Whitworth had four of those, as well as four blown blocks which led to offensive holding flags, which pokes some small holes in his reputation as a redoubt on the blind side. Andre Smith finally approached his lofty draft status, healthy and (relatively) svelte for the first time as a Bengal. He had six false starts, but otherwise was solid opposite Whitworth. Center Kyle Cook is heady but lags behind the division's other stalwarts at the position.

Defensive Front Seven

Defensive Line	Age	Pos	Plays	TmPct	Rk	Stop	Dfts	BTkl	St%	Rk	AvYd	Rk	Sack	Hit	Hur	Runs	St%	Yds	Pass	St%	Yds
Domata Peko	28	DT	65	8.1%	2	43	10	6	66%	60	2.2	47	2.5	1	2	58	66%	2.6	7	71%	-0.9
Geno Atkins	24	DT	49	6.1%	10	42	19	0	86%	11	1.3	12	8	12	19.5	33	85%	2.1	16	88%	-0.4
Michael Johnson	25	DE	45	5.6%	28	33	15	3	73%	58	1.3	38	6.5	6	13	27	70%	2.4	18	78%	-0.4
Frostee Rucker*	29	DE	44	5.5%	30	33	14	1	75%	53	1.3	40	4	3	1	36	75%	1.4	8	75%	0.9
Robert Geathers	29	DE	30	4.3%	57	24	6	0	80%	34	2.4	69	2.5	2	13.5	22	82%	2.0	8	75%	3.6
Carlos Dunlap	23	DE	26	4.3%	56	24	7	2	92%	3	0.4	19	4	13	20.5	15	93%	2.1	11	91%	-1.8
Jonathan Fanene*	30	DE	25	3.1%	72	22	12	1	88%	9	-1.2	2	6.5	6	10.5	16	81%	0.8	9	100%	-4.7
Pat Sims	27	DT	20	3.6%	49	16	4	1	80%	29	1.9	36	1	0	1	19	79%	2.2	1	100%	-5.0
Jamaal Anderson	26	DE	25	3.0%	78	20	7	0	80%	34	2.1	58	3	2	5	20	80%	2.4	5	80%	1.0

Linebackers	Age	Pos	Plays	TmPct	Rk	Stop	Dfts	BTkl	AvYd	Sack	Hit	Hur	Runs	St%	Rk	Yds	Rk	Tgts	Suc%	Rk	AdjYd	Rk
Thomas Howard	29	OLB	101	12.7%	34	41	18	4	6.9	1	3	2	46	52%	104	4.3	94	45	46%	53	6.6	37
Rey Maualuga	25	MLB	90	13.9%	21	54	13	8	4.4	0	0	4	62	66%	53	3.2	43	21	54%	24	4.8	7
Manny Lawson	28	OLB	54	6.8%	96	31	10	2	4.2	1.5	2	4	33	61%	73	3.4	55	18	48%	49	4.7	6
Brandon Johnson*	29	OLB	29	3.6%	--	19	7	1	6.1	0	3	3	8	100%	--	2.1	--	25	53%	30	6.8	43
Dan Skuta	26	OLB	20	2.5%	--	10	1	1	4.8	0.5	0	2	14	57%	--	4.1	--	6	0%	--	11.5	--

Year	Yards	ALY	Rank	Power	Rank	Stuff	Rank	2nd Lev	Rank	Open Field	Rank
2009	3.88	4.35	25	74%	29	16%	27	1.15	18	0.30	1
2010	4.53	4.19	19	73%	32	18%	22	1.17	21	1.05	30
2011	4.09	3.78	5	66%	23	20%	17	1.03	4	0.88	21

CINCINNATI BENGALS

Year	LE	Rank	LT	Rank	Mid	Rank	RT	Rank	RE	Rank	Sacks	ASR	Rank	Short	Long
2009	4.95	26	3.60	6	4.57	27	4.51	26	3.20	4	34	5.4%	28	9	21
2010	3.72	8	3.89	13	4.32	23	4.70	26	3.52	9	27	5.3%	30	6	13
2011	4.28	16	4.28	20	3.63	5	4.30	17	2.82	4	45	7.3%	10	15	20

An agile, slashing defensive line rotation had an excellent season. Tackle Geno Atkins justified his selection to our 2011 Top Prospects list with a Pro Bowl season, and fellow tackle Domata Peko was almost as disruptive inside. The Bengals went from 27 to 45 sacks, despite the fact that top pass rusher Carlos Dunlap was hampered for a large chunk of the year by a balky hamstring, and ranked in the top ten for defensive Adjusted Line Yards for the first time *ever*.

(Seriously, if you want to understand the AFC North, simply consider this stat: Adjusted Line Yards stats go back to 1995. In the 17 years since, Pittsburgh has ranked in the top ten in defensive ALY 13 times, Baltimore has ranked in the top ten 11 times, Cincinnati has ranked in the top ten once, and Cleveland has never ranked in the top ten since returning to the league in 1999.)

A couple of cogs in the machine, Frostee Rucker and Jonathan Fanene, chased free-agent money and more playing time elsewhere. They have been replaced by more than 600 pounds of youthful mass inside, high draft picks Devon Still and Brandon Thompson. Second-rounder Still bluntly admitted that he wore down late in games while at Penn State, so 15-to-20 snaps per game in Mike Zimmer's system should work out well for him. Third-rounder Thompson comes out of Clemson, and turned heads by tossing bodies around at the Senior Bowl. In addition, the Mike Brown Home for Wayward Draft Busts attracted ends Derrick Harvey and Jamaal Anderson to southern Ohio to try and resurrect their careers.

Rey Maualuga's season was defined by the regular-season finale, when Ravens blockers took him out twice, thus releasing Ray Rice for long touchdown runs. Maualuga moved to his more natural middle linebacker slot, and was generally steady, but two or three times per game was either out of position or unable to disengage from lead blocks. Bay Area rejects Manny Lawson and Thomas Howard proved serviceable outside linebackers in the Queen City, with Lawson's coverage ability a bonus. Projected impact pass rusher Dontay Moch missed the season due to severe migraines. His return would add provide an element the team lacks, a standup blitzer who can regularly pressure the passer. However, the most interesting linebacker on the roster is not Moch but an undrafted rookie. Vontaze Burfict's junior year at Arizona State was a miasma of missed assignments and personal fouls, resulting in a nosedive off the league's draft boards. But if Marvin Lewis can contain the crazy, the Bengals may have an undrafted free agent reminiscent of James Harrison in both playmaking ability and wild man tendencies.

Defensive Secondary

Secondary	Age	Pos	Plays	TmPct	Rk	Stop	Dfts	BTkl	Runs	St%	Rk	Yds	Rk	Tgts	Tgt%	Rk	Dist	Suc%	Rk	APaYd	Rk	PD	Int
Reggie Nelson	29	FS	94	11.8%	20	41	16	9	38	39%	37	7.4	48	39	9.0%	15	15.5	60%	24	7.0	27	12	4
Nate Clements	33	CB	67	9.0%	30	34	22	5	10	70%	5	2.3	1	90	22.5%	8	11.6	54%	32	7.1	33	11	2
Chris Crocker	32	SS	66	8.3%	56	23	12	4	29	24%	71	6.6	31	41	9.6%	13	11.5	56%	39	6.5	16	6	0
Leon Hall	28	CB	39	8.7%	35	13	4	5	6	17%	77	5.8	23	46	19.2%	29	13.6	50%	48	8.6	61	6	2
Kelly Jennings*	30	CB	36	5.6%	--	16	8	0	6	33%	--	10.0	--	39	11.2%	--	13.3	61%	--	6.8	--	6	0
Adam Jones	29	CB	34	8.5%	--	12	2	5	10	40%	--	8.9	--	28	13.1%	--	17.9	50%	--	9.3	--	7	0
Gibril Wilson*	31	SS	23	2.9%	--	4	1	3	16	19%	--	10.0	--	2	0.5%	--	10.5	45%	--	7.3	--	1	0
Terence Newman	34	CB	61	9.3%	23	17	7	6	12	33%	53	11.3	75	69	19.0%	31	13.2	43%	73	10.0	76	11	4
Jason Allen	29	CB	48	6.3%	70	15	10	4	11	27%	67	7.8	51	64	14.9%	57	13.7	50%	51	6.3	18	11	4

Year	Pass D Rank	vs. #1 WR	Rk	vs. #2 WR	Rk	vs. Other WR	Rk	vs. TE	Rk	vs. RB	Rk
2009	10	-29.8%	5	-21.5%	4	22.9%	31	-25.7%	2	22.2%	27
2010	14	0.5%	17	-1.7%	14	-5.6%	14	2.8%	14	-25.0%	1
2011	18	14.9%	21	31.9%	28	-5.6%	15	11.4%	19	-11.8%	10

The combination of Leon Hall and Johnathan Joseph was among football's best in 2010. By Thanksgiving 2011, neither was on the field for Cincinnati. Joseph left for Houston and more guaranteed money in last summer's free agent frenzy, a crushing blow to the Bengals made more bitter when Joseph helped shut down A.J. Green in the wild card game. Hall blew out his Achilles tendon at midseason, and his prognosis is uncertain for this season and beyond. Nate Clements had a surprisingly strong season replacing Joseph, but he is 33, and Pacman Jones is Pacman Jones.

The team addressed the corner conundrum by drafting Alabama's Dre Kirkpatrick in the first round. Nick Saban signed off on him, but Kirkpatrick carries concerns about attitude and a penchant for gambling (on the field, that is). Jason Allen was signed away from Houston, but if that's a tit-for-tat move after losing Joseph, then the Texans got Dolly Parton and the Bengals got Olive Oyl. The Bengals also signed Terence Newman, who wants the opportunity to prove last season's disaster in Dallas was due to injury, as he claims. OK, then what was the reason for 2010's disaster?

When last we saw Chris Crocker, he was dropping a sure pick-six and getting run over by Arian Foster in the playoff game against Houston. He was cut mainly as a result of that game, as his regular season was steady, and our game charting crew liked him tons. His replacement looks to be either 49ers washout Taylor Mays, special teams demon Jeremy Miles, or rookie George Iloka. Reggie Nelson holds down the other safety spot after the Bengals fought off several suitors to re-sign him.

Special Teams

Year	DVOA	Rank	FG/XP	Rank	Net Kick	Rank	Kick Ret	Rank	Net Punt	Rank	Punt Ret	Rank	Hidden	Rank
2009	-1.1%	21	-5.0	25	-3.8	24	-4.2	18	-4.5	25	11.0	4	5.4	6
2010	-3.0%	28	-7.4	31	-11.2	29	-3.5	19	8.7	6	-4.3	24	-3.8	18
2011	1.9%	7	3.3	11	10.0	2	-7.5	31	0.7	15	4.8	5	4.8	10

Most discussion about the Bengals surprise playoff run began and ended with Dalton-to-Green, but special teams, in particular kickoffs, were a prime reason for the team's unexpected success. Mike Nugent's booming leg welcomed the new kickoff spot, and a sterling coverage crew led by Miles and Cedric Peerman vaulted the kickoff unit near the top of our rankings. The consistent field position advantage was critical for a young team playing conservative ball. Bengals opponents started their average drive more than 74 yards away from the end zone (sixth in the NFL) while the Bengals themselves started their average drive with less than 70 yards to go (fifth).

Elsewhere, things weren't so special. Kevin Huber remains a below average punter, while Brandon Tate too often ran laterally on both punt and kick returns. He did take a punt back for a key touchdown against Seattle, but otherwise, oy. Tate didn't have a single kick return that passed the 40, and Adam Jones actually had more punt return value on two returns (one of them for 63 yards) than Tate had on 51 returns. Tate was much better with New England in 2010 (+8.4 points on kickoff returns), so all hope is not lost.

Coaching Staff

Andy Dalton and A.J. Green weren't the only rookies who had a strong year in Cincinnati. New offensive coordinator Jay Gruden, fresh from the Florida Tuskers of the United Football League, had no time to properly install his West Coast offense thanks to the lockout, but he still managed to guide his sapling quarterback to the playoffs. Now he will be tasked with improving a basic tenet of the system, yards after catch. Bengals pass grabbers averaged a mere 4.4 YAC, a terribly low figure for a West Coast team. Gruden became a hot commodity for his perceived puppet mastery, and for being Not Bob Bratkowski. But as pointed out earlier in this chapter, Cincinnati's 2011 numbers were virtually identical to Brat's 2010 season in command of the offense. If that doesn't change, even his older brother won't be able to say good things about Jay.

Hue Jackson traded a king's ransom in premium draft picks for Bengals QB-turned *persona non grata* Carson Palmer, and lost his job in Oakland as a result. As a thank you, the Bengals found a job for the Hue-miliated Jackson. He'll help look after the secondary under new defensive backs coach Mark Carrier and the special teams under Darrin Simmons. Jackson has only coached offense in his pro career, so consider this the NFL version of an old-fashioned patronage job, with the Bengals as Tammany Hall and Mike Brown as Boss Tweed.

Cleveland Browns

2011 Record: 4-12

Pythagorean Wins: 5.0 (28th)

DVOA: -14.2% (25th)

Offense: -11.2% (25th)

Defense: 4.2% (22nd)

Special Teams: 1.3% (10th)

Variance: 6.2% (2nd)

2012 Mean Projection: 5.1 wins

On the Clock (0-4): 40%

Mediocrity (5-7): 49%

Playoff Contender (8-10): 11%

Super Bowl Contender (11+): 1%

Postseason Odds: 2.5%

Projected Average Opponent: 3.1% (5th)

2011: Forget the Madden Curse; behold the Football Outsiders Whammy!

2012: You know you've hit bottom when the Bengals are your role model.

In *Football Outsiders Almanac 2011*, we forecast the Browns to battle for a playoff spot. The idea was that this solid defensive team would get just enough offense, powered mainly by a punishing running game, and fatten up on a soft schedule that featured the NFC West and the AFC South. While they figured to struggle with the likes of Baltimore and Pittsburgh down the stretch, a hot start would put the Browns in position for the tournament, even if it meant backing in.

As it happens, that scenario (save for the powerful ground attack part) pretty much describes the journey taken by the other team in Ohio, the Browns' arch-rivals in Cincinnati. In Cleveland, it was (failed) business as usual; a 4-12 finish and the eighth straight season the team has watched the playoffs from home. Since the Browns returned to the NFL in 1999, they have gone 68-140, for an average 5-11 mark. In that span, the Browns have made the playoffs just once, in 2002, and have had winning records just twice (they were 10-6 in 2007). By contrast, the Seahawks had six winning seasons and four playoff appearances in their first thirteen campaigns; the Jags won 45 games in their years two through five; the Panthers were in three conference championships and a Super Bowl by Year 13; and even the hapless Buccaneers were in the NFC Championship game in their fourth year of existence. (Table 1)

Houston's playoff breakthrough is terrible news in Browns Town, where the worst expansion team of the modern era (even if they aren't commonly thought of that way due to the original Browns) plods along. Indeed, the Browns didn't just crash to the basement last season; they are projected to remain a wretched club again in 2012.

What caused such a drastic slide? And can the Browns reverse course and mirror the turnaround achieved in Cincinnati?

In retrospect, the four-game winning streak the Browns put together to close 2009 was a toxic mirage that hindered the franchise, for it convinced team President and shotcaller Mike Holmgren to retain head coach Eric Mangini despite their schematic and stylistic differences. 2010 was thus played at cross-purposes, the inevitable result being a 5-11

Table 1: Records of Last Six Expansion Teams in Their First 13 Seasons

Year	Team	Record	%	Playoffs
1976	Tampa Bay Buccaneers	59-136*	.303	3
1976	Seattle Seahawks	96-100*	.490	4
1995	Jacksonville Jaguars	109-95	.534	6
1995	Carolina Panthers	97-111	.466	3
1999	Cleveland Browns	68-140	.327	1
2002	Houston Texans (10 seasons)	65-95**	.406	1

2012 Browns Schedule

Week	Opp.	Week	Opp.	Week	Opp.
1	PHI	7	at IND	13	at OAK
2	at CIN	8	SD	14	KC
3	BUF	9	BAL	15	WAS
4	at BAL (Thu.)	10	BYE	16	at DEN
5	at NYG	11	at DAL	17	at PIT
6	CIN	12	PIT		

Figure 1. 2011 Cleveland DVOA by Week

season and the transfer of the ManGenius from sideline to ESPN set.

Pat Shurmur, a stout branch of Holmgren's coaching tree, was installed as the top man for 2011, a move that completed the Browns' transition to a traditional West Coast offense in the preferred manner of Holmgren-influenced teams. Mangini's 3-4 defense was likewise junked in favor of new defensive coordinator Dick Jauron's 4-3. With no OTAs and training camps limited thanks to the lockout, some struggle was perhaps inevitable. A full offseason of work can only help the team execute the playbook better.

Cleveland's futility is, of course, directly tied to a historic inability to find a quarterback. You win two free season tickets if you can name the last Browns signal caller to start consecutive opening games (note: second prize is four tickets). Answer: The immortal Charlie Frye in 2006 and 2007. Unsurprisingly, Frye lost both openers. In the rebooted Browns' 13 seasons, no fewer than ten different quarterbacks have taken the season's first snap.

This goes to 11, for the Browns have yet another new man under center. Cleveland's strategy to goose the anemic offense was to attack with the draft. The Browns sacrificed three lower-round picks in order to move up one spot and select Trent Richardson of Alabama, by general consensus (save, notably, for renowned talent evaluator Jim Brown) the finest running back prospect since Adrian Peterson. Cleveland then used a second first-round choice (obtained from Atlanta in the Julio Jones deal) to take Oklahoma State quarterback Brandon Weeden, whose talent runs a distant second in his scouting report to his age.

Weeden is 28, turning 29 in October, which by NFL standards means he has liver spots exploding all over his body. His time is now, and he will almost certainly begin the new season at the helm of the Browns offense. Both of Cleveland's first-round selections are a bit controversial: Weeden because of his age, and Richardson because of evidence that spending such a high choice on a running back isn't the best use of resources, even when that back is as talented as Richardson. Here are the other running backs taken in the top five since 2005: Darren McFadden, Reggie Bush, Ronnie Brown, Cedric Benson, and Cadillac Williams. Draw your own conclusions.

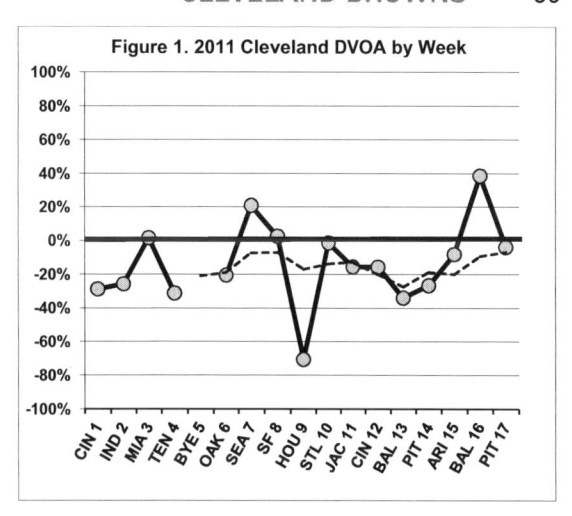

The Browns in a sense are trying to replicate the success those blasted Bengals had with their 2011 draft, with top draft choices Green and Dalton instantly revivifying a moribund offense (at least in perception—the Bengals' offensive DVOA remained static) and catalyzing a shocking playoff berth. Mirroring successful foes is an NFL tradition on the level of Thanksgiving games in Detroit or crappy pregame shows, but can the Browns effectively shove that Cincinnati chili into a dumpling and call it a *pierogi*?

In the last decade, 20 teams have selected skill position players with their first two picks in the top two rounds (Table 2; we included the 2009 Jets, who made Shonn Greene the first pick of round three). Only four of those teams went from missing the postseason to making it after doubling down on rookie skill guys: those 2009 Jets, the 2008 Ravens, and the 2004 Bears, in addition to last year's Bengals. The first three teams had dominating defenses, which allowed them to overcome the shortcomings of their rookies (Ray Rice only ran for 454 yards his first season). Cleveland's defense is nowhere near that strong. Clearly, Cincinnati's playoff run last year was historically fluky, and the Browns are kidding themselves if they think they can catch that particular lightning in a bottle. [1]

Putting aside *realpolitik* achievement in the form of postseason berths, did the teams that took skill players 1-2 actually show any immediate improvement offensively? We created a very simple equation that projected offensive DVOA based solely on offensive DVOA the previous year, to try to isolate how much improvement was simply bad teams regressing towards the mean. Table 2 isolates teams like the 2003 Texans, who had nowhere to go but up, to place any improvement in the context of what was expected. So while these 20 teams averaged a 3.5% rise in offensive DVOA, they also fell short of their projections by an average of 1.5%, taking more of the starch out of the strategy.

In the longer term, there is an obvious risk in investing so much draft value on skill players, which is why we advocate building from the lines outward. While a handful of teams hit pay dirt with both picks, like the 2009 Eagles and the 2008 Ravens, most got multi-season value from only one of the draftees (aside—wouldn't it be just like sports for Richardson to bust and Weeden to break out?). Still, like the 2003 Texans, the 2012 Browns will likely improve offensively simply because they can't get much worse.

Richardson is a mouth-watering blend of power, quickness, vision, durability, and "I think I'll truck you rather than elude you just for the sheer ecstasy of it" attitude. He can only help a running game that was a colossal disappointment in 2011, ranking 31st in DVOA (only the Titans ran it worse). The judgmental finger can be pointed straight at Peyton Hillis, the 2010 folk hero, the second coming of Mike Alstott, who blasted his way over tacklers and beat them to the corner (naturally, Chris Berman added his explosion noises to Hillis highlights even on runs where he wasn't touched by a defender). Just in case we need to highlight the subtext here, we'll tell you that Hillis was the first white running back since Craig James in 1985 to best 1,000 yards in a season.

Unfortunately, Hillis' 2011 campaign was as godawful as James' Texas Senatorial campaign. The back briefly nicknamed "Avalanche" was brought low by a nagging hamstring injury and missed a game with strep throat on the advice of his agent, a move that didn't go over well in the (metaphorically speaking) blue-collar environs of the Cleveland locker room. Meanwhile, Hillis was distracted all season by battles over a contract extension, even as he was turning in an Exhibit A season on why teams are loath to give big dollars to running backs, even totemic ones. It was no coincidence that Cleveland was quite effective (88.1% DVOA, 6.4 yards per play) out of empty backfield sets.

Hillis won a preseason popularity contest to appear on the cover of *Madden NFL 12*. Needless to say, he now believes in the power of the Curse. Hillis has been exiled to Kansas City, and his oft-injured, underwhelming backups (Montario Hardesty, Brandon Jackson) aren't likely to get many carries so long as Richardson remains conscious and vertical.

Weeden's insertion behind center comes at the expense of another ineffective player, Colt McCoy. McCoy's poor play in 2011 (57.2% completion rate, 16 turnovers) would be reason enough for the change, but apparently it was his father Brad who spurred the switch.

Back on a December Thursday night in Pittsburgh, McCoy was nearly beheaded by James Harrison. Despite being knocked cold by the helmet-to-helmet hit, McCoy managed to slip back into the game two plays later. After the game, he admitted he didn't remember getting hit, and the TV cameramen in the locker room were asked to turn off their lights, as Colt was light-sensitive. You didn't have to be a neurologist to understand the implications. McCoy missed the last three games of the season, while the Browns coaching and training staff were pilloried for ignoring the culture's prevailing winds regarding concussions. McCoy *pere* was particularly loud in his criticisms of the front office, and according to Tony Grossi of ESPN Cleveland, the franchise didn't forget. "I've been told that McCoy's fate as a former starter was sealed when his father sounded off about the club's handling of his concussion," Grossi wrote in May. Let that be a lesson to all you football dads out there—if you plan on popping off about your kid, be sure his completion rate tops 60 percent.

---

[1] It should be noted that in 2002, the season before our table's breadth, the Browns went skill 1-2, selecting running back William Green and wideout Andre Davis. That's the year they made their lone playoff appearance, so some history is on their side. Nevertheless, it seems unlikely Holmgren and Heckert were gazing at Fatheads of Green and Davis as the 2012 draft progressed.

Table 2: Teams That Picked Skill Position Players With Top Two Draft Choices, 2003-2011

Year	Team	Players	DVOA Prev Yr	DVOA	Change	Predicted DVOA	Difference
2011	CIN	Green/Dalton	1.7%	-1.4%	-3.1%	0.3%	-1.7%
2011	MIN	Ponder/Rudolph	-15.1%	-10.2%	+4.9%	-7.9%	-2.3%
2010	DEN	Thomas/Tebow	1.3%	2.1%	+0.8%	0.0%	+2.0%
2009	DET	Stafford/Pettigrew	-25.3%	-28.4%	-3.1%	-12.1%	-16.3%
2009	NYJ	Sanchez/Greene*	0.0%	-12.5%	-12.5%	-0.7%	-11.8%
2009	PHI	Maclin/McCoy	6.5%	9.7%	+3.2%	2.9%	+6.8%
2008	BAL	Flacco/Rice	-13.3%	-0.3%	+13.1%	-7.2%	+6.9%
2008	PIT	Mendenhall/Sweed	8.5%	-1.5%	-10.0%	4.1%	-5.6%
2007	OAK	Russell/Miller	-37.0%	-18.0%	+19.0%	-16.0	+2.0%
2007	DET	Johnson/Stanton	-13.4%	-10.3%	+3.1%	-7.2%	-3.1%
2007	MIN	Petersen/Rice	-17.9%	-0.8%	+17.0%	-9.1%	+8.3%
2007	MIA	Ginn/Beck	-10.0%	-6.1%	+3.9%	-5.6%	-0.4%
2006	TEN	Young/White	-8.2%	-9.5%	-1.3%	-4.8%	-4.8%
2006	NE	Maroney/Jackson	17.5%	14.1%	-3.4%	9.6%	+4.5%
2006	DEN	Cutler/Sheffler	26.9%	-4.8%	-31.7%	15.9%	-20.6%
2006	JAX	Lewis/Jones-Drew	5.6%	6.8%	+1.2%	2.4%	+4.4%
2005	CHI	Benson/Bradley	-36.5%	-17.1%	+19.4%	-15.9%	-1.2%
2004	DET	Williams/Jones	-21.7%	-10.1%	+11.6%	-10.7%	+0.6%
2004	BUF	Evans/Losman	-16.1%	-5.9%	+10.2%	-8.4%	+2.5%
2003	HOU	Johnson/Joppru	-43.3%	-14.7%	+28.6%	-17.8%	+3.1%
	AVERAGE		-9.5%	-5.9%	+3.5%	-4.4%	-1.5%

Shonn Greene was taken with the first pick of the third round; the Jets had no second round choice.

If in fact McCoy is finished as a starter in Cleveland, it was a tough way to go out, especially when you recall the way his collegiate career ended: on the sideline, helplessly watching his Texas Longhorns lose to Alabama in the BCS championship game, his injured shoulder in a sling. But this is the NFL, where sentiment is for the losing locker room. Our game charters noted at least a half a dozen times McCoy ran into or tripped over a teammate, slapstick that at least obscured the more subtle comedy of a McCoy passing attempt. McCoy's inaccuracy was a key factor in Cleveland's pathetic YAC average (4.3, tied with Miami for last in the league), which for a West Coast offense is a terminal weakness. Weeden comes equipped with many of the same traits McCoy possessed coming out of the Big 12, but is much bigger and has a stronger arm. He's also three years older than McCoy—not McCoy when he graduated, but McCoy right now.

Cleveland's defense underachieved statistically in 2011, though much can be explained away by the difficulty of having to carry such a lightweight offense. There are solid players at every level on that side of the ball, including Ahtyba Rubin and Jabaal Sheard up front, D'Qwell Jackson at middle linebacker, and Joe Haden and T.J. Ward in the secondary. An offseason injury that could cost defensive tackle Phil Taylor his entire sophomore season hurts, however.

From afar, it sounds promising: a pair of new bluechippers on offense and a strong defensive talent base moving into year two of a new scheme. So why is our 2012 projection so poor, and why is there so little optimism by the Lake? To begin with, there is the AFC North, a relentless cauldron that makes breaking out of the cycle of suckitude difficult. The Browns have won but three division games in *four years*. The rest of the slate figures to stiffen as the NFC East and AFC West make up half the Browns' opposition this season.

Less tangibly, the Browns seem to be following an outdated model in building the team, at least on offense. In a pass-first, -second, and -third league, Cleveland has turned over its offense to a a highly-drafted running back and a rookie quarterback with a closer sell-by date than preferred, two moves that certainly shun modern team-building wisdom. They also ignored the fact that there is little speed and few reliable hands at receiver. Shurmur is on record as believing the run sets up the pass, and you know how we feel about that. At the same time, the Browns are putting all their stock in a bellcow back, when the league has already moved on to a committee model. Heck, the team's signature player is a left tackle, Joe Thomas, which couldn't be more 2006.

And the Browns front office has shown little propensity to be able to turn this battleship around. Despite his championship pedigree as a coach, the 64-year-old Holmgren has yet to show much ability as a CEO, especially one of a company that desperately needs rebranding. As if the losing isn't bad enough, the Big Show's commitment to the organization has been questioned (while his dissing of Richardson as "ordinary" received condemnation, Jim Brown's comments about Holmgren's detachment in the same interview didn't raise many hackles in Cleveland). Before the draft, Holmgren looked bad when he groused about the Redskins getting favored-nation status from St. Louis in the Robert Griffin III sweepstakes. After it, he seemed to admit to panicking after wideout Kendall Wright was taken late in the first round, with the selection of Weeden being cast as Plan B in both scenarios.

In a league engineered to allow everyone to scale the cliffs, the Browns have remained mired down in the lowlands, even as perennial doormats like the Bengals and Saints have tasted success. Matters don't figure to improve in the near future, either. Then again, last year our numbers said the exact opposite. If our projections were proved wrong once, they certainly can be proved wrong twice. But don't count on it.

Robert Weintraub

2011 Browns Stats by Week

Wk	vs.	W-L	PF	PA	YDF	YDA	TO	Total	Off	Def	ST
1	CIN	L	17	27	285	294	-1	-29%	-36%	-10%	-2%
2	@IND	W	27	19	303	285	1	-26%	-25%	12%	11%
3	MIA	W	17	16	280	369	1	2%	6%	1%	-3%
4	TEN	L	13	31	416	332	0	-31%	-4%	31%	3%
5	BYE										
6	@OAK	L	17	24	268	329	0	-20%	1%	5%	-17%
7	SEA	W	6	3	300	137	1	21%	-22%	-61%	-19%
8	@SF	L	10	20	290	348	-2	3%	-5%	3%	11%
9	@HOU	L	12	30	172	380	-1	-71%	-54%	25%	9%
10	STL	L	12	13	335	281	1	-1%	10%	6%	-5%
11	JAC	W	14	10	334	303	-1	-15%	14%	24%	-6%
12	@CIN	L	20	23	274	389	0	-16%	-15%	6%	5%
13	BAL	L	10	24	233	448	0	-34%	-6%	14%	-13%
14	@PIT	L	3	14	304	416	1	-27%	-27%	5%	6%
15	@ARI	L	17	20	333	363	0	-8%	-1%	11%	4%
16	@BAL	L	14	20	256	284	0	39%	10%	4%	33%
17	PIT	L	9	13	240	360	1	-4%	-25%	-17%	4%

Trends and Splits

	Offense	Rank	Defense	Rank
Total DVOA	-11.2%	25	4.2%	22
Unadjusted VOA	-10.7%	24	0.2%	17
Weighted Trend	-8.6%	21	4.5%	21
Variance	10.2%	24	7.5%	25
Average Opponent	-4.5%	1	-4.5%	27
Passing	-3.5%	23	4.7%	17
Rushing	-12.2%	30	3.8%	26
First Down	-4.8%	21	-1.1%	16
Second Down	-23.3%	30	5.0%	19
Third Down	-3.8%	17	11.6%	25
First Half	-8.9%	22	12.0%	28
Second Half	-13.5%	28	-4.0%	8
Red Zone	-36.1%	30	-13.8%	9
Late and Close	-24.8%	28	-5.7%	10

Five-Year Performance

Year	W-L	Pyth	Est W	PF	PA	TO	Total	Rk	Off	Rk	Def	Rk	ST	Rk	Off AGL	Rk	Def AGL	Rk
2007	10-6	8.5	9.8	402	382	-2	9.7%	12	7.9%	10	6.3%	23	8.1%	2	12.6	5	30.5	25
2008	4-12	4.4	5.7	232	350	+5	-20.3%	26	-21.3%	29	3.9%	20	4.9%	4	43.3	26	31.3	23
2009	5-11	4.3	4.8	245	375	-12	-23.1%	16	-16.4%	24	16.4%	30	9.7%	1	37.4	25	43.3	27
2010	5-11	6.1	6.7	271	332	-1	-4.0%	20	-5.0%	22	1.7%	18	2.7%	10	42.7	31	52.0	32
2011	4-12	5	5.5	218	307	+1	-14.2%	25	-11.2%	25	4.2%	22	1.3%	10	45.5	27	26.3	15

CLEVELAND BROWNS

2011 Performance Based on Most Common Personnel Groups

Cleveland Offense					Cleveland Offense vs. Opp.				Cleveland Defense				Cleveland Defense vs. Opp.			
Pers	Freq	Yds	DVOA	Run%	Pers	Freq	Yds	DVOA	Pers	Freq	Yds	DVOA	Pers	Freq	Yds	DVOA
11	39%	4.2	-15.2%	25%	4-3-4	28%	4.4	-17.2%	4-3-4	55%	5.3	7.1%	11	37%	5.5	5.4%
12	25%	5.1	10.9%	36%	4-2-5	24%	4.4	-10.0%	4-2-5	31%	5.2	5.8%	21	21%	5.6	13.5%
21	15%	4.4	-29.0%	50%	3-4-4	20%	4.7	-21.6%	3-3-5	8%	6.0	-17.5%	12	17%	5.6	11.6%
20	8%	4.9	-8.6%	38%	Dime+	10%	5.1	23.3%	Dime+	4%	6.6	1.9%	22	10%	4.8	4.5%
22	5%	2.6	-52.8%	74%	2-4-5	9%	4.2	-15.7%	G-line	1%	0.4	-54.6%	10	3%	4.2	-20.1%
10	4%	6.0	38.1%	25%	3-3-5	7%	5.5	44.4%								

Strategic Tendencies

Run/Pass		Rank	Offense		Rank	Pass Rush		Rank	Defense/Other		Rank
Runs, all plays	40%	19	Form: Single Back	65%	10	Rush 3	3.3%	26	4 DB	55%	7
Runs, first half	44%	11	Form: Empty Back	5%	20	Rush 4	60.3%	21	5 DB	39%	20
Runs, first down	53%	14	Pers: 3+ WR	52%	14	Rush 5	27.4%	7	6+ DB	4%	20
Runs, second-long	33%	19	Pers: 4+ WR	5%	12	Rush 6+	9.0%	11	CB by Sides	82%	14
Runs, power sit.	45%	28	Pers: 2+ TE/6+ OL	33%	15	Zone Blitz	3.6%	22	Go for it on 4th	0.86	22
Runs, behind 2H	26%	25	Play action	18%	16	Sacks by LB	25.8%	17	Offensive Pace	30.5	15
Pass, ahead 2H	47%	8	Max protect	8%	24	Sacks by DB	6.5%	19	Defensive Pace	30.5	19

Cleveland fumbled 18 times on offense and recovered 13 of them. ◉ The Browns were tied with Seattle for the biggest difference gap between passes to the right (48 percent of passes) and the left (31 percent). However, they were better on passes to the left (43.7% DVOA, 18th) than passes to the right (0.8% DVOA, 30th)[2]. ◉ With Peyton Hillis mostly on the sidelines, the Browns went from first to 28th when it came to run-pass ratio in power situations. ◉ Colt McCoy was just brutal against big blitzes, only 2.9 yards per play. ◉ Cleveland receivers dropped 43 passes, eight more than any other offense. ◉ The Browns defense allowed more yardage when they brought more pass rushers: 5.9 yards per play with three or four, 6.3 with five, and 7.2 with six or more.

Passing

Player	DYAR	DVOA	Plays	NtYds	Avg	YAC	C%	TD	Int
C.McCoy	-133	-15.2%	498	2532	5.1	4.6	57.6%	14	11
S.Wallace	-17	-13.6%	111	537	5.1	3.2	52.4%	2	2

Rushing

Player	DYAR	DVOA	Plays	Yds	Avg	TD	Fum	Suc
P.Hillis*	50	-1.7%	161	587	3.6	3	1	55%
M.Hardesty	-79	-32.2%	88	267	3.0	0	1	36%
C.Ogbonnaya	11	-4.9%	76	347	4.6	1	2	47%
C.McCoy	-11	-16.5%	50	216	4.3	0	3	--
T.Clayton	-19	-59.9%	8	12	1.5	0	0	38%
J.Cribbs	-4	-25.4%	7	25	3.6	0	0	29%
S.Wallace	20	53.4%	6	71	11.8	0	0	--

Receiving

Player	DYAR	DVOA	Plays	Ctch	Yds	Y/C	YAC	TD	C%
G.Little	-92	-22.0%	121	62	701	11.3	3.9	2	51%
M.Massaquoi	-77	-26.0%	74	31	384	12.4	2.4	2	42%
J.Cribbs	130	11.9%	67	41	518	12.6	5.6	4	61%
J.Norwood	69	12.0%	34	23	268	11.7	3.7	1	68%
B.Robiskie*	-33	-63.0%	9	3	25	8.3	0.7	0	33%
B.Watson	-47	-17.3%	71	37	410	11.1	5.2	2	52%
E.Moore	59	11.3%	47	34	324	9.5	2.4	4	72%
A.Smith	-1	-7.6%	25	14	131	9.4	4.1	1	56%
J.Cameron	-43	-52.9%	13	6	33	5.5	2.0	0	46%
P.Hillis*	-35	-33.2%	34	22	130	5.9	5.4	0	65%
C.Ogbonnaya	7	-9.4%	31	23	165	7.2	6.3	0	74%
M.Hardesty	24	2.5%	21	14	122	8.7	8.5	0	67%
O.Marecic	-1	-15.9%	6	5	31	6.2	4.6	0	83%

---

[2] If these DVOA numbers seem awfully high to you, it is because when we measure passing by direction, many unsuccessful pass plays (sacks, passes thrown away, passes tipped at the line) are not included.

CLEVELAND BROWNS

Offensive Line

Year	Yards	ALY	Rank	Power	Rank	Stuff	Rank	2nd Lev	Rank	Open Field	Rank	F-Start	Cont.
2009	3.93	4.01	21	65%	14	18%	13	1.10	22	0.50	30	17	28
2010	3.95	4.04	17	74%	4	14%	4	0.93	30	0.55	24	12	31
2011	3.60	3.94	23	66%	9	16%	2	0.85	32	0.41	31	19	39

Year	LE	Rank	LT	Rank	Mid	Rank	RT	Rank	RE	Rank	Sacks	ASR	Rank	Short	Long
2009	5.21	4	3.73	26	3.97	23	4.09	17	2.69	30	30	6.1%	15	14	11
2010	3.34	29	4.56	8	3.84	21	4.74	5	4.00	15	36	7.6%	23	10	17
2011	2.02	31	4.45	13	3.91	22	4.71	6	1.47	32	39	6.4%	15	11	22

One of our central tenets has always been that the line makes the skill players, not the other way around. But the exception that proves the rule is often found in Cleveland, and 2012 was a prime example. The line's run numbers are dragged down by a coalition of running backs unable to turn holes at the line of scrimmage into long gainers. And only three teams had more "long sacks" (over 3.0 seconds), revealing passers who held the ball far too long.

While the skill positions were addressed in radical form, as discussed above, the line appears better as well. The middle chunk of granite fell from the stalwart left side of the Browns line last preseason, when guard Eric Steinbach underwent back surgery. Rookie replacement Jason Pinkston struggled in between reliable center Alex Mack and solid left tackle Joe Thomas. Early reports have him showing improvement in the offseason. The right side of the line was poor, especially tackle Tony Pashos, who blew six blocks and committed seven penalties. The Browns cut him after the season, but in fairness to Pashos, he played on a bad foot for most of the season, and his agent told reporters that Pashos required copious amounts of pain medication and injections to play. Then again, in fairness to the Browns, Pashos wasn't particularly good when he was healthy in 2009 or 2010.

On the right side, second round draft choice Mitchell Schwartz will be expected to start and play right away, even on the High Holidays. Schwartz started at tackle from his first day on campus at Cal, and was on the right side for 16 of his 51 starts, so he should be able to transition to the position with relative ease. Shawn Lauvao was penalty-prone (ten flags, half of them holds), but improved as the season went along, and should hold down the guard spot next to Schwartz.

Defensive Front Seven

Defensive Line	Age	Pos	Plays	TmPct	Rk	Stop	Dfts	BTkl	St%	Rk	AvYd	Rk	Sack	Hit	Hur	Runs	St%	Yds	Pass	St%	Yds
Ahtyba Rubin	26	DT	83	9.8%	1	56	8	2	67%	58	2.8	61	5	8	10	72	65%	3.6	11	82%	-2.1
Phillip Taylor	24	DT	60	7.1%	5	37	11	1	62%	68	2.9	63	4	4	8	52	58%	3.5	8	88%	-1.0
Jabaal Sheard	23	DE	57	6.8%	14	48	22	3	84%	19	0.0	12	8.5	3	18	42	83%	1.4	15	87%	-3.7
Jayme Mitchell*	28	DE	33	4.5%	55	24	10	5	73%	60	2.3	66	1.5	4	6.5	26	69%	2.9	7	86%	0.0
Brian Schaefering	29	DE	29	3.4%	70	17	3	1	59%	79	2.9	75	0.5	1	0	27	59%	2.9	2	50%	4.0
Scott Paxson	30	DT	22	2.6%	67	19	3	0	86%	7	2.0	43	1	1	0.5	16	94%	1.1	6	67%	4.7
Frostee Rucker	29	DE	44	5.5%	30	33	14	1	75%	53	1.3	40	4	3	1	36	75%	1.4	8	75%	0.9

Linebackers	Age	Pos	Plays	TmPct	Rk	Stop	Dfts	BTkl	AvYd	Sack	Hit	Hur	Runs	St%	Rk	Yds	Rk	Tgts	Suc%	Rk	AdjYd	Rk
D'Qwell Jackson	29	MLB	160	19.0%	4	79	27	5	4.7	3.5	4	11	118	53%	100	4.3	99	33	42%	64	7.9	67
Chris Gocong	29	OLB	71	8.4%	73	38	24	8	3.8	3.5	3	7	44	55%	96	3.5	61	19	35%	73	7.4	54
Scott Fujita	33	OLB	53	10.0%	54	33	11	2	4.6	0	1	0	36	69%	37	3.6	73	17	42%	65	11.4	79
Kaluka Maiava	25	OLB	24	2.8%	--	10	5	3	4.5	0	1	2.5	21	43%	--	3.7	--	4	44%	--	7.1	--

Year	Yards	ALY	Rank	Power	Rank	Stuff	Rank	2nd Lev	Rank	Open Field	Rank
2009	4.50	4.61	30	67%	18	13%	31	1.11	14	0.77	16
2010	4.18	4.68	31	68%	28	14%	31	1.00	4	0.44	4
2011	4.55	4.60	31	65%	21	16%	26	1.24	20	0.78	17

Year	LE	Rank	LT	Rank	Mid	Rank	RT	Rank	RE	Rank	Sacks	ASR	Rank	Short	Long
2009	4.86	24	4.10	15	4.73	31	4.24	17	5.75	32	41	7.0%	11	13	18
2010	4.84	25	4.99	30	4.63	30	4.47	21	4.43	26	29	5.9%	21	3	19
2011	4.99	27	4.65	26	4.59	32	4.81	28	3.19	10	32	5.8%	27	12	15

You will have to excuse us for experiencing some cognitive dissonance when it comes to evaluating nose tackle Ahtyba Rubin, because the stats and his play on tape seem to be all over the place. Rubin makes a ton of plays. He's led all defensive tackles in the percentage of team plays for two straight years, and he's a pretty good pass rusher. He has games he seems to dominate, like when he frustrated Miami in Week 3 with nine tackles and 1.5 sacks (plus another sack where he forced Chad Henne out of the pocket so Phil Taylor could clean up). Yet most of the time, Rubin has big problems stopping the run. Last year, Rubin's average run tackle came after a gain of 3.6 yards, the worst figure in the league for defensive tackles. This isn't a one-year problem, either. In 2010, playing in a completely different scheme, Rubin's average run tackle came after a gain of 4.1 yards, again the worst figure in the league for defensive tackles. Rubin hasn't made a run tackle behind the line of scrimmage since his rookie year of 2008. Cleveland coaches would likely argue that the average yardage totals are high because Rubin makes a lot of hustle plays downfield. And he does make some of those, like when he caught Frank Gore after a 26-yard gain in Week 8. But the rest of that game, when he was tackling Gore after four- to six-yard gains, he was just getting pushed back by Mike Iupati. Too often, Rubin is playing on skates, especially against zone blocking. He seems to play finesse even though his body is big and built for clogging, and he's definitely not a pure one-gap shooter.

Rubin plays an even more important role in Cleveland this year because of the loss of Phil Taylor. Taylor had an active rookie season in the middle of Cleveland's retooled 4-3 defense, so it was a significant blow in the offseason when he tore a pectoral muscle while bench pressing a Buick.[3] He is likely done for the year. Veteran Scott Paxson, who incidentally had much better numbers against the run in part-time duty than either Rubin or Taylor, will get the first crack at starting next to Rubin. Taylor was part of Cleveland's 1-2 defensive line combo in the 2011 draft (a stark contrast to this year's draft). The other half of that combo was Jabaal Sheard, who impressed with 8.5 sacks as a rookie. Frostee Rucker, signed away from division rival Cincinnati, starts opposite Sheard. Behind him is former Eagle Juqua Parker; he's always done well in our pass rushing numbers, but how much does he have left at age 34? Depth on the line is a big concern unless rookies like John Hughes (third round, Cincinnati) and Billy Winn (sixth round, Boise State) can match Taylor and Sheard's first-year productivity.

D'Qwell Jackson can soothe some of Taylor's worries about coming back from a torn pec. The middle linebacker lost most of two seasons to the injury, but rebounded with an excellent 2011. Jackson was in on seemingly every play as he turned into Ray Lewis circa 2001, roaming the field untouched behind space eaters Taylor and Rubin. Outside linebacker is a major concern, however. Scott Fujita will miss the first three games thanks to his role in the New Orleans bounty scandal, and when he returns he will still struggle against the pass, probably more than ever. On the other (weak, very weak) side, Chris Gocong was loathed by our game charters—one summed up his play with a pithy "Gocong stinks." Kaluka Maiava will get every chance to make one of the jobs his own.

---

[3] We're kidding, he was lifting normal weights as part of his offseason routine.

Defensive Secondary

Secondary	Age	Pos	Plays	TmPct	Rk	Stop	Dfts	BTkl	Runs	St%	Rk	Yds	Rk	Tgts	Tgt%	Rk	Dist	Suc%	Rk	APaYd	Rk	PD	Int
Joe Haden	23	CB	84	10.6%	12	36	18	3	19	32%	58	6.9	41	81	23.0%	6	13.5	48%	56	9.0	67	18	0
Mike Adams*	31	FS	67	7.9%	59	20	11	4	39	28%	61	10.9	73	17	4.5%	71	15.5	60%	28	8.5	46	6	3
Usama Young	27	FS	66	7.8%	60	21	7	4	37	46%	23	4.9	6	23	6.0%	57	11.3	36%	74	9.4	59	1	1
Sheldon Brown	33	CB	60	7.1%	60	21	7	6	17	29%	63	8.2	56	72	19.3%	28	12.2	55%	30	6.6	22	15	2
T.J. Ward	26	SS	41	9.7%	43	17	5	2	26	46%	22	5.8	18	17	8.8%	18	9.2	59%	31	4.2	3	3	0
Dimitri Patterson	30	CB	37	5.0%	81	20	5	2	3	67%	7	4.3	7	54	16.5%	48	9.7	62%	10	6.4	19	12	0

Year	Pass D Rank	vs. #1 WR	Rk	vs. #2 WR	Rk	vs. Other WR	Rk	vs. TE	Rk	vs. RB	Rk
2009	28	18.3%	23	-20.1%	7	14.5%	28	47.1%	32	34.1%	31
2010	16	12.1%	25	6.7%	18	5.3%	21	-0.8%	12	1.4%	14
2011	17	1.1%	14	20.9%	26	-19.7%	9	22.1%	25	13.8%	25

Joe Haden's problem is that he thinks he is already an All-Pro performer. He struts around and confronts every opposing receiver after incomplete passes. Sure, confidence and a short memory are critical cornerback character traits, but Haden sure talks a lot of yang for a guy with exactly zero interceptions in 2011. That said, Haden certainly has the skill set to reach the upper echelon of corners, and only eight players surpassed his 18 passes defensed in 2011. Haden's struggles have the whiff of sophomore slump, as he ranked in the top 15 in both Success Rate (60 percent) and Adjusted Yards per Pass (6.0) as a rookie. Certainly, the Browns consider Haden a mainstay, and he's already part of the greater Cleveland sports fabric—that was him representing the Cavs at the NBA Draft Lottery.

Looking at stats only, aging Sheldon Brown actually had a better season than Haden, although he had plenty of safety help that Haden usually did not. Brown also had strong numbers against the run. Dmitri Patterson is a quality third corner, but he too is on the wrong side of 30. Buster Skrine, a fifth-rounder in 2011, has some fans in the organization, but depth is a real concern. The Browns will hope to get through the season with their vets and address the position in the 2013 draft.

When intimidating safety T.J. Ward was lost at midseason to a badly sprained foot, the Browns defense took a major hit. The team was forced to use undersized free safety Mike Adams as their primary box safety, hurting the run defense as well as the pass defense. Ward's return to full health is critical, and early reports are promising. Usama Young, a converted corner who can run with receivers but isn't particularly physical, will likely take over as the free safety with Adams gone to Denver, though second-year man Eric Hagg turned heads in spring camps.

Special Teams

Year	DVOA	Rank	FG/XP	Rank	Net Kick	Rank	Kick Ret	Rank	Net Punt	Rank	Punt Ret	Rank	Hidden	Rank
2009	8.2%	1	4.8	6	10.3	4	21.0	1	0.9	15	11.2	3	8.6	4
2010	2.3%	10	-1.1	21	12.5	4	-7.3	24	11.8	3	-2.1	19	2.2	10
2011	1.1%	10	5.0	6	-1.0	23	4.8	4	-2.3	19	-0.1	17	1.2	15

The unit remained tenth overall in our rankings, but there were wild swings within the overall stability. Phil Dawson improved dramatically in placekicking, but his kickoff distance diminished, while the kick gunners also took a major step backwards. In 2010, returns against Cleveland were worth -12.4 points worse than average; in 2011, it was 1.4 points more than average. Similarly, punter Brad Maynard wasn't as effective as Reggie Hodges was in 2010, but it was the coverage team that let the team down, going from allowing returns worth -7.4 points to returns worth 4.7 points. Hodges should be back in 2012 after blowing out his Achilles tendon before last season. Josh Cribbs helped make up for the decline in the coverage teams by rebounding on kickoff returns after a poor 2010.

Coaching Staff

Pat Shurmur and Brad Childress spent seven years together locked in Andy Reid's video room in Philadelphia. Together, they gorged on cheesesteaks and coffee while helping to coach the offenses that put the Eagles in three straight NFC title games and Super Bowl XXXIX. Now, Chilly is Shurmur's offensive coordinator, landing there after being a semi-serious head coaching candidate in Tampa Bay and Miami. Childress didn't call the plays in Philly—that was Reid's bailiwick—and he won't in Browns Town, either, as Shurmur has said he will continue in that duty. Thus we are all spared the image of Childress' bespectacled, balding pate peering out from behind a play chart, a vision that haunted fans when he was in Minnesota. And he surely looks much more sinister in brown than he did in purple.

Meanwhile, Tim Hauck, who wasn't drafted but molded a solid 13-year career in the league as a safety, takes over for Jerome Henderson as defensive backs coach. Hauck was a hard-hitter in the secondary under Holmgren and Jauron in Green Bay in the early-1990s, and was in Philly when Shurmur was there a decade later. But Hauck's pro coaching experience is limited to two seasons as assistant secondary coach in Tennessee, and he was out of football in 2011. Remember, it's not what you know, it's who you know...

Dallas Cowboys

2011 Record: 8-8

Pythagorean Wins: 8.6 (13th)

DVOA: 3.5% (14th)

Offense: 5.9% (12th)

Defense: 0.4% (16th)

Special Teams: -2.1% (25th)

Variance: 11.9% (13th)

2012 Mean Projection: 7.5 wins

On the Clock (0-4): 10%

Mediocrity (5-7): 41%

Playoff Contender (8-10): 40%

Super Bowl Contender (11+): 9%

Postseason Odds: 26.8%

Projected Average Opponent: 4.0% (2nd)

2011: One more win, and maybe that big playoff run could have been theirs.

2012: In a good division, good may not be good enough.

The Dallas Cowboys' 2011 season ended in a 31-14 Week 17 loss to the New York Giants. Both teams entered the game at 8-7, but the loss sent the Cowboys home to watch the playoffs on TV, while New York enjoyed a run to the Super Bowl. The game put a critical Cowboys weakness on fine display, as Victor Cruz and Hakeem Nicks repeatedly burned Dallas cornerbacks for a series of big plays. Knowing how close they had come to beating the eventual Super Bowl champs, the 'Boys went to work patching the enormous holes in their secondary. However, as they fixed that flaw, they ignored another one, one that hurt them all season. And since they did little to address the issue, it's likely to hurt them again in 2012. Given the competitive nature of the NFC East, it could cost them a playoff spot.

Let's get the first weakness out of the way: Dallas' cornerbacks were lousy last season. That's bad for any defense, but especially for a defense with a Ryan in charge. As our strategic tendencies tables show, Rob Ryan likes to blitz, but when he counted on his corners to win one-on-one matchups last year, they usually lost (Table 1).

Four Dallas cornerbacks saw significant action last year—Alan Ball, Terence Newman, Mike Jenkins, and Orlando Scandrick—and none of them ranked in the top 30 in yards per pass allowed. In a league where you really need three good cornerbacks to get by, Dallas had none.

That's especially telling since they play with one of the league's great pass rushers in DeMarcus Ware. It can be hard sometimes to separate the performance of pass rush from coverage, but it Dallas' case the distinction was about as clear as it could be. On all pass plays, including sacks and intentional grounding calls, they gave up 6.7 yards per play, which ranked 24th. Like all teams, they played much better when they got pressure on the quarterback, cutting that down to 3.5 yards per play, which still ranked 26th. However, on those plays where opposing quarterbacks came under pressure but escaped and still managed to get a pass away, Dallas gave up an average of 7.1 yards, and that was the highest such figure in the league.

This weakness in the backfield killed Dallas on third downs, where they ranked sixth against the run, but 30th against the pass and 29th overall. Not surprisingly, they played better on short third downs (13th) than they did in middle distance (32nd) or long (29th) situations.

At the end of the year, the worst of the bunch (Terence Newman) was released, while the others were

Table 1: Live By The Blitz, Die By The Blitz

Rushers	Yards/Play	Rank
3	5.69	11
4	6.55	15
5	7.51	30
6+	7.93	29

2012 Cowboys Schedule

Week	Opp.	Week	Opp.	Week	Opp.
1	at NYG (Wed.)	7	at CAR	13	PHI
2	at SEA	8	NYG	14	at CIN
3	TB	9	at ATL	15	PIT
4	CHI (Mon.)	10	at PHI	16	NO
5	BYE	11	CLE	17	at WAS
6	at BAL	12	WAS (Thu.)		

demoted. Dallas went out and got themselves a shiny new pair of starters, signing Brandon Carr to a five-year, $50.1 million contract in free agency and trading up in the draft to select LSU's Morris Claiborne.

For the past four years, Carr has been the lesser half of one of the league's top cornerback tandems in Kansas City. However, he has steadily improved throughout his career, and in 2011 he actually had better metrics than teammate Brandon Flowers (Table 2).

Carr is only 26 years old, and may not have peaked yet. On the other hand, he's never been the top corner on his team before. Still, he's a clear upgrade over what Dallas had last season, and he should provide the Cowboys with a half-decade of quality starting play. This was a wise signing.

Obviously, we have less of a track record for Claiborne. Draft expert Russ Lande, enamored with Claiborne's coverage ability, ball skills, size (5-foot-11), and speed (4.5-second 40-yard dash), liked him more than former LSU teammate Patrick Peterson and said he would start from Day One for several teams in the league. While his potential may be mile-high, however, he's still a rookie, and history has not always been kind to first-year high-profile corners. Between 2005 and 2011, 26 cornerbacks were drafted in the first round (including guys like Antrel Rolle who started as corners before moving to safety later). The best of those, as a rookie, was Cleveland's Joe Haden, who finished 14th in success rate and 13th in yards per pass. After that, though, the pickings get slim quickly. Seven of these players failed to qualify for the cornerback lead-

Figure 1. 2011 Dallas DVOA by Week

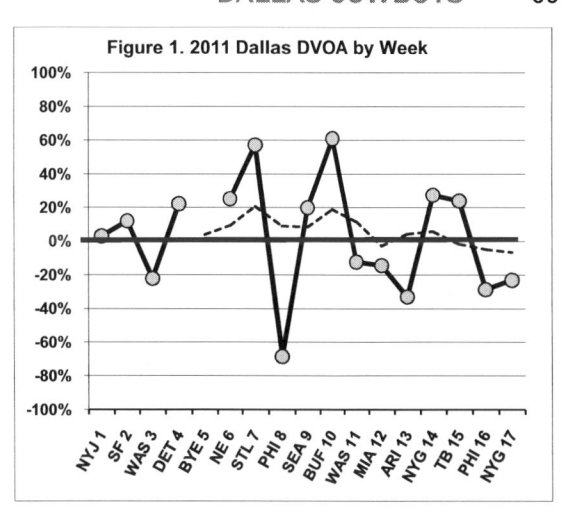

erboards. For the other 19, the average success rate was 49 percent, with an average of 7.9 yards per pass allowed. Only four finished in the top 30 in yards per pass allowed. And that includes many players who only saw nickel action against third and fourth wideouts. If we limit our list to the nine rookies who made 10 or more starts, those who faced the toughest competition, the average success rate falls to 47 percent, and the average yards per pass climbs to 8.5. Claiborne could have a good season for a rookie and still be no better than the subpar veterans he is replacing. Claiborne may well be a Pro Bowler in 2015, but expectations this year should be much, much lower (Table 3).

The Cowboys completely overhauled their cornerback stable, but made few other changes on defense, because few other changes needed to be made. Their front seven was a particular strength. Dallas played excellent run defense, especially after Jason Hatcher returned from a strained calf that cost him three games in October. In the first half of the year, the Cowboys ranked 18th in run defense DVOA. In the second half, that ranking climbed to sixth.

While the Cowboys expect a slew of new defensive backs to lead a turnaround on defense, they've left the offense mostly alone. And why not? This team is stacked at the skill positions. Tony Romo has ranked in the top 10 in passing DVOA in each of his six seasons as a starter, peaking last year when he finished fourth. DeMarco Murray was among the top 10 runners in both DVOA and DYAR despite starting only seven games. They have depth at those positions too. New backup quarterback Kyle Orton has ranked in the top 25 in passing DVOA each of the past four years and could start for a handful of teams. Felix Jones had

Table 2: Brandon Carr, Year-By-Year

Year	Tgt%	Rk	Dist	Suc%	Rk	AdjYd	Rk	PD	Int
2008	18.3%	37	11.6	41%	75	8.3	60	6	2
2009	18.9%	22	13.2	53%	38	7.2	36	19	1
2010	20.5%	7	16.0	59%	15	7.4	48	25	1
2011	20.9%	17	15.0	55%	27	6.2	17	13	4

some fumble issues (three in 127 runs, the second-worst rate of all runners with at least 100 carries), but still averaged 4.5 yards per carry and finished in the top 10 in success rate. Fullback Tony Fiammetta was a crushing blocker, but couldn't stay healthy, missing 14 games in the past three seasons. In his place the Cowboys signed Lawrence Vickers (two missed games in the past three seasons), so expect another heavy dose of I-formation runs.

The top level of the receiver depth chart is just as strong, though the depth is lacking. At wide receiver, Miles Austin took a major step backwards in his age 27 season, hampered by knee and hamstring issues that knocked him out of six games and bothered him all year. Dez Bryant progressed in his second season from situational role player to solid starter, but he had a chance to establish himself as a dominant top-shelf receiver in Austin's absence and couldn't make the jump. The guy who really saved Dallas' season (as much as an 8-8 season can be saved, anyway) was Laurent Robinson, who set new career highs in pretty much everything. Robinson signed with Jacksonville in free agency, but that loss is not as devastating as it sounds. Robinson caught four total touchdowns in his first four seasons before catching 11 last year. Guys who see their production spike like that in one year usually see a similar decline the following season. Who will take Robinson's spot as the third receiver? That's a fine question. The Cowboys will go into training camp 11 men deep at the wide receiver position, including six college free agents from 2011 or 2012. The top two candidates are veteran Kevin Ogletree and fifth-round draftee Danny Coale out of Virginia Tech.

Jason Witten may be showing his age, posting his worst advanced metrics since his rookie season in 2003, but he still ranked among the top ten tight ends in DYAR. Martellus Bennett left for the Giants in free agency. He never lived up to the promise he showed in his rookie season, but the Cowboys have no obvious replacement. John Phillips will get first crack at the No. 2 position, but he has only 22 career receptions, and though he played every game last year he missed all of 2010 with a torn ACL. Sixth-round rookie James Hanna out of Oklahoma will also get a chance to earn playing time.

That leaves only one position group to discuss: the offensive line. Hopefully we can do a better job addressing it than the Cowboys did this offseason. With starting guards Montrae Holland and Kyle Kosier out the door, along with key backup Derrick Dockery, Dallas signed Cincinnati starter Nate Livings and Car-

Table 3: First-round rookie CBs since 2005 (min. 40 targets)

Player	Year	Tm	Suc%	AdjYd
Pacman Jones	2005	TEN	46%	7.2
Carlos Rogers	2005	WAS	51%	7.4
Fabian Washington	2005	OAK	53%	8.0
Tye Hill	2006	STL	48%	9.5
Johnathan Joseph	2006	CIN	53%	7.5
Kelly Jennings	2006	SEA	46%	6.7
Darrelle Revis	2007	NYJ	45%	8.3
Leon Hall	2007	CIN	31%	9.3
Aaron Ross	2007	NYG	47%	8.3
Leodis McKelvin	2008	BUF	44%	7.5
Dominique Rodgers-Cromartie	2008	ARI	53%	6.7
Mike Jenkins	2008	DAL	54%	6.6
Antoine Cason	2008	SD	55%	5.8
Vontae Davis	2009	MIA	47%	10.6
Joe Haden	2010	CLE	60%	6.0
Kareem Jackson	2010	HOU	47%	11.5
Devin McCourty	2010	NE	53%	7.1
Kyle Wilson	2010	NYJ	53%	6.3
Patrick Peterson	2011	ARI	45%	8.9
AVERAGE			**49%**	**7.9**

olina backup Mackenzy Bernadeau to replace them. Simple math will tell you that's a net loss, and that's considering only quantity, not even quality. The Cowboys will also get back a healthy Bill Nagy, but he was lousy last year even before he broke his leg.

That kind of see-what-sticks philosophy is nothing new in Dallas, where they've been just trying to make do on the offensive line for years. This team will spend high draft picks on pass rushers, they'll trade up for corners, they'll deal for wideouts like Roy Williams in the middle of the year, but with the exception of recent first-rounder Tyron Smith, it seems like they've consciously avoided investing resources in their offensive line.

This brings us back to that second weakness we teased at the beginning of this chapter. Dallas had a lot of trouble rushing in key situations, ranking 31st in DVOA on third down and 31st in the red zone. The real problem, though, was in short yardage, and it wasn't just rushing. On third or fourth down with 1 or 2 yards to go, the Cowboys' DVOA was -47.5%. Dallas was only the 18th team since 1991 to dip below -40% in this situation. (St. Louis also qualifies for this group, and Tampa Bay came close.) A look back at history shows that many of those teams rebounded well the next year—but not all of them (Table 4).

The Cowboys tried 22 third- or fourth-down runs with 1 or 2 yards to go last season, and picked up a first down just 59 percent of the time, compared to a league average of 67 percent. Things were even worse when Dallas tried to pass, as they converted just 8 of 19 opportunities, with three sacks and an interception for a whopping 1.9 yards per play.

These struggles contrast sharply with the Cowboys' use of the draw play. Dallas ranked second with 47 running back draws—the fourth straight year they have ranked first or second—and were third with a 7.9-yard average on those plays. What does it take to run a successful draw? Anyone who has watched Tony Romo knows he has great timing and execution of the draw, staring down a receiver and selling the pass, which gets pass rushers looping upfield and out of their run containment lanes. All the Cowboys' blockers have to do is push the defenders in the direction they wish to go. It requires timing and coordination, not brute force. In short-yardage, however, when it's more about muscle, the Dallas line came up woefully short.

Can the Cowboys turn it around this season? Obviously, many of the teams in Table 3 saw dramatic swings in fortune the next year. On the other hand, we have the turn-of-the-century Carolina Panthers, who managed to finish 28th or worse in short-yardage offense five times in eight years between 1995 and 2002. Those Panthers, like these current Cowboys, had a tendency to ignore the offensive line on draft day. After taking Texas tackle Blake Brockermeyer late in the first round of their first draft in 1995, the Panthers didn't add another first-round offensive lineman for eight years. Even in the second round, they added just one blocker. Finally, in 2003, they doubled up on linemen, taking Utah tackle Jordan Gross in the first round and Iowa guard Bruce Nelson in the second. Nelson ended up being a bust with just one start in his career, but the Panthers added Gross to the veterans they had been stockpiling in free agency (former first-rounder Todd Steussie, former third-rounder Kevin Donnalley) and saw enough improvement to reach the Super Bowl.

Let's compare that with what Dallas has done in the past eight years. First of all, they've been too eager to trade away picks, with only 11 picks in rounds one and two since 2006. And when they have picked players, they've taken two defensive backs, four front seven players, four skill position players (including two tight ends) and just one offensive lineman (Smith). You could try to draw a parallel between the Panthers drafting Gross and the Cowboys drafting Smith, but the 2003 Panthers still had a lot more talent on hand. They played that year with two former first-rounders and three other players taken in rounds three through six. The Cowboys' projected starting line has one former first-rounder, two seventh-rounders, and two undrafted players.

This is why the Claiborne trade was a questionable move. The Cowboys gave up a second-round pick, which they could have used to boost their offensive line, to take a cornerback, who will probably play badly in his first season. In all likelihood, that trade makes Dallas a worse team in 2012, even if Claiborne improves them in the long term.

The Cowboys are a talented but flawed bunch this year, with a stacked schedule that includes not only two games each against the Giants and Eagles, but also contests with the powerhouses of the AFC North and NFC South. It will probably be too much for this team to overcome. When Dallas enters the draft next year, they need to avoid trades, and stay away from the so-called playmakers. What this team needs is a couple of big uglies, some powerhouses who will see the door to the postseason and knock it down.

Vince Verhei

Table 4: Teams Below -40% DVOA on Third-and-Short

Year	Team	3rd-Short DVOA	Rk	3rd-Short DVOA Y+1	Rk Y+1
1999	CAR	-70.7%	31	-3.8%	17
2008	PIT	-66.4%	32	-21.5%	28
2002	DAL	-61.6%	32	16.5%	8
2001	CAR	-55.8%	31	-39.8%	31
2006	SF	-55.3%	32	-30.4%	29
2004	ARI	-54.6%	32	-14.0%	24
1992	SEA	-54.3%	28	14.6%	8
1991	PHX	-47.8%	28	11.8%	7
2011	**DAL**	**-47.5%**	**32**	--	--
2005	CHI	-47.4%	32	-15.7%	26
1995	CAR	-46.8%	30	-28.3%	28
1991	SEA	-45.6%	27	-54.3%	28
1998	IND	-45.1%	30	-4.4%	20
1998	DET	-44.9%	29	16.1%	9
2010	NYG	-44.0%	32	6.1%	12
2011	**STL**	**-41.0%**	**31**	--	--
2007	CAR	-40.7%	32	21.7%	6
2001	DAL	-40.3%	30	-61.6%	32
AVERAGE		**-50.5%**		**-11.7%**	

DALLAS COWBOYS

2011 Cowboys Stats by Week

Wk	vs.	W-L	PF	PA	YDF	YDA	TO	Total	Off	Def	ST
1	@NYJ	L	24	27	390	360	-1	3%	17%	-3%	-17%
2	@SF	W	27	24	472	206	-1	12%	15%	-14%	-16%
3	WAS	W	18	16	375	298	0	-22%	-32%	-7%	3%
4	DET	L	30	34	434	303	-2	22%	8%	-10%	4%
5	BYE										
6	@NE	L	16	20	377	371	2	25%	-8%	-31%	2%
7	STL	W	34	7	445	265	1	57%	35%	-22%	0%
8	@PHI	L	7	34	267	495	-1	-68%	-33%	40%	4%
9	SEA	W	23	13	442	381	2	20%	22%	7%	5%
10	BUF	W	44	7	433	271	4	61%	31%	-28%	1%
11	@WAS	W	27	24	353	339	2	-12%	-3%	-5%	-14%
12	MIA	W	20	19	303	352	-1	-14%	1%	13%	-2%
13	@ARI	L	13	19	336	327	0	-33%	-6%	27%	0%
14	NYG	L	34	37	444	510	0	28%	36%	8%	-1%
15	@TB	W	31	15	399	190	0	24%	23%	-6%	-5%
16	PHI	L	7	20	238	386	1	-29%	-21%	12%	4%
17	@NYG	L	14	31	300	437	-2	-23%	-4%	17%	-2%

Trends and Splits

	Offense	Rank	Defense	Rank
Total DVOA	5.9%	12	0.4%	16
Unadjusted VOA	6.7%	12	-0.1%	14
Weighted Trend	7.3%	10	3.5%	20
Variance	8.3%	18	6.7%	19
Average Opponent	-0.8%	12	-1.2%	19
Passing	29.6%	5	8.5%	20
Rushing	-10.4%	27	-10.9%	8
First Down	2.6%	15	-6.1%	11
Second Down	10.3%	8	-3.6%	15
Third Down	5.0%	13	19.9%	29
First Half	11.1%	10	3.1%	20
Second Half	0.7%	14	-2.2%	13
Red Zone	-0.8%	12	-8.5%	18
Late and Close	9.1%	12	-1.8%	15

Five-Year Performance

Year	W-L	Pyth	Est W	PF	PA	TO	Total	Rk	Off	Rk	Def	Rk	ST	Rk	Off AGL	Rk	Def AGL	Rk
2007	13-3	11.2	11.1	455	325	+5	22.9%	4	16.6%	4	-6.8%	9	-0.4%	18	19.6	14	26.2	22
2008	9-7	7.9	8.1	362	365	-11	2.5%	18	1.8%	17	-4.2%	9	-3.6%	27	24.2	17	29.1	19
2009	11-5	11.3	11.9	361	250	+2	25.5%	5	21.7%	3	-2.9%	10	1.0%	14	14.5	11	7.7	2
2010	6-10	7.0	6.8	394	436	0	-10.5%	23	-4.7%	21	6.3%	27	0.6%	15	20.7	12	11.1	7
2011	8-8	8.6	8.4	369	347	+4	3.5%	14	5.9%	12	0.4%	16	-2.1%	25	43.5	25	19.0	11

2011 Performance Based on Most Common Personnel Groups

Dallas Offense					Dallas Offense vs. Opp.				Dallas Defense				Dallas Defense vs. Opp.			
Pers	Freq	Yds	DVOA	Run%	Pers	Freq	Yds	DVOA	Pers	Freq	Yds	DVOA	Pers	Freq	Yds	DVOA
11	32%	5.7	7.8%	15%	4-3-4	33%	6.2	23.5%	3-4-4	38%	5.5	-2.0%	11	43%	5.9	2.3%
12	27%	7.0	28.6%	32%	3-4-4	24%	5.4	-9.4%	Dime+	27%	6.7	22.3%	12	27%	6.0	-3.0%
22	14%	5.3	-5.5%	88%	4-2-5	21%	6.6	24.9%	2-4-5	13%	5.6	-8.9%	21	12%	4.4	-11.0%
21	13%	6.5	23.4%	51%	Dime+	9%	8.0	47.1%	3-3-5	13%	5.4	-1.8%	13	4%	4.9	-34.7%
13	8%	3.4	-30.1%	67%	3-3-5	6%	5.1	-24.3%	4-2-5	3%	7.5	-23.0%	22	4%	4.3	-10.1%
02	4%	8.5	46.2%	0%												

Strategic Tendencies

Run/Pass		Rank	Offense		Rank	Pass Rush		Rank	Defense/Other		Rank
Runs, all plays	39%	23	Form: Single Back	52%	28	Rush 3	18.3%	1	4 DB	41%	26
Runs, first half	41%	21	Form: Empty Back	5%	16	Rush 4	49.0%	28	5 DB	31%	24
Runs, first down	45%	27	Pers: 3+ WR	37%	27	Rush 5	24.8%	11	6+ DB	27%	5
Runs, second-long	30%	24	Pers: 4+ WR	1%	25	Rush 6+	8.0%	14	CB by Sides	94%	4
Runs, power sit.	53%	23	Pers: 2+ TE/6+ OL	53%	3	Zone Blitz	5.2%	16	Go for it on 4th	0.82	24
Runs, behind 2H	23%	28	Play action	14%	30	Sacks by LB	67.9%	3	Offensive Pace	31.9	28
Pass, ahead 2H	44%	16	Max protect	9%	22	Sacks by DB	7.1%	15	Defensive Pace	30.1	7

No defensive coordinator likes to rush three and drop eight into coverage quite like Rob Ryan. The Browns led the league in this category in 2010, and the Cowboys did last season. 🏈 Ryan blitzed much less than he did in Cleveland, but as is usually his custom, he sent the blitz less often on third down (27 percent of pass plays) than he did on first or second down (36 percent of pass plays). He rushed only three on 22 percent of third downs, and that strategy was very successful. The Cowboys allowed an average of 4.6 yards on these plays with a 78 percent Success Rate, compared to 7.9 yards and a 55 percent Success Rate they allowed when sending four or more pass rushers on third down. 🏈 Somewhat connected to those lower blitz rates, the Cowboys' defensive Adjusted Sack Rate ranked fifth on first down and third on second down, but only 27th on third down. 🏈 The Cowboys had the best defensive DVOA in the league against runs from shotgun, -28.8% DVOA and just 4.3 yards per carry. 🏈 Dallas faced 35 running back screens, the third most in the league, but was excellent against this play with -49.0% DVOA. It wasn't just preventing YAC; the Cowboys disrupted screens to force 10 incomplete passes, an interception, and a sack. 🏈 Cowboys opponents committed a league-low 92 opponent penalties. 🏈 Looking only at "standard" plays (i.e. four defensive backs), the Cowboys were far better against 4-3 defenses than they were against 3-4 defenses. Their gap between 4-3-4 and 3-4-4 is 32.9% DVOA, second-highest in the league behind New Orleans (and New Orleans had only 52 plays against 3-4-4, whereas Dallas had at least 240 plays against each of the two formations). Unfortunately, we don't have defensive formation numbers for 2010 to know if this is a fluke or a trend, but we'll watch this closely to see if it continues in 2012.

Passing

Player	DYAR	DVOA	Plays	NtYds	Avg	YAC	C%	TD	Int
T.Romo	1344	26.8%	555	3969	7.2	5.7	66.9%	31	10
S.McGee	3	-10.0%	41	157	3.8	3.6	63.2%	1	0
J.Kitna*	4	-5.3%	10	87	8.7	5.0	60.0%	1	2
K.Orton	97	-5.4%	262	1686	6.4	5.0	60.4%	9	9

Rushing

Player	DYAR	DVOA	Plays	Yds	Avg	TD	Fum	Suc
D.Murray	149	12.6%	164	896	5.5	2	1	58%
F.Jones	-3	-9.1%	127	575	4.5	1	4	52%
S.Morris*	-5	-12.5%	28	98	3.5	0	0	43%
T.Choice*	-55	-59.0%	27	80	3.0	0	2	30%
P.Tanner	-12	-20.2%	22	76	3.5	1	0	45%
T.Romo	-4	-18.0%	12	53	4.4	1	1	--

Receiving

Player	DYAR	DVOA	Plays	Ctch	Yds	Y/C	YAC	TD	C%
D.Bryant	262	20.5%	103	63	931	14.8	4.8	9	61%
L.Robinson*	327	40.0%	81	54	858	15.9	4.9	11	67%
M.Austin	139	11.3%	73	43	579	13.5	4.7	7	59%
K.Ogletree	-13	-19.0%	26	15	173	11.5	4.3	0	58%
J.Holley	72	118.8%	7	7	169	24.1	8.6	0	100%
J.Witten	102	5.6%	117	79	942	11.9	4.6	5	68%
M.Bennett*	-27	-23.7%	26	17	144	8.5	5.6	0	65%
J.Phillips	-6	-11.8%	18	15	101	6.7	6.0	1	83%
F.Jones	28	-3.0%	44	33	231	7.0	7.7	0	75%
D.Murray	-8	-17.8%	35	26	183	7.0	8.6	0	74%
T.Choice*	-22	-45.4%	15	12	66	5.5	6.8	0	80%
S.Morris*	-19	-87.4%	7	5	13	2.6	3.0	0	71%
L.Vickers	-21	-50.3%	8	4	29	7.3	5.3	0	50%

Offensive Line

Year	Yards	ALY	Rank	Power	Rank	Stuff	Rank	2nd Lev	Rank	Open Field	Rank	F-Start	Cont.
2009	5.00	4.48	3	58%	26	17%	10	1.36	3	1.15	5	25	39
2010	3.87	4.14	12	54%	26	18%	13	1.10	20	0.49	26	27	34
2011	4.63	4.26	6	57%	23	19%	16	1.31	8	0.97	9	23	36

Year	LE	Rank	LT	Rank	Mid	Rank	RT	Rank	RE	Rank	Sacks	ASR	Rank	Short	Long
2009	5.21	3	5.03	4	4.19	13	4.16	15	4.87	4	34	6.2%	16	12	15
2010	4.52	12	3.46	29	4.17	11	4.33	9	3.99	16	31	5.8%	11	13	8
2011	4.94	6	4.77	5	4.36	9	3.27	29	3.82	13	39	6.1%	13	10	19

On the whole the Cowboys line played pretty well last year, despite the team's short-yardage problems. There were some struggles running to the right, and our charters noted that many of those troubles began with Tyron Smith, but it's not unusual for rookies to struggle. And the sack rate wasn't great, but a lot of that is because

DALLAS COWBOYS

Tony Romo tended to hang on to the ball for too long—only eight teams gave up fewer short sacks. There will be changes for 2012, as the Cowboys hired a new offensive line coach, Bill Callahan, and chose to jettison a number of veterans. They cut right guard Kyle Kosier after the season, and opted not to re-sign Montrae Holland. That's a bit of a surprise, because the Cowboys' running game improved substantially after Holland replaced rookie Bill Nagy in the lineup, going from 3.65 Adjusted Line Yards per carry through Week 6 to 4.61 ALY afterwards.

Rather than wait to see what line of talent they could get in the draft, the Cowboys made a pair of free agent signings, taking Mackenzy Bernadeau from the Panthers and Nate Livings from the Bengals. Livings has started every game for the past two seasons, while Bernadeau came off the bench 14 times for Carolina after starting 12 contests in 2010. Callahan told Charean Williams of the *Fort Worth Star-Telegram* in May that Bernadeau was penciled in as the starter at right guard with Livings manning the left side. However, Bernadeau had hip surgery in May, which opens things up for Nagy (who played badly in four starts before breaking his ankle last year) to return to the starting lineup. Callahan has also said that Livings and Nagy will have a chance to unseat Phil Costa at center. The tackles are the same as last year, but they're switching spots, with Smith taking over the left tackle spot in his second season and Doug Free moving to the right side.

Defensive Front Seven

Defensive Line	Age	Pos	Plays	TmPct	Rk	Stop	Dfts	BTkl	St%	Rk	AvYd	Rk	Sack	Hit	Hur	Runs	St%	Yds	Pass	St%	Yds
Jay Ratliff	31	DT	41	5.5%	18	30	14	1	73%	50	1.9	37	2	4	15	34	71%	2.1	7	86%	1.1
Kenyon Coleman	33	DE	39	5.2%	39	34	10	2	87%	13	1.4	41	1	1	3	33	85%	1.9	6	100%	-1.5
Jason Hatcher	30	DE	29	4.8%	45	23	9	2	79%	37	1.1	34	4.5	7	6	21	76%	2.6	8	88%	-2.8
Sean Lissemore	25	DT	28	3.7%	45	21	7	0	75%	45	1.4	15	2	3	4.5	25	72%	2.1	3	100%	-4.3
Marcus Spears	29	DE	18	2.4%	--	14	5	0	78%	--	1.7	--	1	2	1	13	77%	1.8	5	80%	1.6

Linebackers	Age	Pos	Plays	TmPct	Rk	Stop	Dfts	BTkl	AvYd	Sack	Hit	Hur	Runs	St%	Rk	Yds	Rk	Tgts	Suc%	Rk	AdjYd	Rk
Sean Lee	26	ILB	109	15.5%	17	65	23	8	4.9	0	3	7	66	67%	48	3.5	66	42	51%	41	5.6	21
Anthony Spencer	28	OLB	66	8.8%	68	45	20	3	3.6	6	12	26	45	71%	29	2.9	33	10	52%	--	9.7	--
DeMarcus Ware	30	OLB	58	7.7%	85	48	28	1	-0.8	19.5	11	23	24	71%	30	2.2	12	7	59%	--	3.3	--
Keith Brooking*	37	ILB	50	6.7%	99	24	4	5	5.9	0	1	1	33	61%	73	4.3	100	17	58%	10	4.4	5
Bradie James*	31	ILB	44	5.9%	104	24	3	3	4.8	0	2	2	32	56%	90	4.1	89	12	53%	--	6.5	--
Victor Butler	25	OLB	17	2.3%	--	17	8	3	1.1	3	4	10	10	100%	--	1.3	--	1	100%	--	0.9	--
Dan Connor	27	ILB	72	9.6%	58	44	6	1	4.1	0	0	0	63	65%	55	2.9	31	6	57%	--	5.8	--

Year	Yards	ALY	Rank	Power	Rank	Stuff	Rank	2nd Lev	Rank	Open Field	Rank
2009	4.02	3.99	13	67%	19	17%	23	1.05	5	0.69	12
2010	4.40	4.27	22	70%	29	14%	29	1.10	14	0.87	19
2011	4.03	3.92	10	57%	10	22%	9	1.13	11	0.66	9

Year	LE	Rank	LT	Rank	Mid	Rank	RT	Rank	RE	Rank	Sacks	ASR	Rank	Short	Long
2009	2.91	4	3.80	10	4.05	17	4.33	22	4.23	22	43	7.0%	12	14	14
2010	4.72	23	3.39	6	4.39	24	4.16	16	4.79	30	35	6.9%	11	14	14
2011	3.51	6	4.81	31	3.58	2	4.04	13	4.04	25	42	7.6%	6	14	18

Is DeMarcus Ware the best defensive player in football? He's certainly the best pass rusher. In the past five seasons, Ware leads all players with 80 sacks, and Jared Allen (77.5) is the only other player over 55. The Cowboys used the franchise tag to stop Anthony Spencer from leaving, which may seem strange for a player who has never had more than six sacks in a season. However, Spencer has 17 quarterback hits and 40 hurries over the last two seasons. He's been a half-step away from making a major impact, and Dallas is banking on him finding that extra half-step.

On the inside, 2010 second-rounder Sean Lee played well in his first season as a starter, but Dallas declined to bring back either Keith Brooking or Bradie James. To start alongside Lee they grabbed Dan Connor from the Carolina Panthers. A third-round pick in 2008, Connor has been a starter for two years (though he missed half the 2010 season). Though he's much younger than James or Brooking, he's still a two-down stopgap. That's fine on a team that already has a strong pass-coverage linebacker like Lee.

On the defensive line, Kenyon Coleman and Jason Hatcher were clear upgrades over Marcus Spears and Igor Olshansky. Jay Ratliff also enjoyed a nice bounceback season, perhaps because he was fresh—backup Sean Lissemore saw some significant action. All three starters (plus Spears and Lissemore) return in 2012, and they'll be joined by third-round pick Tyrone Crawford (Boise State). Crawford lacks elite playmaking athleticism, but has good size and strength at the point of attack, making him an ideal fit for a 3-4 end.

Defensive Secondary

Secondary	Age	Pos	Plays	TmPct	Rk	Stop	Dfts	BTkl	Runs	St%	Rk	Yds	Rk	Tgts	Tgt%	Rk	Dist	Suc%	Rk	APaYd	Rk	PD	Int
Gerald Sensabaugh	29	SS	76	10.1%	37	18	8	6	30	33%	53	10.6	72	26	6.2%	52	12.7	24%	77	14.5	77	3	2
Abram Elam*	31	FS	65	8.7%	53	17	10	4	26	42%	30	5.0	8	25	6.1%	56	14.2	59%	30	5.6	9	0	0
Terence Newman*	34	CB	61	9.3%	23	17	7	6	12	33%	53	11.3	75	69	19.0%	31	13.2	43%	73	10.0	76	11	4
Orlando Scandrick	25	CB	54	8.8%	32	21	14	2	12	50%	27	7.3	47	48	14.2%	64	11.3	48%	59	8.5	60	5	1
Alan Ball*	27	CB	38	5.1%	79	11	5	1	6	33%	53	16.2	81	48	11.6%	72	11.3	44%	71	8.6	62	7	1
Mike Jenkins	27	CB	32	5.7%	75	14	6	4	5	20%	74	7.2	46	48	15.5%	54	12.3	56%	26	7.2	35	9	1
Frank Walker*	31	CB	26	4.0%	--	8	6	3	6	33%	--	10.3	--	20	5.5%	--	8.9	52%	--	6.0	--	2	1
Barry Church	24	SS	20	3.3%	--	6	2	0	7	57%	--	4.3	--	8	2.4%	--	8.1	64%	--	4.3	--	0	0
Brandon Carr	26	CB	60	7.3%	57	26	11	7	12	50%	27	6.8	39	73	20.9%	17	15.0	55%	27	6.2	17	13	4
Brddney Pool	28	FS	36	5.4%	73	13	3	2	16	44%	28	6.9	40	19	5.2%	65	13.3	69%	7	3.9	2	3	1

Year	Pass D Rank	vs. #1 WR	Rk	vs. #2 WR	Rk	vs. Other WR	Rk	vs. TE	Rk	vs. RB	Rk
2009	15	-10.3%	10	-8.7%	9	13.0%	26	22.1%	27	16.1%	24
2010	28	44.1%	32	15.5%	26	2.9%	20	-11.9%	4	-11.2%	6
2011	22	14.0%	19	53.3%	31	-26.9%	6	19.1%	21	-3.6%	15

It's no surprise that all three of Dallas' top cornerbacks were either demoted or fired. Dallas found new starters by paying a king's ransom in money to Brandon Carr, and another king's ransom in draft picks to the Rams in exchange for Morris Claiborne. We already explained why expectations for Claiborne should be held in check, but Carr is a clear upgrade. Even though he was the secondary corner in Kansas City behind Brandon Flowers, he was still a far sight better than anyone in Dallas. Mike Jenkins and Orlando Scandrick will battle each other for the nickel spot, unless Jenkins is (as is often rumored) dealt away.

There's one other new starter in the Dallas backfield, where it's goodbye Abram Elam, hello Brodney Pool. Only seven teams surrendered more 20-yard completions than Dallas, and only six defenses had a worse DVOA on deep passes (16-plus yards through the air). Pool has been top ten among safeties in both success rate and yards per pass in each of the last two years, but on just 41 targets in 29 games, and he was primarily a bench player for the Jets last season.

Gerald Sensabaugh's numbers plummeted after a career year in 2010. We've likely seen the best of him, but there are only so many players you can replace in one offseason. Fourth-rounder Matt Johnson is likely Sensabaugh's future replacement, but the Eastern Washington alum will likely stick to special teams this year.

Special Teams

Year	DVOA	Rank	FG/XP	Rank	Net Kick	Rank	Kick Ret	Rank	Net Punt	Rank	Punt Ret	Rank	Hidden	Rank
2009	0.8%	14	-10.7	29	10.7	3	-5.9	23	0.0	19	10.7	5	-3.2	21
2010	0.5%	15	-5.5	29	1.2	15	-14.6	31	6.3	10	15.3	2	-14.6	30
2011	-1.8%	25	1.6	13	1.6	14	1.2	14	-5.0	23	-9.7	30	3.6	11

The biggest weakness for Dallas came in punt returns. Dez Bryant and Dwayne Harris each had 15 returns, and each was worth roughly -4.0 estimated points of field position. Don't look for many changes here, though. Instead, the Cowboys will hope that Bryant can play like he did in 2010, when he was second to Devin Hester in value on punt returns. Dallas used a committee approach on kickoff returns last year, with nine players getting at least one return and none getting more than eight. Expect Harris and Felix Jones to be the top men for the job in 2012, but there's plenty of flexibility here. Punter Mat McBriar had one of his worst campaigns in 2011, struggling with drop foot that required surgery after the season, and Dallas let him go. Replacement Chris Jones looked good in the last two weeks of last season, and special teams coach Joe DeCamillis has raved about Jones' athleticism, raising at least the threat of a fake punt here and there. Dan Bailey will be back for his second season at kicker, but the Cowboys may want to consider a kickoff specialist. Bailey's gross kickoff value last year was -4.7 points, near the bottom of the league.

Coaching Staff

The Cowboys spent their offseason adding big names and proven commodities on defense, without making a significant addition on offense. While that largely speaks to the team's imbalance in 2011, it also says a lot about Jason Garrett, who clearly feels that he can take what he has and win a championship. Meanwhile, Rob Ryan went on a mini-media blitz after the draft, defending the efforts of his players, taking blame for the failures of 2011 (saying he had tried to teach the team too much, too fast) and telling reporters after one minicamp that "We're gonna be damn good." That's partly because he's a Ryan and talking big is what they do, but the man has been an NFL defensive coordinator for nearly a decade, and he probably wants his name to surface when any head coaching jobs come available at the end of the year.

Denver Broncos

2011 Record: 8-8

Pythagorean Wins: 5.8 (24th)

DVOA: -11.8% (24th)

Offense: -9.9% (23rd)

Defense: 1.6% (18th)

Special Teams: -0.2% (18th)

Variance: 9.5% (9th)

2012 Mean Projection: 8.3 wins

On the Clock (0-4): 6%

Mediocrity (5-7): 29%

Playoff Contender (8-10): 48%

Super Bowl Contender (11+): 16%

Postseason Odds: 43.2%

Projected Average Opponent: 4.5% (1st)

2011: Tebow Time.

2012: Peyton's Place.

In mid-May, a search for "Tim Tebow" on Google produced 60.4 million results. "Peyton Manning" turned up 37.9 million. That's close to 100 million results between Denver's old quarterback and their new one. There are plenty of other magazines out there that will put one (or both) on the cover, and they can have that discussion. If you paid to read *FOA 2012*, you already know the gist of who these men are, and can probably guess what we would say about them. We won't completely avoid them, and we won't stoop to goofy nicknames like "the guy who went to Tennessee" or "the one who's in New York now." But there are 50-some odd other guys on the Denver roster, and those guys are the ones we want to talk about. Those guys are the reason that Denver, according to our simulations, will be in a tight race to win the division despite the addition of Manning.

Though the national media will obsess over Manning's comeback, the Denver front office is much more concerned with the rest of the locker room. Those are the guys who will be playing for their jobs this season. By no means is this a Super Bowl-or-bust year in Denver. Quite the opposite, in fact. Despite the arrival of a Hall of Fame-bound veteran quarterback, Broncos president John Elway is engaged full-bore in a major rebuilding project.

Yes, rebuilding. That may sound surprising for a team that reached the Divisional round and now has a signifi-cantly more accurate passer under center. But the fact of the matter is that Denver was pretty lousy last year, and as their AFC West competition has improved, it will be a tough challenge to get back to the postseason.

The Broncos went just 8-8 last season and gave up 81 more points than they scored, so calling them a bad team is not really breaking new ground. Their streak of seven wins in eight games was exciting, but not as impressive as it looked. Their average DVOA in those seven wins was 9.5%. Tebow's late-game heroics made for great episodes of NFL Gameday, but those heroics were only necessary because the offense had fared so poorly for three quarters. And while that implies that the defense carried the team with dominating play, the fact is that the Broncos' defensive DVOA in those seven games was just -3.6%, only slightly better than their overall performance (1.6%) and not the kind of achievement that will bring back memories of the Steel Curtain. No, the biggest reason Denver won seven of eight games is that they played several bad teams in eight weeks (Table 1).

None of these teams made the playoffs, none had a winning record, and only one (the Jets) could really be called above average. And Denver needed late heroics to beat all of these mid-tier clubs. The overtime win against Pittsburgh in the playoffs wasn't part of a trend. It was an anomaly, the best game they played all year against the best team they played all year. They

2012 Broncos Schedule

Week	Opp.	Week	Opp.	Week	Opp.
1	PIT	7	BYE	13	TB
2	at ATL (Mon.)	8	NO	14	at OAK (Thu.)
3	HOU	9	at CIN	15	at BAL
4	OAK	10	at CAR	16	CLE
5	at NE	11	SD	17	KC
6	at SD (Mon.)	12	at KC		

Figure 1. 2011 Denver DVOA by Week

proved it was a fluke by getting crushed the next week.

Once that was done, the Broncos decided to go with proven skill and ability over rabbit's feet and horseshoes and made a change at quarterback. You all know who Peyton Manning is and what he did during his time with the Colts. You also know what he had to work with in Indianapolis, and at first glance the talent in Denver comes up short. However, considering the guy who was throwing passes last year, we have to cut them some slack.

Which begs the question: Can we separate the performance of those teammates from their quarterback? We can try, because Kyle Orton started the first five games in Denver last year. One of the more underrated players in the league, Orton has ranked in the top 25 in passing DYAR for each of the past four seasons (although, to be fair, the 25.0% DVOA he put up in Kansas City last year was much better than the -7.4% DVOA he produced in Denver). Splitting each receiver's performance by quarterback shows some clear patterns (Table 2).

Orton was willing to check down to his backs and tight ends much more often than Tebow, which partly explains why Orton had a higher completion percentage and lower yards per catch. Regardless of position group, though, Orton completed a lot more passes,

Table 1: Jaywalker's Row: Victims of Denver's Winning Streak

Week	Score	Opp	W-L	DVOA
7	18-15 (OT)	@MIA	6-10	-1.3%
9	38-24	@OAK	8-8	-8.0%
10	17-10	@KC	7-9	-16.9%
11	17-13	NYJ	8-8	13.5%
12	16-13 (OT)	@SD	8-8	0.7%
13	35-32	@MIN	3-13	-22.2%
14	13-10 (OT)	CHI	8-8	1.3%
Average			6.9-9.1	-4.7%

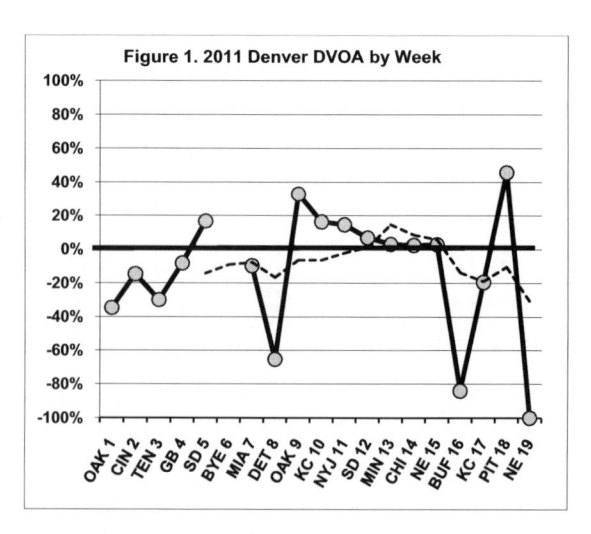

while Tebow hit more big plays. The effect largely evened out (Tebow actually averaged more yards per pass attempt than Orton with Denver last year, 6.4 to 6.3), but it's clear that a change in quarterbacks can have a massive effect on a receiver's numbers. This receiving corps may not be as talented as the one that Manning played with in Indianapolis, but we should expect great improvement across the board. And the Broncos also grabbed some weapons in free agency, adding tight ends Jacob Tamme (Manning's teammate in Indianapolis) and Joel Dreessen and wideout Andre Caldwell. The cupboard here is not bare.

Manning proved in Indianapolis that he doesn't need a dominant defense to win games, just a steady defense that shows up every week. That's good news, because while Denver's defense wasn't particularly good last year, it's hard to find a defense that was more steady. The 2011 Broncos had the second-lowest game-to-game variance of any defense in the 21 years for which we have DVOA stats, behind only the 2001 Chiefs. That's a credit to head coach John Fox and defensive coordinator Dennis Allen (now gone to Oakland) for getting their players to show up and perform every week.

The Denver defense last year was one of the more aggressive units in the league, but they were at their best in passing situations (much like the defenses that helped Manning win so many games in Indianapolis). They were 19th in defensive DVOA overall, but 30th when losing big (by more than a touchdown) and 10th when winning big. They were 21st on first down, 27th on second down, but eighth on third down. When Von Miller and Elvis Dumervil knew they could ignore the run, it was bad news for opposing quarterbacks.

Table 2: 2011 Denver Receiving Numbers by Quarterback

Receiver	\multicolumn{5}{c	}{Orton throwing the ball}	\multicolumn{5}{c	}{Tebow throwing the ball}
	Targets	Tgt%	Yards	Catch%	Avg.	Targets	Tgt%	Yards	Catch%	Avg.
Eric Decker	42	27%	267	52%	12.2	57	21%	371	41%	15.9
Demaryius Thomas	0	--	--	--	--	69	26%	551	46%	17.4
Eddie Royal	10	6%	55	44%	12.5	42	16%	133	37%	8.6
Matt Willis	12	8%	80	55%	12.1	25	9%	208	48%	17.3
Brandon Lloyd	29	18%	263	62%	14.6	2	1%	20	50%	20.0
All WRs	93	59%	665	55%	13.1	195	73%	1283	43%	15.3
All TEs	25	16%	158	56%	11.2	29	11%	244	55%	15.3
All RBs	39	25%	182	72%	6.5	44	16%	256	61%	9.5
All receivers	157	--	1005	59%	10.8	268	--	1783	47%	14.0

(Brandon Lloyd was traded to the Rams during the Broncos' bye week, the same time Tebow was promoted to the starting job. Coincidentally, Demaryius Thomas entered the lineup that same week after missing the first five games with a finger injury. Eddie Royal also missed three games of the Orton era with a groin injury.)

So, the Broncos went and got a new quarterback, hoping that he would be able to turn their offense around despite advanced age (36) and multiple neck surgeries. They already had a defense that seemed to be tailored to play with that quarterback's strengths. Given that they made the playoffs just a few months prior, it seemed like a clear indication the team was going into win-now mode.

But then Denver let both starting defensive tackles (Brodrick Bunkley and Marcus Thomas) leave in free agency, without clear alternatives to replace either of them. They also cut cornerback Andre' Goodman in a salary move, while safety Brian Dawkins finally retired. They didn't do a ton in free agency to replace any of these men. They did add cornerback Tracy Porter from New Orleans, but based on the last several years of our charting stats that's a clear and obvious downgrade (although Porter is also eight years younger than Goodman). They also added safety Mike Adams and cornerback Drayton Florence, but Adams has been a backup for most of his career, and Florence's charting stats have almost always been awful, except for a fluky 2009.

So Denver entered the draft with several glaring needs. Then they traded down out of the first round, which is an awfully strange move for a "win now" team. When they made their first selection, it was Cincinnati tackle Derek Wolfe. Some analysts thought Wolfe was a bad fit for a 4-3 defense, and most felt he would go several rounds later. Things got even weirder when they picked Arizona State quarterback Brock Osweiler later in the round. This was not a "win now" selection. This was a "win in 2015 or later" move. The Broncos went on to add running back Ronnie Hillman and cornerback Omar Bolden, two players who could see a lot of time on passing downs. Still, when the smoke cleared, Denver came out of the draft without a single player who was likely to earn a starting job in 2012. So much for winning now.

The Broncos made more personnel moves after the draft, not among players but among executives. Team president John Elway promoted Matt Russell from director of college scouting to director of player personnel, putting him in charge of players in college and in the pros. Elway also hired former agent Mike Sullivan to manage the team's salary cap. With Russell managing players, Sullivan managing money, and Elway running the show, there was suddenly nothing left for general manager Brian Xanders to do, and he was released. Elway made it clear to Mike Klis of the *Denver Post* that this was a "streamlining" move, and nobody would be hired to fill Xanders' old position.

In short, this is John Elway's team now, maybe even more than when he played. His new career is just beginning, and he's not interested in mortgaging the long-term state of the franchise for short-term benefits. The Manning acquisition was his biggest move, but far from his last move. No matter whether the Broncos are playing next January or not, many of the players on this roster will be replaced in the next year or two as Elway continues to build his team to suit his vision. Elway knows, like we do, that the Broncos are not ready to win championships, no matter how many Google results their quarterback generates.

Vince Verhei

DENVER BRONCOS

2011 Broncos Stats by Week

Wk	vs.	W-L	PF	PA	YDF	YDA	TO	Total	Off	Def	ST
1	OAK	L	20	23	310	289	-2	-35%	-46%	-6%	6%
2	CIN	W	24	22	318	382	-2	-15%	2%	16%	0%
3	@TEN	L	14	17	231	333	0	-30%	-34%	1%	5%
4	@GB	L	23	49	384	507	-2	-8%	-1%	10%	3%
5	SD	L	24	29	275	418	1	17%	5%	-14%	-2%
6	BYE										
7	@MIA	W	18	15	308	267	0	-10%	-7%	-10%	-13%
8	DET	L	10	45	312	376	-3	-65%	-44%	23%	1%
9	@OAK	W	38	24	412	416	3	33%	26%	0%	6%
10	@KC	W	17	10	313	258	0	16%	24%	9%	1%
11	NYJ	W	17	13	229	318	1	15%	-5%	-18%	1%
12	@SD	W	16	13	349	344	0	7%	-17%	-11%	13%
13	@MIN	W	35	32	336	489	1	3%	1%	14%	16%
14	CHI	W	13	10	345	245	-1	2%	-5%	-7%	0%
15	NE	L	23	41	393	451	-3	3%	30%	12%	-15%
16	@BUF	L	14	40	285	351	-3	-84%	-52%	1%	-31%
17	KC	L	3	7	266	281	-1	-19%	-15%	10%	5%
18	PIT	W	29	23	447	400	0	46%	34%	-5%	7%
19	@NE	L	10	45	252	509	1	-101%	-59%	35%	-7%

Trends and Splits

	Offense	Rank	Defense	Rank
Total DVOA	-9.9%	23	1.6%	18
Unadjusted VOA	-10.5%	23	1.2%	19
Weighted Trend	-6.8%	20	1.6%	16
Variance	12.0%	29	2.5%	2
Average Opponent	2.0%	28	1.1%	15
Passing	-16.2%	26	10.2%	22
Rushing	-0.5%	13	-8.0%	13
First Down	3.3%	13	1.0%	19
Second Down	-11.5%	23	12.7%	27
Third Down	-34.7%	29	-16.8%	7
First Half	-21.4%	28	4.7%	22
Second Half	-0.1%	17	-1.6%	15
Red Zone	-7.7%	18	8.5%	27
Late and Close	10.0%	9	-3.8%	12

Five-Year Performance

Year	W-L	Pyth	Est W	PF	PA	TO	Total	Rk	Off	Rk	Def	Rk	ST	Rk	Off AGL	Rk	Def AGL	Rk
2007	7-9	5.6	7.8	320	409	+1	-0.8%	17	9.5%	8	5.2%	21	-5.1%	28	44.3	31	23.4	20
2008	8-8	6.1	6.3	370	448	-17	-8.5%	24	19.2%	1	20.7%	31	-7.0%	31	45.3	28	30.1	22
2009	8-8	8.1	9.2	326	324	+7	10.6%	13	1.3%	18	-9.8%	7	-0.4%	18	16.5	13	3.3	1
2010	4-12	4.9	5.3	344	471	-9	-17.1%	26	2.1%	15	16.6%	30	-2.6%	27	11.0	6	40.8	28
2011	8-8	5.8	7.0	309	390	+1	-11.8%	24	-9.9%	23	1.6%	18	-0.2%	18	15.0	5	40.4	24

2011 Performance Based on Most Common Personnel Groups

Denver Offense				Denver Offense vs. Opp.				Denver Defense				Denver Defense vs. Opp.			
Pers	Freq	Yds	DVOA	Run%	Pers	Freq	Yds	DVOA	Pers	Freq	Yds	DVOA	Pers	Freq	Yds	DVOA
11	47%	5.5	-3.4%	31%	4-3-4	28%	5.5	-3.9%	4-3-4	39%	5.1	-2.3%	11	40%	5.9	12.5%
21	21%	5.0	-10.6%	72%	3-4-4	26%	5.2	4.2%	3-3-5	32%	5.3	1.3%	12	22%	5.5	6.0%
12	17%	4.7	-1.9%	60%	4-2-5	26%	4.4	-28.8%	4-2-5	14%	6.1	16.6%	21	14%	6.5	14.6%
612	3%	4.7	10.6%	81%	3-3-5	8%	5.8	22.3%	3-4-4	7%	7.3	25.8%	22	8%	2.5	-51.1%
22	3%	5.6	24.0%	62%	2-4-5	5%	7.3	-10.2%	Dime+	4%	9.4	18.6%	20	6%	5.1	-19.1%

Strategic Tendencies

Run/Pass		Rank	Offense		Rank	Pass Rush		Rank	Defense/Other		Rank
Runs, all plays	53%	1	Form: Single Back	64%	13	Rush 3	10.8%	8	4 DB	46%	20
Runs, first half	58%	1	Form: Empty Back	7%	10	Rush 4	44.0%	30	5 DB	46%	10
Runs, first down	60%	2	Pers: 3+ WR	51%	15	Rush 5	25.4%	10	6+ DB	4%	19
Runs, second-long	44%	7	Pers: 4+ WR	2%	19	Rush 6+	19.8%	2	CB by Sides	71%	24
Runs, power sit.	78%	2	Pers: 2+ TE/6+ OL	29%	23	Zone Blitz	1.5%	28	Go for it on 4th	0.70	31
Runs, behind 2H	43%	1	Play action	23%	6	Sacks by LB	40.0%	14	Offensive Pace	30.8	20
Pass, ahead 2H	27%	32	Max protect	12%	13	Sacks by DB	15.0%	4	Defensive Pace	30.2	9

You can pretty much toss the first two columns of that strategic tendencies table, since things will change dramatically with Peyton Manning at quarterback. ◉ If Manning wants to hand off from shotgun, at least he knows the line already knows how to block it. The Broncos handed off to a running back on a league-high 20 percent of shotgun plays, with 5.8 yards pas carry and 19.8% DVOA. ◉ Even though they had a new defensive coordinator and moved back to a 4-3 front, the Broncos' split in pass rushers looked very similar to what it was in 2010. They sent four less than half the time, sent three more than you would expect from a 4-3 team, and big-blitzed with at least six guys more than any defense save New Orleans. They were very successful on those big blitzes, allowing just 4.9 yards per pass compared to 7.3 yards per pass otherwise. ◉ Despite the presence of Elvis Dumervil and Von Miller, we marked Denver as bringing significant pass pressure on just 19.3 percent of passes, 27th in the NFL.

Passing

Player	DYAR	DVOA	Plays	NtYds	Avg	YAC	C%	TD	Int
T.Tebow*	-221	-22.7%	301	1507	5.2	4.8	47.0%	12	6
K.Orton*	-95	-20.3%	163	924	5.7	4.2	58.7%	8	7
C.Hanie	-470	-78.7%	118	474	4.0	4.3	51.5%	3	8

Rushing

Player	DYAR	DVOA	Plays	Yds	Avg	TD	Fum	Suc
W.McGahee	131	4.3%	249	1206	4.8	4	3	47%
T.Tebow*	-36	-18.3%	117	668	5.7	6	6	--
L.Ball	42	2.8%	96	408	4.3	1	1	44%
K.Moreno	-9	-16.0%	37	179	4.8	0	1	32%
J.Johnson	11	9.9%	14	77	5.5	0	0	57%
S.Larsen*	6	0.5%	14	44	3.1	0	0	64%
E.Royal*	32	41.6%	7	48	6.9	0	0	--
C.Hanie	25	36.4%	13	98	7.5	0	0	--

Receiving

Player	DYAR	DVOA	Plays	Ctch	Yds	Y/C	YAC	TD	C%
B.Lloyd*	25	-2.2%	31	19	283	14.9	1.9	0	61%
E.Decker	2	-12.4%	98	45	613	13.6	3.9	8	46%
D.Thomas	37	-5.9%	70	32	551	17.2	3.5	4	46%
E.Royal*	-129	-45.3%	50	19	155	8.2	3.5	1	38%
M.Willis	22	-4.7%	36	18	267	14.8	5.2	1	50%
A.Caldwell	-27	-17.9%	67	37	317	8.6	3.1	3	55%
D.Fells*	4	-5.3%	31	19	256	13.5	4.5	3	61%
D.Rosario*	12	10.0%	11	7	117	16.7	4.0	0	64%
J.Thomas	-34	-83.4%	7	1	5	5.0	7.0	0	14%
J.Dreessen	119	40.5%	39	28	353	12.6	5.3	6	72%
J.Tamme	-29	-20.8%	31	19	177	9.3	4.8	1	61%
L.Ball	-9	-19.3%	31	16	148	9.3	7.9	1	52%
W.McGahee	-59	-68.0%	20	12	51	4.3	4.3	1	60%
K.Moreno	37	44.3%	15	11	101	9.2	8.7	1	73%
J.Johnson	13	10.4%	9	7	62	8.9	8.0	0	78%
S.Larsen*	25	32.3%	9	9	76	8.4	4.8	0	100%

Offensive Line

Year	Yards	ALY	Rank	Power	Rank	Stuff	Rank	2nd Lev	Rank	Open Field	Rank	F-Start	Cont.
2009	4.27	4.30	6	58%	27	21%	22	1.29	5	0.61	24	19	26
2010	3.62	3.60	30	52%	27	23%	25	1.12	16	0.45	28	17	32
2011	4.67	4.19	11	56%	26	17%	9	1.31	7	0.94	10	7	48

Year	LE	Rank	LT	Rank	Mid	Rank	RT	Rank	RE	Rank	Sacks	ASR	Rank	Short	Long
2009	4.96	8	3.47	29	4.41	6	3.38	28	5.05	2	34	5.9%	12	10	16
2010	3.51	24	3.75	24	3.78	23	3.30	28	3.40	24	40	6.4%	16	10	20
2011	3.35	26	4.04	21	4.08	15	5.09	2	4.51	5	42	9.5%	29	9	25

Sometime between Labor Day and Halloween, you're going to read an article about how Denver's offensive line is playing much better than they did in 2011. And there's some room for improvement. Ryan Clady led the league with 11 holding penalties. Orlando Franklin was in the top 20 for blown blocks leading to sacks or pressures, and Zane Beadles was in the top five in the same category for interior linemen. All that being said, the biggest improvement will come from the team's new quarterback, not his blockers. To show how one passer can change an entire team, let's break the Broncos' offensive line metrics from last season into the Orton and Tebow eras (Table 3).

Keep in mind that Denver started the same five linemen in all 16 games. You can see how the presence of

DENVER BRONCOS

Table 3: Denver offensive line stats by QB

Time	QB	ALY	Stuff	Power	SLY	OFY	ASR
Weeks 1-5	Orton	3.78	25%	62%	1.12	0.88	5.3%
Weeks 7-17	Tebow	3.95	20%	59%	1.19	0.64	11.2%

Tebow benefited Denver's rushing offense. Defensive ends, forced to watch out for bootlegs and keepers, allowed more running backs to reach the line of scrimmage, and usually for more yards. On the other hand, the difference in ALY works out to about six inches per carry. Further, since opposing safeties were free to crowd the line of scrimmage, big runs became more and more scarce. And then there's the matter of pass protection. With Tebow endlessly scrambling in the backfield, always unsure of what to do and never willing to give up on a play, pass protection would inevitably wear down. Tebow finished 29th in dropbacks, but he was second in football with 21 long sacks. (Cam Newton led the league with 24—in 251 more dropbacks than Tebow.) All told, only eight teams gave up fewer short sacks, but no team surrendered more long sacks.

All five Broncos linemen—left tackle Ryan Clady, left guard Zane Beadles, center J.D. Walton, right guard Chris Kuper, and right tackle Orlando Franklin—will return. (Kuper, who suffered a disgusting broken leg in the Week 17 loss to Kansas City, told Mike Klis of the *Denver Post* in April that he expected to be 100 percent by training camp.) Four of them are 26 or younger, so we should expect them to improve as a group anyway. The biggest difference, though, is that now they will be blocking for Peyton Manning, who simply does not hold onto the football. In each of his last two seasons, Manning's median sack time was just 2.3 seconds, which ranked third in 2009 and first in 2010. The safest bet in all of football in 2012 is that the Denver sack rate will plummet, and that has nothing to do with the linemen themselves.

Defensive Front Seven

Defensive Line	Age	Pos	Plays	TmPct	Rk	Stop	Dfts	BTkl	St%	Rk	AvYd	Rk	Sack	Hit	Hur	Runs	St%	Yds	Pass	St%	Yds
Brodrick Bunkley*	29	DT	43	5.1%	21	35	8	1	81%	25	2.7	60	0	1	1	42	81%	2.6	1	100%	7.0
Elvis Dumervil	28	DE	43	5.8%	25	36	18	1	84%	24	1.0	31	10	8	15.5	29	79%	3.4	14	93%	-4.0
Marcus Thomas*	27	DT	42	6.7%	8	33	8	0	79%	35	1.4	18	0	1	2	40	78%	1.5	2	100%	0.0
Robert Ayers	27	DE	40	4.8%	46	29	7	0	73%	61	1.9	52	3	2	8.5	29	72%	2.2	11	73%	1.1
Ryan McBean*	28	DE	32	3.8%	65	22	11	0	69%	71	2.5	70	4	1	2.5	22	68%	2.7	10	70%	2.1
Jason Hunter	29	DE	20	2.4%	--	15	3	0	75%	--	3.8	--	1	1	7	18	72%	4.5	2	100%	-3.0
Justin Bannan	33	DT	34	4.3%	32	28	5	0	82%	23	1.8	35	0	1	3	29	83%	1.8	5	80%	2.0

Linebackers	Age	Pos	Plays	TmPct	Rk	Stop	Dfts	BTkl	AvYd	Sack	Hit	Hur	Runs	St%	Rk	Yds	Rk	Tgts	Suc%	Rk	AdjYd	Rk
D.J. Williams	30	OLB	92	13.4%	27	49	15	6	4.6	5	2	6	62	56%	88	4.7	108	35	55%	20	5.4	14
Wesley Woodyard	26	OLB	89	11.3%	44	40	14	2	6.2	0	0	2	46	54%	97	4.5	107	41	41%	66	8.0	68
Joe Mays	27	MLB	76	9.0%	63	52	15	9	3.4	0	4	1.5	61	79%	11	2.3	16	14	38%	--	14.8	--
Von Miller	23	OLB	66	8.4%	74	51	29	1	2.0	11	19	17.5	36	75%	13	3.2	45	10	82%	--	6.4	--
Mario Haggan*	32	MLB	22	2.6%	--	15	4	1	3.2	0	0	0	15	80%	--	1.3	--	3	97%	--	1.2	--

Year	Yards	ALY	Rank	Power	Rank	Stuff	Rank	2nd Lev	Rank	Open Field	Rank
2009	4.54	4.13	17	67%	20	18%	21	1.26	26	1.00	24
2010	4.52	4.40	29	57%	9	15%	27	1.11	16	0.99	26
2011	4.26	3.88	9	60%	12	22%	8	1.28	24	0.78	18

Year	LE	Rank	LT	Rank	Mid	Rank	RT	Rank	RE	Rank	Sacks	ASR	Rank	Short	Long
2009	4.52	20	5.02	30	3.93	15	4.58	27	3.49	6	39	7.4%	7	13	18
2010	5.22	31	4.48	23	4.24	22	4.49	23	4.42	23	23	4.6%	32	6	15
2011	4.43	21	4.03	16	3.62	3	4.67	24	3.51	16	41	7.8%	5	18	14

What we have here are two scary young pass rushers, a quietly effective veteran cleanup man, and a bunch of question marks and just-a-guys. Elvis Dumervil and Von Miller were each in the league's top 20 in sacks, although neither made the top 140 in run tackles. Williams, meanwhile, has started at least 11 games every year since the Broncos drafted him in the first round in 2004. Our similarity scores system matches him up with versatile defenders like Karlos Dansby, A.J. Hawk, Will Witherspoon, and former Denver star Al Wilson. That's quite a valuable player, one who will be sorely missed if his six-game suspension for performance-enhancing drugs is upheld. Williams got in further trouble in early June for Tweeting an image of the Broncos' playbook. There was little useful information in the six play diagrams Williams exposed, just that the Broncos are prepared to line up in a 4-3 under shift, but this is not the kind of thing coaches like to expose. Williams also said he had to learn a new position, so perhaps the Broncos plan on using him inside more often.

The rest of the Denver front seven is a bit muddled. Defensive end Robert Ayers and middle linebacker Joe Mays are rotational players, journeymen who will retain starting jobs only because the Broncos failed to bring in anyone to challenge them. Wesley Woodyard, who has started 10 games in the last two seasons, will fill in during Williams' drug suspension; he also comes in for Mays on passing downs. Woodyard is the kind of player who makes for useful depth but will likely be stretched as a starter. And the defensive tackle situation is a mess. Last year's starters, Brodrick Bunkley and Marcus Thomas (quietly one of the more active players at the position last year) were allowed to leave in free agency. So was end/tackle Ryan McBean (partly due to a six-game suspension for PEDs, no doubt). The projected starters are Ty Warren and Kevin Vickerson. Warren has played in only one game in two years after hip and triceps injuries. Vickerson has made 18 starts in his five-year career and missed 11 games last year with an ankle injury. The Broncos signed Justin Bannan away from the Rams, but he's an aging player, and St. Louis is the third team in three years to let him walk away—including the Broncos, who didn't bother to re-sign him after the 2010 campaign. There's also second-round pick Derek Wolfe. Our friend Russ Lande, like most observers, projected Wolfe to go three or four rounds later in the draft, and felt his most natural position was as a 3-4 end, saying that at 6-foot-5, he lacked the leverage necessary to make an effective tackle. Expect a heavy rotation of these guys as the Broncos try to find someone who can stick.

Defensive Secondary

Secondary	Age	Pos	Plays	TmPct	Rk	Stop	Dfts	BTkl	Runs	St%	Rk	Yds	Rk	Tgts	Tgt%	Rk	Dist	Suc%	Rk	APaYd	Rk	PD	Int
Chris Harris	23	CB	71	8.4%	40	32	12	1	22	50%	27	9.3	64	49	11.6%	73	8.1	50%	52	7.7	47	8	1
Andre' Goodman*	34	CB	59	7.0%	63	22	9	6	14	71%	4	4.1	6	87	20.4%	20	12.2	47%	61	6.4	20	9	2
Brian Dawkins*	39	SS	56	7.6%	63	30	13	4	28	54%	12	6.8	37	17	4.6%	70	8.8	62%	16	7.7	38	5	0
Champ Bailey	34	CB	49	7.2%	59	21	5	8	15	40%	44	9.2	62	61	17.7%	37	10.7	49%	55	8.9	64	10	2
Quinton Carter	24	FS	49	5.8%	70	9	2	5	22	27%	64	9.1	64	21	5.0%	67	11.9	40%	72	10.8	69	1	0
Rahim Moore	22	FS	33	4.2%	--	10	4	9	15	27%	--	10.5	--	10	2.4%	--	12.5	23%	--	10.5	--	1	1
Jonathan Wilhite*	28	CB	28	3.5%	--	13	8	1	1	0%	--	8.0	--	31	7.8%	--	8.9	40%	--	8.5	--	2	1
Cassius Vaughn*	25	CB	23	4.9%	--	8	4	1	3	67%	--	0.3	--	26	10.7%	--	14.3	45%	--	8.4	--	4	1
David Bruton	25	SS	16	2.0%	--	7	5	1	6	50%	--	3.5	--	8	2.0%	--	11.3	77%	--	6.4	--	4	0
Mike Adams	31	FS	67	7.9%	59	20	11	4	39	28%	61	10.9	73	17	4.5%	71	15.5	60%	28	8.5	46	6	3
Drayton Florence	32	CB	62	7.7%	53	20	7	3	16	6%	80	11.1	74	69	16.9%	43	15.2	47%	64	9.8	75	13	3
Tracy Porter	26	CB	61	9.0%	29	19	9	6	9	44%	37	7.4	48	61	14.8%	59	10.0	34%	82	8.3	57	10	1

Year	Pass D Rank	vs. #1 WR	Rk	vs. #2 WR	Rk	vs. Other WR	Rk	vs. TE	Rk	vs. RB	Rk
2009	6	-5.6%	11	-25.7%	3	-31.7%	2	21.2%	25	-11.7%	9
2010	31	7.1%	21	16.1%	27	28.9%	32	13.5%	24	8.8%	21
2011	24	21.7%	23	-1.2%	14	2.5%	22	6.1%	14	26.3%	30

The career of Champ Bailey, once one of the game's great players, continues its descent (Table 4).

The Broncos released Andre' Goodman in April. To replace him they signed Tracy Porter, who ranked 82nd in Success Rate in 2011 and 62nd in 2010. In May they added former Bills cornerback Drayton Florence, a 10-year veteran who has ranked 51st or worse in Success Rate four times in the past five years. Those acquisi-

Champ Bailey Charting Stats, 2006-2011

Year	G	Suc%	Rank	PaYd	Rank
2006	16	62%	5	5.8	7
2007	15	59%	7	6.7	25
2008	9	45%	--	9.5	--
2009	16	54%	25	6.1	12
2010	15	52%	42	7.9	56
2011	13	49%	55	8.9	64

tions theoretically shove Chris Harris down the depth chart. Harris, though, played so well as nickelback in 2011 that it will be hard to keep the undrafted rookie off the field. Denver also added one of the draft's most intriguing players in Omar Bolden, who missed two seasons at Arizona State but was very effective when he did play. He's an inconsistent tackler who struggled with press coverage; in short, a poor man's Asante Samuel who can't stay healthy.

Brian Dawkins finally retired, leaving 2009 fourth-rounder David Bruton the incumbent at strong safety. The Broncos also signed Mike Adams (formerly of the Browns and 49ers) for competition. Adams started every game last season in Cleveland, but prior to that made only 34 starts in seven years. On the other hand, Bruton has only four starts in his career. Second-round rookie Rahim Moore opened the season as starter at free safety, but made enough mistakes (nine missed tackles in only 40 attempts) that fourth-round rookie Quinton Carter had taken over by season's end. Both will likely see plenty of time again in 2012.

Special Teams

Year	DVOA	Rank	FG/XP	Rank	Net Kick	Rank	Kick Ret	Rank	Net Punt	Rank	Punt Ret	Rank	Hidden	Rank
2009	-0.3%	18	-1.1	19	9.8	5	-4.2	19	-10.7	31	4.2	10	-3.9	24
2010	-2.2%	27	2.4	11	-4.5	26	2.9	14	-13.0	29	-0.6	16	-17.6	32
2011	-0.2%	18	-6.4	27	1.8	13	0.6	16	-5.3	24	8.2	4	4.8	9

From the Not Fixin' Things That Ain't Broke department: Britton Colquitt and Matt Prater were each within a single point of average on punts and kickoffs, respectively, so they're both back again in 2012. However, Prater is a liability on long field goals. He went 6-of-11 on those kicks last year, and has hit only 59 percent of them over his career. (League average last year on 40-plus-yard field-goal attempts was 71 percent, and most of those kickers didn't get to play half their games a mile high.) Quan Cosby was the top return man on both punts and kickoffs last year, but he's in Indianapolis now. Eric Decker will take over on punt returns; he had six of them last year, including a 90-yard touchdown against Oakland in Week 1. Matt Willis returned eight kickoffs last year for a 20.4-yard average, and he'll probably get the first crack at that job this season.

Coaching Staff

Head coach John Fox and offensive coordinator Mike McCoy deserve a lot of credit for keeping a steady ship as the team's offense went through multiple changes last season. They started as a fairly standard offense under Kyle Orton, then morphed into an option-based attack when Tebow took over. By the end of the year their scheme was much more conventional, though they still leaned heavily on the run. All that being said, they should have little difficulty making whatever changes are required to please Peyton Manning. Speaking of Manning, he's three years older than his new quarterbacks coach, Adam Gase, formerly in charge of the team's wide receivers. Oh, to be a fly on the wall the first time Adam Gase tries to tell Peyton Manning how to play quarterback.

Defensive coordinator Dennis Allen left to take the head coaching job in Oakland, so Jack Del Rio will become Denver's seventh defensive coordinator in the last seven seasons. Del Rio coached Fox's defense in Carolina in 2002 before taking the head job with the Jaguars. His defenses in Jacksonville were somewhat conservative 4-3 units. No Jaguars linebacker ever had more than six sacks in a season under Del Rio, but then again, none of those linebackers had the talents of Von Miller.

Detroit Lions

2011 Record: 10-6

Pythagorean Wins: 10.1 (8th)

DVOA: 10.1% (11th)

Offense: 7.1% (10th)

Defense: -8.1% (9th)

Special Teams: -5.1% (29th)

Variance: 9.9% (11th)

2012 Mean Projection: 7.5 wins

On the Clock (0-4): 10%

Mediocrity (5-7): 40%

Playoff Contender (8-10): 40%

Super Bowl Contender (11+): 10%

Postseason Odds: 20.3%

Projected Average Opponent: -3.4% (27th)

2011: The hot pick to break out actually breaks out.

2012: They'll be in the hunt, but regression is more likely than another leap forward.

This time last year, the Detroit Lions were taking their turn as the NFC's "possible breakout team of 2011." The Lions had finished the 2010 season on a four-game winning streak; there was fresh hope that oft-injured young quarterback Matthew Stafford would be back and healthy; and most encouraging, for the first time in years, the organization seemed to have a cohesive plan. Second-year general manager Martin Mayhew had just spent the 13th overall pick in the draft on Nick Fairley. The somewhat controversial Auburn defensive tackle, who was projected to go first overall at one point, would get to transition to the NFL coming off the bench behind stellar veteran Corey Williams and second-year superstar Ndamukong Suh.

It's rare to see a team coming off a 6-10 season go for a luxury pick like this in the first round. It's even rarer to see that team be applauded for it. But in Detroit's case, the Fairley splurge verified the cohesiveness of Mayhew's plan. The foundation of his club would be the defensive line.

As it turned out, the Lions became one of the few "expected breakout teams" in NFL history to actually break out. After beginning the season 5-0, they finished with a 10-6 record and reached the playoffs for the first time since 1999. Early on, they were the NFL's darlings of 2011, but when Suh stomped on the arm of Packers guard Evan Dietrich-Smith in front of a national Thanksgiving audience, that reputation soured. The Lions' penchant for penalties (they ranked third in the NFL with 128 accepted against them) and a rough playing style that occasionally bordered on dirty invoked parallels to Motown's Bad Boy Pistons of the late '80s. Though unflattering, this reputation was validating, as it had been more than a decade since people respected the Lions enough to hate their style of play.

On the surface, the Lions defense was more undisciplined than rough and tough. As a unit, it ranked 23rd in both points and yards allowed. But as we know, these stats are often incomplete and misleading. The Lions jumped from 22nd in defensive DVOA in 2010 to ninth in 2011, thanks mainly to the fact that they had the league's best defensive DVOA on third and fourth downs. That said, this was a club that lived and died with its offense. Take out the near-meaningless Week 17 shootout loss at Green Bay and the Lions averaged just 16.0 points per game in defeat versus 35.3 points per game in victory.

Stafford was the driving force behind the surging offense. Staying healthy for the first time in his three-year career, he posted video game numbers and led four fourth-quarter comebacks or game-winning drives. The entire season must have been one giant sigh of relief for Mayhew. For we see now that it's not the defensive line he's actually been building around, but the young quarterback. Mayhew is not looking to

2012 Lions Schedule

Week	Opp.	Week	Opp.	Week	Opp.
1	STL	7	at CHI (Mon.)	13	IND
2	at SF	8	SEA	14	at GB
3	at TEN	9	at JAC	15	at ARI
4	MIN	10	at MIN	16	ATL (Sat.)
5	BYE	11	GB	17	CHI
6	at PHI	12	HOU (Thu.)		

Figure 1. 2011 Detroit DVOA by Week

create the second coming of Chuck Daly's Bad Boys. He's looking to create the second coming of Bill Polian's Colts.

Polian's approach was simple: Invest as many resources as possible into maximizing the abilities of his No. 1 overall drafted quarterback. When Peyton Manning arrived in Indianapolis in 1998, waiting for him was wide receiver Marvin Harrison, whom the previous front office had drafted in the first round two years earlier. Also there was rookie receiving target Jerome Pathon, whom Polian had taken with the team's second draft pick that year (32nd overall). In Manning's second year, Polian spent his first-round pick on running back Edgerrin James.

Fast-forward 11 years. When Stafford arrived in Detroit in 2009, waiting for him was wideout Calvin Johnson, whom previous Lions general manager Matt Millen had selected in the first round in 2007. Also there was rookie receiving target Brandon Pettigrew, whom Mayhew took with Detroit's second pick that year (20th overall). In Stafford's second year, Mayhew spent his first-round pick on running back Jahvid Best.

This isn't to say Indy and Detroit's approaches are exactly parallel. The impact of the players certainly hasn't been. Stafford has played far fewer games than Manning did in his first three years. And Best hasn't been asked to be Edgerrin James, of course.

Best, even when healthy—which he hasn't been since suffering his third concussion in two years last October—isn't even a true featured back. Backs in today's NFL, particularly slashing 200-pounders, are niche players more than workhorses like we saw in the late '90s. Mayhew acknowledged this by spending his 2011 second-round pick on Mikel Leshoure, giving Detroit two high drafted backs. Investing mightily in a dual backfield was something Polian actually did in his later Colts years, when, following the departure of James, he used first-round picks on Joseph Addai in 2006 and then Donald Brown in 2009.

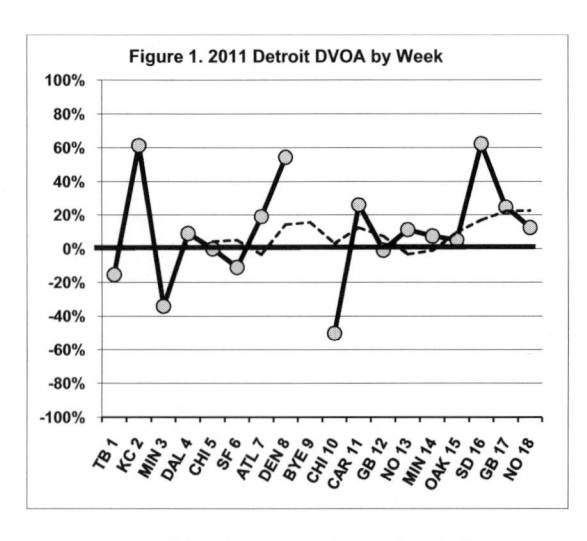

Throughout his 14 years in Indy, Polian never stopped building around Manning, even if the Colts seemingly had needs on defense. If there was so much as a hint of a soft spot looming offensively, Polian addressed it. Hence the first-round picks spent on receiving weapons Reggie Wayne, Dallas Clark, and Anthony Gonzalez, and on offensive tackle Anthony Castonzo. Ensuring that the rock star quarterback had overflowing resources might have left the team with a few extra weaknesses, but it almost always assured that, at the end of the day, opponents had to deal head-on with Indy's greatest strength.

Under this model, the Colts constructed a defense that was schematically simplistic (Tony Dungy's Tampa-2) and often full of young players or fill-in guys in the back seven. Expecting to frequently play with a lead and in shootouts, Polian valued defenders who could simply run well and avoid major mistakes. To hide the soft spots from this vanilla approach, he spent big on pass-rushers Dwight Freeney and Robert Mathis and made sure the Colts had enough defensive line depth to stay fresh for four quarters. An active front four would compensate for an average "rest of the defense."

Mayhew has taken the same approach, only from the inside out. He's stocked the defensive tackle position with stars and sandwiched them with a quality four-man rotation at end. He's made solid but unsexy changes to the speedy linebacking group, and he continues to roll the dice with a subpar secondary. (As in Indianapolis, the star of the secondary is a hard-hitting safety instead of a cornerback, in this case Louis Delmas.) The plan is for all these players to be aided by playing in offensive-oriented contests. Like Polian,

Mayhew continues to address any possible cracks in the offense preemptively. In the last two years, he drafted wideouts Titus Young and Ryan Broyles in the second round and offensive tackle Riley Reiff in the first round.

In all, this leaves Stafford surrounded by six skill position players who were drafted in the first two rounds (Johnson, Young, Broyles, Pettigrew, Leshoure, and Best). He also has viable veteran receiving targets in Nate Burleson and Tony Scheffler. Mayhew's plan is being carried out with tremendous clarity and commitment.

And so the Lions now find themselves in the same position as their fellow Motor City denizens at Chrysler. Having rebounded so emphatically from a downtrodden stretch, they're suddenly facing the unfamiliar challenge of high expectations. The city might not yet be abuzz with Super Bowl chatter, but people aren't just talking hopefully about a mere postseason appearance, either.

However, let's acknowledge how far the Lions still have to go. Yes, this team started 5-0 last season. It also lost seven of its final 12 games, and there are indicators of likely regression on both sides of the ball. Just because Mayhew is working off the Colts blueprint doesn't mean he's built the second coming of the Colts. The plan still has to produce and progress.

Detroit's rise from 22nd to ninth in defensive DVOA is not historic by any means. It doesn't come close to the improvements made last year by Jacksonville and Houston. Nonetheless, even a jump of this moderate size is generally followed by regression towards the mean. Detroit improved last year by 11% defensive DVOA. Since 1992, there are 50 teams that have improved between 9% and 13% in defensive DVOA, a range with the Lions right in the center. The following year, these teams saw their defensive ratings rise (i.e., get worse) by an average of 5% DVOA. The probability of a defensive relapse is even stronger because of the Lions' huge improvement on third downs last year. As we've shown in numerous analyses over the years, teams that are better on third down than they are overall will tend to decline the following season.

On the other side of the ball, the Lions had long expected Stafford to blossom once healthy, but rarely has a young quarterback blossomed by quite so much. Stafford averaged 5.9 yards per attempt if we combine his injury-shortened 2009 and 2010 seasons. He averaged 7.6 yards per attempt in 2011. How likely is Stafford to sustain this big leap forward?

We went through our database looking for quarterbacks who had similarly improved from one year to the next. We limited our search to quarterbacks since 1978 who had three straight seasons with at least 200 pass attempts. There are 55 quarterbacks who qualify and improved by at least 1.0 yards per attempt from one year to the next. In the third season, these quarterbacks saw yards per attempt drop by -.53. There are 26 quarterbacks who qualify and improved by at least 1.2 yards per attempt from one year to the next. In the third season, these quarterbacks saw yards per attempt drop by -.66. Seven of these quarterbacks had four years of experience or less, and they are listed in Table 1.

However, once we compare Stafford to the quarterbacks on that list, we can see why the Lions' signal-caller is more likely to take a small step back than a sizeable one. From a scouting perspective, the most similar quarterbacks to Stafford on that list are Dan Marino and Peyton Manning. Marino only saw his yardage per attempt drop because 9.0 yards per attempt is, frankly, *insane*; the Lions would be perfectly happy if Stafford becomes the quarterback Dan Marino was in 1985. Manning saw his yardage per attempt stay steady after he blossomed in his second season. Stafford, with a strong arm, compact throwing motion, and sufficient reserve of athleticism, might have better raw tools than Manning had. And given the way

Table 1. Young Quarterbacks in Bloom

Player	Team	Years	Year 1	Year 2	Change	Year 3	Change
Drew Brees	SD	2003-2005	5.9	7.9	+2.0	7.2	-0.7
Mark Brunell	JAC	1995-1997	6.3	7.8	+1.6	7.5	-0.3
Brian Griese	DEN	1999-2001	6.7	8.0	+1.3	6.3	-1.7
Peyton Manning	IND	1998-2000	6.5	7.8	+1.3	7.7	0.0
Dan Marino	MIA	1983-1985	7.5	9.0	+1.5	7.3	-1.7
Donovan McNabb	PHI	1999-2001	4.4	5.9	+1.5	6.6	+0.6
Mike Pagel	BALC/IND	1982-1984	5.8	7.2	+1.4	6.7	-0.4

Detroit's offense runs through him—the Lions called passes on a league-leading 67 percent of plays—he might even be on Manning's track.

Of course, there's still a lot of that track to cover before Stafford takes the Lions where Manning took the Colts. Yes, Stafford has been sensational at times. But if he's to be held to superstar standards—which, in Mayhew's plan, he is—then it's fair to say that he's still a tad inconsistent, particularly in his accuracy. His completion percentage was a respectable 63.5 last season, but at times his completions were less effective than they should have been due to erratic ball placement. (47.5 percent of his incomplete passes were listed in our game charting as overthrown, underthrown, thrown ahead, or thrown behind. Only Blaine Gabbert, Cam Newton, and Ben Roethlisberger were higher among regular starting quarterbacks.)

The simplicity of the Lions offense is somewhat striking. There is very little presnap motion or formation versatility. Many of the Lions' route combinations involve rudimentary isolation patterns. In his 10 years as an NFL coach, coordinator Scott Linehan has overseen five different offenses that have ranked in the top 10 in scoring. The fact that he's running a somewhat unsophisticated system in Detroit suggests that he and his staff do not believe the team's key young players can handle much complexity. Whether that's a reflection of Stafford or a reflection of his young receivers is something only the Lions know. Perhaps it's a reflection of both. Regardless, the Lions' youth was apparent last season.

Of course, it's natural for young teams to look young, especially coming off a lockout-condensed offseason. And it's tremendously encouraging that this young offense was as successful as it was. But to continue growing, the Lions will likely have to become more advanced. Stafford will need to be given more presnap responsibilities. This may include more presnap motion and alignment variations, though such tactics are often determined by what a quarterback prefers. Manning, for example, has never liked presnap motion or drastic formation change-ups because, in diagnosing a defense, he prefers to keep the picture as static as possible. That makes sense, but the reason more quarterbacks (including Stafford, most likely) don't do this is they don't have Manning's otherworldly football IQ (less than five quarterbacks in history probably do). Most quarterbacks can't statically dissect a defense all day—they need at least some help from their system.

Thus, to foster mismatches and confuse opponents, many offenses change up their looks and diversify their attack. This is particularly true with teams that have a superstar receiver. The Lions should take note. The numbers don't show it, but opponents at times last season limited Calvin Johnson's impact far too easily. Even when Johnson was producing, he wasn't always dictating the flow of the game the way a player as gifted as he should. Physical press coverage often disrupted his, and thus Detroit's, timing and rhythm. This may have only happened a small handful of times, but Linehan needs to be of the mindset that that's a small handful too much. To make life harder on opponents, the Lions need to use Johnson more in the slot, on the move or on opposite sides of the formation (change up between left and right, weak and strong sides). In the very least, increased diversity will make Johnson more difficult and expensive to double team. Johnson, in turn, needs to aid this diversity by becoming a better intermediary route runner.

It's not all on Johnson; other offensive improvements must be made. Obviously, Stafford must continue to learn from his increasing experience. The front line needs to be at least good enough for the coaches to not fear calling a lot of seven-step drops. Titus Young must mature in all facets. The run game needs to be more of a staple, if for no other reason than to make life a little less stressful for Stafford and his linemen.

With so much high-drafted talent to work with, it's hard to envision improvements not continuing in Detroit. Then again, nothing's easy in the NFL. After all, it took nine years for Polian's near-perfect blueprint to bring a Lombardi Trophy to the Hoosier State.

Andy Benoit

DETROIT LIONS

2011 Lions Stats by Week

Wk	vs.	W-L	PF	PA	YDF	YDA	TO	Total	Off	Def	ST
1	@TB	W	27	20	431	315	1	-15%	4%	7%	-12%
2	KC	W	48	3	411	267	5	61%	6%	-46%	9%
3	@MIN	W	26	23	358	321	0	-34%	-17%	6%	-12%
4	@DAL	W	34	30	303	434	2	9%	-7%	-16%	0%
5	CHI	W	24	13	395	359	-1	0%	37%	37%	0%
6	SF	L	19	25	310	314	2	-11%	-15%	-20%	-16%
7	ATL	L	16	23	263	328	1	19%	0%	-29%	-10%
8	@DEN	W	45	10	376	312	3	55%	35%	-19%	1%
9	BYE										
10	@CHI	L	13	37	393	216	-5	-50%	-50%	-21%	-21%
11	CAR	W	49	35	495	409	1	26%	31%	-18%	-23%
12	GB	L	15	27	409	349	-3	-1%	-2%	-10%	-9%
13	@NO	L	17	31	466	438	-1	11%	34%	14%	-9%
14	MIN	W	34	28	280	425	6	8%	-14%	-20%	2%
15	@OAK	W	28	27	432	477	0	5%	22%	30%	13%
16	SD	W	38	10	440	367	2	62%	38%	-26%	-2%
17	@GB	L	41	45	575	550	-2	25%	26%	9%	7%
18	@NO	L	28	45	412	626	0	13%	35%	25%	2%

Trends and Splits

	Offense	Rank	Defense	Rank
Total DVOA	7.1%	10	-8.1%	9
Unadjusted VOA	10.1%	7	-6.2%	10
Weighted Trend	9.7%	8	-8.6%	13
Variance	4.3%	4	6.1%	18
Average Opponent	2.5%	30	2.4%	7
Passing	20.4%	10	-10.8%	4
Rushing	-4.1%	16	-4.2%	18
First Down	18.4%	4	-7.4%	9
Second Down	4.0%	12	5.0%	20
Third Down	-12.5%	20	-30.1%	1
First Half	0.8%	15	-0.1%	17
Second Half	13.5%	5	15.7%	2
Red Zone	8.3%	5	-5.3%	19
Late and Close	19.7%	6	-11.3%	8

Five-Year Performance

Year	W-L	Pyth	Est W	PF	PA	TO	Total	Rk	Off	Rk	Def	Rk	ST	Rk	Off AGL	Rk	Def AGL	Rk
2007	7-9	5.5	4.9	346	444	-1	-29.0%	29	-10.3%	24	15.2%	32	-3.5%	23	24.5	23	4.7	2
2008	0-16	2.5	2.1	268	517	-9	-48.4%	32	-25.3%	30	24.3%	32	1.3%	15	44.3	27	60.7	32
2009	2-14	2.7	0.0	262	494	-18	-51.6%	32	-28.4%	31	17.9%	32	-5.3%	31	20.4	14	55.1	31
2010	6-10	7.8	7.5	362	369	+4	-1.1%	18	-0.8%	19	2.9%	22	2.6%	11	26.6	16	24.4	17
2011	10-6	10.1	9.4	474	387	+11	10.1%	11	7.1%	10	-8.1%	9	-5.1%	29	13.3	4	14.8	8

2011 Performance Based on Most Common Personnel Groups

Detroit Offense				Detroit Offense vs. Opp.				Detroit Defense				Detroit Defense vs. Opp.			
Pers	Freq	Yds	DVOA	Run%	Pers	Freq	Yds	DVOA	Pers	Freq	Yds	DVOA	Pers	Freq	Yds	DVOA
11	57%	6.0	16.8%	28%	4-2-5	35%	6.1	10.6%	4-3-4	52%	5.2	-11.9%	11	44%	6.0	-15.1%
12	33%	6.4	4.1%	37%	4-3-4	20%	5.8	-2.0%	4-2-5	40%	6.6	-4.1%	12	20%	6.4	11.7%
13	4%	5.3	22.9%	62%	2-4-5	14%	6.4	13.8%	G-line	3%	1.4	-42.8%	21	13%	5.3	-13.9%
01	2%	5.5	21.9%	8%	3-3-5	13%	5.8	29.6%	3-4-4	1%	5.4	30.6%	22	7%	3.0	-54.0%
21	2%	6.5	20.1%	53%	Dime+	10%	6.2	13.1%	3-3-5	1%	6.5	27.1%	13	4%	4.1	-33.4%

Strategic Tendencies

Run/Pass		Rank	Offense		Rank	Pass Rush		Rank	Defense/Other		Rank
Runs, all plays	33%	32	Form: Single Back	81%	2	Rush 3	3.4%	25	4 DB	54%	9
Runs, first half	31%	32	Form: Empty Back	10%	4	Rush 4	77.7%	3	5 DB	42%	18
Runs, first down	43%	30	Pers: 3+ WR	61%	3	Rush 5	11.8%	31	6+ DB	1%	30
Runs, second-long	26%	31	Pers: 4+ WR	3%	17	Rush 6+	7.1%	17	CB by Sides	81%	17
Runs, power sit.	41%	30	Pers: 2+ TE/6+ OL	38%	9	Zone Blitz	2.2%	27	Go for it on 4th	0.79	26
Runs, behind 2H	25%	26	Play action	14%	28	Sacks by LB	12.2%	25	Offensive Pace	29.4	7
Pass, ahead 2H	44%	14	Max protect	7%	28	Sacks by DB	2.4%	26	Defensive Pace	30.5	17

DETROIT LIONS

Detroit used shotgun on 68 percent of offensive plays, the highest rate in NFL history. Shockingly, the Lions were worse in shotgun (4.9% DVOA, 16th) than they were with Matthew Stafford under center (11.0% DVOA, fourth). This doesn't look like a major problem, as the Lions were better in shotgun in 2010. ⬤ Only six percent of Detroit's running back carries came from formations with two players in the backfield, the lowest rate in the league. They averaged a dismal 2.5 yards per carry on these 20 carries, with -41.9% DVOA. ⬤ Detroit's offense was 27th in the league in the first quarter, then ranked fifth from the second quarter on. ⬤ The penalty issue may not just be about the Lions; it may also be about the officials assigned to their games. Detroit had 146 penalties, including declined and offsetting, but their opponents had 149 penalties, the highest figure in the league. ⬤ Surprisingly, given the quality of their defensive line, the Lions were last in the league with just three passes tipped at the line.

Passing

Player	DYAR	DVOA	Plays	NtYds	Avg	YAC	C%	TD	Int
M.Stafford	1170	14.9%	700	4772	6.9	5.3	63.6%	41	16

Rushing

Player	DYAR	DVOA	Plays	Yds	Avg	TD	Fum	Suc
J.Best	38	3.0%	84	390	4.6	2	0	39%
M.Morris*	34	2.1%	80	322	4.0	1	1	48%
K.Smith	42	5.1%	72	356	4.9	4	0	40%
K.Williams	-53	-29.2%	58	194	3.3	2	2	34%
M.Stafford	7	-2.2%	16	83	5.2	0	1	--
J.Harrison*	-12	-26.7%	14	41	2.9	0	0	50%
N.Burleson	58	47.2%	11	85	7.7	0	0	--
S.Logan	13	-14.1%	9	32	3.6	0	0	--

Receiving

Player	DYAR	DVOA	Plays	Ctch	Yds	Y/C	YAC	TD	C%
C.Johnson	570	31.9%	158	96	1680	17.5	5.1	16	61%
N.Burleson	60	-5.7%	110	73	757	10.4	5.5	3	66%
T.Young	70	-2.3%	85	48	607	12.6	2.8	6	56%
B.Pettigrew	-43	-12.6%	126	83	777	9.4	3.7	5	66%
T.Scheffler	66	14.5%	43	26	347	13.3	1.8	6	60%
W.Heller	-32	-43.4%	12	6	42	7.0	3.5	0	50%
J.Best	53	12.0%	40	27	287	10.6	11.4	1	68%
M.Morris*	54	19.0%	35	26	230	8.8	7.7	1	74%
K.Smith	52	19.4%	28	22	180	8.2	8.5	3	79%
K.Williams	34	55.4%	8	8	62	7.8	6.3	0	100%

Offensive Line

Year	Yards	ALY	Rank	Power	Rank	Stuff	Rank	2nd Lev	Rank	Open Field	Rank	F-Start	Cont.
2009	3.72	3.64	29	59%	22	22%	26	1.07	23	0.56	27	24	25
2010	3.46	3.35	32	56%	21	23%	28	1.04	26	0.43	30	22	42
2011	4.22	3.70	31	52%	28	21%	24	1.13	21	0.89	14	19	43

Year	LE	Rank	LT	Rank	Mid	Rank	RT	Rank	RE	Rank	Sacks	ASR	Rank	Short	Long
2009	5.18	6	3.56	28	3.28	31	4.71	3	2.13	32	43	7.0%	21	10	18
2010	4.66	9	3.75	23	3.54	29	2.77	31	1.52	32	27	4.3%	4	10	10
2011	3.67	22	3.65	24	3.71	27	4.22	20	2.44	29	36	5.8%	11	11	19

You wonder if some of Detroit's schematic limitations are due to concerns about the offensive line's pass protection. This unit is not as good as its 2011 numbers suggest. Left tackle Jeff Backus has been a hearty competitor for the past 11 years, but he's 35 and coming off a torn biceps suffered in the wild card loss at New Orleans. Backus was flagged for seven holding penalties last season, tied for third in the NFL, and struggled mightily at times against quality pass-rushers. First-round pick Riley Reiff is obviously Backus' long-term replacement, though Reiff may initially push Gosder Cherilus at right tackle. Cherilus' lack of all-around quickness and penchant for mistakes leaves him regularly on the cusp of being benched. Every season he's told to sit down at least once or twice just due to performance issues.

Inside, guards Rob Sims and Stephen Peterman struggle a bit with power in pass protection, but both are decent enough in the ground game. Peterman is the more mobile run-blocker of the two, which is noteworthy given how important mobility is in a Lions run game that often operates out of single-back sets. Making all the line calls is grizzly veteran center Dominic Raiola. He's not big enough to win a lot of phone booth battles, but he understands the game and is capable of getting out in space. He is, however, nearing his end (he turns 34 on December 30). At this point, there's no plan for succession in place, as top inside backup lineman Dylan Gandy is a far more natural guard.

Defensive Front Seven

Defensive Line	Age	Pos	Plays	TmPct	Rk	Stop	Dfts	BTkl	St%	Rk	AvYd	Rk	Sack	Hit	Hur	Runs	St%	Yds	Pass	St%	Yds
Cliff Avril	26	DE	38	4.5%	51	32	19	5	84%	19	1.3	37	11	6	27	14	79%	4.2	24	88%	-0.5
Ndamukong Suh	25	DT	37	5.0%	23	31	15	2	84%	18	1.4	16	4	7	24	26	85%	2.1	11	82%	-0.2
Kyle Vanden Bosch	34	DE	35	4.2%	59	27	13	3	77%	42	1.4	45	8	8	15.5	26	69%	3.8	9	100%	-5.3
Corey Williams	32	DT	31	3.9%	39	21	6	1	68%	57	2.4	52	2	3	9.5	25	68%	3.1	6	67%	-0.3
Lawrence Jackson	27	DE	26	4.5%	54	22	6	1	85%	18	1.4	44	4.5	5	6.5	21	81%	2.8	5	100%	-4.4
Sammie Lee Hill	26	DT	24	2.9%	60	22	9	1	92%	1	1.1	10	1.5	2	7	22	91%	1.6	2	100%	-4.5
Willie Young	27	DE	15	2.0%	--	13	5	0	87%	--	0.9	--	3	3	13.5	11	82%	2.9	4	100%	-4.8
Nick Fairley	24	DT	15	2.9%	--	10	4	1	67%	--	3.0	--	1	5	3	13	62%	2.8	2	100%	4.5

Linebackers	Age	Pos	Plays	TmPct	Rk	Stop	Dfts	BTkl	AvYd	Sack	Hit	Hur	Runs	St%	Rk	Yds	Rk	Tgts	Suc%	Rk	AdjYd	Rk
Stephen Tulloch	27	MLB	116	13.8%	23	67	18	3	4.6	3	4	6	68	65%	56	3.3	49	25	65%	6	5.9	24
DeAndre Levy	25	OLB	106	12.6%	35	51	19	10	6.1	1	2	3	55	62%	70	3.8	85	41	49%	47	5.9	25
Justin Durant	27	OLB	68	10.0%	55	45	16	5	4.3	1	1	1	35	83%	5	2.1	11	14	32%	--	6.7	--
Bobby Carpenter*	29	OLB	25	3.0%	--	13	4	0	5.2	0	0	1	14	64%	--	3.2	--	12	46%	--	5.7	--

Year	Yards	ALY	Rank	Power	Rank	Stuff	Rank	2nd Lev	Rank	Open Field	Rank
2009	4.66	4.14	18	63%	12	21%	9	1.22	22	1.27	31
2010	4.44	4.07	17	56%	7	20%	13	1.25	26	0.93	23
2011	4.60	3.99	14	52%	5	21%	11	1.23	19	1.16	28

Year	LE	Rank	LT	Rank	Mid	Rank	RT	Rank	RE	Rank	Sacks	ASR	Rank	Short	Long
2009	1.59	1	4.50	24	4.52	26	3.98	14	5.37	30	26	4.4%	30	14	8
2010	3.68	7	3.40	8	4.46	28	4.28	17	3.52	8	44	7.7%	6	14	19
2011	2.22	1	4.74	28	3.69	7	4.42	19	4.62	30	41	6.4%	21	16	16

The Lions' front seven, and particularly the front four, is high on speed and aggression and somewhat low on patience and discipline. It's unusual to see such a high-risk/high-reward style from a defense that plays more Tampa-2 than perhaps any team in the league. The defensive line features a rich eight-man rotation, headlined by the indomitable Ndamukong Suh. He was less consistent as a sophomore than as a rookie, but he remains an overwhelming concern for every offense Detroit will face. Last season, teams became more willing to concede penetration to Suh. Their thinking was that with Detroit's frequent use of wide-9 defensive fronts, inside penetration could be effectively countered with backside pull blocks. In essence, Suh would be taken out of the play by his own over-pursuit.

Expect more offensive approaches like this in 2012. It forces Detroit's linebackers to play with more power, as they must show and fill against the run inside. Detroit can live with this; Stephen Tulloch, DeAndre Levy and Justin Durant are all much better speed and space players than thumpers, but all three have proven capable of providing stout all-around run defense when needed. Overall, this is a quality linebacking corps. In fact, with proficient box safeties like Louis Delmas and Amari Spievey, the Lions actually had a tough run defense in 2011; the reason it ranked a ho-hum 18th in DVOA was that the front seven's aggressive downhill speed too often left them vulnerable to misdirection. It also too often led to over-pursuit or missed tackles. This may explain the drastic split between Detroit's performance between left end and right end runs (first in ALY against left end runs, 30th in ALY against right end runs). In all, the Lions gave up 16 runs of 20-plus yards (tied for fourth most in the NFL) and allowed six runs of 40-plus yards (second most, behind the Rams, who gave up seven).

Of course, Detroit's zone-based defense, like that of the 2000s Colts, is built more to stop the pass than the run. That's why Suh and fellow defensive tackles Corey Williams and Nick Fairley are fire-off-the-ball gap-shooters, and why ends Kyle Vanden Bosch and Cliff Avril (who was franchise-tagged this offseason) align wide and attack upfield. If the Lions' defense can't get pressure from its front four, the whole system fails.

We would be remiss if we didn't also mention defensive end Willie Young, who could make a lot of noise in 2012 depending on how Avril's contract situation shakes out. Young was cut from our annual Top 25 Prospects list when we decided to cap the age at 26, but he brought a ton of pass pressure last year in a limited number of snaps. Under the new SackSEER 2.0 (see page 529), Young's 82.7% SackSEER rating would have been the highest of the entire 2010 draft class regardless of draft position, due to excellent Combine numbers and a high pass-defensed rate at North Carolina State. He's got an explosive initial burst, and while he's a bit undersized, he moves well enough to make that a leverage-gaining advantage as he continues to refine his technique.

Defensive Secondary

Secondary	Age	Pos	Plays	TmPct	Rk	Stop	Dfts	BTkl	Runs	St%	Rk	Yds	Rk	Tgts	Tgt%	Rk	Dist	Suc%	Rk	APaYd	Rk	PD	Int
Eric Wright*	27	CB	91	10.8%	11	41	16	12	14	57%	12	5.6	20	94	21.4%	13	12.1	52%	44	7.2	36	13	4
Amari Spievey	24	SS	72	9.1%	49	24	8	6	34	38%	45	9.1	65	29	7.0%	37	13.1	48%	58	9.4	57	4	3
Chris Houston	28	CB	68	9.2%	24	32	15	2	18	50%	27	15.7	80	83	21.6%	11	13.8	60%	18	7.1	31	12	5
Louis Delmas	25	FS	56	9.7%	44	24	7	8	30	40%	34	9.4	69	21	6.8%	42	15.1	65%	12	6.7	19	3	0
Aaron Berry	24	CB	41	7.1%	--	19	6	2	5	60%	--	3.0	--	37	12.3%	--	12.8	52%	--	7.1	--	8	0
Alphonso Smith	27	CB	27	4.7%	--	10	8	3	2	50%	--	6.0	--	34	11.3%	--	13.8	58%	--	5.8	--	7	3
Brandon McDonald*	27	CB	16	2.3%	--	5	2	1	1	100%	--	3.0	--	13	3.5%	--	12.0	34%	--	11.7	--	1	0
Jacob Lacey	25	CB	74	8.9%	31	30	10	1	19	53%	25	5.1	14	59	16.6%	47	10.0	38%	81	8.0	53	9	1

Year	Pass D Rank	vs. #1 WR	Rk	vs. #2 WR	Rk	vs. Other WR	Rk	vs. TE	Rk	vs. RB	Rk
2009	32	18.2%	22	34.2%	32	11.5%	24	34.2%	30	24.6%	29
2010	19	15.4%	26	-23.4%	2	10.8%	25	23.6%	29	6.9%	20
2011	4	-18.3%	3	-18.5%	5	-4.8%	16	1.1%	9	-12.9%	8

On its best day, this is an average secondary. Safety Louis Delmas is rangy and explosive, but he's a much better box player than centerfielder. Same goes for Amari Spievey, who is basically a less dynamic version of Delmas. Last year, to stabilize the back end of this position, the Lions brought in veteran Erik Coleman, formerly of the Jets and Falcons. He wound up missing the season with an ankle injury. If the 30-year-old can stay healthy, his ability to play both in the box or back deep should fix the safety depth issues that got exposed when Delmas missed five games last season.

When we last saw cornerback Chris Houston, he was getting thrashed by the Saints as he tried to play through an injured shoulder. That tough finish overshadowed what was a decent regular season, but it also underscored the secondary's mediocrity outside. This season Houston is expected to start opposite third-round pick Dwight Bentley (Louisiana-Lafayette), who will replace Eric Wright. Bentley does not have great size and he did not always face elite competition in college. But his draft stock rose after an impressive Senior Bowl showing, where scouts saw that his fluid speed and quickness translated just fine at higher levels of competition. Bentley can play outside as well as slide inside for nickel packages. In line for No. 3 corner duties is Aaron Berry, a finesse player who, like fellow backups Alphonso Smith and ex-Colt Jacob Lacey, has had some bright moments as a mainstream player but not enough of them to make people forget his shortcomings in man coverage. The Lions, of course, hope all these guys can get by with playing frequent off-coverage concepts.

Special Teams

Year	DVOA	Rank	FG/XP	Rank	Net Kick	Rank	Kick Ret	Rank	Net Punt	Rank	Punt Ret	Rank	Hidden	Rank
2009	-4.5%	31	-3.6	23	-9.0	31	-8.0	28	-3.6	24	-2.4	21	-3.5	23
2010	2.2%	11	6.4	5	-1.4	18	10.9	7	-6.8	26	3.7	10	-13.3	29
2011	-4.4%	29	-2.5	21	-8.8	30	-0.6	18	-6.8	26	-7.1	26	-8.6	27

Jason Hanson has been around Detroit long enough to remember the creation of the Model T assembly line. He still has plenty of power and benefits from playing indoors (though four of his five missed field-goal attempts last season came under a roof). This time last year, Hanson was coming off an injury and entering a training camp competition with Dave Rayner. This summer, the job is solely his. Ryan Donahue punted in eight games as a rookie, and had a gross punt value of -5.6 points; pro-rated to an entire season, he would have ranked as the third worst punter in the league. Journeyman veteran Ben Graham replaced Donahue when the rookie pulled a quad at midseason, and the two will compete for the job in 2012. Both kickoff and punt coverage were poor last year, even though the Lions have one of the league's most anonymous special teams studs in John Wendling. Wendling has 64 special teams tackles the past three seasons, 13 more than any other player in the NFL. The tiny (5-foot-6) but electrifying Stefan Logan is slated to handle return duties. He shouldn't face much competition, though last season, coming off an exciting 2010 campaign, Logan failed to register a single punt or kick return longer than 42 yards.

Coaching Staff

Jim Schwartz appears to have his players' backs. In exchange, he gets their respect. This arrangement may be a little too cozy, however, as the Lions lead the NFL in total personal fouls since Schwartz took over in 2009. Schwartz is a defensive coach who has always favored execution over craftiness. In other words, if he has, say, 10 hours of defensive practice time to spend, he's liable to devote 9½ of them to inculcating in his players fundamentals and basic zone technique. Maybe 30 minutes gets dedicated to working on blitz designs or disguised sub-package looks. When Detroit's defense does actually show some wrinkles, chances are that cranky, aggressive throwback coordinator Gunther Cunningham is usually the force behind them. On offense, coordinator Scott Linehan has a lot of autonomy and a natural feel for the passing game. Two of his assistants are ex-NFL players whom you might remember: running backs coach Sam Gash and receivers coach Shawn Jefferson.

Green Bay Packers

2011 Record: 15-1	**2012 Mean Projection:** 11.1 wins
Pythagorean Wins: 12.2 (3rd)	**On the Clock (0-4):** 0%
DVOA: 27.0% (1st)	**Mediocrity (5-7):** 3%
Offense: 33.8% (1st)	**Playoff Contender (8-10):** 32%
Defense: 8.6% (25th)	**Super Bowl Contender (11+):** 64%
Special Teams: 1.8% (8th)	**Postseason Odds:** 88.3%
Variance: 6.7% (3rd)	**Projected Average Opponent:** -5.4% (31st)

2011: Surprisingly one-dimensional, but oh boy, what a dimension.

2012: The clear favorites in the NFC.

Let's start by addressing why this team was unable to defend its Lombardi Trophy in 2011. This part won't take long. The Packers, unlike a lot of unsuccessful defending champions, did not take a step back. They didn't get complacent or "figured out" or anything. They finished the regular season 15-1. *15-1!* Before their Week 15 loss at Kansas City, the Packers were riding a 19-game winning streak—a streak in which 10 of the wins came against playoff teams.

Yet they enter 2012 riding a one-game losing streak because a white-hot Giants team came into Lambeau Field and simply beat them. The Giants didn't do anything tricky. They didn't necessarily lay a blueprint or blaze a new trail. They were just the better team that day.

Giants quarterback Eli Manning took advantage of a 2011 Packers defense that tailed off in the pass-rush department and became strangely susceptible to giving up big plays through the air. The best (or worst) example of this came on the final play of the first half, when the Giants surprised the Packers—though it shouldn't have been that much of a surprise—by heaving a Hail Mary to the end zone. Packers corners Sam Shields and Jarrett Bush absentmindedly stayed with their zone responsibilities on that play instead of just running back to defend the goal line, which was all that mattered in that scenario. This essentially left it up to safety Charlie Peprah to win a jump ball against Hakeem Nicks, which Peprah couldn't do.

On the other side of the ball, New York's tremendous four-man pass rush was able to get to Aaron Rodgers, but that wasn't unusual. The Packers offensive line ranked 23rd in Adjusted Sack Rate last season—and if not for Rodgers' pocket mobility, athleticism and awareness, it would have ranked even worse. The Giants also did a good job applying a physical mixture of man and short-area zone concepts against the Packers receivers, which was a big reason why Rodgers wound up running seven times for 66 yards. The Packers receivers, in turn, helped the Giants by dropping eight passes. Green Bay's running game was not much of a factor and Rodgers uncharacteristically missed two or three big throws that he would normally make. Factor all that together and you get an offense that simply picked the wrong day to suddenly go flat.

The Packers were great in 2011 but certainly did not have a perfect team all season long. They had three games with below-average DVOA during the regular season, and they were particularly stifled by the Kansas City Chiefs when Greg Jennings was out. Their ground game, as the Giants showed, was never anything more than ordinary. Still, very few offenses in NFL history could match this unit when it came to both efficiency and explosiveness. The Packers finished the season with an offensive DVOA of 33.8%, fifth best all-time (Table 1). Their passing DVOA was 67.6%, second only to the 2007 New England Patriots.

GREEN BAY PACKERS

2012 Packers Schedule

Week	Opp.	Week	Opp.	Week	Opp.
1	SF	7	at STL	13	MIN
2	CHI (Thu.)	8	JAC	14	DET
3	at SEA (Mon.)	9	ARI	15	at CHI
4	NO	10	BYE	16	TEN
5	at IND	11	at DET	17	at MIN
6	at HOU	12	at NYG		

Figure 1. 2011 Green Bay DVOA by Week

It all starts with MVP Aaron Rodgers, obviously. Rodgers' own passing DVOA of 46.6% was the fourth-best since 1991. Rodgers is gifted with great arm strength, both in terms of distance and velocity. He has pinpoint accuracy, including from multiple platforms and on the move, along with superb all-around athleticism and pocket mechanics, which allow him to buy time under pressure. But he's not only the most gifted all-round passer in football; he's also one of the game's true masterminds. Rodgers manipulates defenses with hard counts and pre-snap adjustments as astutely as any quarterback in the league. He also has an unparalleled ability to adjust and improvise after the snap. This comes from an innate understanding of how to play the game (lazy analysts inadvertently refer to this frequently, calling it the "it factor") and, more directly, a rich understanding of Mike McCarthy's system.

McCarthy's is a special system. It features a diverse array of formations, many of which can be disguised in the huddle, thanks to the versatility of über-athletic tight end Jermichael Finley. The Packers may line up with three receivers and a tight end on one play; two fullbacks, a running back and two tight ends on the next play; four receivers and a back on the following play; and then base personnel on the play after that.

It's not just the breadth of diversity, it's the volume of the diversity. The Packers do a tremendous job at creating mismatches for players by realigning personnel within the same formations throughout a game. Their wide receivers benefit greatly from this. Greg Jennings, for example, draws an inordinate amount of one-on-one coverage because he's often aligned in the slot or as the lone receiver on the weak side of a spread formation (think a 3x1 set). In a lot of these instances, based on alignment, teams cannot double Jennings without facing blatant one-on-one matchups in at least two other locations. For a defense, that's problematic because players like Finley, Nelson and, to some extent still, Donald Driver, can't be easily defended one-on-one.

McCarthy also designs route options that maximize catch-and-run opportunities, and the Packers were fourth in the NFL with an average of 6.0 yards after catch. One might think that, with the NFL becoming more pass-friendly, powerful offensive teams would stretch the field vertically. In reality, the field stretches horizontally. Horizontal throws are shorter, quicker and easier to spot, making them the perfect response to complex defensive schemes (or any defensive schemes). The Packers understand this as well as any team, and they've trained their quarterback and receivers accordingly. Consequently, the quarterback and those receivers have developed extraordinary chemistry, which allows normally complicated things like option routes, back-shoulder throws and site adjustments to become common features of this offense.

Coming off the 2010 Super Bowl, we waxed as poetically about Dom Capers' defense as we're waxing

Table 1. Best Offensive DVOA, 1991-2011

Year	Team	Off DVOA	Year	Team	Pass Off DVOA
2007	NE	43.5%	2007	NE	72.7%
2010	NE	42.2%	2004	IND	67.6%
2002	KC	35.4%	**2011**	**GB**	**67.6%**
1998	DEN	34.5%	2010	NE	67.5%
2011	**GB**	**33.8%**	1991	WAS	65.0%
2003	KC	33.4%	2009	SD	59.6%
1992	SF	33.1%	2006	IND	55.4%
2011	**NO**	**33.0%**	**2011**	**NE**	**55.3%**
2011	**NE**	**31.9%**	2003	TEN	54.7%
2004	IND	31.8%	2009	NE	53.5%

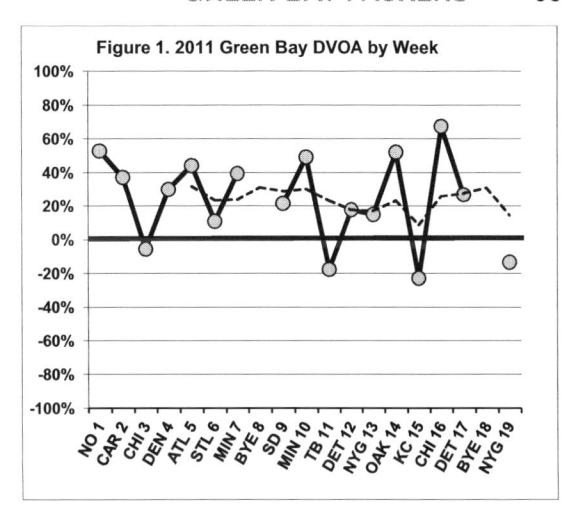

here about McCarthy's offense. That changed last season, though. As mentioned earlier (and as seen by football fans nationwide), the Packers struggled to generate a consistent pass rush in 2011. We recorded Green Bay with pass pressure on just 14.6 percent of pass plays, the lowest rate in the league. And a lot of Capers' Byzantine blitzes simply didn't work; the Packers allowed an average of 8.2 yards on pass plays that our game charters marked as "zone blitzes," as opposed to 7.3 yards otherwise. As a result, Green Bay's secondary got strained and exploited.

The Packers hope that the selection of USC pass-rushing guru Nick Perry in the first round will assuage some of these problems. (We think it will; as you'll learn later in the book, our SackSEER projection system lists Perry as the best edge-rusher prospect in this year's draft class.) However, when it comes to the rest of the defense, they have no choice but to carry on with the program and treat 2011 as an aberration. There weren't a lot of holes on this roster to fill. Charles Woodson is still a superstar. Sam Shields and Tramon Williams are more talented man-defenders than 90 percent of their cornerbacking peers. The middle of the field is manned by safeties and inside linebackers who are just average but certainly not below that. Up front, Clay Matthews is Clay Matthews, B.J. Raji is too talented to fade away as often as he did last season, and the depth around both stars is stellar. This is a loaded defense, and they play in a system that is diverse, complex and big-play oriented.

They also play for a team that is offense-oriented. There are generally two ways teams with great offenses approach defense. One way is to adopt a vanilla scheme that features a star or two but, overall, allows you to make do with fairly mundane players who only have to be good at not screwing up. The Lions take this approach; the Colts took it during the Bill Polian era. The thinking here is that you'll give up some points and yards, but at some point, the opposing offense will inevitably have a few hiccups of which you'll be prepared to take advantage. At the same time, your offense will be keeping the pace of the game up.

The other approach is to build a high-risk, high-reward defense. Because your resources are lopsidedly invested in the offense, you're stuck with mostly average-at-best defensive players. The hope is that an aggressive, attacking scheme can compensate for those players' shortcomings. Teams that do this generally don't have the one or two stars that the vanilla defensive teams have. A good example would be Gregg Williams' Saints or, to a certain degree, Jim Johnson's Eagles of the early 2000s. (Those were solid units, but Brian Dawkins was the only *indisputable* star.) The thinking with these teams is that you'll give up big plays and get gashed at times, but you'll make up for it with a few big plays of your own (sacks, turnovers, blitzing to get a big third down stop, etc.), which, with a juggernaut offense, can lead to multi-score swings with which your opponent can't keep up.

This is the approach the Packers take. What's remarkable, though, is that they're not hiding an average unit. They're hiding a half-average unit that is brilliant in several spots. There are four genuine stars on this defense (Matthews and Woodson, who are both superstars, plus Williams and Raji). Statistically, the Packers defense was lower-echelon in 2011, but the talent they have suggests they're much closer to the top echelon. They're almost like a B-grade version of the Ravens (which is a compliment). But because the Packers offense is so explosive, this defense gets stuck in a lot of shootouts. A team with an inconsistent pass rush is going to take a lot of bullets in a shootout. If the Packers' pass rush were to regain its form, Green Bay would be able to withstand a rash of injuries or unexpected regression from the offense and still remain the best team in the NFC.

This isn't a groundbreaking development. We all saw this same Packers defense in 2010 when it ranked second in DVOA and won the Super Bowl. Maybe the whole point here is just a simple reminder: The Green Bay Packers, on both sides of the ball, are frighteningly stacked.

Andy Benoit

GREEN BAY PACKERS

2011 Packers Stats by Week

Wk	vs.	W-L	PF	PA	YDF	YDA	TO	Total	Off	Def	ST
1	NO	W	42	34	399	477	1	53%	52%	-10%	-9%
2	@CAR	W	30	23	419	475	3	37%	26%	-13%	-2%
3	@CHI	W	27	17	392	291	0	-5%	16%	19%	-2%
4	DEN	W	49	23	507	384	2	30%	50%	17%	-4%
5	@ATL	W	25	14	426	251	1	44%	34%	-8%	2%
6	STL	W	24	3	399	424	0	11%	40%	20%	-9%
7	@MIN	W	33	27	421	435	1	40%	34%	11%	17%
8	BYE										
9	@SD	W	45	38	368	460	3	22%	34%	11%	-1%
10	MIN	W	45	7	356	266	0	49%	29%	2%	23%
11	TB	W	35	26	378	455	1	-18%	19%	40%	3%
12	@DET	W	27	15	349	409	3	18%	21%	0%	-3%
13	@NYG	W	38	35	449	447	1	15%	30%	12%	-3%
14	OAK	W	46	16	391	357	4	52%	5%	-26%	22%
15	@KC	L	14	19	315	438	0	-23%	16%	35%	-4%
16	CHI	W	35	21	363	441	2	67%	76%	16%	7%
17	DET	W	45	41	550	575	2	27%	55%	19%	-9%
18	BYE										
19	NYG	L	20	37	388	420	-3	-13%	-5%	16%	8%

Trends and Splits

	Offense	Rank	Defense	Rank
Total DVOA	33.8%	1	8.6%	25
Unadjusted VOA	34.1%	1	7.8%	23
Weighted Trend	33.0%	2	12.1%	27
Variance	7.3%	14	3.7%	4
Average Opponent	1.7%	26	-2.1%	22
Passing	67.6%	1	10.6%	24
Rushing	5.5%	7	5.6%	29
First Down	22.6%	3	21.4%	31
Second Down	33.9%	2	-6.9%	10
Third Down	58.5%	2	6.6%	21
First Half	33.0%	2	7.9%	26
Second Half	34.7%	1	9.4%	26
Red Zone	29.6%	3	-10.3%	14
Late and Close	52.2%	1	-3.6%	13

Five-Year Performance

Year	W-L	Pyth	Est W	PF	PA	TO	Total	Rk	Off	Rk	Def	Rk	ST	Rk	Off AGL	Rk	Def AGL	Rk
2007	13-3	11.7	11.1	435	291	+4	19.8%	5	15.7%	5	-1.2%	16	3.0%	8	7.6	2	17.1	12
2008	6-10	9.0	8.6	419	380	+7	9.2%	11	7.3%	11	-2.5%	12	-0.5%	19	12.5	6	37.2	26
2009	11-5	12.0	11.0	461	297	+24	29.1%	2	18.8%	5	-17.7%	2	-7.5%	32	22.4	15	25.3	16
2010	10-6	12.1	10.9	388	240	+10	23.0%	4	11.5%	7	-13.9%	2	-2.4%	26	40.4	28	45.9	29
2011	15-1	12.2	13.3	560	359	+24	27.00%	1	33.8%	1	8.6%	25	1.8%	8	21.3	11	37.5	22

2011 Performance Based on Most Common Personnel Groups

Green Bay Offense				Green Bay Offense vs. Opp.				Green Bay Defense				Green Bay Defense vs. Opp.			
Pers	Freq	Yds	DVOA	Run%	Pers	Freq	Yds	DVOA	Pers	Freq	Yds	DVOA	Pers	Freq	Yds	DVOA
11	47%	7.8	55.2%	18%	4-2-5	43%	6.9	41.9%	2-4-5	61%	6.3	2.2%	11	48%	6.4	8.4%
21	14%	7.5	46.9%	55%	4-3-4	32%	6.3	29.2%	3-4-4	27%	6.8	19.8%	12	19%	6.1	-6.0%
12	13%	6.5	34.9%	40%	Dime+	12%	8.3	88.4%	Dime+	7%	6.8	16.8%	21	13%	6.8	42.8%
22	9%	5.9	14.9%	75%	3-3-5	6%	9.1	79.0%	4-4-3	2%	5.6	-16.7%	22	5%	7.6	12.8%
01	5%	6.5	64.1%	2%	3-4-4	2%	6.8	49.5%	G-line	1%	0.2	10.5%	10	4%	7.8	74.8%

Strategic Tendencies

Run/Pass		Rank	Offense		Rank	Pass Rush		Rank	Defense/Other		Rank
Runs, all plays	38%	25	Form: Single Back	58%	22	Rush 3	14.1%	3	4 DB	27%	32
Runs, first half	32%	31	Form: Empty Back	8%	8	Rush 4	43.9%	31	5 DB	63%	2
Runs, first down	47%	24	Pers: 3+ WR	59%	5	Rush 5	36.3%	1	6+ DB	7%	16
Runs, second-long	31%	21	Pers: 4+ WR	7%	6	Rush 6+	5.7%	25	CB by Sides	72%	21
Runs, power sit.	39%	32	Pers: 2+ TE/6+ OL	28%	25	Zone Blitz	9.9%	4	Go for it on 4th	0.96	13
Runs, behind 2H	36%	5	Play action	22%	9	Sacks by LB	63.8%	7	Offensive Pace	29.7	8
Pass, ahead 2H	53%	1	Max protect	11%	15	Sacks by DB	15.5%	3	Defensive Pace	30.8	23

GREEN BAY PACKERS

The more pass rushers you send at Aaron Rodgers, the better he plays: 6.2 yards per pass against three, 8.5 against four, 9.0 against five, and 10.7 against six or more. Rodgers was out of the pocket on 17 percent of pass plays and had 8.1 yards per play with 64.4% DVOA on these plays (including passes, sacks, and scrambles). Green Bay was one of two teams we never saw using an extra offensive lineman. Only 6.5 percent of Packers offensive drives ended in a turnover, the third-lowest figure in our drive stats data that goes back to 1997. The Packers led the league with 91.1% DVOA on running back screens, and were second with 9.3 yards per pass. Perhaps because they had trouble getting pressure with just four pass rushers, the Packers defense was much better when blitzing. The Packers allowed 8.0 yards per pass with three or four pass rushers, but 6.7 yards per pass with five or more. In a related stat, the Packers secondary did a much better job when they had the help of pass pressure. If we remove sacks and scrambles to look only at actual passes where we marked pass pressure, the Packers ranked second in the league with -53.5% DVOA, trailing only Chicago.

Passing

Player	DYAR	DVOA	Plays	NtYds	Avg	YAC	C%	TD	Int
A.Rodgers	2059	46.6%	537	4438	8.4	5.9	68.7%	45	6
M.Flynn*	225	47.3%	54	496	9.4	6.9	67.3%	6	2

Rushing

Player	DYAR	DVOA	Plays	Yds	Avg	TD	Fum	Suc
R.Grant*	63	2.9%	134	561	4.2	2	1	46%
J.Starks	22	-4.5%	132	572	4.3	1	2	49%
A.Rodgers	71	18.7%	48	269	5.6	3	0	--
J.Kuhn	5	-5.7%	30	78	2.6	4	0	43%
B.Saine	0	-8.8%	18	69	3.8	0	0	61%

Receiving

Player	DYAR	DVOA	Plays	Ctch	Yds	Y/C	YAC	TD	C%
G.Jennings	275	20.5%	101	67	949	14.2	4.1	9	66%
J.Nelson	517	52.5%	96	68	1263	18.6	6.0	15	71%
D.Driver	132	17.1%	56	37	445	12.0	3.7	6	66%
J.Jones	234	41.1%	55	38	635	16.7	7.1	7	69%
R.Cobb	127	42.1%	31	25	375	15.0	7.5	1	81%
J.Finley	163	18.0%	92	55	767	13.9	4.1	8	60%
T.Crabtree	1	-6.3%	8	6	38	6.3	3.3	1	75%
J.Starks	39	6.4%	38	30	225	7.5	9.3	0	79%
R.Grant*	99	56.4%	24	19	268	14.1	14.5	1	79%
J.Kuhn	20	2.5%	18	15	77	5.1	4.1	2	83%
B.Saine	11	3.9%	12	10	69	6.9	7.7	0	83%

Offensive Line

Year	Yards	ALY	Rank	Power	Rank	Stuff	Rank	2nd Lev	Rank	Open Field	Rank	F-Start	Cont.
2009	4.17	4.28	9	73%	3	15%	2	1.04	26	0.73	17	19	29
2010	3.52	3.82	23	55%	25	18%	12	0.88	31	0.44	29	20	42
2011	4.06	4.05	17	61%	21	21%	25	1.15	18	0.63	26	28	30

Year	LE	Rank	LT	Rank	Mid	Rank	RT	Rank	RE	Rank	Sacks	ASR	Rank	Short	Long
2009	2.83	30	3.76	24	4.71	1	4.26	11	4.83	5	51	8.6%	30	17	24
2010	2.54	31	3.97	21	4.34	8	4.07	18	3.10	27	38	7.2%	21	10	15
2011	3.57	24	4.12	19	4.36	8	4.61	11	3.42	18	41	7.4%	23	13	19

This is a fairly average unit, but average is all you need when you have a quarterback who can dissect and manipulate a defense as effectively as Aaron Rodgers does. Rodgers, in fact, is so good in this sense that the Packers rarely give tight end help to protect his blind side even if the starting left tackle is a young player who needs help (like say, oh, Marshall Newhouse). With Chad Clifton finally done, Newhouse will likely get the starting job in 2012, as 2011 first-rounder Derek Sherrod is raw and coming off a late-December broken leg.

At right tackle is former first-round pick Bryan Bulaga, who has improved steadily over his first two years in the league. Word out of Green Bay is there are no plans to move Bulaga to guard or left tackle. That's wise. More teams need to realize that a successful right tackle is a plus, not an opportunity to reshuffle your line. Inside, storied veteran Jeff Saturday came aboard as a free agent after the front office decided it wasn't worth spending big money to bring back Scott Wells. This was a risky move; Saturday is highly respected, but he's essentially an older and less dynamic version of Wells. As he ages, he'll only continue to have more trouble blocking powerful nose tackles "in a phone booth."

Right guard Josh Sitton had an unspectacular 2011 campaign after being arguably the best NFL player at his position in 2010. However, as long as Sitton makes just a few less mistakes in pass protection, he'll regain his Pro Bowl form. As a run-blocker, he's uncommonly powerful when delivering on-the-move blows at the second level. Utility lineman T.J. Lang doesn't need the kind of help at left guard that he used to require when lining up outside. He should be able to stay ahead of Evan Dietrich-Smith on the depth chart.

Defensive Front Seven

Defensive Line	Age	Pos	Plays	TmPct	Rk	Stop	Dfts	BTkl	St%	Rk	AvYd	Rk	Sack	Hit	Hur	Runs	St%	Yds	Pass	St%	Yds
Ryan Pickett	33	DE	35	4.8%	44	27	5	0	77%	42	2.5	73	0	0	0.5	31	81%	2.2	4	50%	5.3
C.J. Wilson	25	DE	26	3.1%	74	18	4	0	69%	69	3.5	79	0	0	1	24	71%	3.2	2	50%	7.0
B.J. Raji	26	DT	24	2.9%	59	17	4	0	71%	55	1.8	31	3	0	10	18	67%	2.7	6	83%	-1.0
Jarius Wynn	26	DE	18	2.1%	--	15	7	3	83%	--	0.7	--	3	0	6	11	91%	1.0	7	71%	0.3
Anthony Hargrove	29	DT	16	2.0%	--	13	6	0	81%	--	-0.3	--	3	2	5	10	90%	1.4	6	67%	-3.0

Linebackers	Age	Pos	Plays	TmPct	Rk	Stop	Dfts	BTkl	AvYd	Sack	Hit	Hur	Runs	St%	Rk	Yds	Rk	Tgts	Suc%	Rk	AdjYd	Rk
Desmond Bishop	28	ILB	116	17.0%	9	45	16	4	6.8	5	4	4	67	45%	111	5.5	111	46	31%	78	9.6	73
A.J. Hawk	28	ILB	85	11.6%	43	44	11	6	4.9	1.5	1	5.5	51	55%	94	3.7	76	27	58%	14	6.2	27
Erik Walden	27	OLB	61	7.3%	91	29	11	3	5.2	3	15	9	39	49%	107	4.5	106	12	53%	--	7.9	--
Clay Matthews	26	OLB	58	7.4%	90	44	20	3	1.6	6	23	27.5	33	79%	10	1.6	3	14	64%	--	5.3	--
D.J. Smith	23	ILB	34	4.1%	--	15	5	2	4.8	0	0	3	21	52%	--	4.2	--	13	50%	--	4.3	--
Robert Francois	27	ILB	19	3.3%	--	9	5	2	5.0	0	0	0	6	50%	--	4.2	--	16	47%	51	5.0	10

Year	Yards	ALY	Rank	Power	Rank	Stuff	Rank	2nd Lev	Rank	Open Field	Rank
2009	3.59	3.62	3	68%	21	26%	1	1.03	3	0.50	5
2010	4.02	4.26	21	46%	2	18%	21	1.11	15	0.44	5
2011	4.49	4.50	29	67%	24	16%	30	1.30	27	0.70	12

Year	LE	Rank	LT	Rank	Mid	Rank	RT	Rank	RE	Rank	Sacks	ASR	Rank	Short	Long
2009	3.80	12	4.02	13	3.47	3	3.78	10	3.54	7	37	6.0%	19	6	21
2010	4.58	21	4.82	28	4.03	21	4.60	25	4.00	16	47	8.1%	4	15	24
2011	5.86	32	3.75	11	4.29	22	4.75	27	3.92	22	29	4.8%	32	6	16

This unit was tremendous in 2010 but wildly up-and-down in 2011, partly due to inconsistency from stars Clay Matthews and B.J. Raji. Matthews, with his stunning edge-quickness and supple leverage, is elite in every sense. Last season, even when injuries caused his production to dip at times, he still impacted games in ways that the stats don't show. He also improved as an all-around run-defender. However, the Packers discovered that when Matthews was having an off day, they didn't have the pass-rushing talent elsewhere to compensate. Ted Thompson aimed to change that in April by using his first-round pick on USC's Nick Perry. Perry is expected to instantly beat out athletic but generally very average veterans Erik Walden and Brad Jones for a starting spot. Scouts like Perry's violent hands as an edge rusher, and with his lateral agility in confined areas, he might be a better run defender than expected. A.J. Hawk and Desmond Bishop return as the starting inside linebackers. Hawk has fixed some of his pass coverage shortcomings and, when conditions are sound, he's a pretty good read-and-react run-defender. Overall, though, he's not what you'd expect a former No. 5 overall pick to be. Bishop can be a tad hit-or-miss, but he fits in Dom Capers' scheme because he's one of the better blitzing inside linebackers in football.

Because the Packers use so many nickel groupings and other sub packages, they lined up in a two-man front on 66 percent of defensive plays last year. That was almost twice as often as second-place Arizona at 37 percent.

The two-man front works, but only when Raji is playing like a man-and-a-half. Towards the end of last season, he was much closer to being just one regular man, if not .95 of a man. But Packers fans need not worry about the fourth-year pro. He has the explosiveness and size to be the NFC's version of Haloti Ngata; it's just a matter of consistently tapping into that.

Because 2010 second-round pick Mike Neal has not panned out, Ted Thompson felt it necessary to use his 2012 second-round pick on Michigan State underclassman Jerel Worthy, whom some have compared to Ryan Pickett. Worthy dropped to the second round after a ho-hum Combine showing, but that shouldn't override his body of work in college. When he improved his stamina as a junior at Michigan State, he was a double-team commanding load. Outside of Pickett and Raji, the Packers like to rotate front-line defenders, so Worthy will share playing time with Jarius Wynn, Anthony Hargrove (after he serves an eight-game suspension for his alleged role in the Saints bounty scandal), fourth-round rookie Mike Daniels (Iowa) and either incumbent backup C.J. Wilson or ex-Dolphin Philip Merling. All the veterans listed here are able but not overwhelming run defenders.

Defensive Secondary

Secondary	Age	Pos	Plays	TmPct	Rk	Stop	Dfts	BTkl	Runs	St%	Rk	Yds	Rk	Tgts	Tgt%	Rk	Dist	Suc%	Rk	APaYd	Rk	PD	Int
Morgan Burnett	23	FS	115	13.7%	7	36	13	6	44	30%	59	9.0	63	37	7.2%	36	12.5	60%	27	6.4	14	10	3
Charlie Peprah	29	SS	103	12.3%	14	29	15	7	39	28%	61	5.6	11	45	8.8%	19	12.6	47%	59	10.2	65	10	5
Charles Woodson	36	CB	92	11.7%	5	44	21	9	34	47%	34	5.4	18	70	14.6%	62	10.7	56%	25	5.9	12	18	7
Tramon Williams	29	CB	86	10.9%	10	35	13	7	13	31%	60	7.1	43	102	21.1%	15	15.3	52%	46	9.4	71	22	4
Sam Shields	25	CB	52	6.6%	64	18	9	8	6	33%	53	8.7	59	71	14.8%	60	12.4	47%	62	7.5	42	13	4
Jarrett Bush	28	CB	28	3.3%	--	11	4	2	5	40%	--	5.2	--	31	5.9%	--	13.4	52%	--	9.0	--	7	2

Year	Pass D Rank	vs. #1 WR	Rk	vs. #2 WR	Rk	vs. Other WR	Rk	vs. TE	Rk	vs. RB	Rk
2009	4	-29.2%	6	-5.0%	15	-17.1%	8	-21.7%	3	-12.4%	7
2010	1	-23.5%	3	-18.5%	5	-24.6%	4	12.8%	22	-15.7%	5
2011	23	14.1%	20	-16.2%	7	-28.2%	4	23.2%	26	1.4%	18

The declining pass rush played a huge role in the Packers' pass defense DVOA falling from No. 1 in 2010 to No. 23 in 2011. Without pressure up front, most corners, even outside man-to-man artists as gifted as Sam Shields and Tramon Williams, are bound to give up a few big plays eventually. It didn't help that Shields and Williams were missing rangy centerfielder Nick Collins, who went down last September with a career-threatening neck injury. Collins, still not healthy, was released over the offseason, so Morgan Burnett and Charlie Peprah are once again the starting safeties. Both can play in space or in the box, but in a scheme as demanding as Dom Capers', both need to be more consistent in all facets of the game. (A few opponents, particularly the Giants, were game-planning specifically to attack Peprah last season.)

It seems like every offseason someone floats the idea of Charles Woodson moving to safety. Woodson certainly has the football IQ and tackling prowess for this, but in this scheme, the slot corner is a far more valuable position than safety – and slot corner is a role Woodson fills perfectly. He's capable of handling man-to-man coverage inside (and outside, when the Packers are in a traditional 3-4) and he might be an even better blitzer and run-stopper than pass-defender. Few, if any, players in the NFL understand better than Woodson how to disrupt offensive concepts simply through angles and positioning. This is what makes him mountains better than his younger, respectable backup, Jarrett Bush. If Woodson ever does hit his wall, the Packers hope that this year's second-round pick, Casey Hayward, can fill his shoes. The Vanderbilt product is sort of a B+ in every way: 5-foot-11, fast but not elite, a willing tackler with imperfect technique, and experienced playing man and zone and both outside and in the slot.

Special Teams

Year	DVOA	Rank	FG/XP	Rank	Net Kick	Rank	Kick Ret	Rank	Net Punt	Rank	Punt Ret	Rank	Hidden	Rank
2009	-6.3%	32	-6.1	26	-8.3	30	-3.4	16	-17.4	32	-2.1	20	-1.8	18
2010	-2.1%	26	-0.1	17	-7.0	27	-6.1	23	3.5	15	-2.4	20	-5.7	22
2011	1.5%	8	3.0	12	1.4	15	3.1	8	-2.2	18	3.8	9	-2.8	18

In the return game, Randall Cobb (a.k.a. Antwaan Randall Cobb) has the potential to be a weapon who strikes the type of fear in opposing kickers and punters that swings field position. At the same time, he can make his own coaches just as fearful and swing field position negatively, as fumbles have been a bit of a problem and his habit of taking out kickoffs from very deep in the end zone could eventually come back to bite him.

Despite outstanding depth, the Packers did not have any particularly dominant special teams players in 2011 except for Cobb. Mason Crosby has a strong enough leg to kick from distance in inclement Wisconsin weather. However, accuracy has been somewhat of an issue for him since he came into the league as a sixth-round pick. Last season was the first time in Crosby's five-year career that his field goal success rate was more than 80 percent. He also had positive gross kickoff value for the first time since his rookie season. Punter Tim Masthay was worth 2.5 estimated points of field position last season, but the Packers' net punting value was down due to Green Bay's somewhat shaky coverage units. Fortunately when your quarterback is Aaron Rodgers, punting isn't a major concern. Backup linebackers D.J. Smith and Brad Jones led the club with 10 special teams tackles.

Coaching Staff

The only reason Mike McCarthy is not regarded as an industry superstar is that he's not particularly loquacious or photogenic. His body of work puts him easily in football's top echelon of head coaches. McCarthy is the mastermind behind Green Bay's somewhat-hybrid spread West Coast offense. He's a shrewd game manager and, from what we can tell, a respected locker room voice. McCarthy also has a very good staff, which afforded a lot of benefit of the doubt to his former offensive coordinator, Joe Philbin, during the Dolphins' head coaching search. Promoted to Philbin's job was highly regarded former quarterbacks coach Tom Clements; promoted to Clements' job was rising young assistant Ben McAdoo. Defensively, coordinator Dom Capers has a lot of autonomy; he's practically the head coach on that side of the ball. Assistant head coach Winston Moss (who is in charge of linebackers) has been considered for several head coaching vacancies in recent years, as has secondary coach Darren Perry. Also on staff is five-time Pro Bowl outside linebacker Kevin Greene, who coaches—what else?—outside linebackers.

Houston Texans

2011 Record: 10-6

Pythagorean Wins: 10.9 (7th)

DVOA: 18.6% (5th)

Offense: 8.4% (9th)

Defense: -9.5% (6th)

Special Teams: 0.7% (13th)

Variance: 16.4% (23rd)

2012 Mean Projection: 8.8 wins

On the Clock (0-4): 4%

Mediocrity (5-7): 23%

Playoff Contender (8-10): 52%

Super Bowl Contender (11+): 21%

Postseason Odds: 59.1%

Projected Average Opponent: 2.1% (12th)

2011: It's a brand new era, it feels great.

2012: It's a brand new era, did it come too late?

This one doesn't take a rocket scientist.

Through the first ten weeks of the NFL season, the Texans offense continued to perform at the lofty heights it reached in 2010. Even with Andre Johnson sidelined for much of the year, Matt Schaub and Arian Foster carved up defenses to the tune of a 24.9% DVOA, good for fourth in the NFL at the time of Schaub's injury and very much in line with the 21.7% DVOA the unit posted the previous season.

The difference was all in the defense. The Texans made the sixth-biggest defensive improvement of any team in the DVOA era (Table 1), catapulting themselves from a sideshow seesaw team that could blow or achieve a lead at any moment to one of the most dangerous teams in the NFL. Until Albert Haynesworth, in his one moment of actual effort for the season, forced Schaub's season-ending Lisfranc surgery on a quarterback dive, the Texans were very much in the Super Bowl conversation due to that improvement on defense.

The seeds for Houston's glorious return to the national football scene were sown in the abbreviated 2011 offseason. After years of watching an above-average offense get tripped up by a defense that peaked at mediocre in 2009, owner Bob McNair and general manager Rick Smith finally broke the cycle. They stopped combing through dumpster bins for defensive backs and hiring defensive coordinators that Gary Kubiak personally admired, and instead broke out McNair's Visa at DuhMart to secure the services of Wade Phillips, Johnathan Joseph, and Danieal Manning. Football Outsiders takes a lot of pride in being able to pinpoint the little things that make up a big season—the strength of schedule, avoidance of major injuries, and so on—but a turnaround this monumental wasn't built on little things. This defense improved from next-to-last in DVOA in 2010 to sixth last year mostly because they paired a massive coaching upgrade with one of the five most talented corners in the NFL and improved safety play.

Table 1: Ten Biggest Defensive Improvements in DVOA Era (1991-2011)

Year	Team	Prev Yr DVOA	DVOA	Change	Next Yr DVOA
1998	MIA	11.7%	-22.4%	-34.1%	-9.4%
2009	DEN	20.7%	-9.8%	-30.5%	16.6%
1998	OAK	14.4%	-15.2%	-29.6%	-5.6%
2011	JAC	17.7%	-11.3%	-29.0%	??
2011	HOU	17.5%	-9.5%	-27.0%	??
2001	STL	14.9%	-11.7%	-26.6%	-4.5%
1996	DEN	10.5%	-15.3%	-25.8%	-5.9%
2009	NYJ	-0.8%	-25.5%	-24.7%	-10.9%
1996	GB	5.3%	-19.3%	-24.6%	-10.6%
2001	CLE	9.8%	-13.1%	-22.9%	-5.1%
Averages		12.2%	-15.3%	-27.5%	-4.4%

2012 Texans Schedule

Week	Opp.	Week	Opp.	Week	Opp.
1	MIA	7	BAL	13	at TEN
2	at JAC	8	BYE	14	at NE (Mon.)
3	at DEN	9	BUF	15	IND
4	TEN	10	at CHI	16	MIN
5	at NYJ (Mon.)	11	JAC	17	at IND
6	GB	12	at DET (Thu.)		

Figure 1. 2011 Houston DVOA by Week

So, that wasn't too complicated. The Texans didn't get to complete their dream run because of Schaub's injury, but they still managed to spank Cincinnati on Wild Card Weekend before fifth-round rookie T.J. Yates, their third quarterback, turned into a pumpkin in the divisional round against Baltimore. Schaub is expected to make a complete recovery, and so things looked all set up for the Texans to finish the job next year.

Then the credit card bill arrived in the mail, so to speak, and the Texans were right up against the salary cap limit. That's the tricky thing about those big free-agent signings: There's only so much room to re-sign the players you like when you have to spend big money rectifying situations because other players didn't work out. In Joseph's case, it was necessary because Dunta Robinson never fully recovered from a gruesome 2007 injury where his hamstring tore completely off the bone, and Smith smartly decided to let the veteran walk in free agency. In Manning's case, it was necessary because Manning was the most accomplished safety the Texans had ever employed the second he signed his contract.

So the Texans had themselves an offseason of austerity. Good thing they aren't European. They managed to re-sign running back Arian Foster and Pro Bowl center Chris Myers, but had to chop off almost their entire famed 2006 draft class to do it. Mario Williams fled for Buffalo without so much as an offer. DeMeco Ryans was traded to Philadelphia for a fourth-round pick that eventually became center Ben Jones. Most surprisingly, right tackle Eric Winston was released despite being on rather fair salary terms ($5.5 million base salaries in each of the next two seasons). They were hardly alone. Houston also watched guard Mike Brisiel bolt to the Raiders for a five-year, $20 million deal, stalwart tight end Joel Dreessen sign with the Broncos, and rotation cornerback Jason Allen jump ship to the Bengals.

On defense, at least, the moves made a lot of sense. Williams had notched five sacks in five games before tearing his pectoral muscle, but beneath his immense talent lies a player that has continually struggled to stay healthy. Giving any player $48 million in guaranteed money is a risk, but giving it to a player who has ended the last two years on IR and has a history of having to play through a lot of pain as well? It might not be a popular move, but given Connor Barwin's emergence at his spot last year, letting Williams walk might have been smart even if Houston did have that kind of money available. As for Ryans, he clearly had lost a step in his return from the Achilles tendon surgery that ended his 2010 season. He was noticeably slower and struggled in pass coverage, oft-targeted in the waning weeks of the season as teams tried to spread the base Texans 3-4 out and match slot receivers or running backs against him. There's a chance that he rebounds now that he's another year removed from the surgery, but the second inside linebacker (the Mo) slot isn't a position that sees a lot of investment in today's 3-4 defenses. As for Allen, the Texans invested second- and fourth-round choices on cornerbacks in 2011 on Brandon Harris and Roc Carmichael, respectively. If Kareem Jackson continues to need hand-holding in his third NFL season, there is plenty of draft value behind him on the depth chart.

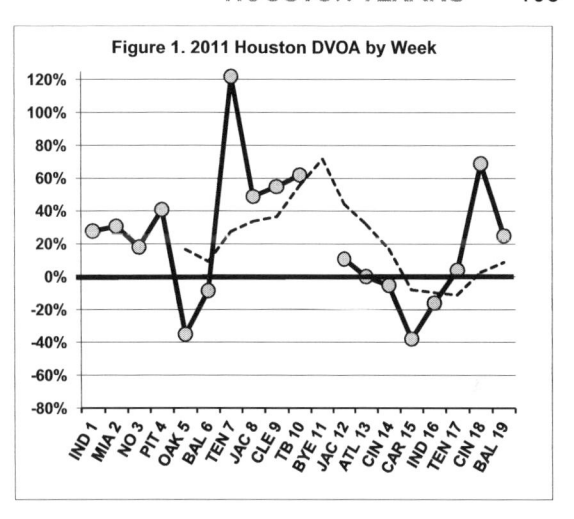

With Brian Cushing re-establishing himself after a down year in 2010 and J.J. Watt looking like an instant mainstay at end, the Texans defense, for the first time since 2004, has fewer questions than their offense.

The curious thing about Houston's offseason moves was the combination of dropping big money on a running back and an interior offensive lineman. It's a very rare thing in the modern NFL for a team to commit that kind of money to two players that are primarily active in the running game. Perhaps the most instructive recent comparison was in Minnesota, where the Vikings signed Steve Hutchinson to a huge deal before the 2006 season, then drafted Adrian Peterson with the fifth overall pick in the 2007 draft. That yielded some pretty inconsistent results despite the investment: The Vikings finished third in rushing DVOA in 2007, but fell to 28th in 2008. In the Vikings' last-gasp romp to the title game on the crocs of Brett Favre in 2009, the Hutchinson-Peterson combo managed just a 23rd place finish in rushing DVOA. That, of course, does not mean that Houston is destined to have the same problems. For instance, the Ryan Kalil-DeAngelo Stewart Panthers handed out some giant contracts and romped to a first-place finish in run DVOA last season. It does, however, illustrate the fact that success in the run game is a bit more fickle than you would expect.

That leaves the passing attack. For years, it was practically the only part of the team that wasn't flawed. Now the Texans may have achieved respectability only to watch the expiration date on their passing game come up. Johnson, now on the wrong side of 30, played in just 20 of 32 possible games the last two years, mostly due to hamstring woes. He's still very productive when he does play, and if receivers like Steve Smith have taught us anything, it's that it is a lot easier to stay healthy and productive in this current era than it once was. But time does have a way taking down even the most elite players. Owen Daniels, who will hit 30 in November, also has a track record of health problems, though he did at least manage to stay on the field for 15 games last season. Add a quarterback coming off of surgery (and Schaub's past record of getting dinged up) and all of the mainstays of the Texans passing attack have question marks at this point.

Instead of slowly graduating players to take over their roles in the system, Houston has spent so much of its draft pick value on defense that the cupboard after those three is pretty barren. Kevin Walter has been a prototypical No. 2 receiver since the very beginning of the Kubiak era, but he started to have problems finding separation last season, as he was targeted just 59 times despite being the nominal No. 1 receiver for over half the season. Jacoby Jones is exactly how you'd build and sculpt a wide receiver—except for the hands, which tend to be pretty important. His punt return ... performance? ... to end the Texans season in Baltimore was very indicative of the low part of the roller coaster ride he takes fans on. Apparently the Ravens came up with a case of Muff-holm Syndrome, as they added him to their receiving corps once the Texans released him. Behind those two, the Texans receiver depth chart was filled with arsonists and kids with mittens pinned to their jerseys. Houston even completed a mid-season trade for Jets wideout Derrick Mason, on the prayer of an idea that he'd remember he wasn't 37. Didn't happen.

The Texans opted not to select a wide receiver with the 26th overall pick, instead fortifying the defense yet again with Illinois endbacker Whitney Mercilus. He will help make up for the loss of Williams, but that left Houston with only a pair of mid-round picks to break in behind Walter: Ohio State third-rounder DeVier Posey and Michigan State fourth-rounder Keshawn Martin. It has become a lot easier to find productive receivers in the middle rounds with the expansion of the passing game, but one wonders if Houston will regret passing on the superb physical attributes of LSU receiver Rueben Randle by trading down from their second-round slot. For now, Houston can operate on the assumption that Johnson will continue to be the end-all and be-all of their passing game, but it would have made all sorts of sense to look for his replacement rather than new players to operate around him.

Then there's the quarterback position. The 31-year-old Schaub enters the year on a lame-duck one-year contract. Despite his strong performance, he has never been an elite arm talent. Yates showed a promising deep ball in his starts, but he tends to force a few too many into coverage. He's certainly graduated to primary backup, but his skills don't scream "protégé being groomed for the starting job." This problem may eventually need to be addressed, and that time may come as soon as 2013.

But, for this year at least, we're projecting that the Texans have enough to hold serve in the AFC South. The tougher schedule puts a big dent in their wins projection. The lack of offensive line continuity, with Rashad Butler and Antoine Caldwell getting the first crack at replacing Winston and Brisiel, takes another chunk out of their offensive projection. For now though, the Texans appear to have lucked into being the best team in a division of flawed ones. That doesn't override any of the long-term concerns about where they've put their money and the health of their passing game, but reaching the playoffs for a second year in a row isn't something to belittle when it took a decade to get there in the first place.

Rivers McCown

HOUSTON TEXANS

2011 Texans Stats by Week

Wk	vs.	W-L	PF	PA	YDF	YDA	TO	Total	Off	Def	ST
1	IND	W	34	7	384	236	-1	28%	3%	-3%	22%
2	@MIA	W	23	13	345	306	2	31%	30%	9%	10%
3	@NO	L	33	40	473	454	1	18%	16%	-5%	-3%
4	PIT	W	17	10	318	296	1	41%	45%	-6%	-10%
5	OAK	W	20	25	473	278	-1	-35%	-35%	-13%	-12%
6	@BAL	L	14	29	293	402	2	-8%	-8%	0%	-1%
7	@TEN	W	41	7	518	148	2	122%	58%	-58%	6%
8	JAC	W	24	14	358	174	0	49%	31%	-14%	4%
9	CLE	W	30	12	380	172	1	55%	26%	-33%	-4%
10	@TB	W	37	9	420	231	4	62%	39%	-38%	-15%
11	BYE										
12	@JAC	W	20	13	215	255	0	11%	-20%	-6%	25%
13	ATL	W	17	10	337	337	1	0%	-9%	-18%	-9%
14	@CIN	W	20	19	412	285	-2	-5%	-3%	-3%	-6%
15	CAR	L	13	28	358	316	-3	-38%	-19%	20%	2%
16	@IND	L	16	19	283	320	0	-16%	-28%	-11%	1%
17	TEN	L	22	23	387	361	0	4%	10%	9%	3%
18	CIN	W	31	10	340	300	3	69%	43%	-21%	5%
19	@BAL	L	13	20	315	227	-4	25%	-17%	-44%	-2%

Trends and Splits

	Offense	Rank	Defense	Rank
Total DVOA	8.4%	9	-9.5%	6
Unadjusted VOA	9.1%	8	-13.4%	4
Weighted Trend	5.3%	12	-10.6%	8
Variance	9.3%	21	8.9%	28
Average Opponent	0.7%	21	-2.7%	24
Passing	20.5%	9	-6.6%	7
Rushing	4.3%	9	-13.4%	6
First Down	16.2%	5	-15.1%	5
Second Down	-0.4%	16	-10.1%	6
Third Down	7.2%	12	1.9%	16
First Half	12.0%	9	-15.3%	6
Second Half	4.3%	11	-4.0%	9
Red Zone	-6.2%	17	-9.0%	17
Late and Close	5.0%	14	4.0%	22

Five-Year Performance

Year	W-L	Pyth	Est W	PF	PA	TO	Total	Rk	Off	Rk	Def	Rk	ST	Rk	Off AGL	Rk	Def AGL	Rk
2007	8-8	7.9	7.5	379	384	-13	-3.6%	18	1.5%	15	12.0%	29	6.9%	3	24.2	20	26.4	23
2008	8-8	7.3	6.4	366	394	-10	-7.4%	22	6.2%	13	13.5%	29	-0.1%	17	20.3	12	22.7	17
2009	9-7	9.5	10.0	388	333	-1	9.7%	14	9.9%	10	2.5%	20	2.4%	7	39.9	28	17.5	7
2010	6-10	7.1	7.9	390	427	0	2.5%	13	21.7%	2	17.5%	31	-1.7%	23	31.0	20	24.2	16
2011	10-6	10.9	10	381	278	+7	18.6%	5	8.4%	9	-9.5%	6	0.7%	13	31.3	17	18.9	10

2011 Performance Based on Most Common Personnel Groups

Houston Offense					Houston Offense vs. Opp.				Houston Defense				Houston Defense vs. Opp.			
Pers	Freq	Yds	DVOA	Run%	Pers	Freq	Yds	DVOA	Pers	Freq	Yds	DVOA	Pers	Freq	Yds	DVOA
12	33%	6.1	17.6%	44%	4-3-4	61%	6.2	14.0%	3-4-4	58%	4.6	-11.4%	11	45%	5.1	-5.2%
21	25%	6.1	19.7%	68%	4-2-5	16%	5.7	15.0%	Dime+	31%	5.4	-9.5%	21	24%	4.2	-23.4%
11	22%	4.9	-7.3%	33%	3-4-4	10%	6.4	43.2%	4-2-5	6%	4.8	-14.5%	12	19%	4.9	-16.4%
22	11%	6.1	18.5%	72%	Dime+	4%	4.5	-18.2%	4-3-4	2%	5.5	-11.2%	22	3%	5.4	22.2%
13	6%	7.0	12.7%	47%	3-3-5	4%	4.9	12.8%	3-3-5	1%	4.9	43.9%	01	2%	6.6	2.2%

Strategic Tendencies

Run/Pass		Rank	Offense		Rank	Pass Rush		Rank	Defense/Other		Rank
Runs, all plays	52%	2	Form: Single Back	55%	26	Rush 3	2.7%	27	4 DB	60%	3
Runs, first half	48%	3	Form: Empty Back	5%	17	Rush 4	47.9%	29	5 DB	8%	32
Runs, first down	59%	3	Pers: 3+ WR	24%	32	Rush 5	33.8%	3	6+ DB	31%	3
Runs, second-long	49%	1	Pers: 4+ WR	0%	30	Rush 6+	15.6%	3	CB by Sides	71%	23
Runs, power sit.	69%	7	Pers: 2+ TE/6+ OL	52%	4	Zone Blitz	6.0%	15	Go for it on 4th	0.96	12
Runs, behind 2H	30%	16	Play action	33%	1	Sacks by LB	61.4%	8	Offensive Pace	30.9	21
Pass, ahead 2H	29%	31	Max protect	10%	18	Sacks by DB	1.1%	29	Defensive Pace	29.1	2

Houston's poor performance with 11 personnel gives evidence of their lack of depth at wide receiver. In a strange quirk based on scheduling and their division rivals, Houston faced a basic 4-3-4 formation on 61 percent of offensive plays. No other offense faced the same defensive formation on more than 44 percent of plays. Houston opponents only ran the ball a lcague-low 14 percent of the time when they spread it out with three or more wide receivers in the formation. The Texans, on the other hand, ran the ball 31 percent of the time when they were spread out with three or more wide receivers. The Texans had by far the biggest gap between usage of five and six defensive backs. Only four other teams used six DBs more than they used five, and with those teams the gap was less than 10 percent. With Houston, it was 23 percent. Houston led the league with 27 passes tipped at the line or batted down, five more than any other defense.

Passing

Player	DYAR	DVOA	Plays	NtYds	Avg	YAC	C%	TD	Int
M.Schaub	701	24.4%	307	2370	7.8	6.6	61.7%	15	6
T.J.Yates	-81	-19.7%	150	893	6.0	5.8	63.4%	3	3
J.Delhomme*	26	2.4%	30	194	6.5	3.1	67.9%	1	0
M.Leinart*	14	4.8%	13	57	4.4	3.9	76.9%	1	0

Rushing

Player	DYAR	DVOA	Plays	Yds	Avg	TD	Fum	Suc
A.Foster	122	2.3%	277	1237	4.5	10	4	44%
B.Tate	151	12.5%	175	949	5.4	4	4	53%
D.Ward*	5	-5.9%	45	154	3.4	2	0	49%
S.Slaton*	-9	-36.2%	7	20	2.9	0	0	43%
T.J.Yates	10	12.7%	8	65	8.1	0	0	--
M.Schaub	10	9.7%	7	16	2.3	2	0	--
J.Forsett	-27	-24.7%	46	145	3.2	1	0	26%

Receiving

Player	DYAR	DVOA	Plays	Ctch	Yds	Y/C	YAC	TD	C%
J.Jones*	41	-4.5%	64	32	515	16.1	4.4	2	50%
K.Walter	91	6.6%	59	39	474	12.2	3.3	3	66%
A.Johnson	118	17.2%	51	33	492	14.9	4.2	2	65%
D.Mason*	-26	-36.9%	13	6	55	9.2	0.7	0	46%
B.Johnson*	1	-12.2%	13	7	91	13.0	2.0	1	54%
O.Daniels	122	14.3%	85	54	677	12.5	5.4	3	64%
J.Dreessen*	119	40.5%	39	28	353	12.6	5.3	6	72%
J.Casey	66	33.3%	24	18	260	14.4	9.1	1	75%
A.Foster	126	18.6%	73	54	621	11.5	11.3	2	74%
B.Tate	11	-3.3%	19	13	98	7.5	6.3	0	68%
L.Vickers*	-21	-50.3%	8	4	29	7.3	5.3	0	50%
J.Forsett	-24	-26.5%	34	23	128	5.6	6.5	0	68%

Offensive Line

Year	Yards	ALY	Rank	Power	Rank	Stuff	Rank	2nd Lev	Rank	Open Field	Rank	F-Start	Cont.
2009	3.73	4.10	15	60%	21	22%	25	1.12	18	0.41	31	16	32
2010	5.12	4.52	4	66%	10	16%	9	1.42	1	1.32	2	12	31
2011	4.66	4.37	4	64%	14	18%	12	1.43	4	0.93	11	15	43

Year	LE	Rank	LT	Rank	Mid	Rank	RT	Rank	RE	Rank	Sacks	ASR	Rank	Short	Long
2009	3.62	25	3.56	27	4.24	11	4.16	14	4.63	9	26	5.2%	8	6	12
2010	4.19	19	4.55	9	4.89	1	4.32	10	4.21	12	32	5.9%	12	14	13
2011	3.75	20	4.16	17	4.57	3	4.60	12	4.15	9	33	7.3%	22	15	15

The Texans had arguably the best offensive line in the NFL by the end of the season, but running up against the salary cap forced the departures of right tackle Eric Winston and right guard Mike Brisiel. Winston fell off a bit in 2011, especially in pass protection, but the decision to let him walk in favor of re-signing center Chris Myers was fascinating. Neither Myers nor Winston is an upper-echelon pass protector. Both excel in the run game, but Myers will turn 31 shortly after the season starts, while Winston will turn 29 in November. Perhaps the Texans valued Myers' line calls more highly than Winston's steady play, or perhaps Winston's drop-off was disconcerting to them.

Those decisions leave the Texans with an entirely new right side of the offensive line: The early pencils have Rashad Butler at right tackle while Antoine Caldwell mans right guard. Both players have some experience in the Texans starting five: Butler played at left tackle in 2010 during Duane Brown's four-game suspension for performance-enhancing drugs, and Caldwell got plenty of reps since Brisiel was a walking injury report. Caldwell struggled last year in pass protection, a fact that the Texans are blaming on high ankle sprains. Butler, on the other hand, needs to work more on his run blocking. He was an adequate pass blocker in 2010, aside from DeMarcus Ware eating his lunch, but he's not as graceful as Winston on combo blocks and cleaning up second-level chaff.

Myers earned a deserved Pro Bowl nod as one of the best run-blocking centers in the league last season. He's agile and heady, but has pass-blocking limitations. Left guard Wade Smith also has some issues in pass protection, but he's terrific at getting to the second level. The Texans reinforced the line with fourth-rounder Ben Jones out of Georgia and third-rounder Brandon Brooks of Miami (Ohio). Brooks has freakish physical potential—according to offensive coordinator Rick Dennison, he runs a sub-5 40-yard-dash … at 350 pounds. He's been mentioned as a fit at right tackle as well as guard. Jones doesn't have those gifts, but may be the more NFL-ready of the two if they are pressed into action this season.

Brown has become one of the three or four best left tackles in the NFL, a far cry from the execrable rookie the Texans fielded in 2008. He's extremely active, is excellent on pulls, and changes directions well while pass blocking. His impending free agency after the season is almost assuredly one of the reasons that Houston took it slow this offseason. Behind Brown and Butler, the Texans spent a sixth-rounder on developmental Purdue tackle Nick Mondek, but last year's seventh-rounder, Derek Newton, probably has the inside track on playing time if an injury arises.

Defensive Front Seven

Defensive Line	Age	Pos	Plays	TmPct	Rk	Stop	Dfts	BTkl	St%	Rk	AvYd	Rk	Sack	Hit	Hur	Runs	St%	Yds	Pass	St%	Yds
J.J. Watt	23	DE	58	7.7%	8	48	19	3	83%	28	1.4	42	5.5	16	21	43	79%	2.5	15	93%	-2.0
Earl Mitchell	25	DT	28	3.7%	46	22	1	3	79%	35	2.6	57	1	0	4	25	76%	2.7	3	100%	1.3
Antonio Smith	31	DE	27	3.6%	68	25	15	1	93%	2	-0.5	8	6.5	14	33	16	94%	0.8	11	91%	-2.4
Shaun Cody	29	DT	25	3.3%	52	20	3	2	80%	29	2.0	39	1	2	4	21	81%	2.3	4	75%	0.0
Tim Jamison	26	DE	21	2.8%	--	17	4	0	81%	--	1.6	--	2	3	4	17	76%	2.9	4	100%	-4.0

Linebackers	Age	Pos	Plays	TmPct	Rk	Stop	Dfts	BTkl	AvYd	Sack	Hit	Hur	Runs	St%	Rk	Yds	Rk	Tgts	Suc%	Rk	AdjYd	Rk
Brian Cushing	25	ILB	119	15.7%	15	79	21	5	3.9	4	10	11.5	82	70%	36	3.0	37	28	58%	11	6.4	33
DeMeco Ryans	28	ILB	67	8.9%	67	41	8	8	3.8	0	2	5	51	61%	72	3.4	53	25	72%	3	3.4	1
Conner Barwin	26	OLB	53	7.0%	95	37	20	4	1.3	11.5	17	26	27	56%	91	3.3	50	5	84%	--	2.9	--
Brooks Reed	5	OLB	47	6.2%	103	40	11	1	1.9	6	5	20	32	88%	2	1.9	6	1	100%	--	4.6	--
Bradie James	31	ILB	44	5.9%	104	24	3	3	4.8	0	2	2	32	56%	90	4.1	89	12	53%	--	6.5	--

Year	Yards	ALY	Rank	Power	Rank	Stuff	Rank	2nd Lev	Rank	Open Field	Rank
2009	4.28	3.65	5	59%	8	23%	7	1.07	7	1.11	28
2010	4.14	4.28	24	62%	15	19%	19	1.32	30	0.53	9
2011	4.04	3.85	7	67%	25	20%	15	1.07	8	0.75	14

Year	LE	Rank	LT	Rank	Mid	Rank	RT	Rank	RE	Rank	Sacks	ASR	Rank	Short	Long
2009	3.18	7	3.10	2	3.79	11	3.62	7	4.04	17	30	6.0%	20	18	8
2010	3.99	14	4.63	26	4.42	25	3.99	15	4.05	19	30	6.3%	17	15	9
2011	2.44	3	3.09	1	4.18	17	3.42	2	3.68	17	44	8.4%	3	14	18

Brooks Reed replaced Mario Williams after his pectoral injury, and while most of his sacks were of the cleanup variety, his high motor was on display from the first snap. Connor Barwin had a phenomenal season under Wade Phillips and will be playing on the last year of his rookie contract come September. The Texans buffered against that potential loss by selecting Illinois defensive end Whitney Mercilus with the 26th overall pick in the draft. Mercilus was a bit of a one-year wonder in college, posting 16 of his 18 sacks in his junior year. Still, he's got the second-highest Sack-SEER projection in a weak pass rusher class and should play sort of an Aldon Smith role this year.

Brian Cushing is an absolute monster in the run game, and the lone linebacker the Texans send out in their dime package. His rebound season made it a lot easier for Phillips to deal with the decline of DeMeco Ryans. Darryl Sharpton was already cutting into Ryans' snaps before going down with a quadriceps injury at midseason, and is penciled into the starting lineup at Mo linebacker. The Texans also signed Bradie James away from the Cowboys and brought back veteran Tim Dobbins, so Sharpton will have decent competition in training camp.

The Texans struck gold with the selection of J.J. Watt with the 10th overall pick last season. He was an instant contributor who ran right through the rookie wall and kept excelling in December and January. Antonio Smith may not get double-digit sacks, but he consistently ranks near the top of the league in quarterback hurries: tied for fifth in both 2010 and 2011, and 16th in 2009. Watt and Smith give Houston the best pair of penetrating 3-4 ends in the league, and they are both excellent on stunts, although Smith is a bit of a non-entity against the run. In the middle stands Shaun Cody, The Devil You Know. Statistically, the Texans were weakest on runs up the middle, outside analysts have called for them to bring in a new nose tackle for years, and yet he still stands like the mush he is. Maybe mush isn't so bad. You can keep stomping on it, but it's all give. It just stays mush. You can't build it up, but you can't break it down either. In a funny way, mush has the edge. Still, if fourth-round rookie Jared Crick (Nebraska) were to be moved inside and given a chance at the position, Texans fans probably wouldn't complain.

Defensive Secondary

Secondary	Age	Pos	Plays	TmPct	Rk	Stop	Dfts	BTkl	Runs	St%	Rk	Yds	Rk	Tgts	Tgt%	Rk	Dist	Suc%	Rk	APaYd	Rk	PD	Int
Glover Quin	26	SS	86	11.4%	26	35	17	7	39	38%	43	5.7	12	47	10.9%	5	9.0	46%	65	8.0	40	9	0
Danieal Manning	30	FS	64	10.4%	35	22	6	3	32	34%	52	8.8	61	28	8.1%	25	11.9	52%	49	7.3	34	7	2
Johnathan Joseph	28	CB	59	8.3%	41	29	12	8	5	60%	11	7.6	50	71	17.7%	38	14.9	53%	38	7.4	40	15	4
Jason Allen*	29	CB	48	6.3%	70	15	10	4	11	27%	67	7.8	51	64	14.9%	57	13.7	50%	51	6.3	18	11	4
Kareem Jackson	24	CB	46	6.5%	66	16	5	2	14	64%	8	5.2	17	55	13.7%	65	16.3	45%	67	10.5	77	7	1
Brice McCain	26	CB	38	5.0%	80	23	12	1	4	50%	27	10.3	70	50	11.6%	71	9.3	64%	5	5.7	11	13	2
Troy Nolan	26	FS	36	5.4%	72	9	4	2	8	13%	77	6.6	33	16	4.3%	73	11.3	48%	57	7.4	35	4	0
Quintin Demps	27	FS	26	6.1%	--	9	5	2	9	22%	--	10.3	--	11	4.6%	--	9.2	68%	--	6.0	--	3	2
Alan Ball	27	CB	38	5.1%	79	11	5	1	6	33%	53	16.2	81	48	11.6%	72	11.3	44%	71	8.6	62	7	1

Year	Pass D Rank	vs. #1 WR	Rk	vs. #2 WR	Rk	vs. Other WR	Rk	vs. TE	Rk	vs. RB	Rk
2009	18	13.4%	19	5.7%	23	-1.8%	13	24.7%	29	-36.3%	1
2010	32	16.0%	27	28.1%	29	0.9%	19	26.3%	30	33.8%	32
2011	9	24.0%	24	-15.9%	8	-14.7%	13	5.1%	12	-12.5%	9

Johnathan Joseph may not have had the best individual stats in our game charting, but he completely changed the way Houston played on defense. He could lock down half of the field, letting Houston give plenty of safety help to Jason Allen (against non-Brandon Marshall players, at least) and Kareem Jackson. Jackson, in fact, finished with the fourth-lowest YAC allowed by any cornerback almost entirely because Phillips stapled Glover Quin to his inside hip on early downs. Allen left for Cincinnati, so should Jackson be exposed again as he was in 2010, the top two candidates to replace him are probably 2011 second-rounder Brandon Harris and 2011 fourth-rounder Roc Carmichael, neither of whom saw much field time last year.

(A note about Joseph and our charting stats: There's a huge gap between Joseph's two worst games and his other 13 games. Anquan Boldin caught all five intended passes in Week 5 for 103 yards, and Steve Smith caught all three intended passes in Week 15 for 67 yards and a touchdown. Without these two games, Joseph had an adjusted Success Rate of 60 percent with just 6.0 yards allowed per pass. Unfortunately, it's hard to use these stats to diagnose if Joseph has a specific hole in his game, because it is hard to think of two No. 1 receivers more different than Smith and Boldin.)

The other major surprise of the 2011 season was the emergence of Brice McCain, ace slot cornerback. The most memorable McCain moment of 2010 was when he played off-coverage against Santonio Holmes on the goal line, leading to one of the easiest touchdowns you'll ever see. That was exemplary of the kind of coverage he offered all season—and this was a guy who played outside because he was a real burner at Utah. Some wondered if he would even make the team in 2011, but he came out and had the best season of any slot corner in the league. In fact, McCain had the highest Success Rate of any qualifying corner (69 percent) before we applied strength of opponent adjustments. His anticipation and technique looked entirely different, and he may be the biggest success secondary coach Vance Joseph produced last year. Quin and Danieal Manning probably had the best two safety seasons the Texans have ever had in their history. They were both great at anticipating the run, and hardly ever got burned by play action. (Only Seattle had a better defensive DVOA than Houston on play action passes.) While the Texans technically play dime on third down, Quin is usually roaming in a linebacker spot on the snap. Quintin Demps also saw the field on those dime packages and the Texans liked him enough to invite him back after initially not tendering him in restricted free agency.

Special Teams

Year	DVOA	Rank	FG/XP	Rank	Net Kick	Rank	Kick Ret	Rank	Net Punt	Rank	Punt Ret	Rank	Hidden	Rank
2009	2.0%	7	-12.1	31	5.5	11	4.7	10	9.6	4	4.0	11	-12.4	30
2010	-1.5%	23	9.2	1	1.6	13	-10.0	30	-4.5	25	-4.9	25	2.2	11
2011	0.6%	13	-3.6	22	3.7	10	-1.9	20	0.9	14	4.6	7	-3.2	20

Houston's special teams were aggressively mediocre in 2011, neither gaining nor losing more than 4.6 points in any one category. Jacoby Jones had a bounce-back year as a punt returner after being a bit too patient in 2010—well, until he visited Baltimore in the playoffs, anyway. Kick returns were handled by Danieal Manning until he fractured his tibia. The Texans played it safe with him after that, opting only to let him return again in the playoffs. Rookie fourth-rounder Keshawn Martin (Michigan State) is the favorite to replace Jones on punt returns, and could factor in on kick returns as well if Houston decides to protect Manning again. In theory, Trindon Holliday is an option to return kicks, but it's more likely that the crowning achievement of his Texans career was when he was forced to ride a pink children's bike in training camp hazing.

Neil Rackers was essentially a replacement-level kicker after his accuracy deserted him down the stretch. The Texans didn't offer him a long-term deal, so he played the butthurt card and took his services to Washington. The Texans responded by drafting Texas A&M kicker Randy Bullock in the fifth round, and he'll compete with (and likely defeat) Shayne Graham for the job. Undrafted free agent Brett Hartmann was excellent on punts before tearing his ACL in December. Hartmann further endeared himself to management by drawing a four-game substance abuse suspension (for Ritalin) to start the year. Donnie Jones was signed to either replace Hartmann or keep his spot warm, depending on if the 2010 version (+6.2 points gross punt value) or the 2011 version (-6.6 points gross punt value) of Jones shows up.

Coaching Staff

The Texans are a litmus test for the Peter Principle. Gary Kubiak and Wade Phillips can create great units on their own, but neither of them demonstrated much head-coaching success until last season. Kubiak couldn't hire a proper defensive mind when given the rope to do so, and Phillips struggled as a head coach even when given great offensive talent in Dallas. With their powers combined, the Texans are an actual contender.

Kubiak was rewarded with a three-year extension after the season. While he's good for a few asinine challenges a season and has gotten the short stick in some incredibly ridiculous defeats, his greatest trait and the thing that has kept him alive in Houston has been the respect he commands from his players. Mario Williams went out of his way to compliment Kubiak on his way out the door, Glover Quin mentioned in an interview that it's a "well-known" fact that Kubiak is one of the "coolest" coaches in the league, and despite the circumstances of 2010, the team never quit on him. Phillips was also given an undisclosed raise after he made some noise about interviewing for Tampa Bay's opening near the end of the season. Still, of the five coaches that have been tenured longer than Kubiak in the NFL, four have made the Super Bowl, and the other one is Marvin Lewis. Kubiak probably needs to change one of those things in the next few years if he wants to see the end of that extension, and turning himself into Marvin Lewis would require massive cosmetic surgery.

Indianapolis Colts

2011 Record: 2-14

Pythagorean Wins: 3.2 (31st)

DVOA: -32.8% (31st)

Offense: -17.2% (27th)

Defense: 9.3% (26th)

Special Teams: -6.2% (31st)

Variance: 13.7% (15th)

2012 Mean Projection: 6.0 wins

On the Clock (0-4): 23%

Mediocrity (5-7): 54%

Playoff Contender (8-10): 21%

Super Bowl Contender (11+): 2%

Postseason Odds: 9.3%

Projected Average Opponent: 1.0% (15th)

2011: Not with a bang, but a Painter.

2012: Press your Luck.

@JimIrsay: *Thundr on the mtn/rolln like a drum/ goin 2 sleep over there/where music comin from*

If you watched an Indianapolis Colts game last season—and given their strong early presence on the national TV schedule, odds are you did—what you witnessed was finality. In *Football Outsiders Almanac 2011*, we predicted that the Colts would lose their division to the Texans ... but that prediction was based on the idea that Peyton Manning would be healthy.

Yes, Peyton Manning. You may have heard of him. In fact, while watching a Colts game last season, you probably saw him in the closest thing he has to street clothes, with his earpiece in, somewhere in the vicinity of 10 times. The team around Manning was already starting to wear down in 2010, the other stars growing old and succumbing to injury just as he did. Without Manning the team collapsed on itself: The passing offense went nowhere under three different quarterbacks, and a defense used to playing with a lead rarely saw one. Colts games themselves were no longer actually games, they were three-hour speculation segments. Rock bottom was reached in Week 7, when the first rematch of Super Bowl XLIV ended with the Saints casually dropping 55 points on Indy's defense during *Sunday Night Football*, then adding seven more on a Curtis Painter interception returned for a touchdown. (Cut to Manning on the sideline, full Manningface in effect.)

Thanks to the general weakness of the AFC South, as well as an identity change that saw the I-formation supplement the existing shotgun-based offense, Indianapolis emerged from the season with the best of both worlds. Not only did they avoid the ignominy of 0-16, but they found themselves with the newly cost-controlled No. 1 pick in the draft. In a draft with two potential franchise quarterbacks, no less. Talk about getting ~~lucky~~ fortunate.

@JimIrsay: *U had a charmin air/all cheap and debonair/My widow mother found so sweet so and so she took u in*

This enabled owner Jim Irsay to gracefully (OK, as gracefully as is allowed in 140 characters most of the time) bid adieu to Manning and his neck woes. Enter Andrew Luck, who is perhaps the most complete quarterback prospect since Manning. Our Lewin Career Forecast projection system, and more than a few other interested observers, spent the draft buildup session knocking Luck down a peg in favor of Robert Griffin III. Luck had one of the top ten scores in LCF history, but Griffin may have had the best.[1]

As usual in this media echo canyon, some people took these opinions a bit far by stripping them of their context. When our friend Greg Cosell says that Luck was not asked to make many tough deep or intermediate throws, and that he favors Griffin III on tape because he made those throws successfully, that does not necessarily mean that Luck isn't a special prospect. Tape and statistical analysis are just two parts of the puzzle, and the fact that Luck wasn't lobbing deep bombs all season at Stanford wasn't necessarily an indictment of his arm strength. Griffin III had a special season last year, one of the best in college football's history. Said season should not be used to trash Luck, who has all of the tools to be the next great Colts quarterback.

But does the team around Luck have enough talent to complete a quick rebuild, à la Manning's Colts? Manning's Colts posted a second straight 3-13 season in his rookie year, then jumped all the way to 13-3 in 1999. While it's always possible that the Colts front office, led by new GM Ryan Grigson, hits a pair of home runs between this year's draft and the 2013 draft that could enable that to happen, there is a stark difference between the talent that 1998 Colts had and the talent that the 2012 Colts will have.

@JimIrsay: *Im a victim of the science age uh/a child of the storm oh yea/i can't remember when i was your age!*

The reason that the Indianapolis machine finally started to slow down in 2010 before sputtering out in 2011 is that the Colts have not drafted well at all over the past six seasons. The core of those strong Manning teams stopped having new stars introduced to them, and instead were handed fairly good players like Joseph Addai, middling contributors like Anthony Gonzalez, and absolute busts like Mike Pollak and Tony Ugoh. While the 1998 Colts were by no means a good team, they had a much stronger base of young talent on the roster than these current Colts have. Especially at the skill positions. Compare the talent on their respective rosters (Table 1).

Let's put the two quarterbacks aside for the moment. Of the other players listed, the three best were almost assuredly on the 1998 team: Marshall Faulk, Marvin Harrison, and Tarik Glenn. Pat Angerer and Jerraud Powers are nice pieces, and Coby Fleener and Dwayne Allen could be a terrific pairing together, but comparing them to two Hall of Famers and a tackle who might have been had he not retired early? That's a bit much.

Although the 1998 Colts didn't improve upon their

Table 1. Indianapolis Colts, 1998 vs. 2012 (projected), Players Under 27 with Significant Roles

1998			2012		
Player	Age	Draft Pos.	Player	Age	Draft Pos.
QB Peyton Manning	22	1-1 (98)	QB Andrew Luck	22	1-1 (12)
RB Marshall Faulk	25	1-4 (94)	RB Donald Brown	25	1-27 (09)
WR Marvin Harrison	26	1-19 (96)	RB Delone Carter	25	4-119 (11)
WR Jerome Pathon	23	2-32 (98)	WR T.Y. Hilton	22	3-92 (12)
TE Marcus Pollard	26	UDFA	TE Coby Fleener	23	2-34 (12)
LT Tarik Glenn	22	1-19 (97)	TE Dwayne Allen	22	3-64 (12)
LG Steve McKinney	23	4-93 (98)	LT Anthony Castonzo	24	1-22 (11)
RT Adam Meadows	24	2-48 (97)	RG Ben Ijalana	23	2-49 (11)
DE Bertrand Berry	23	3-86 (97)	DE Drake Nevis	23	3-87 (11)
DT Ellis Johnson	25	1-15 (95)	ILB Kavell Conner	25	7-240 (10)
CB Tyrone Poole	26	1-22 (95)	ILB Pat Angerer	25	2-63 (11)
CB Jeff Burris	26	1-27 (94)	CB Jerraud Powers	25	3-92 (09)
			CB Kevin Thomas	26	3-94 (10)

3-13 record from the year before, the offense was already starting to hum. They improved from 24th in offensive DVOA to 14th despite Manning's 28 interceptions. If we're measuring the 2012 Colts in baby steps, that is their main task this year. A general manager does not invest his first four picks in the passing game so his quarterback can hand the ball off to Donald Brown. In fact, the instant success of players such as Cam Newton and Matt Ryan goes to show that the level of coaching around the NFL—and the complexity of playing quarterback for many top college teams—has advanced enough to where it wouldn't be out of the question to expect big things from Luck immediately. Well, unless he actually doesn't have anyone to throw it to. The Colts clearly expect to run a two-tight end base offense with Allen and Fleener. They are counting on Reggie Wayne to not fall off a cliff, and somebody from among Austin Collie, Donnie Avery, T.Y. Hilton, and LaVon Brazill has to step up and claim the starting job opposite Wayne. Given Collie's build and concussion history, Avery's multiple injuries, and the draft position of those last two receivers, it's not a complete stretch to say that none of them are going to be starting receivers on the next

---

[1] This year's Lewin Career Forecast numbers are listed near the end of the book in the "Rookie Projections" section; the reasons why we have to qualify Griffin's score with "may have" are explained in the Russell Wilson player comment.

2012 Colts Schedule

Week	Opp.	Week	Opp.	Week	Opp.
1	at CHI	7	CLE	13	at DET
2	MIN	8	at TEN	14	TEN
3	JAC	9	MIA	15	at HOU
4	BYE	10	at JAC (Thu.)	16	at KC
5	GB	11	at NE	17	HOU
6	at NYJ	12	BUF		

Figure 1. 2011 Indianapolis DVOA by Week

Colts playoff team. At 33, Wayne isn't likely to be a part of that team either.

@JimIrsay: *He's got a scar across his face, he wears a hearing aid..sure, he's a Jolly Roger, 'til he answers 4 his crime..Yes, I'll match him win 4 win!*

Defensively, the team has begun the transition from their longtime Tampa-2 scheme to one based out of the 3-4 hybrid style that new head coach Chuck Pagano used in Baltimore. That means that, like Mario Williams for division rival Houston last year, longtime star 4-3 ends Dwight Freeney and Robert Mathis will be transitioning to "outside linebackers." Mathis and Freeney combined for 17 sacks last season, pretty close to the 21 they racked up in 2010, but their hurries were way down. They combined for just 37 of those after notching 57 in 2010. Then again, it's not like the defensive backs were actively giving them much time to rush as the defense slipped into the abyss.

Between safety David Caldwell and the second cornerback slot, which was mainly Jacob Lacey, the Colts fielded two below-average secondary members in their base package, and that's not counting the four games that Jerraud Powers missed with hamstring issues and a dislocated elbow. They gave up at least a 25.5% DVOA to every group of wide receivers (No. 1s, No. 2s, Others), a feat that was matched only by the execrable secondary in Minnesota last year. They had the worst defensive DVOA in the NFL against passes from the shotgun formation, at 36.2%. Worst of all, because of the offensive focus in the draft, the only reinforcement arriving to help in the back four is former Ravens safety Tom Zbikowski, who is more famous for his boxing than his work in coverage. Kevin Thomas, should he manage to stay healthy (which isn't a given), will likely get the first crack at working with Powers, Zbikowski, and Antoine Bethea. It's not exactly a secondary that's going to challenge the 1994 49ers.

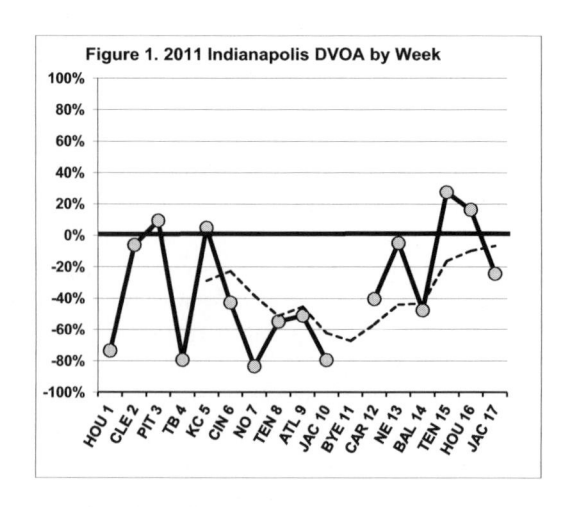

Much like the 1998 Colts, this may be a team that completely bottoms out on defense. Whether you want to blame the decline in Freeney and Mathis' pass pressure on the secondary behind them or their advanced ages (32 and 31, respectively), neither problem has really been addressed. In fact, Mathis was handed a four-year, $36 million contract to stay in Indy solely because it would be impossible to replace what he gives them now on the free agent market.

@JimIrsay: *I'm about to throw a few tomatoes on the griddle to fry...take off your shoes and sit a little....*

That lack of pass defense is really what keeps the rose off the bloom for Indianapolis this year. It doesn't take an incredible amount of wishful thinking to conjure up a best-case scenario where Luck has a Newton-esque rookie season, the offensive line gels quickly, someone establishes himself at the second wide receiver spot, and the run defense is addressed by some of Pagano's Baltimore legacy signings. Turning around the trends of their pass defense is almost entirely reliant on rebound seasons from two players over 30 that are changing positions.

Regardless of their competitive standing this year, Luck and the rest of the draft class should start building some hope as the rest of the Manning Colts hit their expiration dates. Even the most ardent Colts fans can probably admit that this team's upside is showing up somewhere between "Frisky" and "The Good Bad Team" in a Bill Simmons column.

And after last year, that's quite alright. It's nice to have a reason to actually watch the games again.

Rivers McCown

2011 Colts Stats by Week

Wk	vs.	W-L	PF	PA	YDF	YDA	TO	Total	Off	Def	ST
1	@HOU	L	7	34	236	384	1	-73%	-31%	7%	-35%
2	CLE	L	19	27	285	303	-1	-6%	-13%	-11%	-4%
3	PIT	L	20	23	241	408	2	9%	-12%	-29%	-8%
4	@TB	L	17	24	318	466	-1	-79%	-30%	40%	-10%
5	KC	L	24	28	355	436	0	5%	47%	50%	8%
6	@CIN	L	17	27	273	358	-3	-43%	-8%	24%	-11%
7	@NO	L	7	62	252	557	-3	-83%	-39%	45%	1%
8	@TEN	L	10	27	399	311	-2	-55%	-14%	8%	-32%
9	ATL	L	7	31	186	432	-1	-51%	-42%	12%	2%
10	JAC	L	3	17	212	251	-2	-79%	-83%	-5%	-1%
11	BYE										
12	CAR	L	19	27	323	377	-1	-40%	-25%	6%	-10%
13	@NE	L	24	31	437	362	-2	-5%	6%	18%	7%
14	@BAL	L	10	24	167	358	1	-48%	-39%	9%	0%
15	TEN	W	27	13	287	388	2	27%	6%	-21%	0%
16	HOU	W	19	16	320	283	0	16%	-14%	-28%	2%
17	@JAC	L	13	19	298	261	-2	-24%	-8%	7%	-10%

Trends and Splits

	Offense	Rank	Defense	Rank
Total DVOA	-17.2%	27	9.3%	26
Unadjusted VOA	-20.4%	30	10.4%	29
Weighted Trend	-20.0%	27	7.5%	23
Variance	3.6%	2	4.8%	6
Average Opponent	-1.4%	9	1.6%	13
Passing	-16.5%	27	18.2%	27
Rushing	-7.3%	22	1.3%	23
First Down	-13.6%	26	9.3%	26
Second Down	-8.3%	20	8.0%	25
Third Down	-36.4%	31	11.7%	26
First Half	-23.8%	29	9.8%	27
Second Half	-10.6%	25	8.8%	25
Red Zone	-23.4%	26	21.5%	31
Late and Close	-24.2%	27	3.6%	20

Five-Year Performance

Year	W-L	Pyth	Est W	PF	PA	TO	Total	Rk	Off	Rk	Def	Rk	ST	Rk	Off AGL	Rk	Def AGL	Rk
2007	13-3	12.7	12.3	450	262	+18	28.3%	2	22.2%	2	-13.0%	2	-6.9%	32	19.3	12	51.0	32
2008	12-4	10.2	10.4	377	298	+9	15.0%	8	14.2%	5	-3.1%	11	-2.3%	24	31.8	21	39.6	27
2009	14-2	10.9	11.1	416	307	+2	16.5%	8	16.8%	6	-0.8%	16	-1.1%	19	30.1	21	51.9	30
2010	10-6	9.2	8.2	435	388	-4	1.3%	16	13.1%	6	5.5%	24	-6.3%	31	42.5	30	48.1	31
2011	2-14	3.2	3	243	430	-12	-32.8%	31	-17.2%	27	9.3%	26	-6.2%	31	37.5	22	47.2	28

2011 Performance Based on Most Common Personnel Groups

Indianapolis Offense					Indianapolis Offense vs. Opp.				Indianapolis Defense				Indianapolis Defense vs. Opp.			
Pers	Freq	Yds	DVOA	Run%	Pers	Freq	Yds	DVOA	Pers	Freq	Yds	DVOA	Pers	Freq	Yds	DVOA
11	64%	5.1	-14.2%	25%	4-2-5	41%	5.0	-24.3%	4-3-4	62%	5.4	4.6%	11	31%	6.7	16.4%
12	20%	5.3	5.3%	59%	4-3-4	22%	5.1	-7.3%	4-2-5	33%	6.3	16.5%	21	26%	5.5	2.5%
21	10%	4.3	-25.0%	67%	3-4-4	15%	4.5	-13.9%	3-3-5	3%	8.1	23.3%	12	24%	6.1	20.4%
22	3%	3.9	-30.5%	84%	3-3-5	10%	5.0	-11.9%	G-line	1%	0.8	29.4%	22	8%	3.1	-20.1%
611	1%	3.5	-50.1%	77%	Dime+	7%	5.7	24.8%	Dime+	1%	6.0	-56.0%	13	2%	2.8	-43.7%

Strategic Tendencies

Run/Pass		Rank	Offense		Rank	Pass Rush		Rank	Defense/Other		Rank
Runs, all plays	40%	20	Form: Single Back	82%	1	Rush 3	0.4%	32	4 DB	62%	2
Runs, first half	46%	9	Form: Empty Back	1%	31	Rush 4	82.4%	1	5 DB	36%	21
Runs, first down	46%	25	Pers: 3+ WR	65%	2	Rush 5	13.0%	30	6+ DB	1%	30
Runs, second-long	48%	3	Pers: 4+ WR	1%	29	Rush 6+	4.2%	29	CB by Sides	87%	9
Runs, power sit.	55%	21	Pers: 2+ TE/6+ OL	25%	28	Zone Blitz	0.2%	32	Go for it on 4th	0.82	23
Runs, behind 2H	31%	14	Play action	17%	19	Sacks by LB	6.9%	29	Offensive Pace	28.6	2
Pass, ahead 2H	41%	24	Max protect	9%	19	Sacks by DB	0.0%	30	Defensive Pace	31.5	31

The Colts used 11 personnel on 64 percent of plays, the only team in the league to use a personnel package on more than 60 percent of plays. And yet, that was still 12 percentage points lower than when they used 11 personnel on 76 percent of plays in 2010. The Colts also used the same defensive formation (4-3-4) more than any other team used any one defensive formation. The Colts had a league-low 5.5 penalties per game, showing that inexperienced does not necessarily equal undisciplined. Or perhaps the issue was which officials did their games, as the Colts were also tied for 29th in opponent penalties. The Colts only recovered 8 of 23 fumbles on offense. The Colts were one of five teams that ran the running back screen pass less than once per game. The quarterbacks were different, but one strategy was the same: The Colts led the league in wide receiver screens for the second straight season, and it was one of the rare places their offense was above average (6.3 yards per pass, 22.0% DVOA). As bad as the Colts offense was, it looked even worse because of field position. Indianapolis started its average drive 76.3 yards away from a touchdown. Thanks in part to the change in kickoffs, that means the Colts had the worst average starting field position of any offense since at least 1997.

Passing

Player	DYAR	DVOA	Plays	NtYds	Avg	YAC	C%	TD	Int
C.Painter*	-375	-33.3%	261	1412	5.6	5.7	54.5%	6	9
D.Orlovsky*	121	-2.2%	204	1118	5.5	3.1	64.2%	6	4
K.Collins*	-50	-18.9%	102	423	4.4	4.5	50.5%	2	1

Rushing

Player	DYAR	DVOA	Plays	Yds	Avg	TD	Fum	Suc
D.Brown	119	13.9%	134	645	4.8	5	0	37%
J.Addai*	-13	-11.5%	118	433	3.7	1	1	34%
D.Carter	-13	-11.6%	101	377	3.7	2	3	46%
C.Painter*	18	10.3%	13	109	8.4	0	0	--

Receiving

Player	DYAR	DVOA	Plays	Ctch	Yds	Y/C	YAC	TD	C%
P.Garcon*	-48	-17.1%	134	70	950	13.6	5.1	6	52%
R.Wayne	143	1.2%	131	75	960	12.8	3.7	4	57%
A.Collie	-9	-13.8%	97	54	514	9.5	3.9	1	56%
D.Avery	10	-2.6%	11	3	45	15.0	7.0	1	27%
D.Clark*	-84	-25.5%	65	34	352	10.4	4.4	2	52%
J.Tamme*	-29	-20.8%	31	19	177	9.3	4.8	1	61%
B.Eldridge	-12	-24.1%	10	9	45	5.0	1.7	0	90%
J.Addai*	-6	-19.3%	22	15	93	6.2	6.8	0	68%
D.Brown	-6	-19.8%	19	16	86	5.4	5.9	0	84%
D.Carter	-30	-79.3%	8	5	18	3.6	6.8	0	63%
J.Felton*	8	6.6%	7	4	40	10.0	7.3	0	57%

Offensive Line

Year	Yards	ALY	Rank	Power	Rank	Stuff	Rank	2nd Lev	Rank	Open Field	Rank	F-Start	Cont.
2009	3.80	3.92	26	66%	12	22%	29	1.11	21	0.51	29	16	26
2010	3.91	3.82	22	56%	22	20%	20	1.04	24	0.64	21	20	29
2011	4.12	3.91	25	50%	30	20%	17	1.13	20	0.72	23	19	22

Year	LE	Rank	LT	Rank	Mid	Rank	RT	Rank	RE	Rank	Sacks	ASR	Rank	Short	Long
2009	2.63	31	3.97	20	4.39	8	3.92	21	3.91	21	13	3.1%	1	7	5
2010	3.96	21	4.53	12	3.63	26	3.29	29	4.35	11	16	2.8%	1	12	1
2011	4.39	13	2.97	30	3.87	24	4.71	7	3.87	12	35	6.9%	18	17	8

Just three of this year's projected Colts starters were on the team last year: Anthony Castonzo, Joe Reitz, and Ben Ijalana. They combined for just 23 starts, and Ijalana missed all but four games with a torn ACL. That's not the kind of turnover you want on a line tasked with protecting a No. 1 overall pick, but Andrew Luck should have some decent protection on the back side from Castonzo. He isn't very natural-looking at left tackle yet, and he'll take some missteps, but he has terrific lateral agility in pass protection. On the other side of the line, GM Ryan Grigson made an interesting challenge trade, scooping up former first-round tackle Winston Justice from the Eagles for a seventh-round pick. Justice is most well-known for his embarrassing first start against the Giants in 2007, when Osi Umenyiora personally destroyed him. He's grown into an adequate left tackle, but his pass-blocking definitely will play better on the right side of the line. Best of all, the Colts got Justice to take a pay cut after the trade, meaning they're essentially risking nothing on the move. Samson Satele is the new center, moving over from the Raiders to take the spot of longtime incumbent Jeff Saturday. Satele is a solid run blocker, but he did draw seven penalty flags last year, and isn't much in pass protection. Reitz will man the left guard spot, with Ijalana taking the right. Behind them is some functional depth in Mike McGlynn, who the team lured away from Cincinnati in free agency. Once this line is operating on the same wavelength, it has the talent to be the best one the Colts have fielded since Tarik Glenn hung the cleats up. Yes, that is damning with faint praise.

Defensive Front Seven

Defensive Line	Age	Pos	Plays	TmPct	Rk	Stop	Dfts	BTkl	St%	Rk	AvYd	Rk	Sack	Hit	Hur	Runs	St%	Yds	Pass	St%	Yds
Robert Mathis	31	DE	44	4.9%	42	33	18	1	75%	53	0.4	17	9.5	9	19	28	68%	2.3	16	88%	-2.9
Tyler Brayton	33	DE	27	3.0%	77	22	7	1	81%	31	2.3	64	2	2	3	22	82%	2.5	5	80%	1.4
Jamaal Anderson*	26	DE	25	3.0%	78	20	7	0	80%	34	2.1	58	3	2	5	20	80%	2.4	5	80%	1.0
Antonio Johnson	28	DT	23	2.6%	68	17	4	1	74%	48	2.1	44	0	2	5.5	20	70%	2.3	3	100%	0.7
Fili Moala	27	DT	22	2.8%	62	15	6	0	68%	56	2.4	51	2	1	1.5	19	68%	2.5	3	67%	2.0
Ricardo Matthews	25	DT	21	3.1%	54	14	5	0	67%	59	2.6	57	1	1	3	16	56%	3.8	5	100%	-1.4
Dwight Freeney	32	DE	19	2.1%	--	15	12	1	79%	--	-1.9	--	8.5	8	18	9	67%	4.0	10	90%	-7.3
Drake Nevis	23	DT	19	6.8%	--	13	4	0	68%	--	2.2	--	0	1	2.5	14	71%	2.1	5	60%	2.4
Cory Redding	32	DE	44	5.7%	26	36	14	0	82%	29	0.8	21	4.5	6	6.5	37	78%	1.6	7	100%	-3.7

Linebackers	Age	Pos	Plays	TmPct	Rk	Stop	Dfts	BTkl	AvYd	Sack	Hit	Hur	Runs	St%	Rk	Yds	Rk	Tgts	Suc%	Rk	AdjYd	Rk
Pat Angerer	25	MLB	148	16.6%	12	84	20	6	5.1	1	3	4.5	102	64%	62	3.2	44	26	62%	7	6.8	41
Kavell Conner	25	OLB	105	11.8%	41	57	20	8	4.2	0	1	5	70	71%	28	2.1	9	25	34%	75	7.5	60
Philip Wheeler*	28	OLB	80	11.1%	46	45	8	1	4.3	1	0	0	57	63%	63	3.4	58	17	58%	13	5.4	15
Ernie Sims	28	OLB	62	8.6%	72	28	9	5	6.9	0	0	0	22	50%	105	4.3	96	32	42%	63	7.5	56

Year	Yards	ALY	Rank	Power	Rank	Stuff	Rank	2nd Lev	Rank	Open Field	Rank
2009	4.47	4.53	29	57%	6	15%	29	1.21	20	0.63	11
2010	4.58	4.40	28	57%	8	17%	24	1.28	27	0.89	21
2011	4.36	4.41	27	65%	19	17%	24	1.27	22	0.70	11

Year	LE	Rank	LT	Rank	Mid	Rank	RT	Rank	RE	Rank	Sacks	ASR	Rank	Short	Long
2009	4.64	21	4.90	29	4.23	21	4.68	28	5.58	31	34	6.3%	16	17	10
2010	4.14	16	3.83	11	4.48	29	5.10	32	4.30	20	30	5.6%	25	17	7
2011	4.66	24	4.76	29	4.37	27	4.70	25	3.77	19	29	6.8%	15	12	12

Once you get past Robert Mathis and Dwight Freeney, the Colts don't have much in the way of situational pass rushers to put outside. Former first-round pick Jerry Hughes is the top backup at those spots, but he saw most of his time on special teams last year. It says a whole lot about how much confidence the Colts had in him that they'd rather re-sign an aging Mathis than enter a new season with him as a projected starter. Pat Angerer and Kavell Conner take the spots at inside linebacker, with the latter moving over from the weak side. Both of them suffered from what FO's Tom Gower referred to as "DeMeco Ryans Syndrome" last year, where good run-stuffing linebackers on bad teams receive inflated tackle numbers. That goes for Defeats as well, as both of them finished in the top 10 in run Defeats. Angerer was also very solid in pass coverage, where he allowed only three catches of 10 or more yards all season. However, that's not an established level of performance, as he had poor coverage stats in 2010.

Up front, the Colts are shifting a lot of players around. Drake Nevis showed some promise before hitting injured reserve with a back injury at midseason. Then again, his best game was against Pittsburgh, and Pittsburgh's offensive line was capable of producing many highlight reels for defensive linemen early last season. The unit will receive a boost from two Baltimore imports: Cory Redding at end and Brandon McKinney at tackle. Redding should easily secure a starting spot if he's healthy, and he's still rather productive in his old age. McKinney will likely battle incumbent Antonio Johnson for the nose tackle job, with fifth-rounder Josh Chapman (Alabama) waiting in the wings.

Defensive Secondary

Secondary	Age	Pos	Plays	TmPct	Rk	Stop	Dfts	BTkl	Runs	St%	Rk	Yds	Rk	Tgts	Tgt%	Rk	Dist	Suc%	Rk	APaYd	Rk	PD	Int
Antoine Bethea	28	FS	145	16.3%	2	53	21	6	93	38%	46	6.7	36	24	6.3%	50	9.7	75%	3	4.7	6	7	0
Jacob Lacey*	25	CB	74	8.9%	31	30	10	1	19	53%	25	5.1	14	59	16.6%	47	10.0	38%	81	8.0	53	9	1
David Caldwell	25	SS	66	7.4%	64	27	4	6	48	40%	35	5.8	15	13	3.3%	75	12.4	45%	68	9.5	61	3	0
Jerraud Powers	25	CB	57	8.5%	37	23	10	6	20	40%	44	5.6	19	48	16.8%	44	9.0	53%	40	7.9	52	6	2
Kevin Thomas	26	CB	36	7.2%	--	9	5	5	7	14%	--	12.0	--	33	15.5%	--	9.1	41%	--	10.3	--	5	0
Joe Lefeged	24	SS	36	4.0%	--	11	7	3	14	36%	--	6.4	--	12	3.2%	--	16.5	58%	--	6.9	--	5	2
Chris Rucker	24	CB	35	4.2%	--	10	7	0	6	17%	--	10.5	--	23	6.5%	--	10.2	41%	--	7.8	--	2	0
Terrence Johnson	26	CB	32	5.8%	--	12	5	3	13	46%	--	7.2	--	16	6.6%	--	7.5	47%	--	8.6	--	0	0
Cassius Vaughn	25	CB	23	4.9%	--	8	4	1	3	67%	--	0.3	--	26	10.7%	--	14.3	45%	--	8.4	--	4	1
Tom Zbikowski	27	FS	16	2.2%	--	4	2	2	6	17%	--	8.5	--	6	1.5%	--	6.3	52%	--	8.4	--	0	0

Year	Pass D Rank	vs. #1 WR	Rk	vs. #2 WR	Rk	vs. Other WR	Rk	vs. TE	Rk	vs. RB	Rk
2009	11	-0.9%	14	4.1%	20	-1.0%	15	-0.5%	13	-6.2%	12
2010	26	-9.0%	9	-6.0%	10	-2.9%	17	28.8%	31	18.8%	28
2011	28	26.2%	26	25.3%	27	33.7%	32	19.6%	22	-2.5%	17

Jerraud Powers has consistently been an above-average corner by our charting metrics, and his play last season, when healthy, was right in line with his career norms. Antoine Bethea had a fine season despite his lack of interceptions. Any time you can mix that success rate with a high frequency of targets, you're doing something right—even if it is as part of a bad defense.

The other two positions are less settled. Kevin Thomas comes into training camp as the assumed starter at cornerback opposite Powers. He didn't play much in 2011, and when he did, he was a sieve. Against the Falcons in Week 9, he was the target of four separate plays of 20 or more yards, including a 50-yard bomb and an 80-yard catch-and-run where Julio Jones left him in the dust. After allowing Blaine Gabbert three completions of 10 or more yards in Week 10, he saw only intermittent time on the field. Chris Rucker was a fairly reliable tackler, allowing just one play of more than five yards after the catch, but according to our game charting project, opponents completed 77 percent of their passes thrown in his direction. Cassius Vaughn, who was acquired from Denver for Chris Gronkowski over the offseason, could push for playing time. He flashed playmaking skills with a 55-yard pick-six last year, but his overall charting numbers were nothing to get too excited about.

The other safety spot will be manned by Pagano import Tom Zbikowski, who saw his playing time severely reduced in favor of Bernard Pollard and Haruki Nakamura. Zbikowski will likely see the fewest pass attempts in his direction of any member of this secondary, but he doesn't have Ed Reed to help cover his butt on mistakes anymore. David Caldwell started 13 games last year and was noted as the primary target in pass coverage by our charters just 10 times. He'll be around as depth.

One small side stat that could help your belief in this secondary: The Colts were in the middle of the pack in the percentage of defensive plays with a pressure. However, when they did get pressure, they had the seventh-best DVOA allowed.

Special Teams

Year	DVOA	Rank	FG/XP	Rank	Net Kick	Rank	Kick Ret	Rank	Net Punt	Rank	Punt Ret	Rank	Hidden	Rank
2009	-0.9%	19	-2.1	21	1.5	14	-1.6	15	2.8	12	-5.8	26	-11.4	29
2010	-5.4%	31	6.9	4	-3.4	23	-17.6	32	-8.1	27	-9.5	30	-4.2	19
2011	-5.3%	31	-0.1	16	-2.8	25	-9.1	32	-10.9	30	-8.3	28	-5.8	24

The Colts were famously and consistently bad on special teams in the Bill Polian era. Since 1997, they have had above-average special teams DVOA only once (2003), and last year was no different. Adam Vinatieri continues to be as steady as they come on field goals, but his kicking was the only part of the entire unit that was above average last year. There are two extremely revealing stats about the state of Colts return men and coverage teams last year. One is that Joe Lefeged, the only kick returner Indy used all year, averaged just 18.6 yards per return—a full three yards less than any other qualifying kick returner. Yes, the kickoff rule changes had some effect on this, but nobody has had an average that low in the past ten years. Third-rounder T.Y. Hilton out of Florida International may step into Lefeged's shoes as the main returner, which would give Lefeged more time to try to become an NFL safety. The Colts also enter training camp with some retread return candidates like Quan Cosby and Deji Karim on the roster.

The other revealing stat is that the team leader in special teams tackles was punter Pat McAfee, who managed seven. New special teams coach Marwan Maalouf, who is never allowed to eat in public in Sacramento, was an assistant coach with Baltimore's special teams from 2008-2011. Baltimore's special teams ranked in the top 10 in 2009 and 2010 before cratering last year, so this could be an area where the Colts see some actual improvement. No, really!

OK, we're a little skeptical too.

Coaching Staff

Chuck Pagano is just the latest head coach to use the Ravens defensive coordinator springboard to land a lead gig, following in the footsteps of Rex Ryan, Mike Nolan, and Marvin Lewis. He's hung around mostly as a defensive backs coach prior to getting the charge to lead the Ravens last year, so perhaps his experience in that role can help allay concerns about the secondary talent. The switch to 3-4 personnel is in place, but last year Pagano actually flipped around between 3-4 and 4-3, with the distinction largely being "Is Terrell Suggs' hand on the ground?" Look for Indianapolis to play that game with Dwight Freeney. Defensive coordinator Greg Manusky oversaw a very poor pass defense in San Diego last year (30th), and his defenses in San Francisco were only above average once in four years, ranking fifth in 2009. When Manusky left, that defense zoomed up to third in the NFL. Coincidence? Colts fans should hope so.

Offensive coordinator Bruce Arians "resigned" in Pittsburgh. By "resigned," we of course mean "he was let go." The Steelers transformed into a team that ran a much more diverse passing game under Arians, and drafting Coby Fleener and Dwayne Allen has his fingerprints all over it. The Steelers traditionally used a lot of double tight end sets under Arians, despite the fact that they didn't really have an ideal second tight end. Pittsburgh ran 12 personnel 26 percent of the time in 2010 and 17 percent of the time in 2011, and they garnered offensive DVOA ratings of 33.2% and 21.2%, respectively, out of these sets.

Jacksonville Jaguars

2011 Record: 5-11

Pythagorean Wins: 5.3 (26th)

DVOA: -17.4% (27th)

Offense: -26.5% (31st)

Defense: -11.3% (5th)

Special Teams: -2.2% (26th)

Variance: 14.3% (18th)

2012 Mean Projection: 6.1 wins

On the Clock (0-4): 23%

Mediocrity (5-7): 52%

Playoff Contender (8-10): 23%

Super Bowl Contender (11+): 2%

Postseason Odds: 11.1%

Projected Average Opponent: 2.5% (8th)

2011: Another year of MJD's prime wasted.

2012: Fate has no forgiveness for those who dare run against it.

From now on, forget everything you knew about the Jacksonville Jaguars.

Jacksonville, not exactly a major player on the national media scene, had long faced three awkward questions from a media that didn't find their actual team interesting enough to cover. Tarps, half-empty lower bowls, and an owner that was losing money led to questions about when the team would move to Los Angeles. The team's inability to secure a playoff berth since 2007, when they finished third in DVOA, led any logical person to wonder when ninth-year coach Jack Del Rio would finally be relieved of his duties. Finally, there was the icon-driven question of when the Jaguars would make a move for native-ish son Tim Tebow, who would save the franchise with ticket sales, and ... oh, let's say a trident, because he certainly wouldn't have been too much help on the field this past year.

Following a Week 12 loss to the Texans in which rookie first-round quarterback Blaine Gabbert was benched for warmed-over veteran Luke McCown, the changes began. Del Rio was relieved of his duties and replaced on an interim basis by defensive coordinator Mel Tucker. On that same day, long-time owner Wayne Weaver reached an agreement to sell the Jaguars to Pakistani-American businessman Shahid Khan. Khan immediately pledged his desire to keep the team in Jacksonville, which means that the question of when the Jaguars will move to Los Angeles will only be breached three times a year by a sensationalistic hits-grabbing sports media rather than ten. After the season, Tucker was retained as defensive coordinator, but Khan and general manager Gene Smith hired Atlanta offensive coordinator Mike Mularkey as the fourth head coach in Jaguars history.

That left only the Tebow question, and while the Jaguars did put in a bid for him, they ultimately lost out to the New York Jets. It spoke to just how much Jacksonville valued Tebow that they were interested in acquiring him even despite the fact that they'd already signed a fairly capable backup in Chad Henne earlier in the offseason. Or it spoke to spotlight-seeking and the fact that Khan hasn't shied away from his interest in Tebow in interviews. By design or luck, the Jaguars stayed away from letting talk show callers and trolls-masquerading-as-analysts run their team, and that can only be good news for the future of the franchise.

The resolution of this scenario was a commitment to give Gabbert another chance at the helm. It was made clear that Mularkey was hired primarily to help with his development. While it's hard to call sticking with a rookie quarterback in a lost season a controversial move, Gabbert did everything in his power to make it look that way. The -1,009 DYAR he compiled is second only to David Carr's 2002 season among the worst quarterback seasons in the DVOA era (Table 1).

2012 Jaguars Schedule

Week	Opp.	Week	Opp.	Week	Opp.
1	at MIN	7	at OAK	13	at BUF
2	HOU	8	at GB	14	NYJ
3	at IND	9	DET	15	at MIA
4	CIN	10	IND (Thu.)	16	NE
5	CHI	11	at HOU	17	at TEN
6	BYE	12	TEN		

Figure 1. 2011 Jacksonville DVOA by Week

Carr's rookie season was a little easier to stomach since he was piloting an expansion team behind one of the worst offensive lines that has ever been assembled. While the Jaguars had the receiving corps of an expansion team, they weren't exactly handicapped. Expansion teams do not get to employ Maurice Jones-Drew.

Overall, this isn't a list that inspires a lot of hope for Gabbert's future. Trent Dilfer and Alex Smith are the only quarterbacks on it to post a season with positive DVOA at some point in their careers. Jaguars fans can take heart that most of the worst pass offenses of the DVOA era improved greatly the following season. Unfortunately, most of the teams in Table 2 improved by replacing the quarterbacks listed in Table 1. And while the bottom 10 pass offenses in our system improved by an average of 35.9% DVOA, all of them besides last year's Panthers squad were still firmly in the negative numbers.

The only recent team that seems similar to the current Jaguars is the early Alex Smith-era 49ers, who finished in the bottom eleven in the NFL in pass offense DVOA every year from 2005-10 before Jim Harbaugh took over as head coach. The chances that Mularkey can be the Harbaugh who improves Gabbert to the level Smith hit in 2011 seem remote, but stranger things have happened.

Watch Gabbert's tape last year and you will see a boy playing with men. There were a few minor signs of improvement, and a few nice throws down the stretch, but nothing that would lead you to suggest that he had turned a corner. This is a quarterback that made the vast majority of his throws within 10 yards of the line of scrimmage. This is a quarterback that showed signs of panic even when his pocket was relatively clean—though he did get a bit better at this as the season wore on. What was most galling about watching him was his footwork. He correctly stepped into maybe one of every nine throws, and that absolutely killed his accuracy.

There are reasons to expect improvement from the Jacksonville passing game that go beyond just "Gabbert can't possibly be this bad again." Chief among them is their trade up in the first round to select Oklahoma State wide receiver Justin Blackmon. Tape watchers like Greg Cosell have questioned whether Blackmon has the second gear to become a terrific vertical threat in the NFL, but his college production was off the charts. Despite spending most of the last season facing the attention of multiple defensive backs after his coming out party in 2010, Blackmon posted a 76 percent catch rate. Signing the unheralded Laurent Robinson, who finished third among qualifying receivers in DVOA for Dallas last season, will help push the top end of the Jaguars receiving corps of 2011 into better positions for them to succeed. Mike Thomas can be the slot receiver that his skill set clearly says he should be. Marcedes Lewis doesn't

Table 1. Ten Worst Passing Seasons by DYAR, 1991-2011

Name	Team	Year	DVOA	DYAR
David Carr	HOU	2002	-47.4%	-1,129
Blaine Gabbert	JAC	2011	-46.5%	-1,009
Bobby Hoying	PHI	1998	-68.3%	-964
Alex Smith	SF	2005	-88.6%	-866
Kelly Stouffer	SEA	1992	-73.1%	-843
Jimmy Clausen	CAR	2010	-48.0%	-749
Akili Smith	CIN	2000	-51.4%	-700
Trent Dilfer	SF	2007	-55.4%	-681
Craig Krenzel	CHI	2004	-85.4%	-676
Andrew Walter	OAK	2006	-46.2%	-669

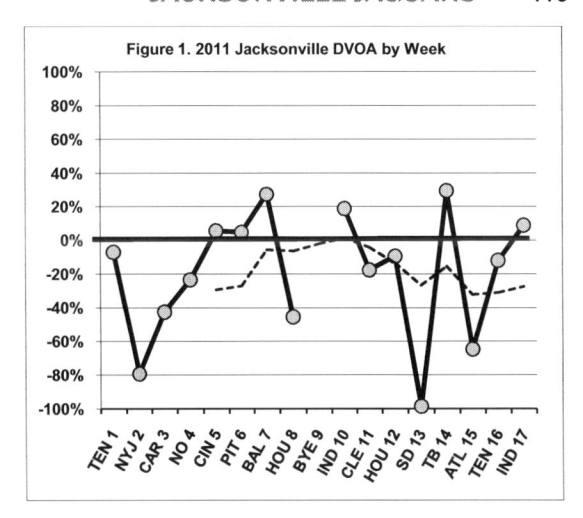

JACKSONVILLE JAGUARS

Table 2. 10 Worst Passing Offenses by DVOA, 1991-2011

Team	Year	Quarterback	DVOA	Quarterback Y+1	DVOA Y+1	Change
SEA	1992	Gelbaugh, Stouffer	-65.3%	Mirer	-19.9%	+45.4%
SF	2005	Rattay, Alex Smith	-56.0%	Alex Smith	-7.0%	+49.0%
CHI	2004	Hutchinson, Krenzel	-50.6%	Orton	-21.2%	+29.4%
ARI	2010	Anderson, Skelton	-46.1%	Kolb, Skelton	-21.7%	+24.4%
OAK	2006	Brooks, Walter	-45.4%	Culpepper, J.McCown	-16.0%	+29.4%
JAC	2011	L.McCown, Gabbert	-45.4%	Gabbert?	--	--
CIN	2000	Mitchell, Akili Smith	-43.9%	Kitna	-11.5%	+32.4%
SF	2007	Dilfer, Alex Smith	-42.1%	O'Sullivan, Hill	-12.5%	+29.6%
NO	1997	Shuler, Wuerffel	-41.4%	Tolliver	-11.8%	+29.6%
CAR	2010	Moore, Clausen	-40.1%	Newton	+13.8%	+53.9%
Average			-47.7%		-11.9%	+35.9%

have to be the go-to-guy and can work on returning to the 2010 version of himself. The rest of the receivers, who were heralded enough to receive spring training invites from the *Major League* Indians, can go back to the anonymity that they deserve.

The Jaguars also made a good under-the-radar move when they signed Chad Henne to be their backup quarterback. Last year, giving up on Gabbert would have put them squarely in the McCown quarterbacking zone, a place where the ceiling is "replacement level." Henne was run out of Miami due to his injury last season and his inconsistency before it, but DVOA has always seen him as a slightly above-average quarterback, similar to what the Jaguars were used to with David Garrard before drafting Gabbert.

If the Jaguars can find the same kind of lightning in a bottle that Carolina found last season—or even just a passing game that borders on competent—they could be a competitor in the AFC South. Maurice Jones-Drew continues to be one of the best running backs in the NFL. Change-of-pace back Deji Karim, who finished with -78 DYAR in just 63 carries, will be replaced by Rashad Jennings, who looked very promising in 2010 before missing last season with a knee injury. While the Jags only finished 21st in rushing DVOA last year, account for the fact that some of that was Karim and some of that was frequent box-stacking by teams unafraid of Gabbert, and it's not far-fetched to see them as a potential top-10 run offense in 2012.

The defense, the main subject of the Jacksonville chapter in last year's book, was completely rejuvenated by the additions of Dawan Landry, Paul Posluszny, and Dwight Lowery. The Jaguars improved from dead last in defensive DVOA to fifth overall, one of the ten biggest year-to-year defensive DVOA improvements of the past two decades. (For the full list, see the Houston chapter.) The Jaguars were one of two defenses, along with the Jets, to be in the top five in both pass defense DVOA and run defense DVOA. Furthermore, they looked even better before a skid of bad injury luck reminiscent of Donald Barthelme's *The School* decimated the unit in the second half of the season. Jacksonville's defense finished with the fourth-worst defensive AGL in 2011, at 52.8. Those injuries accumulated at the positions that tend to hurt pass defense the most: cornerback and defensive end. Injuries to defensive ends Matt Roth (concussion), John Chick (patella tendon), Austen Lane (shoulder), and Aaron Kampman (hamstring) left the Jags with a rotation of Leger Douzable and George Selvie in December. Meanwhile, after Rashean Mathis (torn ACL), Derek Cox (knee), and William Middleton (knee) went down at cornerback, the Jaguars were starting street free agents like Ashton Youboty, Akwasi Owusu-Ansah, and Kevin Rutland down the stretch. Four of their worst six defensive performances, including shreddings at the hands of San Diego and Atlanta, came after Week 10.

That's not to say that the Jacksonville defense is immune to regression (our forecast system expects some when a team goes from 32nd to fifth in one year) or that they didn't make some silly offseason choices (like signing Aaron Ross despite years of evidence in New York that he's nothing better than a slot corner), but they performed very well despite considerable adversity in 2011. Adding Clemson defensive end Andre Branch in the second round should be a boon to their pass rush eventually, and despite a lot of dollars tied up in injury-prone players like Posluszny and Clint

Session, the Jaguars should be a little healthier than they were last year.

The AFC South is hardly a minefield this year, and if the Jaguars can pair adequate quarterback play with a good running game and defense, they could very well be in the thick of it. While the Jaguars haven't exactly given Gabbert an ironclad endorsement, they've done all that they could in one offseason to increase his receiving options and bring in a credible option behind him. Where that adequate play comes from, and how quickly they get it, will go a long way in determining if Jacksonville is involved in the AFC South chase or just factoring into tiebreaker scenarios for the teams that matter.

Rivers McCown

2011 Jaguars Stats by Week

Wk	vs.	W-L	PF	PA	YDF	YDA	TO	Total	Off	Def	ST
1	TEN	W	16	14	323	292	0	-7%	-6%	2%	1%
2	@NYJ	L	3	32	203	283	-2	-79%	-78%	-9%	-10%
3	@CAR	L	10	16	257	265	-1	-42%	-51%	-20%	-11%
4	NO	L	10	23	274	503	1	-23%	-35%	-15%	-3%
5	CIN	L	20	30	296	239	-1	6%	-11%	-23%	-6%
6	@PIT	L	13	17	209	370	0	5%	-17%	-10%	11%
7	BAL	W	12	7	205	146	1	27%	-37%	-60%	5%
8	@HOU	L	14	24	174	358	0	-45%	-33%	4%	-8%
9	BYE										
10	@IND	W	17	3	251	212	2	19%	-29%	-56%	-9%
11	@CLE	L	10	14	303	334	1	-18%	-1%	17%	0%
12	HOU	L	13	20	255	215	0	-9%	-24%	-43%	-29%
13	SD	L	14	38	306	433	-1	-98%	-22%	66%	-10%
14	TB	W	41	14	325	280	5	30%	-30%	-47%	13%
15	@ATL	L	14	41	207	373	-4	-65%	-44%	18%	-3%
16	@TEN	L	17	23	300	407	2	-12%	-16%	0%	4%
17	IND	W	19	13	261	298	2	9%	-16%	-8%	17%

Trends and Splits

	Offense	Rank	Defense	Rank
Total DVOA	-26.5%	31	-11.3%	5
Unadjusted VOA	-23.2%	31	-9.1%	8
Weighted Trend	-23.1%	30	-10.0%	11
Variance	11.0%	28	5.6%	13
Average Opponent	0.3%	17	2.2%	9
Passing	-45.4%	32	-8.2%	5
Rushing	-5.2%	21	-15.0%	5
First Down	-18.4%	28	-9.2%	8
Second Down	-33.1%	32	-12.0%	5
Third Down	-30.6%	28	-14.3%	10
First Half	-20.8%	26	7.9%	26
Second Half	-32.1%	31	-14.0%	3
Red Zone	-37.0%	31	8.9%	28
Late and Close	-30.6%	29	-19.8%	1

Five-Year Performance

Year	W-L	Pyth	Est W	PF	PA	TO	Total	Rk	Off	Rk	Def	Rk	ST	Rk	Off AGL	Rk	Def AGL	Rk
2007	11-5	10.9	11.9	411	304	+9	24.1%	3	21.6%	3	-2.5%	15	0.0%	14	16.8	9	34.3	27
2008	5-11	6.1	8.5	302	367	-7	-1.1%	20	6.0%	14	6.3%	24	-0.8%	21	48.8	29	15.4	11
2009	7-9	5.5	7.0	290	380	+2	-9.3%	23	3.8%	17	11.3%	28	-1.8%	25	4.5	2	43.5	28
2010	8-8	6.3	6.5	353	419	-15	-9.0%	22	3.9%	14	17.7%	32	4.8%	7	19.7	9	17.8	11
2011	5-11	5.3	5.5	243	329	+5	-17.4%	27	-26.5%	31	-11.3%	5	-2.2%	26	20.5	10	52.8	29

2011 Performance Based on Most Common Personnel Groups

Jacksonville Offense					Jacksonville Offense vs. Opp.				Jacksonville Defense				Jacksonville Defense vs. Opp.			
Pers	Freq	Yds	DVOA	Run%	Pers	Freq	Yds	DVOA	Pers	Freq	Yds	DVOA	Pers	Freq	Yds	DVOA
11	39%	4.2	-27.4%	20%	4-3-4	41%	4.3	-28.9%	4-3-4	48%	4.7	-20.5%	11	47%	5.6	-12.3%
21	29%	4.8	-16.2%	63%	3-4-4	21%	4.2	-9.8%	4-2-5	38%	6.0	3.2%	12	19%	4.8	-19.4%
12	16%	4.8	-13.9%	46%	4-2-5	20%	5.1	6.8%	Dime+	9%	7.8	-18.5%	21	17%	5.5	-20.7%
22	10%	2.6	-45.8%	80%	Dime+	8%	3.7	-43.8%	4-4-3	2%	3.1	-27.1%	22	7%	3.7	-19.4%
20	2%	4.7	-48.9%	44%	3-3-5	6%	3.5	-97.3%	3-3-5	2%	4.9	-45.7%	13	3%	5.1	39.8%

JACKSONVILLE JAGUARS

Strategic Tendencies

Run/Pass		Rank	Offense		Rank	Pass Rush		Rank	Defense/Other		Rank
Runs, all plays	47%	4	Form: Single Back	56%	25	Rush 3	3.5%	24	4 DB	48%	16
Runs, first half	46%	7	Form: Empty Back	4%	22	Rush 4	74.3%	4	5 DB	40%	19
Runs, first down	63%	1	Pers: 3+ WR	42%	25	Rush 5	17.1%	25	6+ DB	9%	13
Runs, second-long	37%	13	Pers: 4+ WR	1%	27	Rush 6+	5.1%	26	CB by Sides	66%	26
Runs, power sit.	69%	6	Pers: 2+ TE/6+ OL	29%	24	Zone Blitz	6.9%	11	Go for it on 4th	0.87	17
Runs, behind 2H	40%	3	Play action	22%	8	Sacks by LB	22.6%	18	Offensive Pace	31.0	22
Pass, ahead 2H	37%	27	Max protect	6%	30	Sacks by DB	11.3%	10	Defensive Pace	31.2	28

We know that sacks are somewhat dependent on the quarterback, not just the defense. Is the same true of quarterback hits? Jacksonville provides some evidence that the answer is yes. David Garrard was first or second in QB hits (not counting sacks) every year, but last year, the Jacksonville quarterbacks combined for just 37 hits, 29th in the league. Still, the Jaguars certainly didn't make life easy on their rookie quarterback; only Buffalo and Tennessee were less likely to leave behind extra blockers. After two straight years as the league's most effective offense running the ball on second-and-long, the Jaguars were actually below average, with just 3.99 yards per carry and -25.9% DVOA. Jacksonville significantly decreased its use of the blitz, down from 35 percent of passes in 2010 to 22 percent of passes in 2011. However, they were very successful on the few plays where they did big blitz with six or more, allowing just 2.9 yards per play. Despite the strength of the Jacksonville safeties, opponents threw a league-high 26.4 percent of passes to tight ends.

Passing

Player	DYAR	DVOA	Plays	NtYds	Avg	YAC	C%	TD	Int
B.Gabbert	-1009	-46.5%	457	1888	4.2	5.4	51.1%	12	11
L.McCown*	-250	-73.4%	61	260	4.6	4.7	53.6%	0	4
C.Henne	67	-2.7%	123	801	6.8	5.2	57.1%	4	4

Rushing

Player	DYAR	DVOA	Plays	Yds	Avg	TD	Fum	Suc
M.Jones-Drew	197	5.1%	343	1604	4.7	8	3	49%
D.Karim	-84	-41.0%	63	130	2.1	0	0	29%
B.Gabbert	-35	-38.9%	29	107	3.7	0	3	--
M.Owens	14	25.1%	10	39	3.9	0	0	50%
D.Harris	2	-2.6%	9	42	4.7	0	0	56%
L.McCown*	14	32.9%	5	24	4.8	0	0	--
C.Henne	20	19.0%	14	109	7.8	1	1	--

Receiving

Player	DYAR	DVOA	Plays	Ctch	Yds	Y/C	YAC	TD	C%
M.Thomas	-156	-34.2%	92	44	408	9.3	4.3	1	48%
J.Hill	15	-9.3%	55	25	367	14.7	4.8	4	45%
J.Dillard	2	-12.2%	50	29	292	10.1	1.4	1	58%
C.West	-9	-16.9%	27	13	163	12.5	3.8	2	48%
C.Shorts	-37	-54.3%	11	2	30	15.0	1.5	1	18%
K.Osgood*	-39	-59.7%	11	5	42	8.4	3.6	0	45%
M.Sims-Walker*	-27	-69.3%	6	1	11	11.0	0.0	0	17%
L.Robinson	327	40.0%	81	54	858	15.9	4.9	11	67%
L.Evans	-113	-67.4%	26	4	74	18.5	2.3	0	15%
B.Robiskie	-33	-63.0%	9	3	25	8.3	0.7	0	33%
M.Lewis	-162	-35.7%	85	39	460	11.8	3.9	0	46%
C.Cloherty	-3	-13.9%	8	4	57	14.3	8.3	0	50%
Z.Potter	2	-1.6%	7	5	50	10.0	8.2	0	71%
Z.Miller	-2	-10.6%	7	4	42	10.5	4.3	1	57%
M.Jones-Drew	53	1.9%	63	43	374	8.7	9.3	3	68%
D.Karim	7	-5.7%	19	14	120	8.6	10.7	0	74%
G.Jones	-15	-39.2%	9	4	19	4.8	4.0	0	44%

Offensive Line

Year	Yards	ALY	Rank	Power	Rank	Stuff	Rank	2nd Lev	Rank	Open Field	Rank	F-Start	Cont.
2009	4.55	4.24	11	68%	10	17%	11	1.12	19	1.07	6	14	34
2010	4.62	4.63	2	63%	13	13%	3	1.35	2	0.70	18	13	30
2011	4.28	4.14	13	64%	13	17%	8	1.19	16	0.76	20	10	31

Year	LE	Rank	LT	Rank	Mid	Rank	RT	Rank	RE	Rank	Sacks	ASR	Rank	Short	Long
2009	5.66	1	4.49	8	4.06	19	3.92	20	4.44	11	44	8.5%	29	13	19
2010	4.70	8	4.75	5	4.63	3	4.26	13	4.78	6	38	7.7%	24	11	14
2011	3.81	19	5.11	3	4.25	12	2.56	32	3.81	14	44	8.9%	26	12	19

Jacksonville has for years made running the ball its primary offensive focus. Left tackle Eugene Monroe and right guard Uche Nwaneri are solid, but certainly nothing special, in pass protection. The other constants on the line all struggle when left one-on-one with rushers, and Blaine Gabbert certainly has plenty of his own problems getting rid of the football on time. In fact, per J.J. Cooper's sack project, only eight teams had a lower percentage of short sacks. That shouldn't take away from the fact that this line often couldn't hold blocks on longer drops. Monroe has problems with the top-tier edge rushers, but can hold his own against most of the league. That contrasts nicely with the situation across from him.

Guy Whimper was an absolute travesty at right tackle. In 16 starts, he allowed 12.3 sacks. Of course, he was only pressed into action at right tackle because 2010 second-round pick Eben Britton was going to be moved to guard before he injured his back. As you would expect from a player who might have to move inside, Britton didn't show much aptitude for pass blocking. After Britton was hurt, 2011 third-rounder William Rackley drew the starts at left guard, where he (shockingly!) proved a bit raw in the transition from Lehigh to the NFL. Both Rackley (who allowed 6.5 sacks of his own) and Whimper earned a spot on the All-Keep Chopping Wood team in our Scramble for the Ball column. Assuming Britton is fully healthy—always a dangerous assumption on back injuries—he'll probably push Whimper to the bench. If he's not healthy, things could get dire here in a hurry. The Jaguars didn't spend a single draft pick on the offensive line, and every player on the depth chart beyond the starting five was an undrafted free agent save one: former Packers guard Jason Spitz, who couldn't even beat out Rackley last year.

At center, the ageless Brad Meester is slated to begin his 12th campaign with the Jaguars. He's one of two Jaguars (along with Rashean Mathis) to survive the entire Jack Del Rio era on the Jacksonville roster, and the only current Jaguar who also played under Tom Coughlin. He played in an NFL game before the Playstation 2 came out in America. His pass-blocking moves include holding on for dear life and telling nose tackles to get off his lawn.

Defensive Front Seven

Defensive Line	Age	Pos	Plays	TmPct	Rk	Stop	Dfts	BTkl	St%	Rk	AvYd	Rk	Sack	Hit	Hur	Runs	St%	Yds	Pass	St%	Yds
Jeremy Mincey	29	DE	55	6.9%	12	42	15	2	76%	48	1.2	36	8	12	25	42	71%	2.6	13	92%	-3.4
Tyson Alualu	25	DT	41	5.2%	20	31	10	2	76%	44	3.0	64	2.5	6	7.5	34	76%	3.1	7	71%	2.6
Leger Douzable*	26	DT	39	4.9%	24	30	12	0	77%	43	1.6	26	1	4	5	34	76%	1.6	5	80%	1.6
Terrance Knighton	26	DT	29	4.5%	30	25	7	0	86%	10	1.7	30	0	2	5.5	28	86%	1.9	1	100%	-4.0
Matt Roth*	30	DE	24	5.4%	34	24	10	2	100%	1	0.3	14	3.5	2	9	19	100%	1.2	5	100%	-3.0
C.J. Mosley	29	DT	24	3.2%	53	20	7	0	83%	20	1.5	20	1	0	1	23	83%	1.9	1	100%	-8.0

Linebackers	Age	Pos	Plays	TmPct	Rk	Stop	Dfts	BTkl	AvYd	Sack	Hit	Hur	Runs	St%	Rk	Yds	Rk	Tgts	Suc%	Rk	AdjYd	Rk
Paul Posluszny	28	MLB	128	16.1%	14	73	28	4	4.7	2	5	8.5	75	60%	76	3.8	79	39	51%	39	7.6	65
Daryl Smith	30	OLB	113	14.2%	20	81	21	6	3.0	3.5	8	5	67	81%	8	2.3	15	32	54%	25	5.7	22
Russell Allen	26	OLB	40	5.0%	--	23	6	3	4.9	0.5	0	0	26	54%	--	5.2	--	12	67%	--	3.1	--
Clint Session	28	OLB	30	6.7%	--	22	4	3	4.2	1	0	2	21	90%	--	2.8	--	9	40%	--	10.6	--

Year	Yards	ALY	Rank	Power	Rank	Stuff	Rank	2nd Lev	Rank	Open Field	Rank
2009	4.23	4.07	15	71%	26	17%	24	1.10	10	0.79	17
2010	4.76	3.89	15	68%	26	23%	3	1.22	24	1.43	32
2011	3.94	3.82	6	68%	26	21%	10	1.03	3	0.77	16

JACKSONVILLE JAGUARS

Year	LE	Rank	LT	Rank	Mid	Rank	RT	Rank	RE	Rank	Sacks	ASR	Rank	Short	Long
2009	3.75	11	4.55	25	4.03	16	4.92	30	3.48	5	14	3.8%	31	3	4
2010	3.11	3	4.37	20	3.81	11	5.04	31	4.33	22	26	5.8%	22	10	11
2011	2.96	5	4.33	21	3.95	12	3.64	5	3.93	24	31	7.2%	13	13	12

The real strength of the Jaguars lies in their front seven, and in particular, in the middle of their defense. Middle linebacker Paul Posluszny was a bit of a gamble by Jacksonville in free agency because he'd had problems staying on the field in Buffalo, but he turned in a full 16-game season and was excellent against both the run and the pass. Then he tore his labrum in the final game of the year, which is expected to sideline him through training camp. Nose tackle Terrence Knighton fought injuries (a recurring theme in this section), but continued to be a massive load in the middle of the line when not mouthing off about hating the Texans. Knighton had to have emergency eye surgery in April, and his status for training camp is questionable, though he did do some side work at OTAs. Tyson Alualu took a step back while he dealt with recurring cartilage problems in his right knee, and after the season he had "minor" microfracture surgery. Former third-rounder D'Anthony Smith is hanging around behind Knighton and Alualu on the defensive tackle depth chart after missing the last two seasons with a torn Achilles tendon and a torn ligament in his toe.

Defensive end has been a real problem for the Jaguars for a number of years, but unheralded Jeremy Mincey showed that he was more than just a role player with a breakout eight-sack season. Of course, five of those were against the Colts' execrable offensive line, but he was also just outside of the top 10 with 13 quarterback hits. The Jaguars rewarded him handsomely with a four-year, $20 million contract, then drafted Clemson's Andre Branch in the second round to play opposite him. Branch has an excellent first step, but is still very raw with his pass rush moves. As the SackSEER article later in the book points out, recent Clemson pass rushers do not have a strong NFL track record. Austen Lane and John Chick will be the main backups at end; Lane has one sack in 17 games, and Chick, a 29-year-old undrafted free agent from Utah State, has 2.5 in 11 games.

At outside linebacker, Darryl Smith continued his reign as an excellent all-around linebacker despite moving to accommodate Posluszny. Clint Session, who'd been injury-prone in Indianapolis, missed half of the year with a series of serious concussions after signing a five-year, $27.75 million deal in the abbreviated 2011 offseason. Even when Session was healthy, he didn't add much in pass coverage, and Russell Allen showed plenty of range in his stead, so the Jaguars won't have to bank too hard on him recovering. Fifth-round linebacker Brandon "I'm Not Falling Through That Television" Marshall (Nevada) is a tough competitor who can run with tight ends but tends to "play small" and struggles to make tackles in space.

Defensive Secondary

Secondary	Age	Pos	Plays	TmPct	Rk	Stop	Dfts	BTkl	Runs	St%	Rk	Yds	Rk	Tgts	Tgt%	Rk	Dist	Suc%	Rk	APaYd	Rk	PD	Int
Dawan Landry	30	SS	101	12.7%	12	32	17	8	38	39%	37	7.1	45	45	10.9%	6	8.9	36%	76	8.2	41	4	2
Drew Coleman*	26	CB	51	6.4%	67	31	21	4	7	57%	12	20.3	82	46	11.3%	74	10.8	56%	24	7.3	39	8	2
Dwight Lowery	25	FS	44	6.8%	67	17	14	4	16	25%	68	11.3	75	32	9.5%	14	12.0	68%	9	6.7	20	11	2
Rasheen Mathis	29	CB	38	8.5%	38	20	6	6	11	55%	22	3.8	3	40	17.4%	41	13.4	55%	28	8.4	59	3	1
William Middleton	25	CB	37	6.8%	--	18	3	1	18	61%	--	3.2	--	26	9.3%	--	13.2	47%	--	6.2	--	4	1
Ashton Youboty	28	CB	27	9.1%	--	11	6	1	6	67%	--	4.3	--	30	19.3%	--	14.3	40%	--	12.2	--	3	1
Derek Cox	25	CB	24	8.1%	--	8	3	1	8	38%	--	7.5	--	24	15.4%	--	17.7	74%	--	3.4	--	4	0
Akwasi Owusu-Ansah	24	SS	19	5.5%	--	8	3	1	5	60%	--	4.8	--	3	1.7%	--	10.0	48%	--	14.4	--	0	0
Kevin Rutland	31	CB	18	2.6%	--	3	2	3	4	0%	--	13.5	--	22	6.0%	--	13.3	39%	--	6.5	--	1	1
Morgan Trent	27	CB	18	3.0%	--	6	4	2	1	0%	--	6.0	--	19	6.2%	--	7.8	54%	--	5.7	--	4	2
Aaron Ross	30	CB	72	8.5%	39	25	11	1	13	54%	24	4.9	10	77	16.2%	49	12.0	45%	69	8.9	63	12	4

Year	Pass D Rank	vs. #1 WR	Rk	vs. #2 WR	Rk	vs. Other WR	Rk	vs. TE	Rk	vs. RB	Rk
2009	31	20.1%	27	29.2%	31	13.5%	27	11.2%	19	10.8%	21
2010	30	28.8%	29	8.7%	19	26.3%	30	9.3%	17	5.8%	18
2011	6	-14.4%	4	14.2%	24	2.9%	23	18.5%	20	-38.8%	1

As is the case with the front seven, it all starts up the middle for this unit. Baltimore import Dawan Landry was one of the few players to actually make it through the season unscathed, and he teamed with late trade addition Dwight Lowery to form one of the better safety tandems in the NFL. Neither of them snagged many interceptions, but they both finished in the top 10 in Defeats among safeties, and that's despite Lowery missing three games with a shoulder injury. It was imperative that the Jaguars ante up for Lowery, and they did so by re-signing him to a four-year, $13.6 million deal.

The Jaguars finished 24th in the NFL in DVOA versus No. 2 wideouts, and 23rd in DVOA against other wideouts. While that would nominally point to cornerback depth as an issue, the real problem was injury attrition at the position. Mainstay Rashean Mathis tore his ACL in Week 11, ending his season. Derek Cox was limited to just six games while battling rib, groin, and knee injuries. Reserve William Middleton was also sent to IR with a knee injury. By the end of the season, the Jaguars were starting guys straight off the street, like Ashton Youboty, or off the lowlight reel, like 2010 Jason David Memorial Award winner David Jones.

The Jaguars re-upped Mathis to a one-year "prove it" deal for $5 million, and next to him and Cox will be former Giants cornerback Aaron Ross. Ross was awful last year for New York, allowing 8.9 adjusted yards per pass despite having perhaps the league's best pass rush to agitate the quarterback in front of him. The last time Ross was a full-time corner, in 2008, he also didn't provide the Giants with much to crow about (9.1 yards per pass). He was much better in a nickel role in 2010 though, and though he's already 29, he has a much better pedigree than the now-discarded Drew Coleman. Jacksonville doesn't really have a cornerback that projects to be great, or even good, but as long as Lowery and Landry are patrolling the middle, they need only be cromulent for the Jaguars to boast an above-average pass defense.

Special Teams

Year	DVOA	Rank	FG/XP	Rank	Net Kick	Rank	Kick Ret	Rank	Net Punt	Rank	Punt Ret	Rank	Hidden	Rank
2009	-1.5%	25	-8.2	27	0.4	17	-5.6	22	4.8	7	-0.5	15	-7.6	27
2010	4.1%	7	1.9	13	12.2	5	-1.8	16	8.6	7	3.0	13	-1.8	17
2011	-1.9%	26	5.4	5	3.0	11	-5.3	28	-3.8	21	-10.5	31	15.6	1

Whether it was kick returns or punt returns, the Jaguars had major problems giving themselves good field position. Third-string backs Deji Karim and DuJuan Harris were pedestrian, and the blocking was horrendous in its own right. When he wasn't busy dropping passes, Cecil Shorts added nothing on special teams. Mike Thomas used to be a pretty good return man—we'll see if he actually bothers to care this season. Things would have been even worse for the Jaguars if opposing punters had been able to avoid touchbacks and short punts; notice that the Jags led the league in "hidden" special teams value in 2011.

Two years removed from a season in which he hit just 64 percent of his field goals, the Jaguars decided to franchise kicker Josh Scobee. Losing punter Adam Podlesh to the Bears last offseason probably had something to do with their approach to Scobee's free agency, but we can't help but find it strange that franchising your kicker in the NFL is the new hotness. Scobee was one of five kickers who were franchised this past offseason. Yes, Scobee has a big leg (18-for-29 lifetime from 50 yards or longer, strong kickoffs) but not to the point where he is irreplaceable or worth over $2.5 million.

Horrific punting by Nick Harris and Matt Turk led Smith to spend a third-round selection on Cal punter Bryan Anger. "I think that's an easy decision for me, to get a starter in the third round," Smith said of the pick. It would be easy to criticize the selection with a joke about Blaine Gabbert's offensive ineptitude, but you can find many of those on the Internet. The better way to go is to point out that at least Smith didn't draft a punter from some third-world community college, like he does with every other pick he uses after the second round.

Coaching Staff

The Jaguars' GM and ownership group gambled on Mike Mularkey over a number of more appealing or "hot" choices because they were pot committed to Blaine Gabbert and wanted a quarterback guru who could mold him into something. That's a nice thought, but the last time Mularkey was a head coach, his hands worked the clay of J.P. Losman while the 2004 Bills squandered a middling Drew Bledsoe and the fourth-best defense in DVOA history with a 9-7 campaign that missed the playoffs. Under his watch, Matt Ryan has failed to take the next step for a few years in a row, even after adding Julio Jones to the mix. That's not to say that Mularkey can't coach the Jaguars to the playoffs—it's just that the anecdotal evidence of "offensive mastermind" isn't exactly strong here.

Mel Tucker was coaching for his job last season, and he managed a strong season once the Jaguars finally opened up the pursebook and brought in more talent. He won't be on anyone's head coaching hot list anytime soon, and he may be a bit over-traditional in his schematic choices, but he's a good leader of men. Bob Bratkowski was brought in to key the offense, so expect a lot of five-yard passes on third-and-8, as was his custom in Cincinnati. #RonP4JagsOLCoach

Kansas City Chiefs

2011 Record: 7-9

Pythagorean Wins: 4.1 (29th)

DVOA: -16.9% (26th)

Offense: -19.3% (29th)

Defense: -3.2% (13th)

Special Teams: -0.9% (19th)

Variance: 20.9% (29th)

2012 Mean Projection: 8.3 wins

On the Clock (0-4): 7%

Mediocrity (5-7): 30%

Playoff Contender (8-10): 47%

Super Bowl Contender (11+): 16%

Postseason Odds: 41.0%

Projected Average Opponent: 1.4% (13th)

2011: You can't spell cataclysm without "ACL."

2012: If ever there was a set up for a team to rebound thanks to better health, this is it.

What would you expect from the Patriots if they had to play without Tom Brady, Aaron Hernandez, Rob Gronkowski, *and* Vince Wilfork? What about the Packers without Aaron Rodgers, James Starks, Jermichael Finley, and Charles Woodson? Imagine the Ravens without Joe Flacco, Ray Rice, Anquan Boldin, and Ed Reed, or the Cowboys without Tony Romo, DeMarco Murray, Jason Witten, and DeMarcus Ware.

Well, that's what happened to the Kansas City Chiefs in 2011. By the second quarter of Week 2, they had lost tight end Tony Moeaki, safety Eric Berry, and running back Jamaal Charles for the season with a trio of torn ACLs. Matt Cassel joined them on injured reserve after breaking his hand in Week 10. That's the starting quarterback, two of the three most important offensive weapons, and a Pro Bowl defender. Those four players, critical elements of the success of 2010, missed a combined 52 games in 2011. As a result, the team collapsed. A team that went 10-6 and won the AFC West the year before fell to 7-9, and their total DVOA sank from -0.1% to -15.7%.

The condition of those four key missing pieces from 2011 will likely decide the fate of the Kansas City Chiefs in 2012. Cassel was a full participant in spring OTAs. Moeaki, Berry, and Charles sat out of those drills, but are expected to be fully healthy by the start of the season. Will their return be enough to get the Chiefs back into the playoffs? Let's take them one at a time and examine why their absence hurt so badly last year, and how they'll fit in this season. We'll start at the beginning, which means we must go back to last preseason.

Tony Moeaki

What happened in 2010: A third-round rookie out of Iowa, Moeaki provided a pleasant surprise, ranking 14th among tight ends with 47 receptions and 15th with 556 yards. He had three touchdowns and eight games with at least 40 yards receiving. Moeaki ranked 14th among tight ends with 97 DYAR, and 16th with a 13.9% DVOA.

How he was hurt in 2011: At the start of the second quarter against Green Bay in Kansas City's final preseason game, Moeaki ran a right-to-left crossing pattern. He was tackled at the sideline by sixth-round rookie Ricky Elmore. Moeaki came up limping and headed straight to the sideline. It would be his last play of the year, as he went on injured reserve before the official season opener with a torn ACL.

What we can expect in 2012: Moeaki's statistics in his rookie season were nice, but not dominant. His similarity scores reflect the rookie seasons of a decent crew: Dustin Keller, Randy McMichael, Freddie Jones, Peter Mitchell. Nice players all, but in an era where Rob Gronkowski, Jimmy Graham, Antonio

2012 Chiefs Schedule

Week	Opp.	Week	Opp.	Week	Opp.
1	ATL	7	BYE	13	CAR
2	at BUF	8	OAK	14	at CLE
3	at NO	9	at SD (Thu.)	15	at OAK
4	SD	10	at PIT (Mon.)	16	IND
5	BAL	11	CIN	17	at DEN
6	at TB	12	DEN		

Figure 1. 2011 Kansas City DVOA by Week

Gates, and others are redefining the tight end position, Moeaki's rookie totals don't get the blood rushing.

The special thing about Moeaki isn't how many yards he had as a rookie, though, it's where he was running his routes. Moeaki was the target on 31 passes that went at least 10 yards past the line of scrimmage in 2010. Only six tight ends were thrown so many balls at that distance, and remember that Kansas City ranked 29th in pass attempts last season. His success rate on those throws was 65 percent. The average for tight ends at that range was 52 percent. Moeaki is not the best deep threat among tight ends, but he does have a rare ability to get open downfield.

Without Moeaki, Kansas City's tight ends (primarily Leonard Pope, with Anthony Becht and Jake O'Connell backing up) were basically non-factors as receivers. The Chiefs threw to their tight ends only 50 times, less than any team except Chicago. And those throws usually didn't go far. Only 11 times all season did Kansas City throw to a tight end more than 10 yards beyond the line of scrimmage, easily the lowest total in the league.

Moeaki's downfield ability goes beyond generating big numbers for himself. His presence creates a domino effect, as linebackers and safeties have to guard the middle of the field, leaving the perimeter open for wide receivers and holes underneath for running backs. Without that ability to stretch the interior defense, Kansas City found things much more clogged up in 2011. Moeaki should go a long way towards solving that problem in 2012.

Eric Berry

What happened in 2010: The fifth overall pick out of Tennessee, Berry made the Pro Bowl in his rookie season. According to the Approximate Value system at Pro-Football-Reference.com, he was the most valuable player on the Chiefs' defense. He had 16 total Defeats that year, which tied him for 12th among safeties, and made the top 10 for rookie safeties going back to 1997.

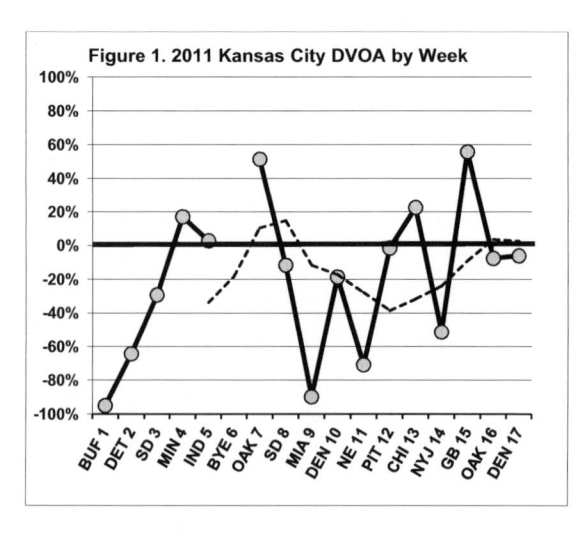

How he was hurt in 2011: On the third play from scrimmage in Week 1, the Bills gave the ball to Fred Jackson on an off-tackle run to the left. Stevie Johnson, lined up in the slot on the right, came across the formation to cut Berry's legs out from under him. Berry left the game but returned in that same series, and was in the area when Ryan Fitzpatrick hit Scott Chandler for a touchdown. On the first play of the Bills' next drive, Berry started to move up on another Jackson run but went down untouched, grabbing at his knee. The Chiefs put him on injured reserve with a torn ACL a few days later. When the New Orleans Saints bounty scandal broke earlier this year, Berry speculated via Twitter that he had been a bounty victim. Johnson denied the charge, telling the hosts of *ProFootballTalk Live* that he had apologized to Berry, and felt so guilty about the incident that he didn't throw another cut block all year. One way or the other, things are sure to be interesting when Kansas City travels to Buffalo in Week 2.

What we can expect in 2012: To get a better idea of what kind of player Berry might be, let's look at the ten rookies most similar to him in our database (Table 1). It's an impressive list. LaRon Landry has been inconsistent, but Louis Delmas and Greg Wesley are at least average players, and the other seven range from Pro Bowler to All-Pro to Hall of Fame candidate.

On the surface, it actually doesn't look like the Chiefs suffered much from having to replace Berry with special-teamer Jon McGraw and journeyman Sabby Piscitelli. Their pass defense was better in nearly every way compared to 2010, and the defensive backs did an excellent job of cutting down on long runs (seventh in Open Field Yards per carry). The

Table 1: Rookie Safeties Most Similar to Eric Berry, 1997-2011

Name	Yr	Tm	G	TmTot	Suc	Dft
Eric Berry	2010	KC	16	12.0%	38	16
Louis Delmas	2009	DET	15	11.8%	41	21
Roy Williams	2002	DAL	16	11.9%	50	23
LaRon Landry	2007	WAS	16	11.7%	34	13
Sean Taylor	2004	WAS	15	11.7%	35	18
Greg Wesley	2000	KC	16	11.0%	36	16
Sammy Knight	1997	NO	16	11.0%	37	15
Nick Collins	2005	GB	16	10.5%	32	14
Ed Reed	2002	BAL	16	10.3%	36	19
Kerry Rhodes	2005	NYJ	16	12.4%	34	11
Erik Coleman	2004	NYJ	16	12.9%	33	17

McGraw-Piscitelli pairing also had very similar play-by-play and charting stats to what Berry had done in 2010, and while that's a little unfair because Kansas City often had both players on the field in nickel and dime formations, it's not as if opponents were constantly exploiting the duo for big plays either.

Does all that mean that Berry's return won't be a significant factor this fall? Not at all. For all that advanced statistics can tell us about the game, they haven't done much to help us evaluate safeties. The responsibilities of the position can change radically from team to team, or even from play to play, and our game charting has done little to add useful information on the subject since they're usually outside the frame anyway. So let's put the numbers aside and use a little common sense. McGraw has played ten years, Piscitelli five, for three teams each, and only once has either of them started 10 or more games in a season. Both remained unsigned as of mid-June, and there's no guarantee that either of them will find work in the league again. The Chiefs declined to bring either one back, and in their place the team will start a Pro Bowler, one of the most promising young safeties of the past decade. It's silly to think that this won't be a tremendous upgrade.

Berry won't just return; he'll return to be part of a very talented young safety tandem. As a rookie alongside Berry in 2010, strong safety Kendrick Lewis averaged 2.9 Plays (defined as any positive appearance in the play-by-play) in 12 games, 10 of them starts. In his second year, that averaged swelled to 4.3 plays per game. If Berry can return to health, and he and Lewis continue to develop, the Chiefs could have one of the league's best secondaries this fall.

Jamaal Charles

What happened in 2010: On a per-carry basis, Charles was the best running back in football. Though Kansas City insisted on using the clearly inferior Thomas Jones as a primary rusher, Charles still rushed for 1,467 yards on only 230 carries. He became the fourth player in NFL history to rush for at least 1,400 yards in a season and average at least 6.0 yards per carry. The others: O.J. Simpson, Barry Sanders, and Jim Brown. In 2010, no player had more carries for 10-plus yards (Charles had 45), but 30 players had more stuffs (29). Advanced stats also loved him. His 382 rushing DYAR were the most since LaDainian Tomlinson's 460 in 2006, and his 35.3% DVOA was the highest since Marshall Faulk's 41.3% in 2000. Oh, and Charles was also ninth among running backs with 468 receiving yards. So there's that.

How he was hurt in 2011: Midway through the first quarter against Detroit in Week 2, Charles took an inside handoff out of a shotgun and ran a sweep to the right. As cornerback Chris Houston moved in to make the tackle, Charles lunged for the first-down marker, striding as far as he could, and came down with all his weight on his left foot. He rolled to the ground clutching his knee, and was eventually carted off the field. An MRI the next day revealed a torn ACL, and noted sports surgeon James Andrews operated on the knee in early October.

What we can expect in 2012: A number of runners have managed to post 1,000-yard seasons after one (or more) ACL tears, including Jamal Anderson, Jamal Lewis, Edgerrin James, Willis McGahee, and Frank Gore. Charles' long-term projections are little different now than they were a year ago.

But can we expect Charles to be the same player he was in 2010? For several reasons, probably not. Only three men (the afore-mentioned Brown, Simpson, and Sanders) have ever gone over 200 carries and 5.5 yards per rush more than once in their careers, and nobody has ever done it twice in a row. The ten backs most similar to Charles in 2010 (excluding Charles himself in 2009) averaged 4.3 yards per rush the following season.

So we should definitely expect a decline from Charles this season. On the other hand, even if he can only average 80 percent of his career rate, that would still leave him at 4.8 yards per carry. The Chiefs added Peyton Hillis in free agency, and he'll take a significant chunk of the team's carries. But Charles is still a special player and a dangerous weapon, a home-run threat that few teams can match.

Matt Cassel

What happened in 2010: Cassel's third season as a starter (including his 2008 fill-in for Tom Brady in New England) was his best. He threw 27 touchdowns and had an NFL passer rating of 93.0, ranking eight in the league in both categories. He also threw only seven interceptions, finishing fourth in interception percentage. His advanced statistics were less impressive, largely because the Chiefs played an easy schedule that season. Cassel ranked ninth with a VOA of 21.9%, but 16th with a DVOA of 15.2%. Still, Cassel seemed to have established himself as a solid enough starter in Kansas City. Nobody was going to put him in the Hall of Fame, but he seemed capable of making regular playoff appearances with the proper talent around him.

How he was hurt in 2011: The Chiefs had a fourth-and-2 down 10 points late in the fourth quarter against Denver in Week 10. Elvis Dumervil beat right tackle Barry Richardson to pressure Cassel. The quarterback stepped up in the pocket, but ran right into the blitzing D.J. Williams, and was eventually taken down by Dumervil and Von Miller. It seemed like an innocuous play at the time, and Cassel casually walked off the field, but cameras caught him favoring his hand on the sideline. Tyler Palko came in to finish the game, and Cassel underwent surgery on his hand the next day. Given how the Chiefs played in the next month with Palko at the helm, and how close the AFC West race proved to be, this injury by itself might have kept Kansas City out of the playoffs.

What we can expect in 2012: Even before his injury, Cassel was pretty lousy last season, with a DVOA of -19.0%. He threw 17 fewer touchdowns than he had the year prior, with two more interceptions, and only four fewer sacks despite missing seven games.

How much of that was Cassel, and how much was the talent (or lack thereof) around him? As we've noted, the Chiefs had big holes at tight end and in the backfield, but were more or less complete at wideout. It may mean something that out of the 47 quarterbacks with at least 100 pass plays, Cassel was 25th in DVOA when throwing to his wide receivers, but 37th throwing to his tight ends and next to last throwing to running backs. The Chiefs also struggled to catch passes, with 31 drops in 495 pass plays, a rate of 6.3 percent that was worse than everyone except the 49ers and Browns. And our game charters noted that there were extenuating circumstances to some of Cassel's interceptions. Two of them should have been receptions, but were dropped by receivers. Three of them were thrown under heavy pressure. Still, sometimes Cassel simply made bad throws (putting the ball right in Eric Weddle's belly on an attempted screen pass, for example) or focused on receivers, telegraphing his passes to defenses.

Our similarity scores tell an interesting story about Cassel. Because Cassel played only nine games in 2011, the standard similarity scores give you a number of other quarterbacks who had a half-season of subpar numbers after a good season. If we limit our list to players close to Cassel in age (i.e. 28 to 30), it is topped by Bubby Brister, Neil O'Donnell, Jim Harbaugh, and Jim Everett (Table 2). Brister and O'Donnell had lower numbers in the third season of their similar spans due to injury. Harbaugh actually started 15 games for the 1993 Bears, but only threw 325 passes because the Bears had a run-pass ratio of more than 2:1. In that same season, the Rams benched Everett halfway through the year.

Another way to look at similarity scores would be to pro-rate Cassel's numbers to 15 starts, the same number he had in both 2009 and 2010. Now our list is topped by the likes of Jim Zorn, Ken O'Brien, Jake Plummer, and Aaron Brooks (Table 3). For the most part, our second similarity list consists of average quarterbacks, and to be honest, that's about what the Chiefs are expecting from Cassel.

However, there's one important difference between Cassel and the quarterbacks he's similar to: era. Our similarity scores are not yet normalized to the offensive environment that each player was in. (We've never gotten it to work quite right.) So Cassel's last three

Table 2. Most Similar QBs to Matt Cassel 2009-11

Player	Years	Team	Age (Y3)
Bubby Brister	1989-91	PIT	29
Neil O'Donnell	1994-96	PIT/NYJ	30
Jim Harbaugh	1991-93	CHI	30
Jim Everett	1991-93	LARM	30
Vinny Testaverde	1989-91	TB	28
Dave Krieg	1986-88*	SEA	30
Kyle Orton	2009-11	DEN/KC	29
Donovan McNabb	2003-05	PHI	29
Jason Campbell	2008-10	WAS/OAK	29
Brian Griese	2001-03	DEN/MIA	28

Limited to players ages 28 to 30 in year three.
*1987 pro-rated for strike

Table 4. Most Similar QB to Matt Cassel 2009-2011 (Cassel 2011 Pro-Rated to 15 Games)

Player	Years	Team	Age (Y3)
Jim Zorn	80-82*	SEA	29
Ken O'Brien	88-90	NYJ	30
Jake Plummer	00-02	ARI	28
Aaron Brooks	03-05	NO	29
Neil O'Donnell	93-95	PIT	29
Dave Krieg	85-87*	SEA	29
Mark Brunell	97-99	JAC	29
Bobby Hebert	87-89*	NO	29
Jim Harbaugh	91-93	CHI	30
Richard Todd	81-83*	NYJ	30

Limited to players ages 28-30 in year three.
*1982 and 1987 pro-rated for strike

years aren't comparable to an average NFL starting quarterback. They're comparable to an average starting quarterback from a decade or two ago. Quarterbacks don't generally put up numbers like that in this century, and when they do, they often lose their jobs.

Even at his best, Cassel has never been particularly good about completing passes or picking up yards. His strengths have been the ability to avoid turnovers and to convert red zone drives into touchdowns. If that's the kind of player that Kansas City gets this fall, they'll need more production from other positions to return to the playoffs. And if Cassel can't even manage that, his time with the Chiefs will likely be done.

Cassel's job won't be the only one at stake in Kansas City this year. Other than the four injured stars, the biggest difference between the 2011 and 2012 Chiefs is the head coach. Last year, the Chiefs let go of the abrasive Todd Haley after a 27-point loss to the Jets in Week 14, Kansas City's fifth loss in six games. He was replaced by Romeo Crennel, who quickly brought stability back to Arrowhead Stadium and won the right to drop "interim" from his title. Nonetheless, Crennel has already failed at one head coaching gig, going 24-40 with no playoff berths in four seasons with the Cleveland Browns. The Chiefs aren't likely to give Crennel four years to make an impression, and he'd best win right out of the gate. The good news is that there's already a sign the locker room respects Crennel. DVOA says the Chiefs played their best football at the end of the year under Crennel, even without their four injured stars. The team's total DVOA in 12 games under Haley was -26.0%, but with Crennel in charge that number soared to 14.1%. That's largely due to a Week 14 upset of then-undefeated Green Bay, but even in close games with Oakland and Denver their DVOA never dipped below -7.5%, still far better than how they performed under Haley.

If there's one thing Crennel can do to improve this club, it's to keep his team focused and playing at their best week in and week out. Under Haley, while they played very well at times, they also tended to get blown out with annoying regularity. They lost five games by at least three touchdowns last year. Even in their 10-win 2010 campaign, they lost four games by 20 or more points (including the Wild Card game against Baltimore). The Chiefs ranked 11th in Football Outsiders' variance stat in Haley's first year in 2009, but 24th and 29th in 2010 and 2011 (including three games under Crennel last year). Their average variance over that three-year period was 17.0 percent. Crennel's 2007 Browns team ranked second in the league with a variance of 5.9 percent, but in other years they were nothing special. Their average variance in four seasons under Crennel was 14.3 percent, not much better than Haley's Chiefs teams.

Crennel will have a few other pieces to play with this season. On offense, they signed Kevin Boss, and will likely pair him with Moeaki for an increased use of two-tight end sets. They promoted second-year lineman Rodney Hudson to starting center, while also grabbing free-agent tackle Eric Winston from Houston. These changes should all boost the team's run blocking, one of Kansas City's biggest weaknesses last season.

On defense, by far the biggest addition is the return of Berry. First-round draft pick Dontari Poe takes over at nose tackle, while free agency's cornerback carousel took Brandon Carr away from the Chiefs, replacing him with Stanford Routt. Both Poe and Routt should be able to hold their own at their new jobs this year.

Like all AFC West teams, the Chiefs have a nasty non-division schedule that includes three playoff teams from the AFC North and two more from the NFC South, plus Cam Newton and the improving Panthers. That's all going to make it difficult to win a Wild Card spot, and that in turn makes Kansas City's divisional games all the more important. Most notably, Denver doesn't visit Arrowhead until Week 12, and Kansas City doesn't go to Mile High until Week 17. Circle those two games, because they will likely decide the championship of the AFC West.

Vince Verhei

KANSAS CITY CHIEFS

2011 Chiefs Stats by Week

Wk	vs.	W-L	PF	PA	YDF	YDA	TO	Total	Off	Def	ST
1	BUF	L	7	41	213	364	-2	-95%	-48%	32%	-16%
2	@DET	L	3	48	267	411	-5	-64%	-51%	2%	-11%
3	@SD	L	17	20	252	375	1	-29%	-38%	-8%	1%
4	MIN	W	22	17	350	341	1	17%	3%	4%	18%
5	@IND	W	28	24	436	355	0	3%	38%	41%	6%
6	BYE										
7	@OAK	W	28	0	300	322	4	51%	-21%	-65%	7%
8	SD	W	23	20	341	447	0	-12%	-40%	-20%	9%
9	MIA	L	3	31	343	351	0	-90%	-13%	68%	-9%
10	DEN	L	10	17	258	313	0	-19%	-4%	16%	2%
11	@NE	L	3	34	334	380	-2	-71%	-63%	-3%	-11%
12	PIT	L	9	13	252	290	-2	-1%	-30%	-18%	11%
13	@CHI	W	10	3	252	181	2	23%	-15%	-50%	-13%
14	@NYJ	L	10	37	221	314	0	-51%	-37%	18%	4%
15	GB	W	19	14	438	315	0	56%	19%	-25%	12%
16	OAK	L	13	16	435	308	0	-8%	-15%	-26%	-19%
17	@DEN	W	7	3	281	266	1	-6%	-13%	-14%	-7%

Trends and Splits

	Offense	Rank	Defense	Rank
Total DVOA	-19.3%	29	-3.2%	13
Unadjusted VOA	-16.8%	27	0.2%	16
Weighted Trend	-18.5%	26	-9.7%	12
Variance	10.0%	23	7.3%	24
Average Opponent	2.5%	29	2.0%	11
Passing	-14.0%	25	-0.3%	12
Rushing	-13.1%	31	-5.9%	17
First Down	-20.7%	29	0.6%	18
Second Down	-16.1%	27	5.7%	21
Third Down	-21.6%	24	-23.0%	3
First Half	-21.1%	27	-4.6%	12
Second Half	-17.5%	29	-1.9%	14
Red Zone	-30.9%	28	-10.0%	15
Late and Close	-4.0%	21	-3.3%	14

Five-Year Performance

Year	W-L	Pyth	Est W	PF	PA	TO	Total	Rk	Off	Rk	Def	Rk	ST	Rk	Off AGL	Rk	Def AGL	Rk
2007	4-12	4.6	5.3	226	335	-11	-19.5%	25	-19.4%	29	-3.8%	14	-4.0%	24	22.8	19	4.2	1
2008	2-14	4.2	3.5	291	440	+5	-29.4%	30	-9.2%	23	13.3%	28	-7.0%	30	30.4	20	16.9	13
2009	4-12	4.6	3.5	294	424	+1	-29.2%	28	-18.0%	25	9.2%	27	-2.1%	27	13.0	9	15.3	6
2010	10-6	9.1	8.3	366	326	+9	0.3%	17	4.4%	13	2.1%	20	-2.1%	24	5.8	2	4.2	1
2011	7-9	4.2	6.3	212	338	-2	-16.9%	26	-19.3%	29	-3.2%	13	-0.9%	19	43.8	26	21.7	13

2011 Performance Based on Most Common Personnel Groups

Kansas City Offense					Kansas City Offense vs. Opp.				Kansas City Defense				Kansas City Defense vs. Opp.			
Pers	Freq	Yds	DVOA	Run%	Pers	Freq	Yds	DVOA	Pers	Freq	Yds	DVOA	Pers	Freq	Yds	DVOA
11	35%	4.9	-29.0%	33%	4-3-4	29%	4.4	-18.5%	3-4-4	52%	5.8	11.4%	11	31%	5.3	-10.8%
21	24%	4.9	-13.8%	59%	3-4-4	23%	4.9	0.3%	Dime+	26%	5.5	-25.3%	12	28%	5.6	3.6%
12	16%	5.2	5.2%	46%	4-2-5	22%	6.0	-6.4%	2-4-5	12%	5.1	-17.6%	21	15%	6.2	9.0%
22	10%	4.3	-10.8%	69%	Dime+	11%	5.6	-24.3%	3-3-5	5%	5.0	-17.8%	10	4%	5.7	-30.3%
10	6%	6.3	11.5%	23%	3-3-5	9%	4.5	-40.7%	4-3-4	3%	5.4	40.4%	22	4%	4.0	-35.9%

Strategic Tendencies

Run/Pass		Rank	Offense		Rank	Pass Rush		Rank	Defense/Other		Rank
Runs, all plays	47%	5	Form: Single Back	57%	24	Rush 3	12.1%	6	4 DB	55%	8
Runs, first half	49%	2	Form: Empty Back	4%	23	Rush 4	54.0%	25	5 DB	17%	31
Runs, first down	56%	6	Pers: 3+ WR	47%	22	Rush 5	26.9%	8	6+ DB	26%	6
Runs, second-long	48%	2	Pers: 4+ WR	6%	7	Rush 6+	7.0%	19	CB by Sides	94%	5
Runs, power sit.	53%	22	Pers: 2+ TE/6+ OL	30%	20	Zone Blitz	3.1%	24	Go for it on 4th	0.99	10
Runs, behind 2H	37%	4	Play action	20%	13	Sacks by LB	67.2%	4	Offensive Pace	30.1	11
Pass, ahead 2H	38%	25	Max protect	24%	1	Sacks by DB	6.9%	18	Defensive Pace	31.0	27

The Chiefs didn't change their run-first philosophy, despite losing their best running back early in the season and killing clock on fewer leads. In fact, in the first half of games, they ran more often than they did in 2010.

When Kansas City was winning or tied, they had the second best defensive DVOA in the league, behind only Baltimore. When they were losing, their defense ranked 28th. ☙ The Chiefs defense got better the more defensive backs they put in the game. ☙ Chiefs opponents started their average drive on the 31.3-yard line, closer than against any other defense. ☙ Chiefs opponents handed off to running backs on a league-high 18 percent of shotgun snaps.

Passing

Player	DYAR	DVOA	Plays	NtYds	Avg	YAC	C%	TD	Int
M.Cassel	-277	-25.9%	291	1586	5.5	4.4	59.9%	10	8
T.Palko	-150	-27.9%	145	718	5.0	4.3	60.9%	2	7
K.Orton*	192	18.4%	96	730	7.6	6.3	60.8%	1	2

Rushing

Player	DYAR	DVOA	Plays	Yds	Avg	TD	Fum	Suc
T.Jones*	-104	-26.1%	153	478	3.1	0	0	35%
J.Battle*	76	4.3%	149	597	4.0	2	0	44%
D.McCluster	27	-2.3%	112	507	4.5	1	1	43%
M.Cassel	25	13.5%	19	104	5.5	0	0	--
L.McClain*	2	-5.5%	15	51	3.4	1	0	47%
J.Charles	2	-4.9%	12	83	6.9	0	1	50%
P.Hillis	50	-1.7%	161	587	3.6	3	1	55%

Receiving

Player	DYAR	DVOA	Plays	Ctch	Yds	Y/C	YAC	TD	C%
D.Bowe	136	-0.5%	141	81	1159	14.3	4.2	5	57%
S.Breaston	100	0.7%	98	61	785	12.9	5.1	2	62%
J.Baldwin	-105	-38.9%	53	21	254	12.1	2.0	1	40%
J.Urban*	-44	-56.7%	13	4	35	8.8	0.8	1	31%
T.Copper	30	20.3%	12	8	114	14.3	4.5	0	67%
K.Colbert	-28	-43.8%	12	9	89	9.9	3.4	0	75%
L.Pope*	19	0.9%	33	24	247	10.3	5.2	1	73%
J.O'Connell	-22	-34.9%	12	7	52	7.4	2.0	0	58%
K.Boss	72	22.3%	39	28	368	13.1	4.7	3	72%
D.McCluster	4	-12.6%	63	47	350	7.4	6.6	1	75%
L.McClain*	-2	-15.2%	22	14	82	5.9	4.4	1	64%
J.Battle*	-17	-37.0%	13	9	68	7.6	8.8	0	69%
T.Jones*	3	-6.3%	7	5	43	8.6	11.2	0	71%
J.Charles	-5	-29.8%	6	5	9	1.8	-0.4	1	83%
P.Hillis	-35	-33.2%	34	22	130	5.9	5.4	0	65%

Offensive Line

Year	Yards	ALY	Rank	Power	Rank	Stuff	Rank	2nd Lev	Rank	Open Field	Rank	F-Start	Cont.
2009	4.39	3.63	30	63%	18	21%	20	1.26	9	1.00	7	22	27
2010	4.82	4.44	5	57%	20	15%	5	1.35	3	1.00	8	17	32
2011	3.89	3.81	28	62%	18	20%	21	1.11	25	0.55	27	26	39

Year	LE	Rank	LT	Rank	Mid	Rank	RT	Rank	RE	Rank	Sacks	ASR	Rank	Short	Long
2009	4.30	16	5.66	1	3.33	30	2.14	32	4.24	15	46	7.8%	25	17	12
2010	4.97	5	4.74	6	4.11	13	4.00	20	5.31	3	32	6.8%	18	6	19
2011	4.88	7	5.67	1	3.39	32	3.43	27	2.94	25	34	7.1%	19	6	20

The Chiefs are going to have two new starters on the offensive line, and both should be pretty substantial upgrades. At center, Casey Wiegmann wasn't getting it done anymore after 227 games in 13 NFL seasons, as the Chiefs' last-place ranking in ALY on runs up the middle points out. He has hung up his pads, clearing the way for Rodney Hudson, the 55th pick of the 2011 draft. Hudson started only one game in his rookie year, playing at left guard against Pittsburgh in Week 12, but he had a stellar career at Florida State, where he was first-team All-ACC three times, first-team All-America twice, and won two Jacobs Blocking Trophies (the ACC's annual award for offensive linemen).

The other new starter is on the right side, where Eric Winston takes over for Barry Richardson (now in St. Louis). Winston was a surprise salary cap cut in Houston, and the Chiefs were all too happy to snap him up and cut ties with Richardson. What kind of improvement will that mean for Kansas City? In pass blocking, it's a pretty lateral move. Richardson led Kansas City last season with 9.0 blown blocks, while Winston led Houston with 7.5. The Chiefs should be much better at run blocking, though. Winston has started every game for Houston since 2007. In that timeframe, the Texans only once ranked in the bottom half of the league in ALY on runs to right tackle, and their average ranking was 12.0. Over that same period, the Chiefs were never higher than 19th, and their average ranking was 27.8.

Winston will pair with Branden Albert to form one of the league's better duos at tackle. Albert had just 5.5 blown blocks last season, and the Chiefs led the league in ALY to his side. Both guards (Ryan Lilja and Jon Asamoah) are also back. Asamoah, a 2010 third-round pick, started every game in his second season, and the Chiefs think he can develop further. Lilja will turn 31 in October, and is likely entering the decline phase of his career. The Chiefs also drafted a pair of linemen in the second and third rounds: Jeff Allen out of Illinois and Donald Stephenson out of Oklahoma. Allen is the more polished of the two (Mike Mayock called him a "day one starter," which couldn't have made Lilja very happy). Lilja and Albert are both free agents after this season, so it's feasible that Allen and Stephenson will both be starting in 2013.

Defensive Front Seven

Defensive Line	Age	Pos	Plays	TmPct	Rk	Stop	Dfts	BTkl	St%	Rk	AvYd	Rk	Sack	Hit	Hur	Runs	St%	Yds	Pass	St%	Yds
Glenn Dorsey	27	DE	59	7.7%	7	48	7	1	81%	32	2.4	67	0	3	0	59	81%	2.4	0	0%	0.0
Tyson Jackson	26	DE	57	7.0%	11	48	9	0	84%	19	2.6	74	1	1	4	52	83%	2.8	5	100%	0.0
Kelly Gregg*	36	DT	38	4.6%	26	32	4	3	84%	16	1.9	38	1	0	1	34	85%	2.2	4	75%	-0.5
Amon Gordon	31	DE	24	2.9%	79	17	3	0	71%	63	2.5	70	2	0	0	20	70%	3.3	4	75%	-1.5

Linebackers	Age	Pos	Plays	TmPct	Rk	Stop	Dfts	BTkl	AvYd	Sack	Hit	Hur	Runs	St%	Rk	Yds	Rk	Tgts	Suc%	Rk	AdjYd	Rk
Derrick Johnson	30	ILB	137	16.7%	10	85	31	9	5.2	2	1	10	90	66%	54	4.3	95	32	54%	23	6.7	39
Jovan Belcher	25	ILB	88	10.8%	49	47	7	4	4.6	0	1	4	71	58%	82	3.8	82	13	53%	--	5.2	--
Tamba Hali	29	OLB	66	8.1%	81	47	18	4	2.0	12	18	40.5	51	69%	44	3.5	62	2	50%	--	5.5	--
Justin Houston	23	OLB	54	6.6%	100	35	17	3	4.0	5.5	6	8	30	73%	20	2.5	22	17	42%	59	11.8	80

Year	Yards	ALY	Rank	Power	Rank	Stuff	Rank	2nd Lev	Rank	Open Field	Rank
2009	4.93	4.70	32	64%	17	13%	32	1.21	21	1.08	26
2010	4.34	4.29	25	66%	22	14%	28	1.12	17	0.67	12
2011	4.13	4.31	24	55%	9	16%	29	1.06	7	0.57	7

Year	LE	Rank	LT	Rank	Mid	Rank	RT	Rank	RE	Rank	Sacks	ASR	Rank	Short	Long
2009	5.42	32	5.24	31	4.63	28	4.27	19	4.13	19	22	3.5%	32	7	8
2010	4.60	22	4.09	17	4.42	27	4.42	20	2.82	2	39	6.5%	12	11	18
2011	4.21	14	4.04	17	4.39	28	4.97	29	3.28	14	29	6.3%	23	12	11

Tamba Hali finished eighth in sacks, first in hurries, and fourth in hits last season. Have the Chiefs found a bookend for him in Justin Houston? Houston drew six holding penalties last year (only three defenders drew more) and ranked fourth on the Chiefs in Defeats even though he rotated in and out of the lineup with Andy Studebaker. It's probably not a coincidence that the Chiefs nearly tripled their sack production after Houston permanently became a starter in Week 11 (1.0 sacks per game through Week 10, 2.9 from that point forward). However, a close look at our charting stats shows that when Houston did get to the quarterback, there were usually extenuating circumstances. Most of them were listed as coverage sacks, or came when Houston was unblocked. The only linemen he beat for sacks were Chicago's Lance Louis (a guard playing out of position at tackle) and New York's Wayne Hunter (one of four linemen last year with more than ten blown blocks).

Derrick Johnson blossomed in his second year playing 3-4 inside linebacker, setting career highs in Plays, Stops, and Defeats against the rush, while making his most total Defeats since 2007. At the other inside linebacker spot, Jovan Belcher will have to hold off a challenge from Brandon Siler. A free-agent signee from the Chargers in 2011, Siler missed all of last season with a torn Achilles tendon.

Like most 3-4 teams, the Chiefs get little in the way of pass rush from their defensive linemen. As a group, they were in the bottom five units in the league in Pass Plays, Successes, Defeats, and Sacks, and last in the league in Hurries. They were more active against the run, but hardly any more effective, ranking 11th in total

Run Plays, but 26th in both Defeats and average yards on run tackles. In short, they get pushed around too much. Dontari Poe—all 6-foot-3, 346 pounds of him—is supposed to change that. Poe should start on opening day, but he's unpolished and thought of as something of a project. Glenn Dorsey and Tyson Jackson, the twin disappointing first-rounders out of LSU, return at the end spots. Allen Bailey, a third-round draft pick who played little as a rookie last year, could see more time as a situational pass rusher.

Defensive Secondary

Secondary	Age	Pos	Plays	TmPct	Rk	Stop	Dfts	BTkl	Runs	St%	Rk	Yds	Rk	Tgts	Tgt%	Rk	Dist	Suc%	Rk	APaYd	Rk	PD	Int
Brandon Flowers	26	CB	78	9.5%	21	40	22	4	19	68%	6	3.7	2	81	23.1%	5	15.0	56%	23	7.5	43	19	4
Kendrick Lewis	24	FS	68	8.3%	55	17	9	9	32	16%	75	11.2	74	25	7.0%	38	19.4	56%	40	10.4	67	9	3
Brandon Carr*	26	CB	60	7.3%	57	26	11	7	12	50%	27	6.8	39	73	20.9%	17	15.0	55%	27	6.2	17	13	4
Jon McGraw*	33	SS	51	10.0%	38	27	16	8	27	63%	2	4.0	1	19	8.5%	21	11.6	61%	20	7.2	33	6	3
Javier Arenas	25	CB	38	5.0%	--	14	10	2	12	33%	--	6.9	--	30	9.0%	--	12.4	58%	--	5.8	--	7	2
Sabby Piscitelli*	29	FS	31	3.8%	77	9	4	1	18	39%	41	6.2	25	18	5.0%	66	13.9	52%	45	9.5	60	1	0
Donald Washington	26	SS	24	3.9%	--	6	3	4	12	25%	--	8.1	--	12	4.6%	--	8.4	36%	--	8.0	--	2	0
Travis Daniels	30	CB	16	2.0%	--	6	4	3	5	20%	--	7.6	--	19	5.4%	--	13.5	69%	--	5.7	--	3	2
Abram Elam	31	FS	65	8.7%	53	17	10	4	26	42%	30	5.0	8	25	6.1%	56	14.2	59%	30	5.6	9	0	0
Stanford Routt	29	CB	64	8.0%	49	25	9	6	10	0%	81	10.8	71	94	20.2%	22	12.7	58%	20	6.1	14	17	4

Year	Pass D Rank	vs. #1 WR	Rk	vs. #2 WR	Rk	vs. Other WR	Rk	vs. TE	Rk	vs. RB	Rk
2009	19	-18.0%	9	26.3%	30	-17.5%	7	-1.1%	12	5.4%	18
2010	18	-12.4%	7	11.2%	22	-3.3%	16	11.3%	20	16.1%	26
2011	13	-22.9%	2	6.8%	19	-27.2%	5	6.5%	16	34.5%	31

With Brandon Carr leaving for Dallas in free agency, the Chiefs raided the Raiders for Stanford Routt, who is something of an enigma. Only once in his first five seasons did he qualify for our cornerback leaderboards, and in that year he was awful, ranking 76th in Success Rate and 78th in Yards per Pass. Then Routt became a starter, and quite unexpectedly a pretty good one. He was sixth in Success Rate in 2010, 32nd in Yards per Pass, and fell somewhere in between on both stats last year. Yes, he led the league in Defensive Pass Interference calls last year, but those seven big plays don't overshadow the other 87 times we charted Routt in coverage. When Routt was released by Oakland, you may have heard a stat quoted in the press that Routt allowed eight touchdowns last season. (Some groups listed him with nine; we have eight.) That stat gives you the impression that Routt was constantly burned deep, but half of these touchdowns were for six yards or less.

Brandon Flowers is coming off his worst season according to both game-charting metrics, which means he's likely to bounce back this year. Javier Arenas, Travis Daniels, and 2011 fourth-rounder Jalil Brown will battle for the nickel spot. Our money is on Arenas, who showed a knack for fighting off blockers on running plays despite standing 5-foot-9 and 195 pounds. (On one play against Oakland in Week 7, Arenas hit the 6-foot-6, 305-pound Khalif Barnes in the open field and actually pushed him backwards.)

Kansas City's top three safeties were banged up as the team went through OTAs. Eric Berry was held out of drills entirely as the team was taking extra caution with his knee. Strong safety Kendrick Lewis sat out too, recovering from January surgery to repair a pectoral muscle that was torn while Lewis tackled Tim Tebow. DeQuan Menzie, a fifth-round pick out of Alabama who can also play corner, sat out with hamstring issues. Though Berry and Menzie are expected to be ready by the start of training camp, there was no timetable for Lewis' return as of late May.

Special Teams

Year	DVOA	Rank	FG/XP	Rank	Net Kick	Rank	Kick Ret	Rank	Net Punt	Rank	Punt Ret	Rank	Hidden	Rank
2009	-1.7%	27	3.9	9	-3.9	25	-7.1	26	3.6	10	-6.7	27	4.9	7
2010	-1.8%	24	-2.8	28	-2.3	21	-9.1	27	-1.5	23	5.3	6	-1.3	15
2011	-0.8%	19	-2.3	20	-1.0	22	-6.6	30	3.2	12	2.1	12	-15.4	32

You may not find a team in the league with less turnover in this department, as kicker Ryan Succop, punter Dustin Colquitt, long snapper Thomas Gafford, and returners Dexter McCluster and Javier Arenas all return. Succop is remarkably mediocre, ranking 18th out of 34 active kickers in career field-goal accuracy. He's equally adequate on kickoffs, where he has been exactly 0.1 points more valuable than the average kicker over the last three years. Former Southern Methodist kicker Matt Szymanski was also invited to training camp. Colquitt was in the top ten in gross punt value in 2009 and 2011, but ranked 21st in 2010. Arenas handles punt returns, and should be the primary kick returner in 2012 as well. Last year he outperformed McCluster, who struggled with fumbles. McCluster is also expected to see more time at wide receiver this year, which would theoretically leave him less time to devote to special teams. Kansas City's league-worst rank in "hidden" special teams is another element pointing towards more wins in 2012; the Chiefs' poor luck was evenly split, as opponents were better than average on kickoff distance, punt distance, and field-goal accuracy.

Coaching Staff

The Chiefs will have one of the league's most experienced coaching staffs. Romeo Crennel, assistant head coach Maurice Carthon, offensive coordinator Brian Daboll, quarterbacks coach Jim Zorn, linebackers coach Gary Gibbs, and defensive backs coach Emmitt Thomas have plied their trade for a combined 116 NFL seasons. Crennel, like his mentor Bill Belichick, will try to find more success in his second gig after washing out with the Browns. He was already defensive coordinator in Kansas City last year, and there is no coordinator now, so we shouldn't expect major changes on that side of the ball. Daboll also comes from a branch of the Bill Parcells coaching tree; he joins Kansas City after running the offenses in Cleveland (after Crennel's tenure there) and Miami. His units have never ranked higher than 20th in DVOA, but he should have more talent this year than he ever has before. He'll work closely with Carthon, former offensive coordinator with the Lions, Cowboys, and Browns. We must also mention offensive quality control coach Jim Bob Cooter, because you should never pass up an opportunity to say "Jim Bob Cooter."

Miami Dolphins

2011 Record: 6-10

Pythagorean Wins: 8.5 (14th)

DVOA: -1.3% (18th)

Offense: -7.5% (20t)

Defense: -3.7% (12th)

Special Teams: 2.5% (6th)

Variance: 9.7% (10th)

2012 Mean Projection: 6.9 wins

On the Clock (0-4): 14%

Mediocrity (5-7): 47%

Playoff Contender (8-10): 33%

Super Bowl Contender (11+): 5%

Postseason Odds: 9.7%

Projected Average Opponent: -2.0% (25th)

2011: Cameron Wake, plus 52 guys who were just kind of there.

2012: Miami has replaced Buffalo as denizens of the AFC East hamster wheel, forever going nowhere.

Jeff Ireland is the new Matt Millen.

Once you accept that simple fact, everything the Dolphins have done in the past three years makes perfect sense. Analyzed logically, their indecision at quarterback, on-and-off flirtation with gadget offenses, incapability of landing premium free agents, indifference toward upgrading their skill positions, and seeming satisfaction with six or seven wins looks like directionless foolishness. Seen through the Prism of Millen, though, the last three years are the clear product of highly directed foolishness. Ireland may have no idea what he is doing, but no one can question his dedication to doing it. He really thinks that his lurching, reactionary managerial approach is the right way to do business.

While the Millen resemblance fits, it is hard to spot at first glance. As Tolstoy once implied, all happy franchises are alike, and every unhappy franchise unhappy in its own way. The Ireland Dolphins and Millen Lions appear to suffer from distinct flavors of misery until you look closely, and more importantly, listen carefully.

In mid-April, after Ireland whiffed on several efforts to sign high-profile free agent quarterbacks, Dolphins fans picketed Ireland's offices with "Fireland" signs. The general manager's response: "I know there are passionate fans out there, and they want results," he said. "I would tell (fans), look, we don't play until August. Let it run its course."

Run its course? Is this football or strep throat? What executive in any industry refers to his decisions as something that has to "run its course?" Ireland's offhand remark encapsulates the Dolphins biggest problem: this is not a franchise that does things, but a franchise that has things done to it.

Ireland's Millienification is most obvious when he engages in self-justification, something he spent a lot of time doing this offseason. Ireland inherited Millen's gift for sounding dismissive and clueless at the same time, projecting a wrongheadedness that scares away everyone from season ticket holders to Peyton Manning. Ireland's Millenosity has its own accent, sounding entitled and aloof, whereas Millen was gruff and old school to a fault. For all his failings, Matt Millen would never ask an incoming rookie receiver if his mother was a prostitute, as Ireland asked Dez Bryant in 2010. Millen would be too busy preparing to draft him. But while Ireland's Millenissitude manifests in other ways, it is undeniably both Millenesque and Millentastic.

Ireland's failure to sign Manning was not the most embarrassing moment of his tenure. No, Ireland's failure to even schedule a face-to-face meeting between Manning and owner Steven Ross, at a time when the quarterback was hanging out in greater Miami, was the most embarrassing moment in the history of sports

MIAMI DOLPHINS

2012 Dolphins Schedule

Week	Opp.	Week	Opp.	Week	Opp.
1	at HOU	7	BYE	13	NE
2	OAK	8	at NYJ	14	at SF
3	NYJ	9	at IND	15	JAC
4	at ARI	10	TEN	16	BUF
5	at CIN	11	at BUF (Thu.)	17	at NE
6	STL	12	SEA		

Figure 1. 2011 Miami DVOA by Week

management. News that Manning later acquiesced to a phone conference conjured sad images of a doomed effort to rekindle a romance: She lives nearby but won't stop over, she cancelled our noon coffee date, she responded to my text message three days later, via e-mail.

Ireland then turned his focus to Matt Flynn. With Packers assistant Joe Philbin as the Dolphins head coach, acquiring Flynn should have been a layup. But Ireland low-balled Flynn, a player who obviously had other suitors among the teams that whiffed on Peyton. Flynn signed with the Seahawks; Ireland shrugged it off with this explanation: "I believe in value. What we try to do is we try to be aggressive in looking at ways to improve the team, but we're not going to be reckless and give up far more than we think we're giving up in return. That goes with any position, not just quarterback."

Meanwhile, Ireland forgot to seal the exits, allowing Chad Henne to slip off to Jacksonville. When the smoke of free agency cleared, one of the greatest redistributions of quarterback wealth in NFL history had taken place, with Hall of Famers, hot prospects, cultural icons, and draft picks extending halfway into the next presidential administration changing hands. All Ireland had to show for it was David Garrard. The non-reckless Dolphins were forced to spend a high draft pick on the third best quarterback in a two-quarterback draft.

Ryan Tannehill, a scrambler who spent two years at wide receiver (Millen!) before taking over the Texas A&M starting job early in the 2010 season, is now the Dolphins quarterback of the most immediate possible future. The Dolphins had not drafted a quarterback in the first round since Dan Marino, and Tannehill has the goods athletically. New offensive coordinator Mike Sherman was previously Tannehill's head coach at A&M, so Tannehill arrived at rookie camp with a basic understanding of the concepts and terminology that should help fast-track his development.

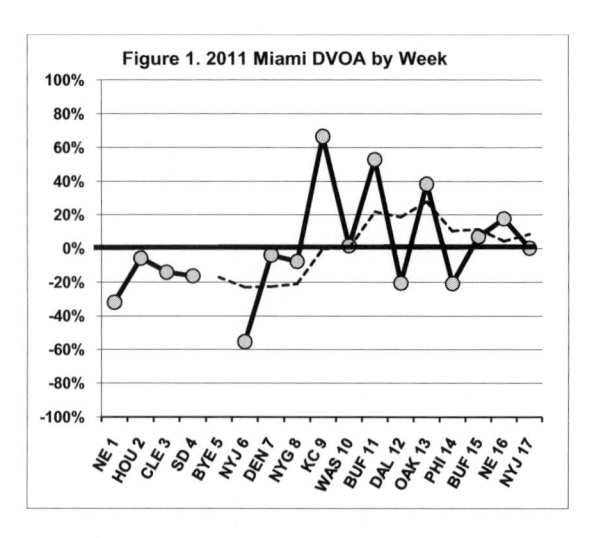

But Tannehill is also raw and mistake-prone, even by rookie standards. Watch the Texas, Oklahoma, or Okie State losses last year, and you will see an unrefined thrower whose Plan A was to lock onto Ryan Swope or Jeff Fuller and ignore the coverage and whose Plan B had not yet developed. Given two seasons on the bench, Tannehill could become Aaron Rodgers, but there is no way in hell that Tannehill will be given two seasons on the bench.

Tannehill's development will be hindered by the Dolphins' receiving corps. The Ireland-as-Millen comparison breaks down at wide receiver: Millen had a fetish, Ireland an allergy. The Dolphins have drafted only one wide receiver in the first three rounds since Ireland's tenure began in 2008: Patrick Turner, a 6-foot-5 square peg who is now a Jets special teamer. Ireland did trade two second-round picks to get Brandon Marshall in 2010, then acquired two third-round picks to get rid of Marshall in March, a fine example of buy-high, sell-low Millen Math.

Ireland claimed in April that he had a plan for replacing Marshall: "Obviously, we got one more piece of the pie to go, in terms of player acquisition." Ireland then forgot about the pie, unless you consider free agent Legedu Naanee and two seventh-round picks to be strawberry and rhubarb. The Dolphins enter camp with Davone Bess and Brian Hartline as their starters, two players who proved themselves as adequate second and third receivers for a sub-.500 team.

The Marshall trade could be interpreted as the start or a rebuilding youth movement, except that Bess will turn 27 at the start of the season and newcomer Naanee is older than Marshall. In fact, the Dolphins roster is full of players like Bess, useful-enough supporting actors who grew into their prime as the nucleus of 6-9 and 7-10 teams and are now at or past peak: Paul Soliai, Randy Starks, Anthony Fasano, Kevin Burnett, and others a year older or younger. Cameron Wake, a "young star" in many minds, started his NFL career late and is already 30 years old.

The Dolphins did get younger at some positions in the offseason, with Jason Taylor retiring, Mark Colombo disappearing, and Yeremiah Bell and Vernon Carey signing elsewhere. (Some people also feel Fasano will be a cap casualty before the end of training camp.) Whether the losses were by design or simply something that ran its course is not clear; tellingly, Bell and Carey will be replaced by backups Chris Clemons and John Jerry, not exciting newcomers. The secondary, with established starters Vontae Davis, Reshad Jones, and Sean Smith at or under 25, is the only unit on the team that can be considered "up and coming."

The Dolphins roster, in short, looks like the product of Millen-level obstinate confusion, an organizational insistence that the core of a good team is in place, despite blinding evidence to the contrary. Meanwhile, the franchise has become free-agent poison. Manning rejected them. Steelers safety Ryan Clark joked on Twitter about "NO ONE" wanting to play for the Dolphins. Former Dolphins linebacker Joey Porter called Ireland "untrustworthy." Porter was a mouthy malcontent, but you have to give his complaints some credence when they fall into line with the opinions of Manning and Clark. Factor in Flynn and Bryant, and the portrait of Ireland's ineptitude, tinged with a nasty streak, is complete. He is a bad boss.

The Tannehill selection is being cast as a make-or-break referendum on Ireland's future as a general manager. Really, the Ireland regime is irrevocably broken. The hope that Tannehill has a Cam Newton rookie season is a pipedream: Imagine how Newton would have fared with Steve Smith traded and Greg Olsen and Jeremy Shockey too dignified to grace the organization with their employment (well, Olsen anyway). Philbin has both Garrard and Matt Moore to fiddle with if he wants to ease Tannehill in gently, but the pressure is on to get Tannehill in the huddle to start selling some tickets.

We know what we can expect from the 2011 Dolphins: a slight variation on the mediocrity that they demonstrated over the past three seasons. They will run Philbin's Packers at the Beach offense, which will not work because they lack the personnel to pull it off. There will be Tannehill highlights and Tannehill interceptions, with Moore and Garrard cameos. The defense, while not great, is solid enough to keep them in some games: Wake will get his sacks, Soliai will hold down the middle, and the young secondary will make some plays. If they can resist the urge to force Tannehill into the lineup immediately, the Dolphins have just enough talent to hover near .500. But this is a problem in itself: most of that talent is in its prime. Another six- or seven-win season will leave the core one year older, with the Dolphins entering next season with a laundry list of needs, a poor draft track record, and zero chance of acquiring free-agent help. Does this cycle of hopelessness sound familiar, Lions fans?

Off the field, we can expect more protests, more recriminations, and more self-justification by Ireland. The sideshow has become more interesting than the team, which is the last thing Ross wanted when he hired Bill Parcells and got Ireland in the bargain.

The Parcells endorsement is Ireland's last shred of credibility. If Ireland begins peppering his justifications with Parcells name-drops, it will become his version of Millen's invocations of his Super Bowl experience as a player, a final cowering behind vicarious qualifications. The circle will then be complete, Ireland will be fired, the ghostly Millen Spirit will haunt another franchise, and Dolphins fans will have a real reason for optimism. With any luck, Tannehill will still be around when it happens.

Mike Tanier

MIAMI DOLPHINS

2011 Dolphins Stats by Week

Wk	vs.	W-L	PF	PA	YDF	YDA	TO	Total	Off	Def	ST
1	NE	L	24	38	488	622	0	-32%	0%	24%	-8%
2	HOU	L	13	23	306	345	-2	-6%	22%	6%	-21%
3	@CLE	L	16	17	369	280	-1	-14%	-12%	7%	5%
4	@SD	L	16	26	248	411	-2	-16%	-12%	10%	6%
5	BYE										
6	@NYJ	L	6	24	308	296	-2	-55%	-39%	16%	0%
7	DEN	L	15	18	267	308	0	-4%	-20%	-10%	6%
8	@NYG	L	17	20	246	402	-1	-8%	4%	17%	6%
9	@KC	W	31	3	351	343	0	67%	67%	9%	9%
10	WAS	W	20	9	303	246	0	2%	-18%	-31%	-11%
11	BUF	W	35	8	242	245	2	53%	0%	-54%	-2%
12	@DAL	L	19	20	352	303	1	-20%	-19%	-4%	-6%
13	OAK	W	34	14	362	304	1	38%	16%	-6%	16%
14	PHI	L	10	26	204	239	-1	-21%	-67%	-37%	9%
15	@BUF	W	30	23	448	404	0	7%	-3%	5%	14%
16	@NE	L	24	27	374	400	-2	18%	1%	-8%	9%
17	NYJ	W	19	17	210	374	1	0%	-18%	-9%	9%

Trends and Splits

	Offense	Rank	Defense	Rank
Total DVOA	-7.5%	20	-3.7%	12
Unadjusted VOA	-5.1%	19	0.9%	18
Weighted Trend	-10.5%	23	-10.5%	10
Variance	6.9%	13	4.5%	5
Average Opponent	1.4%	23	3.2%	4
Passing	3.0%	18	0.4%	13
Rushing	-11.9%	29	-9.4%	11
First Down	-11.0%	24	7.1%	23
Second Down	0.3%	15	-6.1%	13
Third Down	-12.4%	19	-20.8%	5
First Half	-6.4%	19	-11.7%	8
Second Half	-8.7%	23	3.6%	18
Red Zone	-20.1%	22	-16.3%	7
Late and Close	-3.7%	19	6.5%	25

Five-Year Performance

Year	W-L	Pyth	Est W	PF	PA	TO	Total	Rk	Off	Rk	Def	Rk	ST	Rk	Off AGL	Rk	Def AGL	Rk
2007	1-15	3.7	4.4	267	437	-7	-21.4%	27	-6.1%	21	12.6%	31	-2.7%	22	24.4	22	37.8	29
2008	11-5	8.8	8.5	345	317	+17	6.2%	14	12.0%	8	-0.1%	16	-5.9%	29	24.1	16	1.6	1
2009	7-9	7.2	8.4	360	390	-8	4.4%	16	4.1%	16	1.5%	18	1.8%	9	26.9	18	21.2	13
2010	7-9	6.2	8.5	273	333	-12	1.8%	15	0.7%	18	-4.8%	9	-3.7%	29	27.1	19	24.0	15
2011	6-10	8.5	7.7	329	313	-6	-1.3%	18	-7.5%	20	-3.7%	12	2.5%	6	22.1	12	9.6	3

2011 Performance Based on Most Common Personnel Groups

Miami Offense					Miami Offense vs. Opp.				Miami Defense				Miami Defense vs. Opp.			
Pers	Freq	Yds	DVOA	Run%	Pers	Freq	Yds	DVOA	Pers	Freq	Yds	DVOA	Pers	Freq	Yds	DVOA
11	47%	5.5	-8.9%	22%	4-3-4	26%	4.8	-18.2%	4-2-5	42%	5.8	-5.6%	11	40%	5.2	-9.0%
12	15%	4.6	-15.8%	60%	4-2-5	26%	5.8	-3.6%	3-4-4	23%	5.6	1.5%	12	25%	5.8	-2.4%
21	12%	7.1	25.4%	53%	3-4-4	21%	5.9	25.5%	4-3-4	10%	6.0	11.6%	21	14%	5.4	-4.0%
22	10%	4.9	-7.0%	81%	Dime+	11%	5.6	-25.4%	3-3-5	10%	5.3	-5.7%	10	5%	6.3	44.9%
13	4%	3.6	-18.9%	86%	3-3-5	9%	5.8	18.6%	Dime+	10%	6.0	5.2%	20	4%	4.6	-84.1%

Strategic Tendencies

Run/Pass		Rank	Offense		Rank	Pass Rush		Rank	Defense/Other		Rank
Runs, all plays	46%	6	Form: Single Back	75%	5	Rush 3	10.5%	9	4 DB	34%	30
Runs, first half	46%	8	Form: Empty Back	1%	32	Rush 4	52.7%	26	5 DB	53%	3
Runs, first down	57%	5	Pers: 3+ WR	51%	17	Rush 5	26.9%	9	6+ DB	10%	12
Runs, second-long	41%	9	Pers: 4+ WR	2%	22	Rush 6+	10.0%	8	CB by Sides	60%	28
Runs, power sit.	65%	9	Pers: 2+ TE/6+ OL	37%	11	Zone Blitz	5.1%	18	Go for it on 4th	0.79	27
Runs, behind 2H	31%	15	Play action	15%	24	Sacks by LB	53.7%	10	Offensive Pace	30.7	19
Pass, ahead 2H	36%	29	Max protect	12%	10	Sacks by DB	14.6%	5	Defensive Pace	30.3	12

Wildcat, RIP: The Dolphins ran their famous formation just three times all year. The Dolphins ran single-back formations twice as often as they did in 2010, going from last in the NFL to fifth. Joe Philbin has to find himself some receivers who can gain yards after the catch. Miami tied for the league low with 4.3 average yards after the catch, after ranking 28th with 4.3 in 2010 and 31st with 4.1 in 2009. ☞ Looking only at "standard" plays (i.e., four defensive backs), the Dolphins were far better against 3-4 defenses than they were against 4-3 defenses, with a huge gap of 43.6% DVOA and 1.1 yards per play. Unfortunately, we don't have defensive formation numbers for 2010 to know if this is a fluke or a trend, but we'll watch this closely to see if it continues in 2012. ☞ Despite the presence of Reggie Bush, the Dolphins averaged a league-low 2.0 yards per pass on running back screens. ☞ The Dolphins forced 11 fumbles on defense, and only recovered one of them. ☞ Dolphins opponents only threw 20 percent of their passes to their No. 1 receivers, tied with Atlanta for the lowest rate in the league. ☞ Although the Dolphins were low in "CB by Sides," it is difficult to find a pattern for how they decided to move Sean Smith and Vontae Davis around.

Passing

Player	DYAR	DVOA	Plays	NtYds	Avg	YAC	C%	TD	Int
M.Moore	135	-5.7%	388	2266	6.0	4.1	60.6%	16	9
C.Henne*	67	-2.7%	123	801	6.8	5.2	57.1%	4	4
J.P.Losman*	-66	-96.0%	15	22	1.5	3.8	60.0%	0	0

Rushing

Player	DYAR	DVOA	Plays	Yds	Avg	TD	Fum	Suc
R.Bush	51	-2.1%	216	1089	5.0	6	4	44%
D.Thomas	-110	-24.7%	165	581	3.5	0	2	42%
M.Moore	-21	-34.9%	17	75	4.4	2	1	--
S.Slaton	2	-5.3%	17	64	3.8	1	0	35%
L.Hilliard*	15	5.1%	16	41	2.6	1	0	75%
C.Henne*	20	19.0%	14	109	7.8	1	1	--

Receiving

Player	DYAR	DVOA	Plays	Ctch	Yds	Y/C	YAC	TD	C%
B.Marshall*	226	7.4%	143	82	1227	15.0	3.8	6	57%
D.Bess	-79	-24.8%	86	51	537	10.5	4.5	3	59%
B.Hartline	132	11.7%	66	35	549	15.7	2.7	1	53%
C.Gates	-55	-74.8%	12	2	19	9.5	0.5	0	17%
L.Naanee	-16	-15.5%	76	44	483	11.0	3.8	1	58%
A.Fasano	84	16.5%	54	32	451	14.1	3.1	5	59%
R.Bush	4	-12.4%	52	43	296	6.9	6.9	1	83%
C.Clay	118	62.1%	25	16	233	14.6	5.0	3	64%
D.Thomas	20	11.5%	16	12	72	6.0	5.3	1	75%
L.Hilliard*	8	11.5%	7	5	49	9.8	7.4	0	71%

Offensive Line

Year	Yards	ALY	Rank	Power	Rank	Stuff	Rank	2nd Lev	Rank	Open Field	Rank	F-Start	Cont.
2009	4.44	4.51	1	79%	2	14%	1	1.00	28	0.63	22	18	35
2010	3.78	4.07	16	83%	1	16%	7	0.86	32	0.38	32	18	24
2011	4.28	4.05	16	46%	32	18%	13	1.14	19	0.82	17	13	29

Year	LE	Rank	LT	Rank	Mid	Rank	RT	Rank	RE	Rank	Sacks	ASR	Rank	Short	Long
2009	4.99	7	3.46	30	4.59	3	4.36	8	4.12	19	34	6.5%	18	13	14
2010	3.46	25	4.53	10	4.01	14	4.14	15	4.61	7	38	6.3%	15	18	9
2011	4.56	11	4.63	7	4.37	7	2.62	31	1.92	31	52	9.6%	30	22	20

The Dolphins line went from first in the league in Power Success in 2010 to 32nd last year. If you guessed that Reggie Bush had a lot to do with it, you are partially right. The real problem was Daniel Thomas, a rookie who was chided throughout the preseason for tiptoeing in the backfield. Bush converted a reasonable 5-of-9 in short yardage. Thomas was a miserable 3-of-13.

Jake Long is the best player on the Dolphins roster, a perennial Pro Bowler at a vital position, and one of the few players who can honestly be called "Super Bowl caliber" on the line. These being the Dolphins, that means there is trouble brewing. Long is in the final year of his rookie contract, and while Ireland says he will do what it takes to keep the left tackle in Miami, the Dolphins are wedged against the salary cap. There are also concerns that Long, a power-offense mauler, may not be an ideal fit in Joe Philbin's scheme, which requires more zone blocking and more isolated pass protection. But Long is athletic enough to handle the switch, and beggars like the Dolphins cannot be choosers.

MIAMI DOLPHINS

Mike Pouncey had a fine rookie season at center. Richie Incognito committed nine penalties but at least kept his quarterbacks upright. John Jerry has started all over the line in the last two seasons and should be adequate at right guard. Marc Colombo allowed nine sacks and is now pursuing another career. Jonathan Martin was a three-year starter at Stanford and was only credited with allowing one sack in a very run-oriented system. Martin will replace Colombo at right tackle, though he could also move to the left side in 2013 if the Dolphins decide to let Long walk and give up on the whole idea of competition. If Martin is not ready for a starting job by opening day, journeyman Artis Hicks, the starter during minicamps, will hold down the fort.

Defensive Front Seven

Defensive Line	Age	Pos	Plays	TmPct	Rk	Stop	Dfts	BTkl	St%	Rk	AvYd	Rk	Sack	Hit	Hur	Runs	St%	Yds	Pass	St%	Yds
Randy Starks	29	DE	38	4.8%	47	30	13	1	79%	38	0.5	20	4.5	7	15	28	71%	1.9	10	100%	-3.2
Paul Soliai	29	DT	28	3.5%	50	22	5	1	79%	35	1.3	13	0	3	3	26	77%	1.4	2	100%	0.0
Jared Odrick	25	DE	23	2.9%	--	17	10	3	74%	--	0.0	--	6	5	10.5	14	57%	2.4	9	100%	-3.8
Kendall Langford*	26	DE	21	2.6%	--	15	2	1	71%	--	4.0	--	0	2	13.5	17	76%	2.9	4	50%	8.8
Tony McDaniel	27	DE	21	3.5%	--	14	6	1	67%	--	2.8	--	2.5	2	6	11	55%	3.2	10	80%	2.4

Linebackers	Age	Pos	Plays	TmPct	Rk	Stop	Dfts	BTkl	AvYd	Sack	Hit	Hur	Runs	St%	Rk	Yds	Rk	Tgts	Suc%	Rk	AdjYd	Rk
Kevin Burnett	30	ILB	109	13.6%	26	52	20	6	5.6	2.5	1	7.5	62	58%	81	3.5	63	49	42%	61	7.7	66
Karlos Dansby	31	ILB	103	12.9%	32	58	17	5	5.6	2	6	10	65	66%	52	3.7	77	33	53%	31	7.5	58
Cameron Wake	30	OLB	43	5.4%	107	34	17	5	0.4	8.5	20	39	28	68%	47	2.5	20	4	83%	--	4.8	--
Koa Misi	25	OLB	32	5.3%	108	22	7	3	2.7	1	0	4	22	73%	22	2.5	22	6	46%	--	5.4	--
Marvin Mitchell*	28	ILB	20	2.5%	--	12	5	1	3.7	1	1	0	10	50%	--	3.5	--	11	50%	--	7.9	--
Jason Taylor*	38	OLB	20	2.5%	--	13	10	0	1.2	7	9	11.5	8	50%	--	4.8	--	5	86%	--	2.0	--
Gary Guyton	27	OLB	48	7.2%	93	24	7	2	5.5	0	0	1.5	29	62%	67	3.2	46	21	48%	48	6.8	40
Jamaal Westerman	27	OLB	23	3.0%	--	18	8	1	0.9	3.5	7	10	17	82%	--	1.0	--	0	0%	--	0.0	--

Year	Yards	ALY	Rank	Power	Rank	Stuff	Rank	2nd Lev	Rank	Open Field	Rank
2009	4.12	4.33	24	74%	28	17%	25	1.23	24	0.47	3
2010	3.56	3.76	9	61%	12	23%	4	1.03	5	0.41	2
2011	3.79	3.96	13	73%	29	20%	14	1.15	14	0.38	3

Year	LE	Rank	LT	Rank	Mid	Rank	RT	Rank	RE	Rank	Sacks	ASR	Rank	Short	Long
2009	3.25	8	4.74	28	4.09	18	5.17	32	4.17	21	44	9.1%	1	16	14
2010	3.86	11	3.43	10	3.98	19	3.04	2	4.32	21	39	7.1%	9	9	16
2011	4.35	17	3.69	9	4.05	13	4.45	20	3.14	9	41	7.6%	7	15	22

Defensive coordinator Kevin Coyle initially suggested that he would install a hybrid defense with 3-4 and 4-3 looks. By minicamp, it was clear that the Dolphins were switching to a conventional 4-3 scheme. Karlos Dansby is the emotional leader of the Dolphins defense and one of the universe's biggest optimists. "I'm expecting us to win the AFC, period. Point blank," he said during OTAs. Think positive, Karlos! Dansby will start at middle linebacker, with Kevin Burnett moving from inside to the strong side. Burnett has a reputation as a lockdown defender against tight ends, though it may be left over from two employers ago. Newcomer Gary Guyton looked like a top prospect three years ago but slowly faded from the Patriots plans. Guyton started last season as the Patriots middle linebacker but was so poor in run defense that he lost his starting job and saw his role diminish as the season wore on. He will battle Koa Misi for the third spot. Guyton and Misi have had their moments as pass rushers in the past, and Coyle has hinted that he plans to blitz off the weak side.

Cameron Wake held out of April workout sessions before signing a four-year, $33.2 million contract extension that contains up to $15 million in sack-total escalators. "All is well," he said upon returning to camp; the Dolphins should consider using "Point Blank: All Is Well" as their team motto for 2012. (It sounds better than the current motto: "Let It Run Its Course.") Whether Coyle's defense is officially a 3-4 or 4-3, Wake will spend most of his time rushing from the wide-9 position. One of his most impressive statistics doesn't appear in the table above: Wake drew 13 offensive holding flags last year. Eight of those came on pass plays, more than any other defender had on passes and runs combined. Jared Odrick started at end opposite Wake during minicamp, but the 300-pound Odrick is a great candidate to replace Soliai in the middle on passing downs. Paul Soliai is a solid run-stopping defensive tackle. Randy Starks was a 4-3 tackle early in his career and will have no problem transitioning back. Soliai and Starks make interior run defense the least of Miami's problems.

Third-rounder Olivier Vernon is a quick-step pass rusher whose senior year at Miami was ruined by the Nevin Shapiro scandal. Vernon earned praise from Coyle for his motor during minicamp and could come off the bench in a pass rush package.

Defensive Secondary

Secondary	Age	Pos	Plays	TmPct	Rk	Stop	Dfts	BTkl	Runs	St%	Rk	Yds	Rk	Tgts	Tgt%	Rk	Dist	Suc%	Rk	APaYd	Rk	PD	Int
Yeremiah Bell*	34	SS	111	13.9%	6	29	14	5	57	26%	66	6.7	35	38	8.3%	22	12.2	52%	48	8.6	48	4	1
Sean Smith	25	CB	66	8.3%	44	17	8	3	14	29%	64	5.9	24	90	19.5%	26	12.4	48%	57	7.7	49	9	2
Reshad Jones	24	FS	65	8.7%	52	19	8	6	23	30%	57	6.2	24	24	5.6%	61	11.5	47%	60	6.5	17	3	1
Vontae Davis	24	CB	52	8.7%	36	27	11	3	8	63%	9	6.4	30	61	17.6%	40	14.8	57%	21	8.1	54	10	4
Will Allen*	34	CB	46	6.1%	71	25	10	4	16	75%	2	4.1	5	42	9.8%	81	10.0	63%	8	5.6	10	3	0
Nolan Carroll	25	CB	30	4.0%	--	8	4	5	5	40%	--	8.8	--	31	7.2%	--	12.2	47%	--	7.7	--	4	1
Tyrone Culver	29	FS	30	3.8%	--	7	3	1	7	29%	--	9.9	--	14	3.1%	--	10.0	46%	--	6.0	--	1	0
Richard Marshall	28	CB	80	9.2%	25	36	16	2	35	43%	40	5.9	25	52	11.0%	77	11.2	63%	7	7.3	38	9	3
Tyrell Johnson	27	SS	26	4.5%	--	2	0	0	9	11%	--	10.7	--	8	2.8%	--	12.1	41%	--	6.2	--	1	0

Year	Pass D Rank	vs. #1 WR	Rk	vs. #2 WR	Rk	vs. Other WR	Rk	vs. TE	Rk	vs. RB	Rk
2009	13	15.2%	21	2.7%	19	-1.5%	14	16.9%	24	-2.8%	15
2010	23	11.2%	24	-7.2%	8	11.2%	26	20.6%	28	9.0%	22
2011	12	2.0%	15	0.5%	15	13.7%	29	1.7%	10	-13.9%	6

The secondary is the Dolphins' youngest unit, with the most potential to improve into a playoff-caliber group. For that to happen, some young veterans must take their next developmental steps, and everyone has to stay healthy.

Vontae Davis and Sean Smith will remain starters, with Richard Marshall expected to take over the nickel role. Both Davis and Marshall battled injuries during minicamp, Marshall missing time with a pulled hamstring and Davis sitting out numerous practices with an undisclosed ailment. Smith has never developed into the player the Dolphins hoped for when they drafted him in the second round in 2009. He misplays too many deep passes, and though he has the size to be a matchup defender against bigger receivers, he had trouble last year with Plaxico Burress and Vincent Jackson, among others. Kevin Coyle worked extensively with Smith during minicamps. Nickelback Will Allen, who had the best charting stats among Dolphins cornerbacks last year, is now in New England.

Coyle said that he wants two interchangeable free safety types on the field instead of a deep safety and a designated in-the-box defender. Reshad Jones is one likely starter. Jones has a big-play, big-mistake reputation and will whiff on some open-field blocks. Like Smith, he earned some extra attention from Coyle in OTAs. Chris Clemons, a starter in the past, has the inside track to replace Yeremiah Bell, who is now with the Jets. Tyrell Johnson, who started 27 games in four seasons for the Vikings, will also get a look.

Special Teams

Year	DVOA	Rank	FG/XP	Rank	Net Kick	Rank	Kick Ret	Rank	Net Punt	Rank	Punt Ret	Rank	Hidden	Rank
2009	1.6%	9	7.0	5	-2.7	22	4.8	9	3.5	11	-3.4	22	-5.5	25
2010	-3.1%	29	-2.0	24	-7.7	28	-3.6	20	-4.1	24	-1.0	17	-9.5	25
2011	2.2%	6	-0.4	18	2.5	12	1.3	13	8.7	9	0.7	15	11.5	4

Dan Carpenter overcame a midseason groin injury and some early shakiness, becoming much more consistent down the stretch. Carpenter kicked a 58-yarder and three other 40-plus-yarders in the season finale against the Jets. He had to attempt eleven 20-to-29-yard field goals last year, converting ten: just one symptom of the Dolphins' red zone woes. Brandon Fields did not gross below 43.6 yards per punt in a game last year, even though he was often asked to punt six to eight times. Davone Bess and Clyde Gates are adequate return men. Bess is now the No. 1 wide receiver, so it is risky to ask him to return punts, but the only other logical choice on the roster is Reggie Bush, the No. 1 running back, who at press time was skipping OTAs with some undisclosed grudge.

Coaching Staff

Joe Philbin rose through the ranks of the Packers organization. He started as assistant offensive line coach and survived both the head coaching transition from Mike Sherman (now his offensive coordinator) to Mike McCarthy and the offensive switch from a Brett Favre-led West Coast offense to McCarthy's spread-with-benefits scheme. Philbin was advertised as someone who could bring the McCarthy system to Miami, but Sherman is calling most of the shots, which is why Ryan Tannehill understands the terminology Sherman used as the head coach at Texas A&M. While Philbin will certainly have some say, don't expect many signature McCarthy wrinkles, like full house backfields. With Sherman installing the system, Philbin, whose high school nickname was Father Joe, is focusing on organization, motivation, and the Big Picture. Well, someone has to.

Defensive coordinator Kevin Coyle spent nine years as the Bengals defensive backs coach. He helped develop some excellent defenders in that span (Leon Hall, Johnathan Joseph), and he worked extensively with Sean Smith during minicamps. Even Dolphins players admitted that they didn't know much about their new defensive coordinator at the start of OTAs. The fluffy "get to know you" stories out of minicamp describe a "laid back" coach who likes to begin meetings with personal stories but takes a detail-oriented approach to his coaching. His scheme, you will be shocked to learn, emphasizes speed and pass pressure. Coyle sounds professional but nondescript, which makes him a perfect fit for the Dolphins defense.

Minnesota Vikings

2011 Record: 3-13

Pythagorean Wins: 5.3 (27th)

DVOA: -22.2% (29th)

Offense: -10.2% (24th)

Defense: 8.0% (23rd)

Special Teams: -4.1% (27th)

Variance: 14.6% (19th)

2012 Mean Projection: 6.4 wins

On the Clock (0-4): 19%

Mediocrity (5-7): 52%

Playoff Contender (8-10): 26%

Super Bowl Contender (11+): 2%

Postseason Odds: 6.7%

Projected Average Opponent: -5.0% (30th)

2011: Vikings start season losing by small margins, end it losing by large ones.

2012: The afterthought in what is otherwise the NFL's best division.

It's easy to mock the dreadful state of the Minnesota Vikings. They're coming off a 3-13 season and enter 2012 with more holes than Hazeltine National Gold Club. But really, the time to be critical of this club was two years ago. That's when the foundation of this mess (or lack of foundation) was put in place.

Following the 2010 season, the Vikings had a decision to make: They could go out and try to find a young quarterback and build Brad Childress's West Coast offense around him, or they could bring back Brett Favre. Favre had come out of retirement in 2009 to commandeer a team that had wasted three years of a stalwart defense and an explosive rushing attack while trying to groom Tarvaris Jackson or make do with stopgap veteran quarterbacks. Favre in 2009 had arguably the best season of his illustrious career. Bringing him back in 2010 would mean more drama, but that was a small (if not irrelevant) price to pay for one last crack at a Super Bowl run.

The decision was easy. It was so easy, in fact, that no one, perhaps not even the Vikings themselves, paid much attention to just how many eggs this team was placing in its 2010 basket. Just about everyone knew that it would (probably) be Favre's last run. But they didn't seem to realize that, at the same time, the Vikings were essentially ignoring much of their natural rebuilding process for a second consecutive year. Favre's presence masked the fact that the Vikings were nowhere near as good at wide receiver or along the offensive line as they thought. His salary helped dissuade the front office from considering new investments in a defense that was starting to grow old or stale in a few places. And there was no consideration for updating Childress's offense or defensive coordinator Leslie Frazier's Tampa-2. The 2010 season was approached as simply 2009 redux.

We know now that redux failed. Favre battled injuries and off-field drama throughout 2010. His teammates struggled. Childress lost the locker room and got fired before the holidays. When the Metrodome roof collapsed, the season was all but officially declared a disaster. But that doesn't mean the Vikings weren't right in choosing to go all-in in 2010. The NFL is about winning Super Bowls. When you're close enough to jump through the Super Bowl window, you jump—even if the window might be closing.

The risk you run, of course, is that you might discover in midair that the window was closing faster than you thought. In that case, you're liable to come away bruised and bloodied from shattered glass. That leaves you with a cleanup project before you can completely get to your already delayed rebuilding project. In a cleanup project, you get caught in an in-between spot and feel compelled to make foolish short-term decisions (such as plugging your quarterback hole with a twice-dumped wash-up like Donovan McNabb).

2012 Vikings Schedule

Week	Opp.	Week	Opp.	Week	Opp.
1	JAC	7	ARI	13	at GB
2	at IND	8	TB (Thu.)	14	CHI
3	SF	9	at SEA	15	at STL
4	at DET	10	DET	16	at HOU
5	TEN	11	BYE	17	GB
6	at WAS	12	at CHI		

Figure 1. 2011 Minnesota DVOA by Week

To be fair, some of the delays in Minnesota's rebuilding project were caused by the lockout-truncated offseason. And again, it's unfair now to mock the Vikings at the beginning of a massive rebuilding stage, as we all applauded the decisions they made *before* the 2010 season.

Bad as 2011 was, the Vikings are finally in a position to start anew. The nightmarish transition year is in the past; the team's future in the Land of 10,000 Lakes is secure now that the highly politicized new stadium project has finally been green-lighted; and the front office, which up until Childress left, had been headed by a collection of different people with mixed and shared powers (many under the thumb of Childress), is now unquestionably in the hands of one man: Rick Spielman.

Spielman has unhindered control of a roster so full of holes that it's basically a bare lot on which any type of team can be built. Entering this offseason, the Vikings had needs across the board at offensive line, wide receiver, linebacker, cornerback and safety. At this point, it appears that the type of team Spielman wants to construct is one that's traditional. That means sticking with the Tampa-2 scheme on defense and sticking with a balanced, run-oriented scheme on offense. In other words, it's business as usual in Minnesota.

This approach is not surprising. Spielman is choosing to construct this Vikings club using the same blueprint that he had a large hand in drafting for previous Vikings clubs. He's sticking to his core football values, which appear to be staunchly conservative.

But are Spielman's core football values really what's best for Zygi Wilf's club? That's debatable. On defense, staying with Frazier's Tampa-2 is fine for now. Minnesota's two best defensive players, Jared Allen and Kevin Williams, are still in their primes and are perfect fits for the system. And it's a relatively simple system that Frazier and his staff know how to teach. This helps compensate for some of the team's shortcomings at linebacker (veteran Chad Greenway is a stud, but Erin Henderson and Jasper Brinkley are both iffy).

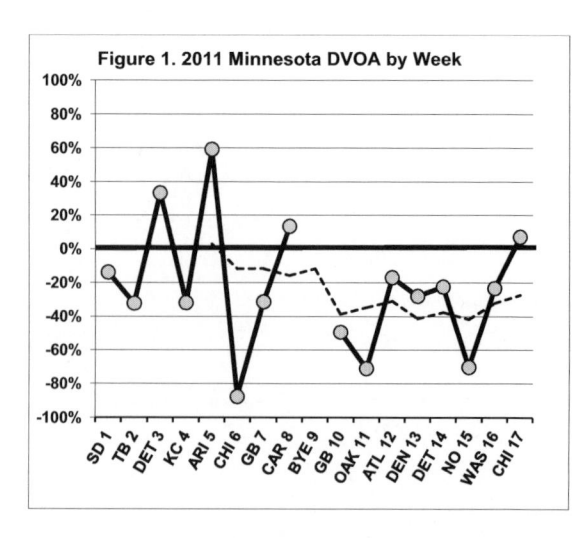

Worth noting is that Frazier's contract expires after 2013. So do those of Jared Allen and highly-paid cornerback Antoine Winfield. Thus, Spielman currently has the option of deciding to change course and go with a whole different defensive approach at some point in the near future. Helping his cause here is that the only major defensive investment he made this offseason was trading up into the late first-round to draft safety Harrison Smith, who can be effective in any scheme.

Offensively, in an era where the best teams are shifting towards spread concepts and wide-open passing attacks, Spielman is going for a ball-control attack. His (hopefully) franchise quarterback, Christian Ponder, is a good young athlete who appears most comfortable with three- and five-step drops and with making throws off play-action and bootlegs. This is how most quarterbacks who have more athleticism than arm strength prefer to play.

The Vikings have an offense that is conducive to Ponder's skill set. Coordinator Bill Musgrave is big on two-back and two-tight end formations. A lot of his passing concepts are based on either/or reads and short area, possession-centric designs. Musgrave's is a system that can put very little on the plate of the quarterback.

The caveat is that a quarterback playing in a system like this is often more dependent on the help around him. With less pre-snap manipulation and fewer dynamic passing targets spread across the field, the offense can't easily out-smart a defense, so it has to out-execute the defense. That's why the Vikings were willing to spend the No. 3 overall pick on left tackle Matt Kalil. The value of the left tackle position is declining in today's NFL, but only for offenses built entirely around a great quarterback (the Packers, Saints, or Giants are good examples). Kalil gives Ponder some much-needed security.

The Vikings will also discover that, even with two stellar receiving tight ends like Kyle Rudolph and ex-Seahawk John Carlson, it's very difficult to sustain drives without a true No. 1 receiver. Jerome Simpson, signed away from Cincinnati in free agency, is not a No. 1 receiver. Neither is gadget weapon Percy Harvin, who needs to be featured in a broader, more diverse ways. Behind Simpson and Harvin is a pair of fourth-round rookies, Jarius Wright and Greg Childs. Both should get a good crack at playing time given that veteran backups Michael Jenkins and Devin Aromashodu plain can't run.

Speaking of running, that's the other glaring caveat. A system like Musgrave's is built around pocket movement and play action. Thus, it's one of the few systems where the old cliché "you have to set up the run in order to execute play action" is not a gross fallacy. Play action can be executed effectively regardless of a rushing attack's prowess, but in the grand scheme of things, if an offense as basic as Minnesota's can't pose a genuine threat on the ground, defenses will eventually construct game plans that easily take away the passing attack.

This is why Spielman's heart must have been lodged in his throat when he saw Adrian Peterson get carted off the field with a torn ACL and MCL last Christmas Eve. Peterson is reportedly on a torrid pace in his rehab and may actually be ready for training camp. The Vikings better pray he's at least ready come September. Toby Gerhardt is a nice player, if you need someone who can spell your superstar for a few carries a game. This offense, however, won't work without its stud back.

On the surface, Spielman is rebuilding the Vikings with a conservative model of running and defense. In today's NFL, however, those conservative values create huge risks. Spielman is trying to win by putting a premium on defense (control the clock, keep the score close and low) but he starts with a defense that is miles away from elite. In Peterson, the Vikings have hitched their wagon to their most vulnerable horse, but as a violent 27-year-old runner with a history of injuries that date back to his college days, Peterson almost certainly has no more than three good seasons left in him. Perhaps the biggest risk is relying on a ground game when the rest of today's NFL recognizes that most games are won and lost through the air. With a strategy that looks like he's playing it safe, Spielman is actually rolling the dice.

Andy Benoit

2011 Vikings Stats by Week

Wk	vs.	W-L	PF	PA	YDF	YDA	TO	Total	Off	Def	ST
1	@SD	L	17	24	187	407	1	-14%	-43%	-9%	21%
2	TB	L	20	24	398	335	0	-32%	15%	37%	-11%
3	DET	L	23	26	321	358	0	33%	6%	-10%	18%
4	@KC	L	17	22	341	350	-1	-32%	-3%	24%	-4%
5	ARI	W	34	10	332	291	3	59%	26%	-28%	5%
6	@CHI	L	10	39	286	377	1	-88%	-11%	38%	-39%
7	GB	L	27	33	435	421	-1	-31%	-9%	22%	0%
8	@CAR	W	24	21	361	405	1	14%	14%	5%	4%
9	BYE										
10	@GB	L	7	45	266	356	0	-49%	-19%	1%	-30%
11	OAK	L	21	27	311	301	-4	-71%	-59%	-7%	-19%
12	@ATL	L	14	24	226	335	1	-17%	-9%	25%	16%
13	DEN	L	32	35	489	336	-1	-28%	-7%	12%	-8%
14	@DET	L	28	34	425	280	-6	-22%	-13%	0%	-10%
15	NO	L	20	42	207	573	1	-70%	-39%	38%	6%
16	@WAS	W	33	26	389	397	2	-23%	21%	31%	-13%
17	CHI	L	13	17	301	209	0	7%	-41%	-50%	-1%

Trends and Splits

	Offense	Rank	Defense	Rank
Total DVOA	-10.2%	24	8.0%	23
Unadjusted VOA	-9.2%	22	10.1%	27
Weighted Trend	-15.7%	25	10.6%	26
Variance	6.9%	12	2.4%	1
Average Opponent	1.5%	24	2.9%	5
Passing	-21.3%	28	22.9%	32
Rushing	11.7%	5	-10.5%	9
First Down	-27.0%	31	-7.1%	10
Second Down	7.0%	11	15.7%	31
Third Down	-2.8%	16	27.0%	31
First Half	-9.6%	23	0.7%	18
Second Half	-10.9%	26	14.5%	30
Red Zone	2.8%	7	7.1%	26
Late and Close	-3.4%	18	17.1%	30

MINNESOTA VIKINGS

Five-Year Performance

Year	W-L	Pyth	Est W	PF	PA	TO	Total	Rk	Off	Rk	Def	Rk	ST	Rk	Off AGL	Rk	Def AGL	Rk
2007	8-8	9.5	8.4	365	311	+1	1.8%	15	-0.8%	16	-0.1%	17	2.5%	9	11.9	4	7.6	4
2008	10-6	9.3	7.1	379	333	-6	1.5%	19	-9.9%	25	-19.3%	4	-7.9%	32	10.0	4	24.0	18
2009	12-4	11.8	10.4	470	312	+6	18.5%	7	12.9%	8	-1.0%	15	4.7%	3	9.4	7	13.1	4
2010	6-10	6.0	6.5	281	348	-11	-13.9%	25	-15.1%	27	-2.5%	12	-1.4%	19	35.7	25	19.7	14
2011	3-13	5.3	4.6	340	449	-3	-22.2%	29	-10.2%	24	8.0%	23	-4.1%	27	20.5	9	28.3	19

2011 Performance Based on Most Common Personnel Groups

Minnesota Offense					Minnesota Offense vs. Opp.				Minnesota Defense				Minnesota Defense vs. Opp.			
Pers	Freq	Yds	DVOA	Run%	Pers	Freq	Yds	DVOA	Pers	Freq	Yds	DVOA	Pers	Freq	Yds	DVOA
11	34%	5.3	-11.7%	22%	4-3-4	39%	5.1	-11.1%	4-2-5	52%	5.9	11.4%	11	42%	6.4	20.2%
12	23%	4.1	-30.1%	44%	3-4-4	22%	6.0	10.2%	4-3-4	43%	5.5	2.3%	21	21%	6.3	20.2%
21	15%	7.4	19.7%	55%	4-2-5	18%	5.2	-15.5%	Dime+	3%	7.4	10.7%	12	15%	4.8	-21.7%
22	9%	3.8	-44.3%	66%	2-4-5	10%	5.3	-12.7%	3-3-5	1%	9.3	80.2%	22	7%	3.6	-27.0%
13	6%	6.5	25.6%	53%	Dime+	6%	7.3	-37.8%	G-line	1%	1.2	70.8%	10	5%	6.6	28.6%
02	5%	8.0	71.7%	37%												

Strategic Tendencies

Run/Pass		Rank	Offense		Rank	Pass Rush		Rank	Defense/Other		Rank
Runs, all plays	44%	10	Form: Single Back	55%	27	Rush 3	4.8%	23	4 DB	43%	23
Runs, first half	48%	4	Form: Empty Back	3%	25	Rush 4	68.9%	9	5 DB	53%	5
Runs, first down	52%	15	Pers: 3+ WR	45%	24	Rush 5	17.6%	23	6+ DB	3%	23
Runs, second-long	47%	4	Pers: 4+ WR	2%	20	Rush 6+	8.7%	12	CB by Sides	79%	18
Runs, power sit.	55%	20	Pers: 2+ TE/6+ OL	45%	6	Zone Blitz	6.4%	13	Go for it on 4th	0.73	30
Runs, behind 2H	34%	8	Play action	29%	2	Sacks by LB	11.2%	27	Offensive Pace	29.9	9
Pass, ahead 2H	42%	20	Max protect	15%	5	Sacks by DB	6.1%	21	Defensive Pace	30.9	25

Note that in the personnel groupings of the table above, Percy Harvin is counted as a wide receiver, even when lined up in the backfield. This explains how the Vikings ran 37 percent of the time without any running backs in the game. The Vikings had -30.1% DVOA (32nd in NFL) and 3.97 yards per carry running from formations with three or four wide receivers. They were also the worst team in the league running out of the shotgun, with just 3.4 yards per carry and -50.7% DVOA (this counts handoffs to Percy Harvin lined up as a running back, but not quarterback runs). The Vikings significantly raised their use of play action compared to 2010. Minnesota quarterbacks left the pocket on 20 percent of pass plays, third in the league behind only Denver and Philadelphia. That's not just Joe Webb; Christian Ponder was also at 20 percent. Ponder averaged 6.1 yards on these plays (higher than average of 5.7) but had -11.2% DVOA (lower than average of 2.2%). 35 percent of passes against Minnesota were marked as being in the middle of the field. No other defense was above 30 percent.

Passing

Player	DYAR	DVOA	Plays	NtYds	Avg	YAC	C%	TD	Int
C.Ponder	-404	-31.5%	321	1698	5.3	5.3	54.7%	13	12
D.McNabb*	70	-4.8%	172	916	5.6	4.5	60.3%	4	2
J.Webb	-12	-13.8%	66	360	5.5	4.1	54.0%	3	2

Rushing

Player	DYAR	DVOA	Plays	Yds	Avg	TD	Fum	Suc
A.Peterson	153	10.4%	208	973	4.7	12	1	47%
T.Gerhart	60	5.4%	109	531	4.9	1	1	40%
P.Harvin	183	30.4%	52	345	6.6	2	0	--
C.Ponder	59	36.5%	25	217	8.7	0	1	--
J.Webb	32	14.1%	22	154	7.0	2	0	--
L.Booker	-29	-68.0%	13	52	4.0	0	2	46%
D.McNabb*	0	-12.7%	11	62	5.6	1	1	--
L.Hilliard	15	5.1%	16	41	2.6	1	0	75%

Receiving

Player	DYAR	DVOA	Plays	Ctch	Yds	Y/C	YAC	TD	C%
P.Harvin	145	2.9%	121	87	961	11.0	6.1	6	72%
D.Aromashodu	-166	-38.0%	84	26	468	18.0	4.4	1	31%
M.Jenkins	96	10.2%	55	38	468	12.3	2.7	3	69%
G.Camarillo*	-22	-25.1%	24	9	121	13.4	1.3	0	38%
B.Berrian*	-72	-54.5%	23	7	91	13.0	1.0	0	30%
J.Simpson	47	-6.7%	105	50	725	14.5	4.6	4	48%
V.Shiancoe*	-52	-18.0%	71	36	409	11.4	3.6	3	51%
K.Rudolph	7	-4.6%	39	26	249	9.6	3.4	3	67%
J.Kleinsasser*	-30	-84.0%	6	1	4	4.0	0.0	0	17%
T.Gerhart	93	46.5%	28	23	190	8.3	7.6	3	82%
A.Peterson	28	9.6%	23	18	131	7.3	6.7	1	78%
L.Booker	27	27.4%	14	8	82	10.3	11.4	0	57%
R.D'Imperio	-23	-72.9%	6	2	7	3.5	2.0	0	33%
L.Hilliard	8	11.5%	7	5	49	9.8	7.4	0	71%
J.Felton	8	6.6%	7	4	40	10.0	7.3	0	57%

Offensive Line

Year	Yards	ALY	Rank	Power	Rank	Stuff	Rank	2nd Lev	Rank	Open Field	Rank	F-Start	Cont.
2009	4.18	4.01	20	59%	23	24%	32	1.18	14	0.94	8	23	32
2010	4.33	4.15	11	70%	6	19%	18	1.25	8	0.82	12	27	30
2011	4.72	4.05	18	73%	1	23%	28	1.43	3	1.15	3	18	33

Year	LE	Rank	LT	Rank	Mid	Rank	RT	Rank	RE	Rank	Sacks	ASR	Rank	Short	Long
2009	3.83	22	4.59	7	4.10	16	3.67	26	3.82	22	34	6.0%	14	9	17
2010	4.50	13	4.56	7	4.22	10	3.72	22	3.73	21	36	6.8%	20	8	18
2011	3.25	28	4.17	16	4.07	16	5.07	3	3.42	19	49	9.8%	32	13	24

You can basically ignore Minnesota's offensive line stats from 2011, as most of this unit has since been revamped. Left tackle Matt Kalil was taken with the third overall pick, which means we're obligated to say that this was a "safe, smart choice" and that the Vikings now have a "10-year bookend player." Maybe so, maybe not. Kalil might have good feet and natural athleticism, but the reality is we won't know what kind of pro he is until we actually see him play in the pros. Just because offensive tackles never touch the ball doesn't mean they automatically transition well to the NFL. (Remember, once upon a time everyone touted No. 2 overall pick Robert Gallery as a "sure thing.") Maybe Kalil will be great. Or, maybe he'll be too soft and complacent like some scouts feared. Time will tell.

Kalil's arrival kicked Charlie Johnson to left guard, where he's a much better fit. Johnson was not horrendous at left tackle last season, but he doesn't have the natural lateral agility and quickness to hold up consistently on an island. At guard, he'll be a downgrade from Steve Hutchinson, but not by much (Hutch was clearly well past his prime by the end of last year). The coaching staff likes the intelligence of center John Sullivan, who has corrected some of his phone booth weaknesses over the past year or two. Sullivan earned a five-year contract extension midway through last season. Right guard Geoff Schwartz was signed away from Carolina, where he missed all of last season with a hip injury. If healthy, he'll give the Vikings more versatility than declining veteran Anthony Herrera (cut in March). At right tackle, Phil Loadholt still doesn't seem to realize that he's 6-foot-8, 343 pounds. Loadholt has poor lateral movement and tends to bend at the waist. If he can't finally become a more reliable force (and *force*, not just *presence*, but *force* ... when you're the size of a small truck, you need to be a *force*), the Vikings may want to consider moving Johnson or Schwartz to right tackle and inserting guards Joe Berger or Chris Degeare into the lineup.

MINNESOTA VIKINGS

Defensive Front Seven

Defensive Line	Age	Pos	Plays	TmPct	Rk	Stop	Dfts	BTkl	St%	Rk	AvYd	Rk	Sack	Hit	Hur	Runs	St%	Yds	Pass	St%	Yds
Jared Allen	30	DE	67	8.0%	5	61	33	3	91%	4	-1.1	3	22	12	21.5	37	86%	1.8	30	97%	-4.8
Brian Robison	29	DE	45	5.4%	33	35	13	3	78%	40	0.8	22	8	6	20.5	31	71%	3.0	14	93%	-4.1
Kevin Williams	32	DT	40	5.5%	17	32	11	3	80%	29	1.6	22	5	5	11	31	77%	2.5	9	89%	-1.7
Fred Evans	29	DT	22	2.6%	65	19	9	1	86%	7	1.4	17	0	3	3.5	21	86%	1.6	1	100%	-2.0
Letroy Guion	25	DT	20	2.4%	69	13	4	0	65%	62	2.7	59	0	2	6	19	68%	2.4	1	0%	8.0
Remi Ayodele	29	DT	15	1.8%	--	12	2	1	80%	--	1.2	--	1.5	1	2	13	77%	2.4	2	100%	-6.5

Linebackers	Age	Pos	Plays	TmPct	Rk	Stop	Dfts	BTkl	AvYd	Sack	Hit	Hur	Runs	St%	Rk	Yds	Rk	Tgts	Suc%	Rk	AdjYd	Rk
Chad Greenway	29	OLB	156	18.7%	5	72	21	7	5.7	2	3	5	92	59%	78	4.5	104	45	43%	58	7.0	45
E.J. Henderson*	32	MLB	111	13.3%	29	56	17	7	6.0	2	3	5	64	75%	13	2.9	32	40	30%	80	9.8	75
Erin Henderson	26	OLB	71	9.1%	62	43	13	3	4.1	1.5	2	2.5	49	69%	38	3.0	38	20	51%	42	6.2	29
Marvin Mitchell	28	ILB	20	2.5%	--	12	5	1	3.7	1	1	0	10	50%	--	3.5	--	11	50%	--	7.9	--

Year	Yards	ALY	Rank	Power	Rank	Stuff	Rank	2nd Lev	Rank	Open Field	Rank
2009	3.86	3.67	7	44%	2	25%	3	1.20	19	0.59	8
2010	3.80	3.64	6	66%	23	22%	8	1.05	9	0.71	14
2011	3.91	3.85	8	62%	16	22%	7	1.26	21	0.51	5

Year	LE	Rank	LT	Rank	Mid	Rank	RT	Rank	RE	Rank	Sacks	ASR	Rank	Short	Long
2009	4.91	25	3.70	8	3.56	5	3.63	8	2.73	2	48	7.8%	4	20	17
2010	3.54	5	4.56	25	3.86	13	3.29	6	2.26	1	31	5.6%	26	13	11
2011	4.05	11	4.63	25	3.79	10	3.97	10	2.94	5	50	8.7%	1	20	21

This is no longer the impenetrable run-stopping group that we came to know during the Williams Wall era. Pat Williams is (hopefully) enjoying his post-football life. Kevin Williams is still around and still as powerfully supple as just about any defensive tackle in the game. Since coming into the league as a first-round pick in 2003, he has led all NFL defensive tackles in sacks (54.5) and balls batted down at the line of scrimmage (55). But with his 350-or-so-pound sidekick retired, Williams naturally faces more double-teams, and the whole front seven suffers. The Vikings are once again counting on Fred Evans and Letroy Guion to capitalize on the attention Williams receives. Evans has shown flashes throughout his career but has never cemented himself into anything greater than a rotational role. Guion has gotten mostly backup minutes since being a fifth-round pick in 2008. Neither is a liability, but neither is a particularly enticing asset.

Having a simple "non-liability" at one of the inside spots may have been enough last season when stalwart middle linebacker E.J. Henderson was patrolling the middle. But the Vikings surprisingly opted not to re-sign the declining-but-still-effective 32-year-old veteran. They're now wishfully hoping that Jasper Brinkley can rebound from a hip injury that cost him the entire 2011 season to fill Henderson's void. Brinkley might—*might*—be able to do this in base defense, despite not having shown natural downhill instincts. Where Henderson was so valuable, though, was in nickel. He and the fleet-footed Chad Greenway were both outstanding at stopping the run as a two-man duo in space. If you're thinking that Henderson's younger brother, Erin, might fill his older brother's nickel shoes, think again. The Vikings might ask him to, but if he were that great in coverage, they would have kept him on the field for more passing downs last season. The Vikings re-signed the younger Henderson almost reluctantly this offseason, giving him a low-paying one-year deal.

The saving grace for this subpar linebacking corps is that it gets to play behind Jared Allen. By just about all statistical measurements, Allen was the most dominant defensive end in football last season. His run-stopping numbers, as well as the plays he made that showed up on film but not in our spreadsheets, were every bit as impressive as his near-record 22 sacks. Opposite Allen is the high-octane Brian Robison, a handful of a pass-rusher who can turn the corner against just about every right tackle. Robison plays ahead of third-year pro

Everson Griffen, who would probably be of more use in a scheme that regularly took advantage of his uncanny athleticism. Griffen is capable of handling some tight ends in coverage, and in minicamp the Vikings were experimenting with him as an outside linebacker. Also providing depth on the line is last year's fourth-round pick, Christian Ballard, who can be used inside or outside.

Defensive Secondary

Secondary	Age	Pos	Plays	TmPct	Rk	Stop	Dfts	BTkl	Runs	St%	Rk	Yds	Rk	Tgts	Tgt%	Rk	Dist	Suc%	Rk	APaYd	Rk	PD	Int
Cedric Griffin*	30	CB	76	9.1%	27	28	8	5	20	40%	44	6.8	38	61	14.6%	61	11.6	41%	78	9.3	69	13	1
Jamarca Sanford	27	SS	76	9.7%	42	24	9	11	32	47%	20	6.5	29	26	6.5%	48	16.0	50%	53	8.3	43	6	2
Husain Abdullah*	27	FS	54	11.5%	23	18	10	3	26	27%	65	6.5	28	21	9.0%	17	14.1	60%	26	9.4	58	3	1
Asher Allen*	24	CB	50	8.0%	50	9	3	6	11	27%	67	9.2	61	50	16.0%	50	10.6	39%	80	8.3	56	3	1
Antoine Winfield	35	CB	41	15.7%	--	24	13	1	11	73%	--	2.2	--	22	16.5%	--	7.2	51%	--	9.0	--	1	1
Benny Sapp*	31	CB	33	7.9%	--	17	11	5	8	63%	--	4.1	--	33	15.6%	--	10.6	49%	--	9.7	--	6	0
Tyrell Johnson*	27	SS	26	4.5%	--	2	0	0	9	11%	--	10.7	--	8	2.8%	--	12.1	41%	--	6.2	--	1	0
Marcus Sherels	25	CB	26	3.1%	--	11	4	1	1	0%	--	2.0	--	24	5.8%	--	8.4	49%	--	6.9	--	3	0
Mistral Raymond	24	FS	25	4.8%	--	6	3	3	13	23%	--	8.5	--	10	3.6%	--	15.8	54%	--	4.3	--	3	1
Chris Cook	25	CB	22	7.0%	--	6	3	0	2	50%	--	5.0	--	25	16.0%	--	13.2	42%	--	6.9	--	4	0
Chris Carr	29	CB	22	4.8%	--	9	5	0	3	67%	--	6.0	--	18	7.7%	--	8.1	32%	--	8.3	--	2	0

Year	Pass D Rank	vs. #1 WR	Rk	vs. #2 WR	Rk	vs. Other WR	Rk	vs. TE	Rk	vs. RB	Rk
2009	22	19.2%	24	-7.5%	11	19.7%	29	16.6%	23	6.7%	20
2010	20	-1.2%	16	14.5%	25	14.0%	27	-6.0%	8	-16.7%	4
2011	32	30.4%	28	41.1%	30	33.6%	31	21.5%	24	15.5%	26

The Vikings could not have earned the No. 3 pick in the draft without the contributions of its secondary last season. Minnesota was the only team to rank in the bottom five in DVOA against opposing No. 1, No. 2 and "other" receivers, and the first defense since the 2008 Broncos to rank in the bottom ten against all five receiver categories. In one particularly rough stretch from Week 6 to Week 14, opposing quarterbacks had a passer rating of 128 against this group. That's only 30 points less than the passer rating you would score against a seven-man defense consisting of no cornerbacks and no safeties.

The cornerbacks were average to begin with, and then got struck by the injury bug. One of the injured players, Antoine Winfield, should be back and starting outside. Whether the sure-tackling 35-year-old can stay healthy is a tossup (he missed six games in 2007, six in 2009 and 11 in 2011). Opposite Winfield is Chris Cook, an unproven third-year pro who finished his rookie 2010 season on IR, got arrested for a handgun issue in the 2011 offseason, and then missed the final 10 games of 2011 after essentially being placed on leave following an ugly domestic violence arrest. Cook was acquitted, but for all intents and purposes, the red flags haven't been lowered. He's getting a second chance because, in the NFL, the only thing worse than a cornerback with off-field violence issues is a cornerback who couldn't break up a pass to Def Leppard's drummer. That's essentially the type of corner Minnesota had last year in Asher Allen, who won't really be missed after his surprising retirement in May. At nickel corner will be either newcomer Chris Carr (versatile but easy to pick on), newcomer Zackary Bowman (physical but stiff) or third-round rookie Josh Robinson (insanely speedy but inexperienced).

Robinson isn't the only rookie with a chance to play serious snaps in 2012. Harrison Smith (first round) and Robert Blanton (fifth round) are both expected to start at safety. Smith, a four-year starter at Notre Dame, is considered by some to be a better downhill thumper than space player. But in a Cover-2 scheme like Leslie Frazier's, athleticism is less important than zone instincts, which Smith has been praised for. Blanton, also a Golden Domer, is not an imposing athlete (he lacks size and runs a 4.66 forty) but he plays with sound technique. Mistral Raymond and Jamarca Sanford serve as the backups. They weren't as responsible as Husain Abdullah was for the defensive backfield's atrociousness in deep coverage last season, but obviously if there was much to like about either guy, the Vikings wouldn't have drafted two players at their position this past offseason.

Special Teams

Year	DVOA	Rank	FG/XP	Rank	Net Kick	Rank	Kick Ret	Rank	Net Punt	Rank	Punt Ret	Rank	Hidden	Rank
2009	4.0%	3	7.7	4	-6.3	28	18.7	2	-0.5	21	3.7	13	2.9	11
2010	-1.2%	19	2.0	12	-15.7	31	4.3	11	6.2	11	-3.7	22	1.8	12
2011	-3.4%	27	-9.1	32	-13.2	31	11.7	1	-6.7	25	-3.0	20	-11.5	31

Thanks to the explosiveness of Percy Harvin and darting quickness of Marcus Sherels, Minnesota boasted the league's No. 1-ranked kick return unit, and that was enough to keep them from ranking dead last in our special teams ratings. Of course, while Harvin is a game-changing threat, he's fragile and very valuable to the offense. In a perfect world, Sherels emerges as the full-time return artist. He did return all punts in 2011 but wasn't as good as he was on kickoffs. Backup safety Eric Frampton leads the coverage and blocking teams, and while Frampton was second in the league with 20 special teams tackles, the coverage teams gave up a lot of big returns. Chris Kluwe is a great Tweeter but a fairly average punter. Ryan Longwell missed six field goals as a 37-year-old in 2011, and finished dead last in our ratings for gross kickoff value. So the Vikings decided to initiate a youth movement at kicker, drafting Blair Walsh out of Georgia in the sixth round. Longwell can now go home and play with his kids until some team inevitably pulls him out of retirement, John Kasay-style.

Coaching Staff

Leslie Frazier is a players' coach who understands all the ins and outs of Tampa-2 defense. He reassumed full control of the defense midway through last season after players reportedly started ignoring the signal calls of coordinator Fred Pagac. (In the NFL, what Pagac experienced is the closest thing to actually being neutered.) Remarkably, Pagac is still on the staff, serving alongside Mike Singletary as the linebackers coach. There were rumors over the offseason that Singletary would be promoted to defensive coordinator and that Minnesota's long-standing Tampa-2 would be remade into a 3-4. Those rumors, however, were put to rest when Alan Williams was promoted to defensive coordinator. Williams hails from the Tony Dungy tree, having served as the defensive backs coach in Indianapolis from 2002-11. Offensively, coordinator Bill Musgrave orchestrates a traditional run-oriented system, with a passing game built largely on play-action. He has a respected offensive line coach in Jeff Davidson.

New England Patriots

2011 Record: 13-3

Pythagorean Wins: 11.9 (4th)

DVOA: 22.8% (3rd)

Offense: 31.9% (3rd)

Defense: 13.2% (30th)

Special Teams: 4.1% (5th)

Variance: 8.6% (6th)

2012 Mean Projection: 12.0 wins

On the Clock (0-4): 0%

Mediocrity (5-7): 1%

Playoff Contender (8-10): 17%

Super Bowl Contender (11+): 83%

Postseason Odds: 94.6%

Projected Average Opponent: -3.6% (28th)

2011: Somewhere, a lonely Patriots fan is holding a cardboard fence and wondering where the guy with the "D" went.

2012: The offense still gives the 1984 Dolphins flashbacks, and the defense still won't give the 1972 Dolphins any nightmares.

With his eighth Super Bowl appearance—five as a head coach of the Patriots, and three working for Bill Parcells on the Patriots and Giants—Bill Belichick's legacy is secure. If he were to retire tomorrow, Belichick would be the all-time winningest coach in New England franchise history, one of the most successful coaches of the modern era and a shoo-in for Canton as soon as he was eligible. Not since Bill Walsh strolled the sidelines in San Francisco has one franchise achieved such consistent and sustained success, and, not coincidentally, not since those 49ers teams has the head coach been such a transcendent star. Those 49ers teams were loaded with some of the greatest players of all time, but their identity was derived from Walsh, the offensive mastermind who invented large chunks of the modern NFL offense. In New England, Belichick is the headliner, the defensive mastermind who can assemble out of spare parts a defense that confounds even the best offenses.

And yet, the last two seasons have complicated Belichick's legacy in this regard. The Patriots have won 27 games in the last two seasons, a run of dominance that nearly matches their output in the back-to-back championship years of 2003-04 and the AFC Championship/16-0 2006-07 years. But they've done it on the shoulders of the offense. Since 2007, the Patriots have been a point-generating machine, finishing atop the league in offensive DVOA in three of the five seasons. Last year's tight end-powered offense was the ninth best of the DVOA era. Yet over that same period, the defense has not kept up, to put it politely. Instead of improvement, there has been stagnation, decline, and finally last year, almost complete disintegration.

Has a defensive mastermind ever fielded a defense this bad? Not in the last two decades, certainly. The worst performance by any Bill Parcells defense was his first season in New England, when he took over the least talented team in the league. New England's defensive DVOA that year was 5.9%. Tony Dungy came to Indianapolis and fitted his Cover-2 scheme to a Colts team that put the bulk of its resources into the offensive side of the ball. His worst season? The 2006 Super Bowl team, which had a DVOA of 8.5% thanks to an extraordinarily bad run defense that allowed 5.3 yards per carry for the season. Neither Bill Cowher nor Rex Ryan ever fielded a defense with a positive DVOA, while Andy Reid's Eagles teams with Jim Johnson running the defense saw their DVOA dip into the black only once, in the 2003 season when Philadelphia finished at 3.0%. New England's defensive DVOA last year was 13.2%, 30th in the league. This shocking state of affairs raises two questions: 1) How did it come to this? and 2) How quickly can Belichick turn this thing around?

Belichick's best defense during his tenure in New

2012 Patriots Schedule

Week	Opp.	Week	Opp.	Week	Opp.
1	at TEN	7	NYJ	13	at MIA
2	ARI	8	at STL (U.K.)	14	HOU (Mon.)
3	at BAL	9	BYE	15	SF
4	at BUF	10	BUF	16	at JAC
5	DEN	11	IND	17	MIA
6	at SEA	12	at NYJ (Thu.)		

Figure 1. 2011 New England DVOA by Week

England was the 2003 Super Bowl team. That group was built around a massive defensive line and oversized outside linebackers who could set the edge, but where it truly excelled was in pass defense, as Belichick's scheme confounded everyone from Kelly Holcomb to Peyton Manning. New England's DVOA against the pass was -26.4%, second-best in the league, and it put the clamps on in the playoffs, shutting down MVPs Steve McNair and Manning in consecutive weeks, and then holding Jake Delhomme almost completely in check for three quarters of the Super Bowl before surrendering a few big plays late.

The blueprint has largely stayed the same since then. The defensive line is stocked with first-round talent and the outside linebackers are still of the jumbo/converted college defensive end variety. Yet the returns have diminished year after year, and in 2011, they diminished to the point of ridiculousness. New England's defense ranked 25th in DVOA against the run and 28th against the pass. The pass defense DVOA against number one receivers was an eye-popping 43.9%, easily the worst mark in the league. In the first two weeks alone, Patriots corners surrendered 17 receptions for 311 yards and 2 touchdowns to the combination of Brandon Marshall and Vincent Jackson, and things never got much better. They also couldn't cover tight ends, and their negligible depth at cornerback was exposed whenever teams used four wide receiver looks. Belichick's exotic schemes didn't faze the likes of Jason Campbell, Vince Young, or Chad Henne. The low point came when Dan Orlovsky—yes, that Dan Orlovsky—went 30-of-37 for 353 yards and two touchdowns in his first start at quarterback for the winless Colts.

The Patriots' defense would have been even worse, perhaps one of the worst defenses of all time, if they didn't continue the Patriots tradition of "bend but don't break." The Pats gave up 37.5 yards per drive, the worst figure of any team in our drive stats (which currently reach back to 1997). However, they stiffened in the red zone, ranking eighth in defensive DVOA once the opposition passed the 20.

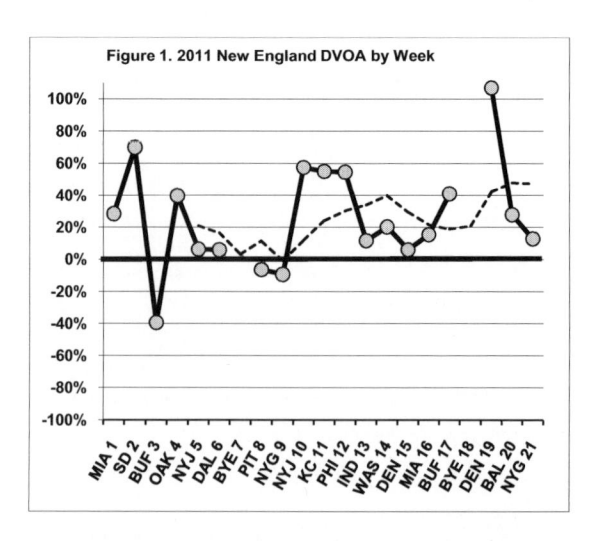

Back in *Pro Football Prospectus 2007*, we introduced a stat called "Points Prevented per Drive," which attempted to measure the "bend but don't break" capability of a defense. It compares how many points a defense gives up to how many points we would expect from a defense that gave up the same number of yards. The 2011 Patriots have the best PP/Dr number of the past 15 seasons, .614. This is not an abnormal result for New England. The 2010 Patriots had the fourth best PP/Dr number in our records, .479. Only once, in 2002, did a Belichick team have a PP/Dr figure below average. Six of the top 17 figures belong to Patriots defenses of the Belichick era. None of the other teams have more than four seasons in the top 50 since 1998.

Injuries obviously played a large part in giving up all those yards. New England had 97.5 Adjusted Games Lost—only Carolina and St. Louis fared worse—and a disproportionate number of those injuries took place in the secondary. Ras-I Dowling was drafted in the second round with the expectation that he would be a starter. Instead, his season was over after two games. Patrick Chung missed eight games with a foot injury, though he was able to return in time for a strong playoff run. Josh Barrett opened the season as the starting safety opposite Chung, but after four games he was done thanks to a calf injury. Belichick was ultimately forced to create a two-headed monster at free safety, playing special teamer James Ihedigbo on early downs and subbing in converted receiver Matt Slater in passing situations. No team is going to come out of that kind of assault on the depth chart unscathed, and Belichick was duly forced to call up guys who were training camp cuts (Sterling Moore) or to go back to the converted receiver well (Julian Edelman) just in order to field a defense.

But the injury situation should not obscure the fact that the talent level on the defense—and in the secondary in particular—is not where it should be. Since the 2008 offseason, when he allowed Pro Bowl cornerback Asante Samuel to leave in free agency, Belichick has expended a great deal of resources on the defensive backfield and has very little to show for it. In 2008, the team drafted cornerback Terrence Wheatley in the second round. Wheatley was considered a major reach at the time, a mid-round prospect with a long medical history. He ended up re-injuring his wrist a month into the season, barely saw the field the following season, was injured again in the 2010 preseason and ultimately released mid-year. His Patriots career ended with with three tackles, two pass defenses and zero interceptions. In 2009, Belichick wheeled and dealed his way to ownership of three second-round picks, and he spent two of them on defensive backs, drafting Oregon safety Patrick Chung and then adding Connecticut cornerback Darius Butler seven picks later. Chung has developed into a good player, but Butler fell apart after a reasonable rookie season. The next year, Belichick went after secondary help yet again, using a first-round pick to select Rutgers corner Devin McCourty. It seemed as if the third time was the charm, as McCourty was an instant sensation, making the Pro Bowl and finishing second in Defensive Rookie of the Year voting. Instead of building on that showing, however, McCourty slumped badly last year, essentially losing his job to Sterling Moore, an undrafted free agent who didn't make it out of training camp with the Raiders. Finally, Belichick used the 33rd overall selection in the 2011 draft on Virginia product Ras-I Dowling. Dowling was widely considered a first-round talent who couldn't stay healthy, and he lived up to his billing.

It's not as if Belichick's record of identifying front seven defenders has been any better. Although there are exceptions such as Jerod Mayo, almost every defensive lineman or linebacker taken since 2007 has failed to pan out. Shawn Crable, a third-round pick in 2008 who was supposed to provide some pass rush, only played in six games before washing out of the league. Ron Brace, a second-rounder in 2009, hasn't turned into the next Richard Seymour or Vince Wilfork. Instead, he's fallen down the depth chart behind marginal talents like Brandon Deaderick, Kyle Love and Myron Pryor. Jermaine Cunningham, another second-round pick brought in to address the continuing need for an edge rusher, saw his playing time reduced and his role replaced by free agent imports Andre Carter and Mark Anderson as well as career journeyman Rob Ninkovich. Brandon Spikes has combined promise with an inability to stay on the field, as he has missed time both to injuries and to a banned substance suspension. Unlike the others, Spikes has clearly shown that he can play, so now it's just a matter of keeping him on the field for a full season.

If Belichick has drafted himself into a hole, he seems determined to draft his way back out of it. New England's 2012 draft went after defense in a major way, emphasizing both quantity and quality with two first-round picks and six picks total used on defensive players. On the face of it, the approach makes perfect sense—there is a line of thinking that it is easier for rookies to make an impact right away on defense, and by building in some redundancy it makes it more likely that you will be able to patch the biggest holes on your roster. Over the past ten years, 15 teams have devoted at least 75 percent of the draft to defensive players. The results have been surprisingly mixed. On average, teams taking this approach lowered their defensive DVOA by just 1.1% in the season immediately after the draft. That's a pretty minimal payoff for such a large investment. While there are some real success stories like last year's Texans or the Colts during Tony Dungy's first year at the helm, there are many cases where the cure of an influx of young talent proved worse than the disease, at least in the short-term (Table 1).

The second half of the equation is quality. After years of trading down to accumulate picks in future drafts, the Patriots finally cashed their chips in, trading up in the first round to select Syracuse defensive end Chandler Jones with the 21st overall selection, and then doing so again to take Alabama linebacker Dont'a Hightower four picks later. Since 1993, teams have dedicated two first-round picks to the defensive side of the ball 15 times (the 2001 Rams used all three of their first-round picks on defense). Unlike the carpet-bombing approach, the results of doubling up on defenders in the first round have been consistently positive. Twelve of those teams showed immediate improvement the following year, and in many cases, the improvement was substantial (Table 2).

Table 1: Teams Dedicating 75 Percent of their Draft to Defense, 2002-2011

Year	Team	Prev Yr DVOA	DVOA	Change
2002	KC	9.5%	14.0%	+4.5%
2002	IND	15.3%	-0.6%	-15.9%
2004	CHI	1.2%	-7.3%	-8.5%
2005	DAL	10.8%	-4.1%	-14.9%
2005	NYG	4.1%	-3.1%	-7.2%
2006	WAS	-11.6%	15.0%	+26.6%
2007	DEN	-2.8%	5.2%	+8.0%
2008	JAC	-2.5%	6.3%	+8.8%
2009	ATL	7.5%	4.1%	-3.4%
2009	NO	7.8%	-0.4%	-8.2%
2010	IND	-0.8%	5.5%	+6.3%
2010	MIA	1.5%	-4.8%	-6.3%
2010	JAC	11.3%	17.7%	+6.4%
2011	NO	-4.3%	10.2%	+14.5%
2011	HOU	17.5%	-9.5%	-27.0%
AVERAGE		4.3%	3.2%	-1.1%

Table 2: Teams Spending Two or More First-Round Picks on Defense in the Same Draft, 1993-2011

Year	Team	Prev Yr DVOA	DVOA	Change
1993	GB	6.1%	-9.3%	-15.4%
1993	SF	2.9%	3.8%	+0.9%
1995	TB	14.0%	4.9%	-9.1%
1996	TB	4.9%	-0.7%	-5.6%
1998	CIN	19.4%	16.6%	-2.8%
2000	NYJ	-3.0%	-14.1%	-11.1%
2000	SF	20.4%	16.0%	-4.4%
2001	STL	14.9%	-11.7%	-26.6%
2002	OAK	0.5%	-6.2%	-6.7%
2003	OAK	-6.2%	9.5%	+15.7%
2004	HOU	11.7%	1.9%	-9.8%
2005	DAL	10.8%	-4.1%	-14.9%
2005	SD	-4.2%	-1.1%	+3.1%
2006	BUF	8.6%	1.7%	-6.9%
2009	GB	-2.5%	-17.7%	-15.2%
AVERAGE		6.6%	-0.7%	-7.3%

With even a modest improvement on defense, there is nothing to keep the Patriots from rolling out another 14-win season, because the offense is humming. The transformation from a shotgun spread offense that relied on Randy Moss to blow the top off the defense and Wes Welker to move the chains to an efficient machine that creates indefensible matchups out of its two-tight end packages is complete. New England's offense distinguishes between the "Y" tight end and the "F" tight end, with the former being a bigger player who can contribute as a receiver but whose job is to be a punishing in-line blocker and the latter being one of the new hybrid tight ends that rarely block and are instead moved around the formation to create matchup problems. As former offensive coordinator Bill O'Brien noted, the "Y" tight end "has to be an adequate receiver, but he doesn't have to be phenomenal." And yet, phenomenal might not be effusive enough to describe Rob Gronkowski, who had what was easily the greatest season of any tight end in the DVOA era and probably in history. In a year when there were several dominant tight ends, Gronk dwarfed all others with 459 DYAR. That was over 200 more than second-place Jimmy Graham, and over 100 more than any tight end had ever scored in a season since 1991. Tom Brady doubled the workload for Gronkowski and teammate Aaron Hernandez, targeting the two 237 times as opposed to 123 times during their rookie year, as the tight ends essentially replaced the running backs and secondary receivers.

Gronkowski and Hernandez didn't replace Wes Welker; they accentuated him. By shifting Hernandez around in the formation, the offense could create favorable matchups for Welker, whose yards per reception jumped from 9.9 to 12.9. And by having two tight ends on the field, the Patriots could punish any defense that put in nickel or dime personnel packages by running the ball, a point that was driven home in the fourth quarter of their October matchup against the Jets when they responded to New York's nickel defense by handing the ball to BenJarvus Green-Ellis on ten out of twelve plays on the drive that sealed the game.

Green-Ellis is gone, but there is no reason to think that the combination of Stevan Ridley, Danny Woodhead, and Shane Vereen will fare any worse running behind a solid offensive line and against defenses that treat the run as an afterthought. New England has finished in the top five in rushing DVOA in four of the last five years, and they will likely do so again. And now that Brandon Lloyd is stepping in to reprise the role of Randy Moss, the passing game is poised to evolve into some terrifying mutant combination of the 2007 and 2011 versions. Yes, there will be days when things aren't clicking, or when a front seven like the Ravens or 49ers plays out of their minds and keeps Brady uncomfortable for four quarters, but most defenses simply don't have the personnel to stop the Patriots from scoring a ton of points. To beat them, most teams are going to take a page out of the Belichick Super Bowl XXV playbook, trying to sustain long drives that keep Brady and all his weapons stuck on the sidelines. It's a strategy that might work, particularly come playoff time when the talent gap is closer. The Patriots dedicated an entire draft class, including two first-round picks, to upgrading the defensive talent. They simply can't get away with allowing 37.5 yards per drive again; that number has to come down. Belichick's legacy as the league's reigning defensive mastermind might depend on it. A return trip to the Super Bowl might depend on it, too.

Sean McCormick

2011 Patriots Stats by Week

Wk	vs.	W-L	PF	PA	YDF	YDA	TO	Total	Off	Def	ST
1	@MIA	W	38	24	622	488	0	28%	57%	22%	-6%
2	SD	W	35	21	504	470	4	70%	65%	3%	8%
3	@BUF	L	31	34	495	448	-2	-39%	-3%	40%	5%
4	@OAK	W	31	19	409	504	2	40%	44%	6%	1%
5	NYJ	W	30	21	446	255	-1	6%	42%	30%	-5%
6	DAL	W	20	16	371	377	-2	6%	0%	-7%	-1%
7	BYE										
8	@PIT	L	17	25	213	427	1	-6%	5%	3%	-8%
9	NYG	L	20	24	438	361	-2	-9%	-4%	4%	-2%
10	@NYJ	W	37	16	389	378	3	58%	50%	2%	9%
11	KC	W	34	3	380	334	2	55%	18%	-21%	16%
12	@PHI	W	38	20	457	466	1	55%	68%	18%	5%
13	IND	W	31	24	362	437	2	12%	44%	40%	7%
14	@WAS	W	34	27	431	463	1	20%	38%	23%	5%
15	@DEN	W	41	23	451	393	3	6%	36%	43%	13%
16	MIA	W	27	24	400	374	2	16%	30%	22%	8%
17	BUF	W	49	21	480	402	3	41%	32%	3%	12%
18	BYE										
19	DEN	W	45	10	509	252	-1	107%	63%	-24%	20%
20	BAL	W	23	20	330	398	-2	28%	27%	-5%	-4%
21	NYG	L	17	21	349	396	-1	13%	20%	9%	2%

Trends and Splits

	Offense	Rank	Defense	Rank
Total DVOA	31.9%	3	13.2%	30
Unadjusted VOA	31.7%	3	10.4%	28
Weighted Trend	31.1%	3	12.2%	28
Variance	7.8%	17	5.9%	16
Average Opponent	-0.4%	13	-1.9%	20
Passing	55.3%	2	19.7%	28
Rushing	12.6%	4	3.6%	25
First Down	28.5%	1	19.5%	30
Second Down	34.9%	1	0.3%	16
Third Down	34.1%	5	20.9%	30
First Half	31.3%	3	14.3%	30
Second Half	32.5%	2	12.2%	29
Red Zone	29.7%	2	-15.4%	8
Late and Close	36.0%	2	0.1%	17

Five-Year Performance

Year	W-L	Pyth	Est W	PF	PA	TO	Total	Rk	Off	Rk	Def	Rk	ST	Rk	Off AGL	Rk	Def AGL	Rk
2007	16-0	14.1	15.2	589	274	+16	52.9%	1	43.5%	1	-5.8%	11	3.6%	7	14.5	7	16.4	10
2008	11-5	10.7	10.4	410	309	+1	13.1%	9	12.5%	7	3.6%	17	4.2%	6	38.6	25	39.9	28
2009	10-6	11.7	11.2	427	285	+6	28.8%	4	26.4%	1	-1.1%	14	1.3%	12	27.1	19	19.1	10
2010	14-2	12.6	14.6	518	313	+28	44.6%	1	42.2%	1	2.3%	21	4.7%	8	32.9	23	39.5	27
2011	13-3	11.9	12.2	513	342	+17	22.8%	3	31.9%	3	13.2%	30	4.1%	5	40.0	23	57.5	31

2011 Performance Based on Most Common Personnel Groups

New England Offense					New England Offense vs. Opp.				New England Defense				New England Defense vs. Opp.			
Pers	Freq	Yds	DVOA	Run%	Pers	Freq	Yds	DVOA	Pers	Freq	Yds	DVOA	Pers	Freq	Yds	DVOA
12	48%	6.2	36.7%	39%	4-2-5	30%	6.9	47.1%	4-3-4	26%	6.3	2.4%	11	49%	6.7	22.7%
11	23%	7.2	40.6%	30%	Dime+	26%	6.8	40.0%	3-3-5	26%	6.2	8.1%	21	15%	5.8	-10.0%
02	7%	7.9	90.8%	5%	3-3-5	12%	6.6	49.6%	4-2-5	26%	6.6	30.4%	12	14%	7.0	19.6%
611	7%	6.6	12.9%	62%	2-4-5	11%	5.7	23.0%	3-4-4	11%	7.3	36.5%	10	7%	7.0	14.7%
612	5%	5.0	34.6%	75%	3-4-4	9%	6.5	31.8%	Dime+	8%	6.9	-5.7%	22	3%	2.4	-37.1%
					4-3-4	8%	5.9	36.7%								

Strategic Tendencies

Run/Pass		Rank	Offense		Rank	Pass Rush		Rank	Defense/Other		Rank
Runs, all plays	40%	21	Form: Single Back	74%	6	Rush 3	13.4%	5	4 DB	37%	29
Runs, first half	37%	26	Form: Empty Back	18%	2	Rush 4	65.5%	15	5 DB	53%	4
Runs, first down	45%	28	Pers: 3+ WR	33%	29	Rush 5	16.3%	27	6+ DB	8%	15
Runs, second-long	29%	27	Pers: 4+ WR	2%	18	Rush 6+	4.8%	27	CB by Sides	87%	8
Runs, power sit.	59%	12	Pers: 2+ TE/6+ OL	74%	1	Zone Blitz	0.5%	31	Go for it on 4th	1.08	5
Runs, behind 2H	27%	24	Play action	16%	21	Sacks by LB	18.8%	20	Offensive Pace	26.4	1
Pass, ahead 2H	51%	2	Max protect	7%	29	Sacks by DB	2.5%	25	Defensive Pace	30.7	22

As you might guess from the fact that two formations show up in their top five, the Patriots led the league in usage of six-OL sets. We listed the Pats using six or more linemen on 15.4 percent of offensive plays; Oakland was the only other team above 8.0 percent. The Patriots passed one-third of the time from these Heavy sets, with as much success as usual, but they struggled to run from Heavy with just 3.4 yards per carry and -5.2% DVOA. The Heavy sets were generally forced by running a tight end-heavy offense with just two tight ends on the roster; there will be a lot fewer of them in 2012 with Nate Solder now starting at left tackle and Daniel Fells or Spencer Larsen available to take his place as the third tight end. ◉ The Patriots targeted running backs on a league-low 9.5 percent of passes, a big change for their offense; they've been at 17 percent or above in every other season we've tracked. In a related note, the running back screen was a longtime staple of the Patriots offense but hasn't been used much lately, just a dozen times in each of the last two seasons. However, the Pats did gain 125 yards on these dozen plays in 2011. ◉ Only nine percent of New England's running back carries came from formations with two players in the backfield, lower than any other NFL team except Detroit. The Patriots had a pathetic 1.7 yards per carry on these runs, with -31.6% DVOA. ◉ Tom Brady was out of the pocket on a league-low 4.1 percent of pass plays, and the Patriots defense forced the opposing quarterback out of the pocket on an also league-low 9.3 percent of pass plays. ◉ The Patriots were the only defense whose opponents threw more passes to No. 2 receivers (21.2 percent) than to No. 1 receivers (20.7 percent). They were also the only defense whose opponents threw more passes to "other receivers" (24.7 percent) than to No. 1 receivers. Because of this, only 13 percent of passes against the Patriots were to tight ends, with every other team at 18 percent or higher. ◉ One reason the Patriots were able to give up so many yards is that New England had more territory to defend than other teams. Patriots opponents started their average drive 75.9 yards away from a touchdown. Only 49ers opponents started in worse field position.

Passing

Player	DYAR	DVOA	Plays	NtYds	Avg	YAC	C%	TD	Int
T.Brady	1997	35.4%	645	5043	7.9	6.4	66.0%	40	12

Rushing

Player	DYAR	DVOA	Plays	Yds	Avg	TD	Fum	Suc
B.Green-Ellis*	106	3.9%	181	667	3.7	11	0	54%
S.Ridley	31	-0.1%	87	441	5.1	1	1	51%
D.Woodhead	100	22.6%	77	351	4.6	1	0	55%
T.Brady	57	10.9%	32	119	3.7	3	0	--
K.Faulk*	-2	-10.8%	17	57	3.4	0	0	59%
S.Vereen	4	-2.1%	15	57	3.8	1	0	40%
A.Hernandez	25	52.1%	5	45	9.0	0	0	--
S.Larsen	6	0.5%	14	44	3.1	0	0	64%

Receiving

Player	DYAR	DVOA	Plays	Ctch	Yds	Y/C	YAC	TD	C%
W.Welker	451	20.4%	173	122	1569	12.9	5.8	9	71%
D.Branch	128	5.2%	90	51	702	13.8	6.5	5	57%
C.Ochocinco	19	-4.9%	32	15	276	18.4	3.5	1	47%
J.Edelman	-19	-46.8%	8	4	32	8.0	2.3	0	50%
T.Underwood*	-3	-19.9%	6	3	30	10.0	2.0	0	50%
B.Lloyd	8	-11.9%	147	70	966	13.8	1.8	5	48%
J.Gaffney	138	2.6%	115	68	948	13.9	2.7	5	59%
D.Stallworth	31	-1.7%	37	22	309	14.0	4.7	2	59%
R.Gronkowski	459	45.9%	125	91	1329	14.6	7.1	18	73%
A.Hernandez	107	6.0%	113	79	910	11.5	6.4	7	70%
D.Fells	4	-5.3%	31	19	256	13.5	4.5	3	61%
D.Woodhead	4	-11.3%	31	18	157	8.7	7.0	0	58%
B.Green-Ellis*	64	72.6%	13	9	159	17.7	15.8	0	69%
K.Faulk*	-7	-26.4%	9	7	34	4.9	4.6	0	78%
S.Larsen	25	32.3%	9	9	76	8.4	4.8	0	100%

Offensive Line

Year	Yards	ALY	Rank	Power	Rank	Stuff	Rank	2nd Lev	Rank	Open Field	Rank	F-Start	Cont.
2009	4.29	4.39	5	68%	9	15%	3	1.22	11	0.59	26	15	29
2010	4.54	4.82	1	68%	8	12%	2	1.30	6	0.56	22	13	34
2011	4.17	4.53	2	61%	19	17%	7	1.22	14	0.45	30	17	24

Year	LE	Rank	LT	Rank	Mid	Rank	RT	Rank	RE	Rank	Sacks	ASR	Rank	Short	Long
2009	4.96	9	4.21	12	4.55	4	3.84	23	3.63	25	18	3.6%	2	4	10
2010	5.04	4	4.08	19	4.82	2	5.25	1	5.35	2	25	4.9%	6	12	8
2011	4.59	9	4.36	14	4.46	5	5.18	1	4.18	8	32	5.4%	9	13	15

While there was hope that Matt Light might return—Tom Brady offered his longtime teammate a season's supply of Kit Kat bars as incentive—there is a strong plan in place to handle the retirement of the 11-year veteran. Nate Solder will slide from right to left, the position he played at the University of Colorado. At 6-foot-8 and 315 pounds, Solder has an ideal combination of size, wingspan and foot speed to protect Tom Brady's blind side, and his impressive play as a rookie suggests that he won't struggle much with the transition. It would certainly help if Logan Mankins is next to him in the lineup, and early indications are that Mankins will be. The four-time Pro Bowler finished up the season playing on a partially torn ACL, but Mankins had a successful surgery and was walking without a knee brace in May, so it's realistic to expect him to be ready for training camp.

The Pats re-signed crafty veteran Dan Koppen to a two-year deal that could be worth up to $5.75 million with playing-time incentives and roster bonuses, but there is some sentiment that the center job is Dan Connolly's to lose. Connolly has started 24 games the last two seasons, and his ability to play any position on the line makes him an asset, but neither he nor Koppen is a standout talents. Of course, you can get away with that when your guard play is superior, and the combination of Mankins and Brian Waters is among the league's best. Waters had another tremendous season, despite the fact that he was playing on a new team and in a new position. There is concern that Waters may opt for retirement, so New England signed former number two overall pick Robert Gallery as insurance. Gallery has never been on a winning team during his eight-year career, and was quick to sign on once the Patriots showed interest. While he is a better interior player, he does provide the versatility to play either guard or tackle. Sebastian Vollmer has experience at both tackle spots and was a second-team All-Pro in 2010. He should start on the right side, though he might be pushed in training camp by promising second-year man Marcus Cannon.

Defensive Front Seven

Defensive Line	Age	Pos	Plays	TmPct	Rk	Stop	Dfts	BTkl	St%	Rk	AvYd	Rk	Sack	Hit	Hur	Runs	St%	Yds	Pass	St%	Yds
Vince Wilfork	31	DT	55	6.7%	7	44	13	1	80%	29	1.6	27	3.5	6	8	41	76%	2.3	14	93%	-0.4
Andre Carter*	33	DE	52	7.2%	10	39	18	0	75%	53	0.3	16	10	15	17	37	70%	2.2	15	87%	-4.3
Kyle Love	26	DT	32	3.9%	42	25	6	2	78%	40	2.0	40	3	3	2	27	74%	2.6	5	100%	-1.2
Mark Anderson*	29	DE	29	3.5%	69	25	16	1	86%	14	-1.6	1	10	6	16	16	75%	2.4	13	100%	-6.6
Brandon Deaderick	25	DE	16	3.1%	--	12	2	1	75%	--	2.3	--	2	0	5	13	77%	2.8	3	67%	-0.3
Jonathan Fanene	30	DE	25	3.1%	72	22	12	1	88%	9	-1.2	2	6.5	6	10.5	16	81%	0.8	9	100%	-4.7

Linebackers	Age	Pos	Plays	TmPct	Rk	Stop	Dfts	BTkl	AvYd	Sack	Hit	Hur	Runs	St%	Rk	Yds	Rk	Tgts	Suc%	Rk	AdjYd	Rk
Jerod Mayo	26	OLB	99	13.8%	24	56	23	5	5.8	1	5	4	54	70%	34	3.8	80	37	45%	54	7.4	53
Rob Ninkovich	28	OLB	75	9.1%	61	40	15	8	3.4	6.5	5	20	45	56%	91	3.3	50	19	52%	37	6.2	30
Brandon Spikes	25	MLB	48	11.7%	42	21	4	0	5.7	0	1	3	26	58%	83	3.1	41	15	39%	--	7.4	--
Gary Guyton*	27	OLB	48	7.2%	93	24	7	2	5.5	0	0	1.5	29	62%	67	3.2	46	21	48%	48	6.8	40
Dane Fletcher	26	MLB	30	5.8%	--	16	6	3	6.3	0	6	6.5	16	63%	--	3.6	--	15	52%	--	7.3	--
Tracy White	31	OLB	26	3.4%	--	13	4	1	7.6	0	0	1	13	62%	--	3.9	--	11	23%	--	9.7	--
Bobby Carpenter	29	OLB	25	3.0%	--	13	4	0	5.2	0	0	1	14	64%	--	3.2	--	12	46%	--	5.7	--

NEW ENGLAND PATRIOTS

Year	Yards	ALY	Rank	Power	Rank	Stuff	Rank	2nd Lev	Rank	Open Field	Rank
2009	4.57	4.39	26	56%	5	16%	28	1.22	23	0.75	15
2010	4.10	4.25	20	71%	30	14%	30	1.06	11	0.52	8
2011	4.48	4.51	30	58%	11	16%	27	1.28	25	0.66	8

Year	LE	Rank	LT	Rank	Mid	Rank	RT	Rank	RE	Rank	Sacks	ASR	Rank	Short	Long
2009	4.30	18	3.11	3	4.72	30	3.81	11	5.20	28	31	6.2%	18	14	11
2010	4.03	15	5.62	32	3.98	17	4.40	19	3.83	14	36	6.3%	15	6	23
2011	5.31	31	3.69	8	4.51	30	5.15	30	3.85	20	40	6.5%	19	9	23

After agreeing to a new five-year, $40 million contract with $25 million in guaranteed money, Vince Wilfork is now the highest paid defensive tackle in the league who is actually currently employed (i.e. non-Haynesworth division). Wilfork deserves his money, as he is arguably the top nose tackle in the league, and at age 28 should still be performing at a high level at the tail end of the deal. Wilfork was forced to spend nearly half his time playing the five-technique last season due to a rash of injuries along the defensive front, and his return to the middle should go a long way towards improving a defense that was gashed up the middle for 4.51 ALY. Wilfork also provides Bill Belichick with the ability to individualize the assignments of the other front seven players in a way that maximizes their strengths. As Chris Brown noted in his Super Bowl preview at Grantland, the Patriots were frequently running a two-gap 3-4 to one side of the field and a one-gap 4-3 to the other on the same play. The Patriots will probably continue to shift back and forth between 3-4 and 4-3 looks, but in either case, they will use hybrid fronts built around Wilfork's ability to control the center. Kyle Love made strides during his second year and will remain as a starter at right end. Looking for an upgrade from Brandon Deaderick, the Pats went out and got Jonathan Fanene, who sparkled as a rotation player in Cincinnati, putting up 6.5 sacks despite playing less than half the defensive snaps. While Fanene should help, the real pass rush is supposed to come from prize rookie Chandler Jones. The Syracuse product flew up draft charts after the Combine, where he measured in at 6-foot-5 and 265 pounds, with the longest arms of any defensive prospect in Indianapolis. NFL draft guru Mike Mayock tabbed Jones as the best defensive player in the draft despite Jones' underwhelming college production. In New England, Jones will likely be used in the "elephant" role, where he would stand up at the line of scrimmage and alternate rushing the passer with dropping into coverage. Third-round pick Jake Bequette is another guy to add into the mix at the "elephant" position. Bequette isn't as pure an athlete as Jones, but he has a similar build, and what's more, he performed better on the field, notching 10 sacks his senior season while playing against SEC competition. Andre Carter, who enjoyed a career resurgence playing as the "elephant" last year, tore his quadriceps late in the year and missed the playoffs. Carter is still unsigned, and he is exactly the sort of savvy veteran the Patriots normally like to keep around, but with the presence of Jones and Bequette on the roster, it stands to reason that Carter will probably not be back.

Jerod Mayo went to the Pro Bowl despite missing two games, and New England locked him up for another five years, making him the literal and symbolic center of the defense. While his numbers were way down from last year, Mayo still led the Patriots in both Stops and Defeats, as he has each of the last three seasons. Mayo's raw stats tend to look better than his rate stats, but that's less a reflection on him than on how Mayo is utilized in the defense. He's a good coverage player, and he may be asked to do even more of it now that Dont'a Hightower is on board. Hightower was a jack of all trades for Nick Saban's defense, and he turned in his best performance his senior year at Alabama, logging 85 tackles, 11 of them for a loss, 4.5 sacks, a forced fumble and a blocked kick. He is a fierce downhill tackler who projects best as an in-the-box defender who can line up as an edge rusher on third downs. That may not be possible, however, as Brandon Spikes is strictly an inside linebacker, and of course Mayo is entrenched in the other inside slot. Hightower's playing time may come at the expense of Rob Ninkovich, particularly when the team comes out in a 4-3 look. Ninkovich got more effective as an edge rusher as the season went along; five of his 6.5 sacks happened after week 10, and he tacked on an additional two sacks in the playoffs. He also contributed some splash plays, picking off Mark Sanchez twice during the November 37-16 victory over the Jets, and running one back for a score.

Defensive Secondary

Secondary	Age	Pos	Plays	TmPct	Rk	Stop	Dfts	BTkl	Runs	St%	Rk	Yds	Rk	Tgts	Tgt%	Rk	Dist	Suc%	Rk	APaYd	Rk	PD	Int
Devin McCourty	25	CB	98	13.6%	3	37	16	7	24	54%	23	5.1	15	95	21.1%	16	13.4	46%	65	10.6	78	13	2
Kyle Arrington	26	CB	91	11.1%	9	24	12	2	15	20%	74	10.2	68	91	17.6%	39	14.2	49%	53	7.8	50	17	7
James Ihedigbo*	29	FS	67	8.2%	57	23	10	7	38	53%	14	5.7	14	32	6.1%	54	9.7	45%	69	7.4	36	3	0
Patrick Chung	25	SS	66	16.1%	3	21	4	1	27	41%	33	7.6	52	25	9.7%	12	10.4	59%	29	6.4	13	4	1
Antwaun Molden*	26	CB	31	3.8%	--	7	3	2	5	40%	--	5.4	--	33	6.3%	--	14.5	29%	--	11.1	--	4	2
Sergio Brown	24	FS	27	3.5%	--	4	1	3	11	18%	--	11.9	--	9	1.9%	--	15.9	42%	--	12.2	--	1	1
Leigh Bodden	31	CB	21	8.2%	--	7	3	0	2	0%	--	19.0	--	21	13.1%	--	13.3	47%	--	10.2	--	4	0
Nate Jones*	30	CB	21	5.8%	--	5	2	1	6	33%	--	9.8	--	15	6.7%	--	6.7	29%	--	10.7	--	1	0
Steve Gregory	29	SS	68	9.3%	47	19	4	5	29	41%	32	6.6	31	25	6.9%	39	16.6	45%	67	10.3	66	5	1
Will Allen	34	CB	46	6.1%	71	25	10	4	16	75%	2	4.1	5	42	9.8%	81	10.0	63%	8	5.6	10	3	0

Year	Pass D Rank	vs. #1 WR	Rk	vs. #2 WR	Rk	vs. Other WR	Rk	vs. TE	Rk	vs. RB	Rk
2009	16	20.1%	26	-14.0%	8	-6.8%	10	12.2%	21	20.1%	26
2010	15	7.9%	23	-5.9%	11	-23.3%	5	11.9%	21	23.0%	30
2011	27	45.4%	32	7.0%	20	6.5%	25	25.8%	29	-14.7%	5

After losing his starting spot to Sterling Moore and finishing out the season playing free safety, Devin McCourty will return to cornerback full time. McCourty's position switch was partly about his own struggles playing press coverage and partly about the atrocious depth at safety and the desire of the coaching staff to get the best four or five defensive backs on the field. An admittedly small sample size suggests that the move worked; the duo of McCourty and Moore gave up 10.4 yards per pass with a 47 percent Success Rate in Weeks 1-to-16, but only 5.0 yards per pass with a 68 percent Success Rate from Week 17 through the Super Bowl. So why go back? Perhaps because McCourty is the best physical talent the team has, and his development and maturation provides the best hope for improving the pass defense long-term. Kyle Arrington led the league with seven interceptions, but his gaudy stat line concealed a distinct drop-off in his play in the second half of the season. Arrington's average yards per pass allowed ballooned from 7.2 to 10.2 after Week 9, and his Success Rate dipped from 57 percent to 40 percent. The one area where Arrington never slacked off was in his tackling—our game charters only credited him with two broken tackles all season despite his being involved in 91 plays. If Ras-I Dowling could ever stay healthy, he could be in the mix for a starting job, but staying healthy is something the former 33rd overall pick has been almost comically inept at. In addition to the torn tendon in his leg that ended his season, Dowling over the past two years has missed time with ankle, hamstring and knee injuries. The coaching staff may need to start wrapping Dowling's legs in bubble wrap if they ever hope on getting a return on their investment. Dolphins veteran Will Allen and Jets castoff Marquis Cole were brought in to upgrade the quality of the nickel and dime packages.

At safety there is Patrick Chung and a bunch of question marks. Chung was in and out of the lineup in 2011, but his return at the end of the regular season aligned closely with a major uptick in team performance. He made his presence felt in the Super Bowl, registering six tackles and making one of the hardest hits in the game when he laid out Hakeem Nicks along the sideline, jarring the ball loose in the process. The other safety spot will probably be manned by either Steve Gregory or surprise second-round pick Tavon Wilson. Gregory is a former undrafted free agent who spent the last six years in San Diego. He's been a reserve for much of his career, but he started 22 games over the past two seasons. Gregory is a cog, a low-ceiling free agent signing who promises competence but not much more. Wilson is much more of a variable. Few draft analysts considered him to be more than a late-round selection at best, but seven NFL teams brought Wilson in for workouts, which suggests that Wilson slipped under the media's radar, perhaps because of his failure to attend the Combine. At six-foot, 203 pounds, Wilson has prototype size, and he was versatile enough to play both corner and safety for the Illini.

Special Teams

Year	DVOA	Rank	FG/XP	Rank	Net Kick	Rank	Kick Ret	Rank	Net Punt	Rank	Punt Ret	Rank	Hidden	Rank
2009	1.1%	12	0.5	18	7.7	8	-5.2	21	-6.6	28	10.1	6	-6.9	26
2010	4.0%	8	1.2	15	-4.1	25	11.4	6	7.3	9	7.7	3	7.6	4
2011	3.5%	5	1.2	14	8.3	3	-3.7	25	15.2	2	-0.3	18	0.0	16

Stephen Gostkowski showed no ill effects from the quad injury that ruined his 2010 campaign. He connected on 28 of his 33 field-goal attempts, and went a perfect five-for-five in the playoffs. He also continues to be a weapon in the kickoff department. Punter Zoltan Mesko may be the most interesting man in the NFL; he spent his childhood in Romania, where his family lived through the overthrow of the Ceausescu regime, then emigrated to the U.S., where Mesko, who was already fluent in Hungarian, German, and Romanian, learned to speak English by watching Barney on TV. Mesko wasn't called on much, only punting 57 times all season, but was worth 9.1 points of estimated field position in gross punt value, tied for fourth in the league. Danny Woodhead and Julian Edelman were generally average on kickoff and punt returns, although Edelman had excellent value in 2010.

Coaching Staff

Coordinator jobs in New England have turned into a springboard to head coaching jobs in other places, so it's nice to see the wheels turning the other way as Josh McDaniels returns to his old stomping grounds after controversial and largely unsuccessful stints in Denver and St. Louis. The offensive system is the same, but McDaniels will have to adapt to the changes in personnel, as there is no more Randy Moss and the tight end position now features the top two playmakers. Belichick has also resurrected the defensive coordinator job, promoting Matt Patricia from linebackers and safeties coach. Patricia called all the plays last season, so the promotion may be more in the way of resume padding than a real change in responsibilities. There is also some shuffling going on among the position coaches, as Pepper Johnson and Patrick Graham will swap duties, with Graham taking over the defensive line duties and Johnson tutoring his old position group at linebacker. Johnson in particular is highly thought of, and he could be next in line to take over coordinating duties should Patricia attract interest as a head coaching candidate in the next two to three years.

New Orleans Saints

2011 Record: 13-3

Pythagorean Wins: 12.4 (1st)

DVOA: 23.8% (2nd)

Offense: 33.0% (2nd)

Defense: 10.2% (28th)

Special Teams: 1.0% (12th)

Variance: 14.1% (17th)

2012 Mean Projection: 9.1 wins

On the Clock (0-4): 3%

Mediocrity (5-7): 19%

Playoff Contender (8-10): 51%

Super Bowl Contender (11+): 26%

Postseason Odds: 52.0%

Projected Average Opponent: 2.7% (7th)

2011: Beautiful football marred by ugly attitudes.

2012: Temps wanted for 16-week project. Dial 1-555-BIG-EASY.

So ... how was *your* offseason?

We could exhaust this essay's word count discussing the legal and ethical ramifications of bounties, or by providing a timeline and accounting of the accusations, punishments, lawsuits, and appeals that dominated the offseason and were still going strong at press time. With whatever tiny space remained, we could touch upon the Drew Brees contract quagmire and the eavesdropping scandal of 2002-04. It would not be a fun chapter to write or read, nor would it help you much when you sat down to watch a Saints game in September.

Instead, let's pick up the pieces, move forward, and try to figure out what we can and cannot predict about this unprecedented state of affairs.

First, let's make sense of the coaching situation. Sean Payton cannot have any meaningful contact with the team at all this season. He cannot game-plan, attend practices, or confer with his once and future assistants. He spent minicamp attending prayer breakfasts in Louisiana parishes. Joe Vitt will serve as interim head coach until the start of the season, with offensive line coach Aaron Kromer taking over while Vitt serves as six-game suspension, after which Vitt will return. This is seriously how the Saints have decided to do things.

Vitt may be the most experienced interim head coach in history. Vitt served as interim head coach of the Rams when Mike Martz had a bacterial infection in 2005. He also took over for Payton when Payton broke his leg last year. If your head coach is in the hospital, or on the outs, Vitt is your man. (Martz was both in the hospital and on the outs; Vitt was in charge during an ugly incident when Rams executive Jay Zygmunt intercepted an in-game call from Martz, who was trying to offer some not-quite-wanted strategic advice).

Vitt's experience makes him a logical interim choice, despite the need for Kromer in a double-deluxe interim role. The Saints are a veteran team whose coordinators can handle scheme installation; the head coach's offseason-preseason roles under such circumstances are organization, depth chart management, and motivation. Players love Jersey Joe, and he's an old coaching hand who can keep practices moving and lines of communication flowing. The younger Kromer can take over when rosters are set and the routine of the season is established. It is not an ideal situation, but under the circumstances, it is far less ridiculous than it sounds.

Offensive coordinator Pete Carmichael takes over as the mastermind of the Saints offense. He has been Payton's assistant since 2009, and like Vitt, he took on additional duties when Payton was recuperating from a broken leg last season. The substitution of Carmichael for Payton, with philosophy and terminol-

2012 Saints Schedule

Week	Opp.	Week	Opp.	Week	Opp.
1	WAS	7	at TB	13	at ATL (Thu.)
2	at CAR	8	at DEN	14	at NYG
3	KC	9	PHI (Mon.)	15	TB
4	at GB	10	ATL	16	at DAL
5	SD	11	at OAK	17	CAR
6	BYE	12	SF		

Figure 1. 2011 New Orleans DVOA by Week

ogy unchanged and most of the offensive personnel returning, is probably not much different from other master-to-protégé transitions in NFL history: Bill Walsh to Mike Holmgren, Holmgren to Mike Sherman, Dick Vermeil to Mike Martz. (Vermeil was not really an offensive guru, but the situations are similar in that the guiding Super Bowl hand is being replaced by a high-level assistant, with no other real changes on offense.)

There was no offensive drop-off when Holmgren replaced Walsh as offensive coordinator of the 1989 49ers. The Packers' DVOA under Holmgren had dipped to 2.9% in his final season; under Sherman, it slowly climbed back up to 18.3%. The Martz Rams did not slip offensively for several years. Carmichael is more of a Sherman than a Martz or Holmgren, but Brees is every bit as good a quarterback as the other coaches had. The scant evidence we have suggests the Saints offense will keep on chuggin', perhaps not at record-breaking 2011 levels, but close.

That the evidence is so scant reminds us of how unusual these circumstances are. Great offensive minds don't suddenly disappear, leaving the reins to assistants. Great offensive minds usually get fired after everything goes kablooey, Martz-style, and the organization goes in a bold new direction. Still, the Walsh, Holmgren, and Vermeil examples provide a little information: if Payton suddenly retired instead of getting suspended, we would point to those examples as evidence that the Saints offense will be just fine.

The Saints are going in a bold new direction on defense. Ironically, the paradigm shift was planned and had nothing to do with bounties or suspensions. Gregg Williams lost his job the old-fashioned way long before we heard creepy audiotapes or saw suspicious ledgers. He coordinated a blitz-heavy defense to a mere 33 sacks last year, with the Saints plunging to 28th in the league in defensive DVOA. Two high-profile defensive failures provided bookends to the 2011 season: Williams' defenders did not seem to know where to line up or who to cover in the 42-34 season-opening loss to the Packers, and the final four minutes of the playoff loss to the 49ers constitute a "What Not to Do" primer for late-game strategy.

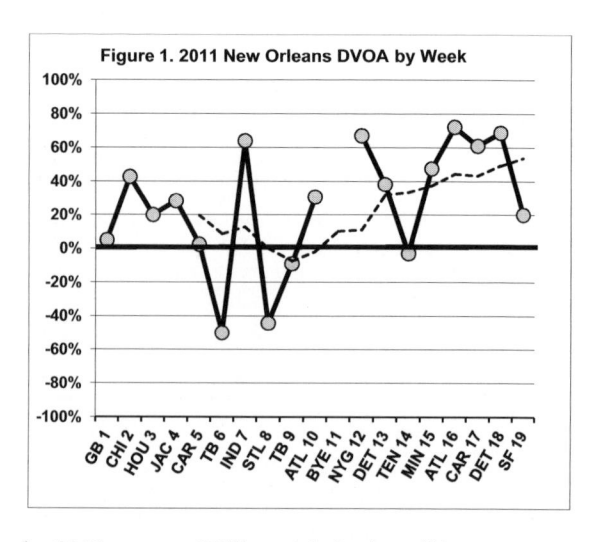

Steve Spagnuolo will replace Williams' complicated hybrid schemes with a more conventional 4-3 approach. Williams liked to apply pressure by blitzing his safeties and corners; Spags prefers mixing-and-matching personnel on his four-man front and using stunts and twists, plus some more judicious blitzing. It's a very different defensive approach, made better by the most distinct advantage Spags has over Williams right now: He is not an indefinitely-suspended pariah.

Spagnuolo flopped as the Rams head coach, of course. Spags could not be expected to rebuild the organization above him or repair the Rams personnel department. There was little he could do about the injuries which crippled the Rams secondary and receiving corps, particularly when the organization has such a poor track record for finding replacements. There are things Spags could have done better, like taking a more active hand in the transition to Josh McDaniels' offense in a season with no minicamps. But whatever his weaknesses as a head coach or supervisor, Spags still has a solid resume as a coordinator. Given Michael Strahan, Osi Umenyiora and Justin Tuck, Spags will give you the 2007 Giants defense. Given Chris Long, James Hall and Robert Quinn, plus some third-stringers in the secondary, he will still give you a defense that ranks 20th to 22nd in the league. Marry a 20th ranked defense to the Saints' usual offense and you get a Super Bowl contender. Spags does not have to be great for the Saints to be great. His conventional (compared to Williams) approach could yield a lot of 35-21 victories.

Spags will feel the effects of the bounty suspensions, but not acutely. The Saints obviously penciled Jonathan Vilma (who is recovering from a knee injury anyway) out of the lineup for a while when they signed Curtis Lofton, a traditional 4-3 linebacker with excellent range. Acquisitions like defensive tackle Brodrick Bunkley and linebackers David Hawthorne and Chris Chamberlain reveal that the switch from Williams' hybrid scheme to a more pure 4-3 had the added advantage of insulating the Saints against potential suspensions. Scott Fujita and Anthony Hargrove were no longer with the team anyway. Will Smith will miss the first four games of the season, but his penalty is similar to a substance-abuse violation, the kind teams routinely work around.

Spags has most of the building blocks for his kind of 4-3 defense. Bunkley and Chamberlain have played for him in the past. Lofton can fill a role occupied by Antonio Pierce and James Laurinaitis in past stops. There are no superstar pass rushers other than Smith, but there are puzzle pieces, like last year's first-round pick Cameron Jordan and converted linebacker Martez Wilson. Spags can go about his business without worrying about arbiters or appeals. He will have something close to a league-average defense installed by September.

If the Saints offense only drops off a little, and the Saints defense steps up a little, they should be right back in the thick of things. But there is one suspension we have not yet discussed: General manager Mickey Loomis will miss the first eight games of the regular season. That means all of the roster decisions made between final cuts and the middle of the year will be made by interim executives.

In-season roster management is the least sexy part of a GM's job, yet it is one of the most important. Two years ago, the Packers reached the Super Bowl because Ted Thompson was able to fill his roster with useful role players like James Starks, Erik Walden, and Howard Green, who started the year on other rosters. The Saints failed to reach the Super Bowl that same year because they were down to their seventh-string running back by the playoffs. Loomis did a great job in 2010 scavenging for Chris Ivory and Julius Jones, but the extent of his 2010 running back salvage operation demonstrates just how important in-season roster management can be: Even a well-run team can suddenly be in the market for a starting running back in Week 6.

Good general managers spend the early weeks of the season evaluating the bottom of their own roster while scanning the waiver wire for useful players, maintaining regular contact with free agents, and holding weekly tryouts. The general manager coordinates his efforts with the head coach, who provides insight on short- and long-term needs while pushing for "his type" (or his coordinators' types) of players. The Saints will undergo this process without their GM or their head coach. For several weeks, they will undergo it with their second-string GM talking to their third-string head coach. Some little things are likely to fall through the cracks. We have to assume that roster depth could be an issue for the Saints, particularly on defense, where fewer positions are set.

The loss of Loomis is one reason to be skeptical of the Saints' Super Bowl chances. There are others, most of them tangential to the bounty scandal and more concrete than concerns about "distractions." There's the tough and improving division, the difficult schedule, the dearth of impact defenders, and the irresistible pull of central tendency. Even if the loss of Payton's vision and creativity amounts to only half a win, there are enough half-wins on the table to pull the Saints down to nine or ten wins, and that assumes that Spags can stabilize the defense.

But those forces can only pull the Saints down so far, and it would be overdramatic to predict some kind of crater season. As long as Drew Brees has Jimmy Graham and Marques Colston to throw to and a stable line to throw behind, the Saints will be competitive, even if Brees is drawing up his own plays. It's possible that the bounty scandal weighs so heavily on so many players' minds that the team collapses, but not likely. By June, Vitt was running a quiet minicamp, and beat writers were back to writing about position battles, with the legal stuff compartmentalized as an "off-field issue."

Of course, if Brees holds out into the season, disregard the last 1,600 words. The Saints are doomed. A team can get by with an interim head coach and Ethel from human resources filling out the practice squad. Hall of Fame quarterbacks are irreplaceable. The Saints would be wise to remember this before Loomis goes on his involuntary vacation.

Mike Tanier

NEW ORLEANS SAINTS

2011 Saints Stats by Week

Wk	vs.	W-L	PF	PA	YDF	YDA	TO	Total	Off	Def	ST
1	@GB	L	34	42	477	399	-1	5%	24%	24%	5%
2	CHI	W	30	13	382	246	0	43%	22%	-9%	12%
3	HOU	W	40	33	454	473	-1	20%	33%	14%	1%
4	@JAC	W	23	10	503	274	-1	28%	30%	-9%	-10%
5	@CAR	W	30	27	444	381	0	3%	15%	12%	0%
6	@TB	L	20	26	453	420	-4	-50%	-11%	40%	0%
7	IND	W	62	7	557	252	3	64%	55%	-8%	0%
8	@STL	L	21	31	283	323	-1	-44%	-18%	11%	-15%
9	TB	W	27	16	453	365	-1	-9%	23%	27%	-4%
10	@ATL	W	26	23	363	481	1	31%	23%	-6%	1%
11	BYE										
12	NYG	W	49	24	577	465	2	67%	73%	8%	2%
13	DET	W	31	17	438	466	1	38%	65%	27%	-1%
14	@TEN	W	22	17	437	373	0	-3%	26%	29%	0%
15	@MIN	W	42	20	573	207	-1	48%	49%	0%	-1%
16	ATL	W	45	16	463	469	-1	72%	58%	5%	19%
17	CAR	W	45	17	617	301	1	61%	50%	-5%	6%
18	DET	W	45	28	626	412	0	35%	62%	27%	0%
19	@SF	L	32	36	472	407	-4	20%	39%	8%	-10%

Trends and Splits

	Offense	Rank	Defense	Rank
Total DVOA	33.0%	2	10.2%	28
Unadjusted VOA	33.1%	2	10.5%	30
Weighted Trend	39.0%	1	10.2%	25
Variance	5.8%	10	5.7%	14
Average Opponent	1.9%	27	-1.0%	18
Passing	50.1%	3	16.7%	26
Rushing	18.5%	2	-0.2%	21
First Down	24.8%	2	19.2%	28
Second Down	27.1%	3	6.9%	23
Third Down	60.9%	1	-3.5%	12
First Half	36.9%	1	16.1%	31
Second Half	29.1%	3	4.6%	20
Red Zone	34.8%	1	6.4%	24
Late and Close	34.5%	3	-4.1%	11

Five-Year Performance

Year	W-L	Pyth	Est W	PF	PA	TO	Total	Rk	Off	Rk	Def	Rk	ST	Rk	Off AGL	Rk	Def AGL	Rk
2007	7-9	7.8	6.3	379	388	-7	-9.7%	22	6.6%	12	12.1%	30	-4.3%	25	21.4	17	13.7	8
2008	8-8	9.7	9.1	463	393	-4	7.6%	13	16.3%	4	7.8%	26	-0.9%	22	24.0	15	33.4	24
2009	13-3	11.8	11.2	510	341	+11	21.3%	6	24.3%	2	-0.4%	17	-3.4%	28	45.6	30	32.9	21
2010	11-5	9.3	9.2	384	307	-6	9.2%	10	6.4%	11	-4.3%	10	-1.5%	21	19.8	10	25.2	18
2011	13-3	12.4	12	547	339	-3	23.8%	2	33.0%	2	10.2%	28	1.0%	12	17.4	7	7.2	1

2011 Performance Based on Most Common Personnel Groups

New Orleans Offense					New Orleans Offense vs. Opp.				New Orleans Defense				New Orleans Defense vs. Opp.			
Pers	Freq	Yds	DVOA	Run%	Pers	Freq	Yds	DVOA	Pers	Freq	Yds	DVOA	Pers	Freq	Yds	DVOA
11	36%	7.5	50.3%	18%	4-3-4	42%	6.2	31.2%	4-3-4	47%	5.9	6.9%	11	41%	6.1	14.8%
21	27%	6.5	29.1%	43%	4-2-5	30%	6.9	39.4%	3-3-5	32%	6.3	18.0%	12	18%	5.6	5.4%
12	14%	6.2	25.3%	41%	Dime+	14%	9.1	75.8%	4-2-5	12%	5.6	9.1%	21	16%	6.2	10.2%
22	9%	5.6	17.4%	67%	2-4-5	5%	6.6	27.8%	3-4-4	4%	6.6	30.4%	22	7%	5.6	-3.7%
20	4%	6.1	6.4%	38%	3-4-4	5%	5.8	-18.9%	Dime+	3%	5.6	16.9%	10	4%	7.3	47.2%

Strategic Tendencies

Run/Pass		Rank	Offense		Rank	Pass Rush		Rank	Defense/Other		Rank
Runs, all plays	38%	28	Form: Single Back	49%	31	Rush 3	17.0%	2	4 DB	51%	14
Runs, first half	32%	30	Form: Empty Back	9%	5	Rush 4	33.4%	32	5 DB	44%	12
Runs, first down	44%	29	Pers: 3+ WR	42%	26	Rush 5	24.3%	12	6+ DB	3%	22
Runs, second-long	31%	22	Pers: 4+ WR	2%	23	Rush 6+	25.3%	1	CB by Sides	84%	12
Runs, power sit.	62%	11	Pers: 2+ TE/6+ OL	30%	19	Zone Blitz	0.5%	30	Go for it on 4th	1.10	4
Runs, behind 2H	29%	18	Play action	23%	5	Sacks by LB	21.2%	19	Offensive Pace	29.0	3
Pass, ahead 2H	48%	5	Max protect	9%	20	Sacks by DB	28.8%	1	Defensive Pace	30.7	21

The Saints will destroy your pathetic dime backs. ☞ 62 percent of Saints RB carries came with two or more players in the backfield, the fifth highest rate in the league. Yet the Saints were much, much better running from single-back sets, leading the league with both 38.0% DVOA and 6.1 yards per carry from single-back sets, compared to 3.4% DVOA and 4.3 yards per carry from multiple-back sets. It was the third straight year they ran more often from multiple-back sets despite having more success from single-back sets. ☞ The Saints had the league's worst fumble recovery rate on offense, 17 percent, but that wasn't such a big deal since they only fumbled six times. ☞ By our count, the Saints led the league with 55 screen passes to running backs, 11 more than any other offense. Their 43.0% DVOA on these plays ranked ninth. ☞ The Saints used six offensive linemen on 5.5 percent of plays and averaged 5.7 yards and 52.3% DVOA on these plays. Both figures led all teams with at least 10 six-OL plays. ☞ Saints opponents rarely big-blitzed Drew Brees—only 4.7 percent of pass plays, lowest rate in the league—but it turned out to be a fairly good strategy, as Brees had a league-high 8.3 yards per play against three or four pass rushers but 7.2 against five and 6.8 against six or more. It was the third straight year that Brees was better against four pass rushers than he was against a blitz. ☞ The Saints had the worst defense in the league against passes marked as "short middle." ☞ Saints opponents committed 72 offensive penalties (second in the NFL) but only 30 defensive penalties (tied for 28th).

Passing

Player	DYAR	DVOA	Plays	NtYds	Avg	YAC	C%	TD	Int
D.Brees	2259	38.3%	678	5303	7.9	5.2	71.7%	46	14

Rushing

Player	DYAR	DVOA	Plays	Yds	Avg	TD	Fum	Suc
M.Ingram	63	2.3%	122	474	3.9	5	1	56%
P.Thomas	180	30.0%	110	562	5.1	5	1	61%
D.Sproles	193	46.2%	87	603	6.9	2	0	53%
C.Ivory	64	10.4%	79	374	4.7	1	0	58%
D.Brees	33	30.5%	16	90	5.6	1	0	--

Receiving

Player	DYAR	DVOA	Plays	Ctch	Yds	Y/C	YAC	TD	C%
M.Colston	390	33.9%	107	80	1143	14.3	3.2	8	75%
L.Moore	234	25.8%	73	52	627	12.1	3.0	8	71%
R.Meachem*	208	30.8%	60	40	620	15.5	2.6	6	67%
D.Henderson	105	14.7%	50	32	503	15.7	5.4	2	64%
J.Graham	244	16.6%	149	99	1310	13.2	4.6	11	66%
D.Thomas	-40	-78.5%	9	5	16	3.2	2.6	0	56%
J.Gilmore*	-8	-23.5%	6	3	20	6.7	4.0	1	50%
D.Sproles	258	25.3%	111	86	710	8.3	8.3	7	77%
P.Thomas	101	15.5%	59	50	425	8.5	9.4	1	85%
J.Collins	17	3.6%	14	11	50	4.5	4.7	2	79%
M.Ingram	-11	-27.5%	13	11	46	4.2	3.6	0	85%

Offensive Line

Year	Yards	ALY	Rank	Power	Rank	Stuff	Rank	2nd Lev	Rank	Open Field	Rank	F-Start	Cont.
2009	4.62	4.48	2	69%	7	18%	14	1.27	8	0.93	9	14	34
2010	4.23	4.42	6	68%	7	19%	17	1.21	10	0.71	17	14	48
2011	5.02	4.95	1	65%	12	15%	1	1.50	1	0.91	13	16	34

Year	LE	Rank	LT	Rank	Mid	Rank	RT	Rank	RE	Rank	Sacks	ASR	Rank	Short	Long
2009	3.67	24	4.18	14	4.65	2	4.63	4	4.87	3	21	4.2%	4	11	6
2010	4.75	7	4.53	11	4.59	4	3.71	23	4.02	14	26	4.7%	5	12	9
2011	5.75	3	5.41	2	4.94	1	4.24	18	4.22	7	24	4.5%	3	10	9

No suspensions, no holdouts, no gaping holes, no upheaval: Welcome to the offensive line, something the Saints can rely upon in an uncertain world.

The Saints were charged with just 15 Blown Blocks in 683 pass plays last year, the third lowest percentage in the NFL. The Saints line remained effective last season despite several personnel changes. Center Brian de la Puente, who spent three seasons bouncing around half the practice squads in North America, was able to hold his own after he suddenly became the starter when Olin Kreutz left the team early in the season. Charles Brown took over at right tackle in Week 4 after Zack Strief suffered an MCL injury. Despite an ugly game in the team-wide pratfall against the Rams (two very bad blown blocks), he played well before suffering a hip injury. Brown and Strief split first-team reps in OTAs, with Strief missing several sessions because of an ankle injury.

Jermon Bushrod has improved steadily at left tackle since his near-death experience as a rookie against DeMarcus Ware in 2009. Bushrod will still get flagged for some sloppy holds but is solid overall. Ben Grubbs replaces Carl Nicks at left guard; although Nicks was All-Pro last year, this isn't as big a downgrade as you might think.

Jahri Evans, who restructured his contract in March to free up cap space so the Saints could continue screwing around with Drew Brees, became the team's unofficial spokesman in Brees' absence. The three-time All-Pro spent the offseason expressing confidence that the Brees dispute would be resolved, supporting Jonathan Vilma in his defamation lawsuit, and projecting professionalism and optimism while Chase Daniel led the first-team offense and Sean Payton spent his OTA mornings hosting Louisiana prayer breakfasts. Evans saved the Saints about two million dollars by renegotiating his contract. After all the heavy lifting he did in April and May, they should give it right back to him.

Defensive Front Seven

Defensive Line	Age	Pos	Plays	TmPct	Rk	Stop	Dfts	BTkl	St%	Rk	AvYd	Rk	Sack	Hit	Hur	Runs	St%	Yds	Pass	St%	Yds
Will Smith	31	DE	36	5.3%	36	25	14	1	69%	68	0.3	15	6.5	5	16	24	63%	1.9	12	83%	-2.8
Cameron Jordan	23	DE	35	4.5%	53	30	5	2	86%	16	1.8	51	1	3	14	28	86%	2.1	7	86%	0.7
Sedrick Ellis	27	DT	33	4.5%	29	24	5	0	73%	52	2.9	62	1	5	8.5	24	67%	3.5	9	89%	1.2
Shaun Rogers*	33	DT	22	2.8%	61	20	2	0	91%	3	1.6	29	0	3	4.5	20	95%	1.5	2	50%	3.0
Junior Galette	24	DE	18	2.3%	--	12	8	1	67%	--	1.6	--	4	6	18	9	56%	3.2	9	78%	-0.1
Aubrayo Franklin*	32	DT	17	2.2%	--	15	5	0	88%	--	2.0	--	0	0	3	15	93%	0.9	2	50%	10.0
Brodrick Bunkley	29	DT	43	5.1%	21	35	8	1	81%	25	2.7	60	0	1	1	42	81%	2.6	1	100%	7.0

Linebackers	Age	Pos	Plays	TmPct	Rk	Stop	Dfts	BTkl	AvYd	Sack	Hit	Hur	Runs	St%	Rk	Yds	Rk	Tgts	Suc%	Rk	AdjYd	Rk
Jo-Lonn Dunbar*	27	OLB	81	10.4%	52	45	8	9	5.1	1	0	5	44	70%	32	2.4	18	28	50%	44	5.2	11
Scott Shanle	33	OLB	72	9.3%	60	32	12	2	6.1	1	1	3	34	47%	110	5.1	110	35	56%	17	6.2	28
Jonathan Vilma	30	MLB	56	10.5%	51	23	6	3	6.3	0	1	2	36	50%	105	5.0	109	17	42%	60	5.3	12
Jonathan Casillas	25	OLB	45	7.1%	--	23	9	4	6.3	3	8	13	20	60%	--	5.4	--	26	41%	67	8.7	70
Ramon Humber*	25	MLB	18	2.9%	--	8	5	3	5.1	1	1	2	7	43%	--	3.3	--	8	33%	--	5.8	--
Curtis Lofton	26	MLB	154	20.0%	2	84	21	6	4.7	1	2	9.5	87	69%	40	3.0	35	64	53%	28	5.3	13
David Hawthorne	27	MLB	121	15.3%	18	60	19	5	4.5	2	1	4	76	54%	99	3.4	60	41	43%	57	5.5	16
Chris Chamberlain	27	OLB	75	9.0%	66	42	10	3	5.4	2	1	4	50	64%	61	4.5	105	17	36%	71	6.5	36

Year	Yards	ALY	Rank	Power	Rank	Stuff	Rank	2nd Lev	Rank	Open Field	Rank
2009	4.51	4.28	22	69%	23	19%	17	1.10	11	0.89	20
2010	4.01	4.00	16	40%	1	21%	12	1.06	12	0.79	17
2011	5.20	4.13	21	73%	30	18%	20	1.42	30	1.45	32

Year	LE	Rank	LT	Rank	Mid	Rank	RT	Rank	RE	Rank	Sacks	ASR	Rank	Short	Long
2009	5.19	29	5.42	32	4.11	19	4.20	16	2.67	1	36	6.3%	17	10	15
2010	2.23	1	4.19	18	3.87	14	4.77	29	4.45	27	33	6.3%	16	17	9
2011	4.24	15	3.99	14	4.29	23	3.83	7	4.08	27	33	6.0%	25	13	16

New defensive coordinator Steve Spagnuolo is known for rotating his defensive linemen and moving defensive ends inside on passing downs to create disruptive rush packages. His lines stunt frequently and zone blitz often. His challenge this season is to cobble together enough quality players to make his schemes effective. The linebackers will all be scrambled, with a number of new names. Curtis Lofton is an old-fashioned vacuum cleaner at middle linebacker whose numbers against the pass were skewed by his assignments in Atlanta. Lofton made 39 plays against wide receivers and tight ends, appearing as the defender of record on passes to Steve Smith,

Marques Colston, Jeremy Maclin and others. Lofton was often isolated in coverage against Brent Celek-Kellen Winslow-Jared Cook caliber tight ends and didn't give up the farm. Fellow newcomer David Hawthorne also has excellent range and is solid in coverage. Chris Chamberlain played for Spagnuolo for three years in St. Louis and could unseat Scott Shanle for the third linebacker job.

Rookie Cameron Jordan recorded just one sack last season but was an effective run defender. Jordan is a prime candidate to start at defensive end but move to tackle on third-and-long. Tackle Brodrick Bunkley comes over from the Denver Broncos, and is a favorite to leave the field in favor of Jordan on third downs. Check out those run-pass statistical splits, which are among the most extreme that we have ever recorded. Yes, Bunkley had 42 run plays and just one pass play, and it wasn't even a sack. It was a tackle of Julian Edelman seven yards downfield on a short third-and-16 completion. Sedrick Ellis, who wore down under constant pounding on the nose last season, should be more effective with Bunkley absorbing some double teams. Third-round pick Akiem Hicks is a 325-pound size-speed marvel who played college football in Canada. He could push Ellis once he learns that there is no 55-yard line, but he projects as a mix-and-match player early in his career.

Martez Wilson has moved from linebacker to defensive end and was praised by Joe Vitt in May as a player who can rush the passer or drop into coverage from the end of the line. Wilson could start the season in place of the suspended Will Smith, then platoon when Smith returns. Junior Galette had four sacks last year and may fit as the pass rushing complement to Jordan.

Defensive Secondary

Secondary	Age	Pos	Plays	TmPct	Rk	Stop	Dfts	BTkl	Runs	St%	Rk	Yds	Rk	Tgts	Tgt%	Rk	Dist	Suc%	Rk	APaYd	Rk	PD	Int
Roman Harper	30	SS	102	13.1%	10	51	15	7	53	57%	6	5.3	9	51	10.9%	7	10.0	59%	35	5.7	10	5	0
Jabari Greer	30	CB	89	11.5%	7	50	18	14	20	55%	20	6.6	32	96	20.3%	21	13.0	58%	19	7.0	29	21	1
Malcolm Jenkins	25	FS	86	11.8%	19	22	11	9	28	14%	76	14.6	77	30	6.8%	41	14.4	66%	11	7.1	29	13	0
Tracy Porter*	26	CB	61	9.0%	29	19	9	6	9	44%	37	7.4	48	61	14.8%	59	10.0	34%	82	8.3	57	10	1
Patrick Robinson	25	CB	60	8.2%	45	28	15	5	7	43%	40	4.0	4	60	13.6%	66	9.6	52%	45	6.1	15	18	4
Leigh Torrence*	30	CB	18	2.9%	--	6	6	0	1	0%	--	12.0	--	19	4.8%	--	10.9	49%	--	10.4	--	3	1

Year	Pass D Rank	vs. #1 WR	Rk	vs. #2 WR	Rk	vs. Other WR	Rk	vs. TE	Rk	vs. RB	Rk
2009	9	-34.9%	2	9.2%	25	9.7%	21	-17.8%	5	6.5%	19
2010	9	2.3%	18	1.8%	16	-14.7%	7	19.4%	27	14.3%	24
2011	26	12.8%	18	-6.6%	11	9.3%	27	9.8%	18	21.5%	28

Jabari Greer allowed 12 broken tackles but finished tied for fourth in the NFL in both Pass Defeats and passes defensed among cornerbacks. Tracy Porter finished second-to-last in the NFL in Success Rate allowed and is now with the Broncos. Patrick Robinson, now the starter opposite Greer, finished sixth-to-last in the league in Yards after Catch allowed and was ineffective in run support, though he did break up his share of passes. There is very little depth, with fifth-round pick Corey White expected to compete for the nickel role. White is a cornerback-safety tweener type from Samford: not the kind of player you expect to step in and play more than half the defensive snaps as a rookie.

Roman Harper led all defensive backs with seven sacks and seven quarterback hits. He will not blitz nearly as often this year, allowing him to spend more time in deep support so Malcolm Jenkins does not have to clean up every mess by himself. Jenkins made tackles at the end of 42-, 41-, 39-, 32-, and 27-yard runs last year. Lots of free safeties have to drag down the likes of Adrian Peterson at the end of a long scamper, but under ideal circumstances, they also get to do other things.

Special Teams

Year	DVOA	Rank	FG/XP	Rank	Net Kick	Rank	Kick Ret	Rank	Net Punt	Rank	Punt Ret	Rank	Hidden	Rank
2009	-2.9%	28	-9.2	28	1.2	16	7.3	7	-8.4	29	-7.8	30	2.3	13
2010	-1.3%	21	-6.1	30	1.4	14	-3.3	17	4.1	14	-3.9	23	-9.6	27
2011	0.8%	12	-4.1	23	-6.2	26	1.9	11	10.2	6	3.0	11	2.3	12

Garrett Hartley and John Kasay will compete for the kicking job in training camp. Hartley spent last season on injured reserve with a hip injury but is in the second year of a pricey five-year deal. Kasay is now shaky from 40 yards out, but the team re-signed him in the offseason as an insurance policy. The Saints needed two or more kickers to get through every season from 2007 to 2010, then scrambled to sign Kasay when Hartley was hurt during last preseason, so keeping two kickers until the final round of cuts makes sense for them. Darren Sproles returned at least one punt 15 or more yards in eight different games last year. He is one of the most consistent return men in the league. Thomas Morstead is an above-average punter, and Isa-Abdul Quddus and Courtney Roby lead excellent kick coverage units.

Coaching Staff

Steve Spagnulo's accent is a Boston burr mixed with a heavy dose of non-denominational East Coast Italian-American city dude. His accent caused problems in some early Saints defensive meetings, because some players just couldn't understand him. "I kind of felt bad because I interrupted him on his meeting, but I didn't understand what he was saying, so I had to ask," said Roman Harper, an Alabama native who may not be used to Northerners who can speak six or seven words in under a minute. Harper even joked that he is doing research on the accent, which probably involves watching *Good Will Hunting*. Let's face it: Saints defensive players want to make really, really sure that they understand every word their coaches say these days.

Sean Payton really did spend his OTAs at prayer breakfasts, sharing the stage with Tulane coach Curtis Johnson at one May 24th event. "We're all faced with different challenges," Payton explained. "They are all hurdles, but they are hurdles we will all overcome," he told the folks at Jefferson Parish. It is not clear why such an event was held on a Thursday (the Feast of the Ascension was a week earlier, catechism snobs) but by a stroke of luck, Payton was available and receptive to a little of that old-time religion. It is doubtful that the commissioner will take time off his sentence for good behavior, but at least the beignets probably rocked.

New York Giants

> **2011 Record:** 9-7
>
> **Pythagorean Wins:** 7.8 (19th)
>
> **DVOA:** 8.5% (12th)
>
> **Offense:** 10.5% (7th)
>
> **Defense:** 2.4% (19th)
>
> **Special Teams:** 0.3% (15th)
>
> **Variance:** 15.0% (20th)
>
> **2012 Mean Projection:** 8.3 wins
>
> **On the Clock (0-4):** 6%
>
> **Mediocrity (5-7):** 29%
>
> **Playoff Contender (8-10):** 48%
>
> **Super Bowl Contender (11+):** 17%
>
> **Postseason Odds:** 43.2%
>
> **Projected Average Opponent:** 3.2% (4th)
>
> **2011:** It's become cliché, but we'll say it: 2007 all over again.
>
> **2012:** 2008 all over again? With this schedule, that may be a bit too optimistic.

How unique was the accomplishment of the 2011 New York Giants? That depends: Do you want to look at a sample size of 46, or a sample size of four?

The Giants were the first team in NFL history to win the Super Bowl despite being outscored in the regular season, and the league's first 9-7 champion. Look at a list of the 46 teams to win the Super Bowl, by nearly any stat, and the Giants stand out—especially when you consider that the second-worst team to win a Super Bowl was this same team four years earlier, with the same head coach, the same quarterback, and most of the same personnel. (That's by standard stats; by DVOA, the 2011 Giants at 8.5% come out better than the 2007 Giants at 1.6%).

On the other hand, the Giants fit perfectly in the larger landscape of American professional sports. Out of the four most recent champions of the four major North American leagues, only one looked like a championship contender wire to wire: the NBA champion Miami Heat, who finished fourth in wins and third in Pythagorean wins.

Even before the Giants won the NFC East in the final game and then went on a magical run through the playoffs, we had the example of baseball's St. Louis Cardinals. They also slipped into the playoffs on the final day of the season, aided significantly by a big month-long collapse from the Atlanta Braves, then went on to win the World Series despite finishing the year at 90-72 (and even worse, 88-74, by the Pythagorean projection).

Hockey's Los Angeles Kings only outscored opponents by 15 goals all season, and they were so bad at midseason that they fired their coach. But they managed to claim the eighth seed in the NHL's Western Conference playoffs and then, like the Giants, suddenly woke up and started walloping on opponents. The Kings dispatched the Western Conference's No. 1, 2, and 3 seeds with a 12-2 record before taking out New Jersey in six games to become the first eighth seed to ever win a Stanley Cup.

Longer seasons and extended playoff series are supposed to deliver a "more deserving" champion. The NFL can't do that, because players need a week to recover from the violent effect the game of football has on the body. Still, if baseball can play three seven-game series and find that the last team standing was the worst of the eight over a 162-game sample, and hockey can play four seven-game series and find that the last team standing was ranked 13th out of those 16 over an 82-game sample, how ridiculous is it to think a team that was one of the worst out of a dozen teams in a 16-game sample can be the best out of those same dozen teams in a four-game sample? Especially when that team actually *wasn't* the worst of that group in the regular season; they may have gone 9-7, but by DVOA the Giants were better than the Bengals or

NEW YORK GIANTS

2012 Giants Schedule

Week	Opp.	Week	Opp.	Week	Opp.
1	DAL (Wed.)	7	WAS	13	at WAS (Mon.)
2	TB	8	at DAL	14	NO
3	at CAR (Thu.)	9	PIT	15	at ATL
4	at PHI	10	at CIN	16	at BAL
5	CLE	11	BYE	17	PHI
6	at SF	12	GB		

Figure 1. 2011 New York Giants DVOA by Week

Broncos, and about as good as the Lions.

For those like us who attempt to forecast the future based on past performance, a team like the 2011 Giants is an enigma wrapped in a riddle, then dipped in salsa. We certainly have faith that our analysis is more accurate than picking every team to go 8-8 or picking every game to end in a tie. Nonetheless, there's a possibility that FO's whole tortured obsession with trying to explain the 2011 Giants is just a case of being fooled by randomness. The Giants certainly played well in the postseason, but they also had great luck. San Francisco dispatched the Saints, who probably were New York's worst possible matchup. New England's best offensive weapon was hobbled in the Super Bowl. The Giants completed a Hail Mary pass at the end of the first half against Green Bay. They recovered eight of ten fumbles, including the two fumbled punts by Kyle Williams that handed them the NFC Championship. And a couple of their own almost-fumbles were nullified by penalties or forward-progress rulings.

Sometimes a mediocre-to-good team gets lucky every week for a month. Sometimes a mediocre-to-good team plays a little bit better during a string of games, based simply on natural human variation. Sometimes a team plays its opponents to a standstill for a few weeks in a row, but wins each game close thanks to a fortuitous break here or there. When the team is closer to mediocre, and the string of luck comes in November and December, you end up with the Tebowmania Broncos. When the team is closer to good, and the string of luck comes in January, you end up with that team winning a Super Bowl. The fact that it has been the same team twice in five years could also just be part of that randomness.

On the other hand, the Giants' championship seems a lot less improbable if we look at the rest of the league rather than the Giants themselves. 2011 was a season without great teams. The Packers certainly looked great when they were 13-0, but they really were just a very good team that had enjoyed good fortune and an easy schedule. They're ranked 20th out of the 21 teams that have led the league in DVOA since 1991, ahead of only the 1993 Cowboys. Based on DVOA, the difference between the Giants and the average playoff team they faced is smaller than a similar measurement for other unexpected Super Bowl participants (Table 1).

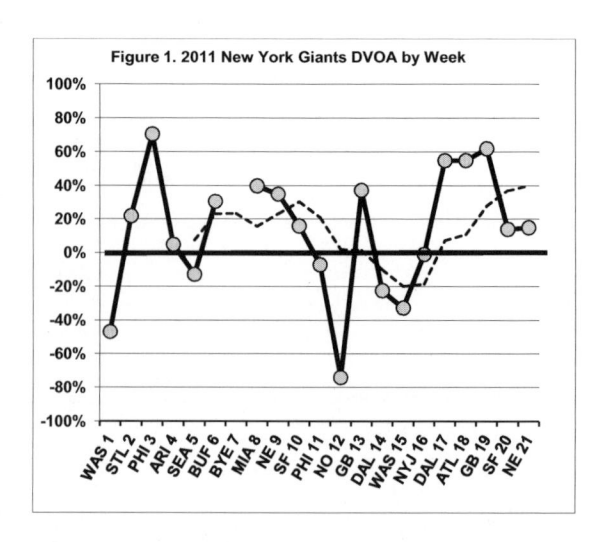

Table 1. Path to a Miracle Super Bowl Berth

Year	Team	DVOA	Avg Playoff Opp.*	Dif
2007	NYG	1.9%	28.4%	26.5%
2008	ARI	-5.0%	20.1%	25.1%
1994	SD	10.4%	24.9%	14.5%
2001	NE	7.9%	20.5%	12.6%
2011	NYG	8.5%	20.6%	12.1%
2003	CAR	0.6%	11.6%	11.0%
1996	NE	10.1%	20.0%	9.9%

*including Super Bowl opponent, regardless of whether team won or lost.

There's also the possibility that we overestimate just how accurately we can evaluate the platonic "quality" of a team when we have just 16 games to look at. Perhaps the Giants simply underperformed in the regular season, and the playoff Giants were the "real" Giants. A 32-game sample instead of a 16-game sample certainly makes the Giants defense look a lot more like the defense we saw in the postseason, because the Giants were third in defensive DVOA in 2010.

This whole question is complicated even further by the fact that the Giants' big playoff run was immediately preceded by the Giants' usual second-half col-

Table 2. Change in Giants' DVOA and Rank between Weeks 1-9 and Weeks 10-17, 2006-2011

Offense	Total	Rk	Run	Rk	Pass	Rk
2006-2010 (DVOA) Avg	-6.1%	4.8	-9.5%	8.6	-7.1%	1.6
2011 (DVOA)	-10.2%	5	-5.6%	6	-20.4%	5
2011 (VOA)	-15.1%	9	-15.0%	15	-22.1%	7

Defense	Total	Rk	Run	Rk	Pass	Rk
2006-2010 (DVOA) Avg	+14.2%	16.0	+4.4%	3.2	+23.9%	14.4
2011 (DVOA)	+23.5%	14	+6.3%	8	+20.5%	15
2011 (VOA)	+24.3%	24	+6.2%	8	+38.7%	25

lapse. Big Blue was riding high at 6-2 after their upset of New England in Week 9, then lost four straight games and five of the next six. This November implosion has become so clockwork that we spent most of last year's Giants chapter trying to figure it out. Over the last six years, the Giants are 36-12 in the first half of the season, 21-27 in the second half. In almost every year, the biggest part of Big Blue's collapse has been pass defense (Table 2). Last year was no different. From 2006 through 2010, the Giants' rank in pass defense DVOA dropped by an average of 14.4 spots between Weeks 1-9 and Weeks 10-17. In 2011, the Giants' rank in pass defense DVOA dropped by 15 spots. Eli Manning and the passing game also declined significantly, although the weaker second-half air attack was still one of the league's top eight.

If Tom Coughlin deserves credit for the way the Giants have played in the postseason, then he also deserves criticism for continual failure and near-failure in the regular season—criticism Giants fans and the New York press were happy to lay on him in December, then totally forgot about in February. The Giants have won two Super Bowls, but they have also had years like 2010, where they could have contended for the title but blew a playoff spot with late-season losses.

With another year of data to analyze, we are honestly no closer to figuring out why the Giants go through this year after year. The most popular explanation for last year's fall and recovery is that the Giants finally improved once they got healthy. There's some truth to that explanation, but not as much as most fans believe, and it may not be related to the players you expect. Many of the Giants' injuries cost players the whole season, so they would have no impact on a second-half collapse. There also was very little difference in the Giants' defensive DVOA or Adjusted Sack Rate if you look at the weeks Justin Tuck was out compared to the weeks he played. You may argue that Tuck wasn't fully healthy when he first returned in Week 8, but if he was getting healthier over the course of the next two months, we didn't see it in the team's total performance, as the Giants had a pass defense DVOA of 0.1% in Weeks 8-12 but 13.6% in Weeks 13-17.

The absences that seemed to really impact the Giants' defense were those of Osi Umenyiora and Michael Boley. Umenyiora missed the first three games of the season as well as Weeks 13-16. When Umenyiora was out of the lineup, the Giants' pass defense DVOA went way up while the Adjusted Sack Rate dropped (Table 3). Boley was listed on the injury report with a hamstring strain for Weeks 11-14, missing two of those games and playing two while hurt. The Giants played horrible pass defense in those four games, even after accounting for the quality of the opponents (which included New Orleans and Green Bay). In particular, the pass defense DVOA against tight ends was worse; again, this is even after accounting for the fact that the Giants were facing guys like Jimmy Graham and Jermichael Finley in those weeks (Table 4). Of course, there's plenty of overlap between when Umenyiora, Boley, and Tuck were or were not healthy in different combinations, so this is far from a definitive analysis.

Table 3. Life without Osi Umenyiora

Weeks	Pass Def DVOA	ASR
Weeks 4-12, 17 (Umenyiora active)	-2.1%	8.5%
Weeks 1-3, 13-16 (Umenyiora out)	18.9%	5.9%

Table 4. Michael Boley's Hamstring Sprain

Weeks	Pass Def DVOA	DVOA vs TE
Weeks 1-10	-2.5%	-8.5%
Weeks 11-14 (Boley hamstring sprain)	34.7%	9.3%
Weeks 15-17	1.0%	-23.2%

Whatever the reason, New York's second half collapses are exacerbated further by the NFL schedule makers, who every year give the Giants a schedule where their toughest opponents come mostly in the final two months of the season. From 2006 through 2010, the average winning percentage of the Giants' first-half opponents was .444, while the average winning percentage of their second-half opponents was

.556. Last year, the dichotomy was even more severe: .430 for the first eight opponents, .609 for the second eight opponents. The distinction would be even stronger if we split things after seven opponents, since the Giants faced the 13-3 Patriots in their eighth game.

The DVOA ratings demonstrate that the Giants' second-half collapses are absolutely real, and can't be blamed solely on the schedule. But a further look at Table 2 shows how the schedule makes the second-half breakdown look even more extreme. It's bad to drop 15 spots in pass defense **DVOA** after midseason, but a 25-spot drop in rank for pass defense *VOA* is completely ridiculous.

Astonishingly, the NFL has done it again, giving the Giants a hugely backloaded 2012 schedule. In the first eight games of the season, the Giants' average opponent has a projected -4.1% DVOA. Their toughest out-of-division game in that stretch is either at Carolina in Week 3 or at San Francisco (a team we forecast to decline) in Week 6. Starting Week 9 with a home game against Pittsburgh, the opponents in the Giants' last eight games have an average projected 11.3% DVOA, by far the NFL's hardest second-half schedule. Besides Pittsburgh, the Giants also have to play Green Bay, New Orleans, at Atlanta, and at Baltimore.

Hopefully there won't be as many injuries as last year, and the Giants will be able to take on these opponents with a lineup that heavily resembles the team that won the Super Bowl. Most of the changes come where over-the-hill veterans left in free agency or were cut, and are being replaced by draft picks from the last two seasons. Among the 2011 picks, James Brewer slides in at right tackle, Greg Jones will play more snaps at linebacker, and Tyler Sash gets first shot at Deon Grant's spot in the "big nickel." This year's first-round pick, David Wilson, replaces Brandon Jacobs in the running back rotation, while second-round pick Rueben Randle takes Mario Manningham's spot in three-wide sets.

Jerry Reese followed his usual modus operandi and avoided big-name (and big-money) veteran acquisitions. The team's most important addition for 2012 comes at no cost whatsoever, as Terrell Thomas returns from a torn ACL to replace the inferior Aaron Ross at cornerback. The only major free-agent signing was Martellus Bennett, the best available tight end in a poor year for free-agent tight ends, and he cost just $2.5 million on a one-year deal. The Giants also took a flier on a couple of oft-injured veterans, tossing a bit of money to defensive tackle Shaun Rogers and then sending a fifth-round pick to Cincinnati for linebacker Keith Rivers. Rogers already looks like he won't pan out, but the Giants may end up with the best backup linebacker in the league if Rivers can luck into an actual healthy season.

Our 2012 projection for the Giants seems low because we tend to think of the team from the playoffs as the "real" Giants. However, the forecast is primarily based off the last two regular seasons, and is basically projecting the Giants to be the same team they were from September through December of last year. The defense is projected to be a little bit better. That's partly due to the expectation of fewer injuries, and partly just a general rebound because the defense was so much better in 2010. There's also projected offensive decline that counters the defensive improvement, a combination of the usual regression towards the mean and a variable accounting for the occasional struggles of teams with a lot of draft value invested in rookies on offense. Put a similar total DVOA together with a similar schedule (fourth last year, projected fourth this year) and you get a similar result, something around 8-8 or 9-7.

Subjectively, though, it feels like the Giants should be better than that. We saw in the postseason what their talent can do when everything's working, especially in the first two rounds when they stomped Atlanta and upset Green Bay. Those were the kind of commanding victories we traditionally associate with Super Bowl champions. It wouldn't be a surprise if the Giants were one of the league's top teams in 2012, demonstrating that the 2011 regular season was just an aberration. But it's more likely that the Giants will appear to dominate the league for two months, hit a losing streak, and see their playoff chances come down to the final week yet again.

And if they get into the tournament, our minds will face yet another battle between objective data and gut instinct.

Aaron Schatz

NEW YORK GIANTS

2011 Giants Stats by Week

Wk	vs.	W-L	PF	PA	YDF	YDA	TO	Total	Off	Def	ST
1	@WAS	L	14	28	315	332	0	-47%	-11%	20%	-15%
2	STL	W	28	16	323	367	1	22%	16%	1%	7%
3	@PHI	W	29	16	334	376	3	71%	48%	-21%	1%
4	@ARI	W	31	27	360	368	0	5%	15%	6%	-4%
5	SEA	L	25	36	464	424	-2	-13%	-14%	-9%	-7%
6	BUF	W	27	24	414	374	2	31%	35%	0%	-5%
7	BYE										
8	MIA	W	20	17	402	246	1	40%	44%	6%	2%
9	@NE	W	24	20	361	438	2	35%	-2%	-30%	7%
10	@SF	L	20	27	395	305	-1	16%	20%	1%	-2%
11	PHI	L	10	17	278	391	1	-7%	-29%	-14%	8%
12	@NO	L	24	49	465	577	-2	-74%	-13%	56%	-5%
13	GB	L	35	38	447	449	-1	37%	17%	-4%	17%
14	@DAL	W	37	34	510	444	0	-22%	19%	43%	2%
15	WAS	L	10	23	324	300	-1	-33%	-24%	14%	5%
16	@NYJ	W	29	14	332	331	2	-1%	-1%	-2%	-2%
17	DAL	W	31	14	437	300	2	55%	40%	-19%	-3%
18	ATL	W	24	2	442	247	0	55%	40%	-25%	-10%
19	@GB	W	37	20	420	388	3	62%	26%	-40%	-4%
20	@SF	W	20	17	352	328	2	14%	5%	-3%	6%
21	NE	W	21	17	396	349	1	15%	7%	0%	8%

Trends and Splits

	Offense	Rank	Defense	Rank
Total DVOA	10.5%	7	2.4%	19
Unadjusted VOA	10.3%	6	5.7%	21
Weighted Trend	9.3%	9	5.2%	22
Variance	4.9%	5	13.9%	32
Average Opponent	-0.3%	14	2.7%	6
Passing	30.2%	4	7.2%	19
Rushing	-4.9%	19	-3.7%	20
First Down	3.2%	14	8.2%	25
Second Down	10.5%	7	-8.1%	8
Third Down	26.3%	7	7.5%	22
First Half	9.9%	11	4.1%	21
Second Half	11.1%	7	0.5%	17
Red Zone	-0.4%	11	9.1%	29
Late and Close	8.2%	13	-1.5%	16

Five-Year Performance

Year	W-L	Pyth	Est W	PF	PA	TO	Total	Rk	Off	Rk	Def	Rk	ST	Rk	Off AGL	Rk	Def AGL	Rk
2007	10-6	8.6	8.2	373	351	-9	1.9%	14	-1.1%	18	-3.8%	13	-0.9%	20	13.8	6	14.5	9
2008	12-4	11.5	11.5	427	294	+9	26.0%	3	18.9%	2	-5.1%	8	1.9%	11	6.2	1	29.6	20
2009	8-8	7.4	8.4	402	427	-7	4.2%	17	8.7%	12	2.4%	19	-2.0%	26	8.5	6	47.2	29
2010	10-6	10.1	10.4	394	347	-3	13.0%	9	7.5%	10	-11.2%	3	-5.8%	30	39.7	26	18.4	13
2011	9-7	7.8	9.1	394	400	+7	8.5%	12	10.5%	7	2.4%	19	0.3%	15	25.2	14	53.1	30

2011 Performance Based on Most Common Personnel Groups

New York Offense					New York Offense vs. Opp.				New York Defense				New York Defense vs. Opp.			
Pers	Freq	Yds	DVOA	Run%	Pers	Freq	Yds	DVOA	Pers	Freq	Yds	DVOA	Pers	Freq	Yds	DVOA
11	44%	7.0	19.5%	18%	3-4-4	28%	5.2	-0.1%	4-2-5	59%	6.4	5.3%	11	43%	5.9	7.3%
21	27%	5.1	6.8%	52%	4-2-5	23%	6.9	15.8%	4-3-4	28%	4.7	-1.4%	12	20%	5.9	-2.4%
12	13%	6.4	16.0%	50%	4-3-4	23%	6.2	23.3%	Dime+	6%	5.6	6.8%	21	17%	5.8	18.2%
22	4%	6.5	15.2%	77%	Dime+	9%	8.0	33.6%	3-3-5	5%	5.6	-12.0%	22	5%	3.7	-5.5%
10	2%	7.7	60.4%	4%	2-4-5	8%	8.3	60.4%	G-line	1%	1.1	23.1%	10	3%	7.7	20.5%
					3-3-5	7%	5.5	-6.7%								

Strategic Tendencies

Run/Pass		Rank	Offense		Rank	Pass Rush		Rank	Defense/Other		Rank
Runs, all plays	39%	24	Form: Single Back	60%	19	Rush 3	6.7%	15	4 DB	28%	31
Runs, first half	37%	28	Form: Empty Back	3%	28	Rush 4	63.3%	18	5 DB	64%	1
Runs, first down	43%	31	Pers: 3+ WR	49%	20	Rush 5	20.8%	17	6+ DB	6%	18
Runs, second-long	43%	8	Pers: 4+ WR	3%	16	Rush 6+	9.1%	10	CB by Sides	53%	31
Runs, power sit.	58%	16	Pers: 2+ TE/6+ OL	25%	29	Zone Blitz	2.9%	25	Go for it on 4th	1.05	7
Runs, behind 2H	33%	9	Play action	14%	29	Sacks by LB	11.5%	26	Offensive Pace	30.2	12
Pass, ahead 2H	48%	6	Max protect	11%	16	Sacks by DB	2.1%	27	Defensive Pace	30.1	8

176 NEW YORK GIANTS

In a massive reversal from 2010, the Giants offense was horrible on play-action passes. In 2010, the Giants' DVOA was 58.1% better with play action than it was without. In 2011, the Giants' DVOA was 62.4% *worse* with play-action than it was without. We honestly have no explanation for this. Manning was superlative against big blitzes, gaining 12.3 yards per play. His performance against big blitzes has improved each of the last four years, and while it used to be the best way to attack him, it is probably no longer the best strategy. Possibly due to the Giants' predilection for option routes, Eli Manning led the league with 14 incomplete passes our charters marked as "miscommunication." Tony Romo was the only other quarterback listed with more than seven. On defense, the Giants were far better against runs from single-back sets (-18.0% DVOA, 4.4 ypc) when compared to runs from multiple-back sets (5.8% DVOA, 4.7 ypc). Although the Giants' defense is predicated on their ability to pressure the quarterback with just four pass rushers, Big Blue is also excellent on the blitz. For the third straight year, the Giants allowed fewer yards per play with five pass rushers (6.5) than with four (7.0), and even fewer yards per play with six or more pass rushers (3.3). The Giants generally moved Corey Webster around and tried to put him against the other team's best receiver. We have Webster covering the other team's No. 1 on 60 percent of his targets, while Aaron Ross covered the No. 1 on just 25 percent. The Giants' defense was second in the league with 22 passes tipped at the line.

Passing

Player	DYAR	DVOA	Plays	NtYds	Avg	YAC	C%	TD	Int
E.Manning	1109	16.2%	618	4686	7.8	5.8	61.4%	29	16

Rushing

Player	DYAR	DVOA	Plays	Yds	Avg	TD	Fum	Suc
A.Bradshaw	80	2.5%	171	659	3.9	9	0	45%
B.Jacobs*	35	-3.2%	152	571	3.8	7	3	49%
D.Ware	3	-7.1%	46	163	3.5	0	0	39%
E.Manning	-18	-43.3%	12	34	2.8	1	1	--
D.Scott	-20	-95.0%	5	16	3.2	0	1	40%

Receiving

Player	DYAR	DVOA	Plays	Ctch	Yds	Y/C	YAC	TD	C%
H.Nicks	274	12.9%	133	76	1192	15.7	4.6	7	57%
V.Cruz	455	32.0%	129	82	1536	18.7	7.2	9	64%
M.Manningham*	44	-5.6%	77	39	523	13.4	2.7	4	51%
R.Barden	-29	-32.1%	19	9	94	10.4	3.0	0	47%
D.Hixon	20	28.2%	6	4	50	12.5	0.0	1	67%
J.Ballard	127	22.5%	61	38	604	15.9	4.8	4	62%
B.Pascoe	21	12.7%	16	12	136	11.3	7.8	0	75%
T.Beckum	-15	-28.5%	10	5	93	18.6	8.0	1	50%
M.Bennett	-27	-23.7%	26	17	144	8.5	5.6	0	65%
A.Bradshaw	39	3.7%	44	34	267	7.9	8.8	2	77%
D.Ware	0	-13.8%	37	27	170	6.3	6.9	0	73%
B.Jacobs*	17	-0.1%	22	15	128	8.5	7.9	1	68%
H.Hynoski	31	17.3%	16	12	83	6.9	6.8	0	75%

Offensive Line

Year	Yards	ALY	Rank	Power	Rank	Stuff	Rank	2nd Lev	Rank	Open Field	Rank	F-Start	Cont.
2009	4.18	4.14	13	60%	20	20%	18	1.23	10	0.68	19	11	32
2010	4.83	4.22	7	59%	18	19%	16	1.31	4	1.25	3	16	23
2011	3.77	3.81	29	53%	27	19%	15	1.05	29	0.49	29	16	26

Year	LE	Rank	LT	Rank	Mid	Rank	RT	Rank	RE	Rank	Sacks	ASR	Rank	Short	Long
2009	4.11	19	4.04	18	4.04	21	4.56	6	4.19	18	32	5.3%	9	8	11
2010	3.44	26	4.31	15	4.48	6	4.39	8	3.89	18	16	3.3%	2	9	2
2011	4.03	17	3.76	23	3.94	19	3.50	26	3.73	16	28	5.0%	6	11	10

The Giants' offensive line struggled from the very beginning of the 2011 season. Half of Eli Manning's 28 sacks came in the first five games, but the pass blocking eventually came around. The same cannot be said for the run blocking. It's hard to pinpoint one or two Giants linemen who were responsible for the running problems. It seemed like on every play, a different lineman was pushed backwards, or missed his block, or seemed to be blocking the wrong player, thus leaving another lineman completely confused. The running backs of course bear some of the responsibility for the collapse of the running game, as the Giants' numbers in Second-Level

Yards and Open-Field Yards declined as much as their numbers in Adjusted Line Yards. And lack of continuity was part of the problem. Center David Baas missed five games in the middle of the year, and left tackle William Beatty went on injured reserve after 10 games.

The Giants will return four-fifths of their starting linemen to the same places where they started 2011, and hope the run-blocking issues work themselves out in training camp. Beatty goes back to left tackle, which will push veteran David Diehl back to left guard. Baas is at center, next to the most consistent member of the Giants' line, right guard Chris Snee. The new face will be at right tackle, where the Giants made no attempt to re-sign Kareem McKenzie in free agency. James Brewer, a 2011 fourth-round pick out of Indiana, gets first crack at the job. Brewer has excellent lateral quickness and impressive size, particularly arm length, but also a poor health record, having lost most of two college seasons to injuries. If he flops or gets hurt, former Washington and Seattle right tackle Sean Locklear was signed as insurance. Meanwhile, Kevin Boothe, who filled in for Baas and then played left guard when Diehl had to move to tackle, will go back to his role as utility lineman. Boothe was the Giants lineman who earned the most accolades from our game charters, with a number of comments complimenting his ability to pull around on runs.

Defensive Front Seven

Defensive Line	Age	Pos	Plays	TmPct	Rk	Stop	Dfts	BTkl	St%	Rk	AvYd	Rk	Sack	Hit	Hur	Runs	St%	Yds	Pass	St%	Yds
Jason Pierre-Paul	23	DE	92	10.9%	1	66	32	2	72%	62	1.3	39	16.5	14	25	55	71%	1.9	37	73%	0.4
Linval Joseph	24	DT	52	6.1%	11	43	8	0	83%	22	1.8	33	2.5	3	3	42	81%	2.7	10	90%	-1.9
Chris Canty	30	DT	47	5.5%	16	37	11	0	79%	34	1.8	32	3.5	3	9	37	76%	2.2	10	90%	0.3
Justin Tuck	29	DE	40	6.3%	20	25	8	2	63%	78	2.2	63	5	5	15.5	26	54%	4.2	14	79%	-1.4
Rocky Bernard	33	DT	33	3.9%	41	21	2	0	64%	65	3.1	66	0	3	2	26	65%	2.5	7	57%	5.1
Osi Umenyiora	32	DE	26	5.5%	32	19	12	2	73%	59	-0.5	7	9	3	11	16	56%	3.3	10	100%	-6.6
Dave Tollefson*	31	DE	20	2.4%	--	14	8	1	70%	--	1.3	--	5	3	4.5	12	50%	4.1	8	100%	-2.9
Shaun Rogers	33	DT	22	2.8%	61	20	2	0	91%	3	1.6	29	0	3	4.5	20	95%	1.5	2	50%	3.0

Linebackers	Age	Pos	Plays	TmPct	Rk	Stop	Dfts	BTkl	AvYd	Sack	Hit	Hur	Runs	St%	Rk	Yds	Rk	Tgts	Suc%	Rk	AdjYd	Rk
Michael Boley	30	OLB	94	12.7%	33	40	16	1	5.8	1	2	3	50	48%	108	4.4	103	47	49%	46	7.6	62
Mathias Kiwanuka	29	OLB	83	9.8%	56	49	26	2	4.2	3.5	6	6.5	56	64%	59	2.8	30	23	34%	76	7.2	51
Jacquian Williams	23	OLB	65	7.7%	86	34	13	2	5.6	1	0	5	29	62%	67	4.3	97	35	55%	21	6.3	31
Greg Jones	24	MLB	25	3.0%	--	10	1	0	6.2	0	0	0	21	48%	--	4.3	--	2	0%	--	17.4	--
Chase Blackburn	29	MLB	23	8.7%	--	12	2	1	5.9	0	1	0	12	67%	--	2.9	--	7	71%	--	3.8	--

Year	Yards	ALY	Rank	Power	Rank	Stuff	Rank	2nd Lev	Rank	Open Field	Rank
2009	4.16	3.63	4	73%	27	25%	2	1.09	9	1.09	27
2010	3.96	3.78	11	65%	20	19%	20	1.03	6	0.75	15
2011	4.49	4.12	20	61%	13	21%	12	1.14	13	1.01	23

Year	LE	Rank	LT	Rank	Mid	Rank	RT	Rank	RE	Rank	Sacks	ASR	Rank	Short	Long
2009	5.39	31	3.65	7	3.32	1	3.00	2	3.88	13	33	6.7%	15	13	11
2010	3.64	6	3.97	15	3.91	16	3.35	7	3.78	13	46	7.6%	7	14	16
2011	4.97	26	3.45	4	4.30	26	4.17	15	3.27	13	48	7.3%	11	8	23

The Giants have become famous for their "Four Aces" package where four defensive ends play along the line at the same time, but right now Big Blue barely has four defensive ends on the roster. Sure, the Giants have the spectacular Jason Pierre-Paul, the steady Justin Tuck, and the finally-happy-with-his-contract Osi Umenyiora. Yet the free-agent departure of Dave Tollefson, combined with the fact that the Giants have not selected a defensive end in the last two drafts, leaves a huge depth problem. Strongside linebacker Mathias Kiwanuka will still play plenty at his old defensive end position, but if injuries strike again, there's nothing left in the cupboard except 2010 sixth-rounder Adrian Tracy, a developmental prospect who never developed, and assorted undrafted free agents like Justin Trattou and Adewale Ojomo. The defensive tackle position has far more depth, with Chris Canty and Linval Joseph backed up by veteran Rocky Bernard and 2011 second-round pick Marvin Austin, who missed his entire rookie season with a torn pectoral. (Austin also was suspended for his senior season at North Carolina for accepting improper benefits, so he hasn't been on the field in a meaningful game since December of 2009.) Veteran Shaun Rogers is also around, but spent minicamp struggling with an elbow injury and was tagged as "a failed experiment" by *New York Post* reporter Bart Hubbuch.

The Giants' linebackers are distinguished by their extremely low broken tackle statistics. For the second straight year, we marked Michael Boley with only one broken tackle, while Kiwanuka and rookie Jacquian Williams had only two apiece. Boley sometimes has trouble sorting through trash to get to the ballcarrier, and his Run Stop Rate has ranked 80th or lower for three years now, but he's regarded as a strong cover player. His charting coverage stats were average last year, but were generally above average in previous seasons. He gets some key assignments such as covering Aaron Hernandez in the Super Bowl, and when he was out of the lineup in Week 12, the Saints whipped up on the Giants with passes to Jimmy Graham and the running backs.

The Giants were a primarily 4-2-5 defense last year, but are expected to go back to more traditional 4-3 sets this year, and the early leader for the starting slot at middle linebacker is playoff hero Chase Blackburn. He has a number of challengers for that role, beginning with Greg Jones, who started five games in the middle as a sixth-round rookie. Jones is another in a long line of tough, instinctive, consistent-tackling linebackers who dropped in the draft because they were undersized and maybe a tad slow. The floor for this type of player is to become a useful special-teamer like H.B. Blades; the ceiling is Zach Thomas, London Fletcher, and Sam Mills. Other possibilities include trade-acquisition Keith Rivers, who has been plagued by injuries since the Bengals made him the ninth overall pick in 2008, and Mark Herzlich, the former Boston College star who worked his way from bone cancer to undrafted free agent to special-teamer to two games in the starting lineup before an ankle injury ended his rookie season.

Defensive Secondary

Secondary	Age	Pos	Plays	TmPct	Rk	Stop	Dfts	BTkl	Runs	St%	Rk	Yds	Rk	Tgts	Tgt%	Rk	Dist	Suc%	Rk	APaYd	Rk	PD	Int
Antrel Rolle	30	FS	100	11.8%	18	44	13	10	40	63%	3	5.7	13	57	11.9%	1	7.8	52%	44	7.2	32	4	2
Kenny Phillips	26	SS	92	11.6%	21	33	12	7	40	45%	27	7.7	53	29	6.5%	47	19.5	60%	23	9.3	55	10	4
Aaron Ross*	30	CB	72	8.5%	39	25	11	1	13	54%	24	4.9	10	77	16.2%	49	12.0	45%	69	8.9	63	12	4
Corey Webster	30	CB	68	8.0%	48	28	16	4	8	25%	70	9.0	60	101	21.3%	14	13.1	54%	36	6.9	27	19	6
Deon Grant*	33	SS	65	7.7%	62	27	10	5	38	39%	37	5.9	19	29	6.1%	55	13.9	57%	37	8.5	47	6	1
Prince Amukamara	23	CB	17	4.6%	--	4	1	0	5	20%	--	15.4	--	17	8.0%	--	18.5	43%	--	12.4	--	3	1
Antwaun Molden	26	CB	31	3.8%	--	7	3	2	5	40%	--	5.4	--	33	6.3%	--	14.5	29%	--	11.1	--	4	2

Year	Pass D Rank	vs. #1 WR	Rk	vs. #2 WR	Rk	vs. Other WR	Rk	vs. TE	Rk	vs. RB	Rk
2009	17	24.6%	30	-0.6%	18	1.9%	17	7.9%	18	-4.2%	14
2010	3	-25.4%	2	-10.1%	7	26.8%	31	-13.0%	3	-0.9%	11
2011	19	0.6%	13	5.7%	17	18.2%	30	5.1%	13	9.0%	23

A zillion Giants cornerbacks went down with injuries last year, but the important one was Terrell Thomas, who has generally had good pass coverage stats (36th in adjusted yards per pass in 2010, seventh in 2009) and makes a lot of run tackles. Thomas will be back in the starting lineup this year, replacing the much weaker Aaron Ross, who signed with Jacksonville. Nickelback Prince Amukamara played like a rookie who had missed half a season with a foot injury, which is appropriate. He should improve with more NFL experience. Antrel Rolle switched from free safety to slot corner much of the time, which is why he leads all safeties in charted targets. Whether playing corner or safety, he had one of his better seasons. Kenny Phillips combines excellent size and athleticism with reasonable zone-coverage skills. Perry Fewell says he still plans on running some of the big nickel package that became the Giants' *de facto* base defense in 2011, but unless the Giants decide to bring back still-unsigned free agent Deon Grant, this sure looks like a team with a lot more depth at linebacker than at safety. 2011 sixth-round pick Tyler Sash is a hitter who was very active on special teams but has coverage deficiencies. Behind him are Chris Horton, who was pretty good as a rookie with the Redskins in 2009 then completely fell out of favor with coaches; Stevie Brown, who has bounced around four teams since the Raiders drafted him in the seventh round of the 2010 draft; and Twitter all-star and college free-agent Will Hill.

Special Teams

Year	DVOA	Rank	FG/XP	Rank	Net Kick	Rank	Kick Ret	Rank	Net Punt	Rank	Punt Ret	Rank	Hidden	Rank
2009	-1.7%	26	-3.0	22	1.2	15	-10.3	30	-5.6	26	7.4	7	-2.6	19
2010	-4.9%	30	-0.7	19	3.4	11	-7.9	25	-15.6	30	-8.2	29	1.5	13
2011	0.3%	15	-1.7	19	4.2	8	-3.4	22	10.9	5	-8.4	29	-3.8	21

Kicker Lawrence Tynes is boring and inoffensive, like a grilled cheese sandwich. If there were football cards for special teams, packs would include 100 Lawrence Tyneses for every one Sebastian Janikowski. This is not necessarily a criticism, because boring and inoffensive is a lot better than being Nick Folk. Speaking of the Jets, punter Steve Weatherford switched locker rooms at MetLife Stadium and was merely very good, instead of superlative like he was the year before. Tynes and Weatherford are helped by strong coverage teams, with both Jacquian Williams and Tyler Sash among the eight NFL players with at least 15 special teams tackles in 2011.

Since Domenik Hixon's first ACL tear in 2010, the Giants have rotated a cast of thousands through the returner spots without finding anyone who is any good on a consistent basis. Over the past two seasons, six different Giants have returned at least eight kickoffs and five different Giants have returned at least three punts. If healthy, Hixon has a shot to take the jobs back; otherwise the Giants will try Jerrel Jernigan or Da'Rel Scott again.

Coaching Staff

As Chris Brown pointed out so well in an article for Grantland before the Super Bowl, offensive coordinator Kevin Gilbride has essentially built the Giants offense as a cross between the power running game favored by Tom Coughlin and a passing game based on option routes that date back to the run-and-shoot that Gilbride ran with the Houston Oilers. Gilbride trusts his receivers to read the defense and know which option will get them open. He did a fine job reacting to the problems of the running game and opening the offense up further in 2011. Like coaches from Buddy Ryan to Mike Shanahan, Gilbride is building a family legacy with his son Kevin Jr. on staff as wide receivers coach.

Sean Ryan is the other name to watch among the Giants' positional coaches. No, he's not the former tight end who bounced around the league in the mid-2000s. This Ryan came up through the coaching ranks at Boston College, Columbia, and Harvard. After three years as offensive quality control, Ryan was wide receivers coach last year, helping Victor Cruz to his breakout year. He was upped to quarterbacks coach when Mike Sullivan left to become the offensive coordinator in Tampa Bay. With experience all around the offense, a coordinator job could be in his future as well.

New York Jets

2011 Record: 8-8

Pythagorean Wins: 8.4 (15th)

DVOA: 13.5% (10th)

Offense: -8.3% (21st)

Defense: -16.1% (2nd)

Special Teams: 5.6% (4th)

Variance: 18.2% (25th)

2012 Mean Projection: 9.2 wins

On the Clock (0-4): 3%

Mediocrity (5-7): 18%

Playoff Contender (8-10): 51%

Super Bowl Contender (11+): 28%

Postseason Odds: 46.4%

Projected Average Opponent: -1.3% (21st)

2011: This was definitely not a fun place to be, Greg McElroy can assure you.

2012: Tim Tebow is in this box. Therefore, this box is a winner.

As a service to readers who have a power drill aimed at their temples right now and will pull the trigger if they read one more lazy Tebow-equals-Jesus joke, a socio-political treatise on the role of religion in sports and culture, or a discussion of how selfish/outspoken locker room personalities poison a team's chances to win a Super Bowl (except when they don't), this essay will strive to remain as analytic as possible.

In the paragraphs to come, we will discuss the viability of the Wildcat as a specialty package in the NFL, assess the strengths and weaknesses of the Jets roster, and explain how a team with such a vicious defensive reputation can record just 35 sacks. There will be sober analysis of Mark Sanchez's strengths and weaknesses and a breakdown of how the Jets offensive line will survive the continued presence of Wayne Hunter.

Please look elsewhere for foot jokes, casual-blasphemy-as-comedy, and clichés about "team chemistry," a "circus atmosphere" or, *shudder*, "all he does is win." There will be some passing acknowledgement of the Jets' organizational personality in the essay's conclusion, and it may be the most successful "passing" you see associated with the Jets this year.

Let's get started.

The Jets enter this season with several obvious assets. First, they possess the best three-deep cornerback corps in the NFL. Darrelle Revis' charting numbers may have fell off in the second half of last season (see the unit comments), but Revis is still the best cornerback in the NFL. Antonio Cromartie has grown into his role as the guy in the crosshairs, and Kyle Wilson is a great fit as a slot cornerback. The Jets finished first in the NFL at stopping No. 1 receivers last year, second in stopping No.2 receivers, and posted respectable DVOA totals against other receivers even though opponents were constantly targeting them to avoid Revis.

Second, the Jets possess a solid foundation of up-the-middle defensive talent, led by tackle Sione Pouha and linebacker David Harris. There is adequate talent around Pouha and Harris, and head coach Rex Ryan still has defensive mastermind bona fides despite an off year in 2011 that forced him to rethink some of his favorite tactics.

The Jets strangely became both more blitz-reliant and blitz-averse last year, relying on blitzes of five or more defenders to provide 18 of their 35 sacks while attempting just 36 blitzes of six or seven defenders in non-goal-to-go situations. So they needed the big blitz to get pressure, yet they were reluctant to use it: a very un-Ryan-like situation. Opponents burned the Jets' big blitzes for 9.1 yards per play, so Ryan adjusted to the fact that he was short on impact pass rushers and opponents were prepared to counter his tactics with max-protect schemes. He became a little more conventional. The Jets held opposing quarter-

2012 Jets Schedule

Week	Opp.	Week	Opp.	Week	Opp.
1	BUF	7	at NE	13	ARI
2	at PIT	8	MIA	14	at JAC
3	at MIA	9	BYE	15	at TEN (Mon.)
4	SF	10	at SEA	16	SD
5	HOU (Mon.)	11	at STL	17	at BUF
6	IND	12	NE (Thu.)		

Figure 1. 2011 New York Jets DVOA by Week

backs to a 54.2 percent completion rate, so Ryan's tactical adjustment paid off, but no coach named Ryan can survive on 35 sacks per year. The Jets pass rush has been bolstered by the return of Bryan Thomas and the selection of rookie Quinton Coples, and Ryan returned to his roots in the offseason by installing some new variations on the family-heirloom 46 defense.

Third, the Jets have four-fifths of a Super Bowl-caliber offensive line. Center Nick Mangold, guard Brandon Moore, and left tackle D'Brickashaw Ferguson are entering their seventh season together, dating back to the Eric Mangini era. Matt Slauson joined them in 2010. Mangold and Ferguson have made multiple Pro Bowls, while Moore has been stalwart as both a blocker and the designated Voice of Reason in the Jets clubhouse.

The fifth amigo, right tackle Wayne Hunter, is an organizational blind spot. He blew 10.5 blocks last year, but instead of replacing Hunter, the Jets are trying to improve his game with a strict regimen of improved coaching and noisy attacks against Hunter's critics. Whether Hunter is a misunderstood hero or a blown piston in need of replacing, however, the Jets still have the capacity to be great on the offensive line.

The Jets' fourth asset is one of circumstance: the AFC has only one offensive superpower, the Patriots, followed by a bunch of teams vying for playoff berths with run-and-defend philosophies. The Bengals made the playoffs with a rookie quarterback last year, the Texans with a power running game and a third-stringer pulling the trigger. The Ravens came within a dropped pass of the Super Bowl with a great defense, a great running back, and an immobile satellite launcher at quarterback. The Broncos dusted off a Wing-T playbook and beat the Steelers, the historic masters of the blitz-now, worry-about-offense-later playoff run. (The Steelers are much more passing-oriented than in years past, of course, but they still have the 16-13 slugfest in their arsenal of winning styles).

Rex Ryan and general manager Mike Tannenbaum recognized that running-and-defense teams can excel in the AFC. They realized that their secondary, scheme, and offensive line give them the potential to be an awesome running-and-defense team. And they quickly whiffed on their attempt to sign Peyton Manning. So they decided to turn the Jets into a hardcore running-and-defense team. Their philosophy evolved slowly through the winter and spring. The Manning courtship suggested that they were just casting around for a short-term solution, a classic Tannenbaum tactic. But by May, a plan had come together, one that made Rex Ryan dream logic crazy sense.

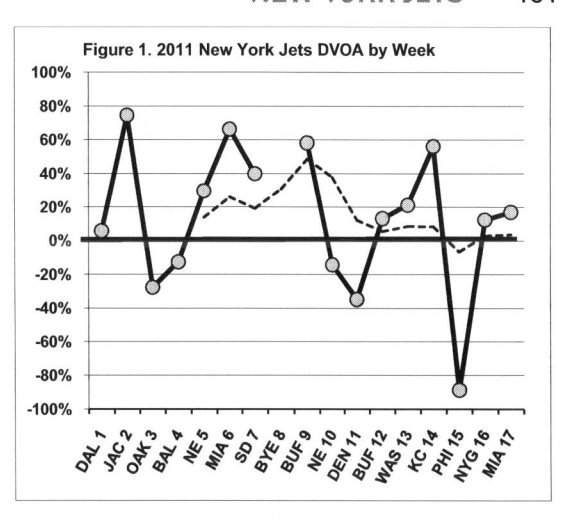

First, Tony Sparano replaced Brian Schottenheimer as offensive coordinator. Schottenheimer's all-things-to-everyone offense was perfect for Chad Pennington and pretty good for Brett Favre, passers who could read a defense pre-snap and thread quick passes across spread formations. With Sanchez at the helm, Schottenheimer's offense became more wrinkles than substance: Wildcats, pistols, six-lineman sets, spread formations, jugglers and stilt-walkers. Sparano also suffered from scheme schizophrenia in Miami; he popularized the Wildcat, then quickly retreated from that success so he could try to build a conventional offense around Chad Henne. But Sparano is a running game guru, and Ryan is a Wildcat lover, so the Sparano hire telegraphed the Jets' newfound commitment to dinosaur football. It should have provided a big clue about what would happen next.

Tim Tebow, acquired with some fanfare from the Broncos in exchange for a pair of draft picks, gives the Jets an excellent trigger man for a Wildcat offense and a likely challenger-usurper to Sanchez. Tebow rushed 85 times for 420 yards (4.9 yards per carry) on designed runs last season, most of which would be better described as option plays than Wildcat plays, but were similar enough for comparison. (We will use "Wildcat" as a generic term for designed runs by special guest snap-recipients for the rest of the essay.) Tebow actually finished among the league's worst running quarterbacks with -39 DYAR, a figure brought down by six fumbles and the Broncos' reliance on quarterback runs in third-and-long situations. There are no questions about Tebow's talent as a runner, repeat, as a runner, and just for emphasis a third time, *as a runner.*

Tebow's negative DYAR, and the rapid marginalization of the Wildcat by Sparano and the rest of the NFL, invite skepticism of the Jets' stated goal of making the scheme a major element of their offense. Sparano's Dolphins used the Wildcat 84 times in the strategy's debut season. Imitators quickly caught on, and the scheme went viral in 2009. As Table 1 shows, however, the fad wore off quickly, for a variety of reasons: It disrupted offensive rhythm, did not follow naturally from most team's offensive strategies, and required direct snaps to rookie cornerbacks and other crimes against logic. By last season, only the Jets and Bills had any regular use for it, with only ten other teams executing any Wildcat-type plays at all.

The data in Table 1 does not tell the whole story, for two reasons. First, it does not include Tebow or Cam Newton, both of whom executed many Wildcat-like plays as starting quarterbacks. Tebow's 22-carry experiments often yielded diminishing returns, but Newton's better-integrated plays did not. Newton rushed 70 times for 354 yards, earning a league-best 190 Rushing DYAR, because a) he did not fumble, and b) his rushes were limited to red-zone carries, short-yardage carries, and the occasional early-down surprise. Designed quarterback runs can be excellent short-yardage weapons: A little confusion can make a big difference in tight quarters, when the defense cannot afford to give up 2 or 3 yards. Newton and Tebow (who was also very effective at the goal-line) demonstrate that judicious use of Wildcat-like strategies can help an offense.

Second, Table 1 only includes one team that made a dedicated, organization-wide commitment to integrating the Wildcat completely into its philosophy: Sparano's 2009 Dolphins. Every other team in the last three seasons was just dabbling. Sparano has been given resources and blessings this year. If the Jets get nowhere on four direct snap plays one week, they are unlikely to scrap it the next week. If the Tebow pack-

Table 1: 'Wildcat' Plays in the NFL

Year	Direct snaps to non-Quarterbacks	Yards Per Play
2009	337	4.83
2010	184	4.44
2011	84	4.04

age is yielding about 4.8 yards per play—Tebow's 2011 designed rush average, and the 2009 Wildcat yards-per-play average—Ryan will be satisfied, assuming those 4.8 yards include a fair share of one-yard touchdowns. Remember the Jets' goal: a grinding offense to complement the defense and facilitate wins with 20-13 final scores, not a scheme that scores 30 points per game.

Where does this commitment to running and Wildcatting leave Sanchez? After three full seasons, Sanchez has not overcome his shortcomings. He's awful against a heavy rush, completing just 30.8 percent of his passes for 3.1 yards per attempt when pressured last season. He was 7-of-28 on passes with an air length of over 25 yards; 12 of those passes came in the fourth quarter with the Jets trailing, demonstrating that Schottenheimer had little faith in Sanchez's deep accuracy until the situation grew desperate. Sanchez is not a high-volume pocket passer, nor is he the kind of ball-protecting, sack-avoiding game manager coaches like Ryan look for when building a defense-oriented team. He is a stopgap, one that the Jets foolishly signed to a contract extension before the Tebow trade.

There's a good chance that all of the Jets' talk about their Wildcat package is just coded language, and Tebow will become the starter after Sanchez's first stalled drive. Keeping Tebow in the game and letting him throw wobblers makes more sense than shuttling Sanchez on and off the bench to attempt passes with slightly less wobble. The threat of a Tebow scramble is more likely to keep the defense honest than the threat of Sanchez suddenly figuring out what he is doing. If the Jets persist in trying to develop a Sanchez-Tebow platoon, they risk the worst of all worlds: Tebow running telegraphed options into a prepared defense; an angry, uncomfortable Sanchez shunting into and out of games; and teammates and fans taking sides in what could become an ugly controversy.

That last point brings us back to the kitchen elephants we have avoided for 1,700 words. Ryan has fostered a bad-boy culture that erupted in outright scapegoating last year. Tebow is a cultural icon whose personality and fan fervidness are potentially divisive.

NEW YORK JETS

The Jets are courting disaster in the name of creating a gimmick offense that can net, in an ideal case, five yards per rush and a red zone advantage. It is easy to imagine the Jets winning a wild card berth and becoming a playoff headache by charting the narrow channel between Revis Island and Cape Tebowmania. It is easier to imagine an entire November episode of *Pardon the Interruption* dedicated to what Cromartie said after Tebow's fumble, how Ryan reacted, and what Sanchez thought when he heard the comments from his new locker room in Arizona.

It is all very crazy, highly unpredictable, and gruesomely interesting, which makes it all quintessentially Jets.

Mike Tanier

2011 Jets Stats by Week

Wk	vs.	W-L	PF	PA	YDF	YDA	TO	Total	Off	Def	ST
1	DAL	W	27	24	360	390	1	6%	-2%	-9%	-1%
2	JAC	W	32	3	283	203	2	75%	-2%	-63%	13%
3	@OAK	L	24	34	439	383	-2	-28%	-1%	31%	5%
4	@BAL	L	17	34	150	267	-1	-12%	-91%	-50%	29%
5	@NE	L	21	30	255	446	1	30%	19%	-2%	9%
6	MIA	W	24	6	296	308	2	66%	19%	-49%	-1%
7	SD	W	27	21	318	268	0	40%	5%	-27%	8%
8	BYE										
9	@BUF	W	27	11	348	287	1	58%	18%	-39%	1%
10	NE	L	16	37	378	389	-3	-14%	-10%	-1%	-5%
11	@DEN	L	13	17	318	229	-1	-35%	-34%	-10%	-11%
12	BUF	W	28	24	318	336	-2	13%	24%	12%	1%
13	@WAS	W	34	19	266	304	2	21%	7%	-14%	-1%
14	KC	W	37	10	314	221	0	56%	25%	-18%	13%
15	@PHI	L	19	45	241	420	0	-89%	-76%	33%	21%
16	NYG	L	14	29	331	332	-2	12%	-20%	-32%	0%
17	@MIA	L	17	19	374	210	-1	17%	-23%	-30%	9%

Trends and Splits

	Offense	Rank	Defense	Rank
Total DVOA	-8.3%	21	-16.1%	2
Unadjusted VOA	-7.5%	20	-14.6%	3
Weighted Trend	-8.8%	22	-14.3%	2
Variance	10.6%	27	13.8%	31
Average Opponent	1.5%	25	2.0%	10
Passing	0.4%	20	-16.0%	2
Rushing	-4.9%	18	-16.2%	4
First Down	-12.9%	25	-19.7%	3
Second Down	-2.7%	17	-6.2%	12
Third Down	-8.4%	18	-25.6%	2
First Half	-7.6%	21	-19.7%	3
Second Half	-9.0%	24	-12.7%	6
Red Zone	4.6%	6	-12.0%	12
Late and Close	-35.2%	31	-6.1%	9

Five-Year Performance

Year	W-L	Pyth	Est W	PF	PA	TO	Total	Rk	Off	Rk	Def	Rk	ST	Rk	Off AGL	Rk	Def AGL	Rk
2007	4-12	5.4	4.9	268	355	-4	-15.3%	24	-9.3%	22	7.6%	25	1.6%	10	19.6	13	18.5	14
2008	9-7	9.3	8.7	405	356	-1	4.0%	17	0.0%	18	-0.8%	14	3.2%	8	7.3	2	10.5	5
2009	9-7	11.4	9.2	342	236	+1	25.8%	9	-12.5%	22	-25.5%	1	2.8%	6	4.1	1	21.0	12
2010	11-5	9.8	10.1	367	304	+9	18.7%	6	2.1%	16	-10.9%	5	5.8%	5	8.9	4	33.0	23
2011	8-8	8.4	8.4	377	363	-3	13.5%	10	-8.3%	21	-16.1%	2	5.6%	4	9.2	2	21.2	12

2011 Performance Based on Most Common Personnel Groups

New York Offense					New York Offense vs. Opp.				New York Defense				New York Defense vs. Opp.			
Pers	Freq	Yds	DVOA	Run%	Pers	Freq	Yds	DVOA	Pers	Freq	Yds	DVOA	Pers	Freq	Yds	DVOA
11	42%	4.9	2.0%	20%	4-3-4	26%	4.8	-9.1%	3-4-4	30%	4.6	-17.2%	11	34%	5.4	-28.8%
21	22%	5.1	-24.1%	53%	4-2-5	24%	5.2	2.3%	Dime	18%	5.9	-13.8%	12	26%	5.6	-3.5%
12	15%	5.1	4.0%	51%	3-4-4	23%	5.4	8.1%	3-3-5	15%	5.3	-17.1%	21	16%	4.7	-12.6%
22	7%	4.2	-0.9%	72%	3-3-5	12%	4.6	-28.7%	Quarter	11%	6.0	-21.3%	10	6%	6.9	13.9%
20	2%	5.5	-6.3%	17%	Dime+	8%	6.4	27.4%	4-3-4	11%	5.0	-24.8%	22	6%	3.5	-23.5%
									4-2-5	9%	5.5	2.0%				

Strategic Tendencies

Run/Pass		Rank	Offense		Rank	Pass Rush		Rank	Defense/Other		Rank
Runs, all plays	42%	15	Form: Single Back	58%	21	Rush 3	13.6%	4	4 DB	41%	25
Runs, first half	43%	18	Form: Empty Back	5%	21	Rush 4	55.9%	23	5 DB	26%	28
Runs, first down	55%	12	Pers: 3+ WR	47%	21	Rush 5	22.9%	13	6+ DB	29%	4
Runs, second-long	29%	29	Pers: 4+ WR	2%	24	Rush 6+	7.5%	15	CB by Sides	55%	30
Runs, power sit.	59%	14	Pers: 2+ TE/6+ OL	31%	17	Zone Blitz	9.7%	5	Go for it on 4th	0.73	29
Runs, behind 2H	31%	12	Play action	20%	14	Sacks by LB	67.1%	5	Offensive Pace	31.6	26
Pass, ahead 2H	31%	30	Max protect	13%	8	Sacks by DB	11.4%	9	Defensive Pace	30.0	6

The Jets are the only team for which we've separated Dime (6 DB) and Quarter (7 DB) formations on the defensive formations table, because they used seven defensive backs so much more often than any other team. Charters listed the Jets using Quarter on 11 percent of pass plays. Dallas, with the other Ryan brother, was the only other team above 1.5 percent. ☞ The Jets went from blitzing on 46 percent of pass plays in 2010 to only 30 percent of pass plays in 2011. As noted in the main essay, bringing big pressure didn't necessarily work for the Jets in 2011. We have the Jets giving up 9.1 yards per play with a big blitz of six or more. ☞ As you would expect, the Jets rank low in "CB by sides" because of Darrelle Revis, who covered the other team's No. 1 receiver on a league-leading 68 percent of his targets. ☞ The Jets offense averaged a league-leading 11.3 yards after catch on passes thrown behind the line of scrimmage, but a below-average 3.8 yards after catch on passes thrown past the line of scrimmage.

Passing

Player	DYAR	DVOA	Plays	NtYds	Avg	YAC	C%	TD	Int
M.Sanchez	-53	-12.5%	581	3220	5.8	4.9	57.2%	26	17
T.Tebow	-221	-22.7%	301	1507	5.2	4.8	47.0%	12	6

Rushing

Player	DYAR	DVOA	Plays	Yds	Avg	TD	Fum	Suc
S.Greene	113	2.2%	252	1053	4.2	6	1	50%
L.Tomlinson*	10	-5.2%	75	280	3.7	1	0	45%
J.McKnight	-11	-14.9%	43	134	3.1	0	0	44%
M.Sanchez	7	-8.2%	26	110	4.2	6	3	--
J.Conner	25	27.0%	13	44	3.4	1	0	69%
B.Powell	-54	-115.1%	13	21	1.6	0	1	15%
J.Kerley	10	-6.0%	6	30	5.0	0	0	--
T.Tebow	-36	-18.3%	117	668	5.7	6	6	--

Receiving

Player	DYAR	DVOA	Plays	Ctch	Yds	Y/C	YAC	TD	C%
S.Holmes	38	-8.0%	101	51	654	12.8	3.7	8	50%
P.Burress*	56	-5.5%	96	45	612	13.6	3.2	8	47%
J.Kerley	6	-11.2%	47	29	314	10.8	3.4	1	62%
D.Mason*	-29	-29.6%	22	13	115	8.8	2.6	0	59%
P.Turner	12	-2.0%	15	8	96	12.0	3.0	1	53%
C.Schilens	72	14.5%	34	23	271	11.8	1.6	2	68%
D.Keller	-11	-8.7%	115	65	815	12.5	4.4	5	57%
M.Mulligan	-28	-53.7%	9	5	58	11.6	8.2	0	56%
L.Tomlinson*	83	15.5%	60	42	449	10.7	9.1	2	70%
S.Greene	12	-8.6%	41	30	211	7.0	6.9	0	73%
J.McKnight	43	31.2%	18	13	139	10.7	8.5	0	72%

Offensive Line

Year	Yards	ALY	Rank	Power	Rank	Stuff	Rank	2nd Lev	Rank	Open Field	Rank	F-Start	Cont.
2009	4.48	4.28	8	70%	6	15%	4	1.11	20	0.87	12	21	48
2010	4.48	4.56	3	76%	2	12%	1	1.15	14	0.56	23	19	43
2011	3.87	4.23	8	66%	10	16%	4	1.06	28	0.32	32	26	41

Year	LE	Rank	LT	Rank	Mid	Rank	RT	Rank	RE	Rank	Sacks	ASR	Rank	Short	Long
2009	3.05	29	4.06	17	4.21	12	5.06	1	3.75	23	30	7.7%	23	8	15
2010	5.04	3	4.06	20	4.52	5	4.90	4	4.37	10	28	5.4%	8	9	15
2011	4.14	16	2.89	31	4.53	4	4.48	15	3.74	15	40	6.7%	17	16	19

New offensive line coach Dave DeGugliemo clearly likes Wayne Hunter. "This guy is the starting right tackle," DeGuglielmo said in May. "Until they tell me otherwise, until they ship him out of this building or until they shoot me dead in my office, that son-of-a-gun is going to be the starting right tackle. And he's going to play well."

Congratulations, Coach DeGugliemo! You officially fit the Jets culture! You invoked graphic violence for no good reason, undermined remarks made by your superiors, and have an insanely over-optimistic opinion of your players' talents!

General manager Mike Tannenbaum said earlier in the offseason that Hunter must compete for his starting job. That makes sense: The Jets may soon have a left-handed starting quarterback, making right tackle the most important position on the field, and Hunter is comically terrible. He had 10.5 blown blocks and 11 penalties last season, problems DeGugliemo laid at the feet of his predecessor. "You'd have to ask Bill Callahan. I think he's in the directory in Dallas."

While DeGugliemo gave his Lunatic with Megaphone at Bus Terminal appraisal of Hunter, center Nick Mangold got his chest hair waxed off on a May episode of *Late Night with Jimmy Fallon*. Jets unit comments aren't like other unit comments, folks. The Jets later added veteran tackle Stephon Heyer, a former starter for the Redskins. Hopefully, DeGugliemo installed metal detectors outside his office.

Mangold, left tackle D'Brickashaw Ferguson, and guards Brandon Moore and Matt Slauson return as starters on the Jets line. All are established and competent-to-great, and as the offensive line stats show, the linemen can't be blamed for the struggles of the running game. Depth is an issue. Sixth-round pick Robert T. Griffin's middle initial stands for "The Other." The Baylor product will back up Moore and Slauson. With Colin Baxter gone, there is no obvious backup center on the roster. Nor is there an obvious starting right tackle, but DeGugliemo will think of something.

Defensive Front Seven

Defensive Line	Age	Pos	Plays	TmPct	Rk	Stop	Dfts	BTkl	St%	Rk	AvYd	Rk	Sack	Hit	Hur	Runs	St%	Yds	Pass	St%	Yds
Sione Pouha	33	DT	61	8.0%	3	51	10	2	84%	19	1.4	19	1	1	4.5	57	82%	1.7	4	100%	-2.8
Muhammad Wilkerson	23	DE	49	6.4%	18	42	15	5	86%	16	0.9	23	3	4	9.5	43	86%	1.3	6	83%	-2.5
Mike DeVito	28	DE	34	6.0%	23	30	5	1	88%	8	2.0	56	1	0	0	32	91%	1.8	2	50%	5.0
Ropati Pitoitua	27	DE	19	2.9%	--	15	6	2	79%	--	1.6	--	1	0	4	18	78%	2.1	1	100%	-6.0
Marcus Dixon	28	DT	17	2.2%	--	13	5	2	76%	--	1.8	--	1.5	5	6	14	71%	2.7	3	100%	-2.7

Linebackers	Age	Pos	Plays	TmPct	Rk	Stop	Dfts	BTkl	AvYd	Sack	Hit	Hur	Runs	St%	Rk	Yds	Rk	Tgts	Suc%	Rk	AdjYd	Rk
David Harris	28	ILB	94	12.4%	37	51	22	4	4.6	5	7	7	59	53%	100	4.4	102	30	75%	1	4.0	2
Calvin Pace	32	OLB	74	9.7%	57	54	20	4	2.6	4.5	9	20	49	73%	19	2.3	14	12	64%	--	2.6	--
Bart Scott	32	ILB	66	8.7%	71	45	14	5	2.3	4.5	3	8	47	72%	25	2.4	17	13	46%	--	6.0	--
Jamaal Westerman*	27	OLB	23	3.0%	--	18	8	1	0.9	3.5	7	10	17	82%	--	1.0	--	0	0%	--	0.0	--
Josh Mauga	25	ILB	17	2.2%	--	10	3	2	3.8	0	0	1	11	73%	--	3.0	--	10	33%	--	5.8	--
Bryan Thomas	33	OLB	15	7.9%	--	9	5	1	5.4	0	1	3	11	55%	--	5.1	--	4	34%	--	14.7	--

Year	Yards	ALY	Rank	Power	Rank	Stuff	Rank	2nd Lev	Rank	Open Field	Rank
2009	3.77	3.55	2	58%	7	23%	5	1.04	4	0.62	10
2010	3.47	3.64	5	67%	25	19%	16	0.88	3	0.42	3
2011	3.86	3.65	2	45%	2	22%	6	1.04	6	0.72	13

Year	LE	Rank	LT	Rank	Mid	Rank	RT	Rank	RE	Rank	Sacks	ASR	Rank	Short	Long
2009	2.92	5	4.17	17	3.35	2	3.40	4	4.41	24	32	6.9%	14	7	18
2010	5.19	30	3.43	9	3.70	8	3.06	3	3.27	5	40	7.0%	10	18	16
2011	4.36	18	3.25	2	3.63	4	3.42	3	3.88	21	35	7.3%	12	6	23

At his first rookie camp, Quinton Coples recorded "about six" simulated sacks during shells practices, according to Rex Ryan's count. His quota of imaginary sacks in minimal-contact drills against practice squad fodder in early May satisfied, Coples was given the next day off by Ryan.

Pre-draft opinions were all over the board for Coples. Some saw a versatile, multi-dimensional pass rusher who could play anywhere from three-tech to outside linebacker. Others saw a rather ordinary block-eating left-end type. Ryan's Jets have whiffed badly on pass rushers in the draft before—imaginary sacks are the only ones Vernon Gholston ever registered—but Ryan has not completely lost his knack for wringing production out of vexing talents. Aaron Maybin was all but invisible in Buffalo. Ryan turned the former first-round pick back into a viable pass rusher last year, though Maybin was strictly a situational player.

Bryan Thomas was running at close to full speed in early spring and is expected to return to the lineup after an Achilles injury erased much of last season. Calvin Pace, who is fading but still effective, will be the other outside linebacker, with Maybin coming off the bench. Coples is in the mix with Mike DeVito, Muhammad Wilkerson, and Marcus Dixon at defensive end, where Ryan likes to mix and match personnel. The Jets plan to use more 46-defense style fronts, so expect to see lots of bodies crowding the line of scrimmage.

Sione Pouha, David Harris, and Bart Scott keep the Jets defense very strong up the middle. Pouha finished third among defensive linemen in Stops on running plays. Harris remains one of the league's best all-around inside linebackers. Scott asked Tim Tebow to baptize him in the cold tub after a minicamp workout in May. Jets unit comments aren't like other unit comments, folks.

Defensive Secondary

Secondary	Age	Pos	Plays	TmPct	Rk	Stop	Dfts	BTkl	Runs	St%	Rk	Yds	Rk	Tgts	Tgt%	Rk	Dist	Suc%	Rk	APaYd	Rk	PD	Int
Eric Smith	29	FS	87	11.4%	25	29	12	5	39	28%	61	6.9	42	44	10.5%	10	12.9	52%	50	11.3	70	4	1
Darrelle Revis	27	CB	73	9.6%	20	32	13	2	18	44%	37	7.2	45	79	19.1%	30	12.6	62%	11	5.5	8	21	4
Antonio Cromartie	28	CB	55	7.2%	58	26	15	5	15	40%	44	8.5	58	78	18.7%	32	16.2	60%	17	6.7	23	14	4
Jim Leonhard*	30	SS	53	8.6%	54	17	8	5	20	30%	58	9.4	68	22	6.5%	46	14.0	62%	17	6.8	23	6	1
Kyle Wilson	25	CB	45	5.9%	72	23	14	3	6	33%	53	6.2	28	56	13.4%	67	10.4	54%	35	8.9	66	8	2
Brodney Pool*	28	FS	36	5.4%	73	13	3	2	16	44%	28	6.9	40	19	5.2%	65	13.3	69%	7	3.9	2	3	1
Donald Strickland*	32	CB	34	4.8%	82	10	3	3	8	25%	70	5.8	21	42	10.7%	79	12.0	56%	22	7.1	32	4	0
Yeremiah Bell	34	SS	111	13.9%	6	29	14	5	57	26%	66	6.7	35	38	8.3%	22	12.2	52%	48	8.6	48	4	1
LaRon Landry	28	SS	49	12.2%	15	26	7	7	33	55%	9	6.0	20	13	6.2%	53	13.2	41%	71	6.7	21	0	0

Year	Pass D Rank	vs. #1 WR	Rk	vs. #2 WR	Rk	vs. Other WR	Rk	vs. TE	Rk	vs. RB	Rk
2009	1	-39.6%	1	-20.4%	6	-29.9%	3	-21.3%	4	-20.9%	2
2010	7	-7.5%	12	12.2%	23	-9.6%	11	-3.4%	9	-6.0%	9
2011	2	-32.5%	1	-25.1%	2	-3.1%	18	23.3%	27	-14.7%	4

Darrelle Revis was his usual self during the first half of the season, leading all cornerbacks in yards allowed per pass (3.9), Success Rate (68 percent), and other indicators of island-ness. But his numbers tailed off in the second half of the season: after Week 9, he averaged 7.8 yards allowed per pass and a 56 percent Success Rate. A nagging knee injury was part of the problem. The Bills also appear to possess some kind of kryptonite, as Revis had a hard time stopping Stevie Johnson. You can picture Chan Gailey cackling as he devised special anti-Revis pass patterns, then forgetting to install the rest of the offense. Rex Ryan referred to Revis as "the best cornerback on the planet" during the Combine, and everyone expects a rebound in 2012. Antonio Cromartie was much more reliable last year than in years past, while Kyle Wilson could start for most teams and is an invaluable nickel defender for a team that faces the Patriots and Revis-killing Bills twice per year.

Free-agent signing LaRon Landry battled groin and hamstring injuries in Washington before finally reinjuring his troublesome left Achilles tendon at the end of last season. Landry opted for an alternative stem-cell related treatment instead of surgery on the chronic ailment in the offseason. (To clarify: "alternative" does not mean "Tim Tebow" and "stem-cell" does not mean "baptize in the ice tub.") When healthy, Landry is an ideal Rex Ryan safety, a defender who can play in the box but who also has range in deep coverage. When lying with incense sticks between his toes and listening to Windham Hill music while some New Age healer massages his ankle's aura, he is of little help to an NFL team. (In fairness, the treatment he opted for sounds slightly more scientific than that.)

Yeremiah Bell led the Dolphins in total plays last year, producing the kind of numbers veteran safeties usually produce for bad teams (lots of clean-up tackles). Bell is almost certain to start ahead of Eric Smith, who was still trying to catch Tim Tebow when we last saw him but will probably get a hand on him during training camp.

Special Teams

Year	DVOA	Rank	FG/XP	Rank	Net Kick	Rank	Kick Ret	Rank	Net Punt	Rank	Punt Ret	Rank	Hidden	Rank
2009	2.4%	6	2.8	12	-2.3	20	7.6	6	0.9	14	5.0	9	1.1	14
2010	4.9%	5	-2.2	25	-0.1	17	19.4	1	14.8	2	-3.2	21	5.9	5
2011	4.8%	4	-0.1	15	11.2	1	10.8	2	13.2	3	-7.0	25	-8.3	26

As if the Jets did not have enough intrigue entering camp: Get ready for a kicker controversy! Josh Brown signed with the Jets after four years in exile with the Rams. Brown subsisted on 16 to 19 extra points per season for most of his Rams tenure, mixing in a disproportionate amount of desperate 50-yard field goals. Brown nailed fifteen 50-plus-yarders in three years before going 0-for-2 last year, as the Rams offense finally sunk to the point where they could not consistently reach the 33.

Incumbent Nick Folk fought off a challenge from Nick Novak after a poor 2010 season (three misses inside 40 yards), and while Folk was better in 2011, Brown is a more serious challenger than Novak. Don't be fooled by the net kickoff value listed above; Folk was below-average on gross kickoffs, but the Jets kick coverage held opponents to -10.7 estimated points worth of field position on returns, the best figure in the league. Coaches are calling the kicker battle an open competition, which is a nice way of saying that they really want Brown to win the job. Actually, a bigger worry for the Jets last year was not their own kicker but the other kickers. Opposing kickers were an absurd 29-for-30 on field-goal attempts against the Jets, with the only miss being by Sebastian Janikowski from 56 yards. That's one bit of bad luck that is almost guaranteed to regress towards the mean in 2012.

Kickoff returner Joe McKnight arrived at minicamp 15 pounds heavier than last season, then explained that he ate lots of unhealthy food at McDonald's in the hope of becoming more durable. If you cover the Jets for a while, statements like that actually make sense. McKnight did lift weights to convert those Big Macs into muscle, so now we can all bask in the brilliance of attempting to avoid injuries by growing heavier, increasing the stress on the knees and ankles (and the heart, fry guy), and making yourself easier to hit squarely.

And of course, Tim Tebow took reps as the Jets' personal protector. Jets unit comments aren't ... you get the idea.

Coaching Staff

New defensive line coach Karl Dunbar has acquired the "guru" label after six years working with Jared Allen and the Williams Wall in Minnesota. The Vikings did not have to blitz much with that personnel, which may be why Dunbar sounded excited to install 46-defense principles in Jets minicamp. "It's attack, it's getting up the field, we're not holding blocks," Dunbar explained in May. "Every man for himself, we're going to get to the quarterback." Sounds like the Jets we know and love.

We heard from offensive line coach Dave DeGugliemo earlier. Oh heck, let's hear from him again, on the difference between him and predecessor/archnemesis Bill Callahan: "The difference between me and Bill: I have a Super Bowl ring, and he doesn't." DeGugliemo earned a ring as an assistant offensive line coach for the Giants. Exactly how meager can a contribution for a coach/player/towel boy be to invoke the "I'm a winner" trump card?

Despite DeGugliemo's arrival, special teams coach Mike Westhoff remains the most lovable, quotable Jets assistant. Few coaches in the league are worse at hiding their feelings than Westhoff. Follow this series of quotes, all from one press conference about the kicking competition, and see how easy it is to read between the lines: "I want to create the most competitive atmosphere that I possibly can"; "We want to have a viable battle here to see who's going to win our job and to get the best possible guy that we can put on the field"; "There were a couple of guys I liked (in the draft), one in particular. We just weren't able to do it. It didn't happen ... (much to) my consternation"; "Actually at this point in time, I believe (Brown's) the most viable candidate."

So, in the spirit of a viable battle, Brown is the most viable candidate, except for the mystery kicker I really wanted (probably Blair Walsh), and if Nick Folk is listening, he should probably start packing his DVD collection into cardboard boxes and calling realtors.

Oakland Raiders

2011 Record: 8-8

Pythagorean Wins: 6.1 (23rd)

DVOA: -8.0% (22nd)

Offense: 2.6% (14th)

Defense: 9.6% (27th)

Special Teams: -1.0% (20th)

Variance: 19.9% (27th)

2012 Mean Projection: 6.9 wins

On the Clock (0-4): 145

Mediocrity (5-7): 47%

Playoff Contender (8-10): 33%

Super Bowl Contender (11+): 5%

Postseason Odds: 17.6%

Projected Average Opponent: 2.2% (11th)

2011: Requiem for Al Davis.

2012: It's a division anyone can win, but they start at the bottom of the pile.

The Oakland Raiders have been involved in a lot of the more interesting events in NFL history. They were witnesses to the Immaculate Reception, the Sea of Hands, and the Tuck Rule. They were the first wild card team to win a Super Bowl. And of course, there was the year Pete Rozelle had to hand the Vince Lombardi Trophy to Al Davis at the same time Davis and the Raiders were suing the NFL.

But 2011 may have been the franchise's most complicated season yet.

It started benignly enough, with a couple vintage Craters moves. The Raiders handed out lavish contracts to very good put perhaps not great players, such as Richard Seymour, Kamerion Wimbley, Michael Huff, and Stanford Routt. They drafted players who run very quickly, such as cornerbacks DeMarcus Van Dyke and Chimdi Chekwa and running back Taiwan Jones. They picked up a legacy Raider, Stefen Wisniewski. There was the typical mortgaging of the future, trading a future second-round pick for the pick to draft Van Dyke and spending a third-round pick in the supplemental draft on raw quarterback Terrelle Pryor. Oh, and Davis also fired head coach Tom Cable, who had led the Raiders to their best season since they made the Super Bowl following the 2002 season, and replaced him with first-time head coach Hue Jackson.

The season started quietly, and the Raiders were 2-2 when Al Davis passed away on October 8.

The Raiders won their next game, beating the eventual AFC South champion Texans despite having only 10 men on the field for the big defensive stop on the final play. There was talk of Davis' death emotionally propelling the Raiders into the playoffs—until quarterback Jason Campbell and running back Darren McFadden, both enjoying the best seasons of their careers, were lost for the year in Oakland's next two games.

When Campbell went down, the Raiders were stuck with Pryor and Kyle Boller at quarterback. With no general manager after Davis' passing, there was some question about who was really in charge of the franchise. Jackson grabbed the reins, went back to his Cincinnati roots, and traded for Carson Palmer. The Raiders gave up a 2012 first-round pick and a 2013 first- or second-round pick for a player who seemed resigned to retiring and who hadn't been the same since a 2008 arm injury. Palmer was forced into the next game with virtually no practice and threw three picks in less than a half.

A series of close wins put the Raiders at 7-4, but they nearly squandered their shot at a playoff berth with a three-game losing streak. In the loss that dropped them to 7-7, Jackson oddly eschewed a two-point conversion up 12 with less than ten minutes to play, and the Raiders then blew their 13-point lead to lose by one.

2012 Raiders Schedule

Week	Opp.	Week	Opp.	Week	Opp.
1	SD (Mon.)	7	JAC	13	CLE
2	at MIA	8	at KC	14	DEN (Thu.)
3	PIT	9	TB	15	KC
4	at DEN	10	at BAL	16	at CAR
5	BYE	11	NO	17	at SD
6	at ATL	12	at CIN		

Figure 1. 2011 Oakland DVOA by Week

That extra-point decision was part of Jackson's seemingly random mix of assertiveness and conservatism. Sometimes he was aggressive on fourth downs, while other times he called 'fraidy-cat punts that would make Jim Caldwell proud. This volatility was matched by Jackson's personality in press conferences. Jackson visibly channeled Davis' spirit in press conferences after his death, claiming Al's legacy as a talisman and his special ability to see like Al did as a symbol of his authority and his right to win the internal power struggle for who would truly inherit Al's role as the man who defined what the Raiders meant.

When the Raiders blew a Week 17 "win and you're in" game against San Diego, Jackson had a tirade in the post-game press conference, describing himself as "pissed off" and claiming the team "needs an attitude adjustment." Perhaps the kind of attitude you might expect to be instilled by, say, a head coach with a stable personality.

It was unclear if Jackson's final post-game press conference was one of the more unusual public claims to a job ever or a snit fit by a coach who knew he was likely to soon be on his way out the door. Mark Davis, Al's son and unfortunately a bit of a ringer for Lloyd Christmas in *Dumb and Dumber*, did indeed hire a new general manager, Packers assistant GM Reggie McKenzie, without consulting Hue, and McKenzie did then send Jackson packing out the door. Jackson of course did not go gracefully, publicly blaming his firing not on his friend McKenzie, but on Davis, specifically because Jackson knew of the low esteem in which Al held Mark's football acumen.

Whatever the true motives for Jackson's firing, the Raiders were in the market for a new head coach. It was clear a new day had dawned when McKenzie selected Broncos defensive coordinator Dennis Allen. Allen was the first head coach with a defensive background hired by the Raiders since Al Davis promoted linebackers coach John Madden to the head job in 1969. He had only one year of experience as a coordinator, but in that year he helped improve Denver's defense from 30th to 18th in DVOA.

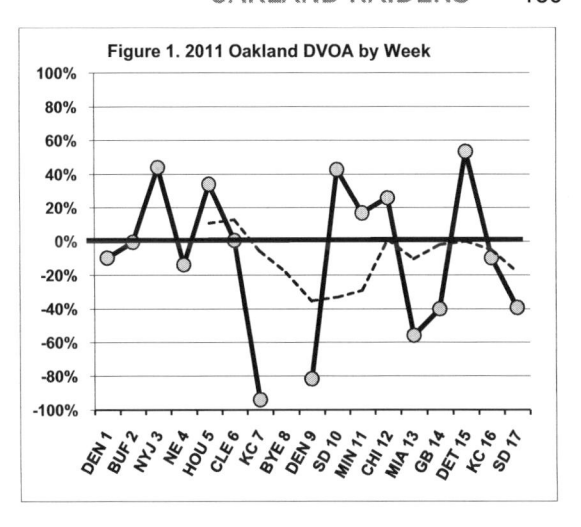

It was clear the Raiders were in serious need of a defensive makeover. Davis' death freed the Raiders from the need to run their traditional aggressive press-man scheme, and defensive coordinator Chuck Bresnahan took full advantage. Unfortunately, Bresnahan's reconceived defensive schemes seemed to be more about doing something new than putting players in the best position to succeed.

Allen and new defensive coordinator Jason Tarver have been deliberately coy about what kind of defense they're going to run. Any attempt to rebuild the defense, like the rest of McKenzie's efforts to reshape the Raiders, was hamstrung by the Raiders' lack of draft picks. When the season ended, the Raiders were missing five draft picks, including their first- (Palmer), second- (Van Dyke), third- (Pryor), fourth- (Campbell), and seventh- (mid-season trade for linebacker Aaron Curry) round selections. They would eventually be awarded three compensatory picks, in the third, fourth, and fifth rounds, prompting McKenzie to exclaim, "Whatever the [compensatory picks] formula is, I love this formula." McKenzie also made it clear that you shouldn't also expect the Raiders to go into future drafts without their first three picks, stating in his pre-draft press conference "I do not want to trade future picks—especially high ones."

It wasn't just the lack of draft picks that hurt McKenzie's attempt at a makeover, though. There also was a lack of cap space. Those big contracts to Seymour, Wimbley, Routt, and Huff all proved to be short-lived. Seymour and Huff restructured their contracts and return to the Raiders for 2012. Wimbley and Routt were cut and departed for greener pastures. Also given their walking papers were tight end Kevin Boss, defensive tackle John Henderson, cornerback Chris "CJ-zero-K" Johnson, and safety Hiram Eugene, while Curry avoided the same fate by restructuring his deal.

Even with all those departures, the Raiders were only able to add two players who were starters in 2011: Philip Wheeler from the Colts, who adds speed and coverage skills to a linebacking unit that was often badly exposed this past season, and offensive guard Mike Brisiel.

Brisiel followed the Raiders' new offensive coordinator Greg Knapp from Houston, where he was a valuable part of the Texans' outstanding running attack. Knapp is a familiar face in Oakland, as he was previously offensive coordinator of the Raiders in 2007-08. The Raiders moved away from the zone-blocking scheme Knapp implemented in his prior stint in Oakland the last couple seasons, but Brisiel will likely help them make the transition back.

Knapp's job will be to meld a crew of receivers mostly assembled for a vertical passing attack into his version of the West Coast offense. In his first go-round, this didn't work out very well, as the Raiders finished 28th and 31st in offensive DVOA. On the other hand, Knapp starts with the 14th-ranked offense instead of the league's worst and Carson Palmer rather than JaMarcus Russell.

Despite his early struggles, Palmer was at times last year a very effective quarterback. Fourth-round rookie Denarius Moore was a sensation and a dynamic vertical threat. Darrius Heyward-Bey, consigned to bust status after an atrocious rookie season, has developed into a reasonable starting receiver and had nearly 1,000 yards last year.

While the Raiders have good depth at receiver, the same is not true at running back, where it's Darren McFadden and a lot of question marks. McFadden is a dynamic player when healthy, but has never remained healthy in the NFL. In four years, he has missed 19 games. Backup Michael Bush is gone as a free agent, and the Raiders replaced him by trading for Mike Goodson. Goodson was the forgotten man in the Panthers' crowded backfield and didn't have a single rushing attempt in 2011 before a hamstring injury sent him to injured reserve. The third-string back is Taiwan Jones, who had 16 carries and missed six games as a rookie.

If all the pieces shake out right, including the line continuing to be effective during the scheme change, the Raiders could be relatively proficient offensively. That means they could be competitive in a potentially complicated AFC West if the defense improves.

That the defense improves at least somewhat is likely. Few defenses are consistently bad unless their personnel is truly awful, and even with the departures, the Raiders have some talented players. The question then becomes how Allen and Tarver will use them.

Before joining the Broncos, Allen worked under Gregg Williams in New Orleans. Tarver comes directly from Stanford, where he led one of the relatively few 3-4 defenses in college football. Will the Raiders make that transition? Given the lack of depth at linebacker, it seems unlikely. It does, however, seem fair to assume the Raiders will show various fronts and formations, especially given that Tarver's early discussions of the defense have indicated a desire to be multiple. What exactly that means is not clear, and may not be clear until the regular season begins.

Also unclear is where exactly the Raiders stand as a franchise. They're coming off their two best seasons in the past nine years. Granted, those seasons were both only 8-8, but after years of four to six wins, that in itself is a great improvement. Those eight wins represented a bit of an overachievement, as the Raiders had 7.5 Estimated Wins and 6.1 Pythagorean Wins. Given the limitations in what they could to this offseason, they're unlikely to be much improved from that, meaning they're a fringe playoff team at best. Both McKenzie's background working for Ted Thompson in Green Bay and his public comments indicate he prefers to build through the draft, probably with the occasional judicious free-agent signing. That's generally the right way to build a consistent winner, but it is also a multi-year process. How that squares with the long-term fate of Palmer, who turns 33 by season's end, is as yet an unanswered question. For now, the Raiders are probably just hoping for a much less dramatic season in 2012 than the one they went through in 2011.

Tom Gower

OAKLAND RAIDERS

2011 Raiders Stats by Week

Wk	vs.	W-L	PF	PA	YDF	YDA	TO	Total	Off	Def	ST
1	@DEN	W	23	20	289	310	2	-10%	-14%	-20%	-16%
2	@BUF	L	35	38	454	481	-1	0%	51%	48%	-4%
3	NYJ	W	34	24	383	439	2	44%	60%	12%	-4%
4	NE	L	19	31	504	409	-2	-14%	4%	19%	1%
5	@HOU	W	25	20	278	473	1	34%	-1%	-21%	14%
6	CLE	W	24	17	329	268	0	1%	-7%	10%	18%
7	KC	L	0	28	322	300	-4	-94%	-80%	11%	-2%
8	BYE										
9	DEN	L	24	38	416	412	-3	-82%	-13%	42%	-26%
10	@SD	W	24	17	489	314	0	43%	21%	-19%	3%
11	@MIN	W	27	21	301	311	4	17%	-8%	-27%	-3%
12	CHI	W	25	20	341	401	2	26%	15%	0%	11%
13	@MIA	L	14	34	304	362	-1	-56%	-19%	27%	-10%
14	@GB	L	16	46	357	391	-4	-40%	-42%	-11%	-9%
15	DET	L	27	28	477	432	0	54%	61%	10%	2%
16	@KC	W	16	13	308	435	0	-10%	-18%	15%	23%
17	SD	L	26	38	520	463	0	-39%	31%	56%	-15%

Trends and Splits

	Offense	Rank	Defense	Rank
Total DVOA	2.6%	14	9.6%	27
Unadjusted VOA	2.9%	13	7.1%	22
Weighted Trend	-2.7%	15	8.9%	24
Variance	10.5%	26	8.5%	27
Average Opponent	0.6%	20	-0.6%	17
Passing	11.1%	17	10.4%	23
Rushing	3.3%	11	8.4%	31
First Down	10.0%	7	6.7%	22
Second Down	-4.7%	18	8.0%	26
Third Down	-1.5%	15	18.3%	28
First Half	4.7%	13	-0.3%	15
Second Half	0.2%	15	18.5%	31
Red Zone	-10.4%	19	-13.1%	10
Late and Close	25.8%	5	13.6%	27

Five-Year Performance

Year	W-L	Pyth	Est W	PF	PA	TO	Total	Rk	Off	Rk	Def	Rk	ST	Rk	Off AGL	Rk	Def AGL	Rk
2007	4-12	4.8	3.3	283	398	-11	-29.2%	30	-18.0%	28	5.7%	22	-5.5%	29	25.1	24	18.2	13
2008	5-11	4.5	5.7	263	388	+1	-23.2%	29	-16.1%	31	3.7%	19	6.5%	2	35.8	23	18.4	14
2009	5-11	2.9	3.9	197	379	-13	-34.0%	30	-25.8%	30	7.9%	24	-0.3%	17	32.4	23	18.9	8
2010	8-8	9.0	7.1	410	371	-2	-4.1%	21	-8.3%	23	-2.3%	13	1.8%	13	15.1	8	15.4	10
2011	8-8	6.1	7.3	359	433	-4	-8.0%	22	2.6%	14	9.6%	27	-1.0%	20	36.7	21	41.4	26

2011 Performance Based on Most Common Personnel Groups

Oakland Offense					Oakland Offense vs. Opp.				Oakland Defense				Oakland Defense vs. Opp.			
Pers	Freq	Yds	DVOA	Run%	Pers	Freq	Yds	DVOA	Pers	Freq	Yds	DVOA	Pers	Freq	Yds	DVOA
21	32%	6.1	14.4%	53%	4-3-4	30%	5.4	12.8%	4-3-4	36%	5.5	2.1%	11	44%	6.6	23.2%
11	31%	6.6	19.1%	33%	3-4-4	27%	6.2	-0.7%	Dime+	32%	7.2	33.2%	12	19%	5.1	-16.7%
20	8%	6.3	-28.5%	23%	4-2-5	15%	6.5	8.9%	4-2-5	26%	5.7	-1.4%	21	12%	5.2	2.2%
12	6%	5.8	3.3%	38%	3-3-5	13%	7.8	34.3%	5-2-4	2%	3.2	-27.0%	22	7%	4.8	-15.5%
10	5%	7.4	12.0%	25%	Dime+	9%	6.6	2.5%	G-line	1%	0.6	21.0%	10	4%	6.2	-4.4%

Strategic Tendencies

Run/Pass		Rank	Offense		Rank	Pass Rush		Rank	Defense/Other		Rank
Runs, all plays	45%	8	Form: Single Back	50%	30	Rush 3	2.6%	28	4 DB	40%	27
Runs, first half	48%	6	Form: Empty Back	1%	30	Rush 4	64.1%	17	5 DB	27%	27
Runs, first down	55%	10	Pers: 3+ WR	46%	23	Rush 5	20.5%	19	6+ DB	32%	1
Runs, second-long	35%	15	Pers: 4+ WR	5%	9	Rush 6+	12.8%	4	CB by Sides	85%	10
Runs, power sit.	79%	1	Pers: 2+ TE/6+ OL	22%	30	Zone Blitz	7.7%	9	Go for it on 4th	0.87	20
Runs, behind 2H	28%	23	Play action	20%	12	Sacks by LB	30.3%	15	Offensive Pace	31.0	23
Pass, ahead 2H	45%	12	Max protect	20%	2	Sacks by DB	10.5%	11	Defensive Pace	29.7	4

Department of What Else is New: The Raiders led the NFL with 181 penalties, including declined and offsetting, exactly one more per game than any other team. In fact, they set NFL records for both penalties and penalty yards. However, as in 2010, part of the issue was the officials who worked their games, as the Raiders also ranked sixth in opponent penalties. Although no six-lineman formation made their top five personnel groups, the Raiders used six or more offensive linemen on 12.6 percent of plays, the only team other than New England to be above 8.0 percent. They had -3.1% DVOA from these sets, slightly below their overall offensive rating. Oakland was fifth in frequency of running back screens, third in DVOA on those plays (85.9%), and second in average yards (10.2). This may not matter under the new regime, but the Raiders zone-blitzed in 2011 much more than they had the year before. Desmond Bryant was the player most likely to drop into coverage, but Kamerion Wimbley also dropped roughly once per game.

Passing

Player	DYAR	DVOA	Plays	NtYds	Avg	YAC	C%	TD	Int
C.Palmer	296	2.5%	344	2627	7.7	5.3	61.2%	13	16
J.Campbell*	340	19.8%	169	1151	6.9	4.5	61.0%	6	3
K.Boller*	-158	-95.4%	32	142	4.4	5.6	53.6%	0	3
M.Leinart	14	4.8%	13	57	4.4	3.9	76.9%	1	0

Rushing

Player	DYAR	DVOA	Plays	Yds	Avg	TD	Fum	Suc
M.Bush*	65	-2.7%	256	980	3.8	7	1	45%
D.McFadden	87	11.6%	113	616	5.5	4	1	44%
M.Reece	38	45.2%	17	112	6.6	0	0	59%
T.Jones	3	-1.6%	16	73	4.6	0	0	38%
J.Campbell*	-6	-19.1%	13	67	5.2	2	2	--
C.Palmer	-16	-32.1%	12	22	1.8	1	0	--
K.Boller	-14	-45.7%	7	34	4.9	0	1	--
L.Murphy	52	133.6%	6	69	11.5	1	0	--
D.Moore	43	164.7%	5	61	12.2	1	0	--

Receiving

Player	DYAR	DVOA	Plays	Ctch	Yds	Y/C	YAC	TD	C%
D.Heyward-Bey	129	1.7%	115	64	975	15.2	3.9	4	56%
D.Moore	74	-0.7%	76	33	618	18.7	3.8	5	43%
C.Schilens*	72	14.5%	34	23	271	11.8	1.6	2	68%
J.Ford	27	-2.3%	33	19	279	14.7	6.6	1	58%
L.Murphy	2	-11.8%	33	15	241	16.1	5.4	0	45%
T.Houshmandzadeh*	14	-2.0%	19	11	146	13.3	2.8	1	58%
D.Hagan*	-1	-13.3%	20	11	114	10.4	1.5	0	55%
K.Boss*	72	22.3%	39	28	368	13.1	4.7	3	72%
B.Myers	-52	-35.0%	27	16	151	9.4	3.4	0	59%
M.Bush*	140	44.0%	47	37	418	11.3	8.6	1	79%
M.Reece	71	20.4%	36	27	313	11.6	8.1	2	75%
D.McFadden	33	12.2%	23	19	154	8.1	8.2	1	83%
R.Cartwright*	-6	-29.2%	6	4	24	6.0	6.5	0	67%
O.Schmitt	5	-0.9%	7	3	32	10.7	9.0	0	43%

Offensive Line

Year	Yards	ALY	Rank	Power	Rank	Stuff	Rank	2nd Lev	Rank	Open Field	Rank	F-Start	Cont.
2009	4.02	3.97	23	72%	4	16%	6	1.03	27	0.63	20	21	25
2010	4.60	4.11	15	61%	15	16%	8	1.10	18	1.15	6	29	33
2011	4.52	4.13	14	67%	8	16%	3	1.12	24	1.05	7	18	37

Year	LE	Rank	LT	Rank	Mid	Rank	RT	Rank	RE	Rank	Sacks	ASR	Rank	Short	Long
2009	4.81	11	3.74	25	3.72	26	4.12	16	4.27	14	49	9.5%	31	15	25
2010	4.41	14	4.92	4	3.98	16	4.03	19	3.71	22	44	8.3%	26	14	21
2011	4.21	15	4.48	11	3.78	25	4.90	4	4.13	10	25	5.0%	5	10	8

In 2011, the Raiders learned the value of continuity in the offensive line. After a year of turmoil, Jared Veldheer, Stefen Wisniewski, Khalif Barnes, and Cooper Carlisle each started 16 games and Samson Satele only missed one game. The biggest key to the improvement in Adjusted Sack Rate was Jason Campbell finally breaking his life-long habit of holding the ball forever and ever until a defender finally brought him down, but over the past three seasons the Raiders have gone from having the second-highest percentage of blown blocks on pass plays to the sixth-fewest. Veldheer is one of the big reasons for that change. 2011 was his first year as a full-time starter, and he reduced his blown block total from six as a rookie to only two. He had a better first half of the season than second, in particular struggling against Tamba Hali in both Chiefs games, but is only 25 and should be a mainstay of the Raiders' offensive line for years to come. Right tackle Khalif Barnes had a surprisingly good season for a player who barely contributed in 2010, but he'll have to battle 2011 third-round pick Joseph Barksdale for the starting job in camp.

The difficulty running up the middle, including fairly underwhelming success rates for both Darren McFadden and Michael Bush, is one reason for a revamp of the interior line. Satele was allowed to walk as a free agent, as he was more active than productive. Stefen Wisniewski, nephew of Raiders great and current assistant offensive line coach Steve, moves to center, and right guard Cooper Carlisle will replace him at left guard. The new right guard should be Mike Brisiel, who was a very good zone-blocking guard for the Texans when he was in the lineup, but was responsible for 19 Adjusted Games Lost over the last three seasons. That means third-round pick Tony Bergstrom (Utah) will see playing time.

Unfortunately, like so many other units on the Raiders, the offensive line was plagued by penalties. Veldheer seemed to mostly solve the false start problem that plagued him as a rookie, but was flagged for holding eight times, second-most in the league. Barnes matched him with 11 total penalties, Wisniewski had five of his own, and while Satele's eight flags are gone, Brisiel was flagged nine times in the 13 games he played for Houston.

Defensive Front Seven

Defensive Line	Age	Pos	Plays	TmPct	Rk	Stop	Dfts	BTkl	St%	Rk	AvYd	Rk	Sack	Hit	Hur	Runs	St%	Yds	Pass	St%	Yds
Lamarr Houston	25	DE	54	6.8%	13	45	12	2	83%	25	1.9	53	1.5	6	21	46	83%	1.9	8	88%	2.0
Tommy Kelly	32	DT	46	5.8%	14	34	13	0	74%	48	1.6	28	7.5	6	11	31	68%	3.2	15	87%	-1.6
John Henderson*	33	DT	40	6.2%	9	30	4	0	75%	45	2.2	46	0	1	2	34	76%	2.0	6	67%	3.2
Desmond Bryant	27	DE	36	4.5%	52	30	10	0	83%	25	1.1	35	5	5	14	29	83%	2.2	7	86%	-3.4
Richard Seymour	33	DT	32	4.0%	36	26	10	2	81%	26	1.2	11	6	9	20.5	21	81%	1.8	11	82%	-0.1
Jarvis Moss*	28	DE	17	2.4%	--	13	4	0	76%	--	1.2	--	1.5	5	10.5	12	83%	1.8	5	60%	-0.4
Dave Tollefson	31	DE	20	2.4%	--	14	8	1	70%	--	1.3	--	5	3	4.5	12	50%	4.1	8	100%	-2.9

Linebackers	Age	Pos	Plays	TmPct	Rk	Stop	Dfts	BTkl	AvYd	Sack	Hit	Hur	Runs	St%	Rk	Yds	Rk	Tgts	Suc%	Rk	AdjYd	Rk
Rolando McClain	23	MLB	113	15.1%	19	68	21	9	4.8	5	3	8.5	54	67%	48	3.8	84	59	52%	32	6.5	35
Aaron Curry	26	OLB	72	9.0%	65	40	13	7	5.1	0	3	6	42	64%	59	3.1	40	27	37%	70	10.4	77
Kamerion Wimbley*	29	OLB	65	8.1%	79	42	19	5	3.7	6.5	15	29	43	72%	26	3.1	42	12	47%	--	11.4	--
Quentin Groves*	28	OLB	21	2.6%	--	13	5	1	5.8	0	1	0	13	77%	--	3.3	--	9	65%	--	6.5	--
Philip Wheeler	28	OLB	80	11.1%	46	45	8	1	4.3	1	0	0	57	63%	63	3.4	58	17	58%	13	5.4	15

Year	Yards	ALY	Rank	Power	Rank	Stuff	Rank	2nd Lev	Rank	Open Field	Rank
2009	4.79	4.07	16	68%	22	19%	15	1.31	30	1.27	30
2010	4.38	3.63	4	62%	13	24%	2	1.09	13	1.17	31
2011	4.87	4.04	18	72%	28	19%	18	1.33	28	1.28	30

Year	LE	Rank	LT	Rank	Mid	Rank	RT	Rank	RE	Rank	Sacks	ASR	Rank	Short	Long
2009	4.25	16	3.44	5	4.18	20	4.39	23	3.56	8	37	7.5%	6	14	15
2010	3.13	4	3.27	4	3.80	10	3.41	8	4.05	18	47	9.5%	1	15	18
2011	3.78	9	4.53	24	4.29	24	3.73	6	3.23	11	39	6.4%	20	12	18

As the defensive tackles went, so went the rest of the Oakland Raiders defense in 2011. The combination of Richard Seymour, John Henderson, and Tommy Kelly could be downright dominant at times, holding the Broncos to only 38 yards rushing and the Chargers to 75 in their first matchups. At other times, though, Henderson, Seymour, and Kelly all looked more like 30-somethings, as the Broncos (now with Tebow) ran for 299 yards and the Chargers for 153 in their respective rematches. Kelly and Seymour will return for 2012, and new defensive line coach Terrell Williams will be looking for more consistency in their play. Desmond Bryant, who spent much of 2011 pressed into duty at defensive end, will be the primary interior backup.

The defensive tackles would benefit most from a return to health by defensive end Matt Shaughnessy, an emerging player who suffered a shoulder injury that ended his season after only three games. Regular left defensive end Lamarr Houston played well, but failed to get to the passer with regularity. Rotational ends Trevor Scott and Jarvis Moss will not return, replaced by free agent acquisition Dave Tollefson and fifth-round pick Jack Crawford (Penn State).

At linebacker, the focus was on Rolando McClain even before his May conviction on assault charges. The eighth overall selection in the 2010 draft may be at a career crossroads. Our game charting project shows he was one of the most-targeted and least-effective cover linebackers in the league. He would probably be at his best in a 3-4 scheme that allowed him to attack downhill and blitz, but be protected in coverage. If McClain is unavailable, either because he's in jail or suspended by the NFL, his backup is 2010 sixth-round pick Travis Goethel, who missed half his rookie season with a back injury and all of 2011 with a knee injury. The rest of the picture at linebacker is not much brighter. Mid-season acquisition Aaron Curry quickly became a starter at weakside linebacker and looked good at times, but sometimes displayed the amazing lack of instincts that made him expendable in Seattle. He restructured his contract and will return. Kamerion Wimbley, who played strongside linebacker and defensive end in sub packages, was poor in coverage and got cut. Philip Wheeler is Wimbley's replacement; while he's not the pass rushing threat Wimbley is and won't play defensive end, he's also not a liability in coverage.

Defensive Secondary

Secondary	Age	Pos	Plays	TmPct	Rk	Stop	Dfts	BTkl	Runs	St%	Rk	Yds	Rk	Tgts	Tgt%	Rk	Dist	Suc%	Rk	APaYd	Rk	PD	Int
Tyvon Branch	26	SS	108	13.5%	9	40	10	4	57	47%	17	6.9	38	53	11.3%	3	9.8	50%	52	7.1	31	6	1
Matt Giordano	30	FS	70	9.4%	46	15	10	9	31	19%	74	12.1	76	20	4.5%	72	22.9	74%	5	9.2	54	5	5
Stanford Routt*	29	CB	64	8.0%	49	25	9	6	10	0%	81	10.8	71	94	20.2%	22	12.7	58%	20	6.1	14	17	4
Lito Sheppard	31	CB	47	10.5%	15	14	6	6	8	25%	70	10.1	67	47	17.9%	36	11.9	50%	49	7.9	51	5	0
Michael Huff	29	FS	42	7.0%	66	19	7	4	16	56%	7	9.2	66	29	8.2%	23	9.7	56%	41	7.7	39	4	2
Mike Mitchell	25	SS	31	4.8%	75	15	7	9	13	54%	10	4.9	7	20	5.3%	63	12.3	57%	36	8.2	42	4	1
Jerome Boyd	26	SS	21	3.0%	--	11	5	2	8	50%	--	5.5	--	11	2.7%	--	14.0	59%	--	7.7	--	3	0
Chris Johnson	33	CB	18	9.0%	--	6	1	1	1	100%	--	2.0	--	20	16.8%	--	12.8	25%	--	11.4	--	5	0
DeMarcus Van Dyke	23	CB	15	2.1%	--	6	2	4	1	0%	--	13.0	--	28	6.9%	--	13.5	68%	--	4.7	--	4	1

Year	Pass D Rank	vs. #1 WR	Rk	vs. #2 WR	Rk	vs. Other WR	Rk	vs. TE	Rk	vs. RB	Rk
2009	26	28.3%	32	22.3%	28	4.5%	19	1.6%	16	-4.6%	13
2010	17	5.0%	20	-3.6%	13	-4.9%	15	14.4%	25	1.0%	13
2011	21	-1.1%	11	20.8%	25	-1.7%	19	-2.3%	5	-2.9%	16

The first year of the post-Nnamdi Asomugha era in Oakland went about how you probably thought it would go. Stanford Routt remained in the starting lineup, and was still targeted a lot. He was still targeted a lot, and generally held up well in coverage notwithstanding a league-leading total of 179 penalty yards, including seven pass interference calls. Chris Johnson was supposed to be the starter opposite him, but only played in 12 games due to a sports hernia injury and some tragic personal issues. Lito Sheppard ended up starting seven games after being signed as a mid-season stopgap. None of the three return for 2012.

Instead, the projected starters are a pair of players who combined for five tackles and zero starts in 2011. Ron Bartell sat out the entire season with a neck injury, but before that was the Rams' best cornerback and finished 12th in Success Rate in 2010. Another NFC West exile, Shawntae Spencer, struggled with a hamstring injury and lost his starting job in San Francisco to Carlos Rogers. He ranked 84th in Success Rate in 2010, so the job loss was pretty deserved. Nickelbacks DeMarcus Van Dyke and Chimdi Chekwa both fit the Raiders stereotype of having speed to burn.

Michael Huff is a free safety. Tyvon Branch is a strong safety. Strong safeties are good against the run and may play a lot of man coverage. Free safeties play less man coverage, though Huff is good enough at that the Raiders talked about moving him to corner early in the offseason. Huff had a good though not great 2011 season in the wake of a 4-year, $32 million extension. So long as Tarver remembers what both players' strengths are, the Raiders should have a very good safety corps. The top backup, famous "who's that" second-round pick Mike Mitchell, has turned out to be a useful depth player.

Special Teams

Year	DVOA	Rank	FG/XP	Rank	Net Kick	Rank	Kick Ret	Rank	Net Punt	Rank	Punt Ret	Rank	Hidden	Rank
2009	-0.3%	17	15.0	1	-6.3	27	-16.3	32	16.3	1	-10.4	31	3.8	9
2010	1.5%	13	3.5	10	0.8	16	5.0	10	9.9	4	-10.2	31	16.2	1
2011	-0.8%	20	16.6	1	-14.0	32	4.0	7	-8.3	28	-3.1	21	9.2	5

Sebastian Janikowski had another phenomenal year on placekicks. He missed four field goals: a 49-yarder that was blocked, a 54-yarder off the infield dirt at O.co Coliseum that went barely wide, a 59-yarder that hit the crossbar, and a 65-yarder that was blocked. His numbers weren't padded with short-range kicks either, as he made a career-high 17 field goals from 40 yards and beyond. Unfortunately, that same leg strength wasn't evident on kickoffs, as he went from being above-average the previous couple seasons to well below it. Then again, Shane Lechler can tell Janikowski that even if you do kick the ball well—Lechler was second in gross punting value—that doesn't mean there won't be long returns. The Raiders ended up 32nd on kickoff coverage and 30th on punt coverage, allowing nearly 20 points of estimated field position between the two.

Rookie Denarius Moore took over Nick Miller's punt return job and was an improvement, though still not that good. When he was healthy and available, Jacoby Ford was again an explosive kick returner. Mid-season acquisition Bryan McCann isn't quite as explosive as Ford but was still good; he could also take over Moore's punt return job with Moore likely to play more receiver snaps.

Coaching Staff

Greg Knapp brought back John DeFilippo, who served as the quarterbacks coach in his previous stint as Raiders offensive coordinator, to fill the same job. DeFilippo was far from the only familiar face Knapp brought with him, though. From Houston came Frank Pollack and Johnny Holland. Pollack was the Texans' assistant offensive line coach and now gets to manage the Raiders' transition back to a zone-blocking scheme. On the other side of the ball, new linebackers coach Holland worked for the Texans for five seasons before spending last year out of football. New defensive backs coach Clayton Lopez retakes a job he previously held in 2004-05; more recently, he coached Ron Bartell in St. Louis.

Philadelphia Eagles

2011 Record: 8-8

Pythagorean Wins: 9.8 (9th)

DVOA: 13.5% (9th)

Offense: 9.8% (8th)

Defense: -3.7% (11th)

Special Teams: 0.0% (17th)

Variance: 16.1% (22nd)

2012 Mean Projection: 8.6 wins

On the Clock (0-4): 5%

Mediocrity (5-7): 25%

Playoff Contender (8-10): 49%

Super Bowl Contender (11+): 20%

Postseason Odds: 48.9%

Projected Average Opponent: 0.7% (17th)

2011: Dream team, my ass.

2012: This is the *Football Outsiders Almanac*. Of course we're projecting a Philadelphia rebound.

There's no point to linger on the nightmare that was the 2011 Philadelphia Eagles season, but let's set the scene quickly. The Eagles were coming off a season where Michael Vick, out of nowhere, re-established himself as one of the top five quarterbacks in the game. To strengthen things on the other side of the ball, the Eagles spent big on high-quality free-agent defenders such as Nnamdi Asomugha, Jason Babin, and Cullen Jenkins. Many preseason publications, including this one, picked the Eagles to represent the NFC in Super Bowl XLVI.

Yet somehow, this ridiculous collection of talent couldn't stop tripping over its own feet. After beating St. Louis in Week 1, the Eagles blew four straight games where the big-money defense gave up an average of 431 yards. The rest of the year, the team kept teasing its fans with games where they looked like they were coming out of their funk, only to fall flat and lose again the next week. Vince Young was horrible when Vick suffered the inevitable injury. The Eagles finished up with four straight wins, but nobody in Philadelphia really noticed because they were too busy calling for the head of Juan Castillo.

Yes, you know Juan Castillo, right? He's the alleged coach who had never seen football defense prior to being named defensive coordinator by Andy Reid last offseason. He had spent his whole life running nothing but 7-on-7 drills without an opponent on the field.

This is how it sounded on WIP, anyway. There was plenty of less-unhinged criticism of Castillo as well, from more reputable sources, and early in the season the Eagles defense was obviously a complete mess. So when the season ended, we all sat and waited for the inevitable decisions that follow a disaster. The Eagles front office would either force Reid to fall on his sword, or they would force Reid to fire his good friend Castillo and bring in a defensive guru with a big name and a lot more experience.

Instead, the Eagles decided to change nothing. Well, almost nothing; they did fire defensive backs coach Johnnie Lynn. But Reid stayed and Castillo stayed. The fact that the Eagles retained Castillo was astonishing, but even more astonishing is the fact that it may have been the right move.

There were some clear signs that the defense was improving during the season. They allowed just seven points to Dallas in Week 8, and just 10 points to the Giants in Week 11. The four-game winning streak in December was certainly a sign of improvement. But casual fans may not have realized just how much the Eagles defense improved over the course of 2011. It improved *a lot*. The Eagles defense was so good in the second half of the season that when we look at their numbers for the entire year, they end up with almost the exact same defensive DVOA that they had the year before: -3.6% in 2010, -3.7% in 2011, 11th

PHILADELPHIA EAGLES 197

2012 Eagles Schedule

Week	Opp.	Week	Opp.	Week	Opp.
1	at CLE	7	BYE	13	at DAL
2	BAL	8	ATL	14	at TB
3	at ARI	9	at NO (Mon.)	15	CIN (Thu.)
4	NYG	10	DAL	16	WAS
5	at PIT	11	at WAS	17	at NYG
6	DET	12	CAR (Mon.)		

Figure 1. 2011 Philadelphia DVOA by Week

in the NFL both years. In their first eight games, the Eagles had 6.3% defensive DVOA, 22nd in the NFL. In their final eight games, they had -13.1% DVOA, sixth in the NFL.

We've done an additional defense-only week-by-week chart for the Eagles (Figure 2), and you can see that while the defense gradually improved throughout the season, there was no clear demarcation point where the defense suddenly "got it." While the Eagles' best defensive games came later in the season, there are also some lousy games like Week 13, when they let the Seahawks score 31 points on them. We often split things into Weeks 1-9 and Weeks 10-17 just because it is the most logical point that works for all 32 teams equally. But there's no reason to believe that anything changed for the Eagles in Week 10 specifically. Week 6, the bye week, seems like a logical break point, but their first good defensive game was actually the week before against Washington. And the only clear lineup change actually came all the way back in Week 4, when the Eagles mercifully euthanized the concept of "Casey Matthews, starting middle linebacker."

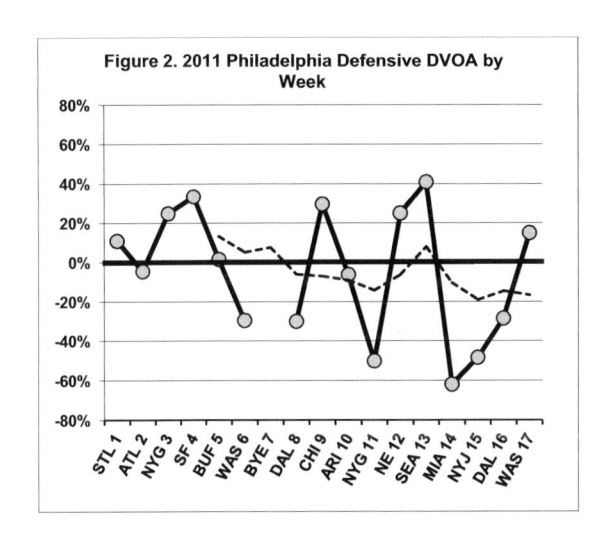

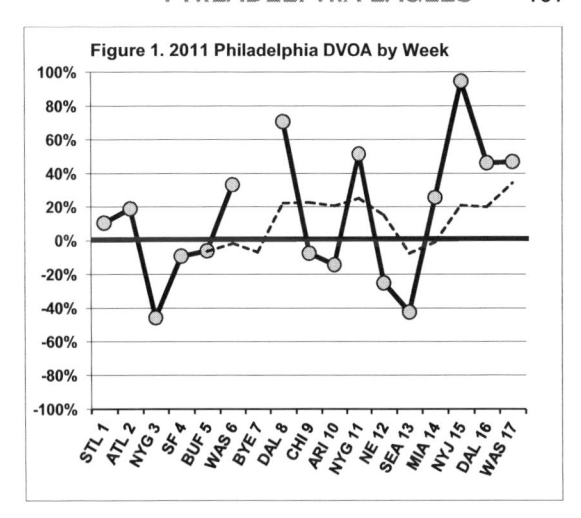

The myriad of Football Outsiders stats don't provide many clues to explain Philadelphia's defensive turnaround. Passing DVOA and rushing DVOA improved equally. DVOA improved equally on first, second, and third down. The Eagles didn't change the number of defenders they sent at the quarterback, although they were able to pressure the passer slightly more often later in the year (23 percent of pass plays before their bye week, 27 percent afterwards). As far as personnel, the Eagles played more nickel and dime later in the year, but that's simply a product of the fact that they were winning more often, and thus opponents were passing the ball more.

We expected to find that the Eagles had fewer broken tackles later in the season, but surprisingly, the opposite is true. The Eagles had better tackling before their Week 6 bye (broken tackles on 7.2 percent of plays) than after their bye (broken tackles on 8.5 percent of plays). Broken tackles were a huge issue for the Eagles all season; Philadelphia ended up with a broken tackle on 8.1 percent of defensive plays, more than any other defense except for Tampa Bay.

Those broken tackles were Philadelphia's biggest problem as far as defensive execution. When it comes to scheme, there were two things clearly wrong with the Eagles defense when it looked discombobulated early in the season: They were leaving a bad linebacker corps massively exposed, and Castillo seemed to have no idea how to use Nnamdi Asomugha.

The wide-9 became a buzzword for what was wrong with the Eagles defense, but the problem was less the wide-9 and more the players behind it. The biggest problem there is the run; when you put the defensive linemen that far apart, you are going to create some

Figure 2. 2011 Philadelphia Defensive DVOA by Week

huge holes for running backs. You need to have quality linebackers behind that, ready to make the tackles when guys come through those holes. When Jim Washburn was coaching the wide-9 in Tennessee, he had guys like Keith Bulluck and Peter Sirmon playing at linebacker. The Eagles, on the other hand, have been going cheap at linebacker for years. They started the season with two seventh-rounders and a fourth-rounder (Matthews) at linebacker. When Matthews was benched, he was replaced by a sixth-round rookie, Brian Rolle.

Gradually, Castillo and the defensive staff came to understand that they needed to limit the use of the wide-9 to protect the linebackers. Starting in the game against Washington after the bye week, the ends were lined up more often in a six-technique, shading the outside of the offensive tackles instead of being way out past where the tight end would usually be. The linebackers had moved closer to the line of scrimmage, in a clear commitment to stop the run. Even when they went back to the wide-9, the Eagles would bring a linebacker very close to the line of scrimmage, almost in a 5-2 setup. All this put less pressure on the linebackers by asking them to cover less space horizontally and vertically.

The aim to stop the run certainly worked. The Adjusted Line Yards numbers show very clear improvement over the course of the year. Surprisingly, the Eagles' ALY numbers went up a little bit on runs marked as left tackle or right tackle. But the defense was better on runs up the middle, and despite the fact that the ends weren't always way out wide, *way* better on runs around the ends (Table 1). Pass defense against tight ends and running backs also improved dramatically after the bye week.

A continued understanding of the limitations of the linebackers should keep the defense playing well in 2012, but the Eagles also finally acknowledged that maybe they can't get away with linebackers on the cheap. This offseason, they dealt a fourth-round pick to Houston for middle linebacker DeMeco Ryans, whose contract is one of the ten most expensive at his position. The Texans wanted to get rid of Ryans for two reasons: first, he was a horrible scheme fit once Wade Phillips showed up, and second, he wasn't the same after an Achilles injury in 2010 which robbed him of some of his mobility. The former won't be a problem in Philadelphia's 4-3 scheme, but the latter may be. The Eagles are planning to use Ryans as a three-down player, but Houston took Ryans off the field in passing situations last year—in part because they felt he was struggling in pass coverage, but in part because they primarily used dime personnel instead of nickel, which meant fewer linebackers anyway. Ironically, Ryans ended up with excellent charting numbers, but he wasn't exactly covering deep routes; 18 of his 25 targets came on passes within three yards of the line of scrimmage. Regardless, even if his pass coverage is subpar, Ryans still represents a clear upgrade on Jamar Chaney; Chaney, in turn, will move to the weak side, where he'll be an upgrade on Brian Rolle.

The problems in the secondary actually lasted longer than the problems with the front seven, which is a bit odd since it was obvious to pretty much anyone who understands football that the Eagles were using Nnamdi Asomugha wrong. The Eagles were so happy about signing one of the best cornerbacks in football that they totally ignored the roster problem they had created for themselves: They now had three cornerbacks who were much better on the outside and only two places to put them. So Castillo decided to use Asomugha as a "joker" defender who could move all over the field. He played slot corner. He played deep safety. He played strong safety, almost like a dime linebacker. He did crossing moves where he started at corner and then switched with a safety. He blitzed a little bit. None of these are things Nnamdi Asomugha is good at.

Asomugha is a classic bump-and-run corner. His best attribute is his ability to use the sideline to control his receiver. Take away the sideline, and you take away that attribute. Castillo was still messing around with Asomugha in different roles into November, but eventually they realized that you need to put him on one side and let him do what he does. Of course, when you put Asomugha back on the outside, you are still stuck with one corner specializing in man coverage and another, Asante Samuel, who can't play press-man at all, and has to play zone or off-man concepts.

The Eagles solved this problem after the season, in a way that is logical but unfortunate. They sent Samuel to the Atlanta Falcons for the low, low price of a seventh-round pick. Samuel is a limited player

Table 1. Philadelphia Defense Adjusted Line Yards, 2011

Weeks	LE	LT	Mid	RT	RE
Weeks 1-5	4.47	3.14	4.47	4.03	5.39
Weeks 7-17	1.85	3.88	3.91	4.22	4.57

when it comes to scheme fit, but when you let him play the way he can play, he delivers. His charting numbers have been superlative over the last couple seasons, with the best adjusted yards per pass allowed among cornerbacks for two straight seasons. That excellent play is now gone from the Eagles defensive backfield. The Eagles hope to replace it with the excellent play Asomugha showed in Oakland, while also counting on his style to free up the safeties a bit more than Samuel's style did. The "trade" of Samuel for Asomugha actually doesn't end up costing the Eagles much money; Asomugha's contract was only about $2 million higher than the one Samuel had in Philadelphia. Meanwhile, Dominique Rodgers-Cromartie can now move back to the outside, where he has much more experience, and the Eagles have Joselio Hanson in the wings, ready to return to the nickelback spot where he played well from 2007 through 2010.

While the defense was shockingly bad early in the season, the offense gave the Eagles pretty much what they expected in 2011. Philadelphia dropped from third to eighth in offensive DVOA last season, but half of that drop came because of the three games started by Vince Young. It looked like 2012 would be more of the same until we found out in March that left tackle Jason Peters had ruptured his right Achilles tendon and would miss the entire season. It was devastating news. Peters made his first All-Pro team in 2011. Our game charting project marked only one sack that came due to a Peters blown block, and he's a very important part of making space for LeSean McCoy.

That being said, let's not overreact to the Peters injury and expect the Eagles to suddenly field a below-average offense. You don't want to lose your best lineman, but this isn't *EAGLES HAZ LOST THEIR LEFT TACKLE ZOMG!* The supreme importance of the left tackle has, like many subjects that Michael Lewis writes about, been a bit exaggerated in the public eye.[1] Plenty of teams have won in recent years with converted guards and last-minute free agents playing left tackle while the Pro Bowl left tackles stay home in January. The left tackle is even less important in the Eagles' scheme because of Michael Vick. Vick is left-handed, so the left side is not his blind side. Plus he's constantly leaving the pocket, and there's only so long that even the best left tackle can hold his block. Anthony Munoz himself wouldn't be able to keep Vick off the ground on one of those plays where he runs around and holds onto the ball for six seconds.

The damage from the Peters injury is also going to be mitigated by the fact that the Eagles didn't throw up their hands and settle for awful backup King Dunlap as his replacement. They signed Demetress Bell, formerly of Buffalo. Bell is nobody's idea of a great tackle, but he's much better than Dunlap. We marked him with only one blown block in six starts last year, and only four blown blocks in 16 starts the year before. That same season, 2010, the Bills led the league in Adjusted Line Yards on runs listed as left tackle.

Other than the change at left tackle, this will be the same offense as 2011, which itself was pretty much the same offense as 2010. The Eagles have a great, well-balanced group of receivers, where the top three guys have very clear roles (Jeremy Maclin as the all-around weapon, DeSean Jackson as the deep threat, and Jason Avant as the short slot guy). Brent Celek is a useful tight end. McCoy is one of the two or three best running backs in the game. He's versatile and very hard to take down, leading the league with 50 broken tackles in 2011. In fact, the Eagles offense as a whole really benefitted from broken tackles about as much as the defense suffered from them. The Eagles were second in the league with 96 broken tackles, and first in the percentage of plays that included broken tackles, at 8.4 percent.[2]

Truthfully, whether the Eagles offense is good or great depends primarily not on the ability of Bell to play left tackle, but on Vick. Can he stay healthy, and can he stick to the consistent, more pocket-aware playing style that helped him dominate games in 2010, rather than improvising before the play has fully developed, the way he did in his youth?

If the Eagles can play as well as they did last year—even if their defense matches their rating for the whole season, not just the second half of the year—there are tons of mathematical indicators that point to improvement. This is a team that went 8-8 despite

---

[1] See also: Baseball players who do nothing but take walks; Germans who enjoy poop.

[2] There are three different charters who regularly do Eagles games, and a number of others who did them here or there, so the Eagles' high total of broken tackles on both sides of the ball is not an issue of charter bias.

outscoring opponents by 68 points. DVOA also provides a strong indicator. From 1991-2010, 15 different teams finished in the top ten in DVOA despite going 8-8 or worse. The following year, these teams averaged 9.9 wins even though the majority of them declined in DVOA (Table 2). Only three of the teams had losing records, and two of those teams were the 1992 Giants and 2000 Cowboys, aging squads whose venerable championship cores finally collapsed. The Eagles don't really fit that model. (Neither do the Jets, who also went 8-8 and were virtually tied with the Eagles in DVOA. Of course, the Jets have their own michegas.)

There are other reasons for optimism, both statistical and otherwise. The Eagles' defense was worse on third down than it was overall, generally an indicator for improvement the next year. A special teams rebound is likely, especially by DeSean Jackson who actually had negative value on punt returns last year. Getting Detroit and (especially) Arizona in their two unique games gives Philadelphia a schedule advantage over the Cowboys and Giants. The young linebackers and safeties should improve with another year of experience.

We're known for our rosy Philadelphia forecasts, and this year is no different. The effect is compounded by the fact that our projections for Dallas and New York ended up surprisingly mediocre. But we won't be the only people suggesting that the Eagles can return to Super Bowl contender status in 2012. This team has a ton of talent. It also still has Juan Castillo, but it looks like he's learned some lessons.

Aaron Schatz

Table 2. Top 10 DVOA with 8-8 Record or Worse, 1991-2011

Year	Team	W-L	DVOA	Rank	W-L Next Yr	DVOA Next Yr	Rank Next Yr
1991	NYG	8-8	6.1%	10	6-10	-7.0%	17
1993	SD	8-8	17.4%	4	11-5	10.6%	8
1994	PHI	7-9	10.9%	7	10-6	-5.3%	18
1995	DEN	8-8	11.3%	8	13-3	26.9%	3
1995	MIN	8-8	12.4%	7	9-7	-14.5%	24
1997	BAL	6-9-1	6.3%	10	6-10	-0.2%	15
1999	DAL	8-8	11.4%	9	5-11	-13.4%	23
1999	OAK	8-8	21.2%	3	12-4	20.8%	5
2002	KC	8-8	24.4%	4	13-3	30.3%	1
2004	KC	7-9	15.1%	10	10-6	24.4%	5
2006	JAC	8-8	22.5%	6	11-5	24.1%	3
2006	NYG	8-8	13.7%	8	10-6	1.9%	14
2006	PIT	8-8	9.3%	10	10-6	19.4%	6
2007	PHI	8-8	11.7%	10	9-6-1	31.8%	1
2008	SD	8-8	15.3%	7	13-3	13.5%	11
2011	PHI	8-8	13.5%	9	--	--	--
2011	NYJ	8-8	13.5%	10	--	--	--
AVERAGE			13.9%		9.9 wins	10.9%	

2011 Eagles Stats by Week

Wk	vs.	W-L	PF	PA	YDF	YDA	TO	Total	Off	Def	ST
1	@STL	W	31	13	403	335	0	11%	24%	11%	-2%
2	@ATL	L	31	35	447	318	-1	19%	19%	-4%	-4%
3	NYG	L	16	29	376	334	-3	-46%	-25%	25%	4%
4	SF	L	23	24	513	442	-2	-9%	37%	33%	-13%
5	@BUF	L	24	31	489	331	-4	-6%	-7%	2%	3%
6	@WAS	W	20	13	422	287	2	33%	-1%	-29%	5%
7	BYE										
8	DAL	W	34	7	495	267	1	71%	45%	-30%	-4%
9	CHI	L	24	30	330	372	0	-7%	21%	30%	1%
10	ARI	L	17	21	289	370	0	-14%	-27%	-6%	7%
11	@NYG	W	17	10	391	278	-1	52%	-10%	-50%	12%
12	NE	L	20	38	466	457	-1	-25%	-1%	25%	1%
13	@SEA	L	14	31	330	347	-4	-42%	-9%	41%	8%
14	@MIA	W	26	10	239	204	1	26%	-19%	-62%	-17%
15	NYJ	W	45	19	420	241	0	95%	56%	-48%	-10%
16	@DAL	W	20	7	386	238	-1	46%	25%	-28%	-7%
17	@WAS	W	34	10	390	377	-1	47%	44%	15%	18%

Trends and Splits

	Offense	Rank	Defense	Rank
Total DVOA	9.8%	8	-3.7%	11
Unadjusted VOA	7.1%	11	-7.0%	9
Weighted Trend	9.7%	7	-10.7%	7
Variance	6.3%	11	5.2%	9
Average Opponent	-2.1%	8	-2.4%	23
Passing	13.5%	16	-3.4%	10
Rushing	17.7%	3	-4.1%	19
First Down	10.0%	8	-1.6%	15
Second Down	15.8%	6	-15.9%	3
Third Down	-1.1%	14	11.0%	24
First Half	12.2%	8	-12.6%	7
Second Half	6.8%	9	5.1%	21
Red Zone	-21.5%	24	3.8%	22
Late and Close	9.2%	11	14.4%	28

PHILADELPHIA EAGLES

Five-Year Performance

Year	W-L	Pyth	Est W	PF	PA	TO	Total	Rk	Off	Rk	Def	Rk	ST	Rk	Off AGL	Rk	Def AGL	Rk
2007	8-8	9.1	9.8	336	300	-8	11.7%	10	12.4%	6	-5.6%	12	-6.4%	31	15.4	8	23.2	19
2008	9-6-1	11.4	11.6	416	289	+3	31.8%	1	6.5%	12	-23.6%	3	1.7%	13	35.5	22	3.5	2
2009	11-5	10.4	11.2	429	337	+15	28.8%	3	9.7%	11	-14.3%	3	4.8%	2	37.4	26	31.5	20
2010	10-6	9.5	11.9	439	377	+9	23.2%	5	17.3%	3	-3.6%	11	2.3%	12	41.4	29	28.7	21
2011	8-8	9.8	9	396	328	-14	13.5%	9	9.8%	8	-3.7%	11	0.0%	17	10.5	3	11.4	5

2011 Performance Based on Most Common Personnel Groups

Philadelphia Offense				Philadelphia Offense vs. Opp.				Philadelphia Defense				Philadelphia Defense vs. Opp.			
Pers	Freq	Yds	DVOA	Run%	Pers	Freq	Yds	DVOA	Pers	Freq	Yds	DVOA	Pers	Freq	Yds	DVOA
11	45%	6.3	12.5%	31%	4-2-5	26%	5.5	-7.7%	4-2-5	46%	5.8	-6.3%	11	36%	5.5	-13.1%
12	25%	6.8	22.1%	53%	2-4-5	16%	4.5	-20.3%	4-3-4	42%	4.9	-7.0%	12	21%	5.4	2.0%
21	11%	5.9	29.1%	33%	3-4-4	15%	7.1	37.8%	Dime+	10%	6.4	30.8%	21	13%	4.5	-37.8%
10	6%	5.4	-10.8%	19%	Dime+	14%	8.8	62.9%	4-4-3	1%	1.3	-30.7%	22	9%	5.9	17.9%
20	4%	7.3	48.5%	21%	4-3-4	14%	7.0	38.1%	G-line	1%	-0.1	-48.2%	10	6%	5.7	23.6%

Strategic Tendencies

Run/Pass		Rank	Offense		Rank	Pass Rush		Rank	Defense/Other		Rank
Runs, all plays	43%	14	Form: Single Back	73%	7	Rush 3	0.6%	31	4 DB	42%	24
Runs, first half	42%	19	Form: Empty Back	8%	7	Rush 4	81.8%	2	5 DB	47%	9
Runs, first down	46%	26	Pers: 3+ WR	61%	4	Rush 5	8.3%	32	6+ DB	10%	11
Runs, second-long	39%	10	Pers: 4+ WR	9%	5	Rush 6+	9.3%	9	CB by Sides	95%	3
Runs, power sit.	64%	10	Pers: 2+ TE/6+ OL	30%	18	Zone Blitz	3.1%	23	Go for it on 4th	0.98	11
Runs, behind 2H	31%	13	Play action	25%	3	Sacks by LB	6.0%	31	Offensive Pace	30.0	10
Pass, ahead 2H	49%	4	Max protect	14%	6	Sacks by DB	2.0%	28	Defensive Pace	30.8	24

Philadelphia ran much more often than in recent years; this is the first time since we started running these tables in 2005 that the Eagles have ranked higher than 23rd in "Runs, all plays." As you might expect, Philadelphia led the league with 24 percent of pass plays where the quarterback was out of the pocket on a bootleg, rollout, or scramble. The Eagles only ran on one-third of plays from 21 personnel; every other team was at 43 percent or higher. Michael Vick struggled against blitzes for the second straight season, with 9.0 yards per pass against three pass rushers, 7.9 against four, 7.0 against five, and 4.5 against six or more. Vince Young's splits were even stronger: 10.2 yards against three pass rushers, 8.1 against four, but 2.6 against five and 1.7 against six or more. Vick tied with Matt Hasselbeck for the most passes tipped or batted down at the line, 19. The Eagles were surprisingly below average on running back screens, gaining just 5.2 yards per pass with 10.6% DVOA. (League average was 6.4 yards and 18.3% DVOA.) Oddly, the Eagles played very well against standard and dime defenses, but struggled against nickel defenses. Juan Castillo dramatically changed the Eagles' philosophy when it came to bringing pressure. The Eagles dropped from 38 percent blitzes in 2010 to just 18 percent blitzes in 2011. They also dropped from second to 23rd in zone blitzes. The Eagles were the league's worst defense against runs from single-back sets (6.3% DVOA, 5.5 yards per carry) but were actually pretty good against runs from multiple-back sets (-15.6% DVOA, 3.6 yards per carry).

Passing

Player	DYAR	DVOA	Plays	NtYds	Avg	YAC	C%	TD	Int
M.Vick	652	11.6%	443	3145	7.1	5.3	60.8%	18	13
V.Young*	-83	-21.7%	122	832	6.8	4.7	57.9%	4	9
M.Kafka	-30	-38.0%	17	101	5.9	3.5	68.8%	0	2

Rushing

Player	DYAR	DVOA	Plays	Yds	Avg	TD	Fum	Suc
L.McCoy	304	15.8%	273	1309	4.8	17	1	51%
M.Vick	131	27.5%	66	599	9.1	1	4	--
R.Brown*	-12	-14.9%	42	136	3.2	1	1	48%
D.Lewis	25	18.3%	23	102	4.4	1	0	52%
V.Young*	2	-10.0%	15	83	5.5	0	0	--
D.Jackson	27	38.3%	7	41	5.9	0	0	--

Receiving

Player	DYAR	DVOA	Plays	Ctch	Yds	Y/C	YAC	TD	C%
D.Jackson	129	3.2%	104	58	961	16.6	3.9	4	56%
J.Maclin	186	12.2%	97	63	859	13.6	4.1	5	65%
J.Avant	92	2.1%	81	52	680	13.1	3.3	1	64%
R.Cooper	32	-1.0%	35	16	315	19.7	3.5	1	46%
S.Smith*	-5	-16.0%	20	11	124	11.3	3.0	1	55%
C.Hall	-40	-70.0%	9	3	20	6.7	3.7	1	33%
B.Celek	70	3.7%	97	62	811	13.1	7.5	5	64%
C.Harbor	30	16.5%	19	13	163	12.5	3.1	1	68%
L.McCoy	45	-2.8%	69	48	315	6.6	8.1	3	70%
O.Schmitt*	5	-0.9%	7	3	32	10.7	9.0	0	43%

Offensive Line

Year	Yards	ALY	Rank	Power	Rank	Stuff	Rank	2nd Lev	Rank	Open Field	Rank	F-Start	Cont.
2009	4.25	4.30	7	63%	19	16%	8	1.05	25	0.61	25	23	31
2010	4.96	4.17	10	76%	3	17%	10	1.25	7	1.35	1	16	21
2011	4.54	3.89	26	67%	6	25%	32	1.43	2	1.10	4	21	31

Year	LE	Rank	LT	Rank	Mid	Rank	RT	Rank	RE	Rank	Sacks	ASR	Rank	Short	Long
2009	4.36	15	5.17	3	4.07	18	4.26	10	4.22	16	40	6.6%	20	10	19
2010	4.56	11	4.46	13	4.28	9	3.57	27	3.82	20	49	8.4%	28	13	28
2011	4.78	8	2.98	29	3.68	28	4.19	21	3.68	17	32	5.8%	10	7	20

When you have Michael Vick as your quarterback, you're going to end up with some long sacks when Vick tries to make something happen and the defense eventually catches up with him. That's certainly not the line's fault, and we attributed only 12 Eagles sacks specifically to blown blocks, the lowest total for any offense in 2011. Three of those were by LeSean McCoy, and right tackle Todd Herremans (5.5) was the only Eagles lineman with more than two blown blocks. When it comes to run blocking, there's a bit of a disagreement between stats and scouting. Most people feel that new Eagles linemen like veteran left guard Evan Mathis and rookie center Jason Kelce did a great job of executing Howard Mudd's zone-oriented blocking scheme. However, even though LeSean McCoy led the league in rushing DYAR, the Eagles' Adjusted Line Yards numbers declined significantly last year. The problem: McCoy got stuffed in the backfield, over and over. McCoy had 22 runs that lost three yards or more, twice as many as any other running back not named Chris Johnson. You can blame McCoy for a couple of those, but you can also thank him for saving some yards with the five broken tackles he had on those 22 runs. Despite all the stuffs, the Eagles were still very good in short-yardage situations for the second straight year. Incidentally, both of these trends—more stuffs on standard downs, and more success in short yardage—were stronger after Danny Watkins finally won the right guard job away from Kyle DeVan in Week 5. Depth is a problem here, which became obvious after the Jason Peters injury. In the Delaware Valley, parents scare their children with tales of King Dunlap being forced into the starting lineup. The Eagles hope to find a diamond in the rough with either fifth-round tackle Dennis Kelly (Purdue), who was ignored by most draftniks, or sixth-round guard Brandon Washington (Miami), a big, athletic, and immature guard who probably cost himself draft position by coming out as a junior.

Defensive Front Seven

Defensive Line	Age	Pos	Plays	TmPct	Rk	Stop	Dfts	BTkl	St%	Rk	AvYd	Rk	Sack	Hit	Hur	Runs	St%	Yds	Pass	St%	Yds
Trent Cole	30	DE	45	6.7%	15	35	19	4	78%	40	0.9	25	11	7	24.5	29	76%	2.0	16	81%	-1.1
Jason Babin	32	DE	41	5.4%	35	34	23	0	83%	27	-0.9	4	18	16	20	17	82%	2.6	24	83%	-3.4
Cullen Jenkins	31	DT	40	5.2%	19	34	19	4	85%	13	0.6	5	5.5	7	13	29	93%	0.7	11	64%	0.4
Mike Patterson	29	DT	35	4.9%	25	25	11	1	71%	54	1.5	21	2.5	1	4.5	31	71%	2.2	4	75%	-3.5
Darryl Tapp	28	DE	29	5.1%	41	20	10	2	69%	70	2.2	62	2.5	5	5	17	71%	1.7	12	67%	2.9
Derek Landri	29	DT	22	3.8%	43	20	8	2	91%	3	0.6	6	2	3	5.5	17	94%	0.6	5	80%	0.4
Trevor Laws*	27	DT	21	3.1%	55	18	6	0	86%	11	2.0	40	1	2	0	16	88%	2.1	5	80%	1.6

Linebackers	Age	Pos	Plays	TmPct	Rk	Stop	Dfts	BTkl	AvYd	Sack	Hit	Hur	Runs	St%	Rk	Yds	Rk	Tgts	Suc%	Rk	AdjYd	Rk
Jamar Chaney	26	MLB	99	12.9%	31	50	18	9	5.2	1	0	1	54	56%	91	3.6	74	44	50%	43	6.4	32
Brian Rolle	24	OLB	57	7.5%	89	42	15	10	3.3	1	3	3.5	33	73%	22	2.6	24	28	54%	22	7.4	55
Casey Matthews	23	MLB	31	4.1%	--	16	5	4	6.0	1	1	1	19	47%	--	5.9	--	12	52%	--	7.6	--
Akeem Jordan	27	OLB	26	3.6%	--	21	2	1	2.8	0	1	1.5	22	82%	--	2.5	--	4	54%	--	5.7	--
Keenan Clayton	25	OLB	23	3.4%	--	10	8	6	8.0	0	0	1	7	43%	--	3.4	--	14	78%	--	5.0	--
Moise Fokou	27	OLB	22	4.2%	--	15	3	1	5.6	0	1	1	12	75%	--	3.2	--	11	47%	--	8.4	--

Year	Yards	ALY	Rank	Power	Rank	Stuff	Rank	2nd Lev	Rank	Open Field	Rank
2009	4.03	3.69	9	59%	9	24%	4	1.07	6	0.83	19
2010	4.03	3.71	8	63%	16	22%	9	1.20	23	0.76	16
2011	4.53	4.02	16	47%	3	23%	3	1.35	29	0.98	22

Year	LE	Rank	LT	Rank	Mid	Rank	RT	Rank	RE	Rank	Sacks	ASR	Rank	Short	Long
2009	2.70	3	4.39	21	3.57	6	3.89	12	4.14	20	44	7.1%	8	16	19
2010	4.19	17	3.04	2	3.36	2	4.55	24	3.69	12	39	7.7%	5	15	11
2011	2.40	2	3.64	7	4.13	15	4.17	16	4.91	31	50	8.3%	4	22	18

Despite all the problems with the players behind them, the Eagles defensive line is still mackin'; there'll be no nose job. The Eagles excelled at stuffing runners at the line of scrimmage, especially in short-yardage situations, and led the league with 22 short sacks. So many indicators suggested that Jason Babin's 12.5-sack season in 2010 was a fluke, but Jason Babin doesn't care about your silly indicators. He set another career high with 18 sacks at age 31.

Babin gets the sacks, and sacks get the glory, but Trent Cole makes more all-around plays. Former Packer Cullen Jenkins fit excellently into the Eagles' one-gap scheme, with the shortest average distance on run tackles of any starting defensive lineman in the league. He headlines an excellent tackle rotation that gets one man stronger with the addition of first-round pick Fletcher Cox. Hopefully, NFL experience will help the aggressive Mississippi State rookie solve the problems he had with double teams, and the excellent teammates beside him will guarantee he doesn't see many of them anyway.

New arrival DeMeco Ryans will be flanked at linebacker by second-round pick Mychal Kendricks on the strong side, and either Jamar Chaney or Brian Rolle on the weak side. Drafting Kendricks in the second round, like the trade for Ryans, showed the Eagles coming to terms with their drastic need for better linebackers. Kendricks started for three years on the inside of California's 3-4 defense, and has outstanding quickness, lateral agility, and closing speed. Those traits should make him ideal in pass coverage, although he had trouble with larger tight ends at Cal. On the weak side, improbably, Chaney and Rolle are cousins fighting over the same job. Rolle may have had a better Run Stop Rate in 2011, but that's because the play-by-play stats can't track the tackles a player doesn't make. Chaney is definitely the better tackler, and at 6-foot-0, 242 pounds has a clear size advantage over the undersized Rolle (5-foot-10, 227 pounds). Akeem Jordan and Moise Fokou, who split the starts on the strong side last year (with Jordan more successful) are around as backups, though they are bit characters in the King Dunlap tales.

Defensive Secondary

Secondary	Age	Pos	Plays	TmPct	Rk	Stop	Dfts	BTkl	Runs	St%	Rk	Yds	Rk	Tgts	Tgt%	Rk	Dist	Suc%	Rk	APaYd	Rk	PD	Int
Kurt Coleman	24	SS	79	11.0%	28	24	10	8	41	41%	31	6.4	27	24	6.5%	45	18.0	47%	63	12.0	71	7	4
Nate Allen	25	FS	64	8.9%	51	29	11	10	30	47%	21	6.5	30	22	5.9%	58	18.2	77%	1	7.0	28	7	2
Nnamdi Asomugha	31	CB	45	5.9%	73	23	12	8	15	47%	36	6.7	37	38	9.7%	82	15.3	61%	15	7.6	46	7	3
Asante Samuel*	31	CB	44	6.6%	65	20	10	8	9	56%	18	11.9	76	62	18.1%	35	13.7	66%	4	4.8	1	12	3
Jarrad Page	28	FS	38	7.2%	--	15	4	7	19	42%	--	7.1	--	14	5.2%	--	10.5	39%	--	8.3	--	2	0
Joselio Hanson	31	CB	33	4.3%	--	13	5	4	7	29%	--	9.0	--	38	9.6%	--	10.1	52%	--	7.3	--	4	0
D. Rodgers-Cromartie	26	CB	30	4.8%	--	15	10	5	6	33%	--	19.3	--	32	10.1%	--	13.4	60%	--	7.3	--	7	0
Jaiquawn Jarrett	23	FS	15	2.6%	--	3	0	2	5	40%	--	8.6	--	10	3.2%	--	16.2	47%	--	11.8	--	0	0

Year	Pass D Rank	vs. #1 WR	Rk	vs. #2 WR	Rk	vs. Other WR	Rk	vs. TE	Rk	vs. RB	Rk
2009	5	-30.0%	3	9.0%	24	-29.8%	4	-9.1%	7	-1.9%	16
2010	11	-8.0%	11	-19.3%	4	-12.6%	9	10.9%	19	27.7%	31
2011	11	-0.5%	12	7.9%	21	-15.2%	12	-8.2%	3	22.5%	29

As noted earlier in this chapter, the Eagles now can clearly use their cornerbacks in defined roles, with Nnamdi Asomugha and Dominique Rodgers-Cromartie on the outside and Joselio Hanson in the slot. But Juan Castillo has to make sure this ends up working in the Eagles' favor, and not to their detriment. Last year, for example, the Eagles lost to Arizona by staying in a bland Cover-2 even when the Cardinals put Larry Fitzgerald in the slot. That led to rookie safety Jaiquawn Jarrett trying to cover Fitzgerald in a deep zone. They need to figure out some way to cover top receivers who move to the slot (hi there, Victor Cruz) without putting Asomugha in a position that doesn't play to his strengths. If one of the top three corners is injured, the Eagles will be able to turn to fourth-round pick Brandon Boykin, a three-year starter at Georgia who has experience playing both inside and outside and is particularly strong in run support. Free safety Nate Allen had excellent coverage stats last year, albeit with a small sample size, and Kurt Coleman is a good box safety. The Eagles expected Jarrett to start when they took him in the second round a year ago, but he hasn't been able to beat out Coleman.

Special Teams

Year	DVOA	Rank	FG/XP	Rank	Net Kick	Rank	Kick Ret	Rank	Net Punt	Rank	Punt Ret	Rank	Hidden	Rank
2009	4.1%	2	3.6	11	9.1	7	-7.5	27	2.6	13	16.3	1	-9.9	28
2010	2.0%	12	3.7	9	8.2	7	-9.9	29	8.6	8	1.1	15	-5.1	20
2011	0.0%	17	3.9	9	7.5	5	-3.5	23	0.1	16	-7.9	27	1.7	14

Up until two years ago, the Eagles consistently had one of the top special teams units in the league. Meanwhile, in Buffalo, Bobby April was renowned as the top special teams coordinator in the NFL. Then April came to work for the Eagles, and a strange thing happened: The special teams declined, becoming worse than either the Eagles or April's Bills were before April came to Philadelphia. The Eagles used twin homophonous rookie specialists, and one of them was not a problem. The decision to let David Akers leave may have looked bad when Akers set an NFL record for field goals in San Francisco, but Alex Henery really wasn't any less efficient than Akers. He just had far less usage. By our metrics, Henery was worth just 0.8 points less than Akers on field goals, and just 1.2 points less on gross kickoff distance. Going forward, the biggest issue with Henery will be extending his range, as he tried only six field goals of 40-plus yards as a rookie.

Unfortunately, we can't be equally nice to punter Chas Henry, who was awful in his rookie season. The gross value of Henry's punts cost the Eagles -11.5 points of estimated field position, worst in the league for any one punter with a single team. (Matt Turk was worse, but played for two teams.) Henry could lose his job in camp to undrafted rookie Ryan Tydlacka out of Kentucky. The Eagles' net punting value was saved only by strong punt coverage, which like the kickoff coverage has remained excellent the last two seasons. Akeem Jordan (13 tackles, 12 forcing a below-average gain) and Colt Anderson (11 tackles, 10 forcing a below-average gain) led the coverage teams. DeSean Jackson had an off-year on punt returns but that's likely to rebound in 2012. Dion Lewis returns kickoffs and was poor as a rookie.

Coaching Staff

Shocking through it may be, there were some Eagles coaches who did not spend the offseason in constant danger of being fired. They are on offense. Coordinator Marty Mornhinweg is still generally lauded for the work he has done tailoring the Eagles offense to fit Michael Vick's strengths. Although an *ESPN the Magazine* article a year ago identified him as the one ex-head coach most likely to find success in a second job, he hasn't been a popular candidate in rumors. One subpar year of ALY numbers isn't going to sully the reputation of offensive line coach Howard Mudd, especially since Mudd has probably never heard of Adjusted Line Yards in the first place. The 70-year-old Mudd has health issues, with back and knee pain to go with hip replacement surgery last October, so he skipped most of OTAs and stayed in Arizona so he would be fresh for the season. In his absence, assistant Eugene Chung (the former Patriots first-rounder) handled the duty of teaching new arrivals like Demetress Bell the preferred Mudd technique of blocking aggressively rather than stepping backwards to cut off pass rushers using the vertical step. Other recent players on the staff include Doug Pederson (quarterbacks) and Duce Staley (assistant running backs and special teams).

Pittsburgh Steelers

2011 Record: 12-4

Pythagorean Wins: 11.1 (6th)

DVOA: 22.6% (4th)

Offense: 11.4% (6th)

Defense: -9.4% (7th)

Special Teams: 1.7% (9th)

Variance: 13.4% (14th)

2012 Mean Projection: 10.1 wins

On the Clock (0-4): 1%

Mediocrity (5-7): 9%

Playoff Contender (8-10): 47%

Super Bowl Contender (11+): 43%

Postseason Odds: 68.6%

Projected Average Opponent: 1.3% (14th)

2011: A farewell tour for the longest-running band in the business.

2012: We're gonna party like it's 2-0-0-7.

The year was 2007. If you said you were a "Belieber," people just thought you had a speech impediment. Tony Soprano was New Jersey's Italian stereotype of the television moment. The original iPhone made its debut. The Dow Jones was over 14,000, and no one outside Wall Street had ever heard of a credit default swap.

In the sports world, Barry Bonds' cap size (and 756th home run) set an all-time record, LeBron James got swept by San Antonio in the NBA Finals, David Beckham came to America (with Posh Spice instead of Arsenio Hall), and Boise State upset Oklahoma in the Fiesta Bowl. Also, Bill Cowher retired as Steelers head coach.

From the hiring of a new leader in January 2007 all the way through the end of last year, seemingly the only thing that hadn't changed in our collective sports consciousness was the Pittsburgh Steelers. General manager Kevin Colbert, head coach Mike Tomlin, defensive coordinator Dick LeBeau, and offensive coordinator Bruce Arians presided over the team in those five years, thereby comprising the longest-tenured quartet of its kind in the NFL. Even Pittsburgh's player lineup was largely the same. Eight of 11 defensive starters in Week 1 of 2011 remained unchanged from Week 1 of 2007. Overall, last year's 22 starters, 17 of which had been drafted by the Steelers, had an average tenure of 6.1 years with the team.

Certainly, you can't argue with that level of continuity given its results. Four playoff berths, two Super Bowl appearances and a Lombardi Trophy speak to consistent winning; their DVOAs over the past five years speak to consistent efficiency. From 2007 to 2011, Pittsburgh was one of three teams to finish in the top 10 in overall DVOA each season (along with New England and Philadelphia), and one of only two teams to finish in the top 10 in defense each season (along with division rivals Baltimore).

Even in a relatively disappointing year by Pittsburgh standards, the Steelers still won 12 games despite producing the worst turnover margin in team history (-13). All five of their losses were at the hands of division champions. Besides, as Thom Brennaman might say, if an NFL team is fortunate enough to spend five minutes or 20 minutes losing to Tim Tebow, their season is better for it. Most teams would follow such a season with small tweaks, not wholesale changes. And given the way the Steelers historically have valued stability, few would have noticed if they did the same. However, as successful as it was, 2011 exposed two major long-term issues in Pittsburgh that needed to be addressed post-haste. First, as much of a warrior as he's been over the past nine years, Ben Roethlisberger's -99 DYAR in the three games after his ankle injury, including the playoff loss to Denver, showed that the Steelers are going to get subpar play from their hero if they can't keep him healthy. Second, injuries and their worst season of run defense since 2002 set off alarm bells that age had

PITTSBURGH STEELERS

2012 Steelers Schedule

Week	Opp.	Week	Opp.	Week	Opp.
1	at DEN	7	at CIN	13	at BAL
2	NYJ	8	WAS	14	SD
3	at OAK	9	at NYG	15	at DAL
4	BYE	10	KC (Mon.)	16	CIN
5	PHI	11	BAL	17	CLE
6	at TEN (Thu.)	12	at CLE		

Figure 1. 2011 Pittsburgh DVOA by Week

finally caught up to the Steelers' front seven. So, rather than standing pat, Pittsburgh embarked on an offseason that was about as close to "retooling" as the franchise is willing to stomach.

Since taking over in Week 3 of 2004, Roethlisberger has been sacked 94 more times than any other active starter, and his total of 2,090 sack yards is the highest by 692. We know from our research that quarterbacks get far too little of the blame for sack numbers, and Roethlisberger has been a prototypical example most of his career. With Kordell Stewart and Tommy Maddox at quarterback from 2001 to 2003, Pittsburgh's Adjusted Sack Rate on offense ranked 12th, 13th, and 19th, respectively. Since then, Pittsburgh's average ranking is 26.5, and it has never gotten back to the (admittedly) mediocre levels of the Stewart/Maddox era.

J.J. Cooper's time-to-sack data cast the spotlight on Big Ben too. In 2009 and 2010 (the numbers only go back three years), Roethlisberger averaged 3.4 seconds per sack in a league where quarterbacks average 3.1. Furthermore, with Roethlisberger at quarterback, the offensive line gave up 45 "long" sacks (i.e., 3.0 seconds or slower) as opposed to only 22 "short" sacks (i.e., 2.5 seconds or faster). In other words, at least through 2010, Roethlisberger was holding onto the ball longer than the amount of time his offensive line should be expected to block. Three-tenths of a second may not seem like much, but it's an eternity for an offensive lineman trying to keep faster pass rushers at bay.

A funny thing happened in 2011, though: Sacks became far less attributable to Roethlisberger. His average sack time decreased to the league norm (3.1), and he only had two more long sacks (18) than short sacks (16). Meanwhile, as a percentage of total sacks, Pittsburgh went from giving up short sacks relatively infrequently in 2009 (30 percent) and 2010 (21 percent) to allowing four out of every 10 sacks in 2011 to occur in a flash. With blame for sacks shifting to the offensive line, and questions surrounding whether or not Roethlisberger could stay healthy enough to finish out the final four years of his contract, Pittsburgh decided that the optimal way to get full value was a modest return to their smash-mouth days of old. It would be a win-win for everyone, including a Pittsburgh fanbase accustomed to lunch pail offense.

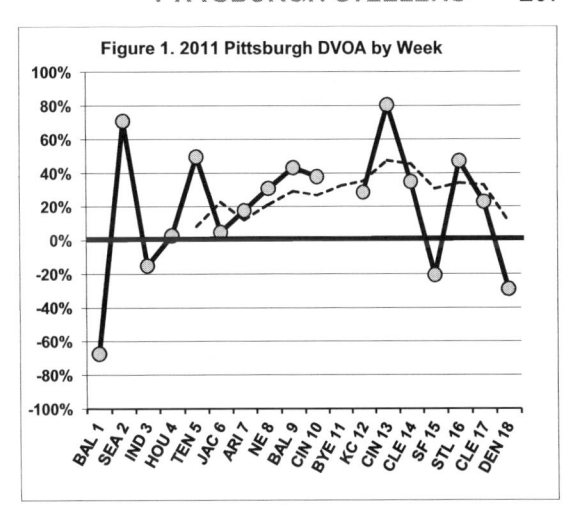

The constant stream of lesser players shuffling through revolving doors on either side of All-Pro center Maurkice Pouncey was a major reason why Roethlisberger's improved pocket presence in 2011 didn't translate to improved overall offense. Therefore, a key component of Pittsburgh's plan was adding talent along the offensive line. Enter the Steelers' first two draft picks, David DeCastro and Mike Adams, who will immediately step in as starters at right guard and left tackle, respectively.

DeCastro was the howitzer in Stanford's arsenal of pulling guard plays, helping lead the Cardinal to more than 200 rushing yards per game in each of his three seasons as a starter. Not only will DeCastro's run-blocking prowess remind fans of that classic Pittsburgh ground-and-pound style, but he'll be wearing the No. 66 jersey once donned by former All-Pro Steelers guard Alan Faneca, to whom DeCastro has drawn comparisons.

Adams isn't a classic blind side protector at left tackle insofar as he's arguably a better run blocker than pass blocker. That's primarily due to getting a ton of practice in the former at Ohio State, where the Buckeyes ran the ball about 70 percent of the time. With starting right tackle Marcus Gilbert also excellent in the running game, the addition of DeCastro and Adams gives the Steelers one of the most talented run-blocking offensive lines in the league. And that's exactly how they want it.

The other main cog in Pittsburgh's offensive retrofit involved not renewing Arians' contract. After five successful years, the band has finally broken up. To replace Arians, the team hired former Chiefs head coach Todd Haley, a move that marked the first time since Kevin Gilbride in 1999 that the team went outside the organization for its offensive coordinator. Of course, "outside the organization" is relative given that Haley served in the same capacity under former Steelers offensive coordinator Ken Whisenhunt when he left to become the Arizona's head coach. The year was—wait for it—2007.

For a team looking to run the ball more, Haley seemed like a curious choice. To the naked eye, his offenses in Arizona and Kansas City—at least when Charlie Weis wasn't around—seemed to be the antitheses of smash-mouth football. Four-wide sets abounded and an elite running talent like Jamaal Charles was relegated to part-time duty. However, when viewed through the prism of keeping Big Ben healthy for the next four seasons, the picture starts to come into focus.

In Haley's two years with the Cardinals, Arizona's offensive line ranked no lower than ninth in Adjusted Sack Rate despite sending exactly zero linemen to the Pro Bowl. True, that didn't continue in Kansas City, but Matt Cassel's had a longer average sack time than even Roethlisberger the past two years (3.6 seconds vs. 3.3 seconds).

More importantly, clearly Haley made no lack of effort in protecting Cassel schematically. It's *that* feature of Haley's offense that gets overlooked in the context of his unexpected move to Pittsburgh. Over the past three seasons with Arians, the Steelers offense ranked 26th, 28th, and 23rd with respect to his use of max protection in the passing game.[1] In contrast, Haley's frequency of max protection in Kansas City ranked eighth in 2009, fifth in 2010, and led the league in 2011.

Furthermore, although Kansas City did use four-wideout sets more than most teams, they only lined up with three wide receivers a league-average portion of the time. If you combine the two percentages, Pittsburgh looks like they've been running an Arena Football League offense in comparison over the past three years. In 2009, the Steelers used three or more wideouts in the formation on 62 percent of plays, whereas Kansas City only went three-wide 52 percent of the time. In 2010, with Weis serving as Haley's 300-pound Quaalude, it was Steelers 54 percent, Chiefs 38 percent. Finally, last season, it was Pittsburgh 58 percent, Kansas City 49 percent.

Haley also protects his quarterbacks by avoiding empty-back sets and using fewer one-back sets. Last season, the Steelers had two running backs in the formation only 21 percent of the time, whereas the Chiefs had two backs 39 percent of the time. As an early indication of switching to the latter tendency, Haley has moved David Johnson from tight-end-qua-novelty-fullback to full-time fullback. Putting all of this together as simply as possible, more bodies in the backfield means more potential blockers on pass plays, which means a longer shelf life for Big Ben.

However, as has been the case over the past 40 years, whether or not the Steelers' offensive moves translate into a seventh Lombardi depends just as much on solidifying the long-term success of their defense. Naturally, then, the other main focus of Pittsburgh's offseason involved getting younger on that side of the ball.

We detailed Pittsburgh's elderly defense in *Football Outsiders Almanac 2011*. We mentioned how their starting lineup projected as the 13th defense since 2000 with an average age over 30 years old, and how 11 of the previous 12 ended the season above average despite their age (including the 2010 Steelers).

Sure enough, that's exactly what happened. Despite having the oldest regular starters in the NFL, Pittsburgh's defense finished above average in efficiency. Nevertheless, for the first time since 2002, their run defense DVOA ranked outside the top 10, and, for the first time since 2000, their Adjusted Line Yards did as well.

Now, age per se doesn't affect DVOA on defense, but injuries do. It's instructive, therefore, to point out the following comparison. When Pittsburgh's starting secondary had an average age of 29.8 years old in 2011, their 0.8 Adjusted Games Lost was the lowest in the NFL, and the pass defense finished with the same DVOA ranking it had in 2010. In contrast, Pittsburgh's starting front seven averaged 31.9 years old, their 26.6 AGL was sixth-highest, and the run defense dropped from first to 15th. In that context, it's hard to completely rule out age as a factor in the Steelers' run defense decline.

We also showed in last year's chapter that, when a defense has an average age over 30, a youth movement tends to happen following the season in question regardless of DVOA. And sure enough, the Steelers'

---

[1] Defined as plays with at least seven blockers, and at least two more blockers than pass rushers.

2012 offseason fell perfectly in line, with almost all of the changes coming where the oldest starters resided (i.e., the front seven). Pittsburgh released 36-year-old defensive end Aaron Smith and 37-year-old inside linebacker James Farrior, and replaced them with Evander Hood and Larry Foote, who are a combined 16 years younger. They also drafted Sean Spence to take over for Foote once the former completes his mandatory redshirt season. Despite being old and injured, nose tackle Casey Hampton (35) and defensive end Brett Keisel (34) barely avoided the reaper this spring, but they may not avoid it this summer if youngsters Cameron Heyward, Alameda Ta'amu, and Steve McLendon develop as advertised. Taken together, the end result is that the front seven's average age will plummet to 28.3 years old this season, and likely drop further to 27.0 in 2013.

So, after an offseason focused on the long view, the Steelers have set themselves up nicely to remain a Super Bowl contender for the foreseeable future. There may be growing pains in 2012, but if there's an NFL franchise that's specifically built for seamless transitions, it's Pittsburgh. There were changes here, but not drastic ones. Haley is bringing back the Steelers offense of 2007, not 1977. On defense, the new starters have been valuable reserves for at least two years, so we're not talking about rookies trying to pick up the system cold turkey. And when players like Heyward, Spence, and Ta'amu take over in 2013, they too will have had a year or two of learning under their belts.

More so than for most teams, past is prologue for Pittsburgh. When they last experienced an offseason this volatile, the year was 2007. The NFL universe didn't collapse in on itself, and the Steelers ended up winning the AFC North with a 10-6 record. While our 10.1-win projection for 2012 gives that narrative a convenient dose of symmetry, it's just a statistical estimate with a bunch of probabilities attached. What's important is that the most likely outcomes involve Pittsburgh once again contending for the AFC Championship.

Danny Tuccitto

2011 Steelers Stats by Week

Wk	vs.	W-L	PF	PA	YDF	YDA	TO	Total	Off	Def	ST
1	@BAL	L	7	35	312	385	-7	-67%	-53%	19%	4%
2	SEA	W	24	0	421	164	0	71%	41%	-33%	-2%
3	@IND	W	23	20	408	241	-2	-15%	-25%	-9%	1%
4	@HOU	L	10	17	296	318	-1	3%	16%	20%	7%
5	TEN	W	38	17	431	306	0	50%	41%	-17%	-9%
6	JAC	W	17	13	370	209	0	5%	14%	-4%	-13%
7	@ARI	W	32	20	445	330	1	18%	25%	20%	13%
8	NE	W	25	17	427	213	-1	31%	10%	-27%	-6%
9	BAL	L	20	23	392	356	-1	43%	33%	-5%	5%
10	@CIN	W	24	17	328	279	1	38%	17%	-19%	2%
11	BYE										
12	@KC	W	13	9	290	252	2	29%	3%	-19%	7%
13	CIN	W	35	7	295	232	2	81%	43%	-22%	15%
14	CLE	W	14	3	416	304	-1	35%	7%	-26%	3%
15	@SF	L	3	20	389	287	-4	-20%	-13%	3%	-5%
16	STL	W	27	0	377	232	-1	47%	35%	-7%	5%
17	@CLE	W	13	9	360	240	-1	23%	-7%	-30%	1%
18	@DEN	L	23	29	400	447	0	-29%	1%	37%	7%

Trends and Splits

	Offense	Rank	Defense	Rank
Total DVOA	11.4%	6	-9.4%	7
Unadjusted VOA	8.8%	9	-13.2%	5
Weighted Trend	13.6%	6	-12.5%	5
Variance	9.1%	20	6.8%	21
Average Opponent	-2.6%	5	-6.2%	32
Passing	24.3%	7	-11.7%	3
Rushing	6.6%	6	-6.6%	15
First Down	-2.0%	18	-29.5%	1
Second Down	20.7%	5	7.8%	24
Third Down	25.0%	8	-0.9%	14
First Half	17.7%	5	-5.2%	11
Second Half	4.4%	10	-13.8%	4
Red Zone	-15.7%	21	-19.9%	6
Late and Close	1.5%	16	-15.4%	3

Five-Year Performance

Year	W-L	Pyth	Est W	PF	PA	TO	Total	Rk	Off	Rk	Def	Rk	ST	Rk	Off AGL	Rk	Def AGL	Rk
2007	10-6	11.4	9.2	393	269	+3	19.4%	6	8.5%	9	-12.5%	3	-1.6%	21	9.1	3	19.7	16
2008	12-4	11.8	11.3	347	223	+4	26.0%	4	-1.5%	21	-29.0%	1	-1.5%	23	37.6	24	16.5	12
2009	9-7	9.2	10.0	368	324	-3	14.2%	10	14.4%	7	-4.6%	9	-4.8%	30	23.9	16	29.2	17
2010	12-4	12.1	12.1	375	232	+17	35.4%	2	14.3%	5	-20.7%	1	0.4%	16	32.0	22	17.9	12
2011	12-4	11.1	11.3	325	227	-13	22.6%	4	11.4%	6	-9.4%	7	1.7%	9	33.2	19	27.3	18

2011 Performance Based on Most Common Personnel Groups

Pittsburgh Offense					**Pittsburgh Offense vs. Opp.**				**Pittsburgh Defense**				**Pittsburgh Defense vs. Opp.**			
Pers	Freq	Yds	DVOA	Run%	Pers	Freq	Yds	DVOA	Pers	Freq	Yds	DVOA	Pers	Freq	Yds	DVOA
11	44%	6.4	20.2%	29%	3-3-5	12%	6.7	19.7%	3-4-4	57%	4.7	-11.1%	11	37%	4.5	-7.0%
12	17%	6.2	21.2%	49%	4-3-4	31%	5.8	13.9%	2-4-5	21%	4.3	-6.3%	12	22%	4.7	-5.1%
13	12%	5.3	14.0%	74%	4-2-5	25%	6.5	24.0%	Dime+	16%	4.6	-13.0%	21	19%	4.6	-11.4%
01	7%	5.4	-4.2%	0%	3-3-5	13%	6.0	-1.2%	3-3-5	2%	5.9	-1.5%	22	6%	4.6	-20.7%
22	7%	4.8	-15.8%	76%	3-4-4	13%	6.8	39.7%	1-5-5	1%	7.2	41.4%	10	4%	5.7	3.5%
21	5%	5.7	26.6%	65%	Dime+	12%	6.5	19.3%								

Strategic Tendencies

Run/Pass		Rank	Offense		Rank	Pass Rush		Rank	Defense/Other		Rank
Runs, all plays	41%	16	Form: Single Back	65%	12	Rush 3	9.1%	11	4 DB	58%	4
Runs, first half	38%	25	Form: Empty Back	14%	3	Rush 4	49.9%	27	5 DB	25%	29
Runs, first down	55%	11	Pers: 3+ WR	57%	7	Rush 5	35.0%	2	6+ DB	16%	8
Runs, second-long	31%	23	Pers: 4+ WR	12%	4	Rush 6+	6.0%	22	CB by Sides	61%	27
Runs, power sit.	58%	17	Pers: 2+ TE/6+ OL	39%	8	Zone Blitz	6.6%	12	Go for it on 4th	0.80	25
Runs, behind 2H	35%	7	Play action	16%	22	Sacks by LB	75.7%	1	Offensive Pace	32.0	31
Pass, ahead 2H	49%	3	Max protect	8%	23	Sacks by DB	5.7%	22	Defensive Pace	28.6	1

The Pittsburgh offense ranked fifth in DVOA through three quarters, but was horrible at the end of games, ranking 27th in the fourth quarter. This wasn't an issue of the Steelers slowing down to hold onto a big lead, either. Their fourth-quarter DVOA was 25.8% when leading by more than a touchdown, but -41.0% otherwise. So why weren't the Steelers blowing games? Their defense stiffened in the fourth quarter as the offense slacked off, ranking second in the fourth quarter after ranking 12th in the first three quarters. The Steelers defense was at its best on those rare occasions where Pittsburgh was losing in the fourth quarter, allowing just 2.2 yards per play. ◉ The Steelers were last in the league with just 18 dropped passes. ◉ The Steelers offense didn't run much from shotgun—just 26 carries by running backs—but had a league-leading 7.8 yards and 71.5% DVOA on these runs. ◉ On defense, the Steelers really struggled against runs from shotgun, allowing 6.6 yards per carry and 30.4% DVOA. However, they faced running back carries on just 6.5 percent of shotgun snaps, the lowest rate in the league. ◉ Pittsburgh was one of three defenses whose opponents threw to tight ends more than 25 percent of the time. ◉ The Steelers allowed 4.0 average yards after catch, up from 3.6 the year before but still the best figure in the NFL. ◉ Ike Taylor covered the opposition's No. 1 receiver on 68 percent of his targets, tied with Darrelle Revis for the highest rate in the league.

Passing

Player	DYAR	DVOA	Plays	NtYds	Avg	YAC	C%	TD	Int
B.Roethlisberger	867	13.3%	555	3806	7.0	5.4	63.6%	21	14
C.Batch	0	-11.1%	26	198	7.6	6.1	62.5%	0	1

Rushing

Player	DYAR	DVOA	Plays	Yds	Avg	TD	Fum	Suc
R.Mendenhall	106	2.3%	228	928	4.1	9	1	52%
I.Redman	55	3.1%	109	478	4.4	3	2	54%
M.Moore*	29	28.5%	22	157	7.1	0	1	68%
J.Dwyer	11	8.8%	16	123	7.7	0	0	38%
B.Roethlisberger	18	9.2%	16	83	5.2	0	0	--
J.Clay	6	10.1%	10	41	4.1	1	0	50%
A.Brown	22	21.8%	7	41	5.9	0	0	--
M.Wallace	38	108.6%	5	57	11.4	0	0	--

Receiving

Player	DYAR	DVOA	Plays	Ctch	Yds	Y/C	YAC	TD	C%
A.Brown	204	9.1%	124	69	1108	16.1	4.9	2	56%
M.Wallace	399	31.4%	113	72	1193	16.6	6.5	8	64%
H.Ward*	3	-12.0%	63	46	381	8.3	3.5	2	73%
E.Sanders	15	-8.0%	43	22	288	13.1	5.8	2	51%
J.Cotchery	63	12.8%	31	17	240	14.1	4.1	2	55%
H.Miller	99	13.2%	76	52	637	12.3	4.8	2	68%
D.Johnson	16	8.9%	14	12	91	7.6	4.7	1	86%
W.Saunders	-8	-23.4%	8	4	29	7.3	2.0	1	50%
L.Pope	19	0.9%	33	24	247	10.3	5.2	1	73%
R.Mendenhall	14	-5.4%	28	18	154	8.6	8.7	0	64%
I.Redman	-11	-21.9%	23	19	79	4.2	6.7	0	83%
M.Moore*	15	3.8%	14	11	104	9.5	8.6	1	79%

Offensive Line

Year	Yards	ALY	Rank	Power	Rank	Stuff	Rank	2nd Lev	Rank	Open Field	Rank	F-Start	Cont.
2009	4.32	4.13	14	72%	5	18%	15	1.18	15	0.87	13	12	37
2010	3.93	3.87	19	64%	12	21%	24	1.04	23	0.73	15	14	31
2011	4.49	4.44	3	57%	24	21%	23	1.32	6	0.82	16	18	22

Year	LE	Rank	LT	Rank	Mid	Rank	RT	Rank	RE	Rank	Sacks	ASR	Rank	Short	Long
2009	4.58	14	4.30	11	4.08	17	3.72	25	4.70	8	50	8.5%	28	15	25
2010	4.85	6	2.89	30	3.91	19	4.08	17	5.02	5	43	8.6%	29	9	26
2011	0.65	32	4.87	4	4.41	6	4.79	5	4.85	3	42	7.2%	20	17	19

We can sit here and talk about how the Steelers made out like bandits by selecting first-round guard David DeCastro (Stanford) and second-round tackle Mike Adams (Ohio State) in the draft. But neither of those additions will mean much of anything if team headquarters can't figure out how to keep their blockers healthy. That's because 2011 marked the fourth straight season in which Pittsburgh had an offensive line that ranked among the eight most injured in the NFL. During that time span, the unit has averaged 24.9 AGL, which is the equivalent of 1.6 player seasons lost to injury. The past two seasons, most of their bad injury luck has befallen Willie Colon, who spent 31 of 32 games on injured reserve. Having slated Colon as their starting left guard in 2012, Pittsburgh is hoping that three's a charm rather than the continuation of an injury curse. The Steelers used four different players at left guard last season (Chris Kemoeatu, Ramon Foster, Trai Essex, and Doug Legursky), so a healthy Colon would at least provide stability at the position. Center Maurkice Pouncey earned Pro Bowl honors for the second straight season, and DeCastro, by almost all accounts the best guard prospect since Steve Hutchinson, replaces Ramon Foster on the right side. DeCastro's straight-ahead run-blocking skills fit perfectly with Pittsburgh's right-handed tendencies, but his athleticism also allows new offensive coordinator Todd Haley to incorporate more right-to-left counters into the Steelers' running game.

Marcus Gilbert gave up only 4.5 sacks on blown blocks last year, a pretty good number for a rookie tackle. In fact, the Steelers were so high on Gilbert that they considered moving him to the left side in 2012 before Adams' draft free-fall forced their hand. A potential first-round pick, Adams fell due to the proverbial "character issues," which included egregious college-student offenses like getting a tattoo and dabbling in the reefer arts. Adams is a better run blocker than pass protector at this stage in his career, but even as a rookie he's probably a better option at left tackle than Jonathan Scott or Trai Essex.

Defensive Front Seven

Defensive Line	Age	Pos	Plays	TmPct	Rk	Stop	Dfts	BTkl	St%	Rk	AvYd	Rk	Sack	Hit	Hur	Runs	St%	Yds	Pass	St%	Yds
Brett Keisel	34	DE	54	8.2%	4	38	10	4	70%	67	2.1	60	3	3	18	41	66%	3.0	13	85%	-0.8
Ziggy Hood	25	DE	32	4.2%	58	21	7	2	66%	77	3.4	78	1.5	2	6.5	26	69%	3.7	6	50%	2.3
Casey Hampton	35	DT	31	5.1%	22	25	7	0	81%	27	2.0	42	0	0	2	31	81%	2.0	0	0%	0.0

Linebackers	Age	Pos	Plays	TmPct	Rk	Stop	Dfts	BTkl	AvYd	Sack	Hit	Hur	Runs	St%	Rk	Yds	Rk	Tgts	Suc%	Rk	AdjYd	Rk
Lawrence Timmons	26	ILB	92	12.2%	40	55	15	4	4.9	2	5	12	57	72%	27	3.4	58	31	48%	50	6.9	44
James Farrior*	37	ILB	81	12.3%	38	44	5	6	5.0	2	3	8.5	49	61%	71	3.6	72	30	42%	62	9.8	76
James Harrison	34	OLB	58	11.2%	45	47	19	2	1.5	9	8	17	41	83%	4	2.4	19	9	54%	--	4.3	--
Larry Foote	32	ILB	46	6.5%	--	23	8	5	4.7	1.5	2	3.5	31	55%	--	4.4	--	10	39%	--	5.5	--
LaMarr Woodley	28	OLB	41	8.7%	70	30	15	2	1.5	9	4	13	25	68%	46	3.6	68	8	58%	--	6.0	--
Jason Worilds	24	OLB	35	6.2%	--	24	6	2	3.5	3	6	16.5	24	71%	--	3.5	--	8	57%	--	6.3	--

PITTSBURGH STEELERS

Year	Yards	ALY	Rank	Power	Rank	Stuff	Rank	2nd Lev	Rank	Open Field	Rank
2009	3.55	3.66	6	82%	32	18%	19	1.00	2	0.37	2
2010	3.07	3.46	1	59%	10	21%	10	0.85	2	0.17	1
2011	3.91	4.00	15	62%	15	18%	22	1.04	5	0.55	6

Year	LE	Rank	LT	Rank	Mid	Rank	RT	Rank	RE	Rank	Sacks	ASR	Rank	Short	Long
2009	2.67	2	3.76	9	3.66	9	3.58	6	4.33	23	47	8.2%	2	15	24
2010	3.89	13	2.98	1	3.47	3	3.82	10	2.99	3	48	8.3%	3	16	16
2011	4.73	25	4.47	23	3.75	8	4.46	22	3.11	8	35	6.8%	14	16	14

Age finally caught up to the Steelers' front seven last season, resulting in their worst ALY since 1999 and worst ASR since 2003. Beginning in 2009, it's been the oldest front seven in the league each season, and in 2011 it was the oldest by *over two years*. Unlike in previous seasons, however, Pittsburgh's ancients couldn't avoid the injury report last year, ending with 26.6 AGL, which was sixth-most among defensive front sevens. Among the six players who contributed to that total, only LaMarr Woodley, who missed six games with a hamstring injury, was younger than 33 years old. Naturally, Pittsburgh commenced with a youth movement during the offseason by releasing the two oldest members of their front seven, inside linebacker James Farrior (36 years old) and defensive end Aaron Smith (35), and drafting an immediate replacement for the third-oldest, nose tackle Casey Hampton (34), who will likely start 2012 on the PUP list after undergoing another ACL surgery. Hampton's heir-apparent, fourth-round pick Alameda Ta'amu (Washington), is an absolute mountain of space-eating humanity (6-foot-3, 348 pounds) ideally suited to be the zero-technique nose tackle that's been a staple of Pittsburgh's defense seemingly forever. Questions about Ta'amu's inconsistency, playing smaller than his size, and lack of success against elite competition are why his draft stock fell so far, but the environment of accountability in Pittsburgh, and practicing against DeCastro for the next few years, should allay those fears. Steve McClendon, who started one game in Hampton's absence last season, provides depth at the nose if Ta'amu falters for whatever reason.

25-year-old Evander "Ziggy" Hood will officially take the reins at left defensive end after starting 21 of the past 25 games. Hood has gotten a lot of positive press since the Steelers selected him in the first round of the 2009 draft, but his advanced stats aren't so great, and Pittsburgh opponents racked up a ton of ALY running in his direction last year. Of course, in this defensive scheme, it's the linebackers who have primary playmaking responsibilities, so we should probably cut Hood some slack. Same goes for the other starting end, Brett Keisel, who has posted a similar statistical profile to Hood's over the past two years. Keisel will be 34 years old in 2012, and hasn't played a full season since 2007, so the Cameron Heyward era may arrive sooner than expected. Heyward got the typical Steelers rookie-redshirt treatment in 2011, but his role will expand this season. His scouting report coming out college read a lot like Ta'amu's: technically sound with prototypical size for his position, but shows inconsistent effort, plays small, and doesn't stand out against elite competition.

Veteran Larry Foote will reprise his role as starting Will linebacker after the Steelers released Farrior, their longtime defensive captain. The 32-year-old Foote is likely just a caretaker at the position until 2012 third-round pick Sean Spence (Miami) is finished putting in his mandatory time on special teams. Mike linebacker Lawrence Timmons saw his advanced stats decline slightly last season, but he remains a young, Pro-Bowl-caliber building block for the foreseeable future. (He's signed through 2016.) On the outside, there's not a better pass-rushing 3-4 duo in the league better than James Harrison and LaMarr Woodley, so it's no surprise that Pittsburgh's ASR dropped in a season where they missed a total of 11 games. If Harrison and Woodley were to miss time again this year, the Steelers are in good hands with backup Jason Worilds, who started seven games in the duo's absence and nearly led the entire unit in quarterback hurries. 2010 fifth-round pick Stevenson Sylvester, who started one game in place of Farrior last season, is the primary backup on the inside, and 2011 redshirt recipient Chris Carter will provide additional depth outside.

Defensive Secondary

Secondary	Age	Pos	Plays	TmPct	Rk	Stop	Dfts	BTkl	Runs	St%	Rk	Yds	Rk	Tgts	Tgt%	Rk	Dist	Suc%	Rk	APaYd	Rk	PD	Int
Ryan Clark	33	FS	105	13.9%	4	39	12	8	55	47%	18	5.8	17	30	6.9%	40	10.0	60%	25	6.5	15	5	1
Troy Polamalu	31	SS	105	13.9%	4	54	26	11	47	62%	4	4.4	3	46	10.7%	9	8.1	59%	33	6.4	12	13	2
William Gay*	27	CB	73	9.7%	19	36	14	4	21	57%	12	5.1	13	74	17.2%	42	10.3	53%	39	6.2	16	12	2
Ike Taylor	32	CB	56	7.4%	55	26	9	4	11	36%	52	7.9	52	94	21.9%	9	13.5	61%	16	5.4	6	15	2
Keenan Lewis	26	CB	40	5.3%	77	11	6	0	4	50%	27	5.8	21	47	11.0%	78	11.2	41%	77	7.5	44	6	1
Ryan Mundy	27	SS	25	3.3%	--	10	3	3	12	58%	--	4.8	--	12	2.7%	--	9.2	48%	--	6.2	--	1	1

Year	Pass D Rank	vs. #1 WR	Rk	vs. #2 WR	Rk	vs. Other WR	Rk	vs. TE	Rk	vs. RB	Rk
2009	14	8.3%	18	-6.0%	12	-3.5%	11	21.7%	26	-6.3%	11
2010	2	-18.5%	4	-23.3%	3	0.2%	18	-9.7%	5	2.0%	15
2011	3	-5.5%	8	-9.9%	10	-0.8%	20	-6.9%	4	-5.1%	14

Pittsburgh repeated as a top-three pass defense last season, and much of the credit goes to Ike Taylor, who was far and away the team's best cornerback according to advanced stats even though he was often shadowing the opponent's No. 1 wide receiver and opposing quarterbacks had no reservations about throwing his way. However, the secondary once again struggled (by Pittsburgh standards) with "other" receivers, and part of the reason was third-year corner Keenan Lewis being thrust into the nickel role after William Gay replaced the banished Bryant McFadden as a starter. The curious thing about Lewis' 2011 season, however, is that, although his coverage success rate was among the worst in the league, he ranked No. 1 in YAC allowed, and didn't have a broken tackle all season. That statistical profile runs contrary to his scouting reports coming out of Oregon State, which cited tackling as one of his biggest weaknesses. With the departures of Gay (who signed with Arizona) and McFadden (currently a free agent), Lewis will start in 2012, and a pair of 2011 draft picks, Cortez Allen and Curtis Brown, will take over nickel and dime duties, respectively. Allen saw limited action last season because the Steelers preferred using three safeties in their dime package, and Brown didn't play a single defensive snap before ending the year on injured reserve. Allen's size and strength are well suited for the perimeter and Brown's athleticism is well suited for the slot, but their lack of experience might lead to a threepeat of Pittsburgh's "other wideouts" problem.

It's hard to argue with Terrell Suggs winning the award last season, but Troy Polamalu was even better in 2011 than when he won Defensive Player of the Year in 2010. He had seven more Defeats than in 2010, his success rate in coverage was up 15 percent, and, most importantly, he played all 16 games—all while maintaining an elite run stop rate. Besides an injury lurking behind every kamikaze attack, the only cause for concern with Polamalu is that, after only one broken tackle in 2009, he's had more than any other Steelers defender over the past two seasons (18). For the second year in a row, Ryan Clark was surprisingly active (and efficient) in run defense for a free safety, and his success rate in coverage returned to 2009 levels after a down year in 2010. Third safety Ryan Mundy was an easy scapegoat in Pittsburgh's soul-crushing playoff loss to Denver, but the Steelers' failure to adjust out of Cover-0 after getting torched by Demaryius Thomas for much of the final three quarters was just as much to blame. Pittsburgh might not have even made it to overtime if not for Mundy's forced fumble in the fourth quarter, which set up the game-tying touchdown.

Special Teams

Year	DVOA	Rank	FG/XP	Rank	Net Kick	Rank	Kick Ret	Rank	Net Punt	Rank	Punt Ret	Rank	Hidden	Rank
2009	-4.1%	30	2.3	14	-34.7	32	5.0	8	4.7	8	-1.3	18	-3.4	22
2010	0.4%	16	-1.9	23	-2.1	20	3.8	13	8.7	5	-6.3	28	-6.3	23
2011	1.5%	9	-7.3	29	8.0	4	-1.1	19	4.5	10	4.6	8	-9.0	28

In two seasons under coordinator Al Everest, Pittsburgh's special teams have gone from a joke to a downright team strength. The biggest success story has been in kickoff coverage, where the Steelers showed continued improvement in 2011 despite Shaun Suisham ranking 22nd in touchback percentage (38.9 percent). Pittsburgh ranked in the top ten for net punting value for the third straight season despite Daniel Sepulveda's knee buckling as frequently as a New York driving instructor. The Steelers finally cut the cord, and will go into 2012 with either Jeremy Kapinos or undrafted free agent Drew Butler as their punter. There was no dropoff when Kapinos replaced Sepulveda in Week 9, but he's more booty call to Pittsburgh than marriage material. At Georgia, Butler was First-Team All-America in both 2009 and 2010. Antonio Brown took over primary kick and punt return duties, finishing ninth (27.3) and 10th (10.8), respectively, in average yards per return.

Coaching Staff

Pittsburgh chose not to retain offensive coordinator Bruce Arians because of "philosophical differences," even though what he deserved was a raise. According to DVOA, Pittsburgh had a top 10 offense in four out of five seasons with Arians at the helm. Unfortunately for him, the front office paid more attention to the fact that the 2008 championship season was his only offense not in the top 10. They probably also noticed that 2008 was the only year in Arians' tenure in which Pittsburgh's run offense was more efficient than its pass offense. To us stat geeks, and almost every other NFL team, those are good things. To the Steelers in 2012, they're fireable offenses (pun intended). Even giving Pittsburgh's front office full benefit of the doubt based on their track record, the man they chose as Arians' replacement, former Kansas City head coach Todd Haley, is hardly known for his smashmouth style. Haley, of course, is the guy who never saw a four-wide passing play he didn't like in Arizona, and drove Charlie Weis out of the NFL because he had the audacity to call an offense that ranked No. 1 in run-pass ratio. Even Ben Roethlisberger doesn't seem to understand how things will change. Luckily, no matter what Haley does, the Steelers still have Dick LeBeau, who will continue his reign as the longest-tenured coordinator in the league. At 74 years old, though, it's a wonder how much longer that will last. Linebackers coach Keith Butler is waiting in the wings, and the Steelers have fought tooth-and-nail to keep him on board as LeBeau's successor.

St. Louis Rams

2011 Record: 2-14

Pythagorean Wins: 2.3 (32nd)

DVOA: -35.4% (32nd)

Offense: -27.2% (32nd)

Defense: 3.4% (21st)

Special Teams: -4.8% (28th)

Variance: 9.4% (8th)

2012 Mean Projection: 4.9 wins

On the Clock (0-4): 42%

Mediocrity (5-7): 50%

Playoff Contender (8-10): 8%

Super Bowl Contender (11+): 0%

Postseason Odds: 5.2%

Projected Average Opponent: -1.7% (23rd)

2011: "Son, your potential is going to get me fired."

2012: Could you kids please try tearing fewer ligaments this year? Thanks.

Life was good for the Rams on Christmas weekend of 2010. They were tied for first place in the NFC West, and held the head-to-head tiebreaker over Seattle by virtue of a 20-3 Week 4 win. Next up on the schedule was a home game against 5-9 San Francisco, which was coming off of a 34-7 loss at San Diego the previous week. Against the 49ers, St. Louis came back from a 14-12 halftime deficit to win 25-17. Amid the glow of that victory, which only got brighter after Seattle lost later in the day, little did they know 10 months would pass before their next win.

The victory that broke the Rams' subsequent seven-game losing streak came at home against the Saints in Week 8 of last season. New Orleans had beaten Indianapolis 62-7 the previous week to go 5-2 on the year, so St. Louis' improbable 31-21 win, coming on Halloween weekend against the only NFL team even tangentially associated with black magic, must have felt like an exorcism of sorts for the Rams.

Unfortunately, the good times didn't roll. The following week, St. Louis blew a 13-6 fourth-quarter lead at Arizona after Josh Brown missed a game-winning 42-yard field goal at the end of regulation, and Patrick Peterson returned a punt 99 yards for a touchdown 90 seconds into overtime. The week after, despite a hard-fought 13-12 win at Cleveland, the Rams lost second-year left tackle Rodger Saffold to a torn pectoral. Another seven-game losing streak ensued, and St. Louis heads into 2012 once again 10 months between regular season wins.

To suggest that Saffold's injury precipitated the Rams' 0-7 finish would be an oversimplification, but a lack of overall health did play a major role over the course of the season. In 2011, St. Louis had a league-high 110.0 Adjusted Games Lost (AGL), the equivalent of losing seven key players for the year in training camp. Only one previous team in our database, which goes back to 2002, had experienced a rash of injuries that bad: the 2009 Buffalo Bills (122.8).

On offense, the Rams' sign-of-the-beast 66.6 AGL was the highest in the NFL last year (a repeat performance) and the highest in our database. Ironically, even though Steven Jackson got hurt on his first run of the season, running back was the only offensive position group that stayed relatively healthy. Injuries to Saffold, his replacement Mike LeVoir, right tackle Jason Smith, and left guard Jacob Bell produced the fifth-highest AGL among offensive lines (24.3). Injuries to quarterback Sam Bradford forced backup A.J. Feeley to make three starts, and injuries to Feeley forced third-stringer Kellen Clemens to make another three starts.

The hardest-hit group, however, was the pass catchers. Their 35.7 AGL was the highest in the NFL for a second straight year, and the highest in our injury database. Slot receiver Danny Amendola dislocated

2012 Rams Schedule

Week	Opp.	Week	Opp.	Week	Opp.
1	at DET	7	GB	13	SF
2	WAS	8	NE (U.K.)	14	at BUF
3	at CHI	9	BYE	15	MIN
4	SEA	10	at SF	16	at TB
5	ARI (Thu.)	11	NYJ	17	at SEA
6	at MIA	12	at ARI		

Figure 1. 2011 St. Louis DVOA by Week

his elbow in Week 1 and then tore his triceps during practice when he was preparing to return in Week 6. Greg Salas broke his right leg in Week 9, and Danario Alexander dealt with a hamstring injury in midseason. At tight end, Lance Kendricks endured foot and concussion issues, and "Illinois Mike" Hoomanawanui landed on injured reserve in Week 11.

The Rams defense ranked 27th in the NFL with 43.5 AGL. However, while the offensive injuries were spread across position groups, the vast majority of St. Louis's defensive injuries were in the secondary (36.6 AGL), mainly at cornerback. In Week 1, the Rams started Bradley Fletcher and Ron Bartell, with Al Harris in nickel. By the start of their losing streak in Week 11, the top three corners were Justin King, Josh Gordy, and Rod Hood. In that light, it's a minor football miracle St. Louis managed a middle-of-the-pack 3.6% pass defense DVOA over their final seven games.

As valiant as that effort was, the accumulation of injuries over time proved too big an obstacle to overcome. Splitting out AGL by week, it's apparent that a lack of health made the Rams' seven-game losing streak almost inevitable. Heading into their first nine games, St. Louis had, on average, a 0.9 AGL disadvantage against their opponents. Missing one more key player than the other team isn't insurmountable. However, in their 0-7 stretch to close the season, St. Louis averaged a 5.7 AGL disadvantage. In other words, they were playing 22-on-16, and this actually understates the problem because the team's most important player, Bradford, missed six games despite never actually being listed as "out."

Normally, an injury epidemic like this would be a reason for optimism in the coming season, but over the last few years, the Rams' training room has been about as busy as Pappy's Smokehouse. From 2007 to 2011, the Rams accumulated 401.5 AGL, which was the highest total of any team; they finished last in AGL twice in that five-year period, and never higher than 21st. Even more troubling is the fact that St. Louis's five-year run of injuries has persisted through personnel changes of all sorts, including two head coaches, two general managers, and two head trainers. After averaging 78.2 AGL in the final three years with long-time head athletic trainer Jim Anderson, they've averaged 83.4 AGL in two years with Reggie Scott in that role. For their two most-injured position groups, maintaining health over the past five seasons has been like playing a marathon game of Whac-A-Mole; seven different linemen and eight different pass catchers have finished the season on IR. Injury totals generally regress towards the mean, but there's no doubt that some teams have a better record of health than other teams, and with a profile like this, the Rams simply can't count on a large health-powered rebound.

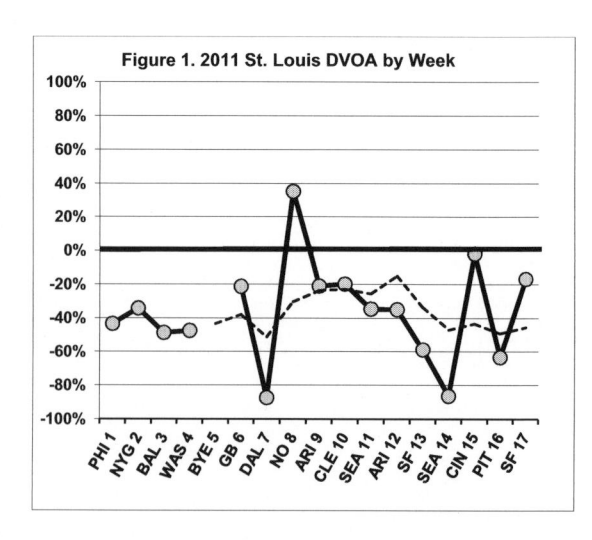

However, there is another factor in last year's 2-14 disaster that does suggest improvement in 2012: strength of schedule. In 2011, St. Louis became the first team in DVOA history (1991-2011) to go from the easiest schedule one season to the hardest schedule the next (Table 1). Before last season, the worst one-year increase in strength of schedule belonged to the 1999 Broncos. Denver had ridden the third-easiest schedule (in a 30-team league) to a Lombardi Trophy in 1998, only to fall apart the next season under the weight of John Elway's retirement, Terrell Davis' Week 4 injury, and—oh, by the way—the toughest schedule in the league.

On average, the 10 teams since 1991 with the biggest year-to-year rise in strength of schedule had 4.1 fewer wins when they had to run a much tougher gauntlet. In that context, the Rams five-loss increase doesn't look so bad. Even better news is that nine of these 10 teams had an easier schedule the following season, and those nine saw an average rebound of 3.4 wins. Our mean projection has St. Louis with the No. 23 schedule in 2012.

The Rams' 2011 schedule wasn't just hard; it was also front-loaded. The average DVOA of their first seven opponents was 12.0%, with games against the entire NFC East as well as the Packers and the team that improbably ended their losing streak, the Saints. The only other team with a similarly difficult schedule through Week 8 was Jacksonville (average opponent: 11.9% DVOA), and they went 2-6 during that period. Basically, the schedule killed the Rams for the first half of the season, and injuries put the nail in their coffin thereafter.

The lockout also hurt the Rams more than most teams. Specifically, they were the only team in the league that hired a new offensive coordinator to *expand* their offense into more of a complex scheme. Rob Chudzinski's offense was certainly more complicated than what Cam Newton ran at Auburn, but that was going to be an issue no matter whether the Panthers hired a new coordinator or not. Mike McCoy, Bill Musgrave, Greg Roman, and Pat Shurmur brought offenses to their new teams that were simpler than what was in place before. Josh McDaniels, however, was tasked with bringing a heady, wide-open passing game to St. Louis. To boot, given McDaniels' track record with quarterbacks, head coach Steve Spagnuolo chose not to replace quarterbacks coach Dick Curl when he retired to a life of that's-what-she-said jokes shortly after the 2010 season ended. Given that the Rams' offensive starters heading into 2011 were the NFL's sixth-youngest at 26.7 years old, the combination of offensive coaching changes and a shortened offseason contributed to the Rams starting the season behind the eight-ball.

After the debacle of 2011, St. Louis fired Spagnuolo and hired Jeff Fisher, who, along with new general manager Les Snead, will helm the Rams' third rebuilding project in seven years. The duo of Spagnuolo and previous general manager Bill Devaney produced a 10-38 record over the past three seasons after the trio of Jay Zygmunt, Scott Linehan, and Jim Haslett went 13-35 from 2006 to 2008. In other words, the bar is set incredibly low.

By season's end, it was apparent among fans that Spagnuolo needed to go, but this was a team that had given Linehan a second chance after going 3-13 in 2007, and had already given Spagnuolo a second chance after his first year ended at 1-15. Anything was possible, especially considering the ready-made excuses detailed earlier.

If recent NFL history is any indication, though, St. Louis seems to have (finally) made the right move. Excluding the expansion Cleveland Browns, 30 teams had a record of 3-13 or worse from 1992 (which preceded the first offseason of free agency) through 2008. Nineteen of them chose to fire their head coach after the season, whereas the other 11 gave him another shot despite the record. Over the subsequent three seasons after their "fish or cut bait" decision, the "cut bait" teams won 44.6 percent of the time under their new head coach, whereas the "fish" teams won only 34.3 percent of the time. Amazingly, that's a statistically significant difference despite the small sample sizes.

When a team held onto a head coach following a

Table 1. Largest Year-to-Year Increase in Strength of Schedule, 1991-2011

Team	Year	Sched Rk	W-L	Year	Sched Rk	W-L	Year	Sched Rk	W-L
STL	2010	32	7-9	2011	1	2-14	2012	??	??
DEN	1998	28	14-2	1999	1	6-10	2000	30	11-5
TB	2005	30	11-5	2006	3	4-12	2007	30	9-7
MIA	2008	29	11-5	2009	3	7-9	2010	3	7-9
NE	2001	29	11-5	2002	4	9-7	2003	10	14-2
NYJ	1991	26	8-8	1992	1	4-12	1993	24	8-8
SD	1992	28	11-5	1993	4	8-8	1994	22	11-5
NO	1997	28	6-10	1998	4	6-10	1999	22	3-13
JAC	2002	28	6-10	2003	4	5-11	2004	10	9-7
CLE	2007	25	10-6	2008	1	4-12	2009	15	5-11
TB	2008	25	9-7	2009	1	3-13	2010	25	10-6

season with three or fewer wins, another person ended up coaching, on average, 39.8 percent of the team's games in the following three seasons. Only two coaches were able to complete three additional seasons with their teams, let alone reverse their fortunes: Jim Mora, Sr., who went 29-19 with the Colts from 1999 to 2001 (thanks, Peyton), and Norval Turner, who went 23-25 with the Redskins from 1995 to 1997. The other 10 incumbents who were retained following a 3-13 or worse season only won 25.7 percent of their remaining games.

The bottom line here is that the vast majority of NFL teams—about 95 percent, to be exact—win more than three games in a season. Almost everything conceivable has to go wrong for a team to be that bad, and among conceivable things is the head coach. So when a team finds itself in that situation, recent NFL history suggests it's better off pulling the trigger on a head coaching change than hoping for the best with a dead man walking. That is, unless he has a long track record of previous success like Jim Mora, the quarterback is like Peyton Manning, and the horrible season came in that quarterback's rookie year.

So now that we've established that St. Louis was correct to fire Spagnuolo, what have Fisher and Snead done with the roster to turn things around? In short, a lot, especially on defense. Of the 44 players currently in the top two spots of each position on the depth chart, 23 weren't even on the team last season.

On offense, although the Rams signed center Scott Wells and right guard Harvey Dahl to start along the line, most of the personnel changes involved prospects acquired in April's draft. Second-round pick Isaiah Pead is Steven Jackson's heir apparent, and the team is hoping fifth-rounder Rokevious Watkins will assume the starting left guard spot sooner rather than later. At wideout, St. Louis selected Brian Quick in the second round and Chris Givens in the fourth round. Given the Rams' perennial injury issues at wide receiver, the Givens pick—he tore both ACLs in high school—makes you wonder if the team needs a lesson in self-awareness.

The overhaul on defense is even more significant, but to the Rams' credit, the five holdovers who will start in 2012 were their five most-talented defenders: defensive ends Chris Long and Robert Quinn, middle linebacker James Laurinaitis, and safeties Quintin Mikell and Darian Stewart. To that group, St. Louis bolstered their secondary by signing Fisher favorite Cortland Finnegan via free agency and drafting Janoris Jenkins in the second round. At defensive tackle, first-round pick Michael Brockers and a pair of free agents (Kendall Langford and Trevor Laws) are the anchors expected to provide an improvement on last year's 27th-ranked run defense.

In the end, though, the team's ultimate fate will lie in the hands of Fisher's first acquisition in St. Louis, new offensive coordinator Brian Schottenheimer. Son-of-Marty's primary task will be to turn Bradford into an efficient NFL quarterback, something he hasn't been in his first two seasons. The jury's still out on Schotty Jr. as a quarterback whisperer, though, because the best DVOA ranking for a quarterback playing in his offense was Chad Pennington finishing 13th in 2006. The past five years, his quarterbacks have ranked no higher than 25th.

There are a lot of reasons to believe the Rams should be better this year: the return of tackles Saffold and Smith, a slightly easier schedule, defensive acquisitions, a full offseason to install schemes, and the simple fact that it is pretty darn difficult to go 2-14 two years in a row. However, a 4-12 or 5-11 season won't get anyone excited unless it is led by development from Bradford. Fisher's two rebuilding projects in Houston/Tennessee each took five years to come to fruition, so 2012 will likely be a transitional year marking the first step towards that end. But in 2016: Look out!

Danny Tuccitto

ST. LOUIS RAMS

2011 Rams Stats by Week

Wk	vs.	W-L	PF	PA	YDF	YDA	TO	Total	Off	Def	ST
1	PHI	L	13	31	335	403	0	-43%	-11%	25%	-7%
2	@NYG	L	16	28	367	323	-1	-34%	-28%	3%	-3%
3	BAL	L	7	37	244	553	-1	-49%	-15%	30%	-4%
4	WAS	L	10	17	172	339	1	-47%	-57%	-11%	-2%
5	BYE										
6	@GB	L	3	24	424	399	0	-21%	-17%	7%	2%
7	@DAL	L	7	34	265	445	-1	-87%	-53%	36%	1%
8	NO	W	31	21	323	283	1	35%	-21%	-53%	3%
9	@ARI	L	13	19	383	262	-1	-21%	-12%	-15%	-23%
10	@CLE	W	13	12	281	335	-1	-20%	-12%	18%	10%
11	SEA	L	7	24	185	289	-1	-35%	-53%	-24%	-5%
12	ARI	L	20	23	272	374	1	-35%	-38%	-7%	-5%
13	@SF	L	0	26	157	389	-2	-59%	-56%	3%	0%
14	@SEA	L	13	30	281	359	0	-86%	-32%	34%	-21%
15	CIN	L	13	20	305	283	1	-2%	-9%	-30%	-23%
16	@PIT	L	0	27	232	377	1	-63%	-27%	26%	-10%
17	SF	L	27	34	311	321	-2	-17%	-9%	17%	9%

Trends and Splits

	Offense	Rank	Defense	Rank
Total DVOA	-27.2%	32	3.4%	21
Unadjusted VOA	-29.2%	32	8.8%	25
Weighted Trend	-27.6%	32	1.1%	15
Variance	5.5%	8	4.8%	7
Average Opponent	-2.7%	4	1.6%	12
Passing	-27.4%	31	2.8%	14
Rushing	-11.5%	28	4.0%	27
First Down	-24.9%	30	-2.3%	13
Second Down	-15.6%	26	6.2%	22
Third Down	-47.1%	32	10.3%	23
First Half	-26.3%	31	-3.7%	13
Second Half	-28.0%	30	11.0%	28
Red Zone	-71.3%	32	5.3%	23
Late and Close	-36.5%	32	6.9%	26

Five-Year Performance

Year	W-L	Pyth	Est W	PF	PA	TO	Total	Rk	Off	Rk	Def	Rk	ST	Rk	Off AGL	Rk	Def AGL	Rk
2007	3-13	3.5	1.8	263	438	-10	-35.5%	32	-22.7%	31	8.2%	26	-4.7%	27	52.4	32	27.4	24
2008	2-14	2.5	1.6	232	465	-5	-47.1%	31	-28.2%	32	18.3%	30	-0.6%	20	50.3	30	29.9	21
2009	1-15	1.6	0.9	175	436	-13	-45.1%	31	-29.5%	32	17.2%	31	1.7%	11	38.4	27	36.3	23
2010	7-9	6.8	5.4	289	328	+5	-19.4%	28	-18.1%	30	2.1%	19	0.8%	14	47.1	32	9.7	4
2011	2-14	2.3	2.2	193	407	-5	-35.4%	32	-27.2%	32	3.4%	21	-4.8%	28	66.6	32	43.5	27

2011 Performance Based on Most Common Personnel Groups

St. Louis Offense				St. Louis Offense vs. Opp.				St. Louis Defense				St. Louis Defense vs. Opp.			
Pers	Freq	Yds	DVOA	Run%	Pers	Freq	Yds	DVOA	Pers	Freq	Yds	DVOA	Pers	Freq	Yds	DVOA
11	47%	4.8	-21.1%	23%	4-3-4	25%	5.0	-5.7%	4-3-4	57%	6.0	6.4%	11	32%	6.0	5.3%
12	32%	4.9	-11.0%	46%	3-4-4	24%	4.3	-22.7%	4-2-5	21%	5.3	-8.4%	12	21%	6.7	11.5%
22	6%	3.5	-28.0%	83%	4-2-5	20%	4.7	-22.0%	Dime+	20%	5.6	-1.8%	21	19%	7.0	22.1%
13	6%	3.8	-29.0%	73%	2-4-5	18%	5.0	-17.9%	G-line	1%	0.9	10.0%	22	13%	4.1	-19.0%
21	5%	3.9	-33.1%	48%	3-3-5	11%	3.6	-50.2%	3-3-5	1%	12.0	110.0%	10	3%	4.9	9.5%

Note: Run%: Runs excluding penalties. Pers: personnel groups are WR-RB-TE or DL-LB-DB. Yds: yards per play.

Strategic Tendencies

Run/Pass		Rank	Offense		Rank	Pass Rush		Rank	Defense/Other		Rank
Runs, all plays	40%	22	Form: Single Back	78%	3	Rush 3	5.2%	20	4 DB	57%	5
Runs, first half	43%	15	Form: Empty Back	6%	13	Rush 4	66.1%	13	5 DB	22%	30
Runs, first down	48%	23	Pers: 3+ WR	50%	19	Rush 5	16.7%	26	6+ DB	20%	7
Runs, second-long	33%	18	Pers: 4+ WR	3%	15	Rush 6+	12.0%	5	CB by Sides	67%	25
Runs, power sit.	46%	27	Pers: 2+ TE/6+ OL	45%	7	Zone Blitz	11.4%	1	Go for it on 4th	1.24	1
Runs, behind 2H	32%	11	Play action	24%	4	Sacks by LB	12.8%	24	Offensive Pace	29.1	4
Pass, ahead 2H	46%	9	Max protect	14%	7	Sacks by DB	12.8%	6	Defensive Pace	30.5	18

The Rams led the league in zone blitzes, with James Hall the most likely lineman to drop into coverage. Chris Long also dropped into coverage roughly once per game. ☙ St. Louis forced 18 fumbles on defense and only recovered five of them. Rams opponents threw 28 percent of passes to their No. 1 receivers, the highest rate in the league. The Rams defense had the best DVOA in the league against passes marked as "short middle." The Rams' low rank in "CB by Sides" comes from the fact that their top two cornerbacks, Justin King and Josh Gordy, are both listed in coverage for more receivers on the offensive right than on the offensive left. St. Louis forced the opposing quarterback out of the pocket on a league-high 18 percent of pass plays. The Rams offense was third in the league with an average of 10.9 yards after catch on passes behind the line of scrimmage, but tied for last with an average of 3.3 yards after catch on passes past the line of scrimmage.

Passing

Player	DYAR	DVOA	Plays	NtYds	Avg	YAC	C%	TD	Int
S.Bradford	-329	-24.2%	396	1884	4.9	4.5	53.7%	6	6
A.Feeley*	-192	-40.7%	107	477	4.5	7.1	54.6%	1	2
K.Clemens	-6	-12.0%	100	466	5.1	3.9	53.3%	2	1

Rushing

Player	DYAR	DVOA	Plays	Yds	Avg	TD	Fum	Suc
S.Jackson	64	-2.3%	259	1146	4.4	5	1	39%
C.Williams*	52	6.2%	87	361	4.1	1	0	41%
J.Norwood*	-15	-27.8%	24	61	2.5	0	0	13%
S.Bradford	-25	-58.6%	9	42	4.7	0	1	--
K.Clemens	3	-3.0%	6	36	6.0	1	1	--
Brit Miller	-4	-24.8%	5	14	2.8	0	0	40%

Receiving

Player	DYAR	DVOA	Plays	Ctch	Yds	Y/C	YAC	TD	C%
B.Lloyd*	-16	-14.5%	116	51	683	13.4	1.8	5	44%
B.Gibson	7	-11.3%	71	36	431	12.0	2.9	1	51%
D.Alexander	1	-12.4%	60	26	431	16.6	5.1	2	43%
A.Pettis	-39	-22.9%	48	27	256	9.5	3.5	0	56%
G.Salas	-64	-36.0%	38	27	265	9.8	8.1	0	71%
M.Sims-Walker*	-54	-37.9%	27	11	139	12.6	2.9	0	41%
D.Amendola	13	12.7%	6	5	45	9.0	5.0	0	83%
S.Smith	-5	-16.0%	20	11	124	11.3	3.0	1	55%
L.Kendricks	-72	-27.2%	58	28	352	12.6	6.6	0	48%
B.Bajema*	-19	-28.7%	14	9	71	7.9	1.9	0	64%
M.Hoomanawanui	-25	-35.4%	13	7	83	11.9	8.7	0	54%
S.Jackson	43	0.1%	58	42	333	7.9	7.4	1	72%
C.Williams*	-40	-42.7%	23	14	97	6.9	6.6	0	61%

Offensive Line

Year	Yards	ALY	Rank	Power	Rank	Stuff	Rank	2nd Lev	Rank	Open Field	Rank	F-Start	Cont.
2009	4.40	3.87	28	56%	30	22%	28	1.34	4	0.88	11	20	27
2010	3.63	3.77	26	58%	19	19%	14	1.03	27	0.51	25	27	37
2011	4.22	3.75	30	48%	31	20%	20	1.25	10	0.72	22	29	27

Year	LE	Rank	LT	Rank	Mid	Rank	RT	Rank	RE	Rank	Sacks	ASR	Rank	Short	Long
2009	4.70	12	5.27	2	3.70	28	3.88	22	2.76	29	44	7.7%	24	23	13
2010	3.55	23	3.75	25	3.62	27	3.69	24	5.91	1	34	5.6%	10	12	14
2011	5.12	4	3.42	28	3.74	26	4.09	23	3.23	22	55	9.1%	28	19	19

With recent highly drafted tackles Rodger Saffold (Indiana) and Jason Smith (Baylor) healthy in 2010, the Rams' offensive line had its best Adjusted Sack Rate since the Greatest Show on Turf, and gave up only 16 blown-block sacks in 642 pass plays. When the duo missed a combined 17 games in 2011, the unit finished 18 spots lower in ASR, and gave up 40 blown-block sacks in 604 pass plays. Injuries regress towards the mean, so everything should be fine in 2012, right? Not exactly. Saffold allowed 9.0 blown block sacks in nine games after allowing only 3.0 in all of 2010. Also, those injuries exposed a lack of depth at tackle, which the Rams nominally addressed by signing former Chiefs turnstile Barry Richardson. Richardson's 7.0 blown block sacks allowed in 2011 were only slightly less than last year's backup, converted guard Adam Goldberg (5.5), although Goldberg started eight fewer games.

Instead, the interior dominated offseason turnover. Harvey Dahl, easily the Rams' best lineman last season, will return to his natural right guard position after starting the final six games at right tackle. St. Louis signed Pro Bowl center Scott Wells (formerly of Green Bay) to replace Jason Brown, who had started 84 consecutive games until he was benched in Week 10. St. Louis also allowed left guard Jacob Bell to leave in free agency, but won't decide on a replacement until training camp. Bryan Mattison, who shuttled on and off of the practice squad before starting four games in a pinch last season, is the current frontrunner, but the current regime sees versatile 2012 fifth-rounder Rokevious Watkins as the long-term answer. In the last two years at South Carolina, Watkins started games at left tackle, right tackle, left guard, and right guard.

Defensive Front Seven

Defensive Line	Age	Pos	Plays	TmPct	Rk	Stop	Dfts	BTkl	St%	Rk	AvYd	Rk	Sack	Hit	Hur	Runs	St%	Yds	Pass	St%	Yds
James Hall*	35	DE	52	6.6%	16	40	14	1	77%	44	1.0	32	6	5	15.5	43	74%	2.2	9	89%	-4.4
Chris Long	27	DE	38	4.5%	50	32	20	5	84%	19	-0.3	9	13	8	33	20	85%	1.7	18	83%	-2.5
Justin Bannan*	33	DT	34	4.3%	32	28	5	0	82%	23	1.8	35	0	1	3	29	83%	1.8	5	80%	2.0
Fred Robbins	35	DT	31	4.0%	38	25	6	1	81%	27	1.6	25	1	1	6	26	85%	1.1	5	60%	4.2
Robert Quinn	22	DE	24	3.1%	75	17	9	1	71%	63	1.4	43	5	6	14	14	64%	3.2	10	80%	-1.2
Darell Scott	26	DT	18	2.6%	--	13	3	1	72%	--	2.6	--	0	0	0	17	71%	2.9	1	100%	-3.0
Gary Gibson*	30	DT	17	2.0%	--	14	5	1	82%	--	0.6	--	3	1	3	12	75%	2.3	5	100%	-3.2
Kendall Langford	26	DE	21	2.6%	--	15	2	1	71%	--	4.0	--	0	2	13.5	17	76%	2.9	4	50%	8.8
Trevor Laws	27	DT	21	3.1%	55	18	6	0	86%	11	2.0	40	1	2	0	16	88%	2.1	5	80%	1.6
William Hayes	27	DE	16	2.9%	--	13	5	1	81%	--	1.3	--	1.5	3	4	14	79%	2.3	2	100%	-6.0

Linebackers	Age	Pos	Plays	TmPct	Rk	Stop	Dfts	BTkl	AvYd	Sack	Hit	Hur	Runs	St%	Rk	Yds	Rk	Tgts	Suc%	Rk	AdjYd	Rk
James Laurinaitis	26	MLB	148	17.7%	7	80	30	2	4.1	3	2	6	103	52%	102	3.8	78	37	69%	4	5.6	18
Chris Chamberlain*	27	OLB	75	9.0%	66	42	10	3	5.4	2	1	4	50	64%	61	4.5	105	17	36%	71	6.5	36
Brady Poppinga*	33	OLB	53	6.8%	97	29	6	5	4.9	0	4	7	36	67%	48	3.6	71	15	45%	--	6.6	--
Jo-Lonn Dunbar	27	OLB	81	10.4%	52	45	8	9	5.1	1	0	5	44	70%	32	2.4	18	28	50%	44	5.2	11
Rocky McIntosh	30	ILB	59	7.9%	84	27	8	7	5.4	1	4	3	34	59%	77	3.8	83	17	34%	77	10.9	78
Mario Haggan	32	MLB	22	2.6%	--	15	4	1	3.2	0	0	0	15	80%	--	1.3	--	3	97%	--	1.2	--

Year	Yards	ALY	Rank	Power	Rank	Stuff	Rank	2nd Lev	Rank	Open Field	Rank
2009	4.36	4.31	23	63%	13	18%	20	1.15	17	0.90	21
2010	4.56	4.07	18	55%	6	21%	11	1.31	28	1.05	29
2011	4.83	4.26	23	55%	8	18%	19	1.21	18	1.26	29

Year	LE	Rank	LT	Rank	Mid	Rank	RT	Rank	RE	Rank	Sacks	ASR	Rank	Short	Long
2009	4.71	23	4.33	20	4.29	24	4.40	24	3.92	15	25	5.4%	27	6	9
2010	5.65	32	3.25	3	3.87	15	3.97	14	3.97	15	43	7.1%	8	20	11
2011	4.42	20	4.79	30	4.28	20	4.34	18	3.02	7	39	7.4%	9	17	16

In Jeff Fisher's final 12 seasons with the Titans, Tennessee's defense had a top 10 Adjusted Sack Rate eight times. And whether it was Jevon Kearse, Kevin Carter, Kyle Vanden Bosch, or Jason Babin, they constantly featured an elite defensive end. So Fisher will feel right at home with St. Louis, where the pass rush features emerging star Chris Long and finished with a top 10 ASR for the second consecutive season. Long ranked fourth in total hurries over the past two seasons (75.5), and his 30.5 sacks through four years exactly matches the beginning of his Hall of Fame father's career. That's either a meaningless statistical oddity or the seventh sign of the apocalypse. (We're not charting 1981-1984 hurries to find out which one.) 2011 first-rounder Robert Quinn (North Carolina) will start at the other end after being a pass-rushing specialist in his rookie season. Quinn has a pair of underrated shoes to fill replacing last year's starter, James Hall, who had 16.5 sacks and 33.5 hurries over the past two seasons. Aside from getting younger (Hall was 34 last year), starting Quinn is a schematic move: Hall dropped into coverage on zone blitzes 31 times last season (fourth in the NFL), but Fisher's defenses rarely zone blitz.

Other than Long, Quinn, and middle linebacker James Laurinaitis, whose statistical profile highly resembles that of Patrick Willis over the past three seasons (high involvement, low run stop rate, high coverage success rate), the

ST. LOUIS RAMS

Rams completely overhauled their starting front seven. At defensive tackle, St. Louis continued their youth movement by replacing 33-year-old Justin Bannan and 35-year-old Fred Robbins with 26-year-old Kendall Langford (formerly of Miami) and 2012 first-round pick Michael Brockers (Louisiana State). Langford wasn't cheap ($5.5 million per year) and will be moving from five-technique end to three-technique tackle, but he was arguably the Dolphins' best run-stopping defensive lineman over the past four years, and has prototypical size for a Fisher tackle. Brockers is more in the mold of Albert Haynesworth, a mountain in the middle with raw pass-rushing skills coaches hope to develop over time. At outside linebacker, St. Louis brought in three new faces via free agency. Jo-Lonn Dunbar is clearly the best of the three, and should be an improvement over last season's outside linebackers, as he was better against both the run and the pass than either Chris Chamberlain or Brady Poppinga in 2011. It's uncertain whether Dunbar will play on the strong side or the weak side, but he'll definitely be in the starting lineup. The other starter will be the winner of a competition between underwhelming veterans Rocky McIntosh and Mario Haggan. After four seasons as a starter in Washington, McIntosh was one of the worst linebackers in the NFL last season, ultimately getting benched after eight games. Haggan was the odd man out in 2011 when Denver switched to a 4-3 defense under John Fox, so he played primarily on special teams. As a starter in 2009 and 2010, he was effective against the run, but rarely got tested in coverage (28 total targets). If Haggan gets the nod, expect him to be a two-down linebacker who leaves the field when St. Louis goes to nickel.

Defensive Secondary

Secondary	Age	Pos	Plays	TmPct	Rk	Stop	Dfts	BTkl	Runs	St%	Rk	Yds	Rk	Tgts	Tgt%	Rk	Dist	Suc%	Rk	APaYd	Rk	PD	Int
Quintin Mikell	32	FS	95	11.4%	27	31	14	12	49	47%	19	7.0	44	27	7.3%	34	15.2	48%	55	8.5	44	4	2
Darian Stewart	24	SS	86	11.0%	30	42	17	19	44	45%	24	6.0	21	34	9.8%	11	9.2	59%	34	5.1	7	10	1
Justin King*	25	CB	63	10.0%	17	23	10	6	23	57%	16	6.1	27	71	25.3%	1	13.1	44%	70	9.7	73	7	1
Craig Dahl	27	FS	52	6.2%	68	16	6	4	23	39%	40	7.6	51	20	5.3%	64	16.3	63%	15	6.8	22	2	1
Josh Gordy	25	CB	47	6.4%	69	14	6	5	11	27%	67	12.5	77	40	12.2%	70	13.0	43%	72	12.3	82	5	3
Rod Hood*	31	CB	24	5.1%	--	14	6	2	8	63%	--	9.4	--	26	12.5%	--	11.2	62%	--	5.1	--	6	1
Bradley Fletcher	26	CB	24	11.5%	--	4	0	1	13	23%	--	10.2	--	19	19.9%	--	13.4	37%	--	7.0	--	1	0
Al Harris*	38	CB	21	4.5%	--	9	4	0	1	100%	--	3.0	--	24	11.3%	--	12.0	72%	--	6.9	--	5	0
Cortland Finnegan	28	CB	86	9.9%	18	43	20	5	25	44%	39	9.8	65	60	12.9%	69	7.7	61%	12	5.0	3	11	1

Year	Pass D Rank	vs. #1 WR	Rk	vs. #2 WR	Rk	vs. Other WR	Rk	vs. TE	Rk	vs. RB	Rk
2009	29	21.0%	29	22.7%	29	12.5%	25	22.8%	28	-15.3%	6
2010	21	-17.0%	5	28.6%	30	7.7%	23	10.0%	18	16.9%	27
2011	15	8.3%	16	6.1%	18	8.5%	26	-11.3%	2	6.9%	22

When a team is starting its fourth- and fifth-string cornerbacks by Week 11, you know they're staring an 0-7 stretch run squarely in the face. Such was the case for St. Louis, which had the second-highest defensive back AGL (36.6) since we've been keeping track. (The 2004 Cleveland Browns' secondary had 40.4 AGL.) Naturally, the new regime cleaned house, allowing longtime starter Ron Bartell and human torch Justin King to leave in free agency, while dreadlock pioneer Al Harris retired. To replace them, St. Louis signed the 2011 league leader in yards allowed per pass (and 2008 first-team All-Pro) Cortland Finnegan, and picked half-baked Janoris Jenkins (Florida via North Alabama) in the second round of April's draft. As with the defensive line, these moves were borne as much out of a philosophy as desperation. In Tennessee, Fisher tended to use two smaller starting corners with a taller nickelback, and you can see him building a similar lineup here. Finnegan and Jenkins are both in the 5-foot-10 range, whereas the top three cornerbacks in 2011 stood at least six feet tall. The Rams retained former starter Bradley Fletcher and drafted Trumaine Johnson (Montana) in the third round, and they'll face off for nickel duties.

St. Louis' top three safeties survived the regime change, and the team didn't add any new competition. Quintin Mikell had a down year statistically after signing a lucrative deal last offseason. The main issue for Mikell is that, after excelling at strong safety in Philadelphia, he's miscast as a free safety in St. Louis. Granted, both Steve Spagnuolo and Jeff Fisher view their safeties as interchangeable, but Mikell has a much bigger impact when he's playing closer to the line of scrimmage. One reason for the position switch was that St. Louis viewed 25-year-old Darian Stewart as their strong safety of the future, and wanted to get him into the starting lineup. Stewart played well in coverage on tight ends last season, but led the league with 19 broken tackles. Craig Dahl, who saw a lot of time in "big nickel" last season, figures to see his role on defense reduced in 2012 because Fisher doesn't employ much nickel.

Special Teams

Year	DVOA	Rank	FG/XP	Rank	Net Kick	Rank	Kick Ret	Rank	Net Punt	Rank	Punt Ret	Rank	Hidden	Rank
2009	1.4%	11	1.5	16	-2.3	21	-6.0	24	13.8	2	1.3	14	-1.6	17
2010	0.5%	14	-2.3	27	2.4	12	-8.8	26	5.6	12	6.0	5	-9.6	26
2011	-4.1%	28	-6.1	26	-0.3	19	-4.4	26	-14.8	31	1.6	13	-4.1	22

With incumbent Josh Brown turning 33 years old and coming off two subpar seasons of field-goal kicking, the Rams drafted Greg Zuerlein (Missouri Western) and cut Brown on the same day. Despite setting an NCAA record for consecutive field goals made (21) last season, and going 9-for-9 beyond 50 yards, the Division II prospect wasn't invited to the combine. If there's one position where being from a small school doesn't matter, it has to be kicker. As Zuerlein put it, "It's you versus the goal post." St. Louis also made a change at punter, preferring to go with Tom Malone, who hasn't kicked a regular-season punt in his fledgling six-year career, over incumbent Donnie Jones, whose performance fell off a cliff in 2011 despite a ton of practice (league-leading 106 punts).

The Rams have handed punt return duties to second-round pick Isaiah Pead (Cincinnati) essentially on the basis of one Senior Bowl MVP performance. Prior to that game, Pead had only returned eight punts in his entire college career, all of which came last season. It's not as if the team has much choice, though, given that both of last year's punt returners (Austin Pettis and Nick Miller) performance-enhanced their way into 2012 suspensions. Whether or not Pead also returns kickoffs is still an open question, but pretty much anything would be better than what the Rams got last year out of Quinn Porter and Jerious Norwood, neither of whom are still with the team.

Coaching Staff

Talk about extremes. In their three hires after Dick Vermeil, St. Louis opted for men who had never previously been head coaches at any level. 112 losses later, the team finally changed tack with Jeff Fisher, who immediately becomes the third-winningest active head coach. Fisher's reputation deteriorated toward the end of his time with Tennessee. In the public's eye, he went from the guy who led the moribund Oilers/Titans franchise to within one yard of an improbable Lombardi trophy to a caricature of mediocrity. Although a 17-year tenure suggests stability, Fisher actually helmed two rebuilding projects in Tennessee, once when he took over in 1994 and again a decade later. The fact that both were successful bodes well for a Rams team that's been trying to rebuild for the past seven years. Both rebuilding projects centered on improving the team's defense, so Fisher hired Gregg Williams in an attempt to rekindle the success they had from 1997 to 2000. One bounty scandal later, Williams is out of the league (possibly for good), and Fisher will go into 2012 without a defensive coordinator. Instead, Fisher set up an ad hoc committee including himself, assistant head coach Dave McGinnis, and defensive backs coach Chuck Cecil. The three coached together in Tennessee from 2004 to 2010, so the strategy might actually work.

Among the rest of the assistants, nepotism and (more) cronyism abounds. There are three sons of well-known head coaches (offensive coordinator Brian Schottenheimer, special teams coordinator John Fassel, and Fisher's own son Brandon as assistant secondary coach); a father-son duo (offensive line coach Paul Boudreau, Sr., and assistant special teams coach Paul Boudreau, Jr.); and a slew of others who coached with Fisher in Tennessee. Perhaps the most valuable addition, though, is a guy without a famous father or previous ties to Fisher: defensive line coach Mike Wauffle. Prior to riding Richard Seymour to a No. 5 ASR in Oakland last season, he helped turn Osi Umenyiora and Justin Tuck into perennial Pro Bowlers during a five-year stint with the Giants. Wauffle's primary task in St. Louis will be to do the same with Chris Long.

San Diego Chargers

2011 Record: 8-8

Pythagorean Wins: 8.7 (11th)

DVOA: 0.7% (16th)

Offense: 13.0% (5th)

Defense: 10.8% (29th)

Special Teams: -1.6% (23rd)

Variance: 20.8% (28th)

2012 Mean Projection: 6.8 wins

On the Clock (0-4): 15%

Mediocrity (5-7): 48%

Playoff Contender (8-10): 32%

Super Bowl Contender (11+): 5%

Postseason Odds: 17.4%

Projected Average Opponent: 3.9% (3rd)

2011: A team less than the sum of its parts.

2012: It just feels like they're set up for disappointment again, doesn't it?

Quietly, one of the NFL's most impressive multi-year team records came to an end in 2011. For the first time since 2003, the San Diego Chargers finished with fewer than 10.0 Pythagorean Wins. That streak of seven consecutive such seasons was the second-longest in the NFL since the expansion to a 16-game season in 1978, trailing only San Francisco's Brobdignagian streak of 16 consecutive years.

One reason the ending of the streak was so quiet was 2011 didn't feel that much different from 2010, or for that matter 2005 or 2008. In each of those seasons, the Chargers underperformed their Pythagorean record and ended up 8-8 or 9-7. While they snuck into the playoffs in 2008, it was only because the other AFC West teams all had poor seasons.

Still, the Chargers in 2011 were clearly worse than they had been the year prior. In 2010, they were every bit as good as the Super Bowl champion Packers on offense and defense, but were undone by historically bad special teams play. In 2011, the offense was on the whole still very good and the special teams play was mediocre, but the defense collapsed.

That defensive collapse was due in large part to abysmal results on third down. The Chargers allowed the highest percentage of third-down conversions by any team since the 1995 Cleveland Browns. This was not a situation where poor play on first or second down put their opponents in position for easy conversions on third; the Chargers were no better than 30th by defensive DVOA whether it was third-and-short, third-and-medium, or third-and-long.

In another down year for the AFC West, though, the Chargers would have won the division with one more victory. Several unfortunate results prevented them from winning more games. Take, for instance, the Monday night affair in Kansas City, when a botched center snap exchange with a minute to play cost them a shot at a game-winning field-goal attempt and sent the game to overtime. The home loss to the division-winning Broncos was more self-inflicted, as in overtime Norv Turner elected to run into the middle of the line three times before settling for a 53-yard field goal attempt. Nick Novak's attempt predictably went wide and gave the Broncos outstanding field position they converted into a game-winning field goal of their own.

Conventional wisdom has portrayed the Chargers as clear AFC West favorites in each of the last two seasons. Whether Turner's fault or simple bad luck, the Chargers did not make it to the postseason either time, effectively wasting two seasons of one of the top half-dozen or so quarterbacks in the league. We've chronicled Turner's apparent ineptness and consistent streak of underperformance in the past (see *Pro Football Prospectus 2007*). He is one of history's worst head coaches at holding a fourth-quarter lead, and 10 of his 14 teams (including four of five Chargers teams)

2012 Chargers Schedule

Week	Opp.	Week	Opp.	Week	Opp.
1	at OAK (Mon.)	7	BYE	13	CIN
2	TEN	8	at CLE	14	at PIT
3	ATL	9	KC (Thu.)	15	CAR
4	at KC	10	at TB	16	at NYJ
5	at NO	11	at DEN	17	OAK
6	DEN (Mon.)	12	BAL		

Figure 1. 2011 San Diego DVOA by Week

have underperformed their Pythagorean projection. Napoleon with his preference for lucky commanders would long since have dismissed him. With the team's worst results in eight years coming on the heels of an offseason filled with controversial decisions—picking a fight with left tackle Marcus McNeill, drafting consensus third-day pick linebacker Jonas Mouton in the second round—it looked like it might be time for Turner and general manager A.J. Smith to be given their walking papers.

Team President Dean Spanos decided otherwise, though, and then a strange thing happened: The Chargers made a number of very intelligent-seeming moves.

• Problem: Defensive coordinator Greg Manusky was unable to manufacture pressure or camouflage individual weaknesses of the personnel. Solution: Manusky was fired, and longtime linebackers coach John Pagano, who led the defense's strongest unit in 2011, took his place.

• Problem: Beyond Antwan Barnes, the defense struggled to get pressure in 2011. Solution: first-round pick Melvin Ingram, one of the draft's top pass rushers.

• Problem: The defensive line wasn't very good at stopping the run. Solution: second-round pick Kendall Reyes, a three-year starter at Connecticut with the ability to beat a back to the corner on outside runs. He played 3-technique in the Huskies' 4-3 but will move to 5-technique in the Chargers' three-man front.

• Problem: The outside linebacker position was neither very deep nor very stout against the run. Solution: free-agent acquisition Jarret Johnson, who excelled in that role for Pagano's brother Chuck in Baltimore.

• Problem: Left tackle was a major question mark, with Brandyn Dombrowski the only returning player with experience at the position. Solution (Maybe): Jared Gaither, who played well in a late-season stint, was re-signed.

Beyond these problem-solving moves, there was an important non-move: Neither Smith nor Turner picked a fight with or otherwise antagonized a key player. Wide receiver Vincent Jackson was allowed to depart as a free agent, but the Chargers' offense had been pretty productive with him in only a limited role while he was feuding the Smith the last couple seasons, and his production should be replaced by a combination of 2011 third-round pick Vincent Brown and free-agent signing Robert Meachem.

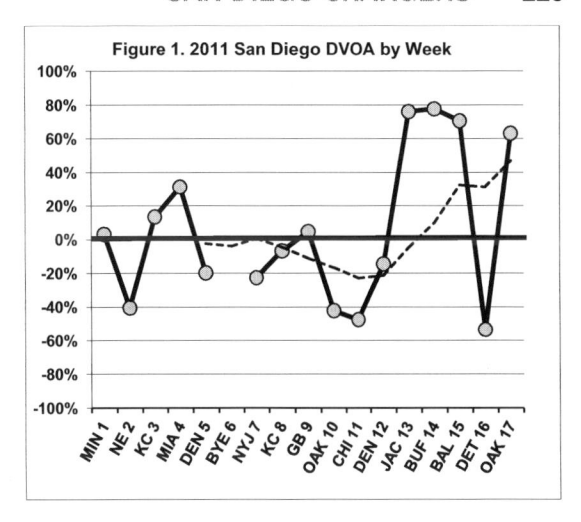

Unfortunately for Pagano, only a limited amount was done to address the Chargers' biggest defensive weakness in 2011, the personnel in the secondary. One of Smith's few good moves in the 2010 offseason was giving free safety Eric Weddle a lucrative contract extension. Beyond him, though, are a lot of question marks. Strong safety Steve Gregory struggled in coverage and was not re-signed. Neither was his backup, Paul Oliver. Smith added Atari Bigby in free agency and Brandon Taylor in the draft, and hopes some combination of the two will prevent quarterbacks from completing lots of passes thrown right to where a safety should be lined up in Cover-2.

The bigger issue lies at cornerback. Antoine Cason, who took a long time to develop into a starter after being a first-round pick, was the relative bright spot notwithstanding a one-game benching for poor play. Mainstay Quentin Jammer was one of the elite few cornerbacks to allow at least ten yards per pass attempt. Rookie Marcus Gilchrist was another in that unfortunate category, and was a particular target for Aaron Rodgers in the home loss to the Packers, allowing seven completions plus a pass interference penalty on the eight plays he was in coverage. Fellow rookie Shareece Wright barely played. Dante Hughes is best suited as a nickelback. Unless Jammer has a career resurgence or Gilchrist and/or Wright make big leaps in their development in their second seasons, Pagano will have to be very creative or hope a much-improved pass rush is able to camouflage the defensive weaknesses.

The broader question is where the Chargers are headed as a franchise. Conventional wisdom has the Chargers as one of the teams poised to be very competitive in what could be a crowded top of the AFC West. The Chargers were one of the best teams in the NFL from 2004 to 2009, going 67-29, but have limped along to a 17-15 record in the past two seasons. With Smith and Turner retained and key players like Philip Rivers, Antonio Gates, and Shaun Phillips returning, plus the offseason moves designed to address immediate weaknesses, San Diego looks like a team that believes it is reloading. Is that a reasonable assumption, though? Have other teams been able to reload with the same core pieces and management?

To try to answer that question, we looked at which teams had followed a similar path and whether there were any historical parallels that might be enlightening. As noted in the introduction, however, the Chargers were in rarified company with at least 10.0 Pythagorean Wins for seven consecutive seasons. Beyond the amazingly consistent 49ers of the '80s and '90s, only three other teams have managed at least 10.0 Pythagorean wins for six consecutive seasons. Even teams that are normally thought of as very good and very consistent, such as the Triplets-era Dallas Cowboys, failed to have that level of consistent success (Table 1).

Unfortunately, Table 1 suggests that once you stop winning, it's very hard to start winning again, especially in the postseason. The Bills, for example, made their fourth and final Super Bowl trip following the 1993 season, had a down year, and then won ten games four of the next five seasons. But they only won one wild card playoff game in that stretch. During that time, the Bills made a coaching change: Wade Phillips succeeded Marv Levy after a down 1997 season, which was also the first season without quarterback Jim Kelly. Philip Rivers is only 31, whereas Kelly was already 34 by the time the Bills began their decline phase. Not the best comparison.

The 49ers are no more enlightening an example. Steve Young helped keep alive an increasingly thin team, and when he was lost for the season early in 1999, shortly before he turned 38, the dynasty was over.

The Cowboys are a difficult comparison, since they came before both the salary cap and free agency.

Table 1. Teams with at Least 10.0 Pythagorean Wins for Six Consecutive Seasons, 1978-2011

Team	Years
Buffalo Bills	1988-1993
Dallas Cowboys	1978-1983 (1982 pro-rated for strike)
New England Patriots	2006-2011 (active)
San Diego Chargers	2004-2010
San Francisco 49ers	1983-1998

Once they entered their decline phase, though, Tom Landry and Tex Schramm continued to stick to their old ways while the rest of the NFL passed them by, and the Cowboys spiraled toward the nadir of 1-15 in 1989. Last offseason was a sign A.J. Smith might have been heading down that same path. While Turner's offense has become staid and predictable after his two decades of top-level NFL experience, most San Diego fans are perfectly happy to take staid and predictable when it ranks in the top five in points scored for five straight years.

The last team on the list is the Patriots, who unfortunately provide no basis for comparison as they're currently in the middle of their streak.

Beyond those examples, it is difficult to find good parallels to the recent run of the Chargers. There are plenty of teams that have watched their win-loss records fluctuate the way San Diego's has the last few years, but those teams didn't have the same underlying consistency in their year-to-year performance. The Monsters of the Midway Bears, for example had seven very good seasons in eight years, but within that time frame they couldn't keep a quarterback healthy, and there's a 6-10 year in the middle of that string of good seasons. After 1991, the Bears went through a period of extended decline where they won no more than nine games a year for nine straight seasons. The '90s Cowboys had four straight great seasons, then two down ones, and then two more good ones before injuries and age meant it was time for a changeover when Aikman was 33 and forced to retire due to concussions.

The most optimistic comparison may be the Favre-era Packers. They had five great seasons, from 1994 through 1998, before that mini-dynasty ended. After a couple down years, they rebounded when Favre was 31, the same age Rivers is now. Just as A.J. Smith has remained in charge in San Diego, Ron Wolf was the man who built the Packers and started the rebuilding process, though he left after the 2002 draft (which would be equivalent to Smith leaving after the 2014 draft). The Packers' down seasons, though, were associated with a change in head coach, as Mike Holmgren departed for Seattle at the conclusion of the five-year run of greatness, replaced first by Ray Rhodes for a season, then by Mike Sherman for a more extended run that saw some success but always ended in disappointment.

The sad thing for Chargers fans is that all of the teams listed above made it to multiple Super Bowls during their streak of success, and most of them won at least one. The Chargers don't even have that to console themselves with. That puts them in particularly unusual company, with only the 1990-93 Houston Oilers in the same ballpark. That Oilers team makes for a depressing example, as a deep and experienced core that had been to the playoffs seven consecutive seasons was blown up in the first year of the salary cap era.

The question for the Chargers is, even if they wanted to rebuild, who would they build around besides Rivers? Gates is still a very good player when healthy, but that's been an increasingly small percentage of the time. He will be 32 this season, and is facing the very harsh aging curve experienced by all tight ends save Tony Gonzalez and Shannon Sharpe. (Since 1978, only nine tight ends have put up seasons of 50 receptions at age 32 or older, and only Gonzalez and Sharpe did it more than once.) Shaun Phillips had a mediocre season in 2011 and, at age 31, is on the downside of his career as well. Ryan Mathews had a promising second season, but has yet to be healthy for a full year—and a dominant running back can't carry a team these days anyway. Neither Meachem nor Malcom Floyd is a top-level receiver who dramatically alters the opposing game plan. Weddle is the Chargers' best defensive player, but it's hard to build a team around a safety and 2011 showed that even with an All-Pro safety you can have a bad pass defense.

No, unless Rivers sees his performance collapse, this incarnation of the Chargers has not yet reached its conclusion. Whether or not A.J. Smith is the right person to be the general manager, the Chargers' best hope for the short- and long-term is to rebuild on the fly and hope they can replicate the peaks and mini-troughs the post-2000 Favre Packers experienced. That's exactly what Smith did this offseason, and it looks like the right move. If only Norv Turner could have the lucky season that's eluded him his entire career, the Chargers could return to the upper echelon of the NFL, win the Super Bowl, and the past eight years of frustration could be forgiven. More likely, though, a still-leaky pass defense and losing two or three games they have no business losing will leave the Chargers on the outside of the playoffs looking in. In that case, expect a similar theme from the Chargers' chapter in *Football Outsiders Almanac 2013*.

Tom Gower

2011 Chargers Stats by Week

Wk	vs.	W-L	PF	PA	YDF	YDA	TO	Total	Off	Def	ST
1	MIN	W	24	17	407	187	-1	3%	-4%	-29%	-21%
2	@NE	L	21	35	470	504	-4	-40%	0%	37%	-4%
3	KC	W	20	17	375	252	-1	14%	10%	-11%	-7%
4	MIA	W	26	16	411	248	2	31%	23%	-2%	7%
5	@DEN	W	29	24	418	275	-1	-20%	-3%	17%	0%
6	BYE										
7	@NYJ	L	21	27	268	318	0	-23%	0%	20%	-2%
8	@KC	L	20	23	447	341	0	-7%	-18%	-5%	6%
9	GB	L	38	45	460	368	-3	5%	20%	18%	3%
10	OAK	L	17	24	314	489	0	-42%	-10%	19%	-13%
11	@CHI	L	20	31	332	378	-2	-47%	3%	42%	-9%
12	DEN	L	13	16	344	349	0	-14%	2%	2%	-14%
13	@JAC	W	38	14	433	306	1	76%	95%	22%	3%
14	BUF	W	37	10	366	281	2	78%	35%	-37%	5%
15	BAL	W	34	14	415	290	2	71%	47%	-31%	-7%
16	@DET	L	10	38	367	440	-2	-53%	-10%	48%	4%
17	@OAK	W	38	26	463	520	0	63%	68%	28%	23%

Trends and Splits

	Offense	Rank	Defense	Rank
Total DVOA	13.0%	5	10.8%	29
Unadjusted VOA	13.9%	5	8.0%	24
Weighted Trend	18.8%	5	12.7%	29
Variance	3.5%	1	9.8%	30
Average Opponent	-1.0%	11	-3.2%	26
Passing	29.1%	6	21.1%	30
Rushing	1.6%	12	0.3%	22
First Down	5.6%	11	-1.7%	14
Second Down	3.3%	13	3.7%	17
Third Down	45.0%	4	47.0%	32
First Half	14.5%	6	13.3%	29
Second Half	11.6%	6	8.1%	24
Red Zone	-2.4%	14	26.7%	32
Late and Close	1.4%	17	17.3%	31

SAN DIEGO CHARGERS

Five-Year Performance

Year	W-L	Pyth	Est W	PF	PA	TO	Total	Rk	Off	Rk	Def	Rk	ST	Rk	Off AGL	Rk	Def AGL	Rk
2007	11-5	11.4	9.4	412	284	+24	18.2%	7	4.6%	14	-8.5%	6	5.1%	5	24.4	21	12.9	7
2008	8-8	10.3	10.3	439	347	+4	15.3%	7	18.8%	3	5.3%	22	1.8%	12	12.4	5	22.2	16
2009	13-3	11.3	10.4	454	320	+8	13.5%	11	19.7%	4	6.5%	23	0.2%	16	26.6	17	29.5	18
2010	9-7	11.0	9.4	441	322	-6	15.4%	8	15.5%	4	-10.0%	7	-10.2%	32	26.8	18	12.7	9
2011	8-8	8.7	7.4	406	377	-7	0.70%	16	13.0%	5	10.8%	29	-1.6%	23	32.6	18	40.0	23

2011 Performance Based on Most Common Personnel Groups

San Diego Offense					San Diego Offense vs. Opp.				San Diego Defense				San Diego Defense vs. Opp.			
Pers	Freq	Yds	DVOA	Run%	Pers	Freq	Yds	DVOA	Pers	Freq	Yds	DVOA	Pers	Freq	Yds	DVOA
12	35%	6.4	12.0%	39%	4-3-4	32%	5.7	10.4%	3-4-4	51%	5.6	9.7%	11	43%	6.6	15.9%
11	33%	7.1	37.9%	17%	4-2-5	18%	6.3	8.6%	3-3-5	20%	7.3	28.8%	12	21%	5.3	4.3%
21	16%	5.8	13.5%	54%	3-4-4	18%	5.6	15.9%	4-2-5	16%	6.0	17.8%	21	15%	5.3	4.8%
22	10%	3.7	-7.6%	79%	Dime+	11%	6.4	17.2%	2-4-5	6%	5.5	-33.8%	22	5%	4.8	-6.3%
13	1%	7.4	24.1%	64%	3-3-5	9%	7.9	35.5%	Dime+	4%	6.6	6.4%	611	3%	6.0	16.7%
					2-4-5	8%	8.5	62.3%								

Strategic Tendencies

Run/Pass		Rank	Offense		Rank	Pass Rush		Rank	Defense/Other		Rank
Runs, all plays	41%	18	Form: Single Back	60%	17	Rush 3	7.7%	12	4 DB	52%	12
Runs, first half	41%	22	Form: Empty Back	3%	27	Rush 4	67.9%	10	5 DB	42%	17
Runs, first down	51%	17	Pers: 3+ WR	35%	28	Rush 5	20.5%	18	6+ DB	4%	21
Runs, second-long	28%	30	Pers: 4+ WR	1%	26	Rush 6+	3.9%	30	CB by Sides	82%	15
Runs, power sit.	51%	25	Pers: 2+ TE/6+ OL	48%	5	Zone Blitz	2.2%	26	Go for it on 4th	1.07	6
Runs, behind 2H	23%	29	Play action	15%	27	Sacks by LB	64.1%	6	Offensive Pace	31.9	29
Pass, ahead 2H	44%	13	Max protect	9%	21	Sacks by DB	0.0%	30	Defensive Pace	31.6	32

The departure of Darren Sproles didn't force a big change in the Chargers offense. They still threw a ton to running backs (29 percent of throws, second behind New Orleans). Although they rarely went empty backfield, the Chargers led the league with 9.7 yards per play and 96.8% DVOA. Philip Rivers had 40 passes thrown away on purpose. No other quarterback in the league had more than 26. Norv Turner was abnormally aggressive on fourth downs in 2011; his career Aggressiveness Index is just .82. San Diego had a league-low nine penalties on special teams. San Diego's defense was far better than rushing five (5.6 yards per play) than when rushing four (7.4) or six or more (8.0). San Diego benefited from a league-low 15 dropped passes, just 3.2 percent of opposing passes.

Passing

Player	DYAR	DVOA	Plays	NtYds	Avg	YAC	C%	TD	Int
P.Rivers	1118	17.0%	610	4414	7.3	5.4	63.3%	27	20
C.Whitehurst	-160	-49.2%	64	254	4.1	4.6	48.2%	1	1

Rushing

Player	DYAR	DVOA	Plays	Yds	Avg	TD	Fum	Suc
R.Mathews	171	10.8%	222	1091	4.9	6	5	50%
M.Tolbert*	30	-3.1%	121	492	4.1	8	1	48%
C.Brinkley	-12	-18.7%	30	101	3.4	1	0	37%
J.Hester	-8	-14.0%	28	90	3.2	0	0	46%
P.Rivers	14	7.5%	11	51	4.6	1	0	--
E.Royal	32	41.6%	7	48	6.9	0	0	--
L.McClain	2	-5.5%	15	51	3.4	1	0	47%

Receiving

Player	DYAR	DVOA	Plays	Ctch	Yds	Y/C	YAC	TD	C%
V.Jackson*	259	15.7%	115	60	1106	18.4	3.2	9	52%
M.Floyd	351	51.4%	70	43	856	19.9	4.2	5	61%
V.Brown	46	1.8%	40	19	329	17.3	4.1	2	48%
P.Crayton*	57	8.4%	34	23	248	10.8	4.3	1	68%
R.Meachem	208	30.8%	60	40	620	15.5	2.6	6	67%
E.Royal	-129	-45.3%	50	19	155	8.2	3.5	1	38%
M.Spurlock	-24	-64.0%	6	2	13	6.5	2.0	0	33%
A.Gates	231	30.9%	88	64	778	12.2	4.0	7	73%
R.McMichael	-19	-14.1%	44	30	271	9.0	6.3	0	68%
D.Rosario	12	10.0%	11	7	117	16.7	4.0	0	64%
M.Tolbert*	51	-2.6%	79	54	433	8.0	8.0	2	68%
R.Mathews	134	27.8%	59	50	455	9.1	8.7	0	85%
J.Hester	-63	-75.0%	18	12	48	4.0	3.8	1	67%
C.Brinkley	-9	-32.3%	9	7	41	5.9	4.9	0	78%
L.McClain	-2	-15.2%	22	14	82	5.9	4.4	1	64%

Offensive Line

Year	Yards	ALY	Rank	Power	Rank	Stuff	Rank	2nd Lev	Rank	Open Field	Rank	F-Start	Cont.
2009	3.54	4.01	18	46%	32	17%	9	0.95	31	0.40	32	16	33
2010	4.18	4.12	14	61%	16	19%	19	1.11	17	0.78	14	11	28
2011	4.42	4.21	9	69%	5	16%	5	1.23	13	0.85	15	15	28

Year	LE	Rank	LT	Rank	Mid	Rank	RT	Rank	RE	Rank	Sacks	ASR	Rank	Short	Long
2009	3.20	27	4.35	10	3.85	25	4.79	2	4.42	12	26	4.5%	5	10	11
2010	4.21	18	3.73	26	4.34	7	4.27	12	3.23	26	38	6.8%	19	10	15
2011	4.99	5	4.48	12	4.14	14	4.57	13	3.14	24	30	5.4%	8	8	13

Usually, a revolving door at left tackle is not a recipe for success on the offensive line, but the Chargers got away with it and finished the year in the top ten of both our main line stats. Veteran Marcus McNeill did a pretty good job of helping Rivers stay upright and opening holes, but committed nine penalties in as many games before being lost for the year with a neck injury. Swing tackle Brandyn Dombrowski was next, but while Dombrowski was a fairly proficient on runs, he had 5.5 blown blocks leading to sacks despite just two starts. So the Chargers signed Jared Gaither off the waiver wire, and he started the final five games. Both Gaither and McNeill were free agents, and the Chargers chose to re-sign Gaither, perhaps because Philip Rivers was sacked only twice in the five games he started. This is called small sample size, kids. The Chargers hope that Gaither remains healthy and avoids the nagging injuries and inconsistency that led to his release by Baltimore and Kansas City.

Beyond Gaither, the two starters who are locked in are right tackle Jeromey Clary and center Nick Hardwick. The Chargers made a financial commitment to Clary before the 2011 season, and he responded by leading the team with 7.0 blown blocks leading to sacks or holding calls. It was the fourth consecutive season he led the Chargers in that category. Hardwick is heading into his ninth season, and is coming off consecutive seasons without missing a game for the first time in his career. When healthy, he's a fine player. The great uncertainty in the lineup comes at left guard. Veteran left guard Kris Dielman's career was prematurely ended by a concussion and ensuing seizure on the flight home. Tyronne Green, a better run blocker than pass blocker, started after Dielman went out and is the favorite to start. Dombrowski is also in the mix, as is veteran journeyman Rex Hadnot. Louis Vasquez started 14 games last year at right guard and like Green is better blocking for runs than for passes.

SAN DIEGO CHARGERS

Defensive Front Seven

Defensive Line	Age	Pos	Plays	TmPct	Rk	Stop	Dfts	BTkl	St%	Rk	AvYd	Rk	Sack	Hit	Hur	Runs	St%	Yds	Pass	St%	Yds
Antonio Garay	33	DT	56	7.2%	4	36	7	4	64%	63	2.5	53	2.5	5	17.5	52	62%	2.8	4	100%	-2.3
Vaughn Martin	26	DE	47	6.0%	22	36	8	1	77%	46	2.4	68	1	0	5	45	78%	2.1	2	50%	8.0
Cam Thomas	26	DT	21	2.7%	64	19	7	0	90%	5	0.0	3	4	3	6.5	15	87%	1.7	6	100%	-4.2
Corey Liuget	22	DE	21	2.9%	--	15	5	0	71%	--	2.1	--	1	0	6	17	71%	2.1	4	75%	2.0

Linebackers	Age	Pos	Plays	TmPct	Rk	Stop	Dfts	BTkl	AvYd	Sack	Hit	Hur	Runs	St%	Rk	Yds	Rk	Tgts	Suc%	Rk	AdjYd	Rk
Takeo Spikes	36	ILB	108	13.8%	22	58	12	8	4.4	1	0	5.5	83	54%	98	4.0	88	32	56%	18	6.0	26
Donald Butler	24	ILB	97	12.4%	36	58	15	5	3.8	2	2	3.5	76	61%	75	3.4	56	20	44%	55	7.6	63
Shaun Phillips	31	OLB	47	8.0%	82	35	17	3	2.7	3.5	3	14.5	27	70%	34	3.4	54	7	86%	--	4.2	--
Na'il Diggs*	34	ILB	40	6.3%	--	25	5	6	4.7	0	0	0	25	84%	--	2.6	--	15	35%	--	8.2	--
Antwan Barnes	28	OLB	38	4.9%	--	32	15	3	0.7	11	4	16.5	24	79%	--	3.5	--	1	0%	--	9.0	--
Travis LaBoy*	31	OLB	38	5.6%	105	21	5	7	2.9	1	4	10	31	55%	95	3.0	36	7	21%	--	9.5	--
Jarrett Johnson	31	OLB	59	7.2%	92	39	11	4	2.9	2.5	6	7.5	45	69%	42	2.6	26	11	58%	--	5.5	--

Year	Yards	ALY	Rank	Power	Rank	Stuff	Rank	2nd Lev	Rank	Open Field	Rank
2009	4.50	4.65	31	54%	4	17%	26	1.36	32	0.55	7
2010	3.74	3.86	14	50%	3	20%	14	1.06	10	0.46	6
2011	4.38	4.32	25	75%	32	16%	28	1.12	10	0.79	19

Year	LE	Rank	LT	Rank	Mid	Rank	RT	Rank	RE	Rank	Sacks	ASR	Rank	Short	Long
2009	4.68	22	4.74	27	4.67	29	3.43	5	5.31	29	35	5.8%	22	14	13
2010	4.28	18	4.73	27	3.65	6	3.96	13	3.41	6	47	9.0%	2	13	25
2011	4.51	22	4.10	18	4.29	21	5.26	31	3.72	18	32	6.5%	18	6	21

It's not that the Chargers' defensive line was terrible in 2011. Rather, it just wasn't very good. Nose tackle Antonio Garay is a good example of that. Severely overmatched when first inserted into the lineup after Jamal Williams was lost to injury in 2009, he had a nice season in 2010 with 6.0 sacks, then dropped to 2.5 last year. While his very high hurries total suggests his sack totals should rebound in 2012, too many of his run tackles came downfield. The defensive end pairing took a big hit when Luis Castillo was lost for the year with a broken leg in the season opener. He was cut and then re-signed this offseason, but if he wants to start he will have to unseat Vaughn Martin, who played decently in his stead. At the other defensive end spot, the Chargers will be looking for sophomore improvement from Corey Liuget, last year's first-round pick. This year's second-round pick, Kendall Reyes, will also be in the mix.

Travis LaBoy led all outside linebackers with 14 games started, which is fairly emblematic of San Diego's mediocrity on defense. This is a player who had not started a game since 2008. LaBoy's main advantage was knowing Greg Manusky's defense, but with Manusky gone, LaBoy was deemed expendable as well. He'll be replaced by Jarret Johnson, a versatile outside linebacker who can drop into coverage, stop the run, or harass the quarterback. Johnson is a good counterpart for Antwan Barnes, a one-trick pony whose trick, rushing the passer, is a very good one. Barnes's 11 sacks were particularly valuable because of the drop-off by Shaun Phillips, who struggled to win one-on-one matchups. 2012 first-round pick Melvin Ingram played all over the formation in college, and should assist the pass rush in a way injury-plagued 2009 first-round pick Larry English has not. Takeo Spikes, another Manusky import at inside linebacker, had a better season than LaBoy but is approaching the point where he needs to be replaced sooner rather than later. Donald Butler had a good "first" season after missing all of 2010 with an injury. His youth showed at times in 2011, but the Chargers are optimistic about his development. 2011 second-round pick Jonas Mouton will have to make the same transition Butler did after he too missed his rookie season with an injury. Free agency acquisition Demorrio Williams is strictly a depth player.

Defensive Secondary

Secondary	Age	Pos	Plays	TmPct	Rk	Stop	Dfts	BTkl	Runs	St%	Rk	Yds	Rk	Tgts	Tgt%	Rk	Dist	Suc%	Rk	APaYd	Rk	PD	Int
Eric Weddle	27	FS	95	12.2%	16	40	22	4	43	37%	47	8.7	59	31	8.2%	24	16.4	76%	2	4.7	5	10	7
Antoine Cason	26	CB	70	9.0%	28	28	10	3	17	41%	43	10.9	73	78	20.5%	19	13.4	49%	54	7.0	28	17	2
Steve Gregory*	29	SS	68	9.3%	47	19	4	5	29	41%	32	6.6	31	25	6.9%	39	16.6	45%	67	10.3	66	5	1
Quentin Jammer	33	CB	60	8.2%	46	23	9	6	14	50%	27	6.7	35	56	15.8%	53	13.5	39%	79	11.1	81	7	0
Dante Hughes	27	CB	37	4.7%	--	18	8	4	11	64%	--	4.6	--	32	8.3%	--	12.2	48%	--	10.7	--	4	0
Marcus Gilchrist	24	CB	32	4.7%	--	8	5	2	7	29%	--	9.6	--	28	8.5%	--	15.7	30%	--	11.5	--	4	2
Paul Oliver*	28	SS	21	3.3%	--	8	4	1	6	33%	--	13.2	--	11	3.4%	--	16.5	67%	--	7.9	--	4	1

Year	Pass D Rank	vs. #1 WR	Rk	vs. #2 WR	Rk	vs. Other WR	Rk	vs. TE	Rk	vs. RB	Rk
2009	21	-2.4%	12	4.5%	21	3.6%	18	-7.8%	9	36.4%	32
2010	4	-35.5%	1	-4.5%	12	-26.9%	3	18.1%	26	15.4%	25
2011	31	32.5%	31	13.5%	23	2.1%	21	32.8%	31	-6.2%	11

We said it in *Football Outsiders Almanac 2010*. We said it in *Football Outsiders Almanac 2011*. We'll say it again this year: free safety Eric Weddle had an outstanding season. An NFL lead-tying seven interceptions finally sent him to the Pro Bowl and put him on the All-Pro team, so somebody else seems to be getting the message as well. Weddle can play centerfield or man coverage, excels in coming up in support against both the run and the pass (he sealed a win over the Chiefs by intercepting a screen pass), and rarely misses a tackle.

Beyond Weddle, the most notable member of the Chargers' secondary is Quentin Jammer, but for how long will Jammer be around? He turned 33 in June and did not play very well in 2011. How much longer can the Chargers expect him to play? According to our defensive similarity scores, the most similar players to Jammer over the last three seasons include:

Player	Team	Years	SimScore
Sam Madison	MIA	03-05	834
Patrick Surtain	KC	05-07	831
Todd Lyght	STL/DET	99-01	830
R.W. McQuarters	CHI/DET/NYG	04-06	830
Jeff Burris	IND/CIN	00-02	821
Ray Crockett	DEN/KC	99-01	820
Ashley Ambrose	ATL/NO	01-03	818

Madison started two years for the Giants and picked up a Super Bowl ring, but for the rest of these players, the future was a whole lot of nothing. Lyght and Burriss each played one more season before retiring, and Crockett, Surtain, McQuarters, and Ambrose each started no more than six games. The Chargers will need 2011 second-round pick Marcus Gilchrist and/or 2011 third-round pick Shareece Wright to be ready to start no later than Week 1 of next season. USC alum Wright essentially had a redshirt as a rookie; he's an intriguing athlete who missed almost all of 2008 with an injury and almost all of 2009 with academic problems. Gilchrist was a more experienced player who played both cornerback and safety at Clemson, but struggled badly as a rookie.

Special Teams

Year	DVOA	Rank	FG/XP	Rank	Net Kick	Rank	Kick Ret	Rank	Net Punt	Rank	Punt Ret	Rank	Hidden	Rank
2009	0.2%	16	7.7	3	-6.1	26	-0.3	12	0.7	17	-0.7	17	10.8	2
2010	-8.6%	32	1.5	14	-17.7	32	-3.5	18	-34.3	32	3.2	12	-7.8	24
2011	-1.3%	23	-0.4	17	-7.0	27	2.8	9	1.6	13	-5.0	22	-3.0	19

A year after having the worst special teams unit in the NFL, the Chargers kicked off 2011 by giving up a touchdown return to Percy Harvin and losing kicker Nate Kaeding for the season on the play. Fortunately, that was rock bottom, and the rest of the season was more mediocre than bad. Kaeding's replacement Nick Novak was average or a little below at both placekicks and kickoffs, which more or less matched Kaeding's 2010 performance. Novak is probably a slight favorite to win the job, not because he can clearly win a kicking competition in training camp but because Kaeding's higher salary and postseason struggles may put him on the outs. Punter Mike Scifres rebounded with a good season after an atrocious 2010, ranking sixth in the league in gross punting value, and both kick and punt coverage units improved from godawful to pedestrian. Reserve wide receiver Richard Goodman inherited the kickoff return job from Darren Sproles and interspersed good returns, like a touchdown in the season finale against the Raiders, with some inexplicably bad decision-making. Patrick Crayton took over punt return duties, and was lousy. Crayton is gone, but Goodman returns and will battle Eddie Royal, Roscoe Parrish, and Micheal Spurlock in the Chargers' version of Thunderdome for the returner jobs and a roster spot.

Coaching Staff

Longtime offensive line coach Hal Hunter is the new offensive coordinator, replacing Clarence Shelmon. Nothing will change offensively or on the offensive line, where Hunter's assistant, Mike Sullivan, received a promotion. The void at linebacker coach created by John Pagano's promotion was filled by Joe Barry. Barry most notably was the Lions' defensive coordinator under Rod Marinelli and led the second-worst defense in DVOA history in 2008. Before that, though, he was Tampa Bay's linebackers coach for six seasons, so he might know what he's doing. The new secondary coach is Ron Meeks, who spent seven seasons as the Colts' defensive coordinator under Tony Dungy before coaching with the Panthers the last three seasons.

San Francisco 49ers

2011 Record: 13-3

Pythagorean Wins: 12.3 (2nd)

DVOA: 18.6% (6th)

Offense: -3.9% (18th)

Defense: -14.6% (3rd)

Special Teams: 7.8% (2nd)

Variance: 6.8% (4th)

2012 Mean Projection: 7.2 wins

On the Clock (0-4): 12%

Mediocrity (5-7): 44%

Playoff Contender (8-10): 38%

Super Bowl Contender (11+): 6%

Postseason Odds: 39.5%

Projected Average Opponent: -2.7% (26th)

2011: Jim Harbaugh, NFL Coach of the Year.

2012: If the 49ers repeat, so should Harbaugh.

"I'm not the fly sweep guru. I took something that I saw that was successful, and I learned about it. And that's one of the great things about Jim Harbaugh. I don't think he will ever get to the point where he'll think he knows it all."

—Sacred Heart Prep head coach Pete Lavorato

On the surface, it's a compliment from one football coach to another and a glimpse into how an effective play at the lower levels makes its way to the NFL. Dig deeper, and that one statement tells you all you need to know about why the 49ers ascended from a decade of mediocrity (or worse) in their first year under Harbaugh.

The story goes like this: Looking for a wrinkle to add to his Stanford offense heading into the 2009 season, and having attended a 2008 high school game between Sacred Heart and King's Academy, Harbaugh sought out Lavorato for an explanation of a bread-and-butter play called the "fly sweep," which involves a wide receiver motioning across the formation at near-full speed and receiving a handoff in stride just after the snap. Harbaugh ended up using the play several times over Stanford's next two seasons, unveiled it in Week 5 with the 49ers, name-checked Lavorato in a press conference, and the rest is history.

The deeper meaning, however, requires a bit of context. Prior to his meeting with Lavorato, Harbaugh had just completed his second season at Stanford, one in which the Cardinal climbed to mediocrity at 5-7 just two years after going 1-11. He had senior running back Toby Gerhart coming off of a 1,136-yard, 15-touchdown season, and redshirt freshman Andrew Luck slated to start at quarterback. At the same time, Harbaugh had played in the NFL for 14 years, quarterbacked his team to an AFC Championship Game, spent time as an NFL assistant, and gone 24-2 in his final two seasons as head coach at the University of San Diego. Many coaches in Harbaugh's position would have simply relied on talent to escape mediocrity. Many coaches in Harbaugh's position would have believed that their wealth of experience and history of success made escaping mediocrity inevitable.

Among top-50 college football programs, however, the landscape is a gridiron version of Lake Wobegon: All the linemen are strong, all the coaching resumes are good looking, and all the bowl participants are above average. For his team to emerge from that box, sometimes a head coach needs to think outside of it, finding a handful of unorthodox tactics that swing a couple of key plays from unsuccessful to successful and a couple of key games from losses to wins.

Relying solely on his existing knowledge base and an influx of Luck, the likeliest outcome for Harbaugh's Stanford teams over the next two years was probably the 12-12 regular season record we predicted across

2012 49ers Schedule

Week	Opp.	Week	Opp.	Week	Opp.
1	at GB	7	SEA (Thu.)	13	at STL
2	DET	8	at ARI (Mon.)	14	MIA
3	at MIN	9	BYE	15	at NE
4	at NYJ	10	STL	16	at SEA
5	BUF	11	CHI (Mon.)	17	ARI
6	NYG	12	at NO		

Figure 1. 2011 San Francisco DVOA by Week

Football Outsiders Almanac 2009 and *Football Outsiders Almanac 2010*. Instead, the Cardinal went 19-5. Obviously, a single, seldom-used play learned in the office of a high school coach didn't add seven wins over two seasons. But it illustrates Harbaugh's understanding that, in a world where every team is basically as good as yours, a continuing education in strategy and tactics is useful for overcoming the typical expectation of continued mediocrity.

In that light, Harbaugh's 30-mile job relocation was a perfect fit for San Francisco, where a fan base accustomed to excellence had suffered for five years through what might as well have been dubbed the "Continued Mediocrity era." From 2006 to 2010, "Win the West" banners and bold ownership proclamations were sound and fury signifying nothing. Despite having a roster talented enough to claim the weak NFC West, the 49ers constantly failed to live up to those lofty expectations.

In particular, Harbaugh's dynamic approach to football strategy was a stark contrast to the stasis of predecessor Mike Singletary, whose idea of what it took to win in the NFL was as set in bronze as his Hall of Fame bust. He infamously ranted about wanting "winners," implored his team to be "physical with an 'F,'" and set a "Formula for Success" as his performance benchmark. The rhetorical question no one bothered asking at the time was, "What team in today's NFL wants a roster full of weak losers who follow a formula for failure?" Cleveland jokes aside, the problem was that, as unorthodox as Singletary's approach *sounded*, it was actually just football boilerplate. And in today's NFL, boilerplate makes you 6-10.

Nevertheless, whether we're talking about Singletary, offensive coordinator Jimmy Raye II, Singletary's predecessor Mike Nolan, or Raye's predecessor Mike Martz, the hallmark of San Francisco's Continued Mediocrity era was a coaching staff set in its ways. Bill Walsh once wrote that "the coach must be willing to change what he is doing if it obviously is destined to fail," and that "coaching is a critical factor in maintaining your position as a team that continually finishes ahead of the curve." In the case of recent 49ers teams, failure in the former led to failure in the latter.

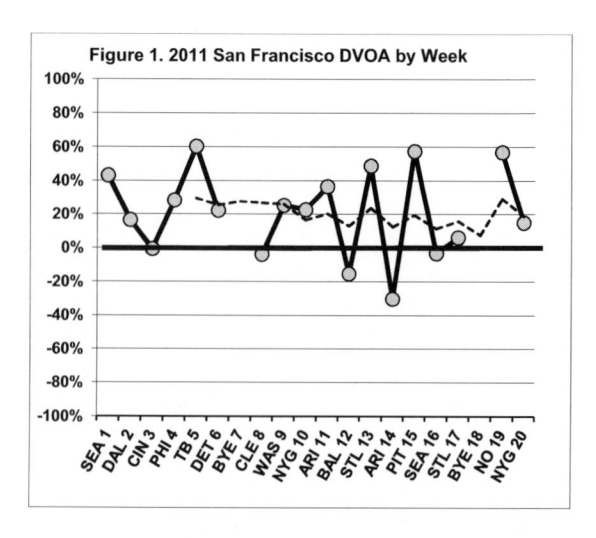

Due in part to a lack of flexibility on the part of their coaches, the 49ers had made a habit of posting a winning record early in the season, only to then suffer a loss that sent them into a death spiral. After starting 2-0 in 2007, an eight-game losing streak began with a 37-16 loss at Pittsburgh in Week 3. In 2008, a 2-1 start was wiped out by a six-game losing streak that began with a 31-17 Week 4 loss at New Orleans. In 2009, the 49ers followed a 3-1 start with a four-game losing streak initiated by a 45-10 home loss to Atlanta.

San Francisco was in a similar situation last season; they blew out Seattle in Week 1 to start 2011 on a high note, but blew a 10-point fourth-quarter lead at home against Dallas in Week 2. The next week at Cincinnati, they were down 6-3 with 8:57 left in the game, and started what ultimately turned into the game-winning drive at their own 28-yard line. Tight end Vernon Davis caught three passes for 36 yards on the drive: 1) a designed "hot" route from a single-back formation against a Bengals blitz; 2) an 8-yard out after feigning a block against another Bengals blitz; and 3) a throw-back play-action screen out of a "we're running right," two-tight-end, strong-I formation. Culminating the drive, San Francisco lined up in a "we're passing left," single-back, bunch left formation, but handed off to Kendall Hunter, who ran behind the bunch for a 7-yard touchdown.

Harbaugh then demonstrated more outside-the-box thinking when he took advantage of ownership's long-standing connection to Youngstown, Ohio, and arranged for the team to stay east in the lead-up to their Week 4 game at Philadelphia. From 2005 to 2010, the 49ers had gone 0-5 against the Eagles, and were outscored 174-90. That day, however, San Francisco came back from a 23-3 third-quarter deficit to win 24-23. Key plays on the game-winning drive took advantage of the athleticism of left tackle Joe Staley, and featured unconventional ways of running up the middle, both of which had been largely ignored in previous years. On a 25-yard inside handoff to Frank Gore out of shotgun, Staley pulled into the middle of the line, which allowed two flexed tight ends (Davis and Delanie Walker) to serve as second-level blockers instead of route runners. A 14-yard run by Kendall Hunter used Staley and Davis in an off-tackle version of the "pin and pull" concept. Finally, on Gore's 12-yard, up-the-middle touchdown, San Francisco lined up with six offensive linemen and nose tackle Isaac Sopoaga as the second lead blocker in a full house backfield, plus Davis split wide just to keep the defense honest.

In past years, lack of flexibility also manifested itself in San Francisco's penchant for following a late-season win to get into the playoff race with a loss to get out of it. For instance, despite an atypical 0-5 start in 2010 (a.k.a. "The Year of the First Sub-.500 Playoff Team"), the 49ers were 5-8 coming off of a home win against division-leading Seattle, and only one game out of first place with three weeks to go. If they beat San Diego on Thursday night of Week 15, they would put pressure on Seattle and St. Louis to win their Sunday games (which they ultimately did not). Instead, the 49ers got blown out, 34-7. The Chargers spent that whole game harassing backup left tackle Barry Sims and rookie right tackle Anthony Davis, yet the 49ers staff refused to help Alex Smith with extra blockers or designed rollouts. The 49ers used just five blockers on 29 of the last 30 pass plays as the Chargers got in Smith's face over and over again. There were no adjustments to account for circumstance or opponent strategies.

Fast-forward a year: After a Thanksgiving night loss to Baltimore in Week 12 of 2011, St. Louis ended up being the opponent that once again stood in the way of a San Francisco playoff berth. Up only 9-0 at halftime against a clearly inferior team, the 49ers had taken on their Continued Mediocrity era look. Unlike previous coaches, however, Harbaugh (and offensive coordinator Greg Roman) unleashed a barrage of varied offensive tactics over an eight-minute span that clinched a playoff spot, and ultimately led to national recognition for the high school coach who taught him one of the key plays.

The sequence began with San Francisco taking over at their 12-yard line with 13 minutes left in the third quarter after Dashon Goldson corralled a red zone interception. On first down, the 49ers lined up with twin wide receivers on the weak side of the formation. Fullback Bruce Miller slid to the weak side pre-snap, both guards pulled left, and Frank Gore ran off the weakside tackle for six yards. The next play was a fly sweep out of an unbalanced line with Ted Ginn, who had experience with the play at Ohio State, running for 16 yards and a first down. Then came an end around to tight end Delanie Walker, which gained 14 yards, and another first down. From the San Francisco 48-yardline, left guard Mike Iupati pulled right, Frank Gore sold the play-fake, and Alex Smith hit Michael Crabtree on a post for a 52-yard touchdown.

After a quick three-and-out by the Rams offense, San Francisco used a Smith bootleg pass, a Kyle Williams end around, and a Gore run behind seven offensive linemen to set up a David Akers 34-yard field goal. In total, it was a stretch of 10 plays with nine different formations, 10 pulling guards, five fake handoffs, three end arounds, and two unbalanced lines that clinched the NFC West for a team that had crumbled in a similar situation the previous year.

Of course, over the course of a full season, Harbaugh made more tactical adjustments than described in the single game above. For instance, to help Alex Smith throw more efficiently against zone blitzes, he replaced complicated sight adjustments used in previous seasons with the easier approach of incorporating a short hot route into every pass play. The result: After finishing 2010 with a worse average on plays on zone blitzes than those without (4.9 yards vs. 6.5 yards), the situation was reversed (6.7 yards per play against zone blitzes vs. 6.0 yards per play otherwise).

Another example was the 49ers Week 6 game against the Lions, in which Harbaugh won both the postgame handshake and the coaching matchup. Recognizing Ndamokung Suh's propensity for naked aggression, Harbaugh and Roman incorporated the "wham" play into their running game plan. The result: 102 yards on two Frank Gore carries.

And there were others. Harbaugh adapted Tom Landry's liberal use of pre-snap shifts into an effective offsides-inducer on third-and-short, managing to even confuse the referees in San Francisco's game against Washington. After using nose tackle Isaac Sopoaga as a lead blocker a handful of times during the regular season, Harbaugh added defensive end Justin Smith as a blocking tight end against New Orleans in the playoffs.

Tactical adjustments were also evident on defense. In 2010, the 49ers brought five or more rushers on 30 percent of the pass plays they faced. In 2011, that frequency dropped to 20 percent. In a microcosm of the differences between coaching staffs, Harbaugh and defensive coordinator Vic Fangio strategized their way into an effective pass rush via a virtually unblockable stunt involving Justin Smith and Aldon Smith rather than using the blunt object of force in numbers.

After reading 1,500-or-so words extolling the coaching virtues of Jim Harbaugh, you're probably asking yourself, "So then why does Football Outsiders have the 49ers winning fewer than eight games this season?" If you're a 49ers fan, that question probably included several expletives. It's a good one, though, with a relatively simple answer. Namely, outside of the usual types of subjective decisions that go into such endeavors, our win projection model is based on general historical trends in NFL statistics, and much of San Francisco's overall statistical profile in 2011 suggests the 49ers are due for a regression in 2012.

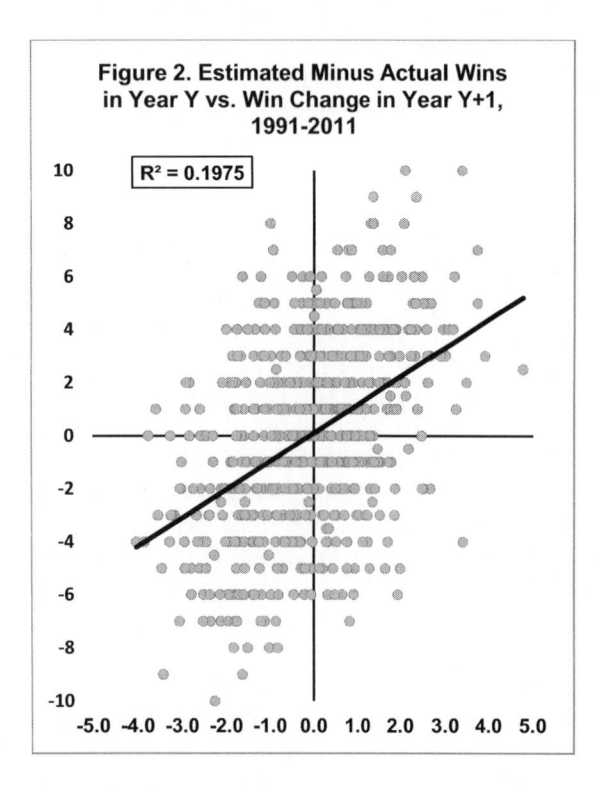

One of the biggest indicators is our Estimated Wins statistic, which is based on DVOA and consistency. As with Pythagorean Wins, which is based strictly on point differential, a team that has more actual wins than Estimated Wins will likely win fewer games the following season, and vice versa. The 49ers actually won 2.2 more games in 2011 than they should have according to Estimated Wins. Since 1991, that discrepancy translates to about two more losses the following season (Figure 1). The 49ers outperformed their Estimated Wins number due in part to a fabulous 7-2 record in close games. We've found that a team's record in close games almost never carries over from one season to the next, so the 49ers can't expect to win as many games in 2012 without getting out to some bigger leads.

A few other statistical indicators from last season chip away at San Francisco's likely win total this season. First, they'll be facing a slightly tougher schedule. Second, among DVOA components, special teams is the least consistent from year to year, which makes a repeat performance of 2011 unlikely. Third, although Alex Smith has posted a better-than-average interception rate in each of the past two seasons, his 1.1-percent rate from 2011 is unsustainable. (Just ask Michael Vick about that.)

Finally, the 49ers are this year's poster children for the "plexiglass principle," which states that a team showing dramatic improvement one season tends to decline the following season. Bill James coined the term for major league baseball, but it works just as well for the NFL. San Francisco's total DVOA was 29.8 percentage points better in 2011 than it was in 2010. If you look at the 41 teams between 1992 and 2010 that showed similar improvement from one year to the next (i.e., between 25 and 35 percentage points), you find that they declined an average of 12.1 DVOA percentage points and 2.3 wins the following season.

That's an average, of course, not a guarantee, and the 49ers hope that continuity in their lineup will help soften the bounce off the plexiglass. Every starter from last year's third-ranked defense remains on the roster. The one change in the starting lineup gets a better player on the field for more snaps, as nominal starter Parys Haralson has officially ceded his right outside linebacker spot to Aldon Smith. Nine of 11 starters return on offense, and again, the 49ers feel that they've improved at the two positions with turnover. After five underwhelming wideouts started games opposite Michael Crabtree in 2011, the 49ers signed veterans Randy Moss and Mario Manningham to add talent

Figure 2. Estimated Minus Actual Wins in Year Y vs. Win Change in Year Y+1, 1991-2011

$R^2 = 0.1975$

and some semblance of stability at the position. The other change is at right guard, but the team has been grooming new starter Alex Boone for three years and feels confident in letting him replace Adam Snyder. Finally, the important special teams nucleus of punter Andy Lee, kicker David Akers, and primary returner Ted Ginn also returns for another season.

Of course, we can look at roster stability, key personnel moves, statistical indicators, and the like, but if Bill Walsh thought coaching flexibility is the key to maintaining success over several seasons, who are we to argue? In Palo Alto, Harbaugh was willing enough to adapt that he sought out the help of a high school coach. Two years later in San Francisco, the play he learned from that high school coach figured prominently in his team's division-clinching win. Both the Cardinal and 49ers were mired in mediocrity (or worse) prior to Harbaugh's arrival, but his continuing education helped both escape.

By all indications, there's been no tactical complacency this offseason. In May, Harbaugh put his players through three weeks of organized team activities not-so-subtly called "Football School." With new offensive weapons like Moss, Manningham, and second-round pick LaMichael James, the question isn't *if* he and his staff have spent the offseason sharpening new strategies, but *where*. Mean projections only give about 16 combined wins to San Francisco's NFC West rivals, so the learning curve won't need to be steep for the 49ers to win another division title.

Danny Tuccitto

2011 49ers Stats by Week

Wk	vs.	W-L	PF	PA	YDF	YDA	TO	Total	Off	Def	ST
1	SEA	W	33	17	209	219	3	43%	-29%	-20%	52%
2	DAL	L	24	27	206	472	1	17%	-9%	-14%	12%
3	@CIN	W	13	8	226	228	2	-1%	-42%	-37%	4%
4	@PHI	W	24	23	442	513	2	28%	54%	8%	-17%
5	TB	W	48	3	418	272	2	60%	26%	-24%	10%
6	@DET	W	25	19	314	310	-2	22%	-22%	-25%	20%
7	BYE										
8	CLE	W	20	10	348	290	2	-4%	-8%	-10%	-5%
9	@WAS	W	19	11	326	303	2	25%	4%	-2%	19%
10	NYG	W	27	20	305	395	1	23%	1%	-9%	12%
11	ARI	W	23	7	431	229	4	37%	6%	-49%	-19%
12	@BAL	L	6	16	170	253	-1	-15%	-22%	6%	13%
13	STL	W	26	0	389	157	2	49%	0%	-44%	5%
14	@ARI	L	19	21	233	325	3	-30%	-51%	-12%	9%
15	PIT	W	20	3	287	389	4	57%	14%	-30%	13%
16	@SEA	W	19	17	349	265	1	-3%	5%	8%	0%
17	@STL	W	34	27	321	311	2	6%	15%	6%	-3%
18	BYE										
19	NO	W	36	32	407	472	4	57%	12%	-19%	26%
20	NYG	L	17	20	328	352	-2	15%	-12%	-28%	-1%

Trends and Splits

	Offense	Rank	Defense	Rank
Total DVOA	-3.9%	18	-14.6%	3
Unadjusted VOA	-17.9%	2	-17.9%	2
Weighted Trend	-3.3%	16	-13.3%	3
Variance	10.3%	25	5.9%	15
Average Opponent	-1.3%	10	-5.8%	29
Passing	15.3%	13	-7.6%	6
Rushing	-7.3%	24	-26.1%	2
First Down	10.5%	6	1.6%	20
Second Down	-11.4%	22	-34.0%	1
Third Down	-19.7%	22	-15.6%	9
First Half	-6.1%	18	-27.2%	1
Second Half	-1.1%	18	-3.3%	11
Red Zone	-31.8%	29	-9.7%	16
Late and Close	-11.1%	25	-17.3%	2

Five-Year Performance

Year	W-L	Pyth	Est W	PF	PA	TO	Total	Rk	Off	Rk	Def	Rk	ST	Rk	Off AGL	Rk	Def AGL	Rk
2007	5-11	3.7	4.1	219	364	-12	-33.4%	31	-32.2%	32	6.3%	24	5.2%	4	31.8	28	19.5	15
2008	7-9	6.8	6.1	339	381	-17	-14.1%	25	-15.6%	27	3.6%	18	5.2%	3	24.9	18	5.4	3
2009	8-8	9.5	7.1	280	390	-8	-1.2%	20	-14.1%	23	-14.0%	5	-1.1%	20	9.5	8	34.1	22
2010	6-10	6.8	6.9	305	346	-1	-11.2%	24	-11.1%	24	-1.4%	15	-1.5%	20	20.7	11	6.8	3
2011	13-3	12.3	10.8	380	229	+2	18.6%	6	-3.9%	18	-14.6%	3	7.8%	2	29.6	16	8.8	2

SAN FRANCISCO 49ERS

2011 Performance Based on Most Common Personnel Groups

San Francisco Offense						San Francisco Offense vs. Opp.					San Francisco Defense					San Francisco Defense vs. Opp.			
Pers	Freq	Yds	DVOA	Run%	Pers	Freq	Yds	DVOA	Pers	Freq	Yds	DVOA	Pers	Freq	Yds	DVOA
12	27%	6.2	28.4%	31%	4-3-4	39%	5.8	11.6%	3-4-4	45%	5.2	-20.6%	11	48%	4.9	-16.8%
11	22%	5.2	-2.0%	20%	3-4-4	24%	4.6	-0.8%	3-3-5	23%	5.4	-16.5%	12	18%	6.5	-2.8%
22	19%	4.2	-16.9%	76%	4-2-5	17%	5.3	3.4%	4-2-5	13%	5.3	-5.7%	21	17%	5.0	-9.5%
21	16%	5.5	4.2%	52%	Dime+	6%	5.4	3.2%	Dime+	10%	6.3	45.6%	10	5%	7.0	7.4%
13	5%	5.6	1.4%	57%	2-4-5	5%	6.0	38.8%	2-4-5	8%	3.9	-37.5%	22	4%	2.7	-55.8%

Strategic Tendencies

Run/Pass		Rank	Offense		Rank	Pass Rush		Rank	Defense/Other		Rank
Runs, all plays	49%	3	Form: Single Back	52%	29	Rush 3	11.7%	7	4 DB	46%	21
Runs, first half	44%	13	Form: Empty Back	4%	24	Rush 4	67.9%	11	5 DB	43%	14
Runs, first down	55%	9	Pers: 3+ WR	24%	31	Rush 5	18.5%	20	6+ DB	10%	10
Runs, second-long	46%	5	Pers: 4+ WR	0%	31	Rush 6+	2.0%	32	CB by Sides	74%	20
Runs, power sit.	70%	5	Pers: 2+ TE/6+ OL	60%	2	Zone Blitz	8.4%	7	Go for it on 4th	1.18	2
Runs, behind 2H	42%	2	Play action	19%	15	Sacks by LB	69.0%	2	Offensive Pace	30.7	18
Pass, ahead 2H	41%	23	Max protect	13%	9	Sacks by DB	0.0%	30	Defensive Pace	31.0	26

The 49ers built a winner on field position. San Francisco started its average drive at its own 33.4-yard line, more than two yards closer to a touchdown than any other offense. On defense, opponents started their average drive on their 24-yard line, also the best figure in the league. ◉ Only 5.4 percent of 49ers offensive drives ended in a turnover, the lowest figure in our drive stats data that goes back to 1997. 23.9 percent of 49ers drives ended in a field goal, the highest figure since 1997. ◉ Jim Harbaugh's offense left in more blockers to protect Alex Smith, going from 26th to ninth in using max protection. ◉ Despite this, as Alex Smith's overall game improved, his ability to beat blitzes declined. In past years, he had always put up strong numbers against big blitzes of six or more. But last year, he had just 5.3 yards per pass against the big blitz, compared to 6.1 yards per play otherwise. ◉ Alex Smith was out of the pocket on 19 percent of pass plays, fifth in the league, and was pretty bad on these plays, with just 4.4 yards per play and -25.1% DVOA. ◉ The 49ers were one of five teams that ran the running back screen pass less than once per game. ◉ The 49ers defense struggled when they dropped eight into coverage, allowing two more yards per pass than they did otherwise.

Passing

Player	DYAR	DVOA	Plays	NtYds	Avg	YAC	C%	TD	Int
A.Smith	442	3.1%	492	2857	5.9	5.2	61.7%	17	5
J.Johnson	-91	-46.8%	39	222	5.7	1.7	52.8%	1	2

Rushing

Player	DYAR	DVOA	Plays	Yds	Avg	TD	Fum	Suc
F.Gore	-17	-10.0%	282	1211	4.3	8	2	42%
K.Hunter	9	-6.5%	112	473	4.2	2	0	46%
A.Smith	38	11.4%	33	195	5.9	2	1	--
A.Dixon	-9	-15.6%	29	87	3.0	2	0	52%
T.Ginn	42	60.0%	8	68	8.5	0	0	--
B.Jacobs	35	-3.2%	152	571	3.8	7	3	49%

Receiving

Player	DYAR	DVOA	Plays	Ctch	Yds	Y/C	YAC	TD	C%
M.Crabtree	154	4.9%	114	73	880	12.1	5.0	4	64%
B.Edwards*	-40	-27.4%	34	15	181	12.1	3.1	0	44%
T.Ginn	5	-10.6%	33	19	220	11.6	2.3	0	58%
K.Williams	56	10.3%	31	20	241	12.1	5.4	3	65%
J.Morgan*	72	32.4%	20	15	220	14.7	6.4	1	75%
B.Swain	-39	-77.6%	7	2	15	7.5	7.5	0	29%
M.Manningham	44	-5.6%	77	39	523	13.4	2.7	4	51%
V.Davis	70	3.9%	95	67	792	11.8	4.9	6	71%
D.Walker	-27	-19.5%	36	20	192	9.6	3.8	3	56%
F.Gore	-8	-18.1%	31	17	114	6.7	6.0	0	55%
K.Hunter	50	21.2%	26	16	195	12.2	11.0	0	62%
B.Miller	11	-0.4%	15	11	83	7.5	5.0	1	73%
B.Jacobs	17	-0.1%	22	15	128	8.5	7.9	1	68%
R.Cartwright	-6	-29.2%	6	4	24	6.0	6.5	0	67%

Offensive Line

Year	Yards	ALY	Rank	Power	Rank	Stuff	Rank	2nd Lev	Rank	Open Field	Rank	F-Start	Cont.
2009	4.24	3.51	32	63%	16	23%	31	0.92	32	1.25	4	16	31
2010	4.05	4.14	13	56%	23	17%	11	1.04	25	0.65	20	20	33
2011	4.17	3.96	21	51%	29	20%	22	1.12	22	0.92	12	28	43

Year	LE	Rank	LT	Rank	Mid	Rank	RT	Rank	RE	Rank	Sacks	ASR	Rank	Short	Long
2009	4.58	13	2.63	32	3.51	29	3.22	31	4.22	17	40	8.1%	26	17	10
2010	4.31	16	5.10	2	3.92	18	4.96	3	3.04	30	44	8.9%	30	15	16
2011	3.68	21	4.56	8	3.57	29	4.24	19	4.59	4	44	8.4%	25	16	13

Finally acknowledging that NFL success these days comes from the passing game, San Francisco made several personnel and strategic changes in 2011 that shifted the focus of their offensive line toward better pass protection. Their ALY and run offense DVOA may have taken a nosedive, but the overall team results are hard to argue with. The first move was replacing David Baas, always better in the running game, with 2009 Pro Bowl center Jonathan Goodwin, who played on one of the best pass offenses in the league (New Orleans) and had only given up one blown block sack in the previous two years. The next personnel move came in Week 4, when Jim Harbaugh benched right guard Chilo Rachal in favor of converted tackle Adam Snyder. On top of these personnel changes, Jim Harbaugh and offensive coordinator Greg Roman relied far more heavily on max protect, frequently using backup tackle Alex Boone as a sixth lineman. (Only New England and Oakland used six-lineman sets more often.) San Francisco based their play-action passing game on pulling athletic left guard Mike Iupati, which, aside from contributing to a 40-percentage point increase in play-action DVOA, had the added benefit of providing help for right tackle Anthony Davis, who led all linemen with 12.0 blown block sacks allowed in 2010. It also didn't hurt that left tackle Joe Staley started all 16 games after playing a total of 18 in the previous two seasons. Finally healthy, Staley responded with a Pro Bowl season in which he had zero holding penalties and the fifth-fewest blown blocks in pass protection (5.5) out of 17 left tackles with 16 starts.

However, there's still plenty to worry about going forward. Regardless of the positive protection changes, the 49ers still ranked in the bottom eight of Adjusted Sack Rate, Davis "improved" to 8.5 blown-block sacks (sixth-most in the league), and San Francisco's interior line never figured out how to handle inside blitzes. In addition, the declines in Power Success Rate and Stuffed Rate are particularly problematic when you consider how often they used jumbo packages featuring six offensive linemen and either a tight end or *defensive* lineman at fullback. Four starters return (Staley, Iupati, Goodwin, and Davis), so it's unclear how any of this will change outside of added experience and the benefit of a full offseason. Boone is the early favorite to replaced Adam Snyder (who signed with Arizona) at right guard, but he's never played guard before in his life, and the move creates a potential hole at backup tackle if Joe Staley should return to his injury-prone ways. The other contenders for right guard are a trio of recent draft picks: 2011 fifth-rounder Daniel Kilgore (Appalachian State) and 2011 seventh-rounder Mike Person (Montana State) were inactive for all 16 games last season, and 2012 fourth-rounder Joe Looney (Wake Forest) is still recovering from a Lisfranc injury he suffered in the Senior Bowl.

Defensive Front Seven

Defensive Line	Age	Pos	Plays	TmPct	Rk	Stop	Dfts	BTkl	St%	Rk	AvYd	Rk	Sack	Hit	Hur	Runs	St%	Yds	Pass	St%	Yds
Justin Smith	33	DE	60	7.7%	6	41	12	1	68%	72	2.3	65	7.5	14	28	45	64%	3.1	15	80%	-0.1
Ray McDonald	28	DE	40	5.5%	31	32	10	2	80%	34	1.0	30	5.5	3	20.5	29	79%	2.3	11	82%	-2.5
Isaac Sopoaga	31	DT	30	4.1%	33	25	0	0	83%	20	2.4	50	0	3	2.5	29	86%	2.3	1	0%	5.0
Ricky Jean-Francois	26	DT	17	2.2%	--	16	1	0	94%	--	2.4	--	0	0	4	15	93%	2.7	2	100%	0.0

SAN FRANCISCO 49ERS

Linebackers	Age	Pos	Plays	TmPct	Rk	Stop	Dfts	BTkl	AvYd	Sack	Hit	Hur	Runs	St%	Rk	Yds	Rk	Tgts	Suc%	Rk	AdjYd	Rk
NaVorro Bowman	24	ILB	143	18.4%	6	89	27	11	4.5	2	4	9	76	75%	13	2.8	29	50	52%	35	7.2	50
Patrick Willis	27	ILB	109	17.2%	8	65	19	2	4.6	2	2	7	56	63%	66	4.0	87	46	65%	5	4.9	8
Ahman Brooks	28	OLB	50	6.4%	102	36	15	2	2.3	7	10	23	29	72%	24	2.7	28	14	51%	--	9.8	--
Aldon Smith	23	OLB	39	5.0%	--	34	21	3	0.5	14	16	31	19	74%	--	6.1	--	3	36%	--	10.5	--
Larry Grant	27	OLB	37	4.7%	--	20	7	2	4.9	2	1	1	17	65%	--	3.9	--	11	63%	--	2.5	--
Parys Haralson	28	OLB	30	3.9%	111	21	4	4	2.5	2	5	10.5	23	83%	6	1.7	4	5	39%	--	7.4	--

Year	Yards	ALY	Rank	Power	Rank	Stuff	Rank	2nd Lev	Rank	Open Field	Rank
2009	3.73	3.68	8	64%	16	20%	14	1.08	8	0.59	9
2010	3.36	3.56	3	61%	11	19%	18	0.78	1	0.48	7
2011	3.49	3.77	4	44%	1	15%	31	0.86	1	0.31	1

Year	LE	Rank	LT	Rank	Mid	Rank	RT	Rank	RE	Rank	Sacks	ASR	Rank	Short	Long
2009	4.15	13	3.09	1	3.72	10	3.66	9	3.56	9	44	7.8%	3	19	16
2010	3.80	9	3.98	16	3.63	5	3.18	4	3.23	4	36	6.4%	14	14	14
2011	4.60	23	3.73	10	3.64	6	4.71	26	2.21	1	42	6.5%	17	15	17

Defensive end Justin Smith, inside linebacker Patrick Willis, and inside linebacker NaVorro Bowman each made last year's Associated Press All-Pro first team. The 2011 49ers joined the 1974 Steelers, 1977 Broncos, 1985 Bears, 1991 Eagles, and 2002 Buccaneers as the only post-merger teams to have three of their front seven receive the honor in the same season. To boot, the combination of Willis and Bowman give San Francisco two of the four inside linebackers since the merger who made first-team All-Pro by their second season. (Brian Urlacher and Jon Beason are the others.) These honors were a long time coming for Smith, however, as he finally entered the national consciousness after toiling in obscurity on a decade's worth of bad teams. Smith's 200 tackles, 29 sacks, and 92 hurries lead all 3-4 defensive linemen over the past four seasons, with his closest rivals lagging 41 tackles (Darnell Dockett), eight sacks (Calais Campbell), and 28.5 hurries (Dockett) behind. As with Smith, Willis' greatness is due to his versatility and seeming omnipresence. In terms of how often he shows up in the play-by-play, Willis has ranked among the top 10 at his position three times in the past four years (Smith too). When the 49ers had little pass rush to speak of in 2009 and 2010, Willis contributed 10 sacks (most among 3-4 inside linebackers). Last season, the 49ers used Willis in coverage more often than years past, and he responded with his best Success Rate since 2008. With respect to size, speed, range, and all-around acumen, Bowman is about as close to a Willis clone as you're going to find. One of the few things separating the two is that Bowman had as many broken tackles in 2011 as Willis did in the past three years *combined*. However, this shouldn't be much of a concern going forward given Bowman's youth and sure-handedness in college.

Fans partial to the 49ers believe the front seven should have received another post-season honor: Defensive Rookie of the Year for right outside linebacker Aldon Smith, who had the seventh-most hurries in 2011 (first among rookies) and the second-most sacks by a rookie since it became an official stat in 1982. (Jevon Kearse had 14.5 in 1999.) A talent like Smith can't be relegated to mere "specialist" status, so he'll start at right outside linebacker in 2012 ahead of Parys Haralson even though Haralson never ranked lower than seventh in run stop rate during his three seasons as a starter. You would think a resume like that makes Haralson a perfect candidate for strong-side duties, but Ahmad Brooks will remain the starter there after re-signing for $37 million over six years.

The defensive line rotation will be exactly the same as last year. Nose tackle Isaac Sopoaga and left defensive end Ray McDonald will start alongside Justin Smith, with a trio of young players (Ricky Jean-Francois, Demarcus Dobbs, and Ian Williams) backing them up.

Defensive Secondary

Secondary	Age	Pos	Plays	TmPct	Rk	Stop	Dfts	BTkl	Runs	St%	Rk	Yds	Rk	Tgts	Tgt%	Rk	Dist	Suc%	Rk	APaYd	Rk	PD	Int
Dashon Goldson	28	FS	73	10.7%	32	20	10	5	16	25%	68	6.9	40	24	5.8%	59	13.9	59%	32	8.9	50	10	6
Donte Whitner	27	SS	71	9.7%	41	29	9	4	25	56%	8	6.2	26	34	7.7%	30	15.9	52%	46	8.5	45	11	2
Carlos Rogers	31	CB	61	7.8%	51	35	21	1	13	38%	50	8.2	55	99	20.9%	18	12.6	62%	9	6.9	26	18	6
Tarell Brown	27	CB	55	7.1%	61	26	11	2	9	56%	18	6.7	33	79	16.7%	45	13.9	55%	31	7.6	45	15	4
Chris Culliver	24	CB	41	5.3%	78	9	7	0	2	0%	81	5.0	11	53	11.1%	75	10.4	53%	41	5.0	4	7	1

Year	Pass D Rank	vs. #1 WR	Rk	vs. #2 WR	Rk	vs. Other WR	Rk	vs. TE	Rk	vs. RB	Rk
2009	7	5.9%	17	-33.2%	1	-18.9%	6	-13.3%	6	15.5%	23
2010	24	31.3%	30	33.3%	31	6.1%	22	-16.9%	1	-2.9%	10
2011	5	-5.7%	7	-17.8%	6	-3.9%	17	-1.1%	6	2.1%	19

Prior to last season, the 49ers turned over two of the top three spots on their cornerback depth chart, giving the third player a promotion. Those changes surprisingly turned a perennial liability into a bona fide strength. For one-fifth the cost, Carlos Rogers gave San Francisco what they expected (but rarely got) from Nate Clements. One reason why the free-agent market for Rogers was so soft last offseason was that, with only eight interceptions through six years, he wasn't thought of as a difference-maker. Let this be a reminder, kids: Defensive interception rates are very inconsistent. A truer test of skill is how often defenders get their hands on the ball in general. Such was the case for Rogers, whose low interception rate masked the fact that he led the league with 24 passes defensed (on 97 targets) in 2008, and averaged 16 (on 72 targets) per season from 2008 to 2010 (seventh-most among corners). The interceptions finally came last season, and the 49ers rewarded Rogers with a four-year deal in March.

It seems like forever ago when we named Brown our No. 4 prospect (*Pro Football Prospectus 2008*), but he spent almost all of the previous four seasons as a reserve not because he lacked talent, but because incumbents were entrenched ahead of him on the depth chart. The new regime decided to end the Shawntae Spencer era, and made Brown the Week 1 starter. (Spencer ultimately fell to fifth-string corner, and has since signed a free-agent deal with Oakland.) Brown's play improved as the season progressed. Before San Francisco's Week 7 bye, he had a 50 percent Success Rate and allowed 8.7 adjusted yards per pass; after the bye, those numbers became 58 percent and 7.5. Completing the trifecta of surprises was Culliver, a third-round pick out of South Carolina who played extensively on the outside of San Francisco's nickel packages (with Rogers moved to the slot). He struggled somewhat on deep passes, benefitting from several overthrows after he was already beaten, but played well overall for a rookie. The 49ers view Culliver as their No. 1 cornerback of the future, so it wouldn't be surprising to see him supplant Rogers in the next season or two. Regardless, based on the lengths of their respective contracts, it will be those three at the top of the depth chart until at least the end of 2013, with free agent signee Perrish Cox (ex-Denver) and 2010 undrafted free agent Tramaine Brock playing in dime personnel packages this season.

San Francisco is far less set at safety, however. Primary backups Reggie Smith and Madieu Williams left in free agency, which means that special-teamer C.J. Spillman and 2012 sixth-rounder Trenton Robinson (Michigan State) are an injury away from starting. There are also questions with Pro Bowl free safety Dashon Goldson; he is seeking a long-term deal and the 49ers aren't likely to oblige, so Goldson will be playing under the franchise tender in 2012. One reason for their hesitation is that Goldson is on the verge of becoming the Bret Saberhagen of NFL safeties. Since joining the starting lineup, he was a ball hawk in 2009 and 2011 (averaging five interceptions, two forced fumbles, and eight passes defensed), but a ball dove in 2010 (one interception, zero forced fumbles, and five passes defensed). Strong safety Donte Whitner played better the closer he got to the line of scrimmage. This was no more evident than in San Francisco's Divisional round win against New Orleans, when his first-quarter goal-line hit caused a turnover and knocked Pierre Thomas out of the game, but his flailing effort as last line of defense on Jimmy Graham put the team 97 seconds away from elimination. Given his contract, and the 49ers drafting his heir apparent (Robinson), Whitner needs a great 2012 season to avoid being a cap casualty next March.

Special Teams

Year	DVOA	Rank	FG/XP	Rank	Net Kick	Rank	Kick Ret	Rank	Net Punt	Rank	Punt Ret	Rank	Hidden	Rank
2009	-0.9%	20	1.9	15	2.6	13	-3.6	17	11.1	3	-17.5	32	-14.7	31
2010	-1.4%	22	-1.3	22	-11.8	30	-5.0	22	4.9	13	5.1	8	-1.6	16
2011	6.6%	2	4.7	7	6.4	6	4.8	3	13.1	4	10.0	3	-2.6	17

I·ron·y ('īrənē): *Incongruity between the actual result of a sequence of events and the normal or expected result.* No word better describes the 49ers' fate last season. After being the only unit to rank in the top 10 for all five components during the regular season, San Francisco's special teams pulled off the most epic heel turn since Sgt. Slaughter abandoned America. By re-signing Ted Ginn and lessening his wide receiver workload, the 49ers have positioned themselves to avoid Kyle Williams' steel chair in 2012. On the coverage units, 49ers fans were disappointed this offseason when the team allowed Blake Costanzo to leave in free agency, but it was actually C.J. Spillman who led the team with 15 return tackles, and 13 of those forced a below-average return. Spillman will be the primary backup at safety in 2012, so San Francisco compensated by signing Rock Cartwright, who had as many return tackles as Costanzo last season (12). In 2011, punter Andy Lee and kicker David Akers became only the third tandem since the merger to earn first-team All-Pro honors in the same season, and the first since Chris Gardocki and Cary Blanchard for the 1996 Colts. Lee signed a six-year extension in May, so his Bay Area ROBOPUNTER battle with Shane Lechler will continue into a ninth season. Despite back-to-back Pro Bowl seasons, vagaries of the new collective bargaining agreement forced Philadelphia to allow Akers a shot at free agency, and their loss was San Francisco's gain. Akers set the single-season record for made field goals (44), and finished third in the league with 3.4 points of gross kickoff value.

Coaching Staff

Jim Harbaugh catches a lot of heat for his repeated inability to properly execute a post-game handshake, but getting the 49ers to properly execute plays on offense was the main catalyst for San Francisco's resurgence in 2011. Although observers viewed predecessor Mike Singletary as the prototypical "motivational coach," his only success story in that regard was Vernon Davis. It was Harbaugh who finally coaxed the best out of an entire team that, by most accounts, was chock-full of talent. Not surprisingly, Harbaugh's influence was most evident on offense, where deceptive tactics like motion, diverse personnel packages, pulling guards, and an occasional offsides-inducing pre-snap shift replaced the predictable 1970s offense run by Jimmy Raye. Getting a career year out of Alex Smith didn't hurt, either. Perhaps the most amazing thing about San Francisco's Harbaugh-led turnaround was that he implemented his schematic changes in an abbreviated offseason. With six months to build on the 2011 foundation, expect the 2012 49ers to better resemble Harbaugh's Stanford teams insofar as their featuring of tight ends, the seeds of which matured at the end of last season when Vernon Davis averaged 103 yards and a touchdown over the final three games (including the playoffs).

Greg Roman may reside in the pigeonhole of offensive-coordinators-in-name-only, but his history coaching offensive lines and tight ends makes him the architect of San Francisco's running and play-action passing games. The latter was one of the best in the league last season, so his primary responsibility in 2012 will be to improve the former. Vic Fangio coordinated a lot of bad defenses between the 1996 Panthers and the 2011 49ers, but his other defenses didn't exactly have the elite talent that San Francisco now has, especially at linebacker. Fangio is an acolyte of disguising rushes, so he prefers stunts and zone blitzes with four rushers rather than trying to overwhelm opponents with all-out blitzes. With Justin and Aldon Smith signed through at least 2013, he should be squarely within his comfort zone for the foreseeable future.

Seattle Seahawks

2011 Record: 7-9

Pythagorean Wins: 8.2 (18th)

DVOA: -1.5% (19th)

Offense: -8.7% (22nd)

Defense: -7.1% (10th)

Special Teams: 0.2% (16th)

Variance: 18.1% (24th)

2012 Mean Projection: 7.2 wins

On the Clock (0-4): 12%

Mediocrity (5-7): 45%

Playoff Contender (8-10): 37%

Super Bowl Contender (11+): 6%

Postseason Odds: 40.9%

Projected Average Opponent: -1.7% (24th)

2011: An injury-prone, stagnant offense squanders the emerging talent on defense.

2012: At least our quarterback competition is way more promising than Arizona's quarterback competition.

Win Forever may be the title of Seattle Seahawks head coach Pete Carroll's book, as well as his offseason corporate workshops, but the driving force behind his philosophy is competition. "If you want to win forever, always compete," Carroll writes, going so far as to place competing ahead of actually winning. The "Always Compete" motto even adorns the scoreboard at the Virginia Mason Athletic Center, the team's Renton, Washington headquarters. How strange it must have been then for Carroll, coming off an NFC West title in his first season back in the NFL, to find himself stuck handing his team's starting job to a new quarterback without any training camp competition to speak of.

Once the Seahawks decided not to bring back veteran Matt Hasselbeck, signing Tarvaris Jackson and installing him as the starter at the beginning of training camp actually made sense. With no OTAs or minicamps due to the lockout, and with only a short period of time to get everybody up to speed in first-year coordinator Darrell Bevell's offense, Jackson's experience with in the system would be beneficial both on the field and in the meeting rooms. The Seahawks presented Jackson with a golden opportunity to cement his status as a starting quarterback in the National Football League. They tossed him the keys to an offense he was familiar with and outfitted it with $75 million in brand-new Pro Bowl receivers by signing Sidney Rice and Zach Miller. Despite all those moves, or perhaps because of some of them, *Football Outsiders Almanac 2011* projected Seattle to have the worst offense in the NFL. We were wrong; the Seahawks didn't have the worst offense in football. Thanks in large part to an improved running game, the offense was merely bad, not dreadful.

There are plenty of explanations for Seattle's offensive struggles in 2011. There was a change at offensive coordinator (Bevell replacing Jeremy Bates). A young, inexperienced offensive line expected to start two rookies on the right side (James Carpenter and John Moffitt) was unable to get any on-field work with first-year offensive line coach Tom Cable before training camp. Injuries were also a factor. The Seahawks were the third least-healthy offense in the NFL last season with 53.4 Adjusted Games Lost. That figure includes 23.7 games lost along the offensive line, which was the sixth-highest total in the league, and 27.8 adjusted games lost at the wide receiver/tight end position, the second-highest total in the league. Tight end John Carlson was lost for the entire season to a torn labrum in his shoulder and Rice missed seven games due to a shoulder injury and multiple concussions. The Seahawks were particularly anemic in the first half of the season, scoring just 122 points in the first eight games. But around midseason, injuries propelled veteran offensive linemen Paul McQuistan and

2012 Seahawks Schedule

Week	Opp.	Week	Opp.	Week	Opp.
1	at ARI	7	at SF (Thu.)	13	at CHI
2	DAL	8	at DET	14	ARI
3	GB (Mon.)	9	MIN	15	at BUF (Tor.)
4	at STL	10	NYJ	16	SF
5	at CAR	11	BYE	17	STL
6	NE	12	at MIA		

Figure 1. 2011 Seattle DVOA by Week

Breno Giacomini into the starting lineup, and Marshawn Lynch entered full-on "Beast Mode." Over the final nine weeks of the season, Lynch averaged over 104.5 rushing yards per game and scored 10 of his 12 touchdowns. The team went from 27th in offensive DVOA through Week 9 to 15th in Weeks 10-17.

In terms of back-of-the-bubblegum-card stats, Jackson put up the best numbers of his NFL career in 2011. Jackson completed 60.2 percent of his pass attempts for 3,091 yards with 14 touchdowns. He accomplished this feat despite playing most of the season with a partially torn pectoral muscle. Jackson deserves toughness points for playing through injury, and certainly earned respect in the locker room. Nonetheless, that same Tarvaris Jackson that prompted Brad Childress to play chauffeur for Brett Favre was too frequently on display in a Seahawks uniform last season. Jackson rarely made the big play when the team needed him to, completing less than 50 percent of his pass attempts with zero touchdowns and six interceptions in the final two minutes of a half. He also took 42 sacks, second only to Alex Smith. Part of that can be attributed to an offensive line that was young and constantly shuffling personnel due to injuries both minor (Max Unger missing one game with a foot injury) and major (Moffitt and Carpenter suffering season-ending knee injuries in the span of five days), but some of that was due to Jackson's indecisiveness. Seventeen of Jackson's sacks were "long sacks," with Jackson holding the ball at least three seconds, and Jackson's median sack time of 3.3 seconds was the sixth worst among quarterbacks with at least 300 pass attempts.

With Jackson failing to prove that he was a viable long-term option at the position, the Seahawks' front office set out to find themselves another quarterback. They ended up with two, but not the one they really wanted. Without invitation, Pete Carroll and general manager John Schneider took the team plane to Denver, hoping to score an impromptu meeting with Peyton Manning and convince him to come to the Pacific Northwest. (The rumors that Schneider stood on the tarmac with a boombox playing "In Your Eyes" may or may not be true.) Manning boarded a plane to visit the Arizona Cardinals instead, so the spurned Seahawks turned their attention to Matt Flynn, the consensus No. 2 quarterback on this year's free-agent market. Schneider knew Flynn well, as he was with the Green Bay Packers in 2008 when they drafted Flynn out of LSU in the seventh round and watched him immediately outplay second-round pick Brian Brohm to become Aaron Rodgers' backup. When the Seahawks hosted Flynn for a free agent visit, they did not attempt to wine-and-dine him. They tossed him some gear and put him through an impromptu workout. "We asked him to do a variety of things that we had questions about," Carroll would say of the throwing session after signing Flynn to a three-year, $19.5 million contract that included $10 million in guarantees. "From throwing the ball in the pocket, to moving around and putting the ball down the field. He was very impressive. He has worked very hard and has improved in many ways. This is based on what John saw way back when to where he is now. He is a better athlete, a better thrower and stronger than he's ever been."

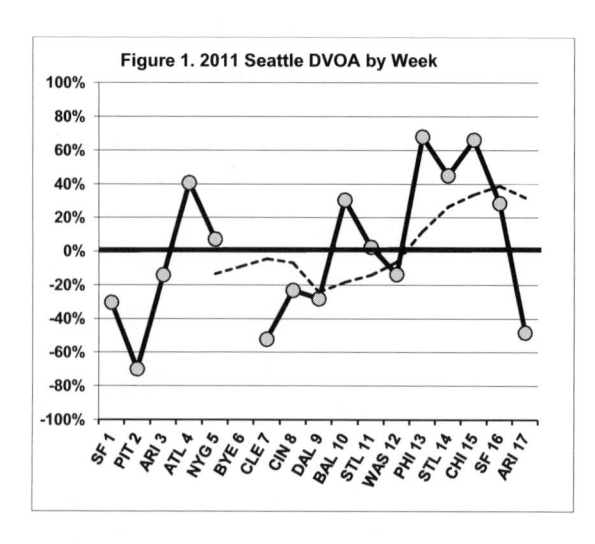

Head coaches are not in the habit of showering their new free-agent signings with derogatory criticism, so Carroll's comments aren't much of a surprise. But they get to the heart of the question everyone has about Flynn: What do we really know about a seventh-round pick with just two starts on his NFL resume? The answer may be "more than you think." Flynn's huge performance against Detroit in Week 17 (31-of-44 for 480 yards and six touchdowns) was good for a

273 DYAR, which makes it one of the 20 best passing performances of the last 20 years. Our own Vince Verhei noted in a January article for ESPN.com that even the worst starting quarterbacks to post a single-game DYAR of 270-plus—Marc Bulger, Randall Cunningham, and Trent Green—made a Pro Bowl. The only one who never made a Pro Bowl, Scott Mitchell, was at least a league average starter for a number of seasons. That puts Flynn's floor at a league average starter who, with the right supporting cast, could perform at a level where he could earn a few trips to the Pro Bowl—in other words, Matt Hasselbeck.

The Seahawks doubled-down on the quarterback position in the third round of the 2012 NFL Draft when they took undersized Wisconsin quarterback Russell Wilson. In his one season with the Badgers after transferring from North Carolina State, Wilson led the nation in passing efficiency in 2011, completing 225-of-309 pass attempts for 3,175 yards with 33 touchdowns and just four interceptions. Wilson has a strong arm and a good release point. His intangibles are off the charts. (So is his Lewin Career Forecast, which we discuss further in the player comments section later in the book.) The only thing keeping Wilson out of the first two rounds of the draft was his height, a shade over 5-foot-10. Doubts about Wilson's size reportedly kept him off some teams' draft boards entirely. Thought to be a developmental prospect behind Flynn and Jackson, Wilson's performance in the team's rookie minicamp so impressed Carroll that he declared the quarterback scramble a three-man race. Carroll tends to be a little excitable, but each player received a third of the reps in the OTAs and it would not be a complete surprise if Wilson made a strong push for the No. 2 job.

Whoever emerges as the starting quarterback—and the smart, i.e. guaranteed, money is on Flynn, even though Jackson is scheduled to take the first-team reps at the start of training camp—could benefit from the collection of current and former Pro Bowlers the front office has acquired over the last three seasons. Lynch ranked second in the league with 201 DYAR after rushing for 1,204 yards and 12 touchdowns in a Pro Bowl season. Lynch has been a key figure in transforming the national image of the Seahawks from a finesse offense under Mike Holmgren to a bigger, more physical offense under Carroll. He was re-signed to a four-year, $30 million contract in March. Improved depth and the healthy returns of Russell Okung and Moffitt to the offensive line should allow Miller to be used for his intended purpose as a receiver, and Rice is expected to be ready for training camp after having both of his shoulders operated on after the season. When the Seahawks want to spread things out, they can count on last year's breakout star, undrafted rookie wide receiver Doug Baldwin, whose emergence was the silver lining around the cloud of injuries. With Seattle desperate for a healthy receiver to step up, Baldwin led the team in every major statistical category despite playing strictly out of personnel groupings with three or more receivers. When the Seahawks prefer to go two-tight end instead of three-wide, they'll now have Kellen Winslow as the "U" tight end, lining up all over the formation as a complement to Miller. Winslow cost the Seahawks just a conditional seventh-round draft choice, and although he has undergone multiple knee operations during his career, he hasn't missed a game in three seasons.

Nevertheless, despite the improvements on offense, the strength of this team is its defense. That's no surprise given Pete Carroll's background. Seattle's defense jumped from 29th in DVOA in 2010 to tenth in 2011, ranking ninth against the pass and 11th against the run, There were a number of reasons, including improved health and the addition of bigger, more physical players better suited to fit Carroll's defensive scheme. Seattle's front seven had just 2.0 Adjusted Games Lost due to injury in 2011, second-fewest in the league behind the Kansas City Chiefs. A full season from Red Bryant and Brandon Mebane, and the addition of Alan Branch, saw the run defense improve from 26th in both Adjusted Line Yards and preventing "Power" runs to 11th and fourth, respectively. Behind them, the Seahawks added 6-foot-4, 246-pound rookie linebacker K.J. Wright, whose emergence allowed them to trade away 2009 No. 4 overall pick Aaron Curry. Whether it was due to the weight of lofty expectations, Curry's immense physical talent could no longer mask his lack of instincts, and the alleged "safest pick in the 2009 NFL Draft" was traded to the Oakland Raiders for a 2012 seventh-round draft choice. ("Who is J.R. Sweezy?" for you *Jeopardy!* fans.)

The improved health of the front seven was not shared by the secondary, but the Seahawks were able to turn injured lemons into lemonade. Normally, injuries force inferior players into the lineup, but sometimes they help a team finally turn things over to better, younger talent, and that's what happened for the Seahawks last season. Nickel corner Roy Lewis opened the season on the PUP list and longtime starter

Marcus Trufant missed the final 12 games with a back injury. Walter Thurmond, Trufant's replacement, suffered a season-ending leg injury just two weeks into his tenure as a starter. The injuries allowed the Seahawks to finally transition from players who fit their old Cover-2 scheme to the kind of cornerbacks that Carroll would prefer: tall, angular players capable of pressing receivers at the line of scrimmage and playing man coverage. The Seahawks had already handed one starting job to 6-foot-4 former CFL star Brandon Browner. When Thurmond went down, the other starting job fell to 6-foot-3 cornerback Richard Sherman, a fifth-round rookie and converted wide receiver out of Stanford. Sherman had just a few dozen NFL snaps under his belt before making his first start, but he would go on to intercept four passes and finish second among cornerbacks in Success Rate. If the scheme works as planned, the strong run defense will force second-and-long situations; then Seattle's tall cornerbacks pressing at the line will force opposing quarterbacks to look down the middle of the field, where young Pro Bowlers Earl Thomas and Kam Chancellor are poised to make big plays from the safety position.

The last step in making the defense work will be improving the pass rush, and that's the deficiency the Seahawks tried to address this offseason. The Seahawks have had an Adjusted Sack Rate of 5.5 percent and 5.3 percent in Carroll's two seasons in Seattle, ranking 28th in the NFL each season. Aside from "Leo" end Chris Clemons, they simply did not have a player capable of getting to opposing quarterbacks with any consistency. The first move on this front was signing former Tennessee Titans defensive end Jason Jones to be a pass-rushing defensive tackle in nickel situations. Jones should be an improvement over Anthony Hargrove, and his addition allows defensive coordinator Gus Bradley to rotate Branch, Mebane, and Bryant as interior pass-rushers in nickel packages this season.

Phase two in improving the pass rush came when the Seahawks used the 15th overall pick in the 2012 NFL Draft on West Virginia defensive end Bruce Irvin, who overcame a checkered past to post 22.5 sacks in 26 games during his two seasons with the Mountaineers. Irvin was a controversial choice for a number of reasons. Many draftniks felt the Seahawks had grabbed him too early, and criticized Irvin as a one-dimensional player who can do nothing *but* rush the passer. There's also the question of his past. Our SackSEER system doesn't like Irvin because that past includes two years of community college. Other observers, a bit less objective than the SackSEER spreadsheets, don't like Irvin's past because it includes Irvin dropping out of high school in the 11th grade and getting mixed up in drugs and crime. Carroll had recruited Irvin when he was head coach at USC, so perhaps he felt he had more familiarity with the person behind the pass-rush specialist than other coaches. The short-term plan is for Irvin to fill the Raheem Brock role, playing about 550 or so snaps opposite Clemons in nickel and dime packages with the hope that his elite speed off the edge will be result in more sacks. Long-term, Irvin is viewed as the "Leo" replacement for Clemons, who turns 31 this season and skipped the team's offseason program in protest of his contract situation.

Winning the division is the No. 1 goal of every team, and the NFC West is once again there for the taking in 2012. The Seahawks have the running game and defense to go toe-to-toe with the San Francisco 49ers and Arizona Cardinals, but the key to beating their mean projection will come down to quarterback play. If Flynn is as ready as the Seahawks think he is, Seattle could post its first winning record under Carroll and return to the playoffs. If he's not, and the Seahawks win another six to seven games and miss the playoffs, Carroll's "Win Forever" mantra will start to ring a bit a hollow. He'll be stuck with three non-winning seasons and a team still searching for the long-term answer at quarterback.

Brian McIntyre

SEATTLE SEAHAWKS 247

2011 Seahawks Stats by Week

Wk	vs.	W-L	PF	PA	YDF	YDA	TO	Total	Off	Def	ST
1	@SF	L	17	33	219	209	-3	-30%	-10%	-16%	-37%
2	@PIT	L	0	24	164	421	0	-70%	-44%	20%	-6%
3	ARI	W	13	10	261	324	1	-14%	-19%	-6%	-1%
4	ATL	L	28	30	372	412	-2	41%	44%	11%	8%
5	@NYG	W	36	25	424	464	2	7%	-22%	-18%	12%
6	BYE										
7	@CLE	L	3	6	137	300	-1	-52%	-79%	-18%	9%
8	CIN	L	12	34	411	252	0	-23%	-7%	-10%	-25%
9	@DAL	L	13	23	381	442	-2	-28%	-1%	24%	-3%
10	BAL	W	22	17	327	323	3	30%	2%	-7%	21%
11	@STL	W	24	7	289	185	1	2%	-42%	-36%	8%
12	WAS	L	17	23	250	416	1	-14%	-1%	19%	6%
13	PHI	W	31	14	347	330	4	68%	40%	-27%	2%
14	STL	W	30	13	359	281	0	45%	13%	-20%	12%
15	@CHI	W	38	14	286	221	4	66%	6%	-49%	12%
16	SF	L	17	19	265	349	-1	28%	30%	-1%	-3%
17	@ARI	L	20	23	369	388	1	-48%	-33%	4%	-11%

Trends and Splits

	Offense	Rank	Defense	Rank
Total DVOA	-8.7%	22	-7.1%	10
Unadjusted VOA	-12.2%	25	-11.3%	7
Weighted Trend	-5.3%	19	-10.5%	9
Variance	9.4%	22	9.5%	29
Average Opponent	-4.0%	2	-5.8%	30
Passing	0.1%	21	-5.8%	9
Rushing	-1.6%	14	-8.5%	12
First Down	-6.8%	23	-12.0%	7
Second Down	0.4%	14	-9.0%	7
Third Down	-25.5%	27	5.5%	19
First Half	-26.0%	30	6.5%	25
Second Half	8.3%	8	-21.7%	1
Red Zone	-10.5%	20	-12.2%	11
Late and Close	2.2%	15	-12.6%	6

Five-Year Performance

Year	W-L	Pyth	Est W	PF	PA	TO	Total	Rk	Off	Rk	Def	Rk	ST	Rk	Off AGL	Rk	Def AGL	Rk
2007	10-6	10.8	9.5	393	291	+10	14.7%	9	6.6%	11	-6.9%	8	1.2%	11	18.9	11	21.9	18
2008	4-12	5.3	5.0	294	392	-7	-30.8%	29	-14.2%	26	11.3%	27	2.9%	9	66.3	32	12.7	6
2009	5-11	4.9	3.1	330	281	+9	-30.8%	29	-19.6%	27	12.0%	29	0.8%	15	44.3	29	30.9	19
2010	7-9	5.4	6.9	310	407	-9	-22.9%	30	-17.3%	29	12.0%	29	6.4%	2	34.3	24	27.2	20
2011	7-9	8.2	8.1	321	315	+8	-1.5%	19	-8.7%	22	-7.1%	10	0.2%	16	53.4	30	25.2	14

2011 Performance Based on Most Common Personnel Groups

Seattle Offense

Pers	Freq	Yds	DVOA	Run%
11	47%	4.9	1.8%	29%
12	21%	5.7	3.1%	41%
21	12%	5.1	-1.3%	73%
22	10%	4.3	-1.9%	77%
02	3%	4.0	-28.5%	0%

Seattle Offense vs. Opp.

Pers	Freq	Yds	DVOA
4-2-5	25%	5.5	7.6%
4-3-4	25%	5.2	-2.2%
3-4-4	22%	4.8	3.3%
2-4-5	13%	4.3	-21.0%
Dime+	8%	5.6	13.0%
3-3-5	6%	3.9	-11.5%

Seattle Defense

Pers	Freq	Yds	DVOA
4-3-4	54%	5.3	-1.3%
4-2-5	34%	4.8	-17.7%
Dime+	6%	8.9	32.4%
G-line	3%	0.6	-27.2%
3-4-4	2%	8.6	34.8%

Seattle Defense vs. Opp.

Pers	Freq	Yds	DVOA
11	31%	5.6	-16.0%
12	25%	5.2	-7.9%
21	17%	6.1	2.2%
22	10%	4.0	-7.0%
10	4%	4.1	-3.5%

Strategic Tendencies

Run/Pass		Rank	Offense		Rank	Pass Rush		Rank	Defense/Other		Rank
Runs, all plays	43%	13	Form: Single Back	68%	9	Rush 3	7.6%	14	4 DB	56%	6
Runs, first half	44%	12	Form: Empty Back	9%	6	Rush 4	63.2%	19	5 DB	35%	22
Runs, first down	52%	16	Pers: 3+ WR	55%	8	Rush 5	22.3%	14	6+ DB	6%	17
Runs, second-long	45%	6	Pers: 4+ WR	5%	11	Rush 6+	6.8%	21	CB by Sides	98%	1
Runs, power sit.	53%	23	Pers: 2+ TE/6+ OL	37%	12	Zone Blitz	9.5%	6	Go for it on 4th	1.00	9
Runs, behind 2H	28%	21	Play action	22%	7	Sacks by LB	27.3%	16	Offensive Pace	29.3	6
Pass, ahead 2H	41%	21	Max protect	12%	12	Sacks by DB	9.1%	13	Defensive Pace	30.7	20

SEATTLE SEAHAWKS

The Seahawks had dramatic splits in their performance before and after halftime. On offense, they went from 30th in DVOA before halftime to eighth after halftime. On defense, they went from 25th in DVOA before halftime to the best defense in the league after halftime. We had a hard time thinking of particular reasons for why such a striking split would exist on both sides of the ball. Maybe they should have had the orange slices before the game instead of at halftime. ☞ Seattle's offense ranked just 30th in yards per drive, but ranked a much better 15th in three-and-outs per drive. ☞ The Seahawks' rank in frequency of play-action fakes went from 28th in 2010 to seventh in 2011. ☞ Only 24 percent of Seattle's throws on third down went to running backs or tight ends (league average was 36 percent). ☞ Seattle allowed 6.8 yards per carry and a league-worst 33.6% DVOA on handoffs to running backs out of the shotgun. ☞ By the count of our game charters, Chris Clemons dropped into coverage on a zone blitz more often than any defensive lineman in the league other than John Abraham.

Passing

Player	DYAR	DVOA	Plays	NtYds	Avg	YAC	C%	TD	Int
T.Jackson	161	-6.0%	495	2790	5.9	5.0	60.8%	15	9
C.Whitehurst*	-160	-49.2%	64	254	4.1	4.6	48.2%	1	1
M.Flynn	225	47.3%	54	496	9.4	6.9	67.3%	6	2

Rushing

Player	DYAR	DVOA	Plays	Yds	Avg	TD	Fum	Suc
M.Lynch	201	8.9%	285	1204	4.2	12	3	46%
L.Washington	-1	-9.1%	53	248	4.7	1	0	36%
J.Forsett*	-27	-24.7%	46	145	3.2	1	0	26%
T.Jackson	-11	-19.1%	29	113	3.9	1	1	--
K.Lumpkin	2	-6.6%	31	105	3.4	0	0	39%

Receiving

Player	DYAR	DVOA	Plays	Ctch	Yds	Y/C	YAC	TD	C%
D.Baldwin	173	14.2%	86	51	788	15.5	6.1	4	59%
B.Obomanu	32	-5.9%	61	37	436	11.8	3.4	2	61%
G.Tate	-10	-14.8%	60	37	385	10.4	4.5	3	62%
S.Rice	45	-3.1%	59	34	485	14.3	3.9	2	58%
M.Williams	21	-5.9%	38	18	236	13.1	3.2	1	47%
D.Butler	15	13.5%	7	6	51	8.5	1.7	0	86%
Z.Miller	-49	-25.4%	44	25	233	9.3	3.2	0	57%
A.McCoy	-41	-32.7%	24	13	146	11.2	5.9	0	54%
C.Morrah	-22	-31.8%	13	6	74	12.3	7.0	0	46%
M.Lynch	16	-7.3%	41	28	212	7.6	7.7	1	68%
J.Forsett*	-24	-26.5%	34	23	128	5.6	6.5	0	68%
M.Robinson	19	5.7%	14	9	74	8.2	7.7	1	64%
L.Washington	-14	-29.8%	14	10	48	4.8	5.2	0	71%
K.Lumpkin	79	16.7%	53	41	291	7.1	5.5	0	77%

Offensive Line

Year	Yards	ALY	Rank	Power	Rank	Stuff	Rank	2nd Lev	Rank	Open Field	Rank	F-Start	Cont.
2009	4.15	3.91	27	56%	29	21%	21	1.19	13	0.72	18	19	30
2010	3.90	3.67	28	48%	29	26%	32	1.06	21	0.84	11	21	21
2011	4.12	4.01	19	73%	2	18%	10	1.11	26	0.72	24	35	27

Year	LE	Rank	LT	Rank	Mid	Rank	RT	Rank	RE	Rank	Sacks	ASR	Rank	Short	Long
2009	1.26	32	4.11	16	4.16	14	4.22	13	4.27	13	41	7.0%	22	24	9
2010	3.00	30	3.48	28	3.60	28	4.24	14	3.06	29	35	6.2%	14	15	14
2011	2.39	30	4.49	10	4.01	18	4.33	16	2.05	30	50	8.3%	24	19	18

After years of offensive line neglect under Tim Ruskell, the Seahawks used back-to-back first round picks on offensive tackles Russell Okung (2010) and James Carpenter (2011), plus a 2011 third-round pick on Wisconsin guard John Moffitt. The plan entering 2011 was to have Okung at left tackle with Moffitt and Carpenter manning the right side. Between them would be Max Unger at center and, for veteran stability purposes, free-agent addition Robert Gallery at left guard. The Seahawks knew that this unit would take some lumps early on due to inexperience, but the hope was that they would come together as the season wore on and provide stability for the years to come. That well-intentioned plan would immediately unravel as Gallery missed four of the first five games with a sprained knee followed by groin surgery. When Gallery returned, Unger was sidelined with a foot injury. Two weeks later, Moffitt tore two knee ligaments (MCL, PCL) and was placed on injured reserve. Four days later, Carpenter, who had eight blown blocks and seven penalties in nine games as a rookie, tore his

ACL in a pass-rush drill during practice and joined Moffitt on injured reserve. In early December, Okung would become the third starting offensive line to land on injured reserve after tearing a pectoral muscle via a post-whistle hip-toss from Philadelphia defensive end Trent Cole. By the regular season finale, Paul McQuistan was the starting left tackle, Lemuel Jeanpierre was at right guard, and Breno Giacomini was at right tackle. This is not how offensive line coach Tom Cable envisioned the season playing out, but he can take comfort in knowing that his system and coaching is sound. Even as the talent level along the line decreased, the unit showed some improvement in the second half of the season in pass protection (29 of the 50 sacks allowed came in the first seven games) and run blocking, with the Seahawks averaging 134.7 yards per game and 4.34 Adjusted Line Yards per carry over the final nine weeks of the season.

For 2012, Okung is expected to be healthy and playing left tackle when training camp opens. The 6-foot-5, 310-pound Okung has All-Pro potential, but to reach it he will need to avoid the fluky injuries that have dogged him over the first two seasons. Unger will be back at center, but the rest of the starting jobs on the line are wide open. Carpenter's knee injury was severe, and he may start the regular season on the Physically Unable to Perform list. When he returns, he'll play right tackle or left guard, where he started for Gallery in the 2011 season-opener. Giacomini's performance at right tackle in the second half of the season gives the Seahawks the freedom to move Carpenter inside. The former Green Bay Packers fifth-round pick had two blown blocks compared to Carpenter's eight, and while Giacomini took nine penalties, several were the result of a playing the game with a nasty disposition that Cable is unlikely to want toned down. The Seahawks signed Giacomini to a two-year, $6 million extension in February and followed that up in March with a two-year, $4 million contract for the versatile McQuistan, who started at three different spots along the line last season. Moffitt is also expected to be ready for training camp, but is not assured of a starting role. To guard against the injuries that hit the line last season, the Seahawks signed versatile offensive linemen Frank Omiyale, who can play four of the five spots along the line, including left tackle, and Deuce Lutui, who played for Pete Carroll at USC and has started 72 games at right guard in the NFL. Lutui has battled weight problems throughout his career, ballooning up to nearly 400 pounds in 2010, but switched to a vegan diet and reported to the Seahawks at a svelte 336.

Defensive Front Seven

Defensive Line	Age	Pos	Plays	TmPct	Rk	Stop	Dfts	BTkl	St%	Rk	AvYd	Rk	Sack	Hit	Hur	Runs	St%	Yds	Pass	St%	Yds
Brandon Mebane	27	DT	57	6.8%	6	41	12	0	72%	53	2.5	54	0	4	8.5	54	72%	2.5	3	67%	2.7
Chris Clemons	31	DE	55	6.5%	17	48	26	3	87%	12	-0.9	5	11	16	24	33	85%	1.1	22	91%	-3.7
Alan Branch	28	DT	36	4.6%	28	28	9	2	78%	41	1.6	23	3	1	12.5	26	81%	1.5	10	70%	1.7
Clinton McDonald	25	DT	35	4.4%	31	22	2	1	63%	66	3.5	68	0	3	4	31	68%	3.0	4	25%	7.0
Red Bryant	28	DE	34	4.0%	62	26	6	3	76%	47	1.9	55	1	4	10.5	28	79%	2.0	6	67%	1.7
Raheem Brock*	34	DE	28	3.3%	71	21	9	1	75%	53	2.1	61	3	6	17.5	21	71%	2.4	7	86%	1.4
Anthony Hargrove*	29	DT	16	2.0%	--	13	6	0	81%	--	-0.3	--	3	2	5	10	90%	1.4	6	67%	-3.0
Jason Jones	26	DE	31	4.1%	61	21	11	6	68%	74	2.5	72	3	5	10.5	19	63%	3.6	12	75%	0.8

Linebackers	Age	Pos	Plays	TmPct	Rk	Stop	Dfts	BTkl	AvYd	Sack	Hit	Hur	Runs	St%	Rk	Yds	Rk	Tgts	Suc%	Rk	AdjYd	Rk
David Hawthorne*	27	MLB	121	15.3%	18	60	19	5	4.5	2	1	4	76	54%	99	3.4	60	41	43%	57	5.5	16
Leroy Hill	30	OLB	89	10.6%	50	45	18	3	5.4	4	1	5.5	48	65%	57	4.2	92	31	47%	52	7.5	57
K.J. Wright	23	OLB	63	7.5%	88	40	14	3	3.5	2	4	4	48	65%	57	3.4	57	21	53%	27	7.5	59
Barrett Ruud	29	MLB	60	12.2%	39	29	11	7	5.7	0	1	0	42	52%	103	4.2	91	28	35%	74	9.6	72

Year	Yards	ALY	Rank	Power	Rank	Stuff	Rank	2nd Lev	Rank	Open Field	Rank
2009	4.24	3.93	10	50%	3	20%	13	1.11	15	0.99	23
2010	4.34	4.29	26	68%	27	16%	26	1.04	7	0.93	24
2011	3.79	3.95	11	49%	4	20%	16	1.11	9	0.49	4

SEATTLE SEAHAWKS

Year	LE	Rank	LT	Rank	Mid	Rank	RT	Rank	RE	Rank	Sacks	ASR	Rank	Short	Long
2009	4.16	14	3.88	12	3.48	4	4.28	20	4.72	26	28	5.3%	29	9	12
2010	4.98	28	3.95	14	4.42	26	3.83	12	4.42	25	36	5.3%	28	21	11
2011	4.20	13	4.01	15	3.77	9	3.85	8	4.35	29	33	5.5%	28	17	12

The Seahawks became one of the toughest defensive fronts to run against in 2011, making dramatic improvements in Adjusted Line Yards, Power, and Stuffs. Red Bryant's transformation from a defensive tackle who couldn't get on the field his first two seasons in the league to a team leader on defense was complete this offseason when he signed a five-year, $35 million extension that included $14.5 million in guaranteed money. Chris Clemons returns as the starting "Leo," a hybrid defensive end/linebacker position in Pete Carroll's defense. Clemons has led the Seahawks in sacks (11) and hurries (27, 24.5) in each of the last two seasons. Raheem Brock had plenty of quarterback hurries but fell from eight sacks to three; he is unlikely to return for the 2012 season. First-round pick Bruce Irvin will take Brock's snaps in pass-rushing situations and could be the long-term option at the "Leo" position. Irvin produced 22.5 sacks in 26 games at West Virginia and will provide a strong test for SackSEER's bias against junior college transfers. Starting a trio of 300-plus-pound run-stuffing defensive linemen (Bryant, Brandon Mebane, and Alan Branch) is going to slow down a team's pass rush, but Branch (three sacks, 12.5 hurries) flashed some pass-rush potential from the defensive tackle position. The Seahawks signed former Tennessee Titans defensive end/tackle Jason Jones to a one-year, $4.5 million contract with the hope that the 6-foot-5, 280-pounder can bring some pressure up the middle in nickel situations. Clinton McDonald returns in a rotational role along with 2012 fourth-round pick Jaye Howard, a penetrating 3-technique tackle who had 11 sacks during his career at Florida.

David Hawthorne replaced Lofa Tatupu as the starting middle linebacker, led the Seahawks in tackles for a third straight year, and showed improvement in pass coverage. That still wasn't enough to get this Seahawks front office to spend money at the linebacker position the way the old regime did, so Hawthorne signed with New Orleans. His replacement is yet to be determined. 2011 fourth-round pick K.J. Wright started the 2011 season-opener at middle linebacker for an injured Hawthorne before replacing former No. 4 overall pick Aaron Curry as the starting strong-side linebacker a few weeks later. Wright has the range and coverage ability to play inside, but also has the long, rangy body to play opposite the "Leo" (Clemons or Irvin) in a 3-4 alignment. A more likely option at middle linebacker is second-round pick Bobby Wagner, a 6-foot, 241-pound tackling machine (445 tackles, 28.5 for a loss in 48 games) from Utah State. Wagner can play all three linebacker positions in a 4-3, but has the size, speed and coverage ability to play in the middle. On the weak side, Leroy Hill rebounded from a 2010 season lost to injury, arrests and suspension to start all 16 games. Hill was arrested for possession of marijuana in February, but those charges were quickly dropped and Seattle re-signed him to a one-year, $1.6 million contract in March. Barrett Ruud (ex-Titans) and the returning Matt McCoy provide linebacker depth for the veteran minimum.

Defensive Secondary

Secondary	Age	Pos	Plays	TmPct	Rk	Stop	Dfts	BTkl	Runs	St%	Rk	Yds	Rk	Tgts	Tgt%	Rk	Dist	Suc%	Rk	APaYd	Rk	PD	Int
Kam Chancellor	24	SS	107	13.6%	8	54	24	10	58	53%	13	5.5	10	36	8.7%	20	11.6	68%	8	5.6	8	13	4
Earl Thomas	23	FS	97	11.5%	22	42	19	6	52	54%	10	6.2	23	35	7.9%	28	13.2	61%	18	6.9	26	7	2
Brandon Browner	28	CB	77	9.1%	26	34	16	1	12	8%	79	9.9	66	89	20.0%	25	15.5	50%	50	9.4	72	23	6
Richard Sherman	24	CB	70	8.3%	42	33	21	4	14	21%	73	6.5	31	81	18.3%	34	13.9	66%	2	5.4	7	19	4
Marcus Trufant	32	CB	26	12.4%	--	7	4	2	7	29%	--	5.1	--	32	28.9%	--	10.2	49%	--	6.1	--	4	1
Roy Lewis	27	CB	21	4.0%	--	5	4	2	3	33%	--	7.3	--	18	6.5%	--	7.3	61%	--	6.0	--	1	0

Year	Pass D Rank	vs. #1 WR	Rk	vs. #2 WR	Rk	vs. Other WR	Rk	vs. TE	Rk	vs. RB	Rk
2009	30	20.7%	28	16.2%	27	23.0%	32	11.5%	20	31.0%	30
2010	29	-3.0%	14	33.8%	32	20.9%	28	-2.8%	10	19.4%	29
2011	8	-3.3%	10	-44.1%	1	-17.8%	11	2.0%	11	35.2%	32

By the end of the 2011 season, the Seahawks were starting four defensive backs in their first or second season in the NFL. Yet three of the four were chosen for the Pro Bowl, and the one player who did not make it to Honolulu may ultimately become the most valuable player in the group. Free safety Earl Thomas has flashed Pro Bowl potential from day one, intercepting five passes and showing off his instincts and range as an undersized centerfielder as a rookie. In his second season, Thomas came down with fewer interceptions, but his Success Rate remained the same and he showed Troy Polamalu-like instincts in making more plays at or behind the line of scrimmage, lowering his Yards per Run from 9.3 to 6.2. The 6-foot-3, 232-pound Chancellor joined Thomas in the Pro Bowl, showing more range than a player his size should reasonably expect to have. He ranked in the Top 10 in Yards per Run, Success Rate and Yards per Pass to go along with four interceptions and a sack in his first season as a starter. Chancellor has room for improvement (he had a team-high 10 broken tackles), but there is little debate that the Seahawks have the best young safety duo in the league. The Seahawks added versatile safety Winston Guy in the sixth round of the 2012 NFL Draft to join Chris Maragos and Jeron Johnson behind Thomas and Chancellor on the depth chart.

The real shocker among the Seahawks' three Pro Bowlers, however, was Brandon Browner, a 6-foot-4, 221-pound street free agent from the Canadian Football League. Nobody could have foreseen Browner locking down a starting job in training camp, pushing former first-round pick Kelly Jennings off the roster, and finishing among the NFL leaders with six interceptions. Browner's lofty interception total may be behind his Pro Bowl nod, as he ranks outside the Top 50 in Success Rate and Yards per Pass. Browner also led the NFL in penalties (19) and was second in penalty yards (167), accounting for six of the ten defensive pass interference flags against the Seahawks. The true bright spot at cornerback was 2011 fifth-round pick Richard Sherman, a lanky, 6-foot-3, 195-pound converted wide receiver from Stanford who was thrust into service in Week 5 after Marcus Trufant and Walter Thurmond suffered season-ending injuries. Sherman made the top ten in both of our cornerback charting stats and was a willing participant in run support. He has the physicality, short memory and cockiness to match-up against the opponents' top receiver. After two stints on injured reserve in the last three seasons, the Seahawks released Trufant in February before re-signing him to a team-friendly contract in April. Trufant will compete with Roy Lewis, 2011 sixth-round pick Byron Maxwell and 2012 sixth-round pick Jeremy Lane for the nickel corner role. Thurmond would be in that mix, but suffered a setback in his return from a broken leg and may not be available at the start of the season.

Special Teams

Year	DVOA	Rank	FG/XP	Rank	Net Kick	Rank	Kick Ret	Rank	Net Punt	Rank	Punt Ret	Rank	Hidden	Rank
2009	0.6%	15	2.4	13	11.8	2	-4.4	20	-2.1	22	-3.9	23	-2.8	20
2010	5.3%	3	-2.3	26	11.6	6	18.3	2	-1.0	22	4.4	9	11.1	2
2011	0.1%	16	3.6	10	-2.0	24	1.9	12	-3.0	20	0.3	16	13.2	3

Steven Hauschka had a good year placekicking, 25-for-29 on reasonable field-goal attempts and 0-for-1 on ridiculous 61-yard end-of-game prayers against the Atlanta Falcons. However, Hauschka can't rival former Seahawks kicker Olindo Mare on kickoffs. Even with the new kickoff rules in place, Hauschka's touchback percentage was 34.7 percent, which ranked 23rd among NFL kickers. (Mare ranked second at 63.1 percent.) A training camp battle will pit Hauschka against undrafted rookie Carson Wiggs, who was 56-of-76 on field goal attempts at Purdue and is known for his strong leg. (He kicked a 67-yard field goal in the Boilermakers' 2011 spring game.)

Punter Jon Ryan had a career-high 46.6 gross average in 2011 and was among the top five punters in gross punt value (9.1 points of estimated field position), but was hindered by Seattle's poor coverage units. That group was negatively impacted by special teams captain Roy Lewis opening the season on the PUP list and core special-teamer Matt McCoy's season-ending knee injury in Week 3. There would be improvement in the second half of the season, due largely to the midseason signings of linebacker Heath Farwell and safety Chris Maragos, who finished 1-2 on the team in special teams tackles.

Leon Washington returned three kickoffs for touchdowns and provided 17.3 estimated points of field position on kick returns in 2010. The Seahawks signed Washington to a four-year, $12.5 million contract extension, then watched as the NFL moved kickoffs to the 35-yard line, significantly reducing the advantage that a dynamic return specialist like Washington provided. Alas.

Coaching Staff

There was a lot of turnover on this staff between 2010 and 2011, but very little between 2011 and the upcoming season. Without a lockout looming over the league, offensive coordinator Darrell Bevell and offensive line coach Tom Cable will get some actual on-field and classroom time with their players during a normal, albeit scaled-down offseason. Gus Bradley enters his fourth season as the Seahawks' defensive coordinator; he actually pre-dates the arrival of Carroll. An interesting addition to the staff is Marquand Manuel, who once replaced Ken Hamlin as a starting safety on the franchise's lone Super Bowl team and now will be a coaching assistant on special teams.

Tampa Bay Buccaneers

2011 Record: 4-12	**2012 Mean Projection:** 7.1 wins
Pythagorean Wins: 3.2 (30th)	**On the Clock (0-4):** 13%
DVOA: -25.1% (30th)	**Mediocrity (5-7):** 45%
Offense: -11.5% (26th)	**Playoff Contender (8-10):** 35%
Defense: 14.2% (31st)	**Super Bowl Contender (11+):** 7%
Special Teams: 0.6% (14th)	**Postseason Odds:** 15.9%
Variance: 22.4% (30th)	**Projected Average Opponent:** 0.2% (19th)

2011: In tribute to the 2011 Bucs, please quit reading halfway through the chapter.

2012: Coaching staff circus hides quality offseason personnel changes. Or vice versa.

'Twas the night before Christmas, and the Buccaneers had just lost their ninth straight game, falling 48-16 to a Panthers team obviously waxing at the same time that the brief Raheem Morris era waned. That loss came on the heels of 38-19, 41-14, and 31-15 defeats. The following week, the Falcons took a 42-7 halftime lead over the Bucs before Mike Smith mercy-cleared his bench.

It was as ugly and futile a stretch of football as modern fans have ever seen. Yet in the days after the Panthers loss, a defiant Morris defended his efforts in a very merry press conference that inspired both snickers and a future hit by indie band Dawes.

"I will never fire myself," Morris said. "You don't go from being a Coach of the Year candidate, to being the worst coach in the league, to get fired within a year. It's about us. It's a little bit of everything."

It was a little bit of everything. The effort and the schemes. Josh Freeman's Desert Eagle. Albert Haynesworth's lazy dreams. The kids who didn't develop and the pressure they could not bring. It was a little bit of everything, which is precisely why Morris deserved to be fired: Systemic collapse falls squarely on the shoulders of the coach, especially when the general manager has earned rave reviews for his recent drafts and salary cap management.

The Glazer family and GM Mark Dominik wanted a "big picture" guy in the wake of Morris' dismissal, so they hired Greg Schiano, the man who made Rutgers football relevant for the first time since the Scarlet Knights' 6-4 win over Princeton in 1869.

Schiano performed the nearly impossible feat of getting New Jersey prospects who traditionally fled to Wisconsin or Miami excited about life off Exit 9. Schiano exhibited both patience and a common-sense approach to talent development. The former Butch Davis defensive disciple arrived in Piscataway with a blitz-happy Miami-style scheme, then quickly adjusted to a more conservative, zone-based philosophy when he discovered what third-team Passaic County All-Stars could and couldn't do. His defense opened up as the talent improved, and his offensive coordinators tinkered with their systems to account for talents like Ray Rice, Brian Leonard, Kenny Britt and Mohammad Sanu.

It was an impressive accomplishment, and the concept of hiring a mid-major collegiate empire builder to get an NFL team full of young talent pointed in the proper direction makes sense on paper. Unfortunately, Schiano started making mistakes in Tampa before he even got his office chair properly adjusted, reminding us again of what Butch Davis, Steve Spurrier, Nick Saban, Lou Holtz, and countless others have taught us: The NCAA and NFL are completely different.

Schiano's organizational skills and his detail-oriented approach are his calling cards, so his disorga-

2012 Buccaneers Schedule

Week	Opp.	Week	Opp.	Week	Opp.
1	CAR	7	NO	13	at DEN
2	at NYG	8	at MIN (Thu.)	14	PHI
3	at BAL	9	at OAK	15	at NO
4	WAS	10	SD	16	STL
5	BYE	11	at CAR	17	at ATL
6	KC	12	ATL		

Figure 1. 2011 Tampa Bay DVOA by Week

nized bungling of the pesky detail of filling out his staff was troubling. Several coveted coordinator candidates turned down interview requests with the Buccaneers. Other potential assistants could not get permission from their teams for interviews. (Sometimes, of course, "I could not get permission," means "I am using my boss as a polite excuse for blowing you off.") One person who was all too eager to get involved in the Schiano regime was Butch Davis himself, who was fired from North Carolina in the wake of the usual NCAA scandals. Davis still receives severance money from North Carolina that disappears the moment he takes a coaching job, so Schiano and the Buccaneers accommodated him with the title "Special Assistant to the Coach," which sounds like something between Dwight Schrute's title on *The Office* and a way to sneak a mistress onto the payroll.

Davis' role in the organization is unclear. In a series of rather apologetic articles, *Tampa Times* columnist Rick Stroud characterized Davis as a "front office ally" for Schaino and someone to help Schiano with the college-to-NFL transition. Everyone insists that Davis will do no coaching (heavens, we would hate to jeopardize that severance) except defensive coordinator Bill Sheridan, who was finally hired one week after Davis. "I view it as a gigantic advantage," Sheridan said at his introductory press conference, while discussing Schaino's defensive background. "That, along with having Butch Davis on our side of the ball." Psst … Bill: Ixnay on the "side of the ball" talk!

Whatever positives Davis might bring as a consigliore or shadow cabinet member, the fact that hiring him and protecting his bank account were prioritized above bringing on actual coordinators sent exactly the wrong message. Schiano's top-down rebuild started with a lateral step, and the master organizer muddled the team's decision structure before there were any decisions to make. Sheridan signed on as a defensive coordinator of last resort, and the man who led the 2009 Giants defense to one of their worst seasons in franchise history sounded a little too eager to subsume his own schemes beneath those of Schiano (and, let's say it, Davis).

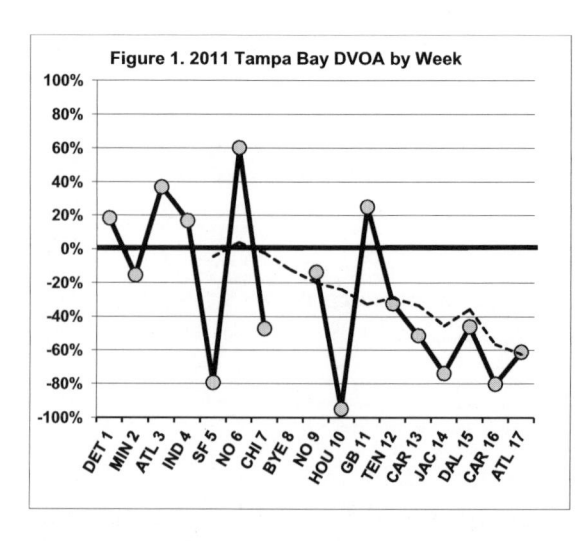

Offensive coordinator Mike Sullivan also arrived to the party late and with the stale whiff of someone who has been settled for. Sullivan took over as the Giants quarterback coach in 2010 and served in that role through their Super Bowl season. If you are Sullivan's agent or wife, you give him credit for "turning Eli around" and ignore the fact that Eli Manning had a Super Bowl ring while Sullivan was coaching another unit in 2007 and that the quarterback was still getting the chorus-of-boos treatment as late as Week 15. Sullivan is an unknown quantity, and he got saddled with a "special assistant" of his own: Jimmy Raye, who was last seen sparring with Alex Smith over the basics of play-calling terminology for the 2010 49ers. Raye, unlike Davis, is actually allowed to coach, which is a bad thing.

Long before the Buccaneers made a single relevant roster move (cutting Albert Haynesworth doesn't count), their coaching staff became a jumble of disparate voices with ill-defined roles and possibly clashing ideologies and agendas. This is the kind of staff the Redskins usually assemble, with comic results. Power struggles are likely, and miscommunications are all but inevitable with Davis whispering in Schiano's ear, Raye mumbling into some headset somewhere, and Sullivan and Sheridan forced to protect the authority they need to do their jobs. Throw in an ownership family that appears more interested in getting the team to play in London than in the Super Bowl and you needed to go into full homer mode to muster any excitement about the Buccaneers' newfound direction before the start of free agency.

When free agency started, however, the Bucs started to look smarter. Wide receiver Vincent Jackson filled the team's biggest need, providing a true top receiver who could move Mike Williams into a complementary role. Guard Carl Nicks infused talent into an offensive line that was overextended to do the basics last year. The draft added late-first-round pick Doug Martin, an all-purpose back who reduces the Bucs' reliance on fumble-prone bulldozer LeGarrette Blount. In May, the Bucs added Dallas Clark and traded away Kellen Winslow. Both Martin and Clark are company men who will supplant/replace talented headaches, showing that Schiano has one eye on team chemistry.

The talent infusion gives Josh Freeman opportunities while taking away excuses. Freeman's public image took an abrupt about-face in the course of a few months last year. During the lockout, he was portrayed as a fiery organizer of player practice sessions and a star on the rise. By the December of Dismemberment, Freeman was an undedicated goof-off whose hand injuries were too serious to allow him to throw straight but not serious enough to keep him away from the pistol firing range on off days. Freeman's interception totals ballooned and his accuracy dropped, but there were many factors involved: the hand injury, some bad bounce luck, receivers who could not get open, backs who could not catch or block, and a fluky 2010 interception total that set expectations a little high for a young quarterback. (Freeman had eight likely interceptions dropped by defenders in 2010, compared to just two in 2011.) Whether he was a cause or product of the late-season malaise is impossible to determine from tape: It's like trying to determine who is drunk from examining crowd footage at a Jimmy Buffett concert. Freeman still has the talent to be a productive starting quarterback. This year, he has something close to the supporting cast.

Defensively, the Bucs will try to improve through youth, health, motivation, and scheme. All heck officially started breaking loose after defensive tackle Gerald McCoy got hurt in Week 6. McCoy is back, joining Adrian Clayborn, Brian Price, Mason Foster, and rookie linebacker Lavonte David to form the nucleus of a front seven that shouldn't allow 2,497 rushing yards once it has decent health luck and an offense that can stay on the field for more than three plays.

Mark Barron gives the Bucs a presence at safety they have lacked since John Lynch left, while free agent Eric Wright takes pressure off Ronde Barber, allowing the future Hall of Famer to ease into a slot-safety role.

The fact that the Bucs spent money on Jackson, Nicks, and Wright at all is interesting in itself. The team was frugal to a fault during the first two seasons of Dominick's tenure, rarely making a peep in free agency. The austerity measures were probably ordered from across the pond, with the Glazers trying to cut their losses from the stagnant Florida economy, make a franchise shift to London appear more palatable and feasible, or both. In Tampa, the penny-pinching was sold as "building through the draft," which is a wise strategy until free agency is totally written out of the script. Morris complained before he was fired that he was only following orders: developing young players and inserting the available bodies into the lineup, a case that was valid up to the point when the 41-14 losses started piling up. The Glazers at least invested some money in giving Schiano a start, Freeman some help, and the defense a chance.

It's now up to Schiano to overcome the bumbling start of his tenure. By May, he was back on message, trading away bad-apple Winslow while symbolically signing Eric LeGrand, a former Rutgers player who was partially paralyzed during a game in 2010. The LeGrand gesture washed away the lingering bad taste left by the circumstances of the Davis hiring. For a team in desperate need of inspiration, an inspirational gesture can work wonders. Of course, the Buccaneers need much more than a human interest angle to become competitive again.

Making the Buccaneers better will be a cinch: It is hard to imagine a team worse than the December Buccaneers. Making them relevant again will be trickier. The Schiano staff must prove it can work in harmony. The Glazers must keep the change purse open. Freeman must rebound, youngsters must develop, and on and on. It is hard to see past a modest improvement in 2012. Like Morris, Schiano could spur a brief improvement, then see the foundation collapse when the owners get thrifty and the feel-good aura wears off. If Schiano, like Morris, finds himself musing aloud about firing himself in two years, he may not appreciate the irony of his first-ever NFL decision: hiring his likely, all too eager successor.

Mike Tanier

TAMPA BAY BUCCANEERS

2011 Buccaneers Stats by Week

Wk	vs.	W-L	PF	PA	YDF	YDA	TO	Total	Off	Def	ST
1	DET	L	20	27	315	431	-1	18%	16%	14%	16%
2	@MIN	W	24	20	335	398	0	-15%	11%	42%	16%
3	ATL	W	16	13	295	325	1	37%	9%	-22%	6%
4	IND	W	24	17	466	318	1	17%	23%	4%	-3%
5	@SF	L	3	48	272	418	-2	-79%	-27%	46%	-5%
6	NO	W	26	20	420	453	4	60%	32%	-28%	1%
7	vs. CHI	L	18	24	280	395	-2	-47%	-44%	4%	1%
8	BYE										
9	@NO	L	16	27	365	453	1	-14%	2%	15%	-1%
10	HOU	L	9	37	231	420	-4	-95%	-56%	43%	4%
11	@GB	L	26	35	455	378	-1	25%	31%	0%	-6%
12	@TEN	L	17	23	308	352	-1	-32%	-34%	-25%	-24%
13	CAR	L	19	38	285	385	-1	-51%	-42%	26%	17%
14	@JAC	L	14	41	280	325	-5	-74%	-46%	11%	-17%
15	DAL	L	15	31	190	399	0	-46%	-18%	29%	2%
16	@CAR	L	16	48	317	433	-4	-80%	-23%	55%	-3%
17	@ATL	L	24	45	294	428	-2	-61%	-34%	31%	4%

Trends and Splits

	Offense	Rank	Defense	Rank
Total DVOA	-11.5%	26	14.2%	31
Unadjusted VOA	-14.2%	26	18.9%	32
Weighted Trend	-21.7%	29	15.3%	31
Variance	5.3%	7	6.8%	20
Average Opponent	0.2%	16	5.7%	2
Passing	-11.6%	24	21.3%	31
Rushing	-2.4%	15	7.6%	30
First Down	-15.1%	27	19.5%	29
Second Down	-6.0%	19	14.0%	28
Third Down	-13.1%	21	1.9%	17
First Half	-12.2%	25	22.5%	21
Second Half	-10.9%	27	4.4%	19
Red Zone	-20.8%	23	1.5%	20
Late and Close	15.9%	7	5.9%	24

Five-Year Performance

Year	W-L	Pyth	Est W	PF	PA	TO	Total	Rk	Off	Rk	Def	Rk	ST	Rk	Off AGL	Rk	Def AGL	Rk
2007	9-7	10.0	10.3	334	270	+15	17.8%	8	5.8%	13	-11.7%	4	0.3%	12	42.0	30	12.6	6
2008	9-7	9.1	8.9	361	323	+4	9.7%	10	-0.5%	20	-10.7%	6	-0.5%	18	27.6	19	15.2	10
2009	3-13	3.7	4.8	244	400	-5	-23.8%	27	-19.3%	26	8.0%	25	3.5%	5	32.3	22	18.9	9
2010	10-6	8.7	8.4	341	318	+9	3.7%	12	8.0%	8	3.7%	23	-0.5%	18	22.9	14	37.9	25
2011	4-12	3.2	5.5	287	494	-16	-25.1%	30	-11.5%	26	14.2%	31	0.6%	14	17.1	6	34.3	20

2011 Performance Based on Most Common Personnel Groups

Tampa Bay Offense					Tampa Bay Offense vs. Opp.					Tampa Bay Defense					Tampa Bay Defense vs. Opp.			
Pers	Freq	Yds	DVOA	Run%	Pers	Freq	Yds	DVOA	Pers	Freq	Yds	DVOA	Pers	Freq	Yds	DVOA
11	52%	5.8	-2.5%	14%	4-3-4	36%	5.1	-20.8%	4-3-4	53%	6.2	12.6%	11	39%	7.0	23.2%
12	19%	4.6	-33.7%	41%	4-2-5	33%	5.7	-3.6%	4-2-5	30%	6.3	6.2%	12	20%	7.1	6.3%
21	19%	5.4	-1.1%	56%	3-4-4	10%	4.6	-18.3%	Dime+	13%	8.0	15.9%	21	17%	6.6	14.7%
22	3%	4.4	10.6%	78%	3-3-5	8%	6.9	20.0%	3-3-5	2%	11.6	197.8%	22	12%	4.8	1.4%
611	2%	8.6	-5.2%	41%	Dime+	6%	6.1	18.0%	G-line	1%	0.9	68.2%	13	4%	7.0	11.2%

Strategic Tendencies

Run/Pass		Rank	Offense		Rank	Pass Rush		Rank	Defense/Other		Rank
Runs, all plays	35%	31	Form: Single Back	75%	4	Rush 3	4.9%	21	4 DB	53%	11
Runs, first half	37%	27	Form: Empty Back	2%	29	Rush 4	65.5%	14	5 DB	33%	23
Runs, first down	41%	32	Pers: 3+ WR	54%	10	Rush 5	17.9%	22	6+ DB	13%	9
Runs, second-long	37%	12	Pers: 4+ WR	2%	21	Rush 6+	11.7%	6	CB by Sides	53%	32
Runs, power sit.	47%	26	Pers: 2+ TE/6+ OL	27%	27	Zone Blitz	4.7%	20	Go for it on 4th	0.92	16
Runs, behind 2H	28%	22	Play action	15%	25	Sacks by LB	13.6%	23	Offensive Pace	33.5	32
Pass, ahead 2H	45%	11	Max protect	8%	27	Sacks by DB	9.1%	13	Defensive Pace	29.8	5

Tampa Bay allowed an average of 6.9 yards after the catch. That's the highest average allowed since 2005, the first year for which we have play-by-play YAC data. ⬤ Tampa Bay allowed 8.1 yards per pass on passes thrown behind the line of scrimmage, nearly a yard more than any other defense. ☞ Tampa Bay's last-place finish in "CB by Sides" has nothing to do with assigning specific cornerbacks to cover the opposition's top target. Instead, it seems to come from a decision at midseason to switch E.J. Biggers from one side to the other. Through Week 9, 70 percent of passes with Biggers as the defender were on the left side. After Week 10, 59 percent of passes with Biggers as the defender were on the right side. ☞ Tampa Bay's offense had one of the biggest gaps in the league between running with one back (5.1 yards per carry, 12.5% DVOA) and running with two backs (4.0 yards per carry, -21.5% DVOA). ☞ Although they didn't use the plays often, Tampa Bay gained more than 7.0 yards per play on draws, running back screens, and wide receiver screens.

Passing

Player	DYAR	DVOA	Plays	NtYds	Avg	YAC	C%	TD	Int
J.Freeman	-96	-13.7%	575	3422	6.0	4.8	63.8%	16	22
J.Johnson*	-91	-46.8%	39	222	5.7	1.7	52.8%	1	2
D.Orlovsky	121	-2.2%	204	1118	5.5	3.1	64.2%	6	4

Rushing

Player	DYAR	DVOA	Plays	Yds	Avg	TD	Fum	Suc
L.Blount	67	0.6%	184	796	4.3	5	3	47%
J.Freeman	70	13.8%	44	238	5.4	4	3	--
E.Graham*	33	13.9%	37	206	5.6	0	1	43%
K.Lumpkin*	2	-6.6%	31	105	3.4	0	0	39%
M.Madu	-4	-14.8%	15	55	3.7	0	0	40%
J.Johnson	2	-8.0%	11	67	6.1	0	1	--
A.Benn	-26	-136.2%	6	-7	-1.2	0	0	--
A.Bradford	-1	-12.2%	5	13	2.6	0	0	0%

Receiving

Player	DYAR	DVOA	Plays	Ctch	Yds	Y/C	YAC	TD	C%
M.Williams	-58	-18.4%	124	65	773	11.9	3.3	3	52%
P.Parker	106	8.2%	65	41	551	13.4	7.0	3	63%
D.Briscoe	121	16.5%	51	35	387	11.1	2.8	6	69%
A.Benn	22	-7.0%	51	30	441	14.7	5.8	3	59%
S.Stroughter	0	-12.3%	7	4	52	13.0	5.0	0	57%
M.Spurlock*	-24	-64.0%	6	2	13	6.5	2.0	0	33%
V.Jackson	259	15.7%	115	60	1106	18.4	3.2	9	52%
K.Winslow	-52	-13.6%	120	75	771	10.3	3.4	2	63%
L.Stocker	-16	-21.1%	17	12	92	7.7	4.3	0	71%
K.Lumpkin*	79	16.7%	53	41	291	7.1	5.5	0	77%
E.Graham*	31	3.0%	31	26	163	6.3	5.3	0	84%
L.Blount	-43	-45.4%	25	15	148	9.9	10.0	0	60%
M.Madu	3	-9.2%	12	10	72	7.2	2.7	0	83%
E.Lorig	4	-6.4%	9	6	53	8.8	6.8	0	67%

Offensive Line

Year	Yards	ALY	Rank	Power	Rank	Stuff	Rank	2nd Lev	Rank	Open Field	Rank	F-Start	Cont.
2009	3.80	3.58	31	65%	13	21%	23	1.06	24	0.62	23	22	40
2010	4.43	3.78	25	60%	17	23%	26	1.18	13	1.21	5	16	24
2011	4.32	3.96	22	65%	11	21%	26	1.23	12	0.79	19	13	32

Year	LE	Rank	LT	Rank	Mid	Rank	RT	Rank	RE	Rank	Sacks	ASR	Rank	Short	Long
2009	4.18	18	4.87	5	3.17	32	4.26	12	2.43	31	33	5.7%	11	10	19
2010	3.41	28	4.25	16	3.81	22	3.57	26	3.40	25	30	6.1%	13	12	12
2011	2.43	29	2.72	32	4.34	10	4.27	17	2.88	26	32	6.2%	14	7	14

The two Jeremys (Zuttah and Trueblood) combined for 17 penalties last season, including seven holds by Jeremy Zuttah. Zuttah was brutal in every way; when he was not clutching or giving up an obvious sack (four Blown Blocks), he could be seen standing around in blitz pickup blocking no one as defenders streamed around him. Zuttah signed a four-year contract in March and is the favorite to replace retired Jeff Faine at center, which is terrifying. Although he has proven himself to be a valuable swing lineman in the past, the move to center suggests that Greg Schiano is looking at the Rutgers alum through scarlet-colored glasses. Ted Larsen is listed as the backup center, but when Faine was hurt last season, Zuttah moved to center with Larsen at guard. Moe Petrus, a 26-year-old undrafted rookie from Connecticut, was the third option.

Jeremy Trueblood committed five false starts last season but was adequate in pass protection. Donald Penn allowed too many sacks and was often outclassed by speed rushers when left alone on the outside. Davin Joseph, the star of the line, had an off year. In fairness, the Bucs linemen were too often given assignments beyond their capabilities: Penn might be isolated one-on-one against a top pass rusher for a whole game, or Joseph would be asked to reach block a defensive end several yards to his right, while Trueblood tried in vain to cut an outside linebacker on a stretch run. Penn, Joseph, and Trueblood are all talented enough to benefit from both the arrival of Carl Nicks and a change of philosophy.

The problems of the Bucs offensive line were exacerbated by some awful pass protection by the backs. LeGarrette Blount often had no idea who to block and was surprisingly easy to toss aside once he figured it out. Fluffy Lumpkin was only a little better. Six-man protection offered Josh Freeman little more than a false sense of security.

Defensive Front Seven

Defensive Line	Age	Pos	Plays	TmPct	Rk	Stop	Dfts	BTkl	St%	Rk	AvYd	Rk	Sack	Hit	Hur	Runs	St%	Yds	Pass	St%	Yds
Adrian Clayborn	24	DE	41	5.2%	38	29	13	5	71%	66	1.5	46	7.5	11	29.5	31	68%	2.9	10	80%	-2.8
Michael Bennett	27	DE	39	5.7%	27	30	15	2	77%	44	1.0	29	4	5	26.5	31	81%	1.0	8	63%	0.8
Roy Miller	25	DT	36	4.6%	27	21	2	2	58%	69	3.6	69	0	1	3	35	60%	3.5	1	0%	6.0
Da'Quan Bowers	22	DE	29	3.7%	66	25	16	3	86%	14	1.0	28	1.5	2	14	21	81%	1.7	8	100%	-0.9
Albert Haynesworth*	31	DT	24	3.8%	44	15	2	3	63%	67	3.2	67	0	6	7.5	19	68%	1.9	5	40%	8.0
Brian Price	23	DT	23	3.1%	56	18	11	0	78%	39	0.6	4	3	2	6	18	72%	1.7	5	100%	-3.6
Frank Okam	27	DT	15	3.4%	--	9	4	1	60%	--	3.7	--	0	0	0	14	57%	3.9	1	100%	1.0
Jayme Mitchell	28	DE	33	4.5%	55	24	10	5	73%	60	2.3	66	1.5	4	6.5	26	69%	2.9	7	86%	0.0
Amobi Okoye	25	DT	28	3.4%	51	22	10	2	79%	35	0.9	7	4	3	11	18	83%	2.3	10	70%	-1.8
Gary Gibson	30	DT	17	2.0%	--	14	5	1	82%	--	0.6	--	3	1	3	12	75%	2.3	5	100%	-3.2

Linebackers	Age	Pos	Plays	TmPct	Rk	Stop	Dfts	BTkl	AvYd	Sack	Hit	Hur	Runs	St%	Rk	Yds	Rk	Tgts	Suc%	Rk	AdjYd	Rk
Mason Foster	23	MLB	85	10.8%	48	43	14	7	5.0	2	2	4	57	63%	63	3.8	86	15	48%	--	6.7	--
Geno Hayes*	25	OLB	65	8.3%	76	40	14	5	3.5	0	0	0	39	69%	39	2.1	8	23	51%	40	7.2	49
Quincy Black	28	OLB	60	8.7%	69	27	9	11	5.3	0	0	1.5	42	48%	109	4.3	98	14	27%	--	7.5	--
Adam Hayward	28	OLB	24	3.0%	--	15	3	0	4.0	0	0	1	19	74%	--	2.8	--	5	23%	--	8.9	--
Dekoda Watson	24	OLB	18	2.6%	--	10	6	1	8.2	1	3	10	8	50%	--	12.3	--	10	52%	--	9.4	--

Year	Yards	ALY	Rank	Power	Rank	Stuff	Rank	2nd Lev	Rank	Open Field	Rank
2009	4.86	4.44	28	80%	31	14%	30	1.31	31	1.06	25
2010	4.92	4.56	30	55%	5	17%	23	1.49	32	1.01	27
2011	5.16	4.37	26	74%	31	23%	4	1.61	32	1.37	31

Year	LE	Rank	LT	Rank	Mid	Rank	RT	Rank	RE	Rank	Sacks	ASR	Rank	Short	Long
2009	3.71	10	4.14	16	4.76	32	4.26	18	3.76	12	28	5.8%	24	9	17
2010	4.83	24	4.40	21	4.67	31	4.71	27	4.04	17	26	4.8%	31	7	14
2011	5.23	29	6.03	32	4.22	19	4.01	11	3.36	15	23	5.2%	30	13	6

Mason Foster was one of the few bright spots of last season. Foster took over at middle linebacker on opening day and was outstanding under the circumstances (rookie starter during lockout year, natural Will linebacker at Mike, defensive line in front of him taking November and December off). There was talk of moving Foster to the weak side before the draft, but defensive coordinator Bill Sheridan was high on Foster since his college days and plans on developing him as the Bucs signal caller on defense. Second-round pick Lavonte David is expected to start on the weak side, though coaches hinted during minicamp that David could get a look at middle linebacker. David recorded 285 tackles in two seasons at Nebraska. He also registered 11.5 sacks, but he is more of a coverage linebacker: He is small and quick, and he defends zones well. Veteran Quincy Black is nothing special on the strong side, but the Bucs don't have anyone to push him.

Eight different defenders started on the Bucs line at various times last season. Gerald McCoy is back from his second torn bicep in two years (different arms) and is usually effective when healthy. Rookie Adrian Clayborn joined Foster on the "bright spot" list, starting every game and playing well against the run and pass. Brian Price also played well all season and cannot be held responsible for the failures of the McCoy replacements lined up next to him. Free agent Amobi Okoye will prevent the Bucs from having to resort to Haynesworth measures.

Da'Quan Bowers earned a late-season starting job and was starting to come around as a run defender, but he tore his Achilles tendon during a May minicamp. Journeyman Michael Bennett returns to the lineup in Bowers' absence. The loss of Bowers was a major blow; the Bucs ignored the defensive line in the draft because they expected the Bowers-Clayborn-McCoy nucleus to develop into a force.

Defensive Secondary

Secondary	Age	Pos	Plays	TmPct	Rk	Stop	Dfts	BTkl	Runs	St%	Rk	Yds	Rk	Tgts	Tgt%	Rk	Dist	Suc%	Rk	APaYd	Rk	PD	Int
Sean Jones*	30	SS	90	11.4%	24	25	7	17	55	31%	55	8.8	60	29	7.9%	27	13.4	49%	54	9.8	63	3	0
Ronde Barber	37	CB	88	11.2%	8	40	18	10	42	55%	21	7.0	42	54	15.0%	56	9.1	52%	43	6.8	24	9	3
E.J. Biggers	25	CB	65	8.3%	43	15	7	9	10	20%	74	10.9	72	84	23.2%	4	12.9	41%	76	9.8	74	13	1
Aqib Talib	26	CB	45	7.0%	62	24	12	4	9	78%	1	5.0	11	47	15.9%	52	12.5	64%	6	5.5	9	11	2
Tanard Jackson*	27	FS	38	7.7%	61	12	3	16	23	22%	73	9.2	67	13	5.6%	62	12.4	63%	14	7.1	30	3	2
Elbert Mack*	26	CB	31	3.9%	--	14	11	5	5	60%	--	13.4	--	32	8.9%	--	8.6	48%	--	8.1	--	5	2
Corey Lynch*	27	FS	24	3.0%	--	9	2	2	9	44%	--	8.9	--	9	2.5%	--	10.0	78%	--	3.9	--	4	1
Eric Wright	27	CB	91	10.8%	11	41	16	12	14	57%	12	5.6	20	94	21.4%	13	12.1	52%	44	7.2	36	13	4

Year	Pass D Rank	vs. #1 WR	Rk	vs. #2 WR	Rk	vs. Other WR	Rk	vs. TE	Rk	vs. RB	Rk
2009	23	4.2%	16	-5.1%	14	11.0%	23	7.0%	17	-9.7%	10
2010	13	-14.2%	6	0.7%	15	-12.0%	10	3.9%	16	12.3%	23
2011	30	-11.1%	5	56.6%	32	12.1%	28	6.4%	15	9.8%	24

The Buccaneers denied rumors that they were shopping Aqib Talib before the draft. Like Asante Samuel, Talib falls under the category of "high-quality cover cornerbacks who had become ibuprofen emergencies for their teams," Samuel because of his tackling and frustration over trade rumors, Talib because of legal problems and injuries. Samuel netted just a seventh-round pick from the Falcons, a sign that the market for players of this type was glutted. Talib finished seventh in the league in yards per pass allowed and can still be excellent when healthy and focused.

Ronde Barber and E.J. Biggers struggled with their roles last season. Barber has lost more than a step to age and was having trouble handling second-tier second receivers like Nate Burleson, who caught four passes in four targets against him. Biggers took a big step back after a fine 2010 season: he sometimes lined up against No. 1 receivers, and he just was not up to the task. Eric Wright is an adequate cornerback-for-hire on his third team in three years, and will take some pressure off Biggers. Undrafted rookie Leonard Johnson (Iowa State) is a pesky, high-effort hitter who will catch coaches' eyes if given a chance. Johnson is an inch short and a step slow but loves contact.

Mark Barron fills a hole at safety that started to open when John Lynch left and nearly swallowed Florida's Gulf Coast last season. Barron tackles well and has great instincts in deep coverage. Cody Grimm showed promise in 2010 before missing most of 2011 with a knee injury. Barber was playing free safety in minicamps, but if Barron and Grimm prove capable as starters, Barber is more likely to play a hybrid-slot role.

Special Teams

Year	DVOA	Rank	FG/XP	Rank	Net Kick	Rank	Kick Ret	Rank	Net Punt	Rank	Punt Ret	Rank	Hidden	Rank
2009	3.0%	5	-11.2	30	6.8	9	9.6	5	0.5	18	11.8	2	14.3	1
2010	-0.4%	18	-0.7	20	-3.1	22	3.9	12	3.3	16	-5.9	27	3.1	8
2011	0.5%	14	7.5	4	1.1	17	0.7	15	4.5	11	-11.0	32	7.2	7

Connor Barth, the Buccaneers' franchise player, attended OTAs in May but had not yet signed his franchise tender. Kickers often receive the franchise tag because it is cheap and expedient, but Barth really was one of the best players on the Buccaneers last season. He went 15-of-17 on field goals beyond 40 yards, with one of his misses bouncing off an upright. The Bucs signed punter Michael Koenen to a six-year, $19.5 million contract in the heady first days after the lockout, when teams were eager to spend money and the Bucs bore some resemblance to playoff contenders who could splurge on a punter. Koenen punted well and finished ninth in the league in touchback percentage as a kickoff specialist. Returner Preston Parker fumbled eight times last season, including a pair of ugly fumbles in that lamentable tar pit of a football game that was Jaguars-Buccaneers. Sammie Stroughter was much more effective on kickoff returns than Parker once he returned from a foot injury in Week 9. On-and-off return specialist Micheal Spurlock, who replaced Parker, is now in San Diego. The Bucs could use additional competition at these positions.

Coaching Staff

We talked a lot about the Bucs coaches in the main essay. LeGarrette Blount praised new running backs coach Earnest Byner in April, calling him "a preaching guy" who dispenses life lessons and philosophy when not offering tips about picking up the blitz. If Byner can reach Blount, he can reach anybody. Gerald McCoy spoke in April about the new philosophy on the defensive line. "It's not that every gap is filled, it's like every gap is destroyed in some way," he told the *Tampa Tribune*. Defensive line coach Randy Melvin will install the gap destruction principles. Melvin worked for Schiano at Rutgers but has coached everywhere from New England to Temple University to British Columbia; only a smart aleck would point out that he hit those three stops in the wrong order. Melvin joined the Buccaneers one day after announcing that he would return to the B.C. Lions as a line coach. Apparently, you can only be on the Buccaneers staff if you are also inconveniencing some other team.

Tennessee Titans

2011 Record: 9-7

Pythagorean Wins: 8.2 (17th)

DVOA: 6.6% (13th)

Offense: 0.6% (15th)

Defense: 0.3% (15th)

Special Teams: 6.3% (3rd)

Variance: 15.9% (21st)

2012 Mean Projection: 7.5 wins

On the Clock (0-4): 10%

Mediocrity (5-7): 39%

Playoff Contender (8-10): 40%

Super Bowl Contender (11+): 10%

Postseason Odds: 31.8%

Projected Average Opponent: 2.8% (6th)

2011: 36-year-old West Coast quarterback + ground-based offense = pass-heavy spread. Wait, what?

2012: Your guess is as good as ours. Or, frankly, theirs.

Jeff Fisher's reign as Titans head coach ended after the 2010 season, following an almost unprecedented 17-year run of coaching the same team. You can count the list of men with a single-team run that long on two hands: Bud Grant, Steve Owen, Chuck Noll, Paul Brown, Don Shula, George Halas, Tom Landry, Curly Lambeau, and Fisher. While Tennessee stayed in-house by promoting offensive line coach Mike Munchak to head coach, removing Fisher swept away the last vestiges of the Floyd Reese-Fisher power structure that prided itself on a power run game and a great defense.

A funny thing happened in its place: A passing game started to grow.

Under Fisher, the Titans had finished in the top 11 in run-pass ratio every single year dating back to 2006, and 14 of the 17 years he was the head coach. Over the last three years, the Titans have gone from running on 46 percent of plays in 2009, to 42 in 2010, to just 37 in 2011. The Titans also used the shotgun more often and more effectively, going from utilizing it the fifth-fewest times in the NFL in 2010 (319) to middle of the pack (13th, 454 times) in 2011 while raising their DVOA out of the shotgun from -16.5% to 24.3%. This is all despite losing their only truly game-breaking wide receiver, Kenny Britt, to a torn MCL and ACL in Week 3. Even the smaller trends showed where Tennessee was heading with their offense. According to our game charters, Chris Johnson split out wide only twice in 2010. In 2011, he did so 41 times. Table 1 shows the evolution of Tennessee's offense over the past few seasons:

Table 1: The Spread Transition

Year	Runs, all plays (Rk)	Runs, first half (Rk)	Runs, first down (Rk)	3+ WR in Formation (Rk)
2009	46% (5)	45% (5)	57% (4)	41% (27)
2010	42% (10)	44% (7)	55% (7)	45% (21)
2011	37% (30)	36% (29)	49% (21)	58% (6)

Most draft experts figured Tennessee would choose a pass rusher or an interior lineman with the 20th overall pick in the draft, but instead they selected Baylor's Kendall Wright, a wideout who thrived mostly in the slot in college. That's a head-scratching pick in the scope of Tennessee's old offensive mantra, but it fits extremely well in the context of what happened last season. Britt accumulated 97 DYAR in his first two games alone, proving that he had turned the corner and become a matchup nightmare. Even accounting for his poor play in Week 3 prior to the knee injury, if he'd played 16 games at his seasonal pace, he would have finished third in wideout DYAR, behind only Calvin Johnson and Jordy Nelson. Journeyman Nate Washington posted a career year, catching more than

2012 Titans Schedule

Week	Opp.	Week	Opp.	Week	Opp.
1	NE	7	at BUF	13	HOU
2	at SD	8	IND	14	at IND
3	DET	9	CHI	15	NYJ (Mon.)
4	at HOU	10	at MIA	16	at GB
5	at MIN	11	BYE	17	JAC
6	PIT (Thu.)	12	at JAC		

Figure 1. 2011 Tennessee DVOA by Week

53 percent of passes his way for the first time despite having to soak up a ton of targets. However, beyond those two, Damian Williams and Lavelle Hawkins combined for -78 DYAR, and the other options on hand, Donnie Avery and Marc Mariani, didn't even merit an extended look. If a team is going to run with three wideouts as often as Tennessee did in 2011, they should at least be three *good* wideouts. Wright is a stab at solving that problem immediately. Offensive coordinator Chris Palmer has always been a proponent of the vertical passing game, but last year Tennessee receivers posted an average of just 4.0 yards after the catch, a number that placed them ahead of only Pittsburgh. A full year of Britt and the emergence of Wright would raise that number significantly.

Many words will be spilled over the Titans' quarterback situation, where second-year quarterback Jake Locker and venerable veteran Matt Hasselbeck will split snaps in training camp. It's a *fait accompli* that Locker will one day claim the throne in Tennessee, but the Titans are in that precarious spot where mistake-free football from Hasselbeck could take them from contender to playoff team this year. Locker's completion percentage was a big problem in college, where he completed just 53 percent of his passes. That showed up again in his limited trials last season, as he completed just 51.5 percent of passes in his rookie year. However, his overall performance was rather impressive: a 22.0% DVOA, four touchdowns, and no interceptions in 70 attempts. It's rather rare for a rookie quarterback to put up a DVOA that high and not get more field time. In fact, the only real comparable quarterbacks in recent history (i.e. rookie quarterbacks with between 20 and 99 passes and a positive DVOA) are Tim Tebow in 2010 and Troy Smith in 2007. Neither Tebow nor Smith is a good comparison for Locker. Tebow was picked in the first round, but didn't have anywhere near the clout that Locker carried with scouts. Smith was only a fifth-round pick.

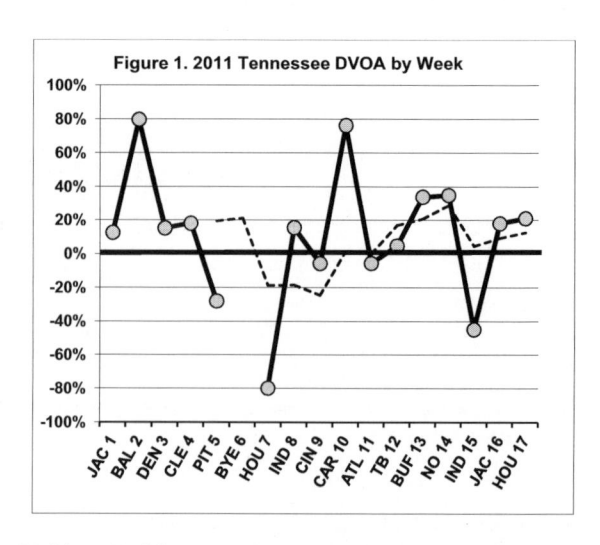

Neither Smith nor Tebow saw significant field time until the last two games of their respective rookie years, nor did they have a quarterback as established as Hasselbeck put in front of them. Tebow is an interesting parallel as a first-round quarterback who has struggled with his accuracy, but Locker has neither the "he just wins" college narrative nor the same questions about his arm talent.

Hasselbeck spent most of his career in Seattle's timing-and-rhythm West Coast offense. He's not someone with the arm strength to hit the seam as often as Palmer would like, especially at the age of 37. On the other hand, Palmer is a big fan of option routes. Hasselbeck will have an edge there, as that's a skill that is often tough for young quarterbacks to learn. The Titans will have to choose: low-risk and low-upside, or high-risk and high-upside. Our KUBIAK projection system likes Hasselbeck over Locker, but it's not exactly a slam dunk. We project Locker with more interceptions and more sacks, but he makes up for some of that with more yards per completion plus 200 yards of rushing value. The difference between the two in projected completion rate is actually less than three percentage points.

Whoever wins the competition will be handing off to Johnson, and how Johnson bounces back will be another key to the Titans' fortunes. While everyone remembers the 2,000-yard season he picked up in 2009, he wasn't exactly a force in 2010. His DVOA slipped from 14.0% (sixth in the NFL) in 2009 to -7.5% in 2010 (33rd). His step back in 2010 was largely ignored due to his still-beefy traditional statistics, but he clearly became a boom-or-bust runner with a low success rate. That only worsened in 2011. Coming off an enormous extension that made him one of the highest-paid backs in the NFL, Johnson cratered to a -15.1% DVOA, which placed him behind every back with more than 100 carries except for Thomas Jones and Daniel Thomas. The Titans finished dead last in rushing offense DVOA.

A lot of excuses were bandied about for Johnson's lack of production. The interior offensive line drew the brunt of the criticism—and some of it was definitely earned—but there was also the time missed in training camp. Some sources within the organization even said they didn't think he came into the season in playing shape. Running the tape back left you with the feeling that Johnson wasn't right at all. He was overly patient, and tended to buckle and brace as soon as he saw contact coming. We're not comfortable jumping into the armchair psychologist's chair, so we won't, but clearly the struggles had as much to do with Johnson as it did with what was going on around him.

Like most NFL contracts, Johnson's deal is year-to-year. The Titans had the opportunity to void the deal and move on this offseason, but chose to stick with Johnson. The Titans may feel optimistic because Johnson improved significantly in the second half of the season. From Week 10 onwards, he averaged 4.83 yards per carry with a 46 percent Success Rate and a -2.2% DVOA. That's a bit more boom-and-bust than we tend to like at FO, but it's a damn sight better than what he did in the first nine weeks (3.02 yards per carry). However, the Titans also may have been emboldened by the fact that they're not locked into Johnson past 2012. Johnson's deal is structured so that next offseason, it doesn't become fully guaranteed until the fifth day of the league year. The Titans could get out of the contract during that small window if he again fails to produce. We are predicting a return to 2010 form, and if Johnson can hit that, it's likely the Titans will keep paying him. The problem is that Tennessee has no real backup plan if they are still stuck with the Johnson of 2011, especially the first half of 2011. Javon Ringer was every bit as bad as Johnson last year, and Jamie Harper didn't show much in his short trial either. The Titans have pinned all of the running game hopes on Johnson resuscitating his career and the free-agent signing of 35-year-old guard Steve Hutchinson. It very well could happen, but this scenario seems to ride an awful lot on the word "could" instead of "should."

Defensively, Titans coordinator Jerry Gray has promised wholesale changes to his unit, emphasizing that last year he utilized a 4-3 defense primarily due to the lockout and the lack of installation time available. Sticking to Gray's interpretation of the 4-3 led Tennessee to move its best pass-rushing tackle (Jason Jones) to defensive end in order to help stop the run. Naturally, with that and the loss of Jason Babin, the Titans plummeted to 31st in Adjusted Sack Rate.

Gray is still well-regarded around the league. He was a candidate for head-coaching gigs in Indianapolis and Tampa Bay this offseason, and rookies Jurrell Casey and Colin McCarthy were instant contributors after he drafted them. When he coached Buffalo earlier in the century, he mostly utilized a 3-4 defense. While Gray hasn't given out the game plan as we head to press, a lot of the recent moves that Tennessee has made are trending in that direction. Casey and Michigan third-rounder Mike Martin both profile as potential nose tackles; North Carolina second-rounder Zach Brown and last year's second-rounder Akeem Ayers give the Titans a pair of athletic linebacker chess pieces to move around; and Tennessee's big stab at improving last year's weak pass rush, free-agent addition Kamerion Wimbley, has primarily operated as a 3-4 endbacker over the course of his career.

The Titans are going to be counting on Gray to keep developing the youngsters, because this offseason's other personnel moves were neutral at best. Wimbley should help the pass rush to some extent, but the loss of Cortland Finnegan will take the air out of the depth Tennessee had accumulated at corner. Finnegan had an amazing season last year according to our charting project, leading all qualifying cornerbacks in yards per pass allowed and allowing just 2.6 yards after catch. Despite his statistical inconsistency—Finnegan had good charting stats in 2009 and terrible stats in 2010 before his awesome 2011—the Titans lost a good one when he joined Fisher in St. Louis this offseason. Alterraun Verner and Jason McCourty should be a respectable starting tandem, if not a great one, but the depth chart behind them is stuffed with question marks. Fourth-round rookie Coty Sensabaugh out of Clemson and 2011 seventh-rounder Tommie Campbell have drawn most of the OTA hype about filling the nickelback position, though former third-rounder Ryan Mouton, coming off an ACL tear, is also in the mix. With nickelbacks drastically increasing in importance these days, it's becoming a bigger risk to entrust the role to a youngster with no track record of playing well. Gray's work as a defensive backs coach should specifically help in this area of his job, but there's no guarantee that Tennessee enters this season with a nickelback worth his salt on this roster.

For a team that we project to win a fair share of games this year, Tennessee sure does walk into the season with a lot unsettled. This is a team that is transitioning into some different ideas on both sides of the ball, a team that doesn't know who its starting quarterback will be, what it will get out of its highest-paid player, or how Gray will mold the defense. Despite their difficult out-of-division schedule against the AFC East and NFC North, there isn't much Tennessee could do to surprise us. It's easy to imagine a sudden AFC South title, or the elevator slamming into the basement like we predicted in *FOA 2011* … or the same frustrating mix of talent, injuries, and weak points that left them on the fringe of contention last year.

This is a team that has fundamentally changed all of its old questions. We're all waiting to see the new answers.

Rivers McCown

2011 Titans Stats by Week

Wk	vs.	W-L	PF	PA	YDF	YDA	TO	Total	Off	Def	ST
1	@JAC	L	14	16	292	323	0	13%	22%	8%	-2%
2	BAL	W	26	13	432	229	2	80%	34%	-59%	-13%
3	DEN	W	17	14	333	231	0	15%	1%	-22%	-8%
4	@CLE	W	31	13	332	416	0	18%	29%	9%	-2%
5	@PIT	L	17	38	306	431	0	-28%	-11%	19%	2%
6	BYE										
7	HOU	L	7	41	148	518	-2	-80%	-39%	40%	0%
8	IND	W	27	10	311	399	2	16%	1%	2%	17%
9	CIN	L	17	24	328	319	-1	-6%	5%	16%	6%
10	@CAR	W	30	3	383	279	1	76%	6%	-46%	24%
11	@ATL	L	17	23	298	432	0	-6%	11%	18%	1%
12	TB	W	23	17	352	308	1	5%	-41%	-24%	22%
13	@BUF	W	23	17	317	386	2	34%	6%	-6%	22%
14	NO	L	17	22	373	437	0	35%	21%	-12%	2%
15	@IND	L	13	27	388	287	-2	-45%	-41%	9%	5%
16	JAC	W	23	17	407	300	-2	18%	12%	9%	14%
17	@HOU	W	23	22	361	387	0	21%	16%	6%	12%

Trends and Splits

	Offense	Rank	Defense	Rank
Total DVOA	0.6%	15	0.3%	15
Unadjusted VOA	1.5%	16	-2.6%	13
Weighted Trend	-4.2%	17	1.7%	17
Variance	18.6%	32	5.6%	12
Average Opponent	-0.2%	15	-2.1%	21
Passing	15.3%	12	8.6%	21
Rushing	-13.4%	32	-9.4%	10
First Down	-2.5%	19	7.9%	24
Second Down	-14.5%	24	-7.9%	9
Third Down	29.5%	6	-1.1%	13
First Half	0.2%	16	-6.1%	10
Second Half	0.9%	13	6.4%	23
Red Zone	17.2%	4	-11.6%	13
Late and Close	-9.7%	24	3.9%	21

Five-Year Performance

Year	W-L	Pyth	Est W	PF	PA	TO	Total	Rk	Off	Rk	Def	Rk	ST	Rk	Off AGL	Rk	Def AGL	Rk
2007	10-6	8.1	9.7	301	297	0	9.9%	11	-4.0%	20	-14.4%	1	-0.4%	17	4.7	1	10.3	5
2008	13-3	12.1	11.8	375	234	+14	23.8%	5	4.0%	16	-18.6%	5	1.3%	14	9.0	3	14.4	9
2009	8-8	6.7	7.9	354	402	-4	-6.6%	21	4.2%	15	9.1%	26	-1.7%	24	7.4	3	14.9	5
2010	6-10	8.5	8.6	356	339	-4	6.6%	11	-4.5%	20	-5.8%	8	5.3%	6	21.0	13	10.6	5
2011	9-7	8.2	8.3	325	317	+1	6.6%	13	0.6%	15	0.3%	15	6.3%	3	20.0	8	17.7	9

2011 Performance Based on Most Common Personnel Groups

Tennessee Offense					Tennessee Offense vs. Opp.				Tennessee Defense				Tennessee Defense vs. Opp.			
Pers	Freq	Yds	DVOA	Run%	Pers	Freq	Yds	DVOA	Pers	Freq	Yds	DVOA	Pers	Freq	Yds	DVOA
11	52%	6.2	15.1%	13%	4-3-4	35%	5.1	-5.9%	4-3-4	47%	5.5	0.8%	11	45%	5.3	1.6%
21	21%	4.9	-17.4%	69%	4-2-5	32%	5.9	13.5%	4-2-5	41%	5.0	0.1%	21	21%	5.6	-2.3%
12	12%	4.9	-15.4%	60%	Dime+	15%	5.4	-7.8%	Dime+	8%	6.2	-2.8%	12	18%	5.1	-0.4%
22	6%	3.8	-12.8%	89%	3-4-4	10%	4.8	-23.6%	3-3-5	2%	7.7	35.3%	22	6%	5.2	-4.3%
10	3%	8.2	43.0%	0%	3-3-5	6%	8.6	71.4%	G-line	1%	2.1	-33.5%	20	3%	4.3	-26.6%

Strategic Tendencies

Run/Pass		Rank	Offense		Rank	Pass Rush		Rank	Defense/Other		Rank
Runs, all plays	37%	30	Form: Single Back	63%	16	Rush 3	10.4%	10	4 DB	48%	18
Runs, first half	36%	29	Form: Empty Back	6%	14	Rush 4	66.1%	12	5 DB	42%	16
Runs, first down	49%	21	Pers: 3+ WR	58%	6	Rush 5	21.1%	16	6+ DB	8%	14
Runs, second-long	36%	14	Pers: 4+ WR	4%	13	Rush 6+	2.5%	31	CB by Sides	82%	16
Runs, power sit.	40%	31	Pers: 2+ TE/6+ OL	21%	31	Zone Blitz	11.3%	3	Go for it on 4th	0.96	14
Runs, behind 2H	23%	31	Play action	12%	31	Sacks by LB	14.3%	22	Offensive Pace	30.5	17
Pass, ahead 2H	43%	17	Max protect	4%	32	Sacks by DB	7.1%	15	Defensive Pace	31.4	29

Tennessee's Adjusted Sack Rate was much lower on third down than on first and second down—on both offense and defense. ☛ Tennessee ran out of 11 personnel less often than any team in the league. ☛ Matt Hasselbeck tied with Michael Vick for the most passes tipped or batted down at the line, 19. ☛ The Titans defense had the NFL's largest gap between defense against runs from multiple-back sets (-25.3% DVOA, 3.8 yards per carry) and defense against runs from single-back sets (6.1% DVOA, 5.2 yards per carry). ☛ The Titans rose from 20th to third in zone blitzes. Derrick Morgan was the lineman most likely to drop into coverage on a zone blitz. ☛ Tennessee was one of the league's better defenses against both draws (-65.7% DVOA, second) and running back screens (-18.3% DVOA, seventh).

Passing

Player	DYAR	DVOA	Plays	NtYds	Avg	YAC	C%	TD	Int
M.Hasselbeck	390	0.5%	536	3410	6.5	5.1	61.8%	18	14
J.Locker	143	22.0%	70	505	7.2	7.8	52.3%	4	0

Rushing

Player	DYAR	DVOA	Plays	Yds	Avg	TD	Fum	Suc
C.Johnson	-67	-15.1%	262	1047	4.0	4	3	41%
J.Ringer	-54	-33.4%	59	185	3.1	1	0	34%
J.Harper	-14	-26.3%	17	46	2.7	1	1	35%
M.Hasselbeck	21	32.1%	9	64	7.1	0	0	--
J.Locker	27	61.4%	7	57	8.1	1	0	--
A.Hall*	-7	-31.8%	6	24	4.0	0	1	67%

Receiving

Player	DYAR	DVOA	Plays	Ctch	Yds	Y/C	YAC	TD	C%
N.Washington	163	5.2%	121	74	1023	13.8	4.3	7	61%
D.Williams	-34	-17.4%	93	45	592	13.2	4.7	5	48%
L.Hawkins	-60	-23.1%	76	47	472	10.0	4.3	1	62%
K.Britt	96	34.1%	26	17	290	17.1	7.4	3	65%
M.Mariani	-54	-68.0%	12	5	24	4.8	3.0	0	42%
J.Cook	100	12.1%	81	49	760	15.5	5.7	3	60%
C.Stevens	35	31.7%	14	9	166	18.4	7.9	1	64%
C.Johnson	40	-4.1%	79	57	418	7.3	5.9	0	72%
J.Ringer	1	-13.2%	36	28	187	6.7	6.7	0	78%
A.Hall*	-15	-31.0%	14	9	46	5.1	5.9	0	64%
J.Harper	-3	-23.0%	6	4	32	8.0	9.0	0	67%

Offensive Line

Year	Yards	ALY	Rank	Power	Rank	Stuff	Rank	2nd Lev	Rank	Open Field	Rank	F-Start	Cont.
2009	5.29	4.01	22	64%	15	21%	24	1.28	7	1.77	1	18	35
2010	4.36	3.47	31	46%	31	26%	31	1.20	12	1.25	4	22	34
2011	3.78	3.39	32	72%	3	24%	29	1.03	31	0.81	18	12	39

Year	LE	Rank	LT	Rank	Mid	Rank	RT	Rank	RE	Rank	Sacks	ASR	Rank	Short	Long
2009	4.11	20	3.45	31	3.71	27	4.44	7	4.81	6	15	3.7%	3	2	9
2010	4.25	17	2.82	32	3.14	32	4.60	6	3.06	28	27	5.6%	9	8	10
2011	3.25	27	3.45	27	3.46	31	3.36	28	3.15	23	24	4.2%	2	11	10

This unit received a substantial bit of blame for Chris Johnson's struggles last year, but the Titans didn't make many fortifications. Michael Roos and David Stewart have been the starting tackles since 2006. Roos has made one All-Pro team, when the Titans went 13-3 in the 2008 season. That it took that kind of season to put him on the team is indicative of his value: He's a very good player, but he's not a top-tier left tackle. Roos is an excellent pass protector who allowed only one sack with a blown block last season, but he also needs to be a little more physical in the running game. On the other side, Stewart's biggest asset is his 6-foot-7 frame: He's a tenacious run blocker and does well in open space. Speed rushers still give him a little more trouble than they probably should. Should either of them get hurt, Mike Otto is still waiting for his first chance at extended playing time. The Titans liked what they saw of Otto, re-signing him to a two-year, $3.2 million deal to remain their swing tackle. If this group has one weakness, it's that they're getting a little old: Roos and Stewart will both turn 30 this year, and Otto is no spring chicken at 29. Regardless, finishing in the top 10 in Adjusted Sack Rate four years running is nothing to be ashamed about.

The interior line was the source of most of Tennessee's problems last year. Leroy Harris wasn't constantly terrible, but our game charters noted some fairly magnificent lowlights.

"Roos has [John] Abraham blocked. Harris comes off and helps and instead shoves Abraham into Hasselbeck as he's throwing."

"Harris clips AND holds [Pat] Sims on the same play. Really impressive."

"RIP Leroy Harris. Fat Albert [Haynesworth] drives him 3 yards backwards at the snap."

The other starters on the interior were worse, particularly right guard Jake Scott. He struggled to reach the second level and would too often get knocked around at the point of attack. Eugene Amano has been a big disappointment at center, working poorly on combo blocks and often having to set up really deep last year to pick up stunts. The Titans flirted heavily with centers Chris Myers and Scott Wells, among others, in free agency. While they didn't land one of those players, they did ink former All-Pro Steve Hutchinson. The soon-to-be-35 Hutchinson is no longer the player he once was, but he should be a big upgrade at left guard, while Harris shifts to the right side. Hutchinson may remind Titans fans of Kevin Mawae, in so much as he's a passable solution right now who needs to be monitored closely going forward.

Behind these three are a bevy of late-round or undrafted players like Fernando Velasco and Kevin Matthews, who get pub in the Tennessee press because they are unknowns rather than known problems. It was a little surprising to see the Titans not target an interior lineman in the draft, and they'll head into the year without a credible solution for replacing Amano if he continues to struggle.

Defensive Front Seven

Defensive Line	Age	Pos	Plays	TmPct	Rk	Stop	Dfts	BTkl	St%	Rk	AvYd	Rk	Sack	Hit	Hur	Runs	St%	Rk	Yds	Pass	St%	Yds
Jurrell Casey	23	DT	53	6.1%	12	42	12	1	79%	33	1.8	34	2.5	3	3	41	80%		1.8	12	75%	1.9
Dave Ball	31	DE	36	4.7%	48	24	13	2	67%	76	1.7	49	4	7	15.5	27	59%		2.9	9	89%	-1.9
Derrick Morgan	23	DE	32	3.9%	64	25	7	1	78%	39	1.5	47	2.5	4	10.5	26	77%		1.9	6	83%	-0.2
Jason Jones*	26	DE	31	4.1%	61	21	11	6	68%	74	2.5	72	3	5	10.5	19	63%		3.6	12	75%	0.8
Shaun Smith	31	DT	25	3.1%	57	16	5	0	64%	64	2.5	56	1	0	1.5	22	64%		3.0	3	67%	-0.7
Sen'Derrick Marks	25	DT	25	2.9%	58	21	8	1	84%	17	2.3	48	0.5	2	4	20	85%		1.4	5	80%	6.2
Karl Klug	24	DT	24	2.8%	63	22	10	0	92%	1	-1.1	1	7	3	3	12	83%		2.1	12	100%	-4.3
William Hayes*	27	DE	16	2.9%	--	13	5	1	81%	--	1.3	--	1.5	3	4	14	79%		2.3	2	100%	-6.0
Leger Douzable	26	DT	39	4.9%	24	30	12	0	77%	43	1.6	26	1	4	5	34	76%		1.6	5	80%	1.6

Linebackers	Age	Pos	Plays	TmPct	Rk	Stop	Dfts	BTkl	AvYd	Sack	Hit	Hur	Runs	St%	Rk	Yds	Rk	Tgts	Suc%	Rk	AdjYd	Rk
Akeem Ayers	23	OLB	72	8.3%	77	47	20	11	4.3	2	2	5	43	74%	17	3.3	47	28	38%	68	7.5	61
Colin McCarthy	24	MLB	68	9.6%	59	43	19	5	4.8	0	2	3.5	42	74%	18	3.0	38	19	52%	33	5.6	20
Barrett Ruud*	29	MLB	60	12.2%	39	29	11	7	5.7	0	1	0	42	52%	103	4.2	91	28	35%	74	9.6	72
Will Witherspoon	32	OLB	57	6.5%	101	32	12	5	3.7	2	3	7	28	75%	13	1.5	2	26	36%	72	7.1	46
Kamerion Wimbley	29	OLB	65	8.1%	79	42	19	5	3.7	6.5	15	29	43	72%	26	3.1	42	12	47%	--	11.4	--

Year	Yards	ALY	Rank	Power	Rank	Stuff	Rank	2nd Lev	Rank	Open Field	Rank
2009	4.49	4.22	20	71%	25	19%	16	1.13	16	0.91	22
2010	3.88	3.71	7	64%	18	22%	7	1.16	19	0.59	11
2011	4.49	4.03	17	53%	6	22%	5	1.18	15	1.09	27

Year	LE	Rank	LT	Rank	Mid	Rank	RT	Rank	RE	Rank	Sacks	ASR	Rank	Short	Long
2009	5.20	30	4.09	14	4.33	25	3.90	13	3.68	11	32	5.7%	25	14	11
2010	5.19	29	3.32	5	3.75	9	3.23	5	3.53	10	40	6.5%	13	22	11
2011	5.16	28	3.63	6	4.15	16	4.02	12	3.01	6	28	5.0%	31	13	12

Tennessee may have handed a big free-agent contract to long-time 3-4 outside linebacker Kamerion Wimbley, but he's something of an outlier on this team. Defensive coordinator Jerry Gray preferred big defensive ends last year, and even moved penetrating defensive tackle Jason Jones to end to try to force a scheme fit. Wimbley, who is listed at 255 pounds, does not fit that model at all, but Gray has vowed to tailor his defense around what he has this year. Tennessee hopes Wimbley can help fix a pass rush that missed Jason Babin dearly. Wimbley is a pure speed edge rusher who finished 10th with 29 hurries per our Game Charting project. However, four of his seven sacks last year came gift-wrapped courtesy of reserve Chargers tackle Brandyn Dombrowski, and in 2010, Wimbley had just nine hurries, with four of his nine sacks that year coming against a Chiefs team that had shut it down for the season in Week 17. Wimbley is clearly a fair stab at improving the pass pressure, but his consistency leaves a little to be desired.

On the other hand, he's head and shoulders above the rest of the pass rushers on this roster. 2010 first-rounder Derrick Morgan contributed less rush than his backup, journeyman Dave Ball. Morgan was dealing with complications from a torn ACL well into the start of the season, but with that injury in the rearview mirror and a real pass-rusher on the other side, this may be a make-or-break year for him. Karl Klug is a nice rotational rusher on passing downs, as he utilizes great leverage and has excellent hand moves, but his seven-to-three sacks-to-hurry ratio suggests that he's probably not going to be that disruptive again. Jurrell Casey was solid against the run in his rookie year, becoming the Titans' most active defensive lineman in a hurry. Third-rounder Mike Martin (Michigan) is primarily known for his run-stuffing capabilities, but a few well-known analysts, including Mike Mayock, think he can get pass pressure in the NFL.

Rookie linebacker Akeem Ayers really struggled to wrap up his tackles, and our game charters constantly lambasted him for being overaggressive against play-fakes and spin moves. He had 11 broken tackles and just 54 solo tackles, a 16.9 percent broken tackle rate. Among linebackers with at least 40 tackles, only Tampa Bay's Quincy Black and Philadelphia's Brian Rolle were worse. However, if he can improve his tackling, Ayers definitely has the speed to stay on the field in the nickel. Middle linebacker Barrett Ruud joined Ayers on the broken tackle leaderboard (his rate of 12.3 percent was sixth-worst in the NFL among linebackers with at least 40 tackles) before being deposed at midseason by 2011 fourth-rounder Colin McCarthy. McCarthy proved an apt tackler and was terrific in coverage from the get-go. He'll be the unquestioned starter this year, with only special teamers and journeyman Zac Diles behind him. Will Witherspoon is a known mediocrity at weakside linebacker at this point. The Titans picked linebacker Zach Brown out of North Carolina in the second round, so he could take over for Witherspoon quickly, as long as he can shed his reputation for being "allergic to contact." A linebacker who is allergic to contact sounds suspiciously like a veterinarian who is allergic to pets.

Defensive Secondary

Secondary	Age	Pos	Plays	TmPct	Rk	Stop	Dfts	BTkl	Runs	St%	Rk	Yds	Rk	Tgts	Tgt%	Rk	Dist	Suc%	Rk	APaYd	Rk	PD	Int
Jason McCourty	25	CB	115	14.1%	1	47	20	4	32	47%	35	7.1	44	103	23.6%	3	10.8	53%	37	7.1	30	15	2
Jordan Babineaux	30	SS	96	11.0%	29	33	10	12	49	39%	42	8.3	56	42	9.0%	16	10.4	51%	51	9.1	52	7	1
Cortland Finnegan*	28	CB	86	9.9%	18	43	20	5	25	44%	39	9.8	65	60	12.9%	69	7.7	61%	12	5.0	3	11	1
Michael Griffin	27	FS	82	9.4%	45	33	12	11	43	37%	47	7.3	47	30	6.4%	49	12.3	66%	10	6.9	25	7	2
Alterraun Verner	24	CB	56	6.4%	68	25	9	5	8	75%	2	4.8	9	51	11.0%	76	9.9	61%	13	5.4	5	10	1
Chris Hope	32	SS	26	4.8%	--	9	1	1	10	50%	--	4.6	--	11	3.8%	--	8.5	46%	--	8.0	--	1	1

Year	Pass D Rank	vs. #1 WR	Rk	vs. #2 WR	Rk	vs. Other WR	Rk	vs. TE	Rk	vs. RB	Rk
2009	25	-1.6%	13	-0.7%	17	10.6%	22	37.8%	31	-18.1%	4
2010	12	4.4%	19	-6.1%	9	-14.3%	8	3.2%	15	6.0%	19
2011	20	30.6%	29	-20.5%	3	-14.1%	14	29.6%	30	-6.2%	12

With Cortland Finnegan's defection to St. Louis, the Titans will enter the year with Jason McCourty and Alterraun Verner as the starting cornerbacks. Verner started over McCourty in 2010, but McCourty won the battle to start in training camp a year ago. As you might expect with how well Finnegan's season went, McCourty was heavily targeted. He was nothing special, but was certainly a passable starting corner. Verner had another strong year in coverage by our statistics, and the Titans may use him in Finnegan's old role, moving to the slot in nickel packages. But they're not going to get Finnegan's 2011 season out of either of these guys, and they do need to know if either McCourty or Verner can be counted on to check top-flight receivers. The other question: Who plays nickelback? The Titans don't have an obvious answer to that question. 2009 third-rounder Ryan Mouton lost 2011 to a torn ACL and has largely been a forgotten man in OTAs. 2012 fourth-rounder Coty Sensabaugh (Clemson) and 2011 seventh-rounder Tommie Campbell seem to have the inside track for the job; neither of those options inspires much short-term confidence.

In Michael Griffin, the Titans have the safety version of Jaguars corner Rashean Mathis. Griffin made a couple of Pro Bowls, and has shown some flashy playmaking skills at times, but isn't consistent enough to scare offenses on a play-by-play basis and is unreliable at best as a deep safety. He's a solid player, so it's hard to blame Tennessee for signing him long-term, but he's hardly a centerpiece. The Titans finally turned the other safety slot over from the aging Chris Hope to scrapheap free-agent signing Jordan Babineaux, and they got about what they paid for. Babineaux was asked in February what would make him feel at home in Tennessee, and he responded with "cha-ching." Two years and $5 million hardly feels cha-ching worthy in today's NFL, but Babineaux will be back in the fold this year. Only 23 NFL players had 10 or more broken tackles in 2011; Babineaux and Griffin were two of them. Sixth-rounder Markelle Martin (Oklahoma State) could be the top reserve coming into the year, as former Utah safety Robert Johnson has struggled to get on the field even despite the vacuum left by the decline of Hope.

Special Teams

Year	DVOA	Rank	FG/XP	Rank	Net Kick	Rank	Kick Ret	Rank	Net Punt	Rank	Punt Ret	Rank	Hidden	Rank
2009	-1.5%	24	11.9	2	-6.7	29	-11.8	31	5.2	6	-7.1	28	0.8	15
2010	4.5%	6	9.0	3	-2.0	19	11.9	5	0.2	18	7.3	4	2.5	9
2011	5.4%	3	13.7	2	1.1	16	4.1	6	9.4	7	3.4	10	7.5	6

The Titans were again among the best in the league on special teams. That starts with kicker Rob Bironas, who has finished in the top five of our FG/XP rankings five years in a row now. Perhaps Bironas is the second recent exception to our general belief that field-goal percentage is almost entirely random. (Matt Stover was the other exception.) Kick returner Marc Mariani regressed in 2011, but it would have taken a lot of fortunate bounces to match his 2010 Pro Bowl year. He's among the best returners in the league, and the blocking in front of him has been excellent since he arrived. Tennessee's coverage teams were both strong, the punt coverage team in particular. Patrick Bailey and Tim Shaw led the way with nine tackles apiece, and both had high stop rates. Even punter Brett Kern improved a bit, though he was still below average on gross punt value. The only real flaw for Tennessee's special teams was their league-leading 33 penalties for 269 yards.

Coaching Staff

Mike Munchak drew nearly universal praise for keeping the Titans competitive in 2011, but he was mostly learning on the job. In fact, he admitted that he'd never seen a seven-on-seven drill prior to last year's training camp. When it comes to personality, Munchak is a chip off the Jeff Fisher block. Munchak rarely screams at his players and tends to be fairly low-key. Reportedly he had some interest in the Penn State opening at the end of last season, but that never really manifested itself.

Offensive coordinator Chris Palmer has a strange resume. After a couple of successful seasons coordinating the Jacksonville offense at its peak (first in DVOA in 1997, eighth in 1998), he attached his name to each of the new expansion teams, becoming head coach of the Browns in 1999 and offensive coordinator of the Texans in 2002. Naturally, given the lack of talent on each roster and a couple of poor No. 1 overall quarterback choices, those teams were not successful. Jerry Gray also has an up-and-down record when it comes to DVOA. In Buffalo between 2001 and 2005 three of his units were in the bottom nine in defensive DVOA, and two of his units were in the top ten, including a 2004 Bills squad that had one of the best defensive DVOA ratings of all-time.

Washington Redskins

2011 Record: 5-11

Pythagorean Wins: 5.7 (25th)

DVOA: -7.0% (21st)

Offense: -7.0% (19th)

Defense: -1.2% (14th)

Special Teams: -1.2% (21st)

Variance: 11.1% (12th)

2012 Mean Projection: 6.8 wins

On the Clock (0-4): 16%

Mediocrity (5-7): 49%

Playoff Contender (8-10): 31%

Super Bowl Contender (11+): 4%

Postseason Odds: 15.7%

Projected Average Opponent: 1.0% (16th)

2011: Yes, it turns out John Beck wasn't the answer.

2012: III is the magic number.

Mike Shanahan was supposed to change things. Shanahan was supposed to be a proven winner who would change the culture of the Washington Redskins. He wouldn't put up with laziness from the likes of Albert Haynesworth. He would avoid big-ticket veterans in free agency and build with younger players, the way he constantly plugged in new running backs in Denver. With the help of his son, he would build a prolific offense to match those that won Super Bowls with the Broncos.

So far, no good.

The Redskins continued to litter their roster with aged free agents like Joey Galloway and Vonnie Holliday. When they did pick up solid free agents, like Stephen Bowen and Barry Cofield, they still overpaid them. They stuck with Santana Moss when he was obviously in his decline phase, and lucked into the fact that London Fletcher doesn't seem to have a decline phase. The Donovan McNabb debacle showed the downside of the Shanahan style; "team sources" badmouthed McNabb to the local press, killing first his confidence and later his trade value. That was followed by a year of futzing around and pretending that Rex Grossman and John Beck were starting-caliber NFL quarterbacks. In two years, the Shanahan Redskins are 11-21.

This summer, the change finally came. Or at least, *a* change—but it was a big one.

It's not unusual for Washington to dominate the headlines with offseason moves. What is unusual is that this time, Washington was finally making headlines by pursuing a young player with outstanding potential instead of an older player who had already reached his. As soon as trade season opened up, the Redskins made a huge deal, trading three first-round picks (this year, 2013, and 2014) plus this year's second-round pick to St. Louis for the No. 2 overall pick and the right to take quarterback Robert Griffin III.

Any discussion of the 2012 Washington Redskins has to start with Griffin, and make no mistake: We are believers. Whether you look through the prism of stats, scouting, or off-field intangibles, Griffin excels. He has the highest score of any first-round pick in the history of our Lewin Career Forecast system. He completed 67 percent of his passes at Baylor, with three years of starting experience plus a couple games in 2009 before he took a medical redshirt. Scouting experts like Greg Cosell and Russ Lande rated him slightly higher than Andrew Luck. Everybody related to the Baylor program speaks glowingly about his leadership skills. He held the press in the palm of his hand with smart and witty answers during his scouting combine press conference. If you want an example of his intelligence on the field, find video of the ESPN Jon Gruden quarterback camp series, where Griffin talks about the way he snaps the ball to catch the de-

WASHINGTON REDSKINS

2012 Redskins Schedule

Week	Opp.	Week	Opp.	Week	Opp.
1	at NO	7	at NYG	13	NYG (Mon.)
2	at STL	8	at PIT	14	BAL
3	CIN	9	CAR	15	at CLE
4	at TB	10	BYE	16	at PHI
5	ATL	11	PHI	17	DAL
6	MIN	12	at DAL (Thu.)		

Figure 1. 2011 Washington DVOA by Week

fense with 12 men on the field while they try to substitute—just like Peyton Manning and Tom Brady do.

Did we mention that he also wears awesome socks?

We want to predict that Griffin can lead the Redskins back to greatness, especially since he seems like a really good guy. There are only two problems with such a prediction: First, the possibility that Robert Griffin won't meet expectations, and second, the stronger possibility that even if Griffin himself meets expectations, he won't have any teammates to help him out.

It's really hard to overstate just how valuable first-round draft picks are in the NFL. Using that classic draft value chart, Washington gave St. Louis more value for the rights to draft Griffin than the Giants gave San Diego for Eli Manning, or the Falcons gave San Diego for Michael Vick. And those picks are worth even more now than they were in 2001 or 2004 because of the new slot-controlled salaries for first-round picks. There's no way Griffin can live up to the hype without making double-digit Pro Bowls. An essay by the Harvard Sports Analysis Collective suggested that for the Redskins to get equivalent value for the picks they gave up, Griffin will need a career as productive as Tom Brady's.

That kind of career isn't guaranteed for anybody, even a prospect as promising as Griffin. Pardon us now for quoting ourselves, but FO's Mike Tanier put things best in the Walkthrough column he wrote after the trade in March:

This is classic Redskins pie in the sky. We're not even penciling in a development period for RG3 with this move. Everyone is expecting a Cam Newton season, followed by a John Elway career. Let me ask you this: What if RG3 is not Elway, but McNabb? McNabb was better than 98 percent of the quarterbacks in NFL history. But would you trade three first-round picks and a second-rounder for him, even in his prime?

You can go fishing for all kinds of similarities between Griffin and Newton, and it doesn't change the fact that we can't count on RG3 repeating Newton's spectacular rookie campaign. So what happens if he's Drew Bledsoe or Sam Bradford instead (in terms of rookie success, not mobility)? Since 1993, 17 teams have gotten at least eight starts from a rookie quarterback chosen in the first dozen picks. On average, those teams have seen their offensive DVOA ratings improve by 6.5%. Of course, a lot of those teams were so bad to begin with that improvement was virtually guaranteed anyway. You may remember that back in the Cleveland chapter, we mentioned a quick and easy equation to project offensive DVOA based simply on last year's offensive DVOA. Using that equation instead, these 17 teams end up with an average offensive DVOA -1.4% below what we would project using simple regression towards the mean. If Griffin has an average season for a top-rated rookie quarterback, the Redskins offense will end up being pretty much equivalent to what it already was last year.

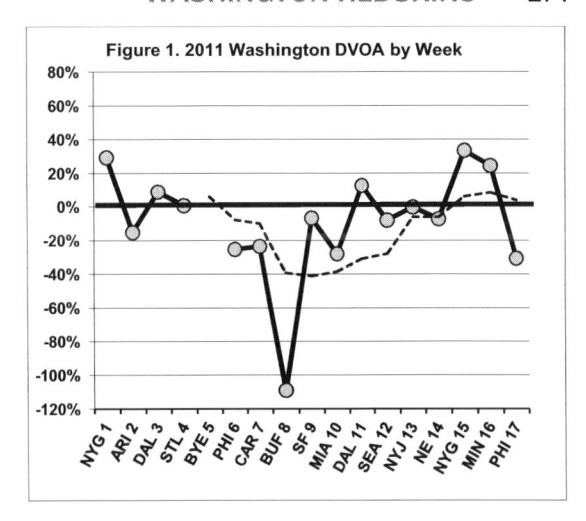

With Griffin, as with any rookie quarterback, the promise of the future is much greater than the promise of the immediate next season. Which brings us to the other problem with trading away those picks: Washington is desperately in need of young playmakers to put around Griffin. Andy Dalton immediately had a young first-round receiver to throw to. Blaine Gabbert and Jake Locker each got one in this year's draft. Perhaps Andrew Luck will get one next year. Robert Griffin won't get one until at least 2015, because the Redskins don't have those first-round picks.

Winning the offseason hype contest with a 22-year-old quarterback doesn't follow the recent Redskins model, but trading away future draft value sure does. And even when they do keep and use draft picks, the Redskins always seem to find a free-agent veteran to take a job instead of giving a shot to some promising youngster.

Washington's reticence to build with young players manifests itself in many different ways. With most franchises, for example, the first place lower-round draft picks get a chance to play is on special teams. Yet five of the top eight Redskins in special teams tackles had at least six years of NFL experience. De-Jon Gomes and Niles Paul were the only rookies with at least three tackles. Compare that to the rest of the NFL, and we find that the Redskins had the oldest coverage teams in the league (Table 1), even if we look at median instead of mean to limit the importance of Mike Sellers and his 17-year career.

A player like Perry Riley, who was nurtured and brought along for a couple years before earning a starting job halfway through his third season, is a real exception in Washington. More frequently, young players either go right into the starting lineup like Griffin, Brian Orakpo, and Ryan Kerrigan, or disappear because the Redskins would rather depend on guys who have been around a few years.

Washington's stars-and-scrubs roster model makes even less sense when you realize that the scrubs aren't really joined by many stars. Only two Redskins made the NFL Network's *Top 100 Players of 2012* countdown this summer, Brian Orakpo and London Fletcher. Now, nobody considers the *Top 100 Players* show to represent authoritative analysis, but think about it further: How many other Redskins would rank among the league's top ten at their positions? Trent Williams might be on the edge. Fred Davis is probably just below the line. If you split cornerbacks up and looked for the top ten left and right, Josh Wilson would have an argument, but now we're really starting to stretch things.

The Griffin trade replaced a huge free-agent move as Washington's biggest headline of the offseason, but the Redskins still made their annual splurge in free agency. Perhaps with an eye on building a team around Griffin, the Redskins at least limited their free-agent forays primarily to players under the age of 30.

The new wide receivers should just be entering their prime, but they still seem like quintessential Washington free-agent pickups. 26-year-old Pierre Garcon is cast perfectly as No. 2 with Good Team Who Will Struggle to Be No. 1, a.k.a. the Alvin Harper Role. Garcon is a player who has consistently put up a lower DVOA and catch rate than his teammates. If we

Table 1. Experience of Core Special Teamers, 2011

Team	Mean	Median	Rookies	6+ Yrs
Most Experience				
Washington	5.45	6.0	2	6
Baltimore	4.86	4.0	1	2
Chicago	4.63	4.5	2	3
NY Giants	4.31	5.0	5	5
NY Jets	4.23	3.0	2	5
Detroit	4.23	3.0	2	4
NFL Average	**3.74**	**3.0**		
Bottom Five				
Dallas	2.90	2.5	3	1
Minnesota	2.90	2.0	2	1
Carolina	2.88	3.0	1	0
Green Bay	2.83	2.5	5	2
Indianapolis	2.81	2.0	5	1

Includes players with at least 3 special teams tackles, except punters and kickers.

rank all the seasons where Peyton Manning threw at least 50 passes to a wide receiver, Garcon's two years as a starter rank 30th and 32nd in DVOA out of 38. 27-year-old Josh Morgan, meanwhile, fits the role of Guy Who Wowed with Small Sample Size. Morgan was a below-average receiver for his first three seasons, with -11.4% DVOA on 204 total passes. Last year, Morgan was phenomenal for five games, catching 15 of 20 passes for 32.4% DVOA. But again, that's *twenty passes*.

The Redskins also filled holes in their secondary with overrated and/or oft-injured veteran free agents. Tanard Jackson finished third in our broken tackle count last year, but since he only played 10 games, his 16 broken tackles work out to a horrid 33.3 percent broken tackle rate. Jackson claims that he'll be better once he recovers from a shoulder injury, but that injury is the main reason Tampa Bay cut him. The current plan is to put Brandon Meriweather next to Jackson, but the Patriots were so sick of his freelancing that they cut him before last season, and the Bears were so sick of his freelancing that they benched him after four games. New nickelback Cedric Griffin suffered ACL tears in successive years, and when he finally returned in 2011, he was one of the worst starting cornerbacks in the league.

This is a team with a lot of mediocrity to hide. Washington wants to hide its secondary behind its front seven, and it wants to hide its lack of real playmakers on offense behind its superlative rookie quarterback. That, in turn, means they are depending on the quarterback being superlative from day one, which is a hard thing to depend on.

Add it all up, and you get a recipe for short-term disappointment. Long-term, things are more optimistic. But to build a winning team around Robert Griffin without first-round picks, the Redskins are going to have to figure out how to mine more talent with their lower-round picks. They're going to need to find diamonds in the rough among undrafted free agents. They're going to need to stop paying for overrated players in free agency. They're going to need to stop the practice of coaches and scouts attacking players through the media, and they're going to need to stoke a more positive atmosphere when they move their training camp and facilities to Richmond, Virginia next year.

In other words, they need to stop being the Redskins.

Aaron Schatz

2011 Redskins Stats by Week

Wk	vs.	W-L	PF	PA	YDF	YDA	TO	Total	Off	Def	ST
1	NYG	W	28	14	332	315	0	29%	12%	-22%	-5%
2	ARI	W	22	21	455	324	0	-15%	5%	19%	-1%
3	@DAL	L	16	18	298	375	0	9%	-12%	-26%	-5%
4	@STL	W	17	10	339	172	-1	1%	-32%	-25%	8%
5	BYE										
6	PHI	L	13	20	287	422	-2	-25%	-35%	-8%	3%
7	@CAR	L	20	33	353	407	-3	-23%	-16%	10%	2%
8	@BUF	L	0	23	178	390	0	-109%	-81%	22%	-5%
9	SF	L	11	19	303	326	-2	-7%	5%	9%	-3%
10	@MIA	L	9	20	246	303	0	-28%	-31%	-13%	-9%
11	DAL	L	24	27	339	353	-2	13%	-7%	-11%	8%
12	@SEA	W	23	17	416	250	-1	-8%	11%	-2%	-21%
13	NYJ	L	19	34	304	266	-2	0%	-1%	11%	11%
14	NE	L	27	34	463	431	-1	-7%	-2%	5%	-1%
15	@NYG	W	23	10	300	324	1	34%	7%	-24%	2%
16	MIN	L	26	33	397	389	-2	25%	25%	17%	16%
17	@PHI	L	10	34	377	390	1	-31%	15%	26%	-20%

Trends and Splits

	Offense	Rank	Defense	Rank
Total DVOA	-7.0%	19	-1.2%	14
Unadjusted VOA	-8.6%	21	4.0%	20
Weighted Trend	-4.9%	18	1.8%	18
Variance	5.1%	6	6.0%	17
Average Opponent	0.5%	19	1.2%	14
Passing	-1.7%	22	4.5%	16
Rushing	-5.0%	20	-7.4%	14
First Down	9.7%	10	11.7%	27
Second Down	-16.7%	28	-14.2%	4
Third Down	-25.4%	26	-5.4%	11
First Half	-7.5%	20	-2.4%	14
Second Half	-6.4%	21	0.0%	16
Red Zone	-22.4%	25	-20.3%	5
Late and Close	-13.7%	26	4.7%	23

Five-Year Performance

Year	W-L	Pyth	Est W	PF	PA	TO	Total	Rk	Off	Rk	Def	Rk	ST	Rk	Off AGL	Rk	Def AGL	Rk
2007	9-7	8.7	7.9	334	310	-5	6.4%	13	-1.0%	17	-7.9%	7	-0.4%	16	36.6	29	16.8	11
2008	8-8	7.0	9.1	265	296	0	9.1%	12	8.2%	10	-3.4%	10	-2.6%	25	12.6	7	42.5	29
2009	4-12	5.8	6.6	266	336	-11	-7.8%	22	-8.3%	21	-2.1%	12	-1.7%	23	55.0	31	20.2	11
2010	6-10	5.9	4.7	302	377	-4	-19.4%	28	-11.3%	25	5.8%	26	-2.3%	25	31.6	21	38.3	26
2011	5-11	5.7	6.3	288	367	-14	-7.0%	21	-7.0%	19	-1.2%	14	-1.2%	21	54.3	31	13.2	7

2011 Performance Based on Most Common Personnel Groups

Washington Offense					Washington Offense vs. Opp.				Washington Defense				Washington Defense vs. Opp.			
Pers	Freq	Yds	DVOA	Run%	Pers	Freq	Yds	DVOA	Pers	Freq	Yds	DVOA	Pers	Freq	Yds	DVOA
11	44%	4.8	-20.6%	19%	4-3-4	30%	5.5	4.5%	3-4-4	52%	5.5	-0.8%	11	32%	5.5	-6.6%
12	20%	6.1	1.5%	52%	4-2-5	21%	5.5	1.0%	2-4-5	31%	6.2	6.9%	12	24%	6.1	0.1%
21	19%	5.6	17.0%	55%	3-4-4	19%	5.0	-10.2%	3-3-5	8%	6.8	23.4%	21	16%	5.9	4.9%
20	5%	6.1	18.7%	50%	Dime+	15%	5.2	-19.2%	4-2-5	4%	5.3	-52.3%	22	9%	5.7	7.9%
22	4%	4.6	4.1%	76%	2-4-5	6%	5.2	17.3%	Dime+	2%	3.4	-86.6%	13	5%	3.6	-34.3%
10	4%	7.5	68.7%	5%	3-3-5	6%	4.9	-30.6%								

Strategic Tendencies

Run/Pass		Rank	Offense		Rank	Pass Rush		Rank	Defense/Other		Rank
Runs, all plays	38%	29	Form: Single Back	60%	20	Rush 3	2.2%	29	4 DB	53%	10
Runs, first half	43%	17	Form: Empty Back	6%	12	Rush 4	60.3%	20	5 DB	43%	15
Runs, first down	50%	19	Pers: 3+ WR	54%	11	Rush 5	30.6%	4	6+ DB	2%	27
Runs, second-long	32%	20	Pers: 4+ WR	5%	10	Rush 6+	6.9%	20	CB by Sides	76%	19
Runs, power sit.	44%	29	Pers: 2+ TE/6+ OL	28%	26	Zone Blitz	4.0%	21	Go for it on 4th	0.93	15
Runs, behind 2H	24%	27	Play action	21%	10	Sacks by LB	50.0%	11	Offensive Pace	30.2	13
Pass, ahead 2H	46%	10	Max protect	8%	26	Sacks by DB	5.0%	23	Defensive Pace	29.5	3

Washington quarterbacks combined for 79 quarterback hits (not including sacks); no other offense was above 70. ● Washington was one of two teams we never saw using an extra offensive lineman. ● The Redskins were near the bottom of the league in offense from empty sets, with just 3.6 yards per play and -42.5% DVOA. ● The Redskins rarely ran from shotgun, handing off on just 5.2 percent of shotgun snaps. They were successful, though, with 39.8% DVOA. On eight shotgun carries, Roy Helu had 67 yards and a touchdown. ● The Redskins' great pass rush doesn't seem to be based on jumping early; Washington was last in the league with just three flags for the various offsides penalties (Defensive Offside, Encroachment, and Neutral Zone Infraction) and one of those came on a punt. ● The Redskins defense had the biggest difference between DVOA with significant pass pressure and DVOA without. They brought pressure on 24.7 percent of pass plays, a little above the league average, but had -127.6% DVOA (first in the NFL) with 2.5 yards per play on these plays, compared to 44.0% DVOA (tied for 26th) with 8.1 yards per play otherwise.

Passing

Player	DYAR	DVOA	Plays	NtYds	Avg	YAC	C%	TD	Int
R.Grossman	96	-8.0%	481	2920	6.1	5.0	58.5%	16	19
J.Beck*	-143	-26.1%	147	764	5.2	5.0	61.5%	2	4

Rushing

Player	DYAR	DVOA	Plays	Yds	Avg	TD	Fum	Suc
R.Helu	25	-4.6%	152	639	4.2	2	2	47%
T.Hightower*	-6	-10.4%	84	321	3.8	1	0	48%
R.Torain*	-60	-34.1%	59	198	3.4	1	1	41%
E.Royster	122	45.7%	56	328	5.9	0	0	64%
J.Beck*	24	36.9%	9	44	4.9	2	0	--
R.Grossman	-14	-42.5%	8	14	1.8	1	1	--
T.Choice*	-23	-76.8%	6	7	1.2	0	3	17%
D.Young	33	74.8%	6	33	5.5	1	0	100%

Receiving

Player	DYAR	DVOA	Plays	Ctch	Yds	Y/C	YAC	TD	C%
J.Gaffney*	138	2.6%	115	68	948	13.9	2.7	5	59%
S.Moss	-41	-18.2%	96	46	584	12.7	4.0	4	48%
D.Stallworth*	31	-1.7%	37	22	309	14.0	4.7	2	59%
A.Armstrong	-67	-45.8%	27	7	103	14.7	1.0	2	26%
T.Austin	-81	-51.6%	26	12	137	11.4	2.8	0	46%
L.Hankerson	21	1.1%	20	13	163	12.5	2.2	0	65%
D.Anderson*	-9	-20.3%	16	7	79	11.3	2.3	1	44%
P.Garcon	-48	-17.1%	134	70	950	13.6	5.1	6	52%
J.Morgan	72	32.4%	20	15	220	14.7	6.4	1	75%
F.Davis	128	15.0%	88	59	798	13.5	5.9	3	67%
L.Paulsen	3	-4.9%	19	11	138	12.5	5.6	0	58%
C.Cooley	-25	-36.4%	13	8	65	8.1	5.3	0	62%
R.Helu	40	-1.3%	59	49	379	7.7	8.6	1	83%
D.Young	33	15.6%	20	15	146	9.7	7.4	0	75%
T.Hightower*	25	14.6%	15	10	78	7.8	7.9	1	67%
E.Royster	5	-7.4%	13	9	68	7.6	6.9	0	69%
R.Torain*	-17	-56.6%	9	6	23	3.8	5.8	0	67%

Offensive Line

Year	Yards	ALY	Rank	Power	Rank	Stuff	Rank	2nd Lev	Rank	Open Field	Rank	F-Start	Cont.
2009	3.73	3.93	25	59%	24	21%	19	1.00	29	0.54	28	18	23
2010	4.19	3.81	24	48%	30	25%	29	1.30	5	0.90	10	22	22
2011	4.19	4.21	10	62%	17	20%	19	1.19	15	0.67	25	11	23

Year	LE	Rank	LT	Rank	Mid	Rank	RT	Rank	RE	Rank	Sacks	ASR	Rank	Short	Long
2009	3.19	28	3.97	19	4.30	9	4.60	5	3.13	27	46	8.5%	27	19	16
2010	3.43	27	4.38	14	3.43	31	4.10	16	4.43	9	46	7.3%	22	18	14
2011	4.02	18	3.64	25	4.58	2	4.49	14	4.23	6	41	6.5%	16	13	15

Washington has had trouble with continuity on the offensive line in recent years, and 2011 was no exception. Center Will Montgomery and right guard Chris Chester each started 16 games, but eight different players started games in the other three slots. Despite this upheaval, the Redskins improved across the board in our offensive line stats, generally going from "poor" to "average." The improvement extended to penalties, where Washington linemen went from 37 flags in 2010 to 24 in 2011. The picture looks even brighter if we only consider the original starting lineup. Washington had only 27 blown blocks leading directly to sacks, grounding, or holding, but half of those came from backups, led by Maurice Hurt and the now-departed Sean Locklear with four apiece. The Redskins need to keep their linemen away from the trainer's table and, in the case of left tackle Trent Williams, their weed dealers.

With their poor depth in mind, the Redskins loaded up on offensive linemen in the draft. Third-round guard Josh LeRibeus out of Southern Methodist has the quickness and agility that the Shanahans crave for their zone-blocking scheme—as long as he can keep his weight down. LeRibeus ballooned to 380 pounds when he was academically ineligible to play his junior year, but shed the weight and had a successful senior campaign. Athletic fifth-round guard Adam Gettis (Iowa) still has room to grow, both in terms of weight and in terms of improving technique. He could eventually move to center. Sixth-rounder Tom Compton (South Dakota) has a base like an oak tree but needs to improve his footwork; he'll likely move from tackle to guard in the pros.

Defensive Front Seven

Defensive Line	Age	Pos	Plays	TmPct	Rk	Stop	Dfts	BTkl	St%	Rk	AvYd	Rk	Sack	Hit	Hur	Runs	St%	Yds	Pass	St%	Yds
Stephen Bowen	28	DE	42	5.2%	37	38	15	1	90%	5	0.4	18	6	3	7.5	32	88%	1.6	10	100%	-3.5
Adam Carriker	28	DE	33	4.1%	60	25	7	1	76%	50	1.0	33	5.5	2	6	26	69%	2.6	7	100%	-4.9
Barry Cofield	28	DT	32	4.0%	37	27	10	2	84%	14	0.9	8	3	4	7	18	78%	1.6	14	93%	0.0
Kedric Golston	29	DE	15	3.3%	--	13	3	0	87%	--	1.3	--	1.5	0	1	11	82%	2.3	4	100%	-1.5

Linebackers	Age	Pos	Plays	TmPct	Rk	Stop	Dfts	BTkl	AvYd	Sack	Hit	Hur	Runs	St%	Rk	Yds	Rk	Tgts	Suc%	Rk	AdjYd	Rk
London Fletcher	37	ILB	173	21.6%	1	95	23	8	4.8	1.5	7	7.5	121	57%	86	3.8	81	47	57%	15	6.7	38
Ryan Kerrigan	24	OLB	66	8.2%	78	49	16	3	2.1	7.5	9	28	38	89%	1	1.3	1	16	38%	69	8.7	71
Perry Riley	24	ILB	65	8.1%	80	48	10	4	3.6	1	2	2	41	85%	3	2.1	10	26	52%	36	6.8	42
Brian Orakpo	26	OLB	64	8.0%	83	48	18	3	1.0	9	4	25.5	45	69%	42	2.6	25	7	40%	--	11.2	--
Rocky McIntosh*	30	ILB	59	7.9%	84	27	8	7	5.4	1	4	3	34	59%	77	3.8	83	17	34%	77	10.9	78

Year	Yards	ALY	Rank	Power	Rank	Stuff	Rank	2nd Lev	Rank	Open Field	Rank
2009	4.11	4.06	14	42%	1	20%	12	1.10	12	0.74	14
2010	4.62	4.37	27	52%	4	17%	25	1.24	25	0.97	25
2011	4.26	4.19	22	54%	7	18%	21	1.14	12	0.76	15

Year	LE	Rank	LT	Rank	Mid	Rank	RT	Rank	RE	Rank	Sacks	ASR	Rank	Short	Long
2009	4.18	15	4.45	23	3.59	7	4.30	21	4.47	25	40	7.5%	5	10	18
2010	3.87	12	5.40	31	3.99	20	4.96	30	4.42	24	29	5.3%	29	8	14
2011	4.40	19	4.46	22	4.21	18	3.86	9	4.06	26	41	7.4%	8	14	18

The Redskins have a prototypical 3-4 defensive line, a solid but unspectacular unit that soaks up blockers without garnering much attention. Although he's one of the smaller nose tackles in the league at 306 pounds, Barry Cofield transitioned seamlessly from the Giants' 4-3 to the Redskins' 3-4. The depth at defensive end gets a boost from the return of Jarvis Jenkins, the 2010 second-round pick out of Clemson who tore his ACL in a preseason game. The versatile Jenkins was projected as a nose tackle by most draftniks, but the Redskins will rotate him with Adam Carriker at left end. Showing their commitment to depth on the line, the Redskins gave Carriker a new four-year deal this offseason even though a healthy Jenkins would have started over him last year, and probably will this year. Stephen Bowen starts at right end, with Kedric Golston spelling him.

When the line does its job, it frees the outside linebackers to get after the quarterback, and it's hard to think of a team with a better pair of bookend pass rushers than Brian Orakpo and Ryan Kerrigan. Among the telling Orakpo stats is one you won't find on the table above; over the last two seasons, he's drawn 16 offensive holding flags, more than any player other than Cameron Wake. Kerrigan took advantage of defenses keying on Orakpo and enjoyed a very productive rookie year. He was also very strong against the run, though it would be nice to see some improvement in pass coverage. On the inside, London Fletcher continues to defy the effects of age, making a higher percentage of team plays than any other defender in the league. His poor advanced stats against the run are more a function of his role in the Washington defense, not a particular difficulty stopping ballcarriers. Against the pass, as in past years, he ranked higher in Success Rate than in yards per pass allowed. Second-year pro Perry Riley replaced Rocky McIntosh as the other starting inside linebacker at midseason. The more physical Riley is also generally better in pass coverage, although he can sometimes get confused when covering tight ends on plays with complicated route combinations. The depth here includes Jonathan Goff, a former starter for the Giants, and Keenan Robinson, a fourth-round pick from Texas whose strength is in pass coverage. He should help the Redskins do a better job against opposing tight ends this year.

Defensive Secondary

Secondary	Age	Pos	Plays	TmPct	Rk	Stop	Dfts	BTkl	Runs	St%	Rk	Yds	Rk	Tgts	Tgt%	Rk	Dist	Suc%	Rk	APaYd	Rk	PD	Int
DeAngelo Hall	29	CB	107	13.4%	4	41	16	6	25	56%	17	6.7	36	88	21.7%	10	11.2	42%	75	9.3	70	18	3
Reed Doughty	30	SS	78	9.7%	40	21	4	4	44	45%	24	5.8	16	20	4.9%	68	16.7	38%	73	13.0	74	1	0
Josh Wilson	27	CB	76	9.5%	22	27	12	6	18	28%	65	12.5	78	81	20.0%	24	13.6	61%	14	6.8	25	15	2
O.J. Atogwe*	31	FS	66	10.1%	36	21	10	1	30	23%	72	10.1	71	16	4.7%	69	14.4	43%	70	9.6	62	5	3
LaRon Landry*	28	SS	49	12.2%	15	26	7	7	33	55%	9	6.0	20	13	6.2%	53	13.2	41%	71	6.7	21	0	0
DeJon Gomes	23	SS	31	4.1%	--	15	1	2	20	60%	--	4.3	--	14	3.6%	--	12.1	50%	--	7.5	--	2	0
Kevin Barnes	26	CB	30	4.0%	--	11	7	6	3	67%	--	3.3	--	38	10.0%	--	9.1	59%	--	6.0	--	6	2
Cedric Griffin	30	CB	76	9.1%	27	28	8	5	20	40%	44	6.8	38	61	14.6%	61	11.6	41%	78	9.3	69	13	1
Tanard Jackson	27	FS	38	7.7%	61	12	3	16	23	22%	73	9.2	67	13	5.6%	62	12.4	63%	14	7.1	30	3	2
Brandon Meriweather	28	FS	34	6.0%	--	8	5	2	8	38%	--	8.0	--	13	3.7%	--	16.3	53%	--	10.5	--	2	0
Leigh Torrence	30	CB	18	2.9%	--	6	6	0	1	0%	--	12.0	--	19	4.8%	--	10.9	49%	--	10.4	--	3	1

Year	Pass D Rank	vs. #1 WR	Rk	vs. #2 WR	Rk	vs. Other WR	Rk	vs. TE	Rk	vs. RB	Rk
2009	20	3.7%	15	10.6%	26	-2.5%	12	0.8%	14	17.1%	25
2010	27	-5.6%	13	12.7%	24	21.7%	29	-9.7%	6	5.8%	17
2011	16	24.6%	25	-15.7%	9	-19.3%	10	23.7%	28	3.6%	20

This is a bad secondary that would look even worse without Orakpo and Kerrigan to harass the opposing quarterback. We can't fault Josh Wilson, who finished in the top 25 in both of our charting stats while starting all 16 games for the first time in his five-year career. However, DeAngelo Hall once again was DeAngelo Hall, only less so, since he managed just three interceptions. To contrast Wilson and Hall, consider this: When covering the opposing team's top receiver, Wilson had a 49 percent Success Rate and allowed 9.4 yards per play. Hall had a 30 percent Success Rate and allowed 11.3 yards per play. To supplement their starters, the Redskins signed Cedric Griffin (ex-Vikings) and Leigh Torrence (ex-Saints) to play nickel and dime. Even before his twin ACL tears, Griffin was 77th in adjusted yards per pass in 2009; last year he was 69th. Torrence has generally come out below average in our charting numbers, although without enough passes to be ranked.

The Redskins thought they were set at safety last season. LaRon Landry had really come into his own after being switched from free to strong safety in 2010. To play next to Landry, the Redskins signed well-regarded former Rams safety O.J. Atogwe. Yes, it was another 30-year-old veteran free agent signing for Washington, but this was a player who had played at a near-Pro Bowl level for four seasons. Unfortunately, the Redskins once again discovered the problem with signing older free agents: Good players tend to go around age 30. That's what happened with Atogwe, as he was benched at midseason and then cut. Meanwhile, Landry experienced more problems with the Achilles tendon that ended his 2010 season early, missing half the season, and was not re-signed. So Washington will have two new starting safeties next year, but as pointed out earlier in this chapter, they aren't necessarily upgrades. If Tanard Jackson can't improve his ability to tackle, or if Washington gets sick of Brandon Meriweather's freelancing the way every other team has, the Redskins can turn to veteran Reed Doughty and youngster DeJon Gomes, who are both strong box safeties but struggle in coverage.

Special Teams

Year	DVOA	Rank	FG/XP	Rank	Net Kick	Rank	Kick Ret	Rank	Net Punt	Rank	Punt Ret	Rank	Hidden	Rank
2009	-1.4%	23	1.4	17	5.8	10	-8.0	29	-0.1	20	-7.5	29	-15.4	32
2010	-1.9%	25	-16.6	32	17.0	1	6.9	9	-22.1	31	3.4	11	4.3	7
2011	-1.0%	21	-7.6	30	4.0	9	-5.1	27	8.8	8	-6.2	23	2.0	13

Washington's special teams have been consistently mediocre, finishing between 21st and 25th in DVOA each of the past four years. The overall results didn't change in 2011, although the specifics did. Punter Sav Rocca was an upgrade on Hunter Smith, but more importantly, Washington's punt coverage improved dramatically from 2010 (9.5 Pts+ allowed on returns) to 2011 (-8.9 Pts+ allowed on returns). On the other hand, Brandon Banks had an egregious sophomore slump after he missed most of training camp due to complications from offseason knee surgery. Washington has to hope that Banks was slowed down by the knee and will be healthier this year, since his only value to the roster comes on kickoff and punt returns. Incumbent kicker Graham Gano faces a training camp competition with free-agent signing Neil Rackers. The two kickers have had similar value on kickoffs the last two years, but Rackers has a better track record and has been better on field goals.

Coaching Staff

Jim Haslett is oft-regarded as a fine defensive coach, but 2011 was the first year since the 2000 New Orleans Saints that a Haslett-coached team had a below-average defensive DVOA. Haslett has a couple of former coordinators on the defensive coaching staff. Raheem Morris is better known as a head coach, but he held both job titles in Tampa Bay. The debacle in Tampa last year didn't stop Morris from getting job offers. He was actually offered the Vikings defensive coordinator one day after accepting a position coaching defensive backs in Washington, but turned down the higher job because he felt he had made a commitment to the Redskins. Morris has been working to broaden the versatility of the Washington secondary, with starting corners Hall and Wilson spending some time as slot corners during OTAs, and Hall and Griffin seeing some time at safety. With Morris coming in to coach defensive backs, Bob Slowik moves over to linebackers coach. Slowik is a coaching lifer who has been defensive coordinator for four different teams, including Mike Shanahan's last Denver squad in 2008.

Quarterbacks

On the following pages, we provide the last three years' statistics for the top two quarterbacks on each team's depth chart, as well as a number of other quarterbacks who played significant time in 2011.

Each quarterback gets a projection from our KUBIAK fantasy football projection system, based on a complicated regression analysis that takes into account numerous variables including projected role, performance over the past two years, performance on third down vs. all downs, experience of the projected offensive line, historical comparables, collegiate stats, height, age, and strength of schedule.

It is difficult to accurately project statistics for a 162-game baseball season, but it is exponentially more difficult to accurately project statistics for a 16-game football season because of the small size of the data samples involved. With that in mind, we ask that you consider the listed projections not as a prediction of exact numbers, but the mean of a range of possible performances. What's important is not so much the exact number of yards and touchdowns we project, but whether or not we're projecting a given player to improve or decline. Along those same lines, rookie projections will not be as accurate as veteran projections due to lack of data.

Our quarterback projections look a bit different than our projections for the other skill positions. At running back and wide receiver, second-stringers see plenty of action, but, at quarterback, either a player starts or he does not start. We recognize that, when a starting quarterback gets injured in Week 8, you don't want to grab your *Football Outsiders Almanac* to find out if his backup is any good only to find that we've projected that the guy will throw 12 passes this year. Therefore, each year we project all quarterbacks to start all 16 games. If Tom Brady goes down in November, you can look up Brian Hoyer, divide the stats by 16, and get an idea of what we think each player will do in an average week.

The exception this year is Tim Tebow because of his planned role as a Wildcat quarterback in New York. Tebow is listed with two projections. One is his projected Wildcat output if Mark Sanchez remains the starter all year; the other what we would forecast over 16 games if Tebow were to become the starter.

The first line of each quarterback table contains biographical data—the player's name, height, weight, college, draft position, birth date, and age. Height and weight are the best data we could find; weight, of course, can fluctuate during the offseason. **Age** is very simple: the number of years between the player's birth year and 2012, but birthdate is provided if you want to figure out exact age.

Draft position gives draft year and round, with the overall pick number with which the player was taken in parentheses. In the sample table, it says that Aaron Rodgers was chosen in the 2005 NFL Draft in the first round with the 24th overall pick. Undrafted free agents are listed as "FA" with the year they came into the league, even if they were only in training camp or on a practice squad.

To the far right of the first line is the player's Risk variable for fantasy football in 2012, which measures the likelihood of the player hitting his projection. The

Aaron Rodgers Height: 6-2   Weight: 223   College: California   Draft: 2005/1 (24)   Born: 2-Dec-1983   Age: 29   Risk: Yellow

Year	Team	G/GS	Att	Comp	C%	Yds	TD	INT	FUM	ASR	NY/P	Rk	DVOA	Rk	DYAR	Rk	YAR	Runs	Yds	TD	DVOA	DYAR
2009	GB	16/16	541	350	64.7%	4434	30	7	8	8.7%	7.1	10	17.8%	9	1106	9	1327	58	316	5	45.7%	136
2010	GB	15/15	475	312	65.7%	3922	28	11	3	6.9%	7.4	2	26.9%	4	1288	4	1241	64	356	4	24.6%	98
2011	GB	15/15	502	343	68.3%	4643	45	6	3	7.2%	8.3	1	46.6%	1	2059	2	2121	60	257	3	18.7%	71
2012	GB		512	334	65.2%	4420	37	13			7.8		34.4%					66	273	4	26.0%	

| 2011: | 43% Short | 36% Mid | 14% Deep | 7% Bomb | YAC: 5.9 (6) | 2010: | 53% Short | 28% Mid | 11% Deep | 8% Bomb | YAC: 5.7 (12) |

default rating for each player is Green. As the risk of a player failing to hit his projection rises, he's given a rating of Yellow or, in the worst cases, Red. The Risk variable is not only based on injury probability, but how a player's projection compares to his recent performance as well as our confidence (or lack thereof) in his offensive teammates. A few players with the strongest chances of surpassing their projections are given a Blue rating. Most players marked Blue will be backups with low projections, but a handful are starters or situational players who can be considered slightly better breakout candidates.

Next, we give the last three years of player stats. The majority of these statistics are passing numbers, although the final five columns on the right are the quarterback's rushing statistics.

The first few columns after the year and team the player played for are standard numbers: games and games started (**G/GS**), pass attempts (**Att**), pass completions (**Cmp**), completion percentage (**C%**), passing yards (**Yds**), passing touchdowns (**TD**), and interceptions (**INT**). These numbers are official NFL totals and therefore include plays we leave out of our own metrics, such as clock-stopping spikes, and omit plays we include in our metrics, such as sacks and aborted snaps. Note that the games total includes all games the player appeared in, not just games started, which is why a backup quarterback who holds on field goals will often be listed with 16 games played. (Other differences between official stats and Football Outsiders stats are described in the "Statistical Toolbox" introduction at the front of the book.)

The next column is fumbles (**FUM**), which adds together all fumbles by this player, whether turned over to the defense or recovered by the offense (explained in the essay "Pregame Show"). Even though this fumble total is listed among the passing numbers, it includes all fumbles, including those on sacks, aborted snaps, and rushing attempts. By listing fumbles and interceptions next to one another we hope to give a general idea of how many total turnovers the player was responsible for.

Next comes Adjusted Sack Rate (**ASR**). This is the same statistic you'll find in the team chapters, only here it is specific to the individual quarterback. It represents sacks per pass play (total pass plays = pass attempts + sacks) adjusted based on down, distance, and strength of schedule. For reference, the NFL average was 6.4 percent in 2009, 6.5 percent in 2010, and 6.7 percent in 2011.

The next two columns are Net Yards per Pass (**NY/P**), a standard stat but a particularly good one, and the player's rank (**Rk**) in Net Yards per Pass for that season. Consider the inclusion of this number our tribute to the godfather of football stats, Bud Goode. It consists of passing yards minus yards lost on sacks, divided by total pass plays.

The five columns remaining in passing stats give our advanced metrics: **DVOA** (Defense-Adjusted Value Over Average), **DYAR** (Defense-Adjusted Yards Above Replacement), and **YAR** (Yards Above Replacement), along with the player's rank in both DVOA and DYAR. These metrics compare each quarterback's passing performance to league-average or replacement-level baselines based on the game situations that quarterback faced. DVOA and DYAR are also adjusted based on the opposing defense. The methods used to compute these numbers are described in detail in the "Statistical Toolbox" introduction at the front of the book. The important distinctions between them are:

• DVOA is a rate statistic, while DYAR is a cumulative statistic. Thus, a higher DVOA means more value per pass play, while a higher DYAR means more aggregate value over the entire season.

• Because DYAR is defense-adjusted and YAR is not, a player whose DYAR is higher than his YAR faced a harder-than-average schedule. A player whose DYAR is lower than his YAR faced an easier-than-average schedule.

To qualify for a ranking in Net Yards per Pass, passing DVOA, and passing DYAR in a given season, a quarterback must have had 100 pass plays in that season. There are 46 quarterbacks ranked for both 2009 and 2010, and 47 quarterbacks ranked for 2011.

If you want to see the effect that normalizing to each season's offensive environment has on our new DVOA ratings, a good example is to look at a list of the best quarterback seasons since 1991. Last year, we noted a number of times that Tom Brady, Drew Brees, and Aaron Rodgers were having three of the best seasons in the history of our numbers, both in DYAR and DVOA. In the new numbers, that's still true as far as DYAR, because all three players were in very pass-heavy offenses (Table 1). However, only Rodgers is now in the top ten for DVOA (minimum 200 passes). Brees is now 17th, and Brady 25th (Table 2).

Returning to a description of our quarterback tables, the final five columns contain rushing statistics, starting with **Runs**, rushing yards (**Yds**), and rushing

QUARTERBACKS

Table 1: Top 10 QB by Passing DYAR (Total Value), 1991-2011

Rk	Player	Team	Year	DYAR
1	Tom Brady	NE	2007	2,674
2	Peyton Manning	IND	2004	2,434
3	Peyton Manning	IND	2006	2,317
4	**Drew Brees**	**NO**	**2011**	**2,259**
5	**Aaron Rodgers**	**GB**	**2011**	**2,059**
6	Tom Brady	NE	2009	2,020
7	**Tom Brady**	**NE**	**2011**	**1,997**
8	Tom Brady	NE	2010	1,918
9	Peyton Manning	IND	2003	1,891
10	Peyton Manning	IND	2000	1,888

Table 2: Top 25 QB by Passing DVOA (Value per Pass), 1991-2011

Rk	Player	Team	Year	DVOA
1	Peyton Manning	IND	2004	58.9%
2	Tom Brady	NE	2007	54.1%
3	Peyton Manning	IND	2006	51.3%
4	Tom Brady	NE	2010	46.7%
5	**Aaron Rodgers**	**GB**	**2011**	**46.6%**
6	Steve Young	SF	1992	45.1%
7	Randall Cunningham	MIN	1998	45.1%
8	Vinny Testaverde	NYJ	1998	42.2%
9	Mark Rypien	WAS	1991	42.0%
10	Philip Rivers	SD	2009	41.7%
11	Peyton Manning	IND	2005	41.7%
12	Chad Pennington	NYJ	2002	40.6%
13	Tom Brady	NE	2009	40.3%
14	John Elway	DEN	1998	39.2%
15	Steve Young	SF	1994	38.8%
16	Peyton Manning	IND	2000	38.3%
17	**Drew Brees**	**NO**	**2011**	**38.3%**
18	Peyton Manning	IND	2007	37.1%
19	Peyton Manning	IND	2003	37.1%
20	Kurt Warner	STL	1999	36.9%
21	Kurt Warner	STL	2001	36.7%
22	Drew Brees	NO	2009	36.7%
23	Steve McNair	TEN	2003	36.3%
24	Ben Roethlisberger	PIT	2005	35.8%
25	**Tom Brady**	**NE**	**2011**	**35.4%**

Minimum 200 passes.

touchdowns (**TD**). Once again, these are official NFL totals and include kneeldowns, which means you get to enjoy statistics such as Matt Flynn rushing 13 times for minus-6 yards. The final two columns give **DYAR** and **DVOA** for quarterback rushing, which are calculated separately from passing. Rankings for these statistics, as well as numbers that are not adjusted for defense (YAR and VOA) can be found on our website, FootballOutsiders.com.

The italicized row of statistics for the 2012 season is our 2012 KUBIAK projection, as detailed above. Again, in the interest of producing meaningful statistics, all quarterbacks are projected to start a full 16-game season, regardless of the likelihood of them actually doing so.

The final line represents data from the Football Outsiders game charting project. First, we break down charted passes based on distance: **Short** (5 yards or less), **Mid** (6-15 yards), **Deep** (16-25 yards), and **Bomb** (26 or more yards). These numbers are based on distance in the air only and include both complete and incomplete passes. Passes thrown away or tipped at the line are not included, nor are passes on which the quarterback's arm was hit by a defender while in motion. We also give Yards after Catch (**YAC**) with the Rank in parentheses for the 47 quarterbacks who qualify.

A number of third- and fourth-string quarterbacks are briefly discussed at the end of the chapter in a section we call "Going Deep."

Table 3: Top 20 QB by Passing DYAR (Total Value), 2011

Rank	Player	Team	DYAR
1	Drew Brees	NO	2,259
2	Aaron Rodgers	GB	2,059
3	Tom Brady	NE	1,997
4	Tony Romo	DAL	1,344
5	Matthew Stafford	DET	1,170
6	Matt Ryan	ATL	1,118
7	Philip Rivers	SD	1,118
8	Eli Manning	NYG	1,109
9	Ben Roethlisberger	PIT	867
10	Matt Schaub	HOU	701
11	Michael Vick	PHI	652
12	Andy Dalton	CIN	575
13	Alex Smith	SF	442
14	Joe Flacco	BAL	409
15	Cam Newton	CAR	404
16	Matt Hasselbeck	TEN	390
17	Jason Campbell	OAK	340
18	Carson Palmer	OAK	296
19	Matt Flynn	GB	225
20	Ryan Fitzpatrick	BUF	189

Table 4: Top 20 QB by Passing DVOA (Value per Pass), 2011

Rank	Player	Team	DVOA
1	Aaron Rodgers	GB	46.6%
2	Drew Brees	NO	38.3%
3	Tom Brady	NE	35.4%
4	Tony Romo	DAL	26.8%
5	Matt Schaub	HOU	24.4%
6	Jason Campbell	OAK	19.8%
7	Matt Ryan	ATL	18.7%
8	Philip Rivers	SD	17.0%
9	Eli Manning	NYG	16.2%
10	Matthew Stafford	DET	14.9%
11	Ben Roethlisberger	PIT	13.3%
12	Michael Vick	PHI	11.6%
13	Andy Dalton	CIN	5.6%
14	Alex Smith	SF	3.1%
15	Carson Palmer	OAK	2.5%
16	Cam Newton	CAR	0.8%
17	Matt Hasselbeck	TEN	0.5%
18	Joe Flacco	BAL	0.0%
19	Dan Orlovsky	IND	-2.2%
20	Chad Henne	MIA	-2.7%

Minimum 100 passes.

One stat we were unable to fit into the quarterback tables was adjusted interception rate, an idea introduced on our website in December 2010 and then expanded on in *Football Outsiders Almanac 2011*. Adjusted interception rate uses game charting data to add dropped interceptions, plays where a defender most likely would have had an interception but couldn't hold onto the ball. We also remove Hail Mary passes and interceptions thrown on fourth down when losing in the final two minutes of the game. And we remove "tipped interceptions," when a perfectly catchable ball deflected off the receiver's hands or chest and into the arms of a defender.

From 2007 through 2011, the year-to-year correlation for interception rate is basically nonexistent (.03) but the year-to-year correlation for adjusted interception rate is a reasonable size (.29). The correlation of both numbers between 2010 and 2011 was really bad; in fact, for quarterbacks with at least 200 pass attempts each season, the correlation of interception rate from 2010 to 2011 was negative.

No quarterback in 2011 came close to Mark Sanchez's league-leading figure of 15 dropped interceptions from 2010. (Sanchez's regular interception rate went up, but his adjusted interception rate actually fell significantly in 2011.) Three quarterbacks tied for the lead with nine dropped picks: Joe Flacco, Carson Palmer, and Matthew Stafford. Palmer's adjusted interception rate of 7.1 percent is the highest of any quarterback since we started counting dropped picks in 2007, although at least he has a good excuse given that the Raiders tossed him into a game about 15 minutes after he showed up in Oakland.

Just in case you needed more evidence of how remarkable Aaron Rodgers was in the 2011 season, he had only four adjusted interceptions. Two of his six picks were tipped by his receivers, and he was the only quarterback who threw more than 200 passes with zero dropped interceptions.

Three of Tarvaris Jackson's 13 interceptions last season were Hail Mary passes; no other quarterback threw more than one pick on a Hail Mary. Ryan Fitzpatrick had four different picks that bounced off his receivers' hands and into the hands of defenders; no other quarterback threw more than two "tipped interceptions."

Table 5 lists the standard and adjusted interception rates for all quarterbacks with at least 200 passes (not including clock-killing spikes) in 2011.

282 QUARTERBACKS

Table 5: Highest Adjusted Interception Rates, 2011

Name	Team	INT	Adj INT	Passes	INT Rate	Adj Rate	Name	Team	INT	Adj INT	Passes	INT Rate	Adj Rate
Carson Palmer	OAK	16	23	326	4.9%	7.1%	Joe Flacco	BAL	12	20	543	2.2%	3.7%
John Skelton	ARI	14	18	274	5.1%	6.6%	Mark Sanchez	NYJ	18	19	539	3.3%	3.5%
Christian Ponder	MIN	13	17	291	4.5%	5.8%	Matt Moore	CAR	9	12	348	2.6%	3.4%
Rex Grossman	WAS	20	25	456	4.4%	5.5%	Sam Bradford	STL	6	12	357	1.7%	3.4%
Kyle Orton	DEN/KC	9	13	252	3.6%	5.2%	Andy Dalton	CIN	13	17	516	2.5%	3.3%
Curtis Painter	IND	9	12	243	3.7%	4.9%	Colt McCoy	CLE	11	15	463	2.4%	3.2%
Cam Newton	CAR	17	24*	514	3.3%	4.7%	Matt Cassel	KC	9	8	268	3.4%	3.0%
Kevin Kolb	ARI	8	11	252	3.2%	4.4%	Eli Manning	NYG	16	17	589	2.7%	2.9%
Philip Rivers	SD	20	25	579	3.5%	4.3%	Jay Cutler	CHI	7	9	314	2.2%	2.9%
Michael Vick	PHI	14	18	418	3.3%	4.3%	Tim Tebow	DEN	6	7	268	2.2%	2.6%
Blaine Gabbert	JAC	11	17	412	2.7%	4.1%	Drew Brees	NO	14	17	653	2.1%	2.6%
Josh Freeman	TB	22	22	546	4.0%	4.0%	Tom Brady	NE	12	15	611	2.0%	2.5%
Ben Roethlisberger	PIT	14	20	514	2.7%	3.9%	Tony Romo	DAL	10	12	519	1.9%	2.3%
Ryan Fitzpatrick	BUF	23	22	566	4.1%	3.9%	Matt Schaub	HOU	6	6	290	2.1%	2.1%
Matt Hasselbeck	TEN	14	20	517	2.7%	3.9%	Matt Ryan	ATL	12	11	561	2.1%	2.0%
Matthew Stafford	DET	16	25	663	2.4%	3.8%	Alex Smith	SF	5	6	447	1.1%	1.3%
Tarvaris Jackson	SEA	13	17	451	2.9%	3.8%	Aaron Rodgers	GB	6	4	501	1.2%	0.8%

Minimum 200 passes.
*Does not include two dropped interceptions that were tipped by Steve Smith before they were dropped by defenders.

Derek Anderson
Height: 6-6   Weight: 229   College: Oregon State   Draft: 2005/6 (213)   Born: 15-Jun-1983   Age: 29   Risk: Red

Year	Team	G/GS	Att	Comp	C%	Yds	TD	INT	FUM	ASR	NY/P	Rk	DVOA	Rk	DYAR	Rk	YAR	Runs	Yds	TD	DVOA	DYAR
2009	CLE	8/7	182	81	44.5%	888	3	10	5	5.5%	4.3	43	-43.6%	44	-398	41	-479	10	8	2	-3.1%	6
2010	ARI	12/9	327	169	51.7%	2065	7	10	5	7.0%	5.4	37	-25.4%	40	-308	41	-245	5	25	0	-9.8%	1
2011	CAR	2/0	0	0	0.0%	0	0	0	--	--	--	--	--	--	--	--	--	2	-2	0	--	--
2012	CAR		437	237	54.3%	2739	15	14			5.5		-5.6%					22	9	0	-26.3%	

2010: 43% Short   35% Mid   17% Deep   5% Bomb   YAC: 4.0 (43)

That period when people talked seriously about Anderson being a viable NFL starting quarterback feels about as ridiculous to us now as the time when people believed bloodletting could cure illness.

Richard Bartel
Height: 6-1   Weight: 200   College: Tarleton State   Draft: 2007/FA   Born: 3-Feb-1983   Age: 29   Risk: Green

Year	Team	G/GS	Att	Comp	C%	Yds	TD	INT	FUM	ASR	NY/P	Rk	DVOA	Rk	DYAR	Rk	YAR	Runs	Yds	TD	DVOA	DYAR
2010	ARI	1/0	28	16	57.1%	150	0	1	0	7.5%	4.6	--	-54.7%	--	-103	--	-86	0	0	0	--	--
2011	ARI	2/0	22	10	45.5%	86	1	1	0	4.0%	3.5	--	-32.2%	--	-32	--	-36	1	9	0	87.9%	2
2012	ARI		524	314	59.8%	3471	16	17			5.5		-8.9%					34	75	0	-10.0%	

2011:   41% Short   27% Mid   27% Deep   5% Bomb   YAC: 1.7 (--)   2010: 64% Short   21% Mid   11% Deep   4% Bomb   YAC: 2.4 (--)

After a few seasons bouncing around practice squads in Dallas, Cleveland, and Jacksonville, Bartel found a home as a backup quarterback with the Cardinals late in the 2010 season. Bartel opened last season as the No. 2 behind Kevin Kolb, but fell behind John Skelton on the depth chart. While Kolb and Skelton battle for the starting job, Bartel will be competing with sixth-round quarterback Ryan Lindley for the No. 3 job and/or a roster spot this summer.

QUARTERBACKS 283

Charlie Batch Height: 6-2 Weight: 220 College: Eastern Michigan Draft: 1998/2 (60) Born: 5-Dec-1974 Age: 38 Risk: Green

Year	Team	G/GS	Att	Comp	C%	Yds	TD	INT	FUM	ASR	NY/P	Rk	DVOA	Rk	DYAR	Rk	YAR	Runs	Yds	TD	DVOA	DYAR
2009	PIT	1/0	2	1	50.0%	17	0	0	0	3.0%	8.5	--	42.2%	--	6	--	7	0	0	0	--	--
2010	PIT	3/2	49	29	59.2%	352	3	3	1	8.2%	6.2	--	-24.0%	--	-43	--	-62	7	30	0	34.4%	9
2011	PIT	4/1	24	15	62.5%	208	0	1	0	7.0%	7.6	--	-11.1%	--	0	--	2	3	-2	0	--	--
2012	PIT		452	284	62.9%	3179	19	11			6.5		6.6%					39	48	1	-24.3%	

2011: 54% Short   29% Mid   13% Deep   4% Bomb   YAC: 6.1 (--)   2010: 45% Short   30% Mid   9% Deep   15% Bomb   YAC: 4.1 (--)

In a numerological quirk, Batch has thrown exactly as many passes as fellow Steelers backup Byron Leftwich since last they held the keys to an NFL franchise (208). What distinguishes the 38-year-old from Leftwich, though, is that he's posted a 5-2 starting record in that time. Being a quarterback who just wins, it's surprising Batch never received interest from the Jets in free agency, instead re-signing with the Steelers as their No. 3 quarterback.

John Beck Height: 6-2 Weight: 215 College: BYU Draft: 2007/2 (40) Born: 21-Aug-1981 Age: 31 Risk: Red

Year	Team	G/GS	Att	Comp	C%	Yds	TD	INT	FUM	ASR	NY/P	Rk	DVOA	Rk	DYAR	Rk	YAR	Runs	Yds	TD	DVOA	DYAR
2011	WAS	4/3	132	80	60.6%	858	2	4	3	11.8%	5.2	37	-26.1%	40	-143	37	-132	10	43	2	36.9%	24
2012	HOU		494	302	61.2%	3472	16	18			5.9		-1.8%					22	30	1	-8.4%	Green

2011: 43% Short   40% Mid   10% Deep   7% Bomb   YAC: 5.0 (26)

Hey, remember when Mike Shanahan was talking about how Beck was his top college quarterback coming out in 2007, and said "I think the world of him?" Yeah, we don't remember either, but apparently this was less than a year ago. Beck will take his poor pocket presence and love of the checkdown to Houston, where fans are really hoping they don't get down to the third-string quarterback again.

Kyle Boller Height: 6-3 Weight: 220 College: California Draft: 2003/1 (19) Born: 17-Jun-1981 Age: 31 Risk: N/A

Year	Team	G/GS	Att	Comp	C%	Yds	TD	INT	FUM	ASR	NY/P	Rk	DVOA	Rk	DYAR	Rk	YAR	Runs	Yds	TD	DVOA	DYAR
2009	STL	7/5	176	98	55.7%	899	3	6	2	8.6%	4.1	44	-39.3%	42	-351	37	-327	13	76	0	-0.1%	1
2010	OAK	5/0	4	2	50.0%	25	0	1	1	20.4%	3.8	--	-268.1%	--	-77	--	-72	7	18	0	-114.6%	-25
2011	OAK	2/1	28	15	53.6%	161	0	3	3	9.7%	4.6	--	-95.4%	--	-158	--	-154	9	38	0	-45.7%	-14

2011: 37% Short   33% Mid   15% Deep   15% Bomb   YAC: 5.6 (--)   2010: 72% Short   25% Mid   0% Deep   4% Bomb   YAC: 1.0 (--)

We predicted in *Football Outsiders Almanac 2011* that if Jason Campbell went down, it wouldn't take long for the Raiders to look for an option other than Boller. Surprise, surprise, that's exactly what happened, as the Raiders traded for Carson Palmer before Boller even had a chance to start a game. He still has a strong arm, but has never had any of the other attributes of an NFL quarterback and has probably taken his last snap.

Sam Bradford Height: 6-4 Weight: 236 College: Oklahoma Draft: 2010/1 (1) Born: 8-Nov-1987 Age: 25 Risk: Green

Year	Team	G/GS	Att	Comp	C%	Yds	TD	INT	FUM	ASR	NY/P	Rk	DVOA	Rk	DYAR	Rk	YAR	Runs	Yds	TD	DVOA	DYAR
2010	STL	16/16	590	354	60.0%	3512	18	15	7	5.6%	5.3	40	-15.6%	34	-178	39	-5	27	63	1	-6.0%	4
2011	STL	10/10	357	191	53.5%	2164	6	6	8	9.1%	4.9	41	-24.2%	38	-329	43	-374	18	26	0	-58.5%	-25
2012	STL		560	350	62.5%	3649	19	16			5.3		-9.2%					41	84	1	-17.7%	

2011: 43% Short   37% Mid   13% Deep   7% Bomb   YAC: 4.5 (38)   2010: 60% Short   29% Mid   7% Deep   4% Bomb   YAC: 5.3 (21)

Most have labeled Bradford's 2011 season a "sophomore slump," but the truth is that his rookie season was successful only in comparison to our general expectations for rookies. Compared to what we expect from an average NFL starter, 2010 was pretty bad and 2011 was only slightly worse. What's more, Bradford's major DVOA splits were also very similar in both seasons.

Sam Bradford DVOA Splits, 2010-2011

DVOA Split	2010	2011
First Down	-23.9%	-34.6%
Second Down	-6.1%	-16.0%
Third Down	-16.6%	-19.7%
Red Zone	-59.3%	-81.0%
Passes with Pressure	-33.8%	-23.7%
Shotgun	-19.2%	-16.0%

Another popular fallacy about Bradford says that his "sophomore slump" was caused by the team's move away from Pat Shurmur's conservative offense, as well as going the entire 2011 season without a quarterbacks coach to help him learn Josh McDaniels' scheme in a shortened offseason. Therefore, as the theory goes, hiring conservative-to-a-fault offensive coordinator Brian Schottenheimer and quarterbacks coach Frank Cignetti will restore order to the Bradford universe. The problem, of course, is that if he wasn't actually that good in 2010, then re-establishing 2010 conditions means nothing. Instead, if Bradford develops into the elite NFL quarterback everyone thought he was going to be coming out of college, it will more likely be due to the simplest explanation of all: time.

Tom Brady
Height: 6-4 Weight: 225 College: Michigan Draft: 2000/6 (199) Born: 3-Aug-1977 Age: 35 Risk: Green

Year	Team	G/GS	Att	Comp	C%	Yds	TD	INT	FUM	ASR	NY/P	Rk	DVOA	Rk	DYAR	Rk	YAR	Runs	Yds	TD	DVOA	DYAR
2009	NE	16/16	565	371	65.7%	4398	28	13	4	3.4%	7.4	5	40.3%	2	2020	1	1649	29	44	1	-20.2%	-13
2010	NE	16/16	492	324	65.9%	3900	36	4	2	5.0%	7.2	3	46.7%	1	1918	1	1771	31	30	1	-12.4%	0
2011	NE	16/16	611	401	65.6%	5235	39	12	6	5.4%	7.9	2	35.4%	3	1997	3	1956	43	109	3	10.9%	57
2012	NE		587	394	67.1%	4939	37	11			7.8		41.9%					38	29	1	-8.5%	

2011: 48% Short 36% Mid 12% Deep 5% Bomb YAC: 6.4 (3) 2010: 55% Short 32% Mid 8% Deep 5% Bomb YAC: 5.8 (9)

Brady set a career high for attempts, including a whopping 459 attempts out of shotgun, as the Patriots took advantage of the matchup difficulties their two-tight end sets created by going no-huddle more than any other team in the league. As Chris Brown noted in *Slate*, Brady actually spends most of his time looking at relatively simple and straightforward defenses, as the no-huddle tempo both prevents the defense from making substitutions and discourages them from doing too much in the way of pre-snap disguise since a quick snap could catch defenders out of position. (Interestingly enough, Brady was actually slightly more effective the few times he slowed down the clock and lined up under center, averaging 8.4 yards per play versus 7.7 from the gun.) There is some thought that the Patriots are going to throttle down a bit this year, emphasizing the run more and then stretching the field vertically with the newly-acquired Brandon Lloyd, but really we're talking about minor tweaks to the scheme, not wholesale changes. This will be the same offense that Brady has run for more than a decade now, and he's gotten rather good at it.

Drew Brees
Height: 6-0 Weight: 209 College: Purdue Draft: 2001/2 (32) Born: 15-Jan-1979 Age: 33 Risk: Yellow

Year	Team	G/GS	Att	Comp	C%	Yds	TD	INT	FUM	ASR	NY/P	Rk	DVOA	Rk	DYAR	Rk	YAR	Runs	Yds	TD	DVOA	DYAR
2009	NO	15/15	514	363	70.6%	4388	34	11	8	4.2%	8.0	2	36.7%	3	1691	4	1730	22	33	2	49.9%	40
2010	NO	16/16	658	448	68.1%	4620	33	22	6	4.6%	6.5	13	13.3%	10	1093	6	1071	18	-3	0	-34.5%	-5
2011	NO	16/16	657	468	71.2%	5476	46	14	1	4.5%	7.9	3	38.3%	2	2259	1	2363	21	86	1	30.5%	33
2012	NO		626	424	67.8%	5130	39	13			7.5		39.6%					20	18	0	-8.3%	

2011: 50% Short 33% Mid 12% Deep 5% Bomb YAC: 5.2 (23) 2010: 54% Short 30% Mid 9% Deep 7% Bomb YAC: 4.6 (34)

Brees is now the all-time NFL career leader in passing yards per game (264.6), completions per game (23.5), and attempts per game (35.6). His 71.2 completion percentage last year broke the previous record, which he set two years ago. Brees' completion percentage over the last three years is an uncanny 69.9 percent; if you turned the last three years into one-mega season for Brees, it would rank fourth on the all-time completion percentage list, surrounded by strike-shortened seasons, fluky one-time performances by Brian Griese and his ilk, and some of the best Steve Young, Joe Montana, and Tom Brady years. Even if you take all of the statistical air you possibly can out of Brees' quality and quantity numbers, accounting for the era and the scheme, you are left with a peak that rivals Young's 1992-1997 run or Otto Graham's AAFC seasons as one of the best sustained multi-year performances a quarterback has ever had. So, yeah, this is a guy to play contract hardball with. Good thinking, Saints organization.

Jason Campbell   Height: 6-5   Weight: 223   College: Auburn   Draft: 2005/1 (25)   Born: 31-Dec-1981   Age: 31   Risk: Yellow

Year	Team	G/GS	Att	Comp	C%	Yds	TD	INT	FUM	ASR	NY/P	Rk	DVOA	Rk	DYAR	Rk	YAR	Runs	Yds	TD	DVOA	DYAR
2009	WAS	16/16	507	327	64.5%	3618	20	15	10	8.4%	6.1	18	-6.1%	25	181	22	219	46	236	1	20.4%	60
2010	OAK	13/12	329	194	59.0%	2387	13	8	9	9.1%	6.1	24	-10.1%	31	23	31	92	47	222	1	1.4%	28
2011	OAK	6/6	165	100	60.6%	1170	6	4	3	3.0%	6.8	15	19.8%	6	340	17	326	18	60	2	-19.1%	-6
2012	CHI		455	260	57.2%	3068	16	14			6.1		-3.5%					63	112	3	-11.8%	

2011: 46% Short   31% Mid   11% Deep   12% Bomb   YAC: 4.5 (39)   2010: 58% Short   24% Mid   10% Deep   7% Bomb   YAC: 6.7 (2)

For the first time in his career, going back to high school, Campbell had the same offensive coordinator he had the year before. He responded with the best half-season of his career. The lower sack rate didn't look like a fluke, as he did a very good job of getting the ball out quickly to open receivers. However, the arrival of Carson Palmer meant he had to find another team, which means yet another offensive coordinator. The Bears snatched him up, and his 2011 improvement in pocket presence will be severely tested if Jay Cutler goes down again.

David Carr   Height: 6-3   Weight: 215   College: Fresno State   Draft: 2002/1 (1)   Born: 21-Jul-1979   Age: 33   Risk: Green

Year	Team	G/GS	Att	Comp	C%	Yds	TD	INT	FUM	ASR	NY/P	Rk	DVOA	Rk	DYAR	Rk	YAR	Runs	Yds	TD	DVOA	DYAR
2009	NYG	6/0	33	21	63.6%	225	1	0	0	5.2%	6.3	--	30.2%	--	83	--	94	9	27	1	69.1%	17
2010	SF	1/0	13	5	38.5%	67	0	1	0	7.5%	4.8	--	-60.1%	--	-31	--	-35	0	0	0	--	--
2012	NYG		529	336	63.5%	3649	17	21			6.2		-2.5%					55	53	2	-26.1%	

2010: 33% Short   17% Mid   50% Deep   0% Bomb   YAC: 9.2 (--)

David Carr is the NFL equivalent of Darren Oliver or Jerry Stackhouse. At some point in August, you're going to turn on NFL Network, and there will be the Giants in a preseason game, and you'll just be gobsmacked to discover that David Carr is still in the league. He even has a Super Bowl ring now.

Matt Cassel   Height: 6-5   Weight: 230   College: USC   Draft: 2005/7 (230)   Born: 17-May-1982   Age: 30   Risk: Green

Year	Team	G/GS	Att	Comp	C%	Yds	TD	INT	FUM	ASR	NY/P	Rk	DVOA	Rk	DYAR	Rk	YAR	Runs	Yds	TD	DVOA	DYAR
2009	KC	15/15	493	271	55.0%	2924	16	16	13	7.9%	5.0	36	-29.2%	37	-619	44	-583	50	189	0	-31.2%	-34
2010	KC	15/15	450	262	58.2%	3116	27	7	2	6.1%	6.3	18	8.4%	16	589	14	793	33	125	0	-13.0%	1
2011	KC	9/9	269	160	59.5%	1713	10	9	5	7.9%	5.5	34	-25.9%	39	-277	41	-169	25	99	0	13.5%	25
2012	KC		513	298	58.1%	3659	22	16			6.4		7.6%					55	133	1	-7.9%	

2011: 45% Short   33% Mid   15% Deep   8% Bomb   YAC: 4.4 (41)   2010: 52% Short   30% Mid   13% Deep   5% Bomb   YAC: 5.7 (13)

What do the Chiefs think of Cassel's pocket presence? Based on their protection patterns, not much. They used seven or more blockers on 34 percent of his pass plays, but only 20 percent of the time for Tyler Palko and 25 percent for Kyle Orton. The more protection Cassel gets, the better he is, throwing longer passes for a much higher DVOA. Cassel's rate of sacks and dumpoffs were essentially unchanged by blocking scheme, so it appears that with five blockers he simply didn't trust his line enough to give him time to try deeper passes. Is this a typical pattern? Yes and no. The average NFL pass last year with five blockers traveled 7.4 yards past the line of scrimmage, compared to 9.5 yards with six blockers and 12.1 yards with seven-plus. However, yardage totals were generally consistent, and league DVOA was actually a little lower with seven or more blockers. But in Cassel's case, it's awfully hard to score touchdowns when you're averaging less than five yards per play, which explains why Kansas City gave him extra protection so often.

Matt Cassel Passing by Number of Blockers, 2011

Blockers	Matt Cassel Yds/Play	Matt Cassel DVOA	Matt Cassel Avg Pass Dist	NFL Average Yds/Play	NFL Average DVOA	NFL Average Avg Pass Dist
5	4.8	-32.1%	5.8	6.3	14.1%	7.4
6	5.7	-19.9%	8.9	6.7	13.4%	9.5
7+	6.1	8.8%	12.5	6.5	3.9%	12.1

Kellen Clemens
Height: 6-2 Weight: 224 College: Oregon Draft: 2006/2 (49) Born: 6-Jun-1983 Age: 29 Risk: Green

Year	Team	G/GS	Att	Comp	C%	Yds	TD	INT	FUM	ASR	NY/P	Rk	DVOA	Rk	DYAR	Rk	YAR	Runs	Yds	TD	DVOA	DYAR
2009	NYJ	10/1	26	13	50.0%	125	0	0	1	13.6%	3.6	--	-38.3%	--	-45	--	-55	12	1	0	-26.6%	-3
2010	NYJ	1/0	2	1	50.0%	6	0	0	0	1.7%	3.0	--	-25.3%	--	-3	--	-2	2	9	1	187.7%	13
2011	2TM	3/3	91	48	52.7%	546	2	1	2	9.7%	4.7	43	-12.0%	28	-6	28	-19	6	37	1	-3.0%	3
2012	STL		509	290	57.0%	3627	11	19		5.8		-15.2%						36	64	2	-13.7%	

2011: 40% Short 38% Mid 17% Deep 5% Bomb YAC: 3.9 (45) 2010: 67% Short 0% Mid 33% Deep 0% Bomb YAC: 2.0 (--)

After being released by Washington in September and Houston in December, Clemens signed on with St. Louis as an injury replacement, and saw his most extensive action since 2007. Unfortunately, Clemens' three starts confirmed what everyone already knew from the previous five years: His arm has all the accuracy of an *Onion* headline. Beyond that, Clemens played about as poorly as you'd expect for a quarterback with matadors in front him: His average sack time (2.4 seconds) was second-fastest among qualifying quarterbacks. Despite all this, Clemens will be Sam Bradford's primary backup in 2012, mostly because the offensive coordinator who ignored his inaccuracy for five seasons with the Jets, Brian Schottenheimer, is now filling that role with the Rams.

Jay Cutler
Height: 6-3 Weight: 220 College: Vanderbilt Draft: 2006/1 (11) Born: 29-Apr-1983 Age: 29 Risk: Yellow

Year	Team	G/GS	Att	Comp	C%	Yds	TD	INT	FUM	ASR	NY/P	Rk	DVOA	Rk	DYAR	Rk	YAR	Runs	Yds	TD	DVOA	DYAR
2009	CHI	16/16	555	336	60.5%	3666	27	26	9	6.0%	5.9	23	-21.4%	30	-390	39	-326	40	173	1	15.4%	41
2010	CHI	15/15	432	261	60.4%	3274	23	16	10	10.5%	6.1	26	-8.5%	30	81	30	54	50	232	1	33.0%	65
2011	CHI	10/10	314	182	58.0%	2319	13	7	7	7.4%	6.4	18	-3.5%	21	157	21	207	18	55	1	-14.5%	-1
2012	CHI		492	300	61.1%	3590	24	17		6.3		4.0%						26	46	2	-0.5%	

2011: 44% Short 38% Mid 13% Deep 5% Bomb YAC: 5.3 (17) 2010: 49% Short 34% Mid 11% Deep 6% Bomb YAC: 5.5 (18)

For the second straight year, Jay Cutler enters training camp having finished the previous season sidelined due to injury. A torn MCL ended Cutler's 2010 season during the second half of the 2010 NFC Championship; a broken right thumb ended is 2011 season in late November. The injury most likely occurred in the third quarter of a win over the Chargers when Cutler tried to make a tackle on cornerback Antoine Cason, who was returning Cutler's seventh (and final) interception on the season. It was the cruelest of fate twists for a Bears team that was 7-3 at that point.

Remarkably, Cutler finished out that game with a broken thumb, putting to rest any of the lingering, ridiculous doubts about his toughness. The thumb surgery should have no impact on Cutler's fastball, which may be the best in the league. Cutler's uncanny raw throwing talent allows him to shoot lasers through tight windows, launch accurate bombs downfield and—something he doesn't get enough credit for—athletically deliver strikes from various platforms while on the move. The problem is that Cutler's dazzling abilities tend to flicker on and off. Poor fundamentals and sloppy pocket mechanics make him inconsistent. He has matured when reading defenses, but those improvements seem to dissipate when he loses trust in his—frankly, untrustworthy—offensive line. A switch from Mike Martz's rigidly structured offense to the presumably more traditional, balanced system of new coordinator Mike Tice should give Cutler more of the free-styling liberty he desires. Whether that's truly the best thing for him (and the Bears) remains to be seen.

Andy Dalton Height: 6-2 Weight: 215 College: TCU Draft: 2011/2 (35) Born: 29-Oct-1987 Age: 25 Risk: Green

Year	Team	G/GS	Att	Comp	C%	Yds	TD	INT	FUM	ASR	NY/P	Rk	DVOA	Rk	DYAR	Rk	YAR	Runs	Yds	TD	DVOA	DYAR
2011	CIN	16/16	516	300	58.1%	3398	20	13	4	4.5%	6.0	23	5.6%	13	575	12	485	37	152	1	-14.6%	-4
2012	CIN		539	336	62.4%	3752	23	15			6.3		11.3%					44	125	2	5.9%	

2011: 47% Short 34% Mid 11% Deep 8% Bomb YAC: 4.4 (40)

Dalton's efficiency numbers were better than Cam Newton's, but we project that to change going forward as the team around Newton gets better. One area Dalton clearly needs to improve is his accuracy. The Bengals' poor YAC numbers, in an offense designed around hitting receivers on the run, can be attributed (at least in part) to Dalton's lack of pinpoint control. Too often, even passes that were caught forced the receiver to break stride or go to ground, limiting potential yardage. Dalton's poise is usually given as the first or second item on his list of attributes, and his numbers in money situations bear that out. Only Aaron Rodgers and Drew Brees had a higher DVOA than Dalton's 38.9% on third and fourth down, and only Rodgers, Brees, Tom Brady, and Tony Romo did better than Dalton's 28.0% DVOA in the red zone. Regression towards the mean, of course, says not to expect splits like that on a regular basis unless Dalton's overall performance improves. The Bengals were exceptionally conservative in 2011, and while some of the shackles on Dalton figure to be removed, the receiving corps is extremely young, and the running back situation remains fluid. Dalton's growth, or lack of it, will define the Bengals' season.

Chase Daniel Height: 6-0 Weight: 225 College: Missouri Draft: 2009/FA Born: 7-Oct-1986 Age: 26 Risk: Yellow

Year	Team	G/GS	Att	Comp	C%	Yds	TD	INT	FUM	ASR	NY/P	Rk	DVOA	Rk	DYAR	Rk	YAR	Runs	Yds	TD	DVOA	DYAR
2010	NO	13/0	3	2	66.7%	16	0	0	1	26.8%	1.5	--	-63.7%	--	-16	--	-17	2	16	0	-109.1%	-16
2011	NO	16/0	5	4	80.0%	29	0	0	0	-0.9%	5.8	--	15.3%	--	8	--	12	3	-3	0	--	--
2012	NO		546	340	62.2%	3998	27	16			6.8		20.9%					75	141	2	28.9%	

2011: 75% Short 0% Mid 25% Deep 0% Bomb YAC: 5.8 (--)   2010: 75% Short 25% Mid 0% Deep 0% Bomb YAC: 5.5 (--)

Drew Brees' absence meant that that Saints OTAs were Chase Daniel love-fests. By all accounts, Daniel ran the offense very well in Brees' absence; because this is Daniel's third year in the system, no one should be surprised that he can complete passes in May. *The Times-Picayune*, or what's left of that dying newspaper, reported that Daniel even scrambled for a 60-yard practice touchdown, admitting that it is impossible to tell how many yards he would have gained if defenders were allowed to touch him but forgetting that quarterbacks are not really supposed to scramble during drills. Despite all of the optimism, everyone was quick to point out that the Saints are Brees' team, even Daniel himself, though he went so far as to call himself a "1-B" quarterback. The takeaway from all of this is that Daniel is probably capable of a Matt Flynn game or two off the bench, and that May can be a miserable time for a beat writer trying to find positive stories about a team full of suspended guys and holdouts.

Jake Delhomme Height: 6-2 Weight: 215 College: Louisiana-Lafayette Draft: 1998/FA Born: 10-Jan-1975 Age: 38 Risk: N/A

Year	Team	G/GS	Att	Comp	C%	Yds	TD	INT	FUM	ASR	NY/P	Rk	DVOA	Rk	DYAR	Rk	YAR	Runs	Yds	TD	DVOA	DYAR
2009	CAR	11/11	321	178	55.5%	2015	8	18	6	6.7%	5.4	31	-23.2%	32	-261	34	-377	17	60	0	-14.6%	-3
2010	CLE	5/4	149	93	62.4%	872	2	7	3	5.2%	5.3	38	-42.7%	42	-313	42	-310	8	-2	0	-90.2%	-26
2011	HOU	1/0	28	18	64.3%	211	1	0	1	8.9%	6.5	--	2.4%	--	26	--	39	0	0	0	--	--

2011: 67% Short 11% Mid 19% Deep 4% Bomb YAC: 3.1 (--)   2010: 57% Short 29% Mid 8% Deep 6% Bomb YAC: 4.1 (42)

With the Texans down to their third-string quarterback and already assured of a playoff berth in Week 17, they turned to Delhomme to absorb all the punishment that the playoff-hungry Titans could throw at him. He actually slung it around a little bit despite having the second-string offensive line protecting him for most of the second half. Considering that was the first positive game Delhomme had since 2008, he'd be wise to stand on it.

A.J. Feeley
Height: 6-3 Weight: 220 College: Oregon Draft: 2001/5 (155) Born: 16-May-1977 Age: 35 Risk: N/A

Year	Team	G/GS	Att	Comp	C%	Yds	TD	INT	FUM	ASR	NY/P	Rk	DVOA	Rk	DYAR	Rk	YAR	Runs	Yds	TD	DVOA	DYAR
2011	STL	5/3	97	53	54.6%	548	1	2	3	9.1%	4.5	44	-40.7%	45	-192	39	-171	3	4	0	1.8%	1

2011: 60% Short 27% Mid 6% Deep 8% Bomb YAC: 7.1 (1)

Last season, Rip Van Feeley woke up from a four-year nap, finally seeing his first game action since 2007. He was probably better off sleeping through his alarm. Van Feeley ended up with more fumbles than touchdowns, was the worst qualifying quarterback in the league on third down (-62.5% DVOA), and broke his right thumb in Week 13. His contract with the Rams completed, Van Feeley can return to his slumber.

Ryan Fitzpatrick
Height: 6-2 Weight: 221 College: Harvard Draft: 2005/7 (250) Born: 24-Nov-1982 Age: 30 Risk: Green

Year	Team	G/GS	Att	Comp	C%	Yds	TD	INT	FUM	ASR	NY/P	Rk	DVOA	Rk	DYAR	Rk	YAR	Runs	Yds	TD	DVOA	DYAR
2009	BUF	10/8	227	127	55.9%	1422	9	10	3	9.1%	5.3	35	-26.7%	36	-239	33	-304	31	141	1	25.2%	51
2010	BUF	13/13	441	255	57.8%	3000	23	15	7	5.6%	6.2	22	-3.6%	27	223	23	139	40	269	0	-3.5%	18
2011	BUF	16/16	569	353	62.0%	3832	24	23	7	3.7%	6.3	20	-6.2%	26	189	19	194	56	215	0	5.2%	38
2012	BUF		538	330	61.4%	3589	25	18		6.0		2.6%						54	226	1	8.5%	

2011: 47% Short 35% Mid 12% Deep 5% Bomb YAC: 5.3 (15)   2010: 47% Short 33% Mid 13% Deep 7% Bomb YAC: 4.8 (30)

There hasn't been much to get excited about at quarterback over the past ten years, so you can forgive Buffalo's front office for throwing money indiscriminately at the first quarterback who looked like he could actually play a little bit. With the six-year, $59 million extension he signed in October, Fitzpatrick became the first Bills quarterback to be re-signed by the team since Doug Flutie in 1999. Naturally, the bottom dropped out almost as soon as the ink was dry. Fitzpatrick's completion percentage dropped six percent over the second half of the season, while his touchdown-to-interception ratio flipped from 15-to-9 in the early going to 9-to-14 down the stretch. Some of the dropoff can be attributed to the (unlisted on the injury report) cracked ribs that Fitzgerald played with in the middle of the season, but no one should discount the role of the law of averages, either. Masking a mediocre offensive line and some fairly pedestrian receiving options is a lot to ask of a quarterback of Fitzpatrick's ilk.

Joe Flacco
Height: 6-6 Weight: 236 College: Delaware Draft: 2008/1 (18) Born: 16-Jan-1985 Age: 27 Risk: Green

Year	Team	G/GS	Att	Comp	C%	Yds	TD	INT	FUM	ASR	NY/P	Rk	DVOA	Rk	DYAR	Rk	YAR	Runs	Yds	TD	DVOA	DYAR
2009	BAL	16/16	499	315	63.1%	3613	21	12	7	6.8%	6.3	17	8.4%	17	668	14	731	35	56	0	-33.5%	-28
2010	BAL	16/16	489	306	62.6%	3622	25	10	9	7.9%	6.3	16	9.4%	15	695	11	686	43	84	1	-27.2%	-21
2011	BAL	16/16	542	312	57.6%	3610	20	12	11	5.6%	5.9	26	0.0%	18	409	14	389	39	88	1	19.3%	34
2012	BAL		515	299	58.1%	3641	23	13		6.2		10.0%						35	64	2	0.0%	

2011: 43% Short 35% Mid 12% Deep 10% Bomb YAC: 5.1 (25)   2010: 49% Short 30% Mid 14% Deep 7% Bomb YAC: 4.9 (29)

Flacco's standard stats over the last three years look remarkably similar to Tom Brady's stats from 2002 through 2004. Brady in those years completed 61.1 percent of passes for 3,667 yards, 26 touchdowns, and 13 interceptions. In comparison, Flacco's 2009-2011 stretch averaged 61.1 percent completions for 3,641 yards, 22 touchdowns, and 11 interceptions. If that's not disturbing enough, Brady's rookie statline was 2,843-18-12, and Flacco's was 2,971-14-12. Obviously, both quarterbacks also won a healthy share of games in those years. But there's a big difference between Brady and Flacco when it comes to development. Brady finally got a high-quality running game in 2004, and he blew up, ranking both fourth in DYAR and DVOA. Flacco, on the other hand, has enjoyed the help of a Pro Bowl running back for his entire career, yet instead of progressing as a quarterback, he had his worst season in year four.

Our KUBIAK projections think that Flacco will rebound in 2012, and he's a better quarterback than a lot of fans give him credit for, but he's not a guy who pulls the team to victory on his own. The only way he could possibly take the leap and become one of the top quarterbacks in the NFL would be to finally solve his problem with holding onto the ball too long in the pocket. His 3.5-second average sack time in 2011 ranked 43rd out of 47 qualifying quarterbacks, and he finished fifth among quarterbacks in long sacks (3.0 seconds or longer) after leading the league in 2010.

Matt Flynn Height: 6-2 Weight: 230 College: Louisiana State Draft: 2008/7 (209) Born: 20-Jun-1985 Age: 27 Risk: Red

Year	Team	G/GS	Att	Comp	C%	Yds	TD	INT	FUM	ASR	NY/P	Rk	DVOA	Rk	DYAR	Rk	YAR	Runs	Yds	TD	DVOA	DYAR
2009	GB	4/0	12	7	58.3%	58	0	1	0	6.8%	4.0	--	-53.7%	--	-38	--	-33	5	-5	0	--	--
2010	GB	7/1	66	40	60.6%	433	3	2	1	9.4%	5.4	--	-15.9%	--	-24	--	-23	9	26	0	-36.2%	-9
2011	GB	5/1	49	33	67.3%	518	6	2	1	9.6%	9.2	--	47.3%	--	225	--	169	13	-6	1	20.9%	5
2012	SEA		491	296	60.3%	3329	19	17			6.0		-11.6%					27	77	0	-7.0%	

2011: 39% Short 39% Mid 12% Deep 10% Bomb YAC: 6.9 (--) 2010: 59% Short 25% Mid 10% Deep 7% Bomb YAC: 6.0 (--)

Flynn essentially made $10 million guaranteed for two impressive late-season performances: his 251-yard, three-touchdown performance at New England in 2010 and his 480-yard, six-touchdown gem against Detroit in 2011. Both starts were intriguing, but two starts obviously do not a career make. Flynn was originally a seventh-round pick for a reason. Though accurate, he doesn't have a dazzling arm and he's not a wunderkind athlete. It's very telling that Flynn's offensive coordinator from Green Bay, Joe Philbin, had only lukewarm interest in bringing him to Miami. The Seahawks offered Flynn decent money (not Kevin Kolb-type money, though) and a chance to operate in a somewhat familiar West Coast offense. Expectations are neither high nor low.

Josh Freeman Height: 6-6 Weight: 248 College: Kansas State Draft: 2009/1 (17) Born: 13-Jan-1988 Age: 24 Risk: Yellow

Year	Team	G/GS	Att	Comp	C%	Yds	TD	INT	FUM	ASR	NY/P	Rk	DVOA	Rk	DYAR	Rk	YAR	Runs	Yds	TD	DVOA	DYAR
2009	TB	10/9	290	158	54.5%	1855	10	18	9	6.6%	5.7	27	-31.1%	39	-393	40	-506	30	161	0	33.9%	51
2010	TB	16/16	474	291	61.4%	3451	25	6	7	6.0%	6.5	14	13.9%	9	816	9	829	68	364	0	18.9%	96
2011	TB	15/15	551	346	62.8%	3592	16	22	8	6.1%	6.0	24	-13.7%	31	-96	34	-84	55	238	4	13.8%	70
2012	TB		539	321	59.6%	3777	20	15			6.2		5.3%					62	212	3	11.6%	

2011: 52% Short 35% Mid 10% Deep 3% Bomb YAC: 4.8 (33) 2010: 54% Short 26% Mid 12% Deep 7% Bomb YAC: 5.2 (24)

Here's a smattering of game charter comments about Josh Freeman's interceptions: "Pass tipped by A. Benn"; "Horribly run route by Spurlock there"; "Kellen Winslow catches the ball, which is then knocked out immediately"; "Thrown a little behind and high but Benn still has to make that catch"; "Well if your receivers aren't even going to try to catch a football it's not easy for you"; and the minimalist classic: "Lumpkin and Winslow collide, allowing an easy interception."

There were plenty of comments blaming Freeman for various errors on interceptions as well, but the moral of the exercise above is that Freeman was both a cause and victim of the Buccaneers malaise. Heading to the firing range to squeeze off a few Desert Eagle rounds with an injured hand may have been stupid, but it didn't cause Lumpkin and Winslow to bump into one another. Freeman had the look of a rising star in 2010, and his interception totals should find a midpoint between 2010 and 2011 once Freeman and 45 of his teammates start taking their profession seriously again.

Blaine Gabbert Height: 6-4 Weight: 234 College: Missouri Draft: 2011/1 (10) Born: 15-Oct-1989 Age: 23 Risk: Yellow

Year	Team	G/GS	Att	Comp	C%	Yds	TD	INT	FUM	ASR	NY/P	Rk	DVOA	Rk	DYAR	Rk	YAR	Runs	Yds	TD	DVOA	DYAR
2011	JAC	15/14	413	210	50.8%	2214	12	11	13	9.1%	4.2	45	-46.5%	46	-1009	47	-895	48	98	0	-38.9%	-35
2012	JAC		496	271	54.6%	2941	16	13			5.0		-17.3%					52	203	1	-4.1%	

2011: 48% Short 34% Mid 13% Deep 5% Bomb YAC: 5.4 (11)

QUARTERBACKS

Blaine Gabbert started 14 games as a rookie and not a single one came out with value over replacement level. Both anecdotal and statistical analysis suggest little improvement down the stretch. (He had -51.2% DVOA in his first seven starts, -44.5% DVOA in his last seven.) The idea that he might improve once the Jaguars give him some real weapons ignores the fact that MJD is one of the best weapons in the game. There's so much invested in Gabbert that pulling the plug didn't make sense after the first year, but unless the signs of improvement are louder than flour this season, he's going to go down with Jimmy Clausen as one of the biggest busts of the decade.

David Garrard
Height: 6-1 Weight: 244 College: East Carolina Draft: 2002/4 (108) Born: 14-Feb-1978 Age: 34 Risk: Red

Year	Team	G/GS	Att	Comp	C%	Yds	TD	INT	FUM	ASR	NY/P	Rk	DVOA	Rk	DYAR	Rk	YAR	Runs	Yds	TD	DVOA	DYAR
2009	JAC	16/16	516	314	60.9%	3597	15	10	14	8.2%	6.1	19	-4.1%	23	249	20	279	77	323	3	4.4%	60
2010	JAC	14/14	366	236	64.5%	2734	23	15	10	8.6%	6.2	19	-1.8%	24	227	22	264	66	279	5	13.5%	79
2012	MIA		450	269	59.7%	3066	19	12			5.9		-2.7%					54	146	2	-4.0%	

2010: 56% Short 26% Mid 12% Deep 6% Bomb YAC: 5.0 (27)

Garrard missed minicamp to deal with some storm damage to his home. The list of things people would rather do than play for the Dolphins just grows and grows ... Think of Garrard in the same light as an accountant or contractor suddenly laid off just days before the busy season. Instead of leaping at whatever offer comes his way, he decides to collect unemployment, eat some savings, and recharge his life batteries before searching for the right opportunity. People who do that usually understand the risks: Those opportunities may never return, and time away from "the game" could be perceived as laziness or a lack of commitment. Then again, Garrard probably would not have helped himself by getting a bench job, half-learning a playbook, and mopping up games for some team like the Chiefs last year. If anything, the year off put his Jaguars release in the rearview mirror and eased the transition to a mentor role that he was about to make anyway. Garrard and Matt Moore are both capable interim starters. Why the Dolphins feel they need two of them is their own business.

Bruce Gradkowski
Height: 6-1 Weight: 220 College: Toledo Draft: 2006/6 (194) Born: 27-Jan-1983 Age: 29 Risk: Red

Year	Team	G/GS	Att	Comp	C%	Yds	TD	INT	FUM	ASR	NY/P	Rk	DVOA	Rk	DYAR	Rk	YAR	Runs	Yds	TD	DVOA	DYAR
2009	OAK	7/4	150	82	54.7%	1007	6	3	5	7.1%	5.9	24	-5.0%	24	63	25	2	18	108	0	7.5%	16
2010	OAK	6/4	157	83	52.9%	1059	5	7	3	6.3%	5.9	34	-21.0%	37	-106	35	-60	12	41	0	-13.2%	-2
2011	CIN	2/0	18	8	44.4%	109	1	1	0	5.2%	5.4	--	-58.5%	--	-51	--	-46	3	1	0	19.2%	2
2012	CIN		493	287	58.2%	3383	20	12			6.0		6.1%					41	153	1	9.1%	

2011: 39% Short 33% Mid 17% Deep 11% Bomb YAC: 8.5 (--) 2010: 51% Short 29% Mid 14% Deep 5% Bomb YAC: 6.3 (5)

Gradkowski replaced an injured Andy Dalton at halftime of the season opener in Cleveland, and beat the Browns thanks to an alert snap-and-throw to an uncovered A.J. Green. Otherwise, he was horrendous, even by his own mediocre spot-starter standards. Durability could be an issue going forward for the slight Dalton, so an upgrade at backup behooves the Bengals, but the job appears to be Gradkowski's for the foreseeable future.

Robert Griffin
Height: 6-2 Weight: 223 College: Baylor Draft: 2012/1 (2) Born: 12-Feb-1990 Age: 22 Risk: Red

Year	Team	G/GS	Att	Comp	C%	Yds	TD	INT	FUM	ASR	NY/P	Rk	DVOA	Rk	DYAR	Rk	YAR	Runs	Yds	TD	DVOA	DYAR
2012	WAS		513	283	55.1%	3604	22	20			6.2		0.6%					108	591	4	4.6%	

The Washington chapter goes into everything we love about Griffin as a passer, but of course he's also wonderfully productive as a runner, with +35.3 career Adj. POE on 11.2 non-sack carries per game. After tearing his ACL in the third game of 2009, he not only finished the half but even carried the ball two more times. He wants to be a passer first and a runner second, but given his lack of experience and the quality of his teammates, there is probably going to be a lot of running in his first couple years. Rookie quarterbacks are almost never a good gamble in fantasy football, but we expect enough rushing yards to make Griffin a big exception to that rule.

QUARTERBACKS

Rex Grossman   Height: 6-1   Weight: 222   College: Florida   Draft: 2003/1 (22)   Born: 23-Aug-1980   Age: 32   Risk: Yellow

Year	Team	G/GS	Att	Comp	C%	Yds	TD	INT	FUM	ASR	NY/P	Rk	DVOA	Rk	DYAR	Rk	YAR	Runs	Yds	TD	DVOA	DYAR
2009	HOU	1/0	9	3	33.3%	37	0	1	1	3.3%	3.7	--	-95.0%	--	-43	--	-25	3	9	0	-78.1%	-11
2010	WAS	4/3	133	74	55.6%	884	7	4	4	7.9%	5.8	36	-24.7%	39	-129	36	-96	3	6	0	-33.9%	-3
2011	WAS	13/13	458	265	57.9%	3151	16	20	7	4.9%	6.1	21	-8.0%	27	96	25	75	20	11	1	-42.5%	-14
2012	WAS		515	303	58.9%	3347	17	17			5.5		-10.9%					30	26	1	-32.0%	

2011: 47% Short   29% Mid   15% Deep   8% Bomb   YAC: 5.0 (30)   2010: 58% Short   25% Mid   14% Deep   3% Bomb   YAC: 5.6 (14)

There's no mystery left when it comes to RG Pick-Six. If you are looking for a replacement-level quarterback, this is the current floor model. Of particular note is that in both of his Washington seasons, Grossman's passing DVOA was a little below average on first and second down but horrible on third down. He'll man the second string in 2012, ready to be ignored when desperate reporters attempt to gin up some sort of ridiculous Robert Griffin-Kirk Cousins quarterback "controversy."

Caleb Hanie   Height: 6-2   Weight: 225   College: Colorado State   Draft: 2008/FA   Born: 11-Sep-1985   Age: 27   Risk: Green

Year	Team	G/GS	Att	Comp	C%	Yds	TD	INT	FUM	ASR	NY/P	Rk	DVOA	Rk	DYAR	Rk	YAR	Runs	Yds	TD	DVOA	DYAR
2009	CHI	2/0	7	3	42.9%	11	0	1	0	0.9%	1.6	--	-151.2%	--	-73	--	-79	0	0	0	--	--
2010	CHI	2/0	7	5	71.4%	55	0	0	0	20.1%	4.4	--	0.7%	--	4	--	-6	1	-1	0	--	--
2011	CHI	6/4	102	51	50.0%	613	3	9	1	16.0%	4.0	47	-78.7%	47	-470	46	-484	13	98	0	36.4%	25
2012	DEN		524	311	59.3%	3689	24	23			6.2		-2.3%					52	72	1	-22.9%	

2011: 38% Short   37% Mid   20% Deep   5% Bomb   YAC: 4.3 (43)   2010: 56% Short   22% Mid   11% Deep   11% Bomb   YAC: 2.4 (--)

The 27-year-old from Colorado State got a chance to showcase himself late last season when he started four games in place of an injured Jay Cutler. That showcase, for all intents and purposes, may have been the death of Hanie's career. Instead of making teams wonder if he might one day develop into a starter, Hanie left teams questioning his viability as a backup. In an effort to help Hanie, the Bears watered down their offense to the point where it practically drowned. Hanie was jittery in the pocket and over-reactive to pressure. Praising him for not making a ton of mistakes would be like praising a monk for not saying the wrong thing; almost never did Hanie let a pass play fully develop. Perhaps working behind Peyton Manning will allow Hanie to one day parlay a Jim Sorgi-like reputation into another backup quarterback contract.

Graham Harrell   Height: 6-2   Weight: 215   College: Texas Tech   Draft: 2009/FA   Born: 22-May-1985   Age: 27   Risk: Yellow

Year	Team	G/GS	Att	Comp	C%	Yds	TD	INT	FUM	ASR	NY/P	Rk	DVOA	Rk	DYAR	Rk	YAR	Runs	Yds	TD	DVOA	DYAR
2012	GB		448	294	65.6%	3420	16	15			6.6		16.8%					28	43	2	23.2%	

Despite his prolific success running Mike Leach's groundbreaking offense at Texas Tech, Harrell went undrafted in 2009. He spent time with the Browns and the Saskatchewan Roughriders before arriving on the Green Bay practice squad. The Packers surprised a lot of people by not signing a veteran quarterback over the offseason, so Harrell is now the man should anything happen to Aaron Rodgers. Over the last ten years, 11 different undrafted quarterbacks with no NFL starting experience have been forced to start games due to injury. Those players have combined to complete 55.6 percent of passes for 6.1 yards per attempt, with a 38-to-48 touchdown-to-interception ratio. Their teams were 10-18 in these starts.

QUARTERBACKS

Matt Hasselbeck Height: 6-4 Weight: 223 College: Boston College Draft: 1998/6 (187) Born: 25-Sep-1975 Age: 37 Risk: Red

Year	Team	G/GS	Att	Comp	C%	Yds	TD	INT	FUM	ASR	NY/P	Rk	DVOA	Rk	DYAR	Rk	YAR	Runs	Yds	TD	DVOA	DYAR
2009	SEA	14/14	488	293	60.0%	3029	17	17	11	6.8%	5.4	30	-24.8%	34	-468	43	-292	26	119	0	-10.2%	1
2010	SEA	14/14	444	266	59.9%	3001	12	17	6	6.4%	6.0	30	-16.8%	35	-173	38	-123	23	60	3	38.5%	46
2011	TEN	16/16	518	319	61.6%	3571	18	14	4	3.7%	6.4	19	0.5%	17	390	16	371	20	52	0	32.1%	21
2012	TEN		509	310	60.9%	3512	21	13			6.3		6.2%					36	28	1	-26.5%	

2011: 52% Short 29% Mid 11% Deep 8% Bomb YAC: 5.1 (24) 2010: 51% Short 30% Mid 12% Deep 7% Bomb YAC: 4.8 (32)

That went about as well as it possibly could have. Hasselbeck saw himself fall from secret stardom to sub-replacement level during his final seasons in Seattle, but he was rejuvenated in Tennessee behind one of the best pass-blocking lines in the NFL. Not only was Hasselbeck effective, but he was also clutch: He had a 34.0% DVOA on third and fourth downs and a 31.6% DVOA in the red zone. It's anyone's guess as to how long he can hold off Jake Locker for the No. 1 spot, but he will easily be the more consistent of the two.

Chad Henne Height: 6-2 Weight: 230 College: Michigan Draft: 2008/2 (57) Born: 2-Jul-1985 Age: 27 Risk: Red

Year	Team	G/GS	Att	Comp	C%	Yds	TD	INT	FUM	ASR	NY/P	Rk	DVOA	Rk	DYAR	Rk	YAR	Runs	Yds	TD	DVOA	DYAR
2009	MIA	14/13	451	274	60.8%	2878	12	14	4	6.1%	5.7	26	3.4%	21	448	17	287	16	32	0	-6.7%	2
2010	MIA	15/14	490	301	61.4%	3301	15	19	5	5.7%	6.0	28	1.0%	22	402	17	291	35	52	0	-61.4%	-55
2011	MIA	4/4	112	64	57.1%	868	4	4	1	8.9%	6.5	16	-2.7%	20	67	27	100	15	112	0	19.0%	20
2012	JAC		474	288	60.8%	3579	21	16			6.4		-5.0%					43	86	0	-22.9%	

2011: 45% Short 28% Mid 18% Deep 8% Bomb YAC: 5.2 (22) 2010: 52% Short 34% Mid 10% Deep 4% Bomb YAC: 4.3 (40)

For a while, our advanced stats said that Chad Henne was a bit underrated. But he ended the 2010 season with a series of bad-to-awful games, then picked up where he left off in 2011 before suffering a shoulder injury in Week 4. Henne has a knack for throwing up 6-of-16, 5-of-18, or 12-of-30 stat lines when faced with a good defense, and after four full seasons, what you see is what you get. At least he's better than the veterans that Jacksonville had pushing Blaine Gabbert last year.

Shaun Hill Height: 6-5 Weight: 210 College: Maryland Draft: 2002/FA Born: 9-Jan-1980 Age: 33 Risk: Green

Year	Team	G/GS	Att	Comp	C%	Yds	TD	INT	FUM	ASR	NY/P	Rk	DVOA	Rk	DYAR	Rk	YAR	Runs	Yds	TD	DVOA	DYAR
2009	SF	6/6	155	87	56.1%	943	5	2	3	11.6%	4.8	40	-36.3%	40	-261	35	-119	8	70	0	80.5%	25
2010	DET	11/10	416	257	61.8%	2686	16	12	2	3.9%	6.0	33	6.7%	19	486	16	372	22	123	0	-9.4%	1
2011	DET	2/0	3	2	66.7%	33	0	0	0	-3.9%	11.0	--	133.9%	--	17	--	13	1	-1	0	--	--
2012	DET		559	324	57.9%	3682	21	17			5.7		-2.7%					38	67	0	-16.7%	

2011: 33% Short 33% Mid 0% Deep 33% Bomb YAC: 0 (--) 2010: 57% Short 26% Mid 13% Deep 3% Bomb YAC: 5.5 (16)

Hill is known for his reliable spot duty quarterbacking and for wearing a helmet that appears to be about two sizes too small (#scrunchedface). He's been with the Vikings, Niners, and now Lions and has always proven capable of keeping the ship afloat for a few weeks if need be. Hill doesn't have a lively enough arm to conjure big plays when things break down, but you can at least still run the bulk of your offense with him. He's more mobile than you would guess, which he's had to be given some of the bad lines he's played behind.

Brian Hoyer Height: 6-2 Weight: 215 College: Michigan State Draft: 2009/FA Born: 13-Oct-1985 Age: 27 Risk: Yellow

Year	Team	G/GS	Att	Comp	C%	Yds	TD	INT	FUM	ASR	NY/P	Rk	DVOA	Rk	DYAR	Rk	YAR	Runs	Yds	TD	DVOA	DYAR
2009	NE	4/0	27	19	70.4%	142	0	0	0	7.8%	4.3	--	-11.6%	--	-1	--	0	10	25	1	10.3%	9
2010	NE	5/0	15	7	46.7%	122	1	1	0	0.0%	8.1	--	16.1%	--	27	--	27	10	-8	0	-116.8%	-5
2011	NE	3/0	1	1	100.0%	22	0	0	0	2.3%	22.0	--	215.2%	--	16	--	16	4	-3	0	--	--
2012	NE		514	338	65.7%	3896	25	16			6.2		11.5%					30	45	2	21.5%	

2011: 0% Short 0% Mid 100% Deep 0% Bomb YAC: 0 (--) 2010: 33% Short 47% Mid 13% Deep 7% Bomb YAC: 5.9 (--)

QUARTERBACKS   293

The Patriots seem poised to replace Green Bay as the team everyone goes to for young developmental quarterback prospects who soak up coaching while stuck on the depth chart behind a legend. Mark Brunell, Aaron Brooks, and Matt Hasselbeck all caddied for Brett Favre before finding starting jobs elsewhere, and Hoyer is poised to follow Matt Cassel as the next Tom Brady understudy to get a starting gig somewhere else. NFL analyst Mike Lombardi loves Hoyer, saying, "I think he's got all the traits you need, in terms of leadership, toughness, the arm strength, the ability to move the team." The Pats tagged Hoyer with a second-round tender and will retain his services for one more year before he hits the open market as an unrestricted free agent.

Tarvaris Jackson   Height: 6-2   Weight: 226   College: Alabama State   Draft: 2006/2 (64)   Born: 21-Apr-1983   Age: 29   Risk: Red

Year	Team	G/GS	Att	Comp	C%	Yds	TD	INT	FUM	ASR	NY/P	Rk	DVOA	Rk	DYAR	Rk	YAR	Runs	Yds	TD	DVOA	DYAR
2009	MIN	8/0	21	14	66.7%	201	1	0	0	0.3%	9.6	--	75.7%	--	106	--	126	17	-10	0	-28.2%	-1
2010	MIN	3/1	58	34	58.6%	341	3	4	1	8.7%	4.7	--	-37.1%	--	-110	--	-148	7	63	0	81.6%	19
2011	SEA	15/14	450	271	60.2%	3091	14	13	8	7.9%	5.7	30	-6.0%	25	161	20	61	40	180	1	-19.1%	-11
2012	SEA		452	271	60.0%	3001	19	14			5.7		-10.6%					40	54	1	-25.3%	
2011:	46% Short	33% Mid	11% Deep	10% Bomb	YAC: 5.0 (27)		2010:	100% Short	0% Mid	0% Deep	0% Bomb										YAC: 3.4 (--)	

Signed to a two-year, $8 million contract by the Seahawks after the lockout, Jackson was instantly installed as the starter due to his familiarity with Darrell Bevell's offense and had his best statistical season as a professional. Jackson rarely made the big play when the Seahawks needed him to, though, posting a -19.3% DVOA on third and fourth downs. Ten of his 13 interceptions came when the Seahawks were already trailing. Jackson deserves credit and earned points in the locker room for playing through a torn right pectoral muscle, which for a right-handed quarterback couldn't have been easy. However, Jackson shouldn't have hopes of remaining the starter after the additions of Matt Flynn and Russell Wilson; he should just hope that his $4 million non-guaranteed contract doesn't get him released.

Josh Johnson   Height: 6-3   Weight: 213   College: San Diego   Draft: 2008/5 (160)   Born: 15-May-1986   Age: 26   Risk: Yellow

Year	Team	G/GS	Att	Comp	C%	Yds	TD	INT	FUM	ASR	NY/P	Rk	DVOA	Rk	DYAR	Rk	YAR	Runs	Yds	TD	DVOA	DYAR
2009	TB	5/3	125	63	50.4%	685	4	8	7	7.5%	4.6	41	-43.2%	43	-265	36	-340	22	148	0	3.4%	15
2010	TB	11/0	16	14	87.5%	111	0	0	0	10.5%	5.7	--	7.0%	--	18	--	19	4	39	0	153.1%	26
2011	TB	9/1	36	19	52.8%	246	1	2	1	8.1%	5.7	--	-46.8%	--	-91	--	-72	11	67	0	-8.0%	2
2012	SF		468	284	60.6%	3118	16	16			5.6		-13.3%					53	149	1	-11.6%	
2011:	40% Short	37% Mid	13% Deep	10% Bomb	YAC: 1.7 (--)		2010:	65% Short	20% Mid	10% Deep	5% Bomb										YAC: 3.6 (--)	

If this were a baseball book, we would call Johnson "toolsy." He is one of the fastest quarterbacks in the league, has a fine arm and quick release, and has shown flashes of brilliance as a passer when asked to do more than run three Wildcat-type plays per month. The tools and flashes make Johnson the kind of player fans scream for, and there will be plenty of "don't be surprised if…" columns about Johnson's ability to wrest a job from Alex Smith. Stranger things have happened. Johnson, like Smith, is essentially a one-read, throw-or-run quarterback. If he proves that he can master Jim Harbaugh's "two plays in the huddle, choose at the line" trick, he could threaten Smith.

Colin Kaepernick   Height: 6-5   Weight: 233   College: Nevada   Draft: 2011/2 (36)   Born: 3-Nov-1987   Age: 25   Risk: Yellow

Year	Team	G/GS	Att	Comp	C%	Yds	TD	INT	FUM	ASR	NY/P	Rk	DVOA	Rk	DYAR	Rk	YAR	Runs	Yds	TD	DVOA	DYAR
2011	SF	3/0	5	3	60.0%	35	0	0	0	0.0%	7.0	--	34.1%	--	14	--	17	2	-2	0	--	--
2012	SF		440	223	50.6%	2697	15	17			5.3		-15.4%					75	346	2	-8.8%	
2011:	20% Short	80% Mid	0% Deep	0% Bomb	YAC: 3.0 (--)																	

In his first NFL preseason, Colin Kaepernick completed 48 percent of passes for just 5.1 yards per attempt, with no touchdowns and five interceptions. Granted, we're talking about preseason, but you don't really want your promising quarterback of the future to be that bad against backups. The 49ers selected Kaepernick knowing full well he's a raw, multi-year project, so the silver lining is that they got a glimpse into just how far away he is from NFL viability. For now, what's important is that he plays better this preseason. Otherwise, he could lose his No. 2 quarterback job to newly-acquired Josh Johnson.

Mike Kafka
Height: 6-3   Weight: 225   College: Northwestern   Draft: 2010/4 (122)   Born: 25-Jul-1987   Age: 25   Risk: Green

Year	Team	G/GS	Att	Comp	C%	Yds	TD	INT	FUM	ASR	NY/P	Rk	DVOA	Rk	DYAR	Rk	YAR	Runs	Yds	TD	DVOA	DYAR
2011	PHI	4/0	16	11	68.8%	107	0	2	0	6.2%	5.9	--	-38.0%	--	-30	--	-32	3	0	0	-57.6%	-2
2012	PHI		550	338	61.6%	3569	20	14			5.7		1.5%					39	51	1	-17.2%	

2011:   60% Short   13% Mid   7% Deep   20% Bomb   YAC: 3.5 (--)

A completion rate of 69 percent with an interception rate of 13 percent is the kind of combination that screams "small sample size," and of course it is. The completion rate was goosed by a lot of wide receiver screens when Kafka had to replace an injured Vick in the Week 2 loss to Atlanta. Still, Kafka is the perfect backup quarterback for the Andy Reid offense: an athletic runner and scholar of the playbook who can be managed with plays that hide his subpar arm strength.

Kevin Kolb
Height: 6-3   Weight: 218   College: Houston   Draft: 2007/2 (36)   Born: 24-Aug-1984   Age: 28   Risk: Yellow

Year	Team	G/GS	Att	Comp	C%	Yds	TD	INT	FUM	ASR	NY/P	Rk	DVOA	Rk	DYAR	Rk	YAR	Runs	Yds	TD	DVOA	DYAR
2009	PHI	5/2	96	62	64.6%	741	4	3	1	5.2%	7.1	8	11.7%	16	151	23	132	5	-1	1	11.6%	5
2010	PHI	7/5	189	115	60.8%	1197	7	7	5	7.9%	5.3	39	-10.2%	32	12	32	21	15	65	0	-25.6%	-7
2011	ARI	9/9	253	146	57.7%	1955	9	8	8	11.0%	6.0	22	-18.5%	33	-133	35	-123	17	65	0	-14.2%	-1
2012	ARI		532	329	61.9%	4047	23	21			6.5		-1.9%					42	93	2	-2.9%	

2011:   46% Short   37% Mid   11% Deep   6% Bomb   YAC: 6.2 (4)   2010:   61% Short   21% Mid   10% Deep   8% Bomb   YAC: 5.0 (28)

Kolb's first season in Arizona was marred by a midseason toe injury and a concussion, his second in as many seasons, which would end his season in December. Kolb said his concussions have been "a freak deal," but he is now wearing a new helmet that is designed to protect the back of his head. Considering the Cardinals' offensive tackle situation, it's a good that something is protecting Kolb. In the eight-plus games Kolb did play, he was progressively worse by down: -4.3% on first down, -23.6% on second down, and -31.7% on third and fourth down. Kolb also had a -61.4% DVOA in the red zone. If finances were the lone determining factor in who starts at quarterback for the Cardinals, Kolb would have the job sewn up. They aren't.

Byron Leftwich
Height: 6-5   Weight: 245   College: Marshall   Draft: 2003/1 (7)   Born: 14-Jan-1980   Age: 32   Risk: Green

Year	Team	G/GS	Att	Comp	C%	Yds	TD	INT	FUM	ASR	NY/P	Rk	DVOA	Rk	DYAR	Rk	YAR	Runs	Yds	TD	DVOA	DYAR
2009	TB	3/3	107	58	54.2%	594	4	3	2	1.3%	5.5	29	1.4%	22	89	24	-13	6	6	0	-7.5%	0
2010	PIT	1/0	7	5	71.4%	42	0	0	0	22.9%	3.9	--	-13.6%	--	-2	--	-1	0	0	0	--	--
2012	PIT		487	298	61.2%	3282	20	11			6.1		7.9%					32	25	1	-22.7%	

2010:   67% Short   33% Mid   0% Deep   0% Bomb   YAC: 3.6 (--)

Once upon a time, some viewed Leftwich as a potential franchise quarterback. In 2012, he's a No. 2 only because Charlie Batch is in his third NFL decade and Pittsburgh didn't re-sign Dennis Dixon. Don't mistake Leftwich's story for a Greek tragedy, though. Since being released by the Jaguars in September 2007, Leftwich has parlayed 208 forward arm motions into $12 million.

QUARTERBACKS

Jake Locker   Height: 6-3   Weight: 231   College: Washington   Draft: 2011/1 (8)   Born: 15-Jun-1988   Age: 24   Risk: Yellow

Year	Team	G/GS	Att	Comp	C%	Yds	TD	INT	FUM	ASR	NY/P	Rk	DVOA	Rk	DYAR	Rk	YAR	Runs	Yds	TD	DVOA	DYAR
2011	TEN	5/0	66	34	51.5%	542	4	0	0	8.3%	7.2	--	22.0%	--	143	--	172	8	56	1	61.4%	27
2012	TEN		480	279	58.2%	3384	25	20			5.8		-5.3%					45	203	3	15.8%	
2011:	49% Short	31% Mid	15% Deep	5% Bomb	YAC: 7.8 (--)																	

You know those commercials where a truck helps a plane with damaged landing gear land? Jake Locker is the NFL equivalent of those trucks; the spectacular things he can do obscure the fact that if you drive him around all the time, the gas mileage sucks. He has is a lack of consistency on his touch throws and, last year, an inability to read more than two options before scrambling. It's obvious why draftniks loved him and the Titans fell for him enough to take him eighth overall despite his horrific college completion percentage, as he oozes raw tools and makes deep balls appear effortless. The Titans need to get him on the field and see if his accuracy is good enough to make him worth driving for 200,000 miles, or if he's just going to be good for driving through rings of fire in a few 30-second spots.

Andrew Luck   Height: 6-4   Weight: 234   College: Stanford   Draft: 2012/1 (1)   Born: 12-Mar-1989   Age: 23   Risk: Yellow

Year	Team	G/GS	Att	Comp	C%	Yds	TD	INT	FUM	ASR	NY/P	Rk	DVOA	Rk	DYAR	Rk	YAR	Runs	Yds	TD	DVOA	DYAR
2012	IND		497	307	61.9%	3453	18	17			6.1		-0.3%					65	267	2	8.4%	

Look, you know what there is to know about Luck at this point: He's one of the best quarterback prospects of the past 15 years, he shows uncommon poise and pocket presence, he turned Stanford (of all places) into a national contender. Let's just throw some random facts out there so you can actually walk away from the capsule with new information. He attended Stratford High School in Houston. His father Oliver was a backup quarterback for the Oilers and, before becoming the athletic director at West Virginia, worked in the Houston Dynamo front office. A homecoming game every year? Not too shabby. He also had +20.3 Adj. POE *running* the football at Stanford, averaging over 8.0 yards per carry once we remove sacks from the numbers.

Eli Manning   Height: 6-4   Weight: 218   College: Mississippi   Draft: 2004/1 (1)   Born: 3-Jan-1981   Age: 32   Risk: Yellow

Year	Team	G/GS	Att	Comp	C%	Yds	TD	INT	FUM	ASR	NY/P	Rk	DVOA	Rk	DYAR	Rk	YAR	Runs	Yds	TD	DVOA	DYAR
2009	NYG	16/16	509	317	62.3%	4021	27	14	13	5.3%	7.1	9	17.3%	10	974	10	845	17	65	0	9.6%	11
2010	NYG	16/16	539	339	62.9%	4002	31	25	6	3.3%	7.0	6	4.2%	20	547	15	609	32	70	0	47.4%	32
2011	NYG	16/16	589	359	61.0%	4933	29	16	8	5.0%	7.6	6	16.2%	9	1109	8	1136	35	15	1	-43.3%	-18
2012	NYG		569	360	63.3%	4501	30	17			7.1		20.4%					19	39	1	-1.2%	
2011:	43% Short	31% Mid	17% Deep	10% Bomb	YAC: 5.8 (7)	2010:	47% Short	32% Mid	14% Deep	6% Bomb	YAC: 4.8 (31)											

During the 2011 preseason, Eli Manning told New York radio host Michael Kay that he considered himself an "elite, top five" quarterback. Everybody in the football commentariat had to spend the entire season having arguments about how good Eli Manning really was and what exactly the word "elite" really meant. Then, when the Giants won the Super Bowl, conventional wisdom spoke loud and clear: Yes, Eli Manning is an "elite" quarterback.

Of course, the idea that one game or even one playoff run marks a player as an "elite" quarterback is a bit silly. If Wes Welker leaps and catches that pass in the fourth quarter, is Eli Manning no longer an elite quarterback? If the Hail Myra pass drops into the hands of Aaron Hernandez, is Eli Manning no longer an elite quarterback? Plays by the other team shouldn't change where Eli Manning stands in the quarterback firmament.

So let's take a step back from the Super Bowl and look at the improvements Eli Manning made to his game over the entire 2011 season. For the first time, Manning couldn't depend on opponents bringing their safeties up; the struggles of the ground game put the weight on his shoulders. He built on his pre-snap skill and became more proficient at moving in the pocket to buy time (or out of the pocket—Manning only left the pocket on six percent of pass plays, but had a league-leading 80.9% DVOA and 10.1 yards per play when he did). He did a better job of going through reads and finding a different receiver when the initial look wasn't there. And in conjunction with Victor Cruz, he turned the option route into poetry.

That being said, statistically it is hard to argue that Manning is one of the top five quarterbacks in the league right now. Manning had a career-high in DYAR because the Giants were depending on him so much more than in previous seasons, but there were still seven quarterbacks ahead of him. On a per-play basis, Manning was no better than he has been since 2008. He's ranked ninth or tenth in DVOA three of the last four years. The other year was 2010, when he had the ridiculous interception total which was, as we pointed out in last year's book, a total fluke, caused by passes tipped off his receivers and a lack of drops by defenders. From a statistical perspective, that's where Eli Manning stands, ninth or tenth.

But of course, there's more to judging a quarterback than just the raw statistics. You have to judge the statistics in context. How dependent was the offense on this quarterback? How good were his receivers and his line? And yes, it does matter if a player can raise his game when the chips are down—or, more accurately, if a player can avoid panic and mistakes when the chips are down.

So again, we're back to the question: "Is Eli Manning elite? Is he top five?" Well, if "elite" means "top tier," then no, Eli Manning is not elite. Right now, the top tier of NFL quarterbacks consists of Tom Brady, Drew Brees, and Aaron Rodgers. The gap between those three players and the rest of the league is simply too large to make up with subjective bonus points. If we assume that Eli's brother will come back from his neck injury close to what he was two years ago, you've got to give him the fourth spot. But if you then want to argue that Eli Manning gets to be number five because of his postseason success and the improvements he made in his game last year, well, we're not going to argue with you.

Peyton Manning Height: 6-5 Weight: 230 College: Tennessee Draft: 1998/1 (1) Born: 24-Mar-1976 Age: 36 Risk: Red

Year	Team	G/GS	Att	Comp	C%	Yds	TD	INT	FUM	ASR	NY/P	Rk	DVOA	Rk	DYAR	Rk	YAR	Runs	Yds	TD	DVOA	DYAR
2009	IND	16/16	571	393	68.8%	4500	33	16	2	2.7%	7.6	4	34.0%	5	1771	3	1849	19	-13	0	-130.4%	-21
2010	IND	16/16	679	450	66.3%	4700	33	17	3	2.8%	6.6	11	19.0%	6	1400	3	1598	18	18	0	81.9%	13
2012	DEN		562	365	65.0%	4380	29	11			7.2		31.0%					16	-10	0	-37.5%	

2010: 54% Short 27% Mid 12% Deep 8% Bomb YAC: 4.2 (41)

We don't have a lot of comparable players for Peyton Manning to help us build a projection. Here's what we do know: He started to decline just the tiniest bit in 2010, before the neck surgery. Beyond that, the most important signs to watch for are his performance in OTAs, training camp, and the preseason. Early reports said his accuracy looked good but the strength on the deep ball was lacking a bit. Other than Denver's tough schedule, the situation is set up for him to succeed. He should be behind the best offensive line he's had in years, and he's never had a receiver as physically dominant as Demaryius Thomas. There are a lot of variables at work here, but the bottom line is that nothing we've seen on the field thus far leads us to believe he'll be anything but excellent if healthy. If healthy, of course, being the $96 million question.

Josh McCown Height: 6-4 Weight: 215 College: Sam Houston State Draft: 2002/3 (81) Born: 4-Jul-1979 Age: 33 Risk: Yellow

Year	Team	G/GS	Att	Comp	C%	Yds	TD	INT	FUM	ASR	NY/P	Rk	DVOA	Rk	DYAR	Rk	YAR	Runs	Yds	TD	DVOA	DYAR
2009	CAR	1/0	6	1	16.7%	2	0	0	0	13.6%	-0.6	--	-93.1%	--	-38	--	-48	0	0	0	--	--
2011	CHI	3/2	55	35	63.6%	414	2	4	2	11.2%	6.0	--	-50.6%	--	-147	--	-110	12	68	0	12.2%	16
2012	CHI		444	268	60.3%	3309	19	16			6.4		-1.0%					72	280	1	-7.6%	

2011: 35% Short 48% Mid 9% Deep 7% Bomb YAC: 4.8 (--)

Until the Bears were forced to drag him off his couch last year, McCown had not started a game in the NFL since 2007. He played well enough at the end of the year to get a contract as this year's third quarterback, but if you are the Bears, doesn't it make sense to replace McCown at the end of training camp with some young passer with upside who couldn't fit on another team's roster? (We're looking at you, Josh Portis.)

QUARTERBACKS

Luke McCown Height: 6-3 Weight: 208 College: Louisiana Tech Draft: 2004/4 (106) Born: 12-Jul-1981 Age: 31 Risk: N/A

Year	Team	G/GS	Att	Comp	C%	Yds	TD	INT	FUM	ASR	NY/P	Rk	DVOA	Rk	DYAR	Rk	YAR	Runs	Yds	TD	DVOA	DYAR
2009	JAC	3/0	3	1	33.3%	2	0	0	0	40.9%	-1.0	--	-144.0%	--	-41	--	-38	0	0	0	--	--
2010	JAC	1/0	19	11	57.9%	120	0	0	0	0.0%	6.3	--	26.0%	--	44	--	28	1	4	0	-53.5%	-2
2011	JAC	4/2	56	30	53.6%	296	0	4	2	7.1%	4.3	--	-73.4%	--	-250	--	-274	7	23	0	32.9%	14
2011:	47% Short	35% Mid	16% Deep	2% Bomb	YAC: 4.7 (--)	2010:	42% Short	32% Mid	16% Deep	11% Bomb	YAC: 5.3 (--)

Against all forms of better judgement, the Jaguars actually entered last season with Luke McCown as their starting quarterback. After contributing a mind-blowing -206 DYAR in roughly three quarters of action against the Jets in Week 2, the Jags quickly decided that Blaine Gabbert couldn't be that raw, and McCown saw only relief action for the rest of the season. In conclusion, Luke McCown : Josh McCown :: Billy Baldwin : Stephen Baldwin. That makes the 2011 Jaguars *Flatliners*.

Colt McCoy Height: 6-1 Weight: 216 College: Texas Draft: 2010/3 (85) Born: 5-Sep-1986 Age: 26 Risk: Red

Year	Team	G/GS	Att	Comp	C%	Yds	TD	INT	FUM	ASR	NY/P	Rk	DVOA	Rk	DYAR	Rk	YAR	Runs	Yds	TD	DVOA	DYAR
2010	CLE	8/8	222	135	60.8%	1576	6	9	1	9.3%	6.0	32	-1.9%	25	146	27	84	28	136	1	48.9%	64
2011	CLE	13/13	463	265	57.2%	2733	14	11	10	6.7%	5.1	38	-15.2%	32	-133	36	-161	61	212	0	-16.5%	-11
2012	CLE		503	313	62.4%	3379	17	16			5.7		-11.9%					51	203	2	-1.8%	
2011:	54% Short	31% Mid	10% Deep	5% Bomb	YAC: 4.6 (35)	2010:	56% Short	27% Mid	10% Deep	7% Bomb	YAC: 5.5 (19)

Despite a solid statistical record, McCoy was available in the third round of the 2009 draft due to size concerns in general and his small hands in particular. Small hands often get linked to fumbling, and indeed, only four quarterbacks put the ball on the ground more often then McCoy (Tim Tebow, Matt Moore, Joe Flacco, and Blaine Gabbert). The one trait Colt was thought to possess for sure was accuracy, but he dipped in that category last season. It probably didn't help that his receivers apparently dip their hands in axle grease before games. Cleveland led the league with 43 drops, eight more than any other team. With Brandon Weeden on hand to take the starting job (unless he completely pratfalls over the summer), McCoy returns to a backup role, be it in Cleveland or somewhere else. It's a job his skill set is better suited for.

Stephen McGee Height: 6-3 Weight: 225 College: Texas A&M Draft: 2009/4 (101) Born: 27-Sep-1985 Age: 27 Risk: Green

Year	Team	G/GS	Att	Comp	C%	Yds	TD	INT	FUM	ASR	NY/P	Rk	DVOA	Rk	DYAR	Rk	YAR	Runs	Yds	TD	DVOA	DYAR
2010	DAL	2/1	44	22	50.0%	238	2	0	1	8.1%	4.8	--	-19.5%	--	-25	--	-39	13	74	0	32.0%	21
2011	DAL	1/0	38	24	63.2%	182	1	0	0	4.6%	3.8	--	-10.0%	--	3	--	-8	4	28	0	24.1%	7
2012	DAL		555	321	57.8%	3908	16	16			5.6		-6.8%					56	127	0	-20.0%	
2011:	61% Short	26% Mid	8% Deep	5% Bomb	YAC: 3.6 (--)	2010:	57% Short	33% Mid	3% Deep	7% Bomb	YAC: 5.5 (--)

All of McGee's action last season came in Week 16 against Philadelphia after Tony Romo hit his hand on a defender's helmet. McGee played exactly how you would expect a veteran third-stringer to play: smart enough to avoid turnovers and take what the defense gave him, but not dangerous enough to generate much productivity. None of his 24 completions gained more than 19 yards. This summer he'll battle Rudy Carpenter (a long-time taxi squad player for Dallas and Tampa Bay) for the third-string spot behind Romo and Kyle Orton.

Donovan McNabb Height: 6-2 Weight: 240 College: Syracuse Draft: 1999/1 (2) Born: 25-Nov-1976 Age: 36 Risk: N/A

Year	Team	G/GS	Att	Comp	C%	Yds	TD	INT	FUM	ASR	NY/P	Rk	DVOA	Rk	DYAR	Rk	YAR	Runs	Yds	TD	DVOA	DYAR
2009	PHI	14/14	443	267	60.3%	3553	22	10	10	7.1%	6.9	12	4.6%	20	485	16	518	37	140	2	42.1%	55
2010	WAS	13/13	472	275	58.3%	3377	14	15	9	7.1%	6.1	25	-6.9%	29	133	28	58	29	151	0	13.4%	26
2011	MIN	6/6	156	94	60.3%	1026	4	2	2	10.1%	5.3	35	-4.8%	22	70	26	35	14	59	1	-12.7%	0
2011:	49% Short	35% Mid	10% Deep	6% Bomb	YAC: 4.5 (36)	2010:	56% Short	27% Mid	9% Deep	8% Bomb	YAC: 5.8 (8)

QUARTERBACKS

McNabb insists that he still has plenty left. The rest of the NFL, and especially his last two coaching staffs, tacitly insist he doesn't. What's interesting here is that with most decade-long stars whose careers are fizzling out, the issue at hand is their physical aptitude. But with McNabb, it seems to be, in large part, his mental aptitude. He struggled to learn the playbook in Washington and impressed no one with his football IQ in Minnesota. His work ethic was also questioned at both stops. That's troubling for the 35-year-old because it essentially eliminates his appeal as a veteran backup.

Matt Moore   Height: 6-3   Weight: 202   College: Oregon State   Draft: 2007/FA   Born: 9-Aug-1984   Age: 28   Risk: Yellow

Year	Team	G/GS	Att	Comp	C%	Yds	TD	INT	FUM	ASR	NY/P	Rk	DVOA	Rk	DYAR	Rk	YAR	Runs	Yds	TD	DVOA	DYAR
2009	CAR	7/5	138	85	61.6%	1053	8	2	2	5.6%	6.7	15	17.1%	11	262	19	278	12	-3	0	-32.5%	-2
2010	CAR	6/5	143	79	55.2%	857	5	10	4	7.9%	4.9	42	-42.8%	43	-324	43	-342	5	25	0	-11.0%	0
2011	MIA	13/12	347	210	60.5%	2497	16	9	13	9.0%	5.9	27	-5.7%	24	135	22	124	32	65	2	-34.9%	-21
2012	MIA		458	276	60.3%	3035	18	12			5.7		1.2%					25	49	1	-5.1%	

2011: 45% Short   30% Mid   15% Deep   11% Bomb   YAC: 4.1 (44)   2010: 55% Short   23% Mid   16% Deep   6% Bomb   YAC: 4.5 (37)

Moore has made a career of being a salvage quarterback who looks great when his team's record is dismal, the starter is injured, and all hope appears lost. He's a viable game manager and pass distributor if he gets the help of a good offensive line, but he's not a natural progression passer because he's uncomfortable in the pocket with bodies around him. Moore also doesn't have a big time arm; his accuracy can be inconsistent, particularly with balls sailing high. There are worse choices to keep the huddle warm until Ryan Tannehill is ready, but Moore may not be the right fit if Joe Philbin wants a quarterback who can make the kind of stick throws and multiple quick progression reads he got used to in Green Bay.

Cam Newton   Height: 6-5   Weight: 248   College: Auburn   Draft: 2011/1 (1)   Born: 11-May-1989   Age: 23   Risk: Yellow

Year	Team	G/GS	Att	Comp	C%	Yds	TD	INT	FUM	ASR	NY/P	Rk	DVOA	Rk	DYAR	Rk	YAR	Runs	Yds	TD	DVOA	DYAR
2011	CAR	16/16	517	310	60.0%	4051	21	17	5	7.3%	6.9	10	0.8%	16	404	15	428	126	706	14	14.5%	188
2012	CAR		469	301	64.3%	3627	24	14			7.0		29.6%					126	608	10	39.6%	

2011: 43% Short   32% Mid   18% Deep   7% Bomb   YAC: 6.2 (5)

Newton from the shotgun: 377 attempts, 9.4% DVOA, 7.2 yards per play. Newton under center: 177 attempts, -15.1% DVOA, 6.4 yards per play. Both DeAngelo Williams and Jonathan Stewart had exceptional rushing DVOA percentages from the shotgun as well. There are a handful of teams further along the road toward a "shotgun only" offense than the Panthers, like the Lions, but there are few teams for whom it makes more sense. What doesn't make sense is that Ron Rivera finished last in the league in Aggressiveness Index. Given Cam Newton's talents, not only should the Panthers be frequently going for it on fourth down, they also should consider going for two after every touchdown.

A *Charlotte Observer* article in mid May noted that local sports-talk callers spent a lot of airtime speculating about whether Cam Newton would leave the Panthers after his contract expires. At the end of the 2014 season. In other words, they are projecting worries three years into the future before the kid even leads the team to a winning record. Someone get this region a decent NBA team, stat!

Dan Orlovsky   Height: 6-5   Weight: 230   College: Connecticut   Draft: 2005/5 (145)   Born: 18-Aug-1983   Age: 29   Risk: Green

Year	Team	G/GS	Att	Comp	C%	Yds	TD	INT	FUM	ASR	NY/P	Rk	DVOA	Rk	DYAR	Rk	YAR	Runs	Yds	TD	DVOA	DYAR
2010	HOU	1/0	0	0	0.0%	0	0	0	--	--	--	--	--	--	--	--	--	0	0	0	--	--
2011	IND	8/5	193	122	63.2%	1201	6	4	7	6.9%	5.5	33	-2.2%	19	121	23	36	6	5	0	4.1%	1
2012	TB		477	264	55.4%	3167	15	18			5.8		-4.5%					27	2	1	-30.3%	

2011: 50% Short   36% Mid   11% Deep   3% Bomb   YAC: 3.1 (47)

Orlovsky finally got his first win as a starter against the Titans in Week 15, and another win over Houston ran his lifetime record to 2-10. He's got the arm to go a little further downfield than Curtis Painter did, but he tends to make some rather doofy choices at times, such as the memorable moment when he took a safety in Detroit by running out of the back of his own end zone. There are three tiers of backup quarterbacks: the ones you wouldn't mind starting, the ones you're not sure about, and the ones that scare you. Orlovsky is somewhere between those first two categories. Josh Freeman has been pretty durable thus far, so look for Orlovsky to do more clipboard holding this year.

Kyle Orton Height: 6-4 Weight: 226 College: Purdue Draft: 2005/4 (106) Born: 14-Nov-1982 Age: 30 Risk: Green

Year	Team	G/GS	Att	Comp	C%	Yds	TD	INT	FUM	ASR	NY/P	Rk	DVOA	Rk	DYAR	Rk	YAR	Runs	Yds	TD	DVOA	DYAR
2009	DEN	16/16	541	336	62.1%	3802	21	12	4	5.3%	6.4	16	8.4%	18	711	12	743	24	71	0	-20.2%	-8
2010	DEN	13/13	498	293	58.8%	3653	20	9	3	6.6%	6.5	15	8.3%	17	663	13	708	22	98	0	6.4%	16
2011	2TM	9/8	252	150	59.5%	1758	9	9	2	5.4%	6.4	17	-5.4%	23	97	24	170	11	13	0	4.9%	3
2012	DAL		533	339	63.6%	3691	21	16			5.8		1.4%					21	31	1	-11.9%	

2011: 47% Short 35% Mid 12% Deep 5% Bomb YAC: 5.0 (28) 2010: 50% Short 30% Mid 13% Deep 8% Bomb YAC: 5.1 (26)

Orton will back up Tony Romo in Dallas even though he could likely outplay at least a half-dozen starters in the league. His potential has been pretty much maxed out, which is why nobody wants to build their franchise around him. Nonetheless, he is an underrated quarterback with a lot of strengths as a timing and rhythm passer. He understands route combinations and how his offensive system correlates to both the game plan and what the defense is playing. This is exactly what you want out of a backup quarterback: a guy you could pull out of bed and hand that week's playbook, and he would be ready to start 30 minutes later. If Romo ends up missing a good chunk of the season again, Orton should be more than capable of keeping Dallas competitive.

Brock Osweiler Height: 6-7 Weight: 242 College: Arizona State Draft: 2012/2 (57) Born: 22-Nov-1990 Age: 22 Risk: Yellow

Year	Team	G/GS	Att	Comp	C%	Yds	TD	INT	FUM	ASR	NY/P	Rk	DVOA	Rk	DYAR	Rk	YAR	Runs	Yds	TD	DVOA	DYAR
2012	DEN		509	245	48.2%	3444	21	21			5.2		-9.8%					37	137	1	1.5%	

Osweiler is basically built for the Lewin Career Forecast to hate. He started one game each as a freshman and sophomore, then one mediocre season as a junior before declaring for the draft. In that brief playing time, he was relatively inconsistent, completing just over 60 percent of his passes. He ranked sixth or worse in the Pac-12 in completion percentage, yards per pass, touchdowns, and passer rating, making him a mediocre passer in a league not known for playing stellar defense. Osweiler measured 6-foot-7 at the Combine. The only other passers that tall in our database are Ryan Mallett and Dan McGwire. Bad company, that.

Curtis Painter Height: 6-4 Weight: 230 College: Purdue Draft: 2009/6 (201) Born: 24-Jun-1985 Age: 27 Risk: Green

Year	Team	G/GS	Att	Comp	C%	Yds	TD	INT	FUM	ASR	NY/P	Rk	DVOA	Rk	DYAR	Rk	YAR	Runs	Yds	TD	DVOA	DYAR
2009	IND	2/0	28	8	28.6%	83	0	2	2	10.0%	2.2	--	-82.5%	--	-140	--	-199	3	4	0	-138.3%	-18
2011	IND	9/8	243	132	54.3%	1541	6	9	5	7.4%	5.5	32	-33.3%	44	-375	44	-312	17	107	0	10.3%	18
2012	BAL		488	270	55.4%	2975	16	17			5.1		-17.3%					48	56	1	-21.4%	Green

2011: 49% Short 31% Mid 13% Deep 7% Bomb YAC: 5.7 (9)

Curtis Painter led the league in "dejectedly staring out into space with hands on hips after incompletions," finishing with 12 more than Kevin Kolb. After years of providing subpar quarterback play in relief of Peyton Manning, we learned in 2011 that Painter can provide subpar quarterback play at all times. He will now continue doing so in Baltimore, where he at least picked a team capable of giving him a victory lap start in Week 17.

300　QUARTERBACKS

Tyler Palko　　Height: 6-1　Weight: 215　College: Pittsburgh　　Draft: 2007/FA　Born: 9-Aug-1983　Age: 29　Risk: N/A

Year	Team	G/GS	Att	Comp	C%	Yds	TD	INT	FUM	ASR	NY/P	Rk	DVOA	Rk	DYAR	Rk	YAR	Runs	Yds	TD	DVOA	DYAR
2010	KC	2/0	6	4	66.7%	35	0	0	0	22.9%	3.1	--	-26.4%	--	-8	--	-13	2	5	0	75.9%	5
2011	KC	6/4	134	80	59.7%	796	2	7	1	7.8%	5.0	40	-27.9%	42	-150	38	-210	5	15	0	-20.3%	-2
2011:	52% Short	31% Mid	13% Deep	4% Bomb	YAC: 4.3 (42)	2010:	78% Short	22% Mid	0% Deep	0% Bomb	YAC: 3.3 (--)

Palko waited three years on practice squads and rosters with the Saints, Steelers, and Chiefs before finally getting a start. When he finally hit the field, it was clear that he does not have the arm strength to play quarterback at the NFL level. His average pass distance last year was 7.2 yards. That's more than a yard short of Matt Cassel (8.3), who will never be confused with Daryle Lamonica. The Chiefs brought in Brady Quinn to battle Ricky Stanzi for the backup job behind Cassel. Palko remained unsigned in early June, and is unlikely to be signed by the time you read this.

Carson Palmer　　Height: 6-5　Weight: 230　College: USC　　Draft: 2003/1 (1)　Born: 27-Dec-1979　Age: 33　Risk: Green

Year	Team	G/GS	Att	Comp	C%	Yds	TD	INT	FUM	ASR	NY/P	Rk	DVOA	Rk	DYAR	Rk	YAR	Runs	Yds	TD	DVOA	DYAR
2009	CIN	16/16	466	282	60.5%	3094	21	13	6	4.9%	6.0	21	7.8%	19	583	15	626	39	93	3	18.6%	48
2010	CIN	16/16	586	362	61.8%	3970	26	20	6	4.8%	6.2	20	7.1%	18	739	10	589	32	50	0	-25.2%	-14
2011	OAK	10/9	328	199	60.7%	2753	13	16	2	5.6%	7.7	5	2.5%	15	296	18	298	16	20	1	-32.1%	-16
2012	OAK		533	332	62.3%	4187	21	17		6.9		10.3%						36	70	0	-9.3%	
2011:	37% Short	35% Mid	20% Deep	8% Bomb	YAC: 5.3 (16)	2010:	48% Short	36% Mid	10% Deep	6% Bomb	YAC: 4.5 (35)

For six weeks, Palmer looked like he might be headed to retirement, then Hue Jackson pulled off the trade with Mike Brown. Thrust into the lineup about five minutes after arriving in Oakland, he looked awful, throwing three interceptions in less than a half. Then he actually got to learn the offense, and if we take out that ridiculous half in Week 7, Palmer's DVOA rating of 9.5% fits nicely into his career path. His arm seemed a bit stronger than it was in those last couple seasons in Cincinnati, and he was particularly successful on first and second downs when operating under center. He struggled badly in the red zone, but the good news is red-zone performance tends to be inconsistent from season to season. New offensive coordinator Greg Knapp will probably have to call fewer bootlegs than he has in the past, but Palmer gives him the ability to attack defenses vertically in a way Matt Schaub could not do in Houston. Palmer also gets to play with Darren McFadden in the backfield for the first time, as the injury-prone back was done for the year before Palmer arrived. We're not going to start discussing Palmer again as one of the league's best quarterbacks, the way we were back in 2005, but Palmer could have a very successful season in 2012.

Christian Ponder　　Height: 6-2　Weight: 229　College: Florida State　　Draft: 2011/1 (12)　Born: 25-Feb-1988　Age: 24　Risk: Green

Year	Team	G/GS	Att	Comp	C%	Yds	TD	INT	FUM	ASR	NY/P	Rk	DVOA	Rk	DYAR	Rk	YAR	Runs	Yds	TD	DVOA	DYAR
2011	MIN	11/10	291	158	54.3%	1853	13	13	6	10.5%	5.3	36	-31.5%	43	-404	45	-378	28	219	0	36.5%	59
2012	MIN		517	311	60.2%	3546	20	16		5.8		-1.6%						57	293	1	14.4%	
2011:	42% Short	38% Mid	11% Deep	9% Bomb	YAC: 5.3 (19)

Ponder took the starting reigns from the ineffective and ill-prepared Donovan McNabb in Week 7. In his debut against the Packers, he had perhaps the best-looking 13-for-32 passing performance we will ever see, sparking some much-needed life into Minnesota's anemic offense with his mobility. It was clear from the start that the Vikings preferred to play with their young quarterback on the move (play-action, bootlegs, etc.) That game, however, wound up being just the first of seven losses for Ponder, as a paucity of receiving talent and mediocre line play hamstrung the Vikings.

There's reason for optimism. Ponder has quick feet and a compact throwing motion. His arm strength is solid but not spectacular. When he's comfortable, he's decisive in his reads. He has flashed the toughness needed to make risky throws from the pocket under pressure, but this is a double-edged sword; many of Ponder's 13 interceptions last season were a result of poor decision-making. Moving forward, the Vikings need to make life easy on Ponder by featuring three- and five-step drops and play-action, as this would highlight the overall quickness that defines his game.

QUARTERBACKS

Terrelle Pryor   Height: 6-6   Weight: 233   College: Ohio State   Draft: 2011/3 (SUP)   Born: 20-Jun-1989   Age: 23   Risk: Yellow

Year	Team	G/GS	Att	Comp	C%	Yds	TD	INT	FUM	ASR	NY/P	Rk	DVOA	Rk	DYAR	Rk	YAR	Runs	Yds	TD	DVOA	DYAR
2011	OAK	1/0	0	0	0.0%	0	0	0	0	--	--	--	--	--	--	--	--	0	0	0	--	--
2012	OAK		498	237	47.5%	3277	26	22			5.1		-13.0%					87	596	3	17.1%	

Pryor's only snap in 2011 was wiped out by his own false start penalty. The last pet project of Al Davis, it's unclear if he has any future in Oakland. He's working on developing consistent footwork, but begins the season behind Carson Palmer and Matt Leinart in an offense that doesn't seem to suit his talents.

Brady Quinn   Height: 6-3   Weight: 235   College: Notre Dame   Draft: 2007/1 (22)   Born: 27-Oct-1984   Age: 28   Risk: Green

Year	Team	G/GS	Att	Comp	C%	Yds	TD	INT	FUM	ASR	NY/P	Rk	DVOA	Rk	DYAR	Rk	YAR	Runs	Yds	TD	DVOA	DYAR
2009	CLE	10/9	256	136	53.1%	1339	8	7	3	6.6%	4.5	42	-22.8%	31	-207	30	-212	20	98	1	41.1%	51
2012	KC		474	261	55.2%	3042	16	21			5.6		-10.1%					27	52	0	-13.4%	

One year ago, there was talk that Quinn might be Denver's starting quarterback in 2011. Obviously, he wasn't, and he leaves the Broncos $1.4 million richer without having ever thrown a regular-season pass for the club. Now he's in Kansas City, reunited with Romeo Crennel, who coached him in Cleveland. Quinn has lost quarterback battles to Charlie Frye, Derek Anderson, Kyle Orton, and Tim Tebow, and now he's dueling Ricky Stanzi for the backup job in Kansas City. Another new teammate for Quinn: Peyton Hillis. You'll recall that the Broncos once traded Hillis and a pair of draft choices to Cleveland for Quinn. In hindsight, that deal didn't do much for the Broncos or Browns. Maybe it will work out better for the Chiefs.

Chris Redman   Height: 6-3   Weight: 223   College: Louisville   Draft: 2000/3 (75)   Born: 7-Jul-1977   Age: 35   Risk: Green

Year	Team	G/GS	Att	Comp	C%	Yds	TD	INT	FUM	ASR	NY/P	Rk	DVOA	Rk	DYAR	Rk	YAR	Runs	Yds	TD	DVOA	DYAR
2009	ATL	5/2	119	69	58.0%	781	4	3	1	6.4%	6.0	22	14.0%	13	196	21	123	6	4	0	3.3%	2
2010	ATL	2/0	6	4	66.7%	20	0	0	0	0.6%	3.3	--	-42.6%	--	-13	--	-16	1	-1	0	--	--
2011	ATL	5/0	28	18	64.3%	188	0	1	0	0.9%	6.7	--	-6.2%	--	8	--	15	5	-6	0	--	--
2012	ATL		511	320	62.5%	3661	21	14			6.8		20.8%					29	30	1	-9.40%	

2011: 33% Short   44% Mid   19% Deep   4% Bomb   YAC: 3.8 (--)   2010: 83% Short   17% Mid   0% Deep   0% Bomb   YAC: 3.8 (--)

Redman re-signed with the Falcons in March. It is hard to get any sense of his current skill level from watching completions against the Buccaneers Quit Brigade, but it is 100 percent certain that Redman is worse than Matt Ryan and better than John Parker Wilson. If he stays with the team through 2012, Redman's Falcons career will have been 50 percent longer than his Ravens career.

Philip Rivers   Height: 6-5   Weight: 228   College: North Carolina State   Draft: 2004/1 (4)   Born: 8-Dec-1981   Age: 31   Risk: Red

Year	Team	G/GS	Att	Comp	C%	Yds	TD	INT	FUM	ASR	NY/P	Rk	DVOA	Rk	DYAR	Rk	YAR	Runs	Yds	TD	DVOA	DYAR
2009	SD	16/16	486	317	65.2%	4254	28	9	6	4.6%	8.0	1	41.7%	1	1776	2	1712	26	50	1	-14.0%	-1
2010	SD	16/16	541	357	66.0%	4710	30	13	6	6.8%	7.8	1	27.9%	3	1430	2	1629	29	52	0	-0.7%	9
2011	SD	16/16	582	366	62.9%	4624	27	20	8	5.4%	7.2	7	17.0%	8	1118	7	1038	26	36	1	7.5%	14
2012	SD		556	350	62.9%	4365	28	15			6.8		16.0%					17	17	1	-14.9%	

2011: 45% Short   31% Mid   16% Deep   8% Bomb   YAC: 5.4 (13)   2010: 54% Short   26% Mid   14% Deep   6% Bomb   YAC: 6.3 (4)

Rivers' average completion was just as far downfield in 2011 as it was the previous couple seasons, but the YAC on his throws went from top-five to league-average. That was partly of a function of a passing game that too often looked like a doughnut, with Rivers throwing deep passes or dumpoffs to the backs and nothing in the middle. The only receiver who consistently showed separation on intermediate to deep routes was Antonio Gates. The higher interception rate was primarily a result of Rivers trying to force more passes downfield, given the lack of better short options. His decision making also seemed to be affected by pressure more than it had been in past years, when he'd been almost completely unflappable. The offensive line should be more consistent than it was in 2011, which would help, but Rivers probably needs either Robert Meachem or Vincent Brown to emerge as a consistent threat to regain the form he had from 2008-2010.

Aaron Rodgers Height: 6-2 Weight: 223 College: California Draft: 2005/1 (24) Born: 2-Dec-1983 Age: 29 Risk: Green

Year	Team	G/GS	Att	Comp	C%	Yds	TD	INT	FUM	ASR	NY/P	Rk	DVOA	Rk	DYAR	Rk	YAR	Runs	Yds	TD	DVOA	DYAR
2009	GB	16/16	541	350	64.7%	4434	30	7	8	8.7%	7.1	10	17.8%	9	1106	9	1327	58	316	5	45.7%	136
2010	GB	15/15	475	312	65.7%	3922	28	11	3	6.9%	7.4	2	26.9%	4	1288	4	1241	64	356	4	24.6%	98
2011	GB	15/15	502	343	68.3%	4643	45	6	3	7.2%	8.3	1	46.6%	1	2059	2	2121	60	257	3	18.7%	71
2012	GB		513	335	65.4%	4270	34	13		7.5		32.1%						66	271	4	33.0%	
2011:	43% Short	36% Mid	14% Deep	7% Bomb	YAC: 5.9 (6)	2010:	53% Short	28% Mid	11% Deep	8% Bomb	YAC: 5.7 (12)

The only Aaron Rodgers debate people can have these days is about whether he's the best quarterback in the entire NFL. His greatness is beyond question. He's as smart as Peyton Manning and as athletically gifted as Ben Roethlisberger (though styles in both examples are different). Rodgers' arm strength and precision accuracy are superb. It's why Packers receivers always perform well after the catch. It's almost unfair that Rodgers is also mobile, both in and out of the pocket. And his is not Michael Vick-like mobility where the quarterback buys time but everything breaks down. When Rodgers buys time, he extends the original design of the play, making life easier (and more productive) for the other Packers. It's the type of quarterbacking genius that can't fully be taught.

Perhaps more impressive is Rodgers' ability to diagnose defenses before the snap (and, if need be, quickly amend his diagnosis after the snap). His innate understanding of the Packers' system has made him a master at adjusting protections and maximizing the effectiveness of route combinations. Rodgers wins as many battles at the line before the snap as any passer in the league.

Ben Roethlisberger Height: 6-5 Weight: 240 College: Miami (Ohio) Draft: 2004/1 (11) Born: 2-Mar-1982 Age: 30 Risk: Yellow

Year	Team	G/GS	Att	Comp	C%	Yds	TD	INT	FUM	ASR	NY/P	Rk	DVOA	Rk	DYAR	Rk	YAR	Runs	Yds	TD	DVOA	DYAR
2009	PIT	15/15	506	337	66.6%	4328	28	14	7	9.0%	7.2	7	23.3%	8	1228	8	1298	40	82	2	11.0%	36
2010	PIT	12/12	389	240	61.7%	3200	17	5	6	8.0%	7.2	4	31.1%	2	1061	7	1013	34	176	2	39.4%	67
2011	PIT	15/15	513	324	63.2%	4077	21	14	8	7.2%	6.9	11	13.3%	11	867	9	841	31	70	0	9.2%	18
2012	PIT		503	322	64.1%	4160	26	13		7.3		20.3%						41	79	2	-4.9%	
2011:	42% Short	36% Mid	15% Deep	7% Bomb	YAC: 5.4 (12)	2010:	48% Short	31% Mid	15% Deep	7% Bomb	YAC: 5.5 (15)

When we think of players suddenly breaking down due to physical punishment, we generally think of running backs, not quarterbacks. But with the punishment Big Ben has taken over the course of his career, it might be time to wonder whether a running-back-style breakdown is nigh. No matter how you slice it, Roethlisberger's sack numbers are rare. His current total of 314 (in 3,627 dropbacks) is 38 more than any other active starter, and the rest of the top five (other than Michael Vick) have at least 2,000 more dropbacks. Since the merger, only Neil Lomax (362 in 3,515 dropbacks) and Randall Cunningham (359 in 3,000 dropbacks) took more sacks than Roethlisberger before turning 30. Only Lomax, Cunningham, and Ken O'Brien (328 in 3,595 dropbacks) were sacked more in their first eight seasons. So what happened to that trio immediately after they set their ignominious standards? Lomax missed all of his age-30 season in 1989, and ultimately retired in 1990, because of a degenerative hip condition. O'Brien retired after throwing only 235 passes in seasons nine and ten. Cunningham infamously broke his leg at age 30, was benched in favor of Rodney Peete, and retired, before coming back to have one great season with Minnesota. Yes, it's a small sample size, and yes, Roethlisberger is a much better quarterback than Lomax or O'Brien, but there's literally no post-merger precedent for a quarterback as sack-prone as Roethlisberger continuing a similar level of production for several years after turning 30. Roethlisberger's late-season high-ankle sprain and subsequent ineffectiveness was a glimpse into what his career could easily turn into very soon.

QUARTERBACKS 303

Tony Romo Height: 6-2 Weight: 219 College: Eastern Illinois Draft: 2003/FA Born: 21-Apr-1980 Age: 32 Risk: Red

Year	Team	G/GS	Att	Comp	C%	Yds	TD	INT	FUM	ASR	NY/P	Rk	DVOA	Rk	DYAR	Rk	YAR	Runs	Yds	TD	DVOA	DYAR
2009	DAL	16/16	550	347	63.1%	4483	26	9	5	6.2%	7.4	6	28.0%	7	1432	7	1333	35	105	1	60.7%	43
2010	DAL	6/6	213	148	69.5%	1605	11	7	0	4.5%	7.2	5	13.3%	11	334	19	359	6	38	0	86.7%	21
2011	DAL	16/16	522	346	66.3%	4184	31	10	5	6.3%	7.2	8	26.8%	4	1344	4	1280	22	46	1	-18.0%	-4
2012	DAL		557	363	65.3%	4302	28	12			6.6		16.6%					20	33	0	-9.0%	

| 2011: | 48% Short | 33% Mid | 12% Deep | 6% Bomb | YAC: 5.7 (10) | 2010: | 49% Short | 36% Mid | 10% Deep | 5% Bomb | YAC: 5.3 (20) |

Statistically, Romo is one of the top-flight quarterbacks of his era. He has ranked 11th or higher in passing DVOA every year since 2006. Among active quarterbacks, only Aaron Rodgers has averaged more yards or touchdowns per pass over his career, and only Rodgers, Brees, and Peyton Manning have higher completion percentages. In December Cowboys owner Jerry Jones said there was no quarterback he'd rather have with the game on the line, and why not? Romo had 36.7% DVOA last year in late-and-close situations (second half, score within a touchdown), fourth in the NFL behind the big three of Aaron Rodgers, Drew Brees, and Tom Brady. If we take out the third quarter from that number, Romo's DVOA goes up to 43.2%. Troy Aikman has said that he was never as good as Romo is now.

Romo is not commonly held in high regard, though, mostly because he has won just one playoff game. That's partly due to tough competition, as the Giants and Eagles have done their share to keep Dallas out of the playoffs. However, Romo has lost three playoff games, two of them close contests in which he played badly and can fairly be blamed for his team's failure. In some ways he is comparable to Bert Jones and Ken Anderson, two 1970s quarterbacks who rarely played in the postseason and did little with the chances they were given. Jones went 0-3 in the playoffs. Anderson finally got a victory and advanced to the Super Bowl in 1981, at age 32. Romo, by the way, turned 32 in April. He does have a habit of throwing a ball up for grabs and cowering when pass rushers get in his face. He averaged 8.6 yards per play without pressure, but just 2.3 yards when under pressure. That's a difference of 6.3 yards, a bigger dropoff than any regular starter except Rex Grossman. That's not quite the same company we were talking about 300 words ago, is it?

Sage Rosenfels Height: 6-4 Weight: 222 College: Iowa State Draft: 2001/4 (109) Born: 6-Mar-1978 Age: 34 Risk: Green

Year	Team	G/GS	Att	Comp	C%	Yds	TD	INT	FUM	ASR	NY/P	Rk	DVOA	Rk	DYAR	Rk	YAR	Runs	Yds	TD	DVOA	DYAR
2010	NYG	12/0	0	0	0.0%	0	0	0	0	--	--	--	--	--	--	--	--	3	-3	0	--	--
2012	MIN		482	284	58.8%	3581	17	18			6.3		-5.8%					27	-9	0	-45.6%	

After beginning the year in Miami, Rosenfels returned to the Vikings at midseason despite the fact that just about everyone in the greater Minneapolis/St. Paul area believes he was the mole in 2009 who kept leaking the Favre-Childress locker room dirt to the media. That drama wound up contributing to Brad Childress's termination in 2010, though by then, Rosenfels was riding the pine for the New York Giants. Why do we dedicate this entire comment to bits of hearsay and mundane details of Rosenfels' recently peripatetic life? Because we have nothing else to say, as the guy hasn't thrown a pass in a regular-season NFL game since 2008.

Matt Ryan Height: 6-4 Weight: 228 College: Boston College Draft: 2008/1 (3) Born: 17-May-1985 Age: 27 Risk: Green

Year	Team	G/GS	Att	Comp	C%	Yds	TD	INT	FUM	ASR	NY/P	Rk	DVOA	Rk	DYAR	Rk	YAR	Runs	Yds	TD	DVOA	DYAR
2009	ATL	14/14	451	263	58.3%	2916	22	14	5	4.1%	6.1	20	12.4%	15	701	13	458	30	49	1	9.0%	23
2010	ATL	16/16	571	357	62.5%	3705	28	9	4	4.1%	6.0	29	18.0%	7	1120	5	1080	46	122	0	-11.0%	6
2011	ATL	16/16	566	347	61.3%	4177	29	12	5	5.3%	6.8	12	18.7%	7	1118	6	1204	37	84	2	19.8%	38
2012	ATL		552	346	62.7%	4216	31	15			7.0		25.6%					32	36	1	-4.7%	

| 2011: | 45% Short | 35% Mid | 14% Deep | 6% Bomb | YAC: 5.0 (29) | 2010: | 50% Short | 32% Mid | 14% Deep | 4% Bomb | YAC: 3.8 (44) |

Ryan seems to improve just a little bit each year. The big change last year was more responsibility at the line of scrimmage, with the Falcons using a no-huddle offense out of three-receiver sets more and more as the season progressed. Ryan is also more mobile than most people give him credit for; he can move in the pocket to avoid pressure, and if he needs to move out of the pocket, he can maintain himself as a threat to pass. Unfortunately, some corners of the blogosphere are rapidly taking notice of Ryan's 0-3 playoff record and shifting from "up and comer" expectations to "justify your existence" treatment. With the exception of his inability to execute a sneak into the mouth of a bloodthirsty Giants defensive line, Ryan does not lack any "winner" attributes. Like the rest of the Falcons franchise, he needs something to break his way one of these postseasons. Ryan is too good to be thrown into the "quarterback expectations" sausage grinder, but that is just where he will be as soon as the Falcons hit a rough patch or lose another playoff game.

Mark Sanchez Height: 6-2 Weight: 227 College: USC Draft: 2009/1 (5) Born: 11-Nov-1986 Age: 26 Risk: Yellow

Year	Team	G/GS	Att	Comp	C%	Yds	TD	INT	FUM	ASR	NY/P	Rk	DVOA	Rk	DYAR	Rk	YAR	Runs	Yds	TD	DVOA	DYAR
2009	NYJ	15/15	364	196	53.8%	2444	12	20	10	7.3%	5.9	25	-26.6%	35	-383	38	-376	36	106	3	12.8%	43
2010	NYJ	16/16	507	278	54.8%	3291	17	13	9	5.4%	5.9	35	-4.3%	28	234	20	219	30	105	3	8.8%	28
2011	NYJ	16/16	543	308	56.7%	3474	26	18	10	6.6%	5.6	31	-12.5%	29	-53	31	-13	37	103	6	-8.2%	7
2012	NYJ		452	258	57.2%	2943	20	14			5.8		-4.8%					46	80	2	-8.4%	

2011: 44% Short 37% Mid 15% Deep 4% Bomb   YAC: 4.9 (31)   2010: 51% Short 30% Mid 11% Deep 8% Bomb   YAC: 4.7 (33)

Take a long, sober look at Sanchez's statistics and try to see anything but unabashed mediocrity. His completion percentages hover five or six points below league average. Yards per attempt and touchdown percentages are consistently below league average, interception percentages above. DVOA nodded at his sophomore improvements in 2010 by proclaiming that he achieved "average," then shrugged at his touchdown rate spike and acknowledged his overall dip last year. Even if you are a "Winners Win Baby" true believer, you have to recognize that one 11-5 record for a defensive juggernaut, fueled by numerous close wins, is hardly the high-water mark you want to hang a "Sanchez is a Winner" argument on.

Now, think of all the time and energy spent analyzing Sanchez, justifying Sanchez, defending Sanchez, and generally trying to prove that Sanchez is anything other than a barely-average player. Think of all the words and broadcast hours spent by our fellow writers, television and radio analysts, former quarterbacks, and other people who should know better (including ourselves once or twice), trying to construct a non-existent Sanchez that was somehow greater than the sum of his 56.7 percent completion-rate parts. It has become almost impossible to think clearly about any starting quarterback, especially a New York quarterback, among the din of attention-seeking opinions, spontaneous "insights," and generally muddled and inane thinking. The Sanchize was, and still is, a high-profile symptom of our industry-wide blathering sickness.

As soon as Sanchez hits the bench this year, the situation will become 7.2 trillion times worse.

Matt Schaub Height: 6-5 Weight: 235 College: Virginia Draft: 2004/3 (90) Born: 25-Jun-1981 Age: 31 Risk: Green

Year	Team	G/GS	Att	Comp	C%	Yds	TD	INT	FUM	ASR	NY/P	Rk	DVOA	Rk	DYAR	Rk	YAR	Runs	Yds	TD	DVOA	DYAR
2009	HOU	16/16	583	396	67.9%	4770	29	15	3	5.3%	7.7	3	29.3%	6	1624	6	1685	48	57	0	-43.7%	-53
2010	HOU	16/16	574	365	63.6%	4370	24	12	8	5.9%	6.9	9	12.2%	13	930	8	926	22	28	0	9.9%	17
2011	HOU	10/10	292	178	61.0%	2479	15	6	3	5.6%	7.8	4	24.4%	5	701	10	690	15	9	2	9.7%	10
2012	HOU		498	314	63.0%	3735	24	12			6.7		17.5%					33	53	1	-0.8%	

2011: 47% Short 31% Mid 14% Deep 8% Bomb   YAC: 6.6 (2)   2010: 54% Short 31% Mid 11% Deep 4% Bomb   YAC: 5.5 (17)

Schaub is not a premium arm talent, but he hangs around the lower portion in the second tier of NFL quarterbacks by throwing an accurate ball, being terrific in the play-action game, and knowing where to find Andre Johnson. Getting injured by Albert Haynesworth, again, in a Week 10 win over the Buccaneers—thus allowing him to miss the playoffs and keep his lack of national renown alive—was arguably the most Matt Schaub thing that Matt Schaub has ever accomplished. One thing he can work on for next season: his red-zone DVOA fell from 48.1% in 2010 to -32.0% in 2011. A little stabilization there would go a long way towards a second division crown for the Texans.

John Skelton
Height: 6-6 Weight: 243 College: Fordham Draft: 2010/5 (155) Born: 17-Mar-1988 Age: 24 Risk: Yellow

Year	Team	G/GS	Att	Comp	C%	Yds	TD	INT	FUM	ASR	NY/P	Rk	DVOA	Rk	DYAR	Rk	YAR	Runs	Yds	TD	DVOA	DYAR
2010	ARI	5/4	126	60	47.6%	662	2	2	3	7.8%	4.5	44	-53.4%	45	-348	45	-281	10	49	0	18.0%	11
2011	ARI	8/7	275	151	54.9%	1913	11	14	4	7.6%	5.9	28	-27.6%	41	-326	42	-349	28	128	0	19.8%	34
2012	ARI		552	305	55.2%	3793	19	20			5.9		-10.9%					63	222	0	-8.6%	

2011: 40% Short 38% Mid 16% Deep 6% Bomb YAC: 5.4 (14) 2010: 52% Short 25% Mid 15% Deep 8% Bomb YAC: 3.3 (46)

Despite ranking outside the top 40 in DYAR and DVOA, and having DVOAs of -41.4% on second down, -38.7% on third down, and -36.6% out of shotgun, the Cardinals won five of Skelton's seven starts (and won a sixth game where Skelton replaced a concussed Kolb in a scoreless game in the first quarter), so he opened the 2012 offseason on equal footing with Kolb in their competition for the starting job. Kolb makes over 15 times more than Skelton, who is third highest-paid quarterback on the roster ($75,000 less than Richard Bartel).

Alex Smith
Height: 6-4 Weight: 212 College: Utah Draft: 2005/1 (1) Born: 7-May-1984 Age: 28 Risk: Red

Year	Team	G/GS	Att	Comp	C%	Yds	TD	INT	FUM	ASR	NY/P	Rk	DVOA	Rk	DYAR	Rk	YAR	Runs	Yds	TD	DVOA	DYAR
2009	SF	11/10	372	225	60.5%	2350	18	12	3	6.5%	5.7	28	-19.5%	27	-209	31	-39	24	51	0	-11.8%	0
2010	SF	11/10	342	204	59.6%	2370	14	10	4	7.8%	6.2	21	-12.2%	33	-26	33	0	18	60	0	-2.9%	6
2011	SF	16/16	445	273	61.3%	3144	17	5	6	8.5%	5.8	29	3.1%	14	442	13	354	52	179	2	11.4%	38
2012	SF		483	293	60.7%	3422	23	11			6.1		0.3%					40	105	2	-0.6%	

2011: 52% Short 32% Mid 10% Deep 6% Bomb YAC: 5.2 (21) 2010: 60% Short 24% Mid 9% Deep 7% Bomb YAC: 6.1 (6)

Don't mock Alex Smith as a game manager, because that's exactly what Jim Harbaugh asked Smith to be: a guy who didn't screw things up. Smith basically led the league in not screwing things up, with a league-low interception rate of 1.1 percent. That happened to be the third-best rate in history for a quarterback with at least 400 pass attempts, behind only Tom Brady in 2010 (0.8%) and Steve DeBerg in 1990 (0.9%). Can Smith possibly repeat such a low interception rate? The short answer is no; he'll almost certainly finish 2012 closer to league average, which was 2.9 percent. The long answer is that Smith's low interception rate may be more sustainable than it seems at first glance. Smith has only had three potential interceptions dropped by defenders over the past two seasons, and had the lowest pass defensed rate in the league last season according to our charting (5.2 percent). His interception rate will be closer to what Brady did the year after (2.0%) than what DeBerg did the year after (3.2%).

However, with offseason improvements at wide receiver and the late-season reappearance of Vernon Davis as an offensive focal point, Harbaugh may be expecting Smith to be more than a game manager this season. Adding a deep threat like Randy Moss, in particular, suggests that the coaching staff will call on Smith to throw the ball downfield more often. Contrary to popular belief, this is not a far-fetched strategy. On throws of 16 yards or more last season, Smith had 88.4% DVOA, which ranked ninth among qualifying quarterbacks.

Matthew Stafford
Height: 6-2 Weight: 225 College: Georgia Draft: 2009/1 (1) Born: 7-Feb-1988 Age: 24 Risk: Green

Year	Team	G/GS	Att	Comp	C%	Yds	TD	INT	FUM	ASR	NY/P	Rk	DVOA	Rk	DYAR	Rk	YAR	Runs	Yds	TD	DVOA	DYAR
2009	DET	10/10	377	201	53.3%	2267	13	20	4	6.0%	5.3	32	-36.6%	41	-652	45	-497	20	108	2	26.2%	32
2010	DET	3/3	96	57	59.4%	535	6	1	2	4.7%	5.0	41	3.0%	21	91	29	80	4	11	1	-22.0%	-3
2011	DET	16/16	663	421	63.5%	5038	41	16	5	5.9%	6.8	13	14.9%	10	1170	5	1312	22	78	0	-2.2%	7
2012	DET		629	384	61.1%	4310	29	21			5.7		2.6%					26	43	1	-5.6%	

2011: 51% Short 30% Mid 10% Deep 8% Bomb YAC: 5.3 (18) 2010: 61% Short 27% Mid 5% Deep 7% Bomb YAC: 5.3 (23)

Staying healthy for the first time in his career, Stafford last season showed why he was the No. 1 overall pick in 2009. Operating out of the shotgun an NFL-record 68 percent of the time, he finished third in the league in passing yards and touchdowns. These numbers weren't buttressed by the garbage time that had long been commonplace in Detroit, either. There is still plenty of room for Stafford to improve. Despite completing a respectable 63.5 percent of his passes, he too often struggled with accuracy. Many of his completions were less effective than they could have been because of poor ball placement. A midseason finger injury, which Stafford played through, may or may not have contributed to these problems. In addition, Stafford wasn't always able to handle extra helpings put on his mental plate. One reason offensive coordinator Scott Linehan used very little pre-snap motion was because he knew his young quarterback needed a static defense in order to make some of the reads. Mind you, this is typical with many young quarterbacks. But the good ones typically grow out of it. Expect that to be the case with Stafford. Let's hope it is. He has one of the best guns in the game. He throws with good velocity and with a compact motion. Best of all, he's willing to play without fear and look down the gun barrel from a muddy pocket.

Drew Stanton   Height: 6-3   Weight: 230   College: Michigan State   Draft: 2007/2 (43)   Born: 7-May-1984   Age: 28   Risk: Yellow

Year	Team	G/GS	Att	Comp	C%	Yds	TD	INT	FUM	ASR	NY/P	Rk	DVOA	Rk	DYAR	Rk	YAR	Runs	Yds	TD	DVOA	DYAR
2009	DET	3/1	51	26	51.0%	259	0	6	1	8.3%	4.2	--	-74.3%	--	-243	--	-296	9	33	1	0.6%	4
2010	DET	6/3	119	69	58.0%	780	4	3	2	5.4%	6.0	27	12.2%	12	174	24	84	18	113	1	20.5%	28
2012	IND		463	271	58.6%	3149	11	12			6.0		-7.1%					43	50	2	-21.6%	

2010: 59% Short   30% Mid   5% Deep   6% Bomb   YAC: 6.1 (7)

OK, so maybe Stanton wasn't worth the second-round pick that Detroit spent on him back in 2007. He's never had the strongest arm, and he has trouble when crowded in the pocket. Stanton also has a tendency to dance around at the top of his drop, which is a symptom of inexperience. But when you're 28, inexperience is a symptom of your coaches thinking you can't really play.

Ryan Tannehill   Height: 6-4   Weight: 221   College: Texas A&M   Draft: 2012/1 (8)   Born: 27-Jul-1988   Age: 24   Risk: Red

Year	Team	G/GS	Att	Comp	C%	Yds	TD	INT	FUM	ASR	NY/P	Rk	DVOA	Rk	DYAR	Rk	YAR	Runs	Yds	TD	DVOA	DYAR
2012	MIA		445	229	51.5%	2870	13	17			5.3		-16.1%					58	261	2	-9.7%	

On September 24, Texas A&M took a 20-3 halftime lead against Oklahoma State, but three Tannehill interceptions helped the Cowboys come back and win a 30-29 game. Later in the year, the Aggies were hanging tough against the Sooners, trailing 13-10 at the half, but two Tannehill interceptions in the third quarter helped Oklahoma reel of 28 unanswered points. The Aggies held a 16-7 halftime lead over Texas, but Tannehill threw two third-quarter interceptions, one of them a pick-six, helping the Longhorns come back to win. These games, plus some other lackluster efforts (against Arkansas, for example) are good reasons for Tannehill skepticism, but they were swept under the rug during the pre-draft silly season, when prospects are broken down into their component parts and the big picture disappears. Tannehill was not ready for the better Big 12 defenses last year, and he won't be ready for NFL defenses this year, no matter what Chris Weinke whispered in his ear. Patience will be the key to unlocking Tannehill's potential; 2012, like 2011, will be a mix of highlights and interceptions by the bunch.

Tyrod Taylor   Height: 6-1   Weight: 216   College: Virginia Tech   Draft: 2011/6 (180)   Born: 3-Aug-1989   Age: 23   Risk: Yellow

Year	Team	G/GS	Att	Comp	C%	Yds	TD	INT	FUM	ASR	NY/P	Rk	DVOA	Rk	DYAR	Rk	YAR	Runs	Yds	TD	DVOA	DYAR
2011	BAL	3/0	1	1	100.0%	18	0	0	0	65.9%	5.0	--	-40.2%	--	-4	--	0	1	2	0	-41.6%	-1
2012	BAL		454	261	57.6%	2951	16	18			5.4		-10.0%					72	388	1	-4.1%	

2011:   0% Short   100% Mid   0% Deep   0% Bomb   YAC: 5.0 (--)

The Internet scouting intelligentsia universally dubbed Taylor "a project" heading into the 2011 draft, but the Ravens don't seem to share that view. When Marc Bulger retired prior to last season, they chose not to sign a veteran replacement, instead making Taylor the primary backup in his rookie season. And when Baltimore signed Curtis Painter in April, they made it a point to re-emphasize Taylor's No. 2 status. Aside from a propensity for holding the ball too long, Flacco and Taylor are as different in size and skill set as any one-two combination in the league, so it's surprising that Baltimore would (again) put themselves one injury away from an in-season overhaul of their offensive scheme.

QUARTERBACKS

Tim Tebow   Height: 6-3   Weight: 236   College: Florida   Draft: 2010/1 (25)   Born: 14-Aug-1987   Age: 25   Risk: Green

Year	Team	G/GS	Att	Comp	C%	Yds	TD	INT	FUM	ASR	NY/P	Rk	DVOA	Rk	DYAR	Rk	YAR	Runs	Yds	TD	DVOA	DYAR
2010	DEN	9/3	82	41	50.0%	654	5	3	1	5.4%	7.3	--	13.6%	--	135	--	143	43	227	6	23.3%	73
2011	DEN	14/11	271	126	46.5%	1729	12	6	12	11.2%	5.0	39	-22.7%	37	-221	40	-276	122	660	6	-18.3%	-36
2012	NYJ		20	12	60.0%	200	3	2			9.0		-7.5%					63	319	5	6.2%	
2012	NYJ		403	215	53.4%	2620	15	16			5.6		-19.0%					127	635	7	13.1%	

| 2011: | 29% Short | 40% Mid | 14% Deep | 17% Bomb | YAC: 4.8 (32) | 2010: | 49% Short | 27% Mid | 14% Deep | 10% Bomb | YAC: 6.2 (--) |

Give Tebow credit for his game-winning drives, but the fact is that over the course of a game this man was not a good NFL quarterback in 2011. Among players with at least 250 dropbacks, he had the worst completion percentage since Akili Smith in 2000, and the worst sack rate since JaMarcus Russell in 2009. And while quarterbacks like Randall Cunningham or Michael Vick have been able to somewhat mitigate their poor passing with stellar rushing play, Tebow's rushes actually had negative value. He gained 5.7 yards per rush, which was almost exactly the league average for his position. However, while the average quarterback's Success Rate on runs was 57 percent, Tebow gained successful yardage only 44 percent of the time, the worst such figure of the 17 quarterbacks with at least 20 runs. In just 11 starts, he led all players, regardless of position, with 29 failed runs on third or fourth down. When Tebow did complete passes, they tended to pick up massive chunks of yardage, and he also had a low interception rate, so he wasn't the worst passer in the league. With such massive holes in his game, however, he's a long way from being a key contributor on a quality team.

What you see above are two projections for Tebow. The first one is a "stab in the dark" estimate of what he'll do as part of a Wildcat package for the Jets. (Let's face it, nobody really knows how often the Jets will actually run that package.) The second projection is the usual 16-game "what if this player was the starter" forecast for backup quarterbacks.

Michael Vick   Height: 6-0   Weight: 215   College: Virginia Tech   Draft: 2001/1 (1)   Born: 26-Jun-1980   Age: 32   Risk: Red

Year	Team	G/GS	Att	Comp	C%	Yds	TD	INT	FUM	ASR	NY/P	Rk	DVOA	Rk	DYAR	Rk	YAR	Runs	Yds	TD	DVOA	DYAR
2009	PHI	12/0	13	6	46.2%	86	1	0	0	0.9%	6.6	--	-7.4%	--	3	--	11	24	95	2	7.5%	21
2010	PHI	12/12	372	233	62.6%	3018	21	6	10	8.7%	7.0	7	14.1%	8	663	12	665	100	676	9	29.0%	192
2011	PHI	13/13	423	253	59.8%	3303	18	14	9	5.6%	7.1	9	11.6%	12	652	11	598	76	589	0	27.5%	131
2012	PHI		518	324	62.6%	3988	26	10			7.0		18.6%					94	479	4	15.6%	

| 2011: | 42% Short | 34% Mid | 17% Deep | 7% Bomb | YAC: 5.3 (20) | 2010: | 57% Short | 24% Mid | 9% Deep | 10% Bomb | YAC: 5.7 (11) |

We had to expect a little bit of regression from Vick's phenomenal 2010 season, especially when it came to that fluky low interception total. At his best, Vick looked as good as he had looked in 2010, but he returned to the inconsistency that had plagued his past career. He didn't fully revert, but he did fall back into old habits, leaving the pocket more often despite a lack of real pressure, or improvising when he really needed to just stay within the structure of the offense, read the defense, and let the route combinations develop. Greg Cosell, as he often does, described it best on a blog post this offseason: The best word to describe Vick is "frenetic." The Eagles have enough talent to make a playoff run with an undisciplined Vick, but they aren't going to win a Super Bowl that way, because there's no way an undisciplined Vick could play three or four straight good games against playoff-quality defenses.

Seneca Wallace   Height: 5-11   Weight: 196   College: Iowa State   Draft: 2003/4 (110)   Born: 6-Aug-1980   Age: 32   Risk: Red

Year	Team	G/GS	Att	Comp	C%	Yds	TD	INT	FUM	ASR	NY/P	Rk	DVOA	Rk	DYAR	Rk	YAR	Runs	Yds	TD	DVOA	DYAR
2009	SEA	13/2	120	78	65.0%	700	3	2	5	7.8%	5.0	39	-13.2%	26	-17	26	-17	13	16	1	-72.8%	-35
2010	CLE	8/4	101	64	63.4%	694	4	2	1	6.3%	6.2	23	11.3%	14	151	25	114	7	9	0	-95.8%	-18
2011	CLE	6/3	107	55	51.4%	567	2	2	1	4.6%	4.8	42	-13.6%	30	-17	29	-89	7	70	0	53.4%	20
2012	CLE		431	251	58.3%	2716	14	13			5.4		-13.8%					27	100	0	-4.7%	

| 2011: | 40% Short | 43% Mid | 10% Deep | 7% Bomb | YAC: 3.2 (46) | 2010: | 50% Short | 32% Mid | 12% Deep | 7% Bomb | YAC: 5.3 (22) |

308 QUARTERBACKS

Wallace's effectiveness as a backup/spot starter nosedived last year after a decent season in 2010. He made Colt McCoy look like a pinpoint passer when he hit the field—that's tough to do. Whether he sticks in Cleveland will depend as much on politics as play. He is a Mike Holmgren fave, and the team has been rumored to be interested in dealing McCoy. In that case, they'd keep the aging little guy who everyone likes. Doug Flutie stuck around the NFL until age 43 in that role.

Joe Webb
Height: 6-3 Weight: 223 College: UAB Draft: 2010/6 (199) Born: 14-Nov-1986 Age: 26 Risk: Green

Year	Team	G/GS	Att	Comp	C%	Yds	TD	INT	FUM	ASR	NY/P	Rk	DVOA	Rk	DYAR	Rk	YAR	Runs	Yds	TD	DVOA	DYAR
2010	MIN	5/2	89	54	60.7%	477	0	3	1	7.7%	4.5	--	-24.7%	--	-86	--	-127	18	120	2	53.1%	56
2011	MIN	11/1	63	34	54.0%	376	3	2	1	5.9%	5.5	--	-13.8%	--	-12	--	-56	22	154	0	14.1%	32
2012	MIN		486	299	61.6%	3277	17	13			5.9		-6.8%					76	278	0	-15.1%	

2011: 45% Short 29% Mid 20% Deep 7% Bomb YAC: 4.1 (--)   2010: 61% Short 28% Mid 5% Deep 7% Bomb YAC: 4.2 (--)

All of the cute analysts who tried to sell Joe Webb's upside and possibly bright future have mostly gone away. Mobility is not nearly a powerful enough trait to make an unskilled passer a starting NFL quarterback, which is why the Vikings have toyed with the idea of using Webb at wide receiver. He's not a wide receiver, though. What he is, on his best day, is a serviceable wildcat threat and reliable (read "semi-experienced") backup signal-caller.

Vikings offensive coordinator Bill Musgrave gets an A for imagination but an F for sensibility in the way he used Webb as a gadget-play quarterback last season. The low point came when Musgrave tried to surprise the Saints in Week 15 by having Webb suddenly line up under center while "actual quarterback" Christian Ponder lined up in a split backfield. There wasn't a soul alive who believed the Vikings would toss/hand/pitch/throw the ball to Ponder from that formation, which made the direction that the play was going in obvious and made Webb perhaps the first man in history to take a snap and be at a disadvantage for having ten teammates on the field instead of a short-handed nine.

Brandon Weeden
Height: 6-4 Weight: 221 College: Oklahoma State Draft: 2012/1 (22) Born: 14-Oct-1983 Age: 29 Risk: Red

Year	Team	G/GS	Att	Comp	C%	Yds	TD	INT	FUM	ASR	NY/P	Rk	DVOA	Rk	DYAR	Rk	YAR	Runs	Yds	TD	DVOA	DYAR
2012	CLE		465	266	57.2%	3010	16	20			5.4		-17.6%					17	74	1	8.3%	

Here are the key stats for Weeden: 19-26, 5.02. Those were his pitching numbers over five seasons in the New York Yankees farm system (he progressed no higher than A ball). His advanced age is a long-term concern. In the short term, scouts worry about his ability to make plays when the pocket isn't clean, as well as his deliberate release. Perhaps the latter is a holdover from his moundsman days? The keys to the franchise have been tossed to Weeden, and KUBIAK forecasts a difficult first season. However, so long as the pass rushers of the AFC North don't turn Weeden into Blaine Gabbert 2.0, he has the tools to compete.

Charlie Whitehurst
Height: 6-4 Weight: 220 College: Clemson Draft: 2006/3 (81) Born: 6-Aug-1982 Age: 30 Risk: Green

Year	Team	G/GS	Att	Comp	C%	Yds	TD	INT	FUM	ASR	NY/P	Rk	DVOA	Rk	DYAR	Rk	YAR	Runs	Yds	TD	DVOA	DYAR
2010	SEA	6/2	99	57	57.6%	507	2	3	1	4.3%	4.8	43	-33.2%	41	-141	37	-167	20	43	1	12.2%	17
2011	SEA	3/2	56	27	48.2%	298	1	1	2	12.3%	4.0	--	-49.2%	--	-160	--	-138	4	13	0	-0.2%	2
2012	SD		472	279	59.2%	3129	17	17			5.6		-7.3%					29	43	1	-15.8%	Green

2011: 35% Short 35% Mid 18% Deep 12% Bomb YAC: 4.6 (--)   2010: 64% Short 22% Mid 9% Deep 6% Bomb YAC: 4.4 (38)

Whitehurst was the only quarterback on the Seahawks roster when the lockout ended, which was the closest he ever came to being "The Man" in Seattle. After a season as a distant backup to Matt Hasselbeck, Whitehurst was once again bumped to the backup role when the Seahawks signed Tarvaris Jackson. Whitehurst had a strong preseason and threw the go-ahead touchdown pass in the fourth quarter of a win over the New York Giants in place of an injured Jackson, but any thoughts of a quarterback controversy would dissipate after a miserable performance in a 6-3 loss to the Cleveland Browns. The following week, Whitehurst was pulled midway the second quarter even though Jackson was nowhere near 100 percent. Those would be the final snaps Whitehurst would take with the Seahawks; the free-agent Whitehurst returned to the Chargers on a two-year, $3.05 million contract and will replace Billy Volek as the No. 2 behind Philip Rivers.

Russell Wilson   Height: 5-11   Weight: 204   College: Wisconsin   Draft: 2012/3 (75)   Born: 29-Nov-1988   Age: 24   Risk: Yellow

Year	Team	G/GS	Att	Comp	C%	Yds	TD	INT	FUM	ASR	NY/P	Rk	DVOA	Rk	DYAR	Rk	YAR	Runs	Yds	TD	DVOA	DYAR
2012	SEA		432	263	60.9%	2843	21	15			5.6		-10.4%					89	414	3	-0.2%	

In March, we posted an article on our website about the Lewin Career Forecast numbers of 2012 quarterback prospects, and we dubbed Russell Wilson "The Asterisk." Wilson's college stats blew LCF away: 48 college games started, a 60.7 percent completion rate, and most importantly, an absurd 64.1 jump in passer rating between his junior and senior seasons. Wilson would have the best LCF forecast of all-time if he were drafted in the first three rounds. But at that point, nobody thought he was going in the first three rounds. Thus, "The Asterisk."

Well, guess what? The Asterisk was drafted in the third round by the Seattle Seahawks and, if you believe Pete Carroll, will even get a shot to compete for the Seahawks' starting job in training camp. So officially, it is now Russell Wilson, not Robert Griffin, who has the highest LCF forecast ever. Nevertheless, he is still The Asterisk, because there are a couple of elements here that the Lewin Career Forecast does not account for. First, that big leap in passer rating was less the product of Wilson's own improvement and more the product of his transfer from North Carolina State to Wisconsin, where defenses were focused on stopping Montee Ball instead of Wilson. Second, we simply have no way to control for Wilson's height. Teams don't draft short quarterbacks unless they are really, really confident in their abilities. Since 1991, Wilson is the only quarterback under six feet tall to be drafted in the first three rounds. Even if we raise that limit to six-foot even, only three quarterbacks have been drafted in the first three rounds: Wilson, Michael Vick, and Drew Brees.

Brees, of course, is the quarterback Wilson is often compared to. The Saints offense built around Drew Brees provides a fine template for designing an offense that takes advantage of Wilson's mobility and perfect throw-and-go timing while minimizing the issue of his height.[1] Wilson's game must focus on manipulation of the pocket and the secondary with the help of movement: play action, short drops, bootlegs, partial rolls, and misdirection. Wilson also excels at delivering the football to a spot where only the receiver has a chance to make a play on it. And if the play breaks down, he can run; he gained 483 yards on just 56 non-sack carries in 2011, and had career +41.3 Adj. POE as a runner.

The Lewin Career Forecast is just a guideline, not a gospel. Nobody would suggest that Russell Wilson is a better quarterback prospect than Andrew Luck and Robert Griffin. But Wilson can win in the NFL if he has an offensive coordinator who knows how to take advantage of his skills.

---

[1] http://www.footballoutsiders.com/nfl-draft/2012/futures-studying-asterisk

T.J. Yates   Height: 6-3   Weight: 195   College: North Carolina   Draft: 2011/5 (152)   Born: 28-May-1987   Age: 25   Risk: Green

Year	Team	G/GS	Att	Comp	C%	Yds	TD	INT	FUM	ASR	NY/P	Rk	DVOA	Rk	DYAR	Rk	YAR	Runs	Yds	TD	DVOA	DYAR
2011	HOU	6/5	134	82	61.2%	949	3	3	4	11.1%	5.9	25	-19.7%	35	-81	32	-15	14	57	0	12.7%	10
2012	HOU		458	285	62.1%	3117	19	16			6.0		1.1%					53	211	1	1.6%	

| 2011: | 48% Short | 35% Mid | 11% Deep | 6% Bomb | YAC: 5.8 (8) |

The book on Yates in college turned out to be mostly true. He's got an NFL arm and isn't afraid to go deep, but he can rush his reads sometimes and will make some throws that scream "gunslinger mentality." Yates threw out of play-action on nearly 40 percent of his snaps last season. Given Matt Schaub's advanced age, Yates is the closest thing this organization has to a quarterback of the future. From that perspective, how he improves on his rookie year will mean a lot for the Texans when it comes time to determine who Schaub's successor will be.

QUARTERBACKS

Vince Young Height: 6-5 Weight: 230 College: Texas Draft: 2006/1 (3) Born: 18-May-1983 Age: 29 Risk: Green

Year	Team	G/GS	Att	Comp	C%	Yds	TD	INT	FUM	ASR	NY/P	Rk	DVOA	Rk	DYAR	Rk	YAR	Runs	Yds	TD	DVOA	DYAR
2009	TEN	12/10	259	152	58.7%	1879	10	7	8	3.8%	6.9	13	13.8%	14	426	18	393	55	281	2	-0.1%	24
2010	TEN	9/8	156	93	59.6%	1255	10	3	6	7.0%	7.0	8	20.5%	5	353	18	358	25	125	0	-1.9%	7
2011	PHI	6/3	114	66	57.9%	866	4	9	2	6.8%	6.8	14	-21.7%	36	-83	33	-56	18	79	0	-10.0%	2
2012	BUF		470	284	60.4%	3076	19	18		5.5			-10.4%					48	240	2	19.5%	Green

2011: 39% Short 34% Mid 17% Deep 10% Bomb YAC: 4.7 (34)   2010: 49% Short 24% Mid 18% Deep 9% Bomb YAC: 4.4 (39)

Every time Vince Young seems to finally get it, he gives it back. When he replaced Kerry Collins in mid-2009 and played well the rest of the way, we were told that Young finally understood that he needed to be professional, that he was finally studying and watching film and working on his game. He had finally improved his pocket presence, too. The next year, the improved pocket presence went away, and so did the improved attitude, with Young missing meetings and openly defying Jeff Fisher in the locker room. He still played well, however, excelling on deep passes with a career-best DVOA. In Philadelphia, he gave back that improvement too. We thought Andy Reid could handle him and that Reid and Marty Mornhinweg could make the same changes that improved Michael Vick's game. Nope. Young caused all kinds of trouble with his "Dream Team" comments, and struggled to learn the wordy West Coast nomenclature in the Eagles playbook. When he finally got into a game, he played "faster" and with less control than ever, the exact opposite of the improved Vick we all wanted him to emulate. On the surface, it looks like Buffalo is a better landing place for him, with a more vertical passing style rather than Philadelphia's WCO. On the other hand, is Vince Young the guy you want to plug in to replace a guy from Harvard?

Going Deep

Tom Brandstater, STL: Brandstater has spent the past two years as the proverbial NFL nomad: waived five times, signed to four practice squads, and eight total weeks on a 53-man roster. In 2011, he finally found a steady paycheck in St. Louis, even playing a handful of snaps in the fourth quarter of Week 11. He'll compete for the third spot with undrafted free agent Austin Davis (Southern Miss) but Brandstater is the better prospect: He's taller (6-foot-5), has a stronger arm with more polished mechanics, throws more often to secondary options, and is more scheme-diverse after having four offensive coordinators in five seasons at Fresno State.

Sean Canfield, NO: Chase Daniel beat Canfield for the No. 3 job in 2010, but Canfield made the practice squad, became the third-stringer last year, and has been hiding out on the back of the depth chart ever since. Canfield is no threat to Daniel's backup job, but he is a threat to break the all-time waiver wire record, as the Saints pull him on and off the roster on seemingly a weekly basis.

Jimmy Clausen, CAR: Clausen tweeted in May that he got a bad haircut at Supercuts just before the Panthers' media guide photos. Clausen did not provide a picture, and Supercuts defended themselves in response, citing their satisfaction guarantee. Great Clips swooped in and tried to lure Clausen over to their grooming services. This is what forgotten prospects-turned-third stringers are forced to do with their smart phones. Clausen did not come with a satisfaction guarantee, and may get a cut in August that he is sure to dislike. (2010 stats: 157-for-259, 3 TD, 9 INT, -749 DYAR, -48.0% DVOA)

B.J. Coleman, GB: Coleman was a highly touted recruit upon arriving at Tennessee, but he left Knoxville for Chattanooga pastures that may not have been greener but were certainly less crowded. Like other "small school" prospects, he's considered to have good raw tools but not much polish. An article on our site in April pointed out how he's developed his style by aping film of Peyton Manning.

Kirk Cousins, WAS: In the days after the draft, numerous television and Internet personalities warned that the Redskins have screwed up Robert Griffin's confidence by selecting Kirk Cousins in the fourth round and creating a quarterback controversy. This media-manufactured hullabaloo is monumentally stupid. The real problem is that the Redskins used a fourth-round pick on a rookie with lousy footwork and pocket presence instead of signing some cheap veteran backup and instead using the pick to strengthen the line or gamble on a high-upside receiver who might help Griffin out.

Dominique Davis, ATL: Davis is a sidearm-throwing scrambler from East Carolina who threw 62 touchdown passes in his final two seasons. He's a one-read-and-throw guy with spotty accuracy and fills D.J. Shockley's old place on the Falcons payroll as the fast camp arm who bounces on and off the practice squad.

Pat Devlin, MIA: A former Penn State transfer who starred at Delaware, Devlin earned five preseason pass attempts for the 2011 Dolphins. He returned as a camp arm in 2012 and could stick as a third quarterback if the Dolphins figure out that keeping David Garrard and Matt Moore is an exercise in redundancy.

Dennis Dixon, FA: After four years on the Steelers bench, the clock on Dixon's NFL career is running out, so he's chosen to search for greener pastures rather than re-signing with Pittsburgh. In 2010, Dixon was given the chance to showcase his abilities by virtue of Ben Roethlisberger's suspension, and responded with a league-leading 10.2 yards per attempt during the preseason, and 9.1 yards per attempt in a Week 1 overtime victory versus Atlanta. In Week 2, however, he suffered a season-ending tear to the lateral meniscus in his left knee, the same one injured during his senior year at Oregon. On the right team, Dixon has the physical ability to compete for a starting job, but the fact that he remains unsigned at this late stage suggests "the right team" doesn't exist. (2010 stats: 22-for-32, 254 yards, 1 INT, -81 DYAR, -45.6% DVOA)

Trent Edwards, PHI: How bad is the situation in Miami? Trent Edwards turned down an offer from the Dolphins last October because he didn't want to play for the organization. This is a guy who had a -39.9% DVOA in his last two seasons and couldn't beat out Kyle Boller for the Oakland backup job in August. Philadelphia signed him in January, but he looked horrible at a May minicamp, and barring injuries he won't make the roster.

Nathan Enderle, JAC: Enderle was drafted because of his prototypical size and analytical football mind, but he didn't face premium college competition playing for Idaho in the Western Athletic Conference. The fifth-round pick spent his rookie offseason locked out and his rookie regular season getting little to no reps in a Mike Martz offense that he'll probably never see again. Cut in June, signed with Jacksonville.

Nick Foles, PHI: A fourth-round rookie out of Arizona, Foles is a tall touch passer with below-average arm strength and no mobility. You know science fiction stories where the scientists are warned not to mix matter and antimatter? Well, putting Nick Foles and Michael Vick in the same locker room may level the entire city of Philadelphia.

Chandler Harnish, IND: Our new Mr. Irrelevant, Harnish is perhaps best-known for his toughness. He played most of the GoDaddy.com Bowl on one ankle, willing Northern Illinois to the victory. Harnish will need to work on stepping into more of his throws to get a chance to step on the field in an actual NFL game.

Jerrod Johnson, PIT: Texas A&M's all-time leader in passing yards went undrafted by the NFL, but was the No. 1 pick in last year's UFL draft by the Hartford Colonials. So, that worked out well. He was in Philadelphia's training camp last year and will be a camp arm for Pittsburgh this year.

Case Keenum, HOU: It seemed like Keenum was at the University of Houston forever thanks to his two redshirt years, but he's still four years younger than Brandon Weeden. The NCAA's new all-time leader in passing touchdowns, completions, and yardage, Keenum will probably have an NFL career similar to that of the man who used to hold those marks: Timmy Chang. He'll battle John Beck for the final quarterback slot on the roster, and could be a favorite based on the fact that he's not John Beck.

312 QUARTERBACKS

Dan LeFevour, FA: One of the original founders of MACtion has had a tough time getting on the field in the NFL—or even staying with a team, for that matter. The Jaguars, his fourth landing spot in two years, cut him in favor of Jordan Palmer. But hey, he was a terrific rusher in college, and he can throw a little. In some circumstances that might land you on the NFL Network's Top 100 Players list.

Matt Leinart, OAK: Texans fans spent two whole weeks getting used to the idea of Matt Leinart, starting quarterback, after Matt Schaub's lisfranc injury. Texans fans spent two quarters watching him throw floaters until he exited with a broken collarbone. After T.J. Yates demonstrated some potential in his end-of-season trial, Houston decided to free up $1.75 million by letting Leinart walk. The Oakland hot tubs (and a chance to back up Carson Palmer again) had the strongest allure to Leinart following the draft. (2011 stats: 5-for-13, 57 yards, 1 TD, 19 DYAR, 10.8% DVOA)

Ryan Lindley, ARI: A four-year starter at San Diego State, Lindley set school records with 12,690 passing yards and 90 touchdowns and is blessed with prototypical NFL size (6-foot-4, 230 pounds) and a strong arm. However, Lindley completed just 55.5 percent of 1,732 pass attempts in college, and just 53 percent of 447 attempts as a senior, and will need to work on his accuracy to stick at the next level. He will likely spend his rookie season working on his mechanics on the Cardinals' practice squad.

J.P. Losman, FA: Losman surfaced on the Dolphins in October of last season, going 6-of-10 in relief of Matt Moore in the December loss to the Eagles. Worst early 2000's Tulane first-round quarterback bust: Losman, or Patrick Ramsey? Yes, we are asking that because we feel Losman's career is over. (Other 2011 stats: 60 yards, -66 DYAR, -96.0% DVOA)

Ryan Mallett, NE: If you watch the NFL Draft long enough, you know the Ryan Mallett pick. It's the one where you look up from your Doritos when the crowd goes, "Ooh!" and the talking heads start gushing about what an incredible steal this guy is and how he could have gone in the first round and you think to yourself, "Hmm, that's really interesting," and then you go back to your Doritos and don't think about it again, and then three years later you happen to catch the fourth quarter of a preseason game and see Mallett playing against Jacksonville's third string and the memory of those Doritos come rushing back at you like Proust's madelines. Mallett has a terrific arm, but he's slower than molasses, and reports that he was partying during the rookie symposium do nothing to alleviate concerns that he's too immature to develop.

Greg McElroy, NYJ: McElroy said in April that the radio interview in which he called out Jets teammates as "extremely selfish individuals" went "out of control." You can picture McElroy and the radio host barreling through Alabama in a '68 Mustang, Molly Hatchet blaring from the speakers, the third-stringer taking shots of nitrous oxide from an inhaler, Blue Velvet-style. "Whoo-ee! My teammates are extremely selfish individuals! Hey, take the wheel for a second. Hold it straight, we're coming on Dead Man's Curve!" Some employers keep malcontent workers around a little longer than they have to, partially to look forgiving and magnanimous, partially to let the worker twist in the wind and limit his professional mobility to teach him a lesson. The Jets appear to be one of those employers.

Kellen Moore, DET: Moore is one of the highest-profile undrafted rookies to enter an NFL training camp in the past 10 years. He had an otherworldly 50-3 record as a starter at Boise State, showing uncanny accuracy and football IQ. Of course, in the NFL, your intelligence and precision are only relevant if you have the physical tools to first stay alive. Being a scrawny 6-foot-0, 197 pounds (give or take) and just barely faster than a glacier, many doubt that Moore is physically capable of thriving at football's highest level.

Jordan Palmer, JAC: Palmer finally found an organization that would sign him without also employing his brother. His relationship with ex-Bengals offensive coordinator Bob Bratkowski is probably the driving force that brought him to North Florida, but now that the Jaguars employ Chad Henne, it's rather unlikely that Palmer sees any field time in Jacksonville. (2010 stats: 3-for-3, 18 yards, -26 DYAR, -86.6% DVOA)

Josh Portis, SEA: Portis had stops at the Florida and Maryland before landing, and dominating, at California University of Pennsylvania, where he passed for over 6,000 yards and a school-record 69 touchdowns. Portis has NFL-caliber size and arm strength, which combined with his speed and athleticism (4.59 forty, 40-inch vertical jump at the Combine) will keep him on an NFL roster. Thanks to Russell Wilson, it may not be Seattle's.

Rusty Smith, TEN: In Rusty Smith's one career start, he managed to single-handedly keep the 2010 Texans from having the worst pass defense in the DVOA era, leading to a verbal confrontation with the late Mike Heimerdinger. He's still tall with a big arm, and the Titans stayed in-house during their recent front office reshuffling, so look for him to continue on with the team until they actually have to watch him play again. (2010 stats: 20-for-40, 200 yards, 4 INT, -196 DYAR, -98.7% DVOA)

Troy Smith, PIT: The Steelers are very used to quarterback injuries, so they are bringing a lot of guys to camp. Smith, the former Ohio State Heisman winner, played for Omaha of the UFL last season. (2010 stats: 73-for-145, 1176 yards, 5 TD, 4 INT, -94 DYAR, -20.0% DVOA)

Ricky Stanzi, KC: In 43 preseason dropbacks, Stanzi had half as many sacks (nine) as he did completions (18). The Chiefs were so impressed that Stanzi didn't play at all in the regular season, and wasn't even put on the active roster until November. Stanzi has a cult following among Chiefs fans who watched him play at nearby Iowa, but he's a fringe NFL player at best.

Tyler Thigpen, BUF: Thigpen had a brief moment of glory (and by glory we mean competence) running the pistol offense for Kansas City back in 2008, and he's been coasting ever since. Thigpen played terribly in Miami when given significant time, and Buffalo's coaching staff evidently preferred trotting out Ryan Fitzpatrick with broken ribs than handing the keys to Thigpen. (2011 stats: 3-for-8, 25 yards, 1 INT, -49 DYAR, -103.0% DVOA)

Scott Tolzien, SF: Tolzien was the surprise winner of the 2010 Johnny Unitas Golden Arm Award, beating out Andy Dalton, Christian Ponder, Ricky Stanzi, and fellow 49ers teammate Colin Kaepernick. Based on the list of previous winners, it should be renamed the Johnny Unitas Noodle Arm Award. Although five current NFL starters show up on the list (Peyton Manning, Carson Palmer, Eli Manning, Matt Ryan, and Andrew Luck), the rest reads like a database of "smart and efficient college quarterback, but lacks arm strength" scouting reports (e.g., Colt McCoy and Graham Harrell in recent years). Tolzien's future in the NFL is as a trusted backup somewhere. For San Francisco in 2012, he'll be a trusted member of the practice squad.

Billy Volek, FA: Volek attempted 44 passes in the regular season over six years in San Diego, then was declared expendable when Charlie Whitehurst became available. At 36, he's probably gone from "a backup who's performed well in a limited role and might be an improvement for your team's terrible backup" to "unlikely to earn another NFL contract."

Adam Weber, DEN: At one point last summer, reports out of Broncos camp said that Weber was throwing better than Tim Tebow. Do not expect similar reports concerning Peyton Manning. Weber started 50 games at the University of Minnesota, and in 2008 he led the Big Ten in completions, attempts, and completion percentage. Other notable Big Ten passers that season include Brian Hoyer, Ricky Stanzi, and Curtis Painter. Somebody had to finish first.

John Parker Wilson, ATL: Wilson threw three interceptions and was sacked six times in 52 preseason attempts in 2011. Dominique Davis has a legitimate shot at the No. 3 job in Atlanta.

Running Backs

In the following section we provide the last three years' statistics, as well as a 2012 KUBIAK projection, for every running back who either played a significant role in 2011 or is expected to do so in 2012.

The first line contains biographical data—each player's name, height, weight, college, draft position, birth date, and age. Height and weight are the best data we could find; weight, of course, can fluctuate during the offseason. **Age** is very simple, the number of years between the player's birth year and 2012, but birthdate is provided if you want to figure out exact age.

Draft position gives draft year and round, with the overall pick number with which the player was taken in parentheses. In the sample table, it says that Matt Forte was chosen in the 2008 NFL Draft in the second round with the 44th overall pick. Undrafted free agents are listed as "FA" with the year they came into the league, even if they were only in training camp or on a practice squad.

To the far right of the first line is the player's Risk for fantasy football in 2012. As explained in the quarterback section, the standard is for players to be marked Green. Players with higher than normal risk are marked Yellow, and players with the highest risk are marked Red. Players who are most likely to match or surpass our forecast—primarily second-stringers with low projections—are marked Blue. Risk is not only based on injury probability, but how a player's projection compares to his recent performance as well as our confidence (or lack thereof) in his offensive teammates.

Next we give the last three years of player stats. The first two numbers are games played (**G**) and games started (**GS**). Games played is the official NFL total and may include games in which a player appeared on special teams, but did not carry the ball or catch a pass. The next four columns are familiar: **Runs**, rushing yards (**Yds**), yards per rush (**Yd/R**) and rushing touchdowns (**TD**). The entry for fumbles (**FUM**) includes all fumbles by this running back, no matter whether they were recovered by the offense or defense. Holding onto the ball is an identifiable skill; fumbling it so that your own offense can recover it is not. (For more on this issue, see the essay "Pregame Show" in the front of the book.) This entry combines fumbles on both carries and receptions.

The next five columns give our advanced metrics for rushing: **DVOA** (Defense-Adjusted Value Over Average), **DYAR** (Defense-Adjusted Yards Above Replacement), and **YAR** (Yards Above Replacement), along with the player's rank (**Rk**) in both **DVOA** and **DYAR**. These metrics compare every carry by the running back to a league-average baseline based on the game situations in which that running back carried the ball. DVOA and DYAR are also adjusted based on the opposing defense. The methods used to compute these numbers are described in detail in the "Statistical Toolbox" introduction in the front of the book. The important distinctions between them are:

• DVOA is a rate statistic, while DYAR is a cumulative statistic. Thus, a higher DVOA means more value per play, while a higher DYAR means more aggregate value over the entire season.

• Because DYAR is defense-adjusted and YAR is not, a player whose DYAR is higher than his YAR faced a harder-than-average schedule. A player whose

Matt Forte
Height: 6-2 Weight: 218 College: Tulane Draft: 2008/2 (44) Born: 10-Dec-1985 Age: 27 Risk: Green

Year	Team	G/S	Runs	Yds	Yd/R	TD	FUM	DVOA	Rk	DYAR	Rk	YAR	Suc%	Rec	Pass	Yds	C%	Yd/C	TD	DVOA	Rk	DYAR	Rk
2009	CHI	16/16	258	929	3.6	4	6	-17.0%	44	-98	49	-146	42%	57	72	471	79%	8.3	0	-1.1%	33	45	25
2010	CHI	16/16	237	1069	4.5	6	3	0.0%	20	88	20	66	41%	51	70	547	73%	10.7	3	10.3%	21	91	11
2011	CHI	12/12	203	997	4.9	3	2	-5.6%	40	24	38	64	45%	52	76	490	68%	9.4	1	-5.7%	35	33	30
2012	CHI		222	1014	4.6	4		3.9%						45	65	380	69%	8.4	1	1.0%			

DYAR is lower than his YAR faced an easier-than-average schedule.

To qualify for ranking in rushing DVOA and DYAR, a running back must have had 100 carries in that season. There are 51 running backs ranked for 2011, 52 backs for 2010, and 50 backs for 2009.

The final rushing statistic is Success Rate (**Suc%**). This number represents running back consistency, measured by successful running plays divided by total running plays. (The definition for success is explained in the "Statistical Toolbox" introduction in the front of the book.) A player with high DVOA and a low Success Rate mixes long runs with plays on which he was stuffed at or behind the line of scrimmage. A player with low DVOA and a high Success Rate generally gets the yards needed, but rarely gets more. The league-average Success Rate in 2011 was 46 percent. Success Rate is not adjusted for the defenses a player faced.

The ten columns to the right of Success Rate give data for each running back as a pass receiver. Receptions (**Rec**) counts passes caught, while Passes (**Pass**) counts total passes thrown to this player, complete or incomplete. The next four columns list receiving yards (**Yds**), Catch Rate (**C%**), yards per catch (**Yd/C**), and receiving touchdowns (**TD**).

Our research has shown that receivers bear some responsibility for incomplete passes, even though only their catches are tracked in official statistics. Catch Rate represents receptions divided by all intended passes for this running back. The average NFL running back caught 72 percent of passes in 2011. Unfortunately, we don't have room to post the best and worst running backs in receiving plus-minus, but you'll find the top 10 and bottom 10 running backs in this metric listed in the statistical appendix.

Finally we have receiving DVOA and DYAR, which are entirely separate from rushing DVOA and DYAR. To qualify for ranking in receiving DVOA and DYAR, a running back must have 25 passes thrown to him in that season. There are 51 running backs ranked for 2011, 54 backs for 2010, and 52 backs for 2009. Numbers without opponent adjustment (YAR, and VOA) can be found on our website, FootballOutsiders.com.

The italicized row of statistics for the 2012 season is our 2012 KUBIAK projection based on a complicated regression analysis that takes into account numerous variables including projected role, performance over the past two years, projected team offense and defense, historical comparables, height, age, experience of the offensive line, and strength of schedule.

For many rookie running backs, we'll also include statistics from our college football arsenal, notably **POE** (Points Over Expected) and **Highlight Yards**. POE analyzes the output of college football running backs by comparing the expected EqPts value of every carry for a given ballcarrier (based on the quality of the rushing defense against which he's running) to the actual output. A positive POE indicates an above-average runner, with an average runner accruing exactly 0 POE. Highlight Yards are yards gained more than 10 yards past the line of scrimmage on a run, those yards not included in Adjusted Line Yards. Anything over 2.50 should be considered good. For more details on these stats, see the college football section of the book (p. TK).

It is difficult to accurately project statistics for a 162-game baseball season, but it is exponentially more difficult to accurately project statistics for a 16-game football season. Consider the listed projections not as a prediction of exact numbers, but the mean of a range of possible performances. What's important is less the exact number of yards we project, and more which players are projected to improve or decline. Actual performance will vary from our projection less for veteran starters and more for rookies and third-stringers, for whom we must base our projections on much smaller career statistical samples. Touchdown numbers will vary more than yardage numbers.

Finally, in a section we call "Going Deep," we briefly discuss lower-round rookies, free-agent veterans, and practice-squad players who may play a role during the 2012 season or beyond.

RUNNING BACKS

Top 20 RB by Rushing DYAR (Total Value), 2011

Rank	Player	Team	DYAR
1	LeSean McCoy	PHI	304
2	Marshawn Lynch	SEA	201
3	Maurice Jones-Drew	JAC	197
4	Jonathan Stewart	CAR	194
5	**Darren Sproles**	**NO**	**193**
6	Pierre Thomas	NO	180
7	Ryan Mathews	SD	171
8	Fred Jackson	BUF	161
9	DeAngelo Williams	CAR	158
10	Adrian Peterson	MIN	153
11	Ben Tate	HOU	151
12	DeMarco Murray	DAL	149
13	Willis McGahee	DEN	131
14	Ray Rice	BAL	129
15	Arian Foster	HOU	122
16	Evan Royster	WAS	122
17	**Donald Brown**	**IND**	**119**
18	Shonn Greene	NYJ	113
19	Rashard Mendenhall	PIT	106
20	BenJarvus Green-Ellis	NE	106

Top 20 RB by Rushing DVOA (Value per Rush), 2011

Rank	Player	Team	DVOA
1	Pierre Thomas	NO	32.7%
2	Jonathan Stewart	CAR	24.5%
3	DeAngelo Williams	CAR	21.0%
4	LeSean McCoy	PHI	17.4%
5	**Donald Brown**	**IND**	**16.8%**
6	Fred Jackson	BUF	16.0%
7	DeMarco Murray	DAL	15.3%
8	Ben Tate	HOU	14.8%
9	Darren McFadden	OAK	14.3%
10	Ryan Mathews	SD	13.8%
11	Adrian Peterson	MIN	12.2%
12	Marshawn Lynch	SEA	10.9%
13	C.J. Spiller	BUF	8.8%
14	Toby Gerhart	MIN	7.4%
15	Maurice Jones-Drew	JAC	7.2%
16	Willis McGahee	DEN	7.1%
17	**Jackie Battle**	**KC**	**6.4%**
18	Ryan Grant	GB	5.8%
19	BenJarvus Green-Ellis	NE	5.7%
20	Shonn Greene	NYJ	4.8%

Minimum 100 carries.

Top 10 RB by Receiving DYAR (Total Value), 2011

Rank	Player	Team	DYAR
1	Darren Sproles	NO	258
2	Ray Rice	BAL	236
3	Michael Bush	OAK	140
4	Ryan Mathews	SD	134
5	**Arian Foster**	**HOU**	**126**
6	Charles Clay*	MIA	118
7	Jonathan Stewart	CAR	102
8	LaRod Stephens-Howling	ARI	101
9	Pierre Thomas	NO	101
10	Ryan Grant	GB	99

Top 10 RB by Receiving DVOA (Value per Pass), 2010

Rank	Player	Team	DVOA
1	Charles Clay*	MIA	62.1%
2	Toby Gerhart	MIN	46.5%
3	Michael Bush	OAK	44.0%
4	Jacquizz Rodgers	ATL	32.1%
5	**Ray Rice**	**BAL**	**29.0%**
6	Ryan Mathews	SD	27.8%
7	Darren Sproles	NO	25.3%
8	Jason Snelling	ATL	24.7%
9	Fred Jackson	BUF	22.5%
10	Kendall Hunter	SF	21.2%

Minimum 25 passes.

Clay, a fullback/tight end hybrid, is listed in the "Going Deep" section of the Tight Ends chapter.

RUNNING BACKS

Joseph Addai   Height: 5-11   Weight: 210   College: Louisiana State   Draft: 2006/1 (30)   Born: 3-May-1983   Age: 29   Risk: Red

Year	Team	G/S	Runs	Yds	Yd/R	TD	FUM	DVOA	Rk	DYAR	Rk	YAR	Suc%	Rec	Pass	Yds	C%	Yd/C	TD	DVOA	Rk	DYAR	Rk
2009	IND	15/15	219	828	3.8	10	1	5.6%	17	139	13	116	53%	51	63	336	81%	6.6	3	9.1%	22	89	10
2010	IND	8/7	116	495	4.3	4	2	8.8%	9	91	19	99	54%	19	26	124	73%	6.5	0	-14.6%	46	-1	46
2011	IND	12/11	118	433	3.7	1	1	-11.5%	47	-13	46	-13	34%	15	22	93	68%	6.2	0	-19.3%	--	-6	--
2012	NE		71	293	4.1	3		2.9%						21	24	156	88%	7.4	0	19.5%			

In his prime, Addai was a terrific complementary weapon to the Colts pass-heavy offense. He's a willing blocker, does well on screens, and works great off the draw and shotgun sweep. Nerve damage in his neck in 2010 and a nagging hamstring injury limited him to just 20 games in the past two seasons, and it left him a shell of his former self. His role in New England is Kevin Faulk's old third-down seat, and his roster spot is just as dispensable if he doesn't have Faulk's work ethic.

Lance Ball   Height: 5-9   Weight: 223   College: Maryland   Draft: 2008/FA   Born: 19-Jun-1985   Age: 27   Risk: Green

Year	Team	G/S	Runs	Yds	Yd/R	TD	FUM	DVOA	Rk	DYAR	Rk	YAR	Suc%	Rec	Pass	Yds	C%	Yd/C	TD	DVOA	Rk	DYAR	Rk
2010	DEN	10/0	41	158	3.9	0	1	-24.1%	--	-25	--	-22	34%	3	6	16	50%	5.3	0	-20.3%	--	-2	--
2011	DEN	16/0	96	402	4.2	1	2	2.8%	--	42	--	43	44%	16	31	148	52%	9.3	1	-19.3%	46	-9	46
2012	DEN		55	207	3.8	1		-7.2%						18	23	133	78%	7.4	0	7.8%			

A former practice squad player for the Rams, Titans, and Colts, Ball finally saw meaningful playing time in 2011. When Willis McGahee and Knowshon Moreno both went down against Kansas City in Week 10, the Broncos gave Ball 30 carries, each with a lead against a Chiefs defense that knew Tim Tebow would not be passing much. Ball amassed a yeoman-like 96 yards without breaking a single run for 10 or more yards. He's not the most talented player in the world, but coaches know that he'll show up, stay healthy, and stay out of trouble. You can't say the same for Knowshon Moreno, which means Ball could beat him out for a roster spot.

Marion Barber   Height: 5-11   Weight: 221   College: Minnesota   Draft: 2005/4 (109)   Born: 10-Jun-1983   Age: 29   Risk: N/A

Year	Team	G/S	Runs	Yds	Yd/R	TD	FUM	DVOA	Rk	DYAR	Rk	YAR	Suc%	Rec	Pass	Yds	C%	Yd/C	TD	DVOA	Rk	DYAR	Rk
2009	DAL	15/15	214	932	4.4	7	2	7.2%	14	147	11	138	53%	26	37	221	73%	8.5	0	-9.7%	41	9	42
2010	DAL	13/10	113	374	3.3	4	0	-11.2%	36	-15	36	-12	48%	11	15	49	73%	4.5	0	-47.9%	--	-27	--
2011	CHI	11/1	114	422	3.7	6	1	-7.9%	42	3	42	6	42%	5	9	50	56%	10.0	0	-23.3%	--	-4	--

From day one, everyone who watched Marion the Barbarian's tenacious running style said, *There's no way the guy will last that long*. Sure enough, everyone was right. Barber retired at age 28, leaving behind a legacy of short-yardage prowess, ferocious pass-blocking effort, and a penchant for converting opponents' would-be tackles into plays eventually blown dead by the whistle.

Jackie Battle   Height: 6-2   Weight: 238   College: Houston   Draft: 2007/FA   Born: 1-Oct-1983   Age: 29   Risk: N/A

Year	Team	G/S	Runs	Yds	Yd/R	TD	FUM	DVOA	Rk	DYAR	Rk	YAR	Suc%	Rec	Pass	Yds	C%	Yd/C	TD	DVOA	Rk	DYAR	Rk
2009	KC	5/0	7	21	3.0	0	0	11.0%	--	5	--	5	43%	2	2	-3	100%	-1.5	0	-157.5%	--	-14	--
2010	KC	16/0	20	50	2.5	1	0	-3.6%	--	3	--	8	45%	1	3	9	33%	9.0	0	-57.1%	--	-10	--
2011	KC	15/4	149	597	4.0	2	0	4.3%	16	76	22	78	44%	9	13	68	69%	7.6	0	-37.0%	--	-17	--

Battle ran a 4.42-second 40-yard dash at the 2007 NFL Combine, giving him a Speed Score of 123.1 that is one of the best we've ever measured. That said, he didn't really demonstrate much speed last year, averaging 0.56 open-field yards per carry. That ranked 40th among qualifying runners. He wasn't much of a power threat either, with a third-down DVOA of -19.1%. The Chiefs made no effort to bring him back. Battle visited with San Diego in March but did not sign a contract at that time.

RUNNING BACKS

Kahlil Bell
Height: 5-11 Weight: 212 College: UCLA Draft: 2009/FA Born: 10-Dec-1986 Age: 26 Risk: Yellow

Year	Team	G/S	Runs	Yds	Yd/R	TD	FUM	DVOA	Rk	DYAR	Rk	YAR	Suc%	Rec	Pass	Yds	C%	Yd/C	TD	DVOA	Rk	DYAR	Rk
2009	CHI	7/0	40	220	5.5	0	0	17.6%	--	37	--	40	55%	1	3	4	33%	4.0	0	-93.6%	--	-10	--
2010	CHI	0/0	0	0	0.0	0	--	--	--	--	--	--	--	0	--	0	--	0.0	0	--	--	--	--
2011	CHI	13/3	79	337	4.3	0	3	-15.1%	--	-20	--	-21	39%	19	23	133	83%	7.0	1	-29.6%	--	-17	--
2012	CHI		57	225	3.9	1		-5.6%						19	26	139	73%	7.3	0	-3.7%			

Bell saw regular playing time in Matt Forte's absence down the stretch last season. He was tremendous in Week 16 against the Packers, rushing for 121 yards on 23 carries. He runs with good balance but not a lot of explosiveness, making him best fit for a zone-based scheme where he can use his patient, one-cut style to get downhill. The Bears used him at times as a passing-down back in 2011, but that was more a function of their attrition at the position. Bell can catch what you throw him, but you wouldn't go out of your way to get him the ball in the flats, and our resident OL expert Ben Muth has referred to him as "the worst chip blocker I've ever seen on film."

Cedric Benson
Height: 5-11 Weight: 222 College: Texas Draft: 2005/1 (4) Born: 28-Dec-1982 Age: 30 Risk: N/A

Year	Team	G/S	Runs	Yds	Yd/R	TD	FUM	DVOA	Rk	DYAR	Rk	YAR	Suc%	Rec	Pass	Yds	C%	Yd/C	TD	DVOA	Rk	DYAR	Rk
2009	CIN	13/13	301	1251	4.2	6	1	2.3%	21	128	15	103	44%	17	24	111	71%	6.5	0	-14.7%	47	-1	47
2010	CIN	16/16	321	1111	3.5	7	7	-12.5%	38	-67	43	-82	45%	28	37	178	76%	6.4	1	-7.8%	40	13	40
2011	CIN	15/15	273	1067	3.9	6	5	-10.4%	45	-21	48	-21	49%	15	22	82	68%	5.5	0	-23.5%	--	-11	--

Benson is the poster back for the utter devaluation of the 1,000-yard season. He's cracked the plateau for three straight years, but in the last two he's averaged under four yards per carry and has been a net negative according to DVOA and DYAR. His sledgehammer approach belies the fact that Benson broke exactly as many tackles (ten) as his replacement in Cincy, BenJarvus Green-Ellis, in nearly a hundred more carries. With that said, it's entirely possible Benson would still be on the Bengals if it weren't for his fumblitis. A 13-to-12 touchdown-to-fumble ratio doesn't do much for job security. As Bill Parcells said, "If you fumble, you're someone else's back." "Someone else" doesn't include any NFL team, as Benson remains unsigned at press time.

Jahvid Best
Height: 5-10 Weight: 199 College: California Draft: 2010/1 (30) Born: 30-Jan-1989 Age: 23 Risk: Yellow

Year	Team	G/S	Runs	Yds	Yd/R	TD	FUM	DVOA	Rk	DYAR	Rk	YAR	Suc%	Rec	Pass	Yds	C%	Yd/C	TD	DVOA	Rk	DYAR	Rk
2010	DET	16/9	171	555	3.2	4	1	-18.6%	44	-77	44	-77	37%	58	80	487	73%	8.4	2	-4.6%	36	41	25
2011	DET	6/6	84	390	4.6	2	0	3.0%	--	38	--	24	39%	27	40	287	68%	10.6	1	12.0%	20	53	18
2012	DET		109	517	4.7	2		4.4%						53	73	495	73%	9.3	1	17.1%			

Best is a perfect fit for a Lions offense that spends a majority of its time in the shotgun. He is a quick-twitch, stop-and-go runner with good initial burst and enough agility to be elusive without having to first build up a lot of momentum. He's a serviceable, willing pass-blocker and a very versatile receiver. These are the traits Best is capable of bringing to the table, anyway. Whether he actually brings them to the table is another story. Durability is an issue, as Best has battled concussions since his college days. He missed the final 10 games of 2011 with a head injury. When Best has been healthy, he's flashed but has also been an inconsistent ballcarrier who leaves yards on the field by (presumably) running too much with his mind and not enough with his instincts. Those Success Rates under 40 percent are a sign of a guy who isn't satisfied just getting a couple of yards when nothing else is available.

LeGarrette Blount
Height: 6-0 Weight: 247 College: Oregon Draft: 2010/FA Born: 5-Dec-1986 Age: 26 Risk: Green

Year	Team	G/S	Runs	Yds	Yd/R	TD	FUM	DVOA	Rk	DYAR	Rk	YAR	Suc%	Rec	Pass	Yds	C%	Yd/C	TD	DVOA	Rk	DYAR	Rk
2010	TB	13/7	201	1007	5.0	6	4	3.9%	14	109	13	101	45%	5	7	14	71%	2.8	0	-95.8%	--	-34	--
2011	TB	14/14	184	781	4.2	5	5	0.6%	28	67	24	54	47%	15	25	148	60%	9.9	0	-45.4%	49	-43	49
2012	TB		85	369	4.4	4		5.3%						32	42	223	76%	7.0	1	2.8%			

Buccaneers coaches stopped pretending to have confidence in Blount after a pair of fumbles against the Jaguars. Following that game, he carried just 17 times for 44 yards in the final three weeks. Blount has terrible hands and awful instincts in pass protection. His only special skills are his Hulk Smash tackle breaking and open-field button mashing—he finished tied for ninth in the league with 30 broken tackles and had a great 15.1 percent rate of broken tackles per touch—but those skills are negated when he forgets to protect the football at the end of long runs. Blount said before the draft that he did not want a Brandon Jacobs-type role as a battering ram off the bench, but once coaches get a long look at Doug Martin, that is what he will be. If a focused Blount fumbles, drops passes, and acts like he is handing out Chinese buffet coupons in pass protection, imagine how much fun a grumpy, dissatisfied Blount could be.

Ahmad Bradshaw   Height: 5-11   Weight: 195   College: Marshall   Draft: 2007/7 (250)   Born: 19-Mar-1986   Age: 26   Risk: Red

Year	Team	G/S	Runs	Yds	Yd/R	TD	FUM	DVOA	Rk	DYAR	Rk	YAR	Suc%	Rec	Pass	Yds	C%	Yd/C	TD	DVOA	Rk	DYAR	Rk
2009	NYG	15/1	163	778	4.8	7	3	8.5%	13	127	16	123	52%	21	30	207	70%	9.9	0	5.8%	26	27	32
2010	NYG	16/11	276	1235	4.5	8	7	2.2%	17	110	12	95	46%	47	59	314	81%	6.7	0	4.0%	26	51	21
2011	NYG	12/9	171	659	3.9	9	1	2.5%	21	80	21	83	45%	34	44	267	77%	7.9	2	3.7%	25	39	29
2012	NYG		185	739	4.0	4		-6.5%						44	60	374	73%	8.5	1	7.4%			

While his outgoing backfieldmate Brandon Jacobs has seen his numbers bounce all over the map these last few years, Bradshaw has been fairly consistent, at least when it comes to DVOA ratings. His DVOA stayed constant in 2011 despite the lower yards per carry average, because a) Bradshaw only fumbled once; b) he needed less yardage to convert for a first down—Bradshaw's carries averaged 8.5 yards to go in 2010, but 8.0 yards to go in 2011; c) his carries in 2011 were more consistent, with fewer losses but also fewer long carries. In 2010, Bradshaw had 29 carries for a loss and 13 carries of 20 or more yards. In 2011, those numbers were 18 and three. Bradshaw played the last few weeks of the season with a stress fracture in his foot, and had bone marrow injected this offseason to try to accelerate healing.

Curtis Brinkley   Height: 5-9   Weight: 208   College: Syracuse   Draft: 2009/FA   Born: 21-Sep-1985   Age: 27   Risk: Green

Year	Team	G/S	Runs	Yds	Yd/R	TD	FUM	DVOA	Rk	DYAR	Rk	YAR	Suc%	Rec	Pass	Yds	C%	Yd/C	TD	DVOA	Rk	DYAR	Rk
2010	SD	3/0	2	11	5.5	0	0	28.5%	--	3	--	4	50%	0	--	0	--	0.0	0	--	--	--	--
2011	SD	10/1	30	101	3.4	1	0	-18.7%	--	-12	--	-7	37%	7	9	41	78%	5.9	0	-32.3%	--	-9	--
2012	SD		36	133	3.8	0		-11.9%						8	9	59	89%	7.4	0	18.3%			

Brinkley is a plodding between-the-tackles runner who's never done anything to distinguish himself in his limited NFL opportunities, and he'll battle Ronnie Brown for the No. 2 spot on the depth chart behind Ryan Mathews. One of them will be in line for carries if Mathews goes down, and Mathews probably will if his first two seasons are an indication of his ability to stay healthy. If that does happen, don't be surprised to see the Chargers scour the waiver wire and mix in some Le'Ron McClain carries as well.

Donald Brown   Height: 5-11   Weight: 210   College: Connecticut   Draft: 2009/1 (27)   Born: 11-Apr-1987   Age: 25   Risk: Green

Year	Team	G/S	Runs	Yds	Yd/R	TD	FUM	DVOA	Rk	DYAR	Rk	YAR	Suc%	Rec	Pass	Yds	C%	Yd/C	TD	DVOA	Rk	DYAR	Rk
2009	IND	11/1	78	281	3.6	3	1	-14.3%	--	-7	--	-26	46%	11	14	169	79%	15.4	0	70.1%	--	63	--
2010	IND	13/8	129	497	3.9	2	0	-4.8%	29	19	29	14	44%	20	28	205	71%	10.3	0	15.8%	17	47	22
2011	IND	16/2	134	645	4.8	5	0	13.9%	5	119	15	101	37%	16	19	86	84%	5.4	0	-19.8%	--	-6	--
2012	IND		184	752	4.1	4		-3.7%						30	42	246	71%	8.2	1	5.1%			

Brown averaged 4.86 yards per carry in two-back sets, and 4.79 yards per carry in one-back sets, so the idea that the Colts helped him by utilizing a fullback more often is a bit of a red herring. Despite the high DVOA, Brown's playing time is limited due to his poor pass-blocking (though it's not as bad as his "Goddammit, Donald!" days) and his lack of value as a receiver. He is what he is at this point: a powerful back who can provide value between the tackles and in the red zone (48.4% DVOA).

RUNNING BACKS

Ronnie Brown
Height: 6-0   Weight: 233   College: Auburn   Draft: 2005/1 (2)   Born: 12-Dec-1981   Age: 31   Risk: Green

Year	Team	G/S	Runs	Yds	Yd/R	TD	FUM	DVOA	Rk	DYAR	Rk	YAR	Suc%	Rec	Pass	Yds	C%	Yd/C	TD	DVOA	Rk	DYAR	Rk
2009	MIA	9/9	147	648	4.4	8	1	12.8%	9	126	18	145	51%	14	20	98	70%	7.0	0	-7.2%	--	8	--
2010	MIA	16/16	200	734	3.7	5	3	-4.6%	28	20	28	7	43%	33	42	242	79%	7.3	0	2.0%	29	38	28
2011	PHI	16/2	42	136	3.2	1	1	-14.9%	--	-12	--	-26	48%	0	2	0	0%	0.0	0	-96.9%	--	-10	--
2012	SD		35	125	3.6	1		-8.7%						8	9	59	89%	7.4	0	17.2%			

Here's a headline you don't want to be associated with: "Ronnie Brown's epic fail personifies Eagles' lost season." That's what our old pal Doug Farrar wrote on Yahoo!'s Shutdown Corner blog after Brown's ridiculously botched Week 4 halfback option on third-and-goal from the 1, where he inexplicably tried to throw a desperate pass while being tackled in a pile of Eagles and 49ers and instead had the ball knocked out of his hand. It's been a long fall for the once-promising Brown. Back in 2007, Brown was second in rushing DVOA and first in receiving DVOA when he tore his ACL at midseason. He came back in 2008, but became known more as the triggerman on the Wildcat than for being a particularly productive back. He went from Miami starter to Philadelphia backup, and the Eagles tried to deal him to Detroit, only to have the trade nixed by Jerome Harrison's health concerns. There was very little interest in him this offseason until San Diego picked him up.

Michael Bush
Height: 6-1   Weight: 245   College: Louisville   Draft: 2007/4 (100)   Born: 16-Jun-1984   Age: 28   Risk: Green

Year	Team	G/S	Runs	Yds	Yd/R	TD	FUM	DVOA	Rk	DYAR	Rk	YAR	Suc%	Rec	Pass	Yds	C%	Yd/C	TD	DVOA	Rk	DYAR	Rk
2009	OAK	16/7	123	589	4.8	3	2	1.0%	25	46	30	71	47%	17	19	105	89%	6.2	0	-8.9%	--	5	--
2010	OAK	14/3	158	655	4.1	8	0	6.4%	12	108	14	108	45%	18	25	194	76%	10.8	0	47.8%	2	83	14
2011	OAK	16/9	256	977	3.8	7	1	-2.7%	33	65	26	45	45%	37	47	418	79%	11.3	1	44.0%	3	140	3
2012	CHI		108	409	3.8	3		-1.8%						36	51	312	71%	8.7	1	9.9%			

Bush began the year as a clear second fiddle to Darren McFadden, but was forced to carry the load the final ten games. He averaged over 5.0 yards per carry his first three starts, then seemed to wear down, averaging under 4.0 yards per carry in every game for the rest of the year save one. He doesn't break many tackles—we only counted 12, a dismal 4.1 percent rate per touch—but was still reasonably effective in all downs and in the red zone, plus he had another very efficient year receiving, and led all running backs with +5.4 plus/minus. His trend suggests he'll be a better back if he splits time with Matt Forte, but Bush has the skills to play every down.

Reggie Bush
Height: 6-0   Weight: 200   College: USC   Draft: 2006/1 (2)   Born: 2-Mar-1985   Age: 27   Risk: Green

Year	Team	G/S	Runs	Yds	Yd/R	TD	FUM	DVOA	Rk	DYAR	Rk	YAR	Suc%	Rec	Pass	Yds	C%	Yd/C	TD	DVOA	Rk	DYAR	Rk
2009	NO	14/8	70	390	5.6	5	2	29.2%	--	97	--	92	44%	47	68	335	69%	7.1	3	2.4%	32	65	21
2010	NO	8/6	36	150	4.2	0	0	-10.8%	--	-3	--	0	42%	34	42	208	81%	6.1	1	-3.2%	33	25	33
2011	MIA	15/15	216	1086	5.0	6	4	-2.1%	30	51	32	91	44%	43	52	296	83%	6.9	1	-12.4%	40	4	40
2012	MIA		173	782	4.5	5		3.2%						43	60	349	72%	8.1	1	-0.1%			

Bush missed minicamp with an undisclosed mystery issue. Helping David Garrard pull tree branches off his roof? Kardashian spawning season? A job stimulus plan for talk radio hosts? Whatever. Tony Sparano worked magic for Bush, mixing slot sweeps and other wrinkles into a diet of conventional runs while remaining calm during some vintage early-season 10-carry, 13-yard efforts. Bush responded with the greatest month of his career, with 518 yards (6.2 yards per carry) and two touchdowns in four December games. Just when the production-to-headache ratio shifted in Bush's favor, Sparano left and the mysterious disappearance began. The Bush of December could be an excellent fit in Joe Philbin's offense. The Bush of All Other Ages keeps one of the sports world's largest noise-to-substance ratios.

Delone Carter
Height: 5-9 Weight: 226 College: Syracuse Draft: 2011/4 (119) Born: 22-Jun-1987 Age: 25 Risk: Green

Year	Team	G/S	Runs	Yds	Yd/R	TD	FUM	DVOA	Rk	DYAR	Rk	YAR	Suc%	Rec	Pass	Yds	C%	Yd/C	TD	DVOA	Rk	DYAR	Rk
2011	IND	16/3	101	377	3.7	2	3	-11.6%	48	-13	45	-20	46%	5	8	18	63%	3.6	0	-79.3%	--	-30	--
2012	IND		119	455	3.8	3		-9.4%						7	9	52	78%	7.4	0	5.9%			

If you're a closet member of the "Peyton Manning is not clutch" club, then note that he bombarded Carter with his anti-clutch rays in his spare time on the sideline. Carter had a 4.0% DVOA on first down, a -15.1% DVOA on second down, and a -29.4% DVOA on third and fourth down. He's got a little more lateral mobility than you'd expect, which is sort of weird given his squatty body type. Like Donald Brown, his pass-catching exploits were non-existent. Step one to doing better than this: stop fumbling three footballs per every 101 attempts you get.

Jamaal Charles
Height: 5-11 Weight: 200 College: Texas Draft: 2008/3 (73) Born: 27-Dec-1986 Age: 26 Risk: Red

Year	Team	G/S	Runs	Yds	Yd/R	TD	FUM	DVOA	Rk	DYAR	Rk	YAR	Suc%	Rec	Pass	Yds	C%	Yd/C	TD	DVOA	Rk	DYAR	Rk
2009	KC	15/10	190	1120	5.9	7	3	19.3%	2	233	2	250	53%	40	55	297	73%	7.4	1	-9.5%	40	14	38
2010	KC	16/6	230	1467	6.4	5	4	32.9%	1	382	1	402	56%	45	64	468	70%	10.4	3	25.7%	8	132	8
2011	KC	2/1	12	83	6.9	0	1	-4.9%	--	2	--	6	50%	5	6	9	83%	1.8	1	-29.8%	--	-5	--
2012	KC		194	1011	5.2	5		12.5%						38	52	359	73%	9.5	1	14.7%			

Is Charles too skinny to stay healthy? His BMI is 27.9, making him one of the 25 men to rush for 1,000 yards in a season with a BMI below 28.0 since 1978. That group includes Tony Dorsett and Eric "Screw The Curse of 370" Dickerson, two durable Hall of Fame performers, but they played in a drastically different league 30-some years ago. A more recent comparison would be Warrick Dunn. At 5-foot-8 and 178 pounds, Dunn put together five 1,000-yard rushing seasons and topped 1,000 yards from scrimmage 11 times with the Buccaneers and Falcons. Besides luck, the key to Dunn's health was a limited workload. He never ran more than 286 times in a season, and he always had a power back teammate (Mike Alstott in Tampa Bay, T.J. Duckett in Atlanta) to pound away at defenses and handle short-yardage runs. To that end, the Charles-Peyton Hillis tag team could be a perfect match in Kansas City. Like Dunn, Charles has proven to be a big-play threat in the passing game as well, and that's a good way to tap his home-run ability without smashing him into 300-pound monsters. It will lengthen his career and pay big short-term dividends. Kansas City's running backs averaged 5.0 yards per target last year, better than only six other teams.

Tashard Choice
Height: 5-10 Weight: 215 College: Georgia Tech Draft: 2008/4 (122) Born: 20-Nov-1984 Age: 28 Risk: Green

Year	Team	G/S	Runs	Yds	Yd/R	TD	FUM	DVOA	Rk	DYAR	Rk	YAR	Suc%	Rec	Pass	Yds	C%	Yd/C	TD	DVOA	Rk	DYAR	Rk
2009	DAL	16/0	64	349	5.5	3	0	24.6%	--	93	--	100	56%	15	22	132	68%	8.8	0	21.7%	--	38	--
2010	DAL	16/0	66	243	3.7	3	1	-4.3%	--	8	--	18	42%	17	22	109	77%	6.4	0	-24.5%	--	-12	--
2011	3TM	13/1	57	152	2.7	1	3	-42.4%	--	-85	--	-96	36%	19	31	124	65%	6.5	0	-62.6%	51	-72	51
2012	BUF		29	131	4.5	1		4.7%						6	8	52	75%	8.7	0	6.2%			

Choice was an awful fine-looking running back in his first two seasons, but the last two years he's been just plain awful. Coaches also feel he's poor on special teams, another reason why he bounced around three teams last year. There's a reasonable chance he won't make the Bills roster.

Anthony Dixon
Height: 6-1 Weight: 233 College: Mississippi State Draft: 2010/6 (173) Born: 24-Sep-1987 Age: 25 Risk: Red

Year	Team	G/S	Runs	Yds	Yd/R	TD	FUM	DVOA	Rk	DYAR	Rk	YAR	Suc%	Rec	Pass	Yds	C%	Yd/C	TD	DVOA	Rk	DYAR	Rk
2010	SF	16/0	70	237	3.4	2	0	-14.2%	--	-14	--	-9	46%	5	5	11	100%	2.2	0	-52.3%	--	-13	--
2011	SF	16/0	29	87	3.0	2	0	-15.6%	--	-9	--	-1	52%	1	1	6	100%	6.0	0	-66.3%	--	-2	--
2012	SF		34	121	3.5	1		-15.9%						5	7	28	71%	5.7	0	-17.5%			

In the past two offseasons, San Francisco has gone from a team bereft of talent on offense to one wishing that the league expanded active rosters to 60 players. Dixon is the most likely skill-position holdover to miss the cut. The most direct threat to his job as a short-yardage back is Brandon Jacobs, who is four inches taller and

RUNNING BACKS

30 pounds heavier. For the sake of Twitter followers everywhere, let's hope @Boobie24Dixon signs on with another team.

Jonathan Dwyer
Height: 5-11 Weight: 229 College: Georgia Tech Draft: 2010/6 (188) Born: 26-Jul-1989 Age: 23 Risk: Green

Year	Team	G/S	Runs	Yds	Yd/R	TD	FUM	DVOA	Rk	DYAR	Rk	YAR	Suc%	Rec	Pass	Yds	C%	Yd/C	TD	DVOA	Rk	DYAR	Rk
2010	PIT	1/0	9	28	3.1	0	0	-43.9%	--	-13	--	-10	33%	0	--	0	--	0.0	0	--	--	--	--
2011	PIT	7/0	16	123	7.7	0	0	8.8%	--	11	--	10	38%	1	1	6	100%	6.0	0	22.6%	--	1	--
2012	PIT		100	430	4.3	2		-3.7%						18	23	125	78%	7.0	1	4.2%			

Dwyer has made most of his limited opportunities since being drafted out of Georgia Tech in 2010. He's led the Steelers in rushing each of the past two preseasons, and had an 11-carry, 107-yard breakout game against Tennessee in Week 6 of last year. Unfortunately, he's only carried the ball in four of his eight career games, and ended last season on injured reserve with a broken left foot. With Rashard Mendenhall's status for 2012 uncertain, Dwyer will get to perform over a larger sample of carries this season, serving as the primary backup to Isaac Redman.

Justin Forsett
Height: 5-8 Weight: 194 College: California Draft: 2008/7 (233) Born: 14-Oct-1985 Age: 27 Risk: Yellow

Year	Team	G/S	Runs	Yds	Yd/R	TD	FUM	DVOA	Rk	DYAR	Rk	YAR	Suc%	Rec	Pass	Yds	C%	Yd/C	TD	DVOA	Rk	DYAR	Rk
2009	SEA	16/2	114	619	5.4	4	3	17.0%	4	106	19	117	46%	41	57	350	72%	8.5	1	-5.9%	37	23	34
2010	SEA	16/5	118	523	4.4	2	0	-7.2%	32	7	31	8	38%	33	51	252	65%	7.6	0	-3.7%	34	25	34
2011	SEA	16/0	46	145	3.2	1	0	-24.7%	--	-27	--	-27	26%	23	34	128	68%	5.6	0	-26.5%	47	-24	47
2012	HOU		27	96	3.6	0		-10.3%						22	34	174	65%	7.9	1	-4.5%			

The top backup to Pro Bowler Marshawn Lynch last season, Forsett saw his playing time and performance both drop significantly. Forsett had a 25 percent Success Rate on a dozen third-down rushing plays and a -19.0% DVOA on running plays out of shotgun, second-lowest among running backs with 15 or more carries. Those aren't good numbers if you are specifically supposed to be a "third-down back." Signed by the Texans during OTAs, Forsett is a natural fit for Houston's "one cut and go" running system and should have the upper hand as he competes with undrafted rookies Jonathan Grimes and Davin Meggett for the No. 3 role behind Arian Foster and Ben Tate.

Matt Forte
Height: 6-2 Weight: 218 College: Tulane Draft: 2008/2 (44) Born: 10-Dec-1985 Age: 27 Risk: Green

Year	Team	G/S	Runs	Yds	Yd/R	TD	FUM	DVOA	Rk	DYAR	Rk	YAR	Suc%	Rec	Pass	Yds	C%	Yd/C	TD	DVOA	Rk	DYAR	Rk
2009	CHI	16/16	258	929	3.6	4	6	-17.0%	44	-98	49	-146	42%	57	72	471	79%	8.3	0	-1.1%	33	45	25
2010	CHI	16/16	237	1069	4.5	6	3	0.0%	20	88	20	66	41%	51	70	547	73%	10.7	3	10.3%	21	91	11
2011	CHI	12/12	203	997	4.9	3	2	-5.6%	40	24	38	64	45%	52	76	490	68%	9.4	1	-5.7%	35	33	30
2012	CHI		222	1019	4.6	3		8.0%						44	64	367	69%	8.3	1	-0.6%			

Matt Forte proved in two different ways last season why he so badly wanted a new contract. First, he averaged 124 yards from scrimmage in the first 12 games, accounting for nearly 50 percent of the Bears' offensive production. Then, in Week 14, he went down with a right knee injury. It was only a sprained MCL, not the dreaded torn ACL, but it still ultimately ended his 2011 campaign. This past offseason, the Bears' new front office slapped Forte with the franchise tag, leaving the 27-year-old still longing for a long-term deal.

At least Forte's franchise tag salary ($7.7 million) is nearly 13 times his 2011 salary. He's worth every penny. Nearly 220 pounds, he's big enough to take a 20-carry-per-week pounding and still maintain his game's defining grace and fluidity. Forte has superb lateral agility when he gets to the second level, and, for a guy with a historically iffy initial burst, he's developed a surprising knack for turning the corner and creating his own space. Just as important as Forte's rushing prowess are his contributions in the pass game. He's caught over 50 balls in each of his four seasons (most of them out of the backfield), and he's willing to block. His negative DVOA numbers are a prime example of why football stats have to be examined in context; he plays behind an awful offensive line, and the opposing defense is designed specifically to try to stop him every single week.

Arian Foster

Height: 6-1 Weight: 225 College: Tennessee Draft: 2009/FA Born: 24-Aug-1986 Age: 26 Risk: Green

Year	Team	G/S	Runs	Yds	Yd/R	TD	FUM	DVOA	Rk	DYAR	Rk	YAR	Suc%	Rec	Pass	Yds	C%	Yd/C	TD	DVOA	Rk	DYAR	Rk
2009	HOU	6/1	54	257	4.8	3	1	22.4%	--	71	--	74	59%	8	9	93	89%	11.6	0	44.1%	--	27	--
2010	HOU	16/13	327	1616	4.9	16	3	18.0%	4	372	2	373	52%	66	86	604	79%	9.2	2	22.2%	10	180	1
2011	HOU	13/13	278	1224	4.4	10	5	2.3%	24	122	14	126	44%	53	73	617	74%	11.6	2	18.6%	14	126	5
2012	HOU		299	1315	4.4	10		7.1%						61	80	548	76%	9.0	2	22.4%			

These things are true: Arian Foster finished below Ben Tate in DYAR and DVOA last year, and he was barely above-average over the course of the season. The missing context, of course, is that Foster struggled early in the season with hamstring woes. From Week 7 on, Foster accumulated 148 DYAR, which would have put him on pace to finish behind only LeSean McCoy on the DYAR leaderboard. The new right side of the offensive line is a cause for minor concern, but so was losing Vonta Leach last season. Foster is as close to a sure thing as a running back can be in today's NFL.

Toby Gerhart

Height: 6-0 Weight: 231 College: Stanford Draft: 2010/2 (51) Born: 18-Mar-1987 Age: 25 Risk: Green

Year	Team	G/S	Runs	Yds	Yd/R	TD	FUM	DVOA	Rk	DYAR	Rk	YAR	Suc%	Rec	Pass	Yds	C%	Yd/C	TD	DVOA	Rk	DYAR	Rk
2010	MIN	15/1	81	322	4.0	1	3	-3.3%	--	15	--	15	42%	21	29	167	72%	8.0	0	-31.5%	51	-27	50
2011	MIN	16/5	109	531	4.9	1	1	5.4%	14	60	30	42	40%	23	28	190	82%	8.3	3	46.5%	2	93	10
2012	MIN		100	438	4.4	2		-4.9%						36	45	321	80%	8.9	0	19.8%			

Comparisons to Peyton Hillis might be tempting, but the only characteristic Gerhart shares with Hillis (besides the obvious one) is a lack of top-end speed. Gerhart is not a bruiser and not even, for all intents and purposes, a quasi-fullback. If you had to pigeonhole him, "third-down back" would make the most sense, though he lacks the quickness and acceleration to be a prototype pass-catcher in this role. This isn't to say Gerhardt isn't worthy of regular touches. He operates effectively north and south and has a hint of lateral agility. He doesn't change tempo dynamically, but he's still a viable spell for Adrian Peterson because he fits Minnesota's style.

Mike Goodson

Height: 5-11 Weight: 208 College: Texas A&M Draft: 2009/4 (111) Born: 23-May-1987 Age: 25 Risk: Green

Year	Team	G/S	Runs	Yds	Yd/R	TD	FUM	DVOA	Rk	DYAR	Rk	YAR	Suc%	Rec	Pass	Yds	C%	Yd/C	TD	DVOA	Rk	DYAR	Rk
2009	CAR	8/0	22	49	2.2	0	1	-77.5%	--	-60	--	-54	23%	2	2	15	100%	7.5	0	62.3%	--	8	--
2010	CAR	16/3	103	452	4.4	3	4	-15.3%	42	-22	38	-6	38%	40	57	310	70%	7.8	0	-11.8%	42	6	42
2011	CAR	4/0	0	0	0.0	0	--							1	3	4	33%	4.0	0	-67.0%	--	-10	--
2012	OAK		110	487	4.4	1		-4.3%						19	23	172	83%	9.0	0	24.8%			

Goodson is a fumble-prone, blown block-prone third-down back who was forced to start a few games for the Panthers in 2010. He has some niftiness, but he was the quintessential late-Fox era Panthers skill position player: an adequate talent with only a vague idea what he was doing. He will try to stick as the third-down back in Oakland this year. If the Raiders give him 143 touches, like the Panthers did in 2010, they will be sorry. If Darren McFadden gets injured again, they may have no choice.

Frank Gore

Height: 5-9 Weight: 215 College: Miami Draft: 2005/3 (65) Born: 14-May-1983 Age: 29 Risk: Green

Year	Team	G/S	Runs	Yds	Yd/R	TD	FUM	DVOA	Rk	DYAR	Rk	YAR	Suc%	Rec	Pass	Yds	C%	Yd/C	TD	DVOA	Rk	DYAR	Rk
2009	SF	14/14	229	1120	4.9	10	4	2.9%	20	97	21	89	42%	52	76	406	70%	7.8	3	4.3%	29	77	18
2010	SF	11/11	203	853	4.2	3	4	-9.3%	34	-3	33	25	48%	46	72	452	64%	9.8	2	-7.2%	39	27	32
2011	SF	16/15	282	1211	4.3	8	2	-10.0%	44	-17	47	3	42%	17	31	114	55%	6.7	0	-18.1%	45	-8	44
2012	SF		216	871	4.0	7		0.2%						17	22	106	77%	6.2	0	-9.7%			

Despite running for over 1,200 yards, 2011 may have marked the beginning of the end for Gore. From an advanced stats perspective, it appears that the 29-year-old is entering the third act of his career. In his first two years, he ranked in the top 15 of rushing DVOA. In the next four, he ranked no higher than 20th. Then, last season, he ranked lower than any other running back with 275 or more carries. He had just 12 broken tackles last year, just 11 the year before, very low totals for a starting back. He finished last among running backs with -6.9 plus/minus as a receiver. Add in that he's shown up on the injury report (or injured reserve) with a lower-body injury for 13 of the past 23 weeks, and San Francisco was correct in adding two running backs to lessen his workload. Expect only about 225 touches in 2012.

Earnest Graham Height: 5-9 Weight: 215 College: Florida Draft: 2004/FA Born: 15-Jan-1980 Age: 32 Risk: N/A

Year	Team	G/S	Runs	Yds	Yd/R	TD	FUM	DVOA	Rk	DYAR	Rk	YAR	Suc%	Rec	Pass	Yds	C%	Yd/C	TD	DVOA	Rk	DYAR	Rk
2009	TB	13/6	14	66	4.7	0	0	18.4%	--	16	--	17	50%	14	22	109	64%	7.8	0	-16.6%	--	-3	--
2010	TB	12/7	20	99	5.0	1	1	-18.2%	--	-7	--	-9	45%	16	19	130	84%	8.1	1	12.7%	--	29	--
2011	TB	7/2	37	206	5.6	0	1	13.9%	--	33	--	29	43%	26	31	163	84%	6.3	0	3.0%	26	31	31

Graham injured his Achilles on the wet grass at Wembley Stadium, then got an infection from the sutures used in surgery. He said in May that he was nearly recovered, but would only return to football if it was the right situation. A battle for a bench role on a 4-12 team is almost certainly not the right situation, so look for him to explore other options if he does return.

Ryan Grant Height: 6-1 Weight: 218 College: Notre Dame Draft: 2005/FA Born: 9-Dec-1982 Age: 30 Risk: N/A

Year	Team	G/S	Runs	Yds	Yd/R	TD	FUM	DVOA	Rk	DYAR	Rk	YAR	Suc%	Rec	Pass	Yds	C%	Yd/C	TD	DVOA	Rk	DYAR	Rk
2009	GB	16/16	282	1253	4.4	11	1	10.9%	11	217	4	228	49%	25	30	197	83%	7.9	0	11.7%	21	41	28
2010	GB	1/1	8	45	5.6	0	0	22.5%	--	9	--	8	38%	0	0	0	--	0.0	0	--	--	--	--
2011	GB	15/14	134	559	4.2	2	1	2.9%	20	63	28	41	46%	19	24	268	79%	14.1	1	56.4%	--	99	--

Grant is a familiar name to NFL fans, but he's never been as good as his 1,200-yard seasons suggest. He's somewhat similar to BenJarvus Green-Ellis, and the opposite of Matt Forte, in that you have to see his numbers in the context of how opponents design game plans to stop Aaron Rodgers and allow the running game. Grant is a mechanical—perhaps even stiff—gaping hole runner. He has good vision and plays smart, but his athletic limitations (the limitations that prevented him from getting drafted) allow him to only gain the yards that are blocked. He's also limited as a veteran back because you can't use him on third downs. He's nothing special as a pass-blocker, and while his receiving numbers have gradually improved with each of his years in the league, one would be hard-pressed to recall a time where Grant ran a meaningful receiver route as the focal point in a play. Though his field vision helps him do a good job of gaining yards after the catch, his receiving skills are really limited to screens and dumpoffs; only one of his passes last year came on third down. That limitation to first and second down is a big reason why Grant is still unsigned as we go to press.

BenJarvus Green-Ellis Height: 5-10 Weight: 219 College: Mississippi Draft: 2008/FA Born: 2-Jul-1985 Age: 27 Risk: Yellow

Year	Team	G/S	Runs	Yds	Yd/R	TD	FUM	DVOA	Rk	DYAR	Rk	YAR	Suc%	Rec	Pass	Yds	C%	Yd/C	TD	DVOA	Rk	DYAR	Rk
2009	NE	12/0	26	114	4.4	0	0	-2.5%	--	2	--	13	58%	2	5	11	40%	5.5	0	-58.9%	--	-13	--
2010	NE	16/11	229	1008	4.4	13	0	26.7%	2	335	3	304	57%	12	16	85	75%	7.1	0	18.3%	--	32	--
2011	NE	16/6	181	667	3.7	11	0	3.9%	18	106	18	115	54%	9	13	159	69%	17.7	0	72.6%	--	64	--
2012	CIN		174	730	4.2	6		1.1%						15	24	118	63%	7.8	1	-8.2%			

Pedestrian is the word that comes to mind when describing Green-Ellis, who averaged 3.7 yards per carry while toting the rock for one of the best offenses of the modern era. The talk in Cincinnati is that the team sees Green-Ellis as a three-down back who can handle the kind of workload that drove Cedric Benson into the ground, which totally goes against the fact that Green-Ellis averaged fewer than 13 touches per game his last two seasons in New England. Green-Ellis was a fairly successful short-yardage back, however, generating a Success Rate of 69 percent on third and fourth downs.

Shonn Greene
Height: 6-0 Weight: 227 College: Iowa Draft: 2009/3 (65) Born: 21-Aug-1985 Age: 27 Risk: Green

Year	Team	G/S	Runs	Yds	Yd/R	TD	FUM	DVOA	Rk	DYAR	Rk	YAR	Suc%	Rec	Pass	Yds	C%	Yd/C	TD	DVOA	Rk	DYAR	Rk
2009	NYJ	14/0	108	540	5.0	2	3	4.0%	19	61	27	67	48%	0	5	0	0%	0.0	0	-120.4%	--	-27	--
2010	NYJ	15/2	185	766	4.1	2	3	7.3%	11	115	11	125	55%	16	24	120	67%	7.5	0	-0.6%	--	20	--
2011	NYJ	16/15	253	1054	4.2	6	1	2.2%	25	113	16	127	50%	30	41	211	73%	7.0	0	-8.6%	37	12	37
2012	NYJ		245	996	4.1	6		-5.2%						33	43	258	77%	7.8	1	7.8%			

Greene carried just six times for 16 yards from the shotgun as a running back last year; he also had eight carries for 38 yards as a direct snap recipient. We suppose Greene could excel in the Willis McGahee role as a shotgun zone-read runner when Tebow plays quarterback, but there is little evidence of that in his professional record so far. Overall, Greene said that he was pleased with Tony Sparano's offense at the end of May minicamps. "It's straight ahead football, and I think it fits for me being that I'm a power back." Apparently, the Jets weren't straight-ahead enough last year, when they used six or seven offensive lineman on 60 plays and ran between the tackles 349 times. Look for Greene to truly come into his own when the Jets finally get rid of those fancy-pants forward passes and dedicate themselves to the 1887 Rutgers playbook.

Montario Hardesty
Height: 6-0 Weight: 225 College: Tennessee Draft: 2010/2 (59) Born: 1-Feb-1987 Age: 25 Risk: Blue

Year	Team	G/S	Runs	Yds	Yd/R	TD	FUM	DVOA	Rk	DYAR	Rk	YAR	Suc%	Rec	Pass	Yds	C%	Yd/C	TD	DVOA	Rk	DYAR	Rk
2011	CLE	10/4	88	266	3.0	0	1	-32.2%	--	-79	--	-77	36%	14	21	122	67%	8.7	0	2.5%	--	24	--
2012	CLE		27	127	4.7	2		13.3%						7	12	50	58%	7.2	0	-21.3%			

On March 14, Peyton Hillis signed with Kansas City. Six weeks later, on April 26, Cleveland traded up to draft Trent Richardson. During the interregnum, Hardesty was the Browns' presumed starting running back. One wonders how Montario spent that time period. Did he order business cards that read "I'm first-string, bitch!"? Or was he knocking around his house in the wee hours, unable to sleep, questioning a world that saw fit to put such an unproductive player in such a prominent role? Either way, Browns fans are no doubt insensate with joy that the Hardesty Era never came to pass. Montario missed all of his rookie season with a knee injury, and missed six more games in 2011. When he was healthy, he was hardly the impactful runner the Browns traded up to draft. He'll have to improve mightily to warrant the scrap carries when Trent Richardson takes a break.

Roy Helu
Height: 5-11 Weight: 216 College: Nebraska Draft: 2011/4 (105) Born: 7-Dec-1988 Age: 24 Risk: Yellow

Year	Team	G/S	Runs	Yds	Yd/R	TD	FUM	DVOA	Rk	DYAR	Rk	YAR	Suc%	Rec	Pass	Yds	C%	Yd/C	TD	DVOA	Rk	DYAR	Rk
2011	WAS	15/5	151	640	4.2	2	3	-4.6%	38	25	37	14	47%	49	59	379	83%	7.7	1	-1.3%	29	40	27
2012	WAS		194	793	4.1	4		-5.4%						43	63	373	68%	8.7	2	5.5%			

As we noted last year, Helu was a favorite of our advanced stats, with 3.19 Highlight Yards per carry at Nebraska and a Speed Score of 114.8. The most impressive part of his rookie year was probably his work as a receiver. Helu was only the fifth rookie since 1990 who had at least 25 percent of his touches as receptions (with a minimum of 100 carries). The others: Terry Kirby (1993), Raymont Harris (1994), Reggie Bush (2006), and Jahvid Best (2010). However, it is interesting to note that backs with Helu's statistical profile don't often become successful starters as sophomores. Of the ten players with the most similar rookie seasons, only LeSean McCoy topped 1,000 rushing yards in his second year, although Ted Brown (of the early '80s Vikings) came close. The Redskins also need to be worried about Helu's ability to stay healthy; he dealt with nagging hamstring and shoulder issues in college, then was limited at the end of his rookie year by toe and ankle injuries.

RUNNING BACKS

Jacob Hester   Height: 5-10   Weight: 226   College: Louisiana State   Draft: 2008/3 (69)   Born: 8-May-1985   Age: 27   Risk: Green

Year	Team	G/S	Runs	Yds	Yd/R	TD	FUM	DVOA	Rk	DYAR	Rk	YAR	Suc%	Rec	Pass	Yds	C%	Yd/C	TD	DVOA	Rk	DYAR	Rk
2009	SD	15/10	21	74	3.5	0	1	-38.0%	--	-33	--	-26	43%	9	11	24	82%	2.7	0	-57.3%	--	-25	--
2010	SD	15/7	26	60	2.3	0	0	-18.2%	--	-14	--	-11	50%	22	26	145	85%	6.6	1	13.3%	19	43	24
2011	SD	16/3	28	90	3.2	0	2	-14.0%	--	-8	--	-8	46%	12	18	48	67%	4.0	1	-75.0%	--	-63	--
2012	SD		19	66	3.4	1		-8.5%						16	18	176	89%	11.0	1	55.8%			

Retained as a free agent even after the acquisition of Le'Ron McClain, Hester will likely see his fairly small role reduced farther. He'll get some snaps at fullback, the occasional pass thrown in his direction, a carry or two, and play special teams as well.

Tim Hightower   Height: 6-0   Weight: 226   College: Richmond   Draft: 2008/5 (149)   Born: 23-May-1986   Age: 26   Risk: Yellow

Year	Team	G/S	Runs	Yds	Yd/R	TD	FUM	DVOA	Rk	DYAR	Rk	YAR	Suc%	Rec	Pass	Yds	C%	Yd/C	TD	DVOA	Rk	DYAR	Rk
2009	ARI	16/16	143	598	4.2	8	5	-9.5%	39	1	38	-7	44%	63	80	428	79%	6.8	0	6.8%	25	89	9
2010	ARI	16/13	153	736	4.8	5	5	-1.4%	23	49	24	49	42%	21	42	136	50%	6.5	0	-61.4%	54	-114	54
2011	WAS	5/5	84	321	3.8	1	0	-10.4%	--	-6	--	9	48%	10	15	78	67%	7.8	1	14.6%	--	25	--
2012	WAS		86	341	4.0	1		-11.1%						15	23	111	65%	7.4	0	-11.3%			

Hightower is essentially a replacement-level back, maybe slightly better, so it seems strange that he keeps getting the opportunity to start. Maybe part of the secret is in something that doesn't appear in our stats: Game charters have constantly called out his excellent pass protection skills. He's coming back from a torn left ACL and you would think that he's competing with Evan Royster for the second spot on the depth chart behind Roy Helu. Still, Hightower does have a habit of impressing his coaches, and Washington sure wants to make sure nobody breaks Robert Griffin.

Peyton Hillis   Height: 6-0   Weight: 240   College: Arkansas   Draft: 2008/7 (227)   Born: 21-Jan-1986   Age: 26   Risk: Yellow

Year	Team	G/S	Runs	Yds	Yd/R	TD	FUM	DVOA	Rk	DYAR	Rk	YAR	Suc%	Rec	Pass	Yds	C%	Yd/C	TD	DVOA	Rk	DYAR	Rk
2009	DEN	14/2	13	54	4.2	1	0	-7.4%	--	5	--	8	54%	4	6	19	67%	4.8	0	-54.7%	--	-17	--
2010	CLE	16/14	270	1177	4.4	11	8	5.0%	13	151	8	152	53%	61	77	477	79%	7.8	2	15.9%	16	126	9
2011	CLE	10/9	161	587	3.6	3	2	-1.7%	29	50	33	48	55%	22	34	130	65%	5.9	0	-33.2%	48	-35	48
2012	KC		172	690	4.0	5		-4.1%						22	30	189	73%	8.6	1	10.5%			

After taking 2010 off to gorge on po' boys with Drew Brees, the Madden Curse was back with a vengeance. Injury, contract trouble, locker room dissension, poor play: Hillis' metamorphosis from handsome prince into ugly duckling came with startling speed. The clearest sign of his tumble came as a receiver, as he fell from 8th among qualifying backs in DYAR to 49th out of 51 players. He wasn't much in the run game, either, breaking a mere four tackles all season as his effort waned. (Compare that to 35 broken tackles the year prior.) Granted a fresh start in Kansas City, Hillis is unlikely to duplicate his breakout season, but he has a decent shot at staying in front of Felix Jones for second place in the "Who was the best player to come out of the 2008 Arkansas Razorbacks backfield?" derby, behind Darren McFadden.

Ronnie Hillman   Height: 5-9   Weight: 200   College: San Diego State   Draft: 2012/3 (67)   Born: 14-Sep-1991   Age: 21   Risk: Green

Year	Team	G/S	Runs	Yds	Yd/R	TD	FUM	DVOA	Rk	DYAR	Rk	YAR	Suc%	Rec	Pass	Yds	C%	Yd/C	TD	DVOA	Rk	DYAR	Rk
2012	DEN		84	382	4.5	1		-0.7%						27	36	212	75%	7.9	1	7.6%			

Hillman rushed for 3,243 yards (5.7 per carry) in college, but his +5.3 Adj. POE, 2.28 Highlight Yards per Carry, and 102.0 Speed Score all put him solidly in the "meh" category of running back prospects. The Broncos took Hillman in the third round hoping he could be their version of Darren Sproles, but he lacks the breakaway speed to be that kind of player. However, Broncos running backs totaled only 46 receptions last season (only two other teams had fewer), so there's certainly a need for a back of this ilk in the Denver offense.

Kendall Hunter
Height: 5-7   Weight: 199   College: Oklahoma State   Draft: 2011/4 (115)   Born: 16-Sep-1988   Age: 24   Risk: Blue

Year	Team	G/S	Runs	Yds	Yd/R	TD	FUM	DVOA	Rk	DYAR	Rk	YAR	Suc%	Rec	Pass	Yds	C%	Yd/C	TD	DVOA	Rk	DYAR	Rk
2011	SF	16/1	112	473	4.2	2	0	-6.5%	41	9	41	31	46%	16	26	195	62%	12.2	0	21.2%	10	50	22
2012	SF		78	378	4.8	1		1.2%						23	29	204	79%	8.9	0	11.7%			

Consistent with his profile coming out of Oklahoma State, Hunter was an above-average receiving option, and ran much less efficiently up the middle (-36.6% DVOA) than elsewhere (3.4% DVOA). Hunter is short and stout like Frank Gore, but he's a third-down back, not an all-purpose runner who can gain yards both inside and outside. However, his surprising ability to pick up blitzes (only one blown block sack allowed all year) should allow him to stave off second-round pick LaMichael James as Gore's change of pace this season.

Mark Ingram
Height: 5-11   Weight: 215   College: Alabama   Draft: 2011/1 (28)   Born: 21-Dec-1989   Age: 23   Risk: Yellow

Year	Team	G/S	Runs	Yds	Yd/R	TD	FUM	DVOA	Rk	DYAR	Rk	YAR	Suc%	Rec	Pass	Yds	C%	Yd/C	TD	DVOA	Rk	DYAR	Rk
2011	NO	10/4	122	474	3.9	5	1	2.3%	22	63	29	47	56%	11	13	46	85%	4.2	0	-27.5%	--	-11	--
2012	NO		165	715	4.3	6		-2.3%						25	36	173	69%	6.9	1	-11.6%			

The Saints used Ingram as a red-zone back last season, and he averaged 3.4 yards per rush on 26 carries, earning an 18.8% DVOA. He also served as a late-game clock muncher, an important job for a team that often has a two-touchdown lead and a defense that will struggle to defend it. Ingram performed his duties well between heel and toe injuries. He had arthroscopic surgery in May but is expected to be ready for training camp. The constant minor ailments, and his lack of receiving chops, will probably limit Ingram to a committee role. He is more likely to be a fantasy leech than a 10-touchdown specialist: The Saints do so many different things at the goal line that it is crazy to depend on any one player to provide touchdowns.

Chris Ivory
Height: 6-0   Weight: 222   College: Tiffin   Draft: 2010/FA   Born: 22-Mar-1988   Age: 24   Risk: Blue

Year	Team	G/S	Runs	Yds	Yd/R	TD	FUM	DVOA	Rk	DYAR	Rk	YAR	Suc%	Rec	Pass	Yds	C%	Yd/C	TD	DVOA	Rk	DYAR	Rk
2010	NO	12/4	137	716	5.2	5	4	13.1%	6	139	9	165	59%	1	1	17	100%	17.0	0	147.8%	--	10	--
2011	NO	6/2	79	374	4.7	1	0	10.4%	--	64	--	74	58%	0	1	0	0%	0.0	0	-84.2%	--	-3	--
2012	NO		34	170	5.0	1		12.4%						5	6	44	83%	8.7	0	23.1%			

The best fourth back in the NFL, Ivory started last season on the PUP list with a sports hernia and a foot injury, but the Saints didn't plan on needing him after signing Darren Sproles and drafting Mark Ingram. Sure enough, heel and toe injuries sidelined Ingram, and Ivory performed well in his role as a carries muncher: 49 of Ivory's 79 carries came in the second halves of games, many of them with the Saints pounding the lumps out of the Vikings or Panthers. The Saints rewarded Ivory by giving him a signing bonus in May that equaled the salary he lost when he was on the PUP list. With Ingram undergoing knee surgery in May, the Saints were wise to keep Ivory happy.

Brandon Jackson
Height: 5-11   Weight: 210   College: Nebraska   Draft: 2007/2 (63)   Born: 2-Oct-1985   Age: 27   Risk: Yellow

Year	Team	G/S	Runs	Yds	Yd/R	TD	FUM	DVOA	Rk	DYAR	Rk	YAR	Suc%	Rec	Pass	Yds	C%	Yd/C	TD	DVOA	Rk	DYAR	Rk
2009	GB	12/0	37	111	3.0	2	1	-16.2%	--	-11	--	-9	38%	21	26	187	81%	8.9	1	40.3%	4	77	17
2010	GB	16/13	190	703	3.7	3	1	-10.3%	35	-8	35	-38	43%	43	50	342	86%	8.0	1	39.8%	3	150	5
2012	CLE		27	98	3.6	0		-16.1%						24	30	168	80%	7.0	0	2.9%			

Jackson missed the 2011 season due to a toe injury. If fully recovered, he should be in a spot to nab any available third-down work in Cleveland from Montario Hardesty. He does have excellent receiving numbers out of the backfield. The *Cleveland Plain-Dealer* expects Jackson to be featured on third down this year. That might be a bit of a stretch, given Trent Richardson's own stellar pass-catching ability, but perhaps he can keep the rook off the field with his blocking prowess.

RUNNING BACKS

Fred Jackson
Height: 6-1 Weight: 215 College: Coe College Draft: 2007/FA Born: 20-Feb-1981 Age: 31 Risk: Green

Year	Team	G/S	Runs	Yds	Yd/R	TD	FUM	DVOA	Rk	DYAR	Rk	YAR	Suc%	Rec	Pass	Yds	C%	Yd/C	TD	DVOA	Rk	DYAR	Rk
2009	BUF	16/11	237	1062	4.5	2	2	1.5%	24	88	22	119	48%	46	60	371	77%	8.1	2	25.5%	9	123	4
2010	BUF	16/13	222	927	4.2	5	5	-0.4%	21	78	21	68	47%	31	54	215	57%	6.9	2	-35.2%	52	-64	52
2011	BUF	10/10	170	934	5.5	6	2	13.7%	6	161	7	165	54%	39	50	442	78%	11.3	0	22.5%	9	95	9
2012	BUF		221	1009	4.6	5		4.6%						44	62	314	71%	7.1	1	-8.5%			

Jackson was coming off a monster five-game stretch where he carried the ball 99 times for 662 yards when he broke his right fibula and landed on injured reserve, opening the door for former ninth-overall pick C.J. Spiller to take his job. That is the story of Jackson's time in Buffalo in a nutshell: Had the organization recognized his ability early and committed to him rather than burning first-round picks on Marshawn Lynch and Spiller, he would be a richer man and would probably be playing on a better team. Instead, at 31, he had to settle for a pithy extension, which will be followed by a training camp battle with the guy Buffalo drafted specifically to replace him. The good news is that Jackson has a lot less mileage on his body than most backs his age, and he is a dangerous enough receiver to keep his career going as a package player after his starting days are over.

Steven Jackson
Height: 6-3 Weight: 229 College: Oregon State Draft: 2004/1 (24) Born: 22-Jul-1983 Age: 29 Risk: Green

Year	Team	G/S	Runs	Yds	Yd/R	TD	FUM	DVOA	Rk	DYAR	Rk	YAR	Suc%	Rec	Pass	Yds	C%	Yd/C	TD	DVOA	Rk	DYAR	Rk
2009	STL	15/15	324	1416	4.4	4	2	6.5%	16	178	7	128	45%	51	75	322	68%	6.3	0	-17.8%	48	-16	50
2010	STL	16/16	330	1241	3.8	6	1	-12.5%	39	-45	40	-28	40%	46	61	383	75%	8.3	0	-5.6%	38	29	31
2011	STL	15/15	260	1145	4.4	5	2	-2.3%	31	64	27	67	39%	42	58	333	72%	7.9	1	0.1%	28	43	24
2012	STL		274	1063	3.9	5		-6.4%						39	58	297	67%	7.6	1	-8.7%			

Jackson once again retained his "Player Who Does the Most With the Least Around Him" title by unanimous decision last season. At this point in his career, and with *another* rebuilding project taking place in St. Louis, the only real question is how much longer he'll wear the belt. One of Jackson's biggest assets as a back is his ability to play through pain. He's been listed as questionable on the injury report 10 times in the past three years, but has only missed two games, which is half as many as you'd expect from historical participation rates. All that wear and tear, though, has steadily degraded his other main asset: breaking tackles. After eluding his way to 50 in 2009, his total fell to 28 in 2010, and then again to 20 in 2011. His contract is up after 2013, and St. Louis drafted his heir apparent, so the champ won't be fighting much longer.

Brandon Jacobs
Height: 6-4 Weight: 264 College: Southern Illinois Draft: 2005/4 (110) Born: 6-Jul-1982 Age: 30 Risk: Green

Year	Team	G/S	Runs	Yds	Yd/R	TD	FUM	DVOA	Rk	DYAR	Rk	YAR	Suc%	Rec	Pass	Yds	C%	Yd/C	TD	DVOA	Rk	DYAR	Rk
2009	NYG	15/15	224	835	3.7	5	2	-9.5%	40	-5	39	-8	45%	18	31	184	58%	10.2	1	-6.5%	38	12	39
2010	NYG	16/5	147	823	5.6	9	3	18.8%	3	183	7	189	54%	7	13	59	54%	8.4	0	-18.4%	--	-3	--
2011	NYG	14/6	152	571	3.8	7	3	-3.2%	35	35	34	29	49%	15	22	128	68%	8.5	1	-0.1%	--	17	--
2012	SF		84	286	3.4	4		-12.0%						8	11	46	73%	5.7	0	-17.1%			

A six-year-old Giants fan sent Jacobs $3.36 this summer in order to try to pay for his favorite player to stay with Big Blue instead of bolting for San Francisco. This was either the entire contents of the boy's piggy bank, or a prediction for Jacobs' yards per carry average in the 2012 season. Jacobs has been so inconsistent over the past few years that it is nearly impossible to guess as to what the 49ers are getting here. Jacobs was third in rushing DVOA in both 2008 and 2010, but below average in 2009 and 2011. The 49ers have made it clear that they want to limit him to what he does best: being a short-yardage specialist who pounds it on the inside.

LaMichael James

Height: 5-8 Weight: 194 College: Oregon Draft: 2012/2 (61) Born: 22-Oct-1989 Age: 23 Risk: Yellow

Year	Team	G/S	Runs	Yds	Yd/R	TD	FUM	DVOA	Rk	DYAR	Rk	YAR	Suc%	Rec	Pass	Yds	C%	Yd/C	TD	DVOA	Rk	DYAR	Rk
2012	SF		57	280	4.9	0		1.7%						9	12	71	75%	7.8	1	0.2%			

With 5,668 yards from scrimmage, 57 touchdowns, and +80.9 Adj. POE, James was the most productive running back in major college football over the past three seasons. Because of his size (5-foot-8, 194 pounds), he draws obvious comparisons to players like Darren Sproles and Dexter McCluster. However, per his Speed Score of 98.9, he's slightly faster for a mighty mite college back than Sproles (93.7) was, and operated at ludicrous speed in comparison to McCluster (78.0). Because of James' playmaking ability in space, almost everyone assumes he'll immediately step in as San Francisco's third-down scatback. Although he very well might, it's important to note that, unlike both Sproles and McCluster, James had very little experience in the passing game at Oregon. He certainly has the talent to do it, as shown by his performance in receiving drills at the Combine, but it will take time for him to learn the nuances of route-running and picking up blitzes.

Rashad Jennings

Height: 6-1 Weight: 231 College: Liberty Draft: 2009/7 (250) Born: 26-Mar-1985 Age: 27 Risk: Yellow

Year	Team	G/S	Runs	Yds	Yd/R	TD	FUM	DVOA	Rk	DYAR	Rk	YAR	Suc%	Rec	Pass	Yds	C%	Yd/C	TD	DVOA	Rk	DYAR	Rk
2009	JAC	15/0	39	202	5.2	1	0	8.6%	--	30	--	34	46%	16	18	101	89%	6.3	0	-17.5%	--	-3	--
2010	JAC	13/3	84	459	5.5	4	0	29.5%	--	140	--	138	52%	26	34	223	76%	8.6	0	-5.1%	37	15	39
2012	JAC		96	454	4.7	0		-1.8%						26	30	263	87%	10.1	1	41.9%			

Jennings fought hard to keep from being placed on injured reserve last season, even admitting that he broke down in tears in GM Gene Smith's office after it happened. Assuming he comes back fully healthy (a safe assumption granted he probably could have played by midseason if he hadn't been placed on IR), look for him to take Maurice Jones-Drew's carries down from 343 to around 300 or so. Jennings is the rarest of all beasts: a productive late-round small-school Jaguars draft pick.

Chris Johnson

Height: 5-11 Weight: 197 College: East Carolina Draft: 2008/1 (24) Born: 23-Sep-1985 Age: 27 Risk: Yellow

Year	Team	G/S	Runs	Yds	Yd/R	TD	FUM	DVOA	Rk	DYAR	Rk	YAR	Suc%	Rec	Pass	Yds	C%	Yd/C	TD	DVOA	Rk	DYAR	Rk
2009	TEN	16/16	358	2006	5.6	14	3	14.0%	6	328	1	307	45%	50	71	503	70%	10.1	2	16.7%	13	113	7
2010	TEN	16/16	316	1364	4.3	11	3	-7.5%	33	18	30	14	39%	44	57	245	77%	5.6	1	-36.9%	53	-70	53
2011	TEN	16/16	262	1047	4.0	4	3	-15.1%	49	-67	49	-51	41%	57	79	418	72%	7.3	0	-4.1%	33	40	26
2012	TEN		273	1163	4.3	7		-0.3%						61	80	446	76%	7.3	0	-4.9%			

Trying to use the Similarity Scores system on Chris Johnson after his 2011 season is like trying to shoot pool with a rope. Four players in the entire database are above a 750 similarity score to Johnson's last three years. Three of them are old-school contemporaries: Ottis Anderson and Earl Campbell in 1982, and Curt Warner in 1988. Warner was pretty much done as an effective back, Campbell had one more great year in his legs, and Anderson had a pair of them before essentially morphing into an effective time-share back (albeit at a younger age). Johnson's only modern comparison, 2008 Frank Gore, was pretty much done as an uber-productive back, for whatever that's worth.

In 2010, Johnson had 154 carries of 3 or less yards, but he mixed that with 37 carries of 10 or more yards. In 2011, he had 164 carries of 3 or less yards, but just 26 carries of 10 or more yards. The "boom" went out and just left Johnson with the busts. We can subjectively debate how much of the blame for that should be assigned to the run blocking, his general lack of conditioning coming out of his contract holdout, or age-based decline. The Titans are trusting that his second-half improvement (he averaged 4.83 yards per carry from Week 10 onwards, with -2.2% DVOA) suggests a return to the Johnson of old, and did nothing to protect against Johnson not returning to form in 2012. We're not so sure that was the optimal path.

RUNNING BACKS

Maurice Jones-Drew
Height: 5-8 Weight: 205 College: UCLA Draft: 2006/2 (60) Born: 23-Mar-1985 Age: 27 Risk: Green

Year	Team	G/S	Runs	Yds	Yd/R	TD	FUM	DVOA	Rk	DYAR	Rk	YAR	Suc%	Rec	Pass	Yds	C%	Yd/C	TD	DVOA	Rk	DYAR	Rk
2009	JAC	16/16	312	1391	4.5	15	2	2.0%	22	147	12	185	49%	53	71	374	75%	7.1	1	4.9%	27	77	16
2010	JAC	14/14	299	1324	4.4	5	3	9.3%	8	223	5	222	51%	34	44	317	77%	9.3	2	24.5%	9	87	12
2011	JAC	16/16	343	1606	4.7	8	5	5.1%	15	197	3	199	49%	43	63	374	68%	8.7	3	1.9%	27	53	19
2012	JAC		295	1345	4.6	9		6.7%						40	53	269	75%	6.7	1	-4.4%			

If you liked the 1976 Buffalo Bills, you must have loved the 2011 Jacksonville Jaguars. Seriously, imagine what it takes to lead the NFL in carries on a team with the worst passing offense in the NFL. Jones-Drew may have ran the ball 400 times if the Jaguars actually had late leads to protect last year. He led the league in rushing anyway, breaking 37 tackles (third in the NFL), and making a terrific wanking-motion-turned-viral .gif on the Jaguars bench following a touchdown run. That motion describes his opinion of Jacksonville's failure to tender him an extension offer, as he sat out OTAs.

Felix Jones
Height: 5-10 Weight: 207 College: Arkansas Draft: 2008/1 (22) Born: 8-May-1987 Age: 25 Risk: Green

Year	Team	G/S	Runs	Yds	Yd/R	TD	FUM	DVOA	Rk	DYAR	Rk	YAR	Suc%	Rec	Pass	Yds	C%	Yd/C	TD	DVOA	Rk	DYAR	Rk
2009	DAL	14/1	116	685	5.9	3	2	14.9%	5	101	20	105	46%	19	22	119	86%	6.3	0	-17.9%	--	-5	--
2010	DAL	16/7	185	800	4.3	1	2	7.6%	10	115	10	112	50%	48	53	450	92%	9.4	1	34.3%	4	135	7
2011	DAL	12/8	127	575	4.5	1	4	-9.1%	43	-3	43	10	52%	33	44	221	75%	6.7	0	-3.0%	32	28	33
2012	DAL		67	274	4.1	1		-10.0%						36	42	410	86%	11.4	1	53.1%			

Despite his low ranking in DVOA, Jones was 10th in Success Rate last season. In fact, in 21 years of DVOA numbers, only Mike Alstott in 2000 had a lower DVOA with a Success Rate above 50%.

Worst Rushing DVOA with Success Rate > 50%, 1991-2011

Year	Player	Team	Runs	Yards	TD	FUM	Suc Rate	DVOA
2000	Mike Alstott	TB	131	465	5	3	54%	-11.4%
2011	**Felix Jones**	**DAL**	**127**	**575**	**1**	**3**	**52%**	**-9.1%**
1995	Leroy Hoard	CLE1	136	547	0	5	50%	-8.7%
1992	Mark Hicks	MIA	256	915	7	4	51%	-7.7%
2003	James Jackson	CLE	102	379	3	3	53%	-7.6%
1993	Brad Baxter	NYJ	173	560	7	0	50%	-7.1%
2009	Knowshon Moreno	DEN	247	947	7	2	50%	-6.6%
1995	Scottie Graham	MIN	110	406	2	0	51%	-6.6%
2002	Tyrone Wheatley	OAK	108	427	2	1	54%	-5.5%
2011	**Ricky Williams**	**BAL**	**108**	**445**	**2**	**2**	**51%**	**-5.2%**

Minimum: 100 carries.

How did this happen? Jones fumbled three times (plus a fourth on a reception) and struggled in the red zone, scoring just one touchdown on 18 carries inside the 20 (ten of them inside the 10).

Jones separated his shoulder twice last season and finished the year with his arm in a sling, so it was no surprise that he underwent shoulder surgery in January, even though the Cowboys didn't reveal the procedure until May. Jones was limited in OTAs, and Jason Garrett said he couldn't catch the ball over his head at the time. There's nobody behind Jones on the roster except college free agents (unless the Cowboys re-sign Sammy Morris), so his job is secure this year. On the other hand, he's also entering the last year of his contract and there seems to be little reason for Dallas to bring him back next year.

RUNNING BACKS 331

Thomas Jones
Height: 5-10 Weight: 220 College: Virginia Draft: 2000/1 (7) Born: 19-Aug-1978 Age: 34 Risk: N/A

Year	Team	G/S	Runs	Yds	Yd/R	TD	FUM	DVOA	Rk	DYAR	Rk	YAR	Suc%	Rec	Pass	Yds	C%	Yd/C	TD	DVOA	Rk	DYAR	Rk
2009	NYJ	16/16	331	1402	4.2	14	2	-2.6%	31	83	23	138	44%	10	18	58	56%	5.8	0	-39.7%	--	-27	--
2010	KC	16/10	245	896	3.7	6	3	-17.5%	43	-90	45	-85	43%	14	20	122	70%	8.7	0	3.8%	--	19	--
2011	KC	16/8	153	478	3.1	0	0	-26.1%	51	-104	50	-98	35%	5	7	43	71%	8.6	0	-6.3%	--	3	--

A strong argument could be made that Jones was the worst first-string player in the league last year, if eight starts qualify a man for first-string. He was last or next-to-last in DVOA, Success Rate, and yards per carry. Some of his DVOA splits were downright gory. Red zone: -41.4% on 19 carries. Third downs: -51.1% on 15 carries. And his days as a receiver are just about through too. This is not a one-year fluke. Jones has averaged 3.8 yards per carry over the last three years, worse than anyone except LaDainian Tomlinson (minimum 300 carries). Jones is a free agent, and should remain a free agent for the rest of his days.

Deji Karim
Height: 5-9 Weight: 210 College: Southen Illinois Draft: 2010/6 (180) Born: 18-Nov-1986 Age: 26 Risk: Green

Year	Team	G/S	Runs	Yds	Yd/R	TD	FUM	DVOA	Rk	DYAR	Rk	YAR	Suc%	Rec	Pass	Yds	C%	Yd/C	TD	DVOA	Rk	DYAR	Rk
2010	JAC	11/0	35	160	4.6	0	1	-6.2%	--	4	--	7	51%	3	7	10	43%	3.3	0	-73.3%	--	-26	--
2011	JAC	12/0	63	130	2.1	0	0	-41.0%	--	-84	--	-90	29%	14	19	120	74%	8.6	0	-5.7%	--	7	--
2012	IND		29	94	3.2	0		-21.2%						7	11	45	64%	6.4	0	-20.9%			

Karim was forced into a bigger role following Rashad Jennings' injury. Clearly he wasn't ready for that. Supposed "speed" backs should probably do better than two carries for 10 or more yards in 63 attempts. Combine his upside as a mediocre runner with his mediocre returns (-3.1 Pts+ on kickoffs) and you've got practice-squad fodder. The only thing promised to him in Indianapolis is a playbook.

John Kuhn
Height: 6-0 Weight: 255 College: Shippensburg Draft: 2006/FA Born: 9-Sep-1982 Age: 30 Risk: Yellow

Year	Team	G/S	Runs	Yds	Yd/R	TD	FUM	DVOA	Rk	DYAR	Rk	YAR	Suc%	Rec	Pass	Yds	C%	Yd/C	TD	DVOA	Rk	DYAR	Rk
2009	GB	14/6	8	18	2.3	1	0	-12.4%	--	-2	--	-3	38%	7	7	47	100%	6.7	2	109.6%	--	45	--
2010	GB	16/2	84	281	3.3	4	1	3.2%	--	55	--	41	60%	15	18	97	83%	6.5	2	31.1%	--	47	--
2011	GB	16/3	30	78	2.6	4	0	-5.7%	--	5	--	13	43%	15	18	77	83%	5.1	2	2.5%	--	20	--
2012	GB		31	89	2.9	2		-8.2%						35	42	161	83%	4.6	1	-9.6%			

In our first few books, we used to include a section with Going Deep-style writeups on fullbacks. We quickly learned that nobody really cared, except for the two or three Vonta Leach-quality blockers and a couple guys who might get actual carries and be useful in very deep fantasy leagues. Kuhn is one of the latter, especially since Green Bay has no established backup behind James Starks, who himself isn't really an established starter.

Brian Leonard
Height: 6-2 Weight: 226 College: Rutgers Draft: 2007/2 (52) Born: 3-Feb-1984 Age: 28 Risk: Green

Year	Team	G/S	Runs	Yds	Yd/R	TD	FUM	DVOA	Rk	DYAR	Rk	YAR	Suc%	Rec	Pass	Yds	C%	Yd/C	TD	DVOA	Rk	DYAR	Rk
2009	CIN	14/1	27	84	3.1	0	1	-24.5%	--	-14	--	-18	41%	30	35	217	86%	7.2	0	12.5%	20	49	23
2010	CIN	11/0	9	61	6.8	0	0	24.8%	--	15	--	15	56%	20	26	137	77%	6.9	1	9.2%	22	36	29
2011	CIN	13/0	17	85	5.0	0	0	18.5%	--	18	--	21	47%	22	31	210	71%	9.5	0	12.7%	19	43	25
2012	CIN		31	157	5.0	0		12.6%						23	29	196	79%	8.5	0	17.6%			

Speak of the devil, here's another one of the few fullbacks that gains actual yardage. Leonard remains a valuable third-down threat, mostly as a receiver, with an admirable yards per touch average, good blocking, and keen situational awareness. The only worry is a declining catch rate, which could spell trouble for such a specialist going forward.

332 RUNNING BACKS

Mikel LeShoure
Height: 6-0 Weight: 227 College: Illinois Draft: 2011/2 (57) Born: 30-Mar-1990 Age: 22 Risk: Yellow

Year	Team	G/S	Runs	Yds	Yd/R	TD	FUM	DVOA	Rk	DYAR	Rk	YAR	Suc%	Rec	Pass	Yds	C%	Yd/C	TD	DVOA	Rk	DYAR	Rk
2012	DET		132	572	4.3	5		2.3%						24	33	132	73%	5.5	0	-18.9%			

Leshoure missed his entire rookie campaign due to a blown Achilles. Such injuries have been known to ruin careers, but if the 22-year-old rebounds fully from the August injury, the Lions expect to have an explosive all-around runner who gets behind his pads inside and flashes the lateral agility to cut outside. Scouts like Leshoure's vision and burst. There were a few questions in college about his character, and those questions resurfaced this past offseason after a marijuana arrest which got him suspended for the first two games of the season.

Dion Lewis
Height: 5-7 Weight: 195 College: Pittsburgh Draft: 2011/5 (149) Born: 27-Sep-1990 Age: 22 Risk: Green

Year	Team	G/S	Runs	Yds	Yd/R	TD	FUM	DVOA	Rk	DYAR	Rk	YAR	Suc%	Rec	Pass	Yds	C%	Yd/C	TD	DVOA	Rk	DYAR	Rk
2011	PHI	15/0	23	102	4.4	1	0	18.3%	--	25	--	23	52%	1	1	-3	100%	-3.0	0	-219.3%	--	-10	--
2012	PHI		58	228	4.0	2		-4.3%						16	21	117	76%	7.3	0	0.9%			

Lewis takes over for Ronnie Brown as LeSean McCoy's primary backup. However, LeSean McCoy's primary backup doesn't get on the field very much. Ronnie Brown had 42 carries a year ago, and Jerome Harrison had just 40 the year before that. When Lewis does get carries, you'll see a deceptively strong back who has the patience to look for the hole and a good burst through it.

Kregg Lumpkin
Height: 5-11 Weight: 226 College: Georgia Draft: 2008/FA Born: 15-May-1984 Age: 28 Risk: Green

Year	Team	G/S	Runs	Yds	Yd/R	TD	FUM	DVOA	Rk	DYAR	Rk	YAR	Suc%	Rec	Pass	Yds	C%	Yd/C	TD	DVOA	Rk	DYAR	Rk
2010	TB	11/0	1	0	0.0	0	0	-94.9%	--	-6	--	-6	0%	1	1	12	100%	12.0	0	104.5%	--	8	--
2011	TB	16/0	31	105	3.4	0	0	-6.6%	--	2	--	-2	39%	41	53	291	77%	7.1	0	16.7%	16	79	13
2012	SEA		27	98	3.6	0		-13.5%						19	28	89	68%	4.7	0	-31.0%			

Last year, Lumpkin's greatest attribute appeared to be that he is not LeGarrette Blount. He can catch, protects the ball, and looks like he is trying in pass protection. Lumpkin caught 14 passes for 115 yards in the final three Buccaneers games, most of them when the Bucs were trailing by 24 or more points. Now in Seattle, Lumpkin will battle Leon Washington for a third-down role and could eat into Michael Robinson's chores as a ball-carrying fullback.

Marshawn Lynch
Height: 5-11 Weight: 215 College: California Draft: 2007/1 (12) Born: 22-Apr-1986 Age: 26 Risk: Yellow

Year	Team	G/S	Runs	Yds	Yd/R	TD	FUM	DVOA	Rk	DYAR	Rk	YAR	Suc%	Rec	Pass	Yds	C%	Yd/C	TD	DVOA	Rk	DYAR	Rk
2009	BUF	13/6	120	450	3.8	2	3	-18.8%	46	-57	45	-42	38%	28	37	179	76%	6.4	0	-25.8%	51	-24	51
2010	2TM	16/14	202	737	3.6	6	4	-14.3%	41	-51	41	-36	44%	22	26	145	85%	6.6	0	-8.0%	41	9	41
2011	SEA	15/15	285	1204	4.2	12	3	8.9%	12	201	2	159	46%	28	41	212	68%	7.6	1	-7.3%	36	16	35
2012	SEA		285	1275	4.5	9		4.2%						37	47	289	79%	7.8	1	12.4%			

Seahawks GM John Schneider spent much of his first season on the job attempting to pry Lynch away from the Buffalo Bills, an acquisition that began to pay dividends in 2011. Starting with his 67-yard touchdown run in a playoff win over the New Orleans Saints in January, Lynch overcame an inefficient passing offense and a young, constantly shuffling offensive line to become the franchise's first 1,000-yard rusher since Shaun Alexander in 2005. Lynch improved significantly in the red zone, going from -39.3% DVOA in 2010 to 35.2% DVOA in 2011. According to our game charters, Lynch had 34 broken tackles in 2011, the fifth-highest total in the league. Lynch has added a physical element to a once "finesse" offense and the front office kept him off the free agent market with a four-year, $30 million contract that included $17 million in guarantees.

Mossis Madu

Height: 6-0　Weight: 197　College: Oklahoma　Draft: 2011/FA　Born: 4-Nov-1987　Age: 25　Risk: Green

Year	Team	G/S	Runs	Yds	Yd/R	TD	FUM	DVOA	Rk	DYAR	Rk	YAR	Suc%	Rec	Pass	Yds	C%	Yd/C	TD	DVOA	Rk	DYAR	Rk
2011	TB	9/0	15	55	3.7	0	0	-14.8%	--	-4	--	0	40%	10	12	72	83%	7.2	0	-9.2%	--	3	--
2012	TB		22	110	4.9	1		12.3%						13	19	18	68%	1.4	0	-61.9%			

Madu is an undrafted rookie from Central Oklahoma who made the Bucs roster when Earnest Graham got hurt and started getting touches when all heck broke loose at the end of last season. Madu is the kind of back a team relies on when it wants to turn a 42-0 halftime deficit into a 42-10 final.

Doug Martin

Height: 5-9　Weight: 223　College: Boise State　Draft: 2012/1 (31)　Born: 13-Jan-1989　Age: 23　Risk: Yellow

Year	Team	G/S	Runs	Yds	Yd/R	TD	FUM	DVOA	Rk	DYAR	Rk	YAR	Suc%	Rec	Pass	Yds	C%	Yd/C	TD	DVOA	Rk	DYAR	Rk
2012	TB		245	991	4.0	4		-3.0%						35	41	292	85%	8.3	0	23.7%			

A tough, hard-working, versatile, likeable little power back, Martin rushed for over 1,200 yards in each of his last two seasons at Boise State, hauling in exactly 28 receptions each year. Martin catches the ball well, can return kickoffs in a pinch, and is a coach's dream in the weight and film rooms. He would have been a mid-first round pick if he were an inch taller or a half-step faster in the open field. The most logical running back rotation for the Bucs would be to use Martin for just about everything but the occasional change-up or short-yardage carry, relegating LeGarrette Blount to a five-touch role. He was truly a special weapon in the passing game, recording an 88 percent catch rate and 10.6 yards per catch over the past two years at Boise.

Ryan Mathews

Height: 6-0　Weight: 218　College: Fresno State　Draft: 2010/1 (12)　Born: 1-May-1987　Age: 25　Risk: Yellow

Year	Team	G/S	Runs	Yds	Yd/R	TD	FUM	DVOA	Rk	DYAR	Rk	YAR	Suc%	Rec	Pass	Yds	C%	Yd/C	TD	DVOA	Rk	DYAR	Rk
2010	SD	12/9	158	678	4.3	7	5	1.2%	18	61	23	66	46%	22	26	145	85%	6.6	0	-22.2%	49	-13	48
2011	SD	14/14	222	1091	4.9	6	5	10.8%	10	171	6	134	50%	50	59	455	85%	9.1	0	27.8%	6	134	4
2012	SD		262	1156	4.4	8		0.0%						59	75	492	79%	8.3	2	16.0%			

The Chargers' frustration with Mathews was palpable at times in 2011. Mike Tolbert got the majority of the red-zone work despite poor results, as well as the majority of the third-down work despite some misadventures in pass blocking. Mathews was the more explosive back, though he did leave some yards on the field with missed reads at the second level. The two big questions about his 2012 production are whether he can earn the trust of the coaching staff to play in all situations and whether he can stay healthy. If the answer to both is in the affirmative, he could join the upper echelon of backs in the league.

Dexter McCluster

Height: 5-9　Weight: 172　College: Mississippi　Draft: 2010/2 (36)　Born: 26-Aug-1988　Age: 24　Risk: Yellow

Year	Team	G/S	Runs	Yds	Yd/R	TD	FUM	DVOA	Rk	DYAR	Rk	YAR	Suc%	Rec	Pass	Yds	C%	Yd/C	TD	DVOA	Rk	DYAR	Rk
2010	KC	11/7	18	71	3.9	0	0	-46.6%	58	-8	70	-4	0%	21	39	209	54%	10.0	1	-18.5%	--	-17	--
2011	KC	16/4	114	516	4.5	1	2	-2.3%	32	27	36	34	43%	46	63	328	75%	7.1	1	-12.6%	41	4	41
2012	KC		20	100	4.9	1		12.7%						26	40	217	65%	8.4	0	-8.2%			

The Chiefs had moved McCluster to wide receiver as of spring OTAs, but not even the head coach knew how long that would last. "We feel like he knows how to play running back, and we can put him over at running back at any point in time, but we felt like he needed the work at wide receiver," Romeo Crennel told reporters. Our game charters listed McCluster as a wide receiver 44 times last year, 14 runs and 30 passes. Four of those runs were reverses or end-arounds to McCluster, one for 24 yards, the others for exactly zero. The Chiefs threw to McCluster eight times out wide, and he only caught four of them for 38 yards. Twice they tried using McCluster on wide receiver screens, and both fell incomplete. McCluster has a lot of work to do before he can be a quality wideout, but the Chiefs need him there much more than they need him at running back. McCluster was also worth -5.6 estimated points on 25 kickoff returns last year, and -3.7 estimated points on 26 punt returns.

334　RUNNING BACKS

LeSean McCoy　　Height: 5-11　Weight: 198　College: Pittsburgh　　Draft: 2009/2 (53)　Born: 12-Jul-1988　　Age: 24　Risk: Green

Year	Team	G/S	Runs	Yds	Yd/R	TD	FUM	DVOA	Rk	DYAR	Rk	YAR	Suc%	Rec	Pass	Yds	C%	Yd/C	TD	DVOA	Rk	DYAR	Rk
2009	PHI	16/4	155	637	4.1	4	2	-6.4%	36	13	37	2	46%	40	55	308	73%	7.7	0	-11.2%	44	8	43
2010	PHI	15/13	207	1080	5.2	7	2	17.5%	5	227	4	205	49%	78	90	592	87%	7.6	2	16.0%	15	158	2
2011	PHI	15/15	273	1309	4.8	17	1	15.8%	4	304	1	262	51%	48	69	315	70%	6.6	3	-2.8%	31	45	23
2012	PHI		232	1071	4.6	12		10.1%						66	104	548	63%	8.3	3	-9.2%			

The most similar backs to LeSean McCoy over the first three years of their careers include Thurman Thomas, Rodney Hampton, Napoleon Kaufman, Ray Rice, and William Andrews. That's some fine company. His increase in touchdowns came from a massive change in Philadelphia strategy, but it was not a fluke of luck. The Eagles gave McCoy 22 carries inside the 5 after giving him just six carries inside the 5 in 2010. However, McCoy only scored 0.6 touchdowns more than we would expect from an average back on those carries. If the Eagles keep giving it to him at the goal line, he should keep scoring for six.

Darren McFadden　　Height: 6-1　Weight: 211　College: Arkansas　　Draft: 2008/1 (4)　Born: 27-Aug-1987　　Age: 25　Risk: Red

Year	Team	G/S	Runs	Yds	Yd/R	TD	FUM	DVOA	Rk	DYAR	Rk	YAR	Suc%	Rec	Pass	Yds	C%	Yd/C	TD	DVOA	Rk	DYAR	Rk
2009	OAK	12/7	104	357	3.4	1	5	-32.7%	49	-91	48	-74	38%	21	35	245	60%	11.7	0	-3.9%	35	20	36
2010	OAK	13/13	223	1157	5.2	7	4	3.4%	15	105	16	112	42%	47	61	507	77%	10.8	3	34.0%	5	151	3
2011	OAK	7/7	113	614	5.4	4	1	11.6%	9	87	20	88	44%	19	23	154	83%	8.1	1	12.2%	--	33	--
2012	OAK		219	1090	5.0	7		10.4%						50	69	480	72%	9.6	2	16.7%			

McFadden has had tremendously exaggerated down-by-down splits the last two years: 22.4% DVOA on first down, -6.1% DVOA on second down, and -49.6% DVOA on third or fourth down (although this is just 17 carries). He's at his best on the edges, looking for a seam he can hit and exploit with his speed, and could be a dominant runner on outside zone if he stays healthy. That's a big if, though, as he's missed at least three games every year he has played in the NFL. Only once has McFadden had more than 113 carries.

Willis McGahee　　Height: 6-0　Weight: 228　College: Miami　　Draft: 2003/1 (23)　Born: 21-Oct-1981　　Age: 31　Risk: Green

Year	Team	G/S	Runs	Yds	Yd/R	TD	FUM	DVOA	Rk	DYAR	Rk	YAR	Suc%	Rec	Pass	Yds	C%	Yd/C	TD	DVOA	Rk	DYAR	Rk
2009	BAL	16/1	109	544	5.0	12	1	18.0%	3	127	17	148	55%	15	22	85	68%	5.7	2	-16.3%	--	-3	--
2010	BAL	15/2	100	380	3.8	5	2	-6.6%	31	6	32	0	49%	14	17	55	82%	3.9	1	-45.9%	--	-30	--
2011	DEN	15/14	249	1199	4.8	4	4	4.3%	17	131	12	117	47%	12	20	51	60%	4.3	1	-68.0%	--	-59	--
2012	DEN		170	710	4.2	5		3.7%						15	21	119	71%	7.9	0	2.3%			

McGahee had his highest yardage total since 2007 and showed surprising burst for a 30-year-old. He had ten 20-yard runs, matching the career high he set way back in 2004 with the Bills. He told reporters he was looking forward to playing with Peyton Manning: "With Peyton coming to Denver, I don't have to worry about nine defenders in the box." However, despite his new quarterback, McGahee is more likely to decline than improve. Two of the three most statistically similar seasons to McGahee's 2011 campaign belonged to Fred Taylor in 2006 and 2007. You'll note that Taylor didn't do much after 2007, when he was 31. McGahee will be 31 this year. He tore up his knee in his final college game, and since then has battled a series of knee, ankle, and hamstring problems. This fall he will try to squeeze one more productive campaign out of an aging, beat-up body. Stranger things have happened.

Joe McKnight　　Height: 6-0　Weight: 198　College: USC　　Draft: 2010/4 (112)　Born: 16-Apr-1988　　Age: 24　Risk: Green

Year	Team	G/S	Runs	Yds	Yd/R	TD	FUM	DVOA	Rk	DYAR	Rk	YAR	Suc%	Rec	Pass	Yds	C%	Yd/C	TD	DVOA	Rk	DYAR	Rk
2010	NYJ	9/1	39	189	4.8	0	0	11.5%	--	30	--	49	59%	3	4	20	75%	6.7	0	38.2%	--	13	--
2011	NYJ	15/0	43	134	3.1	0	0	-14.9%	--	-11	--	-8	44%	13	18	139	72%	10.7	0	31.2%	--	43	--
2012	NYJ		96	427	4.5	1		-3.7%						23	29	189	79%	8.2	0	10.0%			

RUNNING BACKS 335

Failed prospect-turned-special teams ace-turned-Super Size Me human experiment in cheeseburger-chomping nutrition. McKnight should have stopped in phase two of his transformation. As a very good gunner, pretty good return man, and non-embarrassing third running back, he could string together a 12-year career. As a junk food junkie who pigged out to bulk up in the name of "durability," he's just another oddball who plays for the Jets.

Rashard Mendenhall   Height: 5-10   Weight: 225   College: Illinois   Draft: 2008/1 (23)   Born: 19-Jun-1987   Age: 25   Risk: Red

Year	Team	G/S	Runs	Yds	Yd/R	TD	FUM	DVOA	Rk	DYAR	Rk	YAR	Suc%	Rec	Pass	Yds	C%	Yd/C	TD	DVOA	Rk	DYAR	Rk
2009	PIT	16/12	242	1108	4.6	7	3	-3.2%	32	52	29	83	46%	25	32	261	78%	10.4	1	55.6%	1	117	5
2010	PIT	16/16	324	1273	3.9	13	2	-3.0%	25	71	22	79	44%	23	34	167	68%	7.3	0	-3.9%	35	20	37
2011	PIT	15/15	228	928	4.1	9	1	2.3%	23	106	17	88	52%	18	28	154	64%	8.6	0	-5.4%	34	14	36
2012	PIT		109	447	4.1	3		-6.5%						14	17	101	82%	7.2	0	-21.4%			

Mendenhall may not be long for Pittsburgh. Obviously, he's coming off a torn ACL in Week 17 that almost certainly will land him on the PUP list to start this season. There's a reasonable chance one of his replacements will be established as the starter by the time he comes back. (If not, the Steelers could be in trouble.) Add in the fact that Mendenhall's contract expires at the end of the season, and that new offensive coordinator Todd Haley prefers versatile, smaller backs to run-only bigger ones, it's hard to see how Mendenhall fits in the team's long-term plans. Mendenhall's KUBIAK projection assumes that he'll start for half the season.

Lamar Miller   Height: 5-11   Weight: 212   College: Miami   Draft: 2012/4 (97)   Born: 25-Apr-1991   Age: 21   Risk: Blue

Year	Team	G/S	Runs	Yds	Yd/R	TD	FUM	DVOA	Rk	DYAR	Rk	YAR	Suc%	Rec	Pass	Yds	C%	Yd/C	TD	DVOA	Rk	DYAR	Rk
2012	MIA		30	146	4.9	0		2.4%						8	11	54	73%	6.7	1	-2.8%			

Miller is a one-cut slasher who rushed for 1,272 yards at the University of Miami last year, with +14.6 Adj. POE and 2.55 Highlight Yards per carry. His 113.1 Speed Score leads this year's rookie class, and he is a good decision maker who lets blocks develop and sees cutback lanes. The Dolphins are switching to a zone-blocking scheme, and Miller is a natural fit for that style of offense. Reggie Bush has lost carries to far weaker prospects.

Mewelde Moore   Height: 5-11   Weight: 210   College: Tulane   Draft: 2004/4 (119)   Born: 24-Jul-1982   Age: 30   Risk: Yellow

Year	Team	G/S	Runs	Yds	Yd/R	TD	FUM	DVOA	Rk	DYAR	Rk	YAR	Suc%	Rec	Pass	Yds	C%	Yd/C	TD	DVOA	Rk	DYAR	Rk
2009	PIT	16/0	35	118	3.4	0	0	-27.2%	--	-24	--	-23	40%	21	31	153	68%	7.3	2	16.1%	14	49	24
2010	PIT	15/0	33	99	3.0	0	0	-38.2%	--	-36	--	-36	21%	26	31	205	84%	7.9	0	12.0%	20	44	23
2011	PIT	12/0	22	157	7.1	0	2	28.5%	--	29	--	29	68%	11	14	104	79%	9.5	1	3.8%	--	15	--
2012	IND		33	120	3.7	1		-10.8%						20	30	154	67%	7.7	0	-9.1%			

After four years of being Pittsburgh's go-to third-down option, Moore was cut loose and caught on with Indianapolis. He'll compete with Vick Ballard, Deji Karim, and Darren Evans as the Colts look for someone to fill in on passing downs. The third-down back Indy wants stones rushers like Solomon Page, and will work for minimum wage.

Knowshon Moreno   Height: 5-11   Weight: 200   College: Georgia   Draft: 2009/1 (12)   Born: 16-Jul-1987   Age: 25   Risk: Red

Year	Team	G/S	Runs	Yds	Yd/R	TD	FUM	DVOA	Rk	DYAR	Rk	YAR	Suc%	Rec	Pass	Yds	C%	Yd/C	TD	DVOA	Rk	DYAR	Rk
2009	DEN	16/9	247	947	3.8	7	4	-6.6%	37	34	33	44	50%	28	41	213	68%	7.6	2	-13.8%	45	0	45
2010	DEN	13/13	182	779	4.3	5	4	-4.6%	27	34	26	44	43%	37	48	372	77%	10.1	3	29.4%	7	114	10
2011	DEN	7/2	37	179	4.8	0	1	-16.0%	--	-9	--	-5	32%	11	15	101	73%	9.2	1	44.3%	--	37	--
2012	DEN		58	275	4.7	1		5.1%						27	32	222	84%	8.2	0	19.4%			

Three years after the Broncos picked Moreno 12th overall, he has no seasons over 1,000 yards or with a positive DVOA, and only two 100-yard games. He is coming off a torn ACL suffered against Kansas City last November, and facing a DUI trial this October. (Moreno was driving a car with a license plate reading "SAUCED," so we must give him points for honesty.) Willis McGahee is firmly entrenched as Denver's starter, and they added Ronnie Hillman in the draft as a third-down back. In short, this will be a critical training camp for Moreno, who must prove to Denver that his talent still outweighs the risk that he will miss time due to injuries or legal matters.

Maurice Morris
Height: 5-11 Weight: 202 College: Oregon Draft: 2002/2 (54) Born: 1-Dec-1979 Age: 33 Risk: N/A

Year	Team	G/S	Runs	Yds	Yd/R	TD	FUM	DVOA	Rk	DYAR	Rk	YAR	Suc%	Rec	Pass	Yds	C%	Yd/C	TD	DVOA	Rk	DYAR	Rk
2009	DET	14/3	93	384	4.1	2	1	-7.0%	--	-3	--	-11	41%	26	38	210	68%	8.1	0	8.6%	23	44	26
2010	DET	14/7	90	336	3.7	5	1	4.9%	--	45	--	44	46%	25	31	170	81%	6.8	0	8.3%	24	38	27
2011	DET	16/5	80	316	4.0	1	1	2.1%	--	34	--	28	48%	26	35	230	74%	8.8	1	19.0%	13	54	17

At 32, Morris's best days, if not his playing days altogether, are behind him. He's always been an adequate change-of-pace back with third down-type running ability (meaning he's quick enough to get outside or make one cut and go on a draw play). Not many running backs stick around for 10 years in the NFL as pure backups. The ones who do usually have a specific strength they bring to the table. Morris, however, has always just brought reliability.

Sammy Morris
Height: 6-0 Weight: 220 College: Texas Tech Draft: 2000/5 (156) Born: 23-Mar-1977 Age: 35 Risk: N/A

Year	Team	G/S	Runs	Yds	Yd/R	TD	FUM	DVOA	Rk	DYAR	Rk	YAR	Suc%	Rec	Pass	Yds	C%	Yd/C	TD	DVOA	Rk	DYAR	Rk
2009	NE	12/5	73	319	4.4	2	2	-7.7%	--	-3	--	1	51%	19	27	180	70%	9.5	0	30.4%	6	66	20
2010	NE	16/0	20	56	2.8	0	0	0.5%	--	7	--	6	50%	7	12	77	58%	11.0	0	-3.8%	--	8	--
2011	DAL	3/0	28	98	3.5	0	0	-12.5%	--	-5	--	-3	43%	5	7	13	71%	2.6	0	-87.4%	--	-19	--

With DeMarco Murray and Felix Jones both hobbled at the end of the season, the Cowboys signed Morris to play out the string. He was still unsigned in May, but had not formally retired. It wouldn't be a complete shock to see him on an NFL roster this fall. At least ten running backs have played at age 35 this century, most of them fullbacks. Tony Richardson was still getting short-yardage carries for the Jets at age 39 in 2010. If Morris does call it quits, he'll finish with 4,311 yards from scrimmage in 144 games over 11 seasons. Not bad for a guy the Bills grabbed in the fifth round in 2000.

DeMarco Murray
Height: 6-0 Weight: 213 College: Oklahoma Draft: 2011/3 (71) Born: 12-Feb-1988 Age: 24 Risk: Red

Year	Team	G/S	Runs	Yds	Yd/R	TD	FUM	DVOA	Rk	DYAR	Rk	YAR	Suc%	Rec	Pass	Yds	C%	Yd/C	TD	DVOA	Rk	DYAR	Rk
2011	DAL	13/7	164	897	5.5	2	1	12.6%	7	149	11	162	58%	26	35	183	74%	7.0	0	-17.8%	44	-8	45
2012	DAL		246	1115	4.5	6		-2.0%						40	59	321	68%	8.0	1	-3.7%			

Murray averaged 1.43 open-field yards per carry, fifth-best among all running backs with at least 100 attempts. He had the highest Speed Score (112.6) of any running back in last year's draft, so his electrifying rookie performance was not entirely unexpected. Of course, he also had knee, hamstring, and ankle issues at Oklahoma, so it's not a surprise that he ended the year on the sidelines after another ankle injury. Despite Murray's fragile history, Jason Garrett was not afraid to lean on him. Murray didn't see significant action before rushing for a Dallas-record 253 yards against St. Louis in late October, but he still finished five games with 20 or more carries (including four games in a row). That's the most 20-carry games for a Cowboys runner since Julius Jones had seven in 2006. Murray claimed to be 100 percent in spring drills. That's probably true, and he'll probably see plenty of action in September. And then he'll probably get hurt again.

Jerious Norwood
Height: 6-0 Weight: 205 College: Mississippi State Draft: 2006/3 (79) Born: 29-Jul-1983 Age: 29 Risk: N/A

Year	Team	G/S	Runs	Yds	Yd/R	TD	FUM	DVOA	Rk	DYAR	Rk	YAR	Suc%	Rec	Pass	Yds	C%	Yd/C	TD	DVOA	Rk	DYAR	Rk
2009	ATL	10/4	76	252	3.3	0	1	-12.3%	--	-15	--	-13	43%	19	22	186	86%	9.8	1	57.1%	--	86	--
2010	ATL	2/0	2	8	4.0	0	0	76.2%	--	9	--	7	100%	1	3	9	33%	9.0	0	-49.8%	--	-6	--
2011	STL	9/0	24	61	2.5	0	0	-27.8%	--	-15	--	-21	13%	0	1	0	0%	0.0	0	-74.4%	--	-4	--

After six years, it's time to admit that the "Jerious Norwood as a fantasy sleeper" ship has sailed. He had as many kickoff returns as carries in 2011, and was below average in that too (-0.9 estimated points added). Don't walk away mad, folks; just walk away.

Chris Ogbonnaya   Height: 6-0   Weight: 220   College: Texas   Draft: 2009/7 (211)   Born: 20-May-1986   Age: 26   Risk: Green

Year	Team	G/S	Runs	Yds	Yd/R	TD	FUM	DVOA	Rk	DYAR	Rk	YAR	Suc%	Rec	Pass	Yds	C%	Yd/C	TD	DVOA	Rk	DYAR	Rk
2009	STL	2/0	11	50	4.5	0	0	-1.2%	--	4	--	1	45%	1	2	19	50%	19.0	0	30.6%	--	5	--
2011	2TM	13/4	76	340	4.5	1	2	-4.9%	--	11	--	9	47%	23	31	165	74%	7.2	0	-9.4%	38	7	38
2012	CLE		29	111	3.8	0		-13.6%						15	25	87	60%	5.8	0	-32.6%			

Ogbonnaya started the year in Houston, then was picked up by Cleveland after the Texans cut him. He provided a pair of effective performances in relief of an injury-riddled Browns backfield, putting up 90 yards against the Rams and 115 on the Jags. The regulars returned, and Ogbonnaya went to the bench, getting just six carries over the final six games. The small sample numbers indicate he might be a better player than Montario Hardesty, but he wasn't a second-round pick by Mike Holmgren. Hardesty was.

Isaiah Pead   Height: 5-10   Weight: 197   College: Cincinnati   Draft: 2012/2 (50)   Born: 14-Dec-1989   Age: 23   Risk: Green

Year	Team	G/S	Runs	Yds	Yd/R	TD	FUM	DVOA	Rk	DYAR	Rk	YAR	Suc%	Rec	Pass	Yds	C%	Yd/C	TD	DVOA	Rk	DYAR	Rk
2012	STL		80	275	3.4	1		-22.0%						23	30	180	77%	7.8	0	2.8%			

For a St. Louis team with an aging running back and subpar return teams, Pead was the perfect two-birds-with-one-stone pick in April's draft. He can immediately step in as Steven Jackson's heir apparent, and punt returns (which helped him win MVP at the Senior Bowl) give Pead something to do until Jackson's NFL clock runs out. In terms of fantasy football, Pead should be at or near the top of everyone's list as a keeper prospect, but don't believe the easy Jeff Fisher-inspired comparison with Chris Johnson. Pead was productive in college, with +35.1 Adj. POE over three seasons, but Pead's Speed Score of 98.7 was a little low for a second-round pick, whereas Johnson's was off the charts at 121.9.

Adrian Peterson   Height: 6-2   Weight: 217   College: Oklahoma   Draft: 2007/1 (7)   Born: 21-Mar-1985   Age: 27   Risk: Red

Year	Team	G/S	Runs	Yds	Yd/R	TD	FUM	DVOA	Rk	DYAR	Rk	YAR	Suc%	Rec	Pass	Yds	C%	Yd/C	TD	DVOA	Rk	DYAR	Rk
2009	MIN	16/16	314	1383	4.4	18	7	1.8%	23	150	10	108	46%	43	57	436	75%	10.1	0	15.7%	15	90	8
2010	MIN	15/15	283	1298	4.6	12	2	10.7%	7	217	6	224	45%	36	50	341	72%	9.5	1	17.6%	12	87	13
2011	MIN	12/12	208	970	4.7	12	1	10.4%	11	153	9	190	47%	18	23	139	78%	7.7	1	9.6%	--	28	--
2012	MIN		249	1084	4.4	8		2.5%						25	33	179	76%	7.2	1	-4.3%			

Surprisingly, until this past year, we hadn't seen a starting running back go down with a torn ACL since 2007. Peterson's ACL tear came just seven months before the start of 2012 training camps, but in recent years we've seen other stars like Wes Welker and Philip Rivers recover from similar injuries in similar timeframes. The demands on a running back are different than the demands on a receiver or quarterback, but the reports about Peterson have been nothing short of astonishing. He had already resumed sprinting and cutting at full speed by mid-June, and all indications now say that he'll be ready for Week 1, although he may play behind Toby Gerhart for a couple weeks until the Vikings are sure he's close to 100 percent.

Bernard Pierce   Height: 6-0   Weight: 218   College: Temple   Draft: 2012/3 (84)   Born: 10-May-1991   Age: 21   Risk: Green

Year	Team	G/S	Runs	Yds	Yd/R	TD	FUM	DVOA	Rk	DYAR	Rk	YAR	Suc%	Rec	Pass	Yds	C%	Yd/C	TD	DVOA	Rk	DYAR	Rk
2012	BAL		97	475	4.9	1		4.4%						13	19	110	68%	8.5	1	6.1%			

RUNNING BACKS

Baltimore's third-round pick will replace Ricky Williams as Ray Rice's fantasy handcuff. Pierce's combination of size and speed (4.49-second forty at 218 pounds) earned him the third-highest Speed Score (107.3) of this year's rookie running back class, and the highest of the backs taken on the first two days. (This ignores Trent Richardson, who did not run at the Combine.) If you want to toss the 4.34-second forty Pierce ran at his Pro Day into the Speed Score equation, you get an awe-inspiring 122.9. Pierce averaged 20 carries a game over three seasons and was extremely productive, with +60.3 Adj. POE in his college career. This all sounds like Pierce is the perfect backup to Ray Rice, but there are two problems: He has very little experience as a receiver, and his horrific pass-protection attempts at Temple are going to give Joe Flacco nightmares. God forbid Rice gets hurt, the Ravens will be desperate to find a back who can play on third downs.

Bilal Powell
Height: 5-10 Weight: 205 College: Louisville Draft: 2011/4 (126) Born: 27-Oct-1988 Age: 24 Risk: Blue

Year	Team	G/S	Runs	Yds	Yd/R	TD	FUM	DVOA	Rk	DYAR	Rk	YAR	Rk	Suc%	Rec	Pass	Yds	C%	Yd/C	TD	DVOA	Rk	DYAR	Rk
2011	NYJ	2/0	13	21	1.6	0	1	-115.1%	--	-54	--	-57		15%	1	1	7	100%	7.0	0	-22.9%	--	-1	--
2012	NYJ		31	126	4.0	0		-9.2%							8	11	55	73%	6.9	0	-4.3%			

You may remember Powell from the Broncos-Jets game. With Shonn Greene hurt early in the game and LaDainian Tomlinson inactive, Powell became the change-up to Joe McKnight. Powell fumbled at the one-yard line, but Matt Slauson fell on the ball for the Jets' only touchdown. Brian Schottenheimer was so impressed by this feat of goal-line creativity that he gave Powell the ball several more times, including two third-and-long handoffs in the fourth quarter while the Jets waited around for Tim Tebow to figure out how to beat them. Powell finished with seven carries for 11 yards, then got six more carries for ten yards in mop-up duty against the Chiefs. If Powell hoped to prove that he was a better third-and-long option than a Mark Sanchez throw, he probably had to at least crack two yards per carry.

Isaac Redman
Height: 6-0 Weight: 230 College: Bowie State Draft: 2009/FA Born: 10-Nov-1984 Age: 28 Risk: Yellow

Year	Team	G/S	Runs	Yds	Yd/R	TD	FUM	DVOA	Rk	DYAR	Rk	YAR	Rk	Suc%	Rec	Pass	Yds	C%	Yd/C	TD	DVOA	Rk	DYAR	Rk
2010	PIT	16/0	52	247	4.8	0	2	1.7%	--	25	--	21		58%	9	10	72	90%	8.0	2	98.7%	--	54	--
2011	PIT	16/1	110	479	4.4	3	2	3.1%	19	55	31	67		54%	18	23	78	83%	4.3	0	-21.9%	--	-11	--
2012	PIT		158	667	4.2	5		-3.3%							23	27	198	85%	8.6	1	25.7%			

He got a handful of carries each week in 2011, but it wasn't until Rashard Mendenhall got hurt that Redman proved himself as a potential workhorse, running for 213 yards and 5.9 yards per carry in Pittsburgh's last two games (including the postseason). Aside from the obvious (i.e., he gets a starting job), Redman will benefit from Mendenhall's absence by being more of a red-zone presence than he used to be. Despite being a bigger back, Redman has only had 30 red-zone carries over the past two seasons, 63 fewer than Mendenhall. Also of note is that Redman is playing 2012 on a one-year contract, and Pittsburgh is miserly in their free-agent spending, so this season may be an audition for the rest of the league.

Marcel Reece
Height: 6-3 Weight: 240 College: Washington Draft: 2008/FA Born: 23-Jun-1985 Age: 27 Risk: Blue

Year	Team	G/S	Runs	Yds	Yd/R	TD	FUM	DVOA	Rk	DYAR	Rk	YAR	Rk	Suc%	Rec	Pass	Yds	C%	Yd/C	TD	DVOA	Rk	DYAR	Rk
2009	OAK	2/0	0	0	0.0	0	0	--	--	--	--	--		--	2	4	20	50%	10.0	0	2.1%	--	4	--
2010	OAK	16/10	30	122	4.1	1	1	-8.0%	--	-2	--	7		57%	25	43	333	58%	13.3	3	16.8%	14	72	17
2011	OAK	12/6	17	112	6.6	0	1	45.2%	--	38	--	36		59%	27	36	301	75%	11.1	2	20.4%	11	71	14
2012	OAK		30	127	4.2	0		2.0%							32	42	277	76%	8.7	0	13.6%			

Reece is perhaps the league's most versatile fullback. A Swiss-army knife-type player, Reece is a solid lead blocker who spent some time lined up outside as a wide receiver, his collegiate position. He also saw a few snaps at tight end, and may line up there more often with the Raiders' lack of depth and experience at that position. He's not a game-changer at any of those positions, but he's a very useful part.

RUNNING BACKS

Ray Rice Height: 5-8 Weight: 199 College: Rutgers Draft: 2008/2 (55) Born: 22-Jan-1987 Age: 25 Risk: Green

Year	Team	G/S	Runs	Yds	Yd/R	TD	FUM	DVOA	Rk	DYAR	Rk	YAR	Suc%	Rec	Pass	Yds	C%	Yd/C	TD	DVOA	Rk	DYAR	Rk
2009	BAL	16/16	254	1339	5.3	7	3	12.9%	7	227	3	228	51%	78	102	702	77%	9.0	1	7.5%	24	117	6
2010	BAL	16/14	307	1220	4.0	5	0	0.4%	19	97	17	124	46%	63	83	556	76%	8.8	1	5.5%	25	82	15
2011	BAL	16/16	291	1364	4.7	12	2	2.1%	26	129	13	108	45%	76	104	704	73%	9.3	3	29.0%	5	236	2
2012	BAL		291	1375	4.7	10		8.3%						70	92	575	76%	8.2	2	14.3%			

Rice's combination of rushing and receiving skill makes him a very special player. Last year he was the only player in the league with over 200 carries and 60 catches. He's done that now for three straight years, one of only five running backs who has ever accomplished that. (The others: Marcus Allen, Roger Craig, Marshall Faulk, and Priest Holmes.) Our similarity scores say that the most similar backs to Rice over a three-year span have been Thurman Thomas 1989-1991 and Barry Sanders 1990-1992, which is also nice company. Rice became even more valuable in fantasy football when the Ravens jettisoned Willis McGahee and Le'Ron McClain prior to last season and gave him exclusive purview over goal-line duties despite his slight frame. He scored 10 touchdowns on 25 carries inside the seven. Like Matt Forte, Rice's advanced numbers would likely be better if he weren't the primary focus of every opposing defensive coordinator.

Trent Richardson Height: 5-9 Weight: 228 College: Alabama Draft: 2012/1 (3) Born: 10-Jul-1991 Age: 21 Risk: Yellow

Year	Team	G/S	Runs	Yds	Yd/R	TD	FUM	DVOA	Rk	DYAR	Rk	YAR	Suc%	Rec	Pass	Yds	C%	Yd/C	TD	DVOA	Rk	DYAR	Rk
2012	CLE		286	1267	4.4	6		-2.4%						27	35	249	77%	9.2	1	25.0%			

The first time Richardson got significant playing time at Alabama, in the second game of his freshman year, he ran the ball 15 times for 118 yards and two touchdowns. He was generally regarded to be a better prospect than Heisman winner Mark Ingram, who took carries ahead of him and was a first-round pick last year. Production-wise, there are few blemishes on Richardson's record. His +42.6 Adj. POE last season is the third best for a BCS-conference back since 2005, and his 85 percent catch rate suggests that he won't be coming out of the game on many third downs. His 2012 projection would be better if he were teamed with a better passing game to distract the opposing defense.

Stevan Ridley Height: 6-0 Weight: 223 College: LSU Draft: 2011/3 (73) Born: 27-Jan-1989 Age: 23 Risk: Yellow

Year	Team	G/S	Runs	Yds	Yd/R	TD	FUM	DVOA	Rk	DYAR	Rk	YAR	Suc%	Rec	Pass	Yds	C%	Yd/C	TD	DVOA	Rk	DYAR	Rk
2011	NE	16/2	87	441	5.1	1	1	-0.1%	--	31	--	44	51%	3	5	13	60%	4.3	0	-45.5%	--	-9	--
2012	NE		138	628	4.6	7		8.6%						13	20	81	65%	6.2	1	-18.2%			

BenJarvus Green-Ellis is dead. Long live BenJarvus Green-Ellis. Ridley may not be a carbon copy of last year's lead back, but he's close enough. A strong inside runner with patience, excellent pad level, and good balance, Ridley is not a breakaway threat despite his gaudy rookie-year average of 5.1 yards per carry. He also barely registers in the passing game, which means he'll come off the field in favor of Danny Woodhead on third downs. Ridley will fight it out with fellow second-year man Shane Vereen and fading veteran Joseph Addai for carries, and while last year's distribution suggests Ridley has the inside track, the situation is muddy enough to make him a risky fantasy pick.

Javon Ringer Height: 5-9 Weight: 205 College: Michigan State Draft: 2009/5 (173) Born: 2-Feb-1987 Age: 25 Risk: Green

Year	Team	G/S	Runs	Yds	Yd/R	TD	FUM	DVOA	Rk	DYAR	Rk	YAR	Suc%	Rec	Pass	Yds	C%	Yd/C	TD	DVOA	Rk	DYAR	Rk
2009	TEN	7/0	8	48	6.0	0	0	40.4%	--	14	--	14	50%	0	0	0	--	0.0	0	--	--	--	--
2010	TEN	16/0	51	239	4.7	2	0	1.7%	--	17	--	20	37%	7	8	44	88%	6.3	0	13.4%	--	12	--
2011	TEN	12/0	59	185	3.1	1	1	-33.4%	--	-54	--	-46	34%	28	36	187	78%	6.7	0	-13.2%	42	1	42
2012	TEN		57	239	4.2	0		-6.3%						24	30	189	80%	7.9	1	14.3%			

RUNNING BACKS

Were Chris Johnson's struggles in 2011 due to problems on the offensive line? Ringer's regression into the abyss is a strong piece of evidence. Ringer's numbers plummeted across the board and he had the third-worst DVOA of any running back with more than 20 carries. The one thing he did well has nothing to do with the offensive line; he had 16 broken tackles, a very impressive rate of 18.4 percent per touch. He's expected to retain his role behind Johnson this season, but another year like 2011 will likely force the Titans to bring in fresh blood at the position.

Jacquizz Rodgers
Height: 5-6 Weight: 196 College: Oregon State Draft: 2011/5 (145) Born: 6-Feb-1990 Age: 22 Risk: Yellow

Year	Team	G/S	Runs	Yds	Yd/R	TD	FUM	DVOA	Rk	DYAR	Rk	YAR	Suc%	Rec	Pass	Yds	C%	Yd/C	TD	DVOA	Rk	DYAR	Rk
2011	ATL	16/0	57	205	3.6	1	1	-9.8%	--	-3	--	-3	46%	21	28	188	79%	9.0	1	32.1%	4	60	16
2012	ATL		115	489	4.3	3		3.8%						41	52	382	79%	9.3	1	28.9%			

Rodgers led all rookies with 19 broken tackles on just 78 touches. The Falcons didn't appear sure how to use their change-up back last season: after years of Jerious Norwood, they assumed a speed back was someone who fills out the PUP list. Rodgers had six one-carry games and three two-carry games, and he never had more than three catches in a game. The broken tackle data suggests that Rodgers deserves an increased role; any back worth giving one carry per game is worth giving several.

Evan Royster
Height: 6-0 Weight: 218 College: Penn State Draft: 2011/6 (177) Born: 26-Nov-1987 Age: 25 Risk: Green

Year	Team	G/S	Runs	Yds	Yd/R	TD	FUM	DVOA	Rk	DYAR	Rk	YAR	Suc%	Rec	Pass	Yds	C%	Yd/C	TD	DVOA	Rk	DYAR	Rk
2011	WAS	6/2	56	328	5.9	0	0	45.7%	--	122	--	119	64%	9	13	68	69%	7.6	0	-7.4%	--	5	--
2012	WAS		81	372	4.6	1		-3.0%						20	31	166	65%	8.3	0	-5.7%			

Those are some pretty numbers, huh? Royster actually put up the best rushing DVOA ever by a running back with at least 40 carries. He was the sixth back since 1991 with a rushing DVOA over 30% and at least 40 carries. The others were Onterrio Smith (2003), Jerious Norwood (2006), Pierre Thomas (2007), Tashard Choice (2008), and Peyton Hillis (2008). Hillis had that one great year in Cleveland, and Norwood and Thomas have had nice years as part-timers, but in general these players have not turned their fine part-time years into stardom. It is equally unlikely that Royster will do so, but he sure looks like a much better backup than what we all thought Washington was getting with its sixth-round pick.

Brandon Saine
Height: 6-1 Weight: 220 College: Ohio State Draft: 2011/FA Born: 14-Dec-1988 Age: 24 Risk: Yellow

Year	Team	G/S	Runs	Yds	Yd/R	TD	FUM	DVOA	Rk	DYAR	Rk	YAR	Suc%	Rec	Pass	Yds	C%	Yd/C	TD	DVOA	Rk	DYAR	Rk
2011	GB	8/0	18	69	3.8	0	0	-8.8%	--	0	--	2	61%	10	12	69	83%	6.9	0	3.9%	--	11	--
2012	GB		98	479	4.9	3		15.4%						20	25	141	80%	7.0	1	2.1%			

Saine emerged as part of Green Bay's running back committee down the stretch last season, bringing a hint of tempo change to the offense. Though he was never a big-time receiving weapon at Ohio State, the Packers made a point of using Saine in the passing game. Some within the organization have said he may actually have the best hands on the team, but like most backs his age, he is still learning the art of pass protection.

Bernard Scott
Height: 5-11 Weight: 200 College: Abilene Christian Draft: 2009/6 (209) Born: 10-Feb-1984 Age: 28 Risk: Yellow

Year	Team	G/S	Runs	Yds	Yd/R	TD	FUM	DVOA	Rk	DYAR	Rk	YAR	Suc%	Rec	Pass	Yds	C%	Yd/C	TD	DVOA	Rk	DYAR	Rk
2009	CIN	13/2	74	321	4.3	0	1	-10.1%	--	-9	--	-5	43%	5	8	67	63%	13.4	0	69.5%	--	27	--
2010	CIN	16/0	61	299	4.9	1	0	17.6%	--	69	--	70	54%	11	13	60	85%	5.5	0	-10.6%	--	2	--
2011	CIN	16/1	112	380	3.4	3	0	-11.0%	46	-11	44	-6	43%	13	17	38	76%	2.9	0	-62.9%	--	-42	--
2012	CIN		134	544	4.0	3		-5.3%						20	32	125	63%	6.3	1	-26.3%			

It's now or never for Scott, as the departure of Cedric Benson gives him a shot at getting the lion's share of carries. Scott regressed in 2011 after putting up solid numbers in a small sample size in 2010. His speed is mitigated somewhat by the slow tracks in the AFC North, but Scott's ability to get outside and elude tacklers in confined spaces is a weapon that has yet to be fully utilized by the Bengals. He broke 11 tackles in just 112 carries. Scott also has good hands, and he should see most of the early-down screen work over BenJarvus Green-Ellis.

Steve Slaton
Height: 5-9 Weight: 197 College: West Virginia Draft: 2008/3 (89) Born: 4-Jan-1986 Age: 27 Risk: Yellow

Year	Team	G/S	Runs	Yds	Yd/R	TD	FUM	DVOA	Rk	DYAR	Rk	YAR	Suc%	Rec	Pass	Yds	C%	Yd/C	TD	DVOA	Rk	DYAR	Rk
2009	HOU	11/10	131	437	3.3	3	7	-32.9%	50	-122	50	-133	35%	44	55	417	80%	9.5	4	41.8%	3	168	2
2010	HOU	12/1	19	93	4.9	0	0	9.1%	--	15	--	15	47%	3	4	11	75%	3.7	0	-55.9%	--	-9	--
2011	2TM	6/0	24	84	3.5	1	0	-14.6%	--	-6	--	-16	38%	3	4	3	75%	1.0	0	-73.9%	--	-11	--
2012	MIA		32	134	4.1	1		-6.3%						6	8	41	75%	6.9	0	-4.1%			

Slaton signed a one-year contract for $765,000 with the Dolphins in March. The deal is incredibly cap friendly; the Dolphins could cut him and he'd count just $65,000 against the cap. Joe Philbin called Slaton a "good fit" for the offense, and Slaton did have a fine 11-carry, 55-yard game in the season finale, but he hasn't been the same player since his neck required surgery. Rookie Lamar Miller is the favorite to win the third running back job, and the Dolphins should be focused on rebuilding, not reclamation.

Kevin Smith
Height: 6-1 Weight: 217 College: UCF Draft: 2008/3 (64) Born: 17-Dec-1986 Age: 26 Risk: Yellow

Year	Team	G/S	Runs	Yds	Yd/R	TD	FUM	DVOA	Rk	DYAR	Rk	YAR	Suc%	Rec	Pass	Yds	C%	Yd/C	TD	DVOA	Rk	DYAR	Rk
2009	DET	13/13	217	747	3.4	4	3	-12.4%	42	-36	43	-73	44%	4	57	41	72%	10.3	1	25.7%	7	127	3
2010	DET	6/0	34	133	3.9	0	1	-26.4%	--	-23	--	-25	29%	11	16	123	69%	11.2	0	38.4%	--	50	--
2011	DET	7/4	72	356	4.9	4	1	5.1%	--	42	--	72	40%	22	28	179	79%	8.1	3	19.4%	12	52	20
2012	DET		74	343	4.7	2		2.0%						25	30	199	83%	8.0	0	16.5%			

Injuries appeared to have pushed Smith out of football last season, but what injuries taketh away, injuries sometimes giveth back. Smith stayed in close touch with Lions GM Martin Mayhew and was finally granted an opportunity to return midway through 2011, when Detroit's depth chart at running back was decimated. In his second game back, Smith rushed for 140 yards on 16 carries (mad props to the the 2011 Panthers run defense), but he never ran for more than 50 yards in any game after that. To be fair, the Lions never prioritized the run. Smith did contribute in spurts as a receiver, showing his newfound lateral quickness and agility when in space. An ankle injury compromised his rhythm in early December but he returned and contributed down the stretch. With last year's first-round pick Mikel Leshoure back from his Achilles injury, Smith's future in Detroit may depend on the status of Jahvid Best.

Jason Snelling
Height: 5-11 Weight: 235 College: Virginia Draft: 2007/7 (244) Born: 29-Dec-1983 Age: 29 Risk: Green

Year	Team	G/S	Runs	Yds	Yd/R	TD	FUM	DVOA	Rk	DYAR	Rk	YAR	Suc%	Rec	Pass	Yds	C%	Yd/C	TD	DVOA	Rk	DYAR	Rk
2009	ATL	14/2	142	613	4.3	4	2	0.5%	26	62	25	73	46%	30	39	259	77%	8.6	1	25.6%	8	81	13
2010	ATL	14/0	87	324	3.7	2	2	-3.8%	--	26	--	27	44%	44	51	303	86%	6.9	3	1.1%	31	39	26
2011	ATL	15/0	44	151	3.4	0	0	-22.9%	--	-25	--	-22	39%	26	32	179	81%	6.9	1	24.7%	8	60	15
2012	ATL		45	199	4.4	1		7.5%						26	33	206	79%	7.9	1	16.9%			

Snelling saw his role in the offense reduced last season; Jacquizz Rodgers absorbed some of the touches, but the Falcons also threw more passes, and Snelling did not have to replace Michael Turner early in any games, as he did in 2010. Rodgers is likely to play an even larger role in 2012, but Snelling still has a niche as a power back, passing-down blocker, and Turner's stunt double.

342 RUNNING BACKS

C.J. Spiller   Height: 5-11   Weight: 195   College: Clemson   Draft: 2010/1 (9)   Born: 15-Aug-1987   Age: 25   Risk: Green

Year	Team	G/S	Runs	Yds	Yd/R	TD	FUM	DVOA	Rk	DYAR	Rk	YAR	Suc%	Rec	Pass	Yds	C%	Yd/C	TD	DVOA	Rk	DYAR	Rk
2010	BUF	14/1	74	283	3.8	0	2	-11.3%	--	-11	--	-22	43%	24	30	157	80%	6.5	1	3.1%	27	25	35
2011	BUF	16/11	107	561	5.2	4	2	6.4%	13	68	23	62	51%	39	54	269	74%	6.9	2	10.4%	21	79	12
2012	BUF		123	552	4.5	2		-1.0%						43	51	317	84%	7.4	0	8.2%			

After a lost rookie season, Spiller rebounded nicely with a late-season run where he totaled at least 100 all-purpose yards in four of his last five games, sparking some hope that he can justify his high draft spot. No one doubts Spiller's speed, but he doesn't have particularly good instincts as a runner and needs the offensive formation and play call to manufacture space for him. Spiller's four-yard touchdown against Denver in Week 16 was a good example, as the Bills used a spread look to remove defenders from the box, giving Spiller the space to make a quick jump cut and accelerate into the end zone. Spiller will likely lose a training camp battle for the starting spot to Fred Jackson, but he still figures to see the field a lot as both a runner and a receiver because the Bills don't have many players with his skill set. Spiller lined up at wide receiver more often than any other running back, and the identity of the back at number two makes this the perfect place for this table:

Running Backs Most Frequently Used at Wide Receiver, 2011

Player	Team	Plays	Player	Team	Plays	Player	Team	Plays
C.J. Spiller	BUF	139	Steven Jackson	STL	47	Chris Johnson	TEN	38
Darren Sproles	NO	126	Dexter McCluster	KC	44	Matt Forte	CHI	37
Fred Jackson	BUF	83	Marcel Reece	OAK	44	LeSean McCoy	PHI	36
Danny Woodhead	NE	62	Ray Rice	BAL	41	Jahvid Best	DET	34

Includes lining up in the slot or wide; plays cancelled by Defensive Pass Interference included.

Darren Sproles   Height: 5-6   Weight: 181   College: Kansas State   Draft: 2005/4 (130)   Born: 20-Jun-1983   Age: 29   Risk: Green

Year	Team	G/S	Runs	Yds	Yd/R	TD	FUM	DVOA	Rk	DYAR	Rk	YAR	Suc%	Rec	Pass	Yds	C%	Yd/C	TD	DVOA	Rk	DYAR	Rk
2009	SD	16/2	93	343	3.7	3	0	-15.3%	--	-19	--	-5	41%	45	57	497	79%	11.0	4	44.4%	2	181	1
2010	SD	16/3	50	267	5.3	0	1	-20.1%	--	-20	--	-9	34%	59	75	520	79%	8.8	2	21.9%	11	146	6
2011	NO	16/4	87	603	6.9	2	0	46.2%	--	193	--	194	53%	86	111	710	77%	8.3	7	25.3%	7	258	1
2012	NO		76	371	4.9	1		6.6%						74	92	673	80%	9.1	4	27.4%			

Sproles posted a remarkable 67.0% DVOA in 24 red-zone targets, averaging 5.8 yards per red-zone pass. Sproles was able to turn swing passes into touchdowns, picked up positive yardage on red-zone screens (a tricky task), and made the shallow cross a deadly weapon when defenses patrolled the back of the end zone in search of Marques Colston and Jimmy Graham. All of these plays were in the game plan when Reggie Bush played the Sproles role, but while Bush had his moments (he really did, check the highlights!), he never executed them like Sproles. The Saints committee system will limit Sproles to 15 offensive touches per game, and speed backs who average 6.9 yards per carry one year sometimes drop to 2.9 yards per carry the next. As a fantasy option, Sproles is a volatile commodity. As an all-purpose weapon on offense and special teams, Sproles is as reliable as they come.

James Starks   Height: 6-2   Weight: 218   College: Buffalo   Draft: 2010/6 (193)   Born: 25-Feb-1986   Age: 26   Risk: Green

Year	Team	G/S	Runs	Yds	Yd/R	TD	FUM	DVOA	Rk	DYAR	Rk	YAR	Suc%	Rec	Pass	Yds	C%	Yd/C	TD	DVOA	Rk	DYAR	Rk
2010	GB	3/0	29	101	3.5	0	0	6.2%	--	14	--	3	48%	2	4	15	50%	7.5	0	-32.3%	--	-4	--
2011	GB	13/2	133	578	4.3	1	2	-4.5%	37	22	39	6	49%	29	38	216	79%	7.4	0	6.4%	23	39	28
2012	GB		183	758	4.1	5		1.8%						37	46	309	80%	8.3	1	18.1%			

Starks lacks the dynamic qualities of a featured back, but he's proven to be serviceable as a complementary piece. He effectively iced games a few times last season as a fresh-legged, high-volume fourth-quarter ballcarrier. He is a decent pass-blocker and out-of-the-backfield receiver but is by no means a traditional third-down back. Being on the plus side of 215 pounds, Starks can handle short-yardage carries, though he runs naturally a little upright and is fairly tall to begin with. Really, Starks can be whatever the Packers need him to be, just as long as they don't need him to be a star.

LaRod Stephens-Howling Height: 5-7 Weight: 180 College: Pittsburgh Draft: 2009/7 (240) Born: 26-Apr-1987 Age: 25 Risk: Green

Year	Team	G/S	Runs	Yds	Yd/R	TD	FUM	DVOA	Rk	DYAR	Rk	YAR	Suc%	Rec	Pass	Yds	C%	Yd/C	TD	DVOA	Rk	DYAR	Rk
2009	ARI	16/2	6	15	2.5	0	1	-21.9%	--	-3	--	-4	33%	10	18	83	56%	8.3	1	-28.0%	--	-14	--
2010	ARI	13/2	23	113	4.9	1	0	8.9%	--	17	--	20	54%	16	22	111	68%	6.9	0	-6.0%	--	10	--
2011	ARI	14/1	43	167	3.9	0	0	-16.7%	--	-14	--	-17	40%	13	17	234	76%	18.0	2	85.3%	--	101	--
2012	ARI		26	116	4.4	0		-2.2%						38	47	421	81%	11.1	1	42.9%			

Though he played less than Chester Taylor, Stephens-Howling still ranked second on the team in rushing attempts and yards and had a pair of touchdowns that went 50 or more yards as a receiver, including a 52-yarder in overtime against the St. Louis Rams. With Ryan Williams expected back, Stephens-Howling will likely have a lesser role on offense in 2012, but the Cardinals still value his play-making ability: They placed a "second-round" restricted free agent tender (worth $1.927 million in base salary) on him this offseason.

Jonathan Stewart Height: 5-10 Weight: 235 College: Oregon Draft: 2008/1 (13) Born: 21-Mar-1987 Age: 25 Risk: Green

Year	Team	G/S	Runs	Yds	Yd/R	TD	FUM	DVOA	Rk	DYAR	Rk	YAR	Suc%	Rec	Pass	Yds	C%	Yd/C	TD	DVOA	Rk	DYAR	Rk
2009	CAR	16/3	221	1133	5.1	10	3	12.8%	8	184	6	188	50%	18	26	139	69%	7.7	1	14.5%	16	37	30
2010	CAR	14/7	178	770	4.3	2	4	-12.2%	37	-18	37	-14	36%	8	14	103	57%	12.9	1	21.8%	--	28	--
2011	CAR	16/3	142	761	5.4	4	1	23.4%	2	194	4	178	53%	47	61	413	77%	8.8	1	18.2%	15	102	7
2012	CAR		141	733	5.2	4		16.2%						38	46	377	83%	9.9	1	41.8%			

Stewart is fantasy football poison. He did not carry more than 14 times in any game last season, and now that Cam Newton has brought the goal-line option to Carolina, there is no reason to think he will earn any more than the ten scattered goal-to-go carries he received last year. After avoiding Stewart in your fantasy draft, you can enjoy him on the field: He's powerful, catches the ball well, and makes a deadly second counter-punch to Newton and DeAngelo Williams. If the Panthers ever devise a wishbone package, especially now that Mike Tolbert is at fullback, it would be the coolest thing in the world.

Phillip Tanner Height: 6-0 Weight: 214 College: Middle Tennessee Draft: 2011/FA Born: 8-Aug-1988 Age: 24 Risk: Yellow

Year	Team	G/S	Runs	Yds	Yd/R	TD	FUM	DVOA	Rk	DYAR	Rk	YAR	Suc%	Rec	Pass	Yds	C%	Yd/C	TD	DVOA	Rk	DYAR	Rk
2011	DAL	9/0	22	76	3.5	1	0	-20.2%	--	-12	--	-2	45%	2	2	19	100%	9.5	0	93.3%	--	15	--
2012	DAL		45	168	3.7	1		-14.8%						20	23	163	87%	8.2	1	22.9%			

Tanner is best known for losing his helmet and scoring a touchdown against San Diego last year. Officially, the play was blown dead at the spot where Tanner's helmet came off, and Dallas committed a procedural penalty on the play, and it was the preseason anyway, so in many ways, it never really mattered. After Felix Jones was injured, Tanner saw some action as the change-of-pace back behind DeMarco Murray. He had a 17-yard run against St. Louis, but his other 21 carries averaged 2.8 yards apiece before he went on injured reserve with a bad hamstring. He'll compete with a pair of undrafted free agents (South Florida's Darrell Scott and North Texas' Lance Dunbar) to be the Cowboys' third back this fall.

Ben Tate Height: 5-11 Weight: 220 College: Auburn Draft: 2010/2 (58) Born: 21-Aug-1988 Age: 24 Risk: Yellow

Year	Team	G/S	Runs	Yds	Yd/R	TD	FUM	DVOA	Rk	DYAR	Rk	YAR	Suc%	Rec	Pass	Yds	C%	Yd/C	TD	DVOA	Rk	DYAR	Rk
2011	HOU	15/2	175	942	5.4	4	4	12.5%	8	151	10	162	53%	13	19	98	68%	7.5	0	-3.3%	--	11	--
2012	HOU		126	632	5.0	3		12.4%						15	25	131	60%	8.8	0	-5.9%			

You just read Jonathan Stewart's player comment, now you're going to read it again. A highly-drafted back who is buried behind a more-established and better overall runner, Tate will be a must-own handcuff who sends fantasy owners scrambling to the waiver wire if Arian Foster gets hurt. Just don't expect a repeat of last year's usage, which was a function of Foster's hamstring, blowouts, and a meaningless Week 17 game. Tate was the target of trade rumors before the draft, and will likely find himself in that position again (barring injury) next offseason as well.

Daniel Thomas
Height: 6-2 Weight: 228 College: Kansas State Draft: 2011/2 (62) Born: 29-Oct-1987 Age: 25 Risk: Yellow

Year	Team	G/S	Runs	Yds	Yd/R	TD	FUM	DVOA	Rk	DYAR	Rk	YAR	Suc%	Rec	Pass	Yds	C%	Yd/C	TD	DVOA	Rk	DYAR	Rk
2011	MIA	13/2	165	581	3.5	0	2	-24.7%	50	-110	51	-100	42%	12	16	72	75%	6.0	1	11.5%	--	20	--
2012	MIA		191	805	4.2	6		-3.7%						13	21	87	62%	6.7	0	-24.3%			

Thomas had a miserable training camp in 2011, constantly earning Tony Sparano's wrath for tiptoeing to the line and making mistakes in blitz pickup. Thomas later admitted that he "didn't know what the hell [he] was doing" in camp; he started to figure things out early in the season (202 yards in one two-game stretch), but a nagging hamstring injury, and the sudden emergence of "Reggie Bush the Reliable Human," relegated him to a secondary role. Thomas is a 230-pounder who should be a natural complement to Bush as a committee goal-line rusher. If he runs hard and stays healthy, that is.

Pierre Thomas
Height: 5-11 Weight: 210 College: Illinois Draft: 2007/FA Born: 18-Dec-1984 Age: 28 Risk: Yellow

Year	Team	G/S	Runs	Yds	Yd/R	TD	FUM	DVOA	Rk	DYAR	Rk	YAR	Suc%	Rec	Pass	Yds	C%	Yd/C	TD	DVOA	Rk	DYAR	Rk
2009	NO	14/6	147	793	5.4	6	2	24.8%	1	208	5	197	56%	39	45	302	87%	7.7	2	20.1%	12	80	15
2010	NO	6/3	83	269	3.2	2	0	0.6%	--	36	--	24	50%	29	30	201	100%	6.9	0	17.0%	13	56	19
2011	NO	16/7	110	562	5.1	5	1	30.0%	1	180	5	180	61%	50	59	425	85%	8.5	1	15.5%	17	101	8
2012	NO		103	483	4.7	3		5.6%						51	61	432	84%	8.5	3	30.8%			

Thomas received five to ten carries in all but one game last year. He caught a pass in every game, but only caught five or more passes twice. He went 3-for-7 on goal-to-go touchdown conversions, but he wasn't a traditional goal-line back, as the Saints also gave opportunities to Mark Ingram, Darren Sproles, and fullback Jed Collins when they weren't just throwing jumpballs at Jimmy Graham. Thomas puttered through 2011, producing 60 to 100 yards from scrimmage per game while his team kicked the spittle out of opponents, helping the cause with very little fanfare. He can do more if called upon, but the same can be said of about a dozen players in the Saints' offensive caucus.

Mike Tolbert
Height: 5-9 Weight: 243 College: Coastal Carolina Draft: 2008/FA Born: 23-Nov-1985 Age: 27 Risk: Green

Year	Team	G/S	Runs	Yds	Yd/R	TD	FUM	DVOA	Rk	DYAR	Rk	YAR	Suc%	Rec	Pass	Yds	C%	Yd/C	TD	DVOA	Rk	DYAR	Rk
2009	SD	16/3	25	148	5.9	1	1	32.5%	--	48	--	57	72%	17	22	192	77%	11.3	3	19.4%	--	47	--
2010	SD	15/4	182	735	4.0	11	5	-2.0%	24	46	25	66	51%	25	30	216	87%	8.6	0	32.3%	6	76	16
2011	SD	15/1	121	490	4.0	8	2	-3.1%	34	30	35	49	48%	54	79	433	68%	8.0	2	-2.6%	30	51	21
2012	CAR		66	305	4.6	3		13.2%						27	33	178	82%	6.6	1	11.0%			

Tolbert lost some of his workload to an improved Ryan Mathews, but he continued to play frequently on third down and in the red zone. Unfortunately for the Chargers, he was the league's second-worst goal-line back, scoring 2.7 fewer touchdowns than expected, after an above-average year in 2010. He was a reasonably productive runner and receiver on third down. There's not a lot of suddenness or burst to his game, but he plays with good power and tends to end up with more yards than you thought he gained. He passed up more money from San Diego to sign with the Panthers, who sound like they'll use him as a fullback. That's a bit of an odd move, as he didn't really serve as a lead blocker at all his past two seasons in San Diego.

LaDainian Tomlinson
Height: 5-10 Weight: 221 College: TCU Draft: 2001/1 (5) Born: 23-Jun-1979 Age: 33 Risk: N/A

Year	Team	G/S	Runs	Yds	Yd/R	TD	FUM	DVOA	Rk	DYAR	Rk	YAR	Suc%	Rec	Pass	Yds	C%	Yd/C	TD	DVOA	Rk	DYAR	Rk
2009	SD	14/14	223	730	3.3	12	2	-11.9%	41	-21	41	-12	43%	20	30	154	67%	7.7	0	-31.2%	52	-28	52
2010	NYJ	15/13	219	914	4.2	6	4	3.1%	16	107	15	98	44%	52	79	368	66%	7.1	0	-21.8%	48	-35	51
2011	NYJ	14/1	75	280	3.7	1	0	-5.2%	--	10	--	12	45%	42	60	449	70%	10.7	2	15.5%	18	83	11

Requiem for the greatest running back of the last decade, Football Outsiders-style: LaDainian Tomlinson finished in the top five in rushing DYAR for five of six years between 2002 and 2007. His best season was 2006, when he set the NFL record with 28 rushing touchdowns and 31 total touchdowns; his 460 rushing DYAR that season are tenth all-time and his 579 combined rushing and receiving DYAR that season are tied for 11th all-time. His advanced receiving numbers would have been even better if the Chargers hadn't dumped the ball off to him in frustrating, impossible situations so often in his early years. His 137 targets in 2003 represent the highest single-season total for a running back in our database, with Richie Anderson and Larry Centers the only other backs to hit 125.

Ryan Torain
Height: 6-0 Weight: 222 College: Arizona State Draft: 2008/5 (139) Born: 10-Aug-1986 Age: 26 Risk: N/A

Year	Team	G/S	Runs	Yds	Yd/R	TD	FUM	DVOA	Rk	DYAR	Rk	YAR	Suc%	Rec	Pass	Yds	C%	Yd/C	TD	DVOA	Rk	DYAR	Rk
2010	WAS	10/8	164	742	4.5	4	2	-5.9%	30	-6	34	31	44%	18	27	125	67%	6.9	2	9.1%	23	34	30
2011	WAS	8/4	59	200	3.4	1	1	-34.1%	--	-60	--	-53	41%	6	9	23	67%	3.8	0	-56.6%	--	-17	--

Torain started the last four games of the 2010 season, so it was a bit of a surprise when Tim Hightower was installed ahead of him as Washington's 2011 starter. Then Hightower got hurt, and Torain quickly answered the questions about his not starting. Since Mike Shanahan was his biggest booster among NFL coaches, Torain's career is probably done.

Michael Turner
Height: 5-10 Weight: 247 College: Northern Illinois Draft: 2004/5 (154) Born: 13-Feb-1982 Age: 30 Risk: Yellow

Year	Team	G/S	Runs	Yds	Yd/R	TD	FUM	DVOA	Rk	DYAR	Rk	YAR	Suc%	Rec	Pass	Yds	C%	Yd/C	TD	DVOA	Rk	DYAR	Rk
2009	ATL	11/11	178	871	4.9	10	4	9.1%	12	132	14	138	49%	5	7	35	71%	7.0	0	5.4%	--	9	--
2010	ATL	16/15	334	1371	4.1	12	2	-1.3%	22	96	18	128	46%	12	20	85	60%	7.1	0	-28.4%	--	-16	--
2011	ATL	16/15	301	1340	4.5	11	3	-3.4%	36	66	25	101	45%	17	26	168	65%	9.9	0	6.9%	22	31	32
2012	ATL		240	1069	4.5	8		12.0%						13	20	81	65%	6.2	0	-17.5%			

Turner now has just 51 career receptions, the lowest total in NFL history for any receiver with more than 6,000 rushing yards. If he gains 638 more yards before he catches four more passes, he will pass George Rogers as the most one-dimensional running back in history, and he is all but assured of becoming the only running back among the top 50 all-time rushing leaders with fewer than 100 receptions.

For his career, Turner is now two receiving yards above replacement level, though he really belongs in an outlier category: Few featured backs are thrown to so infrequently that their receiving stats drop into "low sample size" territory. Last season's rise from the flat line to something downright measurable represents a real increase in Turner's value: The need to replace him on every single passing down forced the Falcons to rely too much on the talents of Jerious Norwood or Jason Snelling, and it all but eradicated the screen pass from their arsenal over the last few seasons. A 20-carry, two-target Turner beats a 25-carry, zero-target Turner any day, although it looks like the Falcons may instead be moving in the direction of a 15-carry, two-target Turner, making lots of noise this offseason about moving to a more committee-style running back rotation.

We would be remiss if we didn't mention that Turner finished second in our count of broken tackles last season. In fact, though his other stats have declined each year, his broken tackles have gone up from 28 to 38 to 42 since we began tracking that stat in 2009.

346 RUNNING BACKS

Shane Vereen
Height: 5-10 Weight: 205 College: California Draft: 2011/2 (56) Born: 2-Mar-1989 Age: 23 Risk: Yellow

Year	Team	G/S	Runs	Yds	Yd/R	TD	FUM	DVOA	Rk	DYAR	Rk	YAR	Suc%	Rec	Pass	Yds	C%	Yd/C	TD	DVOA	Rk	DYAR	Rk
2011	NE	5/0	15	57	3.8	1	0	-2.1%	--	4	--	1	40%	0	--	0	--	0.0	0	--	--	--	--
2012	NE		120	579	4.8	6		18.5%						27	36	285	75%	10.6	2	34.5%			

Vereen is flying beneath the radar due to a combination of his injury-plagued rookie season, the emergence of draft classmate Stevan Ridley, and the general glut of running backs on the Patriots depth chart. That could be a mistake. Vereen was a higher draft choice than Ridley, and he ran with the first-team during offseason practices. While all signs point to another year of running back-by-committee in New England, Vereen's chances of carving out a slight majority of the carries look about as good as anyone's. His unimpressive college numbers (1.88 Highlight Yards per carry, -3.7 Adj. POE) suggest that Vereen is unlikely to develop into a superstar, but you don't have to be Adrian Peterson to put up decent numbers when you constantly face seven or eight defensive backs.

Derrick Ward
Height: 5-11 Weight: 233 College: Fresno State Draft: 2004/7 (235) Born: 30-Aug-1980 Age: 32 Risk: N/A

Year	Team	G/S	Runs	Yds	Yd/R	TD	FUM	DVOA	Rk	DYAR	Rk	YAR	Suc%	Rec	Pass	Yds	C%	Yd/C	TD	DVOA	Rk	DYAR	Rk
2009	TB	14/1	114	409	3.6	1	0	-20.8%	47	-56	44	-66	36%	20	24	150	83%	7.5	2	49.6%	--	75	--
2010	HOU	16/0	50	315	6.3	4	1	40.6%	--	107	--	101	57%	7	11	61	64%	8.7	0	-15.9%	--	-1	--
2011	HOU	12/1	45	154	3.4	2	0	-5.9%	--	5	--	15	49%	0	1	0	0%	0.0	0	-40.4%	--	0	--

In 2011, the average Derrick Ward carry came with the Texans sporting a 13-point lead. That includes his 12 carries that came throughout a competitive Week 17 game that Houston wasn't trying to win. Unsigned as of press time, this may be the end of the line for Ward, who was one of the key committee backs for the late 2000s Giants. He never truly did get that shot as a team's lead back, but at least he's got a championship ring.

D.J. Ware
Height: 6-1 Weight: 225 College: Georgia Draft: 2007/FA Born: 10-Feb-1985 Age: 27 Risk: Green

Year	Team	G/S	Runs	Yds	Yd/R	TD	FUM	DVOA	Rk	DYAR	Rk	YAR	Suc%	Rec	Pass	Yds	C%	Yd/C	TD	DVOA	Rk	DYAR	Rk
2009	NYG	8/0	13	73	5.6	1	1	19.3%	--	14	--	15	46%	3	4	15	75%	5.0	0	-4.5%	--	1	--
2010	NYG	14/0	20	73	3.7	0	0	3.8%	--	11	--	14	65%	7	9	67	78%	9.6	0	33.8%	--	21	--
2011	NYG	16/1	46	163	3.5	0	0	-7.1%	--	3	--	0	39%	27	37	170	73%	6.3	0	-13.8%	43	0	43
2012	NYG		39	139	3.6	2		-7.7%						32	43	279	74%	8.7	1	11.7%			

Ware finally got a little more playing time in 2011, but didn't do much with it. Along with the disappointing numbers listed above, he had just four carries for 10 yards in the playoffs. Any hope he may have had for an expanded role was dashed when the Giants drafted David Wilson. If the Giants decide to keep just three running backs on the team, they'll have to decide if they prefer power (Ware) or speed (Da'Rel Scott).

Leon Washington
Height: 5-8 Weight: 210 College: Florida State Draft: 2006/4 (117) Born: 29-Aug-1982 Age: 30 Risk: Green

Year	Team	G/S	Runs	Yds	Yd/R	TD	FUM	DVOA	Rk	DYAR	Rk	YAR	Suc%	Rec	Pass	Yds	C%	Yd/C	TD	DVOA	Rk	DYAR	Rk
2009	NYJ	7/0	72	331	4.6	0	1	-16.8%	--	-16	--	-3	35%	15	26	131	58%	8.7	0	-9.4%	39	5	44
2010	SEA	16/0	27	100	3.7	1	0	0.9%	--	13	--	4	44%	9	13	79	69%	8.8	0	14.6%	--	21	--
2011	SEA	16/1	53	248	4.7	1	0	-9.1%	--	-1	--	0	36%	10	14	48	71%	4.8	0	-29.8%	--	-14	--
2012	SEA		31	145	4.8	1		7.1%						13	20	99	65%	7.6	0	-7.5%			

As expected, the new kickoff rules negated much of Washington's value. After tying for the league lead with three kick-return touchdowns and ranking second with 17.8 estimated points of field position on kickoffs in 2010, Washington was held without a touchdown and dropped to 0.8 estimated points of field position in 2011. Washington's role in the Seahawks' backfield remained as the No. 3 behind workhorse Marshawn Lynch and the similarly-skilled Justin Forsett. In considerably less playing time, Washington would distinguish himself from Forsett, posting positive DVOAs on first and second down and showing his home-run potential with a

48-yard touchdown run in the regular season finale against the Cardinals. With the Seahawks moving on from Forsett, Washington will open camp competing with fourth-round pick Robert Turbin and journeyman Kregg Lumpkin for the No. 2 role behind Lynch.

Beanie Wells
Height: 6-1 Weight: 235 College: Ohio State Draft: 2009/1 (31) Born: 7-Aug-1988 Age: 24 Risk: Yellow

Year	Team	G/S	Runs	Yds	Yd/R	TD	FUM	DVOA	Rk	DYAR	Rk	YAR	Suc%	Rec	Pass	Yds	C%	Yd/C	TD	DVOA	Rk	DYAR	Rk
2009	ARI	16/0	176	793	4.5	7	6	-0.6%	29	45	31	36	53%	12	16	143	75%	11.9	0	29.8%	--	44	--
2010	ARI	13/2	116	397	3.4	2	1	-13.8%	40	-23	39	-20	45%	5	8	74	63%	14.8	0	27.3%	--	21	--
2011	ARI	14/14	245	1047	4.3	10	4	1.0%	27	101	19	99	51%	10	16	52	63%	5.2	0	-44.0%	--	-22	--
2012	ARI		158	611	3.9	3		-10.2%						18	25	125	72%	6.9	1	-5.7%			

Ryan Williams was drafted to push Wells, but when Williams suffered a season-ending knee injury, Wells ended up with career bests in rushing yards, touchdowns, DYAR and DVOA. Yet questions remain. According to our game charters, Wells broke more tackles in 2011 (15), but his 5.9 percent broke tackle rate was still the lowest among NFL players with at least 15 broken tackles charted. 52 percent of Wells' rushing yards came in four of the 14 games he played last season and, with the notable exception of a 228-yard performance against the St. Louis Rams (one of the league's worst run defenses), he was less effective after suffering a right knee injury in October. Wells underwent surgery on the joint in January, a procedure he would later describe as "complicated" while refusing to confirm or deny that meant microfracture. The club expects him to be ready for training camp, where he and Williams will compete for carries.

Cadillac Williams
Height: 5-11 Weight: 217 College: Auburn Draft: 2005/1 (5) Born: 21-Apr-1982 Age: 30 Risk: N/A

Year	Team	G/S	Runs	Yds	Yd/R	TD	FUM	DVOA	Rk	DYAR	Rk	YAR	Suc%	Rec	Pass	Yds	C%	Yd/C	TD	DVOA	Rk	DYAR	Rk
2009	TB	16/15	211	823	3.9	4	1	-4.4%	33	37	32	26	38%	28	40	217	73%	7.8	3	20.2%	11	70	19
2010	TB	16/9	125	437	3.5	2	1	-22.4%	45	-65	42	-71	36%	46	64	355	72%	7.7	1	2.5%	28	58	18
2011	STL	11/1	87	361	4.1	1	1	6.2%	--	52	--	49	41%	14	23	93	61%	6.6	0	-42.7%	--	-40	--

Cadillac served admirably as Steven Jackson's backup in 2011, running for 166 yards (4.5 per carry) in two mid-game relief appearances. However, halmstring and calf injuries limited him for the rest of the season, and renewed concerns that the 30-year-old former gruesome-injury sufferer is done.

DeAngelo Williams
Height: 5-8 Weight: 210 College: Memphis Draft: 2006/1 (27) Born: 25-Apr-1983 Age: 29 Risk: Green

Year	Team	G/S	Runs	Yds	Yd/R	TD	FUM	DVOA	Rk	DYAR	Rk	YAR	Suc%	Rec	Pass	Yds	C%	Yd/C	TD	DVOA	Rk	DYAR	Rk
2009	CAR	13/13	216	1117	5.2	7	3	11.3%	10	172	8	159	45%	29	41	252	71%	8.7	0	22.7%	10	87	11
2010	CAR	6/6	87	361	4.1	1	1	-17.2%	--	-16	--	-18	30%	11	13	61	85%	5.5	0	-2.6%	--	8	--
2011	CAR	16/14	155	836	5.4	7	0	18.0%	3	158	8	147	46%	16	25	135	64%	8.4	0	5.3%	24	27	34
2012	CAR		153	764	5.0	5		15.4%						23	30	202	77%	8.8	1	20.7%			

On outside runs (listed as "left end" or "right end"), Williams carried 34 times for 372 yards, 11.3 yards per carry, and three touchdowns. The numbers are skewed by runs of 74, 69, 29, 26, 22, 20 and 20 yards, but when over 20 percent of a player's runs in a given category are big gains, maybe it isn't really "skewing." Williams is four carries away from joining Jim Brown and Joe Perry as the only players in NFL history with 1,000 career carries and over five yards per carry. (Barry Sanders only reaches five yards per carry by rounding). Whether he will stay there very long is another matter: One weak season could push Williams down to 4.9 yards per carry, or below, for his career. Williams is a unique player who is best compared to 1970s backs like Lawrence McCutcheon or Chuck Foreman, speedsters who shared carries for their whole careers. Williams proves that the "little" back can thrive in a 20-touch role if used properly, and that often it is the big back who is better used as the change-up.

RUNNING BACKS

Keiland Williams
Height: 5-11 Weight: 233 College: LSU Draft: 2010/FA Born: 14-Aug-1986 Age: 26 Risk: Red

Year	Team	G/S	Runs	Yds	Yd/R	TD	FUM	DVOA	Rk	DYAR	Rk	YAR	Suc%	Rec	Pass	Yds	C%	Yd/C	TD	DVOA	Rk	DYAR	Rk
2010	WAS	15/3	65	261	4.0	3	1	12.7%	--	52	--	36	51%	39	58	309	67%	7.9	2	-15.1%	47	-4	47
2011	DET	15/0	58	195	3.4	2	2	-29.2%	--	-53	--	-68	34%	8	8	62	100%	7.8	0	55.4%	--	34	--
2012	DET		40	183	4.6	1		7.2%						11	14	76	79%	6.9	0	5.2%			

Williams showed some compactness as an inside runner last season, though he never got a large enough chunk of carries to carve out an identity. His lone fumble (Week 11 against the Panthers) immediately landed him in Jim Schwartz's doghouse. A leash that short is only given to players whom the coaching staff feels are nothing special. Williams has better short-area elusiveness than you might guess, and he caught 39 passes for Washington in 2010. There's probably a No. 3 spot for him on the depth chart of most teams.

Ricky Williams
Height: 5-10 Weight: 226 College: Texas Draft: 1999/1 (5) Born: 21-May-1977 Age: 35 Risk: N/A

Year	Team	G/S	Runs	Yds	Yd/R	TD	FUM	DVOA	Rk	DYAR	Rk	YAR	Suc%	Rec	Pass	Yds	C%	Yd/C	TD	DVOA	Rk	DYAR	Rk
2009	MIA	16/7	241	1121	4.7	11	5	7.1%	15	168	9	176	55%	35	53	264	66%	7.5	2	-10.4%	43	10	40
2010	MIA	16/0	159	673	4.2	2	4	-3.1%	26	32	27	29	53%	19	30	141	63%	7.4	1	-12.7%	43	2	43
2011	BAL	16/0	108	444	4.1	2	2	-5.2%	39	15	40	10	51%	13	20	83	65%	6.4	0	-17.9%	--	-5	--

For such an abnormal individual off the field, the end of Williams' on-field career was about as normal as it comes for a veteran running back: not with a bang, but a whimper. Williams ends his career 26th in lifetime rushing yardage (10,009 yards) and is one of only three backs with more than 8,500 rushing yards but fewer than 100 games started. (Shaun Alexander and Ahman Green are the others.)

Ryan Williams
Height: 5-9 Weight: 212 College: Virginia Tech Draft: 2011/2 (38) Born: 9-Apr-1990 Age: 22 Risk: Green

Year	Team	G/S	Runs	Yds	Yd/R	TD	FUM	DVOA	Rk	DYAR	Rk	YAR	Suc%	Rec	Pass	Yds	C%	Yd/C	TD	DVOA	Rk	DYAR	Rk
2012	ARI		159	724	4.5	4		0.1%						17	21	164	81%	9.6	0	29.9%			

In 2009, Williams had a breakout season as a redshirt freshman at Virginia Tech, rushing for 1,655 yards and 21 touchdowns before missing a portion of 2010 with a hamstring injury. Though he had two years of eligibility remaining, Williams turned pro because his big-play ability earned a first or second-round grade from the NFL Draft Advisory Committee. The only question about Williams was his durability, so naturally, after being selected with the No. 38 pick in the draft, Williams ruptured the patella tendon in his right knee on his fifth preseason carry. After spending the season on IR, Williams is expected to be ready for training camp. If healthy, he'll add a big-play element to a rushing attack that had just seven runs of 20 or more yards in 2011, which tied for the fourth-lowest total in the league.

David Wilson
Height: 5-10 Weight: 206 College: Virginia Tech Draft: 2012/1 (32) Born: 15-Jun-1991 Age: 21 Risk: Green

Year	Team	G/S	Runs	Yds	Yd/R	TD	FUM	DVOA	Rk	DYAR	Rk	YAR	Suc%	Rec	Pass	Yds	C%	Yd/C	TD	DVOA	Rk	DYAR	Rk
2012	NYG		148	614	4.2	6		-1.1%						22	29	215	76%	9.8	1	25.1%			

Wilson has a ton of physical upside—speed, agility, strength, balance—and a strong college record, with +13.7 Adj. POE in 2011 and 2.97 Highlight Yards per Carry. He's going to rack up a lot of broken tackles in the NFL. His biggest problem is that he needs to learn when to take a few yards rather than trying to hit a home run by winding all over the backfield.

Danny Woodhead
Height: 5-9 Weight: 200 College: Chadron State Draft: 2008/FA Born: 25-Jan-1985 Age: 27 Risk: Green

Year	Team	G/S	Runs	Yds	Yd/R	TD	FUM	DVOA	Rk	DYAR	Rk	YAR	Suc%	Rec	Pass	Yds	C%	Yd/C	TD	DVOA	Rk	DYAR	Rk
2009	NYJ	10/0	15	64	4.3	0	0	-4.3%	--	3	--	6	60%	8	14	87	57%	10.9	0	7.5%	--	15	--
2010	2TM	15/3	97	547	5.6	5	1	40.4%	--	190	--	188	57%	34	44	379	77%	11.1	1	53.8%	1	151	4
2011	NE	15/4	77	351	4.6	1	0	22.6%	--	100	--	93	55%	18	31	157	58%	8.7	0	-11.3%	39	4	39
2012	NE		81	387	4.8	2		10.3%						22	28	220	79%	10.0	0	30.5%			

Woodhead wasn't as effective in his second season in New England; surprisingly, he had the second-lowest plus/minus among running backs (-4.5). A lot of his role was usurped by increased usage of Aaron Hernandez. His touches may go up a little with the departure of BenJarvus Green-Ellis, but Stevan Ridley and Shane Vereen are poised to step in and pick up the lost carries. Woodhead was a far superior red zone option to Green-Ellis, averaging 4.39 yards per carry on his 18 touches, although Woodhead had surprisingly poor receiving numbers in the red zone. He caught only one of six passes in the red zone for two yards, after catching all five red zone passes thrown his way in 2010.

Going Deep

Anthony Allen, BAL: At 6-foot-1, 230 pounds, Allen is built like a wrecking ball. The 2011 seventh-round pick out of Georgia Tech was supposed to replace Le'Ron McClain as Baltimore's short-yardage back last year, but ended up spending most of his rookie season inactive due to a thigh injury. (2011 stats: 3 carries for 8 yards, -4 DYAR, -55.4% DVOA)

Armando Allen, CHI: This undrafted Golden Domer was one of Tampa Bay's last preseason cuts. He went to Chicago's practice squad, and injuries to Matt Forte and Marion Barber propelled Allen to the active roster in late December. He made his NFL debut on Christmas Day, carrying the ball 11 times for 40 yards against the Packers. (2011 stats: 15 carries for 48 yards, - 9 DYAR, -23.9% DVOA)

Edwin Baker, SD: A seventh-round pick, Baker would have been better served by staying at Michigan State for another year. Good pad level gives him decent power, but he's not particularly fast (96.9 Speed Score), quick, or elusive, nor does he have much experience catching the ball. He'll enter the season behind both Ryan Mathews and Ronnie Brown at halfback, and with LeRon McClain also in the fold will be lucky to see the ball much if he makes the team.

Vick Ballard, IND: Ballard had a combined +30.8 Adj. POE at Mississippi State over the last two seasons, but he is perhaps best known for tripping during the 40-yard dash at the Scouting Combine and taking out a camera during the spill. He plays faster than his 4.65 forty time, but he doesn't run with a consistent pad level. Neither Delone Carter nor Donald Brown is a textbook third-down back, so if Ballard can improve his blocking, it wouldn't be a shock to see him get on the field in that role.

Joique Bell, DET: As a junior at Fort Wayne State, Bell rushed for 2,084 yards and 29 touchdowns en route to the Harlon Hill Trophy (essentially the Heisman for Division II). He joined the Bills as an undrafted free agent in 2010 and also spent time that year on the practice squads of the Eagles, Colts and Saints, with his only substantial action coming on special teams in Indy. A fun but totally unimportant fact about Bell: Wikipedia lists his height as 5-foot-12.

Lorenzo Booker, MIN: The darting FSU product was originally supposed to blossom into a formidable third-down back with the Dolphins. He didn't. So, he got a chance in Philadelphia. Nothing happened. He fell out of the NFL in 2009 but returned for four games with the Vikings in 2010. In 2011, Booker touched the ball 21 times offensively in 15 games but finished with three fumbles (making him eligible for a cute story in the *Star-*

Tribune about how he was walking around the team's facility with a football tucked high and tight near his chest 24/7). Booker's best chance at maintaining a roster spot is as a return specialist. He has averaged a respectable 23.8 yards per kick return during his two years in Minnesota. (Other 2011 stats: 13 carries for 52 yards, -29 DYAR, -68.0% DVOA; receiving stats: 8-for-14, 82 yards, 27 DYAR, 27.4% DVOA)

Aaron Brown, CIN: Brown was a sixth-round pick of the Lions in 2009 and made an instant impact as a kick returner. He also averaged just under two offensive touches per game as a bottom-of-the-depth chart running back. His 2010 campaign was marred by a broken hand and he had just one run and one catch. Last year, Brown was cut just prior to the start of the season but resurfaced in November due to Jahvid Best's injury.

Andre Brown, NYG: Brown became mildly famous after the Super Bowl for singing "I Got a Ring" in a video that went viral over Twitter. He had plenty of time to compose those witty lyrics when he was spending the entire season on the practice squad. Could we maybe give Brown a ring with a big asterisk on it?

Bryce Brown, PHI: Back in 2008, Rivals.com ranked Brown as the best high school recruit in the country at any position, but the next four years were a mess. Brown committed to Miami, then visited a bunch of other schools anyway and had his scholarship offer revoked. He went to Tennessee, transferred to Kansas State in 2010, sat a year to get his eligibility back and then left the team in early 2011 after a grand total of three carries. The raw talent is still there, though: The 220-pound Brown ran a 4.37 forty at his Pro Day, which works out to a Speed Score of 120.6. Between seventh-rounder Brown and the undrafted Chris Polk, the Eagles probably have one steal with an interesting backstory and one guy who won't make the team.

Eldra Buckley, FA: Buckley signed with Detroit last October after Jerome Harrison was placed on the reserve/non-football injury list. He lasted until mid-November. Before that, he made the Chargers as an undrafted free agent and spent some time with the Eagles. As a compact 5-foot-9, 207-pounder, his touches have come primarily in short-yardage situations, hence his career average of 3.1 yards per carry. (2010 stats: 21 carries for 67 yards, -16 DYAR, -25.7% DVOA)

John Clay, PIT: A former Big Ten Offensive Player of the Year and Doak Walker Award finalist, Clay spent 2011 on Pittsburgh's practice squad until injuries to Jonathan Dwyer and Mewelde Moore got him promoted to the active roster in Week 16. At 248 pounds, Clay projects as a goal-line and short-yardage back for Pittsburgh, and a 10-yard touchdown on his first NFL carry shows he has potential in that role. With three of the four running backs ahead of him on the depth chart coming off of major injuries—including last year's primary goal-line option, Rashard Mendenhall—Clay has a better opportunity to see meaningful carries than most fifth-stringers. (2011 stats: 10 carries for 41 yards, 1 TD, 6 DYAR, 10.1% DVOA)

Shaun Draughn, KC: An undrafted free agent, Draughn was activated from the practice squad and played special teams in Week 17. He had six 100-yard games at North Carolina, including 160 yards in a Music City Bowl win over Tennessee in 2010.

Darren Evans, IND: Evans tore his ACL following a strong freshman year at Virginia Tech, and his NFL prospects were hurt by sharing a backfield with Ryan Williams. He's a bruising between-the-tackles back who duplicates a lot of what Delone Carter brings to the table. If he wants to make the roster again this year, he'll have to show a lot on special teams.

Mario Fannin, DEN: Fannin ran a 4.37-second 40-yard dash at 231 pounds at the 2011 Combine, good enough for an all-time record Speed Score of 125.5. He went undrafted due to injury and fumble issues, landed in Denver, and promptly tore his ACL. He was a full participant in OTAs, and given Denver's desperate need for playmakers, he'll be given every opportunity to succeed.

Kevin Faulk, FA: Faulk didn't dress for the Super Bowl, prompting speculation that he would retire at the end of the season, but the offseason seems to have rejuvenated him. He indicated a desire to return to New England for one more season if they will have him. That's a big if, mostly thanks to the fact that Danny Woodhead already handles all the roles that Faulk filled so capably for many years. What's likely to happen is that Faulk does not make the opening day roster before surfacing later in the season, either as a reserve player or as a newly minted coach. (2011 stats: 17 carries for 57 yards, -2 DYAR, -10.8% DVOA; receiving stats: 7-for-9, 34 yards, 7 DYAR, -21.7% DVOA)

Terrance Ganaway, NYJ: Ganaway is an Ironhead Heyward-type. Heyward was a big cement mixer of a back who did his best work in run-'n'-shoot offenses, where he could just bulldoze nickelbacks on off-tackle runs. At Baylor, Ganaway plowed through defenders too worried about Robert Griffin's Flying Circus to handle a 240-pound running back, gaining 1,547 yards and scoring 21 touchdowns with +30.4 Adj. POE in 2011. Ganaway doesn't catch the ball well and has no moves, so he only fits as a goal-line back, a spread-offense bowling ball, or the piledriver in a caveman running game. It's that third option which brings him to the Jets. He could inherit the five to 10 carries per game LaDainian Tomlinson left behind, and perhaps a little more.

Cyrus Gray, KC: Gray is under six feet tall and can return kicks, so of course the Chiefs drafted him. It's a rule or something. Gray was mediocre in his first two seasons at Texas A&M (+1.8 Adj. POE in 2008-09) then rock-solid for two years (+29.0 Adj. POE in 2010-11). Always part of a committee in college, Gray still managed to go over 900 yards from scrimmage three times, and Romeo Crennel has praised his receiving ability.

Alex Green, GB: Green was mostly a nonfactor before tearing his ACL in late October. In all, he was active for four games, seeing work primarily on special teams while garnering three carries and one catch. The Packers drafted him in the third round presumably to handle the ball out of the heavy backfield sets that Mike McCarthy employs about 10 percent of the time. Coming into the league, scouts described Green as a one-dimensional, tough, physical, downhill runner.

Jamie Harper, TEN: Harper's solid preseason (168 yards, 3 TD, 4.4 YPA) gave some credence to the idea that he could see the field early, and Chris Johnson did him plenty of favors with his decidedly blasé start to the season. With the ability to catch the ball out of the backfield and pass block, Harper should at least compete for more third-down snaps this year. Johnson is facing a prove-it year and Javon Ringer toted a dreadful -31.3% DVOA last season: There are plenty of backs who would kill to be the third man in that rotation. (2011 stats: 17 carries for 44 yards, 1 TD, -14 DYAR, -26.3% DVOA)

DuJuan Harris, JAC: Foxx, as he was nicknamed at birth for his then-red hair, essentially replaced Deji Karim as the Jaguars' backup runner/kick returner. Assuming that he survives this year's crop of Gene Smith Small School UDFAs, the healthy return of Rashad Jennings will probably force Harris into the same role that Karim should have played in 2011: third-string back. (2011 stats: 9 carries for 42 yards, 2 DYAR, -2.6% DVOA)

Dan Herron, CIN: The man known as "Boom" will have to explode in camp to make the cut. He ran a plodding 4.66 at the combine, but was more of a between-the-tackles runner at Ohio State. His advanced numbers were never spectacular and he had his worst year (minus-2.8 Adj. POE) as a senior. His main competition for a roster spot figures to be special teams demon Cedric Peerman, so it will behoove Herron to brush up on his tackling over the summer.

Lex Hilliard, MIN: The Vikings acquired fullbacks Hilliard, Jerome Felton, and rookie Rhett Ellison. Sure, Ellison is more of an H-back (the Vikings have about a dozen of those, too), and Hilliard can absorb some carries in a pinch, but this has gone from depth chart padding to hoarding to an outright fetish. Maybe the Vikings hope to stack them, have the top guy hold up a beach umbrella, and call it a new stadium. (2011 stats: 16 carries for 41 yards, 1 TD, 15 DYAR, 5.1% DVOA)

RUNNING BACKS

Jeremiah Johnson, DEN: After rushing for 1,201 yards and 13 touchdowns in his senior season at Oregon, Johnson joined the Houston Texans as an undrafted rookie in 2009 and promptly tore up his shoulder. He spent the next few years bouncing on and off of practice squads in Washington (for "eight hours," he told Lindsay Jones of the *Denver Post*), Carolina, and Denver, before finally getting real playing time last year. Fifty-one of his 77 yards last year came on just three runs. (Other 2011 stats: 14 carries, 11 DYAR, 9.9% DVOA; receiving stats: 7-for-9, 62 yards, 12 DYAR, 9.1% DVOA)

Taiwan Jones, OAK: As a rookie out of Eastern Washington, Jones was one of the more intriguing later-round players in the 2011 draft. But his collegiate health problems carried over to the pros, and a lingering hamstring injury limited him to only 16 carries. If he can stay healthy, he has the speed to be a difference-maker, but that's a big if. (Other 2011 stats: 73 yards, 3 DYAR, -1.6% DVOA)

Le'Ron McClain, SD: When San Diego owner Dean Spanos talked to his team's website about the pre-draft acquisitions the Chargers had made, the one player he mentioned by name was McClain, not receivers Robert Meachem or Eddie Royal. McClain did go over 1,000 yards from scrimmage with 11 touchdowns with the Ravens in 2008, and he won't turn 28 until December, so the idea that he'll only be a blocker for the Chargers is far from a sure thing. (2011 stats: 15 carries for 51 yards, 1 TD, 2 DYAR, -5.5% DVOA; receiving stats: 14-for-22, 82 yards, 1 TD, -2 DYAR, -15.2% DVOA)

Alfred Morris, WAS: This sixth-round pick has good-looking stats on the surface—4.8 yards per carry, 27 touchdowns in three years—but look specifically at the play-by-play and you find a durable back who has never produced at an average level, even after you factor in the poor blocking he received at Florida Atlantic (career POE: minus-23.0). In the NFL, he's going to be a big hard-to-tackle bowling ball, but he's never shown the speed to be more than a complementary piece.

Cedric Peerman, CIN: A solid special-teamer and popular in the locker room, Peerman has contributed more than his five career carries would indicate. With the Bengals devoted to sharing the wealth in the backfield more in 2012, Peerman might get a few more snaps on offense.

Chris Polk, PHI: Polk is a perfect fit for the Eagles: He gives them the between-the-tackles power back that they lack, but also may be the best receiving back in this year's class. So how did he go undrafted? Blame worries about his shoulder, which has already seen two surgeries. Some teams believe Polk has a "degenerative" shoulder condition, but renowned orthopedist James Andrews has given Polk a clean bill of health. There also may be some questions about his college performance; below-average POE numbers suggest that a lot of backs could have matched the yards he gained given the carries he received.

Tauren Poole, CAR: Poole was on his way to being a mid-round draft pick when he rushed for 1,034 yards and 11 touchdowns for Tennessee in 2010. He backslid last year, however, battling hamstring injuries and hitting the bench a few times for inconsistency and mistakes. The Panthers signed him as a rookie free agent, and he will battle for Mike Goodson's old mop-up role as their third running back. Some experts consider Poole an underrated prospect, but with poor blocking chops, limited receiving value, and no return experience, he will have a hard time sticking behind two established veterans.

Quinn Porter, FA: For hire: Graduate of Stillman College, member of 2010 Super Bowl Champion Green Bay Packers (practice squad), returned 25 kickoffs for the St. Louis Rams in 2011 (-4.1 Pts+). Nickname: "Pom Poms."

Bobby Rainey, BAL: This undrafted free agent from Western Kentucky is a favorite of FO writers Ben Muth and Matt Waldman. Like Maurice Jones-Drew, he's short but not small: 5-foot-7, 208 pounds. He has excellent lateral agility and reads his blocks well, and he's a versatile player who is useful as a receiver or return man.

Those aspects of his game may give him the best shot at a roster spot in Baltimore, which could use a return upgrade on David Reed and at least one back on the depth chart who could fill in the receiving part of Ray Rice's role if Rice were injured.

Chris Rainey, PIT: With two huge backs set for running duties in place of an injured Rashard Mendenhall, Pittsburgh drafted the diminutive Rainey (Florida), who will fill a role similar to that of Dexter McCluster in Kansas City. Here's hoping his fantasy position is less of a headache for commissioners. His college numbers steadily dropped, with 4.5 Highlight Yards per carry as a freshman, 2.7 in his sophomore and junior years, and then 2.0 as a senior.

Daryl Richardson, STL: Despite being one pick away from Mr. Irrelevant, Richardson (Abilene Christian) has an inside track to the Rams' No. 3 running back spot in his rookie season. As the younger brother of Bengals' backup running back Bernard Scott and Dolphins reserve wide receiver Clyde Gates, he has an NFL pedigree, and his 97.0 Speed Score is reasonable for a lower-round pick.

Da'Rel Scott, NYG: Scott has a great combination of speed and strength, and his 118.9 Speed Score led all drafted running backs from the 2011 class. He burst onto the scene with a 97-yard touchdown run in the second preseason game against Chicago. The downside is that Scott has an injury history, and needs to work on both pass blocking and quickness changing directions.

Alfonso Smith, ARI: Undrafted out of Kentucky in 2010, Smith spent most of his rookie season on the Cardinals' practice squad before earning a spot as the No. 3 running back after Ryan Williams' knee injury. With Williams, Beanie Wells, and LaRod Stephens-Howling ahead of him on the depth chart, Smith will need to be indispensable on special teams to earn a roster spot. (2011 stats: 30 carries for 102 yards, 1 TD, 8 DYAR, -3.3% DVOA; receiving stats: 3-for-5, 21 yards, -6 DYAR, -29.2% DVOA)

Antone Smith, ATL: The Falcons' leading preseason rusher in 2010 and 2011, Smith is a scatback who is just good enough to shuffle from the practice squad to the active roster and soak up August carries. In a pinch, he could help as a third-down back, but he is no threat to Jacquizz Rogers. He has just one carry in two seasons, for a loss of two yards, although he's played 21 games on special teams.

Armond Smith, CAR: A mighty mite from tiny Union College in Kentucky, Smith crashed the Cleveland roster with an excellent preseason, including an 81-yard touchdown sprint against Detroit. Alas, he was relegated to the practice squad by October, after three regular-season carries for two yards. Waived and picked up by Carolina in May.

Michael Smith, TB: Smith is a blistering speedster who was timed at 4.32 seconds in his Pro Day forty. He averaged 7.6 yards per carry as Utah State's change-up to Robert Turbin. The Bucs figured 4.32 and 7.6 were decimals worthy of a seventh-round pick, and Smith's speed and bench-role mentality make him an intriguing option as a return man, gunner, and possible third running back.

Chester Taylor, FA: In 2010, Taylor became the first running back since the AFL-NFL merger to average less than 2.4 yards per carry on 100-plus carries. Signed off the scrap heap by the Arizona Cardinals, Taylor actually averaged 3.9 yards on 20 carries in 2011, but if you remove one 34-yard run from the equation, Taylor's average drops to 2.3 yards per carry. Oddly, that 34-yard run came against the San Francisco 49ers, who had a league-best -26.1% DVOA against the run in 2011, and Taylor's scamper was the longest they would allow in the regular or postseason. One run against a great run defense hasn't been enough to land the 33-year-old Taylor a new contract and he remains a free agent. (Other 2011 stats: 77 yards, 1 TD, 2 DYAR, -7.0% DVOA; receiving stats: 14-for-24, 91 yards, -56 DYAR, -65.6% DVOA)

Jordan Todman, MIN: Todman's productive three-year career at Connecticut prompted the Chargers to take a flier on him in the sixth round of last year's draft, but he never got to play, and eventually landed on the Vikings practice squad in December. Though very early, it's been a disappointing pro career for Todman thus far, given that some draft analysts projected him to be as high as a second-round pick prior to the 2011 Combine. There may be some concern around the league that the somewhat undersized Todman was overworked in college.

Robert Turbin, SEA: The 5-foot-10, 222-pound Turbin rebounded from a torn ACL in 2010 to run for 1,517 yards and 19 touchdowns in 2011, with 2.64 Highlight Yards per Carry and +18.9 Adj. POE. Nicknamed "The Hulk" for his massive biceps, Turbin demonstrated a bit more speed than expected when he ran a 4.5 forty at the Combine. Turbin will be a good insurance policy for Marshawn Lynch and his natural receiving (67 receptions, 845 yards, 11 touchdowns at Utah State) and blocking abilities will make him a possible option on third downs.

Harvey Unga, CHI: The Bears invested a seventh-round pick on BYU's all-time leading rusher in the 2010 Supplemental Draft. Unga took that untraditional route to the NFL because in April 2010 he voluntarily withdrew from BYU after violating the school's honor code. He wound up missing all of the 2010 season with a hamstring injury, then created a stir in the 2011 preseason by twice leaving the team for personal reasons. With three capable running backs ahead of him on the depth chart, Unga's chances of making the 2012 roster will likely depend on whether he can contribute on special teams.

Josh Vaughan, CAR: Vaughan replaced Mike Goodson as the Panthers' third running back late last season and earned seven mop-up carries in a late-season blowout of the Buccaneers. He enters camp as the third back this season, but there are no footballs left once DeAngelo Williams and Jonathan Stewart get their shares. (Other 2011 stats: 24 yards, -14 DYAR, -60.2% DVOA)

Johnny White, BUF: White was a regular Jim Thorpe during his time at UNC, playing four different positions during his stay in Chapel Hill, and the Bills drafted him primarily to be a special teams contributor, a role he filled admirably his rookie year. White received very few touches even after Fred Jackson went down, as Chan Gailey opted to ride C.J. Spiller in the final month of the season. With both Spiller and a healthy Jackson clogging up the depth chart, White should again be relegated primarily to special teams duty. (2011 stats: 12 carries for 38 yards, -2 DYAR, -15.8% DVOA)

Javarris Williams, HOU: Williams was exiled from Kansas City due to pass-protection issues; the Texans invited him to training camp and kept him on the practice squad after Chris Ogbonnaya was picked up by the Browns. He has one leg up on the UDFA crop (Jonathan Grimes and Davin Meggett) due to his year in the system.

Wide Receivers

In the following two sections we provide the last three years' statistics, as well as a 2012 KUBIAK projection, for every wide receiver and tight end who either played a significant role in 2011 or is expected to do so in 2012.

The first line contains biographical data—each player's name, height, weight, college, draft position, birth date, and age. Height and weight are the best data we could find; weight, of course, can fluctuate during the off-season. **Age** is very simple, the number of years between the player's birth year and 2012, but birth date is provided if you want to figure out exact age.

Draft position gives draft year and round, with the overall pick number with which the player was taken in parentheses. In the sample table, it says that Calvin Johnson was chosen in the 2007 NFL Draft with the second overall pick of the first round. Undrafted free agents are listed as "FA" with the year they came into the league, even if they were only in training camp or on a practice squad.

To the far right of the first line is the player's Risk for fantasy football in 2012. As explained in the quarterback section, the standard is for players to be marked Green. Players with higher than normal risk are marked Yellow, and players with the highest risk are marked Red. Players who are most likely to match or surpass our forecast—primarily second-stringers with low projections—are marked Blue. Risk is not only based on injury probability, but how a player's projection compares to his recent performance as well as our confidence (or lack thereof) in his offensive teammates.

Next we give the last three years of player stats.

Note that rushing stats are not included for receivers, but that any receiver with at least three carries last year will have his 2011 rushing stats appear in his team's chapter.

Next we give the last three years of player stats. First come games played and games started (**G/GS**). Games played represents the official NFL total and may include games in which a player appeared on special teams, but did not play wide receiver or tight end. Receptions (**Rec**) counts passes caught, while Passes (**Pass**) counts passes thrown to this player, complete or incomplete. Receiving yards (**Yds**) is the official NFL total for each player.

Catch rate (**C%**) includes all passes listed in the official play-by-play with the given player as the intended receiver, even if those passes were listed by our game charters as "Thrown Away," "Tipped at Line," or "Quarterback Hit in Motion." The average NFL wide receiver has caught 57 percent of passes thrown to them in each of the past three seasons; tight ends caught 63 percent of passes in 2011 and 64 percent of passes in 2009 and 2010.

Plus/minus (**+/-**) is a new metric that we introduced in *Football Outsiders Almanac 2010*. It estimates how many passes a receiver caught compared to what an average receiver would have caught, given the location of those passes. Unlike simple catch rate, plus/minus does not consider passes listed as "Thrown Away," "Tipped at Line," or "Quarterback Hit in Motion." Player performance is compared to a historical baseline of how often a pass is caught based on the pass distance, the distance required for a first down, and whether it is on the left, middle, or right side of

Calvin Johnson   Height: 6-5   Weight: 239   College: Georgia Tech   Draft: 2007/1 (2)   Born: 25-Sep-1985   Age: 27   Risk: Yellow

Year	Team	G/S	Rec	Pass	Yds	C%	+/-	Y/C	TD	Drop	YAC	Rk	YAC+	DVOA	Rk	DYAR	Rk	YAR	Short	Mid	Deep	Bomb
2009	DET	14/14	67	138	984	49%	-5.9	14.7	5	5	5.1	19	+0.7	-10.5%	64	24	61	34	24%	41%	17%	18%
2010	DET	15/15	77	138	1120	57%	+2.9	14.5	12	6	3.9	44	+0.1	11.8%	20	265	7	249	20%	46%	19%	14%
2011	DET	16/16	96	158	1681	61%	+8.8	17.5	16	3	5.1	21	+0.9	31.9%	7	570	1	576	25%	38%	18%	18%
2012	DET		98	161	1450	61%	--	14.8	12					17.2%								

the field. Note that plus/minus is not scaled to a player's target total.

Yards per catch (**Yd/C**) and receiving touchdowns (**TD**) are standard stats. Drops (**Drop**) is new to the tables this year and represents the number of dropped passes according to our game charting project. Our totals may differ from the drop totals kept by other organizations.

Next comes Yards After Catch (**YAC**), based on information from the game charting project, rank (**Rk**) in Yards After Catch, and **YAC+**. YAC+ is similar to plus/minus; it estimates how much YAC a receiver gained compared to what we would have expected from an average receiver catching passes of similar length in similar down-and-distance situations. This is imperfect—we don't specifically mark what route a player runs, and obviously a go route will have more YAC than a comeback—but it does a fairly good job of telling you if this receiver gets more or less YAC than other receivers with similar usage patterns.

The next five columns include our main advanced metrics for receiving: **DVOA** (Defense-Adjusted Value Over Average), **DYAR** (Defense-Adjusted Yards Above Replacement), and **YAR** (Yards Above Replacement), along with the player's rank in both DVOA and DYAR. These metrics compare every pass intended for a receiver and the results of that pass to a league-average baseline based on the game situations in which passes were thrown to that receiver. DVOA and DYAR are also adjusted based on the opposing defense and include Defensive Pass Interference yards on passes intended for that receiver. The methods used to compute these numbers are described in detail in the "Statistical Toolbox" introduction in the front of the book. The important distinctions between them are:

- DVOA is a rate statistic, while DYAR is a cumulative statistic. Thus, a higher DVOA means more value per pass play, while a higher DYAR means more aggregate value over the entire season.
- Because DYAR is defense-adjusted and YAR is not, a player whose DYAR is higher than his YAR faced a harder-than-average schedule. A player whose DYAR is lower than his YAR faced an easier-than-average schedule.

To qualify for ranking in YAC, receiving DVOA, or receiving DYAR, a wide receiver must have had 50 passes thrown to him in that season. We ranked 92 wideouts in 2011, 85 wideouts in 2010, and 89 in 2009. Tight ends qualify with 25 targets in a given season; we ranked 47 tight ends in 2011, 45 tight ends in 2010, and 49 in 2009.

The final four columns break down pass length based on the Football Outsiders charting project. The categories are **Short** (5 yards or less), **Mid** (6-15 yards), **Deep** (16-25 yards), and **Bomb** (26 or more yards). These numbers are based on distance in the air only and include both complete and incomplete passes.

The italicized row of statistics for the 2012 season is our 2012 KUBIAK projection based on a complicated regression analysis that takes into account numerous variables including projected role, performance over the past two years, projected team offense and defense, projected quarterback statistics, historical comparables, height, age, and strength of schedule.

It is difficult to accurately project statistics for a 162-game baseball season, but it is exponentially more difficult to accurately project statistics for a 16-game football season. Consider the listed projections not as a prediction of exact numbers, but as the mean of a range of possible performances. What's important is less the exact number of yards we project, and more which players are projected to improve or decline. Actual performance will vary from our projection less for veteran starters and more for rookies and third-stringers, for whom we must base our projections on much smaller career statistical samples. Touchdown numbers will vary more than yardage numbers. Players facing suspension or recovering from injury have those missed games taken into account.

Note that the receiving totals for each team will add up to higher numbers than the projection for that team's starting quarterback, because we have done KUBIAK projections for more receivers than will actually make the final roster.

A few low-round rookies, guys listed at seventh on the depth chart, and players who are listed as wide receivers but really only play special teams are briefly discussed at the end of the chapter in a section we call "Going Deep."

Two notes regarding our advanced metrics: We cannot yet fully separate the performance of a receiver from the performance of his quarterback. Be aware that one will affect the other. In addition, these statistics measure only passes thrown to a receiver, not performance on plays when he is not thrown the ball, such as blocking and drawing double teams.

As with quarterbacks, 2011 was a historic year for great seasons by wide receivers and tight ends. Calvin Johnson finished with the second-highest DYAR total of all-time, with Jordy Nelson also in the top ten. Nelson also came close to the all-time high in DVOA, finishing second to a player (Dennis Northcutt in 2002) who barely makes our usual 50-pass minimum. Two other wide receivers end up in the all-time top 13. For tight ends, Rob Gronkowski set a new tight end DYAR record by leaps and bounds. You'll find these historical tables below along with the tables of the best players from 2011.

There were also some wide receivers and tight ends making DVOA history for the wrong reasons, but we'll get to those players when we hit their player comments.

Top 20 WR by DYAR (Total Value), 2011

Rank	Player	Team	DYAR
1	Calvin Johnson	DET	570
2	Jordy Nelson	GB	517
3	Victor Cruz	NYG	455
4	Wes Welker	NE	451
5	Mike Wallace	PIT	399
6	Marques Colston	NO	390
7	Malcom Floyd	SD	351
8	Laurent Robinson	DAL	327
9	A.J. Green	CIN	284
10	Larry Fitzgerald	ARI	278
11	Greg Jennings	GB	275
12	Hakeem Nicks	NYG	274
13	Dez Bryant	DAL	262
14	Vincent Jackson	SD	259
15	Steve Smith	CAR	239
16	Lance Moore	NO	234
17	James Jones	GB	234
18	Brandon Marshall	MIA	226
19	Roddy White	ATL	219
20	Robert Meachem	NO	208

Top 20 WR by DVOA (Value per Pass), 2011

Rank	Player	Team	DVOA
1	Jordy Nelson	GB	52.5%
2	Malcom Floyd	SD	51.4%
3	James Jones	GB	41.1%
4	Laurent Robinson	DAL	40.0%
5	Marques Colston	NO	33.9%
6	Victor Cruz	NYG	32.0%
7	Calvin Johnson	DET	31.9%
8	Mike Wallace	PIT	31.4%
9	Robert Meachem	NO	30.8%
10	Lance Moore	NO	25.8%
11	Brandon LaFell	CAR	22.3%
12	Greg Jennings	GB	20.5%
13	Dez Bryant	DAL	20.5%
14	Wes Welker	NE	20.4%
15	Andre Johnson	HOU	17.2%
16	Donald Driver	GB	17.1%
17	A.J. Green	CIN	16.9%
18	Dezmon Briscoe	TB	16.5%
19	Vincent Jackson	SD	15.7%
20	Devery Henderson	NO	14.7%

Minimum 50 passes.

All WR, 500-plus DYAR, 1991-2011

Rank	Year	Player	Team	DYAR
1	1995	M.Irvin	DAL	599
2	2011	C.Johnson	DET	570
3	2007	R.Moss	NE	564
4	2001	M.Harrison	IND	547
5	2011	J.Nelson	GB	517
6	2006	M.Harrison	IND	513
7	1995	J.Rice	SF	512
8	1994	J.Rice	SF	512
9	2003	R.Moss	MIN	508
10	2008	A.Johnson	HOU	508
11	2003	T.Holt	STL	508
12	2005	S.Smith	CAR	502

All WR, DVOA over 40%, 1991-2011

Rank	Year	Player	Team	DVOA	Passes
1	2002	D.Northcutt	CLE	60.1%	51
2	2011	J.Nelson	GB	52.5%	96
3	1999	T.Dwight	ATL	51.5%	50
4	2011	M.Floyd	SD	51.4%	70
5	1993	J.Taylor	SF	51.2%	74
6	2001	R.Proehl	STL	49.2%	55
7	2010	M.Wallace	PIT	49.0%	98
8	1999	A.Hakim	STL	46.5%	56
9	2007	A.Gonzalez	IND	43.2%	51
10	2002	J.Porter	OAK	41.9%	70
11	2011	J.Jones	GB	41.1%	55
12	2006	D.Henderson	NO	40.8%	54
13	2011	L.Robinson	DAL	40.0%	81

Minimum 50 passes.

WIDE RECEIVERS

Danario Alexander
Height: 6-5 Weight: 215 College: Missouri Draft: 2010/FA Born: 7-Aug-1988 Age: 24 Risk: Red

Year	Team	G/S	Rec	Pass	Yds	C%	+/-	Y/C	TD	Drop	YAC	Rk	YAC+	DVOA	Rk	DYAR	Rk	YAR	Short	Mid	Deep	Bomb
2010	STL	8/2	20	37	306	54%	+0.5	15.3	1	2	5.7	--	+0.1	1.4%	--	44	--	63	44%	25%	9%	22%
2011	STL	10/5	26	60	431	43%	-4.6	16.6	2	3	5.1	23	+0.9	-12.4%	73	1	73	2	29%	36%	18%	16%
2012	STL		19	40	287	48%	--	15.1	4					-7.2%								

Alexander's 2011 season is probably best remembered for your fantasy league's Week 3 waiver wire. As a no-name wide receiver coming off a three-catch, 122-yard, one-touchdown game, he was a one-man market bubble. Unfortunately, despite playing nine more games, that one performance ended up representing one-third of his fantasy points total for the year. The No. 1 problem for Alexander is that, except for his senior year at Missouri, he's never stayed healthy long enough to produce for extended stretches. Alexander will be fighting for a roster spot this preseason, but already missed an OTA practice because of soreness in his hamstring. Given how snake-bitten his time in St. Louis has been, a change of scenery (or an exorcism) might actually be good for him.

Danny Amendola
Height: 5-11 Weight: 186 College: Texas Tech Draft: 2008/FA Born: 2-Nov-1985 Age: 27 Risk: Yellow

Year	Team	G/S	Rec	Pass	Yds	C%	+/-	Y/C	TD	Drop	YAC	Rk	YAC+	DVOA	Rk	DYAR	Rk	YAR	Short	Mid	Deep	Bomb
2009	STL	14/2	43	64	326	69%	+0.1	7.6	1	3	4.3	41	-0.9	-30.3%	86	-93	85	-66	70%	23%	7%	0%
2010	STL	16/6	85	123	689	69%	+3.6	8.1	3	7	4.3	33	-0.8	-19.3%	76	-64	78	-41	60%	35%	4%	1%
2011	STL	1/1	5	6	45	83%	+0.9	9.0	0	0	5.0	--	+0.5	12.7%	--	13	--	13	67%	33%	0%	0%
2012	STL		69	106	667	65%	--	9.7	4					-7.7%								

Through three quarters of the Rams' Week 1 blowout loss to Philadelphia, Amendola was well on his way to earning vindication for every writer that compared him to Wes Welker. Two plays later, his season was effectively over. It was the first in a series of unfortunate events for St. Louis last season, and it also proved to be one of the most important because of its impact on Josh McDaniels' offense. Not coincidentally, when Amendola entered restricted free agency after the season, one of the only teams rumored to be interested was—wait for it—New England. That would have been a boon for Amendola, as well as the lazy racial-comparison market, but he instead re-signed with St. Louis. Over the past four years, Brian Schottenheimer has employed three wide receivers as rarely as any offensive coordinator in the NFL, but Amendola will surely get used in standard sets given the mess on the depth chart behind him. On a one-year deal, he's almost certain to leave after 2012.

Anthony Armstrong
Height: 5-11 Weight: 183 College: West Texas A&M Draft: 2005/FA Born: 29-Mar-1983 Age: 29 Risk: Green

Year	Team	G/S	Rec	Pass	Yds	C%	+/-	Y/C	TD	Drop	YAC	Rk	YAC+	DVOA	Rk	DYAR	Rk	YAR	Short	Mid	Deep	Bomb
2010	WAS	15/11	44	86	871	51%	+1.3	19.8	3	5	3.6	53	-1.2	7.4%	30	134	32	126	18%	36%	24%	22%
2011	WAS	14/2	7	27	103	26%	-5.4	14.7	2	0	1.0	--	-3.6	-45.8%	--	-67	--	-59	13%	38%	17%	33%
2012	WAS		16	40	246	40%	--	15.4	2					-17.1%								

The Intense Football League-to-National Football League story was a lot of fun in 2010, but last year Armstrong turned back into a pumpkin. If you are supposed to be the deep threat, and you are struggling to get off press coverage, you have a problem. There's some talk that Armstrong won't make the team in 2012, but the Redskins don't really have anyone else to run a nine route if Pierre Garcon gets hurt.

Devin Aromashodu
Height: 6-2 Weight: 202 College: Auburn Draft: 2006/7 (233) Born: 23-May-1984 Age: 28 Risk: Yellow

Year	Team	G/S	Rec	Pass	Yds	C%	+/-	Y/C	TD	Drop	YAC	Rk	YAC+	DVOA	Rk	DYAR	Rk	YAR	Short	Mid	Deep	Bomb
2009	CHI	10/2	24	43	298	56%	-0.5	12.4	4	5	3.5	--	-0.3	1.8%	--	49	--	65	30%	40%	20%	10%
2010	CHI	14/2	10	24	149	42%	-2.3	14.9	0	1	5.1	--	+1.6	-29.1%	--	-31	--	-30	29%	43%	19%	10%
2011	MIN	16/6	26	84	468	31%	-15.3	18.0	1	3	4.4	38	+0.7	-38.0%	90	-166	92	-169	10%	49%	22%	19%
2012	MIN		21	51	310	41%	--	14.7	2					-20.0%								

On the surface, Aromashodu seems like a big, athletic target with some playmaking potential. A closer inspection, however, shows a receiver who doesn't run with fluidity or burst, and can't beat any brand of quality coverage, especially press. Put that together with a rookie quarterback behind an offensive line in decline, and you get the worst catch rate in nearly 20 years for a receiver with at least 50 targets.

Worst Wide Receiver Catch Rate, 1991-2011

Rank	Year	Player	Team	C%	Passes
1	1992	S.Baker	NYG	28.8%	59
2	2011	D.Aromashodu	MIN	31.0%	84
3	1996	M.Pritchard	SEA	33.3%	63
4	1998	E.Kennison	STL	33.3%	51
5	1992	W.Gault	LARD	33.8%	80
6	1991	W.Gault	LARD	33.9%	59
7	1992	L.Clark	SEA	35.1%	57
8	1998	M.Ricks	SD	35.3%	85
9	2000	P.Burress	PIT	35.4%	65
10	2009	L.Murphy	OAK	35.4%	96

Minimum 50 passes.

Worst Wide Receiver DYAR, 1991-2011

Rank	Year	Player	Team	DYAR
1	2006	C.Chambers	MIA	-297
2	2004	B.Wade	CHI	-204
3	2001	P.Warrick	CIN	-187
4	1994	K.Martin	SEA	-184
5	2003	A.Hakim	DET	-182
6	2004	L.Coles	WAS	-169
7	2011	D.Aromashodu	MIN	-166
8	2004	P.Price	ATL	-163
9	2000	P.Burress	PIT	-160
10	1998	I.Fryar	PHI	-157

Looking for the list of all-time worst DVOA ratings for wide receivers? Don't worry, we'll get to that list too. If you can't wait, just page forward to "R."

Miles Austin

Height: 6-3 Weight: 215 College: Monmouth Draft: 2006/FA Born: 30-Jun-1984 Age: 28 Risk: Yellow

Year	Team	G/S	Rec	Pass	Yds	C%	+/-	Y/C	TD	Drop	YAC	Rk	YAC+	DVOA	Rk	DYAR	Rk	YAR	Short	Mid	Deep	Bomb
2009	DAL	16/9	81	124	1320	65%	+6.6	16.3	11	5	7.4	2	+2.9	28.6%	5	399	5	421	31%	46%	15%	7%
2010	DAL	16/16	69	119	1041	58%	-1.6	15.1	7	11	6.2	4	+2.1	12.8%	16	242	12	250	32%	48%	11%	10%
2011	DAL	10/10	43	73	579	59%	-1.0	13.5	7	2	4.7	32	+0.7	11.3%	27	139	32	152	31%	46%	17%	7%
2012	DAL		72	121	974	60%	--	13.5	7					4.9%								

Austin may have never been fully healthy in 2011, as hamstring injuries knocked him out of six games altogether and hampered his play all season. He hinted that the lockout was to blame, as he felt he showed up out of shape for Dallas' abbreviated training camp. "I wasn't prepared for the season in the way I should have been condition-wise," he said in a video interview for *Men's Health* magazine. That may explain why he was much less dangerous with the ball in his hands. He broke only two tackles last year, after breaking 15 total in 2009 and 2010. This season, under the watchful eye of the Cowboys' training staff (historically one of the better such units in the league), he expects to make a full recovery. Austin was at his best on first down last year (25.1% DVOA), but that's probably a meaningless fluke. In 2010, his best down, by far, was third down.

Jason Avant

Height: 6-0 Weight: 210 College: Michigan Draft: 2006/4 (109) Born: 20-Apr-1983 Age: 29 Risk: Green

Year	Team	G/S	Rec	Pass	Yds	C%	+/-	Y/C	TD	Drop	YAC	Rk	YAC+	DVOA	Rk	DYAR	Rk	YAR	Short	Mid	Deep	Bomb
2009	PHI	16/9	41	58	587	71%	+6.7	14.3	3	1	4.6	30	+0.4	21.3%	11	160	29	158	39%	32%	26%	4%
2010	PHI	16/3	51	75	573	68%	+8.5	11.2	1	5	3.1	65	-1.2	6.8%	32	114	40	114	34%	42%	18%	6%
2011	PHI	16/7	52	81	679	64%	+4.0	13.1	1	1	3.3	71	-0.5	2.1%	47	92	51	117	29%	51%	17%	3%
2012	PHI		45	75	542	60%	--	12.1	3					-0.2%								

Avant led the Eagles in third-down targets with 31, and posted a very respectable 19.4% DVOA on third and fourth downs. It was another solid season, but it started with the Eagles signing Steve Smith as their slot receiver and all but handing Avant's slot role to Smith. It was a fine example of fixing something that wasn't broke, and it typified the Eagles' woes last season: the failure to integrate a new player at a position where the old player was still available and effective. Avant will keep his slot role this season, with only rookie Marvin McNutt as a serious challenger. Pencil in 50 more catches, plenty of third-down conversions, and zero controversy.

Donnie Avery
Height: 5-11 Weight: 183 College: Houston Draft: 2008/2 (33) Born: 12-Jun-1984 Age: 28 Risk: Blue

Year	Team	G/S	Rec	Pass	Yds	C%	+/-	Y/C	TD	Drop	YAC	Rk	YAC+	DVOA	Rk	DYAR	Rk	YAR	Short	Mid	Deep	Bomb
2009	STL	16/16	47	98	589	49%	-10.8	12.5	5	9	5.3	16	-0.1	-22.3%	78	-73	80	-46	38%	34%	15%	14%
2011	TEN	8/0	3	11	45	27%	-3.5	15.0	1	2	7.0	--	+3.4	-2.6%	--	10	--	6	42%	33%	8%	17%
2012	IND		16	36	226	44%	--	14.1	1					-19.3%								

Nine of Avery's 11 targets came against the Houston Texans, in Week 7 and Week 17. He picked up two receptions of 20 or more yards, as well as a 30-yard DPI. Despite those gains, he looked completely out of sync in the offense, dropping balls, running routes in the wrong spot, and not showing the wheels that used to help him get deep. Any team that has a significant role planned for him at this point is desperate.

Doug Baldwin
Height: 5-11 Weight: 189 College: Stanford Draft: 2011/FA Born: 21-Sep-1988 Age: 24 Risk: Yellow

Year	Team	G/S	Rec	Pass	Yds	C%	+/-	Y/C	TD	Drop	YAC	Rk	YAC+	DVOA	Rk	DYAR	Rk	YAR	Short	Mid	Deep	Bomb
2011	SEA	16/1	51	86	788	59%	-0.6	15.5	4	2	6.1	10	+1.4	14.2%	21	173	25	183	31%	38%	20%	11%
2012	SEA		54	91	710	59%	--	13.1	4					1.0%								

Despite leading Stanford in receiving in 2010 and running a 4.49 in the 40-yard dash at his pro day, Baldwin went undrafted in 2011. Though he was one of the more sought after undrafted free agents (his $17,500 signing bonus from Seattle was one of the highest given last year), we didn't mention him in last year's book. We hope we made up for it in this year's Top 25 Prospects list. Baldwin quickly earned a role as Seattle's slot receiver, where he led the Seahawks in every major receiving category. Baldwin played almost exclusively in three-plus wide receiver personnel groupings as a rookie and the next step in his development will be to prove to coaches that he can play on the perimeter at the NFL level.

Jonathan Baldwin
Height: 6-5 Weight: 230 College: Pittsburgh Draft: 2011/1 (26) Born: 10-Aug-1989 Age: 23 Risk: Red

Year	Team	G/S	Rec	Pass	Yds	C%	+/-	Y/C	TD	Drop	YAC	Rk	YAC+	DVOA	Rk	DYAR	Rk	YAR	Short	Mid	Deep	Bomb
2011	KC	11/3	21	53	254	40%	-6.8	12.1	1	6	2.0	90	-1.9	-38.9%	91	-105	89	-106	27%	45%	12%	16%
2012	KC		54	98	813	55%	--	15.1	5					4.2%								

In the second quarter against the Broncos in Week 10, the Chiefs ran play-action and Baldwin ran a post-corner route. Brian Dawkins was badly beaten in coverage, and all he could do was raise his arms over his head, never turning back to look for the ball. The pass was underthrown and hit Dawkins in the back between his numbers. However, Baldwin was able to wrap his arms around Dawkins, catch the ball with his hands, and tumble to the ground. It may have been the most spectacular catch of the 2011 season—and technically it never happened, because Kansas City committed a procedural penalty on the play. The catch still served to show Baldwin's spectacular ability, but the above statline shows that he is also mistake-prone. (21 receptions and six drops? Yeesh.) The Chiefs are counting on Baldwin to progress into a starting role this year, moving Steve Breaston into the slot.

Ramses Barden
Height: 6-6 Weight: 229 College: Cal Poly Draft: 2009/3 (85) Born: 1-Jan-1986 Age: 26 Risk: Blue

Year	Team	G/S	Rec	Pass	Yds	C%	+/-	Y/C	TD	Drop	YAC	Rk	YAC+	DVOA	Rk	DYAR	Rk	YAR	Short	Mid	Deep	Bomb
2009	NYG	3/0	1	1	16	100%	+0.3	16.0	0	0	9.0	--	+4.9	143.8%	--	8	--	9	0%	100%	0%	0%
2010	NYG	6/0	5	7	64	71%	+0.8	12.8	0	0	2.0	--	-2.2	-6.2%	--	4	--	13	29%	43%	29%	0%
2011	NYG	8/0	9	19	94	47%	-2.6	10.4	0	0	3.0	--	-0.6	-32.1%	--	-29	--	-32	32%	53%	16%	0%
2012	NYG		4	7	48	57%	--	12.0	0					-5.1%								

WIDE RECEIVERS 361

If height alone made you a great NFL receiver, Chuck Nevitt would have three Super Bowl rings. When asked why Barden doesn't get playing time, Tom Coughlin has pointed out Barden's inconsistency in practice and Kevin Gilbride has complained that he's not fast enough to create separation. Actually, both are correct. New Shimmer is a floor wax *and* a dessert topping!

Arrelious Benn   Height: 6-1   Weight: 219   College: Illinois   Draft: 2010/2 (39)   Born: 8-Sep-1988   Age: 24   Risk: Green

Year	Team	G/S	Rec	Pass	Yds	C%	+/-	Y/C	TD	Drop	YAC	Rk	YAC+	DVOA	Rk	DYAR	Rk	YAR	Short	Mid	Deep	Bomb
2010	TB	15/9	25	38	395	66%	+3.3	15.8	2	1	6.4	--	+1.3	23.7%	--	113	--	112	42%	33%	8%	17%
2011	TB	14/14	30	51	441	59%	-2.0	14.7	3	5	5.8	16	+0.1	-7.0%	64	22	65	20	42%	28%	16%	14%
2012	TB		22	36	285	61%	--	12.9	1					6.0%								

The results of Benn's six carries on various end-arounds last year: gain of three, loss of five, gain of two, loss of four, gain of nine, loss of twelve. There's a "spot the pattern" math problem in there somewhere. Benn was fading from the game plan before a concussion limited him in the final four games of the season. He practiced with the third team during May OTAs and will have to fight for a roster spot.

Earl Bennett   Height: 5-11   Weight: 209   College: Vanderbilt   Draft: 2008/3 (70)   Born: 23-Mar-1987   Age: 25   Risk: Yellow

Year	Team	G/S	Rec	Pass	Yds	C%	+/-	Y/C	TD	Drop	YAC	Rk	YAC+	DVOA	Rk	DYAR	Rk	YAR	Short	Mid	Deep	Bomb
2009	CHI	16/15	54	88	717	61%	-1.7	13.3	2	4	5.6	13	+1.1	-3.4%	52	63	49	60	43%	34%	21%	2%
2010	CHI	14/3	46	70	561	66%	+2.5	12.2	3	1	4.5	31	+0.6	9.9%	22	122	36	128	33%	60%	6%	1%
2011	CHI	11/4	24	43	381	56%	+1.9	15.9	1	0	5.2	--	+0.9	1.0%	--	42	--	48	26%	37%	26%	11%
2012	CHI		36	59	442	61%	--	12.3	2					4.5%								

Bennett and Jay Cutler were at Vanderbilt together for only the 2005 season, but indeed, they seem to have innate chemistry, particularly on third down. Bennett is primarily a slot receiver. He's always been somewhat methodical, although after he returned from a nagging early-season chest injury last year, he showed a new-found burst in all facets. Bennett has good footwork near the sideline. He's effective running routes to the inside or outside, usually of the "short distance" variety. The average pass targeting Bennett in 2010 traveled just eight yards in the air; last season, his average pass traveled 12.2 yards, which is right around league average. That was in Mike Martz's system, though. Under Mike Tice, the Bears are expected to be more traditional (i.e., conservative). Don't be surprised if Bennett goes back to working primarily underneath.

Davone Bess   Height: 5-11   Weight: 193   College: Hawaii   Draft: 2008/FA   Born: 13-Sep-1985   Age: 27   Risk: Yellow

Year	Team	G/S	Rec	Pass	Yds	C%	+/-	Y/C	TD	Drop	YAC	Rk	YAC+	DVOA	Rk	DYAR	Rk	YAR	Short	Mid	Deep	Bomb
2009	MIA	16/2	76	114	758	68%	+5.1	10.0	2	8	4.0	54	-0.9	-0.4%	46	106	41	97	47%	35%	14%	4%
2010	MIA	16/8	79	126	820	63%	+2.2	10.4	5	6	3.9	46	-0.5	-0.8%	53	112	42	82	38%	50%	10%	2%
2011	MIA	16/4	51	86	537	59%	-0.9	10.5	3	2	4.5	36	+0.1	-24.8%	86	-79	87	-77	51%	34%	13%	3%
2012	MIA		61	97	685	63%	--	11.2	5					-0.2%								

Bess had strong third-down numbers in the past, but last year he earned a -25.8% DVOA on 43 third-down targets. His catch rate was just 60 percent, he fumbled once, and he netted just 14 first downs or touchdowns. Essentially, he caught a lot of eight-yard passes on third-and-10. The guys throwing him the ball were part of the problem, and Bess' third-down performance went up when Matt Moore replaced Chad Henne. Some people see Bess as a Wes Welker-type held back by his quarterbacks, but he's really maxed out as a league-average No. 2 receiver. Your go-to guy shouldn't be averaging 10.5 yards per reception.

WIDE RECEIVERS

Armon Binns Height: 6-3 Weight: 209 College: Cincinnati Draft: 2011/FA Born: 8-Sep-1989 Age: 23 Risk: Red

Year	Team	G/S	Rec	Pass	Yds	C%	+/-	Y/C	TD	Drop	YAC	Rk	YAC+	DVOA	Rk	DYAR	Rk	YAR	Short	Mid	Deep	Bomb
2012	CIN		23	40	316	58%	--	13.8	2					2.3%								

At 6-foot-3, Binns fits the Bengals preference for tall wideouts, and as a local kid (he played college ball at UC), he was a natural pickup for the practice squad. With the wide receiver depth chart unsettled, Binns used a strong spring to vault himself into the starting mix, and will compete in the preseason with Brandon Tate and Mohamed Sanu for the right to line up opposite A.J. Green.

Justin Blackmon Height: 6-1 Weight: 207 College: Oklahoma State Draft: 2012/1 (5) Born: 9-Jan-1990 Age: 22 Risk: Red

Year	Team	G/S	Rec	Pass	Yds	C%	+/-	Y/C	TD	Drop	YAC	Rk	YAC+	DVOA	Rk	DYAR	Rk	YAR	Short	Mid	Deep	Bomb
2012	JAC		72	138	786	52%	--	10.9	4					-21.5%								

Blackmon was a statistical monster at Oklahoma State. Even on passing downs, where he was often mugged and marked by multiple players, he accumulated a 78 percent catch rate over the past two seasons. The main concern is that lack of top-end speed will keep him from being the kind of player you have to game-plan around, but he'll certainly break off some big gains on runs after the catch, and it's not like the begging Jaguars can be choosers after the receiving corps they fielded last year. Blackmon was pulled over for a DUI in early June, registering an 0.24 blood alcohol content, which is almost three times the legal limit. At least we know he can hold on to his liquor.

Anquan Boldin Height: 6-1 Weight: 218 College: Florida State Draft: 2003/2 (54) Born: 3-Oct-1980 Age: 32 Risk: Green

Year	Team	G/S	Rec	Pass	Yds	C%	+/-	Y/C	TD	Drop	YAC	Rk	YAC+	DVOA	Rk	DYAR	Rk	YAR	Short	Mid	Deep	Bomb
2009	ARI	15/15	84	128	1024	66%	+9.0	12.2	4	4	4.3	39	+0.2	-0.2%	45	124	38	173	37%	48%	13%	2%
2010	BAL	16/16	64	109	837	59%	+2.8	13.1	7	3	3.5	55	-0.7	5.3%	38	156	29	141	25%	47%	17%	11%
2011	BAL	14/14	57	106	887	54%	-4.6	15.6	3	4	3.9	56	+0.2	8.6%	34	184	23	169	13%	64%	16%	7%
2012	BAL		54	98	752	55%	--	13.9	5					1.3%								

At first glance, Boldin's statistical progression over the past three years looks like a very tidy, predictable pattern for a wide receiver: As short-range targets decrease, catch rate decreases (i.e., longer passes are less accurate) and YAC decreases (i.e., catches are made in closer quarters), whereas DVOA and DYAR increases (i.e., longer gains are more valuable and more efficient). Although that's certainly true, the table is just as much of a testament to Boldin's versatility as it is to his reliability. With Larry Fitzgerald around to gobble up deep passes in Arizona, Boldin feasted on short and intermediate targets. In his first year with the Ravens, the lack of a deep threat forced Boldin to become the intermediate and deep option. Then last year, the emergence of Torrey Smith as a deep threat and two young tight ends as underneath threats allowed Boldin to focus on intermediate routes. Dennis Pitta may be the guy who's "everywhere you want him to be" according to Terrell Suggs, but Boldin is the guy who's "everywhere you *need* him to be." Boldin is probably past his prime, but 32 isn't too old for a receiver, and he's signed through 2013.

Dwayne Bowe Height: 6-2 Weight: 221 College: Louisiana State Draft: 2007/1 (23) Born: 21-Sep-1984 Age: 28 Risk: Green

Year	Team	G/S	Rec	Pass	Yds	C%	+/-	Y/C	TD	Drop	YAC	Rk	YAC+	DVOA	Rk	DYAR	Rk	YAR	Short	Mid	Deep	Bomb
2009	KC	11/9	47	87	589	54%	-2.4	12.5	4	11	3.2	67	-0.9	-4.0%	54	60	50	71	29%	46%	18%	8%
2010	KC	16/16	72	133	1162	54%	+3.4	16.1	15	7	5.1	20	+1.1	12.0%	18	257	8	295	25%	37%	27%	12%
2011	KC	16/14	81	141	1159	57%	+0.6	14.3	5	9	4.2	44	+0.2	-0.5%	52	136	35	161	26%	46%	21%	7%
2012	KC		80	140	1151	57%	--	14.4	8					7.0%								

Despite the chaotic nature of Kansas City's quarterback depth chart last year, Bowe's targets, receptions, and yards remained remarkably consistent with what he had done in 2010. Bowe actually averaged fewer catches per game with Matt Cassel at quarterback than with either Tyler Palko or Kyle Orton (4.6 to 5.7), but with

Cassel he averaged more yards per game (73.7 to 70.9) and per catch (16.0 to 12.4). He also scored four touchdowns in nine games with Cassel, but only one in nearly half a season without him. The Chiefs used the franchise tag on Bowe in the offseason, but as of June he had refused to sign his $9.5 million tender and was holding out of OTAs in search of a long-term deal. Chiefs coach Romeo Crennel responded with the appropriate clichés ("We'll win with whoever we have"), but it's hard to imagine Kansas City winning too many contests without their best downfield weapon.

Deion Branch
Height: 5-9   Weight: 193   College: Louisville   Draft: 2002/2 (65)   Born: 18-Jul-1979   Age: 33   Risk: Red

Year	Team	G/S	Rec	Pass	Yds	C%	+/-	Y/C	TD	Drop	YAC	Rk	YAC+	DVOA	Rk	DYAR	Rk	YAR	Short	Mid	Deep	Bomb
2009	SEA	14/5	45	79	437	57%	-4.3	9.7	2	4	4.3	40	-0.5	-22.1%	76	-57	78	-50	47%	28%	13%	12%
2010	2TM	15/12	61	92	818	66%	+6.2	13.4	6	1	4.5	29	+0.7	21.0%	5	250	10	226	22%	55%	15%	8%
2011	NE	15/15	51	90	702	57%	-1.0	13.8	5	0	6.5	6	+2.6	5.2%	39	128	41	121	37%	49%	11%	4%
2012	NE		15	25	159	60%	--	10.6	2					-2.2%								

Branch's final numbers were right in line with our preseason projection for him, and yet his season ended up feeling like a disappointment. In part that's because Tom Brady ended up throwing the ball 661 times, meaning every Patriot receiver had more opportunities to stir the stat sheet than we anticipated. But it's also because Branch did very little in the last month of the season and in the playoffs, catching only six passes for 74 yards and one touchdown, and showing very little burst in the process. When you are an aging receiver on a stacked roster, any sign of fading is potentially career-threatening, and while Branch's roster spot is probably not in jeopardy, the offseason acquisitions of Brandon Lloyd, Jabbar Gaffney, and Donte Stallworth could push him down the depth chart.

Steve Breaston
Height: 6-1   Weight: 175   College: Michigan   Draft: 2007/5 (142)   Born: 20-Aug-1983   Age: 29   Risk: Green

Year	Team	G/S	Rec	Pass	Yds	C%	+/-	Y/C	TD	Drop	YAC	Rk	YAC+	DVOA	Rk	DYAR	Rk	YAR	Short	Mid	Deep	Bomb
2009	ARI	15/6	55	82	712	67%	+7.9	12.9	3	2	2.9	76	-1.1	13.3%	20	166	27	199	27%	37%	29%	6%
2010	ARI	13/11	47	87	718	54%	-1.5	15.3	1	6	3.4	57	-1.1	-0.2%	50	81	51	98	26%	36%	25%	13%
2011	KC	16/13	61	98	785	62%	+1.9	12.9	2	3	5.1	22	+0.5	0.7%	50	100	48	118	40%	33%	20%	6%
2012	KC		35	62	500	56%	--	14.3	2					1.8%								

Five years into Steve Breaston's career, it's pretty clear that he'll never be more than a complementary receiver. Even when he went over 1,000 yards in 2008 with Arizona, he was the third banana behind Larry Fitzgerald and Anquan Boldin. Now, he's behind Dwayne Bowe and Jonathan Baldwin. The good news is that Breaston's skill set fits that role well. He had a 7.7% DVOA on third downs last season, best of any Kansas City wideout (excepting Terrance Copper, who only had one third-down play).

Dezmon Briscoe
Height: 6-2   Weight: 207   College: Kansas   Draft: 2010/6 (191)   Born: 14-Aug-1989   Age: 23   Risk: Green

Year	Team	G/S	Rec	Pass	Yds	C%	+/-	Y/C	TD	Drop	YAC	Rk	YAC+	DVOA	Rk	DYAR	Rk	YAR	Short	Mid	Deep	Bomb
2010	CIN	2/0	6	7	93	86%	+1.7	15.5	1	0	5.5	--	+1.0	58.6%	--	41	--	39	43%	43%	0%	14%
2011	TB	16/2	35	51	387	69%	+3.7	11.1	6	2	2.8	82	-1.2	16.5%	18	121	43	122	49%	29%	20%	2%
2012	TB		33	57	409	58%	--	12.4	2					-0.4%								

Two of Briscoe's touchdowns came in the Week 17 game when the Falcons let Delta Baggage Handlers of the Month play defense in the second half. Briscoe missed the Bucs offseason workout program for a personal issue, and then was a no-show for OTAs, so we can assume that Greg Schiano is already trying to find a way to end his Bucs career.

WIDE RECEIVERS

Kenny Britt
Height: 6-3   Weight: 218   College: Rutgers   Draft: 2009/1 (30)   Born: 19-Sep-1988   Age: 24   Risk: Red

Year	Team	G/S	Rec	Pass	Yds	C%	+/-	Y/C	TD	Drop	YAC	Rk	YAC+	DVOA	Rk	DYAR	Rk	YAR	Short	Mid	Deep	Bomb
2009	TEN	16/6	42	75	701	56%	+1.2	16.7	3	4	4.2	44	+0.4	11.2%	25	143	36	143	20%	51%	20%	10%
2010	TEN	12/7	42	73	775	58%	+7.7	18.5	9	4	2.9	69	-1.4	29.1%	2	256	9	257	16%	39%	25%	20%
2011	TEN	3/3	17	26	289	65%	+2.6	17.0	3	0	7.4	--	+2.5	34.1%	--	96	--	91	36%	32%	8%	24%
2012	TEN		61	110	999	55%	--	16.4	7					7.9%								

When we talk about the most physically dominant receivers in the NFL, names like Calvin Johnson or Hakeem Nicks pop up first, but Britt has every bit of the talent that they do. He took a big step forward after the lockout last season, playing a Johnson-esque couple of weeks before tearing his ACL and MCL in Week 3. He also took an important step off the field, keeping his nose clean despite plenty of free time in which to cause the kind of chaos he has been known for. Another surgery this spring puts Britt in danger of missing most of training camp and has his Week 1 availability in question, but if he's fully healthy, he could transform the Titans offense in a big way.

Antonio Brown
Height: 5-10   Weight: 186   College: Central Mighican   Draft: 2010/6 (195)   Born: 10-Jul-1988   Age: 24   Risk: Yellow

Year	Team	G/S	Rec	Pass	Yds	C%	+/-	Y/C	TD	Drop	YAC	Rk	YAC+	DVOA	Rk	DYAR	Rk	YAR	Short	Mid	Deep	Bomb
2010	PIT	9/0	16	19	167	84%	+2.2	10.4	0	0	6.9	--	+1.2	27.2%	--	58	--	53	63%	21%	11%	5%
2011	PIT	16/3	69	124	1108	56%	-3.7	16.1	2	6	4.9	27	+0.4	9.1%	33	204	21	183	23%	42%	28%	7%
2012	PIT		74	119	1073	62%	--	14.5	7					13.0%								

Last August, we wrote in our *Four Downs* column for ESPN Insider that the biggest question for Pittsburgh was, "Who will replace Hines Ward?" Brown provided an emphatic answer in his second season. Like Ward earlier in his career, Brown did most of his damage as a receiver in the 6- to 15-yard range, finishing second on the team with 121 receiving DYAR on passes of that length. Also like Ward, Brown was Big Ben's favorite option on third down (a team-high 45 targets), and excelled in those situations (33.8% DVOA). Perhaps pining for the days when more of his opportunities came on short catches in space, Brown showed off his elusiveness on special teams, ranking fifth among primary punt returners with +4.9 expected points added. Emmanuel Sanders may take over kickoff and/or punt returns so that Brown can concentrate on his role in the offense.

Vincent Brown
Height: 5-11   Weight: 184   College: San Diego State   Draft: 2011/3 (82)   Born: 25-Jan-1989   Age: 23   Risk: Yellow

Year	Team	G/S	Rec	Pass	Yds	C%	+/-	Y/C	TD	Drop	YAC	Rk	YAC+	DVOA	Rk	DYAR	Rk	YAR	Short	Mid	Deep	Bomb
2011	SD	14/4	19	40	329	48%	-1.1	17.3	2	1	4.1	--	+0.2	1.8%	--	46	--	49	18%	39%	21%	21%
2012	SD		38	74	658	51%	--	17.3	3					2.5%								

While he lacks explosive deep speed, Brown was targeted frequently on passes thrown 20 or more yards downfield. While Philip Rivers throws more Deep and Bomb passes than most NFL quarterbacks, that's not the best use for Brown's skill set. Unfortunately, he didn't show the ability as a rookie to separate in short areas on intermediate routes. The Chargers think he has a bright long-term future, but that doesn't necessarily mean he'll have 40 catches this year.

Ryan Broyles
Height: 5-10   Weight: 192   College: Oklahoma   Draft: 2012/2 (54)   Born: 9-Apr-1988   Age: 24   Risk: Yellow

Year	Team	G/S	Rec	Pass	Yds	C%	+/-	Y/C	TD	Drop	YAC	Rk	YAC+	DVOA	Rk	DYAR	Rk	YAR	Short	Mid	Deep	Bomb
2012	DET		19	32	245	59%	--	12.9	2					2.0%								

Broyles was very productive and consistent in college, finishing every year with a catch rate between 72 and 76 percent and between 9.1 and 10.9 yards per target. However, he tore his ACL in November, which only added to questions about his raw athletic abilities. Broyles has good-but-not-great speed, which wouldn't be a problem if not for his limited size. The Lions believe he can compensate with competitiveness and well-honed ball skills. Though not fast, he at least has ample quickness, making him a candidate for the slot.

WIDE RECEIVERS

Dez Bryant
Height: 6-2 Weight: 225 College: Oklahoma State Draft: 2010/1 (24) Born: 4-Nov-1988 Age: 24 Risk: Green

Year	Team	G/S	Rec	Pass	Yds	C%	+/-	Y/C	TD	Drop	YAC	Rk	YAC+	DVOA	Rk	DYAR	Rk	YAR	Short	Mid	Deep	Bomb
2010	DAL	12/2	45	73	561	62%	+3.4	12.5	6	2	4.3	34	-0.6	5.8%	35	105	47	93	39%	33%	14%	13%
2011	DAL	15/13	63	103	928	61%	+3.7	14.7	9	3	4.8	29	+0.4	20.5%	13	262	13	255	26%	47%	16%	12%
2012	DAL		67	109	965	61%	--	14.4	8					12.2%								

Most statistically similar player to Bryant over the first two years of his career: Terrell Owens. Their situations are similar; both played with star wide receivers (Jerry Rice and Miles Austin) as rookies, then saw their numbers develop in year two when those stars were injured. Owens caused so many headaches that five NFL teams and one indoor club gave up on him, even though he had nine touchdowns and nearly 1,000 yards in his final NFL season. Bryant was suspended from Oklahoma State for lying to NFL officials, and got into a shouting match with a mall security guard in 2011. Owens made nearly $80 million in his NFL career, but two of his homes are in foreclosure and on *Dr. Phil* he told three of the four mothers of his children that he was broke. Bryant, meanwhile, allegedly got into a brawl with Lil' Wayne in a Miami nightclub in January over debt Bryant owes to a financial company with ties to Wayne's record label, appropriately entitled Young Money Entertainment. Bryant also reportedly racked up $600,000 in debt to a Dallas-area jeweler. Cue The Giant from *Twin Peaks* telling Agent Cooper, "It is happening again."

Nate Burleson
Height: 6-0 Weight: 192 College: Nevada Draft: 2003/3 (71) Born: 19-Aug-1981 Age: 31 Risk: Green

Year	Team	G/S	Rec	Pass	Yds	C%	+/-	Y/C	TD	Drop	YAC	Rk	YAC+	DVOA	Rk	DYAR	Rk	YAR	Short	Mid	Deep	Bomb
2009	SEA	13/12	63	103	812	61%	+1.6	12.9	3	5	4.4	33	+0.4	1.2%	40	113	40	128	31%	40%	22%	7%
2010	DET	14/14	55	86	625	64%	-1.8	11.4	6	4	5.5	13	+1.0	-4.4%	63	57	59	60	44%	36%	19%	1%
2011	DET	16/11	73	110	757	66%	-3.2	10.4	3	6	5.5	19	+0.7	-5.7%	60	60	55	70	64%	25%	8%	4%
2012	DET		58	96	694	60%	--	12.0	3					-0.5%								

Burleson is an experienced veteran who fits extremely well as a No. 2 in Scott Linehan's offense. He's not dynamic enough to be a featured part of a game plan, but he has the necessary speed and change-of-direction quickness to capitalize on opportunities as a complimentary weapon. Though generally reliable, Burleson is not immune to the occasional gaffe (see his three-OPI performance last year against the Saints). A lot of his productivity must be manufactured via play design.

Plaxico Burress
Height: 6-5 Weight: 232 College: Michigan State Draft: 2000/1 (8) Born: 12-Aug-1977 Age: 35 Risk: N/A

Year	Team	G/S	Rec	Pass	Yds	C%	+/-	Y/C	TD	Drop	YAC	Rk	YAC+	DVOA	Rk	DYAR	Rk	YAR	Short	Mid	Deep	Bomb
2011	NYJ	16/13	45	96	612	47%	-7.9	13.6	8	4	3.2	74	-0.4	-5.5%	58	56	56	95	16%	53%	26%	4%

By late May, Plax was reduced to lobbying for himself on talk radio, dropping hints about his willingness to play for just about any team in need of a wide receiver (even the Dolphins!) and the quarterbacks he has friendly social relationships with (Cam Newton!). Unfortunately for Plax, the market for aging, talented, dunderheads was flooded with Roy Williams-Terrell Owens options, and no team will feel compelled to make a move until there is a training camp injury, if at all. Plax's eight touchdowns came mostly as a result of 22 red zone targets; he has little else to offer but a goal-line post-up game, a skill most teams would rather get from a sturdy, younger, and baggage-free tight end.

Deon Butler
Height: 5-10 Weight: 182 College: Penn State Draft: 2009/3 (91) Born: 4-Jan-1986 Age: 27 Risk: Blue

Year	Team	G/S	Rec	Pass	Yds	C%	+/-	Y/C	TD	Drop	YAC	Rk	YAC+	DVOA	Rk	DYAR	Rk	YAR	Short	Mid	Deep	Bomb
2009	SEA	16/0	15	42	175	36%	-8.5	11.7	0	2	3.1	--	-0.5	-39.1%	--	-88	--	-90	20%	60%	3%	18%
2010	SEA	13/8	36	70	385	51%	-6.4	10.7	4	8	3.2	60	-1.3	-21.0%	77	-48	76	-35	43%	31%	13%	13%
2011	SEA	5/0	6	7	51	86%	+1.5	8.5	0	0	1.7	--	-1.9	13.5%	--	15	--	12	29%	57%	14%	0%
2012	SEA		4	8	45	50%	--	11.2	0					-20.9%								

366 WIDE RECEIVERS

Late in his second season, Butler suffered a gruesome broken leg while catching a touchdown pass late in a blowout loss to the San Francisco 49ers. That injury ended Butler's 2010 campaign and forced him to spend the first nine weeks of last season on the PUP list. Activated in Week 10, Butler dressed and played sparingly in the final five games of the season. At 5-foot-10 and 180 pounds, Butler is much smaller than the receivers the Seahawks have brought in under John Schneider and Pete Carroll, but he does bring a speed element to the position that could earn him a spot as a No. 4 or No. 5 receiver.

Andre Caldwell
Height: 6-0   Weight: 190   College: Florida   Draft: 2008/3 (97)   Born: 15-Apr-1985   Age: 27   Risk: Yellow

Year	Team	G/S	Rec	Pass	Yds	C%	+/-	Y/C	TD	Drop	YAC	Rk	YAC+	DVOA	Rk	DYAR	Rk	YAR	Short	Mid	Deep	Bomb
2009	CIN	16/3	51	80	432	64%	-1.7	8.5	3	3	2.6	78	-1.6	-8.1%	59	28	60	23	41%	50%	5%	4%
2010	CIN	15/5	25	37	345	68%	+2.1	13.8	0	3	4.2	--	-0.1	16.8%	--	91	--	87	42%	36%	8%	14%
2011	CIN	13/2	32	67	317	55%	-6.3	9.9	3	4	3.1	78	-1.4	-17.9%	80	-27	79	-58	50%	41%	5%	5%
2012	DEN		54	86	680	63%	--	12.6	3					5.7%								

Bubba fell out of favor with new offensive coordinator Jay Gruden, and was allowed to leave for Denver. His strong 2010 numbers were achieved with a quarterback who had the arm to power in outside throws (Carson Palmer), and now Caldwell will be on the receiving end of fastballs (presumably) from Peyton Manning. Don't be surprised if Caldwell emerges from the chaff competing for the slot job in Denver and establishes himself as a quality NFL wideout.

Greg Camarillo
Height: 6-1   Weight: 190   College: Stanford   Draft: 2005/FA   Born: 18-Apr-1982   Age: 30   Risk: N/A

Year	Team	G/S	Rec	Pass	Yds	C%	+/-	Y/C	TD	Drop	YAC	Rk	YAC+	DVOA	Rk	DYAR	Rk	YAR	Short	Mid	Deep	Bomb
2009	MIA	16/16	50	72	552	69%	+8.9	11.0	0	0	2.0	87	-1.9	10.0%	28	134	37	127	23%	53%	19%	6%
2010	MIN	16/1	20	33	240	61%	-1.0	12.0	1	1	4.4	--	-0.1	2.4%	--	37	--	32	31%	50%	16%	3%
2011	MIN	13/0	9	24	121	38%	-5.1	13.4	0	1	1.3	--	-2.2	-25.1%	--	-22	--	-33	27%	55%	14%	5%

The Vikings never seemed able to figure out why they had traded for Greg Camarillo in the first place. He had been a fine posession receiver in Miami, but the Vikings gave him very little playing time, and thus didn't get much out of him. His numbers last year are awful, but most passes to Camarillo are marked in the game charting as "thrown away" or "what a stupid pass by Joe Webb" or "Ponder still throws a pass he shouldn't be throwing" or some such thing. Camarillo could help a team if he got another chance in the NFL, but we probably will never find out.

Danny Coale
Height: 6-0   Weight: 201   College: Virginia Tech   Draft: 2012/5 (152)   Born: 27-Jun-1988   Age: 24   Risk: Red

Year	Team	G/S	Rec	Pass	Yds	C%	+/-	Y/C	TD	Drop	YAC	Rk	YAC+	DVOA	Rk	DYAR	Rk	YAR	Short	Mid	Deep	Bomb
2012	DAL		19	31	221	61%	--	11.6	2					-1.5%								

Coale started four years in college and had 17.4 yards per catch over the past three seasons, but never produced a 1,000-yard season and caught just eight touchdowns in his career. He has size and speed, but not much YAC ability. On any other roster, a fifth-rounder like this is special teams fodder, but the rest of the Dallas depth chart at wide receiver consists of Miles Austin, Dez Bryant, and 50 guys who answered an ad on craigslist.

Randall Cobb
Height: 5-11   Weight: 190   College: Kentucky   Draft: 2011/2 (64)   Born: 22-Aug-1990   Age: 22   Risk: Blue

Year	Team	G/S	Rec	Pass	Yds	C%	+/-	Y/C	TD	Drop	YAC	Rk	YAC+	DVOA	Rk	DYAR	Rk	YAR	Short	Mid	Deep	Bomb
2011	GB	15/0	25	31	375	81%	+4.0	15.0	1	2	7.5	--	+3.4	42.1%	--	127	--	132	35%	45%	19%	0%
2012	GB		29	46	436	63%	--	15.1	3					19.8%								

Cobb was drafted primarily for his return prowess, though moving forward, the Packers likely plan on using him more as a slot receiver and gadget play specialist. Think Antwaan Randle El, with whom Cobb shares a body type.

Cobb's meaningful offensive snap totals increased as his rookie year wore on. Like the man he's chasing on the depth chart (James Jones), he struggles a bit with holding onto the football. The Packers can live with the risk of some mistakes, though, because the rewards of his sudden speed and powerful shiftiness can be substantial.

Austin Collie   Height: 6-1   Weight: 200   College: BYU   Draft: 2009/4 (127)   Born: 11-Nov-1985   Age: 27   Risk: Green

Year	Team	G/S	Rec	Pass	Yds	C%	+/-	Y/C	TD	Drop	YAC	Rk	YAC+	DVOA	Rk	DYAR	Rk	YAR	Short	Mid	Deep	Bomb
2009	IND	16/5	60	90	676	67%	+3.4	11.3	7	5	4.1	49	-0.5	16.6%	15	215	19	206	44%	28%	24%	3%
2010	IND	9/6	58	71	649	82%	+12.1	11.2	8	4	4.9	23	+0.1	28.0%	3	229	14	259	59%	20%	10%	10%
2011	IND	16/5	54	97	514	56%	-7.9	9.5	1	3	3.9	52	-0.5	-13.8%	74	-9	74	-13	53%	33%	12%	2%
2012	IND		54	89	607	61%	--	11.2	2					-7.1%								

We know, we know, we all thought Collie could repeat that 82 percent catch rate from 2010, but it just wasn't meant to be. His role going forward depends a lot on what the Colts think of his chances of holding up on the outside. After drafting two big and versatile tight ends, the third receiver may not see much field time in Indianapolis unless they go empty. Collie is a fine third receiver either way, but not the kind of player you want to invest much in due to the lack of durability.

Marques Colston   Height: 6-4   Weight: 225   College: Hofstra   Draft: 2006/7 (252)   Born: 5-Jun-1983   Age: 29   Risk: Green

Year	Team	G/S	Rec	Pass	Yds	C%	+/-	Y/C	TD	Drop	YAC	Rk	YAC+	DVOA	Rk	DYAR	Rk	YAR	Short	Mid	Deep	Bomb
2009	NO	16/14	70	107	1074	65%	+6.2	15.3	9	6	5.0	25	+0.9	26.0%	6	337	7	341	31%	47%	17%	5%
2010	NO	15/11	84	132	1023	64%	+4.3	12.2	7	8	3.2	62	-0.6	8.7%	28	221	15	248	35%	46%	15%	4%
2011	NO	14/7	80	107	1143	75%	+15.7	14.3	8	3	3.2	76	-0.6	33.9%	5	390	6	441	22%	51%	20%	8%
2012	NO		78	115	1102	68%	--	14.1	9					25.7%								

Colston is a model of consistency, from game to game and season to season. Colston's stat lines from 2011 are a parade of seven- to eight-catch, 100-yard efforts. His season stats hover around 70 to 80 catches, 1,100 yards, and seven to nine touchdowns whenever he is healthy for a full year. Wind Colston up, and he will give you eight catches and 90-something yards whenever he is healthy. Locking up Colston for five years, as the Saints did at the start of free agency, was one of the safest investments an NFL team can make, and one of the few things that Saints have done since January that does not deserve criticism.

Riley Cooper   Height: 6-4   Weight: 222   College: Florida   Draft: 2010/5 (159)   Born: 9-Sep-1987   Age: 25   Risk: Green

Year	Team	G/S	Rec	Pass	Yds	C%	+/-	Y/C	TD	Drop	YAC	Rk	YAC+	DVOA	Rk	DYAR	Rk	YAR	Short	Mid	Deep	Bomb
2010	PHI	13/2	7	18	116	39%	-1.5	16.6	1	0	2.6	--	-2.0	-9.1%	--	5	--	9	14%	57%	21%	7%
2011	PHI	16/3	16	35	315	46%	+0.3	19.7	1	3	3.5	--	-1.1	-1.0%	--	32	--	32	10%	50%	20%	20%
2012	PHI		4	8	61	50%	--	15.3	0					-2.9%								

Injuries forced Cooper into the starting lineup for Weeks 11 through 13, and he played quite well, especially considering that the quarterback in those weeks was Vince Young rather than Michael Vick. Nonetheless, he went back to playing primarily on special teams when Jeremy Maclin returned in Week 14. For a team that throws so much, the Eagles do surprisingly little with their fourth and fifth receivers.

Jerricho Cotchery   Height: 6-1   Weight: 200   College: North Carolina State   Draft: 2004/4 (108)   Born: 16-Jun-1982   Age: 30   Risk: Yellow

Year	Team	G/S	Rec	Pass	Yds	C%	+/-	Y/C	TD	Drop	YAC	Rk	YAC+	DVOA	Rk	DYAR	Rk	YAR	Short	Mid	Deep	Bomb
2009	NYJ	14/12	57	97	821	60%	+0.1	14.4	3	2	5.3	17	+1.1	12.3%	22	189	22	216	35%	38%	21%	7%
2010	NYJ	14/5	41	86	433	48%	-8.6	10.6	2	6	2.7	75	-1.5	-22.8%	78	-68	81	-76	34%	42%	14%	10%
2011	PIT	13/0	16	31	237	55%	-0.7	14.8	2	1	4.1	--	+0.5	12.8%	--	63	--	50	20%	57%	23%	0%
2012	PIT		27	45	394	60%	--	14.6	2					10.0%								

Although it's possible he's a camp casualty, Cotchery will fill the seldom-used, veteran No. 4 wide receiver role vacated by Hines Ward's retirement. His production has precipitously declined over the past two years, and his main contribution last year was scoring the game-tying touchdown late in Pittsburgh's Wild Card loss to Tim Tebow and the Broncos.

Michael Crabtree   Height: 6-2   Weight: 215   College: Texas Tech   Draft: 2009/1 (10)   Born: 14-Sep-1987   Age: 25   Risk: Green

Year	Team	G/S	Rec	Pass	Yds	C%	+/-	Y/C	TD	Drop	YAC	Rk	YAC+	DVOA	Rk	DYAR	Rk	YAR	Short	Mid	Deep	Bomb
2009	SF	11/11	48	86	625	56%	-2.4	13.0	2	7	4.2	45	-1.0	-19.6%	75	-45	77	-10	38%	32%	18%	12%
2010	SF	16/15	55	100	741	55%	-2.6	13.5	6	7	5.3	15	+0.9	2.9%	43	121	37	116	37%	40%	14%	9%
2011	SF	15/14	72	114	874	64%	+3.1	12.1	4	5	5.0	25	+0.1	4.9%	41	154	28	125	46%	29%	17%	8%
2012	SF		52	98	705	53%	--	13.5	5					-3.1%								

Crabtree had his best season as a pro in 2011, setting career bests in catches, yards, catch rate, DVOA, and DYAR. One area where he needs to improve, though, is in the red zone, where he's had a team-high 26 targets over the past two years, and nearly twice as many as his next-highest teammate in 2011. Nevertheless, he had a -12.3% red zone DVOA in 2010, followed by a -10.7% red zone DVOA last year. Crabtree is entering the fourth of five seasons on his rookie contract, so this will be a make-or-break year for his future in San Francisco. With the additions of Randy Moss and Mario Manningham, he'll no longer have the excuse that he's the only decent wideout in town. The 49ers figure to pass more often this season, so Crabs also won't have the excuse that his receiving numbers are suppressed by a run-first offense. The foot problems that nagged him early in his career seem to be a thing of the past, and he'll have the benefit of a full offseason for the first time in his career. Simply, it's time to go big or go home (to Dallas, where he'll likely sign with his favorite team as a 2014 free agent).

Patrick Crayton   Height: 6-0   Weight: 205   College: NW Oklahoma State   Draft: 2004/7 (216)   Born: 7-Apr-1979   Age: 33   Risk: N/A

Year	Team	G/S	Rec	Pass	Yds	C%	+/-	Y/C	TD	Drop	YAC	Rk	YAC+	DVOA	Rk	DYAR	Rk	YAR	Short	Mid	Deep	Bomb
2009	DAL	16/6	37	67	622	55%	-2.1	16.8	5	5	7.2	3	+3.0	16.1%	16	153	32	154	34%	54%	9%	3%
2010	SD	9/2	28	42	514	67%	+4.5	18.4	1	2	7.6	--	+3.4	41.7%	--	174	--	183	24%	41%	27%	7%
2011	SD	14/1	23	34	248	68%	+2.4	10.8	1	2	4.3	--	+0.3	8.4%	--	57	--	43	45%	45%	6%	3%

A former small-sample size superstar who never made the transition into a high-usage star, Crayton is a valuable third or fourth option who is able to take advantage of depth defensive backs and find holes in zones. At this stage of his career, he won't ever be more than that, but he could still be a useful player for the right team.

Josh Cribbs   Height: 6-1   Weight: 192   College: Kent State   Draft: 2005/FA   Born: 9-Jun-1983   Age: 29   Risk: Green

Year	Team	G/S	Rec	Pass	Yds	C%	+/-	Y/C	TD	Drop	YAC	Rk	YAC+	DVOA	Rk	DYAR	Rk	YAR	Short	Mid	Deep	Bomb
2009	CLE	16/12	20	37	135	54%	+0.4	6.8	1	1	4.4	--	-0.8	-52.0%	--	-113	--	-130	69%	9%	6%	16%
2010	CLE	15/5	23	39	292	59%	-0.2	12.7	1	0	6.0	--	+1.3	-0.3%	--	37	--	21	34%	45%	5%	16%
2011	CLE	16/7	41	67	518	61%	+0.3	12.6	4	4	5.6	17	+0.8	11.9%	25	130	38	117	37%	42%	12%	9%
2012	CLE		27	45	363	60%	--	13.4	2					2.7%								

Cribbs showed notable improvement as a wideout in 2011, especially factoring in the quarterbacks throwing him passes. He still makes his impact on special teams first and foremost, but since the Browns added little in the way of receiving help in the offseason, Cribbs will be asked to take another step forward in the passing game. KUBIAK would be surprised if his numbers measurably improve, however.

Victor Cruz

Height: 6-1 Weight: 200 College: Massachusetts Draft: 2010/FA Born: 11-Nov-1986 Age: 26 Risk: Green

Year	Team	G/S	Rec	Pass	Yds	C%	+/-	Y/C	TD	Drop	YAC	Rk	YAC+	DVOA	Rk	DYAR	Rk	YAR	Short	Mid	Deep	Bomb
2011	NYG	16/7	82	129	1536	64%	+9.1	18.7	9	8	7.2	2	+2.9	32.0%	6	455	3	451	31%	41%	19%	9%
2012	NYG		76	123	1237	62%	--	16.3	8					18.5%								

Why did all the scouts miss on Victor Cruz? Even the Giants passed him up in all seven rounds of the 2010 draft. Perhaps the problem is that Cruz's skills are subtle, and subtle doesn't stand out at the FCS level. Scouts can see a player with size and speed dominate FCS defenses and know that the size and speed will still be there at the NFL level. But if you see a guy like Victor Cruz, and he's dominating FCS defenses with hard cuts and crisp routes, it's easy to write that off as a player who takes advantage of inferior defensive talent at a lower level. You may not even notice Victor Cruz winning the battle of the minds with a cornerback, because his FCS quarterback is not good enough to get the ball to the right place.

That being said, Victor Cruz is not going to repeat his 2011 season. He is not going to have five touchdowns of more than 65 yards again, especially considering that *nobody* had done that since Elroy "Crazy Legs" Hirsch in 1951. Only two players, Marvin Harrison and Andre Johnson, have enjoyed two straight 1,500-yard receiving seasons, and Cruz is not going to become the third. Make sure to temper your fantasy expectations.

Eric Decker

Height: 6-3 Weight: 217 College: Minnesota Draft: 2010/3 (87) Born: 15-Mar-1987 Age: 25 Risk: Red

Year	Team	G/S	Rec	Pass	Yds	C%	+/-	Y/C	TD	Drop	YAC	Rk	YAC+	DVOA	Rk	DYAR	Rk	YAR	Short	Mid	Deep	Bomb
2010	DEN	14/0	6	8	106	75%	+1.2	17.7	1	1	4.0	--	-1.6	56.1%	--	34	--	32	13%	50%	25%	13%
2011	DEN	16/13	44	98	612	46%	-7.4	13.9	8	6	3.9	58	-0.9	-12.4%	72	2	71	-16	30%	34%	16%	20%
2012	DEN		69	113	1013	61%	--	14.7	7					12.5%								

Decker played with Tim Tebow, which largely explains the following split: In the first three quarters of the game, Decker had -121 DYAR, worst of any wide receiver in football. In the fourth quarter and overtime, that number climbed to 123 DYAR, which was in the top ten. Six of his ten 20-plus-yard gains came in the game's final frame. We should expect more consistency with Peyton Manning in town, assuming Decker can hold off Andre Caldwell for a starting spot.

Jarett Dillard

Height: 5-10 Weight: 187 College: Rice Draft: 2009/5 (144) Born: 21-Dec-1985 Age: 27 Risk: Blue

Year	Team	G/S	Rec	Pass	Yds	C%	+/-	Y/C	TD	Drop	YAC	Rk	YAC+	DVOA	Rk	DYAR	Rk	YAR	Short	Mid	Deep	Bomb
2009	JAC	7/0	6	8	106	75%	+1.2	17.7	0	0	3.2	--	-1.4	53.5%	--	37	--	40	13%	50%	25%	13%
2011	JAC	14/5	29	50	292	58%	-0.6	10.1	1	2	1.4	92	-2.9	-12.2%	71	2	72	-9	33%	48%	17%	2%
2012	DET		4	7	42	57%	--	10.5	0					-11.8%								

Dillard lost most of the 2009 and 2010 seasons to injury, and while he finally stayed healthy in 2011, he continued to be a non-factor. He started down the stretch after the Jaguars waived Jason Hill, but that was more about the fact that the Jaguars had nobody at receiver than it was any real indicator of Dillard's talent. He was waived after the season, and caught on with Detroit, but there's no guarantee he'll make the roster.

Early Doucet

Height: 6-0 Weight: 209 College: Louisiana State Draft: 2008/3 (81) Born: 28-Oct-1985 Age: 27 Risk: Blue

Year	Team	G/S	Rec	Pass	Yds	C%	+/-	Y/C	TD	Drop	YAC	Rk	YAC+	DVOA	Rk	DYAR	Rk	YAR	Short	Mid	Deep	Bomb
2009	ARI	9/0	17	24	214	71%	+2.1	12.6	1	4	6.3	--	+1.6	17.6%	--	58	--	64	39%	43%	9%	9%
2010	ARI	10/5	26	59	291	44%	-9.8	11.2	1	6	3.1	66	-1.2	-40.5%	85	-124	83	-108	36%	45%	15%	4%
2011	ARI	16/6	54	97	689	56%	-5.7	12.8	5	4	6.0	12	+1.9	-11.1%	67	12	67	19	49%	33%	15%	2%
2012	ARI		16	27	219	59%	--	13.7	0					-2.5%								

Finally healthy for a full season, Doucet established career-highs in all standard statistics as the No. 3 receiver behind Larry Fitzgerald and Andre Roberts. The Cardinals let him test free agency, but he didn't get much interest from other teams, so the Cardinals brought him back on a two-year, $4 million contract that, with incentives, could be worth up to $5.5 million. Michael Floyd knocks everyone down a slot on the depth chart, so he'll compete with Roberts for snaps from the slot.

Harry Douglas
Height: 5-11 Weight: 176 College: Louisville Draft: 2008/3 (84) Born: 16-Sep-1985 Age: 27 Risk: Green

Year	Team	G/S	Rec	Pass	Yds	C%	+/-	Y/C	TD	Drop	YAC	Rk	YAC+	DVOA	Rk	DYAR	Rk	YAR	Short	Mid	Deep	Bomb
2010	ATL	16/4	22	53	294	42%	-8.1	13.4	1	2	5.6	10	+1.2	-26.3%	80	-57	77	-57	32%	32%	22%	14%
2011	ATL	16/4	39	62	498	63%	+1.8	12.8	1	2	5.9	13	+1.2	-4.9%	57	35	63	35	44%	34%	15%	7%
2012	ATL		28	47	388	60%	--	13.9	1					8.4%								

Douglas played well in relief of injured Julio Jones against the Saints in November, catching eight passes for 133 yards, but his role in the offense shrunk as he battled thigh and groin injuries while Jones caught fire. A new four-year contract indicates that the Falcons are satisfied with Douglas' limited production; the slot receiver does not have a huge role in their offense, so 30 to 40 catches, deep speed, and the ability to start in a pinch will keep Douglas employed for a few seasons.

Donald Driver
Height: 6-0 Weight: 188 College: Alcorn State Draft: 1999/7 (213) Born: 2-Feb-1975 Age: 37 Risk: Green

Year	Team	G/S	Rec	Pass	Yds	C%	+/-	Y/C	TD	Drop	YAC	Rk	YAC+	DVOA	Rk	DYAR	Rk	YAR	Short	Mid	Deep	Bomb
2009	GB	16/16	70	112	1061	63%	+3.8	15.2	6	7	5.4	14	+0.9	13.3%	19	245	14	271	38%	35%	14%	13%
2010	GB	15/15	51	84	565	61%	-1.9	11.1	4	6	3.5	56	-1.0	-7.8%	68	33	68	33	38%	41%	16%	5%
2011	GB	16/15	37	56	445	66%	+1.5	12.0	6	6	3.7	62	-0.1	17.1%	16	132	36	134	28%	56%	14%	2%
2012	GB		26	41	306	63%	--	11.8	3					7.3%								

Driver was essentially Greg Jennings before Greg Jennings. He's always been a fundamentally sound, swift-moving catch-and-run maestro who is capable of both stretching the field and moving the chains over the middle. After averaging over 1,000 yards receiving annually from 2002-09, he settled into an ancillary role in 2010, where he was often listed as a starter but was really the third or fourth option in most of Green Bay's multi-receiver threats. With the rise of Randall Cobb, Driver may be the fifth or sixth option in 2012. In the past two years Driver has shown more wear and tear, though to his credit, he's only missed three regular-season games.

Braylon Edwards
Height: 6-3 Weight: 211 College: Michigan Draft: 2005/1 (3) Born: 21-Feb-1983 Age: 29 Risk: N/A

Year	Team	G/S	Rec	Pass	Yds	C%	+/-	Y/C	TD	Drop	YAC	Rk	YAC+	DVOA	Rk	DYAR	Rk	YAR	Short	Mid	Deep	Bomb
2009	2TM	16/15	45	95	680	47%	-5.8	15.1	4	6	4.1	49	+0.3	-3.5%	53	71	48	61	23%	41%	19%	17%
2010	NYJ	16/15	53	101	904	52%	+2.2	17.1	7	3	5.4	14	+1.4	3.1%	42	131	33	142	27%	37%	13%	23%
2011	SF	9/5	15	34	181	44%	-4.5	12.1	0	1	3.1	--	-0.2	-27.4%	--	-40	--	-50	29%	58%	10%	3%

In San Francisco, Edwards will always be remembered as the 49ers' sneaky answer at split end before Randy Moss became the sneaky answer at split end. Despite missing half of the 2011 season with a torn meniscus, Edwards still finished third on the team with eight red-zone targets. Unfortunately, not a single one resulted in a touchdown. At only 29 years old, Edwards' career need not be over—but when you can't garner interest from the Jets, a team with as putrid a wide receiver corps as any in the league, it might be time to start updating your LinkedIn profile.

Lee Evans
Height: 5-10 Weight: 202 College: Wisconsin Draft: 2004/1 (13) Born: 11-Mar-1981 Age: 31 Risk: Yellow

Year	Team	G/S	Rec	Pass	Yds	C%	+/-	Y/C	TD	Drop	YAC	Rk	YAC+	DVOA	Rk	DYAR	Rk	YAR	Short	Mid	Deep	Bomb
2009	BUF	16/16	44	95	612	46%	-5.9	13.9	7	1	2.2	85	-2.0	-10.2%	63	18	63	-8	20%	46%	18%	16%
2010	BUF	13/13	37	84	578	44%	-3.1	15.6	4	2	3.2	59	-0.9	-16.7%	73	-26	73	-35	15%	37%	24%	23%
2011	BAL	9/2	4	26	74	15%	-8.0	18.5	0	2	2.3	--	-1.6	-67.4%	--	-113	--	-115	13%	38%	21%	29%
2012	JAC		14	32	196	44%	--	14.0	1					-20.7%								

The shelf life of a wide receiver is longer than at other positions, but it's hard not to write off Evans at this point. After ranking 20th in DVOA in 2008, his performance fell off a cliff the following two seasons in Buffalo. Last year, a trade to Baltimore was supposed to resurrect his career, and instead basically ended it. Even when he wasn't injured, he was still ineffective. As further evidence of Evans' steep decline, he'll be competing with Cecil Shorts in training camp for the right to be Jacksonville's No. 4 wide receiver.

Larry Fitzgerald   Height: 6-3   Weight: 225   College: Pittsburgh   Draft: 2004/1 (3)   Born: 31-Aug-1983   Age: 29   Risk: Green

Year	Team	G/S	Rec	Pass	Yds	C%	+/-	Y/C	TD	Drop	YAC	Rk	YAC+	DVOA	Rk	DYAR	Rk	YAR	Short	Mid	Deep	Bomb
2009	ARI	16/16	97	153	1092	63%	+8.9	11.3	13	6	3.2	66	-0.7	9.5%	30	280	11	332	30%	43%	17%	9%
2010	ARI	16/15	90	172	1137	52%	-8.5	12.6	6	5	2.4	79	-1.5	-13.0%	71	-4	71	45	24%	42%	24%	10%
2011	ARI	16/16	80	154	1411	52%	-5.3	17.6	8	3	6.1	8	+1.8	9.7%	31	278	10	245	28%	33%	25%	13%
2012	ARI		86	150	1316	57%	--	15.3	10					10.2%								

Even with two quarterbacks ranking outside the top 32 in DYAR and DVOA, Fitzgerald's DYAR and DVOA in 2011 returned to the levels of Kurt Warner's final seasons in Arizona. Without Anquan Boldin, Fitzgerald has faced more double-teams, and without Warner, his catch rate has dropped by more than 10 percentage points. Perhaps that's why Fitzgerald remained mum during the Cardinals' pursuit of Peyton Manning and openly advocated for the selection of Michael Floyd in the first round of the 2012 NFL Draft. The Cardinals missed out on Manning, but Floyd's arrival could keep opposing defenses more honest in how they defend Fitzgerald.

Malcom Floyd   Height: 6-5   Weight: 201   College: Wyoming   Draft: 2004/FA   Born: 8-Sep-1981   Age: 31   Risk: Green

Year	Team	G/S	Rec	Pass	Yds	C%	+/-	Y/C	TD	Drop	YAC	Rk	YAC+	DVOA	Rk	DYAR	Rk	YAR	Short	Mid	Deep	Bomb
2009	SD	16/9	45	76	776	59%	+5.2	17.2	1	3	2.5	79	-1.8	23.7%	7	222	18	220	16%	36%	28%	20%
2010	SD	11/9	37	77	717	48%	-2.2	19.4	6	1	3.0	67	-1.6	9.6%	23	131	34	149	8%	41%	31%	20%
2011	SD	12/9	43	70	856	61%	+7.4	19.9	5	1	4.2	46	+0.3	51.4%	2	351	7	342	12%	44%	31%	13%
2012	SD		43	80	761	54%	--	17.7	5					11.7%								

In the right role, Floyd is a very valuable receiver, as his second-place finish in DVOA shows. He's a good fit for the Chargers: a big receiver with good downfield speed capable of running the deep routes in Norv Turner's offense effectively. He had a similarly excellent season in a smaller sample size in 2008 (58.9% DVOA on 37 passes). He's never really been targeted like Vincent Jackson though; Floyd is more of a pure vertical threat.

Michael Floyd   Height: 6-3   Weight: 220   College: Notre Dame   Draft: 2012/1 (13)   Born: 27-Nov-1989   Age: 23   Risk: Red

Year	Team	G/S	Rec	Pass	Yds	C%	+/-	Y/C	TD	Drop	YAC	Rk	YAC+	DVOA	Rk	DYAR	Rk	YAR	Short	Mid	Deep	Bomb
2012	ARI		55	91	681	60%	--	12.4	4					-0.3%								

Floyd had some off-field issues in college, but he stayed out of trouble last season and will have the benefit of playing with fellow Minnesota native Larry Fitzgerald as he transitions to the NFL. Fitzgerald had known Floyd since the latter was in high school and, according to Peter King, "badly" wanted the Cardinals to select Floyd in the first round. Floyd had two different college careers: explosive in 2009-2010 with 61 percent catch rate and 16.6 yards per reception, then more of a possession receiver in 2011 with a 66 percent catch rate and 12.1 yards per reception. Floyd should give the Cardinals the legitimate No. 2 receiver they've lacked since the trade of Anquan Boldin after the 2009 season, but which Floyd will it be?

Jacoby Ford
Height: 5-9   Weight: 186   College: Clemson   Draft: 2010/4 (108)   Born: 27-Jul-1987   Age: 25   Risk: Green

Year	Team	G/S	Rec	Pass	Yds	C%	+/-	Y/C	TD	Drop	YAC	Rk	YAC+	DVOA	Rk	DYAR	Rk	YAR	Short	Mid	Deep	Bomb
2010	OAK	16/9	25	54	470	46%	-4.0	18.8	2	4	4.1	39	-0.3	-2.4%	56	41	65	43	30%	26%	24%	20%
2011	OAK	8/3	19	33	279	58%	-1.7	14.7	1	1	6.6	--	+2.4	-2.3%	--	27	--	21	44%	41%	9%	6%
2012	OAK		46	80	687	58%	--	14.9	2					3.0%								

Ford's rookie campaign was very impressive, especially after midseason, but he had an injury-plagued and disappointing second year. Despite his good speed, he was not a great deep threat and he had more success on short passes designed to get him into space. He has been surpassed on the burner depth chart by Denarius Moore and Darrius Heyward-Bey and hasn't shown the skill set of a possession receiver, but the Raiders are planning on using him in the slot.

Jabar Gaffney
Height: 6-1   Weight: 205   College: Florida   Draft: 2002/2 (33)   Born: 1-Dec-1980   Age: 32   Risk: Red

Year	Team	G/S	Rec	Pass	Yds	C%	+/-	Y/C	TD	Drop	YAC	Rk	YAC+	DVOA	Rk	DYAR	Rk	YAR	Short	Mid	Deep	Bomb
2009	DEN	16/7	54	87	732	62%	+0.1	13.6	2	3	4.9	26	+0.4	8.5%	32	148	35	142	43%	32%	22%	3%
2010	DEN	16/11	65	112	875	58%	+0.4	13.5	2	4	3.2	61	-1.2	0.0%	48	111	44	109	32%	39%	21%	8%
2011	WAS	16/15	68	115	947	59%	+2.3	13.9	5	2	2.7	86	-1.4	2.6%	46	138	33	174	27%	39%	22%	12%
2012	NE		24	42	300	57%	--	12.5	2					0.6%								

July 5 was the Patriots player comment deadline and we woke up and couldn't find Gaffney's comment anywhere. So [expletive deleted] this [expletive deleted] ... Broncos and Redskins let Gaffney go after 65 and 68 catch seasons? Feelings are for suckas, never again. Black heart, dead soul, bad teams give mediocre receivers 115 targets ... Lito Sheppard didn't steal this player comment. He is just a [expletive deleted] ... Patriots signed Gaffney for depth in June, because they don't follow The Tweeter, and Gaffney deleted his account anyway ... Home boys will change on you, cut you after a couple of playoff dropped passes, but Gaffney is grateful no matter what.

Er, we regret to inform you that this player comment was hacked.

Pierre Garcon
Height: 6-0   Weight: 210   College: Mount Union   Draft: 2008/6 (205)   Born: 8-Aug-1986   Age: 26   Risk: Green

Year	Team	G/S	Rec	Pass	Yds	C%	+/-	Y/C	TD	Drop	YAC	Rk	YAC+	DVOA	Rk	DYAR	Rk	YAR	Short	Mid	Deep	Bomb
2009	IND	14/13	47	91	765	52%	+0.2	16.3	4	5	6.0	8	+1.8	0.1%	43	95	46	105	32%	29%	17%	22%
2010	IND	14/14	67	119	784	56%	-2.2	11.7	6	12	3.7	49	-0.1	-7.0%	67	55	61	71	37%	37%	13%	13%
2011	IND	16/16	70	134	947	52%	-2.2	13.5	6	4	5.1	24	+0.8	-17.1%	78	-48	82	-59	32%	41%	14%	13%
2012	WAS		55	111	824	50%	--	15.0	6					-7.7%								

Garcon didn't have a great DVOA with Peyton Manning at the helm, so he sure as hell wasn't going to with quarterbacks who needed every ounce of arm strength to utilize his only plus tool. On passes marked as "Deep" (15 or more yards down the field), Garcon actually had a 6.9% DVOA despite just a 28 percent catch rate. The Colts ran him off quick hitches and screens 24 times last season, all but admitting that they wanted the ball in his hands and couldn't actually consistently do that on deep throws. Robert Griffin III could very well do that, and as long as Redskins fans don't expect Garcon to be a No. 1 receiver, they should be happy with the production they get out of him. Now the only problem is that he's getting paid to be a No. 1 receiver.

Clyde Gates
Height: 6-0   Weight: 189   College: Abilene Christian   Draft: 2011/4 (111)   Born: 13-Jun-1986   Age: 26   Risk: Yellow

Year	Team	G/S	Rec	Pass	Yds	C%	+/-	Y/C	TD	Drop	YAC	Rk	YAC+	DVOA	Rk	DYAR	Rk	YAR	Short	Mid	Deep	Bomb
2011	MIA	15/0	2	12	19	17%	-2.3	9.5	0	0	0.5	--	-2.9	-74.8%	--	-55	--	-57	11%	33%	33%	22%
2012	MIA		8	16	127	50%	--	15.8	1					-2.9%								

A fourth-round pick last year, Gates was solid as a kickoff returner but rarely saw the field on offense. Jeff Ireland was lukewarm about Gates' minicamp efforts, praising Roberto Wallace and Marlin Moore instead, so Gates may really have to shine on special teams to stay on the roster.

David Gettis

Height: 6-3 Weight: 217 College: Baylor Draft: 2010/6 (198) Born: 27-Aug-1987 Age: 25 Risk: Yellow

Year	Team	G/S	Rec	Pass	Yds	C%	+/-	Y/C	TD	Drop	YAC	Rk	YAC+	DVOA	Rk	DYAR	Rk	YAR	Short	Mid	Deep	Bomb
2010	CAR	15/13	37	67	508	55%	-1.0	13.7	3	3	4.2	36	-0.8	-0.2%	49	66	57	69	42%	23%	19%	16%
2012	CAR		36	63	467	57%	--	13.0	3					0.3%								

Gettis missed all of last season with an ACL tear. He showed enough during the dog days of 2010, including an eight-reception, 125-yard, two-touchdown game in a win over the 49ers, to suggest that he is a worthy challenger to Brandon LaFell for the Panthers' No. 2 receiver position.

Brandon Gibson

Height: 6-1 Weight: 210 College: Washington State Draft: 2009/6 (194) Born: 13-Aug-1987 Age: 25 Risk: Green

Year	Team	G/S	Rec	Pass	Yds	C%	+/-	Y/C	TD	Drop	YAC	Rk	YAC+	DVOA	Rk	DYAR	Rk	YAR	Short	Mid	Deep	Bomb
2009	2TM	10/4	4	69	34	49%	-5.9	8.5	1	5	3.1	71	-0.8	-28.9%	84	-88	84	-73	34%	45%	12%	9%
2010	STL	10/4	53	91	620	58%	+0.3	11.7	2	7	4.2	35	+0.3	-10.0%	70	20	70	48	33%	50%	12%	6%
2011	STL	15/9	36	71	431	51%	-4.0	12.0	1	7	2.9	80	-1.2	-11.3%	68	7	69	-7	29%	46%	15%	9%
2012	STL		46	82	568	56%	--	12.3	3					-9.9%								

Over two seasons shuffling in and out of the starting lineup, Gibson has established himself as a replacement-level, inefficient wide receiver. In some kind of backhanded compliment, the new regime in St. Louis listed him atop the depth chart, while simultaneously drafting two wide receivers to replace him. At only 25 years old, and in his proverbial contract year, Gibson will spend the 2012 season peacocking for potential mates.

Ted Ginn

Height: 5-11 Weight: 178 College: Ohio State Draft: 2007/1 (9) Born: 12-Apr-1985 Age: 27 Risk: Red

Year	Team	G/S	Rec	Pass	Yds	C%	+/-	Y/C	TD	Drop	YAC	Rk	YAC+	DVOA	Rk	DYAR	Rk	YAR	Short	Mid	Deep	Bomb
2009	MIA	16/12	38	78	454	49%	-2.5	11.9	1	4	1.2	89	-2.8	-15.3%	70	-16	70	-32	12%	49%	16%	22%
2010	SF	13/0	12	35	163	34%	-5.4	13.6	1	5	1.8	--	-2.0	-35.5%	--	-60	--	-68	22%	34%	25%	19%
2011	SF	14/3	19	33	220	58%	+0.3	11.6	0	5	2.3	--	-1.5	-10.6%	--	5	--	6	27%	60%	7%	7%
2012	SF		16	28	196	57%	--	12.2	0					-4.6%								

Thanks to NFL Network, almost every football fan has seen Ginn's 102-yard kickoff return and 55-yard punt return against Seattle in Week 1. He finished fifth in our values for kick returns (+4.9 expected points added), and was even better on punt returns (No. 2 with +10.6 expected points added). With that large of a contribution in the all-important field position battle, which is vital to the 49ers' success, Ginn's roster spot is safe even though he's (at best) listed fifth on the 49ers' wide receiver depth chart.

T.J. Graham

Height: 5-11 Weight: 188 College: North Carolina State Draft: 2012/3 (69) Born: 27-Jul-1989 Age: 23 Risk: Red

Year	Team	G/S	Rec	Pass	Yds	C%	+/-	Y/C	TD	Drop	YAC	Rk	YAC+	DVOA	Rk	DYAR	Rk	YAR	Short	Mid	Deep	Bomb
2012	BUF		16	27	242	59%	--	15.1	1					10.4%								

The Bills traded up to land Graham, a player who few draft experts expected to go anywhere near the third round, which is more proof that NFL front offices and the expert media who cover the draft are engaged in two distinctly different activities. Draftniks saw a thinly-built, underdeveloped receiver who struggles with route running and lacks the size or strength to go over the middle or contribute as a run blocker. Buffalo's front office saw a guy with track speed who can take the top off a defense and open up space for Chan Gailey's intricate short passing game. Football Outsiders saw a guy who was a one-year wonder at N.C. State, with a 48 percent catch rate and just 12.9 yards per catch through his junior year, but a 62 percent catch rate and 16.5 yards per catch as a senior.

A.J. Green

Height: 6-4　Weight: 207　College: Georgia　Draft: 2011/1 (4)　Born: 31-Jul-1988　Age: 24　Risk: Green

Year	Team	G/S	Rec	Pass	Yds	C%	+/-	Y/C	TD	Drop	YAC	Rk	YAC+	DVOA	Rk	DYAR	Rk	YAR	Short	Mid	Deep	Bomb
2011	CIN	15/15	65	115	1057	57%	+3.0	16.3	7	2	4.1	50	-0.6	16.9%	17	284	9	273	30%	31%	18%	21%
2012	CIN		71	128	1169	55%	--	16.5	7					9.6%								

Green lived up to his heralded billing and draft status with a spectacular rookie season, one achieved despite being the team's lone offensive threat by season's end. His signature play was probably a gravity-defying grab of a speculative Andy Dalton pass over Joe Haden in the final minutes against Cleveland, after which he broke away to set up a game-winning chip-shot field goal by Mike Nugent. There were many others to choose from, like his brilliant piece of toe-tapping in the end zone against Denver, or the play where he went flying over Troy Polamalu and Ike Taylor for a score against the Steelers. So long as Green remains healthy and his catch rate improves, he should be among the top receivers in the game.

Green's lone area of poor play was in the red zone, where he posted a surprisingly awful -36.7% DVOA. Too often, Dalton simply defaulted to fade patterns to Green, and it looks like the defense knew this was coming. Given Green's height, leaping ability, and competitiveness in the air, one can understand the temptation. A jolt of coaching creativity and an offseason spent practicing red zone packages should improve those numbers.

Derek Hagan

Height: 6-1　Weight: 205　College: Arizona State　Draft: 2006/3 (82)　Born: 21-Sep-1984　Age: 28　Risk: Green

Year	Team	G/S	Rec	Pass	Yds	C%	+/-	Y/C	TD	Drop	YAC	Rk	YAC+	DVOA	Rk	DYAR	Rk	YAR	Short	Mid	Deep	Bomb
2009	NYG	16/0	8	8	101	100%	+3.1	12.6	1	0	0.3	--	-3.8	74.6%	--	49	--	49	13%	50%	38%	0%
2010	NYG	7/4	24	43	223	58%	+0.2	9.3	1	2	1.3	--	-2.3	-17.5%	--	-16	--	-19	25%	53%	23%	0%
2011	2TM	10/3	24	42	252	57%	-0.8	10.5	1	2	1.8	--	-2.1	-5.7%	--	24	--	40	30%	41%	16%	14%
2012	BUF		12	20	134	60%	--	11.1	1					-3.8%								

Hagan was an emergency midseason signing who barely registered on the stat sheet until perking up with a seven-catch, 89 yard effort in the finale against New England. That was good enough to buy him an extra year in Buffalo, where he will compete for playing time with a bunch of younger receivers with higher upside. Hagan's limitations are obvious to all by now—he is a slow and plodding route runner who doesn't catch the ball especially well but excels on special teams.

Leonard Hankerson

Height: 6-2　Weight: 209　College: Miami　Draft: 2011/3 (79)　Born: 7-May-1988　Age: 24　Risk: Green

Year	Team	G/S	Rec	Pass	Yds	C%	+/-	Y/C	TD	Drop	YAC	Rk	YAC+	DVOA	Rk	DYAR	Rk	YAR	Short	Mid	Deep	Bomb
2011	WAS	4/2	13	20	163	65%	+1.8	12.5	0	0	2.2	--	-1.8	1.1%	--	21	--	20	30%	40%	25%	5%
2012	WAS		21	39	305	54%	--	14.5	2					0.4%								

Washington's third-round pick did not have the best of NFL debuts. Because he was slow to learn the playbook, Hankerson didn't get on the field until Week 7, and his first play was a route miscommunication-turned-John Beck interception. He had one good game, eight catches for 106 yards in a homecoming trip to Miami, but he tore his right hip labrum at the end of the game and went on injured reserve, which was followed by February surgery when rest and rehab couldn't heal the injury. Hankerson and Josh Morgan will battle for the No. 2 receiver position in camp, but whether he's No. 2 or No. 3, Hankerson needs to be used on the outside and not in the slot. He's a size/speed prospect who shows promise when it comes to separating from press coverage but tends to round off his breaks on shorter routes. His projection goes up significantly if the Redskins clear the way for him by dealing Santana Moss.

Brian Hartline

Height: 6-2   Weight: 195   College: Ohio State   Draft: 2009/4 (108)   Born: 22-Nov-1986   Age: 26   Risk: Yellow

Year	Team	G/S	Rec	Pass	Yds	C%	+/-	Y/C	TD	Drop	YAC	Rk	YAC+	DVOA	Rk	DYAR	Rk	YAR	Short	Mid	Deep	Bomb
2009	MIA	16/2	31	56	506	55%	+0.7	16.3	3	2	5.2	18	+1.5	22.4%	9	158	30	146	21%	46%	20%	13%
2010	MIA	12/11	43	73	615	59%	+2.0	14.3	1	2	4.9	21	+0.7	6.0%	34	111	43	89	30%	37%	19%	14%
2011	MIA	16/10	35	66	549	53%	+0.2	15.7	1	3	2.7	85	-1.7	11.7%	26	132	37	130	21%	44%	18%	18%
2012	MIA		51	93	705	55%	--	13.8	5					-1.9%								

Hartline was 8-of-21 for 254 yards on deep passes, plus three pass interference penalties: pretty good numbers considering the quarterback situation. Opponents started paying more attention to Hartline at the end of the year, however, and Antonio Cromartie picked off two errant Matt Moore throws to Hartline in the season finale. Hartline looks like an example of a very good No. 3 receiver who is about to be overextended as a starter.

Percy Harvin

Height: 5-11   Weight: 192   College: Florida   Draft: 2009/1 (22)   Born: 28-May-1988   Age: 24   Risk: Yellow

Year	Team	G/S	Rec	Pass	Yds	C%	+/-	Y/C	TD	Drop	YAC	Rk	YAC+	DVOA	Rk	DYAR	Rk	YAR	Short	Mid	Deep	Bomb
2009	MIN	15/9	60	93	790	67%	+4.4	13.2	6	3	5.8	11	+0.8	12.0%	23	178	26	189	40%	36%	16%	8%
2010	MIN	14/13	71	109	868	65%	+3.1	12.2	5	5	6.0	5	+0.7	5.6%	37	157	26	149	50%	31%	7%	12%
2011	MIN	16/14	87	121	967	72%	+5.3	11.1	6	5	6.1	9	+0.7	2.9%	44	145	29	129	57%	30%	9%	4%
2012	MIN		81	125	908	65%	--	11.2	6					3.0%								

Contrary to popular belief, Harvin does not belong exclusively in the slot. He has speed to burn and, more importantly, the uncommon acceleration to almost instantaneously capitalize on that speed. The Vikings took advantage of this with bubble screens, end arounds and ghost end arounds last season; they must expand on those concepts in 2012. Harvin has proven to be an especially effective receiving target when lining up at the running back position. One reason for this is that his speed and acceleration allow him to attack the seams out of the backfield, something most players aren't physically capable of doing. That's how mismatches against linebackers and safeties are created.

Of course, when you put Harvin in the backfield, you need to have the threat of handing the ball to him, but that doesn't mean you should take your 190-pound wide receiver and try to send him through the tackles. Harvin averaged 6.6 yards per carry last year, which makes you think that handing him the ball in the backfield is a good idea until you look closer at the play-by-play. Harvin averaged 3.1 yards per carry on runs between the tackles, 4.1 yards per carry when he started in the backfield and went around left or right end, and 12.9 yards per carry on end arounds where he was lined up at his usual wide receiver position. So, let Adrian Peterson take the ball up the middle, OK? Harvin's projection includes 34 carries for 147 yards and a touchdown.

Andrew Hawkins

Height: 5-7   Weight: 175   College: Toledo   Draft: 2008/FA   Born: 10-Mar-1986   Age: 26   Risk: Green

Year	Team	G/S	Rec	Pass	Yds	C%	+/-	Y/C	TD	Drop	YAC	Rk	YAC+	DVOA	Rk	DYAR	Rk	YAR	Short	Mid	Deep	Bomb
2011	CIN	13/0	23	34	263	68%	+0.8	11.4	0	0	6.3	--	+0.4	-3.1%	--	23	--	20	55%	33%	9%	3%
2012	CIN		18	29	209	62%	--	11.6	1					0.9%								

This flea-like undrafted free agent finally made an NFL roster in his fourth season and provided the Bengals with a much needed dose of elusiveness at midseason. A handful of plays were installed to maximize his gifts, as he lead the team in YAC, but he was a total liability blocking on runs and had problems getting open deep. The drafting of Mohamed Sanu and Marvin Jones, plus the return to health of Jordan Shipley, means that Hawkins had best put on a show during camp and the preseason if he wants another crack at the roster.

376 WIDE RECEIVERS

Lavelle Hawkins   Height: 5-11   Weight: 187   College: California   Draft: 2008/4 (126)   Born: 12-Jul-1986   Age: 26   Risk: Yellow

Year	Team	G/S	Rec	Pass	Yds	C%	+/-	Y/C	TD	Drop	YAC	Rk	YAC+	DVOA	Rk	DYAR	Rk	YAR	Short	Mid	Deep	Bomb
2009	TEN	10/0	7	14	110	50%	-2.1	15.7	0	1	5.3	--	+1.3	-1.4%	--	12	--	7	36%	43%	14%	7%
2010	TEN	6/0	5	6	61	83%	+1.7	12.2	0	0	1.0	--	-3.5	57.4%	--	36	--	33	33%	33%	17%	17%
2011	TEN	16/2	47	76	470	62%	-0.1	10.0	1	3	4.3	43	-0.2	-23.1%	85	-60	84	-40	48%	32%	12%	8%
2012	TEN		35	53	348	66%	--	9.9	2					-3.9%								

Hawkins had an interesting offseason. Despite the Titans being stacked with middling receivers, they re-signed Hawkins to a three-year deal worth $7.2 million, then drafted Kendall Wright in the first round. Assuming Kenny Britt is healthy and Marc Mariani has a stranglehold on the returner spot, he and Damian Williams are battling for one game day spot. Hawkins has the money, but Williams is younger, has more upside, and was (barely) more productive last year.

Devery Henderson   Height: 5-11   Weight: 200   College: Louisiana State   Draft: 2004/2 (50)   Born: 26-Mar-1982   Age: 30   Risk: Green

Year	Team	G/S	Rec	Pass	Yds	C%	+/-	Y/C	TD	Drop	YAC	Rk	YAC+	DVOA	Rk	DYAR	Rk	YAR	Short	Mid	Deep	Bomb
2009	NO	16/11	51	83	804	61%	+2.7	15.8	2	4	5.8	12	+1.4	11.3%	24	151	34	159	36%	30%	14%	19%
2010	NO	16/11	34	59	464	58%	-0.4	13.6	1	5	3.8	48	-0.9	-5.3%	64	33	67	47	34%	31%	17%	17%
2011	NO	16/13	32	50	503	64%	+2.9	15.7	2	2	5.4	20	+1.6	14.7%	20	105	47	107	35%	35%	17%	13%
2012	NO		27	50	501	54%	--	18.6	2					16.8%								

Henderson was 6-of-14 for 202 yards on deep passes, with a 79-yard touchdown against the Bears but just a handful of other highlights. Robert Meachem and Jimmy Graham ate into Henderson's role as the designated deep threat in New Orleans last season, and while Meachem is now in San Diego, Graham is still a matchup nightmare. Life can be precarious for a 30-year-old field stretcher, but the Saints have so many weapons that they may be comfortable keeping Henderson as a 30-catch starter for another year or two.

Devin Hester   Height: 5-10   Weight: 185   College: Miami   Draft: 2007/2 (57)   Born: 4-Nov-1982   Age: 30   Risk: Yellow

Year	Team	G/S	Rec	Pass	Yds	C%	+/-	Y/C	TD	Drop	YAC	Rk	YAC+	DVOA	Rk	DYAR	Rk	YAR	Short	Mid	Deep	Bomb
2009	CHI	13/12	57	91	757	64%	+2.9	13.3	3	4	5.0	24	+0.2	-0.2%	44	90	47	101	38%	36%	11%	15%
2010	CHI	16/13	40	73	475	55%	-3.5	11.9	4	5	5.5	12	+1.2	-3.4%	60	53	62	45	37%	40%	11%	11%
2011	CHI	16/8	26	56	369	46%	-8.2	14.2	1	5	5.6	18	+0.9	-29.6%	88	-70	85	-57	40%	38%	15%	8%
2012	CHI		29	48	403	60%	--	13.9	2					10.9%								

It's no longer an experiment; Hester has now spent four full seasons as a de facto starting wide receiver. At age 30, it's time to judge him as a finished product, and the finished product sure looks a lot like the unfinished product from 2008. To be fair, his mechanics and hands have surely improved, and he's developed a much broader understanding of the route tree. Still, he remains fairly raw. He executes deep routes with aplomb but is not a down-to-down threat within the confines of a regular offense. The fact that his reps at receiver seem to occasionally compromise his effectiveness as a return artist begs the never-ending question of why the Bears don't limit him to gadget plays and special sub packages.

Darrius Heyward-Bey   Height: 6-2   Weight: 210   College: Maryland   Draft: 2009/1 (7)   Born: 26-Feb-1987   Age: 25   Risk: Green

Year	Team	G/S	Rec	Pass	Yds	C%	+/-	Y/C	TD	Drop	YAC	Rk	YAC+	DVOA	Rk	DYAR	Rk	YAR	Short	Mid	Deep	Bomb
2009	OAK	11/11	9	40	124	23%	-10.5	13.8	1	7	1.3	--	-2.5	-45.0%	--	-105	--	-126	21%	21%	36%	23%
2010	OAK	15/14	26	64	366	41%	-5.0	14.1	1	6	3.9	45	+0.3	-28.8%	82	-83	82	-64	19%	44%	19%	19%
2011	OAK	15/14	64	115	975	56%	+1.9	15.2	4	7	3.9	55	-0.2	1.7%	48	129	40	120	23%	39%	24%	15%
2012	OAK		59	108	887	55%	--	15.0	5					2.4%								

Everything you once knew was wrong. Darrius Heyward-Bey is now an actual starting-caliber NFL receiver and would have gained 1,000 yards if Hue Jackson had not inexplicably benched him in Week 9 for no apparent reason. He's continuing to work on his consistency and hands, but that above-average +/- figure is a sign he's not the joke he used to be. For the first time in his career, you saw glimpses of skills commensurate with being a top-level pick, such as the combination of size and speed he showed off in Week 15 with a 43-yard touchdown catch-and-run against the Lions that included two broken tackles.

Jason Hill Height: 6-1 Weight: 204 College: Washington State Draft: 2007/3 (76) Born: 20-Feb-1985 Age: 27 Risk: Red

Year	Team	G/S	Rec	Pass	Yds	C%	+/-	Y/C	TD	Drop	YAC	Rk	YAC+	DVOA	Rk	DYAR	Rk	YAR	Short	Mid	Deep	Bomb
2009	SF	11/0	9	17	90	53%	-0.7	10.0	2	0	6.0	--	+1.6	-13.0%	--	-1	--	6	60%	27%	7%	7%
2010	JAC	8/1	11	21	248	52%	+0.6	22.5	1	3	3.8	--	-0.5	22.3%	--	56	--	55	10%	40%	30%	20%
2011	JAC	10/10	25	55	367	45%	-7.3	14.7	3	6	4.8	28	+1.0	-9.3%	66	15	66	1	25%	53%	15%	7%
2012	DEN		19	33	308	58%	--	16.2	2					12.8%								

The Jaguars waived Jason Hill in November, three months after naming him a starter on the other side of Mike Thomas, once they realized that he was Jason Hill. Regardless, just the act of convincing the Jaguars it was finally time to bring in some new receivers had some value, so there's a bit of faint praise to damn him with.

Stephen Hill Height: 6-4 Weight: 215 College: Georgia Tech Draft: 2012/2 (43) Born: 25-Apr-1991 Age: 21 Risk: Red

Year	Team	G/S	Rec	Pass	Yds	C%	+/-	Y/C	TD	Drop	YAC	Rk	YAC+	DVOA	Rk	DYAR	Rk	YAR	Short	Mid	Deep	Bomb
2012	NYJ		28	63	458	44%	--	16.4	3					-8.2%								

In case you missed all of the sirens, claxons, and flashing highway beacons, here's a scoop: The Jets plan to run some kind of Option-Wildcat-Tebophiliac offense this year, and they will get around to formally admitting it as soon as camp starts and fans begin booing Mark Sanchez in earnest. Exhibit Q in their transformation is Hill, a 6-foot-5 burner who caught just 28 passes in 2011 because he was busy blocking in Georgia Tech's wingbone option offense. The last Georgia Tech wide receiver to break big in the NFL was Demaryius Thomas, who spent 2011 blocking for Tebow options and occasionally sneaking downfield to catch bombs. Hill is a very similar player; if anything, with his outstanding blocking reputation and career average of 25.5 yards per catch, he is more of a block-and-bomb specialist than Thomas. As explained later in the book, our Playmaker Score 3.0 projection system likes Hill more than any other receiver in this year's draft class, for his fabulous Combine numbers (4.36 forty, 39.5-inch vertical jump) as much as his college production.

T.Y. Hilton Height: 5-10 Weight: 183 College: Florida International Draft: 2012/3 (92) Born: 14-Nov-1989 Age: 23 Risk: Green

Year	Team	G/S	Rec	Pass	Yds	C%	+/-	Y/C	TD	Drop	YAC	Rk	YAC+	DVOA	Rk	DYAR	Rk	YAR	Short	Mid	Deep	Bomb
2012	IND		14	24	161	58%	--	11.5	1					-7.9%								

Hilton has great speed and elusiveness, and his hands will dictate whether he becomes a high-target slot option or an outside speed threat. (Statements Ryan Grigson made on the Colts website seem to suggest the former.) He also has the weaknesses you would expect from a receiver his size, starting with durability concerns. His stats were dinged last year as he played through a hamstring injury, and again because he was the only real target at Florida International. He still managed a 66 percent catch rate and 13.4 yards per catch.

Domenik Hixon Height: 6-2 Weight: 182 College: Akron Draft: 2006/4 (130) Born: 8-Oct-1984 Age: 28 Risk: Red

Year	Team	G/S	Rec	Pass	Yds	C%	+/-	Y/C	TD	Drop	YAC	Rk	YAC+	DVOA	Rk	DYAR	Rk	YAR	Short	Mid	Deep	Bomb
2009	NYG	14/2	15	28	187	54%	-1.7	12.5	1	0	6.7	--	+2.4	-7.2%	--	12	--	6	21%	61%	4%	14%
2010	NYG	0/0	0	--	0	--	--	--	0	--	--	--	--	--	--	--	--	--	--	--	--	--
2011	NYG	2/0	4	6	50	67%	+0.9	12.5	1	0	0.0	--	-3.6	28.2%	--	20	--	20	0%	80%	20%	0%
2012	NYG		30	50	515	60%	--	17.2	3					19.4%								

Hixon has now torn his right ACL in consecutive seasons. When he re-signed with the Giants for one year at $615,000, it looked like a no-risk flier on a player at a salary that could easily be cut if he showed up to training camp at less than 100 percent. And then—surprise, surprise—Hixon was running with the ones at Giants mini-camp after Hakeem Nicks broke his foot. Nicks will likely be back by Week 1, so Hixon won't be a starter, but it does look like he'll be able to contribute to the 2012 Giants as both a depth receiver and a return man. Until he tears his right ACL for the third time, that is.

Santonio Holmes   Height: 5-10   Weight: 185   College: Ohio State   Draft: 2006/1 (25)   Born: 3-Mar-1984   Age: 28   Risk: Green

Year	Team	G/S	Rec	Pass	Yds	C%	+/-	Y/C	TD	Drop	YAC	Rk	YAC+	DVOA	Rk	DYAR	Rk	YAR	Short	Mid	Deep	Bomb
2009	PIT	16/16	79	138	1248	57%	+0.8	15.8	5	9	6.0	9	+1.8	13.2%	21	284	10	294	26%	48%	18%	8%
2010	NYJ	12/10	52	96	746	54%	-1.1	14.3	6	5	4.2	37	+0.3	5.1%	39	135	31	146	21%	49%	20%	10%
2011	NYJ	16/16	51	101	564	50%	-7.3	11.1	8	5	3.7	64	-0.2	-8.0%	65	38	61	65	27%	47%	22%	5%
2012	NYJ		50	91	674	55%	--	13.5	6					1.0%								

The official party line is that Holmes has put 2011 behind him, that he is completely with the program and will no longer be chairman and founder of the Sulking Malcontent Society. So let's change the "plays well with others" box on his report card from "cause for concern" to "satisfactory." We are still left with an alleged No. 1 receiver whose career line consists of five 800-yard type seasons with gradually descending yards-per-catch averages, wrapped around one 1,248-yard effort that was so magical his team traded him for a mid-round pick the following summer. Holmes is the quintessential Jets offensive player in many ways: talented, mind-bogglingly overrated, and more trouble than most other franchises would think he was worth.

T.J. Houshmandzadeh   Height: 6-1   Weight: 197   College: Oregon State   Draft: 2001/7 (204)   Born: 26-Sep-1977   Age: 35   Risk: N/A

Year	Team	G/S	Rec	Pass	Yds	C%	+/-	Y/C	TD	Drop	YAC	Rk	YAC+	DVOA	Rk	DYAR	Rk	YAR	Short	Mid	Deep	Bomb
2009	SEA	16/16	79	135	911	59%	-1.3	11.5	3	2	3.7	59	-0.4	-8.7%	60	44	55	71	34%	45%	14%	7%
2010	BAL	16/2	30	57	398	53%	-1.3	13.3	3	0	2.6	77	-1.8	7.0%	31	90	49	89	23%	44%	21%	12%
2011	OAK	9/0	11	19	146	58%	-0.7	13.3	1	1	2.8	--	-1.3	-2.0%	--	14	--	2	26%	37%	32%	5%

Brought in as a familiar face for Carson Palmer, Houshmandzadeh had six of his 11 catches in one game. That meant he had five catches in the other eight games he played, which accurately reflected the impact he made in Oakland. He's at the stage in his career where he's no longer a good possession receiver, and he hasn't been able to stretch the field in years. Unsigned at press time, his NFL career is at or very close to its end.

DeSean Jackson   Height: 5-9   Weight: 169   College: California   Draft: 2008/2 (49)   Born: 1-Dec-1986   Age: 26   Risk: Yellow

Year	Team	G/S	Rec	Pass	Yds	C%	+/-	Y/C	TD	Drop	YAC	Rk	YAC+	DVOA	Rk	DYAR	Rk	YAR	Short	Mid	Deep	Bomb
2009	PHI	15/15	62	116	1156	53%	-3.1	18.6	9	6	6.4	6	+1.9	9.5%	29	203	20	192	31%	33%	17%	19%
2010	PHI	14/14	47	96	1056	49%	-2.0	22.5	6	10	7.2	1	+2.9	2.1%	45	107	46	112	23%	38%	14%	24%
2011	PHI	15/15	58	104	961	56%	+4.0	16.6	4	10	3.9	54	-0.8	3.2%	43	129	39	145	25%	35%	18%	22%
2012	PHI		63	117	1180	54%	--	18.7	5					13.5%								

Armed with a new five-year, $48.5 million contract which features $18 million in guarantees, DeSean Jackson promises to be a good team player from now on. No more missing team meetings, no more skipping training camp, no more badmouthing the front office. All that pouting coincided with a bit of an abnormal season for Jackson. Although he still dropped a lot of balls, he had a positive plus/minus rating for the first time in his career—but his yards after catch dropped significantly. One thing that did stay constant for Jackson in 2011: He's consistently awful in the red zone. His strength is going deep, of course, and he has trouble getting open when the field gets small. He has a negative DVOA on red-zone passes in each year of his career, and for the four years in total he has -40.4% DVOA and a 38 percent catch rate.

Vincent Jackson
Height: 6-5 Weight: 241 College: Northern Colorado Draft: 2005/2 (61) Born: 14-Jan-1983 Age: 29 Risk: Red

Year	Team	G/S	Rec	Pass	Yds	C%	+/-	Y/C	TD	Drop	YAC	Rk	YAC+	DVOA	Rk	DYAR	Rk	YAR	Short	Mid	Deep	Bomb
2009	SD	15/15	68	109	1167	63%	+11.4	17.2	9	2	2.8	77	-1.3	39.6%	1	456	2	459	15%	44%	18%	23%
2010	SD	5/5	14	23	248	61%	+3.9	17.7	3	1	3.4	--	-0.5	39.2%	--	97	--	104	16%	47%	26%	11%
2011	SD	16/16	60	115	1106	52%	+2.7	18.4	9	5	3.2	74	-1.0	15.7%	19	259	14	247	13%	38%	26%	23%
2012	TB		65	121	1087	54%	--	16.7	7					11.8%								

At his best, Jackson is a valuable combination of size, speed, and the ability to separate in tight areas. That ability to separate showed itself only occasionally in 2011; two of his three biggest games came against the Patriots and Packers, bad pass defenses who were concentrating their best resources on Antonio Gates. The Bucs are hoping that performance was partially a result of his contract battle with A.J. Smith, and that he'll be able to thrive despite being the focus of every defense and every fan's eye.

Alshon Jeffery
Height: 6-3 Weight: 216 College: South Carolina Draft: 2012/2 (45) Born: 14-Feb-1990 Age: 22 Risk: Red

Year	Team	G/S	Rec	Pass	Yds	C%	+/-	Y/C	TD	Drop	YAC	Rk	YAC+	DVOA	Rk	DYAR	Rk	YAR	Short	Mid	Deep	Bomb
2012	CHI		30	51	458	59%	--	15.3	4					15.0%								

If he cares, he's amazing. Comparisons to Seattle's "Big" Mike Williams are easy to make, and that can be both positive and negative. Jeffery has the size to box out and wear down opponents. He also offers surprisingly effective run-after-catch ability. But all this is contingent on that size not becoming too sizeable (if you catch our drift). In 2010, Jeffery had a 67 percent catch rate with 17.2 yards per reception. He disappeared for large swaths of 2011, with a 56 percent catch rate and 15.6 yards per catch. Then he had four catches for 148 yards in the Capital One Bowl. Again, if he cares, he's amazing. Good luck, Chicago.

A.J. Jenkins
Height: 6-0 Weight: 190 College: Illinois Draft: 2012/1 (30) Born: 8-Sep-1989 Age: 23 Risk: Red

Year	Team	G/S	Rec	Pass	Yds	C%	+/-	Y/C	TD	Drop	YAC	Rk	YAC+	DVOA	Rk	DYAR	Rk	YAR	Short	Mid	Deep	Bomb
2012	SF		10	21	131	48%	--	13.1	1					-14.6%								

The 49ers' selection of Jenkins was right out of the Bill Walsh playbook. Walsh wanted scouts to be decisive in their evaluations, putting their money where their mouths are rather than hedging as a CYA tactic. Walsh didn't mind reaching if he was convinced about a player, and boy was this a reach. Jenkins is the quintessential boom-or-bust pick. In terms of skills, he has great speed (4.39 forty at the Combine), he has great hands (64 percent catch rate the past two years), is a polished route-runner, and knows how to exploit zone coverages. He also saw the lion's share of targets in a run-first offense at Illinois (42.1 percent of their targets in 2011). At the same time, he's a smallish one-year wonder with a questionable work ethic, a bit of a diva streak, and the one trait that most unsuccessful NFL wideouts possess: an inability to get off the line in press coverage. Already, he's shown up to minicamp out of shape, and looked horrible in OTAs. However, with Randy Moss, Michael Crabtree, and Mario Manningham ahead of him on the depth chart, and the 49ers having used exactly zero four-wide receiver packages last season, Jenkins will get plenty of time to hone his skills before having to come through on game day.

Michael Jenkins
Height: 6-4 Weight: 217 College: Ohio State Draft: 2004/1 (29) Born: 18-Jun-1982 Age: 30 Risk: Green

Year	Team	G/S	Rec	Pass	Yds	C%	+/-	Y/C	TD	Drop	YAC	Rk	YAC+	DVOA	Rk	DYAR	Rk	YAR	Short	Mid	Deep	Bomb
2009	ATL	15/9	50	90	635	56%	-0.7	12.7	1	7	3.2	69	-1.9	-11.0%	65	11	65	8	22%	36%	31%	11%
2010	ATL	11/9	41	73	505	56%	+1.9	12.3	2	1	2.0	84	-2.2	6.3%	33	111	45	89	20%	39%	32%	9%
2011	MIN	11/7	38	55	466	69%	+5.0	12.3	3	0	2.7	84	-1.2	10.2%	29	96	49	103	30%	48%	13%	9%
2012	MIN		34	53	377	65%	--	12.9	3					-3.8%								

Possession catches and run blocking are important in Minnesota's offense, although in Jenkins' case, the "possession receiver" description has become too much of a euphemism for "slow, plodding and unable to sepa-

380 WIDE RECEIVERS

rate." Jenkins is lanky and strong, but he can't consistently beat physical coverage. His lack of initial explosiveness limits how he can be used and hinders an offense that, with Christian Ponder under center, should be built around more three- and five-step drops in 2012.

Greg Jennings Height: 5-11 Weight: 195 College: Western Michigan Draft: 2006/2 (52) Born: 21-Sep-1983 Age: 29 Risk: Green

Year	Team	G/S	Rec	Pass	Yds	C%	+/-	Y/C	TD	Drop	YAC	Rk	YAC+	DVOA	Rk	DYAR	Rk	YAR	Short	Mid	Deep	Bomb
2009	GB	16/13	68	119	1113	57%	+5.2	16.4	4	3	6.8	5	+2.4	11.1%	26	229	17	261	30%	42%	14%	14%
2010	GB	16/16	76	125	1265	61%	+7.9	16.6	12	5	5.3	16	+1.1	19.4%	7	328	3	327	25%	44%	14%	17%
2011	GB	13/13	67	101	949	66%	+8.1	14.2	9	2	4.1	49	-0.2	20.5%	12	275	11	306	28%	45%	19%	9%
2012	GB		80	121	1205	66%	--	15.1	10					28.2%								

Jennings has emerged as an elite wide receiver in part because his strengths are practically tailor-made for Mike McCarthy's offense. He is a tremendous route runner, in particular with his first steps immediately after the snap, where the quick-hit nature of McCarthy's catch-and-run system demands that receivers win battles. The Packers do a wonderful job of manufacturing mismatches for Jennings. Often, this is achieved by aligning him in the slot (where he's more likely to face third corners or safeties, and where he can't be jammed) or as the lone receiver on the weak side of Green Bay's frequently-used 1x3 spread sets (a formation that all but assures Jennings will face one-on-one man coverage). Statistically, the most similar receivers to Greg Jennings in the past three years include Steve Largent from 1980-1982 and Derrick Mason at his peak, 2000-2002. Packers fans will appreciate that the most similar receiver over a two-year span, after Largent, is Antonio Freeman 1999-2000.

Andre Johnson Height: 6-3 Weight: 219 College: Miami Draft: 2003/1 (3) Born: 11-Jul-1981 Age: 31 Risk: Yellow

Year	Team	G/S	Rec	Pass	Yds	C%	+/-	Y/C	TD	Drop	YAC	Rk	YAC+	DVOA	Rk	DYAR	Rk	YAR	Short	Mid	Deep	Bomb
2009	HOU	16/16	101	172	1569	59%	+4.2	15.5	9	8	5.4	15	+0.6	6.6%	35	265	13	298	33%	39%	16%	12%
2010	HOU	13/13	86	139	1216	63%	+5.6	14.1	8	6	4.1	38	-0.5	12.9%	15	281	5	242	39%	30%	20%	12%
2011	HOU	7/7	33	51	492	65%	+3.9	14.9	2	3	4.2	47	-0.5	17.2%	15	118	44	126	31%	39%	16%	14%
2012	HOU		82	140	1190	59%	--	14.5	8					7.5%								

He's still one of the three most talented receivers in the NFL, along with Larry Fitzgerald and Calvin Johnson, but Andre Johnson has started to spend a little too much time on the sideline as he's creeped past his 30th birthday. After undergoing another arthroscopic surgery on his knee in May, the Texans still expect Johnson to be ready for training camp. It's a masochist version of poetic justice that sees Johnson's health hogtied to the Texans playoff aspirations after years where he was the only reason to watch the team, but that's the media cycle we live in. Prepare the pitchforks.

Calvin Johnson Height: 6-5 Weight: 239 College: Georgia Tech Draft: 2007/1 (2) Born: 25-Sep-1985 Age: 27 Risk: Yellow

Year	Team	G/S	Rec	Pass	Yds	C%	+/-	Y/C	TD	Drop	YAC	Rk	YAC+	DVOA	Rk	DYAR	Rk	YAR	Short	Mid	Deep	Bomb
2009	DET	14/14	67	138	984	49%	-5.9	14.7	5	5	5.1	19	+0.7	-10.5%	64	24	61	34	24%	41%	17%	18%
2010	DET	15/15	77	138	1120	57%	+2.9	14.5	12	6	3.9	44	+0.1	11.8%	20	265	7	249	20%	46%	19%	14%
2011	DET	16/16	96	158	1681	61%	+8.8	17.5	16	3	5.1	21	+0.9	31.9%	7	570	1	576	25%	38%	18%	18%
2012	DET		98	161	1450	61%	--	14.8	12					17.2%								

Megatron has blossomed into the most dangerous wide receiver in the NFL. Johnson's mixture of size, speed and raw athleticism are unparalleled. His catching radius is larger than most zip codes. Skill-wise, Johnson still has room to grow. His route running has improved over his first five years in the league, but it's still nothing special. He must get better at the intermediate level. Last season, quality defenses that built their game plan around coverage were often able to limit Johnson's impact. The numbers didn't always show it, but the film did. That's partly a commentary of the whole Lions offense, but still. Teams were able to disrupt Johnson's flow with press-man concepts involving aggressive safety help. Aiding the defense's cause was the fact that the

Lions ran a fairly basic system, featuring little pre-snap deception and a lot of rudimentary route combinations. With the young offense being more experienced in 2012, don't be surprised if coordinator Scott Linehan uses Johnson in a wider variety of ways. There needs to be more effort in creating mismatches for the superstar. But that can't happen until Johnson becomes a more proficient all-around route runner.

We're nitpicking a bit with Johnson only in an effort to help explain how he can progress from "great" to "legendary". We could easily go the other way and praise Johnson for all the minor things he does well (his blocking, for example, borders on Hines Ward, or at least Michael Jenkins, caliber). If Johnson continues at his current rate of development, he'll ultimately fulfill his once-in-a-generation potential.

Fun fact for Detroit fans: By far the most similar three-year span to Johnson's last three seasons belongs to Herman Moore from 1993 through 1995.

Steve Johnson
Height: 6-2 Weight: 202 College: Kentucky Draft: 2008/7 (224) Born: 22-Jul-1986 Age: 26 Risk: Yellow

Year	Team	G/S	Rec	Pass	Yds	C%	+/-	Y/C	TD	Drop	YAC	Rk	YAC+	DVOA	Rk	DYAR	Rk	YAR	Short	Mid	Deep	Bomb
2009	BUF	5/0	2	3	10	67%	-0.1	5.0	0	0	0.0	--	-3.7	-41.2%	--	-7	--	-6	100%	0%	0%	0%
2010	BUF	16/13	82	142	1073	58%	-2.5	13.1	10	7	4.8	24	+1.1	8.9%	27	239	13	216	30%	49%	14%	7%
2011	BUF	16/16	76	134	1004	57%	-5.8	13.2	7	4	4.2	45	+0.2	0.0%	51	137	34	138	34%	43%	19%	4%
2012	BUF		77	126	1005	61%	--	13.1	7					7.0%								

The most remarkable thing about Steve Johnson's 2011 season is the way he completely owned the otherwise nigh-untouchable Darrelle Revis. We charted 16 passes with Revis covering Johnson. Thirteen of those were complete, for 9.9 yards per pass. Against the rest of the NFL, Revis only allowed 4.6 yards per pass and a 36 percent completion rate. Johnson commemorated this performance which a ridiculous "fake shooting myself in the leg" celebration routine. A new $36.25 million contract in the offseason will keep Johnson in Buffalo for another five years.

Donald Jones
Height: 6-0 Weight: 214 College: Youngstown State Draft: 2010/FA Born: 17-Dec-1987 Age: 25 Risk: Yellow

Year	Team	G/S	Rec	Pass	Yds	C%	+/-	Y/C	TD	Drop	YAC	Rk	YAC+	DVOA	Rk	DYAR	Rk	YAR	Short	Mid	Deep	Bomb
2010	BUF	15/5	18	41	213	44%	-5.2	11.8	1	1	4.8	--	-1.0	-34.9%	--	-74	--	-74	53%	19%	14%	14%
2011	BUF	8/7	23	46	231	50%	-3.4	10.0	1	3	3.0	--	-1.9	-36.4%	--	-86	--	-80	30%	35%	22%	13%
2012	BUF		53	102	636	52%	--	12.0	5					-9.8%								

Jones was a key component in the Week 3 upset of New England, where he went off for 101 yards on five catches, but it was more than balanced out by putrid performances against Kansas City (two catches for three yards) and the Jets (one catch for six yards). Despite his abject lack of production, the club seems high on Jones, and did nothing to replace him or even provide significant competition for him in the offseason.

Jacoby Jones
Height: 6-3 Weight: 192 College: Lane Draft: 2007/3 (73) Born: 11-Jul-1984 Age: 28 Risk: Green

Year	Team	G/S	Rec	Pass	Yds	C%	+/-	Y/C	TD	Drop	YAC	Rk	YAC+	DVOA	Rk	DYAR	Rk	YAR	Short	Mid	Deep	Bomb
2009	HOU	14/1	27	40	437	68%	+6.0	16.2	6	4	5.1	--	+0.1	42.3%	--	172	--	176	20%	40%	23%	17%
2010	HOU	15/7	51	78	562	65%	+0.3	11.0	3	10	4.5	28	+0.5	-4.2%	62	52	63	47	38%	51%	7%	4%
2011	HOU	16/10	31	64	512	50%	-0.7	16.5	2	1	4.4	40	+0.0	-4.5%	56	41	60	48	27%	27%	29%	17%
2012	BAL		28	56	428	50%	--	15.3	2					-2.9%								

It takes a strange confluence of events for a player to manage nine fewer charted drops than he did a season ago and *lower* his catch rate, but Jacoby Jones managed that feat last season. Only 11 percent of his targets in 2010 came on deep balls thrown 16 or more yards past the line of scrimmage, but the Texans bumped that up to nearly 50 percent in 2011. That was actually a better use of Jones' talents, as he had a 46 percent catch rate and a 29.7% DVOA on those passes. On short passes, he had a -29.2% DVOA. Simply put: Jones' inability to work underneath effectively limits him to sub package work. The Ravens know this, and this year he'll likely work in that role when he's not busy returning kicks.

WIDE RECEIVERS

James Jones   Height: 6-1   Weight: 208   College: San Jose State   Draft: 2007/3 (78)   Born: 31-Mar-1984   Age: 28   Risk: Green

Year	Team	G/S	Rec	Pass	Yds	C%	+/-	Y/C	TD	Drop	YAC	Rk	YAC+	DVOA	Rk	DYAR	Rk	YAR	Short	Mid	Deep	Bomb
2009	GB	16/3	32	61	440	52%	-4.2	13.8	5	6	6.1	7	+1.8	-6.1%	55	30	59	35	37%	47%	9%	7%
2010	GB	16/3	50	87	679	57%	+3.2	13.6	5	6	5.8	8	+1.2	-3.4%	59	63	58	78	34%	34%	19%	13%
2011	GB	16/0	38	55	635	69%	+4.2	16.7	7	4	7.1	3	+2.5	41.1%	3	234	17	219	39%	32%	16%	13%
2012	GB		28	49	412	57%	--	14.7	4					8.9%								

The sixth-year pro from San Jose State would have everyone drinking the Kool-Aid if not for a habit of untimely mistakes. With instant speed and better-than-expected body control, Jones can be a lethal big-play weapon inside or outside. Problem is, he doesn't consistently hold onto the football. Perhaps no game better exemplifies Jones than Super Bowl XLV. Against the Steelers, he had five catches for 50 yards (two were quick-hitters on first down, two others moved the chains downfield) but he also dropped what would have been a breakaway touchdown in the third quarter. Jones doesn't necessarily drop more passes than a typical receiver, but when he does drop them, they seem to sting, and the same goes for his four fumbles over the past two years. Jones started losing a few snaps last year to Randall Cobb. If he wants to prevent that from snowballing, Jones must be more consistent in the slot and more effective against man coverage outside.

Julio Jones   Height: 6-3   Weight: 220   College: Alabama   Draft: 2011/1 (6)   Born: 3-Feb-1989   Age: 23   Risk: Yellow

Year	Team	G/S	Rec	Pass	Yds	C%	+/-	Y/C	TD	Drop	YAC	Rk	YAC+	DVOA	Rk	DYAR	Rk	YAR	Short	Mid	Deep	Bomb
2011	ATL	13/13	54	95	959	57%	+0.9	17.8	8	4	7.5	1	+2.8	9.9%	30	164	26	155	33%	32%	20%	15%
2012	ATL		64	117	1103	55%	--	17.2	8					18.0%								

Jones ended the year on a tear: 20 catches, 393 yards, and six touchdowns in his final four regular-season games, then seven catches for 64 yards in the playoff loss. He typically looks like the most athletic player on the field; with a full camp under his belt, he could quickly develop into the best No. 2 receiver in the NFL. It is hard to seriously argue that the Jones trade hurt the Falcons, and ridiculous to suggest that Jones was somehow responsible for the playoff loss, but a "statistical analyst" did just that in *Sports Illustrated* in January, based essentially on the logic that if the Falcons lost, then their decisions (especially ones that do not gibe with some crowd-pleasing definition of "tough-guy" football) must have been bad.

Jeremy Kerley   Height: 5-9   Weight: 188   College: TCU   Draft: 2011/5 (153)   Born: 3-May-1989   Age: 23   Risk: Blue

Year	Team	G/S	Rec	Pass	Yds	C%	+/-	Y/C	TD	Drop	YAC	Rk	YAC+	DVOA	Rk	DYAR	Rk	YAR	Short	Mid	Deep	Bomb
2011	NYJ	14/1	29	47	314	62%	+2.2	10.8	1	2	3.4	--	-0.6	-11.2%	--	6	--	29	41%	39%	14%	7%
2012	NYJ		12	20	126	60%	--	10.5	1					-7.9%								

A fun-to-watch Wildcat-type who was solid on returns and had his moments as a slot receiver, Kerley did a fine job filling Brad Smith's former role as the one Jets skill position player who didn't grate on your nerves. Kerley could do a lot of things in a Tebow offense: grab bubble screens, motion to take pitches or jet-sweep handoffs, attempt the occasional option pass. None of this amounts to much for fantasy football players, because Kerley is strictly a slot guy for a team that wants to run-Run-RUN, but Kerley is going to pop up on the highlight reels a few times.

Johnny Knox   Height: 6-1   Weight: 185   College: Abilene Christian   Draft: 2009/5 (140)   Born: 3-Nov-1986   Age: 26   Risk: Blue

Year	Team	G/S	Rec	Pass	Yds	C%	+/-	Y/C	TD	Drop	YAC	Rk	YAC+	DVOA	Rk	DYAR	Rk	YAR	Short	Mid	Deep	Bomb
2009	CHI	15/0	45	80	527	56%	+0.9	11.7	5	5	3.9	55	-0.8	-9.9%	61	17	64	34	32%	40%	17%	11%
2010	CHI	16/16	51	100	960	51%	-1.9	18.8	5	5	4.7	27	+0.6	14.7%	11	207	18	201	17%	44%	24%	16%
2011	CHI	14/11	37	69	727	54%	+1.7	19.6	2	2	4.4	39	+0.1	9.2%	32	116	45	123	18%	42%	26%	14%
2012	CHI		4	7	65	57%	--	16.1	1					14.4%								

Knox was on track to eventually earn a hefty contract as a darting, fairly multidimensional receiver and dynamic return artist. But a horrific back injury in Week 15 last season has put his career in serious question. When healthy, Knox's quick feet and tempo-changing shiftiness make him arguably Chicago's top target. He's gets in and out of breaks with good efficiency and has a natural ability to stretch the field, but his availability for 2012 is very much up in the air. If he's cleared to play, it will then be his physical capability that's up in the air.

Brandon LaFell
Height: 6-3 Weight: 211 College: LSU Draft: 2010/3 (78) Born: 4-Nov-1986 Age: 26 Risk: Yellow

Year	Team	G/S	Rec	Pass	Yds	C%	+/-	Y/C	TD	Drop	YAC	Rk	YAC+	DVOA	Rk	DYAR	Rk	YAR	Short	Mid	Deep	Bomb
2010	CAR	14/2	38	77	468	49%	-7.0	12.3	1	3	3.5	54	-0.8	-18.9%	75	-38	75	-25	33%	46%	11%	10%
2011	CAR	16/6	36	56	613	64%	+4.2	17.0	3	1	6.5	5	+2.2	22.3%	11	144	30	145	26%	37%	28%	9%
2012	CAR		41	69	557	59%	--	13.6	3					6.1%								

Ron Rivera said in a May interview with the *Charlotte Observer* that "Brandon LaFell encapsulates who we are." By "we," Rivera meant the Panthers, not humans or society, because it is terrifying to think of all human culture encapsulated by a fairly unknown receiver from a 7-9 team. Rivera used LaFell as an object lesson for a team that cannot feel like it has "arrived," one which flashed a lot of potential and pulled itself off the scrap heap in 2011, but still has much room for growth. A few days later, LaFell dropped three passes in a minicamp practice, which probably made Rivera think for a second about contacting Plaxico Burress, a player who encapsulates many, many things.

Greg Little
Height: 6-2 Weight: 220 College: North Carolina Draft: 2011/2 (59) Born: 30-May-1989 Age: 23 Risk: Green

Year	Team	G/S	Rec	Pass	Yds	C%	+/-	Y/C	TD	Drop	YAC	Rk	YAC+	DVOA	Rk	DYAR	Rk	YAR	Short	Mid	Deep	Bomb
2011	CLE	16/12	61	121	709	51%	-11.2	11.6	2	13	3.9	53	-0.3	-22.0%	84	-92	88	-108	47%	31%	14%	8%
2012	CLE		62	118	795	53%	--	12.8	5					-11.3%								

As debut seasons go, Little's wasn't quite *Cop Rock*, but it wasn't *Mad Men*, either. He had 13 drops, second-most in the league behind Roddy White (who dropped 16, but also was targeted 180 times). That's what happens when Mohamed Massaquoi is your spirit guide in practice. Little became a target of fan venom, mainly because it seemed that when Cleveland's quarterbacks were actually on target with a throw, Little dropped it. Still, there is reason for optimism. Little did lead the team in receptions and yards as a rookie, no small accomplishment despite his shortcomings. Presumed new quarterback Brandon Weeden had a great on-field relationship with a similarly sized-wideout, Justin Blackmon. Little missed his senior season at North Carolina after a suspension for taking illegal benefits and missed crucial NFL practice time thanks to the lockout. A full offseason of consistent work could do wonders for his game, and he reportedly showed up to minicamps in terrific shape.

Brandon Lloyd
Height: 6-0 Weight: 192 College: Illinois Draft: 2003/4 (124) Born: 5-Jul-1981 Age: 31 Risk: Yellow

Year	Team	G/S	Rec	Pass	Yds	C%	+/-	Y/C	TD	Drop	YAC	Rk	YAC+	DVOA	Rk	DYAR	Rk	YAR	Short	Mid	Deep	Bomb
2009	DEN	2/1	8	18	117	44%	-2.1	14.6	0	1	1.8	--	-3.9	-18.9%	--	-9	--	-9	28%	33%	33%	6%
2010	DEN	16/11	77	152	1448	51%	+2.7	18.8	11	5	2.4	80	-1.8	20.1%	6	415	2	402	11%	48%	20%	22%
2011	2TM	15/14	70	147	966	48%	-10.4	13.8	5	6	1.8	91	-2.2	-11.9%	69	8	68	-20	14%	49%	24%	13%
2012	NE		58	99	939	59%	--	16.2	7					17.7%								

On the surface, Lloyd's advanced-stat decline last season looks exactly like what you'd typically see from someone thought of as a one-year wonder. However, it's important to keep in mind that 80.2 percent of his targets in 2011 were thrown by Tim Tebow, A.J. Feeley, Kellen Clemens, and a hobbled Sam Bradford. He had -1.0% DVOA with Kyle Orton, -13.5% DVOA with the other guys. After signing with New England this offseason, he'll have Tom Brady at quarterback, so his numbers should rebound considerably, although probably not back to 2010 levels. The presence of other viable receiving options in New England means that Lloyd will be able to return to his devastating role as a deep threat. In 2011, he dropped from seventh to 18th in percentage of targets that travelled 16 or more yards in the air.

WIDE RECEIVERS

Jeremy Maclin   Height: 6-0   Weight: 198   College: Missouri   Draft: 2009/1 (19)   Born: 11-May-1988   Age: 24   Risk: Green

Year	Team	G/S	Rec	Pass	Yds	C%	+/-	Y/C	TD	Drop	YAC	Rk	YAC+	DVOA	Rk	DYAR	Rk	YAR	Short	Mid	Deep	Bomb
2009	PHI	15/13	56	92	773	61%	+1.2	13.8	4	5	4.4	34	+0.0	9.4%	31	158	31	150	31%	44%	12%	12%
2010	PHI	16/16	70	115	964	61%	+8.1	13.8	10	7	3.7	52	-0.6	15.2%	8	249	11	244	32%	36%	14%	18%
2011	PHI	13/13	63	97	859	65%	+6.6	13.6	5	5	4.1	48	-0.2	12.2%	23	186	22	176	30%	40%	23%	8%
2012	PHI		74	127	999	58%	--	13.5	8					5.8%								

He hasn't been transcendent like Larry Fitzgerald or Calvin Johnson, but otherwise we're not sure what more you could ask of a first-round reciever than to be as good and consistent as Jeremy Maclin has been in his first three seasons. The six most similar receivers in their first three years include, in order, Darrell Jackson (62 catches for 877 yards and four touchdowns in his third year), Santonio Holmes, Koren Robinson, Art Monk, Bert Emanuel, and Marvin Harrison. Unlike a couple of those guys, Maclin has been a solid citizen, so we expect more of the same in 2012.

Mario Manningham   Height: 5-11   Weight: 181   College: Michigan   Draft: 2008/3 (95)   Born: 25-May-1986   Age: 26   Risk: Red

Year	Team	G/S	Rec	Pass	Yds	C%	+/-	Y/C	TD	Drop	YAC	Rk	YAC+	DVOA	Rk	DYAR	Rk	YAR	Short	Mid	Deep	Bomb
2009	NYG	14/10	57	99	822	58%	-0.1	14.4	5	4	4.6	28	+0.1	8.4%	33	165	28	149	24%	47%	19%	10%
2010	NYG	16/8	60	92	944	65%	+8.8	15.7	9	4	5.8	7	+1.1	12.5%	17	188	20	214	32%	38%	15%	15%
2011	NYG	12/10	39	77	523	51%	-0.4	13.4	4	3	2.7	83	-1.3	-5.6%	59	44	59	50	23%	36%	24%	17%
2012	SF		50	94	692	53%	--	13.8	4					-4.1%								

It's hard to blame Manningham for losing his job to Victor Cruz when Cruz was so stunningly good last season, but it isn't like Manningham really stepped up to try to grab it back. He simply couldn't get open as often as Nicks and Cruz. The catch that put the Giants in position to win the Super Bowl, which will go down as the signature play of his career, was amazing precisely because he *wasn't* open; he practically had Sterling Moore draped all over him. The Giants didn't really make an attempt to re-sign him after the season, and you have to worry when a guy tells reporters there are "things floating" in his knees and then goes without surgery in the offseason. The 49ers got him for a reasonable price, two years at $7.5 million. He'll get more snaps than he did in New York, but don't get excited about his fantasy football value; the 49ers aren't suddenly going to start slinging it all over the field next year.

Brandon Marshall   Height: 6-4   Weight: 229   College: UCF   Draft: 2006/4 (119)   Born: 23-Mar-1984   Age: 28   Risk: Red

Year	Team	G/S	Rec	Pass	Yds	C%	+/-	Y/C	TD	Drop	YAC	Rk	YAC+	DVOA	Rk	DYAR	Rk	YAR	Short	Mid	Deep	Bomb
2009	DEN	15/13	101	155	1120	66%	+5.4	11.1	10	6	5.1	21	+0.2	2.6%	38	181	24	178	50%	30%	11%	9%
2010	MIA	14/14	86	146	1014	59%	+5.5	11.8	3	11	2.8	73	-1.2	-1.8%	54	127	35	85	36%	40%	16%	8%
2011	MIA	16/16	81	143	1214	57%	+0.9	15.0	6	10	3.8	61	-0.7	7.4%	36	226	18	223	33%	36%	15%	16%
2012	CHI		86	163	1172	53%	--	13.6	9					1.4%								

Marshall in the red zone last year: 21 targets, six catches, four touchdowns, a -40.5% DVOA, and one pick-six the other way by Darrelle Revis. The Dolphins had few other red-zone options, so they developed the early-season habit of lobbing fades and jump balls to Marshall and crossing their fingers. Marshall has the ability to be a post-up player in the end zone, but not when the whole defense knows what's coming. In essence, Marshall is a younger, slightly better Roy Williams. The talent is undeniable, as are the headaches that make players like these hot potatoes. Why the Bears keep bellying up to the bar for Williams-Marshall types is not clear: Recreating the magic of the 2008 Broncos does not sound like a logical roster strategy.

Derrick Mason

Height: 5-10 Weight: 190 College: Michigan State Draft: 1997/4 (98) Born: 17-Jan-1974 Age: 38 Risk: N/A

Year	Team	G/S	Rec	Pass	Yds	C%	+/-	Y/C	TD	Drop	YAC	Rk	YAC+	DVOA	Rk	DYAR	Rk	YAR	Short	Mid	Deep	Bomb
2009	BAL	16/16	73	134	1028	54%	+1.8	14.1	7	6	3.6	60	-0.0	5.0%	36	187	23	182	13%	54%	20%	13%
2010	BAL	16/15	61	100	802	61%	+8.5	13.1	7	4	2.1	83	-1.6	13.6%	14	217	16	225	16%	53%	21%	10%
2011	2TM	12/2	19	35	170	54%	-2.1	8.9	0	3	2.0	--	-1.6	-32.4%	--	-56	--	-52	45%	39%	12%	3%

Mason will go down as the Jimmy Smith of the 2000s: a sturdy possession receiver who compensated for his lack of breakaway speed with pinpoint routes, guile, and an ability to create separation. Last year, after he escaped the Jets media circus for Houston in a mid-season trade, we discovered that he no longer had those things. Gary Kubiak did the best thing for all parties by making sure he was only targeted 13 times in a Texans uniform, because six of those passes were defensed and another was dropped.

Mohamed Massaquoi

Height: 6-2 Weight: 210 College: Georgia Draft: 2009/2 (50) Born: 24-Nov-1986 Age: 26 Risk: Green

Year	Team	G/S	Rec	Pass	Yds	C%	+/-	Y/C	TD	Drop	YAC	Rk	YAC+	DVOA	Rk	DYAR	Rk	YAR	Short	Mid	Deep	Bomb
2009	CLE	16/11	34	95	624	36%	-12.2	18.4	3	5	4.6	29	+0.6	-22.9%	79	-76	81	-83	21%	33%	24%	22%
2010	CLE	15/14	36	73	483	49%	-1.3	13.4	2	5	3.9	43	+0.0	-13.8%	72	-6	72	-11	28%	43%	12%	17%
2011	CLE	14/13	31	74	384	42%	-11.3	12.4	2	4	2.4	88	-1.3	-26.0%	87	-77	86	-93	33%	46%	11%	10%
2012	CLE		21	48	265	44%	--	12.6	2					-25.9%								

Three seasons into his career, it has been definitively established that Massaquoi is not an NFL-quality receiver. His career catch rate is a dreadful 42 percent. You would have a better chance at completing a pass to the Venus de Milo than to Massaquoi. There's no shame in that; plenty of folks have gone on to successful careers in public service and the arts once they realized their shortcomings at catching a football.

Robert Meachem

Height: 6-2 Weight: 210 College: Tennessee Draft: 2007/1 (27) Born: 28-Sep-1984 Age: 28 Risk: Green

Year	Team	G/S	Rec	Pass	Yds	C%	+/-	Y/C	TD	Drop	YAC	Rk	YAC+	DVOA	Rk	DYAR	Rk	YAR	Short	Mid	Deep	Bomb
2009	NO	16/7	45	64	722	70%	+10.6	16.0	9	0	3.8	56	-0.8	39.3%	2	268	12	250	29%	32%	10%	30%
2010	NO	16/7	44	66	638	67%	+8.6	14.5	5	4	3.0	68	-1.8	23.2%	4	190	19	193	43%	23%	8%	26%
2011	NO	16/8	40	60	620	67%	+6.4	15.5	6	3	2.6	87	-1.8	30.8%	9	208	20	216	27%	35%	18%	20%
2012	SD		44	82	698	54%	--	15.9	6					5.0%								

It is hard to project Saints receivers out of their highly-defined roles. Meachem has been a designated deep threat for four years. He is usually part of the Saints two-back, two-receiver personnel group, splitting wide and running deep routes when Sean Payton wants to hand off or threaten the defense with play-action. Nineteen of Meachem's 60 targets came on play-action passes; most of them were listed as "deep" passes, typically from the I-formation, according to our game charters. Sometimes he ran the fly, sometimes a comeback or an out-route off the fly, but you get the idea: This was a pretty specialized role. Meachem will be targeted more often in San Diego, and it is not clear how well he will perform against defenses who don't have a dozen other things to worry about. On the plus side, San Diego is the perfect place for an I-formation play-action deep threat to wind up: Norv Turner has a big role for that kind of player.

Denarius Moore

Height: 6-0 Weight: 191 College: Tennessee Draft: 2011/5 (148) Born: 9-Dec-1988 Age: 24 Risk: Red

Year	Team	G/S	Rec	Pass	Yds	C%	+/-	Y/C	TD	Drop	YAC	Rk	YAC+	DVOA	Rk	DYAR	Rk	YAR	Short	Mid	Deep	Bomb
2011	OAK	13/10	33	76	618	43%	-3.7	18.7	5	5	3.8	59	-0.9	-0.7%	53	74	53	64	18%	36%	18%	28%
2012	OAK		67	114	1063	59%	--	15.9	7					12.7%								

2011's later-round rookie sensation, Moore benefited from the presence of a quarterback who could throw the ball downfield and in his general vicinity, as much of his value came from doing a very good job on bombs (passes thrown 30 or more yards downfield). That's a good fit for Carson Palmer's skill set, and Moore will have some value even if he never improves beyond that. Talk in the offseason, though, is that Moore is making strides on becoming a more complete receiver. If that's accurate—and KUBIAK is optimistic that it is—expect his receiving totals to take a big step forward in his second season.

Lance Moore
Height: 5-9 Weight: 177 College: Toledo Draft: 2005/FA Born: 31-Aug-1983 Age: 29 Risk: Green

Year	Team	G/S	Rec	Pass	Yds	C%	+/-	Y/C	TD	Drop	YAC	Rk	YAC+	DVOA	Rk	DYAR	Rk	YAR	Short	Mid	Deep	Bomb
2009	NO	7/0	14	19	153	74%	+2.8	10.9	2	1	2.9	--	-1.2	24.3%	--	57	--	57	53%	29%	18%	0%
2010	NO	16/1	66	94	763	70%	+6.3	11.6	8	2	4.4	32	-0.0	15.1%	9	208	17	221	46%	40%	5%	9%
2011	NO	14/7	52	73	627	71%	+6.0	12.1	8	2	3.0	79	-0.9	25.8%	10	234	16	252	36%	45%	14%	5%
2012	NO		51	77	645	66%	--	12.6	6					17.0%								

Moore has caught 16 touchdown passes in the last two years, more than Larry Fitzgerald, Anquan Boldin, Steve Smith, Miles Austin, Andre Johnson, Reggie Wayne, DeSean Jackson, or Brandon Marshall, among other big names. Moore is, at best, the fifth or sixth guy you name when you rattle off Saints skill position stars, yet there he is, scoring seven touchdowns in 15 red-zone passes last year and somehow finding 52 receptions left over after Marques Colston, Jimmy Graham, Darren Sproles, and others gobbled up their shares. Moore's role may increase with Robert Meachem gone, but even if it doesn't, he has found a very productive niche.

Josh Morgan
Height: 6-0 Weight: 219 College: Virginia Tech Draft: 2008/6 (174) Born: 20-Jun-1985 Age: 27 Risk: Green

Year	Team	G/S	Rec	Pass	Yds	C%	+/-	Y/C	TD	Drop	YAC	Rk	YAC+	DVOA	Rk	DYAR	Rk	YAR	Short	Mid	Deep	Bomb
2009	SF	16/15	52	81	527	64%	+3.1	10.1	3	3	4.8	27	-0.0	-17.6%	72	-31	73	9	53%	32%	9%	5%
2010	SF	16/11	44	80	698	55%	+0.8	15.9	2	3	6.8	2	+2.3	-3.5%	61	57	60	52	28%	39%	19%	14%
2011	SF	5/5	15	20	220	75%	+2.6	14.7	1	0	6.4	--	+2.5	32.4%	--	72	--	83	37%	53%	11%	0%
2012	WAS		38	67	542	57%	--	14.3	4					4.8%								

From a pay perspective, the Morgan signing adds to the annals of horrible free-agent acquisitions during the Dan Snyder era. You would think the market was as buyer-friendly as could be for a wideout coming off a broken leg who had done very little until one five-game stretch. Instead, the Redskins gave Morgan a 1,000 percent raise. The optimistic viewpoint says that Morgan was just starting to reach his potential when he got hurt, and broken bones are generally easy to recover from. He is a big, physical receiver with above-average hands, and he's still only 27. He has a lot of upside depending on a) how real last year's improvement truly was and b) whether the Redskins do finally get rid of Santana Moss.

Randy Moss
Height: 6-4 Weight: 215 College: Marshall Draft: 1998/1 (21) Born: 13-Feb-1977 Age: 35 Risk: Red

Year	Team	G/S	Rec	Pass	Yds	C%	+/-	Y/C	TD	Drop	YAC	Rk	YAC+	DVOA	Rk	DYAR	Rk	YAR	Short	Mid	Deep	Bomb
2009	NE	16/16	83	137	1264	61%	+8.0	15.2	13	4	4.1	51	+0.1	22.3%	10	400	4	351	24%	42%	14%	20%
2010	3TM	16/11	28	63	391	44%	-3.4	14.0	5	3	2.3	81	-1.9	2.3%	44	73	54	64	20%	39%	19%	22%
2012	SF		34	57	494	60%	--	14.5	5					13.5%								

When Moss signed with the 49ers after giving up on 2010, and skipping 2011, statheads went scrambling to find examples of historically similar wide receiver situations, and what they mean for Moss' expectations in 2012. That kind of analysis, though, applies sampling variability and selection bias to one of NFL history's most transcendent talents, and tells you absolutely nothing. Among the public, performance expectations are—and should be—all over the place for Moss this season. However, what the 49ers expect from him is very precise, and it has nothing to do with statistics. All they want is for him to fill a schematic need they lacked last season: a legitimate deep threat who gets opposing safeties out of the way for their running and underneath passing games. In that context, fulfilling expectations means being the NFL's No. 1 decoy. Questions about Moss's motivation, therefore, only matter in the context of whether or not he'll be happy in that role.

WIDE RECEIVERS

Santana Moss   Height: 5-10   Weight: 185   College: Miami   Draft: 2001/1 (16)   Born: 1-Jun-1979   Age: 33   Risk: Red

Year	Team	G/S	Rec	Pass	Yds	C%	+/-	Y/C	TD	Drop	YAC	Rk	YAC+	DVOA	Rk	DYAR	Rk	YAR	Short	Mid	Deep	Bomb
2009	WAS	16/16	70	120	902	58%	-0.9	12.9	3	7	5.1	20	+0.1	-11.9%	67	7	67	16	40%	34%	14%	12%
2010	WAS	16/16	93	145	1115	64%	+2.7	12.0	6	5	5.1	19	-0.1	-2.3%	55	116	39	131	46%	34%	11%	9%
2011	WAS	12/12	46	96	584	48%	-10.4	12.7	4	7	4.0	51	-0.7	-18.2%	82	-41	81	-29	43%	29%	18%	10%
2012	WAS		36	73	482	49%	--	13.4	3					-9.5%								

Long the most dangerous weapon in the Washington offense, Moss seems to be nearing the end. The top-end speed is gone; last year Moss was the intended receiver on 11 passes of over 20 yards, and the only one he caught was the gadget-play touchdown thrown by Brandon Banks. We spent the offseason waiting for the Redskins to cut Moss and his $2.65 million salary, but as of press time he was still on the roster. He still has a place in the Washington passing game, but it will be a smaller one. Ironically, our similarity scores say the most similar three-year span to Moss in 2009-2011 belongs to the receiver he once replaced and then was traded for, Laveranues Coles. Coles was two years younger during his span (2005-2007).

Louis Murphy   Height: 6-3   Weight: 203   College: Florida   Draft: 2009/4 (124)   Born: 11-May-1987   Age: 25   Risk: Green

Year	Team	G/S	Rec	Pass	Yds	C%	+/-	Y/C	TD	Drop	YAC	Rk	YAC+	DVOA	Rk	DYAR	Rk	YAR	Short	Mid	Deep	Bomb
2009	OAK	16/9	34	96	521	35%	-15.6	15.3	4	7	3.4	62	-0.9	-26.1%	81	-104	88	-130	22%	35%	27%	16%
2010	OAK	14/9	41	78	609	53%	-2.9	14.9	2	6	5.1	18	+0.8	-8.7%	69	24	69	40	22%	47%	19%	12%
2011	OAK	11/1	15	33	241	45%	-2.9	16.1	0	2	5.4	--	+1.0	-11.8%	--	2	--	9	26%	32%	32%	10%
2012	OAK		30	55	428	55%	--	14.3	1					-2.5%								

Murphy was one of the few Raiders receivers who was more productive on third downs in 2011, but he has posted a below-average catch rate in every season of his career. That's not a good sign for a possession receiver. Like the rest of the plethora of young Raiders receivers, he needs to become more consistent with his route-running and hands. With new offensive coordinator Greg Knapp likely featuring less of a deep-oriented passing attack, Murphy has an opportunity to pick up more catches if he sees the field.

Legedu Naanee   Height: 6-2   Weight: 225   College: Boise State   Draft: 2007/5 (172)   Born: 16-Sep-1983   Age: 29   Risk: Green

Year	Team	G/S	Rec	Pass	Yds	C%	+/-	Y/C	TD	Drop	YAC	Rk	YAC+	DVOA	Rk	DYAR	Rk	YAR	Short	Mid	Deep	Bomb
2009	SD	15/1	24	29	242	83%	+4.9	10.1	2	1	5.4	--	+0.4	33.5%	--	104	--	109	59%	30%	11%	0%
2010	SD	10/9	23	46	371	50%	-2.4	16.1	1	3	4.6	--	+0.4	-6.7%	--	21	--	28	29%	40%	21%	10%
2011	CAR	15/10	44	76	467	58%	-3.1	10.6	1	3	3.8	60	-1.1	-15.5%	76	-16	76	-12	33%	35%	23%	9%
2012	MIA		25	38	271	66%	--	10.8	1					1.0%								

Last year, Naanee was flagged three times for holding, and once for a face mask penalty. He is a very good, aggressive blocker, and one of the penalties was a bit tacky, but if Naanee hoped to stick as a "system fit" who made up for his low catch totals by springing DeAngelo Williams on outside runs, he needed to be a little smarter on the toss crack. Naanee is now with the Dolphins, who need receivers who can get open and catch, not bargain-bin Muhsin Muhammad wannabes, but there is no reason to speculate on what the Dolphins were thinking because they made it clear this offseason that *they* have no idea what they are thinking.

David Nelson   Height: 6-5   Weight: 217   College: Florida   Draft: 2010/FA   Born: 7-Nov-1986   Age: 26   Risk: Yellow

Year	Team	G/S	Rec	Pass	Yds	C%	+/-	Y/C	TD	Drop	YAC	Rk	YAC+	DVOA	Rk	DYAR	Rk	YAR	Short	Mid	Deep	Bomb
2010	BUF	15/3	31	47	353	66%	+2.6	11.4	3	0	2.5	--	-1.2	15.5%	--	96	--	93	13%	67%	20%	0%
2011	BUF	16/13	61	98	658	62%	-1.9	10.8	5	3	3.3	73	-0.8	3.3%	42	122	42	116	36%	50%	11%	3%
2012	BUF		55	86	612	64%	--	11.1	3					1.1%								

Nelson doesn't look like your average slot receiver, which has both its advantages and its disadvantages. He towers over most nickel corners, which makes him a particularly attractive red-zone target; Ryan Fitzpatrick

388   WIDE RECEIVERS

looked for Nelson 15 times inside the 20-yard line, with five of those passes going for touchdowns. Nelson has very little run-after-the-catch ability, however, and he hasn't stepped up when given opportunities to be more involved. Despite almost doubling his receptions in his second year, Nelson doesn't look to have a whole lot of upside. He's a safety valve who will produce in his specific role, nothing more.

Jordy Nelson   Height: 6-2   Weight: 217   College: Kansas State   Draft: 2008/2 (36)   Born: 31-May-1985   Age: 27   Risk: Green

Year	Team	G/S	Rec	Pass	Yds	C%	+/-	Y/C	TD	Drop	YAC	Rk	YAC+	DVOA	Rk	DYAR	Rk	YAR	Short	Mid	Deep	Bomb
2009	GB	13/0	22	31	320	71%	+4.6	14.5	2	2	4.0	--	-0.3	40.1%	--	130	--	133	28%	45%	14%	14%
2010	GB	16/4	45	64	582	70%	+6.4	12.9	2	5	5.6	11	+0.8	9.5%	24	113	41	119	39%	38%	13%	10%
2011	GB	16/9	68	96	1263	71%	+11.5	18.6	15	2	6.0	11	+1.6	52.5%	1	517	2	525	31%	40%	14%	14%
2012	GB		65	95	966	68%	--	14.9	8					24.2%								

Statistically speaking, as we note in the opening to the wide receivers section, Nelson is coming off one of the greatest seasons in wide receiver history. His success is a function of many things. He plays with a special quarterback in a wide receiver-friendly offense, opposite a star (Greg Jennings) whom defenses tend to fixate on. However, Nelson himself is a very skilled player. Besides being fast for his build, he has tremendous body control both in and out of breaks, as well as in the air. He has good mechanics and an understanding of angles and timing (hence his brilliance on back-shoulder catches). It helps that he doesn't just catch balls but plucks them out of the air. Pure hands-catchers always have an advantage. Though Nelson struggled against the Chiefs as a true No. 1 when Jennings was out last season, there were occasions down the stretch where defenses made him their top concern. Don't be surprised to see more of that in 2012.

Hakeem Nicks   Height: 6-3   Weight: 212   College: North Carolina   Draft: 2009/1 (29)   Born: 14-Jan-1988   Age: 24   Risk: Red

Year	Team	G/S	Rec	Pass	Yds	C%	+/-	Y/C	TD	Drop	YAC	Rk	YAC+	DVOA	Rk	DYAR	Rk	YAR	Short	Mid	Deep	Bomb
2009	NYG	14/6	47	74	790	64%	+2.9	16.8	6	4	8.8	1	+3.6	18.2%	14	180	25	159	40%	34%	13%	13%
2010	NYG	13/12	79	128	1052	62%	+5.1	13.3	11	7	3.7	51	-0.4	14.5%	13	276	6	301	30%	40%	18%	11%
2011	NYG	15/15	76	133	1192	57%	+3.8	15.7	7	5	4.6	34	+0.2	12.9%	22	274	12	277	28%	33%	21%	18%
2012	NYG		77	135	1121	57%	--	14.6	8					7.3%								

Like his classmate Jeremy Maclin, Nicks has been consistently good in his first three seasons, giving the Giants pretty much everything they could have asked for when they took him 29th overall in 2009. Nicks broke the fifth metatarsal of his right foot while running routes during late May OTAs, but the expected 12-week recovery period puts him back on the field in time for the Giants to open the season on September 5. His KUBIAK projection is slightly lowered to reflect the likelihood that he'll take a couple weeks to get up to full speed, and his Risk is Red to reflect the possibility he'll have a setback before then.

Jordan Norwood   Height: 5-11   Weight: 179   College: Penn State   Draft: 2009/FA   Born: 29-Sep-1986   Age: 26   Risk: Yellow

Year	Team	G/S	Rec	Pass	Yds	C%	+/-	Y/C	TD	Drop	YAC	Rk	YAC+	DVOA	Rk	DYAR	Rk	YAR	Short	Mid	Deep	Bomb
2011	CLE	14/4	23	34	268	68%	+1.6	11.7	1	2	3.7	--	-0.1	12.0%	--	69	--	60	38%	44%	9%	9%
2012	CLE		18	34	226	53%	--	12.5	1					-12.8%								

After two seasons of practice squadding, Norwood's first taste of Sunday play was quite promising. Norwood is a racehorse owner, something he has in common with Browns punter Reggie Hodges and Patriots back Danny Woodhead, among others. It's a natural fit, as Norwood is the size of a jockey. He can fly, but newly drafted Travis Benjamin is very similar in size and is even faster.

WIDE RECEIVERS

Ben Obomanu Height: 6-0 Weight: 203 College: Auburn Draft: 2006/7 (249) Born: 30-Oct-1983 Age: 29 Risk: Green

Year	Team	G/S	Rec	Pass	Yds	C%	+/-	Y/C	TD	Drop	YAC	Rk	YAC+	DVOA	Rk	DYAR	Rk	YAR	Short	Mid	Deep	Bomb
2009	SEA	14/0	4	5	41	80%	+0.7	10.3	0	1	3.8	--	+0.5	31.0%	--	19	--	20	60%	40%	0%	0%
2010	SEA	15/6	30	49	494	61%	+1.4	16.5	4	0	5.6	--	+0.1	15.6%	--	109	--	111	47%	27%	13%	13%
2011	SEA	16/7	37	61	436	61%	+2.4	11.8	2	5	3.4	69	-1.1	-5.9%	61	32	64	34	35%	39%	11%	16%
2012	SEA		23	42	284	55%	--	12.3	1					-8.3%								

With Mike Williams and Sidney Rice missing stretches of the season due to injury, and Doug Baldwin playing solely in three-plus wide receiver personnel groupings, Obomanu, the team's longest-tenured player on offense, led Seahawks receivers in playing time in 2011. Obomanu's -24.4% DVOA on third and fourth downs was the lowest on the team, however, and he'd yield playing time to Golden Tate as the season progressed. With Williams coming off a serious leg injury, the competition for the No. 2 receiver role opposite Rice is wide open and Obomanu will certainly be in the mix.

Chad Ochocinco Height: 6-1 Weight: 192 College: Oregon State Draft: 2001/2 (36) Born: 9-Jan-1978 Age: 35 Risk: Red

Year	Team	G/S	Rec	Pass	Yds	C%	+/-	Y/C	TD	Drop	YAC	Rk	YAC+	DVOA	Rk	DYAR	Rk	YAR	Short	Mid	Deep	Bomb
2009	CIN	16/15	72	129	1047	57%	-1.6	14.5	9	6	3.7	57	-0.3	10.4%	27	241	15	246	20%	52%	19%	8%
2010	CIN	14/12	67	126	831	53%	-3.2	12.4	4	8	2.8	71	-0.9	-0.4%	52	120	38	94	21%	55%	16%	8%
2011	NE	15/3	15	32	276	47%	-0.5	18.4	1	1	3.5	--	-0.0	-4.9%	--	19	--	28	3%	52%	29%	16%
2012	MIA		40	71	484	56%	--	12.1	3					-6.3%								

In retrospect, the amount of virtual ink that was spilled over Ochocinco's lone year in New England seems even more ridiculous than it did at the time. Ochocinco left such a small statistical footprint that there's really not much to dissect. His -50.8% DVOA on first downs came from only catching 27 percent of the passes intended for him. On second and third downs, Ochocinco performed competently the few times Tom Brady looked his way. Ocho was supposed to help out in the red zone, an area where he had performed well as a Bengal in 2008 and 2009, but Rob Gronkowski and Aaron Hernandez soaked up all the targets. In the end, Brady only threw three passes to Ochocinco down inside the 20, and Ocho didn't catch a single one of them. Early word out of Miami says that Ochocinco is having an easier time learning the Dolphins playbook than he had learning the Patriots playbook, but we're skeptical that he'll have a big rebound year.

Kevin Ogletree Height: 6-2 Weight: 196 College: Virginia Draft: 2009/FA Born: 5-Dec-1987 Age: 25 Risk: Yellow

Year	Team	G/S	Rec	Pass	Yds	C%	+/-	Y/C	TD	Drop	YAC	Rk	YAC+	DVOA	Rk	DYAR	Rk	YAR	Short	Mid	Deep	Bomb
2009	DAL	11/0	7	8	96	88%	+1.2	13.7	0	0	9.9	--	+3.3	54.9%	--	37	--	39	63%	25%	13%	0%
2010	DAL	6/0	3	6	34	50%	-1.1	11.3	0	1	2.0	--	-2.2	-14.3%	--	-1	--	-3	50%	17%	33%	0%
2011	DAL	14/1	15	26	164	58%	-0.8	10.9	0	0	4.3	--	+0.0	-19.0%	--	-13	--	-13	35%	50%	8%	8%
2012	DAL		27	48	347	56%	--	12.8	1					-5.5%								

Ogletree's brother Calvin was shot in the head last January. He survived and is recovering, but Ogletree told Carlos Mendez of the *Fort Worth Star-Telegram* that the incident "really forced me to look in the mirror and dig deep and find out what I want to be," and "specifically has changed my attitude and work ethic." There's a wide-open opportunity for Ogletree with the Cowboys, who are in desperate need for a third receiver. They liked Ogletree enough to re-sign him in March, but not enough to stop him from hitting the open market in the first place, so take that for what it's worth.

Preston Parker Height: 6-0 Weight: 200 College: North Alabama Draft: 2010/FA Born: 13-Feb-1987 Age: 25 Risk: Green

Year	Team	G/S	Rec	Pass	Yds	C%	+/-	Y/C	TD	Drop	YAC	Rk	YAC+	DVOA	Rk	DYAR	Rk	YAR	Short	Mid	Deep	Bomb
2010	TB	9/0	4	10	42	50%	-0.9	10.5	0	0	8.4	--	+2.4	-30.4%	--	-15	--	-14	67%	11%	11%	11%
2011	TB	16/0	40	65	554	63%	+1.0	13.9	3	1	7.0	4	+2.8	8.2%	35	106	46	109	44%	51%	5%	0%
2012	TB		25	42	310	60%	--	12.4	2					2.9%								

Fumble-prone as a return man, Parker was intermittently effective as a slot receiver after taking the role from injured Sammie Stroughter early in the season. He became Josh Freeman's favorite third-down target, producing a respectable 4.1% DVOA on 38 third-down passes. The Bucs gave Parker a new one-year contract and plan to continue using him as a third receiver, which is wise, and as a punt returner, which is definitely not (he was worth -8.9 estimated points of field position on punt returns last season).

Austin Pettis Height: 6-3 Weight: 209 College: Boise State Draft: 2011/3 (78) Born: 7-May-1988 Age: 24 Risk: Green

Year	Team	G/S	Rec	Pass	Yds	C%	+/-	Y/C	TD	Drop	YAC	Rk	YAC+	DVOA	Rk	DYAR	Rk	YAR	Short	Mid	Deep	Bomb
2011	STL	12/3	27	48	256	56%	-1.3	9.5	0	3	3.5	--	-0.8	-22.9%	--	-39	--	-43	49%	40%	2%	9%
2012	STL		4	7	38	57%	--	9.5	0					-20.9%								

Although a 2011 third-round pick, Pettis is destined to be cut before Week 1. Exhibit A: He only played last year because first- and second-string slot receivers (Danny Amendola and Greg Salas) suffered season-ending injurires. Exhibit B: New offensive coordinator Brian Schottenheimer doesn't give a rat's ass about slot receivers. Exhibit C: Pettis was a below-average punt returner (-2.6 estimated points added), and the Rams drafted Senior Bowl punt-return wunderkind Isaiah Pead.

DeVier Posey Height: 6-2 Weight: 211 College: Ohio State Draft: 2012/3 (68) Born: 15-Mar-1989 Age: 23 Risk: Green

Year	Team	G/S	Rec	Pass	Yds	C%	+/-	Y/C	TD	Drop	YAC	Rk	YAC+	DVOA	Rk	DYAR	Rk	YAR	Short	Mid	Deep	Bomb
2012	HOU		16	30	218	53%	--	13.7	1					-5.3%								

Posey will likely be brought along slowly in the Houston offense. He fits the standard West Coast mold: physical, can make catches in traffic, can block a little. He does have some untapped vertical skill, and was very solid for the Buckeyes in 2010, averaging 9.6 yards per target. Posey was caught in the tattoos-for-cash scandal, which he claimed in a sports radio interview was done to keep the bills paid at home, so he missed most of the 2011 season. That's a very rare combination for any third-round pick, let alone one for the image-conscious Texans. He eventually projects to replace Kevin Walter outside.

Brian Quick Height: 6-4 Weight: 220 College: Appalachian State Draft: 2012/2 (33) Born: 5-Jun-1989 Age: 23 Risk: Red

Year	Team	G/S	Rec	Pass	Yds	C%	+/-	Y/C	TD	Drop	YAC	Rk	YAC+	DVOA	Rk	DYAR	Rk	YAR	Short	Mid	Deep	Bomb
2012	STL		39	79	476	48%	--	12.1	3					-21.2%								

Quick, name a 6-foot-3, 220-pound NFL wide receiver who runs a 4.5-second 40-yard dash, and was selected by a Jeff Fisher team between picks 30 and 35 of the draft? If you answered Kenny Britt, congratulations. The only thing standing in between Quick and a starting job is the underwhelming, injury-prone Brandon Gibson. Keeper league alert!

Rueben Randle Height: 6-3 Weight: 210 College: Louisiana State Draft: 2012/2 (63) Born: 7-May-1991 Age: 21 Risk: Red

Year	Team	G/S	Rec	Pass	Yds	C%	+/-	Y/C	TD	Drop	YAC	Rk	YAC+	DVOA	Rk	DYAR	Rk	YAR	Short	Mid	Deep	Bomb
2012	NYG		30	47	399	64%	--	13.3	3					10.9%								

The Giants were ecstatic when Randle fell to them with the final pick of the second round. Apparently, two things caused him to go later than expected: an off day at the Combine, where he ran a 4.55 forty, and the fact that he's more of a raw potential guy than a finished product. Hey, that's OK with the Giants, who were actually considering Randle with their first-round pick. Randle is gifted with height, speed, and big, sturdy hands. He's still learning nuances of route running, and was only a bit player for LSU in 2009-2010 before catching 56 balls for 16.6 yards per catch as the Tigers' No. 1 receiver in 2011. Randle will fit right into the role vacated by Mario Manningham, and at OTAs was already impressing the Giants a lot more than recent receiver picks Ramses Barden and Jerrel Jernigan.

Sidney Rice

Height: 6-4 Weight: 200 College: South Carolina Draft: 2007/2 (44) Born: 1-Sep-1986 Age: 26 Risk: Yellow

Year	Team	G/S	Rec	Pass	Yds	C%	+/-	Y/C	TD	Drop	YAC	Rk	YAC+	DVOA	Rk	DYAR	Rk	YAR	Short	Mid	Deep	Bomb
2009	MIN	16/14	83	121	1312	69%	+11.8	15.8	8	2	4.4	32	+0.6	36.1%	3	483	1	493	23%	52%	13%	12%
2010	MIN	6/5	17	42	280	40%	-3.3	16.5	2	1	2.5	--	-1.1	-1.7%	--	36	--	18	13%	42%	18%	26%
2011	SEA	9/9	32	59	484	58%	+2.6	15.1	2	2	3.9	57	-1.2	-3.1%	55	45	58	49	21%	41%	10%	28%
2012	SEA		60	118	904	51%	--	15.1	6					-3.1%								

Even though Rice had only one season of elite production on his resume, and was coming off a 2010 that was mostly lost to hip surgery, the Seahawks backed up the Brinks truck after the lockout ended and dropped a five-year, $41 million contract that included $18.5 million in guarantees on his doorstep. Signs of trouble first appeared in the first two weeks of the season, which Rice missed with a shoulder injury that was rumored to be a torn labrum. Rice would play through the shoulder injury, and a foot injury, before suffering multiple concussions that prompted the team to shut him down in December. Rice underwent surgery on both shoulders in the offseason, but is expected to be a full go for training camp. If healthy, and catching passes from a former Packers quarterback whose last name begins with an "F," Rice has shown the ability to produce at an elite level. Unfortunately for the Seahawks, Matt Flynn becoming the next Brett Favre is as likely as Rice staying healthy for a full season.

Andre Roberts

Height: 5-11 Weight: 195 College: The Citadel Draft: 2010/3 (88) Born: 9-Jan-1988 Age: 24 Risk: Green

Year	Team	G/S	Rec	Pass	Yds	C%	+/-	Y/C	TD	Drop	YAC	Rk	YAC+	DVOA	Rk	DYAR	Rk	YAR	Short	Mid	Deep	Bomb
2010	ARI	15/2	24	49	307	49%	-6.7	12.8	2	2	5.8	--	+0.8	-39.0%	--	-99	--	-66	49%	32%	15%	4%
2011	ARI	16/16	51	97	586	53%	-5.3	11.5	2	4	4.4	37	+0.5	-15.5%	77	-22	78	-40	37%	47%	11%	5%
2012	ARI		28	53	381	53%	--	13.6	1					-11.5%								

The free-agent departure of Steve Breaston after the lockout vaulted Roberts into a starting role and KUBIAK darling status in 2011. The 2010 third-round pick out of The Citadel played in over 90 percent of the Cardinals' offensive snaps in 2011, but failed to out-produce Early Doucet. Among the team's top three wideouts, Roberts had the lowest DVOA rating on second (-32.3%) and third down (-18.0%). Roberts' performance in 2011 led the Cardinals to use their 2012 first-round pick on Michael Floyd. All he'll be given this year is a shot to compete for the slot receiver job.

Laurent Robinson

Height: 6-2 Weight: 192 College: Illinois State Draft: 2007/3 (75) Born: 20-May-1985 Age: 27 Risk: Green

Year	Team	G/S	Rec	Pass	Yds	C%	+/-	Y/C	TD	Drop	YAC	Rk	YAC+	DVOA	Rk	DYAR	Rk	YAR	Short	Mid	Deep	Bomb
2009	STL	3/3	13	23	167	57%	-0.7	12.8	1	0	3.3	--	-0.7	-1.2%	--	21	--	31	27%	55%	5%	14%
2010	STL	14/11	34	75	344	45%	-6.6	10.1	2	4	3.1	64	-0.8	-36.5%	84	-140	84	-116	35%	44%	14%	8%
2011	DAL	14/4	54	81	858	67%	+5.0	15.9	11	3	4.9	26	+0.7	40.0%	4	327	8	332	28%	41%	18%	12%
2012	JAC		44	82	577	54%	--	13.1	3					-9.5%								

Fluke alert! Fluke alert! Forty-one of the 50 receivers most statistically similar to Robinson declined the next season, by an average of 391 yards. That's a dropoff of greater than 50 percent. And that's without mentioning the touchdowns. Robinson was the target on 11 red-zone passes last year, catching nine of them for eight touchdowns. The year before, the St. Louis Rams threw Robinson nine red-zone passes, and he only scored twice. Now he's supposed to be the proven receiver on a team whose quarterback was woefully inept last year, with a rookie at the other receiver spot. The Risk factor here would be "Red," except the decline is already built into his projection.

Naaman Roosevelt

Height: 6-0   Weight: 189   College: Buffalo   Draft: 2010/FA   Born: 24-Dec-1987   Age: 25   Risk: Blue

Year	Team	G/S	Rec	Pass	Yds	C%	+/-	Y/C	TD	Drop	YAC	Rk	YAC+	DVOA	Rk	DYAR	Rk	YAR	Short	Mid	Deep	Bomb
2010	BUF	6/1	9	17	139	53%	+1.3	15.4	0	0	3.7	--	-0.3	2.0%	--	20	--	19	6%	69%	25%	0%
2011	BUF	10/0	16	26	257	62%	+0.3	16.1	1	1	8.2	--	+3.7	3.4%	--	32	--	36	29%	46%	25%	0%
2012	BUF		4	7	53	57%	--	13.3	0					1.0%								

Roosevelt didn't make the opening day roster, but he came up from the practice squad after Roscoe Parrish went on injured reserve and hung onto his spot for the rest of the year. Aside from brief flashes against the Eagles and Giants, Roosevelt didn't contribute much, and he was frequently inactive on game days. A Buffalo native who stayed home and played his college ball at the University of Buffalo, Roosevelt is a fan favorite, but he is going to have a hard time making the team.

Eddie Royal

Height: 5-9   Weight: 184   College: Virginia Tech   Draft: 2008/2 (42)   Born: 21-May-1986   Age: 26   Risk: Yellow

Year	Team	G/S	Rec	Pass	Yds	C%	+/-	Y/C	TD	Drop	YAC	Rk	YAC+	DVOA	Rk	DYAR	Rk	YAR	Short	Mid	Deep	Bomb
2009	DEN	14/12	37	79	345	47%	-6.8	9.3	0	3	3.4	64	-0.9	-34.8%	89	-138	89	-133	43%	46%	7%	3%
2010	DEN	16/10	59	106	627	57%	-6.3	10.6	3	2	6.6	3	+0.8	-17.2%	74	-37	74	-29	49%	35%	11%	4%
2011	DEN	12/8	19	50	155	38%	-8.1	8.2	1	3	3.5	68	-1.5	-45.3%	92	-129	90	-150	33%	41%	13%	13%
2012	SD		39	67	409	58%	--	10.5	2					-12.1%								

As a rookie in 2008, Royal caught 91 passes for 920 yards and ranked 45th in DVOA. He hasn't sniffed any of those numbers since, and to say that he didn't mesh with Tim Tebow is an understatement. How on earth does a player who catches only 38 percent of targets average just 8.1 yards per reception? And it's not just the quarterback—Royal had similar numbers whether Tebow or Kyle Orton was under center. The end result: Royal came within .078% of setting a new record for worst DVOA by a wide receiver.

Worst Wide Receiver DVOA, 1991-2011

Rank	Year	Player	Team	DVOA	Passes
1	1991	T.B.Jones	HOIL	-45.3%	53
2	**2011**	**E.Royal**	**DEN**	**-45.3%**	**50**
3	2000	P.Burress	PIT	-44.5%	65
4	2004	B.Wade	CHI	-43.5%	89
5	2010	E.Doucet	ARI	-40.5%	59
6	2007	J.Webb	KC	-40.0%	57
7	1993	G.McMurtry	NE	-39.3%	52
8	2002	M.Robinson	CHI	-38.9%	53
9	**2011**	**J.Baldwin**	**KC**	**-38.9%**	**53**
10	**2011**	**D.Aromashodu**	**MIN**	**-38.0%**	**84**

Minimum 50 passes.

Fortunately, Royal has great value as a punt returner. Among active qualifying players, only Devin Hester and Roscoe Parrish can top Royal's 11.9 yards per return. Both Royal and Parrish were signed by San Diego, but Royal is four years younger and has been healthier in recent years, so he should win the battle for playing time on offense and special teams.

Greg Salas

Height: 6-1   Weight: 206   College: Hawaii   Draft: 2011/4 (112)   Born: 25-Aug-1988   Age: 24   Risk: Green

Year	Team	G/S	Rec	Pass	Yds	C%	+/-	Y/C	TD	Drop	YAC	Rk	YAC+	DVOA	Rk	DYAR	Rk	YAR	Short	Mid	Deep	Bomb
2011	STL	6/0	27	38	264	71%	+0.0	9.8	0	3	8.1	--	+1.7	-36.0%	--	-64	--	-52	83%	8%	6%	3%
2012	STL		14	25	158	56%	--	11.3	0					-13.0%								

The Rams drafted Salas in last year's fourth round because they figured Josh McDaniels and his reliance on slot receivers would be around longer than one year. With McDaniels gone, the most prolific wide receiver in University of Hawaii history is once again a man on an island—but instead of the Pacific Ocean, Salas is surrounded by competition. He's behind at least six receivers on the Rams' depth chart, including two 2012 draft picks. Nevertheless, he showed enough in his rookie season to be able to find a job elsewhere if released.

Emmanuel Sanders Height: 5-11 Weight: 186 College: SMU Draft: 2010/3 (82) Born: 17-Mar-1987 Age: 25 Risk: Green

Year	Team	G/S	Rec	Pass	Yds	C%	+/-	Y/C	TD	Drop	YAC	Rk	YAC+	DVOA	Rk	DYAR	Rk	YAR	Short	Mid	Deep	Bomb
2010	PIT	13/1	28	50	376	56%	+0.1	13.4	2	3	2.5	78	-1.4	5.7%	36	69	55	53	19%	46%	27%	8%
2011	PIT	11/0	22	43	288	51%	-2.9	13.1	2	0	5.8	--	+1.5	-8.0%	--	15	--	23	29%	38%	21%	12%
2012	PIT		37	65	483	57%	--	13.0	1					-3.5%								

In his rookie year, Sanders was an efficient No. 4 wide receiver who needed to improve his catch rate. Then he broke his foot in the Super Bowl, and the resulting recovery and overcompensation made most of his lower half (knee, both feet) uncooperative in 2011. He's declared himself fully healthy in 2012, but even his head coach is skeptical. "You can't anticipate [Sanders' injuries] are going to stop," Tomlin said. With Hines Ward now spending Sundays terrorizing Bob Costas, Sanders is firmly entrenched as the Steelers' No. 3 wideout, and his role on returns may expand if the Steelers want to make sure Antonio Brown isn't distracted from his offensive duties.

Mohamed Sanu Height: 6-2 Weight: 211 College: Rutgers Draft: 2012/3 (83) Born: 22-Aug-1989 Age: 23 Risk: Red

Year	Team	G/S	Rec	Pass	Yds	C%	+/-	Y/C	TD	Drop	YAC	Rk	YAC+	DVOA	Rk	DYAR	Rk	YAR	Short	Mid	Deep	Bomb
2012	CIN		47	74	496	64%	--	10.6	2					-3.4%								

Sanu earned his post-game jacuzzi treatments while at Rutgers. He was the targeted 176 times, second-most in the country, and caught 115 of them, a Big East Conference record. A well-rounded athlete and willing blocker, he suffered from puny quarterback play as a senior. Sanu's catch rate improved to 65 percent while his yards per catch dwindled to 10.5. However, in his entire college career, Sanu never averaged as much as seven yards per target, which is a red flag even with an iffy quarterback. His maturity and good attitude were on display during the draft, when he was the victim of a prankster who called him with "good news" in the first round, pretending to be a Bengals coach. Cincy got him in the third instead, and Sanu laughed off the incident.

Dane Sanzenbacher Height: 5-10 Weight: 182 College: Ohio State Draft: 2011/FA Born: 13-Oct-1988 Age: 24 Risk: Green

Year	Team	G/S	Rec	Pass	Yds	C%	+/-	Y/C	TD	Drop	YAC	Rk	YAC+	DVOA	Rk	DYAR	Rk	YAR	Short	Mid	Deep	Bomb
2011	CHI	16/1	27	54	276	50%	-8.7	10.2	3	5	2.1	89	-1.6	-17.9%	81	-22	77	-27	38%	53%	9%	0%
2012	CHI		16	29	166	55%	--	10.4	1					-13.2%								

Sanzenbacher emerged as a back-of-the-rotation contributor in his rookie year. Scouts liked how when he was at his best, he showed good lateral agility and quickness coming in and out of his breaks. Sanzenbacher has the physical tools to get separation on intermediate and shorter routes. It's just a matter of matching those traits with the right role in the lineup. He had 27 receptions last season but had a six-week stretch in November and December where he didn't catch a single pass.

Chaz Schilens Height: 6-4 Weight: 225 College: San Diego State Draft: 2008/7 (226) Born: 7-Nov-1985 Age: 27 Risk: Green

Year	Team	G/S	Rec	Pass	Yds	C%	+/-	Y/C	TD	Drop	YAC	Rk	YAC+	DVOA	Rk	DYAR	Rk	YAR	Short	Mid	Deep	Bomb
2009	OAK	8/8	29	51	365	57%	-1.2	12.6	2	5	3.2	70	-1.0	-2.9%	49	37	57	32	33%	37%	24%	6%
2010	OAK	5/0	5	9	40	56%	+0.1	8.0	1	0	2.6	--	-0.9	4.8%	--	13	--	10	56%	22%	11%	11%
2011	OAK	15/5	23	34	271	68%	+2.6	11.8	2	3	1.6	--	-1.8	14.5%	--	72	--	59	29%	38%	26%	6%
2012	NYJ		16	29	189	55%	--	11.8	2					-7.5%								

394 WIDE RECEIVERS

Schillens was an outstanding receiver in the red zone in both 2010 and 2011, catching every pass thrown his direction. Of course, that was only five catches over two years, so we may not be talking about a reliable sample size. 2011 was one of his infrequent healthy seasons, and he was a useful possession receiver when he was on the field. He'll likely fill a similar role with the Jets.

Jordan Shipley
Height: 5-11 Weight: 193 College: Texas Draft: 2010/3 (84) Born: 23-Dec-1985 Age: 27 Risk: Red

Year	Team	G/S	Rec	Pass	Yds	C%	+/-	Y/C	TD	Drop	YAC	Rk	YAC+	DVOA	Rk	DYAR	Rk	YAR	Short	Mid	Deep	Bomb
2010	CIN	15/4	52	74	600	70%	+4.8	11.5	3	0	4.0	42	-0.2	14.7%	10	160	25	142	49%	43%	6%	3%
2011	CIN	2/0	4	5	14	80%	+0.4	3.5	0	0	0.0	--	-4.6	-92.5%	--	-35	--	-38	67%	17%	17%	0%
2012	CIN		64	96	749	67%	--	11.7	2					4.2%								

When Shipley was drafted in 2010, the first thing everyone said was that he was a "Wes Welker clone." The second thing everyone said was: "...if he doesn't get hurt." Unfortunately, he did. Ship blew out his ACL and MCL in the second game of the season. Having already lost two full seasons in college to knee and hamstring injuries, we can probably deem him injury-prone at this point. Certainly, Shipley's determination isn't in question, and he participated at full speed during spring OTAs. But at age 27, with legs apparently better suited for scuba diving or some other low-impact sport, Shipley needs to rebound and put in a full, quality season—or the Bengals will be looking for the next Welker clone.

Cecil Shorts
Height: 6-0 Weight: 200 College: Mount Union Draft: 2011/4 (114) Born: 22-Dec-1987 Age: 25 Risk: Red

Year	Team	G/S	Rec	Pass	Yds	C%	+/-	Y/C	TD	Drop	YAC	Rk	YAC+	DVOA	Rk	DYAR	Rk	YAR	Short	Mid	Deep	Bomb
2011	JAC	10/0	2	11	30	18%	-4.1	15.0	1	2	1.5	--	-2.3	-54.3%	--	-37	--	-37	18%	36%	18%	27%
2012	JAC		9	19	145	47%	--	16.1	1					-6.8%								

A training camp standout for the Jaguars, Shorts was given sporadic playing time early on, and the first eight passes targeting him were incomplete. Two of the next three weren't. Jacksonville mercifully decided to acquire actual receivers this offseason, so next year we'll again get to try to glean more about this receiver in a Shorts Sample Size.

Jerome Simpson
Height: 6-2 Weight: 199 College: Coastal Carolina Draft: 2008/2 (46) Born: 4-Feb-1986 Age: 26 Risk: Yellow

Year	Team	G/S	Rec	Pass	Yds	C%	+/-	Y/C	TD	Drop	YAC	Rk	YAC+	DVOA	Rk	DYAR	Rk	YAR	Short	Mid	Deep	Bomb
2009	CIN	2/0	0	1	0	0%	-0.6	0.0	0	0	--	--	+0.0	-66.0%	--	-4	--	-7	0%	100%	0%	0%
2010	CIN	5/3	20	25	277	80%	+4.3	13.9	3	0	3.9	--	+0.0	44.1%	--	109	--	95	20%	60%	12%	8%
2011	CIN	16/14	50	105	725	48%	-8.8	14.5	4	6	4.6	33	+0.6	-6.7%	63	47	57	27	24%	52%	13%	10%
2012	MIN		41	79	606	52%	--	14.8	3					-3.7%								

There are two Jerome Simpsons. There is the wondrous athlete whose full-front somersault for a touchdown against Arizona in December will live in NFL Network promotional history forever, and then there is the clueless route-runner with a deplorable catch rate. Bengals offensive coordinator Jay Gruden summed it up by saying, "Jerome had moments of greatness and moments of 'What is going on?'" Cincinnati probably would have kept Dr. Jekyll in stripes and lived with the Mr. Hyde appearances if it weren't for Simpson's arrest for marijuana trafficking after the season (he got 15 days in the clink, and three years probation). That was the cannabis plant that broke the camel's back, as it were, and Simpson has signed with Minnesota, where he will miss the first three games of the season thanks to his Saul Silver impression and Herr Goodell. He should fill a deep threat role in Minnesota, as they were 28th in yards per attempt in 2011.

Mike Sims-Walker
Height: 6-2 Weight: 208 College: UCF Draft: 2007/3 (79) Born: 11-Nov-1984 Age: 28 Risk: N/A

Year	Team	G/S	Rec	Pass	Yds	C%	+/-	Y/C	TD	Drop	YAC	Rk	YAC+	DVOA	Rk	DYAR	Rk	YAR	Short	Mid	Deep	Bomb
2009	JAC	15/14	63	111	869	57%	+2.6	13.8	7	5	4.0	53	+0.1	1.1%	41	120	39	107	33%	39%	21%	7%
2010	JAC	14/13	43	79	562	53%	-1.5	13.1	7	3	2.9	70	-0.9	11.9%	19	156	28	137	20%	54%	21%	6%
2011	2TM	6/4	12	33	150	36%	-3.9	12.5	0	2	2.7	--	-0.5	-43.6%	--	-81	--	-83	27%	54%	12%	8%

Sims-Walker left Jacksonville with a lengthy injury history and a history as a bit of a malcontent. He spent two whole months in St. Louis before his release, and decided that maybe the grass wasn't greener after all by joining the Jaguars again. Knee surgery sent him to IR shortly thereafter, and he now finds himself as a hungry young receiver as training camp approaches. He'll literally play for a sandwich.

Brad Smith
Height: 6-2 Weight: 210 College: Missouri Draft: 2006/4 (103) Born: 12-Dec-1983 Age: 29 Risk: Yellow

Year	Team	G/S	Rec	Pass	Yds	C%	+/-	Y/C	TD	Drop	YAC	Rk	YAC+	DVOA	Rk	DYAR	Rk	YAR	Short	Mid	Deep	Bomb
2009	NYJ	13/2	7	12	63	58%	-1.1	9.0	0	1	4.1	--	-0.4	-47.1%	--	-33	--	-28	58%	33%	8%	0%
2010	NYJ	16/2	4	7	44	57%	-0.1	11.0	0	2	2.5	--	-1.5	-36.3%	--	-13	--	-11	83%	0%	17%	0%
2011	BUF	15/5	23	42	240	55%	-3.2	10.4	1	3	4.6	--	-0.6	-25.5%	--	-41	--	-56	44%	32%	15%	10%
2012	BUF		19	33	215	58%	--	11.3	3					-4.3%								

Smith's game logs read like a tale of two seasons. For the first eight games of the season, Smith was used primarily as a runner in the Wildcat package, and he logged carries in six of the games. He only carried the ball one more time for the rest of the year, as mounting injuries forced the Bills to utilize Smith primarily as a receiver. He performed reasonably well, catching 18 passes for 197 yards over the final two months. All indications are that the Bills would like to use Smith more like they did in the first half of the season. They're listing him on the depth chart at quarterback, but that has to be a joke, right? His projection also includes 27 carries for 208 yards and a touchdown.

Steve Smith
Height: 5-9 Weight: 185 College: Utah Draft: 2001/3 (74) Born: 12-May-1979 Age: 33 Risk: Yellow

Year	Team	G/S	Rec	Pass	Yds	C%	+/-	Y/C	TD	Drop	YAC	Rk	YAC+	DVOA	Rk	DYAR	Rk	YAR	Short	Mid	Deep	Bomb
2009	CAR	15/15	65	128	982	51%	-7.4	15.1	7	4	5.1	22	-0.1	-7.2%	57	55	52	41	39%	32%	15%	15%
2010	CAR	9/7	48	99	529	46%	-8.6	11.0	3	6	4.7	25	-0.2	-32.4%	83	-150	85	-154	40%	36%	18%	6%
2011	CAR	16/16	79	129	1394	61%	+3.6	17.6	7	7	5.8	14	+0.7	12.1%	24	239	15	242	30%	32%	23%	15%
2012	CAR		81	137	1222	59%	--	15.1	7					11.9%								

Smith on passes marked "deep" in the play-by-play (15 or more yards in the air): 23-of-47, 711 yards, 15.1 yards per pass, four touchdowns. When your rookie quarterback and deep receiver are connecting on nearly half their deep passes, they are doing something right. Smith's career statistics read like the growth rings of an old oak tree. Look at his year-by-year totals, and you can see the Panthers' early-2000s heyday; the rise and slow, long descent of the Jake Delhomme era; the devastation of 2010; and the sudden rebirth of 2011. On the one hand, the Smith growth rings prove just how dependent even a great receiver is on his quarterbacks. On the other hand, anyone who can gain 982 receiving yards with Matt Moore and a 34-year-old Delhomme throwing to him deserves some kind of lifetime achievement award.

Steve Smith
Height: 6-0 Weight: 195 College: USC Draft: 2007/2 (51) Born: 6-May-1985 Age: 27 Risk: Red

Year	Team	G/S	Rec	Pass	Yds	C%	+/-	Y/C	TD	Drop	YAC	Rk	YAC+	DVOA	Rk	DYAR	Rk	YAR	Short	Mid	Deep	Bomb
2009	NYG	16/15	107	157	1220	68%	+13.8	11.4	7	5	2.3	84	-1.8	13.7%	18	325	8	311	32%	41%	16%	10%
2010	NYG	9/7	48	75	529	64%	+4.8	11.0	3	4	2.2	82	-1.5	1.8%	46	87	50	98	26%	49%	14%	11%
2011	PHI	9/1	11	20	124	55%	+0.2	11.3	1	3	3.0	--	-0.9	-16.0%	--	-5	--	-3	35%	41%	12%	12%
2012	STL		24	38	271	63%	--	11.3	0					-2.4%								

If you like talented football players, Smith's descent should make you sad. He was a stud possession receiver, with phenomenal catch rates and plus/minus numbers. But although the articular cartilage knee injury he suffered in

WIDE RECEIVERS

2010 didn't fully end his NFL career, it at least seems to have ended his career time as a quality player. He didn't do much for the Eagles, who were playing Riley Cooper ahead of him. Eventually he had to go on injured reserve with a bone bruise in the same knee that underwent microfracture surgery. Jeff Fisher told the media that Smith's free-agent workout with St. Louis was "extraordinary," but teams weren't exactly running to sign Smith this offseason.

Torrey Smith
Height: 6-1 Weight: 204 College: Maryland Draft: 2011/2 (58) Born: 26-Jan-1989 Age: 23 Risk: Yellow

Year	Team	G/S	Rec	Pass	Yds	C%	+/-	Y/C	TD	Drop	YAC	Rk	YAC+	DVOA	Rk	DYAR	Rk	YAR	Short	Mid	Deep	Bomb
2011	BAL	16/14	50	96	841	54%	+0.8	16.8	7	6	4.7	30	+0.1	11.3%	28	180	24	173	19%	34%	18%	29%
2012	BAL		51	97	828	53%	--	16.2	8					8.6%								

Since John Harbaugh and Cam Cameron arrived in Baltimore, the Ravens have used play-action as much as any team in the league. Of course, the whole point of a play fake is to make defensive backs flinch for a moment, and then beat them over the top. Previous No. 2 wideouts were either old (Derrick Mason) or pedestrian (Mark Clayton), so the addition of Smith marked the first time that the Harbaugh-era Ravens could maximize their strategic tendency. 22 percent of Smith's targets, and three of his seven touchdowns, were out of play-action.

Donte' Stallworth
Height: 6-0 Weight: 197 College: Tennessee Draft: 2002/1 (13) Born: 10-Nov-1980 Age: 32 Risk: Red

Year	Team	G/S	Rec	Pass	Yds	C%	+/-	Y/C	TD	Drop	YAC	Rk	YAC+	DVOA	Rk	DYAR	Rk	YAR	Short	Mid	Deep	Bomb
2010	BAL	8/0	2	5	82	40%	-0.3	41.0	0	1	11.0	--	+6.2	20.9%	--	13	--	12	20%	20%	20%	40%
2011	WAS	11/0	22	37	309	59%	+1.6	14.0	2	1	4.7	--	+0.2	-1.7%	--	31	--	51	31%	47%	13%	9%
2012	NE		10	16	127	63%	--	12.7	1					9.1%								

Maybe the Patriots decided to bring Stallworth back because he had four catches for 96 yards against them in Week 14, but that happens to be the best game Stallworth has had since he left New England in 2008. He goes into camp essentially competing for a roster spot with fellow D.C.-to-Foxboro refugee Jabar Gaffney, but Gaffney has been more productive in recent years and had a better rapport with Tom Brady back in 2007.

Golden Tate
Height: 5-10 Weight: 199 College: Notre Dame Draft: 2010/2 (60) Born: 2-Aug-1988 Age: 24 Risk: Green

Year	Team	G/S	Rec	Pass	Yds	C%	+/-	Y/C	TD	Drop	YAC	Rk	YAC+	DVOA	Rk	DYAR	Rk	YAR	Short	Mid	Deep	Bomb
2010	SEA	11/0	21	40	227	55%	-2.8	10.8	0	2	5.3	--	+0.5	-26.4%	--	-41	--	-35	46%	31%	10%	13%
2011	SEA	16/5	35	60	382	62%	+2.6	10.9	3	0	4.5	35	-0.1	-14.8%	75	-10	75	-19	39%	39%	11%	11%
2012	SEA		18	36	187	50%	--	10.4	0					-25.9%								

Even though the lockout deprived Tate of a full NFL offseason, 2011 was supposed to be the year he justified the team using a second-round pick on him in 2010. With just 16 receptions for 173 yards and no role in the return game entering December, Tate appeared headed towards Bustville. A season-ending concussion to Sidney Rice propelled Tate into a starting role and he began to show some play-making ability, finishing with 19 receptions for 209 yards in the final five weeks of the season. Tate was strongest on third and fourth downs (8.2% DVOA) and though he's only 5-foot-10, his ability to high-point the ball led to him leading the team in red-zone targets (13), with three of his five receptions resulting in touchdowns. A full NFL offseason would have been beneficial to Tate, but he suffered a broken hand early in OTAs. Tate is expected to be ready for training camp, but the injury is a setback.

Demaryius Thomas
Height: 6-3 Weight: 224 College: Georgia Tech Draft: 2010/1 (22) Born: 25-Dec-1987 Age: 25 Risk: Red

Year	Team	G/S	Rec	Pass	Yds	C%	+/-	Y/C	TD	Drop	YAC	Rk	YAC+	DVOA	Rk	DYAR	Rk	YAR	Short	Mid	Deep	Bomb
2010	DEN	10/2	22	39	283	56%	-2.5	12.9	2	1	6.2	--	+0.7	-4.4%	--	25	--	9	42%	26%	26%	5%
2011	DEN	11/5	32	70	551	46%	-2.4	17.2	4	3	3.5	67	-0.4	-5.9%	62	37	62	40	16%	51%	14%	19%
2012	DEN		70	122	1077	57%	--	15.4	7					10.2%								

In two seasons, Thomas has missed 11 games due to a broken foot, sprained ankle, concussion, torn Achilles tendon, and broken thumb. When he was on the field, though, he showed some scary big-play ability. Only five men had three 30-yard plays in a single game last year: Vincent Jackson, Reggie Wayne, Rob Gronkowski, Calvin Johnson, and Thomas. And then in the playoffs, Thomas topped them all with four 30-yard plays (including a 32-yard DPI call) in the Wild Card win over Pittsburgh. Thomas was a project coming out of Georgia Tech's triple-option attack and remains greatly unknown in the NFL, but 2012 will be his third season in the league, and his ceiling in Denver is (ahem) mile-high.

Mike Thomas
Height: 5-8 Weight: 195 College: Arizona Draft: 2009/4 (107) Born: 4-Jun-1987 Age: 25 Risk: Green

Year	Team	G/S	Rec	Pass	Yds	C%	+/-	Y/C	TD	Drop	YAC	Rk	YAC+	DVOA	Rk	DYAR	Rk	YAR	Short	Mid	Deep	Bomb
2009	JAC	14/4	48	62	453	77%	+6.6	9.4	1	2	4.3	37	-1.0	8.0%	34	101	43	104	60%	28%	12%	0%
2010	JAC	16/11	66	102	820	66%	+3.6	12.4	4	2	4.5	30	-0.4	11.1%	21	185	22	179	41%	30%	18%	10%
2011	JAC	15/13	44	92	415	48%	-12.3	9.4	1	1	4.3	41	-0.9	-34.2%	89	-156	91	-191	40%	39%	16%	6%
2012	JAC		27	54	271	50%	--	10.0	1					-30.2%								

We'll put as much effort into this comment as Mike Thomas put into the 2011 season. The thing abou

Nick Toon
Height: 6-2 Weight: 215 College: Wisconsin Draft: 2012/4 (122) Born: 4-Nov-1988 Age: 24 Risk: Red

Year	Team	G/S	Rec	Pass	Yds	C%	+/-	Y/C	TD	Drop	YAC	Rk	YAC+	DVOA	Rk	DYAR	Rk	YAR	Short	Mid	Deep	Bomb
2012	NO		23	39	313	59%	--	13.6	2					7.1%								

Toon is the son of Al Toon, a three-time Pro Bowler for the Jets in the 1980s. Toon is pretty fast, pretty tall, has good hands and plenty of experience (he was a three-year starter at Wisconsin), but has a long history of foot injuries and surgeries, including an injury that limited his participation in pre-draft activities. His college stats show a clear dichotemy: explosive on standard downs (11.5 yards per target) but iffy in clear passing situations (6.9 yards per target). The Saints have enough weapons to bring him along slowly if they so choose.

Mike Wallace
Height: 6-0 Weight: 199 College: Mississippi Draft: 2009/3 (84) Born: 1-Aug-1986 Age: 26 Risk: Green

Year	Team	G/S	Rec	Pass	Yds	C%	+/-	Y/C	TD	Drop	YAC	Rk	YAC+	DVOA	Rk	DYAR	Rk	YAR	Short	Mid	Deep	Bomb
2009	PIT	16/4	39	72	756	54%	+0.5	19.4	6	3	3.4	63	-1.3	30.3%	4	235	16	227	18%	35%	21%	25%
2010	PIT	16/16	60	98	1257	61%	+7.2	21.0	10	5	6.0	6	+0.9	49.0%	1	458	1	445	26%	32%	15%	27%
2011	PIT	16/14	72	113	1193	64%	+6.1	16.6	8	6	6.5	7	+1.9	31.4%	8	399	5	374	35%	38%	8%	19%
2012	PIT		72	126	1246	57%	--	17.3	7					14.5%								

For Wallace to have sustained such a high average over so many receptions at the beginning of his career is quite improbable, historically speaking. Through their first three seasons, Wallace's 18.8-yard receiving average was higher than that of Randy Moss (18.4) and Jerry Rice (17.9). In fact, among all wideouts since 1978 with 150 or more catches in their first three years, Wallace's average ranks first. What's interesting is that, over time, his average has relied more and more on YAC on short passes. As we detailed in *Football Outsiders Almanac 2011*, Wallace's catches (and targets) came closer to the line of scrimmage as his second season progressed. That trend continued last season, with the average pass length of his targets dropping from 15.9 in 2010 to 13.4 in 2011. However, with new offensive coordinator Todd Haley adding more play-action into the passing game (Pittsburgh ranked 27th in play-action frequency last year), it probably won't continue into a third season.

Kevin Walter

Height: 6-3 Weight: 221 College: Eastern Michigan Draft: 2003/7 (255) Born: 4-Aug-1981 Age: 31 Risk: Green

Year	Team	G/S	Rec	Pass	Yds	C%	+/-	Y/C	TD	Drop	YAC	Rk	YAC+	DVOA	Rk	DYAR	Rk	YAR	Short	Mid	Deep	Bomb
2009	HOU	14/14	53	70	611	76%	+9.0	11.5	2	2	2.2	86	-1.5	23.4%	8	200	21	216	33%	45%	19%	3%
2010	HOU	16/16	51	80	621	64%	+5.9	12.2	5	4	2.6	76	-1.2	14.6%	12	187	21	182	34%	45%	15%	6%
2011	HOU	15/14	39	59	474	66%	+2.6	12.2	3	2	3.3	70	-0.7	6.6%	37	91	52	106	34%	41%	16%	9%
2012	HOU		49	83	624	59%	--	12.7	4					0.8%								

Walter used to be one of the real unheralded receivers in the NFL: a speedy technician who could sit in a zone and also catch a few deep play-action bombs each year. Father Time started to take the wind out of his sails last season though, and he agreed to a paycut to stay with Houston before free agency started. As a receiver, at this point, he makes a great blocker. How long he'll get to keep DeVier Posey's seat warm depends mostly on how long he can hang on to this version of himself.

Hines Ward

Height: 6-0 Weight: 205 College: Georgia Draft: 1998/3 (92) Born: 8-Mar-1976 Age: 36 Risk: N/A

Year	Team	G/S	Rec	Pass	Yds	C%	+/-	Y/C	TD	Drop	YAC	Rk	YAC+	DVOA	Rk	DYAR	Rk	YAR	Short	Mid	Deep	Bomb
2009	PIT	16/16	95	137	1167	69%	+8.8	12.3	6	6	4.2	42	-0.6	14.6%	17	287	9	272	35%	41%	19%	5%
2010	PIT	16/15	59	95	755	64%	+1.8	12.8	5	6	3.9	47	-1.3	9.1%	25	157	27	154	34%	36%	27%	3%
2011	PIT	15/9	46	63	381	73%	+3.5	8.3	2	1	3.5	66	-1.6	-12.0%	70	3	70	-14	57%	30%	10%	3%

We have plus/minus numbers for six seasons, and only six players have had a plus/minus above +1.0 in all six: Antonio Gates, Andre Johnson, Kevin Walter, Wes Welker, Jason Witten, and Ward. With Pittsburgh's move toward a more wide-open offense the past couple of seasons, Ward's role became smaller and smaller behind three bigger and faster wideouts. Ward never had a high receiving average, but his catches at age 35 looked more like extended handoffs. Perhaps the aging Ward needed to take Satchel Paige's advice: "Don't look back; something might be gaining on you, and that something might be an exploding football field." With his 1,000 career receptions ranked seventh all-time among wide receivers, Ward will be the cause of headaches among Hall of Fame voters everywhere six years from now.

Nate Washington

Height: 6-1 Weight: 185 College: Tiffin Draft: 2005/FA Born: 28-Aug-1983 Age: 29 Risk: Green

Year	Team	G/S	Rec	Pass	Yds	C%	+/-	Y/C	TD	Drop	YAC	Rk	YAC+	DVOA	Rk	DYAR	Rk	YAR	Short	Mid	Deep	Bomb
2009	TEN	16/15	47	95	569	49%	-1.4	12.1	6	8	1.9	88	-2.0	-9.9%	62	20	62	26	20%	40%	24%	16%
2010	TEN	16/16	42	94	687	45%	-6.1	16.4	6	4	2.7	74	-1.2	-3.0%	58	74	53	71	19%	40%	21%	21%
2011	TEN	16/15	74	121	1023	61%	+3.0	13.8	7	6	4.3	42	-0.1	5.2%	40	163	27	199	41%	34%	16%	10%
2012	TEN		42	82	603	51%	--	14.3	3					-6.9%								

Washington had a neat little late-career renaissance last year, raising his catch rate over 60 percent for the first time. He soaked up a lot of targets for the Titans and performed admirably under the conditions, especially since he was limping off the field often by the end of the season. Call it a small sample size, but 100 of his 175 DYAR on the season came on 18 Jake Locker throws. Look for him to be a lot less involved this year if Kenny Britt is able to stay on the field.

Reggie Wayne

Height: 6-0 Weight: 198 College: Miami Draft: 2001/1 (30) Born: 17-Nov-1978 Age: 34 Risk: Green

Year	Team	G/S	Rec	Pass	Yds	C%	+/-	Y/C	TD	Drop	YAC	Rk	YAC+	DVOA	Rk	DYAR	Rk	YAR	Short	Mid	Deep	Bomb
2009	IND	16/16	100	149	1264	67%	+16.9	12.6	10	3	4.1	47	-0.1	18.6%	13	377	6	385	38%	37%	14%	11%
2010	IND	16/16	111	175	1355	63%	+5.8	12.2	6	10	3.7	50	-0.8	0.4%	47	182	23	220	43%	30%	14%	13%
2011	IND	16/16	75	131	960	57%	-1.6	12.8	4	3	3.7	63	-0.4	1.2%	49	143	31	121	26%	44%	23%	7%
2012	IND		62	114	848	54%	--	13.7	4					-5.2%								

The end of a wide receiver's career is a very fickle thing to judge. How many years did Derrick Mason and Jimmy Smith defy the odds to keep putting up big seasons? Wayne slipped a bit statistically last season, but it's almost impossible to tell how much because of the confines of the Indianapolis offense. You are probably going to get more short balls thrown at you when your quarterback crew is Kerry Collins, Curtis Painter, and Dan Orlovsky. Either Andrew Luck's arm talent opens up his deep throws again, or Wayne has truly lost something and will find himself out of the league in a couple of years.

Wes Welker
Height: 5-9   Weight: 190   College: Texas Tech   Draft: 2004/FA   Born: 1-May-1981   Age: 31   Risk: Green

Year	Team	G/S	Rec	Pass	Yds	C%	+/-	Y/C	TD	Drop	YAC	Rk	YAC+	DVOA	Rk	DYAR	Rk	YAR	Short	Mid	Deep	Bomb
2009	NE	14/13	123	162	1348	76%	+14.3	11.0	4	4	5.9	10	+0.9	21.1%	12	434	3	372	58%	35%	6%	2%
2010	NE	15/11	86	124	848	69%	+1.4	9.9	7	13	4.7	26	+0.1	4.1%	40	164	24	120	58%	38%	3%	1%
2011	NE	16/15	122	173	1569	71%	+9.4	12.9	9	6	5.8	15	+1.4	20.4%	14	451	4	464	46%	39%	11%	4%
2012	NE		108	149	1325	72%	--	12.3	8					22.5%								

One year removed from his ACL surgery, Welker showed his form immediately, opening the season against Miami with an eight-catch, 160-yard performance that included a 99-yard touchdown catch that tied the NFL record for longest play from scrimmage. By the end of the year, Welker was atop the leader chart in receptions with 122, one short of his career high, and his DYAR ranked behind only Calvin Johnson and Jordy Nelson. It was the diminutive Welker, not either of the big tight ends, who was New England's top red-zone threat, with a DVOA of 61.8% on the strength of an astounding 87 percent catch rate.

That red-zone performance, like Welker's ongoing contract squabble, is wrapped up in the question of how much Welker's production is because he's a special player, and how much it comes from the offense around him and opponents' need to concentrate on other weapons like Rob Gronkowski. Welker has signed his franchise tender and is currently slated to play for one year at $9.5 million, but the negotiations about a longer-term deal have been surprisingly unpleasant, with both sides sniping back and forth in the press, and the Patriots not only standing firm on their initial two-year, $16 million offer, but reducing it. The team just committed to Gronkowski with a mammoth new deal, and they may no longer be interested in making that same kind of long-term commitment to an undersized receiver on the wrong side of 30, no matter how good he is.

Chastin West
Height: 6-1   Weight: 216   College: Fresno State   Draft: 2010/FA   Born: 1-May-1987   Age: 25   Risk: Blue

Year	Team	G/S	Rec	Pass	Yds	C%	+/-	Y/C	TD	Drop	YAC	Rk	YAC+	DVOA	Rk	DYAR	Rk	YAR	Short	Mid	Deep	Bomb
2011	JAC	12/1	13	27	163	48%	-1.0	12.5	2	0	3.8	--	+0.3	-16.9%	--	-9	--	6	32%	41%	23%	5%
2012	JAC		4	7	40	57%	--	10.1	0					-17.8%								

West jumped from the Packers practice squad to the Jaguars active roster, where he saw significant time after Jason Hill was waived. A lot of his production was muted by the fact that Blaine Gabbert wasn't a very good quarterback, but he also doesn't get much separation. Five of his 14 incomplete targets were listed as defensed by our charting project. With the new changes to the receiving corps, he'll have trouble making the roster again this year, and he's now played too many games to be practice squad-eligible.

Roddy White
Height: 6-1   Weight: 201   College: Alabama-Birmingham   Draft: 2005/1 (27)   Born: 2-Nov-1981   Age: 31   Risk: Green

Year	Team	G/S	Rec	Pass	Yds	C%	+/-	Y/C	TD	Drop	YAC	Rk	YAC+	DVOA	Rk	DYAR	Rk	YAR	Short	Mid	Deep	Bomb
2009	ATL	16/16	85	165	1153	52%	-9.1	13.6	11	8	4.5	31	+0.3	-0.9%	48	151	33	89	30%	43%	20%	7%
2010	ATL	16/16	115	180	1389	64%	+7.4	12.1	10	6	3.2	63	-0.9	8.9%	26	303	4	299	36%	40%	19%	5%
2011	ATL	16/16	100	180	1296	56%	+0.3	13.0	8	16	3.6	65	-0.2	2.7%	45	219	19	235	24%	46%	21%	8%
2012	ATL		93	150	1276	62%	--	13.7	9					17.0%								

Even with Julio Jones in town, the Falcons still depended on Roddy White a ton. He was targeted on 31 percent of passes, the highest rate for any receiver in the league and the fourth straight year the Falcons targeted White on at least 30 percent of passes. White also led the NFL with 30 red-zone targets; all of those passes resulted in just 13 receptions and seven touchdowns. The incomplete passes were a mix of Matt Ryan overthrows and defensed passes, with a drop and a few throw-aways in White's general direction mixed in. As the Falcons look for ways to optimize the potential of their offensive stars, they should find an alternative to forcing the ball to White from around the 15-yard line. Julio Jones' development should help.

Damian Williams   Height: 6-1   Weight: 197   College: USC   Draft: 2010/3 (77)   Born: 26-May-1988   Age: 24   Risk: Green

Year	Team	G/S	Rec	Pass	Yds	C%	+/-	Y/C	TD	Drop	YAC	Rk	YAC+	DVOA	Rk	DYAR	Rk	YAR	Short	Mid	Deep	Bomb
2010	TEN	16/1	16	28	219	57%	+0.7	13.7	0	0	2.5	--	-1.7	-3.7%	--	18	--	18	19%	42%	27%	12%
2011	TEN	15/13	45	93	592	48%	-7.4	13.2	5	5	4.7	31	+0.3	-17.4%	79	-34	80	-23	36%	31%	20%	12%
2012	TEN		16	29	200	55%	--	12.5	1					-8.2%								

When 64 of your 93 targets are marked less than 15 yards from the line of scrimmage, and you still can't even muster a 50 percent catch rate, that's a red flag. Williams had five drops according to our game charting project, and also had quite a few passes easily defensed. As the 77th overall pick in 2010, he'd normally get a few more cracks at improvement. With Kendall Wright now on board though, his upside is something like fourth on the depth chart.

Kyle Williams   Height: 5-10   Weight: 188   College: Arizona State   Draft: 2010/6 (206)   Born: 19-Jul-1988   Age: 24   Risk: Yellow

Year	Team	G/S	Rec	Pass	Yds	C%	+/-	Y/C	TD	Drop	YAC	Rk	YAC+	DVOA	Rk	DYAR	Rk	YAR	Short	Mid	Deep	Bomb
2010	SF	5/0	1	1	8	100%	+0.2	8.0	0	0	4.0	--	-0.2	39.5%	--	4	--	3	100%	0%	0%	0%
2011	SF	13/1	20	31	241	65%	+3.8	12.1	3	1	5.4	--	+1.3	10.3%	--	56	--	50	32%	64%	0%	4%
2012	SF		22	36	266	61%	--	12.1	2					1.7%								

Two untimely turnovers in the NFC Championship game ruined what was otherwise a promising second season for Williams. A fast but raw project out of Arizona State, Williams was on the slow road to NFL-caliber wide receiver play, learning the nuances of route-running and whatnot, when injuries thrust him into duty before he was ready. People remember how Ted Ginn's injury impacted San Francisco's special teams on that unforgettable January day, but immediately forgotten was that Williams, a natural slot receiver, was forced to start at split end even though he had only played one game there all season. The 49ers have speculated that they might keep six receivers on their active roster this season. If it's only five, then Williams will compete with Ginn for the final spot. Given what happened last year, choosing the former would be a hard sell, regardless of how much potential he has.

Mike Williams   Height: 6-5   Weight: 235   College: USC   Draft: 2005/1 (10)   Born: 4-Jan-1984   Age: 29   Risk: Green

Year	Team	G/S	Rec	Pass	Yds	C%	+/-	Y/C	TD	Drop	YAC	Rk	YAC+	DVOA	Rk	DYAR	Rk	YAR	Short	Mid	Deep	Bomb
2010	SEA	14/13	65	110	751	59%	+0.6	11.6	2	5	3.3	58	-0.7	-6.7%	66	50	64	60	35%	42%	16%	8%
2011	SEA	12/10	18	38	236	47%	-1.8	13.1	1	2	3.2	--	-0.5	-5.9%	--	21	--	25	20%	57%	11%	11%
2012	SEA		19	37	241	51%	--	12.7	2					-10.3%								

Seattle's leading receiver in 2010, Williams found himself back on the side of the proverbial milk carton in 2011. Williams won't gain separation from opposing defensive backs, but has the size, length and hands to make the contested catch and be a red-zone threat. A broken leg suffered last December in Chicago kept Williams out of the OTAs and minicamps, which could affect his ability to develop a rapport with the new quarterbacks in Seattle.

Mike Williams   Height: 6-2   Weight: 221   College: Syracuse   Draft: 2010/4 (101)   Born: 18-May-1987   Age: 25   Risk: Green

Year	Team	G/S	Rec	Pass	Yds	C%	+/-	Y/C	TD	Drop	YAC	Rk	YAC+	DVOA	Rk	DYAR	Rk	YAR	Short	Mid	Deep	Bomb
2010	TB	16/16	65	128	964	50%	-5.7	14.8	11	6	4.9	22	+0.5	-6.1%	65	66	56	63	22%	41%	23%	13%
2011	TB	16/15	65	124	771	52%	-7.6	11.9	3	7	3.3	72	-1.0	-18.4%	83	-58	83	-66	31%	48%	15%	6%
2012	TB		59	102	792	58%	--	13.4	5					4.8%								

The Bucs targeted Williams 40 times on passes that traveled five yards or less in the air: a mix of screens, hitches, smoke routes, and miscellaneous "here, take this!" hot potato passes. Williams caught 24 of them for

156 yards and 3.9 yards per pass, a rotten haul for one-third of a player's targets. The good news, as Williams tries to avoid following Mark Clayton's career trajectory, is that most of Williams' production came before the Bucs' December of Dismemberment, so his season totals are not padded by tons of garbage production. Williams just could not consistently beat top cornerbacks and was miscast as a No. 1 receiver last year. Vincent Jackson's arrival will move him into a more appropriate role.

Roy Williams

Height: 6-3 Weight: 215 College: Texas Draft: 2004/1 (7) Born: 20-Dec-1981 Age: 31 Risk: N/A

Year	Team	G/S	Rec	Pass	Yds	C%	+/-	Y/C	TD	Drop	YAC	Rk	YAC+	DVOA	Rk	DYAR	Rk	YAR	Short	Mid	Deep	Bomb
2009	DAL	15/13	38	86	596	44%	-10.3	15.7	7	8	5.1	23	+1.2	-7.8%	58	32	58	42	20%	54%	18%	8%
2010	DAL	15/9	37	64	530	58%	+0.3	14.3	5	6	5.6	9	+1.6	3.1%	41	77	52	65	27%	45%	22%	7%
2011	CHI	15/9	37	63	507	59%	+1.9	13.7	2	4	3.2	77	-0.6	6.4%	38	96	50	119	20%	56%	16%	8%

If not for mistakes and an unusual ability to later expound publicly on said mistakes, Roy Williams would be considered just another run-of-the-mill starting wide receiver. Instead, he's everybody's favorite whipping boy. Detroit fans don't like him because, aside from a prolific 2006 season, he never lived up to his billing there. Dallas fans don't like him because he never remotely lived up to his billing there (the Cowboys traded a first- and third-round pick to acquire Williams, then gave him a contract worth $26 million guaranteed). Chicago fans don't like Williams because, well, he came to town known as a guy who is easy to dislike.

In reality, Williams is an affable teammate and gifted split end target. His huge hands allow him to pluck balls at odd angles. He can be surprisingly balletic for a man with fishing boat-sized feet. Those fishing boats prevent him from changing directions quickly on routes, but in a vertical, slow-developing pass system, Williams is a legitimate threat. That is, if he's playing with consistency. That's proven to be a big *if* the past several years. Still unsigned as of press time.

Matt Willis

Height: 5-11 Weight: 185 College: UCLA Draft: 2007/FA Born: 13-Apr-1984 Age: 28 Risk: Blue

Year	Team	G/S	Rec	Pass	Yds	C%	+/-	Y/C	TD	Drop	YAC	Rk	YAC+	DVOA	Rk	DYAR	Rk	YAR	Short	Mid	Deep	Bomb
2009	DEN	1/1	0	0	0	--	--	--	0	0	--	--	--	--	--	--	--	--	--	--	--	--
2010	DEN	6/0	1	2	17	50%	+0.5	17.0	0	0	0.0	--	-2.2	17.9%	--	4	--	3	0%	0%	100%	0%
2011	DEN	16/0	18	36	267	50%	-2.2	14.8	1	1	5.2	--	+1.0	-4.7%	--	22	--	28	24%	50%	18%	9%
2012	DEN		5	9	58	56%	--	11.6	1					-7.3%								

Willis is as responsible as anyone for starting the Broncos' midseason winning streak, as he recovered a fumble on a punt against the Dolphins in Week 7 and later caught a 42-yard pass in the fourth quarter to set up the first of Denver's miracle touchdowns. A well-rounded athlete, Willis ran track and played football at UCLA, and during the NFL lockout of 2011 he completed the obstacle course on American Ninja Warrior (though he did so too slowly to advance in the competition). The Broncos tried to tap into that athleticism by using Willis on kick returns last year, and he'll enter camp as their first option for that job.

Kendall Wright

Height: 5-10 Weight: 196 College: Baylor Draft: 2012/1 (20) Born: 12-Nov-1989 Age: 23 Risk: Red

Year	Team	G/S	Rec	Pass	Yds	C%	+/-	Y/C	TD	Drop	YAC	Rk	YAC+	DVOA	Rk	DYAR	Rk	YAR	Short	Mid	Deep	Bomb
2012	TEN		47	73	618	64%	--	13.1	4					8.6%								

Wright was a key cog in Baylor's coming out party, with a 75 percent catch rate and 15.5 yards per catch to help deliver the Heisman to Robert Griffin. He shows the most promise in the slot, but reportedly showed aptitude at all three receiver slots during Titans OTAs.

WIDE RECEIVERS

Titus Young   Height: 5-11   Weight: 174   College: Boise State   Draft: 2011/2 (44)   Born: 21-Aug-1989   Age: 23   Risk: Green

Year	Team	G/S	Rec	Pass	Yds	C%	+/-	Y/C	TD	Drop	YAC	Rk	YAC+	DVOA	Rk	DYAR	Rk	YAR	Short	Mid	Deep	Bomb
2011	DET	16/9	48	85	607	56%	+0.3	12.6	6	3	2.8	81	-1.6	-2.3%	54	70	54	91	29%	45%	10%	16%
2012	DET		37	68	497	54%	--	13.4	3					-3.1%								

It was somewhat of an up-and-down rookie season for the ex-Boise State star. Young flashed the swift playmaking prowess that made him a second-round pick, especially when the Lions prioritized getting him the ball in catch-and-run scenarios (something they did more of as the season progressed). He looked much more comfortable in the slot and against zone coverage than he did as a traditional outside receiver. When going inside, Young attacks the ball in the air and plays with his maximum quickness (including his impressive change-of-direction quickness). If he can apply those skills to all areas of the field, and also cut down on mental mistakes (which, if anything, actually increased as his rookie season went along), he'll develop into a sound second option opposite Calvin Johnson.

Going Deep

Darvin Adams, CAR: Adams went undrafted out of Auburn in 2011, then spent half of last season on the Panthers practice squad before getting activated for a handful of late games. There's a crowded receiver mix in Carolina, but he's a bit of a sleeper: He did very well in our Playmaker Score metric, and the Panthers coaches really like his work ethic.

Joe Adams, CAR: Adams is a tiny slot receiver/return man best known for two highlight-reel plays at Arkansas: a long, looping punt return against Tennessee and a 92-yard end-around against Auburn. Adams is likely to supplant Armanti Edwards as a return man, and he could become the slot weapon that the Panthers have lacked since Steve Smith stopped playing the slot. He had a 71 percent catch rate as a senior.

Kris Adams, MIN: Adams turned some heads in Bears training camp in 2011 and may have a shot at cracking Minnesota's final roster in 2012. Though originally undrafted, he has compelling size, which is something the Vikings seem to value in reserve wide receivers. He also runs around a 4.4 forty.

Kamar Aiken, BUF: Aiken flashed in preseason action, catching seven passes for 97 yards, which made him something of a fan favorite. He didn't make the final roster but was called up from the practice squad after Donald Jones landed on IR. Aiken has good speed and could get in the mix for playing time on a team that regularly throws four receivers onto the field.

Seyi Ajirotutu, CAR: A former Norv Turner project in San Diego who caught one pass for the Panthers last year, Ajirotutu has the size to be a red-zone option and block-first receiver. The Panthers have a history of employing block-first receivers, so Ajirotutu has a legitimate chance to stick down on the depth chart.

David Anderson, FA: This one-time seventh-round pick from Colorado State carved out a reasonable six-year career as a possession receiver, but it's probably time to figure out what to do with that college degree. Unfortunately, a killer Ron Jaworski impression can only take you so far in the business world. Anderson took the field last year for both Houston and Washington but is currently unsigned. (2011 stats: 7-for-16, 79 yards, 1 TD, -9 DYAR, -20.3% DVOA)

Adrian Arrington, NO: Arrington is entering his fifth season with the Saints but has only been active for six games, including two playoff games last year. Most of his career production came from his seven-catch mop up effort in Week 16 of the 2010 season. With rookie Nick Toon in the fold, Arrington may find his roster spot in jeopardy. (2011 stats: 2-for-3, 31 yards, 12 DYAR, 33.2% DVOA)

Terrence Austin, WAS: If the Redskins want to save a roster spot, they could waive Brandon Banks and give the return roles to Austin, who has the advantage of four more inches, 25 more pounds, and a lot more receiving experience. Otherwise, he may not make the team, and if he does he won't see as many offensive snaps as he did a year ago. (2011 stats: 12-for-26, 137 yards, -81 DYAR, -51.6% DVOA)

Brandon Banks, WAS: Banks has only three career catches. He's a return specialist who followed up a strong rookie season (9.7 Pts+ in 2010) with a terrible sophomore campaign (-11.7 Pts+). The biggest problem was a case of the dropsies; Banks had four fumbled returns plus three muffed punts, and got lucky when Washington recovered all seven balls.

Arnaz Battle, FA: God bless Arnaz Battle for living football's version of the American Dream. Despite a lack of production at receiver and returner over the course of nine years in the NFL, Battle managed to earn upwards of $8 million thanks primarily to his acumen as ... just another guy on special teams. With one receiving target and four special teams tackles for Pittsburgh in what was likely his retirement tour last season, Battle closed his career by providing viewers five final chances to ask, "Arnaz Battle is still in the league?"

Travis Benjamin, CLE: A burner who ran a 4.36 forty-yard dash at the combine, Benjamin had a 55 percent catch rate and 17.3 yards per catch at Miami in 2009 and 2010. He's seen by many people as a one-dimensional deep threat. However, this fourth-round pick improved as a more well-rounded receiver in 2011 (77 percent catch rate, 14.9 yards per catch). He may also be the heir to Josh Cribbs' kick-returning duties.

Bernard Berrian, FA: We've probably seen the last of the sometimes-effective-but-usually-disappointing string-bean receiver. Berrian was released last October after putting up just a 30 percent catch rate. The year before, he caught just 28 passes in 14 games. Ten of these 19 games were starts. In his heyday, Berrian was a long-striding downfield weapon (he averaged 20.1 yards per catch in 2008) but consistency was always an issue, mainly because he's always struggled to separate against quality man coverage. (2011 stats: 7-for-23, 91 yards, -72 DYAR, -54.5% DVOA)

LaVon Brazill, IND: This Ohio product was given high praise by our own Matt Waldman, who claims that his only real flaw is his lack of size. Brazill is a willing blocker, had a 71 percent catch rate over the past three seasons, and should have plenty of advancement potential in a Colts receiving corps that looks to be seriously considering Donnie Avery as a starting flanker. Smells like a sleeper to us.

Stephen Burton, FA: Burton made a cameo appearance on Minnesota's active roster last October after the dismissal of Bernard Berrian, but got IR'ed with an MCL strain after three games. There may not be room for this 2011 seventh-rounder on the 2012 roster, but uphill battles are not unfamiliar to the Lakewood, Calif., native. After no scholarship offers, Burton began his collegiate career at Long Beach Community College before eventually making it to Texas A&M.

Michael Calvin, ATL: The undrafted Calvin was not very productive at Cal (10 career starts, 42 catches) until his Pro Day, when he ran a 4.32 forty and posted impressive broad and vertical jumps. We'll let D. Orlando Ledbetter of the *Atlanta Journal-Constitution* take it from here: "I'm thinking there's a pretty hot 4 X 100 relay team in the wide receiver meeting room. Here it is: Calvin (4.32), Cody Pearcy (4.3 to .35), Julio Jones (4.39) and Harry Douglas (4.42)," Ledbetter wrote in May. "The Olympics are this summer, you know. Rule number one for the relay team: CLEAN EXCHANGES AND DON'T DROP THE BATON!" Oh, and no more quarterback sneaks on fourth-and-1.

Greg Childs, MIN: Childs, who played opposite fellow Vikings rookie receiver Jarius Wright at Arkansas, has impressive size and measurables but is far from guaranteed to make it in the NFL. Scouts think his separation skills and change-of-speed tactics need improvement. There's the feeling that Childs got away with certain habits and forms of contact in college that he won't get away with in the NFL.

Mark Clayton, FA: Teams haven't shown much free agent interest in Clayton, which is understandable considering he ended his last two seasons on injured reserve. To make matters worse, Clayton's career appears to have peaked in 2006 (2.1% DVOA), his second year in the league. Since then, his catches and targets have decreased with each season, and his receiving DVOA has been no better than -7.5% (2008). (2010 stats: 23-for-42, 306 yards, 2 TD, 4 DYAR, -11.5% DVOA)

Toney Clemons, PIT: There isn't much roster space for this seventh-round pick, but the former Colorado track star's size (6-foot-2, 210 pounds) and speed (4.36 forty at his pro day) make him an ideal practice squad candidate. His college stats are unimpressive, with just a 54 percent catch rate and 13.5 yards per catch over the last two seasons.

David Clowney, BUF: Clowney was recently clocked running a 4.38 forty, which goes a long way towards explaining why NFL teams keep giving him a look despite his stone hands. That speed will likely make him look good as he blows past third-stringers in preseason, but at this point in his career, there is no reason to expect him to show much once he is matched up against better (faster) competition. (2010 stats: 7-for-16, 124 yards, 7 DYAR, -6.4% DVOA)

Keary Colbert, FA: In *FOA 2009*, we noted that Colbert had played for three NFL teams in 2008, and those teams had lost a combined 36 games, then said fans could be forgiven for weeping if he ended on their roster the next season. Colbert followed this with stints in the UFL and on the USC coaching staff before somehow landing on the Kansas City roster. He caught nine passes before the Chiefs came to their senses and released him in November. There are no circumstances, none, where he should ever play in the NFL again. (2011 stats: 9-for-12, 89 yards, -28 DYAR, -43.8% DVOA)

Kevin Cone, ATL: Here's a player with a fascinating background. Cone played one year at Shorter College in 2007, catching 12 passes for 83 yards. He transferred to Georgia Tech in 2008, started five games without a catch in the Yellow Jackets option attack in 2009, then caught five passes for 89 yards for Georgia Tech in 2010. He then spent 16 weeks in the Falcons practice squad before earning a Week 17 activation. This may be the least impressive resume of any receiving prospect, ever. According to our latest projections, Cone will play 11 more years and catch negative 37 passes.

Terrance Copper, KC: 76 catches, 939 yards, and six touchdowns. Sounds like the kind of second or third wideout who could really help the Chiefs out, right? Unfortunately, that's not a single season for Copper. Those are his total numbers over his nine-year, four-team career. Copper has special teams value, but he turned 30 in March and is going to struggle to stay in the league. (2011 stats: 8-for-12, 114 yards, 30 DYAR, 20.3% DVOA)

Juron Criner, OAK: Even in the sixth round, Al Davis probably wouldn't have drafted a receiver who ran a 4.68 forty. Criner probably doesn't have either deep speed or quickness to separate, but is a very good route-runner (71 percent catch rate in 2011) with excellent hands. As the only Raiders receiver with those traits, he has a chance to contribute early.

B.J. Cunningham, MIA: One of two receivers the Dolphins selected in the seventh round, Cunningham is Michigan State's all-time receptions leader with 218 career catches. He is a possession-type receiver, but several dropped passes during Shrine Game practices raised questions about him since he doesn't have elite size or great speed.

Dominique Curry, STL: After a torn ACL cost him 14 games of his rookie year, Curry returned to play a full season in 2011. Curry was a core member of the Rams' special teams, making six tackles on coverage units, but had no pass targets. After a slew of draft picks and free agent signings this offseason, St. Louis' stable of wide receivers is crowded to the point where there isn't any room for a one-trick pony. The 24-year-old Curry has to develop skills as a receiver—or become a Pro-Bowl-caliber special teams ace—to justify his spot on an NFL roster.

Rashied Davis, FA: Davis has always been touted as a former Arena League star who scrapped his way into the NFL. Indeed, it's a nice story, but also an outdated one. The soon-to-be-33-year-old has now been in the league—the big league, that is—since 2005. He spent his first six seasons in Chicago, where sheer speed made him an occasional star on special teams and spot duty playmaker on offense. Limiting Davis' ceiling is the fact that he doesn't have the size to consistently operate outside of the slot.

Tandon Doss, BAL: Doss came out of Indiana as a junior with injury issues, so the Ravens essentially redshirted him as a rookie. His NFL destiny is as a slot receiver and kick returner, but with Jacoby Jones around to play that role, Doss gets to be the fourth receiver on a team that never uses more than three.

Kris Durham, SEA: A fourth round pick out of Georgia in 2011, Durham was active for three of Seattle's first eight games before undergoing surgery to repair a torn labrum in an unspecified shoulder in November. Durham missed his 2009 season at Georgia after having surgery to repair a torn labrum in his left shoulder. If healthy, Durham's size and speed (4.46-40 at his Pro Day) could make him an effective target on the perimeter. Two shoulder surgeries in three years make that a fairly big "if."

Marcus Easley, BUF: Easley has yet to play in a professional football game, and he spent last year on injured reserve with a serious heart condition. Now he's been given a clean bill of health, and Buddy Nix and Chan Gailey reportedly are high him as a player. He has a chance to rise as high as number two on the depth chart if things break right.

Jeremy Ebert, NE: Ebert is the latest in the line of Wes Welker clones that the Patriots horde as either insurance against an injury or leverage against a potential Welker departure, depending on your point of view. Ebert is a shifty, undersized (and yes, let's say it, white) receiver with a lot of experience in a spread offense. Unlike the other Welker clones, Ebert can fly; he ran a sub-4.4 forty-yard dash during Northwestern's Pro Day, and he ran a lot of vertical routes during his college days (and had an impressive 74 percent catch rate). Ebert is probably headed to the practice squad, but that speed could conceivably get him a spot on the active roster.

Julian Edelman, NE: Edelman started off being touted as a poor man's Wes Welker after successfully subbing for the injured Welker at the start of the 2009 season. Then he morphed into a poor man's Troy Brown, as Bill Belichick pressed Edelman into service as a defensive back to match up against slot receivers. In the 2011 AFC Championship game, Edelman logged an even 27 snaps on offense and 27 on defense. He's supposed to play less defense this year, but his role in the offense has been almost entirely usurped by the Gronkowski-Hernandez-Woodhead trio. (2011 stats: 4-for-8, 32 yards, -19 DYAR, -46.7% DVOA)

Armanti Edwards, CAR: Through two seasons, Edwards has not caught an NFL pass. He's averaged 5.2 yards per punt return, rushed twice for 12 yards, and completed two passes for 11 yards. This is not what the Panthers hoped for when they drafted Edwards as a playmaking "Slash" type out of Appalachian State. Sometimes, the skills of a small-college spread quarterback don't immediately translate to the role of NFL slot receiver and punt returner. We apologize if we ever gave you the impression that such a transition is easy and automatic.

Chris Givens, STL: After a couple of non-descript seasons at wide receiver, Givens (Wake Forest) exploded for 83 catches, 1,330 yards, and nine touchdowns in his junior year, and left early for the draft. Givens fell into the fourth round because of fear that he's a one-year wonder. In reality, he projects as the St. Louis equivalent of former Jeff Fisher wideout Damian Williams, a fast, smaller receiver. The main concern with Givens is that, as is recent Rams tradition, he's well acquainted with tearing his ACL.

WIDE RECEIVERS

Anthony Gonzalez, FA: Ouch, I just broke myself again. (2010 stats: 5-for-9, 67 yards, -11 DYAR, -29.7% DVOA)

Richard Goodman, SD: Virtually all of Goodman's value came on special teams, both as a kick returner and gunner. Unfortunately for him, the Chargers signed two other receiver-returners in Eddie Royal and Roscoe Parrish, so Goodman may not even make it through training camp.

Chad Hall, PHI: Hall is small (5-foot-8, 187 pounds) but hard-working. The Eagles keep futzing around with him, thinking they can make him into some sort of all-purpose weapon, like a destitute man's Percy Harvin. (2011 stats: 3-for-9, 20 yards, 1 TD, -38 DYAR, -67.5% DVOA)

Dwayne Harris, DAL: The Cowboys drafted Harris as a returner, but he was pretty lousy at it, particularly on punts. On only 15 returns, he averaged 5.3 yards and was worth -4.0 estimated points of field position. By December, Dallas gave that job back to Dez Bryant. Bryant's important role on offense could mean Harris is back returning punts again this fall, and he's also part of the cast of thousands seeking a place on the Dallas wide receiver depth chart.

Joe Hastings, SF: Almost every NFL team has an undersized, small-school player that conventional wisdom says has no business being on their active roster. For the 49ers, the (lift-aided) 6-foot, 185-pound Hastings is that player. Signed as an undrafted free agent in 2011, Hastings played his college ball for the Washburn Ichabods—surprisingly not located in Sleepy Hollow. After spending the first 15 weeks on San Francisco's practice squad, the release of Braylon Edwards and injuries to Ted Ginn and Kyle Williams allowed Hastings to banish the Headless Horseman once and for all, and earn a promotion to the gameday roster in Week 16. San Francisco's acquisitions at wide receiver this offseason mean Hastings is once again practice-squad fodder, and allow us to make literary jokes in a football book.

Junior Hemingway, KC: Playing with Denard Robinson (58.3 percent completion rate, but 8.5 yards per attempt in his career) no doubt skewed Hemingway's numbers at Michigan. He never gained more than 700 yards or four touchdowns in his career, but averaged 18.6 yards per catch. He was also used sparingly as a returner, but the Chiefs have other options there. Limited athleticism but promising size (6-foot-1, 225 pounds) could make him an effective possession guy.

Jesse Holley, NE: Where to begin? Holley won a national championship at North Carolina as a backup point guard on the basketball team in 2005. He also played four years on the football team, but was overshadowed by Hakeem Nicks. He then spent several years on practice squads and in the CFL before landing a spot on Michael Irvin's reality show, where he won a training camp roster spot with the Cowboys, and surprised everyone by making them team. And then came Week 2 against San Francisco, when Holley caught three balls for 96 yards, including a 77-yard gain to set up the winning field goal in overtime. The Cinderella story ends there—Holley caught only four more passes the rest of the year, and the Cowboys opted not to re-sign him after the season. (2011 stats: 7-for-7, 169 yards, 72 DYAR, 120.0% DVOA)

Andre Holmes, DAL: The most productive wide receiver in the history of Hillsdale College, Holmes spent most of 2011 on the practice squads of Minnesota and Dallas. He's tall (6-foot-5) but ran a 4.51 forty at the 2011 Combine, which is below average for an NFL wide receiver. He's one of many guys who might stick on a very thin Dallas depth chart behind Miles Austin and Dez Bryant.

Jeremy Horne, KC: Horne was an All-CAA player in his junior season at UMass in 2008—a third-team All-CAA player, but still. His teammate at UMass, a two-time first-team All-CAA wideout, also went undrafted, and ended up signing with the Giants. That man's name was Victor Cruz, and his story has a much happier ending. Horne caught a touchdown pass for Kansas City in the 2010 preseason, but he has yet to catch a ball in a regular season game. No word on his salsa skills.

LeStar Jean, HOU: Jean is a physical receiver who went undrafted out of Florida Atlantic in 2011 and spent last year on injured reserve after an impressive preseason. Texans receivers coach Larry Kirksey praised him heavily, saying that his attention to detail was excellent and that he'd "engulfed himself" in the offense. That may be a bit much, but nature does abhor a vacuum, and right now the bottom of the Texans receiving depth chart is that.

Jerrel Jernigan, NYG: When the head coach nicknames you "One-Play J.J.," this does not signal a good chance of getting extensive playing time. Jernigan is a little waterbug whose speed and agility in the open field wowed scouts, but has very little experience running complicated routes. His natural role on the team is now completely blocked by Victor Cruz, so he'll primarily be used for returns.

Bryant Johnson, FA: Bryant Johnson had seven catches for 91 yards last season, and sat on the depth chart behind a washed-up 37-year-old Derrick Mason. His career is probably done. (Other 2011 stats: 7-for-13, 2 DYAR, -10.5% DVOA)

Damaris Johnson, PHI: At Tulsa, Johnson became the all-time NCAA leader in kickoff return and all-purpose yardage in only three years. Then he got suspended for his entire senior season after police discovered he had been effectively stealing thousands of dollars in goods from the Macy's where his girlfriend worked. (In one instance, Johnson took home over $1,200 of merchandise and was charged 34 cents.) The Eagles took a shot on him as an undrafted free agent and he was the talk of minicamps, showing speed, elusiveness, and great hands. An interesting prospect to watch, unless he's too small (5-foot-8, 170 pounds) for the naked eye to see.

Jaymar Johnson, ARI: Waived by the Minnesota Vikings in September, Jackson spent most of the 2011 season on the Cardinals' practice squad, appearing in one game and playing exactly one snap before he was released and re-signed to the practice squad. Johnson has just one reception for nine yards in his career and missed 2010 with a broken thumb, but he was a versatile weapon at Jackson State and, perhaps most importantly, works out with Larry Fitzgerald in the offseason.

Marvin Jones, CIN: Greg Cosell says that Jones "displayed the widest catching radius of any wide receiver I evaluated," so he may force his way out of the Going Deep ghetto in *FOA 2013*. Many were surprised the strong (22 bench press reps at the combine) and productive (62 receptions his senior season at Cal despite horrendous quarterbacks) Jones was still available in the fifth round, especially after Jones impressed at the Senior Bowl. Jones blocked effectively on many a bubble screen for electrifying fellow Cal wideout Keenen Allen, and that talent could also get him on the field.

Ricardo Lockette, SEA: A track star at Division II Fort Valley State, Lockette spent most of his rookie season on the practice squad before being activated to the 53-man roster in December. On his first NFL play, Lockette beat San Francisco 49ers Pro Bowl cornerback Carlos Rogers for a 44-yard reception. The following week, Lockette showed off his speed and concentration by tipping and then hauling in a deep ball from Tarvaris Jackson with Arizona's Marshay Green draped all over him for a 61-yard, game-tying touchdown in the fourth quarter. The Seahawks like Lockette's size and athleticism; now he needs to show more polish as a receiver and route-runner.

Stefan Logan, DET: Logan (5-foot-6, 180) is a guy you have to squint in order to see, which is both good and bad. It's bad in that it means he's good for just a few touches a game. It's good in that he can be electrifyingly elusive on those touches. Logan's a threat to go the distance on any kick return. In the mainstream offense, Detroit has used him not so much as a reserve receiver, but rather as a backfield gadget player. He'll take a direct snap, catch a uniquely designed screen, or even get a traditional running back type carry. The Lions like to use him in the backfield against man-to-man defenses, as that often forces an ill-prepared middle linebacker to deal directly with Logan's speed.

WIDE RECEIVERS

Jeff Maehl, HOU: After 14 weeks of waiting for a chance to crack Houston's weak receiving corps, Maehl was signed to replace Derrick Mason. Jake Delhomme threw a football at Maehl in Week 17, during what was essentially an abandoned game against the Titans. He dropped it. (Other 2011 stats: -5 DYAR, -101.6% DVOA)

Marc Mariani, TEN: Selected to the Pro Bowl in 2010 for his fine return skills, he regressed in 2011. Perhaps the plan to try to let him work in the slot was too much for Mariani. Or perhaps we shouldn't build narratives with small sample sizes. (2011 stats: 5-for-13, 24 yards, -51 DYAR, -64.4% DVOA)

Keshawn Martin, HOU: This fourth-round rookie's combination of speed and vision make him a big threat in the open field, and he could develop into a nice slot receiver given a little time. He had a 70 percent catch rate in his last two years at Michigan State. With Jacoby Jones sent packing, Martin comes into training camp as the favorite to return punts and kicks for Houston.

Ruvell Martin, BUF: The Bills re-signed Martin to be a special teams player, a role he filled adequately last year. However, Martin turns 30 before the start of the season, and there are a large number of younger developmental receivers on the roster with more upside. (2011 stats: 7-for-16, 82 yards, -17 DYAR, -25.5% DVOA)

Rishard Matthews, MIA: Matthews is a spread-option type who caught 91 passes at Nevada in his senior year. His catch rate went from 60 percent to 69 percent even though his quarterback went from Colin Kaepernick to freshman Cody Fajardo. Matthews is well-built, makes plays after the catch, and can return punts, but he lacks long speed and was a spot-on-the-field route runner. His special teams value may give him a leg up on fellow seventh-round pick B.J. Cunningham, and on the many veteran practice squanders vying for roster spots in Miami.

Scotty McKnight, NYJ: Mark Sanchez's childhood bestie landed a practice squad job at the start of the 2011 season, then wound up on injured reserve with an ACL injury. He was healthy enough to participate in Sanchez' "Jets West," a desperate attempt by the quarterback to assert some leadership thinly disguised as an OTA. McKnight has a chance to win the fifth receiver role, where he may get more playing time than Sanchez.

Marvin McNutt, PHI: Our Playmaker Score system likes McNutt because he led the Big Ten with 101.2 yards per game, and scored 28 career touchdowns at Iowa. However, the Playmaker Score system doesn't know that McNutt is a bit of a diva who refused to even practice with special teams units at the Senior Bowl. He can be a solid underneath option in spread sets but sixth-rounders who don't want to play special teams don't last long in the NFL.

Kerry Meier, ATL: A big, tough special-teamer with zero career receptions, Meier is best known for blindsiding Vikings long snapper Cullen Loeffler in a late-season game. Meier drew a $20,000 fine and the wrath of Vikings punter/Twitterati Chris Kluwe, who called him a "douchepickle." The Syfy Channel immediately picked up the rights to *Douchepickle*, which will star Mark-Paul Gosselaar as the heroic park ranger trying to save campers from the 30-foot pickle of too-creepy-to-mention origins, and for *Sharktodouchepickle*, with a cameo by Freddie Mitchell.

Nick Miller, FA: Miller played for Oakland and St. Louis last year, and scored an 88-yard punt return touchdown in Week 12. Then he was suspended for PEDs in February, and the Rams released him in March.

Carlton Mitchell, CLE: A good size/speed combo, but so far, Mitchell's athletic ability hasn't translated to getting open at the NFL level. He barely dressed as a rookie in 2010, and skipped his senior season at South Florida to enter the draft, so a problem may be a simple lack of reps. His website, carltonmitchell.net, has tabs for Mitchell's highlights from 2007-09, but ends there. At this point, the site is more likely to be shut down than to add a "2012 Highlights" tab.

Marlon Moore, MIA: Moore and Roberto Wallace are a matched set. Both made the Dolphins roster as undrafted rookies in 2010, both caught six passes that year, and both were limited to a handful of games last year. Any article that mentions one automatically mentions the other, and they co-starred in various "Top Ten Dolphins We Will Pretend To Know Something About" slideshows during the offseason. Even Jeff Ireland mentions them in the same breath; in fairness, it is not clear that Ireland knows more about football than the average slideshow producer. Moore is the smaller, quicker one, and Wallace is the tall one. One or both of them could earn a 20-catch role now that the Dolphins are opening up their offense, but they are little more than roster fodder for a sub-.500 team.

Jamar Newsome, KC: The two knocks on Newsome coming out of Central Florida were that he had problems getting separation at the line and that nearly all of his passes were caught within five yards of the line of scrimmage. A new knock emerged last year: failure to separate from the pedestrian Jaguars wideout group. He'll try his luck in Kansas City this year.

Kassim Osgood, FA: The Jaguars fell from seventh in special teams DVOA in 2010 to 26th in 2011. On opposing returns in 2010, they saved a combined 20.8 points. In 2011, -0.5. When that happens, and you are the gunner who will be 32 before the 2012 season starts, job security is usually at a minimum. (2011 stats: 5-for-11, 42 yards, -37 DYAR, -56.9% DVOA)

Chris Owusu, SF: Stanford's Owusu ran the fastest 40-yard dash of any wide receiver at this year's NFL combine, but a concussion history in college rendered him undraftable. The presence of Jim Harbaugh made San Francisco his inevitable landing spot. However, with all of the 49ers' wide receiver acquisitions this offseason, and other teams showing interest, Owusu may very well end up on a different team's practice squad this season.

Roscoe Parrish, SD: Roscoe only suited up for two games in 2011, and he has only caught 37 passes since 2009. With Eddie Royal locked in as the slot receiver in San Diego, Parrish will have to battle for a roster spot as a fifth receiver and punt returner. His days as a regular contributor are likely over.

Kealoha Pilares, CAR: Last year's fifth-round pick from Hawaii, Pilares returned a punt for a touchdown and was among the best of the Panthers kick gunners (such as they are), but he never caught a pass. Pilares was a dynamic rusher and receiver at Hawaii, and he is as good a fifth receiver option as the Seyi Ajriotutu types around him at the bottom of the depth chart.

Taylor Price, JAC: Price was a third-round pick for New England in 2010, but he only appeared in four games before falling off the depth chart. He caught two passes in Jacksonville for 39 yards before being sidelined by a stress fracture in his left foot. Price may not be healthy in time for training camp, which will make it hard for him to make the final roster even for the receiver-starved Jags.

Julius Pruitt, MIA: Pruitt drew high praise for his special teams work last year and could stick with the Dolphins in a Courtney Roby role. Pruitt attended Ouachita Baptist University, a school of about 1,500 students outside of Little Rock, Ark. The Ouachita mascot is the tiger. It should be the Cheetah, so they could be the Ouachita Cheetahs.

Raymond Radway, DAL: A former track star from Abilene Christian, Radway might have made the Cowboys roster last year as an undrafted rookie had he not broken his leg in the final preseason game. He's yet another of the many anonymous receivers vying for playing time behind Miles Austin and Dez Bryant.

David Reed, BAL: In 2010, Reed led the NFL in kick return yardage (29.3), and finished seventh in kick return value (7.8 Pts+) as a rookie. Things were proceeding nicely through nine games in 2011 (29.7-yard average), but in Week 10 against Seattle, things fell apart. Reed's two lost fumbles, which led directly to six points in a 22-17 Ravens loss, ended his tenure as primary returner. Six weeks later, an ACL tear ended his season. That injury, combined with his lack of offensive contribution and Baltimore's signing of Jacoby Jones, means Reed will have a hard time making the final roster.

Eron Riley, NYJ: A former standout at Duke, Riley has bounced from the practice squads of the Ravens to the Panthers to the Broncos to the Jets since 2009. His NFL highlights begin and end with a pair of preseason touchdowns for the Broncos in 2011. He is one of many players vying for the fourth and fifth receiver slots for a team that may run the Wildcat 30 times per game.

Gerell Robinson, DEN: Long-term sleeper alert: Of 57 receivers targeted at least 100 times at the FBS level last year, only three had at least a 64 percent catch rate with at least 16.5 yards per catch: Jarius Wright at Arkansas (drafted by Minnesota), Marquess Wilson at Washington State (still in school), and Robinson at Arizona State. Good part-time player out of the slot, then exploded with 1,397 yards in 2011. Signed with Denver as a free agent.

Brian Robiskie, JAC: It's a long fall from beloved second-round pick and life-long Ohioan to being buried on the Jacksonville depth chart, but it sure didn't *take* long. Speaking of not taking long: Robiskie averaged 2.0 YAC on 29 catches in 2010, then 0.7 YAC on his three receptions last year. (2011 stats: 3-for-9, 25 yards, -32 DYAR, -60.9% DVOA)

DeMarco Sampson, ARI: Sampson's big-play potential (23.0 yards per catch in the preseason) earned him a spot on the Cardinals' 53-man roster last summer. Sampson dressed for the first 13 games of the season, playing primarily on special teams before he was a healthy scratch down the stretch. His roster competition is primarily coming from Jaymar Johnson. (2011 stats: 3-for-8, 36 yards, 4 DYAR, -6.6% DVOA)

Micheal Spurlock, SD: The longtime Buccaneers return man has landed in San Diego, where the Chargers are lousy with free agent slot receiver/return man types (Spurlock, Eddie Royal, Roscoe Parrish). Spurlock is a notch below Royal but more consistent than Parrish; at any rate, a team only needs one of these guys, so the battle for second place behind Royal may be irrelevant. (2011 stats: 2-for-6, 13 yards, -24 DYAR, -64.4% DVOA)

Brandon Stokley, DEN: When Peyton Manning signed with the Broncos, it was only a matter of time before Brandon Stokley followed him there. Stokley was reasonably useful for the Broncos back in 2007-2008, but how much can you really expect from a 36-year-old coming off a season with one catch?

Maurice Stovall, DET: It's not often that a former third-round pick who wound up catching just 51 passes in five years with his first team sticks around too long on his second team. This is especially true when said former third-round pick caught just one pass in 15 games for his second team. But Stovall is an exception to the rule because he's developed into one of the better special-teams gunners in the NFL. Like other accomplished gunners (Kassim Osgood comes to mind), Stovall benefits from lanky but sturdy size.

Rod Streater, OAK: An undrafted free agent out of Temple, Streater surprisingly stepped in with the starting receivers when Denarius Moore suffered a hamstring injury in OTAs and earned good reviews from head coach Dennis Allen for his explosiveness, route running, and ability to get open. Moore should be healthy by training camp, though, and Streater's far from a lock to make the team.

Tommy Streeter, BAL: Streeter (Miami) is a ridiculous physical specimen (6-foot-5, 215 pounds, 4.40-second 40-time) who happens to have virtually no experience playing wide receiver. He played only one meaningful season in college, and then left early for the NFL. He's a "project" if there ever was one. He'll almost certainly spend 2012 on special teams.

Sammie Stroughter, TB: Stroughter excelled on kick returns in between foot injuries; his four receptions all came in the Christmas Eve loss to the Panthers, and he was targeted only two other times all season. The Bucs extended his contract and expect him to contend for the fourth receiver spot. He was ahead of Arrelious Benn on the depth chart during May minicamps. (2011 stats: 4-for-7, 52 yards, 2 DYAR, -9.4% DVOA)

Chansi Stuckey, FA: Stuckey led the Cleveland Browns wide receivers in receptions (40) in 2010, but averaged less than nine yards per catch and had a DVOA of -26.5%. Signed to a two-year, $3.2 million contract by the Arizona Cardinals following the lockout, Stuckey caught just four passes for 39 yards in nine games last season. Stuckey also lost a fumble on a potential game-winning drive in a 22-21 loss to the Washington Redskins in Week 2 which was followed by three weeks on the shelf with a hamstring injury. The Cardinals released Stuckey on March 16 and he remains a free agent. (Other 2011 stats: 4-for-8, -20 DYAR, -46.1% DVOA)

Brett Swain, SF: After playing a full season with the Packers in 2010, Swain signed with the 49ers in October, and eventually saw meaningful action at wide receiver due to a myriad of San Francisco injuries. The 49ers re-signed him in April at the veteran minimum, but he's no higher than seventh on the depth chart heading into training camp. (2011 stats: 2-for-7, 15 yards, -38 DYAR, -75.0% DVOA)

Brandon Tate, CIN: Tate was purely a returner for Cincinnati in 2011, but with the wideout position in flux, he'll get a chance to attend some offense meetings and play hooky from the special teams rooms, which are located in a sub-basement next to a clanking boiler in Paul Brown Stadium.

Devin Thomas, CHI: Thomas was a complete flop as the 34th overall pick in the 2008 draft, but give him credit—instead of disappearing in shame, he's worked hard to establish a career for himself on special teams. He can wear his Super Bowl ring with pride after recovering both of Kyle Williams' muffed punts in the NFC Championship game. Chicago, which knows something about special teams talent, signed Thomas to replace Corey Graham as their top gunner.

Patrick Turner, NYJ: A 6-foot-5 square peg drafted in 2009 by a Dolphins team with no idea what to do with him, Turner finally worked his way up to No. 5 wideout and special-teamer for the Jets last year, excelling at neither. Rookie Stephen Hill has a similar skill set, but is also younger and faster. (2011 stats: 8-for-15, 96 yards, 1 TD, 12 DYAR, -2.0% DVOA)

Tiquan Underwood, TB: Last year, Underwood bounced back and forth between New England's practice squad and active roster three times, most famously getting cut on the eve of the Super Bowl so Bill Belichick could get another defensive lineman on the roster. He will probably spend 2012 in the same way, this time in Tampa. (2011 stats: 3-for-6, 30 yards, -3 DYAR, -18.6% DVOA)

Jerheme Urban, FA: Kansas City had a unique theme among their wideouts in 2011, collecting as many guys as they could who had played multiple seasons in the NFL without ever being any good. Urban fit right in with the Keary Colberts and Terrance Coppers in Missouri. Even among that weak field, Urban was the sixth wideout in Kansas City, and he played like it, with three of his four catches gaining six or fewer yards. (2011 stats: 4-for-13, 35 yards, 1 TD, -44 DYAR, -56.7% DVOA)

Roberto Wallace, MIA: Wallace is a 6-foot-4 specimen who made the Dolphins roster as an undrafted rookie in 2010 and has hung around the roster fringes for two years, catching six passes in 2010 but seeing action in just two games last year. His size makes him intriguing, and the change to a more receiver-friendly offense increases his chances of finding a role. He will battle Clyde Gates, Marlon Moore, and about a dozen others for playing time.

Bryan Walters, MIN: It looked like Walters might have a solid season after a kickoff return for a touchdown in the preseason and a couple catches in the regular-season opener, but he only had one more catch and barely cracked the lineup. He's a non-undersized slot receiver with the ability to return both punts and kicks. Apparently the two catches against them impressed the Vikings enough to offer him a two-year deal; who knows what more catches would have earned him.

Eric Weems, CHI: There's speculation in Chicago that the Bears will replace punt returner Devin Hester with Weems, which is utterly bonkers, though it does reflect the peculiar neurosis Bears fans have regarding Hester. ("He's the best punt returner of his generation but … shouldn't he be better? Or shouldn't he be doing something else? Or…?") Weems was a Phil Emery project when Emery was in Atlanta, so the new GM acquired Weems as a possible fourth receiver, gunner, and kickoff returner. Weems' offensive value may be untapped, because the Falcons never really knew what to do with their slot receivers. He has returned enough punts to prove that he's adequate, but no sane person's challenger to Hester. (2011 stats: 11-for-14, 90 yards, 9 DYAR, -4.4% DVOA)

Ryan Whalen, CIN: Whalen's 2012 role will depend greatly on Jordan Shipley's knee. If Ship shrugs off the effects of his torn ligament, the second-year man from Stanford will watch more than he plays. But if the Bengals' first choice slot receiver struggles in rehab, the sure-handed Whalen will duke it out with Andrew Hawkins to make the position his, especially with Andre Caldwell gone to free agency.

Jordan White, NYJ: This seventh-round compensatory pick is Playmaker Score's sleeper of the year (see page 541). He was targeted an absurd 203 times at Western Michigan in 2011, and made 140 catches. (Since 2005, only Freddie Barnes had more, 224 targets for the 2009 Bowling Green Falcons.) He was also on his sixth year of eligibility after losing two years to torn ACLs, and he promptly went out and broke his foot at Jets OTAs.

LaQuan Williams, BAL: Signed as an undrafted free agent out of Maryland in 2011, the highlight of Williams' season was simply making the 53-man roster. On the field, his main contributions were on special teams, spending time as a part-time returner and forcing a fumble in the AFC Championship Game that allowed Baltimore to take a four-point lead heading into the fourth quarter. Williams also served as the Ravens' No. 3 wide receiver during Lee Evans' injury absence, but the team's offseason acquisitions make it unlikely he'll be called on to do the same in 2012. (2011 stats: 4-for-12, 46 yards, -34 DYAR, -45.7% DVOA)

Stephen Williams, ARI: As a rookie in 2010, the 6-foot-5, 208-pound Williams took advantage of an injury to Early Doucet and started three of his first five games in the NFL. Williams' playing time steadily decreased that season and Williams has been unable to claw his way back onto the 46-man active roster. He watched most of the 2011 season from the sidelines, often in street clothes, appearing in just two games.

Jarius Wright, MIN: The fourth-round rookie is considered by scouts to be a solid all-around receiver with no dynamic strengths but no major weaknesses. Wright doesn't have elite size or measurables but he is durable and instinctive, which is why he left Arkansas as the most productive receiver in school history. His 2011 stats are detailed in Gerell Robinson's comment above.

Devon Wylie, KC: The Chiefs already have Dexter McCluster and Javier Arenas, but apparently somebody in Kansas City has an affection for undersized returner types. Wylie couldn't stay healthy in college and maxed out at 716 yards receiving, though he did lead the nation with 446 punt return yards as a senior while scoring twice. This may surprise you, but he missed time in minicamp with a sore hamstring.

Tight Ends

Top 10 TE by DYAR (Total Value), 2011

Rank	Player	Team	DYAR
1	Rob Gronkowski	NE	459
2	Jimmy Graham	NO	244
3	Antonio Gates	SD	231
4	Tony Gonzalez	ATL	181
5	Jermichael Finley	GB	163
6	Fred Davis	WAS	128
7	Jake Ballard	NYG	127
8	Owen Daniels	HOU	122
9	Joel Dreessen	HOU	119
10	Scott Chandler	BUF	113

Top 10 TE by DVOA (Value per Play), 2011

Rank	Player	Team	DVOA
1	Rob Gronkowski	NE	45.9%
2	Joel Dreessen	HOU	40.5%
3	Antonio Gates	SD	30.9%
4	Scott Chandler	BUF	27.0%
5	Jake Ballard	NYG	22.5%
6	Kevin Boss	OAK	22.3%
7	Jermichael Finley	GB	18.0%
8	Jimmy Graham	NO	16.6%
9	Anthony Fasano	MIA	16.5%
10	Tony Gonzalez	ATL	15.6%

Minimum 25 passes.

Top 10 TE by DYAR (Total Value), 1991-2011

Rank	Year	Player	Team	DYAR
1	**2011**	**R.Gronkowski**	**NE**	**459**
2	1993	S.Sharpe	DEN	358
3	2010	A.Gates	SD	358
4	2000	T.Gonzalez	KC	357
5	2009	A.Gates	SD	336
6	2004	T.Gonzalez	KC	335
7	2004	A.Gates	SD	309
8	1996	S.Sharpe	DEN	303
9	2005	A.Gates	SD	279
10	1999	R.Dudley	OAK	275

Top 10 TE by DVOA (Value per Play), 1991-2011

Rank	Year	Player	Team	DVOA	Passes
1	2010	A.Gates	SD	76.3%	65
2	1999	R.Dudley	OAK	62.3%	59
3	2010	R.Gronkowski	NE	51.7%	59
4	2008	V.Shiancoe	MIN	51.7%	59
5	1997	T.Drayton	MIA	50.1%	50
6	1995	K.Dilger	IND	48.3%	55
7	**2011**	**R.Gronkowski**	**NE**	**45.9%**	**125**
8	1995	M.Chmura	GB	43.9%	74
9	1999	K.Dilger	IND	43.1%	51
10	1994	B.Jones	SF	40.8%	74

Minimum 50 passes.
Note: With a minimum of 25 passes, Gronkowski ranks 13th.

TIGHT ENDS

Dwayne Allen
Height: 6-3 Weight: 255 College: Clemson Draft: 2012/3 (64) Born: 24-Feb-1990 Age: 22 Risk: Green

Year	Team	G/S	Rec	Pass	Yds	C%	+/-	Y/C	TD	Drop	YAC	Rk	YAC+	DVOA	Rk	DYAR	Rk	YAR	Short	Mid	Deep	Bomb
2012	IND		33	53	357	62%	--	10.8	2					-4.8%								

FO's Matt Waldman actually prefers Allen to Coby Fleener, noting that Allen was an elite blocker in both the run and the pass game. He's not the same kind of player Fleener is, nor is he the fantasy threat that Fleener could be, but Allen is definitely the more complete player of the two coming out of college. One thing to watch for though: While Allen looks very smooth as a receiver, he only had a 54 percent catch rate at Clemson. In fairness, he did spend a lot of time pass blocking and dealing with mediocre quarterbacks before Tahj Boyd arrived in 2011, but his catch rate was still 54 percent with Boyd.

Jake Ballard
Height: 6-6 Weight: 275 College: Ohio State Draft: 2010/FA Born: 2-Dec-1987 Age: 25 Risk: N/A

Year	Team	G/S	Rec	Pass	Yds	C%	+/-	Y/C	TD	Drop	YAC	Rk	YAC+	DVOA	Rk	DYAR	Rk	YAR	Short	Mid	Deep	Bomb
2011	NYG	14/13	38	61	604	62%	+2.3	15.9	4	3	4.8	16	+0.7	22.5%	5	127	7	136	30%	37%	27%	7%

In last year's "Going Deep" section, we wrote that "Ballard swears he would be a great receiver if someone just gave him the chance." Guess what: the Giants did, and he was. Unfortunately, Ballard tore up his left knee so badly in the Super Bowl that he required not just ACL reconstruction but also microsurgery to repair the cartilage. The Giants tried to sneak him through waivers in June so he wouldn't take up a 90-man roster spot, but the Patriots snapped him up, so he'll get to sit on their IR for the 2012 season.

Gary Barnidge
Height: 6-6 Weight: 243 College: Louisville Draft: 2008/5 (141) Born: 22-Sep-1985 Age: 27 Risk: Red

Year	Team	G/S	Rec	Pass	Yds	C%	+/-	Y/C	TD	Drop	YAC	Rk	YAC+	DVOA	Rk	DYAR	Rk	YAR	Short	Mid	Deep	Bomb
2009	CAR	16/3	12	21	242	57%	+1.1	20.2	0	0	8.2	--	+3.7	4.0%	--	14	--	21	30%	20%	25%	25%
2010	CAR	16/3	0	9	0	0%	-3.8	0.0	0	1	0.0	--	+0.0	-87.9%	--	-49	--	-51	14%	29%	57%	0%
2012	CAR		23	43	191	53%	--	8.3	0					-33.1%								

Barnidge is the best baseball player on the Panthers. He played first base in high school, and he always puts on the best show when the Panthers take their annual promotional batting practice at Charlotte's Knights Stadium. Barnidge was also a prospect as a receiving tight end before suffering an ankle injury in the second preseason game last year. Barnidge was healthy enough to hit a batting practice home run in June, and his potential as a second tight end allowed the Panthers to play hardball with Jeremy Shockey.

Martellus Bennett
Height: 6-6 Weight: Too Much College: Texas A&M Draft: 2008/2 (61) Born: 10-Mar-1987 Age: 25 Risk: Yellow

Year	Team	G/S	Rec	Pass	Yds	C%	+/-	Y/C	TD	Drop	YAC	Rk	YAC+	DVOA	Rk	DYAR	Rk	YAR	Short	Mid	Deep	Bomb
2009	DAL	14/6	15	30	159	50%	-4.1	10.6	0	2	3.5	39	-1.2	-29.0%	43	-41	41	-47	41%	52%	3%	3%
2010	DAL	16/11	33	47	260	70%	+1.4	7.9	0	2	5.5	13	+0.0	-28.6%	42	-64	42	-70	71%	26%	2%	0%
2011	DAL	14/7	17	26	144	65%	-0.2	8.5	0	1	5.6	8	-0.1	-23.7%	41	-27	34	-16	65%	22%	9%	4%
2012	NYG		29	40	292	73%	--	10.1	3					14.7%								

In his rookie season of 2008, Bennett led all tight ends in receiving DVOA. He has not made the top 40 since then. The Giants signed him so they could increase their use of two-tight end sets, but Bennett, listed at 265 pounds, weighed 291 when he showed up for OTAs. (That's the listed weight for William Beatty, who started ten games for the Giants at left tackle last year.) Bennett soon injured his hamstring during a conditioning drill. Giants tight ends coach Mike Pope said that Bennett was "probably a little too big for his legs to carry." Indeed.

Kevin Boss

Height: 6-7　Weight: 255　College: Western Oregon　Draft: 2007/5 (153)　Born: 11-Jan-1984　Age: 28　Risk: Green

Year	Team	G/S	Rec	Pass	Yds	C%	+/-	Y/C	TD	Drop	YAC	Rk	YAC+	DVOA	Rk	DYAR	Rk	YAR	Short	Mid	Deep	Bomb
2009	NYG	15/15	42	69	567	61%	-0.3	13.5	5	1	5.5	13	+0.5	9.7%	13	76	17	61	41%	41%	19%	0%
2010	NYG	15/13	35	70	531	50%	-7.4	15.2	5	6	7.0	3	+2.6	-8.9%	33	-8	32	-4	44%	31%	25%	0%
2011	OAK	14/11	28	39	368	72%	+3.2	13.1	3	1	4.7	19	+0.7	22.3%	6	72	17	98	33%	50%	17%	0%
2012	KC		21	35	249	60%	--	11.9	2					5.2%								

Signed to a big contract in the offseason, Boss had little impact in his first and only season in Oakland. He had nearly half the targets he received in New York two years ago. Overpaid at his salary, the Raiders cut him and he signed with the Chiefs as insurance for Tony Moeaki. He fits the Moeaki mold: a better receiver than blocker, but more decent than great in both roles.

John Carlson

Height: 6-4　Weight: 255　College: Notre Dame　Draft: 2008/2 (38)　Born: 12-May-1984　Age: 28　Risk: Green

Year	Team	G/S	Rec	Pass	Yds	C%	+/-	Y/C	TD	Drop	YAC	Rk	YAC+	DVOA	Rk	DYAR	Rk	YAR	Short	Mid	Deep	Bomb
2009	SEA	16/16	51	83	574	61%	-2.8	11.3	7	2	5.1	21	+0.2	-5.3%	28	11	25	36	41%	47%	11%	1%
2010	SEA	15/13	31	58	318	53%	-3.1	10.3	1	3	4.1	32	-0.2	-35.3%	44	-110	44	-100	50%	31%	15%	4%
2012	MIN		37	59	364	63%	--	9.8	2					-10.5%								

Carlson had back-to-back 50-catch seasons and a dozen touchdowns over his first two seasons with the Seattle Seahawks before disappearing when Jeremy Bates took over as offensive coordinator in 2010. Carlson's targets dropped from 80-plus his first two seasons to just 58, and though those targets were closer to the line of scrimmage, his catch rate fell eight percentage points. A torn labrum in his shoulder during training camp ended his 2011 season and, after the Seahawks had tepid interest in bringing him back as the No. 2 tight end behind Zach Miller, Carlson signed a five-year, $25 million contract with his hometown Minnesota Vikings. He will compete with fellow Notre Dame alum Kyle Rudolph for the starting job.

James Casey

Height: 6-3　Weight: 246　College: Rice　Draft: 2009/5 (152)　Born: 22-Sep-1984　Age: 28　Risk: Green

Year	Team	G/S	Rec	Pass	Yds	C%	+/-	Y/C	TD	Drop	YAC	Rk	YAC+	DVOA	Rk	DYAR	Rk	YAR	Short	Mid	Deep	Bomb
2009	HOU	15/0	6	12	64	50%	-1.2	10.7	0	1	4.0	--	-1.2	-19.9%	--	-10	--	-6	55%	27%	18%	0%
2010	HOU	16/4	8	14	98	57%	-1.6	12.3	0	1	7.6	--	+2.3	-13.0%	--	-5	--	-8	69%	15%	15%	0%
2011	HOU	14/7	18	24	260	75%	+3.1	14.4	1	0	9.1	--	+3.7	33.3%	--	66	--	60	68%	9%	14%	9%
2012	HOU		23	33	260	70%	--	11.3	1					8.7%								

Casey played more fullback than tight end last year, but may see time at both positions this year following the departure of Joel Dreessen. As a fullback, he's a matchup nightmare who can get lost at the line of scrimmage and re-appear wide open for a big gain. As a tight end, he's a plain 'ol move guy with no elite skills. So naturally, the Texans split him out wide 23 times last year. Casey is a Swiss army knife that has the best damn pair of scissors you've ever seen surrounded by a bunch of dull blades.

Brent Celek

Height: 6-4　Weight: 261　College: Cincinnati　Draft: 2007/5 (162)　Born: 25-Jan-1985　Age: 27　Risk: Yellow

Year	Team	G/S	Rec	Pass	Yds	C%	+/-	Y/C	TD	Drop	YAC	Rk	YAC+	DVOA	Rk	DYAR	Rk	YAR	Short	Mid	Deep	Bomb
2009	PHI	16/15	76	112	971	68%	+3.9	12.8	8	12	5.4	15	+0.7	15.5%	11	169	5	179	43%	39%	16%	2%
2010	PHI	16/15	42	79	511	53%	-7.7	12.2	4	5	5.7	10	+1.1	-11.9%	35	-25	35	-33	49%	29%	12%	11%
2011	PHI	16/16	62	97	811	64%	-0.5	13.1	5	5	7.5	1	+2.2	3.7%	22	70	19	99	51%	29%	17%	2%
2012	PHI		61	91	696	67%	--	11.4	5					13.8%								

Brent Celek is a reminder of what a good tight end looked like before Four G's of the Apocalypse (Gonzalez, Gates, Graham, and Gronk) came around to completely redefine stardom at the position. He's a useful receiver and a reasonable blocker, but nobody the opposition has to game-plan around. He's also never missed a game despite a series of nagging injuries. Celek was awful on third and fourth downs last year, -39.0% DVOA with only nine conversions on 31 passes (including a DPI), but that looks like a one-year fluke; he was fine on third down the year before.

Scott Chandler   Height: 6-7   Weight: 270   College: Iowa   Draft: 2007/4 (129)   Born: 23-Jul-1985   Age: 27   Risk: Yellow

Year	Team	G/S	Rec	Pass	Yds	C%	+/-	Y/C	TD	Drop	YAC	Rk	YAC+	DVOA	Rk	DYAR	Rk	YAR	Short	Mid	Deep	Bomb
2010	2TM	13/1	1	3	8	33%	-0.7	8.0	0	0	5.0	--	+0.3	-46.8%	--	-8	--	-9	33%	33%	0%	33%
2011	BUF	14/9	38	46	389	83%	+7.9	10.2	6	0	4.0	31	-0.1	27.0%	4	113	10	115	57%	39%	5%	0%
2012	BUF		36	54	406	67%	--	11.3	4					13.6%								

The tight end position in the Buffalo offense had been in the dead zone since the days of Pete Metzelaars, but Chandler changed that in 2011. Chandler fits the mold of the current crop of Bills receiving threats in that he is not an explosive athlete and instead has to rely on being big and having the scheme spring him. He was a terror in the red zone, hauling in six touchdowns and compiling a 56% DVOA as he caught nine of the 13 passes intended for him. The tight end isn't on the field for more than 40 percent of the snaps in Chan Gailey's offense, which limits Chandler's fantasy upside.

Dallas Clark   Height: 6-3   Weight: 257   College: Iowa   Draft: 2003/1 (24)   Born: 12-Jun-1979   Age: 33   Risk: Yellow

Year	Team	G/S	Rec	Pass	Yds	C%	+/-	Y/C	TD	Drop	YAC	Rk	YAC+	DVOA	Rk	DYAR	Rk	YAR	Short	Mid	Deep	Bomb
2009	IND	16/16	100	133	1106	75%	+12.9	11.1	10	6	4.8	23	+0.3	15.9%	10	204	3	243	52%	32%	13%	2%
2010	IND	6/6	37	53	347	70%	+1.5	9.4	3	3	3.7	38	-0.5	1.3%	22	31	25	40	52%	40%	6%	2%
2011	IND	11/10	34	65	352	52%	-9.9	10.4	2	9	4.4	27	+0.2	-25.5%	43	-84	46	-83	61%	34%	5%	0%
2012	TB		29	48	324	60%	--	11.2	3					3.6%								

The clock is ticking down to the end to Clark's career, and he feels more like a Hall of Very Good member than a Hall of Famer. He made just one Pro Bowl and one All-Pro team (both in 2009), and despite his longevity for the Manning-era Colts, he's going to need another few games to pick up 5,000 receiving yards. That used to be a much bigger deal for a tight end, but things are changing, given that Rob Gronkowski is on pace to reach that milestone by his age-27 season. Clark's biggest legacy at FO will probably be his contribution to re-shaping the game charting project, since he spent practically the last five years split into the slot and we used to count tight ends in the slot as wideouts. Clark's last gasp will come in Tampa, where professionalism is needed and Luke Stocker needs someone to duel for the starting job.

Jared Cook   Height: 6-6   Weight: 246   College: South Carolina   Draft: 2009/3 (89)   Born: 7-Apr-1987   Age: 25   Risk: Green

Year	Team	G/S	Rec	Pass	Yds	C%	+/-	Y/C	TD	Drop	YAC	Rk	YAC+	DVOA	Rk	DYAR	Rk	YAR	Short	Mid	Deep	Bomb
2009	TEN	14/0	9	15	74	60%	-0.7	8.2	0	0	4.0	--	-0.2	-18.7%	--	-12	--	-11	46%	38%	15%	0%
2010	TEN	16/1	29	45	361	64%	+1.8	12.4	1	4	4.7	21	+0.1	14.9%	13	59	19	75	37%	44%	15%	5%
2011	TEN	16/5	49	81	759	60%	+3.9	15.5	3	1	5.7	7	+1.7	12.1%	17	100	13	88	30%	58%	9%	3%
2012	TEN		45	71	587	63%	--	13.1	4					14.3%								

The top man on last year's Top 25 Prospects list was quite frustrating to own in fantasy football. He had seven games where he accumulated seven or more targets, then seven games where he was targeted three times or less. There was little discernable pattern. What we do know is that Cook's a mid-tier tight end with a lower catch rate than you'd like, but the size and strength to be a factor underneath and in the red zone. Surprisingly, in light of those facts, Cook caught just one of six balls in the red zone last year. Cook is facing a crossroads season. He has the talent to be a top-10 NFL tight end. Is he going to keep improving enough to utilize it?

Chris Cooley
Height: 6-3 Weight: 252 College: Utah State Draft: 2004/3 (81) Born: 11-Jul-1982 Age: 30 Risk: Red

Year	Team	G/S	Rec	Pass	Yds	C%	+/-	Y/C	TD	Drop	YAC	Rk	YAC+	DVOA	Rk	DYAR	Rk	YAR	Short	Mid	Deep	Bomb
2009	WAS	7/7	29	45	332	64%	-0.0	11.4	2	2	7.1	3	+1.7	-3.6%	26	10	27	28	53%	40%	8%	0%
2010	WAS	16/15	77	126	849	61%	-1.4	11.0	3	9	4.8	20	+0.1	-11.6%	34	-34	37	-28	48%	42%	10%	0%
2011	WAS	5/5	8	13	65	62%	+1.4	8.1	0	0	5.3	--	-0.0	-36.4%	--	-25	--	-26	70%	30%	0%	0%
2012	WAS		25	48	275	52%	--	11.0	1					-16.8%								

Chris Cooley had his knee drained 15 times between the start of training camp and the October game where he broke a finger. At that point, the Redskins had a tight end who couldn't catch or run, so they put him on injured reserve. Cooley showed up to OTAs 15 to 20 pounds lighter than usual, and has admitted that he's now slower than he was before the knee injury. Fred Davis is now the main man at tight end, so Cooley will need to show he can still block if he wants to keep the job as No. 2.

Owen Daniels
Height: 6-3 Weight: 245 College: Wisconsin Draft: 2006/4 (98) Born: 9-Nov-1982 Age: 30 Risk: Yellow

Year	Team	G/S	Rec	Pass	Yds	C%	+/-	Y/C	TD	Drop	YAC	Rk	YAC+	DVOA	Rk	DYAR	Rk	YAR	Short	Mid	Deep	Bomb
2009	HOU	8/8	40	58	519	69%	+3.0	13.0	5	2	5.6	9	+1.0	26.3%	4	130	11	112	41%	43%	13%	4%
2010	HOU	11/10	38	68	471	56%	-1.8	12.4	2	5	6.6	5	+1.7	-2.0%	26	24	26	19	45%	37%	18%	0%
2011	HOU	15/15	54	85	677	64%	+2.0	12.5	3	3	5.4	9	+1.2	14.3%	14	122	8	109	35%	51%	12%	3%
2012	HOU		59	90	706	66%	--	12.0	3					11.1%								

Fully healthy for the first time since his ACL tear in 2009, Daniels absorbed the vast majority of Andre Johnson's targets and became T.J. Yates' main dumpoff guy down the stretch. Daniels isn't much of a blocker, and is never going to be a Gronkowski-type field stretcher, but he's a pain in the butt for other teams to cover underneath. At least until his knees catch up with him again.

Fred Davis
Height: 6-4 Weight: 248 College: USC Draft: 2008/2 (48) Born: 15-Jan-1986 Age: 26 Risk: Green

Year	Team	G/S	Rec	Pass	Yds	C%	+/-	Y/C	TD	Drop	YAC	Rk	YAC+	DVOA	Rk	DYAR	Rk	YAR	Short	Mid	Deep	Bomb
2009	WAS	16/10	48	76	509	63%	+0.3	10.6	6	8	5.2	19	+0.5	8.1%	15	76	16	73	46%	46%	9%	0%
2010	WAS	16/9	21	30	316	70%	+3.0	15.0	3	2	8.0	1	+3.1	34.9%	5	86	15	92	56%	30%	11%	4%
2011	WAS	12/12	59	88	796	67%	+4.4	13.5	3	3	5.9	6	+1.5	15.0%	11	128	6	113	39%	40%	14%	6%
2012	WAS		57	94	744	61%	--	13.0	4					10.7%								

Davis blossomed after Chris Cooley's injury put the focus on him, and he got franchise-tagged for his trouble. He signed the tender, so he'll make $5.4 million and then be a free agent in 2013. He's put up strong numbers since he came into the league, and his yards after the catch really stand out compared to other tight ends, but let's not go overboard about what Fred Davis can do with a rookie quarterback. Some people are talking about him becoming a top-five fantasy tight end, but we just don't see it unless your league is playing in 1992.

Kellen Davis
Height: 6-6 Weight: 262 College: Michigan State Draft: 2008/5 (158) Born: 11-Oct-1985 Age: 27 Risk: Green

Year	Team	G/S	Rec	Pass	Yds	C%	+/-	Y/C	TD	Drop	YAC	Rk	YAC+	DVOA	Rk	DYAR	Rk	YAR	Short	Mid	Deep	Bomb
2009	CHI	16/2	9	14	75	64%	+0.4	8.3	3	1	1.9	--	-1.8	9.8%	--	17	--	18	46%	38%	15%	0%
2010	CHI	16/3	1	2	19	50%	+0.5	19.0	1	0	2.0	--	-2.8	61.1%	--	19	--	20	0%	0%	100%	0%
2011	CHI	16/15	18	35	206	51%	-2.4	11.4	5	1	3.3	41	-1.1	-2.9%	26	10	26	11	31%	47%	19%	3%
2012	CHI		20	35	201	57%	--	10.0	4					-1.6%								

Davis has the potential to be an excellent blocking tight end—it's just a matter of honing his technique and becoming more consistent. He's proven capable of handling defensive ends one-on-one at times, but he's also proven susceptible to gaffes and penalties. Davis doesn't run with enough fleetness or agility to be a big-time receiving weapon, but he can catch what you throw him. Overall, it still remains to be seen just what he can be

418   TIGHT ENDS

in the NFL. Is he a full-time contributor or just a fringe role player? The Bears don't yet seem to quite know for sure. They re-signed Davis over the offseason but only to a two-year contract (worth $6 million).

Vernon Davis   Height: 6-3   Weight: 250   College: Maryland   Draft: 2006/1 (6)   Born: 31-Jan-1984   Age: 28   Risk: Green

Year	Team	G/S	Rec	Pass	Yds	C%	+/-	Y/C	TD	Drop	YAC	Rk	YAC+	DVOA	Rk	DYAR	Rk	YAR	Short	Mid	Deep	Bomb
2009	SF	16/16	78	129	965	60%	+5.4	12.4	13	12	4.2	27	-0.5	3.9%	19	91	14	119	47%	29%	15%	10%
2010	SF	16/16	56	93	914	60%	+0.7	16.3	7	5	7.5	2	+2.7	23.1%	10	181	3	186	37%	34%	20%	9%
2011	SF	16/16	67	95	792	71%	+7.3	11.8	6	4	4.9	14	+0.1	3.9%	21	70	18	24	53%	23%	15%	10%
2012	SF		67	90	805	74%	--	12.0	5					28.0%								

With 18 catches for 410 yards (158 YAC) and two touchdowns, the last three games of San Francisco's season (including playoffs) finally unleashed Davis' potential in Jim Harbaugh's tight-end-friendly offense. Davis was once again among the league leaders in targets 16 or more yards downfield, but what made those deep balls more effective was Harbaugh setting them up with a short-route frequency even higher than Davis' breakout 2009 season. Davis didn't crack the top five in fantasy value last season only because of his 10th-ranked target total. The 49ers take full advantage of Davis' elite blocking skills, so he simply doesn't go out for a pass nearly as much as most receiving tight ends. With the return of blocking tight end Nate Byham from injury, and Harbaugh looking to open up the offense, lack of targets shouldn't be a problem in 2012.

Ed Dickson   Height: 6-4   Weight: 249   College: Oregon   Draft: 2010/3 (70)   Born: 25-Jul-1987   Age: 25   Risk: Green

Year	Team	G/S	Rec	Pass	Yds	C%	+/-	Y/C	TD	Drop	YAC	Rk	YAC+	DVOA	Rk	DYAR	Rk	YAR	Short	Mid	Deep	Bomb
2010	BAL	15/3	11	23	152	48%	-2.4	13.8	1	2	6.5	--	+1.4	-29.5%	--	-31	--	-28	45%	35%	10%	10%
2011	BAL	16/16	54	89	528	61%	-1.0	9.8	5	6	2.9	45	-1.1	-1.7%	25	31	24	13	41%	38%	16%	5%
2012	BAL		33	56	369	59%	--	11.2	3					-0.6%								

Dickson's involvement in Baltimore's offense got more and more fleeting as the season progressed, to the point where, come playoff time, he had fully become the dreaded "nominal starter" ahead of Dennis Pitta.

Weeks	E.Dickson Targets	D.Pitta Targets
Weeks 1-4	32	7
Weeks 6-11	39	31
Weeks 12-17	18	18
Playoffs	8	12

The problem for Dickson is that the only thing that separates him from Pitta is that Dickson is more of a downfield threat, yet he could only muster a -31.8% DVOA on 18 deep and bomb targets. Otherwise, he and Pitta personify "skill redundancy," so the Ravens will have an even shorter leash on Dickson if he can't improve that split.

Joel Dreessen   Height: 6-4   Weight: 260   College: Colorado State   Draft: 2005/6 (198)   Born: 26-Jul-1982   Age: 30   Risk: Yellow

Year	Team	G/S	Rec	Pass	Yds	C%	+/-	Y/C	TD	Drop	YAC	Rk	YAC+	DVOA	Rk	DYAR	Rk	YAR	Short	Mid	Deep	Bomb
2009	HOU	16/11	26	39	320	67%	+2.7	12.3	1	1	5.3	17	+1.6	5.4%	18	35	19	45	53%	38%	9%	0%
2010	HOU	16/10	36	54	518	67%	+3.8	14.4	4	6	5.1	17	+1.0	25.4%	9	110	8	107	32%	54%	12%	2%
2011	HOU	16/10	28	39	353	72%	+4.2	12.6	6	1	5.3	10	+0.8	40.5%	2	119	9	116	44%	39%	11%	6%
2012	DEN		33	47	380	70%	--	11.5	2					13.8%								

Dreessen was a reliable secondary cog in a good offense, and his numbers benefited as such. Take away a couple of long play-action plays where he went uncovered and a desperation heave near the end of the Oakland game, and you're left with a credible underneath threat who can block a little, but isn't going to beat anyone in coverage. In Denver he'll be playing the Marcus Pollard role in the Peyton Manning fast-break offense. It's a good scheme fit as long as Dreessen doesn't tire; Jacob Tamme is still the one you'd rather own in a fantasy league.

TIGHT ENDS

Michael Egnew
Height: 6-5 Weight: 252 College: Missouri Draft: 2012/3 (78) Born: 1-Nov-1989 Age: 23 Risk: Green

Year	Team	G/S	Rec	Pass	Yds	C%	+/-	Y/C	TD	Drop	YAC	Rk	YAC+	DVOA	Rk	DYAR	Rk	YAR	Short	Mid	Deep	Bomb
2012	MIA	16	27	161	59%	--	10.0	1						-13.0%								

Egnew, the Dolphins' third-round pick, is a spread-offense tight end who caught 140 passes in two seasons at Missouri, a school that also produced tight ends Martin Rucker and Chase Coffman. Remember them? Egnew is a similar player: a small forward with good leaping ability and little blocking experience who earned his scholarship by running to a spot on the field and posting up a linebacker. At Senior Bowl practices, he looked like the guy on the scout team who pretends to be Jermichael Finley. The Dolphins must have mistook him for another Finley, but he is probably another Rucker.

Brody Eldridge
Height: 6-5 Weight: 261 College: Oklahoma Draft: 2010/5 (162) Born: 31-Mar-1987 Age: 25 Risk: Yellow

Year	Team	G/S	Rec	Pass	Yds	C%	+/-	Y/C	TD	Drop	YAC	Rk	YAC+	DVOA	Rk	DYAR	Rk	YAR	Short	Mid	Deep	Bomb
2010	IND	14/8	5	9	39	56%	-1.2	7.8	0	1	4.4	--	-0.7	-31.3%	--	-15	--	-17	56%	22%	22%	0%
2011	IND	13/8	9	10	45	90%	+1.6	5.0	0	1	1.7	--	-2.5	-24.1%	--	-12	--	-11	90%	10%	0%	0%
2012	STL		8	12	72	67%	--	9.0	1					-10.8%								

Much like Gijon Robinson before him, Brody Eldridge made the mistake of being a blocking Colts tight end who couldn't really block all that well. After making sure he'd never see the field by drafting Dwayne Allen and Coby Fleener, new GM Ryan Grigson decided to bring in his own bottom-of-the-roster blocker by claiming Andre Smith off waivers from Chicago. Now in St. Louis, Eldrige will battle Matthew Mulligan for a chance to discretely blow blocks that will be credited to Jason Smith or Rodger Saffold instead.

Anthony Fasano
Height: 6-4 Weight: 255 College: Notre Dame Draft: 2006/2 (53) Born: 20-Apr-1984 Age: 28 Risk: Green

Year	Team	G/S	Rec	Pass	Yds	C%	+/-	Y/C	TD	Drop	YAC	Rk	YAC+	DVOA	Rk	DYAR	Rk	YAR	Short	Mid	Deep	Bomb
2009	MIA	14/14	31	53	339	58%	-0.5	10.9	2	3	3.8	33	-0.5	-18.2%	37	-40	39	-41	37%	45%	14%	4%
2010	MIA	15/15	39	60	528	65%	+2.8	13.5	4	4	5.1	16	+0.6	27.0%	7	136	6	126	40%	45%	13%	2%
2011	MIA	15/15	32	54	451	59%	+3.4	14.1	5	0	3.1	43	-0.9	16.5%	9	84	15	85	34%	28%	34%	4%
2012	MIA		31	55	383	56%	--	12.4	4					3.6%								

Fasano is a block-first tight end with a cap number over $4 million for a team that is opening up its offense. Therefore, his "cap casualty" probability is rather high. Fasano is productive as a short receiver and red zone target, so he can help the Dolphins if they do not expect him to be Jermichael Finley. If released, Fasano will find a home on a team like the Panthers or Giants that has a big role for a thumping blocker.

Daniel Fells
Height: 6-4 Weight: 252 College: California-Davis Draft: 2006/FA Born: 23-Sep-1983 Age: 29 Risk: Yellow

Year	Team	G/S	Rec	Pass	Yds	C%	+/-	Y/C	TD	Drop	YAC	Rk	YAC+	DVOA	Rk	DYAR	Rk	YAR	Short	Mid	Deep	Bomb
2009	STL	14/4	21	35	273	60%	-1.4	13.0	3	5	6.2	7	+0.8	1.9%	21	22	23	26	41%	41%	19%	0%
2010	STL	16/6	41	65	391	63%	+1.8	9.5	2	5	6.5	6	+1.4	-7.5%	31	-1	31	1	67%	30%	4%	0%
2011	DEN	16/15	19	31	256	61%	+1.3	13.5	3	1	4.5	23	-0.2	-5.3%	28	4	28	11	43%	29%	14%	14%
2012	NE		14	20	143	70%	--	10.2	1					9.1%								

Fells made a curious decision in signing a three-year contract with New England. In four years, he has 88 catches for 1,001 yards and eight touchdowns, all of which Rob Gronkowski surpassed in just one season in 2011. With Aaron Hernandez also around, Fells' role in Foxboro is clearly that of a blocking specialist. The Patriots also signed Spencer Larsen and Tony Fiammetta, so Fells probably won't be making cameo appearances at fullback. He was signed for a very small, very specific purpose: Seal the edge on third-and-1. Any receiving value he brings should be thought of as an unexpected bonus.

TIGHT ENDS

Jermichael Finley
Height: 6-4   Weight: 243   College: Texas   Draft: 2008/3 (91)   Born: 26-Mar-1987   Age: 25   Risk: Green

Year	Team	G/S	Rec	Pass	Yds	C%	+/-	Y/C	TD	Drop	YAC	Rk	YAC+	DVOA	Rk	DYAR	Rk	YAR	Short	Mid	Deep	Bomb
2009	GB	13/10	55	72	676	76%	+8.0	12.3	5	4	5.3	18	+1.3	25.6%	5	164	6	148	48%	38%	11%	3%
2010	GB	5/5	21	26	301	81%	+4.7	14.3	1	1	4.6	22	-0.1	51.8%	2	99	11	101	32%	40%	24%	4%
2011	GB	16/13	55	92	767	60%	+0.4	13.9	8	9	4.1	29	+0.1	18.0%	7	163	5	153	26%	45%	21%	8%
2012	GB		54	86	744	63%	--	13.8	6					28.4%								

Athletically speaking, Finley is probably the most gifted tight end to ever play the game. He's big not just in terms of thickness (like most tight ends) but also length. This gives him an enormous catching radius. He runs like a wide receiver, especially when he can work the seams and not have to change direction much. Most impressive of all of Finley's athletic blessings is his body control, which is buttressed by sinewy strength. Unfortunately, Finley is not a finished product, as evidenced by his mental gaffes, blown blocks, and especially dropped passes. Most teams would probably prefer to treat Finley as a wide receiver, but few teams have the cornerback size or depth to do so. The Chiefs pulled it off in their upset of the Packers last season, though they gave corner Travis Daniels help via bracket coverage concepts inside. It helped that they didn't have to worry about defending Greg Jennings, who was injured that game.

By our count, Finley was split wide on 152 plays last year, more than any other tight end in the league. Aaron Hernandez was second at 123, and Jimmy Graham third at 78. No other tight end was above 32 plays.

Coby Fleener
Height: 6-6   Weight: 247   College: Stanford   Draft: 2012/2 (34)   Born: 20-Sep-1988   Age: 24   Risk: Red

Year	Team	G/S	Rec	Pass	Yds	C%	+/-	Y/C	TD	Drop	YAC	Rk	YAC+	DVOA	Rk	DYAR	Rk	YAR	Short	Mid	Deep	Bomb
2012	IND		53	90	706	59%	--	13.3	5					0.2%								

Coby Fleener can run the seam routes, but does he have elite elusiveness in the open field? That's the question that separates Rob Gronkowski and Jimmy Graham from an Owen Daniels-type player. Then again, if that's the worst of Fleener's problems going forward, then Indianapolis will probably be pretty happy with this pick. Reunited with Andrew Luck, with whom he put up a 67 percent catch rate and 17.8 yards per catch over the past few years at Stanford, there are few rookie tight ends in history who seem as set up for success as Fleener.

Antonio Gates
Height: 6-4   Weight: 260   College: Kent State   Draft: 2003/FA   Born: 18-Jun-1980   Age: 32   Risk: Red

Year	Team	G/S	Rec	Pass	Yds	C%	+/-	Y/C	TD	Drop	YAC	Rk	YAC+	DVOA	Rk	DYAR	Rk	YAR	Short	Mid	Deep	Bomb
2009	SD	16/16	79	114	1157	69%	+9.7	14.6	8	8	6.1	8	+1.6	35.6%	2	336	1	326	43%	35%	16%	6%
2010	SD	10/10	50	65	782	77%	+11.1	15.6	10	2	6.2	8	+2.0	76.3%	1	358	1	355	43%	31%	25%	2%
2011	SD	13/13	64	88	778	73%	+8.0	12.2	7	0	4.0	32	+0.3	30.9%	3	231	3	264	36%	48%	16%	1%
2012	SD		69	99	827	70%	--	12.0	9					31.7%								

Antonio Gates is aging. We know this because the same plantar fasciitis injury that prematurely ended his 2010 season also bothered him in 2011. There were games where he was clearly hobbled, thus the reduced YAC number you see above. In the games where he wasn't hobbled, though, it could have been 2004. He used his size to pluck passes out of the air over overmatched defenders and his speed to gain separation from linebackers, safeties, and slot corners. He's no more of a blocker than he used to be, and is now almost exclusively a slot receiver. That hasn't seemed to hurt his production, though. Pencil him in for another five catches and 55 to 75 yards in every game he's healthy for, and yes, he's still a favored (and efficient) target in the red zone.

Tony Gonzalez
Height: 6-5   Weight: 251   College: California   Draft: 1997/1 (13)   Born: 27-Feb-1976   Age: 36   Risk: Yellow

Year	Team	G/S	Rec	Pass	Yds	C%	+/-	Y/C	TD	Drop	YAC	Rk	YAC+	DVOA	Rk	DYAR	Rk	YAR	Short	Mid	Deep	Bomb
2009	ATL	16/16	83	134	867	62%	+0.9	10.4	6	3	2.8	45	-1.0	9.4%	14	150	9	106	29%	61%	9%	1%
2010	ATL	16/16	70	109	656	64%	+0.3	9.4	6	7	2.7	43	-1.2	-0.4%	25	52	21	41	41%	49%	10%	1%
2011	ATL	16/16	80	116	875	69%	+6.8	10.9	7	4	3.0	44	-0.7	15.6%	10	181	4	183	37%	49%	13%	1%
2012	ATL		71	108	735	66%	--	10.4	6					13.8%								

Gonzo is the greatest tight end in history; anyone who thinks otherwise is just being argumentative and playing the "real tight ends block" card to make themselves feel more like tough guys. He is also the greatest player in NFL history to never win a playoff game, with all due respect to Archie Manning. He may be the greatest player in North American professional team sports history to never win a playoff game, though there is no good way to compare him to someone like Ernie Banks.

We first speculated that Gonzo was about to break down back in *Pro Football Prospectus 2005*. We stopped harping on his age and accepted him as a force of nature in *Football Outsiders Almanac 2010*. The Falcons remain dangerously dependent on Gonzalez completely blowing the aging curve at his position: He is a major facet of their offense, and there is no depth behind him. But who cares? At this rate, we will be saying the same thing in the *Football Outsiders Straight to Brain Application* in 2016.

Jimmy Graham
Height: 6-6 Weight: 260 College: Miami Draft: 2010/3 (95) Born: 24-Nov-1986 Age: 26 Risk: Green

Year	Team	G/S	Rec	Pass	Yds	C%	+/-	Y/C	TD	Drop	YAC	Rk	YAC+	DVOA	Rk	DYAR	Rk	YAR	Short	Mid	Deep	Bomb
2010	NO	15/5	31	43	356	72%	+3.9	11.5	5	2	4.5	26	+0.0	22.6%	11	91	14	83	43%	38%	12%	7%
2011	NO	16/11	99	149	1310	66%	+6.5	13.2	11	6	4.6	20	+0.3	16.6%	8	244	2	273	39%	40%	18%	3%
2012	NO		85	117	1107	73%	--	13.0	10					41.6%								

Graham, on passes of 16 or more air yards: 30 targets, 20 catches, 550 yards, four touchdowns. There are other awesome Graham stats we could cite, but once you realize that he catches two-thirds of the long passes thrown to him, you really have all the information you need.

Jermaine Gresham
Height: 6-5 Weight: 261 College: Oklahoma Draft: 2010/1 (21) Born: 16-Jun-1988 Age: 24 Risk: Yellow

Year	Team	G/S	Rec	Pass	Yds	C%	+/-	Y/C	TD	Drop	YAC	Rk	YAC+	DVOA	Rk	DYAR	Rk	YAR	Short	Mid	Deep	Bomb
2010	CIN	15/10	52	83	471	63%	-3.2	9.1	4	6	7.0	4	+1.1	-17.4%	37	-57	41	-47	67%	28%	5%	0%
2011	CIN	14/13	56	92	596	61%	-2.0	10.6	6	3	3.4	39	-1.3	-8.5%	30	-8	31	-4	45%	40%	15%	0%
2012	CIN		58	87	599	67%	--	10.3	5					4.6%								

Gresham was solid in the red zone (18.6% DVOA), where you would expect him to be targeted, but poor on third downs (-26.2%), where option routes proved a struggle. He showed a penchant for making the sensational catch, then dropping an easy one. The other tight ends on the roster are stronger blockers, so hopefully Gresham can focus on his path toward becoming an elite pass catcher.

Rob Gronkowski
Height: 6-6 Weight: 264 College: Arizona Draft: 2010/2 (42) Born: 14-May-1989 Age: 23 Risk: Yellow

Year	Team	G/S	Rec	Pass	Yds	C%	+/-	Y/C	TD	Drop	YAC	Rk	YAC+	DVOA	Rk	DYAR	Rk	YAR	Short	Mid	Deep	Bomb
2010	NE	16/11	42	59	546	71%	+5.4	13.0	10	2	4.4	28	+0.1	51.7%	3	243	2	229	42%	33%	19%	5%
2011	NE	16/16	90	125	1327	73%	+12.0	14.7	17	4	7.1	2	+2.4	45.9%	1	459	1	469	36%	43%	18%	3%
2012	NE		84	122	1127	69%	--	13.4	12					37.1%								

Gronkowski's rookie year, where he finished second in the league in DYAR and third in DVOA, gave some indication that he might be a special player. No one could have foreseen that Gronk would suddenly morph into a 265-pound version of Jerry Rice in his prime. Gronkowski's stat line in the divisional playoffs against Denver (10 catches on 12 attempts, 145 yards, three touchdowns) was the best single-game performance by any tight end last year, but in truth it wasn't that far removed from what he was doing on most weeks. Gronkowski was literally unstoppable in the red zone, where he caught 19 of 27 passes and scored 13 touchdowns. His DVOA in those situations was 51.8%, right in line with his overall performance. How often do you see a third-year player have his rookie deal torn up and replaced with a six-year, $54 million deal? Not often, and in this case, the Patriots got themselves a bargain.

422   TIGHT ENDS

Todd Heap   Height: 6-5   Weight: 252   College: Arizona State   Draft: 2001/1 (31)   Born: 16-Mar-1980   Age: 32   Risk: Red

Year	Team	G/S	Rec	Pass	Yds	C%	+/-	Y/C	TD	Drop	YAC	Rk	YAC+	DVOA	Rk	DYAR	Rk	YAR	Short	Mid	Deep	Bomb
2009	BAL	16/16	53	75	593	71%	+7.3	11.2	6	3	3.4	41	-1.1	23.5%	6	151	8	153	43%	35%	18%	4%
2010	BAL	13/13	40	64	599	63%	+1.5	15.0	5	2	5.6	12	+1.2	21.5%	12	116	7	117	43%	30%	17%	10%
2011	ARI	10/4	24	36	283	67%	+3.2	11.8	1	1	4.6	22	+0.8	-8.7%	32	-3	30	16	39%	52%	10%	0%
2012	ARI		35	54	381	65%	--	10.9	4					10.0%								

After 10 seasons with the Baltimore Ravens, Heap was released for salary cap purposes but landed on his feet when the Cardinals signed him to a two-year, $5.5 million contract on August 1. By signing Heap and Jeff King, the Cardinals hoped to increase production from a position that averaged 27 receptions for 262 yards and two touchdowns in the first four seasons of the Ken Whisenhunt era. Heap alone would nearly match that production, despite missing six games in the heart of the season to a hamstring injury.

Aaron Hernandez   Height: 6-3   Weight: 245   College: Florida   Draft: 2010/4 (113)   Born: 6-Nov-1989   Age: 23   Risk: Yellow

Year	Team	G/S	Rec	Pass	Yds	C%	+/-	Y/C	TD	Drop	YAC	Rk	YAC+	DVOA	Rk	DYAR	Rk	YAR	Short	Mid	Deep	Bomb
2010	NE	14/7	45	64	563	70%	+1.3	12.5	6	5	6.5	7	+2.0	27.1%	6	144	5	146	50%	39%	11%	0%
2011	NE	14/12	79	113	910	70%	+4.2	11.5	7	4	6.4	4	+1.7	6.0%	19	107	11	117	66%	22%	6%	5%
2012	NE		77	112	957	69%	--	12.4	6					24.5%								

Hernandez, the "other" Patriots tight end, would be the main attraction in many offenses around the league. While he may be slightly under the radar in New England (or under the Gronk, more specifically), don't tell that to opposing defensive coordinators. In a league that increasingly features multidimensional athletes that don't cleanly fit into one position, Hernandez is arguably the most problematic matchup of them all. He lines up all over the field, sometimes as a standard in-line tight end, sometimes as a slot receiver, sometimes as an outside receiver, and sometimes as a fullback in shotgun and full house sets. Near the end of the season, Hernandez even began to take handoffs as a halfback; between Week 15 and the AFC Championship game, Hernandez gained 113 rushing yards on 12 carries. Hernandez broke 21 tackles in the regular season, by far the most by a tight end, and then another six in the postseason. His projection also includes 16 carries for 123 yards and a touchdown.

Rob Housler   Height: 6-6   Weight: 249   College: Florida Atlantic   Draft: 2011/3 (69)   Born: 17-Mar-1988   Age: 24   Risk: Green

Year	Team	G/S	Rec	Pass	Yds	C%	+/-	Y/C	TD	Drop	YAC	Rk	YAC+	DVOA	Rk	DYAR	Rk	YAR	Short	Mid	Deep	Bomb
2011	ARI	12/2	12	26	133	46%	-3.4	11.1	0	4	4.1	30	-0.3	-39.7%	47	-47	40	-58	29%	50%	17%	4%
2012	ARI		20	32	213	69%	--	10.6	1					-6.0%								

Housler began his college career at Florida Atlantic as a wide receiver, and due to his limited abilities as a blocker, his role as a rookie was to be the No. 3 tight end behind Todd Heap and Jeff King. An opportunity for more playing time opened up when Heap suffered a hamstring injury, but Housler injured his groin and couldn't take full advantage of the opening. Seven of Housler's 12 receptions came on third down, where he had a DVOA of 16.4%. A full offseason could lead to Housler playing a larger role in the Cardinals offense in 2012.

Dustin Keller   Height: 6-2   Weight: 242   College: Purdue   Draft: 2008/1 (30)   Born: 25-Sep-1984   Age: 28   Risk: Green

Year	Team	G/S	Rec	Pass	Yds	C%	+/-	Y/C	TD	Drop	YAC	Rk	YAC+	DVOA	Rk	DYAR	Rk	YAR	Short	Mid	Deep	Bomb
2009	NYJ	16/12	45	81	522	56%	-6.1	11.6	2	5	3.9	32	-0.6	-8.7%	30	-7	31	-9	38%	41%	19%	2%
2010	NYJ	16/13	55	100	687	55%	-4.1	12.5	5	8	3.9	35	-0.3	-4.7%	29	17	27	8	41%	40%	15%	3%
2011	NYJ	16/12	65	115	815	57%	-5.0	12.5	5	5	4.4	25	+0.3	-8.7%	31	-11	32	10	41%	41%	14%	5%
2012	NYJ		53	91	682	58%	--	12.9	4					4.1%								

Keller's Catch Rate of 57 percent was the lowest of any tight end with over 100 targets; it was lower than Kellen Winslow's, which is remarkable. Keller dropped six passes with 13 defensed and 11 overthrown, but the overarching issue is that Keller isn't the caliber of tight end who should be targeted 115 times, serve as his team's top third-down target, and so on. Tony Sparano likes to use his tight ends as blockers and on the occasional "mesh" route in the middle: Anthony Fasano averaged 50 to 60 targets per year, and he thrived in that role. Keller deserves more touches than Fasano, but not the near-Gronkowski role he had last season.

Lance Kendricks
Height: 6-3   Weight: 243   College: Wisconsin   Draft: 2011/2 (47)   Born: 30-Jan-1988   Age: 24   Risk: Yellow

Year	Team	G/S	Rec	Pass	Yds	C%	+/-	Y/C	TD	Drop	YAC	Rk	YAC+	DVOA	Rk	DYAR	Rk	YAR	Short	Mid	Deep	Bomb
2011	STL	10/1	28	58	352	48%	-7.6	12.6	0	4	6.6	3	+1.4	-27.2%	44	-72	45	-82	56%	25%	19%	0%
2012	STL		54	81	668	67%	--	12.4	4					10.4%								

Like most everything associated with the Rams last year, we can probably set aside Kendricks' 2011 season. He did struggle with drops, but, in the bigger picture, the quarterback situation was a mess, early-season snaps as a flexed tight end fell off after tackle injuries required more max protect, and he was dealing with concussion symptoms late in the season. The situation is much more favorable heading into 2012. St. Louis took steps to shore up their offensive line, so Kendricks will be on the field more in his natural receiving role, and hopefully he won't be trying to catch passes from backup quarterbacks. Most importantly, offensive coordinator Brian Schottenheimer and tight ends coach Rob Boras have a much better track record with tight ends (Dustin Keller, Greg Olsen, Desmond Clark, and the 2010 version of Marcedes Lewis) than their predecessors ever did.

Jeff King
Height: 6-5   Weight: 250   College: Virginia Tech   Draft: 2006/5 (155)   Born: 19-Feb-1983   Age: 29   Risk: Green

Year	Team	G/S	Rec	Pass	Yds	C%	+/-	Y/C	TD	Drop	YAC	Rk	YAC+	DVOA	Rk	DYAR	Rk	YAR	Short	Mid	Deep	Bomb
2009	CAR	16/15	25	33	200	76%	+2.1	8.0	3	2	2.5	47	-1.9	-1.6%	24	13	24	16	61%	30%	3%	6%
2010	CAR	16/16	19	31	121	61%	-0.4	6.4	2	2	1.8	45	-2.3	-20.5%	40	-29	36	-33	59%	41%	0%	0%
2011	ARI	16/10	27	34	271	79%	+4.1	10.0	3	0	4.8	17	+0.2	14.6%	12	53	22	43	58%	33%	6%	3%
2012	ARI		19	29	165	66%	--	8.7	2					-6.2%								

King was expected to be more of a blocker, but played a larger role in the offense than expected as Todd Heap missed a good portion of the season with a hamstring injury. While many tight ends are there to help move the chains, 30 of King's 34 targets were on first or second down. King underwent surgery in May after suffering a torn quadriceps tendon during the offseason workout program, but is expected to be ready for training camp. As long as Heap stays healthy, King will be the Cardinals' No. 2 tight end, which means he'll probably be starting by November.

Marcedes Lewis
Height: 6-6   Weight: 255   College: UCLA   Draft: 2006/1 (28)   Born: 19-May-1984   Age: 28   Risk: Red

Year	Team	G/S	Rec	Pass	Yds	C%	+/-	Y/C	TD	Drop	YAC	Rk	YAC+	DVOA	Rk	DYAR	Rk	YAR	Short	Mid	Deep	Bomb
2009	JAC	15/15	32	59	518	54%	-1.9	16.2	2	3	5.2	19	+0.5	1.7%	22	34	20	32	35%	22%	39%	4%
2010	JAC	16/16	58	88	700	66%	+1.2	12.1	10	6	4.5	25	+0.2	8.5%	19	96	12	108	58%	26%	14%	1%
2011	JAC	15/15	39	85	460	46%	-10.2	11.8	0	4	3.9	33	-0.7	-35.7%	46	-162	47	-176	43%	34%	19%	4%
2012	JAC		54	96	662	56%	--	12.3	4					-4.6%								

The signature moment of Lewis' season came in Week 12 against the Texans, when a play-fake left him completely uncovered in the end zone and he still dropped the pass. The Jaguars kept trying to throw him the ball week after week, so with the new normalized stats he now ends up with the worst DYAR season of all-time by a tight end. (See tables, next page.)

Worst Tight End DYAR, 1991-2011

Rank	Year	Player	Team	DYAR
1	2011	M.Lewis	JAC	-162
2	1998	F.Jones	SD	-158
3	2010	D.Graham	DEN	-139
4	2004	B.Williams	NO	-139
5	1997	J.Asher	WAS	-132
6	1996	K.Cash	KC	-125
7	2004	S.Alexander	DET	-124
8	1998	H.Cross	NYG	-124
9	2007	B.Scaife	TEN	-120
10	2008	D.Clark	CHI	-119

Worst Tight End DVOA, 1991-2011

Rank	Year	Player	Team	DVOA	Passes
1	2008	R.Royal	BUF	-36.4%	57
2	2011	M.Lewis	JAC	-35.7%	85
3	2004	B.Williams	NO	-35.3%	75
4	2010	J.Carlson	SEA	-35.3%	58
5	2004	B.Troupe	TEN	-32.0%	54
6	2007	Q.Sypniewski	BAL	-32.0%	52
7	2004	S.Alexander	DET	-31.6%	76
8	2009	D.Lee	GB	-31.1%	54
9	2008	D.Clark	CHI	-30.6%	73
10	2007	B.Scaife	TEN	-30.5%	78

Minimum 50 passes.
Note: With a minimum of 25 passes, Lewis ranks 33rd.

Lewis blamed his poor performance on legal battles with the mother of his child. The talent is there for Lewis to repeat 2010, when he was a slower Jimmy Graham who could actually block. The opportunity? That all rides on Blaine Gabbert.

Randy McMichael
Height: 6-3 Weight: 250 College: Georgia Draft: 2002/4 (114) Born: 28-Jun-1979 Age: 33 Risk: Green

Year	Team	G/S	Rec	Pass	Yds	C%	+/-	Y/C	TD	Drop	YAC	Rk	YAC+	DVOA	Rk	DYAR	Rk	YAR	Short	Mid	Deep	Bomb
2009	STL	16/16	34	62	332	55%	-7.2	9.8	1	6	4.1	30	-0.2	-19.9%	38	-52	43	-62	45%	43%	12%	0%
2010	SD	16/11	20	27	221	74%	+2.2	11.1	2	1	4.2	31	-0.3	26.5%	8	61	18	65	38%	50%	12%	0%
2011	SD	16/14	30	44	271	68%	+2.3	9.0	0	3	6.3	5	+0.3	-14.1%	36	-19	33	-29	70%	22%	8%	0%
2012	SD		16	27	161	59%	--	10.1	0					-13.1%								

The Chargers liked enough of the veteran reliability McMichael showed in 2010 and 2011 to re-sign him to another two-year deal. He'll continue to play in-line so Gates can play the slot, and he's good at catching the 8-yard pass on third-and-7, though not very good at turning that 8 yards into 10.

Heath Miller
Height: 6-5 Weight: 256 College: Virginia Draft: 2005/1 (30) Born: 22-Oct-1982 Age: 30 Risk: Green

Year	Team	G/S	Rec	Pass	Yds	C%	+/-	Y/C	TD	Drop	YAC	Rk	YAC+	DVOA	Rk	DYAR	Rk	YAR	Short	Mid	Deep	Bomb
2009	PIT	16/16	76	98	789	78%	+11.4	10.4	6	3	5.6	11	+0.9	14.9%	12	142	10	141	61%	30%	9%	0%
2010	PIT	14/14	42	67	512	63%	-0.0	12.2	2	3	5.4	14	+0.6	-3.7%	28	15	28	22	38%	43%	16%	3%
2011	PIT	16/16	51	76	631	68%	+1.9	12.4	2	3	4.8	18	+0.4	13.2%	15	99	14	99	39%	47%	14%	0%
2012	PIT		36	55	466	65%	--	12.9	5					26.8%								

After a statistical rebound in 2011, Miller's prospects in 2012 are wholly dependent on trying to read tea leaves about new offensive coordinator Todd Haley. In the past five seasons, the only time one of Haley's tight ends had 25 or more catches was in 2010 (Tony Moeaki), which also happens to be the year he ceded Kansas City's offense to Charlie Weis (before running him out of town, of course). Despite platitudes in front of reporters, perhaps the best indicator of Haley's current thinking is that Pittsburgh signed Leonard Pope, his tight end during those other four seasons.

TIGHT ENDS

Zach Miller
Height: 6-5 Weight: 256 College: Arizona State Draft: 2007/2 (38) Born: 11-Dec-1985 Age: 27 Risk: Yellow

Year	Team	G/S	Rec	Pass	Yds	C%	+/-	Y/C	TD	Drop	YAC	Rk	YAC+	DVOA	Rk	DYAR	Rk	YAR	Short	Mid	Deep	Bomb
2009	OAK	15/15	66	99	805	67%	+5.8	12.2	3	3	5.6	10	+1.1	1.7%	23	56	18	77	41%	36%	20%	3%
2010	OAK	15/15	60	92	685	65%	-0.2	11.4	1	6	4.6	24	+0.4	-0.3%	24	42	23	75	55%	31%	13%	0%
2011	SEA	15/15	25	44	233	57%	-1.0	9.3	0	3	3.2	42	-1.5	-25.4%	42	-49	41	-68	41%	38%	18%	3%
2012	SEA		40	64	411	63%	--	10.3	3					-2.9%								

In his first season in Seattle, Miller spent a good portion of his time as a sixth offensive lineman, setting career lows in receptions, touchdowns, and receiving yards. Miller had been Oakland's top target in the red zone, but was thrown at just six times in that part of the field in 2011. The Seahawks paid Miller handsomely after the lockout, signing the 2010 Pro Bowler to a five-year, $34 million contract that contained $17 million in guaranteed money. An improved offensive line should allow for Miller to run more routes, and the expected change at quarterback from deep-ball oriented Tarvaris Jackson to the more accurate Matt Flynn could help Miller's receiving numbers.

Tony Moeaki
Height: 6-3 Weight: 245 College: Iowa Draft: 2010/3 (93) Born: 8-Jun-1987 Age: 25 Risk: Yellow

Year	Team	G/S	Rec	Pass	Yds	C%	+/-	Y/C	TD	Drop	YAC	Rk	YAC+	DVOA	Rk	DYAR	Rk	YAR	Short	Mid	Deep	Bomb
2010	KC	15/15	47	72	556	65%	+3.9	11.8	3	5	4.0	33	-0.1	10.4%	16	82	16	76	36%	48%	14%	2%
2012	KC		48	77	535	62%	--	11.2	4					2.5%								

Kansas City ranked third in two-tight end sets in 2010, but 20th last season. Obviously, Moeaki's torn knee ligaments had a lot to do with that. With Moeaki back on the field and veteran Kevin Boss signed in free agency, the Chiefs should once again use that formation often. Even with Boss on board, the Chiefs need Moeaki at full strength. Only about half the teams in the league have a tight end who can get open down the field at all. Those that do can not only exploit defensive mismatches, but as linebackers and safeties are forced to clog the middle of the field to take away the seam route, opportunities will open for receivers on the outside and running backs underneath. Moeaki's projection may look modest, but his impact will go far beyond his individual numbers.

Evan Moore
Height: 6-6 Weight: 247 College: Stanford Draft: 2008/FA Born: 3-Jan-1985 Age: 28 Risk: Yellow

Year	Team	G/S	Rec	Pass	Yds	C%	+/-	Y/C	TD	Drop	YAC	Rk	YAC+	DVOA	Rk	DYAR	Rk	YAR	Short	Mid	Deep	Bomb
2009	CLE	5/0	12	23	158	52%	-1.3	13.2	0	2	5.4	--	+1.1	-7.1%	--	0	--	2	23%	50%	27%	0%
2010	CLE	12/4	16	26	322	62%	+1.9	20.1	1	3	5.6	11	+1.0	38.4%	4	78	17	72	32%	24%	24%	20%
2011	CLE	16/4	34	47	324	72%	+2.9	9.5	4	2	2.4	46	-1.9	11.3%	18	59	21	40	47%	43%	9%	2%
2012	CLE		32	50	353	64%	--	11.0	3					3.3%								

Moore, a former basketball player at Stanford, is getting better as he's given more opportunity. As might be expected given his cager background, Moore was frequently targeted in the red zone. His steep drop in yards per catch is more attributable to Cleveland's quarterbacks than a lack of downfield ability. Although Benjamin Watson's contract ends after this season, Moore isn't really an heir apparent, as he's generally a receiving option only.

Brandon Myers
Height: 6-4 Weight: 250 College: Iowa Draft: 2009/6 (202) Born: 4-Sep-1985 Age: 27 Risk: Red

Year	Team	G/S	Rec	Pass	Yds	C%	+/-	Y/C	TD	Drop	YAC	Rk	YAC+	DVOA	Rk	DYAR	Rk	YAR	Short	Mid	Deep	Bomb
2009	OAK	11/2	4	6	19	67%	-0.3	4.8	0	0	3.8	--	-2.3	-63.0%	--	-19	--	-20	67%	17%	17%	0%
2010	OAK	15/3	12	16	80	75%	+0.8	6.7	0	1	3.2	--	-1.3	-20.7%	--	-14	--	-19	75%	25%	0%	0%
2011	OAK	16/7	16	27	151	59%	-0.1	9.4	0	1	3.4	37	-1.3	-35.0%	45	-52	44	-48	57%	26%	13%	4%
2012	OAK		24	35	272	69%	--	11.3	3					15.1%								

A solid blocker, Myers is the Raiders' number-one tight end by default with the release of Kevin Boss. He's a limited receiver who hasn't done anything impressive in that area since his first training camp and preseason. Don't expect anything in terms of fantasy value from him.

426 TIGHT ENDS

Greg Olsen
Height: 6-6　Weight: 254　College: Miami　Draft: 2007/1 (31)　Born: 11-Mar-1985　Age: 27　Risk: Green

Year	Team	G/S	Rec	Pass	Yds	C%	+/-	Y/C	TD	Drop	YAC	Rk	YAC+	DVOA	Rk	DYAR	Rk	YAR	Short	Mid	Deep	Bomb
2009	CHI	16/15	60	108	612	56%	-5.1	10.2	8	5	2.9	44	-1.3	-12.6%	32	-41	40	-40	47%	28%	19%	6%
2010	CHI	16/13	41	70	404	59%	+0.3	9.9	5	3	3.8	36	-0.6	-19.6%	39	-57	40	-46	44%	32%	21%	3%
2011	CAR	16/13	45	89	540	51%	-8.0	12.0	5	1	4.4	26	-0.0	-13.9%	35	-38	37	-47	27%	52%	15%	6%
2012	CAR		49	82	524	60%	--	10.7	5					-2.6%								

Olsen caught 34 passes through the first nine games of last season, with four touchdowns and a two-point conversion. Then, a serious of strange accidents and injuries befell him. He collided with a teammate during pregame warm-ups before facing the Colts, and while he played in that game, he soon began missing practice time with knee and back injuries. Olsen's role in the offense gradually dwindled until he was ultimately knocked out the season finale with a head injury. Olsen is a very good blocker who can line up all over the offensive formation, but after two seasons of 40-something catches and five touchdowns per year, what you see is what you get, statistically.

Brandon Pettigrew
Height: 6-6　Weight: 263　College: Oklahoma State　Draft: 2009/1 (20)　Born: 23-Feb-1985　Age: 27　Risk: Green

Year	Team	G/S	Rec	Pass	Yds	C%	+/-	Y/C	TD	Drop	YAC	Rk	YAC+	DVOA	Rk	DYAR	Rk	YAR	Short	Mid	Deep	Bomb
2009	DET	11/11	30	54	346	56%	-4.8	11.5	2	6	6.3	6	+1.6	-15.6%	34	-29	35	-20	45%	43%	10%	2%
2010	DET	16/16	71	111	722	64%	-2.9	10.2	4	8	4.9	18	+0.2	0.9%	23	58	20	45	61%	31%	8%	1%
2011	DET	16/16	83	126	777	66%	+1.0	9.4	5	6	3.7	35	-0.8	-12.6%	33	-43	38	-18	54%	34%	12%	0%
2012	DET		73	106	802	69%	--	11.0	5					9.5%								

Though a former first-round pick, Pettigrew's emergence as one of the best all-around tight ends in the NFL has gone largely unnoticed. He's always been an effective blocker, both in-line and in space (he's every bit as thick as his listed size suggests). Last season, despite coming off a torn ACL suffered on Thanksgiving 2010, Pettigrew improved noticeably as a receiver. He was less of a plodder and more attack-oriented as a route runner. This isn't to say he's a Jermichael Finley-type athlete. Far from it, in fact. Pettigrew is, and always will be, methodical. That's fine because he's fundamentally complete and has very good chemistry with Matthew Stafford. The Lions believe Pettigrew can win a one-on-one matchup against any NFL linebacker. This makes him a go-to option on most weeks and, in the very least, a safety valve on all the other weeks.

John Phillips
Height: 6-5　Weight: 265　College: Virginia　Draft: 2009/6 (208)　Born: 11-Jun-1987　Age: 25　Risk: Green

Year	Team	G/S	Rec	Pass	Yds	C%	+/-	Y/C	TD	Drop	YAC	Rk	YAC+	DVOA	Rk	DYAR	Rk	YAR	Short	Mid	Deep	Bomb
2009	DAL	16/4	7	9	62	78%	+0.4	8.9	0	0	6.4	--	+1.2	0.3%	--	4	--	2	67%	33%	0%	0%
2011	DAL	16/7	15	18	101	83%	+1.7	6.7	1	0	6.0	--	-0.4	-11.8%	--	-6	--	-10	88%	12%	0%	0%
2012	DAL		26	45	226	58%	--	8.7	2					-20.1%								

Phillips was second on the Cowboys in special teams tackles, and he hit a home run at Rangers Ballpark in a charity event in May. So he's got the kickoff coverage and baseball taken care of; now the Cowboys need him to be a more reliable receiver. Martellus Bennett's escape to New York opens a key spot in the Dallas lineup, as only New England and San Francisco used more two-tight end sets than the Cowboys last year. In the past, Phillips has mostly been a blocker; we counted him lining up in the backfield 123 times last season, the most of any tight end in the NFL:

Tight Ends Most Frequently Lined Up in Backfield, 2011

Player	Team	Backfield Plays	Player	Team	Backfield Plays
John Phillips	DAL	123	Will Heller	DET	47
Randy McMichael	SD	101	Kyle Rudolph	MIN	47
Greg Olsen	CAR	63	Heath Miller	PIT	44
David Johnson	PIT	57	Chris Cooley	WAS	43
Jim Kleinsasser	MIN	57	Tom Crabtree	GB	40

Plays cancelled by Defensive Pass Interference included.

Dennis Pitta

Height: 6-5　Weight: 245　College: BYU　Draft: 2010/4 (114)　Born: 29-Jun-1985　Age: 27　Risk: Yellow

Year	Team	G/S	Rec	Pass	Yds	C%	+/-	Y/C	TD	Drop	YAC	Rk	YAC+	DVOA	Rk	DYAR	Rk	YAR	Short	Mid	Deep	Bomb
2010	BAL	11/0	1	5	1	20%	-1.9	1.0	0	0	0.0	--	-5.2	-69.8%	--	-25	--	-25	20%	20%	60%	0%
2011	BAL	16/2	40	56	405	71%	+3.6	10.1	3	1	4.5	24	-0.2	12.2%	16	72	16	78	46%	41%	13%	0%
2012	BAL		42	70	470	60%	--	11.2	2					-8.2%								

The second of Baltimore's mid-round tight end selections in 2010, Pitta emerged towards the end of 2011 as a more reliable option than the guy drafted before him. From Week 12 through the AFC Championship game, he had more third-down targets (17) than Ed Dickson (12), and scored on four of his five red zone targets. (Unfortunate timing fact: His unsuccessful red-zone target immediately preceded Billy Cundiff's shank.) One part of the reason for Pitta's increased playing time is that he has much better hands than Dickson. The other part is that he's skillfully ingratiated himself with teammates, even going so far as being brothers-in-fu-manchu with Joe Flacco.

Leonard Pope

Height: 6-6　Weight: 250　College: Georgia　Draft: 2006/3 (72)　Born: 9-Sep-1983　Age: 29　Risk: Green

Year	Team	G/S	Rec	Pass	Yds	C%	+/-	Y/C	TD	Drop	YAC	Rk	YAC+	DVOA	Rk	DYAR	Rk	YAR	Short	Mid	Deep	Bomb
2009	KC	13/8	20	30	174	67%	-0.9	8.7	1	3	4.2	28	-1.2	-27.6%	42	-38	38	-19	63%	27%	10%	0%
2010	KC	16/6	10	19	76	53%	-2.2	7.6	2	3	3.4	--	-0.7	-26.8%	--	-28	--	-18	67%	22%	11%	0%
2011	KC	16/10	24	33	247	73%	+2.1	10.3	1	3	5.2	13	+0.3	0.9%	24	19	25	25	53%	38%	6%	3%
2012	PIT		17	26	204	65%	--	12.0	2					14.7%								

The Steelers will be Pope's third team since 2007, but in that time Todd Haley has always been his offensive coordinator or head coach, so he should have little trouble adjusting to the Pittsburgh offense. Pope is 6-foot-6, but that does not mean he's useful in the red zone. In the past two years Kansas City threw him a total of four passes inside the opponents' 20. On the other hand, three of those were caught for touchdowns, so perhaps they should have used him down there more often.

Kyle Rudolph

Height: 6-6　Weight: 265　College: Notre Dame　Draft: 2011/2 (43)　Born: 9-Nov-1989　Age: 23　Risk: Red

Year	Team	G/S	Rec	Pass	Yds	C%	+/-	Y/C	TD	Drop	YAC	Rk	YAC+	DVOA	Rk	DYAR	Rk	YAR	Short	Mid	Deep	Bomb
2011	MIN	8/1	26	39	249	67%	+2.3	9.6	3	1	3.4	40	-0.9	-4.6%	27	7	27	5	53%	28%	19%	0%
2012	MIN		63	102	804	62%	--	12.8	6					14.1%								

The Vikings need to make Rudolph a more prominent part of their offense in 2012, and we're betting that they will. His rookie season was somewhat hindered by the lack of offseason and the team's shortcomings under center. Those shouldn't be issues now, though, and the lithe, ball-plucking 265-pounder is expected to be the clear-cut No. 1 tight end, if not Christian Ponder's No. 1 overall target. One problem: Tight ends must contribute as blockers in coordinator Bill Musgrave's offense, and coming out of Notre Dame, scouts noted that Rudolph's blocking technique needed help, though size alone should make him at least somewhat effective from the get-go.

Tony Scheffler

Height: 6-5　Weight: 255　College: Western Michigan　Draft: 2006/2 (61)　Born: 15-Feb-1983　Age: 29　Risk: Green

Year	Team	G/S	Rec	Pass	Yds	C%	+/-	Y/C	TD	Drop	YAC	Rk	YAC+	DVOA	Rk	DYAR	Rk	YAR	Short	Mid	Deep	Bomb
2009	DEN	15/9	31	50	416	62%	+1.2	13.4	2	2	5.6	12	+1.3	17.2%	9	84	15	71	34%	47%	13%	6%
2010	DET	15/4	45	72	378	63%	+0.1	8.4	1	4	3.3	40	-1.1	-17.4%	38	-46	39	-53	55%	38%	5%	3%
2011	DET	15/5	26	43	347	60%	+1.6	13.3	6	1	1.8	47	-2.4	14.5%	13	66	20	92	23%	53%	15%	10%
2012	DET		30	52	356	58%	--	11.9	4					4.2%								

Scheffler may not quite be good enough to justify the elaborate nature of some of his touchdown dances, but he's at least one of the most wideout-like receiving tight ends in the NFL. Is that a compliment? Sort of. Scheffler poses matchup problems in dual tight end sets because defenses must decide whether to defend him with a linebacker/safety or a nickel corner. The Lions make things harder by moving Scheffler around like a queen on a chess board. He'll line up in the slot, at natural tight end, as an H-back or receiver split outside. Defenses can often get away with going nickel against him because Scheffler is not a fervid blocker, but his size alone can be enough to neutralize most nickel corners in the run game. Durability has always been a concern; Scheffler has only played one 16-game season, though he's never missed more than three games in any season. Offseason injuries have been more of a problem.

Visanthe Shiancoe   Height: 6-4   Weight: 250   College: Morgan State   Draft: 2003/3 (91)   Born: 18-Jun-1980   Age: 32   Risk: N/A

Year	Team	G/S	Rec	Pass	Yds	C%	+/-	Y/C	TD	Drop	YAC	Rk	YAC+	DVOA	Rk	DYAR	Rk	YAR	Short	Mid	Deep	Bomb
2009	MIN	16/13	56	79	566	71%	+4.3	10.1	11	6	3.6	37	-0.5	30.8%	3	210	2	212	53%	29%	17%	1%
2010	MIN	16/9	47	79	530	59%	-2.4	11.3	2	6	3.7	37	-0.8	-8.8%	32	-8	33	-19	39%	41%	16%	4%
2011	MIN	16/14	36	71	409	51%	-5.3	11.4	3	3	3.6	36	-0.4	-18.0%	38	-52	43	-28	45%	42%	6%	8%

When Brett Favre was in Minnesota, Shiancoe was a highly productive safety valve and a movable chess piece, which is all you could want in a veteran tight end. But after a mistake-filled 2010 campaign in which he dropped too many passes and led the league with 15 penalties (an astounding number for any non-offensive lineman), the Vikings used a second-round pick on Kyle Rudolph and let Shiancoe play out his contract. Though not ferociously powerful, Shiancoe is a good enough blocker to serve in a No. 2 role (as long as he's not asked to block defensive ends one-on-one as often as he was last year in Minnesota). He's versatile enough to set the edge outside or be a movement blocker out of the backfield. In the passing game, Shiancoe is somewhat of a body-catcher, which limits his receiving dimensionality, but he's serviceable enough to run basic routes off the line or out of the slot. He can still help a team and we're a bit surprised he was unsigned as of press time.

Jeremy Shockey   Height: 6-5   Weight: 253   College: Miami   Draft: 2002/1 (14)   Born: 18-Aug-1980   Age: 32   Risk: N/A

Year	Team	G/S	Rec	Pass	Yds	C%	+/-	Y/C	TD	Drop	YAC	Rk	YAC+	DVOA	Rk	DYAR	Rk	YAR	Short	Mid	Deep	Bomb
2009	NO	13/12	48	67	569	72%	+5.8	11.9	3	1	2.7	46	-1.1	17.3%	8	109	13	126	31%	52%	17%	0%
2010	NO	13/11	41	59	408	69%	+4.2	10.0	3	3	3.0	41	-1.0	4.1%	21	46	22	56	38%	48%	13%	2%
2011	CAR	15/13	37	62	455	60%	-0.6	12.3	4	2	5.3	11	+0.7	1.6%	23	36	23	31	35%	42%	23%	0%

Warren Sapp claimed on NFL Network that Shockey was the "snitch" in the Saints bounty scandal. Shockey vehemently denied the claim, and one of the ugliest sidebars to one of the ugliest stories in NFL history was born. Shockey's reputation as a nincompoop probably led to the use of the term "snitch"—Drew Brees would have been called a "whistleblower" and a "hero"—and Shockey ceded the moral and intellectual high ground by claiming that the story was made up because the New York media needed something to write about, at a time when those of us who weren't on 24-7 Tebow Alert were following Jeremy Lin around with a sweat rag. It was all irrelevant and a little skeezy, and we only recount it here because it happened and there is no other place to mention it. On the field, Shockey's reception total dropped for the fifth consecutive year, but he posted his highest per-catch average since 2005 and blocked as well as he always does. For a 40-catch tight end, Shockey has a unique ability to draw attention to himself, even when he isn't doing anything. It sometimes diverts attention away from the things he still does very well.

Luke Stocker   Height: 6-5   Weight: 258   College: Tennessee   Draft: 2011/4 (104)   Born: 17-Jul-1988   Age: 24   Risk: Green

Year	Team	G/S	Rec	Pass	Yds	C%	+/-	Y/C	TD	Drop	YAC	Rk	YAC+	DVOA	Rk	DYAR	Rk	YAR	Short	Mid	Deep	Bomb
2011	TB	9/1	12	17	92	71%	-0.0	7.7	0	2	4.3	--	-0.7	-21.1%	--	-16	--	-23	65%	29%	6%	0%
2012	TB		25	38	270	66%	--	10.8	3					10.0%								

Stocker is an H-back type who will have to battle Dallas Clark for the Bucs' starting tight end spot. Stocker caught four 4-yard passes and two 1-yard passes last season, none of them touchdowns. The Bucs just liked to motion him across the formation, send him into the flat for a super-short pass, and watch him get tackled ... often while trailing 27-10. Bucs tape was not a lot of fun to watch.

TIGHT ENDS

Jacob Tamme
Height: 6-3 Weight: 236 College: Kentucky Draft: 2008/4 (127) Born: 15-Mar-1985 Age: 27 Risk: Green

Year	Team	G/S	Rec	Pass	Yds	C%	+/-	Y/C	TD	Drop	YAC	Rk	YAC+	DVOA	Rk	DYAR	Rk	YAR	Short	Mid	Deep	Bomb
2009	IND	16/1	3	10	35	30%	-2.7	11.7	0	0	4.0	--	-1.2	-36.4%	--	-18	--	-25	22%	56%	22%	0%
2010	IND	16/8	67	93	631	72%	+5.2	9.4	4	5	4.6	23	-0.2	8.0%	20	95	13	105	56%	30%	11%	3%
2011	IND	16/5	19	31	177	61%	-1.8	9.3	1	0	4.8	15	-0.0	-20.8%	40	-29	36	-33	73%	17%	10%	0%
2012	DEN		40	54	432	74%	--	10.8	5					25.3%								

After using Tamme to cover for Dallas Clark's maladies over the past two years, the Colts let him walk to Denver without much of a fight. Being a move tight end in a Peyton Manning offense means that you will find yourself as a hot read fairly often. It also means that you catch passes by the bushel. Tamme showed that he could be every bit as productive as Clark in that role in 2010, and Tamme's experience with Manning should make him a focal point in the offense.

Delanie Walker
Height: 6-1 Weight: 241 College: Central Missouri Draft: 2006/6 (175) Born: 12-Aug-1984 Age: 28 Risk: Green

Year	Team	G/S	Rec	Pass	Yds	C%	+/-	Y/C	TD	Drop	YAC	Rk	YAC+	DVOA	Rk	DYAR	Rk	YAR	Short	Mid	Deep	Bomb
2009	SF	16/8	21	33	233	64%	-0.2	11.1	0	0	7.6	1	+1.9	-21.7%	40	-33	37	-43	59%	19%	19%	3%
2010	SF	14/8	29	46	331	65%	-0.3	11.4	0	5	5.8	9	+0.2	-3.4%	27	12	29	10	65%	21%	7%	7%
2011	SF	15/7	19	36	198	56%	-1.3	10.4	3	3	3.8	34	-1.3	-19.5%	39	-27	35	-32	61%	26%	6%	6%
2012	SF		16	25	139	64%	--	8.7	1					-10.9%								

Walker is the Godot of NFL tight ends. We've been waiting for his physical talent to translate into gaudy receiving numbers, but it never shows up. When the 49ers hired noted tight end enthusiast Jim Harbaugh, many envisioned that 2011 would be the year Walker finally played a major role in San Francisco's passing game. Instead, when blocking tight end Nate Byham got hurt in training camp, Harbaugh combined all of Walker's previous roles (wide receiver, fullback, H-back, and blocking tight end) and made him a jack-of-all-trades lynchpin of offensive formation diversity. Byham's return allows Walker to spend less time blocking, but offseason wide receiver additions mean more competition for targets.

Benjamin Watson
Height: 6-3 Weight: 255 College: Duke Draft: 2004/1 (32) Born: 18-Dec-1980 Age: 32 Risk: Green

Year	Team	G/S	Rec	Pass	Yds	C%	+/-	Y/C	TD	Drop	YAC	Rk	YAC+	DVOA	Rk	DYAR	Rk	YAR	Short	Mid	Deep	Bomb
2009	NE	16/7	29	41	404	71%	+5.4	13.9	5	2	3.2	42	-0.8	47.8%	1	157	7	153	33%	28%	30%	10%
2010	CLE	16/16	68	103	763	67%	+3.4	11.2	3	5	3.9	34	-0.5	8.9%	18	108	9	86	37%	44%	15%	3%
2011	CLE	13/11	37	71	410	52%	-7.9	11.1	2	4	5.2	12	+0.3	-17.3%	37	-47	39	-66	57%	31%	9%	3%
2012	CLE		43	72	494	60%	--	11.5	4					0.4%								

Whoo, baby, does that 2010 season scream "career year" or what? Watson is an effective supporting tight end at this point, but that specific class doesn't tend to age gracefully.

Kellen Winslow
Height: 6-4 Weight: 254 College: Miami Draft: 2004/1 (6) Born: 21-Jul-1983 Age: 29 Risk: Red

Year	Team	G/S	Rec	Pass	Yds	C%	+/-	Y/C	TD	Drop	YAC	Rk	YAC+	DVOA	Rk	DYAR	Rk	YAR	Short	Mid	Deep	Bomb
2009	TB	16/14	77	127	884	61%	+3.5	11.5	5	7	3.2	43	-0.8	7.7%	16	121	12	104	37%	40%	19%	4%
2010	TB	16/11	66	97	730	68%	+7.0	11.1	5	3	3.5	39	-0.8	9.4%	17	102	10	113	40%	41%	16%	3%
2011	TB	16/15	75	120	763	63%	+1.9	10.2	2	4	3.4	38	-0.6	-13.6%	34	-52	42	-56	42%	48%	11%	0%
2012	SEA		46	77	445	60%	--	9.7	2					-15.3%								

Winslow is a good candidate to respond to Pete Carroll's brand of rah-rah motivation: The talent is there, and the old "f---ing soldier" routine suggests that he likes a little noisy showmanship. Winslow has milked a long career out of his name and a lot of empty receiving calories (Winslow caught 30 passes for 280 yards last year when the Bucs were trailing by 14 or more points.) The move to Seattle is his last chance to do something relevant.

TIGHT ENDS

Jason Witten   Height: 6-6   Weight: 265   College: Tennessee   Draft: 2003/3 (69)   Born: 6-May-1982   Age: 30   Risk: Green

Year	Team	G/S	Rec	Pass	Yds	C%	+/-	Y/C	TD	Drop	YAC	Rk	YAC+	DVOA	Rk	DYAR	Rk	YAR	Short	Mid	Deep	Bomb
2009	DAL	16/16	94	124	1030	76%	+11.1	11.0	2	3	4.5	25	+0.2	17.8%	7	198	4	183	49%	38%	11%	2%
2010	DAL	16/16	94	128	1002	73%	+10.7	10.7	9	3	4.2	30	-0.2	13.8%	14	173	4	186	47%	43%	9%	1%
2011	DAL	16/16	79	117	942	68%	+5.5	11.9	5	2	4.6	21	+0.2	5.6%	20	102	12	75	47%	38%	12%	3%
2012	DAL		69	105	824	66%	--	11.9	6					14.5%								

Witten needs 72 yards to pass Jackie Smith and Ozzie Newsome for third place in career yardage for tight ends. He'll still be about 2,000 yards short of Shannon Sharpe at that point, and at least 5,000 yards behind Tony Gonzalez. He's actually ahead of Gonzalez (and everyone else) through age 29, but it's hard to imagine he'll keep up with Gonzo's absurd longevity. Regardless, the one-time third-round pick should join those other names in Canton someday. For now, we must accept that Witten is beginning to show his age. After ranking fourth or better among tight ends in DYAR every season since 2002, Witten was just 10th last year. His DYAR and DVOA were both the worst since his rookie season. The glut of prolific young tight ends will make Witten's inevitable decline look even steeper when it really hits.

Going Deep

Kyle Adams, CHI: Adams made the Bears as an undrafted rookie because of his H-back work and special teams contributions. There was a specific demand for H-back abilities in Mike Martz's offense—an offense that the Bears scrapped after last season. Adams may have to prove himself all over again in Mike Tice's system. Perhaps helping Adams' cause is the fact that Chicago's other tight ends are known for blocking, while he's known for his soft hands and receiving aptitude.

David Ausberry, OAK: A 2011 seventh-round pick out of USC, Ausberry was converted from oversize collegiate receiver to tight end. He has the athleticism to make an impact, but only had two catches in 12 games as a rookie. Carson Palmer said nice things about his performance in offseason workouts. Ausberry has Owen Daniels-like upside in Greg Knapp's offense, but he also may just be another athletic tight end with upside who never does anything.

Billy Bajema, FA: A seventh-round pick by the 49ers out of Oklahoma State in 2005, Bajema has parlayed the H-back position into a seven-year NFL career worth about $5 million. Still unsigned at this late juncture, his eight-season parlay is looking like a loser. (2011 stats: 9-for-14, 71 yards, -19 DYAR, -28.7% DVOA)

Josh Baker, NYJ: Baker impressed the Jets with a six-catch preseason as an undrafted rookie in 2011, then made the active roster after Jeff Cumberland's Achilles injury. He joins Cumberland and several others in the mix for the second tight end role, which will be large (but blocking-oriented) in Tony Sparano's offense.

Anthony Becht, FA: Becht gained 20 yards receiving against Green Bay last year. It was his first 20-yard game since Week 1 of 2006, which coincidentally was also the last year that he caught more than seven passes in a season. A first-round pick in 2000, Becht was considering retirement, but he might find a roster spot on some team desperate for blocking and special teams help.

Travis Beckum, NYG: Like Jake Ballard, Beckum tore his ACL in the Super Bowl. His recovery has been much faster, since he didn't also require microfracture surgery; he'll start the season on PUP but should eventually play as an occasional receiving option. He's not much of a blocker. (2011 stats: 5-for-10, 93 yards, 1 TD, -15 DYAR, -28.5% DVOA)

Richie Brockel, CAR: Brockel is best known as the guy who scored on the *Little Giants* play against the Texans, taking a sneaky between-the-legs handoff from Cam Newton and slipping off to the left as the defense chased Newton to the right. It was a fun play, but not the kind of thing that happens more than once a career. Brockel's H-back role will be eaten up by Mike Tolbert at fullback and Gary Barnidge and others at tight end, so hopefully he owns a good recording of last year's touchdown.

Nate Byham, SF: It's not often that a training camp injury to a team's third tight end has major consequences for an offense, but Byham's torn ACL was that rare case, as it forced former college wide receiver Delanie Walker into more of a blocking role than expected. Therefore, although Byham will be the primary beneficiary of his own health in 2012, Walker's target total (only 35 last year) will be a close second.

Jordan Cameron, CLE: When the Browns drafted this combine all-star last year, they mistakenly called Cameron Jordan, the New Orleans defensive end, with the good news. "Uh, the Saints already picked me," laughed the first-rounder. This Cameron, a fourth-round pick, is extremely athletic but raw, like many former basketball players (Cameron played at BYU before switching to football, USC, and presumably, a non-Mormon lifestyle). (2011 stats, 6-for-13, 33 yards, -43 DYAR, -52.9% DVOA)

Mike Caussin, BUF: Caussin is a small school prospect, a 243-pound tight end who needs to add bulk before he has a chance to see the field regularly. He had a six-game stint on the active roster where he caught a few passes and acquitted himself well on special teams, and if he hits the weight room, he could be in line for an increased role in 2012. (2011 stats: 5-for-6, 41 yards, 5 DYAR, 4.3% DVOA)

Orson Charles, CIN: Charles knocked over Florida's 2007 BCS National Championship trophy while in Gainesville on a recruiting visit, shattering the crystal football. Needless to say, he attended Georgia instead. He showed much more consistency with his hands in 2011 (2009-10 catch rate: 58 percent; 2011 catch rate: 67 percent), and he was a frequent target of his quarterback and high school teammate Aaron Murray. Charles was in the mix to be a first-rounder when he first declared for the draft, but a DUI arrest in March and a mediocre Combine resulted in a spill to the fourth round.

Charles Clay, MIA: Tony Sparano liked to line Clay up outside Anthony Fasano in twin-tight end sets and send Clay up the seam while Fasano blocked or ran a drag. Clay produced some big plays from this look, including back-to-back 21- and 22-yard receptions against the Chiefs, and a 49-yard catch against the Bills where Clay ran a corner route instead of a seamer. Clay also lined up at fullback and in the slot. He doesn't have great speed, but he runs good routes and blocks well enough. He can be a very useful H-back, and if the Dolphins try to clear cap space by releasing Fasano, Clay would be an adequate replacement. (2011 stats: 16-for-25, 233 yards, 3 TD, 118 DYAR, 62.1% DVOA)

Colin Cloherty, JAC: Brown alum Cloherty will face a bit of a roster crunch in Jacksonville this season with the return of (the other) Zach Miller. After spending the 2010 season with the Colts practice squad, unnamed Colts officials told ESPN's Len Pasquarelli that Cloherty had "Dallas Clark-like abilities." His skills are definitely similar to Clark's, in so much as he can play tight end and sometimes catch a football. (2011 stats: 4-for-8, 0 DYAR, -7.4% DVOA)

Colin Cochart, CIN: The Jackrabbit from South Dakota State beat out Chase Coffman for a roster spot because he was a willing blocker. When pressed into receiving duty, he proved he had decent hands as well, with a touchdown and a 25-yard gain among his five grabs. The addition of Orson Charles means Cochart will battle Donald Lee for a spot on the roster. (2011 stats: 5-for-9, 44 yards, 1 TD, 7 DYAR, 3.7% DVOA)

Tom Crabtree, GB: Crabtree is not cut out to be a mainstream NFL tight end, but he can be very effective as a role player in the right packages. Green Bay uses him frequently as a finesse blocker out of the backfield, where he can lead inside and, more effectively, help create specific angles on the outside. In the passing game, Crabtree contributes as that eligible receiver defenses tend to forget about in short-yardage situations. (2011 stats: 6-for-8, 38 yards, 1 TD, 6 DYAR, 1.4% DVOA)

Jeff Cumberland, NYJ: A converted wide receiver, Cumberland caught a 33-yard pass against the Cowboys and a 2-yard pass against the Jaguars, then blew out his Achilles tendon against the Raiders and was lost for the year. The Jets see him as a possible seam-stretcher at tight end.

Jim Dray, ARI: Dray established a career-high when he caught two passes for 25 yards in a Week 9 win over the St. Louis Rams. Dray's production outburst was rewarded the following week against the Philadelphia Eagles when quarterback John Skelton targeted him three times, with all three falling incomplete. Perhaps reminded that Dray's best attribute is his blocking ability, Dray was not thrown to over the next seven weeks.

Drake Dunsmore, TB: The Buccaneers' seventh-round pick, Dunsmore is a long, lean, spread-style tight end best known for his four-touchdown effort for Northwestern against Indiana. He has the Poor Man's Jimmy Graham profile: tall, fast, limited football background, none of Graham's elite athleticism. With Kellen Winslow gone, the tight end position is pretty open for the Bucs, so Dunsmore will get a chance.

Collin Franklin, TB: Franklin led Iowa State in receiving in 2010 and had an impressive Pro Day performance before the 2011 draft, but pity the plight of an undrafted rookie in a lockout year. The Jets signed him in late July, then waived him. The Bucs signed him, activated him for two games, then released him. Franklin is back with the Buccaneers, and participation in a training camp that doesn't resemble doorbuster savings at a Walmart off the turnpike will help establish if he is truly an NFL-caliber player.

John Gilmore, FA: Gilmore started three games as a blocking tight end for the Saints after David Thomas went down. The 32-year-old was a free agent at press time, but could still catch on somewhere as a special teams contributor. (2011 stats: 3-for-6, 20 yards, 1 TD, -5 DYAR, -18.4% DVOA)

Richard Gordon, OAK: The rare non-undersized young tight end, Gordon played a mix of blocking tight end and fullback in 2011. His play probably helped make Rock Cartwright expendable. He probably won't see the ball much again (only one catch in 2011), but should see a good amount of work at both tight end and fullback as a pure blocker.

Daniel Graham, FA: With Craig Stevens taking most of the snaps at blocking tight end for Tennessee, Graham was relegated to a supporting role in big packages despite his three-year, $8.6 million contract. The Titans cut him this offseason, but if someone still needs a blocker, he can still do the job.

Garrett Graham, HOU: Graham saw some time in three-tight end sets, but sterling health from the guys ahead of him limited his opportunities. He's looked very solid in the preseason each of the last couple years; how much playing time he can take away from James Casey will probably depend on how much his blocking has improved this offseason.

Ladarius Green, SD: A fourth-round pick, Green is an intriguing move tight end prospect and potential heir to Antonio Gates in a couple years. To be that, he'll have to improve his strength, blocking, and route-running. At Louisiana-Lafayette, he became much more of a possession receiver as defenses started to key on him. He averaged 18.0 yards per catch with a 53 percent catch rate as the team's top target in 2010, then 11.9 yd/rec with a 64 percent catch rate as the No. 2 target in 2011.

Virgil Green, DEN: A seventh-round selection last year, Green was facing an uphill battle to get on the field after Denver signed Jacob Tamme and Joel Dreesen in free agency. Then Green was suspended four games for using performance-enhancing drugs. He only caught three passes all season, so perhaps his performance was not enhanced enough.

Chris Gronkowski, DEN: This Gronkowski brother is most well-known for blowing the assignment on Michael Boley that led to Tony Romo's fractured clavicle in 2010. Dallas let him go after the preseason, and the Colts claimed him on waivers. He was a part of the one thing Indianapolis was actually OK at last season, at least down the stretch: running the football. Besides, who hasn't gotten Tony Romo hurt at this point?

Dan Gronkowski, CLE: The eldest Gronk was nominated for a Rhodes Scholarship at Maryland, which, given his brother Rob's doltishness, leads one to question the family mailman's whereabouts in the late 1980s. Didn't catch a ball for either the Browns or the Pats in 2011; at this point, a career switch to Rob's marketing team seems prudent.

James Hanna, DAL: Hanna led all tight ends with a 4.49-second 40-yard dash at the Combine, and he flashed big-play potential as a junior at Oklahoma, averaging 16.2 yards per catch with 64 percent catch rate and seven touchdowns. Those numbers sank in his senior season (to 61 percent catch rate, 14.1 yards per catch), and concerns about his hands and blocking ability left him on the board for Dallas to take in the sixth round.

Clay Harbor, PHI: Harbor is an athletic H-back type who fits well in the Eagles' offense, very similar to (but not as good as) Brent Celek. (2011 stats: 13-for-19, 163 yards, 1 TD, 30 DYAR, 16.5% DVOA)

Ben Hartsock, CAR: Hartsock has caught five passes for 35 yards and one touchdown in his last four seasons. Worse yet, he no longer gets to play tambourine in Hunter Smith's band (which has been renamed The Hunter Smith Band). He is milking the last drops of veteran special teamer career value. Soon, you will not be able to find him: not here in "Going Deep," and not where quality Christian rock albums by NFL punters are sold.

Will Heller, DET: Heller is a veteran complimentary piece who has spent his career providing blocks. He can effectively chip on the outside or from an H-back like position in the run front. He has a good overall understanding of all blocking principles. He's not a feared receiving threat, which is why he usually surprises about one unsuspecting defense each year with a touchdown catch. (2011 stats: 6-for-12, 42 yards, -32 DYAR, -43.4% DVOA)

Mike Higgins, NO: The Saints promoted Higgins from the practice squad after David Thomas suffered a concussion in November. The undrafted rookie from Nebraska-Omaha caught a 4-yard pass in the regular season and a 10-yarder against the Niners in the playoffs. He could stick with the Saints as a special teamer this year.

Michael Hoomanawanui, STL: "Illinois Mike" led the Rams in receiving during the 2010 preseason, but then promptly turned into "Injured Mike," missing 16 out of 32 games in his first two years. With 2011 second-round pick Lance Kendricks figuring to fill the Dustin Keller role in new offensive coordinator Brian Schottenheimer's system, Hoomanawanui will be relegated to the Matthew Mulligan role, which doesn't bode well for his receiving production. (2011 stats: 7-for-13, 83 yards, -25 DYAR, -35.4% DVOA)

David Johnson, PIT: Johnson might be listed as a backup to starting tight end Heath Miller, but he spent plenty of time in the backfield (57 plays, by our count) and actually started all 16 games. Nevertheless, Todd Haley makes his role for 2012 uncertain. In 2011, Haley's Chiefs used two or more tight ends at a frequency that ranked in the bottom half of the NFL, and Kansas City tight ends only played 30 snaps in the backfield combined. Also foreboding for Johnson is that Haley's personal sidekick, second tight end Leonard Pope, signed with the Steelers in April. (2011 stats: 12-for-14, 91 yards, 1 TD, 16 DYAR, 8.9% DVOA)

Reggie Kelly, FA: Kelly has developed a line of Southern-style specialty foods called Kyvan: barbecue sauces, salsas, pecan pies, and so on. Between Kelly's delicacies and Tony Gonzalez's health-conscious cookbook, Falcons tight ends may be the NFL's biggest foodies. Kelly had just two receptions last year, and he was a free agent at press time, so it may be time to kick those pecan pies into high gear.

Donald Lee, CIN: Provided veteran smarts and hands as Jermaine Gresham's backup, and re-signed in April for another year as the No. 2 tight end in Cincy. Age and injury history are a concern, but he's effective enough in two-tight end sets. (2011 stats: 11-for-13, 115 yards, 15 DYAR, 9.3% DVOA)

Jeron Mastrud, MIA: Mastrud has started five games in two years and caught one 8-yard pass against the Chargers last season. The team re-signed him as an exclusive rights free agent for 2012, because no matter what else goes wrong for the Dolphins, they will never be stuck without an experienced, slow-footed H-back.

Anthony McCoy, SEA: John Carlson landing on injured reserve and Cameron Morrah opening the season on the PUP list pressed McCoy into service as the No. 2 tight end behind Zach Miller. With Carlson gone to Minnesota, McCoy has the inside track on the No. 2 job again, but we have a feeling that might mean fewer two-tight end sets and more three-wide sets from Darrell Bevell's offense. (2011 stats: 13-for-24, 146 yards, -41 DYAR, -32.7% DVOA)

Zach Miller, JAC: The bad news for this sure-handed move tight end is that he missed most of last season with a shoulder injury that required surgery. The good news is that with Seattle Zach Miller becoming irrelevant in fantasy football, nobody will accidentally draft this version. (2010 stats: 20-for-26, 216 yards, 1 TD, 35 DYAR, 13.5% DVOA)

Cameron Morrah, SEA: Morrah opened the 2011 season on the PUP list with a toe injury before catching six passes for 74 yards in nine games, including four starts. Morrah was a bit raw coming out of Cal in 2009; better health and a full offseason make him the favorite over Anthony McCoy for the third spot on the depth chart. (Other 2011 stats: 6-for-13, -22 DYAR, -31.8% DVOA)

Matthew Mulligan, STL: A career practice-squader who served stints with the Titans and Dolphins, Mulligan finally earned a regular role in his third season with the Jets, starting nine games as the Jets second tight end after Jeff Cumberland injured his Achilles. Mulligan caught a 41-yard pass in the season finale, which must have impressed the Rams enough to sign him as a free agent. (2011 stats: 5-for-9, 58 yards, -23 DYAR, -45.6% DVOA)

Jake O'Connell, KC: O'Connell had more games played (eight) than receptions (seven) in 2011, but the Chiefs thought enough of his blocking ability that they signed him to an extension in February. (2011 stats: 7-for-12, 52 yards, -22 DYAR, -34.9% DVOA)

Michael Palmer, ATL: The Falcons appear convinced that Palmer can step right into a starting role when Tony Gonzalez retires. They have been developing him for two seasons, and they have studiously avoided all of the "next Jermichael Finley" types in the last two draft classes. Palmer has responded with pedestrian production, but there just aren't many footballs to go around for role players in the Falcons offense. Palmer has never caught a pass longer than 11 yards in his career; the longest pass even thrown to him last season traveled just 13 yards in the air. It is hard to project Palmer as a worthy successor to Gonzo, but the Falcons may be banking that they will not have to make that decision for another decade or so. (2011 stats: 10-for-16, 72 yards, 1 TD, -23 DYAR, -28.8% DVOA)

Bear Pascoe, NYG: Not many players get to set career highs in the Super Bowl, but that's what happened for Pascoe when he had four catches for 33 yards after the Giants' other two tight ends went down with injury. He re-signed as an exclusive rights free agent in April, but the addition of Martellus Bennett may not leave him with a space on the roster. (2011 stats: 12-for-16, 136 yards, 21 DYAR, 12.7% DVOA)

Niles Paul, WAS: This 2011 fifth-round pick out of Nebraska played mostly on special teams as a rookie. The Redskins are moving him to tight end for 2012, but he's very small for the position. At 6-foot-1, he'll be tied with Richard Brockel and Delanie Walker as the league's shortest tight end, and at roughly 230 pounds he'll be second behind Jordan Cameron as the league's lightest tight end.

Logan Paulsen, WAS: Injury and suspension turned Paulsen into Washington's first-string tight end for the last month of the season, but the return of Fred Davis and Chris Cooley knocks him back down the depth chart. He didn't catch a pass last year in a game where both Davis and Cooley were active. (2011 stats: 11-for-19, 138 yards, 3 DYAR, -4.9% DVOA)

David Paulson, PIT: For your convenience, here is a condensed version of Paulson's scouting report: He isn't big, he isn't fast, he isn't agile, he didn't do much damage in the passing game at Oregon, but man does he work hard! You know, the kind of seventh-round pick who will either end up on the trash heap of NFL draft history or overcome it all to star in a Bob Costas video essay on *Sunday Night Football* three years from now.

Justin Peelle, FA: Peelle's football career, which began in the Bay Area as a high school freshman, came full circle in 2011 when he signed with San Francisco. The 49ers acquired him to help fill the hole created when blocking tight end Nate Byham tore his ACL during training camp, but Peelle ended up spending additional time as an injury replacement at fullback in wins against Arizona and Seattle. Byham's return in 2012 means Peelle's career is likely over unless a bull market for 33-year-old blocking tight ends emerges in the coming months. (2011 stats: 1-for-4, 19 yards, -11 DYAR, -50.3% DVOA)

Zack Pianalto, TB: Pianalto missed most of his senior season at North Carolina with a broken fibula. He was cut after training camp with the Bills but caught on with the Bucs and had four catches in very occasional action as a third tight end. (2011 stats: 4-for-5, 40 yards, 12 DYAR, 24.7% DVOA)

Zach Potter, JAC: Primarily a blocking tight end, Potter was on the field more than ever due to Zach Miller's shoulder injury and Marcedes Lewis' subpar play. Being the lone survivor of the three-man Jaguars tight end unit is really more of a *Hunger Games* trope though, so we're all a bit disappointed. (2011 stats: 5-for-6, 50 yards, 2 DYAR, -1.6% DVOA)

Andrew Quarless, GB: Quarless proved in the absence of Jermichael Finley in 2010 that he can be an adequate starter ... as long as he's the fourth or fifth option in a sophisticated, well-oiled offense. Quarless can split into the slot as a short-area receiver, and he's comfortable enough coming out of the backfield as a quasi H-back. As a traditional line-of-scrimmage tight end, he may not have a dynamic enough initial burst to consistently create separation off the line, and his blocking has never been characterized as "overpowering." (2010 stats: 21-for-33, 1 TD, 2 DYAR, -6.6% DVOA)

Richard Quinn, WAS: This blocking specialist is another piece of evidence in the case of Josh McDaniels vs. Reasonable Drafting. Denver blew the 64th overall pick on him in 2009, then cut him after two years. Quinn missed most of 2011 with a torn MCL and is probably just training camp fodder.

Allen Reisner, MIN: Because Reisner is essentially the opposite of a marquee name and only appeared in five games last season (registering one reception for five yards and zero of everything else), we'll let his hilariously choppy Wikipedia bio from May do the work here: "Minnesota Vikings Reisner was signed by the Minnesota Vikings as an undrafted free agent following the end of the NFL lockout on July 26, 2011. He was born and raised in Marion, Iowa. Allen is laid back and enjoys interactions with fans. Reisner was released from the Vikings on October 4, 2011. Reisner was signed back to the Vikings October 5, 2011 and placed on practice squad. He was signed to the Minnesota Vikings on November 26, 2011." Couldn't have said it better ourselves.

Adrien Robinson, NYG: After the draft, Giants GM Jerry Reese referred to Robinson as "the JPP of tight ends." Like JPP, he has freakish physical attributes; he's 6-foot-5, 270 pounds, and runs a 4.57 forty. Also like JPP, he had limited college production, with only 12 catches in his senior year at Cincinnati. Tight ends coach Mike Pope needs to spend a while polishing this raw gem, but he could be a fantasy player to watch in 2013 and beyond.

Evan Rodriguez, CHI: Character concerns were Rodriguez's biggest red flag coming out. He began his collegiate career at West Virginia but transferred to Temple after being accused of felony assault from an alleged confrontation with a female residence hall advisor. The Bears, not surprisingly, say they've done extensive research on the athletic hybrid player and are confident in his maturity. They're more confident in his running ability. They plan on using Rodriguez as a fullback-slash-"move player", which, in essence, is an H-back (or a poor man's Aaron Hernandez).

Dante Rosario, SD: Rosario was released by the Dolphins after two games in 2011. Luckily for him, John Fox could not bear to see one of his former mediocre skill position players out on the street, so Fox brought Rosario to Denver to catch about one pass per game during the Tebow Silliness portion of the season. Rosario is now in San Diego, where Norv Turner is talking seriously about keeping four tight ends on the roster, because if there is one force in the universe stronger than Fox's obsession with underwhelming tight ends, it's Turner's gift for absurdity. (2011 stats: 7-for-11, 117 yards, 12 DYAR, 10.0% DVOA)

Weslye Saunders, PIT: If we were to build a model that predicts training camp cuts, Saunders would be the perfect test case this year. He entered the league as an undrafted free agent in 2011 after obstruction of NCAA justice cost him his senior season at South Carolina. In his rookie season with the Steelers, he played more than the typical third-stringer thanks to Pittsburgh's propensity for multiple-tight end sets, but a PED suspension will cost him the first four games of 2012. In April, Pittsburgh put the writing on the wall by signing Leonard Pope and drafting David Paulson. The only way Saunders makes the final roster is if Pittsburgh cuts "Wesley" Saunders by accident.

Brad Smelley, CLE: 21 of his 27 regular-season receptions as a Crimson Tide senior moved the chains, tipping off his likely role should he find a way through the thicket of tight end/H-back types amassed by Mike Holmgren in Cleveland. Smelly amassed a 74 percent career catch rate on passing downs, so he's got the hands to stick in that role. His older brother is Chris Smelley, who washed out as South Carolina's quarterback, thus at least positioning Brad as the least pungent Smelley.

Alex Smith, CLE: Smith was a star tight end at Stanford long before Andrew Luck showed up, but nowadays, the Bahamanian will be hard pressed to hang on to a roster spot with the tight end-rich Browns. The Freeport Falcons beckon. (2011 stats: 14-for-25, 131 yards, 1 TD, -1 DYAR, -7.6% DVOA)

Andre Smith, IND: Great example of how a person's behavior can unfairly impact others: When you Google "Andre Smith Bears," near the top of first page search results you get one of those infamous pictures of Bengals offensive tackle Andre Smith running his pro day forty-yard dash topless. This Andre Smith weighs about 1½ Olsen Twins less than the former Alabama tackle, but he's in the NFL for the same reason: to block. At 6-foot-4, 270 pounds, Smith (who was elevated from Chicago's practice squad to the active roster in Week 10 last year) is a thumper of a tight end, cut somewhat in the shape of former Bear Brandon Manumaleuna. Picked up off waivers by Indianapolis in May.

Lee Smith, BUF: There's a glut of tight ends circling around the bottom of the Buffalo roster, but Smith is the most likely to see significant playing time in 2012 because he is far and away the best in-line blocker. Of course,

TIGHT ENDS

those same skills that will get Smith on the field will keep him off the stat sheet; he has only caught four passes in his career and is currently averaging a whopping 1.2 yards per game.

Stephen Spach, FA: When a tight end has seven times as many fullback assignments (21) as receiving targets (3), you know he's the definition of "blocking tight end." After languishing in the free-agent market for several months at age 30, you know Spach is approaching the definition of "former blocking tight end."

Matt Spaeth, CHI: In Chicago Spaeth has been essentially a lighter version of what he was in Pittsburgh: a lanky red-zone target and fairly versatile blocking specialist. His frame is as long as his 6-foot-7 size suggests. This helps him as a short-area receiver but can compromise his blocking power in a phone booth. Spaeth doesn't always bring the dynamic energy typical of a No. 2 blocking tight end, but he's experienced in the role. (2011 stats: 7-for-11, 50 yards, 2 TD, 5 DYAR, -0.3% DVOA)

Kory Sperry, SD: Sperry re-signed with the Chargers despite not being tendered as a restricted free agent. The talk before 2011 that he could have a breakout season didn't pan out, as he only had one catch despite the opportunity created by Antonio Gates' injury struggles. Ladarius Green may cost him his roster spot.

Craig Stevens, TEN: Stevens is the rare Cal product worthy of being called "a hell of a player" by FO's resident Stanford alum Ben Muth. He's a superb blocking tight end and has solid enough hands to be an underneath threat if he needs to. Stevens snagged a four-year, $15 million deal from Titans brass after the season and should continue to be a big (if fantasy-irrelevant) part of what they do on offense going forward. (2011 stats: 9-of-14, 166 yards, 1 TD, 39 DYAR, 35.5% DVOA)

Ryan Taylor, GB: Taylor is cut in that H-back mold that the Packers like. His versatility at North Carolina, where he played tight end, linebacker and special teams, was appealing enough to inspire the Packers to take a shot with him in the seventh round. In order to make the active roster, Taylor will have to a) thrive on special teams and b) present more value as an offensive player than 2011 fifth-round pick D.J. Williams (no easy task).

David Thomas, NO: Thomas missed most of the season with concussion issues. His role in the passing game will be scaled back even if he is healthy; there is no sense giving 30 passes per year to the second tight end when Jimmy Graham is the first tight end. Thomas made himself useful during minicamps by throwing passes for the quarterback-thin Saints during drills. Don't get too good at it, Dave, or they will start playing hardball with your contract. (2011 stats: 5-for-9, 16 yards, -36 DYAR, -71.4% DVOA)

Julius Thomas, DEN: Jimmy Graham, raw athleticism, basketball experience, Antonio Gates, seam route, blah blah blah. Thomas missed most of his rookie year with an ankle injury, and finally had surgery in April, which makes him a 50-50 bet to be ready for training camp. (2011 stats: 1-for-7, 5 yards, -31 DYAR, -77.6% DVOA)

D.J. Williams, GB: It will be difficult for Williams to carve out a niche in Green Bay's loaded offense this season. He contributed in sub packages midway through last season but wasn't able to keep a firm grasp on his role when Andrew Quarless returned from a knee injury. Gritty and versatile, Williams doesn't have the size to be a traditional every-down tight end, but he'd fit in an offense that needs a movement player who can handle H-back duties.

Will Yeatman, MIA: Yeatman was a) born in Italy; b) part of a family of dedicated lacrosse players; c) a two-sport football and lacrosse star in high school; d) arrested for driving on the sidewalk while intoxicated at Notre Dame in 2008; e) signed just after the lockout by lacrosse-loving Patriots coach Bill Belichick; f) waived by the Patriots, a team with few needs at tight end, in early September; and g) signed by the Dolphins, a team that is always in need of a new midfielder, a few weeks later. The lacrosse press follows Yeatman's every NFL move, because nothing validates the popularity of one sport like glomming onto a player's minimal success in another.

2012 Kicker Projections

Listed below are the 2012 KUBIAK projections for kickers. Because of the inconsistency of field-goal percentage from year to year, kickers are projected almost entirely based on team forecasts, although a handful of individual factors do come into play:

• More experience leads to a slightly higher field-goal percentage in general, with the biggest jump between a kicker's rookie and sophomore seasons.

• Kickers with a better career field-goal percentage tend to get more attempts, although they are not necessarily more accurate.

• Field-goal percentage on kicks over 40 yards tends to regress to the mean.

Kickers are also listed with a Risk of Green, Yellow, or Red, as explained in the introduction to the section on quarterbacks.

Fantasy Kicker Projections, 2012

Kicker	Team	FG	Pct	XP	Pts	Risk
Robbie Gould	CHI	34-40	85%	39	141	Yellow
Mason Crosby	GB	27-30	90%	55	136	Green
Stephen Gostkowski	NE	25-29	86%	60	135	Green
Jason Hanson	DET	32-38	84%	35	131	Green
Matt Bryant	ATL	27-32	84%	46	127	Green
Rian Lindell	BUF	29-34	85%	37	124	Yellow
Nick Folk	NYJ	29-34	85%	36	123	Red
Lawrence Tynes	NYG	27-32	84%	40	121	Green
Sebastian Janikowski	OAK	29-36	81%	34	121	Green
Matt Prater	DEN	27-32	84%	40	121	Yellow
Rob Bironas	TEN	29-34	85%	32	119	Green
Bill Cundiff	BAL	26-32	81%	41	119	Yellow
David Akers	SF	28-36	78%	34	118	Green
Ryan Succop	KC	28-35	80%	33	117	Green
Adam Vinatieri	IND	28-34	82%	32	116	Green
Garrett Hartley	NO	22-28	79%	50	116	Red
Shaun Suisham	PIT	24-30	80%	44	116	Green
Randy Bullock	HOU	24-32	75%	41	113	Red
Mike Nugent	CIN	26-32	81%	35	113	Green
Olindo Mare	CAR	21-25	84%	50	113	Green
Alex Henery	PHI	21-25	84%	46	109	Green
Jay Feely	ARI	25-30	83%	34	109	Green
Dan Bailey	DAL	24-30	80%	37	109	Green
Ryan Longwell	MIN	24-30	80%	36	108	Yellow
Graham Gano	WAS	24-32	75%	34	106	Green
Josh Scobee	JAC	24-29	83%	27	99	Green
Steven Hauschka	SEA	23-29	79%	29	98	Yellow
Nate Kaeding	SD	19-25	76%	40	97	Red
Connor Barth	TB	21-29	72%	32	95	Green
Phil Dawson	CLE	23-29	79%	24	93	Green
Dan Carpenter	MIA	21-28	75%	28	91	Green
Greg Zuerlein	STL	19-24	79%	25	82	Red

Other kickers who may win jobs

Kicker	Team	FG	Pct	XP	Pts	Risk
Shayne Graham	HOU	24-33	73%	41	113	Red
Josh Brown	NYJ	27-33	82%	35	116	Green
John Kasay	NO	26-31	84%	49	127	Green
Nick Novak	SD	21-27	78%	40	103	Green

2012 Fantasy Defense Projections

Listed below are the 2012 KUBIAK projections for fantasy team defense. The projection method is discussed in an essay in *Pro Football Prospectus 2006*, the key conclusions of which were:

• Schedule strength is very important for projecting fantasy defense.

• Categories used for scoring in fantasy defense have no consistency from year-to-year whatsoever, with the exception of sacks and interceptions.

Fumble recoveries and defensive touchdowns are forecast solely based on the projected sacks and interceptions, rather than the team's totals in these categories from a year ago. This is why the 2012 projections will look very different from the fantasy defense values from the 2011 season. Safeties and shutouts are not common enough to have a significant effect on the projections. Team defenses are also projected with Risk factor of Green, Yellow, or Red; this is based on the team's projection compared to performance in recent seasons.

In addition to projection of separate categories, we also give an overall total based on our generic fantasy scoring formula: one point for a sack, two points for a fumble recovery or interception, and six points for a touchdown. Special teams touchdowns are listed separately and are not included in the fantasy scoring total listed.

Fantasy Team Defense Projections, 2012

Team	Fant Pts	Sack	Int	Fum Rec	Def TD	Risk	ST TD
NYJ	126	43.6	18.7	11.9	3.5	Yellow	0.9
BUF	124	40.7	19.9	11.9	3.3	Red	0.7
NE	121	42.0	20.7	10.4	2.9	Green	0.7
GB	121	41.5	21.3	9.8	2.9	Green	0.6
HOU	119	43.3	18.6	10.5	2.9	Red	0.6
BAL	118	38.0	17.5	8.2	4.8	Yellow	0.5
CIN	118	39.7	18.5	10.8	3.3	Red	0.7
CHI	117	38.9	18.1	13.3	2.6	Yellow	2.1
MIN	116	43.5	16.5	14.0	1.9	Red	0.8
PHI	116	44.4	15.4	13.4	2.3	Yellow	0.5
SEA	116	42.0	18.0	11.6	2.4	Yellow	0.8
ATL	115	38.5	17.1	10.8	3.5	Yellow	1.0
MIA	115	40.5	17.7	12.0	2.4	Red	0.8
DET	113	40.7	17.7	11.5	2.3	Green	0.9
NYG	112	44.2	14.4	12.3	2.5	Green	0.5
SF	111	43.0	17.3	8.4	2.8	Yellow	0.6
TEN	106	34.7	17.7	9.5	2.8	Red	0.8
PIT	105	45.4	13.7	12.0	1.4	Red	0.8
CAR	104	33.6	15.7	9.8	3.3	Red	0.7
DAL	104	37.8	14.5	10.0	2.9	Yellow	0.3
NO	101	34.3	14.6	10.6	2.8	Red	0.9
ARI	100	39.0	15.2	10.6	1.6	Yellow	2.6
KC	99	32.8	17.0	8.1	2.7	Yellow	0.3
WAS	98	36.8	16.5	8.9	1.8	Yellow	0.7
CLE	98	30.6	16.0	9.9	2.6	Red	1.0
STL	98	35.8	15.0	9.7	2.1	Red	0.6
DEN	97	35.4	13.6	9.1	2.7	Yellow	0.9
SD	95	30.2	14.9	9.8	2.6	Yellow	0.7
IND	92	32.5	11.9	11.5	2.0	Yellow	0.5
OAK	90	28.7	16.8	6.7	2.3	Green	0.7
JAC	86	33.9	14.7	9.8	0.5	Yellow	0.5
TB	79	24.0	13.1	6.4	2.6	Green	1.0

Projected Defensive Leaders, 2012

Solo Tackles			Total Tackles			Sacks			Interceptions		
Player	Team	Tkl	Player	Team	Tkl	Player	Team	Sacks	Player	Team	INT
N.Bowman	SF	103	C.Greenway	MIN	149	D.Ware	DAL	15.8	E.Reed	BAL	5.0
J.Laurinaitis	STL	101	N.Bowman	SF	146	J.Pierre-Paul	NYG	13.5	D.Revis	NYJ	4.3
D.Jackson	CLE	101	J.Anderson	CAR	145	J.Allen	MIN	13.1	A.Samuel	ATL	4.3
C.Greenway	MIN	93	L.Fletcher	WAS	144	J.Babin	PHI	12.8	N.Clements	CIN	4.1
C.McCarthy	TEN	92	P.Angerer	IND	132	A.Smith	SF	12.7	C.Tillman	CHI	4.0
J.Anderson	CAR	92	P.Willis	SF	132	T.Hali	KC	12.6	T.J.Ward	CLE	3.9
D.Washington	ARI	92	D.Jackson	CLE	130	M.Williams	BUF	12.2	C.Rogers	SF	3.7
P.Willis	SF	91	J.Mayo	NE	129	V.Miller	DEN	11.5	C.Bailey	DEN	3.7
S.Tulloch	DET	91	D.Sharpton	HOU	127	C.Barwin	HOU	11.5	A.Cromartie	NYJ	3.7
D.Johnson	KC	91	J.Laurinaitis	STL	125	C.Avril	DET	11.2	T.Jennings	CHI	3.6
D.Sharpton	HOU	91	C.McCarthy	TEN	125	C.Wake	MIA	11.1	C.Woodson	GB	3.3

College Football Introduction and Statistical Toolbox

College football is simultaneously surging and dealing with more negativity than ever before. At this point, fans can find just about every notable game on television, the value of television contracts is somewhere between "lucrative" and "ridiculous," and, quite simply, the depth of talent and entertainment potential are off the charts. Just look at what college football will be offering in 2012:

In the southeast, Alabama and LSU return quite a few important pieces from their respective 2012 BCS Championship Game runs, Georgia and Florida are well-positioned to take steps forward, and after a couple of years of fits and starts, it appears Florida State could very well be a Top 10 team this season.

In the midwest, Brady Hoke has already taken Michigan to more BCS bowls than his predecessor, Rich Rodriguez, did; in his second year, he welcomes back oft-electrifying quarterback Denard Robinson and is putting together Michigan's best recruiting class in recent history. Meanwhile, Urban Meyer is taking the reins at Ohio State, and Wisconsin looks to once again plug in a new quarterback and keep running over opponents with Montee Ball.

West Virginia joins the Big 12 Conference and may be an immediate contender for the conference title. What this move lacks in geographic continuity, it makes up for in stylistic congruity. Head coach Dana Holgorsen's Mountaineers will fit right in with the offense-heavy Big 12, while Texas and its unforgiving defense will attempt to tame every explosive "O" that comes its way.

Out west, Oregon could be just as dangerous as ever and USC appears to be back among the elite (and off of a two-year postseason ban). The Pac-12 North welcomes former Texas Tech coach Mike Leach to Washington State, and welcomes back a wealth of exciting offensive talent. Washington quarterback Keith Price, California receiver Keenan Allen, Stanford running back Stepfan Taylor, and Oregon State receivers Markus Wheaton and Brandin Cooks will all be fun to watch.

Throughout the country, one can find intriguing plotlines. Plus, perhaps the most appealing recent plot twist of all (to some, anyway), took place in conference rooms in June: Beginning in the 2014 season, college football will be implementing a four-team playoff. It is far from a perfect fix. It might not help undefeated mid-major teams much, and if you thought differentiating between the No. 2 and No. 3 teams was hard, the difference between No. 4 and No. 5 could be even smaller. Still, for much of the college football fanbase, this is a wonderful development.

So why, then, are there so many negative feelings in the land of college football? Easy: Not only were many turned off by last year's BCS Championship Game (Alabama was a controversial choice to face undefeated LSU in the championship, since No. 3 Oklahoma State was also 11-1, and LSU had already defeated Alabama in Tuscaloosa), but off the field, the sport has had one of its worst years ever. In July, Butch Davis was fired by North Carolina for his role in a long series of improper benefits. In August, imprisoned Miami booster Nevin Shapiro "named names," so to speak, and attempted to take down the Miami football program with his admission of an incredible series of improper benefits to Miami players. In April, successful Arkansas head coach Bobby Petrino was fired for lying about an "inappropriate relationship" with a former Razorbacks volleyball player following a motorcycle wreck. And of course, anybody reading this book knows about the nightmare of the Jerry Sandusky scandal at Penn State. The story of the 2011 encompassed as much off-the-field negativity as it did any sort of on-field excitement. If the story of the 2012 season sticks to what takes place on the gridiron, the narrative could be much more positive.

For nine years, Brian Fremeau has been developing and tweaking the drive-based Fremeau Efficiency Index (FEI) and its companion statistics; for the last five years, Bill Connelly's research has explored play-by-play data, developing measures of efficiency and ex-

COLLEGE FOOTBALL INTRODUCTION AND STATISTICAL TOOLBOX

plosiveness and creating his system, the S&P+ ratings. Both systems are schedule-adjusted and effective in both evaluating teams and uncovering strengths and weaknesses. The combination of the two ratings, the F/+, provides the best of both worlds.

The College Statistical Toolbox section that follows this introduction explains the methodology of FEI, S&P+, F/+ and other stats you will encounter in the college chapters of this book. There are similarities to Football Outsiders' NFL-based DVOA ratings in the combined approach, but college football presents a unique set of challenges different from the NFL. All football stats must be adjusted according to context, but how? If Team A and Team B do not play one another and don't share any common opponents, how can their stats be effectively compared? Should a team from the SEC or Big 12 be measured against that of an average team in its own conference, or an average FBS team? With seven years of full data, we are still only scratching the surface with these measures, but the recent progress has been both swift and exciting.

This book devotes a chapter to each of the six BCS conferences, and a seventh chapter covering the best of the independents and non-AQ teams. For each team detailed, we give a snapshot of the statistical profile from 2011 and projections for 2012, along with a summary of that team's keys to the upcoming season. Player and coaching personnel changes, offensive and defensive advantages and deficiencies, and schedule highlights and pitfalls are all discussed by our team of college football writers. The top prospects for the 2013 NFL draft are listed at the end of each team segment. An asterisk denotes a player who may or may not enter the draft as a junior eligible.

Each chapter concludes with a Win Probability table. For each of the 124 FBS teams, we project the likelihood of every possible regular season record, both overall and in conference games only. We hope the Win Probability tables provide a broader understanding of our projections and the impact of strength of schedule on team records.

By taking two different statistical approaches to reach one exciting series of answers to college football's most important questions, we feel we are at the forefront of the ongoing debates. Enjoy the college football section of *Football Outsiders Almanac 2012*, and join us at www.FootballOutsiders.com/college throughout the season.

College Statistics Toolbox

Regular readers of FootballOutsiders.com may be familiar with the FEI and Varsity Numbers columns and their respective stats published throughout the year. Others may be learning about our advanced approach to college football stats analysis for the first time by reading this book. In either case, this College Statistics Toolbox section is highly recommended reading before getting into the conference chapters. The stats that form the building blocks for F/+, FEI, and S&P+ are constantly being updated and refined.

Each team profile in the conference chapters begins with a statistical snapshot (defending BCS champion Alabama is presented here as a sample). Within each chapter, teams are organized by division (or conference in the final chapter) and Projected F/+ rank. The projected overall and conference records —rounded from the team's projected Mean Wins— are listed alongside the team name in the header. Estimates of offensive and defensive starters returning in 2012 were collected from team websites, spring media guides, and other reliable sources. All other stats and rankings provided in the team snapshot are explained below.

No. 1 Alabama Crimson Tide (11-1, 7-1)
2011: 12-1 (7-1) / F/+ #1 / FEI #3 / S&P+ #1

Program F/+	-199.7	1	Returning Starters: 7 OFF, 4 DEF		2-Yr Recruiting Rank		1
2011 Offense			**2011 Defense**		**2011 Field Position**		
Offensive F/+	+13.6%	7	**Defensive F/+**	+22.5%	1	Field Position Advantage	0.528	19
Offensive FEI:	0.418	11	Defensive FEI	-0.78	1	**2012 Projections**		
Offensive S&P+	113.7	8	Defensive S&P+	199.8	1	**Mean Wins**	11.1	
Rushing S&P+	145.3	3	Rushing S&P+	170.2	1	Proj. F/+	+35.4%	1
Passing S&P+	149.0	3	Passing S&P+	187.2	1	Offensive F/+	+14.2%	6
Standard Downs S&P+	144.4	1	Standard Downs S&P+	156.4	2	Defensive F/+	+21.2%	1
Passing Downs S&P+	137.7	10	Passing Downs S&P+	210.5	1	Strength of Schedule	0.094	9

Drive-by-Drive Data

Fremeau Efficiency Index: Fremeau Efficiency Index (FEI) analysis begins with drive data instead of play-by-play data and is processed according to key principles. A team is rewarded for playing well against a strong opponent, win or lose, and is punished more severely for playing poorly against bad teams than it is rewarded for playing well against bad teams.

To calculate FEI, the nearly 20,000 possessions in every season of major college football are filtered to eliminate first-half clock-kills and end-of-game garbage drives and scores. A scoring rate analysis of the remaining possessions then determines the baseline possession efficiency expectations against which each team is measured. Game Efficiency is the composite possession-by-possession efficiency of a team over the course of a game, a measurement of the success of its offensive, defensive, and special teams units' essential goals: to maximize the team's own scoring opportunities and to minimize those of its opponent. Finally, each team's FEI rating synthesizes its season-long Game Efficiency data, adjusted for the strength of its opposition; special emphasis is placed on quality performance against good teams, win or lose.

Offensive and Defensive FEI: Game Efficiency is a composite assessment of the possession-by-possession performance of team over the course of a game. In order to isolate the relative performance of the offense and defense, more factors are evaluated.

First, we ran a regression on the national scoring rates of tens of thousands of college football drives according to starting field position. The result represents the value of field position in terms of points expected to be scored by an average offense against an average defense—1.4 points per possession from its own 15-yard line, 2.3 points per possession from its own 40-yard line, and so on. These expected points are called Field Position Value (FPV).

Next, we ran a regression on the value of drive-ending field position according to national special teams scoring expectations. To determine the true national baseline for field-goal range, we took into account not only the 2,200 field goals attempted annually, but also the 1,400 punts kicked from opponent territory each year. In other words, if a team has an average field goal unit and a coach with an average penchant for risk-taking, the offensive value of reaching the opponent's 35-yard line is equal to the number of made field goals from that distance divided by the number of attempts plus the number of punts from that distance.

Touchdowns credit the offense with 6.96 points of drive-ending value, the value of a touchdown adjusted according to national point-after rates. Safeties have a drive-ending value of negative two points. All other offensive results are credited with a drive-ending value of zero.

Offensive efficiency is then calculated as the total drive-ending value earned by the offense divided by the sum of its offensive FPV over the course of the game. Defensive efficiency is calculated the same way using the opponent's offensive drive-ending value and FPV. Offensive and defensive efficiency are calibrated as a rating above or below zero—a good offense has a positive rating and a good defense has a negative one. These numbers are represented in the college chapters as Unadjusted Offense and Unadjusted Defense.

Offensive FEI and Defensive FEI are the opponent-adjusted values of offensive and defensive efficiency. As with FEI, the adjustments are weighted according to both the strength of the opponent and the relative significance of the result. Efficiency against a team's best competition is given more relevance weight in the formula.

Field Position Advantage (FPA): FPA was developed in order to more accurately describe the management of field position over the course of a game. For each team, we calculate the sum of the FPV for each of its offensive series. Then, we add in a full touchdown value (6.96 points) for each non-offensive score earned by the team. (This accounts for the field position value of special teams and defensive returns reaching the end zone versus tripping up at the one-yard line.) Special teams turnovers and onside kicks surrendered have an FPV of zero. The sum of the FPV of every possession in the game for both teams represents the total field position at stake in the contest. FPA represents each given team's share of that total field position.

FPA is a description of which team controlled field position in the game and by how much. Two teams that face equal field position over the course of a game will each have an FPA of .500. Winning the field position battle is quite valuable. College football teams that play with an FPA over .500 win two-thirds of the time. Teams that play with an FPA over .600 win 90 percent of the time.

Other Drive-Based Data: The conference chapters and team capsules include references to other possession efficiency statistics we track that further break down offensive, defensive, and special teams performance.

• Available Yards represent yards earned by the offense divided by total possible yardage measured from starting field position on each drive to the end zone.

• Explosive Drives are the percentage of drives that average at least 10 yards per play.

• Methodical Drives are the percentage of drives that run 10 or more plays.

• Value Drives are the percentage of drives beginning on the offense's own side of the field that reach at least the opponent's 30-yard line.

• Special Teams Efficiency is the composite expected value generated by a team's field goal, punt, punt return, kickoff, and kickoff return units.

Play-by-Play Data

Success Rates: Our play-by-play analysis was introduced throughout the 2008 season in Bill Connelly's Varsity Numbers columns. More than 600,000 plays over five seasons in college football have been collected and evaluated to determine baselines for success for every situational down in a game. Similarly to DVOA, basic success rates are determined by national standards. The distinction for college football is in defining the standards of success. We use the following determination of a "successful" play:

• First down success = 50 percent of necessary yardage
• Second down success = 70 percent of necessary yardage
• Third/Fourth down success = 100 percent of necessary yardage

On a per play basis, these form the standards of efficiency for every offense in college football. Defensive success rates are based on preventing the same standards of achievement.

Equivalent Points and Points per Play: All yards are not created equal. A 10-yard gain from a team's own 15-yard line does not have the same value as a 10-yard gain that goes from the opponent's 10-yard line into the end zone. Based on expected scoring rates similar to FPV described above, we can calculate a point value for each play in a drive. Equivalent Points (EqPts) are calculated by subtracting the value of the resulting yard line from the initial yard line of a given play. This assigns credit to the yards that are most associated with scoring points, the end goal in any possession.

With EqPts, the game can be broken down and built back up again in a number of ways. With the addition of penalties, turnovers and special teams play, EqPts provides an accurate assessment of how a game was played on a play-by-play basis. We also use it to create a measure called Points per Play (PPP), representative of a team's or an individual player's explosiveness.

S&P: Like OPS (on-base percentage plus slugging average) in baseball, we created a measure that combines consistency with power. S&P represents a combination of efficiency (Success Rates) and explosiveness (Points per Play) to most accurately represent the effectiveness of a team or individual player.

A boom-or-bust running back may have a strong yards per carry average and PPP, but his low Success Rate will lower his S&P. A consistent running back who gains between 4 and 6 yards every play, on the other hand, will have a strong Success Rate but possibly low PPP. The best offenses in the country can maximize both efficiency and explosiveness on a down-by-down basis. Reciprocally, the best defenses can limit both.

S&P+: As with the FEI stats discussed above, context matters in college football. Adjustments are made to the S&P unadjusted data with a formula that takes into account a team's production, the quality of the opponent, and the quality of the opponent's opponent. To eliminate the noise of less-informative blowout stats, we filtered the play-by-play data to include only those that took place when the game was "close." This excludes plays where the score margin is larger than 24 points in the first quarter, 21 points in the second quarter, or 16 points in the second half.

The result is S&P+, representing a team's efficiency and explosiveness as compared to all other teams in college football. S&P+ values are calibrated around an average rating of 100. An above-average team, offensively or defensively, will have an S&P+ rating greater than 100. A below-average team will have an S&P+ rating lower than 100.

In the team capsules in each conference chapter, the S&P+ ratings are broken down further as follows:

• Rushing S&P+ includes only running plays, and unlike standard college statistics, does not include sacks.
• Passing S&P+ includes sacks and passing plays.

- Passing Downs S&P+ includes second-and-8 or more, third-and-5 or more, and fourth-and-5 or more. These divisions were determined based on raw S&P data showing a clear distinction in Success Rates as compared with Standard Downs.
- Standard Downs S&P+ includes all close-game plays not defined as Passing Downs.

POE and Adjusted POE: The collegiate stepchild of DYAR, POE stands for Points Over Expected. It is a running back-specific measure that compares a runner's EqPts output to what an average back would have done with carries in the same situations against the same opponents. The Adjusted POE figure, used most in these chapters, adjusts POE to account for the relative strength (or weakness) of the offensive line.

Adjusted Score: Taking a team's single-game S&P+ for both offense and defense, and applying it to a normal distribution of points scored in a given season, can give us an interesting, descriptive look at a team's performance in a given game and season. Adjusting for pace and opponent, Adjusted Score asks the same question of every team in every game: if Team A had played a perfectly average opponent in a given game, how would they have fared? Adj. Score allows us to look at in-season trends as well, since the week-to-week baseline is opponent-independent.

Combination Data

F/+: Introduced in *Football Outsiders Almanac 2009*, the F/+ measure combines FEI and S&P+. There is a clear distinction between the two individual approaches, and merging the two diminishes certain outliers caused by the quirks of each method. The resulting metric is both powerfully predictive and sensibly evaluative.

Program and Projected F/+: Relative to the pros, college football teams are much more consistent in year-to-year performance. Breakout seasons and catastrophic collapses certainly occur, but generally speaking, teams can be expected to play within a reasonable range of their baseline program expectations. The idea of a Football Outsiders program rating began with the introduction of Program FEI in *Pro Football Prospectus 2008* as a way to represent those individual baseline expectations.

As the strength of the F/+ system has been fortified with more seasons of full drive-by-drive and play-by-play data, the Program F/+ measure has emerged. Program F/+ is calculated from five years of FEI and S&P+ data. The result not only represents the status of each team's program power, but provides the first step in projecting future success.

The Projected F/+ found in the following chapters starts by combining Program F/+ (weighted more toward recent seasons) with measures of two-year recruiting success (using Rivals.com ratings for signees who actually ended up enrolling at each school) and offensive and defensive performance. We adjust that baseline with transition factors like returning offensive and defensive starters, talent lost to the NFL Draft, and disproportional success on passing downs. The result, Projected F/+, is a more accurate predictor of next-year success than any other data we have tested or used to date.

Strength of Schedule: Unlike other rating systems, our Strength of Schedule (SOS) calculation is not a simple average of the Projected FEI data of each team's opponents. Instead, it is calculated from a "privileged" perspective, representing the likelihood that an elite team (typical top-five team) would win every game on the given schedule. The distinction is valid. For any elite team, playing No. 1 Alabama and No. 124 Texas State in a two-game stretch is certainly more difficult than playing No. 60 Oregon State and No. 61 Louisiana Tech. An average rating might judge these schedules to be equal.

The likelihood of an undefeated season is calculated as the product of Projected Win Expectations (PWE) for each game on the schedule. PWEs are based on an assessment of five years of FEI data and the records of teams of varying strengths against one another. Roughly speaking, an elite team may have a 65 percent chance of defeating a team ranked No. 10, a 75 percent chance of defeating a team ranked No. 20, and a 90 percent chance of defeating a team ranked No. 40. Combined, the elite team has a 44 percent likelihood of defeating all three ($0.65 \times 0.75 \times 0.90 = 0.439$).

A lower SOS rating represents a lower likelihood of an elite team running the table—a stronger schedule. For our calculations of FBS versus FCS games, the likelihood of victory is considered to be 100 percent for top-40 teams and gradually declines from there to around 85 percent for the worst FBS teams.

Mean Wins and Win Probabilities: To project records for each team, we use Projected F/+ and PWE formulas to estimate the likelihood of victory for a given team in its individual games. The probabilities for winning each game are added together to represent the average number of wins the team is expected to tally over the course of its scheduled games. Potential conference championship games and bowl games are not included.

The projected records listed next to each team name in the conference chapters are rounded from the mean wins data listed in the team capsule. Mean Wins are not intended to represent projected outcomes of specific matchups, rather they are our most accurate forecast for the team's season as a whole. The correlation of mean wins to actual wins is 0.69 for all games, 0.61 for conference games.

The Win Probability tables that appear in each conference chapter are also based on the game-by-game PWE data for each team. The likelihood for each record is rounded to the nearest whole percent.

Brian Fremeau and Bill Connelly

Atlantic Coast Conference

For a conference mocked for so long as a one-man show, the extended absence of a real national power hasn't done much for the ACC's reputation. Since the collapse of Florida State's reign of terror over the rest of the league a decade ago, the ACC champion is 1-10 in BCS games, and the conference as a whole joins the MAC, Conference USA and Sun Belt as the only leagues that have failed to put a team in the top five of the final polls. Seven of those 11 years, the ACC has failed to put a team in the top ten. In 2011, on the heels of another dismal postseason punctuated by Clemson's 70-33 Orange Bowl incineration at the hands of West Virginia, it failed to put a team in the top 20. Altogether, ACC teams were 2-6 last winter in bowl games and 0-2 in BCS games, extending their failure to beat a single ranked team from another conference (based on the final polls) all season. The power void has yawned so wide for so long, it's beginning to seem permanent.

Such a mediocre state of affairs has positioned the league as the Sick Man of college football in the ongoing wars of realignment. The waves of chaos rippling across the continent in search of increasingly lucrative television money have left the ACC straddling the divide between the Haves and Have Nots—an ironic twist, considering the ACC's bold move to solidify its place at the adult's table by poaching Miami, Virginia Tech, and Boston College at the Big East's expense back in 2003. With the dominoes continuing to fall at a rapid pace last year, the ACC made another night-time raid into Big East territory to annex Pittsburgh and Syracuse, both scheduled to expand the league's ranks to 14 members in 2013. But it may have been too little, too late: When the ACC's newly renegotiated, $3.6 billion television deal with ESPN this spring failed to match the record sums in recently renegotiated deals by the Big 12, Pac-12, and SEC, several Florida State officials began nakedly lobbying for a move to the Big 12.

If Florida State leaves the fold, though, the ACC will lose its most valuable asset in its most vulnerable sport, and it will almost certainly lose another (either Clemson or Virginia Tech) to give the Big 12 the even dozen teams it needs under NCAA rules to reboot its conference championship game. That, in turn, will diminish the ACC's influence in the ongoing process of converting the BCS into a four-team playoff by 2014, and make it exponentially more difficult to place a team in that playoff (or to reap the as yet undetermined financial benefits certain to come with it). Once that happens, its seat at the table may be permanently removed.

As of publication, that scenario remains speculative. And in the murky game of brinksmanship that is conference realignment, much surer machinations have come and gone or fallen apart at the last minute. But if FSU follows through on its threat, and the ACC watches its BCS birthright slip through its fingers as a result, there will be no shortage of postmortems looking over the last ten years and wondering what took so long.

ATLANTIC

No. 7 Florida State Seminoles (10-2, 7-1)
2011: 9-4 (5-3) / F/+ #8 / FEI #12 / S&P+ #11

Program F/+	-199.9	16	Returning Starters: 6 OFF, 8 DEF		2-Yr Recruiting Rank		3
2011 Offense			**2011 Defense**		**2011 Field Position**		
Offensive F/+	+4.9%	32	**Defensive F/+**	+10.4%	6	Field Position Advantage	0.560	3
Offensive FEI:	0.052	54	Defensive FEI	-0.51	10	**2012 Projections**		
Offensive S&P+	89.5	56	Defensive S&P+	150.5	5	**Mean Wins**	10.3	
Rushing S&P+	103.8	56	Rushing S&P+	134.6	9	Proj. F/+	+22.2%	7
Passing S&P+	105.1	54	Passing S&P+	129.8	12	Offensive F/+	+7.0%	30
Standard Downs S&P+	108.1	41	Standard Downs S&P+	127.7	7	Defensive F/+	+15.2%	4
Passing Downs S&P+	114.6	35	Passing Downs S&P+	134.7	15	Strength of Schedule	0.370	56

Many years ago, when some brilliant, overworked hack coined the phrase "on paper" to describe the gap between potential and reality, he probably had Florida State football in mind. A full decade after ceding their crown as perennial ACC overlords, the Seminoles are still pulling in first-rate recruiting classes, still rolling out blue-chip lineups that command respect from the preseason polls, and still finding ways to fall short of their potential. Since the league expanded to twelve teams in 2006, the 'Noles have failed to win the ACC championship they used to take for granted and have dropped at least two games to unranked opponents in every season. In three of those six years, they've finished outside of the polls their own selves. For prognosticators, Florida State is the team that cried "wolf."

This is useful to remember when scanning another depth chart that appears too stacked to fail. There's the senior quarterback, E.J. Manuel, surrounded by a familiar corps of veteran skill players and a mostly intact offensive line. There are ten returning starters from the best overall defense in the conference, four of them on a nasty-looking defensive line, where a handful of five-star backups threaten to hijack the rotation. (Behind NFL-bound starters Brandon Jenkins, Bjoern Werner and Everett Dawkins are a number of highly-regarded recruits, including sophomore Timmy Jernigan and incoming freshmen Mario Edwards and Eddie Goldman.) The schedule is as friendly as ever, featuring not just one but *two* FCS patsies out of the gate as well as both Clemson and Florida coming to Tallahassee. The stench of decay that defined the end of the Bobby Bowden era has been replaced by an air of energy and momentum under Bowden's successor, Jimbo Fisher. And after all, three of FSU's four regular season losses last year *did* come with Manuel either on the bench or severely limited by a shoulder injury.

That's how easy it is. But even with a healthy quarterback and a nightmarish D, the Seminoles won't be turning any corners without a leap forward from the offensive line, a unit so inconsistent and besieged by injuries by the end of the year that it was forced to conscript four true freshmen into the starting lineup for the bowl game. The all-important left tackle spot was won this spring—at least temporarily—by a new convert from the defensive line, sophomore Cameron Erving. As always, talent and expectations here are a given. Until there's stability up front, FSU stock remains *caveat emptor.*

Top 2013 NFL Prospects: CB Xavier Rhodes* (1), DE-OLB Brandon Jenkins (1-2), DE Bjoern Werner* (1-2), QB E.J. Manuel (2-3), CB/KR Greg Reid (4-5), K Dustin Hopkins (6), DT Everett Dawkins (6-7).

No. 21 Clemson Tigers (9-3, 6-2)

2011: 10-4 (6-2) / F/+ #36 / FEI #32 / S&P+ #48

Program F/+		-199.9	18	Returning Starters: 6 OFF, 7 DEF			2-Yr Recruiting Rank		9
2011 Offense				**2011 Defense**			**2011 Field Position**		
Offensive F/+		+7.7%	20	Defensive F/+		-2.3%	76	Field Position Advantage	0.501	59
Offensive FEI:		0.326	22	Defensive FEI		-0.134	50	**2012 Projections**		
Offensive S&P+		101.4	20	Defensive S&P+		110.4	69	Mean Wins	8.7	
Rushing S&P+		106.8	47	Rushing S&P+		94.4	82	Proj. F/+	+13.9%	21
Passing S&P+		131.1	12	Passing S&P+		99.3	65	Offensive F/+	+12.0%	10
Standard Downs S&P+		113.0	25	Standard Downs S&P+		96.0	80	Defensive F/+	+1.9%	51
Passing Downs S&P+		127.3	19	Passing Downs S&P+		119.4	31	Strength of Schedule	0.295	44

With a different ending, 2011 might have been a triumph for Clemson. Fueled by an 8-0 start, the Tigers climbed as high as fifth in the BCS standings, spent nearly half the season ranked in the top 10, clinched their first conference championship in two decades and finished the year in their first-ever BCS game. And yet, on the heels of the Orange Bowl debacle against West Virginia, the whole exercise felt like just another missed opportunity. With visions of a dark horse national title run beginning to form in late October, Clemson proceeded to drop four of its last six, all by double digits, including back-to-back blowouts at the hands of lowly N.C. State and archrival South Carolina that stung even more than the most lopsided rout in BCS history. For lack of a better term, it was a very *Clemson* collapse.

So the lack of momentum for the 2012 bandwagon is fairly easy to grasp, despite the usual trappings on the depth chart. Junior Tajh Boyd was the best quarterback in the conference as a first-year starter, thanks in no small part to the up-tempo spread attack imported by new offensive coordinator Chad Morris and the emergence of the most productive freshman in the nation, dreadlocked dynamo Sammy Watkins (1,225 receiving yards, 9.9 yards per target). By himself, Watkins is a cruise missile awaiting launch from anywhere on the field; as part of an arsenal that also includes All-ACC tailback Andre Ellington (1,178 rushing yards, plus-7.3 Adj. POE) and veteran targets Jaron Brown and DeAndre Hopkins, he'll have plenty of opportunities to strike against man coverage. The question on offense isn't one of firepower, but of consistency.

The question on defense, on the other hand, is one of evolution. The historic embarrassment in the Orange Bowl sounded the death knell for coordinator Kevin Steele, who ceded the title a few days later to longtime Oklahoma defensive coordinator Brent Venables. First priority: rebuilding a defensive line that lost two seniors, sack master Andre Branch and defensive tackle Brandon Thompson, who went on the second day of the draft. Then it's on to a veteran but oft-victimized secondary, which found itself on the wrong end of too many career games by opposing quarterbacks. Not that Venables didn't have his share of long afternoons in the pass-happy Big 12, but given the current state of ACC offenses, another string of shootouts in his new job will carry a slightly different connotation.

Top 2013 NFL Prospects: RB Andre Ellington (2-3); C Dalton Freeman (3-4); DE Malliciah Goodman (3-4); DB Rashard Hall (7-FA).

No. 45 Boston College Eagles (6-6, 4-4)

2011: 4-8 (3-5) / F/+ #69 / FEI #64 / S&P+ #82

Program F/+		-199.9	36	Returning Starters: 9 OFF, 9 DEF			2-Yr Recruiting Rank		44
2011 Offense				**2011 Defense**			**2011 Field Position**		
Offensive F/+		-5.2%	88	Defensive F/+		+1.8%	48	Field Position Advantage	0.536	14
Offensive FEI:		-0.26	95	Defensive FEI		-0.187	40	**2012 Projections**		
Offensive S&P+		74.5	99	Defensive S&P+		114.9	59	Mean Wins	6.4	
Rushing S&P+		90.9	95	Rushing S&P+		98.7	65	Proj. F/+	+5.8%	45
Passing S&P+		85.1	98	Passing S&P+		112.7	28	Offensive F/+	-1.5%	64
Standard Downs S&P+		85.3	109	Standard Downs S&P+		101.4	54	Defensive F/+	+7.3%	22
Passing Downs S&P+		99.9	72	Passing Downs S&P+		119.9	30	Strength of Schedule	0.284	40

At one point last season, Boston College was 1-6 with losses to Northwestern, Central Florida, Duke, and Wake Forest, and coach Frank Spaziani was beginning to catch glimpses of the grim reaper around every corner. He wasn't the only one: Normally patient B.C. fans and blogs, frustrated by the impending end of a 12-year bowl streak, spent the rest of the year openly rooting for the reaper.

Few of the skeptics were swayed by three wins in the last five games, which still left the Eagles with a depressing 4-8 record and the most anemic offense in the conference. But it was enough for athletic director Gene DeFillipo, who apparently felt that Spaziani was owed another year out of either a) Loyalty, for filling the void in early 2009 after DeFillipo followed through on his promise to fire popular head coach Jeff Jagodzinski for interviewing with the New York Jets, or b) Sympathy, for presiding over a lineup plagued by injuries and youth. The offense played the entire season without its best running back or receiver, and the defense largely held its own despite being forced to rely on 26 starts from six different true freshmen.

At any rate, the prospect of a more seasoned, stable lineup doesn't make for much of a silver lining in an offseason already filled with its share of clouds: All-Universe linebacker Luke Kuechly left early for the draft, career rushing leader Montel Harris was booted from the team and a pair of returning defensive starters (defensive end Max Holloway and safety Hampton Hughes) turned down the standard fifth year of eligibility to get on with life. Among those who decided to stick it out, the most notable is junior quarterback Chase Rettig, who enters his third season as a starter with last year's top three rushers, top four receivers and four-fifths of the starting offensive line in tow. That group didn't do much together in 2011—the Eagles failed to crack 30 points against FBS competition, and cracked 20 just once without the help of a defensive score—and it will be adjusting to its third new coordinator in as many years. But there is nowhere to go but up.

Top 2013 NFL Prospects: DT Kaleb Ramsey (6), TE Chris Pantale (7-FA).

No. 53 N.C. State Wolfpack (6-6, 3-5)
2011: 8-5 (4-4) / F/+ #67 / FEI #50 / S&P+ #77

Program F/+	-200.0	58	Returning Starters: 7 OFF, 7 DEF			2-Yr Recruiting Rank		62
2011 Offense			**2011 Defense**			**2011 Field Position**		
Offensive F/+	+0.7%	57	**Defensive F/+**	-2.0%	73	Field Position Advantage	0.484	81
Offensive FEI:	0.012	58	Defensive FEI	-0.314	25	**2012 Projections**		
Offensive S&P+	75.3	98	Defensive S&P+	115.2	57	**Mean Wins**	6.0	
Rushing S&P+	78.2	115	Rushing S&P+	95.8	76	Proj. F/+	+2.4%	53
Passing S&P+	96.0	74	Passing S&P+	105.0	45	Offensive F/+	+2.2%	46
Standard Downs S&P+	85.7	108	Standard Downs S&P+	101.6	52	Defensive F/+	+0.2%	62
Passing Downs S&P+	103.0	60	Passing Downs S&P+	108.3	48	Strength of Schedule	0.389	61

A few years back, pop philosopher Malcolm Gladwell introduced the pseudo-intellectuals, self-help gurus and aspiring Earl Woodses of America to the "10,000-hour rule," the idea that mastering any complex skill at an elite level requires 10,000 hours of dedicated practice. If you or someone you know subscribes to this idea, or some variant thereof, have I got the college football team for you: Entering year six under head coach Tom O'Brien, N.C. State's fate is more dependent on fourth- and fifth-year vets than any other outfit in the ACC, and maybe the country.

The starting quarterback, Mike Glennon, is a senior with draft-worthy measurables and now a full season as a starter under his belt; ditto the leading returning rusher (James Washington) and receiver (Tobais Palmer). The offensive line returns five old hands who have combined for 111 career starts. On defense, the top four members of the secondary have combined for 114 career starts. Other seniors and fourth-year juniors are atop the depth chart at receiver, tight end, two of the three linebacker slots and both ends of the defensive line. These guys have played *a lot* of football together.

The line from quantity to quality, though, is still a little shaky—especially on the offensive line, whose venerable members presided over an attack last year that finished 115th in Rushing S&P+ and 98th in sacks allowed, barely avoiding the ACC cellar on both counts. Despite a relatively forgiving schedule, at various points the Wolfpack were blown out by

Cincinnati, shut out by Florida State, and upset by division doormats Wake Forest and Boston College. If not for an unsustainably high turnover margin (plus-14 for the year, best in the ACC and easily the best of the O'Brien era), they would have likely fallen short of the postseason for the third time in five years and subjected their coach to an offseason of incessant "hot seat" chatter.

Still, the fact that a struggling outfit did rally with a pair of November upsets over North Carolina and Clemson and an incredible fourth quarter comeback against Maryland to score a bowl bid does speak to a general upward trend over the course of the season, as does the bowl win over Louisville. Glennon, in particular, showed up late with 11 touchdown passes in the three-game winning streak to close the year, arguably the three best games of his career. Given a little run support, enough time in the pocket and a go-to target to replace the departed T.J. Graham, it's not out of the question for Glennon to pass the Pack into dark horse contention in the Atlantic Division. But it would require a leap well beyond the natural progression.

Top 2013 NFL Prospects: CB David Amerson* (1), QB Mike Glennon (3-4), DB Brandan Bishop (6-7), OT R.J. Mattes (6-7).

No. 72 Maryland Terrapins (4-8, 2-6)
2011: 2-10 (1-7) / F/+ #96 / FEI #81 / S&P+ #95

Program F/+	-200.0	61	Returning Starters: 5 OFF, 8 DEF			2-Yr Recruiting Rank		47
2011 Offense			**2011 Defense**			**2011 Field Position**		
Offensive F/+	-5.1%	87	**Defensive F/+**	-3.0%	83	Field Position Advantage	0.494	68
Offensive FEI:	-0.102	75	Defensive FEI	0.148	74	**2012 Projections**		
Offensive S&P+	80.8	79	Defensive S&P+	99.6	94	**Mean Wins**	3.9	
Rushing S&P+	109.1	41	Rushing S&P+	83.0	112	Proj. F/+	-3.9%	72
Passing S&P+	86.9	93	Passing S&P+	100.1	61	Offensive F/+	-5.1%	82
Standard Downs S&P+	100.8	63	Standard Downs S&P+	94.1	85	Defensive F/+	+1.2%	54
Passing Downs S&P+	109.9	45	Passing Downs S&P+	97.0	72	Strength of Schedule	0.324	48

Randy Edsall arrived in College Park last January touting Maryland as his "dream job," and immediately found himself in a nightmare. On the field, the Terps dropped their last ten against FBS competition, eight of them by double digits, including blowout losses at the hands of Temple and Wake Forest and blown fourth quarter leads against Clemson and N.C. State. Off the field, holdovers from the Ralph Friedgen regime rejected the coaching transplant en masse—a staggering 24 players transferred out of the program during Edsall's first 14 months on the job, led by Wisconsin-bound quarterback Danny O'Brien and fellow starters at left tackle and safety. One venerable columnist in Washington compared Edsall to Captain Queeg in *Mutiny on the Bounty*; another skipped the literary pretense and called for his head after just one year.

None of which has seemed to throw Edsall, who has brushed off the attrition with a kind of "those who stay will be champions" resolve, even if, for now, he'll settle for a middling bowl game. To kick off the reboot, he ditched both coordinators in favor of Mike Locksley (a dysfunctional flop in his own right as head coach at New Mexico, but a proven recruiter in his native D.C.) on offense and former Houston defensive coordinator Brian Stewart to resuscitate the most generous defense in the conference. On paper, this group also happens to be one of the most promising in 2012: The front seven alone boasts at least three future draft picks at defensive end (senior Joe Vellano, a two-time All-ACC pick) and linebacker (seniors Kenny Tate and Demetrius Hartsfield), along with four other regulars (tackles Andre Monroe and Keith Bowers and linebackers Alex Twine and L.A. Goree) who were thrown into the fire as freshmen. Tate and Monroe are also two of five likely starters on defense who missed at least three full games in 2011 to injury, which should be more than enough—at minimum—to pull the stat line out of the gutter.

It's harder to say the same about an offense that now rests on the unpredictable arm of junior C.J. Brown, a scrambly junior who completed just south of 50 percent of his passes last year and probably necessitates a full-time emphasis on the zone read. Whatever they do scheme-wise, the Terps are in desperate need of someone who fits the description of "playmaker." Even with three fairly reliable senior targets in the passing game (Kevin Dorsey, Kerry Boykins and tight end Matt Furstenburg), the best hope for a breakthrough is five-star freshman Stefon Diggs, a DeSean Jackson type who passed on national offers to become Maryland's biggest local recruiting victory in ages. If Diggs or prep teammate Wes Brown can't produce an immediate spark, it may be a short-lived trend.

Top 2013 NFL Prospects: LB Kenny Tate (2-3), DT Joe Vellano (3-4), LB Demetrius Hartsfield (6).

No. 81 Wake Forest Demon Deacons (4-8, 2-6)

2011: 6-7 (5-3) / F/+ #66 / FEI #55 / S&P+ #71

Program F/+	-200.0	57	Returning Starters: 3 OFF, 7 DEF			2-Yr Recruiting Rank		90
2011 Offense			**2011 Defense**			**2011 Field Position**		
Offensive F/+	+2.3%	47	**Defensive F/+**	-3.4%	86	Field Position Advantage	0.483	83
Offensive FEI:	0.178	36	Defensive FEI	0.012	62	**2012 Projections**		
Offensive S&P+	86.6	62	Defensive S&P+	109.6	72	**Mean Wins**	3.8	
Rushing S&P+	97.4	78	Rushing S&P+	95.6	77	Proj. F/+	-6.7%	81
Passing S&P+	107.5	47	Passing S&P+	94.3	77	Offensive F/+	-3.0%	69
Standard Downs S&P+	99.2	69	Standard Downs S&P+	92.9	89	Defensive F/+	-3.7%	84
Passing Downs S&P+	112.9	39	Passing Downs S&P+	106.3	51	Strength of Schedule	0.287	41

Jim Grobe once won an ACC championship at Wake Forest, which might as well have come with a guarantee of lifetime tenure. In the meantime, though, Grobe has managed the equally unprecedented task of keeping the Demon Deacons mostly in the black. Last year's trip to the Music City Bowl was their fourth bowl bid in six years, a run that quietly stands as Wake's best since World War II. Few coaches in the ACC or anywhere else have done as much with so little, or with so little credit.

So if there's anyone in the business with patience enough to handle, say, a chaotic overhaul of the entire offensive line, it's Jim Grobe. Not only is senior center Garrick Williams the only Deacon who's started a game up front, but aside from a few garbage snaps in last year's win over Gardner-Webb, only one other returning lineman (sophomore guard Colin Summers) has even set foot on the field, turning the spring into an impromptu round of *Winston-Salem Idol* for the 300-pound set. Given the beating he's already taken over his first two years on the job, junior quarterback Tanner Price may want to consider employing his redshirt year, or at least an insurance policy.

But seriously, folks, despite the reassuring presence of Price and steady junior receiver Michael Campanaro, this is a "rebuilding" year for the offense, to put it mildly. The defense is in significantly better shape, largely thanks to cornerbacks Merrill Noel and Kenny Okoro (42 combined career starts), a long-in-the-tooth linebacker corps and All-ACC nose guard Nikita Whitlock, an undersized junior who was reportedly set to join the Army before landing a late scholarship offer from Wake in 2009; he's repaid the favor by emerging as the most improbably disruptive lineman in the conference at a relatively bite-sized 260 pounds. (According to the school's scales, anyway, which means he's probably slightly smaller in reality.) That's the kind of underdog story programs like Wake Forest thrive on. But it's going to take a few more we haven't heard yet to get the Deacons back to .500.

Top 2013 NFL Prospects: CB Kenny Okoro (7).

COASTAL

No. 18 Virginia Tech Hokies (9-3, 5-3)
2011: 11-3 (7-1) / F/+ #22 / FEI #27 / S&P+ #18

Program F/+	-199.8	10	Returning Starters: 3 OFF, 9 DEF			2-Yr Recruiting Rank		28
2011 Offense			**2011 Defense**			**2011 Field Position**		
Offensive F/+	+5.9%	25	**Defensive F/+**	+5.4%	21	Field Position Advantage	0.504	52
Offensive FEI:	0.196	35	Defensive FEI	-0.286	31	**2012 Projections**		
Offensive S&P+	94.0	44	Defensive S&P+	140.1	11	**Mean Wins**	8.8	
Rushing S&P+	105.9	51	Rushing S&P+	114.1	27	Proj. F/+	+16.6%	18
Passing S&P+	110.9	37	Passing S&P+	137.5	9	Offensive F/+	+4.3%	34
Standard Downs S&P+	104.6	53	Standard Downs S&P+	114.9	23	Defensive F/+	+12.3%	11
Passing Downs S&P+	106.1	54	Passing Downs S&P+	152.0	4	Strength of Schedule	0.330	50

Virginia Tech hasn't settled comfortably enough in the penthouse yet to start taking 11-win seasons that end in a BCS game for granted. But it has spent enough time at the top of the ACC standings to discern a great campaign from a merely good one, and the 2011 edition—sullied by an 0-3 record against ranked teams—clearly fell into the latter category. The Hokies' 38-10 flop against Clemson in December was the most lopsided score in the history of the ACC Championship Game, and their final poll position (21st) following an overtime Sugar Bowl loss to Michigan was Tech's worst since joining the conference in 2004. Stranger still, BeamerBall fell 67 spots in our special teams efficiency rankings last season after leading the nation in 2010.

Years from now, in fact, it's entirely possible that the 2011 Hokies will be best remembered for introducing America to quarterback Logan Thomas, a 6-foot-6, 250-pound specimen whose first season as a starter resulted in a school record for total yards (3,482) and swoons from pro scouts over his combination of size and mobility. Thomas is still relatively raw as a passer, and will be asked to take on more responsibility in a traditionally run-oriented scheme with first-rounder David Wilson yielding the tailback job to a pair of freshmen (redshirt Michael Holmes and early enrollee J.C. Coleman) who have never touched the ball in a college game. He'll also be working behind four new starters on a totally rebuilt offensive line. Given a little time and a senior-laden receiving corps, though, the ceiling for the passing game is as high as it's been in ages.

The other notable development was the return of the vaunted "Lunch Pail" defense to its usual form after a year in the wilderness: The Hokies finished among the top dozen defenses nationally in both total and scoring D for the seventh time in eight years and ranked in the Top 25 of Defensive F/+ for the fourth time in five years—despite losing three starters (defensive tackle Antoine Hopkins and linebackers Bruce Taylor and Jeron Gouveia-Winslow) for the entire second half of the season. All three are back this fall, giving Tech nine players with significant starting experience along the front seven to go with a pair of two-year starters (Kyle Fuller and Antone Exum) at the corners. As long as there are two safeties somewhere on the roster who aren't prone to major breakdowns, and they're identified in time for the opener against Georgia Tech, the offense can take its sweet time revving up. As usual.

Top 2013 NFL Prospects: QB Logan Thomas* (1), DE James Gayle* (3), LB Bruce Taylor (3-4), CB Kyle Fuller* (4).

No. 30 Georgia Tech Yellow Jackets (8-4, 5-3)

2011: 8-5 (5-3) / F/+ #48 / FEI #43 / S&P+ #33

Program F/+	-199.9	37	Returning Starters: 8 OFF, 7 DEF			2-Yr Recruiting Rank		42
2011 Offense			**2011 Defense**			**2011 Field Position**		
Offensive F/+	+6.8%	23	**Defensive F/+**	-1.0%	62	Field Position Advantage	0.484	82
Offensive FEI:	0.4	16	Defensive FEI	0.01	61	**2012 Projections**		
Offensive S&P+	105.7	16	Defensive S&P+	113.9	62	**Mean Wins**	7.7	
Rushing S&P+	125.2	11	Rushing S&P+	86.9	101	Proj. F/+	+10.5%	30
Passing S&P+	117.4	25	Passing S&P+	105.1	43	Offensive F/+	+9.6%	19
Standard Downs S&P+	115.3	24	Standard Downs S&P+	92.5	93	Defensive F/+	+0.9%	58
Passing Downs S&P+	127.8	17	Passing Downs S&P+	92.5	79	Strength of Schedule	0.249	34

Paul Johnson isn't going to say it in public, and would just as soon have no one else notice—in general, Paul Johnson is the kind of coach who'd just as soon have outsiders ignore his team altogether—but when he collapses on his office desk at night, this is the offense he dreams about. The quarterback, Tevin Washington, is a fifth-year senior with 17 career starts in Johnson's throwback triple-option scheme. The leading rushers at both "A-Back" (Orwin Smith) and "B-Back" (David Sims) are back. Five regular starters return up front, each heading into his fourth or fifth year in the program, who have grown up together over the course of 79 combined starts the last two years. Essentially the same group last year returned Georgia Tech to the top of the conference in terms of both yards and points per game.

The glaring exception is in the role of resident deep threat, where Stephen Hill left a 6-foot-5, 215-pound void en route to the second round of the draft. Wide receiver may not seem like a priority for an offense that keeps the ball on the ground roughly 80 percent of the time, year-in, year-out, but Hill and All-ACC predecessor Demaryius Thomas have amply demonstrated how much more dangerous the Yellow Jackets can be with a big target to exploit secondaries obsessed with stopping the run. Hill led the nation by a mile last year by averaging more than 29 yards per catch and played a central role in the Jackets' biggest wins, over North Carolina and Clemson. Forty percent of Georgia Tech's drives qualified as either explosive or methodical, third-most nationally. Among the returnees, sophomores Jeff Greene and Darren Waller have the same intimidating size, but no receiver on the roster has caught a pass in a college game.

Unlike last year's backloaded schedule, there's no learning curve, either, with a season-defining trip to Virginia Tech (the winner of the Tech-Tech game has gone on to win the Atlantic Division all seven years there has been an Atlantic Division) set for opening night and critical division dates with Virginia and Miami hot on its heels. If the Jackets come out of that stretch in the driver's seat, this has the makings of Johnson's best team in his five years in Atlanta. If not, another second- or third-tier bowl game is par for the course.

Top 2013 NFL Prospects: G Omoregie Uzzi (3), LB Jeremiah Attaochu* (3-4), CB Rod Sweeting (4).

No. 33 North Carolina Tar Heels (9-3, 5-3)

2011: 7-6 (3-5) / F/+ #49 / FEI #41 / S&P+ #44

Program F/+	-199.9	38	Returning Starters: 8 OFF, 5 DEF			2-Yr Recruiting Rank		23
2011 Offense			**2011 Defense**			**2011 Field Position**		
Offensive F/+	+4.7%	33	**Defensive F/+**	+0.2%	56	Field Position Advantage	0.475	98
Offensive FEI:	0.108	46	Defensive FEI	-0.304	26	**2012 Projections**		
Offensive S&P+	95.6	36	Defensive S&P+	118.9	48	**Mean Wins**	8.8	
Rushing S&P+	98.9	72	Rushing S&P+	108.8	42	Proj. F/+	+10.1%	33
Passing S&P+	121.1	20	Passing S&P+	102.8	53	Offensive F/+	+8.6%	23
Standard Downs S&P+	109.9	36	Standard Downs S&P+	105.1	44	Defensive F/+	+1.6%	52
Passing Downs S&P+	128.7	14	Passing Downs S&P+	102.0	61	Strength of Schedule	0.591	84

North Carolina hired Butch Davis in late 2006 to rescue the program from a decade of obscurity, and in a way it got its wish: Amid two utterly nondescript seasons on the field—8-5 in 2010, 7-6 last year, with a pair of middling bowl games—Davis' administration lay in the path of a sweeping NCAA probe that made UNC one of the most scrutinized teams in college football. By time the smoke finally cleared this spring, 16 Tar Heel wins had been wiped from the books, 14 players (almost all starters) had missed at least one game as a result of the scandal, six had been ruled permanently ineligible, both Davis and short-lived successor Everett Withers had been kicked to the curb, former assistant coach John Blake had been effectively excommunicated from the profession and the program had been slapped with sanctions, including scholarship losses and a one-year bowl ban. In terms of drama and intrigue, it may have been the most memorable run in school history.

On the field, however... well, nothing has really changed. The "Return to Normalcy" phase will be overseen by new head coach Larry Fedora, fresh from a four-year stint at Southern Miss that ended with a Conference USA championship and a school record for wins in a season. The bar won't be nearly that high in Chapel Hill, at least not right away, though there's plenty of reason for quiet optimism on offense. First, there's junior quarterback Bryn Renner, who led the ACC in pass efficiency as a first-year starter, and All-ACC tailback Giovani Bernard, who bounced back from a torn ACL in 2010 to churn out 1,615 yards from scrimmage. Then, there's the officially "grizzled" offensive line, returning four full-time starters. And there's Fedora himself, an evangelist for the kind of fast-paced spread scheme Carolina fans have been clamoring after for years.

Still, there is still no proven, reliable game-breaker on offense on the order of departed wide receiver Dwight Jones, and there's considerably less hype over a defense that had earned a reputation—especially along the front four—as a steady pipeline to the NFL. Raw-yet-promising defensive tackle Sylvester Williams may extend that trend another year, but minus all-conference sack leaders Quinton Coples (first round to the Jets) and Zach Brown (second round to the Titans), the once-formidable pass rush is suddenly looking for answers, and the secondary doesn't offer much cushion to find them.

Top 2013 NFL Prospects: G Jonathan Cooper (1-2), LB Kevin Reddick (2), DT Sylvester Williams (2-3), RB Giovani Bernard* (2-3), OT James Hurst* (4).

No. 36 Miami Hurricanes (6-6, 4-4)

2011: 6-6 (3-5) / F/+ #32 / FEI #26 / S&P+ #51

Program F/+	-199.9	31	Returning Starters: 4 OFF, 6 DEF			2-Yr Recruiting Rank		25
2011 Offense			**2011 Defense**			**2011 Field Position**		
Offensive F/+	+9.8%	15	**Defensive F/+**	-3.5%	87	Field Position Advantage	0.478	91
Offensive FEI:	0.563	3	Defensive FEI	0.121	71	**2012 Projections**		
Offensive S&P+	99.8	23	Defensive S&P+	110.0	70	**Mean Wins**	6.2	
Rushing S&P+	110.1	38	Rushing S&P+	109.7	41	Proj. F/+	+8.4%	36
Passing S&P+	124.2	16	Passing S&P+	78.2	109	Offensive F/+	+10.2%	15
Standard Downs S&P+	118.2	17	Standard Downs S&P+	95.9	81	Defensive F/+	-1.8%	68
Passing Downs S&P+	109.6	46	Passing Downs S&P+	101.2	64	Strength of Schedule	0.279	38

Under anything resembling normal circumstances, the exodus from Miami last December might have felt like a bittersweet but well-deserved graduation. Under the actual circumstances in coach Al Golden's first season—a debut defined by mass suspensions, nagging injuries, humbling upsets and looming NCAA sanctions—it must have felt more like a purge. Within a few days of their season-ending loss to Boston College, the 'Canes had sworn off a bowl game, bid farewell to nearly two-thirds of the starting lineup—including six of the eight veterans suspended at least one game for allegedly accepting cash and prizes as recruits from a former booster turned convicted Ponzi schemer—and commenced the Golden era in earnest.

Of course, this is still a program facing an uncertain future at the end of an expansive NCAA investigation, as well as the unenviable task of replacing six draft picks and its starting quarterback in the meantime. Any pretense of an open competition for the job was derailed in February by a back injury to junior Stephen Morris, who didn't take a snap during spring practice but still emerged in front of Memphis transfer Ryan Williams on the post-spring depth chart. There were key absences everywhere: Starting guard Jon Feliciano hurt his knee during a scrimmage, fellow guard Jermaine Johnson missed the spring game and starting linebacker Ramon Buchanan sat out to continue rehabbing the injured knee that cost him the last eight games of 2011. Massive (and massively hyped) offensive lineman Seantrel Henderson, a victim of back and knee injuries as a sophomore, was one of three players suspended for the entire spring for the proverbial violation of team rules, prompting Golden to complain about "constantly weeding" at the start of year two: "When you're trying to improve the program and move the program forward, you can't just weed your garden, you've got to water your garden, too."

On that front, there is a potentially refreshing recruiting class that's already supplied a handful of early enrollees—most notably offensive lineman Ereck Flowers, linebacker Raphael Kirby and junior college transfer Ladarius Gunter, who left the spring listed as a starter at cornerback—and will add a pair of five-star locals this summer at tailback (Duke Johnson) and cornerback (Tracy Howard). But there is no shortage of blue-chip talent among the holdovers, either, which has yet to produce corresponding results on scoreboards, stat sheets, all-conference teams or otherwise. Whatever seeds Golden manages to plant this fall, they'll have to take root amid an ongoing championship drought, with pitch-black clouds forming just over the horizon.

Top 2013 NFL Prospects: S Ray-Ray Armstrong (2), OT Seantrel Henderson* (3-4), S Vaughn Telemaque (4-5).

No. 52 Virginia Cavaliers (6-6, 4-4)

2011: 8-5 (5-3) / F/+ #65 / FEI #56 / S&P+ #57

Program F/+	-200.0	62	Returning Starters: 6 OFF, 5 DEF			2-Yr Recruiting Rank		24
2011 Offense			**2011 Defense**			**2011 Field Position**		
Offensive F/+	+0.6%	58	**Defensive F/+**	+0.1%	57	Field Position Advantage	0.462	106
Offensive FEI:	0.062	51	Defensive FEI	-0.171	45	**2012 Projections**		
Offensive S&P+	83.5	73	Defensive S&P+	121.1	44	**Mean Wins**	5.9	
Rushing S&P+	97.1	81	Rushing S&P+	110.0	40	Proj. F/+	+2.8%	52
Passing S&P+	96.7	70	Passing S&P+	103.0	52	Offensive F/+	+1.9%	50
Standard Downs S&P+	94.2	86	Standard Downs S&P+	116.7	21	Defensive F/+	+0.9%	55
Passing Downs S&P+	98.8	76	Passing Downs S&P+	99.9	65	Strength of Schedule	0.326	49

As remarkable as Virginia's progress was in 2011 under second-year coach Mike London, it was at least as notable for how *unremarkable* it was: The Cavaliers doubled their 2010 win total despite averaging fewer yards and points per game and failing to rank among the top 30 nationally in any major standard statistical category. What to make of an eight-win team that simultaneously a) came within a game of its first ever division title, and b) was slightly outscored over the course of the season?

After four consecutive years in the red, of course, UVA fans aren't about to start asking tough questions about a winner. But by any measure, the step forward in the win column was a precarious one. It took a fourth-quarter comeback to beat hapless Indiana on the final snap of the game, and overtime to put away Idaho; later, the optimism forged in narrow upsets of Georgia Tech, Miami and Florida State in conference play was offset by season-ending flops against Virginia Tech—a 38-0 rout in Charlottesville that extended the Hokies' streak of in-state dominance to eight years and counting—and Auburn in the Chick-Fil-A Bowl. With a dozen starters on their way out, the only relevant number that doesn't point toward a regression in 2012 is an unsightly, minus-7 turnover margin.

The recruiting trail paints a more sustainable picture. Last year, the five highest-ranked signees in London's first full recruiting class—all projected as four-star skill types—all saw the field as true freshmen and are expected to move into the starting lineup as sophomores. (One of them, cornerback Demetrious Nicholson, is already there after starting every game right out of the chute.) This year's crop offers immediate potential on the front seven, courtesy of four-star defensive ends Eli Harold and Michael Moore and linebacker Kwontie Moore (no relation). It also brings the return of prodigal quarterback Phillip Sims, a former Virginia prep star who's transferring home after two years at Alabama and still hoping for an NCAA waiver that will allow him to challenge incumbent Michael Rocco this fall. Not that Sims or anyone else on the current roster is likely to emerge as a messiah for the low-octane offense, regardless of his eligibility. If his defection plays any role in improving the program's

No. 73 Duke Blue Devils (4-8, 2-6)
2011: 3-9 (1-7) / F/+ #77 / FEI #72 / S&P+ #92

Program F/+	-200.1	83	Returning Starters: 8 OFF, 8 DEF			2-Yr Recruiting Rank		79
2011 Offense			**2011 Defense**			**2011 Field Position**		
Offensive F/+	+0.3%	61	Defensive F/+	-6.3%	105	Field Position Advantage	0.522	27
Offensive FEI:	0.155	40	Defensive FEI	0.355	99	**2012 Projections**		
Offensive S&P+	84.3	67	Defensive S&P+	99.2	98	**Mean Wins**	4.2	
Rushing S&P+	96.1	85	Rushing S&P+	89.2	95	Proj. F/+	-4.1%	73
Passing S&P+	103.5	58	Passing S&P+	91.8	87	Offensive F/+	+1.3%	52
Standard Downs S&P+	97.9	78	Standard Downs S&P+	87.7	104	Defensive F/+	-5.4%	98
Passing Downs S&P+	109.2	47	Passing Downs S&P+	85.6	93	Strength of Schedule	0.183	26

At Duke, which hasn't had a winning record since 1994, "success" in football means winning a few here and there and otherwise not doing anything that might embarrass the basketball team. By that standard, the Devils are doing just fine under coach David Cutcliffe, even if they continue to wallow in the conference basement by almost every relevant measure after four unremarkable years. The notable exception is in Cutcliffe's specialty, the passing game, which propelled former quarterback Thaddeus Lewis to the top of the school record books and has senior Sean Renfree nipping at his heels—if for no other reason than that the impotent running game and defense leave no other choice but to keep the ball in the air. Cutcliffe insists Renfree's job is safe after 23 starts over the last two seasons, but a trio of backup QBs (sophomores Anthony Boone and Brandon Connette and true freshman Thomas Sirk) all spent the spring rotating in at other positions in an effort to find someone, *anyone,* who can keep defenses from ganging up on All-ACC receiver Conner Vernon.

The single brightest spot of Cutcliffe's fifth team is its experience: Twenty returning players have at least seven career starts under their belt, all of whom have spent at least three years in the program. The back-loaded schedule sets up for a possible 4-1 start in September (four of the first five games are against Florida International, North Carolina Central, Memphis and Wake Forest), which is probably still not enough to carry the Devils out of their desperate bowl drought once they've gone through the thick of the conference slate. Under the circumstances, though, it may be another 18 years before they get a better chance.

Top 2013 NFL Prospects: QB Sean Renfree (6-7), WR Conner Vernon (7).

Matt Hinton

Projected Win Probabilities For ACC Teams

	Overall Wins											Conference Wins							
ACC Atlantic	12-0	11-1	10-2	9-3	8-4	7-5	6-6	5-7	4-8	3-9	2-10	1-11	0-12	8-0	7-1	6-2	5-3	4-4	3-5	2-6	1-7	0-8
Boston College	-	-	1	7	15	25	26	17	7	2	-	-	-	-	1	4	17	30	29	15	4	-
Clemson	-	3	11	23	28	21	10	3	1	-	-	-	-	3	19	35	28	12	3	-	-	-
Florida State	13	33	32	16	5	1	-	-	-	-	-	-	-	26	43	24	6	1	-	-	-	-
Maryland	-	-	-	-	-	2	9	20	29	25	13	2	-	-	-	-	1	7	21	36	28	7
N.C. State	-	-	-	3	11	21	28	23	11	3	-	-	-	-	-	3	11	27	32	20	6	1
Wake Forest	-	-	-	-	-	2	7	18	30	28	13	2	-	-	-	-	1	4	17	33	33	12
ACC Coastal	12-0	11-1	10-2	9-3	8-4	7-5	6-6	5-7	4-8	3-9	2-10	1-11	0-12	8-0	7-1	6-2	5-3	4-4	3-5	2-6	1-7	0-8
Duke	-	-	-	-	-	3	10	25	32	22	7	1	-	-	-	-	1	4	15	32	34	14
Georgia Tech	-	1	7	19	29	26	13	4	1	-	-	-	-	1	6	21	33	26	11	2	-	-
Miami	-	-	1	6	13	22	25	19	10	3	1	-	-	-	2	10	23	30	23	10	2	-
North Carolina	1	8	21	29	24	12	4	1	-	-	-	-	-	3	16	30	29	16	5	1	-	-
Virginia	-	-	-	3	10	20	27	23	12	4	1	-	-	-	1	6	19	31	27	13	3	-
Virginia Tech	2	8	21	28	23	13	4	1	-	-	-	-	-	3	16	30	29	16	5	1	-	-

Big East Conference

Say what you will about the Big East Conference. The conference has earned most of the negative sentiments it has received.

Yes, it did turn away Penn State 20 years ago.

Yes, it did lose three of its more storied programs (Miami, Virginia Tech, Boston College) about a decade ago.

Yes, it has made curious decisions regarding its awkward football-to-basketball relationship.

Yes, it turned down what, in retrospect, would have been a fantastic new television deal.

Yes, its new lineup makes absolutely no geographic sense. West Virginia is now gone to the Big 12, and it will lose Pittsburgh and Syracuse to the ACC soon. In response, the conference added Temple, a school it once kicked out, and will be adding Central Florida, SMU, Houston, Memphis, Boise State and San Diego State in different capacities (some for football only, some in all sports).

Yes, that means that San Diego State will be playing football in a conference called the Big East.

Yes, the conference's status as what one considers a "major conference" is now in severe jeopardy.

All of these statements are true. However, one also has to admit this: This conference produces some crazy, dramatic, unpredictable title races. The conference has long been called a "torso conference" because of the fact it rarely has elite teams and rarely has terrible ones. This should be the case again in 2012, as five teams, over half the conference, are projected to rank between 29th and 43rd in F/+ and finish either 5-2 or 4-3 in conference play. Of course, there is not a single Top 25 team in the bunch, which means that, once again, odds are good that the Big East champion will be far inferior to, say, whichever Big 12 and SEC teams end up playing in the non-BCS Cotton Bowl. But we're not here to talk about elite play; we're just here to talk about competition. And the Big East does indeed have that going for it.

No. 29 South Florida Bulls (9-3, 5-2)

2011: 5-7 (1-6) / F/+ #40 / FEI #34 / S&P+ #36

Program F/+	-199.9	32	Returning Starters: 8 OFF, 8 DEF			2-Yr Recruiting Rank		51
2011 Offense			**2011 Defense**			**2011 Field Position**		
Offensive F/+	+1.6%	49	**Defensive F/+**	+5.0%	24	Field Position Advantage	0.495	67
Offensive FEI:	0.036	56	Defensive FEI	-0.445	14	**2012 Projections**		
Offensive S&P+	95.4	37	Defensive S&P+	121.9	40	**Mean Wins**	8.5	
Rushing S&P+	126.8	9	Rushing S&P+	114.1	28	Proj. F/+	+11.1%	29
Passing S&P+	100.0	62	Passing S&P+	96.3	71	Offensive F/+	+3.2%	42
Standard Downs S&P+	107.6	43	Standard Downs S&P+	107.2	40	Defensive F/+	+7.8%	21
Passing Downs S&P+	102.8	61	Passing Downs S&P+	109.8	46	Strength of Schedule	0.503	76

Behold the power of close games: In both of Skip Holtz's first two years in charge at South Florida, his Bulls ranked 40th in overall F/+. In Year One, they went 8-5, seemingly resuming the momentum the program experienced through most of Jim Leavitt's run as head coach. In Year Two, they flat at 5-7. The difference? In 2010, they went 3-2 in one-possession games. In 2011, they went 1-5. In the Big East, teams are quite evenly matched in terms of talent, it seems, and your down-the-stretch execution means an incredible amount. With a relatively new cast of characters in place last fall, Holtz and his staff just couldn't quite figure out the right buttons to press. In 2012, however, USF brings to the table one of the most experienced rosters in the conference. Is that alone a recipe for a turnaround?

Fifth-year senior B.J. Daniels returns for yet another season as USF's starting quarterback in 2012. He has slowly morphed from an all-or-nothing quarterback into a reasonably decent game manager, and he will have quite a deep batch of skill position players at his disposal. Senior running back Demetris Murray (503 yards, plus-3.3 Adj. POE) takes over the full-time No. 1 spot after Darrell Scott's early departure to the pros, and junior receiver Sterling Griffin (530 receiving yards, 9.1 per target) might be one of the country's more underrated receivers. If the Bulls can find capable replacements for two three-year starters on the line, an offense that improved from 87th in Offensive F/+ to 49th last year could see another solid step forward.

The Bulls' defense was not particularly deep last year, and it showed: USF ranked 32nd in first-quarter S&P+, 34th in the second quarter, 51st in the third and 60th in the fourth. Eight starters return, and for the Bulls' sake, one hopes that some interesting newcomers can make their way into the rotation. The linebacking corps is one of the best in the country; junior DeDe Lattimore (13 tackles for loss) joins a trio of steady seniors (Mike Lanaris, Sam Barrington, Mike Jeune). Up front, tackles Cory Grissom and Elkino Watson are strong, but end Ryne Giddins needs a pass-rushing partner. The secondary must replace two starters, but corner Kayvon Webster is a keeper.

Top 2013 NFL Draft Prospects: LB Mike Lanaris (6-7), CB Kayvon Webster (6-7), S John Lejiste (6-7).

No. 37 Rutgers Scarlet Knights (8-4, 4-3)
2011: 9-4 (4-3) / F/+ #34 / FEI #24 / S&P+ #59

Program F/+	-200.0	44	Returning Starters: 6 OFF, 8 DEF			2-Yr Recruiting Rank		29
2011 Offense			**2011 Defense**			**2011 Field Position**		
Offensive F/+	+1.5%	50	Defensive F/+	+3.9%	29	Field Position Advantage	0.519	31
Offensive FEI:	0.056	52	Defensive FEI	-0.596	4	**2012 Projections**		
Offensive S&P+	71.7	108	Defensive S&P+	132.2	19	Mean Wins	8.3	
Rushing S&P+	85.3	104	Rushing S&P+	110.1	39	Proj. F/+	+8.0%	37
Passing S&P+	84.4	100	Passing S&P+	126.7	16	Offensive F/+	+1.1%	53
Standard Downs S&P+	83.0	111	Standard Downs S&P+	113.1	28	Defensive F/+	+6.9%	27
Passing Downs S&P+	99.9	71	Passing Downs S&P+	140.6	8	Strength of Schedule	0.479	72

The results of the 2011 season were very, very important for the overall trajectory of the Rutgers football program. The Scarlet Knights had seen the level of their product either stagnate or diminish for four consecutive years following their brilliant 2006 campaign; they ranked 11th in F/+ in 2006 (11-2), 26th in 2008 (8-5) and 82nd in 2010 (4-8). But with a predominantly young team and an occasionally brilliant defense, Rutgers rebounded to 34th last fall, with a 9-4 record. Head coach Greg Schiano then took the Tampa Bay Buccaneers job, leaving for new coach Kyle Flood a program with a bit of momentum. Floyd locked down a stellar recruiting class, kept quite a few familiar faces on the staff, and enters 2012 with a defense that threatens to be even stronger than it was last year.

Rutgers was well-rounded at every level of the defense last year—eighth in Adjusted Line Yards, 16th in Passing S&P+, eighth in Passing Downs S&P+—and that should remain the case. Linebacker Khaseem Green, the conference's co-defensive player of the year, rolled up 14 tackles for loss and made 16 percent of Rutgers' tackles; he should be 100 percent healthy this fall after suffering a gruesome leg injury in the Scarlet Knights' bowl win over Iowa State. He is surrounded by playmakers: cornerback Logan Ryan (17 passes defended, 5.5 tackles for loss), middle linebacker Steve Bauharnais (16 tackles for loss), and tackle Scott Vallone (8.5 tackles for loss), to name three.

Of the 23 players who recorded at least 5.0 tackles last season, 18 return. Joining them this fall: five-star defensive end Darius Hamilton and four-star linebacker Quanzell Lambert. There is no reason why the Scarlet Knights shouldn't continue to field one of the best defenses in the eastern time zone.

Offense, on the other hand? Call it a work in progress. Sophomore running backs Jawan Jamison and Savon Huggins each had their moments last fall despite poor blocking (Rutgers ranked 118th in Adjusted Line Yards). But quarterbacks Chas Dodd and Gary Nova have struggled to stand out, go-to receiver Mohamed Sanu is gone, and the aforementioned iffy line must replace four starters.

Top 2013 NFL Draft Prospects: CB Logan Ryan (2-3), LB Khaseem Green (2-3), DT Scott Vallone (6-7), OT R.J. Dill (6-7).

No. 38 Pittsburgh Panthers (8-4, 4-3)

2011: 6-7 (4-3) / F/+ #47 / FEI #36 / S&P+ #62

Program F/+	-199.9	27	Returning Starters: 8 OFF, 5 DEF			2-Yr Recruiting Rank		48
2011 Offense			**2011 Defense**			**2011 Field Position**		
Offensive F/+	-1.1%	67	**Defensive F/+**	+4.3%	27	Field Position Advantage	0.507	50
Offensive FEI:	-0.04	66	Defensive FEI	-0.321	24	**2012 Projections**		
Offensive S&P+	83.9	70	Defensive S&P+	118.2	50	**Mean Wins**	7.7	
Rushing S&P+	117.6	23	Rushing S&P+	105.1	47	Proj. F/+	+7.8%	38
Passing S&P+	91.2	82	Passing S&P+	101.8	55	Offensive F/+	+1.4%	51
Standard Downs S&P+	101.6	59	Standard Downs S&P+	99.4	64	Defensive F/+	+6.4%	29
Passing Downs S&P+	103.0	59	Passing Downs S&P+	122.2	27	Strength of Schedule	0.413	65

The next time you read about a team learning to adapt to a new coach's style, roll your eyes and think of Pittsburgh. The Panthers have been led by four head coaches since December 2010; they fired Dave Wannstedt, hired Miami (Ohio)'s Mike Haywood, fired Haywood two weeks later after a domestic assault charge, hired Tulsa coach Todd Graham, lost Graham to Arizona State after a single season, then hired Wisconsin offensive coordinator Paul Chryst. After a season of switching to a spread offense and a 3-4 defense, Chryst will bring back many aspects of Wannstedt's pro-style offense and 4-3 defense.

Chryst was a wonderful success at Wisconsin; his Badgers ranked fourth in Offensive F/+ in 2010, lost seven starters, and improved to first the next year. He brings to Pittsburgh a modern version of the old, grind-it-out Wisconsin running attack. That should suit the personnel quite well. Senior running back Ray Graham returns after missing the final five games of 2011 with a knee injury. He gained 1,164 rushing and receiving yards in his eight games and, assuming full health, could become a nice Montee Ball-style option for Chryst's offense. He will be running behind an enormous, if slightly inexperienced line. When Pitt has to pass, quarterback Tino Sunseri will find two strong downfield weapons in junior Devin Street (754 receiving yards, 8.3 per target in 2011) and senior Mike Shanahan (493 yards, 7.8 per target); meanwhile, tight end Hubie Graham should be much more effective in this system than in the spread.

The Pitt defense, which has ranked 32nd or better in Defensive F/+ for each of the past five seasons, faces quite a bit of turnover in the front seven. Depth could be a concern, but there is still quality upside to be found in players like tackle Aaron Donald (16 tackles for loss in 2011), sophomore linebackers Todd Thomas and Ejuan Price, corner K'Waun Williams, and a large set of quality safeties, led by Jarred Holley.

One has to assume there will be issues when it comes to the offense and defense each learning a third system in three years, but there is decent upside on both sides of the ball, and the offense could quickly thrive under Chryst's approach.

Top 2013 NFL Draft Prospects: RB Ray Graham (3-4), WR Devin Street (5-6), G Chris Jacobson (5-6), FS Jarred Holley (6-7).

No. 41 Louisville Cardinals (8-4, 4-3)

2011: 7-6 (5-2) / F/+ #44 / FEI #30 / S&P+ #66

Program F/+	-200.0	59	Returning Starters: 7 OFF, 7 DEF			2-Yr Recruiting Rank		34
2011 Offense			**2011 Defense**			**2011 Field Position**		
Offensive F/+	+3.2%	41	**Defensive F/+**	+0.6%	53	Field Position Advantage	0.517	33
Offensive FEI:	0.158	39	Defensive FEI	-0.191	38	**2012 Projections**		
Offensive S&P+	83.7	71	Defensive S&P+	116.0	55	**Mean Wins**	7.6	
Rushing S&P+	102.2	62	Rushing S&P+	102.8	54	Proj. F/+	+6.5%	41
Passing S&P+	104.9	56	Passing S&P+	90.5	90	Offensive F/+	+4.1%	35
Standard Downs S&P+	100.7	64	Standard Downs S&P+	100.5	61	Defensive F/+	+2.4%	49
Passing Downs S&P+	105.3	55	Passing Downs S&P+	90.3	84	Strength of Schedule	0.595	85

The word "future" should be applied judiciously to anything relating to the Big East. But one needs to make an exception when it comes to discussing Charlie Strong's Louisville Cardinals. It took Strong 50 years to land a head coaching job, but he ended a three-year bowl drought in 2010, then sustained his gains with a ridiculously young squad in 2011. His team will *still* be quite young this fall, but there is reason for excitement at Papa John's Stadium.

The No. 1 reason for optimism in 2012: quarterback Teddy Bridgewater. The sophomore from Miami took far too many hits last fall (10 percent sack rate), but he managed a healthy 132.4 passer efficiency rating (strong for a true freshman), and over his last six starts he completed 66 percent of his passes and threw nine touchdowns to six interceptions. He will be protected by a line that returns six players with starting experience, including three sophomores.

The No. 2 reason: Eli Rogers, Michaelee Harris and DeVante Parker. The trio of sophomore receivers combined for 94 catches, 1,183 yards and a per-target average of 8.3 yards. Rogers was the Cardinals' leading receiver as a freshman, and while the Cardinals might miss tight end Josh Chichester a bit, it is difficult not to be excited about this trio. An enhanced pass attack will go a long way to improve upon Louisville's No. 107 ranking in explosive drive percentage last season.

The No. 3 reason: The defense was almost as young and just as interesting as the offense last year. Sophomores like end B.J. Dubose, linebacker Deionterez Mount, free safety Calvin Pryor and cornerback Andrew Johnson got their feet wet last year, and the defense remained average to above average most of the year. Throw in juniors like tackle Roy Philon, linebacker Preston Brown, strong safety Hakeem Smith and cornerback (and Florida transfer) Adrian Bushell, and you've got a defense that will improve in 2012, then improve again in 2013 when almost all of them return.

Louisville is built to improve in 2012, even as they continue life as one of the younger teams in the country.

Top 2013 NFL Draft Prospects: S Hakeem Smith (3-4), C Mario Benavides (5-6), CB Adrian Bushell (5-6).

No. 43 Cincinnati Bearcats (8-4, 4-3)
2011: 10-3 (5-2) / F/+ #27 / FEI #23 / S&P+ #39

Program F/+	-199.9	23	Returning Starters: 4 OFF, 6 DEF			2-Yr Recruiting Rank		45
2011 Offense			**2011 Defense**			**2011 Field Position**		
Offensive F/+	+5.0%	31	**Defensive F/+**	+3.1%	39	Field Position Advantage	0.542	10
Offensive FEI:	0.297	25	Defensive FEI	-0.289	30	**2012 Projections**		
Offensive S&P+	91.5	52	Defensive S&P+	124.1	37	**Mean Wins**	7.9	
Rushing S&P+	120.7	17	Rushing S&P+	110.7	35	Proj. F/+	+6.1%	43
Passing S&P+	99.3	65	Passing S&P+	96.6	69	Offensive F/+	+2.3%	43
Standard Downs S&P+	105.6	50	Standard Downs S&P+	90.8	100	Defensive F/+	+3.8%	42
Passing Downs S&P+	123.9	23	Passing Downs S&P+	134.2	17	Strength of Schedule	0.607	88

Entering his third season in control of the Cincinnati Bearcats, Butch Jones has improbably become one of the deans of the conference; only Syracuse's Doug Marrone has been at his school for a longer period of time. Jones led Cincinnati back to a bowl game in 2011, but he faces quite a bit of offensive transition in 2012.

It only seemed like quarterback Zach Collaros, running back Isaiah Pead and receiver D.J. Woods had been playing for the Bearcats since they were in the Missouri Valley Conference. All three finally ran out of eligibility following the 2011 season, as did three starting offensive linemen (including all-conference guard Randy Martinez). But fans got a peek at their intriguing potential replacements in 2011. Exciting quarterback Munchie Legaux took the reins of the offense when Collaros was hurt, and while he is certainly much further along as a runner (6.6 yards per non-sack carry) than he is as a passer (5.8 yards per pass attempt with a 47 percent completion rate), he has a lot of potential. At the end of spring practice, Marrone listed Legaux and senior Brendon Kay, a more conventional passer, as "tied" atop the depth chart. But this is really just to motivate Legaux; nobody in Cincinnati seems to believe that Kay actually has a chance to be the starter.

Senior George Winn and highly-touted sophomore Jameel Poteat (combined: 327 yards, 5.2 per carry, plus-2.9 Adj. POE in 2011) will take over for Pead in the backfield. Pead was an underrated, explosive runner through his years at Cincinnati, but Winn and Poteat each bring potential to the table. Cincinnati should be fine at receiver thanks to the emergence of two receivers: junior Anthony McClung (683 yards, 7.9 per target) and senior Kenbrell Thompkins (536 yards, 7.1 per target). McClung is an explosive option, but the key for success if Legaux wins the quarterback job will be finding some decent efficiency options.

The Cincinnati defense struggled to leverage opponents into passing downs in 2011, but when they did, they quickly turned the lights out. The Bearcats ranked 100th in Standard Downs S&P+ and 17th in Passing Downs S&P+, one of the larger spreads in the country. They must replace their three leaders in tackles for loss this fall, however. Gone are linebacker J.K. Schaffer (13 tackles for loss, nine passes defended) and tackles Derek Wolfe and John Hughes, whose combined 34 tackles for loss were absurdly high for interior linemen. Players like end Walter Stewart, linebacker Maalik Bomar and corner Deven Drane have potential, but they will face pressure to make plays.

Top 2013 NFL Draft Prospects: CB Dominique Battle (6-7), S Drew Frey (6-7), DE Walter Stewart (6-7).

No. 57 Connecticut Huskies (6-6, 3-4)
2011: 5-7 (3-4) / F/+ #61 / FEI #48 / S&P+ #79

Program F/+	-199.9	42	Returning Starters: 7 OFF, 9 DEF		2-Yr Recruiting Rank		98
2011 Offense			**2011 Defense**		**2011 Field Position**		
Offensive F/+	-4.7%	83	**Defensive F/+**	+3.4%	36	Field Position Advantage	0.510	42
Offensive FEI:	-0.209	91	Defensive FEI	-0.325	23	**2012 Projections**		
Offensive S&P+	68.9	111	Defensive S&P+	120.8	45	**Mean Wins**	6.4	
Rushing S&P+	88.6	100	Rushing S&P+	132.0	10	Proj. F/+	+0.8%	57
Passing S&P+	81.1	108	Passing S&P+	92.2	84	Offensive F/+	-5.7%	87
Standard Downs S&P+	90.1	97	Standard Downs S&P+	101.6	51	Defensive F/+	+6.5%	28
Passing Downs S&P+	83.6	106	Passing Downs S&P+	117.3	34	Strength of Schedule	0.601	86

Sometimes dazzling hires don't work out. Sometimes hires that make no sense end up fantastic. Connecticut fans are left hoping that the hire of Paul Pasqualoni falls into the latter category. Unless your last name is Pasqualoni, you probably were not blown away by the hire of this 62-year-old veteran and former Syracuse head coach, and a year later, he has not done much to prove skeptics wrong.

Actually, that isn't entirely fair. The Huskies only regressed from 54th in F/+ to 61st in 2011, but after going 3-1 in one-possession games on their way to a 2010 conference title, UConn went just 2-4 in 2011 and, as a result, fell to 5-7 overall. A rebound in 2012 will depend on both finding a reliable quarterback among five candidates (the leader in the clubhouse: Illinois transfer Chandler Whitmer) and a couple of sturdy defensive tackles to replace the departed Kendall Reyes and Twyon Martin.

First, the quarterbacks: Whitmer, senior Johnny McEntee (last year's starter), sophomore Mike Nebrich, run-heavy sophomore Scott McCummings and incoming freshman Casey Cochran all bring different traits to the table, but Whitmer had the best spring. Whoever wins this derby will hand off to sophomore running back Lyle McCombs (1,151 yards, minus-13.3 Adj. POE) quite a bit. McCombs averaged 23 carries per game as a freshman, and he could find the going a bit easier if the line can quickly break in a couple of new starters, and if the passing game has more to offer. Michael Smith, UConn's leading receiver in 2010, is back after missing a season with academic ineligibility, and Boston College transfer Shakim Phillips had a nice spring.

The UConn defense ranked a respectable 36th in Defensive F/+ last fall, mostly because of a tremendous line that ranked fourth in Adjusted Line Yards. Unfortunately, with the departures of Reyes and Martin, the defense's biggest strength could now be a weakness. Pass-rush specialist Trevardo Williams (12.5 sacks last year) returns at end, and every linebacker of consequence is back, but it is difficult to see the UConn defense avoiding a dropoff without stellar tackle play.

Top 2013 NFL Draft Prospects: LB Sio Moore (3-4), CB Blidi Wreh-Wilson (6-7), TE Ryan Griffin (6-7), WR Michael Smith (6-7).

No. 77 Temple Owls (4-7, 2-5)

2011: 9-4 (5-3) / F/+ #24 / FEI #38 / S&P+ #27

Program F/+	-200.0	70	Returning Starters: 2 OFF, 5 DEF			2-Yr Recruiting Rank		102
2011 Offense			**2011 Defense**			**2011 Field Position**		
Offensive F/+	+2.9%	44	Defensive F/+	+4.8%	26	Field Position Advantage	0.550	9
Offensive FEI:	0.03	57	Defensive FEI	-0.158	47	**2012 Projections**		
Offensive S&P+	95.7	35	Defensive S&P+	129.4	23	**Mean Wins**	4.1	
Rushing S&P+	112.2	33	Rushing S&P+	108.6	43	Proj. F/+	-5.7%	77
Passing S&P+	106.6	50	Passing S&P+	104.3	47	Offensive F/+	-6.8%	93
Standard Downs S&P+	105.6	49	Standard Downs S&P+	100.8	59	Defensive F/+	+1.1%	56
Passing Downs S&P+	88.3	100	Passing Downs S&P+	125.1	23	Strength of Schedule	0.567	81

Six years ago, Temple was destitute. Homeless until the Mid-American Conference took them in before the 2007 season, the Owls went 4-42 from 2003-05 and didn't finish with a winning season from 1987-2009. There are redemption tales, and then there are *redemption tales*. In five years in Philadelphia, Al Golden transformed the worst program in the country into one of the best programs in the MAC; he won just 10 games in his first three seasons, then won 17 in his last two. He left to take the Miami job a year ago, and his replacement, embattled former Florida offensive coordinator Steve Addazio, actually took the Owls to an even higher level. They won nine games for just the fourth time ever and ranked 24th in the final F/+ rankings. The success earned them a bid back into the conference that spurned them eight years ago, the Big East.

Addazio faces a good news, bad news situation this fall.

The good news: He's got more of his personnel in place, and he can begin to put together his offensive dream scenario of hybrids on hybrids on hybrids (quarterbacks who can run, running backs who can catch, receivers who can take handoffs, et cetera). Junior quarterback Chris Coyer was fantastic last year, although his place in the offense was run-first, run-second, and pass-somewhere around 25th. Running backs Matt Brown (5-foot-5, 170 pounds) and Kenny Harper (6-foot-0, 215 pounds) are versatile, and a couple of interesting receivers (Deon Miller, Jalen Fitzpatrick) were unearthed this spring.

The bad news: Addazio had one of the most experienced offensive lines in the country last year; now, only one starter returns. He must find a way to replace his two best defensive linemen, two best linebackers and two best defensive backs from last year's squad. Safety Justin Gildea, linebackers Ahkeem Smith and Blaze Caponegro, and tackle Levi Brown are solid, but it is hard to say whether Temple has the necessary defensive depth as they move back to a BCS conference. The Owls ranked No. 2 nationally in preventing value drives, but did so against the 117th ranked defensive strength of schedule.

Top 2013 NFL Draft Prospects: RB Matt Brown (6-7), DE John Youboty (6-7).

No. 79 Syracuse Orange (3-9, 2-5)

2011: 5-7 (1-6) / F/+ #71 / FEI #62 / S&P+ #76

Program F/+	-200.1	85	Returning Starters: 6 OFF, 6 DEF			2-Yr Recruiting Rank		70
2011 Offense			**2011 Defense**			**2011 Field Position**		
Offensive F/+	-1.2%	68	Defensive F/+	-1.1%	65	Field Position Advantage	0.482	86
Offensive FEI:	-0.015	62	Defensive FEI	-0.188	39	**2012 Projections**		
Offensive S&P+	81.7	76	Defensive S&P+	111.0	67	**Mean Wins**	3.5	
Rushing S&P+	98.5	73	Rushing S&P+	102.1	55	Proj. F/+	-6.4%	79
Passing S&P+	99.1	66	Passing S&P+	95.8	72	Offensive F/+	-3.3%	72
Standard Downs S&P+	100.0	68	Standard Downs S&P+	93.8	87	Defensive F/+	-3.1%	73
Passing Downs S&P+	103.3	57	Passing Downs S&P+	115.5	36	Strength of Schedule	0.354	54

Doug Marrone faces a "Get busy livin', or get busy dyin'" year in upstate New York. The fourth-year Syracuse head coach experienced a nice breakthrough in 2010, leading his Orange to an 8-5 record and their first bowl win since 2001, but Syracuse regressed to 5-7 in 2011. Marrone has brought respectability back to a program that won just 10 games in four awful seasons under Greg Robinson, but in program building, as in weight loss, you tend to hit a wall after signs of progress. The Orange should have a solid running game and one of the best linebacking corps in the conference, but a tough non-conference schedule and turnover in the trenches could lead to another down year up north.

In his second year as Syracuse's starting quarterback, Ryan Nassib lived a contradictory life. On one hand, he completed a healthy 62 percent of his passes, and put together a solid 22-to-9 touchdown-to-interception ratio. On the other hand, most of his completions didn't really go anywhere, and he got sacked far too much for what was supposed to be an efficiency offense. Nassib loses four of his top five targets from last fall, but in Alec Lemon (834 yards, 8.7 per target) and Marcus Sales (414 yards, 10.4 per target in 2010; suspended in 2011), he still has some potentially strong weapons at his disposal. The graduation of running back Antwon Bailey (1,051 rushing yards, 200 receiving yards) means that the run game will shift hands to an interesting threesome of Jerome Smith, Prince-Tyson Gulley, and Adonis Ameen-Moore.

The Syracuse offense improved a decent amount in 2011, but it couldn't offset regression on the defensive side of the ball. The Orange defense actually improved on passing downs, but they were unable to consistently force passing downs, sinking from 50th in Standard Downs S&P+ to 87th. As a result, their overall Defensive F/+ ranking plummeted from 35th to 65th. Newcomers at tackle and middle linebacker softened the defense up a bit, but the strengths and weaknesses should flip. Gone are the top three defensive ends, but tackles Jay Bromley and Cory Boatman return, and so does every linebacker of significance, including sophomore Dyshawn Davis (10.5 tackles for loss). Free safety Phillip Thomas (4.5 tackles for loss, nine passes defended) will be missed, but the back seven should be sturdy.

Top 2013 NFL Draft Prospects: OT Justin Pugh (2-3), WR Marcus Sales (6-7), QB Ryan Nassib (6-7).

Bill Connelly

Projected Win Probabilities For Big East Teams

Big East	12-0	11-1	10-2	9-3	8-4	7-5	6-6	5-7	4-8	3-9	2-10	1-11	0-12	7-0	6-1	5-2	4-3	3-4	2-5	1-6	0-7
Cincinnati	-	3	10	22	27	22	11	4	1	-	-	-	-	2	12	25	31	21	8	1	-
Connecticut	-	-	1	6	15	24	26	18	8	2	-	-	-	-	1	7	20	33	27	11	1
Louisville	-	2	8	18	26	24	14	6	2	-	-	-	-	2	10	27	33	20	7	1	-
Pittsburgh	-	2	7	20	29	25	13	3	1	-	-	-	-	2	13	29	31	18	6	1	-
Rutgers	-	3	13	27	30	19	7	1	-	-	-	-	-	2	10	28	33	20	6	1	-
South Florida	1	7	18	27	25	15	6	1	-	-	-	-	-	9	28	34	21	7	1	-	-
Syracuse	-	-	-	-	-	1	6	15	26	29	18	5	-	-	-	-	3	14	30	36	17
Temple	-	-	-	1	2	10	22	30	23	10	2	-	-	-	-	1	5	18	35	32	9

Big Ten Conference

The Big Ten was the first major conference to form way back in 1896, and with the addition of Nebraska last season, it now features four of the top 10 teams in all-time winning percentage. Three of the four largest college football stadiums host Big Ten teams. The conference boasts the most profitable conference sports cable network and rakes in cash from its broadcast network contracts as well. Forbes recently ranked seven Big Ten programs among the top 20 most valuable in all of college football.

These assets are the main reason why the Big Ten has wielded so much influence in the battles being waged over a new college football playoff system this summer. However, that power hasn't led to superior performance on the field of late. The Big Ten hasn't participated in a BCS championship game or placed a team in the top four of the Associated Press final poll since 2006. For as fiercely as league commissioner Jim Delany has protected the conference's stake in the future of the Rose Bowl, the Big Ten's recent participation in that game has been underwhelming. Ohio State's victory in the Rose Bowl in 2010 is the Big Ten's only victory there in the last 12 seasons.

Our projections don't give the conference much of a shot to improve that profile too significantly this year either. Ohio State and Penn State are introducing new head coaches, and the Buckeyes will be sitting out the postseason due to NCAA infractions. The defending Big Ten Leaders and Legends division champs, Michigan State and Wisconsin, are both starting new quarterbacks this fall. The Michigan Wolverines are getting the most attention from preseason polls, but a tough schedule will make it more difficult this year for them to get back to a BCS bowl game.

Nebraska and Iowa are intriguing possibilities for 2012 as teams that have demonstrated in the past that they belong among the league's upper tier. There may not, however, be an elite tier in the Big Ten this fall. Instead, it looks like a crowded clump of conference title contenders will beat one another up. Seven teams project to win between 8.0 and 9.6 wins in the Big Ten according to our ratings. A legitimate run at a national championship is likely another year away, but a wide-open league will make for intriguing games throughout the season.

LEADERS

No. 13 Ohio State Buckeyes (10-2, 6-2)
2011: 6-7 (3-5) / F/+ #38 / FEI #35 / S&P+ #52

Program F/+	-199.8	9	Returning Starters: 7 OFF, 9 DEF			2-Yr Recruiting Rank		6
2011 Offense			**2011 Defense**			**2011 Field Position**		
Offensive F/+	-0.4%	63	**Defensive F/+**	+5.4%	22	Field Position Advantage	0.533	15
Offensive FEI:	-0.037	65	Defensive FEI	-0.357	22	**2012 Projections**		
Offensive S&P+	83.6	72	Defensive S&P+	126.0	33	**Mean Wins**	9.5	
Rushing S&P+	111.7	35	Rushing S&P+	119.1	19	Proj. F/+	+18.1%	13
Passing S&P+	82.4	106	Passing S&P+	112.6	29	Offensive F/+	+3.7%	36
Standard Downs S&P+	101.5	60	Standard Downs S&P+	113.5	27	Defensive F/+	+14.4%	6
Passing Downs S&P+	106.8	53	Passing Downs S&P+	114.1	40	Strength of Schedule	0.354	53

There aren't any sure things in college football, but Urban Meyer's track record of success at every stop in his career is as reliable as it gets. After Jim Tressell's resignation last offseason amidst an NCAA investigation, the Buckeyes drifted through a disappointing but not entirely unexpected 6-7 swoon under interim head coach Luke Fickell. It was a season that can be easily be forgotten by the Buckeyes faithful as long as Meyer succeeds in restoring the elite status of the program.

Major strides are expected on offense under Meyer, but it could take time. He isn't inheriting a team of speedsters like the one he assembled at Florida, but he does a have young dual-threat weapon at quarterback to build around. Sophomore Braxton Miller was named Big Ten freshman player of the year, demonstrating his elite potential in a shootout loss to rival Michigan last season (100 yards rushing, 235 yards passing, 8.2 yards per play). The offensive roster as a whole still has a lot to prove, with three new offensive linemen and many skill position players who have seen limited action. The only player with more than a season of starting experience under his belt, fullback Zach Boren, was used almost exclusively as a blocker for three years.

The Buckeyes offense can make a big impact this year simply by sustaining drives. Ohio State ranked 101st nationally in generating value drives (possessions that start on a team's own side of midfield and reach the opponent's 30-yard line). Any improvement will depend on Miller's development and Meyer's ability to find ways to get the ball into the hands of every athlete he has to work with.

Unlike the offense, the Ohio State defense has strong experience at every position. Eight of the team's ten leading tacklers from a year ago are back on the field this fall. Defensive tackles John Simon (seven sacks, 16 tackles for loss) and Johnathon Hankins are a fearsome, athletic duo and among the best at the position in the Big Ten. The secondary has a wealth of talent back as well, and the competition to get on the field will likely spill over and benefit special teams play. Defense and special teams play have the biggest impact on field position, and Meyer's Florida teams were consistently dominant in Field Position Advantage in the past. Ohio State has historically been strong as well. The offense doesn't need to explode out of the gate if Ohio State can generate punt and kickoff exchanges that maximize scoring opportunities.

Four non-conference home games that should heavily favor the Buckeyes will help get the Meyer era off to a good start as well. Ohio State can't qualify for postseason play due to NCAA sanctions, but they have the best chance according to F/+ to be the top dog in the league and set the stage for a true championship run in 2013.

Top 2013 NFL Prospects: DT Johnathon Hankins* (1-2), DE John Simon (1-2), TE Jake Stoneburner (3-4), S C.J. Barnett (3-4), FB Zach Boren (4-5), CB Travis Howard (5-6), LB Nathan Williams (5-6), LB Etienne Sabino (6-7), OT Reid Fragel (6-7).

No. 19 Wisconsin Badgers (10-2, 6-2)

2011: 11-3 (6-2) / F/+ #6 / FEI #5 / S&P+ #6

Program F/+	-199.9	14	Returning Starters: 4 OFF, 6 DEF			2-Yr Recruiting Rank		41
2011 Offense			**2011 Defense**			**2011 Field Position**		
Offensive F/+	+19.1%	1	Defensive F/+	+2.4%	43	Field Position Advantage	0.531	17
Offensive FEI:	0.745	2	Defensive FEI	-0.139	49	**2012 Projections**		
Offensive S&P+	140.1	1	Defensive S&P+	118.1	51	Mean Wins	9.6	
Rushing S&P+	146.4	2	Rushing S&P+	96.9	70	Proj. F/+	+15.4%	19
Passing S&P+	174.8	1	Passing S&P+	97.7	67	Offensive F/+	+14.7%	3
Standard Downs S&P+	143.6	2	Standard Downs S&P+	96.1	78	Defensive F/+	+0.7%	59
Passing Downs S&P+	164.7	1	Passing Downs S&P+	126.3	19	Strength of Schedule	0.482	73

After back-to-back trips to the Rose Bowl and three consecutive seasons with ten or more victories, you would think that the Badgers would have clearly established themselves as the best program in the conference and one of the nation's elite. That's not the case, however. The record is glossy, but the midseason hiccups and losses in Pasadena have kept Wisconsin from truly breaking through. And it looks like another strong, but not strong enough season is in store this fall.

There were question marks before last season about transfer quarterback Russell Wilson's ability to seamlessly step into the Badgers offense, but those concerns were immediately relieved. The Badgers led the nation in points per drive (4.0), and Wilson was very efficient (73 percent completions, a huge leap from 59 percent a year earlier at NC State). The key was that he didn't have to carry the load for the entire offense. That should help the new starter, Maryland transfer Danny O'Brien, who like Wilson was asked to do more for his old team than he will be at Wisconsin.

A new quarterback and a new offensive coordinator might be a problem at other programs, but Wisconsin is expected to remain dominant due to running back Montee Ball's consistent production. His 39 total touchdowns (two or more in 13 straight games) drove the bus last season and will again this fall. although Peter Konz and Kevin Zeitler are gone to the NFL, the Badgers return all-conference guard Travis Frederick and tackle Ricky Wagner, a potential NFL first-round pick next spring

The defense was a weak link in 2011, especially considering the Badgers rarely played tough offenses (73rd in defensive strength of schedule according to FEI). Wisconsin was susceptible to big plays, allowing explosive drives (over 10 yards per play) on 27 percent of opponent possessions and giving up 6.9 points per explosive drive (111th nationally). Two end-of-game touchdown heaves allowed to Michigan State and Ohio State in back-to-back weeks eliminated the Badgers from the national championship race. Six starters return this year, led by linebackers Chris Borland and Mike Taylor (293 tackles combined last season), but Wisconsin replaces multiple starters along the defensive line and in the secondary. The Badgers have yet to produce a top-20 defense according to F/+ (a consistent threshold for elite contenders), and that won't change in 2012.

The Badgers haven't lost a regular season non-conference game since 2003, but the collective strength of those opponents is one of the weakest in college football over that span. This year's slate features a features an away game at Oregon State, Wisconsin's first trip to an AQ opponent stadium in the Bret Bielema era (2006 to present). The Big Ten schedule includes a tough road opener at Nebraska, but Ohio State and Michigan State both make the trip to Madison where the Badgers are 20-1 in the last three seasons. Since the Buckeyes can't play in the Big Ten title game, the Leaders division spot will likely belong to Wisconsin once again.

Top 2013 NFL Prospects: OT Ricky Wagner (1-2), RB Montee Ball (2-3), LB Mike Taylor (4-5), CB Devin Smith (5-6), DE David Gilbert (6-7), CB Marcus Cromartie (6-7).

No. 32 Penn State Nittany Lions (8-4, 5-3)

2011: 9-4 (6-2) / F/+ #31 / FEI #39 / S&P+ #26

Program F/+	-199.9	15	Returning Starters: 5 OFF, 5 DEF			2-Yr Recruiting Rank		38
2011 Offense			**2011 Defense**			**2011 Field Position**		
Offensive F/+	-2.2%	75	**Defensive F/+**	+9.8%	7	Field Position Advantage	0.513	37
Offensive FEI:	-0.148	81	Defensive FEI	-0.437	15	**2012 Projections**		
Offensive S&P+	80.7	80	Defensive S&P+	144.8	9	**Mean Wins**	8.0	
Rushing S&P+	106.4	49	Rushing S&P+	129.4	14	Proj. F/+	+10.3%	32
Passing S&P+	88.8	87	Passing S&P+	147.4	3	Offensive F/+	-2.0%	67
Standard Downs S&P+	92.8	90	Standard Downs S&P+	137.1	4	Defensive F/+	+12.2%	9
Passing Downs S&P+	114.0	38	Passing Downs S&P+	137.1	12	Strength of Schedule	0.458	69

New head coach Bill O'Brien has a lot to deal with this year: the shadows cast by the Jerry Sandusky scandal, the pressure of living up to the Paterno legend, and question marks on both sides of the ball with only 10 starters returning. The State College community is desperate for winning football to dominate the headlines, but they'll have to wait a year or longer to contend for a conference crown.

O'Brien's success as an assistant with several prolific New England Patriots offenses is notable, though the track record of first-time head coaches in college football isn't a glossy one. He inherits a very inexperienced offensive line (center Matt Stankiewitch is the only returning starter). Penn State also graduated its leading receiver for the past three years, Derek Moye. After working one-on-one with the Patriots' Tom Brady for the last three seasons, O'Brien's biggest challenge will be dealing with unreliability at the quarterback position. Senior Matt McGloin has been named the starter, but he has struggled with accuracy issues that have bogged down the offense. Penn State ranked 106th nationally in offensive drive efficiency and 108th in points per possession (1.4).

Last year's secondary was very effective (third in S&P+ defending the pass) and allowed the front seven to pressure opposing offenses. Now all four starters must be replaced. The linebackers (who else at Penn State?) will anchor the defense this fall, led by junior Glenn Carson and seniors Gerald Hodges and Michael Mauti. As poor as the Nittany Lions offense was at generating points per drive, the defense picked up the slack by being even stingier. They were especially effective at limiting opponent big plays. Penn State gave up only 10 plays all season of 30 or more yards (tied with Alabama and USC for fewest nationally), and allowed only five percent of opponent drives to average at least 10 yards per play (third fewest nationally).

A year ago, Penn State carried an undefeated conference record into November, but their Leaders division edge had been built on a very thin resume and they lost three of their last four games on the season. This year may not be much different. Penn State's conference strength of schedule is second-weakest in the Big Ten according to our projections, however, so bowl eligibility should be a given.

Top 2013 NFL Prospects: LB Gerald Hodges (2-3), LB Michael Mauti (4-5), DT Jordan Hill (4-5), C Matt Stankiewitch (6-7), DE Pete Massaro (6-7).

No. 51 Illinois Fighting Illini (7-5, 4-4)

2011: 7-6 (2-6) / F/+ #62 / FEI #61 / S&P+ #45

Program F/+	-200.0	46	Returning Starters: 6 OFF, 7 DEF		2-Yr Recruiting Rank		54
2011 Offense			**2011 Defense**		**2011 Field Position**		
Offensive F/+	-7.2%	98	**Defensive F/+**	+9.3%	9	Field Position Advantage	0.452	111
Offensive FEI:	-0.435	108	Defensive FEI	-0.53	8	**2012 Projections**		
Offensive S&P+	73.9	104	Defensive S&P+	139.5	12	**Mean Wins**	6.9	
Rushing S&P+	87.0	102	Rushing S&P+	131.6	11	Proj. F/+	+3.4%	51
Passing S&P+	85.4	96	Passing S&P+	129.3	13	Offensive F/+	-9.0%	101
Standard Downs S&P+	89.3	100	Standard Downs S&P+	127.1	9	Defensive F/+	+12.4%	10
Passing Downs S&P+	103.2	58	Passing Downs S&P+	123.5	25	Strength of Schedule	0.346	52

The ups-and-downs of the Ron Zook era at Illinois came to a fitting end last fall. After racing out to a 6-0 start (their first since 1951), the Illini sputtered and fell into a tailspin, dropping each of their final six games of the regular season to finally send Zook packing. The program doesn't have the historical pedigree to expect to regularly contend for conference championships, but the success Zook had on the field fell far short of the level of the talent he brought to Champaign. New coach Tim Beckman arrives from a successful rebuilding project in Toledo, and will have a chance to find the consistency that has eluded the program for years.

Quarterback Nathan Scheelhaase has a decent skill set to beat defenses through the air and on the ground, but Illinois needs to fill a major gap in the receiving corps with the departure of A.J. Jenkins, now with the San Francisco 49ers. Jenkins received 45 percent of Scheelhaase's completions. Beckman's teams were very productive offensively at Toledo (eighth nationally in points per game, ninth in yards per game last year), but almost every skill position at Illinois lacks experience. Scheelhaase led the team in rushing in 2011, though his yards per carry declined from his first year due to the lack of another major threat in the Illini backfield. Illinois' rushing S&P+ dropped significantly last year as well.

The defense returns lots of experience to a unit that ranked in the top 10 in standard downs S&P+. They are led by junior linebacker Jonathan Brown, who tallied 14.5 tackles for loss in a year ago (best in the Big Ten), and averaged better than 10 tackles per game in conference play. The Illini defense was particularly tough near its own end zone, ranking third in the nation in points allowed per value drive (3.7).

Special teams were a major hole that contributed to poor field position disadvantages throughout the year. If the Illini can keep teams honest and force opponents to beat them over the length of the field, Illinois will find itself competing in every game.

Top 2013 NFL Prospects: DE Michael Buchanan (1-2), LB Jonathan Brown* (2-3), DT Akeem Spence* (3-4), C Graham Pocic (3-4), CB Terry Hawthorne (4-5).

No. 69 Purdue Boilermakers (5-7, 2-6)

2011: 7-6 (4-4) / F/+ #73 / FEI #78 / S&P+ #84

Program F/+	-200.0	67	Returning Starters: 8 OFF, 7 DEF			2-Yr Recruiting Rank		75
2011 Offense			**2011 Defense**			**2011 Field Position**		
Offensive F/+	-4.7%	85	**Defensive F/+**	-1.6%	70	Field Position Advantage	0.529	18
Offensive FEI:	-0.177	86	Defensive FEI	0.216	79	**2012 Projections**		
Offensive S&P+	80.1	86	Defensive S&P+	107.6	77	**Mean Wins**	4.8	
Rushing S&P+	97.1	80	Rushing S&P+	99.6	63	Proj. F/+	-3.4%	69
Passing S&P+	88.5	88	Passing S&P+	92.6	81	Offensive F/+	-3.3%	73
Standard Downs S&P+	100.1	66	Standard Downs S&P+	97.5	71	Defensive F/+	-0.1%	60
Passing Downs S&P+	99.5	74	Passing Downs S&P+	110.4	44	Strength of Schedule	0.282	39

The Boilermakers posted their first winning season since 2007 last year, finished third in the Leaders division, and won the Little Caesars Pizza Bowl. These modest accomplishments could be the foundation for progress in West Lafayette, but our projections don't agree. Only one of the Boilermakers' seven victories last year came against a top-40 F/+ opponent (a 26-23 victory versus No. 38 Ohio State), and five wins came by less than a touchdown. Purdue was crushed by three solid opponents last year and will face six top 40 teams this fall. This is not the profile of a team ready to make a leap.

The roster on offense includes multiple quarterbacks with starting experience, though senior Caleb TerBush (13 touchdowns, six interceptions) is expected to take the majority of snaps this fall. Running back Ralph Bolden (1,620 career yards) has led the team in rushing twice in the last three seasons, but is recovering from a third knee surgery and may not return to peak condition.

Defensive tackle Kawaan Short tallied 17.5 tackles for loss last season, including 6.5 sacks, and was a bright spot on an otherwise underwhelming defense. Purdue had difficulty getting opposing offenses off the field, allowing first-down conversions on 44 percent of all third-down rushing attempts. Special teams were relatively strong, keyed by the nation's leading kick returner Raheem Mostert (33.5 yards per kickoff return). That helped Purdue earn a top-20 season-long field position advantage.

The Boilermakers have been known to steal a game or two unexpectedly in recent years, especially at home, but our projections don't expect that to happen early on in the year. Their conference schedule kicks off against their three toughest Big Ten opponents (Michigan, Wisconsin, and Ohio State). Unless they do pull an early upset, Purdue will be struggling to get back to .500 down the stretch.

Top 2013 NFL Prospects: DT Kawann Short (1-2).

No. 92 Indiana Hoosiers (3-9, 1-7)

2011: 1-11 (0-8) / F/+ #112 / FEI #105 / S&P+ #115

Program F/+	-200.1	94	Returning Starters: 8 OFF, 9 DEF			2-Yr Recruiting Rank		60
2011 Offense			**2011 Defense**			**2011 Field Position**		
Offensive F/+	-8.2%	103	**Defensive F/+**	-9.0%	117	Field Position Advantage	0.464	104
Offensive FEI:	-0.08	69	Defensive FEI	0.493	112	**2012 Projections**		
Offensive S&P+	73.7	105	Defensive S&P+	82.7	117	**Mean Wins**	3.5	
Rushing S&P+	103.6	57	Rushing S&P+	78.5	114	Proj. F/+	-10.1%	92
Passing S&P+	79.5	110	Passing S&P+	70.0	119	Offensive F/+	-5.4%	83
Standard Downs S&P+	100.4	65	Standard Downs S&P+	82.5	113	Defensive F/+	-4.7%	93
Passing Downs S&P+	82.7	108	Passing Downs S&P+	80.1	107	Strength of Schedule	0.484	74

The Hoosiers have only three Big Ten victories in the last four seasons, and another hapless campaign is likely in store for 2012. There were glimmers of hope early on—Indiana was competitive in each of its first four losses—but the wheels came off defensively down the stretch. The young Hoosiers gave up a total of 326 points over the final seven games, a humiliating skid that soured Kevin Wilson's debut in Bloomington. The expectations aren't very lofty at Indiana, and progress can be made this fall, if only incrementally.

It begins with a slew of returning starters, featuring dual-threat sophomore quarterback Tre Robinson, who carried the offense in brief spurts a year ago. All of the primary playmakers last year were freshmen or sophomores, including running back Stephen Houston (5.3 yards per carry, +10.7 Adj. POE) and wide receiver Kofi Hughes (15.3 yards per reception). The offense wasn't much of a scoring threat, but 18 percent of Indiana's drives lasted at least 10 plays (19th-most nationally). Finishing long drives can be a modest point of emphasis for the Indiana offense to build upon this season. The young defense couldn't get anyone off the field themselves, of course, but a ball-control offense could help mitigate that weakness.

The Hoosiers face their weakest Big Ten opponents (Northwestern and Purdue) on the road, so it will be a struggle to earn any conference victories. By our projections, the Hoosiers don't have any sure FBS non-conference victories either, though wins over Massachusetts and Ball State are expected.

Top 2013 NFL Prospects: None.

LEGENDS

No. 16 Michigan Wolverines (8-4, 6-2)
2011: 11-2 (6-2) / F/+ #12 / FEI #9 / S&P+ #14

Program F/+	-199.9	39	Returning Starters: 7 OFF, 7 DEF		2-Yr Recruiting Rank		15
2011 Offense			**2011 Defense**		**2011 Field Position**		
Offensive F/+	+10.6%	14	**Defensive F/+**	+4.9%	25	Field Position Advantage	0.523	26
Offensive FEI:	0.472	9	Defensive FEI	-0.414	16	**2012 Projections**		
Offensive S&P+	112.0	10	Defensive S&P+	124.7	35	**Mean Wins**	8.3	
Rushing S&P+	141.7	4	Rushing S&P+	110.5	37	Proj. F/+	+16.7%	16
Passing S&P+	125.0	15	Passing S&P+	107.8	35	Offensive F/+	+11.5%	13
Standard Downs S&P+	124.4	9	Standard Downs S&P+	114.3	25	Defensive F/+	+5.3%	31
Passing Downs S&P+	140.5	8	Passing Downs S&P+	106.0	55	Strength of Schedule	0.098	11

Brady Hoke's debut season in Ann Arbor was nearly pitch-perfect, exceeding expectations of fans and observers across the country. After Rich Rodriguez's ouster, Hoke arrived in Ann Arbor with a blue-collar Michigan Man attitude, leaned on similarly hard-nosed coordinators, and pushed all the right buttons to get the most out of a roster presumed to be thin on playmakers. Michigan also drummed up more than a bit of unusually good fortune at opportune moments throughout the season. They'll need even more of that magic to post another double-digit winning season this fall.

There may not be superstars all over the field for the Wolverines, but senior quarterback Denard Robinson certainly ranks as one of the most dynamic athletes in the country. The key to his success has been Michigan's commitment to running as much of the offense as possible through him. In the last two seasons, 74 percent of the Wolverines' total offensive output was produced by the quarterback, ninth-most nationally and second-most among AQ conference teams. His improvisation skills and lightning-quick speed are threats defenses must account for on every play. His accuracy in the air is much less reliable, and his 15 interceptions last year could have been even worse if not for several lucky ricochets.

Michigan was the biggest beneficiary of turnover luck last season, according to our Adjusted Turnover Margin data. If we compare turnovers for and against Michigan to standard rates of fumble recovery and interceptions to passes defensed, we find that the Wolverines gained an additional 3.97 points per game. It wasn't just Robinson's good fortune that ran up that tally. Michigan recovered 75 percent of fumbles in games last season, the highest percentage nationally by a wide margin. The pendulum doesn't just swing back and forth year to year when it comes to luck, but there's going to be some regression towards the mean.

Robinson lost his top target from a year ago to graduation, but senior wide receiver Roy Roundtree was featured in 2010 and is expected to step back into a leadership role this year. Michigan also returns junior running back Fitzgerald Toussaint, who added 1,041 rushing yards on his own (+13.3 Adj. POE) and led the Wolverines ground attack down the stretch last season. The offensive line has a couple of holes to fill, but should be stable enough for Michigan's backfield to shine again (fourth nationally in Rushing S&P+ in 2011).

The weakness on defense this fall is along the line, after losing three starters to graduation from a unit that anchored Michigan's dramatic rise last season. The Wolverines gave up only 1.6 points per drive in 2011 (25th fewest nationally), nearly half as many as they had a year earlier (2.9 points per drive, 106th nationally). Linebacker Kenny Demens and safety Jordan Kovacs were the leading tacklers last season and both return, but Michigan may have trouble getting pressure with young players up front.

Hoke has a good thing going so far, but it's hard not to expect a setback in terms of record this fall. The Wolverines face Alabama in Dallas on opening weekend, and there are road trips to Notre Dame, Nebraska, and Ohio State. Still, our projections favor Michigan to win the Legends division, which would be another step forward for the program's return to glory.

Top 2013 NFL Prospects: DE Craig Roh (2-3), QB/WR Denard Robinson (3-4), WR Roy Roundtree (4-5), RB Fitzgerald Toussaint* (4-5), LB Kenny Demens (5-6), CB J.T. Floyd (6-7).

No. 23 Nebraska Cornhuskers (8-4, 5-3)

2011: 9-4 (5-3) / F/+ #26 / FEI #31 / S&P+ #29

Program F/+	-199.9	28	Returning Starters: 7 OFF, 7 DEF			2-Yr Recruiting Rank		17
2011 Offense			**2011 Defense**			**2011 Field Position**		
Offensive F/+	+5.6%	28	**Defensive F/+**	+2.9%	41	Field Position Advantage	0.525	22
Offensive FEI:	0.226	31	Defensive FEI	-0.112	53	**2012 Projections**		
Offensive S&P+	92.7	46	Defensive S&P+	129.4	24	**Mean Wins**	8.2	
Rushing S&P+	106.7	48	Rushing S&P+	113.4	29	Proj. F/+	+13.5%	23
Passing S&P+	110.7	39	Passing S&P+	126.9	15	Offensive F/+	+7.9%	25
Standard Downs S&P+	108.1	40	Standard Downs S&P+	106.9	42	Defensive F/+	+5.6%	30
Passing Downs S&P+	100.8	65	Passing Downs S&P+	135.5	14	Strength of Schedule	0.315	47

Though our projections were much more modest, the Cornhuskers were an Associated Press preseason top 10 team in each of the last two seasons and failed to deliver on lofty expectations. Now that it appears that the national media may have given up on Nebraska, might they finally make a breakthrough return to the top? Our projections suggest they are in for another year of decent, but far from spectacular success, testing the patience of a demanding fan base.

Last year wasn't a complete disaster by any means, but the Cornhuskers did suffer a pair of uncompetitive road losses to Wisconsin and Michigan that placed them definitively in the second tier of the conference. Those games (and others) were marked by significant defensive breakdowns, uncharacteristic of Bo Pelini's previous teams in Lincoln. The Cornhuskers gave up 2.0 points per drive last season (56th nationally) after ranking among the top 10 in each of the previous two seasons.

The returning defense this fall has experience, but little in the way of star power. Defensive ends Cameron Meredith (5.0 sacks in 2011) and Jason Ankrah will be focal points on the line, and linebacker Will Compton is the team's leading returning tackler (82 tackles). Nebraska forced three-and-outs on only 30 percent of opponent drives last season (82nd nationally) and gave up 120 first downs on the ground. The famed "Blackshirts" defense must be much tougher than that in order for the Cornhuskers to compete for a conference championship.

The offense hasn't performed up to expectations either, and fans are still waiting for quarterback Taylor Martinez to demonstrate his full potential with consistency. Martinez has racked up eight career games with more than 100 yards on the ground (all Huskers victories), but only three of those games came in conference play. Sustaining drives is key—Nebraska is merely average in generating value drive opportunities, but has ranked in the top 10 in points per value drive each of the last two seasons. Martinez is joined in the backfield by bruising senior running back Rex Burkhead (1,357 yards, 15 touchdowns, +4.5 Adj. POE), giving Nebraska the most proven one-two punch in the Big Ten. But Nebraska's lack of a passing game threat and new faces along the offensive line at center and both tackles will keep the Cornhuskers from dominating offensively.

Nebraska faces the toughest conference strength of schedule in the Big Ten according to our projections, with games against all six of the other top-seven conference teams lined up. The first two Big Ten games come against Wisconsin and Ohio State and have the potential to either set the stage for a conference title run or knock the Huskers out of the race immediately.

Top 2013 NFL Prospects: DE Cameron Meredith (4-5), DT Baker Steinkuhler (5-6), LB Sean Fisher (6-7), TE Kyler Reed (6-7), LB Will Compton (6-7), RB Rex Burkhead (6-7), K Brett Maher (6-7), TE Ben Colton (6-7).

No. 24 Michigan State Spartans (8-4, 5-3)
2011: 11-3 (7-1) / F/+ #10 / FEI #11 / S&P+ #12

Program F/+	-199.9	29	Returning Starters: 4 OFF, 8 DEF		2-Yr Recruiting Rank		35
2011 Offense			**2011 Defense**			**2011 Field Position**	
Offensive F/+	+7.6%	21	Defensive F/+	+7.9%	13	Field Position Advantage	0.539	11
Offensive FEI:	0.15	41	Defensive FEI	-0.542	6	**2012 Projections**		
Offensive S&P+	92.4	48	Defensive S&P+	147.0	8	Mean Wins	8.3	
Rushing S&P+	96.9	83	Rushing S&P+	138.2	8	Proj. F/+	+13.5%	24
Passing S&P+	114.3	32	Passing S&P+	135.4	11	Offensive F/+	+3.7%	37
Standard Downs S&P+	102.0	58	Standard Downs S&P+	135.1	5	Defensive F/+	+9.8%	16
Passing Downs S&P+	114.1	37	Passing Downs S&P+	142.5	6	Strength of Schedule	0.288	42

Posting back-to-back 11-win seasons for the first time in school history, Michigan State appears to have shed its second-class citizenship status in the Big Ten. MSU's upward trajectory under Mark Dantonio has been fueled by a reliable offense, fierce defense, and an uncanny ability to seize opportunities in a handful of spectacular moments. Among the highlights last season was a 50-yard touchdown completion to beat Wisconsin as time expired, which capped Michigan State's fifth double-digit comeback victory in the last four years. Still, a BCS bowl berth remains an elusive goal and the Spartans' staying power as one of the conference's leaders is in doubt this fall after the departure of several key players.

Three-year starting quarterback Kirk Cousins was a reliable winner for Michigan State, and the loss of his leadership isn't an asset our metrics can quantify. The data does tell us that the offense rarely led the way in Michigan State's recent success, and in fact, the Spartans' Offensive FEI regressed somewhat each season Cousins was at the helm. Running backs Le'Veon Bell and Edwin Baker combined for more than 1,500 yards last year, but Baker averaged only 3.9 yards per carry with a minus-13.2 Adj. POE. He perhaps foolishly left for the NFL, but the Spartans' rushing game shouldn't miss a beat with senior Larry Caper getting more carries. Four offensive line starters return as well, so the ground game will be an area of strength as long as a new faces in the passing game can keep defenses honest. Michigan State struggled on third down last year (38 percent, 84th nationally) and rarely put together methodical drives (10 percent, 106th nationally).

The Spartans were at their best on the defensive side of the ball and may be even better this year. Michigan State ranked among the top 10 in S&P+ standard downs, S&P+ passing downs, limiting opponent available yards, and forcing three-and-outs. Eight starters are back, including six all-conference players. Three underclassmen—linebacker Denicos Allen along with stud defensive ends William Gholston and Marcus Rush—combined to tally 46.5 tackles for loss last season. In a bowl game victory over Georgia, Michigan State generated more drive value defensively (17.4 points) than any SEC defense did against the Bulldogs all year. If the Spartans do return to a conference championship game, it will be powered by the defense.

Michigan State's non-conference schedule is challenging, but home games against Boise State and Notre Dame give the Spartans a chance to make an immediate impression in the polls, for better or for worse. A brutal midseason swing will pose an even bigger test—consecutive weeks at Michigan, at Wisconsin, and then home versus Nebraska. If Michigan State can win more than two of those five games, the season will have to be considered a major success.

Top 2013 NFL Prospects: DE William Gholston (1-2), CB Johnny Adams (2-3), RB Le'Veon Bell* (5-6), DT Anthony Rashad White (5-6), CB Mitchell White (6-7), G Chris McDonald (6-7).*

No. 34 Iowa Hawkeyes (9-3, 5-3)

2011: 7-6 (4-4) / F/+ #42 / FEI #37 / S&P+ #50

Program F/+	-199.9	24	Returning Starters: 6 OFF, 5 DEF			2-Yr Recruiting Rank		33
2011 Offense			**2011 Defense**			**2011 Field Position**		
Offensive F/+	+3.9%	39	Defensive F/+	+1.1%	50	Field Position Advantage	0.492	71
Offensive FEI:	0.127	45	Defensive FEI	-0.172	44	**2012 Projections**		
Offensive S&P+	93.7	45	Defensive S&P+	117.0	53	**Mean Wins**	8.6	
Rushing S&P+	108.5	44	Rushing S&P+	111.6	34	Proj. F/+	+9.3%	34
Passing S&P+	112.1	35	Passing S&P+	89.8	92	Offensive F/+	+6.3%	29
Standard Downs S&P+	110.2	35	Standard Downs S&P+	99.9	63	Defensive F/+	+3.1%	46
Passing Downs S&P+	119.7	28	Passing Downs S&P+	90.6	81	Strength of Schedule	0.471	71

Kirk Ferentz is the longest-tenured head coach in the Big Ten conference, and his teams have posted at least six wins in each of the last 11 years. Nevertheless, elements of the fan base are growing restless with what appears to be a downward trend line. The Hawkeyes have been one of the Big Ten's best at times under Ferentz, but it certainly feels like they've been pushed firmly back into the middle of the second tier for the time being.

The Iowa offense was productive at times last year, but the offseason has not been kind. The graduation of top receiver Marvin McNutt and three starting offensive linemen, the transfer of top rusher Marcus Coker, and an ACL injury suffered by No. 2 rusher Jordan Canzeri all leave the Hawkeyes desperate to find playmakers this fall. If they don't become too one-dimensional, the accuracy of senior quarterback James Vandenberg may continue to be a reliable barometer for Iowa's success. In games in which Vandenberg completed 60 percent of his passes, the Hawkeyes went 7-1 last year, and they lost all five games in which he failed to complete 60 percent of his throws. After McNutt, Vandenberg's favorite target was wide receiver Keenan Davis (713 yards, 58 percent catch rate, 4 touchdowns), and he'll expect to see the lion's share of targets this fall.

The Iowa defense has experience issues too, losing three defensive linemen and 75 percent of the team's sacks to graduation. Linebackers James Morris and Christian Kirksey each chipped in 110 tackles a year ago, and will be the key upperclassmen to watch this fall along with defensive backs Tanner Miller and Micah Hyde. The Hawkeyes defense had only two above-average games last year according to our drive value splits, and really struggled to get opponents off the field. Iowa ranked dead last nationally in methodical drives, allowing 34 opponent possessions to last at least 10 plays. Those drives helped push Iowa into a field position deficit in five games (all losses).

Top 2013 NFL Prospects: CB Micah Hyde (2-3), WR Keenan Davis (3-4), C James Ferentz (4-5), QB James Vandenberg (5-6).

No. 68 Northwestern Wildcats (5-7, 2-6)

2011: 6-7 (3-5) / F/+ #59 / FEI #51 / S&P+ #60

Program F/+	-200.0	66	Returning Starters: 5 OFF, 5 DEF			2-Yr Recruiting Rank		71
2011 Offense			**2011 Defense**			**2011 Field Position**		
Offensive F/+	+5.4%	29	Defensive F/+	-4.5%	93	Field Position Advantage	0.475	95
Offensive FEI:	0.353	20	Defensive FEI	0.242	85	**2012 Projections**		
Offensive S&P+	99.5	24	Defensive S&P+	102.8	87	**Mean Wins**	4.5	
Rushing S&P+	112.1	34	Rushing S&P+	95.9	74	Proj. F/+	-3.3%	68
Passing S&P+	116.9	27	Passing S&P+	74.8	116	Offensive F/+	+3.9%	41
Standard Downs S&P+	116.4	22	Standard Downs S&P+	87.6	105	Defensive F/+	-7.1%	109
Passing Downs S&P+	109.0	48	Passing Downs S&P+	80.2	106	Strength of Schedule	0.376	59

The Wildcats just graduated the winningest class in school history, a group that racked up 30 wins in four years and made four bowl trips. The program has been revived a bit under Pat Fitzgerald, but consistent success simply isn't part of Northwestern's DNA. The trendline is stagnant, if not drifting downward, and bowl eligibility in 2012 is no guarantee.

Quarterback Kain Colter started in place of an injured Dan Persa in a handful of games last fall, including a victory over Nebraska. Colter demonstrated his versatility the rest of the year at other positions, leading the team in rushing (654 yards) and ranking third in receiving (458 yards). Fitzgerald's offenses have frequently confounded Big Ten defenses, and Colter's playmaking ability will be leaned on heavily this fall. Northwestern quarterbacks racked up 73 percent of the Wildcats' total offensive yardage last year, the second-highest percentage in the Big Ten.

The defense needs a major overhaul if the Wildcats expect to be more competitive this fall. Northwestern had only two games last year in which the defense allowed fewer points than expected based on field position, against Rice and Minnesota, two of the worst offenses in college football. Northwestern forced a three-and-out on only 22 percent of opponent drives last year, good for 112th nationally. The front seven this fall is experienced, but the secondary returns only one starter, safety Ibraheim Campbell, who earned Freshman All-American honors last year and led the team in tackles.

Our projections favor the Wildcats in only two FBS games this fall (Indiana and Minnesota), and the Big Ten schedule will be a challenge. The potential for bowl eligibility hinges on non-conference games against similarly weak opponents—at Syracuse, then home versus Vanderbilt and Boston College in the first three weeks.

Top 2013 NFL Prospects: None.

No. 84 Minnesota Golden Gophers (4-8, 1-7)

2011: 3-9 (2-6) / F/+ #99 / FEI #104 / S&P+ #94

Program F/+	-200.1	82	Returning Starters: 6 OFF, 5 DEF			2-Yr Recruiting Rank		53
2011 Offense			**2011 Defense**			**2011 Field Position**		
Offensive F/+	-6.9%	94	**Defensive F/+**	-5.0%	95	Field Position Advantage	0.491	73
Offensive FEI:	-0.188	87	Defensive FEI	0.442	106	**2012 Projections**		
Offensive S&P+	79.8	91	Defensive S&P+	101.1	91	**Mean Wins**	4.3	
Rushing S&P+	96.3	84	Rushing S&P+	91.7	93	Proj. F/+	-7.7%	84
Passing S&P+	97.7	68	Passing S&P+	99.8	63	Offensive F/+	-4.6%	81
Standard Downs S&P+	94.1	87	Standard Downs S&P+	93.8	86	Defensive F/+	-3.1%	72
Passing Downs S&P+	92.8	90	Passing Downs S&P+	110.1	45	Strength of Schedule	0.386	60

The highlights of Jerry Kill's 3-9 debut season at Minnesota were few and far between, but the year did end on a strong note, a 20-point victory over Illinois in Minneapolis. Actually, the high note may have been a two-point loss on the road to the USC Trojans in Week 1, one of the most inexplicable results of the year considering where each team ended up.

To take another step forward as a program, the Golden Gophers will look again to senior quarterback MarQueis Gray to lead the way. His 51 percent completion rate is a huge liability, but he picked up 966 yards rushing out of the quarterback position and was responsible for 14 of Minnesota's 24 touchdowns a year ago. He's also pretty much the only skill position player this fall with significant experience. The fresh faces on offense have nowhere to go but up. The Golden Gophers ranked 105th in points per drive (1.5) and struggled to finish value drives with any kind of consistent success. Defensively, the results weren't much better and the outlook for 2012 isn't any more promising. Minnesota collected only nine opponent turnovers all year, tied for fewest in the nation. The leading tacklers and playmakers have all graduated.

Minnesota's shot to improve on its record from a year ago is to grab a few easy victories against one of the weakest non-conference schedules in the nation, and possibly pick up another win against the bottom of the Big Ten. A winless conference slate is well within reach, however.

Top 2013 NFL Prospects: None.

Brian Fremeau

Projected Win Probabilities For Big Ten Teams

Big Ten Leaders	12-0	11-1	10-2	9-3	8-4	7-5	6-6	5-7	4-8	3-9	2-10	1-11	0-12	8-0	7-1	6-2	5-3	4-4	3-5	2-6	1-7	0-8
Illinois	-	-	2	9	21	29	23	12	3	1	-	-	-	-	1	5	22	36	26	9	1	-
Indiana	-	-	-	-	-	1	4	14	29	33	16	3	-	-	-	-	-	-	4	17	40	39
Ohio State	5	18	30	27	14	5	1	-	-	-	-	-	-	6	23	34	25	10	2	-	-	-
Penn State	-	3	10	22	28	22	11	3	1	-	-	-	-	1	6	19	31	27	13	3	-	-
Purdue	-	-	-	-	1	7	19	31	27	13	2	-	-	-	-	-	2	9	25	37	23	4
Wisconsin	5	18	32	27	13	4	1	-	-	-	-	-	-	6	23	34	25	10	2	-	-	-

Big Ten Legends	12-0	11-1	10-2	9-3	8-4	7-5	6-6	5-7	4-8	3-9	2-10	1-11	0-12	8-0	7-1	6-2	5-3	4-4	3-5	2-6	1-7	0-8
Iowa	1	6	19	30	26	13	4	1	-	-	-	-	-	1	8	25	34	23	8	1	-	-
Michigan	-	3	13	29	31	17	6	1	-	-	-	-	-	6	26	37	23	7	1	-	-	-
Michigan State	-	4	15	26	28	18	7	2	-	-	-	-	-	2	10	28	33	20	6	1	-	-
Minnesota	-	-	-	-	1	3	13	27	30	19	6	1	-	-	-	-	-	2	11	32	39	16
Nebraska	-	4	15	25	27	19	8	2	-	-	-	-	-	1	6	20	31	26	13	3	-	-
Northwestern	-	-	-	-	2	5	16	26	27	17	6	1	-	-	-	-	3	12	29	35	18	3

Big 12 Conference

One has to hand it to the Big 12: It is never, ever boring. Whether we are talking about the five consecutive seasons of conference-wide offensive fireworks or the three straight offseasons of extreme realignment drama, there is never a dull moment when the Big 12 is involved, never an instance where either defensive coordinators or conference commissioners can feel comfortable with their lots in life.

Thus far, 2012 has promised no drop-off in drama. West Virginia and TCU replace new SEC members Texas A&M and Missouri on the conference roster, bringing with them a pair of exciting offenses and recently successful defenses. Although the conference took a hit with the departures of players like Baylor quarterback Robert Griffin III, Oklahoma State receiver Justin Blackmon and Oklahoma receiver Ryan Broyles, it is still not lacking for offensive star power. Quarterbacks Landry Jones (Oklahoma), Geno Smith (West Virginia) and Collin Klein (Kansas State) lead the way, while TCU, Oklahoma State and Texas should all field exciting, deep stables of running backs.

Off the field, meanwhile, the rumor-mongering and realignment talk have continued. Only this time, the Big 12 is the aggressor. Despite losing one-third of its original members in a two-year period, and despite many considering it on life support on a couple of different occasions, the conference has thrived, forged a certain level of unity and, with recent moves, reestablished itself as a stable player in the world of college sports. Rumors of Florida State, Clemson, and others joining the Big 12's ranks were stunning at first and have become more realistic over time.

Regardless of who will or will not be a conference member in the future, the Big 12 promises to put one of the most consistently exciting college football products on the field in 2012. The SEC may have won the last six national titles, but the Big 12 is still the No. 2 conference in terms of quality and No. 1 in terms of entertainment.

No. 3 Oklahoma Sooners (10-2, 8-1)

2011: 10-3 (6-3) / F/+ #7 / FEI #4 / S&P+ #7

Program F/+	-199.8	2	Returning Starters: 8 OFF, 7 DEF			2-Yr Recruiting Rank		12
2011 Offense			**2011 Defense**			**2011 Field Position**		
Offensive F/+	+11.4%	11	**Defensive F/+**	+9.7%	8	Field Position Advantage	0.559	4
Offensive FEI:	0.386	18	Defensive FEI	-0.464	12	**2012 Projections**		
Offensive S&P+	105.5	17	Defensive S&P+	150.1	6	**Mean Wins**	10.4	
Rushing S&P+	124.2	14	Rushing S&P+	145.9	6	Proj. F/+	+27.5%	3
Passing S&P+	115.2	29	Passing S&P+	135.4	10	Offensive F/+	+14.9%	4
Standard Downs S&P+	116.8	21	Standard Downs S&P+	137.2	3	Defensive F/+	+12.6%	8
Passing Downs S&P+	123.6	25	Passing Downs S&P+	138.0	11	Strength of Schedule	0.198	29

In five-year F/+ rankings, Oklahoma places second, ahead of LSU, Florida, Ohio State, Boise State, and every other recent power not named Alabama. They have produced two Heisman winners in the last decade, they have won four of the last six Big 12 titles, and they have ranked No. 1 at some point in five of the last 12 seasons.

So why the bad mood?

Most of the stories coming out of Norman in recent months have had little to do with the product on the field. Instead, they have dealt more with transfers, suspensions, and players' parents telling recruits not to come to OU on Twitter.

Negativity has seeped into the Oklahoma program, and it doubled when the Sooners got pummeled by longtime whipping boy Oklahoma State last December. For Bob Stoops, the solution was simple: Bring in new blood, even if it's old blood. Some players were shown the door, others were suspended, and a host of (hopeful) instant-impact recruits were brought to Norman. But the biggest change could come on the coaching staff; Stoops reintroduced his brother Mike as defensive coordinator after Mike spent the last eight seasons as Arizona's head coach.

Oklahoma's defense struggled with injuries and personnel issues last fall, and it showed. A depleted, iffy secondary suffered a series of breakdowns in losses to Texas Tech, Baylor and Oklahoma State. The Sooners ranked sixth in the nation in forcing three-and-outs, but ranked No. 64 in allowing explosive drives. Corner Demontre Hurst and free safety Tony Jefferson will lead what is likely a rejuvenated unit, but the biggest question mark for 2012 will be the pass rush. Ends Ronnell Lewis and Frank Alexander combined for 40 percent of the Sooners' 2011 sacks, and both are gone.

Since bottoming out in 2009 following Sam Bradford's season-ending injury, the Oklahoma offense has improved steadily in each of the last two seasons. The Sooners rose to 11th in Offensive F/+ in 2011 despite losing their best running back (Dom Whaley) to injury in October and their all-world receiver (Ryan Broyles) in November. Whaley returns and will run behind a line that has combined for 102 career starts, but the passing game is a question mark. No true go-to receiver emerged in Broyles' absence, and three of the Sooners' top four returning wideouts are suspended to start the season. Junior Kenny Stills is a keeper, but he will be flanked by a host of newcomers, most notably blue-chip freshman Trey Metoyer who wowed in the spring.

Top 2013 NFL Draft Prospects: QB Landry Jones (1), CB Demontre Hurst (2-3), FS Tony Jefferson* (2-3), FB Trey Millard* (4-5).

No. 5 Oklahoma State Cowboys (10-2, 7-2)
2011: 12-1 (8-1) / F/+ #3 / FEI #2 / S&P+ #5

Program F/+	-199.9	13	Returning Starters: 6 OFF, 8 DEF			2-Yr Recruiting Rank		30
2011 Offense			**2011 Defense**			**2011 Field Position**		
Offensive F/+	+14.0%	5	Defensive F/+	+11.3%	3	Field Position Advantage	0.558	5
Offensive FEI:	0.414	12	Defensive FEI	-0.728	3	**2012 Projections**		
Offensive S&P+	126.2	2	Defensive S&P+	135.1	16	Mean Wins	9.9	
Rushing S&P+	159.6	1	Rushing S&P+	114.2	26	Proj. F/+	+22.4%	5
Passing S&P+	130.8	13	Passing S&P+	127.1	14	Offensive F/+	+10.9%	14
Standard Downs S&P+	132.5	6	Standard Downs S&P+	113.7	26	Defensive F/+	+11.4%	13
Passing Downs S&P+	139.1	9	Passing Downs S&P+	135.9	13	Strength of Schedule	0.181	25

The 2012 Oklahoma State Cowboys are perfectly designed to confuse projections. OSU has made wonderful strides in its seven seasons under Mike Gundy, and it culminated in 2010 (11-2, 12th in F/+) and 2011 (12-1, third). The Cowboys were an overtime loss to Iowa State away from facing LSU in the BCS title game, and they return upwards of 14 starters, eight on a defense that ranked third in Def. F/+ last fall. So they're going to be great again in 2012, right?

Then again, here are some of the 2011 starters they must replace: quarterback Brandon Weeden (a first-round draft pick), receiver Justin Blackmon (a two-time Biletnikoff Award winner), receiver Josh Cooper (139 receptions in two years), offensive linemen Grant Garner and Levy Adcock (each first-team all-conference performers), defensive ends Jamie Blatnick and Richetti Jones (a combined 20.0 tackles for loss) and safety Markelle Martin (5.0 tackles for loss, 11 passes broken up). Oklahoma State returns a solid amount of depth but loses perhaps eight of its 11 or 12 best players from last year's Fiesta Bowl championship squad.

It is likely that OSU's offense will still be solid in 2012, though it will also be redefined. A trio of exciting running backs (Joseph Randle, Jeremy Smith and Herschel Sims, who combined for 2,104 yards, 6.4 per carry, and a plus-60.2 Adj. POE) will share the backfield with new starting quarterback (and true freshman) Wes Lunt. Randle and Sims also combined for 65 targets and 54 catches last year, so expect to see a lot of hand-offs and safe passes while Lunt develops a rapport with receivers like seniors Tracy Moore and Isaiah Anderson and sophomore Josh Stewart.

Defensively, OSU seemed to pull off a magic act in 2011, taking the bend-but-don't-break philosophy to extremes. The Cowboys ranked 10th in the country in Defensive PPP+ and third in DFEI despite ranking a whopping 107th in yards allowed. They faced a series of explosive offenses, but they defended 87 passes, picked off 24 interceptions, and forced 18 fumbles (each a Top 10 total). Whether this magic act is replicable without the Cowboys' two best pass rushers and their best ball-hawk safety, we don't know. But corners Brodrick Brown and Justin Gilbert are among the best in America, Shaun Lewis is an exciting linebacker, and tackle Nigel Nicholas is a force in the middle.

Top 2013 NFL Draft Prospects: RB Joseph Randle* (2-3), G Lane Taylor (5-6), CB Broderick Brown (5-6).

No. 9 Texas Longhorns (9-3, 6-3)
2011: 8-5 (4-5) / F/+ #19 / FEI #28 / S&P+ #22

Program F/+	-199.9	11	Returning Starters: 10 OFF, 7 DEF			2-Yr Recruiting Rank		2
2011 Offense			**2011 Defense**			**2011 Field Position**		
Offensive F/+	-0.2%	62	**Defensive F/+**	+10.7%	4	Field Position Advantage	0.501	57
Offensive FEI:	-0.081	70	Defensive FEI	-0.523	9	**2012 Projections**		
Offensive S&P+	82.0	75	Defensive S&P+	149.2	7	**Mean Wins**	9.2	
Rushing S&P+	106.2	50	Rushing S&P+	151.5	3	Proj. F/+	+19.9%	9
Passing S&P+	85.2	97	Passing S&P+	138.6	8	Offensive F/+	+4.0%	39
Standard Downs S&P+	101.3	61	Standard Downs S&P+	127.5	8	Defensive F/+	+15.8%	3
Passing Downs S&P+	88.4	99	Passing Downs S&P+	156.7	2	Strength of Schedule	0.166	24

Texas makes more money from its athletic department than any other university in the country. It is the elite recruiting power in probably the most football-rich state. It has some of the best athletic facilities the world has ever seen and spends more money on its football team than anybody.

In other words, Texas is supposed to be really, really good. But while the defense has mostly held up its end of the bargain in recent years, the offense simply vanished. Colt McCoy, Jordan Shipley and company kept the Longhorns afloat for a few years, but once they were gone, the Texas offense fell to unacceptable levels: 110th in 2010 and, after bringing in an almost entirely new offensive staff, 62nd in 2011.

Texas utilized a run-heavy attack in returning to offensive mediocrity in 2011, and they will likely do so again this fall. Though his sack rate (8.5 percent) and interception rate (4.6) definitely left something to be desired, quarterback David Ash's running ability made him at least a reasonably decent game manager last fall. If a hefty batch of blue-chip running backs—sophomores Malcolm Brown and Joe Bergeron, senior D.J. Monroe, incoming blue-chipper Johnathan Gray—can actually stay healthy this year, the run game should improve once again, especially with a line that returns six players with starting experience and 65 career starts. But what about the passing game? Ash's right arm is far from NFL-quality, and of the top three returning targets (Mike Davis, Jaxon Shipley, Marquise Goodwin), only one had even a 57 percent catch rate or averaged better than 7.5 yards per target (Shipley).

As iffy as the offense might remain, the defense could pick up the slack even more capably than it did last season. In Manny Diaz's first year as defensive coordinator, the Longhorns ranked first in the country in Adjusted Line Yards, third in Rushing S&P+ and eighth in Passing S&P+. With seven of their top eight linemen returning, including perhaps the best pair of ends in the country (Jackson Jeffcoat and Alex Okafor combined for 35 tackles for loss and 15 sacks in 2011), the Longhorns may have the best defensive line in college football. An exciting pair of cornerbacks (Carringtom Byndom and Quandre Diggs) return as well, but Texas will need to find replacements for a pair of playmaking linebackers, Emmanuel Acho and Keenan Robinson.

Top 2013 NFL Draft Prospects: DE Alex Okafor (1), DE Jackson Jeffcoat* (1), SS Kenny Vaccaro (2-3), CB Carrington Byndom* (2-3).

No. 12 TCU Horned Frogs (9-3, 6-3)

2011: 11-2 (7-0) / F/+ #17 / FEI #21 / S&P+ #13

Program F/+	-199.8	6	Returning Starters: 6 OFF, 7 DEF			2-Yr Recruiting Rank		31
2011 Offense			**2011 Defense**			**2011 Field Position**		
Offensive F/+	+9.1%	16	Defensive F/+	+3.9%	30	Field Position Advantage	0.538	13
Offensive FEI:	0.333	21	Defensive FEI	-0.184	42	**2012 Projections**		
Offensive S&P+	108.1	13	Defensive S&P+	128.8	25	**Mean Wins**	8.7	
Rushing S&P+	122.5	16	Rushing S&P+	142.4	7	Proj. F/+	+18.8%	12
Passing S&P+	122.8	18	Passing S&P+	95.2	75	Offensive F/+	+11.4%	12
Standard Downs S&P+	111.2	29	Standard Downs S&P+	118.5	17	Defensive F/+	+7.5%	24
Passing Downs S&P+	137.7	11	Passing Downs S&P+	94.9	76	Strength of Schedule	0.157	21

It's go time for the purple and white. After three and a half seasons of elite football (2008-10, plus the second half of 2011), the TCU Horned Frogs once again find themselves in a major conference. They've got a new stadium and a new lease on life, and now they face their toughest schedule in years. TCU has grown accustomed to playing between about two and four solid teams per year, but now they begin life in what was perhaps the deepest conference in the country last year.

Despite their reputation as defensive stalwarts, TCU began to figure out how to play offense in recent years. They improved to 16th in Offensive F/+ last fall, and while offensive co-coordinator Justin Fuente is gone (he is now Memphis' head coach), a good amount of personnel returns for co-coordinators Jarrett Anderson and Rusty Burns. Junior quarterback Casey Pachall had a lovely debut replacing Andy Dalton in 2011: 2,921 yards, a 67-percent completion rate, 25 touchdowns and only seven interceptions. The former four-star recruit returns three of his top four targets from last year (Josh Boyce, Skye Dawson and Brandon Carter, who combined for 129 catches, 1,850 yards and a per-target average of 9.8 yards), along with a trio of explosive running backs (Matthew Tucker, Waymon James and Ed Wesley, who combined for 2,303 yards and a plus-29.5 Adj. POE). The line returns just two starters and 28 career starts, however. That is a rather obvious red flag.

Following some serious turnover in personnel, the TCU defense took a hefty step backwards at the start of the 2011 season, but it eventually rounded into its normal form; the Horned Frogs allowed an average of 30.5 Adj. Points per Game in the first five contests and just 21.5 over the final eight. Six starters return, including explosive end Stansly Maponga; but depth in the secondary, where five of the top seven tacklers are gone, could be an issue. TCU runs one of the fastest defenses in the country out of a 4-2-5 alignment—a defense seemingly custom-made for handling the spread offenses of the Big 12—and it probably goes without saying that you need a healthy number of strong defensive backs to make the clock tick in this defense.

Even when outmatched, TCU is a threat in every game due to its consistency in managing field position advantages under Gary Patterson. The Horned Frogs have ranked in the top 15 for FPA in each of the last five seasons, and no Big 12 program was able to do so more than once.

Top 2013 NFL Draft Prospects: QB Casey Pachall* (3-4), G Blaize Foltz (3-4), WR Josh Boyce* (3-4), RB Matthew Tucker (6-7).

No. 20 West Virginia Mountaineers (8-4, 5-4)

2011: 10-3 (5-2) / F/+ #23 / FEI #17 / S&P+ #28

Program F/+	-199.9	12	Returning Starters: 8 OFF, 6 DEF			2-Yr Recruiting Rank		43
2011 Offense			**2011 Defense**			**2011 Field Position**		
Offensive F/+	+10.7%	13	Defensive F/+	+0.9%	52	Field Position Advantage	0.490	75
Offensive FEI:	0.53	4	Defensive FEI	-0.216	35	**2012 Projections**		
Offensive S&P+	105.8	15	Defensive S&P+	118.7	49	**Mean Wins**	8.2	
Rushing S&P+	124.5	13	Rushing S&P+	94.8	80	Proj. F/+	+15.1%	20
Passing S&P+	123.7	17	Passing S&P+	100.3	60	Offensive F/+	+13.5%	8
Standard Downs S&P+	115.7	23	Standard Downs S&P+	101.0	56	Defensive F/+	+1.5%	53
Passing Downs S&P+	160.0	2	Passing Downs S&P+	99.4	67	Strength of Schedule	0.164	22

The concept of geography may have taken a hit when West Virginia joined the Big 12, a conference in which its closest rival (Iowa State) is 875 miles away. But there's no question that the Mountaineers have found kindred spirits from a stylistic perspective. Head coach Dana Holgorsen made a name for himself as the offensive coordinator at both Texas Tech (2005-07) and Oklahoma State (2010), and he will bring his own version of the famed Air Raid offense to "rival" towns like Austin, Lubbock (distance: 1,500 miles), Stillwater and Ames this fall.

Holgorsen's shift from OSU offensive coordinator to West Virginia's head-coach-in-waiting to West Virginia's head coach took just a few months, but he handled himself well in his first year in charge. The Mountaineers went 10-3, advanced to their first BCS bowl since 2007, and made an enormous statement by posting 70 points on Clemson in the Orange Bowl. Now they return most of the personnel that was only beginning to learn the offense last year.

Quarterback Geno Smith is one of the more exciting quarterbacks in the country; he completed 66 percent of his passes and threw 31 touchdowns to just seven picks last fall, and he has an incredible 1-2 combination at his disposal. Receivers Tavon Austin and Stedman Bailey combined to catch 172 passes last year for 2,459 yards and a per-target average of 10.2 yards. Though obviously a pass-first offense, the Mountaineers were able to run effectively as well—backs Dustin Garrison and Shawne Alston combined for a plus-24.9 Adj. POE last year in 18 carries per game. If the line can overcome the loss of two starters, including three-year starter (and all-conference tackle) Don Barclay, the Air Raid machine should hum.

The defense does face a hefty transition, however. After nine seasons in Morgantown, defensive coordinator Jeff Casteel left for Arizona and was replaced by former Oklahoma State safeties coach Joe DeForest. He will attempt to shift a longtime 3-3-5 defense toward more 3-4 and 4-3 looks, and he will do so despite losing important veterans at each level of the defense. Gone are defensive linemen Julian Miller and Bruce Irvin, who combined for 26 tackles for loss last year. Gone, too, are linebacker Najee Goode and safety Eain Smith. Safeties Terence Garvin and Darwin Cook are strong building blocks, however, assuming they don't miss too much time following a May shoplifting arrest.

Top 2013 NFL Draft Prospects: QB Geno Smith (2-3), WR Tavon Austin (2-3), SS/OLB Terence Garvin (6-7), OLB Josh Francis (6-7).

No. 31 Texas Tech Red Raiders (7-5, 4-5)

2011: 5-7 (2-7) / F/+ #76 / FEI #77 / S&P+ #74

Program F/+	-199.9	34	Returning Starters: 9 OFF, 10 DEF			2-Yr Recruiting Rank		20
2011 Offense			**2011 Defense**			**2011 Field Position**		
Offensive F/+	+2.0%	48	Defensive F/+	-6.7%	106	Field Position Advantage	0.476	94
Offensive FEI:	0.209	33	Defensive FEI	0.555	116	**2012 Projections**		
Offensive S&P+	98.4	29	Defensive S&P+	95.3	107	Mean Wins	7.4	
Rushing S&P+	108.9	43	Rushing S&P+	92.3	91	Proj. F/+	+10.3%	31
Passing S&P+	112.8	33	Passing S&P+	82.0	104	Offensive F/+	+10.0%	16
Standard Downs S&P+	106.3	48	Standard Downs S&P+	91.5	94	Defensive F/+	+0.4%	61
Passing Downs S&P+	127.6	18	Passing Downs S&P+	84.0	100	Strength of Schedule	0.166	23

In theory, Tommy Tuberville has done things just about right in Lubbock. His star power was able to assuage a decent percentage of Texas Tech fans still angry over Mike Leach's dismissal, and he made the hires necessary to both continue Tech's pass-happy ways on offense and take steps forward on defense.

In practice, however, things haven't quite worked out. The Red Raiders have slipped from 11th in Offensive F/+ in 2009, Leach's final season, to 48th in both 2010 and 2011. And unexpectedly, the defense has completely fallen apart, slipping from 37th in 2009 to 106th in 2011.

Tuberville attempted to flip from a 4-3 to a 3-4 defense in 2010, then made another switch, to a 4-2-5, in 2011, and the lack of continuity has been devastating. Tech slipped to 5-7 last fall, their first losing season since 1992.

The natives are getting justifiably restless, but Tuberville will at least have one of the most experienced teams in the country as he attempts to right the ship in 2012. Quarterback Seth Doege (4,004 passing yards in 2011) returns, as do Tech's leading rusher (Eric Stephens), six of last year's top eight receivers (including the top three), and four offensive linemen with starting experience, including a potential all-conference tackle in LaAdrian Waddle. The continuity should help an offense that certainly had its moments last year (580 yards against Kansas State, 572 against Oklahoma in a stunning upset win, 523 against Texas A&M) but just didn't have enough of them.

The problem, then, is the defense. Tuberville brought in *another* new defensive coordinator (Art Kaufman) to install *another* new alignment (4-3) this spring. Kaufman has some interesting pieces with which to work. Safety Terrance Bullitt (four passes broken up, 9.5 tackles for loss in 2011) and linebacker Daniel Cobb (7.5 tackles for loss) are both stellar, and there is disruptive potential in players like end Dartwan Bush and tackle Kerry Hyder. But to put it kindly, the burden of proof is on Tech to prove their defense should eventually be taken seriously.

Top 2013 NFL Draft Prospects: OT LaAdrian Waddle (6-7), QB Seth Doege (6-7).

No. 46 Baylor Bears (6-6, 3-6)

2011: 10-3 (6-3) / F/+ #29 / FEI #29 / S&P+ #20

Program F/+		-200.0	74	Returning Starters: 6 OFF, 8 DEF			2-Yr Recruiting Rank		40
2011 Offense				**2011 Defense**			**2011 Field Position**		
Offensive F/+		+15.0%	2	**Defensive F/+**		-4.4%	92	Field Position Advantage	0.482	88
Offensive FEI:		0.865	1	Defensive FEI		0.244	86	**2012 Projections**		
Offensive S&P+		125.0	3	Defensive S&P+		106.9	79	**Mean Wins**	5.9	
Rushing S&P+		130.2	7	Rushing S&P+		99.8	62	Proj. F/+	+5.1%	46
Passing S&P+		148.8	4	Passing S&P+		90.3	91	Offensive F/+	+10.2%	11
Standard Downs S&P+		134.5	4	Standard Downs S&P+		92.8	90	Defensive F/+	-5.1%	107
Passing Downs S&P+		143.5	6	Passing Downs S&P+		98.6	70	Strength of Schedule	0.103	14

It was one hell of a year for the Baylor athletic program. Men's basketball made the Elite Eight, women's basketball went undefeated and won the national title, and baseball spent much of the season in the nation's top five. More notable than all of that, however, was what happened at Floyd Casey Stadium last fall. Art Briles' reclamation project reached its climax with a 10-win season (Baylor's first since 1980 and second ever) and a Heisman Trophy win by charismatic, athletic quarterback Robert Griffin III. The Bears beat Texas for the second consecutive season, pulled off a late-night, last-second win over Oklahoma, won their final six games of the season, and played in quite a few of the season's most exciting games.

So what happens now? Griffin (4,293 passing yards, 848 pre-sack rushing yards) is now the starting quarterback for the Washington Redskins. Star receiver Kendall Wright (1,672 receiving yards) is a Tennessee Titan. Running back Terrance Ganaway (plus-30.4 Adj. POE) and all-conference offensive linemen Robert T. Griffin and Philip Blake are also gone. Briles has done a stunning job of improving Baylor's team speed, and the Bears' foundation is too strong to completely collapse upon these stars' departures. But a step backwards is still inevitable this fall.

The 2012 Baylor offense will be built around quarterback Nick Florence, who showed flashes of excellence filling in for Griffin through the years, and a couple of familiar wideouts: Terrence Williams (957 receiving yards in 2011) and ultra-fast Tevin Reese (877 yards). Former blue-chip running back Lache Seastrunk makes his Baylor debut as well. This team will still be fast and exciting, if a bit less successful.

It is up to the defense, then, to pick up the slack. Part of the reason Baylor games were so exciting last year was because opponents were racking up almost as many yards and points as the Bears were. Defensive coordinator Phil Bennett was able to engineer only marginal improvement; Baylor ranked 106th in Defense F/+ in 2010, 92nd in 2011. Almost everybody returns, for better or worse, including potentially high-caliber players like ends Terrance Lloyd and Gary Mason, Jr., cornerbacks Mike Hicks, K.J. Morton and Joe Williams (combined: 31 passes defended) and nickelback Ahmad Dixon. Still, another season of only minor improvement will result in quite a few more shootouts, and Baylor isn't quite as well-equipped to win those this year, especially if the Bears continue to struggle in special teams (five straight seasons ranked 100th or worse).

Top 2013 NFL Draft Prospects: WR Terrance Williams (2-3), G/T Cyril Richardson (2-3), C Ivory Wade (6-7).*

No. 47 Kansas State Wildcats (6-6, 3-6)

2011: 10-3 (7-2) / F/+ #33 / FEI #18 / S&P+ #64

Program F/+	-200.0	63	Returning Starters: 9 OFF, 7 DEF			2-Yr Recruiting Rank		61
2011 Offense			**2011 Defense**			**2011 Field Position**		
Offensive F/+	+5.3%	30	**Defensive F/+**	+0.9%	51	Field Position Advantage	0.528	21
Offensive FEI:	0.256	29	Defensive FEI	-0.397	19	**2012 Projections**		
Offensive S&P+	87.0	60	Defensive S&P+	113.6	63	**Mean Wins**	5.5	
Rushing S&P+	109.6	39	Rushing S&P+	111.7	33	Proj. F/+	+4.9%	47
Passing S&P+	92.3	81	Passing S&P+	103.8	50	Offensive F/+	+5.9%	32
Standard Downs S&P+	103.1	57	Standard Downs S&P+	107.8	37	Defensive F/+	-1.0%	63
Passing Downs S&P+	99.8	73	Passing Downs S&P+	101.6	62	Strength of Schedule	0.103	13

As fun as it may be when numbers tell you a true story—Team A is overrated, Team B is a title sleeper, Player C is poised for a huge year—it is almost as much fun to be really, really wrong, at least occasionally. In the *Football Outsiders Almanac 2011*, we projected Kansas State to rank 62nd and win just five games. An offense led by big quarterback Collin Klein was expected to thrive (they were projected to rank 22nd in Offensive F/+ and finished 30th), but the defense was, to put it politely, a question mark. The Wildcats had ranked 101st in Defensive F/+ in 2010, but Bill Snyder pulled a couple of Bill Snyder Moves™ and turned things around. He signed a lightly-regarded junior college cornerback named Nigel Malone, and Malone turned into a star, defending 17 passes in 2011. He also brought in former blue-chip linebacker Arthur Brown, a career backup at Miami; Brown recorded 9.5 tackles for loss, logged an enormous interception against Baylor, and became the heart and soul of a defense that improved to 51st in Defensive F/+.

As incorrect as our projections were, our week-to-week rankings were also no match for Snyder's brand of sorcery. K-State ranked just 33rd in F/+ for the season but won close game after close game. They went 8-1 in one-possession games in 2011, won 10 games in all, and attended their biggest bowl (the Cotton) since the 2004 Fiesta Bowl. It was an incredibly enjoyable story; it is also going to be incredibly difficult to replicate.

It probably goes without saying that the numbers are skeptical of Kansas State after such a smoke-and-mirrors success story. Quite a few of last year's stars (Klein, running back John Hubert, Brown, Malone, defensive ends Adam Davis and Meshak Williams) return, but there are holes, particularly in the trenches. The Wildcats must replace four starters on the offensive line, and three of their better defensive playmakers (end Jordan Voelker, linebacker Emmanuel Lamur, cornerback David Garrett) are gone. When you rely to a degree on bailing yourself out with turnovers and bend-don't-break defense, you need every playmaker you can get. Last year proved that it is foolish to bet against Bill Snyder and Kansas State, but the Wildcats' margin for error this fall will be even smaller than last season.

Top 2013 NFL Draft Prospects: MLB Arthur Brown (2-3), CB Nigel Malone (4-5), FB Braden Wilson (6-7).

No. 83 Iowa State Cyclones (3-9, 1-8)

2011: 6-7 (3-6) / F/+ #72 / FEI #60 / S&P+ #90

Program F/+	-200.1	92	Returning Starters: 7 OFF, 5 DEF			2-Yr Recruiting Rank		72
2011 Offense			**2011 Defense**			**2011 Field Position**		
Offensive F/+	-4.3%	82	**Defensive F/+**	+0.6%	55	Field Position Advantage	0.490	74
Offensive FEI:	-0.151	82	Defensive FEI	-0.197	37	**2012 Projections**		
Offensive S&P+	75.4	97	Defensive S&P+	109.8	71	**Mean Wins**	2.7	
Rushing S&P+	100.4	68	Rushing S&P+	100.2	59	Proj. F/+	-6.8%	83
Passing S&P+	83.3	104	Passing S&P+	106.8	39	Offensive F/+	-5.9%	88
Standard Downs S&P+	88.2	103	Standard Downs S&P+	107.5	38	Defensive F/+	-1.0%	66
Passing Downs S&P+	100.3	69	Passing Downs S&P+	106.0	56	Strength of Schedule	0.110	16

No coach picks his spots better than Paul Rhoads. The Iowa State head coach engineered a stunning upset at Nebraska in 2009, pulled off an upset at Texas in 2010, took out Iowa in 2011, then painted his masterpiece, an overtime win over No. 2 Oklahoma State last November. The game kept the Cowboys out of the BCS title game and solidified Rhoads' reputation as a giant killer. Iowa State has already logged more huge wins in three years under Rhoads than it did in 14 years under Dan McCarney and Gene Chizik. Of course, the Cyclones have also gone just 18-20. One big upset per year is not the same as sustained success, something which has eluded Rhoads and the Cyclones of late.

To reach six wins in 2012, Iowa State might need a *few* upsets. A brutal nine-game Big 12 slate, combined with non-conference games against solid Tulsa and Iowa teams, creates a pretty steep hill for the Cyclones to climb, especially after quite a bit of attrition in the trenches. ISU must replace its top two offensive linemen (including all-conference tackle Kelechi Osemele) and three of its four starting defensive linemen.

The complexion of Iowa State's teams have shifted dramatically in Rhoads' three seasons. They have improved each year on the defensive side of the ball (from 106th in Defensive F/+ in 2009 to 55th in 2011) and regressed with similar velocity on offense (from 34th in Offensive F/+ in 2009 to 82nd in 2011). Hope for a rebound on offense lies in the backfield; quarterback Jared Barnett proved himself a decent runner and game manager as a redshirt freshman last fall, and junior running back James White showed occasional explosiveness. Alas, the passing game was, and should remain, a disaster.

The defense must overcome the losses of ends Jake Lattimer and Patrick Neal and tackle Steven Ruempolhamer, but there is both hope and depth. Linebackers Jake Knott and A.J. Klein (combined: 11.5 tackles for loss, 12 passes defended, and more than 23 percent of ISU's tackles) somehow still have eligibility remaining after what seems like 16 years each in Ames, and undersized cornerback Jeremy Reeves is interesting and disruptive.

Top 2013 NFL Draft Prospects: OLB Jake Knott (5-6), MLB A.J. Klein (5-6).

No. 91 Kansas Jayhawks (3-9, 1-8)
2011: 2-10 (0-8) / F/+ #113 / FEI #114 / S&P+ #109

Program F/+	-200.0	77	Returning Starters: 8 OFF, 6 DEF			2-Yr Recruiting Rank		49
2011 Offense			**2011 Defense**			**2011 Field Position**		
Offensive F/+	-9.9%	107	**Defensive F/+**	-7.2%	111	Field Position Advantage	0.448	114
Offensive FEI:	-0.322	102	Defensive FEI	0.337	96	**2012 Projections**		
Offensive S&P+	79.9	90	Defensive S&P+	88.2	114	**Mean Wins**	2.8	
Rushing S&P+	98.2	75	Rushing S&P+	92.6	89	Proj. F/+	-9.9%	91
Passing S&P+	95.9	75	Passing S&P+	82.9	103	Offensive F/+	-5.1%	91
Standard Downs S&P+	88.1	104	Standard Downs S&P+	91.0	99	Defensive F/+	-4.9%	81
Passing Downs S&P+	110.4	44	Passing Downs S&P+	82.6	104	Strength of Schedule	0.117	18

Charlie Weis must be the best job interviewee of all time. An outstanding assistant coach in the NFL, Weis has struggled at the college level, but he keeps receiving new opportunities. In his final three years as Notre Dame's head coach, he went 16-21. After a successful season as the Kansas City Chiefs' offensive coordinator, he took the same position at the University of Florida, and the once-explosive Gators ranked 65th in Offensive F/+. Somehow Weis fell up, landing a second chance at a head coaching position. He inherits what has been an absolutely hopeless Kansas program over the last couple of seasons.

Around the same time Weis' tenure was falling apart at Notre Dame, Kansas was thriving under Mark Mangino. The Jayhawks went 12-1 and won the Orange Bowl in 2007, but things have headed downhill since. They ranked 14th in F/+ that season, fell to 56th in 2009, and then ranked an abhorrent 113th in both 2010 and 2011 as Turner Gill took over for Mangino, then was fired. Weis has done his best to restock a bare cupboard with transfers, but improvement should be minimal in the short term. Former Notre Dame quarterback (and Weis signee) Dayne Crist is the presumptive starting quarterback; he has a decent weapon in sophomore running back Tony Pierson, but that's about it. Running back James Sims is serviceable, as are receivers D.J. Beshears and Kale Pick, but the explosiveness is mostly limited to Pearson.

Defensive coordinator Dave Campo (yes, *that* Dave Campo) has quite a bit of work to do to restore a defense that ranked 111th in Defensive F/+ last fall and must replace its best player, linebacker Steven Johnson. End Toben Opurum is an exciting pass rusher, safety Bradley McDougald is a playmaker, and linebacker Darius Willis was second on the team with eight tackles for loss last year. Beyond that? Good luck.

Top 2013 NFL Draft Prospects: DE Toben Opurum (6-7), QB Dayne Crist (6-7), OT Tanner Hawkinson.

Bill Connelly

Projected Win Probabilities For Big 12 Teams

Big 12	12-0	11-1	10-2	9-3	8-4	7-5	6-6	5-7	4-8	3-9	2-10	1-11	0-12	9-0	8-1	7-2	6-3	5-4	4-5	3-6	2-7	1-8	0-9
Baylor	-	-	-	2	8	21	32	25	10	2	-	-	-	-	-	-	2	11	26	35	21	5	-
Iowa State	-	-	-	-	-	-	1	4	16	32	32	14	1	-	-	-	-	-	1	9	28	41	21
Kansas	-	-	-	-	-	-	-	4	19	39	31	7	-	-	-	-	-	-	-	2	16	49	33
Kansas State	-	-	-	1	6	16	28	29	16	4	-	-	-	-	-	-	2	8	24	34	24	7	1
Oklahoma	16	35	30	14	4	1	-	-	-	-	-	-	-	20	39	28	11	2	-	-	-	-	-
Oklahoma State	6	27	35	22	8	2	-	-	-	-	-	-	-	6	29	36	21	7	1	-	-	-	-
TCU	1	6	20	31	27	12	3	-	-	-	-	-	-	1	6	22	33	26	10	2	-	-	-
Texas	2	12	29	32	18	6	1	-	-	-	-	-	-	2	12	31	32	17	5	1	-	-	-
Texas Tech	-	-	3	14	28	31	18	5	1	-	-	-	-	-	-	3	14	28	31	18	5	1	-
West Virginia	-	2	12	26	32	20	7	1	-	-	-	-	-	-	3	12	28	32	19	5	1	-	-

Pac-12 Conference

Back in the summer of 2009, Larry Scott didn't strike many people as a particularly revolutionary figure in college football. The new Pac-10 commissioner was a French-speaking, tennis-playing Ivy Leaguer who'd spent the previous decade living in London as CEO of the Women's Tennis Association, and hadn't attended a college football game of any stripe since Harvard-Yale in 1997. He arrived in his new job talking, bizarrely, about taking the Pac-10 brand to China.

Three years later, it would be hard to find anyone in the sport who doesn't view Scott as either a visionary or a threat, or both. In year one, he put the Pac-10 on the offensive in the early stages of the realignment wars, adding Colorado and Utah to the ranks and very nearly destroying the Big 12 in the process. In year two, he oversaw the creation of a conference championship game, negotiated a new television contract that roughly quintupled annual payouts to member schools, and laid plans for multiple cable networks owned entirely by the conference. (Subsequently presented with a second opportunity to carve up the Big 12 by poaching Oklahoma and Texas, Scott and a majority of Pac-12 presidents decided to pass.) He appointed a new officiating czar to improve the conference's reputation for fielding dubious refs, and to clean house if necessary. (Surprise: They decided it was.) Then, his league's slice of the ever-expanding pie secured, he took a week-long business trip to China.

From the logo down, the Pac-12 of 2012 is virtually unrecognizable from the stagnant conference Scott found three years ago, and nowhere more so than on the sidelines. Taking a cue from the new conference overlords in Eugene, Arizona hired Rich Rodriguez to install the "Spread 'n Shred" scheme that made West Virginia a national power in the middle of the last decade. Washington State turned to Mike Leach to import the "Air Raid" system that once forced the outside world to acknowledge the existence of Texas Tech. Arizona State is going up-tempo under new coach Todd Graham. UCLA is going outside the Bruin family for the first time in half a century with Jim Mora. Jon Embree and David Shaw are beginning their second seasons on opposite ends of the spectrum at Colorado and Stanford, respectively. Lane Kiffin is hitting year three at USC, bowl ban finally behind him. Already Chip Kelly and Steve Sarkisian, entering their fourth years at Oregon and Washington, must be beginning to feel like old hands.

At the same time, the only head coaches who were in their current positions when Scott was hired—Oregon State's Mike Riley and Jeff Tedford at Cal—both saw their stock plummet last year due to rare losing seasons. After more than a decade apiece at schools that have never had much sustained success in football, they know the value of patience when it comes to building something. At this rate, though, it's just uncertain how much longer they'll be able to afford that patience.

NORTH

No. 4 Oregon Ducks (11-1, 8-1)
2011: 12-2 (8-1) / F/+ #5 / FEI #6 / S&P+ #4

Program F/+	-199.8	7	Returning Starters: 5 OFF, 6 DEF			2-Yr Recruiting Rank		11
2011 Offense			**2011 Defense**			**2011 Field Position**		
Offensive F/+	+14.2%	4	**Defensive F/+**	+8.8%	10	Field Position Advantage	0.508	44
Offensive FEI:	0.461	10	Defensive FEI	-0.549	5	**2012 Projections**		
Offensive S&P+	121.9	4	Defensive S&P+	144.2	10	**Mean Wins**	10.9	
Rushing S&P+	137.4	5	Rushing S&P+	121.2	17	Proj. F/+	+25.0%	4
Passing S&P+	133.0	11	Passing S&P+	142.7	6	Offensive F/+	+14.3%	5
Standard Downs S&P+	136.2	3	Standard Downs S&P+	125.9	10	Defensive F/+	+10.8%	14
Passing Downs S&P+	112.6	40	Passing Downs S&P+	138.5	10	Strength of Schedule	0.396	62

Chip Kelly has only been a head coach for three years, and only been involved in Division I football in any capacity for five. By any measure, though, he doesn't have much left to accomplish: Since Oregon promoted Kelly from offensive coordinator in 2009, the Ducks are 26-2 in conference games with three consecutive conference championships—as many as Oregon won in the previous 89 years combined—and have taken up residence near the top of the national polls. Their 12-0 run to the BCS title game in 2010 was the first undefeated regular season in school history; their 45-38 shootout with Wisconsin on January 2 was Oregon's first Rose Bowl win since the U.S. entered World War I. When the Tampa Bay Buccaneers came calling a few weeks later, it's no wonder Kelly was at least briefly intrigued by the challenge.

The challenge he embraced instead was the slightly more familiar burden of adapting the Pac-12's most prolific offense to a new quarterback. All eyes in the spring were on the race to replace two-year starter Darron Thomas, whose bizarre decision to forego his senior season and a degree for a shot at the NFL (he went undrafted in April) left sophomore Bryan Bennett and redshirt freshman Marcus Mariota to duel to an apparent draw heading into the summer. There doesn't seem to be much distinction between the two: Bennett and Mariota both fit into the "dual threat" template that propelled their predecessors to stardom in Kelly's up-tempo, spread-option scheme, and both will be blessed with the usual fleet of versatile, blazing skill threats out of the backfield. Senior Kenjon Barner (939 rushing yards, plus-15.0 Adj. POE) and sophomore De'Anthony Thomas (595 rushing yards, 605 receiving yards) combined for more than 2,300 yards from scrimmage last year behind All-America workhorse LaMichael James, capped by a 315-yard, two-touchdown eruption by Thomas in the Rose Bowl that guaranteed "Black Mamba" his place among the most feared players in the country from virtually anywhere on the field. If the new quarterback commands even the slightest respect for his arm, the offense will be (quite literally) full-speed ahead.

But then, as long as Kelly is pulling the strings, points are kind of a given. Barring a collapse at quarterback, the difference between a solid "rebuilding" year and another year on the Pac-12 throne is the progress of an impressive (on a per-play basis) defense bringing back eight returning starters. Because of the offense's pace, the defense has posted underrated numbers, but three of the Ducks' four regular season losses under Kelly have come with at least 38 points on the board for the opposition, including a 38-35 loss to USC last November that may have cost Oregon a rematch with opening-night foil LSU for the BCS title.

USC quarterback Matt Barkley bombed the Ducks in that game for 323 yards and four touchdowns passing, arguably the high point of his late-season surge onto Heisman lists and draft boards. This year, the winner of Oregon's November 3 trip to Los Angeles has the inside track to host the Pac-12 Championship Game a month later, and quite possibly a trip to the BCS Championship in Miami a month after that. If a more experienced group can do to Barkley what it did to Andrew Luck in last year's blowout win at Stanford, the rest of the schedule is merely avoiding land mines. Oregon plays the weakest regular season schedule of any projected top-15 team and ranks only behind Alabama in projected mean wins.

Top 2013 NFL Prospects: DE/OLB Dion Jordan (3), RB Kenjon Barner (4-5), FS John Boyett (4-5), G Carson York (6), P Jackson Rice (6-7).

No. 11 Stanford Cardinal (9-3, 7-2)

2011: 11-2 (8-1) / F/+ #9 / FEI #7 / S&P+ #9

Program F/+	-199.9	21	Returning Starters: 6 OFF, 7 DEF			2-Yr Recruiting Rank		16
2011 Offense			**2011 Defense**			**2011 Field Position**		
Offensive F/+	+14.4%	3	**Defensive F/+**	+3.4%	37	Field Position Advantage	0.493	70
Offensive FEI:	0.505	6	Defensive FEI	-0.446	13	**2012 Projections**		
Offensive S&P+	115.5	6	Defensive S&P+	129.5	22	**Mean Wins**	9.5	
Rushing S&P+	119.5	20	Rushing S&P+	114.2	25	Proj. F/+	+19.4%	11
Passing S&P+	134.2	9	Passing S&P+	122.2	20	Offensive F/+	+14.8%	2
Standard Downs S&P+	125.3	8	Standard Downs S&P+	118.8	16	Defensive F/+	+4.6%	36
Passing Downs S&P+	120.0	27	Passing Downs S&P+	114.9	39	Strength of Schedule	0.222	32

Most accounts of Stanford's Lazarus-like ascent over the last three years begin and end—justifiably so—with quarterback Andrew Luck's ascent to the top of draft boards as one of the most coveted pro prospects in a generation. But the handwringing over the Cardinal's fate hardly stops at replacing the star quarterback: It's also a matter of losing the nimble giants up front who made his job about as easy as it could be. Luck spent his entire college career behind a pair of All-American classmates. Left tackle Jonathan Martin and guard David DeCastro arrived with Luck as part of the unheralded recruiting class of 2008, started every game of the best two-year run in school history, and joined Luck in the top 50 picks of April's draft. So did All-American tight end Coby Fleener.

Before them all, though, there was coach Jim Harbaugh, who built the program on the same foundation of old-school, between-the-tackles brawn that he brought last year to the San Francisco 49ers. Stanford out-muscled opponents on both sides of the line of scrimmage, leading the nation in net points per methodical drive each of the last two years. That remains the default setting for the post-Luck rebuild. Even with the steadiest arm in college football at its disposal, the Cardinal continued to run more than they passed in 2011, churning out well over 200 yards per game on the ground and producing a 1,000-yard rusher (Stepfan Taylor) for the fourth year in a row. Taylor (1,330 yards, minus-2.4 Adj. POE) returns, along with three starting offensive linemen (David Yankey, Sam Schwartzstein and Cameron Fleming), the starting fullback (Ryan Hewitt) and two oversized tight ends (Levine Toilolo and Zach Ertz) who are no strangers to run blocking. Defensively, Stanford returns six starters from a front seven that finished 25th in Rushing S&P+, including all-conference picks Ben Gardner and Chase Thomas—and *not* including linebacker Shayne Skov, a future pro who missed the last ten games with a knee injury. Just to emphasize the point, Stanford also signed a beefed-up, blue-chip recruiting class with multiple five-star behemoths on both sides of the line of scrimmage.

Still, once the ball is in the air, all bets are off. The top candidates to replace Luck in the spring, sophomore Brett Nottingham and junior Josh Nunes, have attempted ten collegiate passes between them, all in garbage time. Except for sophomore Ty Montgomery (355 receiving yards, 73 percent catch rate), the receivers are even more nondescript. Coach David Shaw bluntly insisted after the spring game that the quarterback position "was not played well enough for us today to win a football game," which shouldn't be a very high bar most of the time. On the occasions that it is, though, it's an open question who's going to get the Cardinal over the top.

Top 2013 NFL Prospects: LB Shayne Skov* (1-2), LB Chase Thomas (2-3), TE Zach Ertz* (4), RB Stepfan Taylor (6-7).

No. 40 California Golden Bears (7-5, 5-4)

2011: 7-6 (4-5) / F/+ #45 / FEI #49 / S&P+ #35

Program F/+	-200.0	43	Returning Starters: 6 OFF, 5 DEF			2-Yr Recruiting Rank		18
2011 Offense			**2011 Defense**			**2011 Field Position**		
Offensive F/+	+1.0%	54	**Defensive F/+**	+3.5%	35	Field Position Advantage	0.482	84
Offensive FEI:	-0.037	64	Defensive FEI	-0.175	43	**2012 Projections**		
Offensive S&P+	89.2	57	Defensive S&P+	128.4	26	**Mean Wins**	6.5	
Rushing S&P+	100.9	67	Rushing S&P+	108.3	44	Proj. F/+	+6.9%	40
Passing S&P+	101.3	60	Passing S&P+	125.0	17	Offensive F/+	+1.9%	48
Standard Downs S&P+	98.1	76	Standard Downs S&P+	118.9	15	Defensive F/+	+5.0%	33
Passing Downs S&P+	92.5	92	Passing Downs S&P+	110.6	43	Strength of Schedule	0.195	28

By any reasonable measure, Jeff Tedford's first decade at Cal was the best in Berkeley since the post-World War II heyday of Lynn "Pappy" Waldorf, culminating in a massive, multiyear renovation of on-campus facilities and Tedford's passing Waldorf as the winningest coach in school history. With the construction finally coming to an end, it's also reasonable for Cal fans to wonder if the next facelift is going to come on the sideline: On the field, the Golden Bears haven't beaten a team that finished in the top 25 in three years and haven't landed in the final polls themselves in five.

In the same span, they've been lapped by Oregon and Stanford in the Pac-12 pecking order and ceded the mantle of upward mobility on the West Coast to Washington, which successfully lured ace recruiter Tosh Lupoi from Tedford's staff in January at the expense of what was shaping up as a blockbuster class for Cal. (The most hyped recruit in the state, Sacramento safety Shaq Thompson, followed Lupoi to Seattle; fellow blue-chips Ellis McCarthy and Jordan Payton defected from Cal to UCLA.) The Bears are scheduled to return to a refurbished Memorial Stadium this fall with big bills coming due, relatively new coaching staffs overseeing almost every conference rival, and the momentum of the first half of the Tedford era an increasingly distant memory.

Ironically enough, given Tedford's well-documented reputation as a quarterback guru, the ongoing gridlock in the standings is a direct result of ongoing inconsistency under center. On the other side of the ball, in fact, defensive coordinator Clancy Pendergast has produced the No. 1 total defense in the Pac-12 two years running (the Bears ranked 38th in Defensive F/+ in 2010, 35th in 2011), while the offense has yielded diminishing returns. Tedford personally reclaimed offensive play-calling duties last year, but has little hope of turning pedestrian Zach Maynard (a former transfer from the University of Buffalo) into the second coming of Aaron Rodgers as a fifth-year senior. He does, however, have freakish wide receiver Keenan Allen (66 percent catch rate, 9.1 yards per target), who made good on his five-star recruiting buzz with an All-Pac-12 breakthrough as a sophomore and should continue to raise the ceiling for the entire offense on a weekly basis.

Top 2013 NFL Prospects: WR Keenan Allen* (1), DE/DT Aaron Tipoti (3-4), G Brian Schwenke (6), RB Isi Sofele (6-7), C Matt Summers-Gavin (6-7).

No. 55 Washington Huskies (6-6, 4-5)

2011: 7-6 (5-4) / F/+ #64 / FEI #68 / S&P+ #67

Program F/+	-200.0	75	Returning Starters: 7 OFF, 7 DEF			2-Yr Recruiting Rank		21
2011 Offense			**2011 Defense**			**2011 Field Position**		
Offensive F/+	+4.1%	35	**Defensive F/+**	-6.2%	104	Field Position Advantage	0.482	85
Offensive FEI:	0.306	24	Defensive FEI	0.41	103	**2012 Projections**		
Offensive S&P+	98.6	28	Defensive S&P+	101.0	93	**Mean Wins**	5.5	
Rushing S&P+	105.7	52	Rushing S&P+	84.9	107	Proj. F/+	+2.0%	55
Passing S&P+	117.4	26	Passing S&P+	101.1	58	Offensive F/+	+6.9%	27
Standard Downs S&P+	108.1	39	Standard Downs S&P+	100.8	58	Defensive F/+	-4.9%	92
Passing Downs S&P+	123.8	24	Passing Downs S&P+	84.1	98	Strength of Schedule	0.077	5

Employees rarely get the axe for a bad day at the office, or even an historically awful day, so it's worth pointing out that head coach Steve Sarkisian's decision to fire Washington's entire defensive coaching staff last December wasn't exactly sudden. The 2011 Huskies finished the year ranked 107th nationally in total defense, 108th in scoring D and 104th in Defensive F/+. They allowed more yards per game (453.3) than any defense in school history. They yielded at least 38 points in all six of their losses. But if there was any doubt about coordinator Nick Holt's future before his unit's turnstile-like turn in the Alamo Bowl, the Huskies' 67-56 loss to Baylor was certainly the falling piano that broke the camel's back. In one night, the Bears ripped off 777 yards of total offense on 9.1 yards per play, earned 33 first downs, and sent three different rushers over 100 yards on the ground. Facing a 42-24 deficit at the start of the third quarter, the Bears responded by scoring six touchdowns on their last 21 offensive snaps.

Thus marks the first major reboot of the Sarkisian era, a tacit admission that the project is beginning to stagnate after two-and-a-half years of relative progress out of the pit of despair that greeted him in 2009. Largely because of the defense, Washington dropped five of its last seven in 2011—all by double digits—on the heels of a 5-1 start, spiraling into its second consecutive 7-6 finish. For new blood, Sarkisian opened the pursestrings for 35-year-old Justin Wilcox, an ex-Oregon linebacker who spent the last six years coordinating defenses at Boise State and Tennessee, and California's 30-year-old recruiting ace, Tosh Lupoi, at a combined salary of nearly $1.2 million. Within weeks, the Huskies were beginning the transition to a 3-4 scheme on defense and boasting the signature of the most sought-after prospect on the West Coast, one-time Cal commit Shaq Thompson.

While the defense is getting a facelift, the offense is setting into a familiar comfort zone with junior quarterback Keith Price, whose brilliant turn in the Alamo shootout (478 total yards, seven touchdowns) left him with single-season UW records for touchdown passes, completion percentage, and pass efficiency as a first-year starter. Somehow, he managed almost all of that on two sore knees, which makes the first priority finding two new tackles to replace a pair of departing seniors. The second priority is cobbling together a viable running game in the absence of enormously productive tailback Chris Polk. If junior Jesse Callier and/or sophomore Bishop Sankey can fill that void, the graduation of Price's top two receivers may be a minor footnote. If not, the spotlight will move to touted sophomore targets Kasen Williams and Austin Seferian-Jenkins—whether they're ready or not.

Top 2013 NFL Prospects: CB Desmond Trufant (3-4).

No. 60 Oregon State Beavers (5-7, 3-6)

2011: 3-9 (3-6) / F/+ #86 / FEI #91 / S&P+ #87

Program F/+	-199.9	33	Returning Starters: 6 OFF, 7 DEF			2-Yr Recruiting Rank		45
2011 Offense			**2011 Defense**			**2011 Field Position**		
Offensive F/+	-6.8%	91	**Defensive F/+**	-1.3%	67	Field Position Advantage	0.508	45
Offensive FEI:	-0.321	100	Defensive FEI	0.148	73	**2012 Projections**		
Offensive S&P+	78.8	94	Defensive S&P+	107.2	78	**Mean Wins**	4.8	
Rushing S&P+	91.1	94	Rushing S&P+	96.5	73	Proj. F/+	+0.1%	60
Passing S&P+	90.8	84	Passing S&P+	110.1	33	Offensive F/+	-3.7%	77
Standard Downs S&P+	90.2	96	Standard Downs S&P+	107.8	36	Defensive F/+	+3.9%	35
Passing Downs S&P+	108.6	50	Passing Downs S&P+	106.1	53	Strength of Schedule	0.309	46

At Oregon State, the virtues of a consistent ground game border on religious, as established by a succession of indefatigable workhorses: Ken Simonton begat Steven Jackson, who begat Yvenson Bernard, who begat Jacquizz Rogers, a lineage that gave the Beavers a 1,000-yard rusher in 12 of 13 seasons from 1998-2010, easily among the most impressive streaks in college football. By that standard, or almost any other, 2011 was a catastrophe: Four different players drew starting assignments at tailback, falling well short of 1,000 yards *combined* as part of an impotent rushing attack that ranked 94th in Rushing S&P+. (Excluding the season opener against Sacramento State, OSU averaged a grim 2.8 yards per carry for the year and failed to reach 100 yards rushing in any of its eight subsequent losses.) Every member of the rotation returns in 2012, but could all wind up looking up the depth chart at either a true freshman, incoming Chris

Brown, or a redshirt freshman, spring mover Storm Woods, who spent all of last season on the bench.

It was that kind of year in Corvallis, besieged by injury, attrition and youth. In all, 14 projected starters missed a combined 59 games to assorted ailments, yielding to 23 first-time starters and a school-record ten true freshmen pressed into immediate action. The resulting record, 3-9, was the worst since coach Mike Riley inherited a desperate program in 1997, and marked the first back-to-back losing seasons (following a 5-7 flop in 2010) since he returned from a stint in the NFL in 2003. Worse, seven of those nine losses came by double digits; besides the depressing running game, the Beavers finished last or next-to-last in the Pac-12 in scoring offense, rushing defense, pass efficiency and turnover margin, and fell from 23rd in Offensive F/+ to 91st—a startlingly un-Riley-like effort across the board after nearly a decade of consistent overachieving.

Barring a similar exodus to the disabled list, there's a silver lining in the fact that the investment in all those wide-eyed freshmen and sophomores may begin to pay off now that they've grown into relatively seasoned sophomores and juniors. Most notably, that applies to redshirt sophomore quarterback Sean Mannion, who took over for good in the second game of 2011 and wound up alongside defensive end Scott Crichton on a few Freshman All-America teams. Frankly, that may say more about his competition for the honor (or lack thereof) than it does about Mannion, who served up a league-worst 18 interceptions trying to pass OSU out of a string of lost causes. But Mannion has the size (6-foot-5, 215 pounds) and arm of a future pro, and enough of a supporting cast in receivers Markus Wheaton, Jordan Bishop, and Brandin Cooks to get the Beavers back within striking distance of the postseason with just a little bit of support in the trenches.

Top 2013 NFL Prospects: CB Jordan Poyer (2-3), WR Markus Wheaton (4).

No. 100 Washington State Cougars (3-9, 1-8)

2011: 4-8 (2-7) / F/+ #100 / FEI #89 / S&P+ #104

Program F/+	-200.2	114	Returning Starters: 5 OFF, 9 DEF			2-Yr Recruiting Rank		66
2011 Offense			**2011 Defense**			**2011 Field Position**		
Offensive F/+	-0.5%	64	Defensive F/+	-9.3%	118	Field Position Advantage	0.464	105
Offensive FEI:	0.038	55	Defensive FEI	0.312	93	**2012 Projections**		
Offensive S&P+	80.6	83	Defensive S&P+	94.7	109	**Mean Wins**	3.1	
Rushing S&P+	75.1	118	Rushing S&P+	96.7	71	Proj. F/+	-13.5%	100
Passing S&P+	104.6	57	Passing S&P+	77.8	111	Offensive F/+	-3.6%	71
Standard Downs S&P+	105.3	51	Standard Downs S&P+	86.7	106	Defensive F/+	-9.8%	117
Passing Downs S&P+	77.2	111	Passing Downs S&P+	90.5	83	Strength of Schedule	0.335	51

On the day he fired coach Paul Wulff last November, Washington State athletic director director Bill Moos not-so-subtly hinted at his preference for a "flashy, high-octane offense" that will boost sagging attendance and make Wazzu "a destination, not a stepping stone." Within 24 hours he had the man for both. In a decade at Texas Tech, Mike Leach emerged from among his mostly buttoned-down, CEO-like peers in the major college coaching ranks as a kind of savant: a mumbling, unpolished cultivator of pirate swords, magic tricks, Geronimo memorabilia, rambling press conferences, wildly tattooed linemen, place-kickers pulled from the stands, unlikely friendships with the likes of Donald Trump, and a play sheet the size of a cocktail napkin holding the secrets of the most consistently prolific offense in the country.

As second chances go, Leach could do a lot worse than Washington State, where he'll inherit an offense that finished among the top ten nationally in passing yards and improved to 57th in Passing S&P+ despite playing virtually the entire season with starting quarterback Jeff Tuel on the bench. All three of last year's starting quarterbacks will be back, along with a legitimate star in Marquess Wilson (1,383 receiving yards, 11.3 per target), who ranked among the most productive and underrated receivers in the nation as a sophomore. The Cougars are going to come in passing, go out passing and spend as much time as possible passing in between.

For an outfit with four conference wins in four years and consistently atrocious pass protection, that doesn't guarantee an immediate turnaround in the standings. But it does promise an immediate uptick in attendance—barely 16,000 people showed up for the Cougars' home finale against Utah, officially, and the real number is probably worse—and exposure. After nearly a decade of languishing in mediocrity and worse, it means being a Washington State fan is going to be kind of fun.

Top 2013 NFL Prospects: WR Marquess Wilson (1-2), DE Travis Long (3-4), QB Jeff Tuel (5).*

SOUTH

No. 6 USC Trojans (10-2, 7-2)
2011: 10-2 (7-2) / F/+ #11 / FEI #10 / S&P+ #17

Program F/+	-199.8	8	Returning Starters: 8 OFF, 7 DEF			2-Yr Recruiting Rank		4
2011 Offense			**2011 Defense**			**2011 Field Position**		
Offensive F/+	+12.9%	10	Defensive F/+	+2.0%	46	Field Position Advantage	0.524	23
Offensive FEI:	0.487	8	Defensive FEI	-0.295	29	**2012 Projections**		
Offensive S&P+	109.6	12	Defensive S&P+	126.3	32	**Mean Wins**	10.1	
Rushing S&P+	114.5	30	Rushing S&P+	115.3	24	Proj. F/+	+22.3%	6
Passing S&P+	130.4	14	Passing S&P+	116.7	23	Offensive F/+	+17.7%	1
Standard Downs S&P+	120.3	12	Standard Downs S&P+	107.1	41	Defensive F/+	+4.6%	34
Passing Downs S&P+	125.1	21	Passing Downs S&P+	115.5	35	Strength of Schedule	0.307	45

Not many 21-year-olds get a glimpse of a multimillion-dollar contract to begin their professional careers, and even fewer have the luxury of turning it down in favor of another year of school. But then, unlike USC quarterback Matt Barkley, almost none of them stand to parlay an extra semester of two into a Heisman Trophy, the No. 1 slot in the NFL Draft or the undying adulation of not just an entire campus, but most of the second-largest media market in America. (Which just so happens to be filled with legions of aspiring models and actresses and no NFL franchise to monopolize the local spotlight, if you're into, you know, the *scene*.) Aside from all of the obvious perks of stardom, though, there is also the fact that Barkley has more incentive than any college player in recent memory to finish what he started on the field.

Even before he took his first snap as a true freshman starter in 2009, Barkley was the heir apparent to a line of five-star Orange County quarterbacks—Carson Palmer, Matt Leinart, Mark Sanchez—who had combined for two Heisman Trophies, two national championships and a grand total of five losses as starters over the previous seven years. Along with John David Booty, they'd led USC to seven consecutive Pac-10 titles and six wins in BCS bowls. By comparison, the narrative during Barkley's first two-and-a-half years at USC was one of steady decline: By the start of his sophomore season, the Trojans had lost four games in 2009 alone, lost coach Pete Carroll to the NFL, appointed an unpopular successor in Lane Kiffin, and been blindsided by the most severe NCAA sanctions of the last 20 years. They subsequently lost five games in 2010, didn't go to a bowl game, and jogged into last season as an afterthought. They spent six of the first eight weeks of 2011 unranked, suffering through close calls against Minnesota, Utah and Arizona and a 20-point loss at Arizona State.

The subsequent November surge—capped by Barkley's six-touchdown turn in an emphatic, 50-0 obliteration of rival UCLA – reinstated both Barkley and USC among the national elite, but also brought the empty lines on his resumé into even sharper focus: Leaving his senior season on the table for the draft would mean leaving as the first Trojan quarterback in more than a decade without at least a conference championship or BCS bowl to his credit.

That will change in 2012. And if for some reason it doesn't, the blame certainly isn't going to fall on the supporting cast. On the other end of Barkley's bombs, junior Robert Woods and sophomore Marqise Lee finished their first season together as the most lethal 1-2 receiving punch in the nation, bringing down more than 2,400 yards and 28 touchdowns between them on 184 catches. Behind them, sophomore George Farmer and incoming freshman Nelson Agholor—hyped, five-star athletes in their own right—will be lucky to get a few snaps in edgewise. Senior tailback Curtis McNeal turned in a 1,000-yard season on the ground despite spending the first half of it relegated to third string. Tight ends Randall Telfer and Xavier Grimble had nine touchdowns on 39 grabs as redshirt freshmen. Four of five starters are back on the offensive line. The defense returns two senior starters up front, all three starting linebackers and the entire secondary, headed by another future first-rounder, All-American safety T.J. McDonald. Even the kicker, Andre Heidari, was a first-team All-Pac-12 pick as a true freshman.

The lineup isn't as strong as it would be if it included left tackle Matt Kalil and defensive end Nick Perry, both of whom followed the first-round money with a year of eligibility remaining. Kalil's decision, especially, leaves Barkley without the best offensive lineman in the Pac-12 protecting his blind side, the most glaring issue on the two-deep by far. First crack in the spring went to colossal sophomore Aundrey Walker, who has all the makings of another first-round giant in two years, but for now has yet to start a college game. If he's merely competent at keeping his quarterback clean, the path to the national championship is wide open.

Top 2013 NFL Prospects: QB Matt Barkley (1), FS T.J. McDonald (1), WR Robert Woods* (1), DE Wes Horton (2), C Khaled Holmes (2), CB Nickell Robey* (3), DE/OLB Devon Kennard (5-6).

No. 35 Utah Utes (9-3, 6-3)

2011: 8-5 (4-5) / F/+ #54 / FEI #54 / S&P+ #54

Program F/+	-199.9	26	Returning Starters: 9 OFF, 7 DEF			2-Yr Recruiting Rank		35
2011 Offense			**2011 Defense**			**2011 Field Position**		
Offensive F/+	-6.9%	95	**Defensive F/+**	+8.2%	11	Field Position Advantage	0.523	24
Offensive FEI:	-0.425	107	Defensive FEI	-0.412	17	**2012 Projections**		
Offensive S&P+	72.1	106	Defensive S&P+	135.0	17	**Mean Wins**	8.8	
Rushing S&P+	83.3	108	Rushing S&P+	127.4	16	Proj. F/+	+9.3%	35
Passing S&P+	84.1	102	Passing S&P+	122.6	19	Offensive F/+	-4.0%	79
Standard Downs S&P+	88.7	102	Standard Downs S&P+	121.9	14	Defensive F/+	+13.3%	7
Passing Downs S&P+	75.1	113	Passing Downs S&P+	125.2	22	Strength of Schedule	0.609	89

2011 was a year of dramatic change for Utah, from the new offense to the new conference, yet it somehow wound up feeling awfully familiar. Despite the apparent step up in class from the Mountain West to the Pac-12, an eight-win campaign capped by a December bowl victory was close to the exact average of the Utes' last decade in the MWC. As the season unfolded, in fact, it probably qualified as a missed opportunity: With a win over fellow newcomer/South Division doormat Colorado in the final game of the regular season, Utah would have clinched a spot in the first Pac-12 Championship Game in place of probation-saddled USC. Instead, the Utes missed three field goals in a 17-14 loss, ceded the championship bid to underachieving UCLA, and slinked into the postseason virtually unnoticed.

The late stumble was doubly disappointing considering the efforts of the defense, which mastered the learning curve with league-best marks in takeaways and points allowed. (Nationally, the Utes ranked 19th in Passing S&P+.) At the center of the push was junior college transfer Star Lotulelei, the best defensive lineman in the conference according to opposing blockers and a likely top-10 pick in next year's draft according to pro scouts. But there are also third-year starters Dave Kruger and Brian Blechen at defensive tackle and safety, respectively, and four other regulars from last year's starting 11 to carry the banner in the absence of veteran tackle machines Chaz Walker and Matt Martinez.

By contrast, the offense was lost in translation under first-year coordinator Norm Chow, who left in December for the top job at Hawaii after overseeing an attack that languished at the bottom of the league in both yards and points per game. That was due in no small part to the absence of junior quarterback Jordan Wynn, victim of a September shoulder injury that kept him out of the last nine games. With junior Jon Hays filling in, Utah lagged well behind the rest of the conference in completions covering at least 15 yards (47, compared to a Pac-12 average of 80) or resulting in first downs (93; Pac-12 average: 157).

As much mileage as the Utes got out of juco transfer John White IV at tailback (1,520 yards, 15 touchdowns on 24 carries per game), they also averaged just 3.8 yards per carry for the season and failed to crack the century mark on the ground in any of their five losses. Even if White's workhorse numbers make him the headliner, with a healthy Wynn, a fresh-faced new coordinator—24-year-old Brian Johnson, less than four years removed from leading Utah to a 13-0 finish capped by a Sugar Bowl ambush of Alabama in 2008—and last year's top six receivers back in the fold, it will be the passing game that decides the offense's fate.

Top 2013 NFL Prospects: DT Star Lotulelei (1), DT Dave Kruger (7).

No. 56 UCLA Bruins (6-6, 4-5)

2011: 6-8 (5-4) / F/+ #83 / FEI #93 / S&P+ #65

Program F/+	-200.0	65	Returning Starters: 7 OFF, 7 DEF			2-Yr Recruiting Rank		32
2011 Offense			**2011 Defense**			**2011 Field Position**		
Offensive F/+	-1.0%	66	**Defensive F/+**	-4.5%	94	Field Position Advantage	0.499	60
Offensive FEI:	0.065	50	Defensive FEI	0.483	111	**2012 Projections**		
Offensive S&P+	95.2	40	Defensive S&P+	104.9	84	**Mean Wins**	5.7	
Rushing S&P+	109.4	40	Rushing S&P+	86.5	102	Proj. F/+	+1.2%	56
Passing S&P+	121.7	19	Passing S&P+	104.3	48	Offensive F/+	+2.2%	45
Standard Downs S&P+	112.8	26	Standard Downs S&P+	98.5	68	Defensive F/+	-0.9%	65
Passing Downs S&P+	101.9	63	Passing Downs S&P+	103.2	60	Strength of Schedule	0.430	66

Since its last conference championship in 1998, UCLA has dropped 12 of 13 against USC, failed to sniff a major bowl game and landed in the final polls just once. But of all the unsavory streaks associated with Bruin football, none is more revealing than this: When Jim "Don't Call Me Junior" Mora arrived as the new head coach last December, he did so as the first outsider in charge of the program in more than 50 years.

Mora's immediate predecessors over the last decade were all either Bruin-born as players (Karl Dorrell was a part of three Rose Bowl teams from 1982-85, two of which included his future successor, Rick Neuheisel) or Bruin-bred as assistants (Bob Toledo was promoted from offensive coordinator to replace longtime boss Terry Donahue in 1996), and all three rode a wave of mediocrity to the chopping block. The previous six head coaches before them came with the same pedigree, a lineage dating back to Harry R. "Red" Sanders in 1957. By the end, both Dorrell and Neuheisel seemed to be presiding over a wilting hemophiliac.

No wonder Mora has seemed more preoccupied with forcing a sort of cultural revolution—he was particularly hostile to the annual "tradition" of seniors leading the rest of the team out of a practice session during spring drills and/or bowl prep—than with, say, who's going to be the starting quarterback. In fact, if healthy, personnel may turn out to be an immediate asset: The roster Mora inherits from Neuheisel is the most veteran outfit in the Pac-12, and arguably the most talented this side of USC. (If there's one thing "Slick Rick" did on a championship level, it's recruit.) The defense alone features a dozen players who have started at least five games in their careers, including five seniors who have started at least 20 games. At least half the starting defense has some kind of future in the NFL.

As for the quarterback, the sentimental choice would be fifth-year senior Kevin Prince, who's won the starting job each of the last three seasons and paid for it at various points with a broken jaw, a strained oblique, two separated shoulders, a season-ending knee injury and at least two concussions. Based on the spring, though, the best bet is on the gem of the 2011 recruiting class, Brett Hundley, who emerged from his redshirt season looking like the most dynamic playmaker (if not necessarily the most consistent) in a wide-open, six-man race. If growing pains are inevitable under the new administration, an occasional spark from the future might be a good investment.

Top 2013 NFL Prospects: TE Joseph Fauria (2), DT Cassius Marsh* (2), DE Datone Jones (4-5), LB Patrick Larimore (5), RB Johnathan Franklin (5-6), CB Aaron Hester (6-7), CB Sheldon Price (7).

No. 58 Arizona State Sun Devils (5-7, 4-5)

2011: 6-7 (4-5) / F/+ #41 / FEI #42 / S&P+ #46

Program F/+	-200.0	45	Returning Starters: 4 OFF, 4 DEF			2-Yr Recruiting Rank		55
2011 Offense			**2011 Defense**			**2011 Field Position**		
Offensive F/+	+4.4%	34	**Defensive F/+**	-0.1%	58	Field Position Advantage	0.507	49
Offensive FEI:	0.227	30	Defensive FEI	0.018	63	**2012 Projections**		
Offensive S&P+	97.9	30	Defensive S&P+	114.3	61	**Mean Wins**	5.4	
Rushing S&P+	116.3	26	Rushing S&P+	98.3	66	Proj. F/+	+0.5%	58
Passing S&P+	109.2	42	Passing S&P+	105.9	40	Offensive F/+	+2.9%	44
Standard Downs S&P+	110.6	31	Standard Downs S&P+	100.0	62	Defensive F/+	-2.4%	67
Passing Downs S&P+	121.6	26	Passing Downs S&P+	106.8	50	Strength of Schedule	0.278	37

No one celebrates a 6-7 finish as a campaign to remember, but even by the standards of mediocrity, the swoon that overtook Arizona State last November left an especially bitter taste of missed opportunity. In August, the Devils' veteran lineup made them the chic pick to win the new Pac-12 South, a destiny they seemed well on their way to fulfilling during a 6-2 start that included the biggest win of Dennis Erickson's tenure as head coach, a 43-22 romp over USC. By December, they'd been ejected from the polls and the division lead by a four-game losing streak, and the 64-year-old Erickson had been ejected from his job.

At least the beginning of the Todd Graham era isn't going to be saddled with high expectations. To some extent, that's a reflection of Graham himself, who only emerged after a ramshackle search for Erickson's successor last winter and didn't win any converts for abandoning the top job in Pittsburgh—after a single, unremarkable season there—with a generic text message to Pitt players. But he's also inheriting an attrition-ravaged depth chart that returns just four starters on each side of the ball, the best of whom, junior defensive end Junior Onyeali, was promptly suspended by the new staff in January.

Spring practice shed precious little light on the three-man quarterback derby between sophomores Mike Bercovici and Taylor Kelly and redshirt freshman Michael Eubank, none of whom figures to quite fill the shoes of NFL-bound Brock Osweiler (though the 6-foot-5, 240-pound Eubank *can* fill the Osweiler-sized void for freakish size at the center of the huddle). That leaves the spotlight to bruiser Cameron Marshall (1,050 rushing yards, plus-18.3 Adj. POE) at tailback. Still, if hyped freshman D.J. Foster happens to steal a little of it for himself after he arrives this summer, ASU fans probably aren't going to mind.

Top 2013 NFL Prospects: DE/OLB Junior Onyeali* (4-5), RB Cameron Marshall (6-7), FS Keelan Johnson (7).

No. 62 Arizona Wildcats (5-7, 3-6)

2011: 4-8 (2-7) / F/+ #79 / FEI #74 / S&P+ #68

Program F/+	-199.9	41	Returning Starters: 6 OFF, 5 DEF			2-Yr Recruiting Rank		52
2011 Offense			**2011 Defense**			**2011 Field Position**		
Offensive F/+	+3.9%	37	**Defensive F/+**	-7.0%	108	Field Position Advantage	0.486	79
Offensive FEI:	0.257	28	Defensive FEI	0.482	110	**2012 Projections**		
Offensive S&P+	95.2	39	Defensive S&P+	103.7	86	**Mean Wins**	4.9	
Rushing S&P+	92.4	92	Rushing S&P+	97.7	67	Proj. F/+	-1.1%	62
Passing S&P+	115.3	28	Passing S&P+	98.3	66	Offensive F/+	+5.9%	31
Standard Downs S&P+	107.5	44	Standard Downs S&P+	100.7	60	Defensive F/+	-7.1%	113
Passing Downs S&P+	118.9	29	Passing Downs S&P+	86.8	91	Strength of Schedule	0.156	20

Rich Rodriguez has been around the block. He's circled it three or four times now, in fact, from early stops at Appalachian backwaters Salem and Glenville State to the cauldron of Michigan, at least one time too many to start aiming for some kind of reinvention at age 48. His new employer isn't plunking down $9.5 million over five years for a "new" RichRod. Trading on more than a decade as the de facto Father of the Spread Offense, Rodriguez sold Arizona last winter on a familiar promise: Give him three years and a viable athlete at quarterback, and you'll reap the rewards of one of the most explosive attacks in college football.

For an undistinguished program crawling out of a disappointing 4-8 crater, that qualifies as a coup. Even the dysfunctional marriage in Ann Arbor—doomed from Rodriguez's first press conference in December 2007, if not sooner—managed to produce the Big Ten's most prolific offense in his final season there, 2010. That mirrored his previous efforts as offensive coordinator at Tulane and Clemson and head coach at West Virginia, where he confirmed his bona fides as the nation's leading spread evangelist in the process of leading his alma mater to three consecutive top-10 finishes. (As a reminder of Rodriguez's reputation in those years, recall that he once backed out of an apparent deal to take over at Alabama in late 2006, forcing the down-on-their-luck Crimson Tide to settle for Nick Saban instead.) The learning curve should be significantly smoother in Tucson, where Rodriguez inherits a fifth-year senior at quarterback (Matt Scott, a better fit for the spread option than outgoing starter Nick Foles), credible threats at running back (sophomore Ka'Deem Carey) and receiver (senior Dan Buckner, a former transfer from Texas) and five returning offensive linemen who paid their dues last year as first-time starters.

No, the real construction job here is on defense, which the new staff found unconscious in the Pac-12 basement after being assaulted last year for a league-worst 460 yards and 35 points per game. Its recuperation is in the hands of an old Rodriguez hand, defensive coordinator Jeff Casteel, whose decision to remain in West Virginia after his boss' departure in 2007 haunted Rodriguez for the next three years: RichRod's attempt to transplant Casteel's unique 3-3-5 scheme to Michigan without its architect yielded the worst succession of defenses in Wolverine history. That won't be the case this time around, for three reasons. First, because Casteel is back on board. Second, because of the addition of a pair of veteran tackle machines at linebacker, Akron transfer Brian Wagner and 2011 injury casualty Jake Fischer. And third, because there's no way it could be any worse.

Top 2013 NFL Prospects: WR Dan Buckner (3-4), QB Matt Scott (4-5), LB Brian Wagner (6-7).

No. 98 Colorado Buffaloes (3-9, 1-8)
2011: 3-10 (2-7) / F/+ #108 / FEI #108 / S&P+ #106

Program F/+	-200.1	87	Returning Starters: 6 OFF, 6 DEF			2-Yr Recruiting Rank		67
2011 Offense			**2011 Defense**			**2011 Field Position**		
Offensive F/+	-7.0%	96	**Defensive F/+**	-7.2%	112	Field Position Advantage	0.451	112
Offensive FEI:	-0.174	85	Defensive FEI	0.519	114	**2012 Projections**		
Offensive S&P+	79.1	93	Defensive S&P+	94.3	110	**Mean Wins**	3.0	
Rushing S&P+	92.9	90	Rushing S&P+	88.1	98	Proj. F/+	-12.5%	98
Passing S&P+	95.5	77	Passing S&P+	91.7	88	Offensive F/+	-6.7%	92
Standard Downs S&P+	89.1	101	Standard Downs S&P+	102.2	49	Defensive F/+	-5.9%	101
Passing Downs S&P+	100.3	70	Passing Downs S&P+	72.9	118	Strength of Schedule	0.200	30

No program in college football reinvented itself in 2011 with quite the vengeance of Colorado, which enthusiastically embarked for a new conference (goodbye Big 12; hello Pac-12) with a new head coach (goodbye Dan Hawkins; hello Jon Embree) and a renewed emphasis on restoring the glory of Embree's playing days in the late '80s and early '90s. Then the games started, and the reality of the rebuilding job began to set in.

"When are they gonna get tired of losing?" Embree seethed on October 4, two days after watching his team fall to 1-4 by blowing a late 10-point lead against fellow doormat Washington State. "When are they gonna get tired of finding a way of losing? Because you know what, this staff, we've been here for five frickin' weeks and we're tired of it. And if I've been here for five years, I gotta be tired of it myself too." By November he was an exhausted man indeed; from there, the Buffs dropped their next five by an average of 34 points per game and ultimately finished dead last in the conference in both points scored and points allowed.

The eternal consolation of such ineptitude, of course, is that it leaves nowhere to go but up. That makes the loss of starting quarterback Tyler Hansen and 86 percent of the offense's total production—including top receiver Paul Richardson, victim of a spring ACL injury that will cost him his entire junior season—a little easier to swallow. So, too, does the promotion of sophomore quarterback Connor Wood after a mandatory season on the bench following his transfer from Texas. Wood closed the spring with a brief but impressive effort in the spring game that not only solidified him as the starter, but also as the only realistic hope of pulling the Buffs out of their rut.

Top 2013 NFL Prospects: LB Jon Major (6-7), FS Ray Polk (6-7), DT Will Pericak (7).

Matt Hinton

Projected Win Probabilities For Pac-12 Teams

Pac 12 North	12-0	11-1	10-2	9-3	8-4	7-5	6-6	5-7	4-8	3-9	2-10	1-11	0-12	9-0	8-1	7-2	6-3	5-4	4-5	3-6	2-7	1-8	0-9
California	-	-	1	5	17	29	27	15	5	1	-	-	-	-	1	4	17	31	29	14	4	-	-
Oregon	25	46	23	5	1	-	-	-	-	-	-	-	-	25	47	23	5	-	-	-	-	-	-
Oregon State	-	-	-	-	2	9	19	27	25	14	4	-	-	-	-	1	5	14	27	30	18	5	-
Stanford	2	15	33	31	14	4	1	-	-	-	-	-	-	6	29	39	20	5	1	-	-	-	-
Washington	-	-	-	1	6	16	29	28	15	4	1	-	-	-	-	1	5	19	32	28	12	3	-
Washington State	-	-	-	-	-	-	2	8	24	36	24	6	-	-	-	-	-	-	2	9	30	42	17

Pac 12 South	12-0	11-1	10-2	9-3	8-4	7-5	6-6	5-7	4-8	3-9	2-10	1-11	0-12	9-0	8-1	7-2	6-3	5-4	4-5	3-6	2-7	1-8	0-9
Arizona	-	-	-	-	2	8	22	31	24	11	2	-	-	-	-	-	2	11	26	33	21	6	1
Arizona State	-	-	-	1	5	14	26	28	18	7	1	-	-	-	-	1	5	19	31	28	13	3	-
Colorado	-	-	-	-	-	-	2	10	22	32	25	9	-	-	-	-	-	-	2	10	27	39	22
UCLA	-	-	-	2	9	19	26	24	14	5	1	-	-	-	-	3	12	25	31	21	7	1	-
USC	9	29	34	20	7	1	-	-	-	-	-	-	-	12	35	34	15	4	-	-	-	-	-
Utah	1	8	22	29	23	12	4	1	-	-	-	-	-	2	12	28	30	19	7	2	-	-	-

Southeastern Conference

To those of you still refusing to bow before the throne of Southern football, 2011 was the firmest reminder yet: Resistance is futile, y'all. So unstoppable was the SEC juggernaut—in the minds of pundits and pollsters as much as on the field—that the league managed not only to extend its six-year stranglehold on the BCS championship, but to monopolize the stage entirely by claiming *both* teams in the championship game, an unprecedented sequel to LSU's overtime win at Alabama in early November. Think about it long enough, and the coronation starts to carry the whiff of self-fulfilling prophecy: How did two teams from the same conference wind up playing for the title? The SEC is *that* good. How do you know the SEC is that good? It produced *both* teams playing for the title, didn't it?

As it turns out, the only team good enough to beat the SEC champion in the main event was the SEC runner-up: Alabama's 21-0 revenge romp over LSU marked the conference's first loss in the title game in nine appearances since the BCS lurched into existence in 1998. And fair or not, it's increasingly obvious that the only way any other league is going to turn back the tide of Dixie dominance is to take the crystal football back for itself.

The question in 2012 is whether the next challenger will actually have to slay the beast face-to-face. Appropriately enough, the end of the SEC's reign is at least as likely to come from within the conference from without. LSU may be the consensus favorite to top the preseason polls in August, but the Tigers are facing a new starting quarterback and a significant exodus of talent to the NFL. Between them, LSU and Alabama lost 13 players in April's draft, eight of them in the first two rounds. Arkansas is replacing its adulterous head coach and the better half of its already-mediocre defense. South Carolina has no passing game. Georgia has lost nine straight against teams that finished in the final polls. Auburn and Florida are both starting over with new coordinators on both sides of the ball, and no notable stars on either.

Along with newcomers Missouri and Texas A&M, that may well add up to better *depth* than the conference has boasted in years. But there is no team—even LSU and Alabama, loaded as they still are—that looks invulnerable or destined to run the table. At some point, the carousel of powerhouses must give way to parity, and this may be the year that the SEC goes back to eating its own.

WEST

No. 1 Alabama Crimson Tide (11-1, 7-1)

2011: 12-1 (7-1) / F/+ #1 / FEI #3 / S&P+ #1

Program F/+	-199.7	1	Returning Starters: 7 OFF, 4 DEF		2-Yr Recruiting Rank		1
2011 Offense			**2011 Defense**		**2011 Field Position**		
Offensive F/+	+13.6%	7	Defensive F/+	+22.5%	1	Field Position Advantage	0.528	19
Offensive FEI:	0.418	11	Defensive FEI	-0.78	1	**2012 Projections**		
Offensive S&P+	113.7	8	Defensive S&P+	199.8	1	**Mean Wins**	11.1	
Rushing S&P+	145.3	3	Rushing S&P+	170.2	1	Proj. F/+	+35.4%	1
Passing S&P+	149.0	3	Passing S&P+	187.2	1	Offensive F/+	+14.2%	6
Standard Downs S&P+	144.4	1	Standard Downs S&P+	156.4	2	Defensive F/+	+21.2%	1
Passing Downs S&P+	137.7	10	Passing Downs S&P+	210.5	1	Strength of Schedule	0.094	9

Forecasting a college football season is not a science. But there is something like the law of gravity when it comes to departing talent: Under normal conditions, the fate of every team is inversely proportional to the number of players it sends to the NFL Draft. Alabama just lost five members of last year's BCS championship team in the first two rounds alone—four of them starters on the most apocalyptic college defense in memory—the result of which should be an automatic "rebuilding" year in the cutthroat SEC West. Theoretically, anyway.

That's assuming, however, that there is anything normal about the pipeline of talent Nick Saban has constructed to Tuscaloosa over the last five years, which in fact is beginning to resemble not just a factory but a monopoly. Since 2008, four of Bama's last five recruiting classes have been ranked by at least one of the major recruiting sites as the best incoming crop in the nation, producing a perennial contender regardless of the turnover in a given season. Last year's title run came in spite of the loss of four first-rounders from the 2010 team (not to mention the starting quarterback, Greg McElroy), and the noobs in the lineup this fall come with the full accoutrement of blue-chip accolades. The most hyped of the lot, incoming tailback T.J. Yeldon, has already announced his presence as MVP of the spring game, and still he figures to split carries at best in a crowded backfield—not that it particularly matters who's carrying the ball at any given time behind four future draft picks on the front line.

Again, the defense will be an issue only by comparison to the 2011 unit, which set a new cosmic standard by leading the nation in Defensive F/+, total defense, scoring defense, rushing defense, passing defense, pass efficiency defense and third-down defense, then wrapping it all up in a bow made of LSU's entrails in the BCS title game. Alabama obliterated defensive efficiency standards, forcing three-and-outs on 60 percent of opponent drives and giving up zero touchdowns on drives begun at or inside the opponent's own 25-yard line. Most of that bloodthirsty group is gone, but given the overall talent level and Saban's track record on that side of the ball—the Crimson Tide have led the SEC in both yards and points allowed four years running—even the inevitable step back leaves them running at the front of the pack.

Top 2013 NFL Prospects: OT D.J. Fluker* (1), G Barrett Jones (1), CB Dee Milliner* (1-2), LB Nico Johnson (1-2), LB C.J. Mosley* (1-2), DB Robert Lester (1-2), G Chance Warmack (2), RB Eddie Lacy* (2-3), DT Jesse Williams (2-3), TE Michael Williams (4), DE Damion Square (5).

No. 2 LSU Tigers (10-2, 7-1)

2011: 13-1 (8-0) / F/+ #2 / FEI #1 / S&P+ #2

Program F/+	-199.8	5	Returning Starters: 7 OFF, 5 DEF			2-Yr Recruiting Rank		8
2011 Offense			2011 Defense			2011 Field Position		
Offensive F/+	+13.9%	6	Defensive F/+	+17.7%	2	Field Position Advantage	0.572	2
Offensive FEI:	0.391	17	Defensive FEI	-0.747	2	2012 Projections		
Offensive S&P+	112.3	9	Defensive S&P+	177.1	2	Mean Wins	10.5	
Rushing S&P+	135.3	6	Rushing S&P+	169.8	2	Proj. F/+	+30.6%	2
Passing S&P+	154.9	2	Passing S&P+	160.6	2	Offensive F/+	+13.7%	7
Standard Downs S&P+	133.5	5	Standard Downs S&P+	159.8	1	Defensive F/+	+16.9%	2
Passing Downs S&P+	152.7	3	Passing Downs S&P+	142.7	5	Strength of Schedule	0.099	12

From a distance, the first thing you'll notice about LSU is just how much it's seemed to lose since the calendar turned to 2012. First, it lost the sense of invincibility forged by last fall's 13-0 run to the SEC title, demolished by Alabama in a lopsided BCS grudge match. Then came April's NFL Draft, where five Tigers were snapped up in the first four rounds. At the same time, spring practice anointed a new quarterback who has never started a Division I game, Zach Mettenberger, in place of a pair of outgoing seniors, Jordan Jefferson and Jarrett Lee, who combined for 50 starts over the last four years.

All of which, when you look closer, turns out to be beside the point: Just as the flop against Alabama obscured the fact that LSU was the best team in college football over the course of the entire 2011 season, the few notable departures obscure just how *young* that team really was. Not only are the Tigers bringing back 16 players who started at least three games last year, but a whopping 13 of them were freshmen and sophomores—a number that included the top four tailbacks, top two pass rushers, eight of the top 11 tacklers and the program's first Heisman Trophy finalist in 35 years, electric cornerback/punt returner Tyrann Mathieu. LSU's defensive and special teams units racked up 146.7 points in field-position scoring value, more than the total value added by 104 different offenses. Among the few first-time starters this fall are a pair of former five-star recruits, La'El Collins on the offensive line and Anthony Johnson on the defensive line, who were both honored as Freshman All-Americans off the bench.

For sheer talent and depth across the roster, the Tigers are again matched only by Alabama—if at all—and they get the Crimson Tide in Baton Rouge this time after prevailing in last November's epic, overtime field goal fest in Tuscaloosa for the regular season crown. Not surprisingly, they're also likely to start the season atop the major polls, which confirms both the high expectations awaiting the new quarterback and the mixed reviews of his predecessors. If Mettenberger is the answer there—even if it's in a more with-in-the-offense context than his fireballing reputation suggests—there aren't many relevant questions left.

Top 2013 NFL Prospects: OT Chris Faulk* (1), CB/KR Tyrann Mathieu* (1), DE/LB Barkevious Mingo* (1), DE Sam Montgomery* (1), DB Eric Reid* (1), OT Alex Hurst (1-2), QB Zach Mettenberger* (1-2), DT Bennie Logan* (2), DB Craig Loston* (2-3), G Josh Williford* (2-3), RB Spencer Ware* (3-4), DT Josh Downs (4), DE Lavar Edwards (5), WR Russell Shepard (5-6).

No. 15 Arkansas Razorbacks (8-4, 4-4)
2011: 11-2 (6-2) / F/+ #14 / FEI #14 / S&P+ #21

Program F/+	-199.9	19	Returning Starters: 7 OFF, 6 DEF			2-Yr Recruiting Rank		26
2011 Offense			**2011 Defense**			**2011 Field Position**		
Offensive F/+	+10.9%	12	Defensive F/+	+2.4%	44	Field Position Advantage	0.532	16
Offensive FEI:	0.408	14	Defensive FEI	-0.185	41	**2012 Projections**		
Offensive S&P+	111.1	11	Defensive S&P+	120.1	46	**Mean Wins**	7.9	
Rushing S&P+	124.9	12	Rushing S&P+	100.0	61	Proj. F/+	+16.8%	15
Passing S&P+	135.8	8	Passing S&P+	107.0	38	Offensive F/+	+13.2%	9
Standard Downs S&P+	122.8	10	Standard Downs S&P+	101.3	55	Defensive F/+	+3.6%	43
Passing Downs S&P+	147.5	5	Passing Downs S&P+	126.0	20	Strength of Schedule	0.090	7

OK, let's face it: Given his nomadic resumé, even the most rosy-eyed Arkansas partisans might have guessed Bobby Petrino would someday exit Fayetteville as quickly and unexpectedly as he arrived back in December 2007, with the ink still drying on the brief "Dear John" notes he left in the Atlanta Falcons' lockers with three games left in the season. Still, it would have taken a true cynic to conjure up the circumstances that actually forced Petrino out this spring, beginning with a motorcycle accident on April 1 and ending ten days later with his termination for failing to disclose an "inappropriate relationship" with his passenger in the crash, a 25-year-old ex-Razorback volleyball player Petrino had just helped land a job in the athletic department. The search for an interim replacement unfolded amid records requests for university-issued cell phones that made for offseason reading straight out of a supermarket checkout line.

Before their head coach's literal crash-and-burn, the Razorbacks had the makings of a chic dark horse pick in the SEC West, which these days qualifies them as automatic contenders in the national race as well. With that "win now" mandate in mind, Arkansas recalled outgoing special teams coach John L. Smith from the top job at his alma mater, Weber State, in the name of continuity: Before taking the Weber job last December, Smith had spent three years on Petrino's staff in Fayetteville, on the heels of two decades as a head coach at Idaho, Utah State, Louisville (where he was succeeded by Petrino in 2003) and Michigan State. For his loyalty in a crisis, Smith was rewarded with a 10-month contract and implicit instructions to keep the trains running on Petrino Time.

The conductor in this metaphor is All-SEC quarterback Tyler Wilson, a sturdy (6-foot-3, 225 pounds) fifth-year senior who passed on a likely first-round grade for another round at the helm of the league's most productive offense. The engine—assuming he's healthy—is tailback Knile Davis, another All-SEC type who lost his entire junior campaign to a preseason ankle injury. Fellow backs Dennis Johnson and Ronnie Wingo, Jr., have combined with wide receiver Cobi Hamilton and tight end Chris Gragg for well over 4,200 yards of total offense over the last two years. The defense gets back eight full-time starters. Even with the loss of three top receivers, the top two tacklers and an All-SEC pass rusher, the individual pieces of last year's 11-2, top-five finish are largely intact.

Top 2013 NFL Prospects: QB Tyler Wilson (1), WR Cobi Hamilton (2), G Alvin Bailey* (2-3), RB Knile Davis* (2-3), C Travis Swanson* (3-4), LB Alonzo Highsmith (4), RB Dennis Johnson (4-5), DT DeQuinta Jones (6).

No. 22 Auburn Tigers (7-5, 4-4)

2011: 8-5 (4-4) / F/+ #52 / FEI #66 / S&P+ #58

Program F/+	-199.9	22	Returning Starters: 7 OFF, 9 DEF			2-Yr Recruiting Rank		7
2011 Offense			**2011 Defense**			**2011 Field Position**		
Offensive F/+	+0.7%	55	**Defensive F/+**	-1.1%	64	Field Position Advantage	0.552	7
Offensive FEI:	0.096	47	Defensive FEI	0.31	92	**2012 Projections**		
Offensive S&P+	95.8	34	Defensive S&P+	108.8	75	**Mean Wins**	7.3	
Rushing S&P+	118.7	22	Rushing S&P+	100.1	60	Proj. F/+	+13.6%	22
Passing S&P+	114.3	31	Passing S&P+	92.8	80	Offensive F/+	+6.5%	28
Standard Downs S&P+	117.1	20	Standard Downs S&P+	97.9	70	Defensive F/+	+7.1%	26
Passing Downs S&P+	124.8	22	Passing Downs S&P+	89.0	88	Strength of Schedule	0.053	3

There have been harsher hangovers than the one that afflicted Auburn on its post-championship tour in 2011, and certainly more unexpected ones—given the mass exodus of talent from the Tigers' 2010 title run, the 8-5 encore actually *exceeded* most preseason predictions. Beyond the respectable record, though, there was more than a hint of putrid aftertaste: The offense sunk from first to 55th in Offensive F/+, and was even worse (100th) in yards per game. The defense came up last or next-to-last in the conference in every major category, and the five losses came by an average of four touchdowns per game. (The final insult came in a 42-14 rout at the hands of Alabama in which the Auburn offense failed to score.) By December, coordinators Gus Malzahn and Ted Roof were both on their way out, with All-SEC tailback Michael Dyer hot on their heels in the midst of a postseason suspension.

So despite 18 returning starters, 2012 arrives with a palpable sense of reinvention, even if its exact shape is uncertain. On offense, the overhaul hinges on the preferences of a new play-caller, Scott Loefler, whose experience in both spread and "pro style" schemes makes handicapping the three-man quarterback derby between junior Clint Moseley, scrambly sophomore Kiehl Frazier and fireballing freshman Zeke Pike that much harder. There's a new guru on the other side of the ball, too, former Atlanta Falcons defensive coordinator Brian Van Gorder, but the really dramatic change on defense is old-fashioned experience: The growing pains of last year's untenably green lineup should yield ten returning regulars this fall—all of them juniors or seniors—who have combined for 147 career starts.

Add second-year blue-chips Gabe Wright and Kris Frost at defensive tackle and linebacker, respectively, and you have the foundation for the most improved unit in the league on either side of the ball. Just how much better it has to be relative to the new-look offense is very much to be determined.

Top 2013 NFL Prospects: DE Corey Lemonier (2), TE Philip Lutzenkirchen (3-4), WR Emory Blake (4), RB/KR Onterio McCalebb (6-7).*

No. 25 Texas A&M Aggies (7-5, 4-4)

2011: 7-6 (4-5) / F/+ #16 / FEI #16 / S&P+ #16

Program F/+	-200.0	51	Returning Starters: 9 OFF, 6 DEF			2-Yr Recruiting Rank		22
2011 Offense			**2011 Defense**			**2011 Field Position**		
Offensive F/+	+8.8%	17	**Defensive F/+**	+5.2%	23	Field Position Advantage	0.507	46
Offensive FEI:	0.359	19	Defensive FEI	-0.298	27	**2012 Projections**		
Offensive S&P+	102.8	18	Defensive S&P+	133.3	18	**Mean Wins**	7.3	
Rushing S&P+	123.7	15	Rushing S&P+	128.6	15	Proj. F/+	+13.5%	25
Passing S&P+	110.6	40	Passing S&P+	121.4	21	Offensive F/+	+9.3%	20
Standard Downs S&P+	110.8	30	Standard Downs S&P+	117.0	20	Defensive F/+	+4.1%	39
Passing Downs S&P+	142.9	7	Passing Downs S&P+	141.7	7	Strength of Schedule	0.057	4

Under different circumstances, Texas A&M might have been able to take some solace in its sixth-place swan song from the Big 12, if for no other reason than that it was so *close*. Five of the Aggies' six losses in 2011 came by a combined 17 points, two of them in overtime, four of them against teams ranked in the top 16 of the final polls. Five of the six came after A&M led by at least two scores in the second half. Against arguably the toughest schedule in the country, the Aggies outscored opponents by 11 points per game, outgained them by an average of 112 yards and were in every game except one (a 41-25 loss at Oklahoma in November) down to the final snap. If not for a handful of untimely turnovers, they might have been on the verge of a BCS nod.

As it was, a series of fourth-quarter collapses by a team that opened the season in the top 10 was enough to cost head coach Mike Sherman his job after four years. But SEC types expecting easy pickings against the new kid in class would be advised to look past the uninspiring record: Man for man, A&M still looks more like an aspiring national contender than a rebuilding mediocrity. That starts with the offensive line, anchored by a pair of future first-rounders at tackle—juniors Luke Joeckel and Jake Matthews, spawn of Hall-of-Famer Bruce Matthews—and senior center Patrick Lewis, who's started 35 consecutive games over the last three years. There's also proven, draft-worthy talent at receiver (seniors Ryan Swope and Uzoma Nwachukwu), linebacker (senior Sean Porter), defensive end (junior Damontre Moore), cornerback (senior Dustin Harris) and running back (senior Christine "It's Pronounced 'Christian'" Michael). And just in case Michael's health remains a concern after two season-ending knee injuries, there's unproven but immensely hyped talent behind him in the form of incoming freshman Trey Williams and Oklahoma transfer Brandon Williams (no relation), who dominated spring practice while waiting on word of his eligibility in the fall. Physically, the Aggies hold up and then some.

Instead, the nagging questions are the usual ones for a team attempting a coaching transplant, specifically: a) How quickly can the Kevin Sumlin administration bridge the gap between potential and results? and b) How steep is the learning curve for the new quarterback? For now, first crack at replacing first-rounder Ryan Tannehill belongs to sophomore Jameill Showers, who ended the spring in the pole position of a four-man race. Judging from Sumlin's preferences at Houston—the Cougars put the ball in the air more often during his four-year tenure than any other team in college football—A&M is going to come out of the chute firing in true Big 12 fashion. How long it's willing to keep it up against the considerably prouder defenses of the SEC is anyone's guess.

Top 2013 NFL Prospects: OT Luke Joeckel* (1), OT Jake Matthews* (1), LB Sean Porter (1), DE Damontre Moore* (2-3), WR Ryan Swope (3), RB Christine Michael (3-4), WR Uzoma Nwachukwu (5), CB Dustin Harris (5-6), C Patrick Lewis (6-7).

No. 44 Mississippi State Bulldogs (7-5)

2011: 7-6 (2-6) / F/+ #43 / FEI #47 / S&P+ #40

Program F/+	-200.0	47	Returning Starters: 5 OFF, 7 DEF		2-Yr Recruiting Rank		37
2011 Offense			**2011 Defense**		**2011 Field Position**		
Offensive F/+	-1.4%	72	Defensive F/+	+5.7%	18	Field Position Advantage	0.511	38
Offensive FEI:	-0.191	88	Defensive FEI	-0.297	28	**2012 Projections**		
Offensive S&P+	89.0	58	Defensive S&P+	126.5	30	Mean Wins	6.5	
Rushing S&P+	107.1	46	Rushing S&P+	110.6	36	Proj. F/+	+6.0%	44
Passing S&P+	115.0	30	Passing S&P+	110.2	32	Offensive F/+	-2.8%	68
Standard Downs S&P+	112.7	27	Standard Downs S&P+	103.4	46	Defensive F/+	+8.8%	18
Passing Downs S&P+	99.5	75	Passing Downs S&P+	121.4	28	Strength of Schedule	0.039	2

You don't have to paint a "Before" and "After" portrait for Mississippi State fans to appreciate the energy coach Dan Mullen has injected into the once-moribund program. But one year removed from the Bulldogs' big breakthrough in Mullen's second season, the scope of the project is beginning to become clear: Of their ten losses over the last two seasons, nine have come at the hands of conference rivals that went on to finish in the top 20 of the final polls, seven of whom finished in the top ten. In the rough-and-tumble reality of the SEC West, even tangible on-field progress hasn't been enough to lift MSU out of fifth place.

If any team was going to make the leap, it was the 2011 edition, a reunion of the gang that turned in a 9-4, top-15 finish in 2010 and subsequently found itself in the preseason polls for the first time in recent memory. That kind of optimism is harder to come by for this fall's outfit, which safely falls under the "rebuilding" category with at least 11 new starters in the regular rotation. Most prominent among them is the new quarterback, junior Tyler Russell, the more traditional half of last year's haphazard platoon with bullish athlete Chris Relf. Mullen's run-oriented spread scheme has always preferred a quarterback who can function as a second tailback out of the shotgun—think Tim Tebow at Florida, where Mullen was offensive coordinator under head coach Urban Meyer—but the less mobile Russell and a long-in-the-tooth receiving corps may force a little more balance.

Russell's recruiting class was Mullen's first to Starkville back in 2009, and has raised the bar, talent-wise: Defensive tackle Fletcher Cox left early to become Mississippi State's first top-ten draft pick since 1983, and senior cornerback Johnthan Banks may command the same lofty status next year. Former classmates Gabe Jackson, Nickoe Whitley and Chad Bumphis could hear their names called, too. Against another murderer's row of a schedule, though, the sobering fact is that Alabama, Arkansas and LSU still eat diamonds in the rough for breakfast.

Top 2013 NFL Prospects: CB Johnthan Banks (1), DB Nickoe Whitley* (3), G Gabe Jackson* (5-6), WR Chad Bumphis (6).

No. 59 Mississippi Rebels (4-8, 2-6)
2011: 2-10 (0-8) / F/+ #95 / FEI #98 / S&P+ #101

Program F/+	-200.0	53	Returning Starters: 8 OFF, 7 DEF			2-Yr Recruiting Rank		27
2011 Offense			**2011 Defense**			**2011 Field Position**		
Offensive F/+	-12.2%	111	**Defensive F/+**	+0.6%	54	Field Position Advantage	0.466	102
Offensive FEI:	-0.524	114	Defensive FEI	0.174	77	**2012 Projections**		
Offensive S&P+	77.3	96	Defensive S&P+	101.2	90	**Mean Wins**	4.4	
Rushing S&P+	107.1	45	Rushing S&P+	88.5	96	Proj. F/+	+0.2%	59
Passing S&P+	90.5	86	Passing S&P+	96.7	68	Offensive F/+	-7.2%	99
Standard Downs S&P+	97.9	77	Standard Downs S&P+	95.1	83	Defensive F/+	+7.5%	17
Passing Downs S&P+	108.6	49	Passing Downs S&P+	88.9	89	Strength of Schedule	0.017	1

For some indication of just how depressing Ole Miss was offensively in 2011, look no further than the quarterback competition in the spring: Given their choice of three veterans with significant experience—Randall Mackey, Barry Brunetti, and Zack Stoudt—the new coaching staff opted for d) None of the above, elevating incoming junior college transfer Bo Wallace to the top of the depth chart instead after a few weeks of practice. Now consider this: From a yardage perspective, the Rebel defense was even *worse*.

Wallace's emergence is only the most notable development in the full-scale hope offensive waged by first-year head coach Hugh Freeze, who (at least for now) has the rare advantage of inheriting both an experienced roster and exceedingly low expectations. The Rebels go into the season having dropped 14 straight SEC games under Freeze's predecessor, Houston Nutt, all but one of them by double digits. It was so pitiful at the end that Nutt, immediately following a 29-24 loss to Arkansas last October, felt vindicated enough by the final score to declare victory over a local reporter who'd predicted a blowout. (The fact that his team had just blown a 17-point lead by allowing the Razorbacks to score 29 unanswered had somehow failed to register.) At one point, LSU resorted to taking knees on offense with nearly half a quarter remaining to prevent running up the score even further in the most lopsided massacre in the 100-year history of the series.

Obviously, improvement under Freeze—a big winner last year in his only turn as a Division I head coach, leading traditionally hapless Arkansas State on an unprecedented run to the Sun Belt Conference title—is a given. And with a new quarterback throwing to a promising pair of sophomore receivers (Donte Moncrief and Tobias Singleton) in a more wide-open scheme, there's a glimmer of a foundation for the future, albeit a slightly less sturdy one after rising two-way star Nickolas Brassell was declared academically ineligible in the spring and transferred. Fortunately for Freeze, in this division, a glimmer is all even the most diehard Rebel fans will need.

Top 2013 NFL Prospects: None.

EAST

No. 8 Georgia Bulldogs (10-2, 6-2)
2011: 10-4 (7-1) / F/+ #15 / FEI #19 / S&P+ #8

Program F/+	-199.9	17	Returning Starters: 6 OFF, 9 DEF			2-Yr Recruiting Rank		5
2011 Offense			**2011 Defense**			**2011 Field Position**		
Offensive F/+	+8.4%	18	**Defensive F/+**	+6.9%	17	Field Position Advantage	0.498	63
Offensive FEI:	0.201	34	Defensive FEI	-0.469	11	**2012 Projections**		
Offensive S&P+	94.6	42	Defensive S&P+	151.4	4	**Mean Wins**	9.9	
Rushing S&P+	92.6	91	Rushing S&P+	129.7	13	Proj. F/+	+21.8%	8
Passing S&P+	147.4	5	Passing S&P+	139.6	7	Offensive F/+	+10.7%	18
Standard Downs S&P+	118.7	15	Standard Downs S&P+	130.4	6	Defensive F/+	+11.1%	12
Passing Downs S&P+	110.9	43	Passing Downs S&P+	134.2	16	Strength of Schedule	0.293	43

If you really wanted to, it's no major task to find an asterisk or two to attach to Georgia's 2011 run to the SEC East title, its first since 2005. Thanks to the quirks of the conference schedule, the Bulldogs didn't have to face any of the "Big Three" from the SEC West (Alabama, LSU or Arkansas) during the regular season, didn't beat an opponent that finished with fewer than five losses and—by virtue of their come-from-ahead, triple-overtime loss to Michigan State in the Outback Bowl—ultimately dropped all four dates with teams that landed in the final polls. For a program that delivered a pair of SEC titles and the highest winning percentage in the league over Mark Richt's first eight years as head coach, it didn't exactly qualify as a breakthrough.

Still, on the heels of an unthinkable slide to 6-7 in 2010—and especially following an 0-2 start last September that shoved Richt onto one of the hottest seats in the country—there's a distinct feeling in Athens that the clouds have parted and brighter days are ahead. The optimism begins with a rehabilitated defense that surged in its second year under coordinator Todd Grantham, improving from 47th in Defensive F/+ to 17th, and should have no problem holding at the top of the charts: Twelve of last year's top 13 tacklers are back, including a pair of All-Americans (linebacker Jarvis Jones and safety Bacarri Rambo) with first-round potential next April and at least four others likely to come off the board. Even considering a handful of key suspensions over the first four games, on paper there's not a better returning group in the country. It doesn't hurt that Alabama, Arkansas and LSU are still absent from the dance card, either.

The only persistent question: Georgia's consistency in big games, particularly the offense, which occasionally struggled to come out of its shell against competent defenses. All the pieces are there: Junior quarterback Aaron Murray has 27 career starts under his belt, more than twice as many as any other quarterback in the conference, and the brightest star in the supporting cast—wide receiver Malcolm Mitchell—only scratched the surface of his potential as a freshman All-American. The running back position is in flux, however, with the dismissal of former blue-chipper Isaiah Crowell, and the offensive line is more of a work in progress. Still, if they can survive trips to Missouri and South Carolina in the top half of the schedule, there's no reason the Bulldogs can't run the table en route to the SEC title game. After nine consecutive losses against ranked teams, though, that's still a very long bridge to cross.

Top 2013 NFL Prospects: OLB Jarvis Jones* (1), FS Bacarri Rambo (1-2), QB Aaron Murray* (2), DT Jonathan Jenkins (2), DT Kwame Geathers* (2-3), WR Tavarres King (2-3), CB Branden Smith (3), OLB Cornelius Washington (5-6), MLB Christian Robinson (6).

No. 10 Florida Gators (8-4, 5-3)

2011: 7-6 (3-5) / F/+ #30 / FEI #44 / S&P+ #41

Program F/+	-199.8	3	Returning Starters: 7 OFF, 10 DEF		2-Yr Recruiting Rank		9
2011 Offense			**2011 Defense**		**2011 Field Position**		
Offensive F/+	-0.7%	65	**Defensive F/+**	+5.6%	20	Field Position Advantage	0.502	55
Offensive FEI:	-0.155	84	Defensive FEI	-0.238	33	**2012 Projections**		
Offensive S&P+	91.7	50	Defensive S&P+	123.8	38	**Mean Wins**	8.4	
Rushing S&P+	112.8	32	Rushing S&P+	111.9	32	Proj. F/+	+19.5%	10
Passing S&P+	120.5	21	Passing S&P+	101.6	57	Offensive F/+	+5.2%	38
Standard Downs S&P+	118.2	16	Standard Downs S&P+	107.3	39	Defensive F/+	+14.3%	5
Passing Downs S&P+	100.7	67	Passing Downs S&P+	118.9	32	Strength of Schedule	0.112	17

Rocky debut notwithstanding, it would be unfair to coach Will Muschamp, to his celebrated predecessor, and especially to Florida players to suggest Muschamp found the cupboard bare last year after taking the keys from Urban Meyer. That may have been true at quarterback, where once-touted John Brantley cemented his legacy as a monumental flop in the role of heir apparent to Tim Tebow, and it was reflected in April's draft, where only two Gators came off the board, and none until the fourth round. But the underachievement narrative also risks overlooking the sheer *inexperience* of the project: Fifteen full-time starters in 2011 were freshmen or sophomores, led by a first-time head coach into the teeth of a schedule featuring five teams that finished in the final polls.

The immediate result, predictably, was Florida's worst record in 25 years. As far as 2012 is concerned, though, think of it as an investment: The starting lineup this fall will be made up almost exclusively of blue-chip types from Meyer's last two recruiting classes in 2009 and 2010, massively hyped hauls on the verge of a collective bloom after two years of growing pains. The defense alone boasts six starters who arrived in Gainesville with five-star billing from the scouts, not including incoming defensive ends Jonathan Bullard and Dante Fowler, Jr., or junior end Ronald Powell, whose season is in the air after a major knee injury in the spring. Along with Powell, former five-stars Sharrif Floyd, Dominique Easley, Jelani Jenkins, and Matt Elam all settled into the starting lineup last year as sophomores for a defense that finished 20th in Defensive F/+, and all could potentially hear their name called by Roger Goodell next April.

Not that there's any shortage of latent talent on the other side of the ball, including sophomore quarterbacks Jacoby Brissett and Jeff Driskel, who spent the spring vying to replace Brantley full-time after being thrown into the fire—and burned badly—as true freshman backups. But whoever wins the job, he'll have to deal with a new scheme imported by ex-Boise State coordinator John Pease and a startling dearth of proven playmakers in the supporting cast. As little chance as there is of going backwards, the familiar firepower necessary to keep the Gators from merely running in place remains purely hypothetical.

Top 2013 NFL Prospects: DT Sharrif Floyd* (1-2), SS Matt Elam* (2-3), DT Dominique Easley* (2-3), LB Jelani Jenkins* (3), OT Xavier Nixon (4-5), LB Jonathan Bostic (6), FS Josh Evans (6-7), K Caleb Sturgis (6-7).

No. 17 South Carolina Gamecocks (8-4, 5-3)

2011: 11-2 (6-2) / F/+ #21 / FEI #13 / S&P+ #19

Program F/+	-199.9	25	Returning Starters: 7 OFF, 6 DEF		2-Yr Recruiting Rank		19
2011 Offense			**2011 Defense**		**2011 Field Position**		
Offensive F/+	+5.8%	26	**Defensive F/+**	+8.1%	12	Field Position Advantage	0.490	76
Offensive FEI:	0.139	43	Defensive FEI	-0.541	7	**2012 Projections**		
Offensive S&P+	95.1	41	Defensive S&P+	139.0	13	**Mean Wins**	8.1	
Rushing S&P+	115.4	29	Rushing S&P+	104.6	49	Proj. F/+	+16.7%	17
Passing S&P+	106.4	51	Passing S&P+	146.4	4	Offensive F/+	+7.1%	26
Standard Downs S&P+	110.4	33	Standard Downs S&P+	123.6	12	Defensive F/+	+9.6%	15
Passing Downs S&P+	115.7	33	Passing Downs S&P+	118.4	33	Strength of Schedule	0.084	6

If you were only checking in on a week-to-week basis, South Carolina's most anticipated campaign in ages seemed to be teetering on the brink of collapse: At various points, the 2011 Gamecocks narrowly escaped an upset bid from Navy, lost their starting quarterback to a career-ending suspension, lost their All-American tailback to a season-ending knee injury, and subsequently fell into an offensive funk that left them impotent for most of October and November. The sum of which makes the final results—school records for both wins (11) and final ranking in the major polls (ninth), capped by South Carolina's first New Year's Day bowl win in a decade—that much more of a revelation. After seven years under Steve Spurrier, the Gamecocks have finally reached the point that they can compete among the SEC's elite even when things are going actively *wrong*.

Last year, that was mostly due to a stacked defense that came in 12th in Defensive F/+, and paid the price in attrition: All-American defensive end Melvin Ingram, top cover man Stephon Gilmore and leading tackler Antonio Allen all went in the draft—the former two in the first round—and veteran coordinator Ellis Johnson leapt at the head coaching vacancy at Southern Miss. Versatile as he was, Ingram may be actually the most dispensable of that group thanks to equally freakish bookends Devin Taylor and Jadeveon Clowney, a Freshman All-American who gave every indication of fulfilling his massive recruiting hype coming off the bench. (More quietly, fellow freshman Kelcy Quarles emerged as an equally promising run stuffer over the second half of the season.) Uncovering another blue-chip corner to plug in for Gilmore looks like a much taller task by comparison.

Still, all offseason intrigue eventually returns to the reconstructed knee of Marcus Lattimore, who was personally accounting for more than a third of the Gamecocks' total offense when he went down with a torn ACL in the seventh game. At full speed, Lattimore is a unique, punishing talent who can hold his own against any back in the country as an every-down workhorse, a short-yardage bulldozer or a receiver out of the backfield. If not, the offensive weight falls disproportionately on the shoulders—and legs—of junior quarterback Connor Shaw. Shaw kept the offense on an even keel down the stretch (South Carolina averaged 29.3 Adj. PPG before Lattimore's injury, 29.8 Adj. PPG after) but now lacks the proven downfield threat he had last year in departed receiver Alshon Jeffery. Not surprisingly, Lattimore avoided contact drills in the spring out of an abundance of caution. With the East Division title well within its reach, Carolina can't afford another year of living dangerously.

Top 2013 NFL Prospects: RB Marcus Lattimore* (1), SS/OLB DeVonte Holloman (2), DE Devin Taylor (2-3), C T.J. Johnson (6-7).

No. 27 Tennessee Volunteers (7-5, 4-4)

2011: 5-7 (1-7) / F/+ #57 / FEI #57 / S&P+ #43

Program F/+	-199.9	40	Returning Starters: 10 OFF, 8 DEF			2-Yr Recruiting Rank		13
2011 Offense			**2011 Defense**			**2011 Field Position**		
Offensive F/+	+0.5%	60	**Defensive F/+**	+2.2%	45	Field Position Advantage	0.474	99
Offensive FEI	-0.109	77	Defensive FEI	-0.285	32	**2012 Projections**		
Offensive S&P+	94.4	43	Defensive S&P+	120.1	47	**Mean Wins**	7.3	
Rushing S&P+	103.2	59	Rushing S&P+	110.2	38	Proj. F/+	+12.1%	27
Passing S&P+	133.5	10	Passing S&P+	103.8	49	Offensive F/+	+5.9%	33
Standard Downs S&P+	107.2	46	Standard Downs S&P+	104.4	45	Defensive F/+	+6.2%	25
Passing Downs S&P+	133.8	13	Passing Downs S&P+	108.5	47	Strength of Schedule	0.109	15

By the start of last season, Tennessee fans had seen enough dysfunction since their last bid for SEC relevance, back in 2007, to know there were no miracles on the horizon. And there weren't: UT dropped its first six in SEC play by an average of 22 points per game against a murderer's row of the conference elite. During one midseason stretch, following injuries to quarterback Tyler Bray and receiver Justin Hunter, LSU, Alabama and South Carolina combined to keep the Volunteers out of the end zone in ten consecutive quarters. Miserable, yes, but predictable under the circumstances.

By the final gun, though, even the realists had run out of patience. With Bray back in the lineup and a bowl game on the line against their traditional November whipping boys, the Vols barely survived an overtime scare at Vanderbilt and let a 26-year winning streak against Kentucky slip away in a listless, 10-7 flop in Lexington, ensuring a new school record for SEC losses (7) and denying UT a token bowl game. No combination of excuses—youth, injuries or otherwise—can excuse a last-place finish at Tennessee.

At least this time around, you can finally scratch "youth" from the list. Bray is now a junior with a dozen career starts to his name and NFL scouts marveling over his barely tapped potential; ditto receiver Da'Rick Rogers, who picked up an All-SEC nod as a sophomore and joins Hunter (if healthy) among the most potent deep threats in the country. Up front, there are four veteran offensive linemen (Dallas Thomas, Alex Bullard, Zach Fulton and Ja'Wuan James) who started every game last year, and two others (James Stone and Marcus Jackson) who split an assignment at right guard. The defense brings back an incredible seven players who started multiple games last year in their first season in the program, including linebackers Curt Maggitt and A.J. Johnson and safety Brian Randolph, who found themselves thrust into full-time roles as true freshmen. It also returns a pair of senior corners (Marsalis Teague and Prentiss Waggner) who have combined for 48 career starts and seasoned linebacker Herman Lathers, who lost all of 2011 to a preseason Achilles injury.

Altogether, Tennessee's starting lineup has played more football at this level than any other lineup in the SEC. Unless it has some tangible progress to show for it by the end of Derek Dooley's third season as head coach, though, the next phase of the rebuilding job will be bequeathed to new management.

Top 2013 NFL Prospects: QB Tyler Bray* (1-2), WR Justin Hunter* (1-2), WR Da'Rick Rogers* (1-2), SS Prentiss Waggner (2-4), G James Stone* (4-5), OT Dallas Thomas (4-5).

No. 28 Missouri Tigers (6-6, 3-5)
2011: 8-5 (5-4) / F/+ #25 / FEI #20 / S&P+ #31

Program F/+	-199.9	20	Returning Starters: 5 OFF, 6 DEF		2-Yr Recruiting Rank		39
2011 Offense			**2011 Defense**		**2011 Field Position**		
Offensive F/+	+8.3%	19	**Defensive F/+**	+1.7%	49	Field Position Advantage	0.503	53
Offensive FEI:	0.411	13	Defensive FEI	-0.165	46	**2012 Projections**		
Offensive S&P+	99.0	26	Defensive S&P+	121.9	41	**Mean Wins**	6.4	
Rushing S&P+	119.5	19	Rushing S&P+	116.5	22	Proj. F/+	+11.2%	28
Passing S&P+	106.6	49	Passing S&P+	109.5	34	Offensive F/+	+8.7%	24
Standard Downs S&P+	118.9	14	Standard Downs S&P+	108.0	35	Defensive F/+	+2.5%	47
Passing Downs S&P+	100.7	66	Passing Downs S&P+	139.7	9	Strength of Schedule	0.091	8

Here's one way to get the attention of your new conference rivals: Beat them out for the most coveted recruit in the country. Missouri's late push to sign in-state wide receiver Dorial Green-Beckham—a record-breaking, 6-foot-6 freak of nature hotly pursued by Alabama and Arkansas, among others, all the way up to National Signing Day—was an unprecedented coup for the Tigers and a satisfying opening salvo at skeptics of their ability to run with the league's big dogs. Now, it's time to start running.

In terms of overall talent and pedigree (Green-Beckham notwithstanding), Mizzou stacks up against the Alabamas, LSUs and Georgias of its new neighborhood about as well as it traditionally has against the Nebraskas, Oklahomas and Texases of its old one, which isn't saying much. Despite their progress under coach Gary Pinkel, the Tigers haven't won a conference championship or played in a major bowl game since 1969. Along with Texas A&M, though, they do bring an up-tempo, balanced spread attack that until now has been largely foreign to SEC defenses, and more than enough to weapons to make it go. With 2,872 yards passing and 981 rushing (after sacks), quarterback James Franklin came up just shy of joining the exclusive 3,000/1,000 club in his first year as a starter; with All-Big 12 tailback Henry Josey and senior receiver T.J. Moe, he has proven threats at his disposal before Green-Beckham ever sets foot on the field. As a system, in terms of total yards, Missouri's output would have ranked No. 1 in the SEC five of the last seven seasons.

Of course, that says at least as much about the unflattering state of Big 12 defenses as it does about the lack of offensive fireworks in the SEC, where reputations still tend to be made along the line of scrimmage. Not that the Tigers are shrinking violets in the trenches—senior Sheldon Richardson has first-round potential in the middle of the defensive line, though it went almost entirely untapped in his first season out of junior college—but coming from the most spread-friendly conference in America, it's hard to imagine a scenario in which the culture shock works in their favor the first time around.

Top 2013 NFL Prospects: DT Sheldon Richardson (2-3), OLB Zaviar Gooden (4), WR T.J. Moe (4-5), DE Brad Madison (5-6).

No. 50 Vanderbilt Commodores (6-6, 3-5)

2011: 6-7 (2-6) / F/+ #46 / FEI #45 / S&P+ #37

Program F/+	-200.0	73	Returning Starters: 9 OFF, 7 DEF			2-Yr Recruiting Rank		56
2011 Offense			**2011 Defense**			**2011 Field Position**		
Offensive F/+	+0.6%	59	Defensive F/+	+4.2%	28	Field Position Advantage	0.497	65
Offensive FEI:	0.148	42	Defensive FEI	-0.145	48	**2012 Projections**		
Offensive S&P+	88.1	59	Defensive S&P+	128.1	28	**Mean Wins**	5.8	
Rushing S&P+	125.8	10	Rushing S&P+	108.2	45	Proj. F/+	+4.0%	50
Passing S&P+	92.3	80	Passing S&P+	116.3	24	Offensive F/+	+0.2%	59
Standard Downs S&P+	97.7	79	Standard Downs S&P+	117.6	18	Defensive F/+	+3.8%	41
Passing Downs S&P+	134.2	12	Passing Downs S&P+	111.1	42	Strength of Schedule	0.273	36

Almost by definition, Vanderbilt football has always been and always will be a Sisyphean ordeal, but few coaches have ever attacked the boulder with the gusto of James Franklin. In his first year in Nashville, Franklin's Commodores broke even in the regular season; came within a hair's breadth of upsetting Arkansas, Georgia and Tennessee; played in a bowl game; and signed the most celebrated recruiting class in school history. Franklin personally talked trash with opposing coaches, buzzed recruits in a helicopter and helped sell the university on both renovations of Vanderbilt Stadium and a new indoor practice facility, while also securing a contract extension and raise for himself. It may be too early to tell, but it's entirely possible he made the league's most apathetic culture actually *care* about football.

Now comes the hard part: Keeping the ball from rolling back to the bottom of the hill. The last time Vanderbilt played in a bowl game, ending a 25-year drought in 2008, it immediately reverted to form with a 2-10 flop in 2009 that shoved coach Bobby Johnson into an abrupt retirement. Franklin isn't going anywhere, but he's hardly vanquished the disadvantages that have limited the Commodores to just two winning seasons in the last 35 years—namely, the yawning talent gap relative to the rest of the SEC. With the exception of a few true freshmen, not a single player on the Vandy depth chart arrived with more than three stars from the recruiting gurus, which means they were ignored completely by at least half the league.

If there's anyone on the team who clearly defies that pedigree, it's senior tailback Zac Stacy, who set a school record with 1,193 yards rushing last year while backfield mate Warren Norman (a former SEC Freshman of the Year in 2009) nursed the same nagging knee injury that cut short his sophomore campaign in 2010. Even if Norman fails to crack the rotation again, the combination of Stacy, incoming freshman Brian Kimbrow and the top three receivers from 2011 give the Commodores as potent a collection of skill threats as they've boasted in decades. Still, without a quantum leap from senior quarterback Jordan Rodgers—who was rarely reminiscent of older brother Aaron in his first season out of junior college, and was seriously pushed in the spring by Wyoming transfer Austyn Carta-Samuels—the attack will be driving sideways, at best.

Top 2013 NFL Prospects: CB Trey Wilson (6-7), QB Jordan Rodgers (7).

No. 64 Kentucky Wildcats (4-8, 1-7)

2011: 5-7 (2-6) / F/+ #89 / FEI #88 / S&P+ #98

Program F/+	-200.0	55	Returning Starters: 6 OFF, 6 DEF		2-Yr Recruiting Rank		50
2011 Offense			**2011 Defense**		**2011 Field Position**		
Offensive F/+	-11.9%	110	**Defensive F/+**	+3.0%	40	Field Position Advantage	0.475	96
Offensive FEI:	-0.45	110	Defensive FEI	-0.116	52	**2012 Projections**		
Offensive S&P+	65.8	113	Defensive S&P+	113.5	64	**Mean Wins**	4.1	
Rushing S&P+	96.9	82	Rushing S&P+	97.6	68	Proj. F/+	-2.7%	64
Passing S&P+	72.3	115	Passing S&P+	105.0	44	Offensive F/+	-10.3%	107
Standard Downs S&P+	87.6	106	Standard Downs S&P+	99.2	65	Defensive F/+	+7.6%	20
Passing Downs S&P+	82.9	107	Passing Downs S&P+	99.0	68	Strength of Schedule	0.194	27

By mid-October, the attention of Kentucky fans tends to be monopolized by that *other* winter sport. Still, it's not like they don't have a good excuse: Where the UK offense is concerned, actually caring may be hazardous to their health. Last year, token emotional investments were rewarded with a toxic attack that ranked 110th in Offensive F/+ and finished dead last in the SEC in virtually every major category, including total offense, scoring offense, passing offense, pass efficiency, third down conversions and sacks allowed. (It was merely next-to-last in rushing offense, narrowly outpacing Tennessee.) The Wildcats topped 16 points just once in conference play, in a 30-13 win over lame-duck Ole Miss, which promptly fired head coach Houston Nutt the next day.

So it wasn't just the top-ranked basketball team that kept the partisans from fretting over the greenest lineup in the conference this spring. Even with a largely rebuilt offensive line, an unresolved quarterback situation—the pole position belongs to sophomore Maxwell Smith, thanks in part to an injury that kept senior Morgan Newton out of spring drills—and no proven playmakers anywhere, there is nowhere to go but up. The only semblance of buzz surrounds the pending arrival of freshman quarterback Patrick Towles, the most touted prospect in the state, who already looks the part of a future draft pick at 6-foot-5, 230 pounds, and will have the opportunity to seize the reins immediately.

As usual, the schedule is designed to get Kentucky into a bottom-rung bowl game at the expense of a handful of non-conference patsies (Kent State, Western Kentucky and Samford) and two or three victims in conference play; before last year's dip to 5-7, the Wildcats had quietly qualified for a bowl in five consecutive seasons. Barring a complete collapse, coach Joker Phillips is at least a year away from any ultimatums. Another sideways step that fails to get the final record out of the red, though, and the clock will be officially ticking.

Top 2013 NFL Prospects: G Larry Warford (2-3).

Matt Hinton

Projected Win Probabilities For SEC Teams

	Overall Wins												Conference Wins							
SEC East	12-0	11-1	10-2	9-3	8-4	7-5	6-6	5-7	4-8	3-9	2-10	1-11	0-12	8-0	7-1	6-2	5-3	4-4	3-5	2-6	1-7	0-8
Florida	1	4	16	28	28	16	6	1	-	-	-	-	-	2	12	27	31	20	7	1	-	-
Georgia	8	25	33	23	9	2	-	-	-	-	-	-	-	10	28	34	20	7	1	-	-	-
Kentucky	-	-	-	-	-	2	8	23	34	25	7	1	-	-	-	-	-	2	8	27	40	23
Missouri	-	-	1	4	15	27	29	17	6	1	-	-	-	-	-	2	10	24	34	24	6	-
South Carolina	-	2	12	24	30	21	9	2	-	-	-	-	-	-	5	20	32	27	13	3	-	-
Tennessee	-	-	3	14	26	29	19	8	1	-	-	-	-	-	1	5	18	31	29	13	3	-
Vanderbilt	-	-	-	2	9	19	27	25	13	4	1	-	-	-	-	1	5	15	28	30	17	4
SEC West	12-0	11-1	10-2	9-3	8-4	7-5	6-6	5-7	4-8	3-9	2-10	1-11	0-12	8-0	7-1	6-2	5-3	4-4	3-5	2-6	1-7	0-8
Alabama	33	45	18	4	-	-	-	-	-	-	-	-	-	37	46	15	2	-	-	-	-	-
Arkansas	-	1	8	22	31	24	11	3	-	-	-	-	-	-	2	10	27	33	21	6	1	-
Auburn	-	-	4	14	26	28	19	7	2	-	-	-	-	-	1	7	21	32	25	11	3	-
LSU	16	37	31	13	3	-	-	-	-	-	-	-	-	16	37	31	13	3	-	-	-	-
Mississippi	-	-	-	-	-	3	14	29	33	18	3	-	-	-	-	-	-	3	14	33	36	14
Mississippi State	-	-	1	4	16	29	29	16	4	1	-	-	-	-	-	1	6	19	31	28	13	2
Texas A&M	-	-	4	14	27	29	18	7	1	-	-	-	-	-	1	5	17	30	28	15	4	-

Non-AQs and Independents

Over the last eight seasons, non-AQ college football programs have racked up seven BCS bowl appearances (winning five times), multiple undefeated and one-loss seasons, and ten combined top-10 rankings in the final Associated Press poll. But even with all of that success, it still feels as though the efforts of college football's mid-major programs have been largely underappreciated. No non-AQ team ever participated in a BCS championship game. None were given the opportunity to compete for the sport's top prize.

We now stand on the precipice of a new era in college football, with conference realignment finally settling down and a four-team playoff on the horizon. The elimination of the term "automatic qualifier" and "BCS" from the college football lexicon is around the corner, and it feels as though the have-nots in the lesser conferences may have even less access to the championship than before. Utah and TCU have already moved up to major conferences, and Boise State is expected to follow suit. The non-AQ era may officially be over before it ever ultimately triumphed.

There will be strong seasons, and a few non-AQs may sneak in and out of the top 25 throughout the year. But according to our projections, none will sniff the top 10. The two best non-AQs according to F/+ have an elite quarterback to replace. We don't project a single non-AQ in our top 25, and only two appear in our projected top 40.

The key independents this year, Notre Dame and BYU, will feature more prominently in attention-grabbing matchups, but there are too many pitfalls to consider either one a legitimate national contender this year. Non-AQs and independents may have to get comfortable in the role of spoiler. There won't be any BCS busters this season, and the future postseason isn't offering any guarantees either.

No. 14 Notre Dame Fighting Irish (8-4, -)

2011: 8-5 (—) / F/+ #13 / FEI #15 / S&P+ #10

Program F/+	-199.9	35	Returning Starters: 8 OFF, 6 DEF			2-Yr Recruiting Rank		14
2011 Offense			**2011 Defense**			**2011 Field Position**		
Offensive F/+	+7.4%	22	Defensive F/+	+7.6%	15	Field Position Advantage	0.498	64
Offensive FEI:	0.281	26	Defensive FEI	-0.407	18	**2012 Projections**		
Offensive S&P+	102.4	19	Defensive S&P+	138.5	14	**Mean Wins**	8.2	
Rushing S&P+	129.5	8	Rushing S&P+	148.3	4	Proj. F/+	+17.6%	14
Passing S&P+	112.5	34	Passing S&P+	111.6	31	Offensive F/+	+8.9%	21
Standard Downs S&P+	120.7	11	Standard Downs S&P+	122.7	13	Defensive F/+	+8.7%	19
Passing Downs S&P+	125.4	20	Passing Downs S&P+	121.2	29	Strength of Schedule	0.097	10

Five famed head coaches in Notre Dame's illustrious history have statues erected in their honor outside Notre Dame Stadium. Each produced a national champion by the end of his third year at the helm. None of the other men who have had the job ever won a championship, and none of them lasted much longer than three years either.

Rationally, such lofty expectations are completely unfair to place upon head coach Brian Kelly as he enters his third season in South Bend. And after the Irish posted back-to-back winning seasons for only the second time in more than a decade, Kelly is in no danger of losing his job after this season. To ramp up enthusiasm for the future of the program, however, he needs to demonstrate that the program isn't treading water.

Notre Dame can start by limiting turnovers. Few teams cost themselves more on turnovers in crucial situations last season. The Irish coughed up the football nine times in the red zone (four fumbles, five interceptions) and two of those turnovers were returned for touchdowns on the same play. Notre Dame lost four games last year—against South Florida, Michigan, USC, and Florida State—in which the adjusted turnover value lost in the game was greater than the margin of defeat. Bad luck was in play a bit, but they can't simply count on the turnover pendulum naturally swinging back in their favor this fall. Above all else, the Irish need to find some consistency at the quarterback position to correct the turnover plague.

Four quarterbacks competed for the starting job in the spring game and three have a decent shot at seeing the field this fall since Kelly has been willing to mix multiple quarterbacks into game action. Tommy Rees has the experience, but his performance ceiling may already have been reached (32 touchdowns, 22 interceptions in his first two seasons). Sophomore Andrew Hendrix has a strong arm and adds mobility out of the backfield. Freshman Everett Golson appears to have the brightest upside and is the most dynamic athlete of the three.

Regardless of who gets the nod, he'll need to find a new No. 1 receiver after the departure of superstar Michael Floyd to the Arizona Cardinals. There's no one on the roster that can match Floyd's physical talents at the position, and tight end Tyler Eifert (803 yards, five touchdowns) might be the team's biggest and best downfield threat. Kelly's spread attack should be more dynamic this season (especially with Golson or Hendrix under center) since Notre Dame has an arsenal of backfield and slot receiver weapons to deploy. Running back Cierre Wood (1,102 yards, 9 touchdowns) and speedster George Atkinson (two kickoff return touchdowns) should figure more prominently into the running game.

The defense is solid, though the departure of defensive end Aaron Lynch leaves the front seven a bit thin on playmakers. Senior linebacker Manti Te'o (128 tackles) is a leading candidate for the Butkus Award. The secondary is a weak link with limited experience and depth. The Irish were generally good at keeping opponents off the scoreboard last season, but a lack of aggressiveness limited turnover opportunities and allowed opponents to milk the clock (96th in allowing methodical drives).

The schedule is brutal, with road games at Michigan State, Oklahoma, and USC, and virtually no breathers throughout the year. Even if Notre Dame fixes its turnover issues and plays like a legitimate top-15 team week in and week out, they'll still have trouble winning more than nine games.

2013 NFL Prospects: LB Manti Te'o (1-2), TE Tyler Eifert* (1-2), RB Cierre Wood* (3-4), WR Theo Riddick (6-7).

No. 39 BYU Cougars (8-4)

2011: 10-3 (—) / F/+ #37 / FEI #46 / S&P+ #34

Program F/+	-199.9	30	Returning Starters: 8 OFF, 7 DEF			2-Yr Recruiting Rank		68
2011 Offense			**2011 Defense**			**2011 Field Position**		
Offensive F/+	+1.2%	51	**Defensive F/+**	+3.8%	33	Field Position Advantage	0.515	35
Offensive FEI:	-0.014	61	Defensive FEI	-0.13	51	**2012 Projections**		
Offensive S&P+	90.0	54	Defensive S&P+	127.9	29	**Mean Wins**	8.5	
Rushing S&P+	105.2	53	Rushing S&P+	120.5	18	Proj. F/+	+7.0%	39
Passing S&P+	105.4	53	Passing S&P+	99.6	64	Offensive F/+	+1.7%	49
Standard Downs S&P+	103.2	56	Standard Downs S&P+	108.7	34	Defensive F/+	+5.3%	32
Passing Downs S&P+	112.1	42	Passing Downs S&P+	107.4	49	Strength of Schedule	0.430	67

The Cougars enter the season with solid experience on both sides of the ball and a schedule that will give them several opportunities to make the kind of big-win statement that eluded them a year ago. BYU won 10 games in 2011, but none of those wins came against F/+ top-30 teams. The lack of a signature win was aggravated by an embarrassing 44-point loss to rival Utah, another reminder that no matter how well BYU plows through the weakest parts of its schedule, there's still a ways to go get back into the national consciousness.

The offense stabilized a bit when quarterback Riley Nelson reclaimed the starting job midseason, but that stability didn't threaten many opposing defenses. When BYU did move the ball into scoring range, they had trouble finishing, ranking 90th in points per value drive. Wide receiver Cody Hoffman is the team's best playmaker (15.5 yards per reception, three touchdowns in a bowl game victory over Tulsa). Leading rusher J.J. Di Luigi has graduated, but junior running back Michael Alisa led the team in Adjusted POE (+2.8) and was the featured back over the second half of the year. The offensive line has holes to fill, but BYU has a strong track record of working new bodies into the mix.

The defensive leadership comes from the linebacker position, especially Kyle Van Noy on the weak side, who lit up Tulsa in the bowl game with five tackles for loss. He is one of only a few bright spots, however. The defense was solid in terms of raw performance (13th in forcing three-and-outs, 19th in surrendering available yards), but none of their 2011 games were remarkable in terms of opponent-adjusted performance. Cornerback Preston Hadley anchors the secondary, a unit that ranked 19th nationally in total passes defended.

As mentioned, there are opportunities to impress this year, including road games at Notre Dame, Boise State, Utah, and Georgia Tech. The Broncos won't be favored in those games and we give them a 32 percent chance of losing all four.

2013 NFL Prospects: G Braden Hansen (5-6).

Other Independents

Navy failed to qualify for a bowl last year, and though our projections like their chances to bounce back a bit this season, there are plenty of concerns to address. First and foremost, Navy has to find a way to win more defensive battles. The Midshipmen ranked near the bottom of our raw play and drive efficiency stats and played one of the weakest overall sets of opponent offenses in the country (107th in defensive strength of schedule). By design, they aim to contain, limit game possessions, and seize occasional big-play moments, but Navy couldn't manufacture those opportunities last year. The departure of standout defensive end Jabaree Tuani won't help matters this fall.

The Navy triple-option offense rarely lit up the scoreboard last year, but the Midshipmen did rank among the top 20 in terms of points per drive. New starting quarterback Trey Miller saw limited action last season. He's joined in the backfield by Gee Gee Green (501 yards, 7.8 yards/attempt, +7.1 adjusted POE). The rarely-used receiving corps (only 16 percent of Navy's plays are passes) remains largely intact. The Army Black Knights haven't beaten Navy since 2001, but their best shot may come at the end of this season with an experienced backfield that may be Army's best in years. Quarterback Trent Steelman and running backs Raymond Maples and Malcolm Brown combined to rush for more than 2,200 yards last season. Even if Army doesn't ramp up its scoring rates, the offense can help out the weak defense and special teams by controlling field position. Army played only one game last season with a field position advantage, and rode that advantage to a 45-6 victory over Tulane.

2013 NFL Prospects: None

Projected Win Probabilities For Independent Teams

Independents	12-0	11-1	10-2	9-3	8-4	7-5	6-6	5-7	4-8	3-9	2-10	1-11	0-12
Army	-	-	-	-	1	5	11	22	27	22	10	2	-
BYU	-	3	13	32	35	14	3	-	-	-	-	-	-
Navy	-	1	6	20	30	25	13	4	1	-	-	-	-
Notre Dame	-	3	15	26	28	18	8	2	-	-	-	-	-

MOUNTAIN WEST CONFERENCE

No. 26 Boise State Broncos (10-2, 8-0)
2011: 12-1 (6-1) / F/+ #4 / FEI #8 / S&P+ #3

Program F/+	-199.8	4	Returning Starters: 4 OFF, 3 DEF			2-Yr Recruiting Rank		83
2011 Offense			**2011 Defense**			**2011 Field Position**		
Offensive F/+	+13.2%	9	**Defensive F/+**	+10.4%	5	Field Position Advantage	0.611	1
Offensive FEI:	0.308	23	Defensive FEI	-0.357	21	**2012 Projections**		
Offensive S&P+	113.8	7	Defensive S&P+	159.2	3	**Mean Wins**	10.3	
Rushing S&P+	112.8	31	Rushing S&P+	146.2	5	Proj. F/+	+12.6%	26
Passing S&P+	137.8	7	Passing S&P+	142.9	5	Offensive F/+	+9.7%	17
Standard Downs S&P+	117.6	19	Standard Downs S&P+	124.8	11	Defensive F/+	+2.9%	48
Passing Downs S&P+	128.6	15	Passing Downs S&P+	128.2	18	Strength of Schedule	0.689	98

We don't have data to explain why the Boise State Broncos emerged as the most consistently successful program in college football over the last decade. They can't recruit like the big boys, and their resources aren't anywhere near as robust as the elite teams from the major conferences. But since we base our projections fundamentally in consistent program success, we can continue to expect Boise State to be a winner, no matter how much their roster turns over.

Boise State needs to replace 16 starters this offseason, including six NFL draft picks, but head coach Chris Petersen has already met such a challenge in his career. Four years ago, Boise State entered the 2008 season as one of the youngest and inexperienced teams in the country, and a freshman quarterback named Kellen Moore rattled off 12 straight victories to propel Boise State into a BCS bowl game. Now Moore is gone, and his replacement will likely be Joe Southwick, though true freshman Nick Patti is being billed as the future star of the program. Running back D.J. Harper was productive as the backup option out of the backfield (+10.2 adjusted POE, 557 yards, 9 touchdowns) and should slide into the starting role this year.

The secret to Boise State's success over the years has been their ability to be multidimensional. The Broncos ranked first in special teams efficiency last year, led by returning wide receiver and punt returner Mitch Burroughs (17.2 yards per return) and punt and kickoff units that helped generate the best field position advantage in football.

They also have been quietly dominant on the defensive end. Boise State forced three-and-outs on 51 percent of opponent drives last year, the third best rate nationally behind only Alabama and Georgia. They ranked in the top 10 in points surrendered per opponent possession in each of the last four years. Those marks will also be difficult to duplicate with new faces up front, but a step back may still position the Broncos with the best defense in the league. The secondary has the most experience, led by cornerbacks Jerrell Gavins and Jamar Taylor.

The schedule is the biggest reason Boise State hasn't ever broken through to a BCS title game, and the schedule will be the reason they post another gaudy record this fall. They've made a habit out of making an early splash with a first weekend road victory, and this year's target is Michigan State in East Lansing on August 31st. By our projections, Boise State has a 64 percent chance of running the table in the Mountain West, and while the non-conference schedule has a few pitfalls, they'll be favored in every game if they knock out the Spartans.

2013 NFL Prospects: RB D.J. Harper (4-5).

Other Mountain West

The Mountain West welcomes in several new faces from the WAC, familiar foes for Boise State who dominated that league for years. Fresno State, Hawaii, and Nevada should each be part of the Mountain West's middle-to-upper tier alongside Air Force and San Diego State. None of those teams has proven to have what it takes to derail the Broncos and each has experience issues to deal with as well, but there are players that can make things interesting.

Due to five-year program success, our numbers give the Air Force Falcons the second-best conference win likelihood, but they are rebuilding their entire offensive attack. The only player in the Falcons backfield with extensive experience is running back Mike Dewitt (12 touchdowns, +4.7 adjusted POE). Air Force does play the easiest conference schedule in the Mountain West, dodging Boise State in the regular season and hosting Nevada. Their unique up-tempo option may also pose a threat in a non-conference road trip to Michigan in the second week of the season.

Nevada is anchored by quarterback Cody Fajardo who, in addition to completing 69 percent of his pass attempts, ran the ball 12 times per game as well (6.6 yards per carry, +16.1 adjusted POE). Fresno State boasts the most experience among teams looking to dethrone the Broncos, led by quarterback Derek Carr (26 touchdowns, 9 interceptions) and running back Robbie Rouse (1544 yards rushing). They have a long way to go defensively, however, having surrendered at least 35 points in eight games last year.

2013 NFL Prospects: San Diego State CB Leon McFadden (5-6), Nevada OT Jeffrey Nady (5-6).

Projected Win Probabilities For Mountain West Teams

Mountain West	12-0	11-1	10-2	9-3	8-4	7-5	6-6	5-7	4-8	3-9	2-10	1-11	0-12	8-0	7-1	6-2	5-3	4-4	3-5	2-6	1-7	0-8
Air Force	-	2	9	20	27	23	13	5	1	-	-	-	-	4	18	31	28	14	4	1	-	-
Boise State	10	33	35	17	4	1	-	-	-	-	-	-	-	64	31	5	-	-	-	-	-	-
Colorado State	-	-	1	2	10	20	27	23	12	4	1	-	-	-	-	4	16	30	31	16	3	-
Fresno State	-	-	-	4	13	26	28	19	8	2	-	-	-	-	3	15	30	30	16	5	1	-
Hawaii	-	-	-	-	3	14	27	31	19	5	1	-	-	-	-	3	14	28	33	18	4	-
Nevada	-	1	9	22	31	24	10	3	-	-	-	-	-	2	18	34	30	13	3	-	-	-
New Mexico	-	-	-	-	-	-	2	10	23	33	24	8	-	-	-	-	-	1	6	23	41	29
San Diego State	-	-	2	9	21	28	23	12	4	1	-	-	-	-	2	11	26	32	21	7	1	-
UNLV	-	-	-	-	-	1	3	10	23	32	23	8	-	-	-	-	-	3	16	35	36	10
Wyoming	-	-	-	-	3	11	21	28	23	11	3	-	-	-	-	2	10	25	33	22	7	1

*New Mexico and UNLV will play 13 regular season games; for projected overall records, 12-0 means 12-1, 11-1 means 11-2, etc.

CONFERENCE USA

The Houston Cougars ran out to a 12-0 regular season start behind senior quarterback Case Keenum last season, and nearly qualified for a BCS bowl. They were Conference USA's best shot at generating the kind of mid-major buzz that propelled non-AQ contenders into the limelight in past years, but the Cougars flopped in their big moment, losing the conference championship game to Southern Mississippi on their own field by three touchdowns.

That kind of big-moment disappointment has characterized many of Conference USA's best teams over the last few seasons. The league is certainly competitive—we project four teams to win six or seven games this fall—but we don't have much confidence in their ability to make a significant impression outside of league play.

The Cougars have the edge in our projections due to the program data boosted by Keenum's stellar career, but they'll need to replace both his high production and head coach Kevin Sumlin. New starter David Piland played significantly in 2010 after Keenum went down with an injury, and though the offense that year was serviceable (30th in F/+), it wasn't enough to cover up for defensive deficiencies and Houston failed to qualify for a bowl. The defense this year returns seven starters, including almost every significant contributor along the line and in the secondary. To win the West division again, they'll need to get opponents off the field more quickly (94th in allowing methodical drives).

Southern Mississippi also lost its head coach and starting quarterback this offseason, but the nucleus of the team, an experienced offensive line led by guard Joe Duhon and right tackle Jason Weaver, does return. Southern Miss was also particularly good last year at distributing the ball to a number of weapons in the receiving corps and in the backfield. Sophomore running back Jamal Woodyard (6.7 yards per attempt) is a potential breakout star.

Tulsa and Central Florida field the only other teams that should threaten to win the conference crown. The Golden Hurricane played and struggled through the nation's toughest non-conference schedule last year before ripping off seven straight victories in October and November. They have to replace … you guessed it … their starting quarterback. The early season non-conference tests aren't a cakewalk (at Iowa State, Fresno State, at Arkansas), but Tulsa should get off to another hot start in league play.

Central Florida is garnering some attention as a national contender, but those hopes should be derailed in non-conference games against Ohio State and Missouri, the toughest non-conference schedule faced by Conference USA's contenders. They do have an experienced offense led by quarterback Jeff Godfrey and a trio of players (Godfrey, and running backs Brynn Harvey and Latavius Murray) who each ran for more than 500 yards and combined for 20 touchdowns on the ground. They were terribly weak at finishing drives, however (113th in points per value drive).

SMU welcomes ex-Texas quarterback Garret Gilbert to lead an offense that hasn't yet clicked under head coach June Jones. Running back Zach Line (+25.2 adjusted POE) is an underappreciated workhorse, but he'll be playing behind an entirely new offensive line.

2013 NFL Prospects: SMU DE Margus Hunt (1-2), Tulsa S Dexter McCoil (6-7), SMU FB Zach Line (6-7).

Projected Win Probabilities For Conference USA Teams

Conf USA East	12-0	11-1	10-2	9-3	8-4	7-5	6-6	5-7	4-8	3-9	2-10	1-11	0-12	8-0	7-1	6-2	5-3	4-4	3-5	2-6	1-7	0-8
Central Florida	1	5	20	31	26	13	3	1	-	-	-	-	-	12	34	33	16	4	1	-	-	-
East Carolina	-	-	-	2	11	24	30	22	9	2	-	-	-	-	3	15	32	31	15	4	-	-
Marshall	-	-	1	4	11	22	28	22	10	2	-	-	-	-	-	3	13	28	32	19	5	-
Memphis	-	-	-	-	-	1	6	17	29	28	15	4	-	-	-	-	1	6	20	36	29	8
Southern Miss.	-	4	17	28	28	16	6	1	-	-	-	-	-	13	40	33	12	2	-	-	-	-
UAB	-	-	-	-	-	-	2	10	25	33	23	7	-	-	-	-	1	6	19	36	30	8
Conf USA West	12-0	11-1	10-2	9-3	8-4	7-5	6-6	5-7	4-8	3-9	2-10	1-11	0-12	8-0	7-1	6-2	5-3	4-4	3-5	2-6	1-7	0-8
Houston	10	28	32	20	8	2	-	-	-	-	-	-	-	25	41	25	8	1	-	-	-	-
Rice	-	-	-	-	-	1	4	12	24	29	21	8	1	-	-	-	2	7	22	33	27	9
SMU	-	-	1	6	17	28	27	15	5	1	-	-	-	-	3	12	28	32	19	5	1	-
Tulane	-	-	-	-	-	1	5	13	24	28	20	8	1	-	-	-	4	15	29	32	17	3
Tulsa	-	4	17	29	28	16	5	1	-	-	-	-	-	5	22	36	26	9	2	-	-	-
UTEP	-	-	-	-	-	-	2	12	27	35	19	4	1	-	-	-	2	9	29	38	19	3

SUN BELT CONFERENCE

After having been a one-horse league for years, the Sun Belt finally featured breakthrough wins from a handful of conference contenders, making for an exciting title race that was ultimately claimed by Arkansas State. This year, we project a three-team race between the Red Wolves, Troy Trojans, and Florida International Golden Panthers.

The Red Wolves have an experienced and productive quarterback in Ryan Aplin, who ranks among the nation's leading returning passers in yards per game (276). He'll be playing behind a relatively inexperienced line, however, and he'll be looking for a new No. 1 receiving target. The defense has been decimated by graduation as well. They took a big leap in production last season (from 80th in points per opponent drive to 19th) and a significant step back may be in store this year.

Florida International is our best bet to win the conference this year due to a loaded defense that returns all but one of its top 15 tacklers from last season. Linebackers Winston Fraser and Jordan Hunt and defensive end Tourek Williams (13 tackles for loss) are the senior leadership of a unit that allowed few big plays (15th in opponent explosive drives) and ranked No. 1 in points surrendered per methodical drive (2.1). The offense won't need to put up many points themselves with that kind of production. That's good, because running back Kedrick Rhodes (1,159 yards, eight touchdowns) is one of the few weapons with experience on that side of the ball.

Troy is one of the most experienced offenses in the country in terms of skill position players—every significant contributor in the backfield and in the receiving corps is back this fall. But quarterback Corey Robinson (21 touchdowns, 15 interceptions) has a long ways to go and the offensive line is replacing four starters. Troy is awfully thin on defensive line experience as well, a bad combination for a team looking to bounce back to the top of the league.

2013 NFL Prospects: Arkansas State RB Michael Dyer* (3-4), Western Kentucky TE Jack Doyle (6-7).

Projected Win Probabilities For Sun Belt Conference Teams

Sun Belt	12-0	11-1	10-2	9-3	8-4	7-5	6-6	5-7	4-8	3-9	2-10	1-11	0-12	8-0	7-1	6-2	5-3	4-4	3-5	2-6	1-7	0-8
Arkansas State	-	-	4	15	29	28	17	6	1	-	-	-	-	3	17	31	29	15	4	1	-	-
Florida Atlantic	-	-	-	-	-	2	7	18	28	27	14	4	-	-	-	1	7	18	30	28	13	3
Florida Int'l	-	2	11	22	28	22	11	3	1	-	-	-	-	12	31	32	18	6	1	-	-	-
La. Lafayette	-	-	-	1	7	17	26	26	16	6	1	-	-	-	-	2	9	20	29	25	12	3	-
Louisiana Monroe	-	-	-	1	5	14	26	28	18	7	1	-	-	-	4	18	31	29	14	4	-	-
Middle Tennessee	-	-	-	-	1	6	17	27	27	16	5	1	-	-	-	3	12	26	31	20	7	1
North Texas	-	-	-	-	1	5	15	26	28	18	6	1	-	-	1	4	15	27	29	18	5	1
South Alabama	-	-	-	-	-	-	1	7	17	31	30	11	3	-	-	-	-	1	9	25	40	25
Troy	-	-	1	5	13	23	25	19	10	3	1	-	-	2	10	24	29	22	10	3	-	-
Western Kentucky	-	-	-	1	7	17	27	26	15	6	1	-	-	-	3	13	27	31	19	6	1	-

*South Alabama will play 13 regular season games; for projected overall records, 12-0 means 12-1, 11-1 means 11-2, etc.

MID-AMERICAN CONFERENCE

There aren't national championships to contend for in conferences at the bottom of the FBS heap, but there are hashtags. #MACtion was a thrilling brand of college football in 2011, featuring weekday games throughout the season that lit up the scoreboard (and Twitter) with wild offensive outbursts. We expect another fun race for the conference crown once again with five teams projected to win between 5.3 and 6.1 league games.

The defending champion Northern Illinois Huskies need to replace one of the most productive and efficient quarterbacks in the nation, Chandler Harnish, along with 2,200 yards of running game production, and four starters along the offensive line. Yikes. Their biggest threat in the West division, Toledo, also has heavy personnel losses to deal with and their coach was snagged by Illinois. Western Michigan quarterback Alex Carder should be one of the top passers in the league and Western Michigan ranked seventh nationally in avoiding three-and-outs. But the defense has a long way to go for the Broncos to be a legitimate conference threat (48 percent of opponent drives crossed Western Michigan's 30-yard line).

Things change annually in the MAC, and it looks like the East division may have the edge this year due primarily to strong defenses. The Ohio Bobcats are the defending East division champs and return one of the most experienced defenses in the MAC. Junior quarterback Tyler Tettleton was very efficient (8.0 yards per attempt) in his first season as a starter and was also the team's second-leading rusher. Bowling Green brings back 10 defensive starters, and may be able to squeeze a bit more offense out of the running game with four offensive linemen and the top four rushers back in the fold as well. The Falcons were consistent offensively, but not consistently good (No. 2 in FEI offensive variance, No. 87 in offensive FEI).

2013 NFL Prospects: Western Michigan QB Alex Carder (6-7), Central Michigan S Jahleel Addae (6-7).

Projected Win Probabilities For Mid-American Conference Teams

MAC East	12-0	11-1	10-2	9-3	8-4	7-5	6-6	5-7	4-8	3-9	2-10	1-11	0-12	8-0	7-1	6-2	5-3	4-4	3-5	2-6	1-7	0-8
Akron	-	-	-	-	-	-	-	2	10	27	39	20	2	-	-	-	-	2	9	28	43	18
Bowling Green	-	-	2	14	29	30	18	6	1	-	-	-	-	2	13	31	31	17	5	1	-	-
Buffalo	-	-	-	-	-	1	5	15	27	29	18	4	1	-	-	1	3	14	28	32	18	4
Kent State	-	-	-	1	4	12	22	27	21	10	3	-	-	-	1	6	17	28	28	16	4	-
Massachusetts	-	-	-	-	-	-	-	1	5	18	32	31	13	-	-	-	-	3	14	30	36	17
Miami (OH)	-	-	-	2	11	23	30	22	10	2	-	-	-	1	9	23	31	24	10	2	-	-
Ohio	1	7	20	29	25	13	4	1	-	-	-	-	-	10	29	33	20	7	1	-	-	-

MAC West	12-0	11-1	10-2	9-3	8-4	7-5	6-6	5-7	4-8	3-9	2-10	1-11	0-12	8-0	7-1	6-2	5-3	4-4	3-5	2-6	1-7	0-8
Ball State	-	-	-	-	1	3	8	17	25	25	15	5	1	-	-	2	9	20	29	26	12	2
Central Michigan	-	-	1	3	13	24	28	20	9	2	-	-	-	1	6	18	31	27	13	4	-	-
Eastern Michigan	-	-	-	-	1	3	11	22	28	23	10	2	-	-	-	1	5	12	26	31	20	5
Northern Illinois	1	7	19	28	25	14	5	1	-	-	-	-	-	7	25	34	23	9	2	-	-	-
Toledo	-	2	9	20	27	23	13	5	1	-	-	-	-	3	15	31	30	15	5	1	-	-
Western Michigan	-	3	10	20	26	22	13	5	1	-	-	-	-	5	20	31	26	13	4	1	-	-

WESTERN ATHLETIC CONFERENCE

This will be the final year of existence for the once proud WAC, and there's little chance the league will go out with anything more than a whimper. Only seven teams are in the conference this year after an exodus of teams to the Mountain West. Two of the seven are FBS newcomers Texas State and UT-San Antonio, and none of the other five programs has had much national acclaim. Someone has to win the final WAC football championship, of course, and perhaps it is befitting that the Western Athletic Conference will likely be dominated by the team furthest east—Louisiana Tech.

Senior quarterback Colby Cameron played the final seven games of the season last year, coinciding with the Bulldogs' surge down the stretch to claim the WAC crown. In addition to 1,667 yards through the air and 13 touchdowns, he protected the football (three interceptions) and chipped in 200 yards on the ground. Top receiver Quinton Patton (1,177 yards, 8.5 yards per target) is back. Running back Hunter Lee was the second-best weapon behind Cameron in terms of yards per attempt (4.8), and the offensive line is sturdy. Louisiana Tech's defense has a few holes to fill in the front seven, but the secondary is solid. The Bulldogs were especially good at generating field position advantages—punter Ray Allen ranked fifth nationally in yards per punt and Louisiana Tech ranked No. 2 in punt efficiency.

Utah State is the only other WAC team that might threaten the Bulldogs, having come within a whisker of notching a few marquee victories last season behind a dynamic rushing attack. But the Aggies are rebuilding their offensive line and have to replace their top two running backs. They were terrible on special teams last season as well, a contributing factor in their five losses that came by a touchdown or less.

2013 NFL Prospects: Louisiana Tech WR Quinton Patton (6-7).

Projected Win Probabilities For Western Athletic Conference Teams

WAC	12-0	11-1	10-2	9-3	8-4	7-5	6-6	5-7	4-8	3-9	2-10	1-11	0-12	6-0	5-1	4-2	3-3	2-4	1-5	0-6	0-7
Idaho	-	-	-	-	-	2	10	25	32	22	8	1	-	-	3	19	38	29	10	1	-
Louisiana Tech	-	2	11	30	36	17	4	-	-	-	-	-	-	64	31	5	-	-	-	-	-
New Mexico State	-	-	-	-	-	1	6	17	30	28	14	3	1	-	-	6	22	38	27	7	3
San Jose State	-	-	-	-	2	7	20	29	25	13	4	-	-	1	7	27	36	22	6	1	-
Texas State	-	-	-	-	-	-	-	3	14	30	34	17	2	-	-	1	10	30	40	19	-
Utah State	-	-	1	8	25	34	22	8	2	-	-	-	-	8	41	37	12	2	-	-	38
UTSA	-	-	-	2	9	20	29	24	12	3	1	-	-	-	-	5	20	37	31	7	1

Top 2013 NFL Prospects, FCS Level

Elon WR Aaron Mellette (2-3), Southern Utah QB Brad Sorensen (3-4), Glenville State OT Mark Jackson (3-4), McNeese State S Malcolm Bronson (5-6), Jacksonville State RB Washaun Ealey (5-6), William & Mary CB B.W. Webb (6-7).

Brian Fremeau

NCAA Teams, No. 1 to No. 124

Rk	Team	Conf	Proj F/+	MW	Rec	Conf	SOS	Rk
1	Alabama	SEC	0.353	11.1	11-1	7-1	0.094	9
2	LSU	SEC	0.305	10.5	10-2	7-1	0.099	12
3	Oklahoma	Big 12	0.274	10.4	10-2	8-1	0.198	29
4	Oregon	Pac 12	0.250	10.9	11-1	8-1	0.396	62
5	Oklahoma St.	Big 12	0.223	9.9	10-2	7-2	0.181	25
6	USC	Pac 12	0.222	10.1	10-2	7-2	0.307	45
7	Florida State	ACC	0.221	10.3	10-2	7-1	0.370	56
8	Georgia	SEC	0.217	9.9	10-2	6-2	0.293	43
9	Texas	Big 12	0.198	9.2	9-3	6-3	0.166	24
10	Florida	SEC	0.194	8.4	8-4	5-3	0.112	17
11	Stanford	Pac 12	0.193	9.5	9-3	7-2	0.222	32
12	TCU	Big 12	0.187	8.7	9-3	6-3	0.157	21
13	Ohio State	Big Ten	0.181	9.5	10-2	6-2	0.354	53
14	Notre Dame	Ind.	0.175	8.2	8-4	-	0.097	10
15	Arkansas	SEC	0.167	7.9	8-4	4-4	0.090	7
16	Michigan	Big Ten	0.167	8.3	8-4	6-2	0.098	11
17	South Carolina	SEC	0.167	8.1	8-4	5-3	0.084	6
18	Virginia Tech	ACC	0.166	8.8	9-3	5-3	0.330	50
19	Wisconsin	Big Ten	0.153	9.6	10-2	6-2	0.482	73
20	West Virginia	Big 12	0.150	8.2	8-4	5-4	0.164	22
21	Clemson	ACC	0.139	8.7	9-3	6-2	0.295	44
22	Auburn	SEC	0.135	7.3	7-5	4-4	0.053	3
23	Nebraska	Big Ten	0.135	8.2	8-4	5-3	0.315	47
24	Michigan State	Big Ten	0.134	8.3	8-4	5-3	0.288	42
25	Texas A&M	SEC	0.134	7.3	7-5	4-4	0.057	4
26	Boise State	MWC	0.125	10.3	10-2	8-0	0.689	98
27	Tennessee	SEC	0.120	7.3	7-5	4-4	0.109	15
28	Missouri	SEC	0.112	6.4	6-6	3-5	0.091	8
29	South Florida	Big East	0.110	8.5	9-3	5-2	0.503	76
30	Georgia Tech	ACC	0.105	7.7	8-4	5-3	0.249	34
31	Texas Tech	Big 12	0.102	7.4	7-5	4-5	0.166	23
32	Penn State	Big Ten	0.102	8.0	8-4	5-3	0.458	69
33	North Carolina	ACC	0.101	8.8	9-3	5-3	0.591	84
34	Iowa	Big Ten	0.092	8.6	9-3	5-3	0.471	71
35	Utah	Pac 12	0.092	8.8	9-3	6-3	0.609	89
36	Miami	ACC	0.083	6.2	6-6	4-4	0.279	38
37	Rutgers	Big East	0.079	8.3	8-4	4-3	0.479	72
38	Pittsburgh	Big East	0.077	7.7	8-4	4-3	0.413	65
39	BYU	Ind.	0.069	8.5	8-4	-	0.430	67
40	California	Pac 12	0.069	6.5	7-5	5-4	0.195	28
41	Louisville	Big East	0.064	7.6	8-4	4-3	0.595	85
42	Houston	C-USA	0.061	10.1	10-2	7-1	0.902	122
43	Cincinnati	Big East	0.060	7.9	8-4	4-3	0.607	88
44	Mississippi St.	SEC	0.059	6.5	7-5	3-5	0.039	2
45	Boston College	ACC	0.057	6.4	6-6	4-4	0.284	40
46	Baylor	Big 12	0.050	5.9	6-6	3-6	0.103	14
47	Kansas State	Big 12	0.048	5.5	6-6	3-6	0.103	13
48	Central Florida	C-USA	0.047	8.7	9-3	6-2	0.570	83
49	Southern Miss.	C-USA	0.045	8.4	8-4	6-2	0.623	91
50	Vanderbilt	SEC	0.040	5.8	6-6	3-5	0.273	36
51	Illinois	Big Ten	0.034	6.9	7-5	4-4	0.346	52
52	Virginia	ACC	0.027	5.9	6-6	4-4	0.326	49
53	N.C. State	ACC	0.023	6.0	6-6	3-5	0.389	61
54	Tulsa	C-USA	0.023	8.4	8-4	6-2	0.628	92
55	Washington	Pac 12	0.020	5.5	6-6	4-5	0.077	5
56	UCLA	Pac 12	0.012	5.7	6-6	4-5	0.430	66
57	Connecticut	Big East	0.007	6.4	6-6	3-4	0.601	86
58	Arizona State	Pac 12	0.004	5.4	5-7	4-5	0.278	37
59	Mississippi	SEC	0.002	4.4	4-8	2-6	0.017	1
60	Oregon State	Pac 12	0.001	4.8	5-7	3-6	0.309	46
61	Louisiana Tech	WAC	-0.007	8.3	8-4	6-0	0.657	97
62	Arizona	Pac 12	-0.012	4.9	5-7	3-6	0.156	20
63	Nevada	MWC	-0.027	7.9	8-4	6-2	0.723	101
64	Kentucky	SEC	-0.028	4.1	4-8	1-7	0.194	27
65	Navy	Ind.	-0.029	7.7	8-4	-	0.644	95
66	N. Illinois	MAC	-0.031	8.6	9-3	6-2	0.861	119
67	Toledo	MAC	-0.033	7.8	8-4	5-3	0.907	123
68	Northwestern	Big Ten	-0.033	4.5	5-7	2-6	0.376	59
69	Purdue	Big Ten	-0.034	4.8	5-7	2-6	0.282	39
70	W. Michigan	MAC	-0.037	7.8	8-4	6-2	0.898	121
71	Ohio	MAC	-0.039	8.7	9-3	6-2	0.824	114
72	Maryland	ACC	-0.040	3.9	4-8	2-6	0.324	48
73	Duke	ACC	-0.042	4.2	4-8	2-6	0.183	26
74	Florida Int'l	Sun Belt	-0.046	7.9	8-4	6-2	0.850	117
75	SMU	C-USA	-0.048	5.6	6-6	4-4	0.568	82
76	Air Force	MWC	-0.055	7.7	8-4	6-2	0.700	100
77	Temple	Big East	-0.058	4.1	4-7	2-5	0.567	81
78	East Carolina	C-USA	-0.062	6.1	6-6	4-4	0.523	78

NON-AQS AND INDEPENDENTS

Rk	Team	Conf	Proj F/+	MW	Rec	Conf	SOS	Rk	Rk	Team	Conf	Proj F/+	MW	Rec	Conf	SOS	Rk
79	Syracuse	Big East	-0.065	3.5	3-9	2-5	0.354	54	102	Colorado State	MWC	-0.142	5.9	6-6	4-4	0.785	110
80	Arkansas State	Sun Belt	-0.066	7.4	7-5	5-3	0.375	58	103	UTEP	C-USA	-0.144	3.3	3-9	2-6	0.397	63
81	Wake Forest	ACC	-0.068	3.8	4-8	2-6	0.287	41	104	Army	Ind.	-0.147	4.1	4-8	-	0.822	113
82	Bowling Green	MAC	-0.069	7.3	7-5	5-3	0.470	70	105	E. Michigan	MAC	-0.148	4.1	4-8	2-6	0.768	108
83	Iowa State	Big 12	-0.069	2.7	3-9	1-8	0.110	16	106	Wyoming	MWC	-0.150	5.0	5-7	3-5	0.563	80
84	Minnesota	Big Ten	-0.077	4.3	4-8	1-7	0.386	60	107	Buffalo	MAC	-0.163	3.5	3-9	2-6	0.527	79
85	Fresno State	MWC	-0.084	6.3	6-6	4-4	0.371	57	108	Rice	C-USA	-0.171	3.3	3-9	2-6	0.826	115
86	Central Mich.	MAC	-0.085	6.2	6-6	5-3	0.750	103	109	North Texas	Sun Belt	-0.175	4.4	4-8	3-5	0.256	35
87	San Diego St.	MWC	-0.085	6.9	7-5	4-4	0.762	105	110	UAB	C-USA	-0.182	3.2	3-9	2-6	0.403	64
88	Marshall	C-USA	-0.085	5.1	5-7	3-5	0.634	94	111	Tulane	C-USA	-0.186	3.3	3-9	2-6	0.794	111
89	Miami (OH)	MAC	-0.088	6.0	6-6	5-3	0.515	77	112	Mid. Tenn. St.	Sun Belt	-0.189	4.6	5-7	3-5	0.763	106
90	Utah State	WAC	-0.099	7.0	7-5	4-2	0.620	90	113	San Jose St.	WAC	-0.190	4.8	5-7	3-3	0.603	87
91	Kansas	Big 12	-0.100	2.8	3-9	1-8	0.117	18	114	Memphis	C-USA	-0.202	3.6	4-8	2-6	0.886	120
92	Indiana	Big Ten	-0.102	3.5	3-9	1-7	0.484	74	115	Florida Atlantic	Sun Belt	-0.207	3.7	4-8	3-5	0.125	19
93	Troy	Sun Belt	-0.111	6.2	6-6	5-3	0.758	104	116	Idaho	WAC	-0.232	4.1	4-8	3-3	0.232	33
94	W. Kentucky	Sun Belt	-0.116	5.6	6-6	4-4	0.201	31	117	Massachusetts	MAC	-0.235	1.8	2-10	1-7	0.651	96
95	Hawaii	MWC	-0.117	5.3	5-7	3-5	0.458	68	118	UNLV	MWC	-0.241	3.1	3-10	2-6	0.773	109
96	La. Monroe	Sun Belt	-0.121	5.3	5-7	5-3	0.631	93	119	Akron	MAC	-0.249	2.3	2-10	1-7	0.768	107
97	Ball State	MAC	-0.122	3.7	4-8	3-5	0.695	99	120	New Mexico	MWC	-0.263	3.1	3-10	1-7	0.487	75
98	Colorado	Pac 12	-0.126	3.0	3-9	1-8	0.200	30	121	New Mexico St.	WAC	-0.268	3.6	4-8	2-4	0.729	102
99	Kent State	MAC	-0.128	5.2	5-7	4-4	0.856	118	122	UTSA	WAC	-0.273	5.9	6-6	2-4	0.951	124
100	Washington St.	Pac 12	-0.135	3.1	3-9	1-8	0.335	51	123	South Alabama	Sun Belt	-0.293	2.7	3-10	1-7	0.848	116
101	La. Lafayette	Sun Belt	-0.139	5.5	6-6	4-4	0.368	55	124	Texas State	WAC	-0.309	2.5	2-10	1-5	0.812	112

Turning the Tide: Big Plays and Psychological Momentum in the NFL

Matthews changed momentum with textbook hit
—Headline in a *Sporting News* story discussing Rashard Mendenhall's fumble on the opening play of the fourth quarter in Green Bay's Super Bowl XLV victory over Pittsburgh

"Yeah, I think it changed the momentum completely of the game."
—Texans linebacker Brian Cushing, discussing J.J. Watt's pick-six right before halftime of Houston's 31-10 playoff win over Cincinnati

"Whenever you get a turnover on downs, especially the situation being they're a power team [...] We stoned it in the backfield and our offense came on the field. It's a huge momentum builder and I think we rallied off of it."
—Saints linebacker Jonathan Casillas on the Saints' fourth-and-1 stop of LaGarrette Blount in the fourth quarter of Week 9's 27-16 New Orleans victory over Tampa Bay

The belief in "psychological momentum"—the idea that a big play can motivate teams to perform better during subsequent plays—is ubiquitous in the NFL. In post-game analyses, NFL coaches, players, fans, and the media all point to interceptions, fumbles, fourth-down stops, and other big defensive plays that turned the tide of the game. But does psychological momentum truly exist, or is it simply a cognitive illusion? And, if it does exist, can it be transferred from a team's defense to its offense, which had nothing to do with the turnover? Furthermore, do coaches on the sidelines show a belief in psychological momentum, calling aggressive plays immediately after they gain possession through a turnover?

In 1994, in the *Journal of Applied Sport Psychology*, authors Jim Taylor and Andrew Demick constructed a multidimensional model of momentum in sports—the "Momentum Chain"—that posits the factors influencing whether an athlete's perception of momentum translates into a change in his performance. These are organized into six steps that they theorize all must occur in sequence for momentum to have a noticeable effect.

1) A precipitating event or events
2) Change in cognition, affect, and physiology
3) Change in behavior
4) Change in performance consistent with the above changes
5) A continuous and opposing change in the previous factors on the part of the opponent (for sports with head-to-head competition)
6) A resultant change in the immediate outcome

These factors are highly individualized—their impact on a player's performance depends on his experience, self-efficacy ("a situation-specific form of self-confidence"), perceptions of control, and attitude.

Researchers have quantitatively investigated psychological momentum in many sports, but there is still conflicting evidence as to whether precipitating events translate into observable changes in performance. In an analysis of Wimbledon tennis matches between 1992 and 1995, professors Franc Klaassen and Jan Magnus did find that there were small positive and negative effects of momentum. Another study by Terry Appleby in 2012 found evidence for psychological momentum in hockey. According to his analysis, a fight increases the momentum (as defined by the number of shots on goal per second) of at least one of the teams involved 76 percent of the time.

Other researchers have found no effect of psychological momentum. The seminal study of "the hot hand" in basketball was appeared in *Cognitive Psychology* in 1985. It found that while players and fans believed "a player's chances of hitting a shot are greater following a hit than following a miss on the previous shot," neither a statistical analysis of two NBA teams' shooting records nor a controlled experiment with collegiate basketball players lent support to this idea. S. Christian Albright performed a similar study for hot and cold hitting streaks in baseball, finding that the behavior of all MLB players as a whole did not differ significantly from a model of randomness. Therefore, he also discounted the average effect of psychological momentum.

Research into psychological momentum in the NFL has also shown evidence for and against momentum. Berkeley professor David Romer, in his famous 2006 paper on fourth-down decisions, looked at both "bad" and "good" plays and their effect on the three subsequent plays. Bad plays were defined as changes in possession where the ball advanced less than ten yards, and good plays were touchdowns. Romer found that there was no significant momentum effect; rather, there was a slight effect of "counter-momentum." As Romer stated, "From the situation immediate following a bad play to the next, the team that lost possession does somewhat better than average." On the Advanced NFL Stats Community website, Andy Steiner investigated this transfer of psychological momentum, investigating how much more likely an intercepting team was to score afterwards. His analysis of the 2002-09 NFL seasons suggests that there was no positive effect of momentum, but he did not test for statistical significance either.

For our analysis, we used a data set comprising all 2,921 games during the 2000-10 NFL seasons, including the postseason. We are interested in two different categories of drives: those that followed a big defensive play ("BD drives"), and those that did not ("NBD drives", or "Normal drives"). We identified six types of big defensive plays:

1) Interception
2) Fumble recovered by the defense
3) Fourth-down stop (turnover on downs)
4) Safety
5) Blocked field goal or punt
6) Muffed punt recovered by the kicking team

If a turnover resulted in a defensive touchdown, we removed this play from our analyses. We are interested in the transfer of momentum between a given team's defense and offense on the drive following a big defensive play. When a defensive touchdown is scored, the offense that gave up the turnover regains possession.

There are a number of confounding variables that anecdotally change a team's overall strategy and may affect an offense's success. These factors include:

1) The score differential
2) The time left in the game
3) The starting line of scrimmage on the drive

To remove the effects of the first two confounding variables, we only considered first-, second-, and third-quarter drives (except for those in the last two minutes of the first half) with a score differential of less than 10 points. During this phase of the game, we assume the coaches' general strategy to be constant. The third factor listed above, however, is a larger problem. Obviously, play-calling and potential outcomes change depending on the line of scrimmage that starts a drive. Some outcomes that are of interest (say, a gain of 50-plus yards) are only possible at certain yard lines. Since the distributions of the starting line of scrimmage are not equal between BD and NBD drives, we must modify the dataset to create a fair comparison.

To ensure a symmetrical comparison of BD and NBD drives with respect to the starting line of scrimmage, both the BD and NBD data subsets were divided into 10 groups of evenly spaced 10-yard increments (e.g. 0-10, 11-20, etc.). For the statistical analysis of psychological momentum, equal numbers of samples were randomly drawn from each group, ensuring that we analyzed the same number of BD and NBD drives from each 10-yard portion of the field. The resultant final data set for the offensive performance analysis comprised 8,032 total changes of possession, split evenly between BD and NBD drives. The final data set for the offensive play-calling analysis comprised 5,692 changes of possession, once again split evenly between BD and NBD drives. (This number is less than for the analysis of offensive performance, due to missing play-calling data on some drives.) Since we are randomly sampling from a population of plays, it is possible that a particular sample could be unusual and not well representative of the overall trends. To prevent this from impacting the findings, we used a methodology called "bootstrapping," performing the random sampling 1,000 times and then averaging the counts, in order to gain a better representation of the population.

To account for effects of psychological momentum over a number of time horizons, we selected three dependent variables (DV) for our analyses of offensive performance. Increasing in time, these are:

1) The result of the first play after a change of possession
2) The result of the first set of downs after a change of possession
3) The result of the entire drive after a change of possession

Statistical analyses on the effect of a big defensive play on the DVs were performed using contingency tables. These DVs are designed to be unaffected by psychological momentum within an offense, a debatable but separate issue. Within the first two DVs, the offense has run at most four plays, a short time for offensive momentum to build up. Furthermore, if there are any "big plays" greater than 10 yards in the first set of downs, any potential momentum from these will not affect the first two DVs. The third DV is not influenced by offensive momentum because it does not care how a team scored—if they ground it out with short plays or successfully gambled on long plays—but rather whether or not they eventually scored. A long kick or punt return may have an effect on the offense's performance, but special teams' effect on momentum is left for future studies.

The analysis of offensive play-calling had one dependent variable: the type of play called on the first play after a change in possession. As with the analysis of offensive performance, we constructed a contingency table to compare coaches' play-calling on plays that were immediately preceded by a big defensive play and those that were not.

For the analysis of a DV, the counts of each outcome in the final data set were tallied. The resultant contingency tables were analyzed for a significant association between the presence of a preceding big defensive play and the outcomes of interest using a statistical test called Pearson's Chi Square Test of Independence, with a level of significance of $\alpha = 0.05$. This test compares two distributions of counts in a contingency table, and determines if there is enough evidence to say that these are significantly different. In our analyses, Pearson's Chi Square test will tell us if the distribution of outcomes for each particular DV are different for BD and NBD drives. If the distributions are different, then we can conclude that psychological momentum is having an effect on performance or play-calling.

Table 1 shows the average counts (± standard error) of each of the outcomes considered for the result of the first play of a new drive. The first play of BD drives shows higher counts of touchdowns and gains of 50-plus yards. Additionally, plays succeeding a big defensive play show a decrease in turnovers as compared to NBD drives. But are these differences large enough for us to confidently say they truly exist, or are they simply caused by random variations? Using Pearson's Chi Square test, we found the differences between BD and NBD drives to be insignificant (p = 0.295 ± 0.007). We do not find strong enough evidence to say that an offense is performing differently on the first play after a big defensive play.

Table 1. First Play of Drive Based on BD/NBD Samples

Outcome	Big Defensive Play	Normal Play
Gain of 0-3 yards	1608.84 ± 0.46	1614.27 ± 0.87
Gain of 4-6 yards	736.43 ± 0.35	687.84 ± 0.66
Gain of 7-9 yards	416.48 ± 0.29	415.61 ± 0.56
Gain of 10-30 yards	550.45 ± 0.28	601.46 ± 0.64
Gain of 30-50 yards	51.75 ± 0.05	49.34 ± 0.22
Gain of 50+ yards	15.00 ± 0.00	10.80 ± 0.10
Touchdown	71.35 ± 0.23	56.65 ± 0.13
Loss of yards	277.91 ± 0.26	282.01 ± 0.44
Turnover	58.00 ± 0.14	68.36 ± 0.22
Safety	2.00 ± 0.00	1.15 ± 0.04

Numbers shown are the mean counts +/- standard error.

Similarly, Table 2 shows the contingency table for the result of the first set of downs after a change of possession. Having a successful set of downs, judged by either achieving a first down or scoring, was slightly more likely after a big defensive play. However, this was not significant as determined by Pearson's Chi Square test (p = 0.477 ± 0.008).

Table 2. Success on First Set of Downs Based on BD/NBD Samples

Outcome	Big Defensive Play	Normal Play
Successful	2873.65 ± 0.36	2841.55 ± 0.82
Unsuccessful	1131.51 ± 0.35	1157.79 ± 0.82

Numbers shown are the mean counts ± standard error.

Table 3 shows the contingency table associated with the outcome of the drive, quantified as the points scored on that drive. BD drives show slightly higher proportions of defensive safeties, field goals, and touchdowns; and a lower proportion of defensive touchdowns. However, once again this potential association is not significant by Pearson's Chi Square test ($p = 0.564 \pm 0.008$).

Table 3. Result of Drive Based on BD/NBD Samples

Outcome	Big Defensive Play	Normal Play
Defensive Touchdown	34.73 ± 0.06	39.74 ± 0.18
Defensive Safety	9.00 ± 0.00	7.16 ± 0.08
No Points Scored	2152.88 ± 0.41	2178.82 ± 0.83
Field Goal	769.46 ± 0.46	777.79 ± 0.59
Touchdown	1049.93 ± 0.49	1012.49 ± 0.71

Numbers shown are the mean counts ± standard error

Next, we turn from the performance of the offense to the play-calling strategy of the offensive coordinator. Table 4 shows the contingency table for the type of play called on the first play of a possession. We see that there are differences between the two distributions. There are fewer short passes and more runs (of every type except off the tackle) called after a big defensive play. However, when analyzed with Pearson's Chi Square test, we find these differences to be insignificant ($p = 0.068 \pm 0.003$). While we are seeing trends in the data, we cannot be sure that these are the result of big defensive plays, and not random variations.

So overall, there were differences in the frequencies of outcomes between BD and NBD plays, sets of downs, and drives. However, these differences were not large enough to find a statistically significant association. This implies that any effects of psychological momentum being transferred from a team's offense to a defense are no greater than random chance. Potential reasons for this result can be understood through Taylor and Demick's Momentum Chain. For a precipitat-

Table 4. First Called Play of Drive Based on BD/NBD Samples

Outcome	Big Defensive Play	Normal Play
Run, off the end	558.61 ± 0.32	532.75 ± 0.58
Run, off the tackle	582.70 ± 0.33	585.18 ± 0.62
Run, off the guard	468.36 ± 0.28	437.88 ± 0.55
Run, up the middle	587.56 ± 0.33	551.43 ± 0.58
Short pass (<15 yards)	499.44 ± 0.30	591.95 ± 0.60
Long pass (≥15 yards)	167.33 ± 0.18	164.80 ± 0.36

Numbers shown are the mean counts +/- standard error.

ing event to have an effect on an individual's performance, a number of factors and internal attitudes must line up perfectly. This is not to say that psychological momentum does not exist at all. It can certainly occur in an NFL game—a running back who loses a fumble can start paying attention to his ball security and not lose another fumble. However, there are three factors that we believe may prevent a big defensive play from changing an offensive's subsequent performance.

For noticeable outcomes of psychological momentum to be visible on the field, multiple offensive players must complete the full Momentum Chain and alter their performance. Granted, there are specific players whose individual performance is more important to the team, such as the quarterback. A future analysis of quarterback-specific metrics might show an influence of psychological momentum. However, if the center, right guard, wide receiver, and tight end change their performance, there may be no visible effect.

The players on offense also had nothing to do with the prior big defensive play; they were on the sideline when it happened (unless Bill Belichick was feeling frisky that day). While the offense will undoubtedly be happy with their teammates' performance, they may not have additional encouragement to do better than they otherwise would have. Furthermore, the opposing defense whose team just gave up the ball may be frustrated and angry with their teammates, but they may not feel like there is any change they're able to make. They weren't the ones who messed up! Therefore, the players on either side of the ball may not feel that they have control over the performance of their team's other unit who created the precipitating event.

If enough offensive players *do* change their performance after a big defensive play, the effects of psychological momentum may still not be observable. As Taylor and Demick note, in head-to-head sports the Momentum Chain requires "a continuous and opposing change in the previous factors on the part of the opponent." In other words, the offense must undergo positive momentum and the opposing defense must undergo negative momentum to see a change in performance. If, like the offense, the opposing defense also increases their performance after a big defensive play, no effects of momentum will be seen.

Just as psychological momentum did not significantly affect the offense's performance, neither did it affect the coach's play-calling. If this were true, we would have expected to see coaches trying to capitalize on their team's advantage and calling for riskier deep passes more often. On the contrary, trends in the data actually suggest the opposite. Coaches appear to be more conservative immediately after a big defensive play, tending to call more running plays and fewer short pass plays. However, these trends were statistically insignificant. The first play called immediately after a big defensive play does not significantly differ from the first play called after a normal change of possession.

Aaron Johnson
Alexander Stimpson
Torin Clark

This essay is adapted from an academic paper originally presented at the MIT Sloan Sports Analytics Conference in March 2012. We would like to thank ArmchairAnalysis.com for providing us with NFL play-by-play data and Dr. Jaime Mateus for advice on the statistical analysis.

Bilbliography

Taylor, Jim, and Andrew Demick. "A Multidimensional Model of Momentum in Sports." Journal of Applied Sport Psychology 6 (1994): 51-70.

Klaassen, Franc J.G.M., and Jan R. Magnus. "Are Points in Tennis Independent and Identically Distributed? Evidence From a Dynamic Binary Panel Data Model." Journal of American Statistical Association 96.454 (2001): 500-509.

"Examining the Value of Fighting in the NHL." PowerScoutHockey.com, 6 Jan 2012. http://powerscouthockey.com/blog/examining-value-fighting-nhl

Litke, Jim. "Need some momentum? Just drop the gloves." Boston.com. Boston Globe, 6 Jan 2012. http://articles.boston.com/2012-01-06/sports/30598504_1_hockey-fans-fighting-momentum

Gilovich, Thomas, Robert Vallone, and Amos Tversky. "The Hot Hand in Basketball: On the Misperception of Random Sequences." Cognitive Psychology 17 (1985): 295-314.3

Albright, S. Christian. "A Statistical Analysis of Hitting Streaks in Baseball." Journal of American Statistical Association 88.424 (1993): 1175-1183.

Romer, David. "Do Firms Maximize? Evidence from Professional Football." Journal of Political Economy 114.2 (2006): 340-365.

Steiner, Andy. "Interception and counter-momentum?" Advanced NFL Stats Community. Advanced NFL Stats, 25 Oct 2010. http://community.advancednflstats.com/2010/10/interception-and-counter-momentum.html

The Curse of 25 Carries and Questionable

A decade ago, Ricky Williams had as many carries as any running back ever had in a two-year span, and then he temporarily walked away from the game. It turns out he also took more of a pounding while already playing hurt than anyone else in the last decade. Ricky Williams had four of six games in 2003 where he appeared on the official injury report entering the week and still carried the ball at least 25 times anyway, and averaged 26.0 carries in those games. To put that in perspective, that's the same rate of carries per game that Larry Johnson averaged in his record-setting 416-carry season.

No other back in the last decade has had four different high-workload games when already appearing on the injury report. The only others to have three were Rudi Johnson in 2005 (11 weeks on injury report while playing with knee injury) and Eddie George in 2001 (listed seven different weeks with an ankle injury). Those two backs aren't exactly poster boys for the aging gracefully club. George plodded along for three more seasons, while Johnson had fewer than 750 career rushing yards after his 28th birthday. Whatever his personal reasons, Ricky Williams probably had the right idea taking a year off, and after returning to the NFL, he was able to play four different seasons where he had between 150 and 250 carries as part of a platoon.

While we don't know how Ricky Williams would have done in 2004 after consecutive high-carry and injury-filled seasons, we can look at whether playing hurt has an impact the next year on other feature running backs.

Using the Football Outsiders' injury report database, I went through every season between 2001 and 2010 where a back had 300 or more carries, and reviewed his appearances on the injury report. (We left off Ricky Williams' 2003 season, since he "retired" before the next year.)

Eighty-four seasons appear on the list, and the back made it through without being listed on the injury report 27 percent of the time. Twenty-five others involved backs who played while on the injury report at least once, but had their carries limited to less than 25 when they were injured (Table 1).

Table 1: Workload vs. Injury Report Appearance for 300+-Carry Backs

Type	No.	Avg Rush, Yr N	GP, Yr N+1	8 or fewer GP, Yr N+1
One or more high-carry games while hurt	36	331.6	13.8	4
Played hurt, but no high-carry games	25	327.7	14.7	1
Never appeared on injury report	23	337.1	14.7	0

I also looked at what happened two years later for those backs at the top of the list who had at least two high-carry games while appearing on the injury report. That includes, in addition to George and Johnson, Cedric Benson (2009), Priest Holmes (2003), Jamal Lewis (2003), Deuce McAllister (2002), Clinton Portis (2008), Lamar Smith (2001), Chester Taylor (2006), and LenDale White (2007). I also included Ricky Williams from 2005 (but not 2004 when he sat out, as Ricky Williams was on the list twice).

These backs had a variety of skill levels and were a variety of ages, so to create comparisons, I found the five most similar seasons at the same age for other backs in the same time period, and looked at what the comp group did two years later.

Those that ran for multiple high-carry games while injured averaged 747 yards from scrimmage and 4.7 touchdowns two years later. The comparable backs without those high-carry games while injured averaged 934 yards from scrimmage and 5.3 touchdowns two years later. The yards per carry numbers showed the most significant dropoff. The "high-carry while injured" backs averaged 3.69 yards per carry two seasons later, while the comparable backs averaged 4.19 yards per carry two seasons later. Of the 11 seasons reviewed, only Cedric Benson in 2011 and Eddie George in 2003 had better overall volume numbers than their list of comps. Of course, Eddie George showed up as better because he continued to get opportunities and played 16 games at age 30; he wasn't particularly good.

So perhaps it is no surprise that Williams walked away after head coach Dave Wannstedt kept calling his number carry after carry, game after game. Those injuries may have shelved lesser players, and they probably sapped any remaining will to keep playing from Williams. He quit the game in part because of a failed drug test, though as Williams stated at the time, he didn't quit football because he failed a drug test, he failed a drug test because he wanted to quit football.

That Ricky Williams—who played through six appearances on the injury report, and was one of only two players to cross 370 carries in consecutive years—was the centerpiece of the original Football Outsiders article that established the idea which became known as the "Curse of 370."

Since that original article on Football Outsiders, we have seen the number of high-carry seasons decrease. Only four backs have eclipsed the 370-carry mark in a single season since 2004, and those backs averaged 10.25 games played the following season. In the eight years prior to Ricky walking away, there were nine seasons where a back had at least 370 carries. Last year, Maurice Jones-Drew led the league with 343 carries, while Michael Turner led the year before with 334. Both of those totals would have ranked only sixth in 2003.

Still, when we talk about the Curse of 370, there are criticisms. The first is the sample size, and that the numbers do not lend themselves to certainty. This is true; only 23 different men in 28 seasons have reached the milestone in the history of the league. The outcome of 28 seasons would likely never prove anything, unless the results were extremely drastic.

Another issue, one that Football Outsiders has tried to warn against, is taking the Curse of 370 too literally as a hard number, where anything up to 369 carries is acceptable. In reality, the issue isn't the specific number 370, but the things that backs who reach 370 rush attempts have in common. They were good enough for their team to get them lots of carries, and they were healthy enough to continue to play for at least 15 games.

Cadillac Williams had the most rushing attempts of any rookie through the first three games of a career, and the third most ever to start a season behind our protagonist, Ricky Williams. In Cadillac's fourth game, he hurt his foot, missed two games, and struggled for much of the middle of the year. He would never again have a 1,000-yard rushing year.

What about Willie Parker in 2007? His 307 carries through 13 games had him leading the league in that category and on pace to surpass the 370-carry mark, but a fractured fibula that occurred on the first carry of Week 16, without contact, left him way short.

Perhaps you remember the brief sensation that was Samkon Gado in 2005. He came out of nowhere and had 136 rush attempts over six games, including four with at least 25 carries. In his next to last game that year, he had a career high 29 carries in an overtime win over Detroit. On the sixth carry of the next game, he tore up his knee.

If you took the "Curse" too literally, you might think that those backs (and dozens of others like them) were fortunate that they never got to 370. In reality, the same issues and risks claimed them. Cadillac Williams was never the same back after his early foot injury. Willie Parker missed five more games the next year and never came close to his totals from 2005 to 2007. Samkon Gado bounced around the league as a backup, averaging 3.2 yards per carry the rest of his career.

This is real life and teams do not do things just to allow for proper scientific experimentation. Teams don't wait to see if something has a p-value of .05 to make decisions on whether one course is better than the other. We can't just ask teams to give running backs enough carries to reach 370 in a season so we can get adequate sample sizes, and even if we did, some of the subjects might smoke pot and walk away before the data was collected.

Another way to look at the issue is to sub-divide smaller groups to see if similar patterns emerge, where the highest workload groups fare the worst. I did this in the past, looking at both the highest-carry groups during the first six games of a season as well as the last six games of a season, then measuring how those players did in the games that followed. The nine backs who had 150 or more carries in the first six games of a season (1995-2006) averaged 7.9 games the rest of the year. Twenty-four backs with between 138 and 149 carries averaged 8.5 games the rest of the year. The remaining starting running backs who had at least 90 carries at the start of a season? They averaged 9.0 games played (n= 179). Small sample sizes at the top, but again a similar pattern where those backs, many who never got to 370 carries, showed up injured more frequently.[1]

The same thing was true for the high-carry backs at the end of a season. Those 14 backs who averaged 25.0 or more carries over the last six weeks played in an average of 11 games the next year. The twenty-three backs who averaged 23.0 to 24.9 carries at season's end averaged 13.3 games played the following season. The remaining backs who averaged at least 15 carries played in 13.7 games a year later. More noticeable was the early-season serious injury rate. Four of the 14 highest-carry backs suffered season-ending injuries in the first six weeks the following year, while five percent of others suffered the same fate. Again, small sample sizes at the top, and again, a similar pattern. Those who received a high-carry rate turned up injured more frequently than their peers afterward.[2]

Why would high-carry games at the end of one season lead to higher injury rates at the start of another, when a back has had opportunity to recover? I suppose this is the same logic that the Curse of 370 applies in looking at seasonal totals. Perhaps it's because running backs aren't running at the same stress level in the offseason, so the next time they run with regular-season effort, you see the decline or injuries. Microtears of ligaments or injuries to tendons that do not heal fully may later materialize as a full tear or noticeable injury 20, 40, or 60 sharp cuts later.

After looking at those increased injury rates from high-carry backs in shorter periods of time than a full season, I posited that single-game rush attempt totals, like game pitch counts in baseball, were at issue. That while simply counting rush attempts as a proxy for "overworking one's self physically to the point of greater injury risk" is inexact, the injuries seemed to pick up in the aftermath of games with 25 or more carries. Last year, I did an exhaustive study where I went back through history to 1978, and looked at how frequently games missed occurred after certain rushing totals in single games.[3] Again, the games missed due to injury increased within 40 touches of the highest workload games.

The backs who suffered an injury within 40 touches of a 30-plus-carry game missed 4.9 games per injury, compared with 3.9 games for injuries following a 24- to 29-carry game, and 2.7 games missed after an 18- to 23-carry game.

You might recall from earlier Curse of 370 analysis that rushing attempts matter in measuring workload, while receptions do not. Why then did I measure touches, including receptions, for injury rates? Because rushing attempts, particularly high-carry games, are highly correlated with winning, playing with the lead, and running the ball late in games in a way that receptions are not. However, if we are measuring the per-play injury risk in the aftermath of a suspected overuse period, we want to account for all the potential hits that could have resulted in injury. A back with 20 touches had twice the opportunity to get hurt as one with 10 touches. Even accounting for the likelihood that "workhorse" backs continue to get greater touches, the serious injury rate on a per-touch basis was higher.

Those previous studies matched up games missed in each player's career logs. Of course, players can and do suffer injuries and play through them, but the onset of injuries themselves can be identified with more specific data. The injury report data that Football Outsiders has accumulated is so exhaustive that for the last decade alone, there are more than 6,000 lines of data for running backs. I would have loved to have gone through every player and match them up with the game logs and rush attempt totals. Ultimately, so I could spend some time with my family before Christmas, I settled on analyzing each back from the last decade who had one of the 25 best single seasons in terms of yards from scrimmage. That list includes all the backs who had elite seasons, from LaDainian Tomlinson to Chris Johnson to Shaun Alexander, and includes every player who had at least 1,750 yards from scrimmage in a season between 2001 and 2010.

---

[1] "Running Back Overuse and Injuries," July 11, 2007: http://www.pro-football-reference.com/blog/?p=328

[2] "Running Back Overuse and Injuries, Part II," July 12, 2007: http://www.pro-football-reference.com/blog/?p=330

[3] "Single Game Carries Are The Problem," September 23, 2010: http://thebiglead.com/index.php/2010/09/23/analysis-of-running-back-injuries-single-game-carries-are-the-problem/

I then looked at every game, and injury report, for those players before their 29th birthday, for the period between 2001 and 2010 for which we have injury report data. (I limited it by age so that backs who begin to break down due to age would not pollute the results.)

I measured how frequently the player first appeared on the injury report, and what the rushing attempt total was in the previous game. For games where the player suffered an injury noted in the play-by-play, and had 12 or fewer carries, I reverted to the previous game the player finished without injury. For example, when Willie Parker broke his fibula on the first carry and showed up on the injury report the next week, I used the 21-carry game in Week 15, and not the one-carry game in Week 16, to represent the week before injury onset.

Also, these backs were categorized by the result, so "Probable" means "played, but listed as probable on injury report", and "Questionable" means "played, but listed as questionable or worse". (Adrian Peterson played while being listed as Out in Week 3 of 2008, the only such case for this group). Out means the player missed the game due to injury, and includes those who were listed as Questionable/Probable on the injury report, but sat out (Table 2).

Table 2. Injury Rates for Elite Backs, Based on Previous Game Carry Totals and Injury Report Appearance

Rush Attempts	Probable	Questionable	Out	Overall
30 or more carries	0.076	0.010	0.038	0.124
27 to 29 carries	0.079	0.016	0.031	0.126
24 to 26 carries	0.067	0.029	0.033	0.129
21 to 23 carries	0.073	0.032	0.012	0.117
18 to 20 carries	0.035	0.012	0.004	0.050
15 to 17 carries	0.038	0.017	0.004	0.059

What do we see with our elite backs from the last decade? Just as we had seen in other groups, the amount of games missed increased as they crossed toward the 25-carry barrier. They rarely first appeared on the injury report and missed a game due to injury following a more moderate workload. In fact, it happened less than one percent of the time when these top backs had between 15 and 20 carries a week earlier.

Based on observation of other running back injury report rates, this sample of backs, who represented the elite of the last decade, appeared on the injury report with less frequency overall than their peers. Perhaps staying healthy with a standard NFL-starter workload is a skill just like vision and cutting ability. Perhaps we are just observing the lucky ones, and other backs with similar health skill happened to take that one bad hit. The truth is probably somewhere in between, though I suspect that even if the ability to maintain health is a skill, we could not identify it beforehand. Any skill is probably related not to bulk, but to stamina and genetics and being able to keep tissue oxygenated while working through a game with 300-pound guys hitting you repetitively. Players such as Emmitt Smith and Curtis Martin were not the largest players on the field, but they made it through the gauntlet where others did not.

The other thing about these results is that the high-carry games also show up as leading to more outcomes where the player shows up on the injury report but still takes the field. The percentage of players who played despite being listed as injured on the official report doubled above 20 carries. Why does this matter? We already saw that the future outcomes for players can be affected by continuing with higher workloads while injured, so playing through injury for the team may not be the best long term outcome.

We would expect some slight increase in injury report rates with increased carries simply due to the increased number of opportunities on each hit to get that injury. However, the fact that it more than doubles compared to the games where these backs had between 15 and 20 carries suggests that both "any given hit" and overuse factors are at work as carries increase.

Individual differences exist within the group. We would probably guess that Brian Westbrook has a lower injury threshold than other backs given his running style and personal history, for example. Still, even among guys with an injury reputation, we see that injury rates seem to correspond with single-game usage. Fred Taylor garnered the nickname "Fragile Fred" early in his career for frequent injuries from 1998 to 2001. How much of that came from his usage rate early in his career? Taylor was injured right after a 25-carry game in 1998 and had two separate injuries after 24-carry and 27-carry games in 1999. The injury that cemented his reputation in 2001 came after multiple 30-plus-carry games at the end of the previous season, and 24 carries in Week 1.

Steven Jackson is another back with an injury reputation, and his injuries have almost always coincided with periods of higher workload. In his first year, he tore his MCL immediately after a 26-carry game. In 2006, he went through a season without once appearing on the injury report, and was consistently getting between 18 and 23 carries a game. At season's end, though, he had two 30-carry games, and then another one in Week 3 of the following season. He tore his groin at the end of that game and labored through the rest of the year after missing a month. In 2008, his strained quad in Week 8 came right after a 25-carry game against Dallas. In 2009, he first appeared on the report with back spasms after a two-game stretch with 50 carries.

I could provide other examples, but the data shows that the best backs, while maybe lasting longer and enduring more, are still more subject to injuries, missing games with injuries, and suffering career-altering injuries when they have high-carry games. The best strategy, then, may not be to go to an even platoon, but for teams to give their most-talented back a decent but not excessive number of carries. After that, the remaining carries can be siphoned off in short-yardage, late-game, or low-leverage situations.

The number of 30-plus carry games has dropped dramatically in the last decade. There were 36 such games in 2003, and 44 games in 2004. In the last four years, this total has never topped 12.

There is no Curse of 370, *per se*, but the original research that showed that elite backs who surpassed that mark got hurt or declined more frequently was just part of a larger picture. All backs get hurt more frequently if they carry the ball more. It is a self-perpetuating cycle. Those who survive high-carry games get more opportunities to break down in the future. They tend to not get their carries reduced, unless acted upon by an external force—namely, a blown-out knee or a worn-out body.

This year brings us one of the most heralded running back prospects in a decade, Trent Richardson. The temptation will be there for Cleveland to ride him, just as it was there for Tampa Bay with Cadillac Williams and Miami with Ricky Williams. Cleveland needs to recognize that Richardson is a valuable asset, and to not overuse him early in his career. This does not mean limiting him to 12 carries, but it does mean trying to target 17 to 23 carries a game consistently. They cannot assume that anything short of 370 is acceptable. The greater risk of higher carries comes in a variety of doses, from a single game to the pounding of playing through injuries and running excessively.

Jason Lisk

FO Rookie Projections

Over the years, Football Outsiders has developed four different methods for forecasting the NFL success of highly-drafted players at various positions. Here is a rundown of those four methods and what they say about the NFL's Class of 2011.

Quarterbacks: Lewin Career Forecast

The Lewin Career Forecast, named after original designer David Lewin, was first introduced in Pro Football Prospectus 2006. A newer version was introduced in 2011. Despite the NFL success of such quarterbacks as Cam Newton (14 games started) and Aaron Rodgers (25 games started) in recent seasons, games started remains the most important factor in forecasting highly-drafted college quarterback prospects. LCF also includes variables that analyze completion percentage, a player's improvement or decline in their senior year, and how often a quarterback scrambles or gets sacked. Plays from non-AQ conferences receive a penalty.

The dependent variable projected by LCF v2.0 is the quarterback's total DYAR in seasons 3-5. Here are the projections for quarterbacks chosen in the first three rounds of the 2012 draft:

Name	Team	Rnd	Pick	Projection
Russell Wilson	SEA	3	75	2,650 DYAR
Robert Griffin III	WAS	1	2	2,530 DYAR
Andrew Luck	IND	1	1	1,749 DYAR
Nick Foles	PHI	3	88	1,391 DYAR
Brandon Weeden	CLE	1	22	1,011 DYAR
Ryan Tannehill	MIA	1	8	730 DYAR
Brock Osweiler	DEN	2	57	248 DYAR

The Lewin Career Forecast is extremely high on the quarterbacks of 2012. Russell Wilson and Robert Griffin have the two highest projections in LCF history, and Andrew Luck ranks seventh. Wilson's forecast comes with a bit of an asterisk, however, discussed in his player comment in the quarterbacks section. Some of the other players also have their forecasts discussed in their respective player comments.

Running Backs: Speed Score

Speed Score was created by Bill Barnwell and introduced in Pro Football Prospectus 2008. The basic theory is simple: not all 40-yard dash times are created equal. A fast time means more from a bigger running back, and the range of 40 times for backs is so small that even a miniscule difference can be meaningful. The formula for Speed Score is:

(Weight x 200) / 40 time ^4

Unlike in 2011, the order of drafted running backs this year falls much closer to the order of Speed Score, although the two players with the best Speed Scores among backs who ran at the Combine did not go until the fourth round. However, no back taken in the first three rounds had a particularly low Speed Score.

Third overall selection Trent Richardson did not run at the Combine and therefore does not officially have a Speed Score; if were to consider the 4.49 forty he ran at Alabama's Pro Day, his Speed Score would be 112.2.

Here are the Speed Scores for all backs chosen in the first three rounds, except for Richardson, as well as the top five Speed Scores for backs chosen in the final four rounds:

Name	Team	Rnd	Pick	40 time	Weight	Speed Score
Bernard Pierce	BAL	3	84	218	4.49	107.3
Doug Martin	TB	1	31	223	4.55	104.1
Ronnie Hillman	DEN	3	67	200	4.45	102.0
David Wilson	NYG	1	32	206	4.49	101.4
LaMichael James	SF	2	61	194	4.45	98.9
Isaiah Pead	STL	2	50	197	4.47	98.7
Lamar Miller	MIA	4	97	212	4.40	113.1
Robert Turbin	SEA	4	106	222	4.50	108.3
Cyrus Gray	KC	6	182	206	4.47	103.2
Terrance Ganaway	NYJ	6	202	239	4.67	100.5
Edwin Baker	SD	7	250	204	4.53	96.9

Wide Receivers: Playmaker Score

An essay by Vince Verhei exploring the latest version of our Playmaker Score metric was available in the original version of this book online, but we are unable to include it here due to printing issues. To read this essay, please visit: http://www.footballoutsiders.com/files/playmaker.pdf.

The new version of Playmaker Score incorporates both college stats and Combine data into one metric. The NCAA portion of the metric incorporates receptions, yards, and touchdowns in the receiver's best college season, adjusted for his team's total pass attempts. The Combine portion of the metric incorporates the vertical jump and the 10-yard split, which is the first 10 yards of the 40-yard dash.

Over the past decade, wide receivers from the SEC and ACC are more likely to exceed their Playmaker projections, and wide receivers from the Big 12 and non-AQ conferences are likely to fall short.

Players drafted from 2005-2009 with Playmaker Score over 400 have averaged 499 yards per season. Those with Playmaker Score between 200 and 400 have averaged 271 yards per season. Those with Playmaker Score under 200 have averaged 91 yards per season.

Jets second-round pick Stephen Hill establishes a new Playmaker Score record this year with 660, surpassing Calvin Johnson (621). There may be an asterisk on this because Hill's numbers were skewed by Georgia Tech's triple-option offense, but Hill had better receiving stats and Combine numbers than Demaryius Thomas, who came out of the same offense two years ago.

Here are projections for wide receivers chosen in the first three rounds of the 2011 draft, along with the highest-scoring later-round receivers:

Edge Rushers: SackSEER

An essay by Nathan Forster exploring the latest version of SackSEER was available in the original version of this book online, but we are unable to include it here due to printing issues. To read this essay, please visit: http://www.footballoutsiders.com/files/sackseer.pdf.

SackSEER is a method that projects sacks for edge rushers, including both 3-4 outside linebackers and 3-4 defensive ends, using the following criteria:

- An "explosion index" that measures the prospect's scores in the forty-yard dash, the vertical jump, and the broad jump in pre-draft workouts.
- Sacks per game, adjusted for factors such as early entry in the NFL Draft and position switches during college.
- Passes defensed per game.
- Missed games of NCAA eligibility due to academic problems, injuries, benchings, suspensions, or attendance at junior college.

The new SackSEER outputs two numbers. The first, SackSEER rating, solely measures how high the prospect scores compared to players of the past. The second, SackSEER projection, represents a forecast of sacks for the player's first five years in the NFL. It synthesizes metrics with conventional wisdom by adjusting based on the player's expected draft position (interestingly, not his actual draft position) based on pre-draft analysis at the site NFLDraftScout.com.

Here are the SackSEER numbers for players drafted in the first three rounds of the 2011 draft, along with later-round picks with a high SackSEER rating. Defensive ends drafted by 3-4 teams are not included.

Player	Tm	Rnd	Pick	College	Conf	PM Score
Stephen Hill	NYJ	2	43	Georgia Tech	ACC	660
Kendall Wright	TEN	1	20	Baylor	Big 12	502
A.J. Jenkins	SF	1	30	Illinois	Big Ten	418
Justin Blackmon	JAC	1	5	Oklahoma St.	Big 12	407
Alshon Jeffery	CHI	2	45	South Carolina	SEC	315
DeVier Posey	HOU	3	68	Ohio St.	Big Ten	286
T.Y. Hilton	IND	3	92	Florida Intl.	Non-AQ	282
Rueben Randle	NYG	2	63	LSU	SEC	277
Michael Floyd	ARI	1	13	Notre Dame	--	248
Brian Quick	STL	2	33	Appalachian St.	Non-AQ	203
Ryan Broyles	DET	2	54	Oklahoma	Big 12	161
Mohamed Sanu	CIN	3	83	Rutgers	Big East	157
T.J. Graham	BUF	3	69	N.C. State	ACC	102

Name	College	Team	Rnd	Pick	S.SEER Proj.	S.SEER Rating
Nick Perry	USC	GB	1	28	24.5	90.6%
Shea McClellin	Boise St.	CHI	1	19	23.5	62.9%
Whitney Mercilus	Illinois	HOU	1	26	21.5	51.3%
Chandler Jones	Syracuse	NE	1	21	20.1	60.6%
Andre Branch	Clemson	JAC	2	38	19.5	54.9%
Melvin Ingram	S. Carolina	SD	1	18	18.4	21.6%
Courtney Upshaw	Alabama	BAL	2	35	17.2	15.5%
Bruce Irvin	W. Virginia	SEA	1	15	13.0	26.4%
Vinny Curry	Marshall	PHI	2	59	11.5	16.9%
Jake Bequette	Arkansas	NE	3	90	8.9	48.7%
Olivier Vernon	Miami	MIA	3	72	2.9	18.7%
Ronnell Lewis	Oklahoma	DET	4	125	16.7	64.2%
Jack Crawford	Penn St.	OAK	5	158	10.0	51.3%
Frank Alexander	Oklahoma	CAR	4	103	9.4	77.9%
Tim Fugger	Vanderbilt	IND	7	214	7.9	48.2%

Top 25 Prospects

Here it is: Football Outsiders' sixth annual list of under-the-radar, lower-drafted prospects who could have a big impact on the NFL in the coming seasons. In the past, Rotoworld has referred to our Top 25 Prospects list as "an all-star team of waiver pickups" after we used it to promote young players such as Miles Austin, Jamaal Charles, and Arian Foster. Last year, however, the "skill players" who get used in fantasy football weren't the stars of the list. Instead, it was the defensive players who made the biggest impact. Geno Atkins (sixth) made the Pro Bowl. Lardarius Webb (ninth) started 15 games and had 22 passes defensed, earning a huge contract from Baltimore in the offseason. Morgan Burnett (second) and Erik Walden (16th) started most of the year for a team that nearly went undefeated (although Walden will likely lose his starting job to rookie Nick Perry in 2012). Even one of last year's honorable mention defenders, Seattle safety Kam Chancellor, made the Pro Bowl as an injury replacement.

We're expecting to see some big stars from this year's list on both the offensive and defensive sides of the ball. Of course, there will also be some duds. We can't get them all right. Just ask last year's No. 8 prospect, Tashard Choice.

For the uninitiated, this list is not like the prospect lists you read about in the world of baseball. Because the top prospects in college football are stars on national television before they get taken in the first round of the NFL Draft, there's not much utility in listing them here. Everyone knows Andrew Luck is a top prospect who is likely to succeed in the NFL. Instead, we use a combination of statistics, measurables, context, and expected role to compile a list of under-the-radar players whom we expect to make an impact in the NFL, both in 2012 and beyond. To focus on these players, we limit the pool to guys who fit the following criteria:
- Drafted in the third round or later, or signed as an undrafted free agent
- Entered the NFL between 2009 and 2011
- Fewer than five career games started
- Still on their initial contract
- Age 26 or younger in 2012

That last item is new for this season, and is meant to ensure that we list players who could play a significant role in the NFL over the next few years, not just in 2012. To give two examples, running backs Bernard Scott and Isaac Redman are definitely important to their teams' plans this season. But, as each of them is already 28, they aren't really promising players for the long term. Other players who would have made the list if not for the age limit include Jacksonville running back Rashad Jennings, Detroit defensive end Willie Young, and Baltimore tight end Dennis Pitta.

For the third season out of four, we've chosen a wide receiver as our top prospect, following Miles Austin (2009) and Mike Wallace (2010). This time, however, it isn't a player who has looked impressive in limited action. It's a player who already is the leading receiver on his team, even though he's started only one game.

1. Doug Baldwin, WR, Seahawks

It feels like cheating to include Baldwin on our Top Prospects List; after all, this is the guy who led Seattle receivers in receptions, yards, and touchdowns. He was the first player since the AFL-NFL merger to lead his team in receiving yards as an undrafted rookie. Just for good measure, Baldwin also had 14.2% DVOA while every other Seattle receiver with at least 10 targets was below zero. Nevertheless, Baldwin only started one game last year, because he was used strictly as a slot receiver. Out of Baldwin's 86 targets, only two came with just two wide receivers in the formation—and on one of those plays, Baldwin was actually in the backfield, so the personnel was still three wide receivers. Baldwin is tough going for passes over the middle despite his small size (5-foor-10, 190 pounds). He's good at running precise routes and finding soft spots in zones. The next test is working on the perimeter from two-receiver sets against starting corners instead of nickelbacks.

2. Martez Wilson, DE-LB, Saints

Wilson played sparingly in 2011. He produced just one major highlight, sacking Cam Newton on a blitz up the middle for a 16-yard loss. The old regime used Wilson as a situational blitz-package player, when they used him at all. Steve Spagnuolo has moved Wilson from linebacker to defensive end, a more natural position for a player with a Jevon Kearse-meets-Jason Pierre-Paul body type. Wilson, a third-round pick in 2011, played middle linebacker at Illinois, a sign that college and pro coaches have been baffled about what to do with a 6-foot-4, 250-pounder with 4.4-range 40-times, 36-inch arms, and an over 10-foot standing broad jump. If any coach knows how to get the most out of that kind of player, it's Spags.

3. Everson Griffen, DE-LB, Vikings

Once thought to be a second- or even first-round talent, Griffen ended up falling to Minnesota in the fourth round of the 2010 draft. He probably can blame worries about his off-field decorum more than worries about his raw technique. The former still may be a problem (he was arrested for public intoxication in January 2011) but the latter is becoming more polished. That means it may finally be time for Griffen's breakout. As a part-time pass rusher in 2011, Griffen had four sacks, nine hurries, three quarterback hits, and two forced fumbles. He's supremely talented, with an explosive burst of the edge and good inside quickness. He provides coverage almost as readily as pass-rushing prowess, which is very important for a team that likes to drop defensive ends into coverage as often as Minnesota does. The Vikings are trying to figure out ways to get Griffen on the field more often, and may use him as a linebacker in some packages next season.

4. Cortez Allen, CB, Steelers

When the Steelers drafted Allen in the fourth round out of the Citadel, he was considered by many to be a long-term project at corner. The Steelers had success picking Ike Taylor in the fourth round in similar circumstances. As a rookie, it was Allen who saw playing time in dime packages while third-round cornerback Curtis Brown stuck to special teams. In the Steelers' Week 8 win over the Patriots, Pittsburgh used Allen regularly to cover New England's athletic tight ends. Allen has long limbs and a very smooth backpedal, and he can play physical. He should move up to the nickelback role this year, but don't be surprised if he beats out Keenan Lewis for a starting job in training camp.

5. Stevan Ridley, RB, Patriots

Ridley has good lower-body control and balance with a powerful stride, although he's not the fastest back out there (Speed Score: 95.4). The Pats really started to use him in the last five weeks of the regular season, when he had 5.2 yards per carry and a 57 percent Success Rate. He needs work on blocking and receiving, which limits his ability to play on third downs but also makes him a nice complement to Shane Vereen and Danny Woodhead. Of course, he also needs work on his hands after fumbling in back-to-back games near the end of his rookie season, which put him on the bench for most of the playoffs. But he didn't have fumble problems at LSU, and there's a good chance that the back-to-back fumbles were just random chance, not evidence of a real issue.

6. Pernell McPhee, DE, Ravens

As a rookie in 2011, McPhee took advantage of offenses worrying about Terrell Suggs to score six sacks as a situational pass rusher. McPhee primarily came on the field in clear passing situations, particularly on third downs, and really came alive in the second half of the year. Although he had three sacks through Week 9 and his other three sacks afterwards, 15 of his 16.5 regular-season hurries came in Baltimore's final eight games. McPhee is all about motor, motor, motor, and his technique is still developing. He came out of Mississippi State as a better athlete than football player. (He also came to Mississippi State from community college, which puts a bit of a red flag on him as far as SackSEER is concerned.) McPhee had minor arthroscopic surgery this offseason but should be healthy in time for training camp, where he will battle Arthur Jones for the starting spot at defensive end vacated by Cory Redding. It will be interesting to see how McPhee fits as a five-technique in the Ravens base defense, because he's much more suited to the more conventional way the Ravens use their defensive ends in nickel packages.

7. Allen Bailey, DE, Chiefs

Bailey, a third-round rookie, made only eight plays last year, but five of them were Defeats. He's a two-time All-ACC player who twice led the Miami Hurricanes in sacks, a versatile talent who was an outside linebacker as a freshman, then later started at both defensive end and tackle. The pessimistic term for this, of course, would be "tweener," as he's too slow to play defensive end in a 4-3, and not quite big enough to be an NFL defensive tackle. Romeo Crennel has a pretty good history with "tweeners" like Bailey who have smarts and a non-stop motor. The Chiefs occasionally used him last year as a situational pass rusher on passing downs. This year, they'll likely use him a lot more often, and it isn't far-fetched to think he could earn a starting job in 2013. Bailey also has a fascinating personal story; he hails from Sapelo Island, Georgia, population 49, as part of the African-American Gullah (also known as Geechee) community which has maintained much of its West African cultural heritage for 200 years.

8. James Brewer, OT, Giants

The Super Bowl champs were perfectly happy to let Kareem McKenzie leave in free agency this offseason because they're fairly confident that Brewer can take over the right tackle spot in his sophomore year. (If he fails in training camp, there is a backup plan: Kevin Boothe at left guard with David Diehl at right tackle.) Brewer has long arms and good balance with a strong lower base. Unfortunately, he also has a history of knee and ankle injuries, which helped knock him down to the fourth round of last year's draft.

9. Akeem Dent, LB, Falcons

Dent was trapped behind Curtis Lofton last season, but he was the Falcons' top special teams player. The 2011 third-round pick recorded 19 special-teams tackles and 16 Return Stops[1], tying Heath Farwell of the Seahawks for the league lead. Special teams coach Keith Armstrong often singled Dent out as the hardest worker on his units. Dent worked behind Lofa Tatupu at middle linebacker during minicamps, but Tatupu has had numerous knee injuries and concussions, and is coming off what amounts to a year of family leave. Dent could develop into a star if he gets his chance.

10. DeMarcus Van Dyke, CB, Raiders

Van Dyke barely makes the list; he was a third-round pick, and started four games as a rookie. Our game charting project shows him with only 4.6 adjusted yards per pass and a Success Rate of 67 percent. Those numbers are among the league's best, but come with the small sample size caveat. In the past, small sample size charting numbers have picked out some soon-to-breakout stars (Cortland Finnegan) but also some busts (Ronnie Prude, anyone?). Van Dyke has the athletic talent to be a starting corner if he can work on his technique and discipline. At Miami, he was more potential than performance, and even got benched halfway through his senior season because he was struggling on the field. The Raiders signed free agents Ron Bartell and Shawntae Spencer to be their starting cornerbacks, but Van Dyke could grab one of those jobs if he shows enough in training camp.

11. Evan Royster, RB, Redskins

Royster, a sixth-rounder from Penn State, put up the best rushing DVOA ever by a running back with at least 40 carries. In the player comments, we pointed out that similar small-sample size studs had not developed into star backs. However, they did generally develop into useful part-time players, and Mike Shanahan certainly does have a history of getting the best out of his running backs. Royster also brings blocking skills and good hands as a receiver to the table. It's enough to make us actually set aside our usual pessimism about Big Ten running backs.

12. Brice McCain, CB, Texans

Putting together this list, we were stuck with a bit of a quandary when it came to a number of talented young nickelbacks. More and more each year, nickelback has essentially become a "starting" position. Players may not get more than a 1 or 2 in the "GS" column of the stat sheet, but they play almost as many snaps as the starting cornerbacks. Some teams even move their starters inside to that nickel position, so the "backup" is actually an outside cornerback. But while these nickelbacks have already had a big impact on their teams, many of them are also limited. Covering the slot is what they do best; good numbers as a nickelback don't necessarily forecast a player who would be successful as a starting corner who had to cover vertical routes on the outside.

In the end, we mostly tried to keep our Top 25 Prospects list to cornerbacks who we feel have the biggest chance to develop into every-down starters who can play both slot and outside. But we did make this one exception, because Brice McCain's numbers last season were so phenomenal. McCain actually ended up first in Success Rate among all corners with at least 40 targets; he's listed as fifth in the Houston chapter because of adjustments for the quality of the receivers he covered. He also finished 11th with just 5.7 adjusted yards per pass allowed. In retrospect, it's almost incredible that the Texans even bothered to try

---

[1] Plays which end a return short of what our special teams rating system considers league average.

McCain on the outside in 2010. Freed from the oppressive regime of Frank Bush, McCain's reading and recognition skills were much better utilized, and he even made a couple of nice plays off the blitz. He's never going to be a shutdown outside corner, but you don't need to be one to be important in today's NFL. The same goes for the other nickelbacks we list below under honorable mention, who would have made our list if we expanded it to 35 guys instead of 25.

13. Jeremy Kerley, WR, Jets

Ignore the way the Jets messed around with Kerley in the Wildcat last year. He's really a Wes Welker type: a small, quick, slot receiver who's elusive enough to ring up yards after the catch. Right now he's ticketed to be the third receiver when the Jets go three-wide, but considering how raw rookie Stephen Hill is, it wouldn't be a surprise to see Kerley as a starter who then moves inside to the slot when the Jets go three-wide. He's also likely to run all kinds of fun reverses and end-arounds when the Jets go to their Tebow package of wackiness (or, if you prefer, wackness). Incidentally, he had 17 of his 29 catches and 226 of his 314 yards against AFC East opponents. This is good because the Jets have to play those teams each twice; it's bad because they weren't particularly hard defenses to put up yards against.

14. O'Brien Schofield, LB, Cardinals

Schofield had 12 sacks as a senior defensive end at Wisconsin, but fell down draft boards when he tore his ACL at the Senior Bowl. The Cardinals snatched him in the fourth round and it was a perfect match; Schofield wasn't going to make it as a defensive end in the pros at just 240 pounds, but he has the ideal body type for a 3-4 outside linebacker. Schofield has 6.5 sacks in a year and a half of part-time play. (He didn't take the field as a rookie until Week 8 because of the ACL recovery.) He also led the Cardinals with 12 tackles on special teams last year. Although the Cardinals did decide to re-sign veteran Clark Haggans, the plan is for Schofield to take his spot as the starting strongside linebacker with Haggans as the backup.

15. Karl Klug, DT, Titans

We're not going to pretend that Klug, a 2011 fifth-round pick out of Iowa, isn't limited as a player. He's probably too undersized (275 pounds) to become an every-down defensive tackle in the NFL. And admittedly, his rookie total of seven sacks looks like a bit of a fluke, since it was only accompanied by three hits and three hurries. Looking through his sacks, there are a couple where he just got a garbage sack after the ends did the real work or the quarterback held the ball too long. However, he also made a couple of great plays on stunts, and sometimes he just ran through guards both unknown (Seth Olsen) and famous (Carl Nicks). Plus, there are the plays you won't find in his sack total, like four passes batted away at the line, or the tackles of Donald Brown and Jason Snelling that forced no gain on second-and-1. Klug has great hands, leverage, and a nice repertoire of rush moves, and he should be bringing the pain on Andrew Luck for the next few years.

16. Ryan Mallett, QB, Patriots

Even though Mallett didn't step on the field during the regular season, everything that scouts said about him a year ago is still true. He's still a tall, classic pocket passer with elite arm strength who can drop the deep ball in with a beautiful touch pass. He also can't throw well on the run and will take a ton of sacks. He's had a year under the tutelage of Bill O'Brien and Tom Brady, and hopefully they helped him work on improving his decision-making skills, both on and off the field. Mallett is still likely to earn a job as an NFL starter someday, and it is still likely to be somewhere other than New England.

17. Buster Skrine, CB, Browns

The fifth-round rookie out of Tennessee-Chattanooga earned more playing time as season went along, eventually snagging his first NFL interception in Week 15. Our charting numbers have him with 5.7 adjusted yards per pass on 14 targets. He's a smaller guy, 5-foot-10, but quickly got a reputation around the Browns for his aggressive nature. Skrine can be physical in press and strong in run support. He's got a good backpedal but lacks top-end straight speed. If he develops a bit more, he may replace Sheldon Brown in the starting lineup as early as next season.

18. Cam Thomas, DT, Chargers

Thomas was generally hailed as a steal when the Chargers snagged him in the fifth round of the 2010 draft, but played in just six games as a rookie and had just seven tackles (although two of those were sacks). Last year, we saw a bit more of what Thomas can do, with four sacks, three quarterback hits, and 6.5 hurries, plus an 87 percent Stop Rate on run tackles. He has rare natural strength and can both get to the quarterback in a one-gap and stuff up the run in a two-gap. It's unlikely Thomas will take a starting job away from Antonio Garay, but he's a useful piece when San Diego goes to four linemen (which they did on nearly 20 percent of snaps last year).

19. Marcus Cannon, OL, Patriots

Cannon was a flat-out steal by the Patriots. He's a huge guy with quick feet, and draftniks expected him to go as early as the second round before he was diagnosed with non-Hodgkins Lymphoma before the draft. The Pats were perfectly happy to take him in the fifth round and wait for him to complete chemotherapy, and by Week 11 he was getting snaps in a regular-season game. Cannon was a right tackle at TCU and could spell Sebastian Vollmer in a pinch if necessary, but he's much better suited for guard in the pros because he has trouble with bull rushers. He will likely replace Brian Waters at right guard whenever Waters decides he feels like retiring.

20. Victor Butler, LB, Cowboys

Victor Butler was a fourth-round pick out of Oregon State in 2009. He's been hiding under the surface in Dallas, with only one game started in three years but eight total sacks as a backup linebacker. His playing time has gone up a little bit each year, and in 2011 Butler had three sacks, 10 hurries, and four quarterback hits. He also got a Stop on all 10 of his run tackles. Rob Ryan wants to get a heavy pass rush from his outside linebackers, and that's what Butler brings to the table. Actually, his biggest task going forward may be gaining experience doing other things, since the outside linebackers in Dallas (especially the ones who are not DeMarcus Ware) do drop into coverage sometimes. Anthony Spencer will be playing on the franchise tag this year, so perhaps Butler will get more playing time to test if he's ready to start in 2013.

21. Vincent Brown, WR, Chargers

The Chargers love this local third-round pick (out of San Diego State) who has drawn comparisons to Derrick Mason. He has good hands and quick feet, but isn't great at getting separation on vertical routes. The trick is to use him right: He should be the possession receiver with Robert Meachem and Malcom Floyd as the deep threats, but the Chargers sent him 20 or more yards on 14 of his 40 targets, plus a 27-yard DPI. He also needs to work on getting open against NFL corners, as an awful lot of his passes as a rookie were either defensed or saw Brown immediately tackled without yards after the catch. Once he improves, he could be the dynamic intermediate option they were lacking last year when Antonio Gates was out of the lineup.

22. Phillip Hunt, DE, Eagles

Phillip Hunt left the University of Houston in 2009. When he couldn't stick on the Cleveland Browns as an undrafted free agent, he went north to Winnipeg and led the CFL with 16 sacks in 2010. The Eagles brought him back down south last year, hoping to get Cameron Wake Part II. They didn't get that, partly because Hunt was deep in the defensive end rotation. However, in limited time, Hunt had two sacks, 6.5 hurries, four quarterback hits, and drew two holding flags. Hunt isn't in our SackSEER database, which doesn't include undrafted players, but if we looked at the appropriate variables, he would end up with one of the best SackSEER ratings ever at 94.6 percent. He had a +0.82 explosion index, no missed games, a .61 SRAM, and .34 passes defensed per game. Scouts might be confused because he's built like a 244-pound square, not like the athletic stud suggested by his workout numbers. But he's a good power and leverage guy, and he's flashed a bit as an inside crasher. The strange thing is that there may not be room for Hunt on the roster after the Eagles drafted Vinny Curry and picked up Monte Taylor off waivers. If they cut him, there's going to be a pretty darn promising pass rusher out on the open market for almost no cost. Anybody looking for one of those?

23. D.J. Smith, LB, Packers

Ted Thompson is known for finding contributors amidst the ranks of undrafted free agents, but this one he actually found on draft day. A sixth-rounder from Appalachian State, Smith was inconsistent as a rookie but showed intriguing potential in his three starts. Greg Cosell noted that Smith showed more juice and explosiveness than Desmond Bishop, who started ahead of him. He just wasn't as reliable. Smith moves with good athleticism in tight areas and can sift through traffic to get to the ballcarrier. Scouts generally considered him weak in pass coverage coming out of college, but the Packers were unafraid to use him in nickel and dime packages.

24/25. Kris Durham and Ricardo Lockette, WR, Seahawks

The Seahawks are swimming in receivers with as-yet unrealized potential, but these two are our favorites. Lockette was a track star at Fort Valley State, and spent most of last season on the practice squad before catching two passes for 105 yards and a touchdown in the final two weeks of the season. The team appears high on him but he's raw like sushi. If he can learn more than one route and show more consistency as a receiver, he could be a big-play guy in Seattle.

Durham was Seattle's fourth-round pick last year out of Georgia. He averaged more than 20 yards per catch as a senior, but just can't stay healthy. He's torn a shoulder labrum twice, once in college and then again last year after just three games. (The Seahawks weren't clear about which shoulder he tore, so we don't know if Durham has torn each one once or the left one twice.) If he can stay healthy, Durham is a big receiver (6-foot-5, 215 pounds) who could take over the role Mike Williams played in Pete Carroll's first two seasons in Seattle.

Honorable Mention

Darvin Adams, WR, Panthers
Joe Barksdale, OT, Raiders
Junior Galette, DE, Saints
Andre Neblett, DT, Panthers
Da'Rel Scott, RB, Giants

Honorable Mention, Special Nickelbacks Unit

Chris Culliver, 49ers
Chris Harris, Broncos
D.J. Moore, Bears
Justin Rogers, Bills

Aaron Schatz

Statistical Appendix

Broken Tackles by Team, Offense

Rk	Team	Plays	Plays w/ BTkl	Pct	Total BTkl
1	PHI	1018	86	8.4%	96
2	ATL	1046	82	7.8%	99
3	PIT	995	78	7.8%	93
4	TEN	969	70	7.2%	78
5	CHI	967	66	6.8%	73
6	BUF	976	64	6.6%	73
7	NE	1068	65	6.1%	75
8	CAR	987	60	6.1%	64
9	DAL	1001	60	6.0%	68
10	DET	1052	62	5.9%	73
11	HOU	1027	60	5.8%	65
12	NO	1104	64	5.8%	81
13	SEA	993	57	5.7%	68
14	MIN	999	57	5.7%	63
15	NYG	1006	57	5.7%	67
16	JAC	984	55	5.6%	63
17	DEN	1004	55	5.5%	62
18	TB	950	50	5.3%	67
19	OAK	999	54	5.4%	59
20	ARI	979	49	5.0%	55
21	SD	1026	51	5.0%	65
22	SF	971	48	4.9%	58
23	GB	962	47	4.9%	52
24	MIA	978	48	4.9%	52
25	KC	1005	46	4.6%	51
26	CLE	1012	44	4.3%	56
27	BAL	1016	44	4.3%	49
28	IND	938	39	4.2%	44
29	WAS	1018	38	3.7%	45
30	CIN	1004	37	3.7%	39
31	NYJ	1019	34	3.3%	41
32	STL	1004	29	2.9%	33

Broken Tackles by Team, Defense

Rk	Team	Plays	Plays w/ BTkl	Pct	Total BTkl
1	NYG	1056	40	3.8%	41
2	SF	965	37	3.8%	42
3	CLE	1016	43	4.2%	52
4	BAL	992	42	4.2%	48
5	ARI	1077	46	4.3%	54
6	BUF	986	44	4.5%	50
7	MIA	1028	49	4.8%	58
8	GB	1038	50	4.8%	64
9	SEA	1031	51	4.9%	56
10	DEN	1043	52	5.0%	60
11	PIT	956	48	5.0%	59
12	DAL	959	49	5.1%	55
13	CIN	993	51	5.1%	61
14	IND	1040	54	5.2%	60
15	CHI	1038	54	5.2%	60
16	MIN	1010	53	5.2%	64
17	NYJ	977	52	5.3%	58
18	WAS	974	52	5.3%	62
19	JAC	958	53	5.5%	59
20	NE	1052	59	5.6%	65
21	HOU	946	54	5.7%	58
22	OAK	1048	61	5.8%	72
23	KC	979	57	5.8%	66
24	ATL	957	57	6.0%	62
25	DET	1044	65	6.2%	74
26	TEN	1065	67	6.3%	82
27	NO	998	63	6.3%	72
28	SD	939	60	6.4%	65
29	CAR	955	62	6.5%	71
30	STL	1008	66	6.5%	75
31	PHI	968	78	8.1%	97
32	TB	981	88	9.0%	106

STATISTICAL APPENDIX

Top 20 Defenders in Broken Tackles

Rk	Player	Team	BTkl
1	D.Stewart	STL	19
2	S.Jones	TB	17
3	T.Jackson	TB	16
4	J.Greer	NO	14
5	S.Weatherspoon	ATL	13
6	S.Martin	CAR	12
6	E.Wright	DET	12
6	Q.Mikell	STL	12
6	J.Babineaux	TEN	12
10	Q.Black	TB	11
10	A.Ayers	TEN	11
10	J.Sanford	MIN	11
10	M.Griffin	TEN	11
10	C.Godfrey	CAR	11
10	T.Polamalu	PIT	11
10	N.Bowman	SF	11
17	B.Rolle	PHI	10
17	N.Allen	PHI	10
17	R.Barber	TB	10
17	K.Chancellor	SEA	10
17	A.Rolle	NYG	10
17	D.Levy	DET	10
17	D.Washington	ARI	10

Top 20 Defenders, Broken Tackle Rate

Rk	Player	Team	BTkl	Tkl	Rate
1	B.Mebane	SEA	0	46	0.0%
1	T.Jackson	KC	0	42	0.0%
1	A.Carter	NE	0	40	0.0%
4	M.Boley	NYG	1	76	1.3%
5	C.Harris	DEN	1	60	1.6%
5	P.Wheeler	IND	1	60	1.6%
7	J.Laurinaitis	STL	2	119	1.7%
7	D.Connor	CAR	1	58	1.7%
9	J.Senn	CAR	1	53	1.9%
10	J.Lacey	IND	1	52	1.9%
10	V.Miller	DEN	1	52	1.9%
12	B.Browner	SEA	1	51	1.9%
12	A.Ross	NYG	1	51	1.9%
14	D.Ware	DAL	1	48	2.0%
14	J.Smith	SF	1	48	2.0%
16	P.Taylor	CLE	1	47	2.1%
17	J.Hall	STL	1	45	2.2%
18	O.Atogwe	WAS	1	44	2.2%
18	J.Casey	TEN	1	44	2.2%
18	H.Ngata	BAL	1	44	2.2%

Broken Tackles divided by Broken Tackles + Solo Tackles.
Special teams not included; min. 40 Solo Tackles

Most Broken Tackles, Running Backs

Rk	Player	Team	BTkl
1	L.McCoy	PHI	50
2	M.Turner	ATL	42
3	Drew	JAC	37
4	M.Forte	CHI	36
5	M.Lynch	SEA	34
5	R.Mendenhall	PIT	34
7	F.Jackson	BUF	33
8	A.Foster	HOU	32
9	L.Blount	TB	30
9	C.Johnson	TEN	30
11	R.Bush	MIA	29
11	R.Rice	BAL	29
13	A.Peterson	MIN	26
14	R.Mathews	SD	24
15	W.McGahee	DEN	22
15	I.Redman	PIT	22
17	A.Bradshaw	NYG	21
17	J.Stewart	CAR	21
19	S.Jackson	STL	20
19	P.Thomas	NO	20

Bottom 20 Defenders, Broken Tackle Rate

Rk	Player	Team	BTkl	Tkl	Rate
1	D.Stewart	STL	19	65	22.6%
2	B.Rolle	PHI	10	44	18.5%
3	S.Jones	TB	17	75	18.5%
4	C.Gamble	CAR	9	41	18.0%
5	S.Martin	CAR	12	55	17.9%
6	N.Allen	PHI	10	46	17.9%
7	D.Robinson	ATL	9	43	17.3%
8	Q.Black	TB	11	53	17.2%
9	A.Ayers	TEN	11	54	16.9%
10	J.Greer	NO	14	69	16.9%
11	J.Sanford	MIN	11	56	16.4%
12	J.Joseph	HOU	8	43	15.7%
13	E.Biggers	TB	9	51	15.0%
13	K.Lewis	KC	9	51	15.0%
15	B.Grimes	ATL	7	40	14.9%
15	L.Landry	WAS	7	40	14.9%
17	M.Griffin	TEN	11	64	14.7%
18	L.Delmas	DET	8	47	14.5%
18	D.Ryans	HOU	8	47	14.5%
20	M.Giordano	OAK	9	53	14.5%

Broken Tackles divided by Broken Tackles + Solo Tackles.
Special teams not included; min. 40 Solo Tackles

STATISTICAL APPENDIX

Most Broken Tackles, WR/TE

Rk	Player	Team	BTkl
1	A.Hernandez	NE	21
2	M.Wallace	PIT	14
3	R.Gronkowski	NE	13
3	G.Little	CLE	13
5	N.Burleson	DET	12
5	C.Johnson	DET	12
7	D.Bowe	KC	11
7	V.Cruz	NYG	11
7	J.Witten	DAL	11
10	D.Bryant	DAL	10
10	M.Crabtree	SF	10
12	S.Breaston	KC	8
12	B.Celek	PHI	8
12	J.Cribbs	CLE	8
12	V.Davis	SF	8
12	L.Fitzgerald	ARI	8
12	T.Gonzalez	ATL	8
12	J.Graham	NO	8
12	L.Hawkins	TEN	8
12	J.Jones	ATL	8
12	S.Smith	CAR	8
12	G.Tate	SEA	8
12	R.White	ATL	8

Most Broken Tackles, Quarterbacks

Rk	Player	Team	Behind LOS	Beyond LOS	BTkl
1	T.Tebow	DEN	12	10	22
1	M.Vick	ATL	17	5	22
3	C.Newton	CAR	6	7	13
4	J.Freeman	TB	7	4	11
5	A.Smith	SF	5	3	8
5	J.Webb	MIN	5	3	8
7	D.Brees	NO	5	2	7
8	C.McCoy	CLE	3	3	6
8	A.Rodgers	GB	4	2	6
10	M.Cassel	KC	3	2	5

Best Broken Tackle Rate, Offensive Players (min. 80 touches)

Rk	Player	Team	BTkl	Touch	Rate
1	A.Hernandez	NE	21	84	25.0%
2	J.Ringer	TEN	16	87	18.4%
3	T.Tebow	DEN	22	122	18.0%
4	I.Redman	PIT	22	128	17.2%
5	F.Jackson	BUF	33	209	15.8%
6	L.McCoy	PHI	50	321	15.6%
7	J.Best	DET	17	111	15.3%
8	L.Blount	TB	30	199	15.1%
9	R.Gronkowski	NE	13	91	14.3%
10	N.Burleson	DET	12	84	14.3%
11	M.Forte	CHI	36	255	14.1%
12	K.Smith	DET	13	94	13.8%
13	R.Mendenhall	PIT	34	246	13.8%
14	D.Bowe	KC	11	82	13.4%
15	V.Cruz	NYG	11	83	13.3%
16	M.Turner	ATL	42	318	13.2%
17	P.Thomas	NO	20	160	12.5%
18	C.Johnson	DET	12	97	12.4%
19	C.J.Spiller	BUF	17	146	11.6%
20	A.Peterson	MIN	26	226	11.5%

Top 20 Defenders in Passes Defensed

Rk	Player	Team	PD
1	B.Browner	SEA	23
2	L.Webb	BAL	22
2	T.Williams	GB	22
4	J.Greer	NO	21
4	D.Revis	NYJ	21
6	B.Flowers	KC	19
6	R.Sherman	SEA	19
6	C.Webster	NYG	19
9	J.Haden	CLE	18
9	D.Hall	WAS	18
9	P.Robinson	NO	18
9	C.Rogers	SF	18
9	C.Woodson	GB	18
14	K.Arrington	NE	17
14	A.Cason	SD	17
14	S.Routt	OAK	17
17	C.Williams	BAL	16
18	8 tied with		15

Note: Based on the definition given in the Statistical Toolbox, not NFL totals.

STATISTICAL APPENDIX

Top 20 Defenders in Defeats

Rk	Player	Team	Dfts
1	J.Allen	MIN	33
2	J.Pierre-Paul	NYG	32
3	D.Johnson	KC	31
3	T.Suggs	BAL	31
5	J.Laurinaitis	STL	30
5	D.Washington	ARI	30
7	V.Miller	DEN	29
8	C.Campbell	ARI	28
8	P.Posluszny	JAC	28
8	D.Ware	DAL	28
11	N.Bowman	SF	27
11	D.Jackson	CLE	27
13	N.Barnett	BUF	26
13	L.Briggs	CHI	26
13	C.Clemons	SEA	26
13	M.Kiwanuka	NYG	26
13	T.Polamalu	PIT	26
13	S.Weatherspoon	ATL	26
19	K.Chancellor	SEA	24
19	C.Gocong	CLE	24

Top 20 Defenders in Run Tackles for Loss

Rk	Player	Team	Dfts
1	K.Conner	IND	16
2	M.Kiwanuka	NYG	15
3	J.Laurinaitis	STL	11
4	P.Angerer	IND	10
4	C.Johnson	CAR	10
4	J.Sheard	CLE	10
4	M.Wilkerson	NYJ	10
8	J.Anderson	CAR	9
8	D.Bowers	TB	9
8	L.Briggs	CHI	9
8	D.Dockett	ARI	9
8	E.J.Henderson	MIN	9
8	D.Jackson	CLE	9
8	C.Jenkins	PHI	9
8	D.Johnson	KC	9
8	B.Mebane	SEA	9
8	J.Pierre-Paul	NYG	9
8	D.Washington	ARI	9
8	S.Weatherspoon	ATL	9
20	20 tied with		8

Top 20 Defenders in Quarterback Hits

Rk	Player	Team	Hits
1	C.Matthews	GB	23
2	C.Wake	MIA	20
3	V.Miller	DEN	19
4	T.Hali	KC	18
5	C.Barwin	HOU	17
6	J.Babin	PHI	16
6	C.Clemons	SEA	16
6	D.Dockett	ARI	16
6	A.Smith	SF	16
6	J.Watt	HOU	16
11	A.Carter	NE	15
11	E.Walden	GB	15
11	K.Wimbley	OAK	15
14	J.Pierre-Paul	NYG	14
14	A.Smith	HOU	14
14	J.Smith	SF	14
14	T.Suggs	BAL	14
18	C.Dunlap	CIN	13
19	J.Allen	MIN	12
19	G.Atkins	CIN	12
19	J.Mincey	JAC	12
19	A.Spencer	DAL	12

Adjusted based on official scorer tendencies

Top 20 Defenders in QB Knockdowns (Sacks + Hits)

Rk	Defender	Team	KD
1	J.Allen	MIN	35
2	J.Babin	PHI	34
3	V.Miller	DEN	33
4	J.Pierre-Paul	NYG	32
4	A.Smith	SF	32
4	D.Ware	DAL	32
7	C.Barwin	HOU	31
7	T.Hali	KC	31
9	C.Matthews	GB	29
9	C.Wake	MIA	29
11	C.Clemons	SEA	28
11	T.Suggs	BAL	28
13	A.Carter	NE	26
14	C.Long	STL	22
14	J.Smith	SF	22
14	J.Watt	HOU	22
14	K.Wimbley	OAK	22
18	J.Abraham	ATL	21
18	G.Atkins	CIN	21
18	J.Mincey	JAC	21
18	A.Smith	HOU	21

Full credit for whole and half sacks; includes sacks cancelled by penalty.

Top 20 Defenders in Drawing Offensive Holding Flags

Rk	Player	Team	Total	Pass	Run
1	C.Wake	MIA	13	8	5
2	L.Houston	OAK	7	5	2
2	B.Orakpo	WAS	7	4	3
4	J.Abraham	ATL	6	5	1
4	C.Clemons	SEA	6	3	3
4	J.Houston	KC	6	3	3
4	B.Robison	MIN	6	4	2
8	J.Harrison	PIT	5	4	1
8	A.Haynesworth	2TM	5	3	2
8	C.Johnson	CAR	5	5	0
8	J.Ratliff	DAL	5	2	3
8	K.Wimbley	OAK	5	4	1
13	D.Bryant	OAK	4	4	0
13	J.Casey	TEN	4	1	3
13	C.Jenkins	PHI	4	2	2
13	C.Matthews	GB	4	3	1
13	J.Peppers	CHI	4	4	0
13	A.Rubin	CLE	4	2	2
13	J.Sheard	CLE	4	0	4
13	J.Smith	SF	4	1	3
13	N.Suh	DET	4	3	1
13	V.Wilfork	NE	4	1	3

Top 20 Defenders in Hurries

Rk	Defender	Team	Hur
1	T.Hali	KC	40.5
2	C.Wake	MIA	39
3	T.Suggs	BAL	38.5
4	J.Abraham	ATL	35
5	C.Long	STL	33
5	A.Smith	HOU	33
7	J.Peppers	CHI	31
7	A.Smith	SF	31
9	A.Clayborn	TB	29.5
10	K.Wimbley	OAK	29
11	R.Kerrigan	WAS	28
11	J.Smith	SF	28
13	C.Matthews	GB	27.5
14	C.Avril	DET	27
15	M.Bennett	TB	26.5
16	C.Barwin	HOU	26
16	A.Spencer	DAL	26
18	B.Orakpo	WAS	25.5
19	J.Mincey	JAC	25
19	J.Pierre-Paul	NYG	25

Top 20 Quarterbacks in QB Hits

Rk	Player	Team	Hits
1	M.Ryan	ATL	68
2	R.Grossman	WAS	66
3	T.Jackson	SEA	60
4	E.Manning	NYG	53
5	C.McCoy	CLE	52
6	M.Vick	PHI	50
7	R.Fitzpatrick	BUF	49
7	J.Flacco	BAL	49
9	M.Stafford	DET	48
10	T.Brady	NE	43
10	A.Dalton	CIN	43
10	B.Roethlisberger	PIT	43
13	A.Smith	SF	42
14	S.Bradford	STL	40
15	C.Newton	CAR	39
15	P.Rivers	SD	39
15	T.Romo	DAL	39
18	J.Freeman	TB	36
19	J.Cutler	CHI	34
19	M.Hasselbeck	TEN	34

Adjusted based on official scorer tendencies

Top 20 Quarterbacks in QB Knockdowns (Sacks + Hits)

Rk	Player	Team	Adj KD
1	T.Jackson	SEA	102
2	M.Ryan	ATL	95
3	R.Grossman	WAS	92
4	A.Smith	SF	89
5	C.McCoy	CLE	86
5	B.Roethlisberger	PIT	86
5	M.Stafford	DET	86
8	J.Flacco	BAL	81
8	E.Manning	NYG	81
10	T.Brady	NE	77
10	B.Gabbert	JAC	77
12	S.Bradford	STL	76
12	T.Romo	DAL	76
14	C.Newton	CAR	75
15	M.Vick	PHI	74
16	R.Fitzpatrick	BUF	72
16	M.Sanchez	NYJ	72
18	A.Rodgers	GB	71
19	P.Rivers	SD	70
20	M.Moore	MIA	69

Includes sacks cancelled by penalties
Does not include "self sacks" with no defender

STATISTICAL APPENDIX

Top 10 Quarterbacks in Knockdowns per Pass

Rk	Player	Team	KD	Pct
1	C.Hanie	CHI	29	23.8%
2	C.Henne	MIA	27	21.1%
3	T.Jackson	SEA	102	19.5%
4	T.Tebow	DEN	60	19.0%
5	J.Beck	WAS	28	18.2%
6	R.Grossman	WAS	92	18.1%
7	S.Bradford	STL	76	18.1%
8	M.Moore	MIA	69	17.2%
9	A.Smith	SF	89	17.1%
10	C.McCoy	CLE	86	16.3%

Min. 120 passes; includes passes cancelled by penalty

Most Passes Tipped at the Line, Defenders

Rk	Player	Team	Total
1	C.Campbell	ARI	8
1	G.Hardy	CAR	8
3	B.Cofield	WAS	7
3	J.Pierre-Paul	NYG	7
5	H.Ngata	BAL	6
6	C.Barwin	HOU	5
6	B.Keisel	PIT	5
6	B.Orakpo	WAS	5
6	S.Phillips	SD	5
6	J.J.Watt	HOU	5

Top 20 Players, Pct. Passes Dropped

Rk	Player	Team	Drops	Passes	Pct
1	M.Hardesty	CLE	6	21	28.6%
2	F.Gore	SF	7	31	22.6%
3	A.McCoy	SEA	5	24	20.8%
4	T.Ginn	SF	5	33	15.2%
5	D.Murray	DAL	5	35	14.3%
6	D.Clark	IND	9	65	13.8%
7	J.Baldwin	KC	6	53	11.3%
8	J.Hill	JAC	6	55	10.9%
9	G.Little	CLE	13	121	10.7%
10	D.Driver	GB	6	56	10.7%
11	B.Gibson	STL	7	71	9.9%
12	A.Benn	TB	5	51	9.8%
13	J.Finley	GB	9	92	9.8%
14	D.Jackson	PHI	10	104	9.6%
15	D.Sanzenbacher	CHI	5	54	9.3%
16	C.J.Spiller	BUF	5	54	9.3%
17	D.Hester	CHI	5	56	8.9%
18	R.White	ATL	16	180	8.9%
19	L.Tomlinson	NYJ	5	60	8.3%
20	B.Obomanu	SEA	5	61	8.2%

Min. five drops

Most Passes Tipped at Line, Quarterbacks

Rk	Player	Team	Total
1	M.Hasselbeck	TEN	19
1	M.Vick	PHI	19
3	M.Sanchez	NYJ	17
4	A.Dalton	CIN	15
4	R.Grossman	WAS	15
6	K.Kolb	ARI	14
6	C.McCoy	CLE	14
8	S.Bradford	STL	13
8	R.Fitzpatrick	BUF	13
8	M.Stafford	DET	13
11	B.Gabbert	JAC	12
11	B.Roethlisberger	PIT	12

Bottom 10 Quarterbacks in Knockdowns per Pass

Rk	Player	Team	KD	Pct
1	D.Brees	NO	53	7.5%
2	M.Hasselbeck	TEN	53	9.4%
2	J.Freeman	TB	66	10.8%
4	P.Rivers	SD	70	10.9%
5	K.Orton	DEN/KC	31	10.9%
6	T.Brady	NE	77	11.4%
7	R.Fitzpatrick	BUF	72	11.5%
8	M.Sanchez	NYJ	72	11.6%
9	A.Dalton	CIN	67	11.6%
10	M.Stafford	DET	86	11.7%

Min. 120 passes; includes passes cancelled by penalty

Top 20 Players, Passes Dropped

Rk	Player	Team	Total
1	R.White	ATL	16
2	G.Little	CLE	13
3	D.Jackson	PHI	10
3	B.Marshall	MIA	10
5	D.Bowe	KC	9
5	D.Clark	IND	9
5	J.Finley	GB	9
8	V.Cruz	NYG	8
9	B.Gibson	STL	7
9	F.Gore	SF	7
9	D.Heyward-Bey	OAK	7
9	S.Moss	WAS	7
9	S.Smith	CAR	7
9	M.Williams	TB	7
15	18 tied with		6

2011 Quarterbacks with and without Pass Pressure

Rank	Player	Team	Plays	Pct Pressure	DVOA with Pressure	Yds with Pressure	DVOA w/o Pressure	Yds w/o Pressure	DVOA Dif	Rank
1	M.Schaub	HOU	312	33.3%	-25.8%	4.5	70.4%	9.4	-96.2%	7
2	T.Tebow	DEN	335	31.3%	-90.6%	1.8	30.0%	7.0	-120.6%	15
3	B.Roethlisberger	PIT	572	29.0%	-36.6%	3.8	51.1%	8.3	-87.7%	4
4	A.Smith	SF	521	28.6%	-76.0%	2.0	53.5%	7.5	-129.5%	21
5	K.Kolb	ARI	294	28.6%	-130.1%	2.6	30.9%	7.5	-161.0%	31
6	J.Freeman	TB	608	27.3%	-51.7%	3.6	13.6%	7.0	-65.3%	1
7	M.Vick	PHI	494	27.1%	-39.1%	4.5	61.9%	8.6	-101.0%	9
8	J.Cutler	CHI	347	26.5%	-76.0%	3.3	41.9%	7.6	-117.9%	13
9	S.Bradford	STL	404	26.5%	-109.9%	0.5	11.4%	6.6	-121.3%	16
10	B.Gabbert	JAC	477	26.4%	-120.9%	1.4	-4.5%	5.4	-116.4%	12
11	C.Ponder	MIN	345	26.4%	-95.0%	1.9	-1.6%	6.9	-93.4%	6
12	T.Jackson	SEA	519	25.6%	-97.0%	2.1	47.9%	7.1	-144.9%	27
13	D.Orlovsky	IND	208	25.5%	-103.7%	2.2	40.1%	6.7	-143.7%	26
14	R.Grossman	WAS	488	24.6%	-108.9%	1.2	44.7%	7.7	-153.6%	29
15	M.Cassel	KC	312	24.4%	-135.0%	1.3	22.9%	6.9	-157.9%	30
16	C.Palmer	OAK	351	24.2%	-134.3%	3.4	49.5%	9.0	-183.8%	35
17	M.Sanchez	NYJ	605	23.6%	-123.6%	1.0	42.1%	7.3	-165.7%	33
18	J.Skelton	ARI	316	23.4%	-118.5%	2.4	8.1%	7.1	-126.5%	17
19	C.McCoy	CLE	541	22.9%	-81.1%	2.0	25.8%	6.1	-106.9%	11
20	J.Flacco	BAL	594	22.7%	-84.6%	3.0	43.1%	7.4	-127.6%	18
21	C.Newton	CAR	599	22.5%	-62.0%	4.3	44.2%	7.8	-106.2%	10
22	T.Romo	DAL	567	22.0%	-79.9%	2.3	63.0%	8.6	-142.9%	25
23	M.Ryan	ATL	609	22.0%	-82.8%	2.6	55.6%	8.1	-138.4%	24
24	P.Rivers	SD	626	21.7%	-77.5%	3.4	59.0%	8.4	-136.5%	23
25	A.Dalton	CIN	576	21.5%	-52.9%	2.6	39.6%	7.2	-92.5%	5
26	M.Moore	MIA	401	21.2%	-134.2%	1.5	41.3%	7.4	-175.5%	34
27	M.Stafford	DET	714	20.9%	-43.4%	4.7	37.9%	7.5	-81.2%	3
28	T.Brady	NE	659	20.6%	-38.0%	3.8	80.1%	8.9	-118.0%	14
29	E.Manning	NYG	637	20.4%	-69.7%	3.4	58.0%	8.9	-127.7%	19
30	C.Painter	IND	271	19.6%	-127.6%	1.8	1.7%	7.0	-129.3%	20
31	D.Brees	NO	696	17.4%	-13.8%	4.7	65.5%	8.5	-79.3%	2
32	K.Orton	DEN/KC	268	17.2%	-136.8%	2.2	25.2%	7.4	-162.0%	32
33	R.Fitzpatrick	BUF	625	16.6%	-99.7%	2.9	30.0%	7.3	-129.7%	22
34	A.Rodgers	GB	590	16.1%	-57.9%	3.0	91.8%	9.2	-149.6%	28
35	M.Hasselbeck	TEN	547	13.9%	-72.4%	3.6	27.0%	6.9	-99.4%	8

Includes scrambles and Defensive Pass Interference. Does not include aborted snaps.
Minimum: 200 passes.

STATISTICAL APPENDIX

Top 10 Teams, Pct Passes Dropped

Rk	Team	Drops	Passes	Pct
1	PIT	18	539	3.3%
2	DET	23	665	3.5%
3	SD	20	578	3.5%
4	ARI	19	544	3.5%
5	NE	22	610	3.6%
6	MIN	19	508	3.7%
7	DAL	22	567	3.9%
8	WAS	24	584	4.1%
9	CIN	22	534	4.1%
10	NO	28	657	4.3%

Top 10 Plus/Minus for Running Backs

Rk	Player	Team	Pass	+/-
1	M.Bush	OAK	47	+5.4
2	P.Thomas	NO	59	+5.2
3	D.Sproles	NO	111	+4.7
4	R.Mathews	SD	59	+4.3
5	K.Lumpkin	TB	53	+4.2
6	R.Bush	MIA	52	+3.5
7	E.Graham	TB	31	+2.7
8	A.Foster	HOU	73	+2.6
9	T.Gerhart	MIN	28	+2.5
10	J.Rodgers	ATL	28	+2.3

Min. 25 passes; totals adjusted for passes tipped/thrown away.

Bottom 10 Plus/Minus for Running Backs

Rk	Player	Team	Pass	+/-
1	F.Gore	SF	31	-6.9
2	D.Woodhead	NE	31	-4.5
3	L.Blount	TB	25	-3.4
4	L.Ball	DEN	31	-3.1
5	M.Forte	CHI	76	-3.1
6	D.Williams	CAR	25	-2.9
7	R.Rice	BAL	104	-2.4
8	V.Leach	BAL	27	-2.4
9	J.Best	DET	40	-1.8
10	T.Choice	DAL/WAS/BUF	31	-1.8

Min. 25 passes; totals adjusted for passes tipped/thrown away.

Top 20 Intended Receivers on Interceptions

Rk	Player	Team	Total
1	K.Winslow	TB	10
2	L.Fitzgerald	ARI	9
2	V.Jackson	SD	9
4	D.Bowe	KC	7
4	A.Caldwell	CIN	7
4	D.Jackson	PHI	7
4	S.Johnson	BUF	7
4	D.Moore	OAK	7
4	S.Moss	WAS	7
4	D.Nelson	BUF	7
4	A.Roberts	ARI	7
4	R.White	ATL	7
13	D.Aromashodu	MIN	6
13	F.Davis	WAS	6
13	E.Decker	DEN	6
13	B.Lloyd	DEN/STL	6
13	S.Smith	CAR	6
18	9 tied with		5

Bottom 10 Teams, Pct Passes Dropped

Rk	Team	Drops	Passes	Pct
23	BAL	28	544	5.1%
24	NYJ	28	542	5.2%
25	TB	32	581	5.5%
26	ATL	35	588	6.0%
27	GB	34	551	6.2%
28	STL	34	549	6.2%
29	PHI	34	546	6.2%
30	KC	31	495	6.3%
31	SF	29	451	6.4%
32	CLE	43	567	7.6%

Top 10 Plus/Minus for Wide Receivers

Rk	Player	Team	Pass	+/-
1	M.Colston	NO	107	+15.7
2	J.Nelson	GB	96	+11.5
3	W.Welker	NE	173	+9.4
4	V.Cruz	NYG	129	+9.1
5	C.Johnson	DET	158	+8.8
6	G.Jennings	GB	101	+8.1
7	M.Floyd	SD	70	+7.4
8	J.Maclin	PHI	97	+6.6
9	R.Meachem	NO	60	+6.4
10	M.Wallace	PIT	113	+6.1

Min. 50 passes; totals adjusted for passes tipped/thrown away.

Top 10 Plus/Minus for Tight Ends

Rk	Player	Team	Pass	+/-
1	R.Gronkowski	NE	125	+12.0
2	A.Gates	SD	88	+8.0
3	S.Chandler	BUF	46	+7.9
4	V.Davis	SF	95	+7.3
5	T.Gonzalez	ATL	116	+6.8
6	J.Graham	NO	149	+6.5
7	J.Witten	DAL	117	+5.5
8	F.Davis	WAS	88	+4.4
9	J.Dreessen	HOU	39	+4.2
10	A.Hernandez	NE	113	+4.2

Min. 25 passes; totals adjusted for passes tipped/thrown away.

Bottom 10 Plus/Minus for Wide Receivers

Rk	Player	Team	Pass	+/-
1	D.Aromashodu	MIN	84	-15.3
2	M.Thomas	JAC	92	-12.3
3	M.Massaquoi	CLE	74	-11.3
4	G.Little	CLE	121	-11.2
5	B.Lloyd	DEN/STL	147	-10.4
6	S.Moss	WAS	96	-10.4
7	J.Simpson	CIN	105	-8.8
8	D.Sanzenbacher	CHI	54	-8.7
9	D.Hester	CHI	56	-8.2
10	E.Royal	DEN	50	-8.1

Min. 50 passes; totals adjusted for passes tipped/thrown away.

Bottom 10 Plus/Minus for Tight Ends

Rk	Player	Team	Pass	+/-
1	M.Lewis	JAC	85	-10.2
2	D.Clark	IND	65	-9.9
3	G.Olsen	CAR	89	-8.0
4	B.Watson	CLE	71	-7.9
5	L.Kendricks	STL	58	-7.6
6	V.Shiancoe	MIN	71	-5.3
7	D.Keller	NYJ	115	-5.0
8	R.Housler	ARI	26	-3.4
9	K.Davis	CHI	35	-2.4
10	A.Smith	CLE	25	-2.2

Min. 25 passes; totals adjusted for passes tipped/thrown away.

Most Dropped Interceptions, 2011

Rk	Player	Team	Drops
1	T.Jennings	CHI	4
1	T.Newman	DAL	4
3	D.Caldwell	IND	3
3	B.Grimes	ATL	3
3	J.Haden	CLE	3
3	R.McClain	OAK	3
3	T.Williams	GB	3
8	27 tied with		2

Most Dropped Interceptions, 2009-2011

Rk	Player	Team	Drops
1	T.Jennings	IND/CHI	9
2	D.Florence	BUF	7
2	S.Smith	MIA	7
2	A.Talib	TB	7
2	T.Williams	GB	7
6	A.Bethea	IND	6
6	N.Collins	GB	6
6	Q.Mikell	PHI/STL	6
6	T.Newman	DAL	6
6	C.Rogers	WAS/SF	6

Top 20 First Downs/Touchdowns Allowed in Coverage

Rk	Player	Team	Total
1	C.Tillman	CHI	44
2	D.McCourty	NE	42
3	D.Hall	WAS	41
3	P.Peterson	ARI	41
3	T.Williams	GB	41
6	E.J.Biggers	TB	39
7	K.Arrington	NE	36
7	C.Webster	NYG	36
9	A.Goodman	DEN	35
9	A.Ross	NYG	35
11	A.Cason	SD	34
12	N.Clements	CIN	33
12	A.J.Jefferson	ARI	33
12	T.Newman	DAL	33
12	S.Smith	MIA	33
12	C.Williams	BAL	33
17	E.Wright	DET	32
18	B.Browner	SEA	31
19	J.Greer	NO	29
19	C.Houston	DET	29
19	Q.Jammer	SD	29
19	J.King	STL	29
19	S.Shields	GB	29

Includes Defensive Pass Interference.

Top 20 Passing Yards Allowed in Coverage

Rk	Player	Team	Yards
1	D.McCourty	NE	873
2	T.Williams	GB	865
3	E.J.Biggers	TB	778
4	C.Tillman	CHI	757
5	D.Hall	WAS	731
6	P.Peterson	ARI	673
7	K.Arrington	NE	634
8	A.Ross	NYG	632
9	T.Newman	DAL	625
10	B.Browner	SEA	619
11	C.Williams	BAL	597
12	J.King	STL	591
13	Q.Jammer	SD	570
14	A.J.Jefferson	ARI	563
15	J.Haden	CLE	557
16	B.Flowers	KC	548
17	C.Webster	NYG	542
18	J.Greer	NO	540
19	C.Rogers	SF	539
20	N.Clements	CIN	537

Includes Defensive Pass Interference.

Fewest Yards After Catch Allowed in Coverage

Rk	Player	Team	YAC
1	K.Lewis	PIT	1.3
2	K.Jackson	HOU	2.1
3	A.Cromartie	NYJ	2.1
4	R.Sherman	SEA	2.2
5	A.Samuel	PHI	2.2
6	J.McCourty	TEN	2.3
7	A.J.Jefferson	ARI	2.3
8	C.Williams	BAL	2.3
9	D.Revis	NYJ	2.3
10	L.Hall	CIN	2.3
11	N.Asomugha	PHI	2.5
12	A.Verner	TEN	2.5
13	I.Taylor	PIT	2.5
14	C.Finnegan	TEN	2.5
15	J.Joseph	HOU	2.5
16	J.Allen	HOU	2.6
17	A.Ball	DAL	2.6
18	A.Cason	SD	2.6
19	K.Arrington	NE	2.6
20	C.Culliver	SF	2.7

Min. 40 passes or 8 games started.

Most Yards After Catch Allowed in Coverage

Rk	Player	Team	YAC
1	C.Bailey	DEN	7.2
2	C.Munnerlyn	CAR	6.5
3	K.Wilson	NYJ	5.9
4	E.J.Biggers	TB	5.9
5	J.Haden	CLE	5.6
6	C.Rogers	SF	5.6
7	P.Robinson	NO	5.5
8	D.Butler	CAR	5.5
9	T.Newman	DAL	5.4
10	A.Talib	TB	5.2
11	J.Gordy	STL	5.2
12	J.Powers	IND	5.2
13	R.Mathis	JAC	5.0
14	D.Hall	WAS	4.9
15	L.Sheppard	OAK	4.9
16	T.Williams	GB	4.7
17	J.Greer	NO	4.6
18	B.Grimes	ATL	4.6
19	C.Griffin	MIN	4.6
20	D.Patterson	CLE	4.5

Min. 40 passes or 8 games started.

Fewest Avg Yards on Run Tackle, DL

Rk	Player	Team	Tkl	Avg
1	C.Jenkins	PHI	29	0.7
2	M.Bennett	TB	31	1.0
3	C.Clemons	SEA	33	1.1
4	D.Dockett	ARI	36	1.1
5	F.Robbins	STL	26	1.1
6	I.Idonije	CHI	40	1.3
7	M.Wilkerson	NYJ	43	1.3
8	J.Sheard	CLE	42	1.4
9	P.Soliai	MIA	26	1.4
10	F.Rucker	CIN	36	1.4
11	M.Thomas	DEN	40	1.5
12	A.Branch	SEA	26	1.5
13	C.Redding	BAL	37	1.6
14	L.Douzable	JAC	34	1.6
15	S.Bowen	WAS	32	1.6
16	C.Johnson	CAR	27	1.7
17	S.Pouha	NYJ	57	1.7
18	J.Casey	TEN	41	1.8
19	J.Bannan	STL	29	1.8
20	J.Allen	MIN	37	1.8

Min. 25 run tackles

Fewest Avg Yards on Run Tackle, LB

Rk	Player	Team	Tkl	Avg
1	R.Kerrigan	WAS	38	1.3
2	W.Witherspoon	TEN	28	1.5
3	C.Matthews	GB	33	1.6
4	T.Suggs	BAL	47	1.8
5	B.Reed	HOU	32	1.9
6	S.Weatherspoon	ATL	57	2.0
7	G.Hayes	TB	39	2.1
8	K.Conner	IND	70	2.1
9	P.Riley	WAS	41	2.1
10	J.Durant	DET	35	2.1
11	C.Kelsay	BUF	30	2.2
12	C.Pace	NYJ	49	2.3
13	D.Smith	JAC	67	2.3
14	J.Mays	DEN	61	2.3
15	B.Scott	NYJ	47	2.4
16	J.Dunbar	NO	44	2.4
17	J.Harrison	PIT	41	2.4
18	C.Wake	MIA	28	2.5
19	J.Houston	KC	30	2.5
20	B.Rolle	PHI	33	2.6

Min. 25 run tackles

Fewest Avg Yards on Run Tackle, DB

Rk	Player	Team	Tkl	Avg
1	J.McGraw	KC	27	4.0
2	B.Pollard	BAL	42	4.3
3	D.Gomes	WAS	20	4.3
4	T.Polamalu	PIT	47	4.4
5	A.Wilson	ARI	47	4.4
6	D.Searcy	BUF	24	4.4
7	U.Young	CLE	37	4.9
8	A.Elam	DAL	26	5.0
9	W.Gay	PIT	21	5.1
10	D.McCourty	NE	24	5.1
11	R.Harper	NO	53	5.3
12	C.Woodson	GB	34	5.4
13	K.Chancellor	SEA	58	5.5
14	J.Powers	IND	20	5.6
15	C.Peprah	GB	39	5.6
16	G.Quin	HOU	39	5.7
17	A.Rolle	NYG	40	5.7
18	J.Ihedigbo	NE	38	5.7
19	D.Caldwell	IND	48	5.8
20	R.Doughty	WAS	44	5.8

Min. 20 run tackles

Top 20 Players in Blown Blocks

Rk	Player	Team	BB
1	G.Whimper	JAC	12.3
2	J.Webb	CHI	11.5
3	L.Brown	ARI	10.5
3	W.Hunter	NYJ	10.5
5	L.Louis	CHI	9.5
6	R.Clady	DEN	9.0
6	M.Columbo	MIA	9.0
6	A.Davis	SF	9.0
6	P.Loadholt	MIN	9.0
6	M.Newhouse	GB	9.0
6	B.Richardson	KC	9.0
6	R.Saffold	STL	9.0
13	J.Backus	DET	8.5
13	D.Diehl	NYG	8.5
13	D.Free	DAL	8.5
13	D.Penn	TB	8.5
17	E.Monroe	JAC	8.3
18	J.Carpenter	SEA	8.0
18	O.Franklin	DEN	8.0
18	T.Smith	DAL	8.0
18	A.Whitworth	CIN	8.0

Includes blown blocks which lead to sacks, intentional grounding, or offensive holding calls

STATISTICAL APPENDIX

Most False Starts

Rk	Player	Team	Pen
1	J.Webb	CHI	8
2	W.Hunter	NYJ	7
2	T.J.Lang	GB	7
2	B.Pettigrew	DET	7
5	B.Albert	KC	6
5	M.McNeill	SD	6
5	M.Mulligan	NYJ	6
5	R.Okung	SEA	6
5	F.Omiyale	CHI	6
5	B.Richardson	KC	6
5	R.Saffold	STL	6
5	A.Smith	CIN	6
5	J.Staley	SF	6
5	J.Thomas	CLE	6

Top 10 Kickers, Gross Kickoff Value over Average

Rk	Player	Team	Kick Pts+	Net Pts+	Kicks
1	B.Cundiff	BAL	+6.4	-6.1	74
2	O.Mare	CAR	+4.5	-0.8	79
3	D.Akers	SF	+3.4	+6.4	91
4	P.McAfee	IND	+3.4	-2.8	60
5	M.Nugent	CIN	+3.1	+10.0	79
6	S.Gostkowski	NE	+2.8	+8.4	99
7	J.Scobee	JAC	+2.7	+3.0	62
8	A.Henery	PHI	+2.3	+7.5	81
9	S.Hauschka	SEA	+2.3	-2.0	75
10	R.Gould	CHI	+2.1	+0.8	79

Min. 20 kickoffs; squibs and onside not included

Bottom 10 Kickers, Gross Kickoff Value over Average

Rk	Player	Team	Kick Pts+	Net Pts+	Kicks
1	R.Longwell	MIN	-7.9	-12.6	75
2	M.Bosher	ATL	-6.1	-8.0	87
3	S.Janikowski	OAK	-5.1	-14.0	77
4	D.Bailey	DAL	-4.7	+0.3	65
5	N.Folk	NYJ	-4.0	+11.2	79
6	R.Lindell	BUF	-3.8	+2.7	42
7	P.Dawson	CLE	-2.9	-1.0	55
8	G.Gano	WAS	-2.0	+4.0	69
9	J.Hanson	DET	-1.8	-7.6	93
10	N.Rackers	HOU	-1.7	+1.4	33

Min. 20 kickoffs; squibs and onside not included

Most Penalties, Offense

Rk	Player	Team	Pen	Yds
1	J.Webb	CHI	15	82
2	R.Clady	DEN	13	80
3	B.Bell	CAR	12	80
4	R.Grossman	WAS	12	78
5	J.Veldheer	OAK	11	84
6	B.Pettigrew	DET	11	81
7	W.Hunter	NYJ	11	80
8	K.Barnes	OAK	11	65
9	J.Backus	DET	11	55
10	L.Pope	KC	10	84
11	M.Oher	BAL	10	79
12	B.Albert	KC	10	75
12	D.Free	DAL	10	75
14	J.Clary	SD	10	65
14	P.Loadholt	MIN	10	65
14	A.Whitworth	CIN	10	65
17	S.Lauvao	CLE	10	60
18	R.Saffold	STL	10	56
19	11 with		9	

Min. 20 run tackles

Most Penalties, Defense

Rk	Player	Team	Pen	Yds
1	S.Routt	OAK	17	167
2	B.Browner	SEA	15	124
3	J.Babin	PHI	12	57
4	R.Seymour	OAK	11	90
5	C.Avril	DET	11	86
6	D.Florence	BUF	11	78
7	J.Haden	CLE	10	87
8	D.Ware	DAL	10	65
9	C.Griffin	MIN	10	63
10	A.Smith	HOU	10	55
11	P.Peterson	ARI	9	122
12	I.Taylor	PIT	9	67
13	C.Woodson	GB	9	63
14	T.Kelly	OAK	9	50
15	C.Munnerlyn	CAR	8	113
16	Y.Bell	MIA	8	93
17	R.Harper	NO	8	89
18	E.Wright	DET	8	84
19	N.Suh	DET	8	65
20	R.Sherman	SEA	8	58
21	J.Abraham	ATL	8	36
22	C.Johnson	CAR	8	35
23	A.Brooks	SF	8	30
24	C.Williams	DET	8	25

Includes declined and offsetting, but not special teams

STATISTICAL APPENDIX

Top 10 Punters, Gross Punt Value over Average

Rk	Player	Team	Punt Pts+	Net Pts+	Punts
1	A.Lee	SF	+15.2	+13.1	79
2	S.Lechler	OAK	+11.5	-8.3	78
3	B.Fields	MIA	+10.1	+8.7	78
4	J.Ryan	SEA	+9.1	-3.0	95
5	Z.Mesko	NE	+9.1	+15.2	57
6	M.Scifres	SD	+8.0	+1.6	47
7	D.Colquitt	KC	+7.5	+3.2	89
8	S.Weatherford	NYG	+7.4	+10.9	82
9	J.Kapinos	PIT	+3.7	+4.1	34
10	T.Masthay	GB	+2.5	-2.2	55

Min. 20 punts

Bottom 10 Punters, Gross Punt Value over Average

Rk	Player	Team	Punt Pts+	Net Pts+	Punts
1	M.Turk	HOU/JAC	-12.3	-8.9	44
2	C.Henry	PHI	-11.5	+0.1	67
3	M.Bosher	ATL	-9.2	-1.4	71
4	N.Harris	JAC	-8.6	+4.9	72
5	K.Huber	CIN	-6.7	+0.7	91
6	J.Baker	CAR	-6.6	-19.6	66
7	D.Jones	STL	-6.6	-14.8	106
8	R.Donahue	DET	-5.6	-3.5	49
9	M.McBriar	DAL	-4.5	-8.6	59
10	B.Hartmann	HOU	-4.0	+1.1	58

Min. 20 punts

Top 10 Kick Returners, Value over Average

Rk	Player	Team	Pts+	Returns
1	J.McKnight	NYJ	+13.2	34
2	P.Harvin	MIN	+10.2	16
3	R.Cobb	GB	+6.4	34
4	J.Ford	OAK	+5.2	11
5	T.Ginn	SF	+4.6	29
6	K.Pilares	CAR	+4.3	23
7	J.Rogers	ATL	+3.7	13
8	B.McCann	OAK	+3.7	13
8	J.Cribbs	CLE	+3.4	39
10	M.Sherels	MIN	+2.8	16

Min. eight returns

Bottom 10 Kick Returners, Value over Average

Rk	Player	Team	Pts+	Returns
1	J.Lefeged	IND	-7.9	30
2	B.Tate	CIN	-7.5	41
2	B.Banks	WAS	-5.7	51
4	D.McCluster	KC	-5.6	25
5	L.Stephens-Howling	ARI	-4.2	36
6	Q.Porter	STL	-4.1	25
7	D.Lewis	PHI	-3.1	31
8	D.Karim	JAC	-3.1	27
9	M.Mariani	TEN	-2.9	31
10	A.Cromartie	NYJ	-2.7	16

Min. eight returns

Top 10 Punt Returners, Value over Average

Rk	Player	Team	Pts+	Returns
1	P.Peterson	ARI	+21.0	44
2	T.Ginn	SF	+10.6	38
3	D.Hester	CHI	+10.6	28
4	E.Royal	DEN	+6.4	12
5	L.McKelvin	BUF	+5.6	8
6	N.Miller	OAK/STL	+5.6	8
7	J.Jones	HOU	+5.4	49
8	A.Brown	PIT	+4.9	30
9	M.Mariani	TEN	+4.8	46
10	R.Cobb	GB	+4.7	26

Min. eight returns

Bottom 10 Punt Returners, Value over Average

Rk	Player	Team	Pts+	Returns
1	P.Parker	TB	-8.9	23
2	A.Edwards	CAR	-6.7	32
3	S.Logan	DET	-6.0	37
4	B.Banks	WAS	-6.0	36
5	M.Thomas	JAC	-5.6	19
6	D.Bryant	DAL	-4.6	15
7	A.Ross	NYG	-4.4	14
8	P.Garcon	IND	-4.1	16
9	D.Harris	DAL	-4.0	15
9	D.Jackson	PHI	-3.6	16

Min. eight returns

STATISTICAL APPENDIX

Top 20 Special Teams Plays

Rk	Player	Team	Plays
1	H.Farwell	SEA	21
2	E.Frampton	MIN	20
3	A.Dent	ATL	19
4	N.Bellore	NYJ	17
4	J.Wendling	DET	17
6	J.Williams	NYG	16
7	T.Sash	NYG	15
7	C.J.Spillman	SF	15
9	L.Alexander	WAS	14
9	C.Brown	PIT	14
9	J.Cribbs	CLE	14
9	J.Miles	CIN	14
13	A.Jordan	PHI	13
13	C.McIntyre	BUF	13
13	M.Slater	NE	13
13	J.Trusnik	MIA	13
17	14 tied with		12

Min. 40 passes or 8 games started.

Top 10 Offenses, 3-and-out per drive

Rk	Team	Pct
1	NO	13.2%
2	SD	13.9%
3	PHI	15.5%
4	GB	16.1%
5	NE	16.8%
6	DAL	17.3%
7	WAS	17.8%
8	DET	18.8%
8	PIT	18.8%
10	ATL	19.8%

Top 10 Defenses, 3-and-out per drive

Rk	Team	Pct
1	CIN	31.3%
2	JAC	30.3%
3	PIT	30.1%
4	SF	27.4%
5	CHI	27.4%
6	MIA	26.6%
7	KC	26.4%
8	NYJ	26.4%
9	PHI	26.2%
9	BAL	26.1%

Bottom 10 Offenses, 3-and-out per drive

Rk	Team	Pct
23	TEN	26.7%
24	SF	27.2%
25	KC	27.3%
26	CIN	27.9%
27	STL	28.9%
28	JAC	29.3%
29	NYJ	30.3%
30	CHI	31.4%
31	DEN	32.2%
32	IND	32.8%

Bottom 10 Defenses, 3-and-out per drive

Rk	Team	Pct
23	WAS	21.1%
24	IND	20.7%
25	NYG	20.6%
26	MIN	20.4%
27	STL	19.5%
28	NO	18.6%
29	GB	18.0%
30	TB	17.6%
31	CAR	15.9%
32	OAK	15.7%

Top 10 Offenses, Yards per drive

Rk	Team	Yds/Dr
1	NO	42.44
2	NE	39.53
3	GB	39.43
4	SD	38.17
5	PIT	35.58
6	CAR	35.11
7	PHI	34.01
8	ATL	33.21
9	NYG	32.95
10	DET	32.74

Bottom 10 Offenses, Yards per drive

Rk	Team	Yds/Dr
23	SF	26.69
24	CLE	26.51
25	KC	25.83
26	DEN	25.78
27	IND	25.72
28	NYJ	25.59
29	CHI	25.02
30	SEA	24.33
31	STL	23.07
32	JAC	22.05

Top 10 Offenses, Points per drive

Rk	Team	Pts/Dr
1	GB	3.05
2	NO	2.98
3	NE	2.79
4	SD	2.32
5	CAR	2.26
6	DET	2.20
7	ATL	2.10
8	DAL	2.02
9	NYG	1.98
10	HOU	1.97

Top 10 Defenses, Yards per drive

Rk	Team	Yds/Dr
1	BAL	24.63
2	NYJ	24.78
3	HOU	24.97
4	CIN	25.48
5	PIT	25.66
6	JAC	26.12
7	SF	26.41
8	CHI	27.03
9	PHI	27.46
10	SEA	27.94

Bottom 10 Defenses, Yards per drive

Rk	Team	Yds/Dr
23	DAL	31.98
24	IND	32.47
25	NO	32.71
26	BUF	32.73
27	SD	34.20
28	OAK	34.97
29	GB	35.64
30	TB	36.35
31	CAR	36.87
32	NE	37.49

Top 10 Defenses, Points per drive

Rk	Team	Pts/Dr
1	SF	1.19
2	BAL	1.29
3	PIT	1.33
4	HOU	1.47
5	SEA	1.48
6	NYJ	1.55
7	CHI	1.56
8	MIA	1.57
9	CIN	1.59
10	PHI	1.64

STATISTICAL APPENDIX

Top 10 Offenses, avg LOS to start drive

Rk	Team	LOS
1	SF	33.4
2	SEA	31.2
3	NYJ	30.9
4	HOU	30.4
5	CIN	30.1
6	GB	30.0
7	MIA	29.3
8	DAL	29.2
9	NE	28.9
10	MIN	28.9

Top 10 Defenses, avg LOS to start drive

Rk	Team	LOS
1	SF	24.0
2	NE	24.1
3	DAL	25.6
4	GB	25.7
5	NO	25.8
6	CIN	26.0
7	TEN	26.1
8	OAK	26.2
9	SD	26.4
10	SEA	26.6

Top 10 Offenses, Better DVOA with Shotgun

Rk	Team	% Plays Shotgun	DVOA Shot	DVOA Not	Yd/Play Shot	Yd/Play Not	DVOA Dif
1	CAR	57%	34.9%	-1.6%	7.0	5.5	36.6%
2	GB	52%	51.3%	17.3%	7.4	6.2	34.0%
3	TEN	46%	17.5%	-12.1%	6.5	4.8	29.5%
4	CLE	34%	6.4%	-18.4%	5.1	4.4	24.7%
5	NE	51%	44.7%	20.8%	7.2	5.5	23.9%
6	NYJ	33%	7.8%	-14.5%	5.7	4.7	22.3%
7	NO	38%	47.7%	25.6%	7.8	6.1	22.2%
8	SD	47%	25.5%	3.6%	7.3	5.2	21.8%
9	ATL	36%	20.8%	-0.7%	6.4	5.5	21.4%
10	CHI	15%	-4.9%	-23.8%	6.7	4.9	18.8%

Bottom 10 Offenses, avg LOS to start drive

Rk	Team	LOS
23	TB	27.0
24	CHI	26.9
25	PIT	26.6
26	DEN	26.5
27	BUF	26.5
28	STL	26.4
29	NYG	26.0
30	ARI	25.7
31	KC	24.5
32	IND	23.6

Bottom 10 Defenses, avg LOS to start drive

Rk	Team	LOS
23	CLE	29.5
24	STL	29.7
25	JAC	29.7
26	MIN	30.1
27	CHI	30.6
28	WAS	30.7
29	TB	30.7
30	ARI	30.8
31	IND	30.9
32	KC	31.3

Bottom 10 Offenses, Better DVOA with Shotgun

Rk	Team	% Plays Shotgun	DVOA Shot	DVOA Not	Yd/Play Shot	Yd/Play Not	DVOA Dif
23	MIN	32%	-13.7%	-8.8%	5.4	5.3	-4.9%
24	DET	68%	4.9%	11.0%	6.2	5.8	-6.1%
25	BUF	58%	-3.1%	4.2%	6.3	5.4	-7.3%
26	ARI	46%	-23.0%	-15.1%	5.7	4.9	-7.9%
27	SEA	35%	-18.4%	-4.5%	5.1	4.9	-13.9%
28	OAK	25%	-9.2%	6.0%	5.7	6.2	-15.2%
29	HOU	19%	-5.7%	10.9%	5.5	5.9	-16.5%
30	KC	34%	-32.2%	-13.6%	5.2	4.8	-18.7%
31	JAC	37%	-40.0%	-20.4%	4.0	4.4	-19.5%
32	WAS	32%	-22.9%	-1.2%	5.2	5.3	-21.7%

Bottom 10 Offenses, Points per drive

Rk	Team	Pts/Dr
23	ARI	1.48
24	CHI	1.48
25	SEA	1.48
26	TB	1.47
27	DEN	1.38
28	IND	1.24
29	CLE	1.22
30	JAC	1.15
31	KC	1.06
32	STL	0.92

Bottom 10 Defenses, Points per drive

Rk	Team	Pts/Dr
23	GB	1.94
24	NYG	1.99
25	WAS	2.01
26	SD	2.06
27	OAK	2.08
28	BUF	2.21
29	IND	2.21
30	MIN	2.23
31	CAR	2.46
32	TB	2.62

Top 10 Defenses, Better DVOA vs. Shotgun

Rk	Team	% Plays Shotgun	DVOA Shot	DVOA Not	Yd/Play Shot	Yd/Play Not	DVOA Dif
1	BUF	37%	-2.9%	14.1%	6.2	6.1	-17.0%
2	GB	45%	-1.2%	15.4%	6.5	6.2	-16.6%
3	KC	37%	-11.6%	1.4%	5.9	5.2	-13.0%
4	STL	31%	-4.6%	6.5%	5.6	5.8	-11.1%
5	PHI	40%	-9.0%	-0.8%	5.5	5.4	-8.2%
6	TEN	38%	-4.0%	2.5%	5.3	5.4	-6.5%
7	CIN	40%	-1.1%	1.8%	5.1	5.2	-2.9%
8	MIA	45%	-5.0%	-2.7%	6.0	5.0	-2.3%
9	PIT	38%	-10.3%	-9.0%	4.7	4.5	-1.3%
10	SD	36%	11.3%	10.5%	6.2	5.8	0.8%

Bottom 10 Defenses, Better DVOA vs. Shotgun

Rk	Team	% Plays Shotgun	DVOA Shot	DVOA Not	Yd/Play Shot	Yd/Play Not	DVOA Dif
23	BAL	40%	-6.0%	-23.1%	5.4	4.2	17.1%
24	ATL	43%	2.2%	-16.4%	6.0	5.3	18.6%
25	NE	45%	24.3%	5.5%	7.2	5.7	18.8%
26	DEN	39%	14.3%	-5.3%	6.5	4.8	19.7%
27	NO	45%	22.5%	1.6%	6.4	5.5	20.9%
28	HOU	45%	3.4%	-18.7%	5.5	4.5	22.1%
29	TB	36%	30.9%	5.9%	7.7	5.8	25.0%
30	MIN	43%	23.4%	-2.7%	6.7	5.0	26.1%
31	OAK	44%	26.4%	-2.1%	7.0	5.2	28.5%
32	IND	33%	29.3%	0.7%	7.3	4.9	28.7%

Top 10 Offenses, Better DVOA with Play Action

Rk	Team	% PA	DVOA PA	DVOA No PA	Yd/Play PA	Yd/Play No PA	DVOA Dif
1	DEN	23%	39.2%	-28.9%	7.3	5.0	68.2%
2	ARI	15%	30.3%	-26.7%	8.3	5.6	57.0%
3	DET	14%	61.0%	13.9%	9.8	6.5	47.1%
4	ATL	17%	60.3%	14.8%	8.7	6.5	45.5%
5	SF	19%	50.5%	7.5%	7.8	5.5	43.0%
6	KC	20%	21.1%	-19.5%	6.8	5.5	40.6%
7	HOU	33%	47.3%	8.5%	10.0	5.7	38.8%
8	CIN	16%	42.2%	12.4%	7.8	5.8	29.9%
9	MIA	15%	31.5%	3.4%	7.7	6.0	28.1%
10	WAS	21%	17.6%	-5.3%	7.6	5.5	22.9%

Bottom 10 Offenses, Better DVOA with Play Action

Rk	Team	% PA	DVOA PA	DVOA No PA	Yd/Play PA	Yd/Play No PA	DVOA Dif
23	BUF	11%	2.9%	7.4%	7.0	6.5	-4.4%
24	GB	22%	58.3%	71.3%	10.0	7.8	-13.0%
25	OAK	20%	-0.2%	14.6%	6.5	7.4	-14.7%
26	NO	23%	40.3%	55.8%	8.0	7.8	-15.5%
27	BAL	17%	1.4%	18.6%	6.7	6.3	-17.2%
28	PHI	25%	9.3%	28.0%	8.3	6.9	-18.7%
29	TB	15%	-25.1%	-2.3%	7.2	5.9	-22.8%
30	PIT	16%	3.9%	30.3%	7.6	6.9	-26.4%
31	JAC	22%	-60.9%	-29.6%	3.4	4.7	-31.3%
32	NYG	14%	-21.1%	41.3%	6.3	8.0	-62.4%

Top 10 Defenses, Better DVOA vs. Play Action

Rk	Team	% PA	DVOA PA	DVOA No PA	Yd/Play PA	Yd/Play No PA	DVOA Dif
1	SEA	22%	-26.0%	4.2%	6.0	6.3	-30.2%
2	HOU	17%	-21.6%	-1.3%	5.7	5.4	-20.3%
3	IND	24%	4.7%	23.5%	6.9	6.9	-18.8%
4	OAK	16%	3.2%	15.2%	7.1	6.6	-12.0%
5	TB	18%	15.5%	23.8%	8.9	7.4	-8.3%
6	MIA	15%	-4.2%	2.7%	6.9	6.3	-6.9%
7	ATL	20%	-5.4%	0.9%	8.4	6.0	-6.3%
8	DAL	17%	7.7%	9.0%	8.0	6.5	-1.3%
9	NO	19%	17.9%	18.0%	6.5	6.3	-0.1%
10	CHI	21%	-5.5%	-5.5%	6.7	6.1	0.0%

Bottom 10 Defenses, Better DVOA vs. Play Action

Rk	Team	% PA	DVOA PA	DVOA No PA	Yd/Play PA	Yd/Play No PA	DVOA Dif
23	PHI	17%	14.6%	-5.8%	7.6	5.8	20.5%
24	SF	19%	10.5%	-10.5%	9.2	5.4	20.9%
25	MIN	19%	40.9%	19.2%	8.2	6.7	21.7%
26	KC	19%	18.0%	-3.8%	6.8	6.7	21.8%
27	PIT	15%	9.6%	-14.0%	5.7	4.9	23.6%
28	BUF	20%	31.4%	7.2%	8.5	6.9	24.3%
29	NYJ	16%	9.4%	-19.0%	6.7	5.9	28.5%
30	CIN	20%	33.4%	-0.8%	7.9	5.5	34.1%
31	DEN	17%	44.4%	5.6%	8.2	6.2	38.9%
32	CAR	26%	50.9%	9.1%	9.2	7.2	41.8%

2011 Defenses with and without Pass Pressure

Rank	Team	Plays	Pct Pressure	DVOA with Pressure	Yds with Pressure	DVOA w/o Pressure	Yds w/o Pressure	DVOA Dif	Rank
1	HOU	606	33.2%	-67.4%	3.0	28.7%	6.7	-96.1%	22
2	BAL	610	29.2%	-75.7%	2.4	14.3%	6.7	-90.0%	24
3	SF	654	28.6%	-65.9%	3.3	21.6%	7.3	-87.5%	25
4	OAK	667	28.0%	-78.6%	3.2	44.0%	8.0	-122.6%	11
5	TB	525	27.4%	-55.6%	5.0	46.9%	8.7	-102.5%	20
6	STL	561	26.9%	-80.2%	1.9	37.8%	8.2	-117.9%	14
7	MIA	660	26.5%	-59.2%	2.3	26.7%	7.9	-85.9%	26
8	ATL	621	26.4%	-40.5%	4.3	17.7%	7.3	-58.2%	31
9	PIT	586	26.1%	-83.4%	1.5	18.3%	6.2	-101.8%	21
10	DAL	617	25.6%	-84.6%	3.5	40.7%	7.9	-125.2%	10
11	NYJ	559	24.9%	-51.9%	2.8	5.9%	7.2	-57.8%	32
12	PHI	587	24.7%	-97.6%	1.7	28.0%	7.5	-125.6%	9
13	WAS	571	24.7%	-127.6%	2.5	44.0%	8.1	-171.6%	1
14	DET	672	24.4%	-68.4%	3.6	15.7%	7.0	-84.1%	29
15	ARI	662	23.7%	-84.0%	2.1	34.5%	7.4	-118.5%	13
16	KC	502	23.5%	-89.2%	2.7	29.6%	8.0	-118.8%	12
17	SD	542	23.4%	-100.1%	3.6	51.6%	8.3	-151.7%	5
18	CIN	606	23.3%	-68.9%	3.2	24.2%	6.8	-93.0%	23
19	CHI	680	22.9%	-87.7%	2.3	21.0%	7.4	-108.6%	17
20	NO	685	22.6%	-67.2%	2.8	39.7%	7.4	-107.0%	18
21	SEA	621	22.4%	-66.9%	3.4	15.2%	7.0	-82.1%	30
22	MIN	615	20.8%	-116.0%	2.1	54.9%	8.2	-171.0%	2
23	NE	697	20.8%	-99.9%	2.6	46.0%	8.7	-145.9%	6
24	JAC	567	20.6%	-86.1%	2.0	20.4%	7.4	-106.4%	19
25	NYG	666	20.4%	-122.1%	1.3	39.3%	7.8	-161.4%	4
26	CAR	545	19.4%	-71.1%	3.2	39.9%	8.8	-111.0%	16
27	DEN	601	19.3%	-97.9%	2.0	38.4%	7.6	-136.3%	7
28	IND	543	18.2%	-119.7%	2.1	44.7%	8.0	-164.4%	3
29	CLE	532	17.3%	-88.9%	2.4	23.1%	6.8	-112.0%	15
30	TEN	640	16.9%	-63.9%	3.8	21.1%	6.4	-85.0%	27
31	BUF	558	15.1%	-60.3%	3.3	24.7%	7.9	-85.0%	28
32	GB	698	14.6%	-98.0%	3.7	30.1%	7.8	-128.1%	8
NFL AVERAGE			23.2%	-80.0%	2.8	30.9%	7.6	-110.9%	

Includes scrambles and Defensive Pass Interference. Does not include aborted snaps.

Author Bios

Editor-in-Chief and Statistician

Aaron Schatz is the creator of FootballOutsiders.com and the proprietary NFL statistics within *Football Outsiders Almanac,* including DVOA, DYAR, Adjusted Line Yards, and the KUBIAK fantasy football projections. He writes regularly for ESPN.com and ESPN the Magazine, and appeared regularly and he has done custom research for a number of NFL teams. *The New York Times Magazine* has referred to him as "the Bill James of football." Before creating Football Outsiders, he was a radio disc jockey and spent three years tracking search trends online as the writer and producer of the Internet column "The Lycos 50." He has a B.A. in Economics from Brown University and lives in Framingham, Massachusetts with his wife Kathryn and daughter Mirinae.

Layout and Design

Vince Verhei is a freelance writer and editor, and has been a writer and editor for Football Outsiders since 2007. In addition to writing for *Football Outsiders Almanac 2012*, he did all layout and copy editing on the book. A regular contributor to the pro and college football sections of Rumor Central at ESPN.com, he also writes the "Any Given Sunday" column covering the week's top upset using Football Outsiders metrics. His writings have also appeared in *ESPN the Magazine* and in Maple Street Press publications, and he has done layout for a number of other books for Football Outsiders and for Prospectus Entertainment Ventures. He is also a writer and podcast host for pro wrestling/MMA website Figurefouronline.com. He is a graduate of Western Washington University.

Contributors

Andy Benoit is an NFL analyst for CBSSports.com and the *New York Times* Fifth Down Blog, and will begin writing FO's "Cover-2'" column for the 2012 season. He has also contributed to NBC Sports, USA Today, and a variety of NFL magazines and websites, and he is a frequent panelist on the NFL Network's *Top 10* series. He has been writing about the NFL since he began his annual preview book *NFL Touchdown* as a summer hobby at age 11. Over the years, the project evolved from scrapbook (1997-2002) to self-publication (2003-2004) to national publication (Random House 2005-2006) and eventually to the website NFLTouchdown.com. Andy graduated with a business degree from the College of Idaho and currently resides in Boise.

Bill Connelly analyzes the ins and outs of college football play-by-play data in the weekly Football Outsiders column, "Varsity Numbers." He is also the College Sports Editor and Analytics Director for SB Nation, where he runs the college football blog Football Study Hall. He grew up a numbers and sports nerd in western Oklahoma, but now lives in Missouri with his wife, pets, and young daughter.

Brian Fremeau contributes the Fremeau Efficiency Index (FEI) and other college football stats, analysis, and data visualization design to FootballOutsiders.com, ESPN Insider, and Maple Street Press college football publications. He recently launched bcftoys.com, a personal archive of his stat analysis and graphics work. He lives in South Bend, Indiana, with his wife and daughter.

AUTHOR BIOS

Tom Gower joined the writing staff in 2009 after being a game charter for three seasons. He co-wrote "Scramble for the Ball" this past season, and his work also appeared on ESPN.com. He has degrees from Georgetown University and the University of Chicago, whose football programs have combined for an Orange Bowl appearance and seven Big Ten titles but are still trying to find success after Pearl Harbor. When not practicing law in the Chicago area or writing for FO, he keeps a keen eye on Tennessee for the blog Total Titans.

Matt Hinton lives in Austin, Texas, and will contribute biweekly college football columns to Football Outsiders this fall. He writes daily for the Eye on College Football blog on CBSSports.com. Previously, he was the editor of Yahoo! Sports' college football blog, Dr. Saturday, or: How I Learned to Stop Worrying and Love the BCS, and he has also written for Lindy's, Maple Street Press and The Baffler. He does not love the BCS.

Sean McCormick is a graduate of the University of Pennsylvania and holds an MFA in Creative Writing from Arizona State University. In addition to being a regular contributor at FootballOutsiders.com, his draft coverage has appeared at FOXSports.com. He also indulges his inner masochist as a contributing writer for TheJetsBlog.com and is the proud owner of the lone Richard Todd jersey still in existence. He lives in Brooklyn, New York.

Rivers McCown started charting games for Football Outsiders in 2007 on a lark and soon found himself engrossed in football writing, statistics, and the idea that Phil Simms was often wrong about things. A lifelong Houstonian by choice, he has built up a tolerance to humidity and bad football teams. Prior to joining Football Outsiders as an assistant editor, Rivers was Managing Editor for SB Nation Houston; he still contributes sparingly to Battle Red Blog and his personal blog, From Mom's Basement.

Brian McIntyre may be from Clinton, Massachusetts, but he grew up a fan of the Seattle Seahawks. Brian caught the football bug early, passionately following the sport even after having his six-year-old heart broken when the NFL went on strike six days before he was to attend his first NFL game (Seahawks-Patriots at Schaefer Stadium) in 1982. He now writes for NFL.com's Around the League blog, but previously covered the NFL since 2005 on his own site (Mac's Football Blog) as well as for Scout.com and the *Tacoma News-Tribune.*

Mike Tanier has been part of the Football Outsiders team since 2005. In addition to his "Walkthrough" column at FO, Mike writes the weekly NFL matchups for the *New York Times*, contributes to *ESPN the Magazine*, and has provided content for everyone from *Sports Illustrated Kids* to *Maxim*. His first solo book, *The Philly Fan's Code*, covers the history of Philadelphia sports and was published in 2011.

Football Outsiders assistant editor **Danny Tuccitto** holds a Masters in Sport Psychology from the University of Florida. Before coming to Football Outsiders, he was the resident statistics nerd at SB Nation's 49ers blog, Niners Nation. He lives in Miami.

Robert Weintraub bleeds orange, both because of his inexplicable passion for the Cincinnati Bengals (he grew up in suburban New York, not Ohio) and because of his alma mater, Syracuse University. Robert also works as a freelance television producer and writes for Slate and *The Guardian*. His first book, *The House That Ruth Built: A New Yankee Stadium, the First Championship, and the Redemption of 1923*, was published in 2011. His second book, *The Victory Season: World War II, The Homecoming, and the Birth of Baseball's Golden Age*, will be published in the spring of 2013. He lives in Atlanta.

Research Articles

Torin Clark is a Ph.D. student in the Department of Aeronautics and Astronautics at the Massachusetts Institute of Technology, studying astronaut sensorimotor adaptation to spaceflight. He grew up in Boulder, Colo., and has a bachelor's degree in aerospace engineering from the University of Colorado.

Nathan Forster played wide receiver for his freshman football team, but unfortunately graduated before Matt Millen left the broadcast booth. He graduated with a B.A. in English from the University of Michigan and a J.D. from Boston College Law School, which naturally lead him to develop a regression model to project the professional sack totals of college edge rushers. Nathan and his love-hate relationship with the Detroit Lions currently reside in the greater Boston area with wife Sarah and daughter Lily.

Jason Lisk has been covering the NFL for thebiglead.com since 2010. His circuitous route from lawyer to full-time writer began when he was an early commenter and avid reader of Football Outsiders, and from there discovered the pro-football-reference blog and Doug Drinen. He contributed football research pieces to pro-football-reference.com for four years before moving to the Big Lead. A life-long fan of heartbreak in sports, Jason grew up a Chiefs fan and also attended the University of Missouri, where he learned to hate both Tyus Edney and Matt Davison. He lives in the Kansas City area now with his wife and four children.

Aaron Johnson is a Ph.D. student in the Department of Aeronautics and Astronautics at the Massachusetts Institute of Technology, studying human-automation task allocation for human spaceflight. Originally from Pittsburgh, Pa., he has a bachelor's degree in aerospace engineering from the University of Michigan.

Alexander Stimpson is a Ph.D. student in the Department of Aeronautics and Astronautics at the Massachusetts Institute of Technology, studying machine learning applications to proceduralized training. A longtime football fan, he has a bachelor's degree in biological engineering from the University of Florida.

Acknowledgements

We want to thank all the Football Outsiders readers, all the people in the media who have helped to spread the word about our website and books, and all the people in the NFL who have shown interest in our work. This year, instead of the never-ending long list naming everyone who's ever acknowledged our existence, we wanted to give a few specific acknowledgements:

- FO techmasters Elias Holman and Erik Stieringer.

- Jason Beattie for cover design.

- Mike Harris for help with the season simulation, and Dr. Ben Alamar for help with previous season simulations.

- Programmers Pat Laverty and Sean McCall, Excel stat report guru John Argentiero, and drive stats guru Jim Armstrong.

- FO writers who did not write for the book, including Mike Kurtz, Ben Muth, and Matt Waldman.

- J.J. Cooper, who has compiled and generously shared his data on quarterback sack times.

- David Lewin, creator of the Lewin Career Forecast and Jason McKinley, creator of O-Line Continuity Score.

- Chris Povirk, the greatest Internet data-scraper in the history of Internet data-scraping.

- Jeremy Snyder, our incredibly prolific transcriber of old play-by-play gamebooks. Redskins fans who have been dying to see 1991 DVOA stats should be particularly grateful.

- Roland Beech of the Dallas Mavericks, formerly of TwoMinuteWarning.com, who came up with the original ideas behind our individual defensive stats.

- Our editors at ESPN.com and *ESPN the Magazine*, including Daniel Kaufman, Chris Sprow, and Ben Fawkes.

- Jamie Horowitz and Kevin Wildes, for putting Football Outsiders on television on a weekly basis, and the rest of the staff of ESPN2's *Numbers Never Lie*: Michael Smith, Charissa Thompson, David Arnold, Matt Ketaineck, and many others we're surely forgetting.

- Bill Simmons, for constantly promoting us on his podcast, and Peter King, for lots of promotion in his SI.com column.

- Ron Jaworski, Greg Cosell, and the entire *NFL Matchup* production team, for the annual film-study lessons.

- Chris Hoeltge at the NFL, for responding to our endless questions about specific items in the official play-by-play, and for collecting old gamebooks and making them available to us.

- All the media relations people at various NFL teams who have helped with our search for old play-by-play, plus Jon Kendle at the Hall of Fame for filling the gaps.

- All the friends we've made on coaching staffs and in front offices across the National Football League, who generally don't want to be mentioned by name. You know who you are.

- Russ Lande, whose draft guide was extremely helpful in researching this year's rookies.

- Our comrades in the revolution: Doug Drinen (creator of the indispensible pro-football-reference.com), Bill Barnwell, Doug Farrar, Neil Paine, Chris Brown, Chase Stuart, and K.C. Joyner, plus our friends at Prospectus Entertainment Ventures.

- The Seadar Inn in Harwich, Mass., for use of their wifi network in the crucial final week of book preparation. (The Seadar Inn, where our motto is "You just might find a professional football writer staying at that old house next door.")

- Interns who helped prepare data over the past year or for this book specifically, including Kurt Chipps, Zack Feffer, Sam Hendrickson, and Mike Ridley.

- All those who have volunteered their time and effort for the Football Outsiders game charting project, particularly those people who have been consistently charting for multiple seasons. Our regular charters last year included: Chris Berney, Michael Bonner, Frank Brown, Andy DeMambro, Dave DuPlantis, Nathan Eagan, Kwame Flaherty, Van Gutenson, David Heck, Bo Hurley, Steve Kaneb, Shawn Krest, Bin Lee, Ryan Marsh, Aaron McCurrie, Braden Moore, Matt Morrow, Sander Philipse, Matthew Raymond, Nate Richards, Augie Salick, John Scappini, Alex Schaefer, Matt Scribbins, Navin Sharma, Derek Snyder, Robert Stevick, Rob Stewart, John Sullivan, Fred Tobin, Abe vander Bent, Bobby Wilson, and Chris Young. Weekly data collection was handled by Peter Koski.

Infinite gratitude goes to our wives, girlfriends, and children, for putting up with this silliness.

Follow Football Outsiders on Twitter

Follow the official account announcing new Football Outsiders articles at **@fboutsiders**.

You can follow other FO writers at these Twitter addresses:

Andy Benoit: **@Andy_Benoit**
Bill Connelly: **@SBN_BillC**
Brian Fremeau: **@bcfremeau**
Tom Gower: **@ThomasGower**
Matt Hinton: **@MattRHinton**
Rivers McCown: **@FO_RiversMcCown**
Brian McIntyre: **@brian_mcintyre**
Ben Muth: **@FO_WordofMuth**
Aaron Schatz: **@FO_ASchatz**
Mike Tanier: **@FO_MTanier**
Danny Tuccitto: **@FO_DTuccitto**
Vince Verhei: **@FO_VVerhei**
Robert Weintraub: **@robwein**

Printed in Great Britain
by Amazon.co.uk, Ltd.,
Marston Gate.